Oxford American Large Print Thesaurus

Oxford American Large Print Thesaurus

OXFORD
UNIVERSITY PRESS

OXFORD UNIVERSITY PRESS

Oxford University Press, Inc., publishes works that further
Oxford University's objective of excellence
in research, scholarship, and education.

Oxford   New York
Auckland   Cape Town   Dar es Salaam   Hong Kong   Karachi
Kuala Lumpur   Madrid   Melbourne   Mexico City   Nairobi
New Delhi   Shanghai   Taipei   Toronto

With offices in
Argentina   Austria   Brazil   Chile   Czech Republic   France   Greece
Guatemala   Hungary   Italy   Japan   Poland   Portugal   Singapore
South Korea   Switzerland   Thailand   Turkey   Ukraine   Vietnam

The *Oxford American Large Print Thesaurus* is based on the *Oxford American Minithesaurus*, 2004

Published by Oxford University Press, Inc.
198 Madison Avenue, New York, New York, 10016
www.oup.com/us
www.askoxford.com

Oxford is a registered trademark of Oxford University Press

Library of Congress Cataloging-in-Publicaion Data
Oxford American large print thesaurus.
       p. cm.
    "The Oxford American Large Print Thesaurus is based on the Oxford American
Minithesaurus, 2004"—T.p. verso.
    ISBN 0-19-530077-7
    1. English language—Synonyms and antonyms.   2. English language—United States—
Synonyms and antonyms.   3. Large type books.   I. Title: American large print thesaurus.   II.
Oxford American minithesaurus.

    PE1591.0884 2006
    423'.12—dc22

                                2005025172

ISBN-10: 0-19-530077-7
ISBN-13: 978-0-19-530077-2

10   9   8   7   6   5   4   3   2   1
Printed in the United States of America on acid-free paper

Contents

Staff

Editor in Chief	Erin McKean
Managing Editor	Constance Baboukis
Senior Editor	Christine Lindberg
Editors	Richard Goodman
	Alan H. Hartley
Assistant Editor	Grant Barrett
Editorial Assistant	Elizabeth Jerabek

Preface

The *Oxford American Large Print Thesaurus* is intended as a helpful, easy-to-read thesaurus for the home, school, or office. The thesaurus, in a simple A-Z format, includes many compound terms and idiomatic expressions in American English. Special sections at the back of the book provide clear and helpful information on punctuation, capitalization, and clichés to avoid.

This book's clear page layout, designed in association with Lighthouse International, offers enlarged fonts, larger margins, generous line spacing, and good quality paper for minimum glare and show-through.

The *Oxford American Large Print Thesaurus*, with its attention to quality, thoroughness, and currency, continues the tradition of Oxford—the world's most trusted name in dictionaries.

This thesaurus has been produced in cooperation with Lighthouse International, which made recommendations on design and layout. A percentage from the sale of each thesaurus will be made to Lighthouse International to support its work helping people with vision loss remain productive and independent. For more information about Lighthouse International, please visit www.lighthouse.org.

Aa

abandon ▸ *n.* **recklessness,** lack of restraint/inhibition, unrestraint, carelessness, wildness, impulse, impetuosity, immoderation, wantonness.

abandoned *adj.* **1 deserted,** forsaken, cast aside, vacated, evacuated, unoccupied, empty, unused. **2 reckless,** unrestrained, uninhibited, impetuous, wild, careless, wanton,dissipated, debauched, profligate, dissolute, immoral, corrupt, depraved, reprobate, wild, reckless.

abashed *adj.* **embarrassed,** ashamed, shamefaced, mortified, humiliated, taken aback, disconcerted, nonplussed, discomfited, perturbed, confounded, dismayed, dumbfounded.

abbreviate *v.* **shorten,** reduce, cut, cut short/down, contract, condense, compress, abridge, truncate, clip, crop, shrink, constrict, summarize, abstract, synopsize. ***Ant.*** lengthen; expand; elongate.

abdicate *v.* **1 resign,** stand down, retire, quit, give up, renounce, resign from, relinquish, abjure, cede, *Law* disclaim. **2 give up,** renounce, relinquish, abjure, repudiate, reject, disown, waive, yield, forgo, refuse, abandon, surrender, cast aside, drop, turn one's back on, wash one's hands of.

abduct *v.* **kidnap,** carry off, run away/off with, make off with, seize, hold as hostage, hold for ransom, *inf.* snatch.

abhorrent *adj.* **detestable,** loathsome, hated, abominable, repellent, repugnant, repulsive, revolting, disgusting, distasteful, horrible, horrid, heinous, obnoxious, odious, offensive, *inf.* yucky.

abide *v.* **1 keep to,** comply with, observe, follow, obey, agree to, hold to, conform to, adhere to, stick to, stand by. **2 stand,** tolerate, bear, put up with, endure, stomach, suffer, accept, brook.

ability *n.* **1 talent,** competence, competency, proficiency, skill, expertise, expertness, adeptness, aptitude, dexterity, adroitness, qualification, cleverness, flair, gift, knack, savoir faire, *inf.* know-how. **2 capacity,** capability, potential, potentiality, power, aptness, facility, faculty, propensity. ***Ant.*** inability; incapacity.

ablaze *adj.* **1 on fire,** burning, blazing, alight, flaming, *lit.* afire, aflame. **2 lit up,** alight, gleaming, glowing, aglow, illuminated, brilliant, radiant, shimmering, sparkling, flashing, incandescent. **3 passionate,** aroused, excited, stimulated, animated, impassioned, ardent, fervent, frenzied.

able *adj.* **competent,** capable, talented, skillful, skilled, clever, intelligent, accomplished, gifted, proficient, apt, fit, expert, adept, efficient, effective, qualified, adroit. ***Ant.*** incompetent; incapable; inept.

abnormal *adj.* **unusual,** strange, odd, peculiar, uncommon, curious, queer, weird, eccentric, extraordinary, unexpected, exceptional, irregular, unnatural, erratic, singular, atypical, nontypical, anomalous, deviant, deviating, divergent, aberrant, *inf.* oddball, off the wall, wacko. ***Ant.*** normal; regular; typical.

abolish *v.* **do away with,** put an end to, end, stop, terminate, eliminate, eradicate, exterminate, destroy, annihilate, stamp out, obliterate, wipe out, extinguish, quash, expunge, extirpate, annul, cancel, invalidate, nullify, void, rescind, repeal, revoke, vitiate, abrogate, *inf.* ax. ***Ant.*** keep; retain; maintain.

abominable *adj.* **hateful,** loathsome, detestable, odious, obnoxious, base, despicable, contemptible, damnable, cursed, disgusting, revolting, repellent, repulsive, offensive, repugnant, abhorrent, reprehensible, foul, vile, wretched, horrible, nasty, disagreeable, unpleasant, execrable, *inf.* yucky, god-awful.

aboriginal *adj.* **indigenous,** native, original, earliest, first, ancient, primitive, primeval, primordial.

abortive *adj.* **failed,** unsuccessful, nonsuccessful, vain, futile, useless, worthless, ineffective, ineffectual, fruitless, unproductive, unavailing. ***Ant.*** successful; productive; fruitful.

abound *v.* **be plentiful,** proliferate, superabound, thrive, flourish.

abrasive *adj.* **1 erosive,** eroding, corrosive, chafing, rubbing, coarse, harsh. **2 caustic,** cutting, grating, biting, rough, harsh, irritating, sharp, nasty.

abridge *v.* **shorten,** cut down, condense, contract, compress, abbreviate, reduce, decrease, diminish, curtail, truncate, lessen, trim, summarize, abstract, epitomize, synopsize, digest.

abrupt *adj.* **1 sudden,** quick, hurried, hasty, swift, rapid, headlong, instantaneous, surprising, unexpected, unanticipated, unforeseen. **2 curt,** blunt, brusque, short, terse, brisk, crisp, gruff, snappish, unceremonious, rough, rude. **3 steep,** sheer, precipitous, sudden, sharp. **4 jerky,** uneven, irregular, disconnected, discontinuous, broken, rough, inelegant. *Ant.* gradual; unhurried; smooth.

abscond *v.* **run away,** bolt, clear out, flee, make off, escape, take flight, fly, decamp, disappear, slip/steal/sneak away, take to one's heels, make a quick getaway, beat a hasty retreat, run for it, *inf.* cut and run, skedaddle, skip, beat it.

absent *adj.* **1 away,** off, out, gone, missing, truant, lacking, unavailable, nonexistent, nonattendant. **2 absentminded,** distracted, preoccupied, daydreaming, dreaming, faraway, blank, empty, vacant, inattentive, vague, absorbed.

absentminded *adj.* **distracted,** preoccupied, absorbed, abstracted, inattentive, forgetful, oblivious.

absolute *adj.* **1 complete,** total, utter, out and out, outright, perfect, entire, undivided, unqualified, unadulterated, unalloyed, downright, undiluted, solid, consummate, unmitigated. **2 certain,** positive, definite, unquestionable, undoubted, unequivocal, decisive, unconditional, categorical, conclusive, confirmed, infallible. **3 fixed,** independent, nonrelative, nonvariable, rigid, established, set, definite. **4 unlimited,** unrestricted, unrestrained, unbounded, boundless, infinite, ultimate, total, supreme, unconditional, full, utter, sovereign, omnipotent. **5 despotic,** dictatorial, autocratic, tyrannical, authoritarian, arbitrary, autonomous, sovereign. *Ant.* qualified; conditional; limited.

absolve *v.* **1 acquit,** exonerate, discharge, release, free, deliver, liberate, let off, clear, exempt, exculpate. **2 forgive,** pardon, excuse, reprieve, give amnesty to, give dispensation/indulgence to, clear, set free, vindicate. *Ant.* blame; charge; condemn.

absorb *v.* **1 soak up,** suck up, draw up/in, take up/in, blot up,

mop, sponge up, sop up.
2 consume, devour, eat up,
swallow, assimilate, digest, ingest.
3 take in, incorporate, assimilate,
appropriate, co-opt, *derog.*
swallow up. **4 occupy,** engage,
preoccupy, captivate, engross,
monopolize, rivet.

absorbent *adj.* **spongelike,**
spongy, porous, permeable,
pervious, penetrable, assimilative,
receptive, blotting.

absorbing *adj.* **fascinating,**
gripping, interesting, captivating,
engrossing, riveting, spellbinding,
intriguing. *Ant.* boring;
uninteresting; dull.

abstain *v.* **1 refrain,** decline,
forbear, desist, hold back, keep
from, refuse, renounce, avoid,
shun, eschew. **2 decline/refuse to
vote. 3 be teetotal,** be/stay sober,
refrain, take the pledge, *inf.* be on
the wagon. *Ant.* join in (see join);
vote; indulge.

abstemious *adj.* **moderate,**
temperate, abstinent, self-
denying, austere, sober, self-
restrained, ascetic, puritanical,
nonindulgent, self-abnegating.

abstract *adj.* **1 theoretical,**
conceptual, notional, intellectual,
metaphysical, philosophical.
2 nonrepresentational,
nonrealistic, unrealistic.
3 complex, abstruse, recondite,

obscure, deep. *Ant.* actual;
concrete.
▶ *n.* **summary,** synopsis, précis,
résumé, outline, abridgment,
condensation, digest.

abstruse *adj.* **obscure,** deep,
profound, complex, hidden,
esoteric, mysterious,
incomprehensible, unfathomable,
inscrutable, enigmatic,
perplexing, puzzling, recondite,
arcane.

absurd *adj.* **ridiculous,** foolish,
silly, idiotic, stupid, nonsensical,
senseless, inane, crazy, ludicrous,
funny, laughable, comical,
preposterous, farcical,
harebrained, asinine, *inf.* daft.

abundance *n.* **plenty,**
plentifulness, profusion,
copiousness, amplitude,
affluence, lavishness,
bountifulness, *inf.* heaps, lots,
stacks, loads, tons, oodles. *Ant.*
lack; scarcity.

abundant *adj.* **plentiful,** large,
great, huge, ample, well-supplied,
well-provided, profuse, copious,
lavish, bountiful, teeming,
overflowing, *inf.* galore.

abuse *v.* **1 misuse,** misapply,
misemploy, mishandle, exploit.
2 mistreat, maltreat, ill-use, ill-
treat, manhandle, injure, hurt,
harm, beat, damage, wrong,

oppress, torture. **3 assault sexually. 4 insult,** swear at, curse, scold, rebuke, upbraid, reprove, castigate, revile, vilify, slander.
▶ *n.* **1 misuse,** misapplication, misemployment, mishandling, exploitation. **2 mistreatment,** maltreatment, ill-use, ill-treatment, manhandling, injury, hurt, harm, beating, damage, oppression, torture. **3 sexual assault. 4 corruption,** wrongdoing, wrong, misconduct, misdeeds, offense, crime, fault, sin. **5 swearing,** cursing, scolding, rebuke, upbraiding, reproval, invective, castigation, revilement, vilification, vituperation, defamation, slander, insults, curses, expletives, swearwords.

abusive *adj.* **1 insulting,** rude, blasphemous, offensive, vulgar, vituperative, reproachful, reproving, derisive, scornful, castigating, slanderous, defamatory, calumniating. **2 violent,** cruel.

abysmal *adj.* **extreme,** utter, complete, thorough, profound, deep, endless, immeasurable, boundless, incalculable, unfathomable, bottomless.

abyss *n.* **1 chasm,** gorge, cavity, void, pit, bottomless pit, hole, gulf, depth, ravine, canyon, crevasse. **2 chasm,** void, bottomless pit, hell, hellhole, depths.

academic *adj.* **1 educational,** scholastic, instructional, pedagogical. **2 scholarly,** studious, literary, well-read, intellectual, erudite, learned, cultured, bookish, highbrow, pedantic, professorial, cerebral, *inf.* brainy. **3 theoretical,** hypothetical, abstract, conjectural, notional, impractical, unrealistic, speculative, ivory-towerish.
▶ *n.* **scholar,** lecturer, teacher, tutor, professor, fellow, pedant, pedagogue, *inf.* bookworm, egghead.

accelerate *v.* **speed up,** go faster, pick up speed, hasten, hurry, quicken, advance rapidly, expedite, step up, advance, forward, further, spur on, facilitate, precipitate, stimulate, *inf.* open up. **Ant.** decelerate; slow down (see slow); delay.

accent *n.* **1 pronunciation,** intonation, enunciation, articulation, inflection, tone, modulation, utterance. **2 stress,** emphasis, accentuation, force, beat, prominence, primary stress, secondary stress. **3 emphasis,** stress, prominence, importance, accentuation, priority, underlining, underscoring.
4 accent mark, mark, diacritic,

diacritical (mark), sign, circumflex, acute accent, grave accent, cedilla, umlaut, tilde.

▸ *v.* **1 stress,** put/lay the stress on, emphasize, put/lay the emphasis on, accentuate. **2 accentuate,** emphasize, highlight, underline, draw attention to.

accentuate *v.* **1 emphasize,** stress, highlight, underline, draw attention to, give prominence to, heighten, point up, underscore, accent. **2 stress,** put the stress/emphasis on, emphasize, accent.

accept *v.* **1 receive,** take, take receipt of, get, gain, obtain, acquire, come by. **2 accede to,** agree to, consent to, acquiesce in, concur with, endorse, comply with, go along with, defer to, put up with, recognize, acknowledge, cooperate with, adopt, admit. **3 take on,** undertake, assume, bear, tackle, be responsible for. **4 believe,** trust, credit, be convinced of, have faith in, count/rely on. **5 welcome,** receive, receive favorably, embrace, offer friendship to, integrate. **6 say yes to,** reply in the affirmative, comply with. *Ant.* refuse; reject; deny.

accepted *adj.* **1 approved,** recognized, sanctioned, authorized, received, allowable, acceptable. **2 usual,** customary, normal, expected, standard, conventional, recognized, acknowledged, established, traditional, confirmed.

access *n.* **1 entry,** entrance, way in, means of entry/entrance, admittance, admission, approachability, accessibility, approach, means of approach, gateway, driveway, road, path, avenue, passage. **2 admission,** admittance, entrée, right of entry, permission/opportunity to enter/reach/use, accessibility, attainability.

▸ *v.* **gain access to,** retrieve, gain, acquire.

accessible *n.* **1 attainable,** reachable, available, approachable, obtainable, achievable. **2 approachable (by),** available, easygoing, informal, friendly, pleasant, agreeable, obliging, congenial, affable, cordial. **3 understandable,** comprehensible, intelligible, penetrable, fathomable. *Ant.* inaccessible; unapproachable.

accessory *n.* **1 accomplice,** associate, confederate, abettor, helper, assistant, partner. **2 attachment,** extra, addition, adjunct, appendage, supplement. **3 adornment,** trimming, ornament, ornamentation,

embellishment, trappings, handbag, shoes, gloves, hat, belt, ribbon, jewelry.
▸ *adj.* **additional,** extra, supplementary, contributory, subsidiary, ancillary, auxiliary, secondary, assisting.

accident *n.* **1 mishap,** casualty, misfortune, misadventure, injury, disaster, tragedy, blow, catastrophe, calamity. **2 crash,** collision, *inf.* pile-up. **3 chance,** mere chance, fate, twist of fate, fortune, good fortune, luck, good luck, fortuity, hazard, *inf.* fluke.

accidental *adj.* **1 chance,** occurring by chance/accident, unintentional, unintended, inadvertent, unexpected, unforeseen, unlooked-for, fortuitous, unanticipated, unplanned, uncalculated, unpremeditated, unwitting, adventitious. **2 nonessential,** inessential, incidental, extraneous, extrinsic, supplementary, subsidiary, subordinate, secondary, accessory, irrelevant. ***Ant.*** intentional; calculated.

acclaim *v.* **1 applaud,** cheer, celebrate, salute, welcome, approve, honor, praise, commend, hail, extol, laud, eulogize, exalt. **2 declare,** announce, proclaim, hail.

▸ *n.* **applause,** ovation, praise, commendation, approval, approbation, homage, tribute, extolment, laudation, cheers, congratulations, plaudits, bouquets.

acclimatize *v.* **acclimate,** adjust, adapt, accustom, get used, accommodate, accustom/ habituate oneself, become seasoned, familiarize oneself, become inured, become naturalized.

accommodate *v.* **1 put up,** house, cater for, board, lodge, provide shelter for, shelter, harbor, billet. **2 adapt,** adjust, modify, reconcile, fit, harmonize, conform. **3 provide,** supply, furnish, serve, grant. **4 help,** assist, aid, lend a hand to, oblige, meet the needs/wants of, do a favor for, indulge.

accommodating *adj.* **obliging,** cooperative, helpful, adaptable, pliable, compliant, complaisant, considerate, unselfish, willing, polite, kindly, hospitable, kind, friendly, agreeable.

accommodation *n.*
1 adaptation, adjustment, modification, reconciliation, fitting, harmonization.
2 provision, supply, supplying, furnishing, serving. **3 help,**

assistance, aid, obliging, indulgence.

accompany *v.* **1 escort,** go with, go along with, keep company, squire, usher, conduct, convoy, chaperon. **2 go with,** go along with, go together with, coexist/occur/coincide with, supplement. **3 play a musical accompaniment with,** play with/for, back up, support.

accomplice *n.* **confederate,** accessory, collaborator, abettor, associate, partner, ally, assistant, helper, aider, henchman, right hand, right-hand man, fellow conspirator, partner in crime, friend, *inf.* sidekick.

accomplish *v.* **1 achieve,** carry out, fulfill, perform, attain, realize, succeed in, bring off, bring about, effect, execute, effectuate. **2 finish,** complete, carry through, do, perform, conclude, effect, execute, consummate. **Ant.** fail; give up (see give).

accomplished *adj.* **1 skilled,** skillful, expert, gifted, talented, proficient, adept, masterly, polished, practiced, capable, able, competent, experienced, professional, deft, consummate. **2 achieved,** fulfilled, realized. **3 finished,** completed, executed.

accomplishment *n.* **1 ability,** skill, talent, gift, attainment, achievement, capability, proficiency. **2 achievement,** act, deed, exploit, performance, attainment, feat, coup, triumph. **3 achievement,** fulfillment, attainment, realization, success, effecting, execution. **4 finishing,** completion, performance, conclusion, execution, consummation.

accord *v.* **1 agree,** concur, fit, correspond, match, conform, harmonize, be in tune. **2 give,** grant, confer, bestow, tender, offer, present, award, vouchsafe, concede. **Ant.** disagree; contrast; withhold.

▸ *n.* **agreement,** harmony, rapport, unison, concord, amity, sympathy, unanimity, accordance.

account *n.* **1 statement,** report, description, record, narration, narrative, story, recital, explanation, tale, chronicle, history, relation, version. **2 bill,** invoice, charges, debts. **3 bank account,** checking account, savings account. **4 ledger,** balance sheet, financial statement, books. **5 importance,** consequence, significance.

▸ *v.* **consider,** regard, reckon, believe, think, look upon, view as, judge, count, deem.

accumulate v. **gather,** pile/build up, collect, amass, stockpile, store, hoard, increase, augment, accrue.

accumulation n. **stockpile,** pile, heap, mass, collection, buildup, gathering, stock, store, hoard, stack, cumulation, aggregation, amassing, building up, stockpiling, accrual.

accurate adj. **correct,** precise, exact, right, errorless, without error, valid, close, faithful, true, truthful, authentic, factual, literal, veracious, strict, careful, meticulous, painstaking. **Ant.** inaccurate; inexact.

accusation n. **charge,** allegation, attribution, incrimination, imputation, denouncement, indictment, arraignment, impeachment, citation, inculpation, blame.

accuse v. **blame,** condemn, arraign, impeach, charge, indict, censure, attack, denounce. **Ant.** absolve; exonerate; defend.

accustomed adj. **usual,** normal, customary, habitual, regular, routine, ordinary, fixed, set, typical, established, common, general.

ache n. **1 pain,** dull pain, soreness, pang, throb, twinge, smarting, gnawing, stabbing, spasm, suffering. **2 suffering,** sorrow, misery, distress, grief, anguish, affliction, woe, mourning. **3 longing,** yearning, craving, desire, hunger, hungering, pining, hankering.
▶ v. **1 hurt,** be sore, be painful, be in pain, pain, throb, pound, twinge, smart. **2 grieve,** be sorrowful, be distressed, be in distress, be miserable, mourn, agonize, suffer.

achieve v. **1 attain,** reach, arrive at, gain, earn, realize, win, acquire, obtain, procure, get, wrest. **2 complete,** finish, accomplish, carry through, fulfill, execute, conclude, perform, effect, consummate.

acid adj. **1 sour,** tart, bitter, sharp, biting, acrid, pungent, acerbic, vinegary, vinegarish, acetic, acetous, acidulous. **2 acerbic,** sarcastic, sharp, caustic, trenchant, vitriolic, mordant.

acknowledge v. **1 admit,** grant, allow, recognize, accept, subscribe to, approve, agree to, acquiesce in, concede. **2 greet,** salute, address, hail, recognize, notice. **3 answer,** reply to, respond to, react to. **4 show appreciation for/of,** express gratitude for, give thanks for, thank.

acquaint v. **familiarize,** make familiar/conversant, make known to, make aware of, advise of, inform, apprise of, enlighten, let know.

acquaintance *n.* **1 associate,** colleague, contact. **2 association,** relationship, contact, social contact, fellowship, companionship. **3 familiarity,** knowledge, awareness, understanding, cognizance.

acquire *v.* **obtain,** come by, get, receive, gain, procure, earn, win, secure, take possession of, gather, collect, pick up, achieve, attain, appropriate, amass.

acquisition *n.* **gain,** purchase, buy, possession, accession, addition, accretion, property, obtaining, procurement, collecting, collection, attainment, appropriation.

acquit *v.* **clear (of charges),** absolve, exonerate, discharge, release, vindicate, liberate, free, deliver, *fml.* exculpate. *Ant.* convict; find guilty; blame.

acrid *adj.* **1 pungent,** sharp, sour, bitter, tart, harsh, acid, stinging, burning, irritating, vinegary, acerbic, acetic. **2 acerbic,** sarcastic, sharp, stinging, caustic, astringent, trenchant, vitriolic, virulent.

acrimonious *adj.* **bitter,** caustic, cutting, sarcastic, harsh, sharp, acid, acerbic, virulent, trenchant, stringent, spiteful, crabbed, vitriolic, venomous, irascible.

act *n.* **1 deed,** action, feat, performance, undertaking, operation, execution, exploit, enterprise, achievement, accomplishment. **2 bill,** law, decree, statute, edict, dictum, enactment, resolution, ruling, judgment, ordinance, measure, ukase. **3 division,** part, section, segment. **4 performance,** turn, routine, show, sketch, skit. **5 pretense,** sham, fake, make-believe, show, feigning, affectation, counterfeit, front, posture, pose.

▶ *v.* **1 take action,** do, move, be active, perform, function, react, behave, be employed, be busy, work, take effect, operate, function, be efficacious. **2 perform,** play, play a part, be an actor/actress, be one of the cast, portray, enact, represent, characterize, personify, stage, *inf.* tread the boards. **3 pretend,** fake, feign, pose.

acting *n.* **1 the theater,** drama, the performing arts, dramatics, stagecraft, theatricals, performing, portraying. **2 taking action,** moving, functioning, reacting, action, working, taking effect. **3 performance,** playing, portrayal, enacting. **4 pretending,**

pretense, faking, feigning, play-acting, posturing.

▸ *adj.* **deputy,** substitute, temporary, interim, provisional, pro tem, pro tempore, *inf.* fill-in.

action *n.* **1 act,** deed, move, effort, operation, performance, undertaking, maneuver, endeavor, exertion, exploit, acting, activity, doing, movement, motion, operating, work, working, functioning. **2 activity,** energy, vitality, vigor, forcefulness, spirit, liveliness, vim, *inf.* get-up-and-go. **3 effect,** influence, power, result, consequence. **4 activity,** events, happenings, incidents, episodes, excitement, bustle, *inf.* goings-on. **5 conflict,** combat, warfare, fighting, battle, engagement, clash, encounter, skirmish, affray. **6 lawsuit,** case, prosecution, litigation, legal proceedings.

activate *v.* **switch on,** turn on, start, set going, trigger (off), set in motion, energize, actuate, motivate, stimulate, move, drive, rouse, prompt.

active *adj.* **1 working,** functioning, operating, operative, in action, in operation, in force, effective, effectual, operational, powerful, potent, nonpassive, noninert. **2 mobile,** energetic, vigorous, vital, sprightly, lively, spry, busy, bustling, occupied, involved, *inf.* on the go/move. **Ant.** inactive; dormant; inert.

activity *n.* **1 action,** bustle, hustle and bustle, liveliness, movement, life, stir, animation, commotion, flurry, tumult, functioning, mobility, effectiveness, vigor, strength, potency, *inf.* comings and goings. **2 interest,** hobby, business, pastime, pursuit, occupation, venture, undertaking, enterprise, project, scheme.

actual *adj.* **real,** true, factual, genuine, authentic, verified, confirmed, veritable, existing.

acute *adj.* **1 sharp,** keen, penetrating, discerning, sensitive, incisive, astute, shrewd, clever, smart, discerning, perceptive, perspicacious, piercing, discriminating, sagacious, judicious. **2 severe,** critical, crucial, grave, serious, urgent, pressing, vital, dangerous, precarious. **3 sharp,** shooting, piercing, keen, penetrating, stabbing, intense, excruciating, fierce, racking, *fml.* exquisite. **4 intense,** severe, short and sharp, short-lasting. **Ant.** dull; chronic.

adapt *v.* **1 adjust,** tailor, convert, change, alter, modify, transform, remodel, reshape. **2 adjust,** conform, acclimatize, accommodate, familiarize oneself with, habituate oneself.

add *v.* **1 include,** put on/in, attach, append, affix, *fml.* adjoin. **2 add up,** add together, total, count, count up, compute. **3 go on to say,** state further, *inf.* tack on. **Ant.** deduct; remove; subtract.

addict *n.* **1 abuser,** user, *inf.* junkie, head, fiend. **2 fan,** enthusiast, devotee, follower, adherent, *inf.* buff, freak, nut.

addiction *n.* **dependency,** craving, devotion, obsession, dedication, enslavement, habit.

addition *n.* **1 inclusion,** adding on, attachment, appendage. **2 adding up,** counting, totaling, computation, calculation. **3 increase,** increment, extension, augmentation, gain, supplement, appendage.

additional *adj.* **extra,** supplementary, further, more, other, over and above, fresh, supplemental.

address *n.* **1 inscription,** label, superscription, directions. **2 house,** home, location, place, residence, abode, domicile, dwelling, situation, whereabouts. **3 speech,** lecture, talk, dissertation, discourse, oration, sermon, harangue, diatribe. ▸ *v.* **1 direct,** label, inscribe, superscribe, send, communicate, convey, forward, remit. **2 talk to,** speak to, give a talk to, make a speech to, lecture, give a discourse/dissertation/oration to, preach to, declaim to, harangue, greet, hail, salute. **3 name,** call, speak to, write, describe, designate, *fml.* denominate. **4 take aim at,** aim at, face.

adept *adj.* **expert,** clever, proficient, skillful, accomplished, brilliant, talented, first-rate, masterly, *inf.* top-notch, A-1.

adequate *adj.* **1 sufficient,** enough, ample, reasonable, satisfactory, requisite. **2 passable,** tolerable, acceptable, fair, middle-of-the-road, mediocre, unexceptional, indifferent, average, so-so, minimal, *inf.* nothing to write home about, no great shakes. **Ant.** inadequate; insufficient.

adhere *v.* **stick,** cling, hold fast, be fixed, be pasted/glued.

adherent *n.* **supporter,** follower, upholder, advocate, disciple, votary, partisan, sectary, member, fan, admirer, follower, enthusiast, devotee, lover, addict, aficionado, *inf.* hanger-on, buff, freak, fiend. ▸ *adj.* **sticky,** sticking, adhering, clinging, viscous, adhesive.

adjacent *adj.* **adjoining,** neighboring, next door, abutting, close, near, bordering, alongside, contiguous, proximate, attached, touching, conjoining.

adjourn *v.* **1 break off,** discontinue, interrupt, suspend, dissolve, postpone, put off, defer, delay, shelve, break, pause, take a recess. **2 withdraw,** retire, retreat, *fml.* repair.

adjournment *n.* **1 breaking-off,** discontinuation, interruption, suspension, postponement, deferment, deferral, delay, shelving, break, pause, recess. **2 withdrawing,** retirement, retreat, *fml.* repairing.

adjust *v.* **1 adapt,** become accustomed, get used (to), accommodate, acclimatize, reconcile oneself, habituate oneself, assimilate. **2 adapt,** rearrange, alter, modify, change, remodel, regulate, modify, fix, repair, rectify, put in working order, set to rights, tune.

administer *v.* **1 manage,** direct, control, conduct, run, govern, operate, superintend, supervise, oversee, preside over. **2 dispense,** hand out, discharge, allot, deal, distribute, mete out, disburse, bestow, provide. **3 apply,** give, dispense, provide, treat with.

admirable *adj.* **worthy,** commendable, praiseworthy, laudable, good, estimable, honorable, excellent, superb, brilliant, first-rate, first-class, supreme, great, fine, masterly, marvelous.

admiration *n.* **1 approval,** regard, high regard, respect, approbation, appreciation, praise, esteem, veneration. **2 object of admiration,** pride, pride and joy, wonder, delight, marvel, sensation.

admire *v.* **approve of,** respect, think highly of, appreciate, applaud, praise, hold in high regard/esteem, venerate, like, compliment, sing the praises of, be taken with, adore, love, be enamored of, idolize, *inf.* carry a torch for. **Ant.** disapprove; despise.

admissible *adj.* **allowable,** allowed, permissible, permitted, acceptable, passable, justifiable, tolerable.

admission *n.* **1 admittance,** entry, right of entry, entrance, access, entrée, *fml.* ingress. **2 entrance fee,** entry charge, ticket, cover charge. **3 acknowledgment,** confession, revelation, disclosure, divulgence, expression, declaration, utterance, avowal.

admit *v.* **1 let in,** allow/permit entry to, give access to. **2 acknowledge,** confess, reveal, make known, disclose, divulge, declare, avow, concede, accept, grant, acknowledge, agree, allow, concur. *Ant.* exclude; prohibit; deny.

admonish *v.* **reprimand**, rebuke, scold, reprove, upbraid, chide, censure, berate, advise, urge, caution, warn, counsel, exhort.

adopt *v.* **1 take as one's own child,** be adoptive parents to, take in, take care of. **2 assume**, take on, take over, affect, embrace, espouse, appropriate. **3 select,** choose, vote for. **4 approve,** endorse, accept, ratify, sanction, support, back.

adore *v.* **1 love,** be devoted to, dote on, cherish, hold dear, idolize, worship, like, be fond of, enjoy, delight in, take pleasure in, relish. **2 worship,** glorify, praise, revere, reverence, exalt, magnify, laud, extol, esteem, venerate. *Ant.* hate; loathe; detest.

adorn *v.* **decorate,** embellish, add ornament to, ornament, trim, enhance, beautify, enrich, bedeck, deck, array, grace, emblazon.

adrift *adj.* **1 drifting,** unmoored, unanchored. **2 aimless,** purposeless, without purpose/goal, directionless, unsettled, rootless. **3 wrong,** awry, amiss, astray, off course.

adult *adj.* **1 mature,** grown-up, fully grown, full-grown, fully developed, *fml.* of age. **2 sexually explicit,** obscene, pornographic.

adulterate *v.* **make impure,** debase, degrade, spoil, contaminate, taint, doctor, water down, weaken, bastardize, *fml.* vitiate.

advance *v.* **1 go/come/move forward,** proceed, go ahead, move along, press on, push forward, make progress, make headway, forge ahead, gain ground. **2 speed up,** accelerate, step up, hasten, expedite, hurry, quicken, forward. **3 further,** forward, help, assist, facilitate, promote, boost, improve, benefit, foster. **4 put forward,** suggest, propose, submit, recommend, present, introduce, offer, proffer. **5 lend,** supply on credit. *Ant.* retreat; postpone; impede.
▸ *n.* **1 progress,** headway. **2 progress,** development, advancement, movement forward, headway, improvement, betterment, furtherance. **3 development,** discovery, breakthrough, finding, invention. **4 down payment,** deposit, retainer.

advanced *adj.* **progressive,** forward, highly developed, modern, ultramodern, avant-garde, ahead of the times.

advantage *n.* **1 benefit,** asset, good point, boon, blessing.

2 benefit, superiority, dominance, ascendancy, supremacy, power, mastery, upper hand, trump card.
3 benefit, profit, gain, good. *Ant.* disadvantage; handicap; detriment.

advantageous *adj.* **1 favorable,** superior, dominant, powerful.
2 beneficial, of benefit, helpful, of assistance, useful, valuable, of service, profitable.

adventure *n.* **1 risk,** hazard, danger, peril, gamble, gambling, uncertainty, precariousness.
2 exploit, deed, feat, experience, incident.

adventurous *adj.* **daring,** daredevil, bold, intrepid, audacious, *fml.* adventuresome, venturesome.

adverse *adj.* **1 unfavorable,** unlucky, disadvantageous, inauspicious, unpropitious, unfortunate, untoward. **2 hostile,** unfriendly, unfavorable, antagonistic, negative, opposing, inimical, antipathetic. **3 harmful,** dangerous, injurious, detrimental, disadvantageous, hurtful. *Ant.* favorable; auspicious; beneficial.

adversity *n.* **1 misfortune,** ill luck, bad luck, trouble, hardship, distress, disaster, suffering, affliction, sorrow, misery, tribulation, woe, hard times.
2 misfortune, mishap, accident, shock, reverse, setback, disaster, catastrophe, tragedy, calamity, trial.

advertise *v.* **1 make known/public,** publicize, give publicity to, announce, broadcast, proclaim, call attention to.
2 promote, publicize, give publicity to, call attention to, display, tout, promulgate, *inf.* push, plug.

advertisement *n.* **1 notice,** announcement, *inf.* ad, display ad, want ad, classified ad.
2 promotion, commercial, blurb, *inf.* ad, plug. **3 advertising,** promotion, publicizing, touting, *inf.* plugging, pushing.

advice *n.* **1 guidance,** counseling, counsel, help, recommendations, suggestions, hints, tips, ideas, opinions, views. **2 notification,** communication, information, data.

advisable *adj.* **desirable,** best, wisest, sensible, sound, prudent, proper, appropriate, suitable, fitting, apt, judicious, recommended, suggested, expedient, politic.

advise *v.* **1 give guidance to,** guide, counsel, give counsel to, give recommendations to, offer suggestions/opinions to, give hints/tips to, instruct, suggest, recommend, urge. **2 inform,**

notify, give notice to, apprise,
acquaint with, warn.

advocacy *n.* **advising,**
recommending, support (for),
backing, arguing/argument (for),
promotion.

advocate *v.* **recommend,** advise,
favor, support, uphold, back,
subscribe to, champion, speak
for, campaign on behalf of, argue/
plead/press for, urge, promote.
▸ *n.* **1 supporter,** upholder,
backer, champion, spokesman,
spokeswoman, spokesperson,
speaker, campaigner, pleader,
promoter, proponent, exponent,
apostle, apologist. **2 counsel,**
lawyer, attorney.

affable *adj.* **friendly,** amiable,
genial, congenial, cordial,
pleasant, agreeable, easygoing,
good-humored, good-natured,
kindly, courteous, civil,
approachable, sociable.

affair *n.* **1 concern,** business,
matter, responsibility. **2 event,**
happening, occurrence, incident,
episode, circumstance, adventure,
case. **3 party,** function, reception,
gathering, *inf.* get-together, do.
4 love affair, extramarital affair,
relationship, romance, liaison,
affair of the heart, intrigue,
amour.

affect¹ *v.* **1 have an effect on,**
influence, act on, work on, have
an impact on, change, alter,
transform. **2 attack,** strike at,
infect, take hold of. **3 move,**
touch, upset, disturb, trouble,
perturb, agitate, stir, tug at the
heartstrings.

affect² *v.* **1 assume,** put on,
adopt, like, have a liking for,
espouse. **2 pretend,** feign, fake,
simulate.

affectation *n.* **pretense,**
pretension, pretentiousness,
affectedness, artificiality,
insincerity, posturing, airs,
posing, façade, show, appearance,
false display, pretense, feigning,
simulation.

affected *adj.* **1 pretentious,**
artificial, unnatural, assumed,
high-flown, ostentatious,
contrived, studied, pompous,
mannered. **2 put on,** pretended,
feigned, fake, counterfeit, sham,
simulated.

affecting *adj.* **moving,** touching,
poignant, upsetting, pathetic,
heart-rending.

affection *n.* **love,** liking,
fondness, warmth, devotion,
caring, attachment, friendship,
amity, warm feelings.

affectionate *adj.* **loving,** fond,
devoted, caring, tender, doting,
friendly.

affinity *n.* **1 likeness,** similarity,
resemblance, correspondence,

analogy, similitude, relationship, connection. **2 liking,** fondness, attraction, inclination, rapport, sympathy, partiality, penchant, predilection.

affirm *v.* **state,** assert, declare, aver, proclaim, pronounce, swear, attest.

affirmation *n.* **statement,** assertion, declaration, averment, proclamation, pronouncement, swearing, attestation.

affirmative *adj.* **assenting,** consenting, agreeing, concurring, corroborative, favorable, approving, positive. ***Ant.*** dissenting; negative.

afflict *v.* **trouble,** burden, distress, beset, harass, oppress, torment, plague, rack, smite.

affluence *n.* **wealth,** prosperity, opulence, fortune, richness, riches, resources.

affluent *adj.* **rich,** wealthy, prosperous, opulent, well off, moneyed, well-to-do, comfortable, *inf.* well-heeled, in the money, loaded.

afford *v.* **1 pay for,** meet the expense of, spare the price of, manage. **2 bear,** sustain, stand. **3 provide,** supply, offer, give, impart, bestow, furnish.

afraid *adj.* **1 frightened,** scared, terrified, apprehensive, fearful, nervous, alarmed (at), intimidated (by), terror-stricken. **2 sorry,** regretful, apologetic, unhappy.

aftermath *n.* **aftereffects,** effects, consequences, results, end result, outcome, upshot, issue, end.

age *n.* **1 number of years,** lifetime, duration, stage of life, generation, years. **2 maturity,** seniority, elderliness, oldness, old age, advancing years, declining years, *fml.* senescence. **3 era,** epoch, period, time.
▶ *v.* **mature,** ripen, grow up, come of age, grow old, decline, wither, fade, become obsolete.

aged *adj.* **old,** elderly, superannuated, *fml.* senescent, *inf.* as old as the hills.

agent *n.* **1 representative,** negotiator, emissary, envoy, factor, go-between, *inf.* rep. **2 spy,** secret agent, *inf.* mole. **3 factor,** cause, instrument, vehicle, means, power, force.

aggravate *v.* **1 worsen,** make worse, exacerbate, inflame, intensify, increase, heighten, magnify. **2 annoy,** irritate, anger, exasperate, provoke, irk, vex, get on one's nerves, rub the wrong way, *inf.* needle. ***Ant.*** alleviate; improve; calm; mollify.

aggressive *adj.* **1 quarrelsome,** argumentative, belligerent, pugnacious, militant, warring, hostile, combative, bellicose, invasive, intrusive. **2 hostile,** belligerent, warring, combative, bellicose, invasive, intrusive. **3 assertive,** forceful, insistent, vigorous, energetic, dynamic, bold, enterprising, zealous, *inf.* pushy. **Ant.** peaceable; friendly; retiring.

aggrieved *adj.* **1 upset,** resentful, angry, distressed, disturbed, piqued, *inf.* peeved, miffed. **2 wronged,** injured, abused, harmed, mistreated, ill-used.

agile *adj.* **active,** nimble, spry, lithe, fit, supple, sprightly, lively, quick-moving, limber, alert, sharp, acute, clever, quick-witted. **Ant.** inactive; stiff.

agitate *v.* **1 upset,** work up, perturb, fluster, ruffle, disconcert, disquiet, flurry, trouble, worry. **2 stir,** whisk, beat, churn, shake, toss. **3 stir up,** rouse, arouse, disturb, perturb, excite, inflame, incite, foment.

agitator *n.* **troublemaker,** instigator, agent provocateur, inciter, rabble-rouser, provoker, fomenter, firebrand, revolutionary, demagogue.

agonizing *adj.* **excruciating,** harrowing, racking, painful, acute, searing, insufferable, piercing, unendurable, torturous, tormenting, *lit.* exquisite.

agony *n.* **suffering,** pain, hurt, distress, torture, torment, anguish, misery, woe, pangs, throes.

agreeable *adj.* **1 pleasant,** pleasing, delightful, enjoyable, pleasurable, to one's liking, likable, charming, amiable, nice, friendly, good-natured. **2 willing,** amenable, compliant, consenting, assenting, accommodating, tractable. **Ant.** disagreeable; unpleasant; unwilling.

agreement *n.* **1 accord,** assent, concurrence, harmony, accordance, unity, concord. **2 contract,** compact, treaty, covenant, pact, bargain, settlement, proposal, *inf.* deal, *fml.* concordat. **3 matching,** similarity, accordance, correspondence, conformity, coincidence, harmony.

agriculture *n.* **farming,** husbandry, animal husbandry, cultivation, tillage, horticulture, agribusiness, agronomics, agronomy.

aground *adv./adj.* **beached,** grounded, ashore, stuck, shipwrecked, on the ground/bottom.

aid *v.* **help,** assist, support, lend a hand, succor, sustain, second, speed up, hasten, facilitate, expedite, encourage, promote. **Ant.** hinder; impede; discourage.

▸ *n.* **1 help,** assistance, support, a helping hand, succor, encouragement. **2 contribution,** subsidy, gift, donation. *Ant.* hindrance; obstruction.

ailing *adj.* **ill,** unwell, sick, sickly, poorly, weak, indisposed, under the weather.

ailment *n.* **illness,** disease, disorder, sickness, complaint, infection.

aim *v.* **1 point,** direct, take aim, train, sight, focus, position. **2 plan,** intend, resolve, propose, purpose, design.
▸ *n.* **1 pointing,** directing, training, line of sight. **2 goal,** ambition, objective, object, end, target, intention, plan, purpose, aspiration, resolve, proposal, design, desire, wish.

aimless *adj.* **purposeless,** pointless, goalless, futile, undirected, objectless, unambitious, drifting, wandering. *Ant.* purposeful; determined.

air *n.* **1 atmosphere,** sky, heavens, aerospace. **2 breeze,** breath of air, gust/movement of wind, zephyr, draft. **3 impression,** appearance, look, atmosphere, mood, quality, ambience, aura, manner, bearing, character, feeling, flavor, effect, tone. **4 tune,** melody, song, theme, strain.
▸ *v.* **1 ventilate,** aerate, freshen.

2 make public, publicize, express, voice, publish, vent, disseminate, circulate, communicate, broadcast, reveal, proclaim, divulge.

airless *adj.* **stuffy,** close, stifling, suffocating, unventilated, sultry, muggy, oppressive.

airy *adj.* **1 breezy,** windy, gusty. **2 well-ventilated,** spacious, open. **3 delicate,** insubstantial, ethereal, flimsy, wispy, incorporeal, vaporous. **4 lighthearted,** breezy, flippant, blithe, gay, jaunty, nonchalant, insubstantial, cheerful.

aisle *n.* **passageway,** passage, corridor, path, lane, alley.

akin *adj.* **similar,** related, close, near, alike, comparable, equivalent, corresponding. *Ant.* unlike.

alacrity *n.* **readiness,** promptness, willingness, eagerness, enthusiasm, haste, swiftness.

alarm *n.* **1 warning sound/device,** alarm signal, alarm bell, danger/distress signal, siren, alert. **2 fear,** fright, terror, apprehension, panic, trepidation, nervousness, anxiety, unease, distress, consternation, disquiet, perturbation.
▸ *v.* **1 frighten,** scare, terrify, panic, startle, unnerve, distress,

intimidate. **2 warn,** alert, arouse, signal.

alcohol *n.* **strong drink,** liquor, intoxicating liquor, spirits, *inf.* booze, firewater, hooch, rotgut, hard stuff.

alcoholic *adj.* **intoxicating,** inebriating, strong, hard.
▸ *n.* **alcohol addict,** dipsomaniac, hard/heavy drinker, drunk, drunkard, tippler, sot, toper, inebriate, imbiber, *inf.* boozer, lush, alky, wino.

alert *adj.* **wide awake,** sharp, bright, quick, keen, perceptive, *inf.* on the ball, on one's toes. **Ant.** slow; inattentive; oblivious.

alibi *n.* **defense,** plea, justification, explanation, reason, vindication, excuse, pretext.

alien *adj.* **1 foreign,** overseas, nonnative, unnaturalized, strange, unfamiliar, unknown, outlandish, remote, exotic.
2 opposed, conflicting, contrary, adverse, incompatible, unacceptable, repugnant, hostile, antagonistic, inimical.
▸ *n.* **1 foreigner,** outsider, stranger. **2 extraterrestrial,** *inf.* E.T., little green man.

alight[1] *adj.* **1 on fire,** ablaze, burning, lighted, lit, blazing, flaming, ignited. **2 lit up,** shining, bright, brilliant, illuminated.

alight[2] *v.* **get off,** dismount, disembark, descend, land, come down, come to rest, touch down, settle, perch. **Ant.** get on (see get); board; fly off (see fly).

align *v.* **1 line up,** arrange, arrange in line, put in order, straighten. **2 affiliate,** ally, associate, join, cooperate, side, sympathize, agree.

alike *adj.* **like,** similar, the same, indistinguishable, resembling, identical, interchangeable, corresponding.
▸ *adv.* **similarly,** the same, just the same, in the same way, identically, in like manner.

alive *adj.* **1 living,** live, breathing, *inf.* in the land of the living, alive and kicking, kicking, *fml.* animate. **2 active,** continuing, going on, existing, extant, prevalent, functioning, in the air/wind, in existence, in operation, *fml.* existent. **3 full of life,** lively, active, energetic, alert, animated, vivacious, vigorous, spry, sprightly, vital, zestful, spirited. **4 alert to,** awake to, aware/cognizant of. **5 overflowing,** teeming, crowded, packed, bristling, swarming, thronged, bustling, *inf.* crawling, hopping. **Ant.** dead; extinct; inactive.

allay *v.* **lessen,** diminish, reduce, relieve, calm, lull, alleviate, assuage, appease, quell, check, mitigate.

allegation *n.* **claim,** charge, accusation, professing, declaration, statement, assertion, averment, avowal, deposition, plea, affirmation.

allege *v.* **claim,** profess, declare, state, assert, aver, avow, affirm.

alleged *adj.* **supposed,** so-called, claimed, professed, declared, stated, designated.

allegiance *n.* **loyalty,** obedience, fidelity, faithfulness, duty, devotion, constancy, adherence, homage, *fml.* fealty.

allergic *adj.* **1 hypersensitive,** sensitive, susceptible. **2 averse,** opposed, loath, hostile, antagonistic, disinclined.

alleviate *v.* **reduce,** lessen, diminish, relieve, ease, allay, abate, mitigate, assuage, palliate.

alliance *n.* **1 union,** association, coalition, league, confederation, federation, partnership, affiliation. **2 affinity,** association, relationship.

allot *v.* **1 set aside,** designate, earmark, assign, appropriate. **2 allocate,** distribute, give out, dispense, apportion.

allow *v.* **1 permit,** give permission to, let, authorize, sanction, *inf.* give the go-ahead to, give the green light to. **2 allocate,** allot,

grant, give, assign, remit, spare. **3 admit,** acknowledge, concede, grant, own, confess, agree. *Ant.* prevent; forbid; deny.

allowance *n.* **1 remittance,** payment, subsidy, grant, contribution. **2 allocation,** quota, share, ration, portion. **3 rebate,** discount, deduction, reduction, concession.

alloy *n.* **compound,** mixture, amalgam, blend, combination, admixture, composite.

allude *v.* **refer to,** suggest, hint at, imply, make an allusion to.

allure *v.* **attract,** fascinate, entice, seduce, charm, enchant, bewitch, beguile, captivate, tempt, lure.

allusion *n.* **reference,** citation, mention, hint, intimation, suggestion.

ally *n.* **confederate,** partner, associate, accomplice, colleague, friend, helper, accessory, abettor. *Ant.* enemy; opponent; adversary.
▸ *v.* **unite,** join, join forces, band together, go into partnership, combine, go into league, affiliate, form an alliance.

almighty *adj.* **1 all-powerful,** omnipotent, supreme, most high. **2 terrible,** awful, dreadful, great, extreme.

almost *adv.* **nearly,** close to, just about, not quite, all but, not far from, approximately, practically, as good as, virtually, approaching, verging on, bordering on.

alone *adj./adv.* **1 by oneself,** solitary, unaccompanied, unattended, unescorted, companionless, solitary, lonely, deserted, abandoned, forsaken, forlorn, desolate, isolated, by itself, separate, detached, apart, unconnected. **2 by oneself,** single-handed, single-handedly, unassisted, unaided. **3 unique,** unparalleled, unequaled, unsurpassed, matchless, peerless. **4 only,** solely, just, exclusively, no one else but, nothing but.

aloof *adv.* **at a distance,** apart, separately, distanced, at arm's length.
▸ *adj.* **distant,** detached, unresponsive, remote, unapproachable, standoffish, indifferent, unsympathetic, unsociable, unfriendly, cold, chilly.

aloud *adv.* **out loud,** audibly, clearly, distinctly, plainly, intelligibly.

already *adv.* **1 by this time,** by now, before, before now, previously. **2 as early as this,** as soon as this, so soon, so early.

also *adv.* **too,** as well, besides, in addition, additionally, on top of that, to boot, besides, furthermore, moreover, and, plus.

alter *v.* **change,** make different, adjust, adapt, modify, convert, reshape, remodel, vary, transform, transfigure, diversify, metamorphose.

alteration *n.* **change,** adjustment, adaptation, modification, conversion, variation, revision, amendment, transformation, transfiguration, metamorphosis.

alternate *adj.* **1 every other,** every second. **2 in rotation,** rotating, occurring in turns, interchanging, following in sequence, sequential.
3 alternative, different.
▸ *v.* **take turns,** rotate, interchange, oscillate.

alternative *adj.* **1 another,** other, second, different. **2 nonstandard,** unconventional, nonconventional.
▸ *n.* **choice,** option, preference, election, substitute.

alternatively *adv.* **on the other hand,** otherwise, instead, if not, or, as an alternative.

although *conjunction* **though,** even though, even if, even supposing, despite the fact that, while, albeit, notwithstanding the fact that.

altogether *adv.* **1 completely,** thoroughly, totally, entirely, absolutely, fully, utterly, perfectly, quite. **2 on the whole,** all things considered, all in all, by and large, in general, in the main. **3 in all,** all told, in toto, taken together, in sum. *Ant.* partially; relatively.

always *adv.* **1 every time,** on every occasion, consistently, invariably, without exception, regularly, repeatedly, unfailingly. **2 continually,** constantly, forever, repeatedly, perpetually, incessantly, eternally, forever and ever, evermore, ever, everlastingly, endlessly. **3 whatever the circumstances,** no matter what, in any event, in any case, come what may. *Ant.* seldom; never; temporarily.

amalgamate *v.* **combine,** merge, unite, integrate, fuse, blend, mingle, intermingle, mix, intermix, incorporate, *lit.* commingle.

amass *v.* **collect,** gather, accumulate, pile/heap up, hoard, store up, assemble, garner, *inf.* stash away.

amateur *n.* **nonprofessional,** dilettante, layman, tyro, dabbler. *Ant.* professional; expert.

amateurish *adj.* **unprofessional,** unskillful, inexperienced, inexpert, incompetent, clumsy, crude, bungling.

amaze *v.* **astonish,** astound, surprise, dumbfound, flabbergast, daze, shock, stun, startle, bewilder, stupefy, *inf.* bowl over, strike dumb.

amazement *n.* **astonishment,** surprise, shock, bewilderment, stupefaction, wonder.

ambassador *n.* **diplomat,** consul, envoy, emissary, legate, attaché, plenipotentiary, representative, deputy.

ambiguous *adj.* **1 equivocal,** ambivalent, two-edged. **2 cryptic,** obscure, doubtful, dubious, unclear, vague, uncertain, indefinite, abstruse, puzzling, perplexing, enigmatic, paradoxical, nebulous. *Ant.* clear; unequivocal; definite.

ambition *n.* **1 desire,** aspiration, drive, striving, force, enterprise, eagerness, zeal, longing, yearning, hankering, *inf.* get-up-and-go, oomph. **2 goal,** aim, objective, purpose, intent, desire, wish, design, end, dream, hope.

ambitious *adj.* **1 aspiring,** forceful, enterprising, zealous, purposeful, assertive, designing, *inf.* pushy. **2 challenging,** demanding, exacting, formidable, arduous, difficult, bold. *Ant.* aimless; apathetic; easy.

ambivalent *adj.* **equivocal,** uncertain, doubtful, indecisive, inconclusive, irresolute, unresolved, hesitating, fluctuating, vacillating, mixed, opposing, conflicting, clashing. *Ant.* unequivocal; certain; conclusive.

ambush *n.* **1 hiding,** concealment, cover, shelter. **2 trap,** snare, pitfall, lure.
▸ *v.* **waylay,** lay a trap for, lie in wait for, trap, entrap, ensnare, decoy.

amenable *adj.* **1 tractable,** agreeable, responsive, pliant, flexible, persuadable, adaptable, acquiescent, manageable, susceptible. **2 accountable,** answerable, subject, liable, responsible. *Ant.* inflexible; obstinate.

amend *v.* **1 revise,** alter, correct, modify, change, adjust. **2 improve,** remedy, ameliorate, better, fix, set right, repair, enhance.

amenity *n.* **1 facility,** service, convenience, resource, advantage. **2 pleasantness,** agreeableness, pleasurableness, enjoyableness, niceness.

amiable *adj.* **friendly,** pleasant, agreeable, pleasing, charming, delightful, good-natured, sociable, genial, congenial. *Ant.* unfriendly; disagreeable.

amnesty *n.* **general pardon,** pardon, pardoning, reprieve, absolution, forgiveness, dispensation, indulgence.

amorous *adj.* **loving,** passionate, sexual, lustful, erotic, amatory.

amorphous *adj.* **formless,** unformed, shapeless, unshaped, structureless, unstructured, indeterminate, ill-organized, vague, nebulous, *fml.* inchoate.

amount *v.* phrase: **amount to 1 add up to,** total, come to, run to. **2 equal,** add up to, be equivalent to, correspond to, approximate to. **3 become,** grow/develop/mature into, progress/advance to.
▸ *n.* **1 quantity,** measure, mass, volume, bulk, expanse, extent. **2 total,** grand/sum total, aggregate, *inf.* whole kit and caboodle, whole shebang.

ample *adj.* **1 enough,** sufficient, adequate, plenty (of), more than enough, enough and to spare. **2 plentiful,** abundant, copious, lavish, generous, liberal, profuse, bountiful, plenteous. **3 large,** big, substantial, extensive, wide, spacious, roomy, capacious, commodious. *Ant.* insufficient; scanty; meager.

amplify *v.* **1 increase,** boost, magnify, intensify, heighten, augment, supplement. **2 expand,** enlarge on, elaborate on, add to, develop, flesh out, go into detail about, expound on, explicate. *Ant.* reduce; condense.

amputate *v.* **cut off,** sever,

remove, excise, lop, lop off, dismember.

amuse *v.* **1 entertain,** gladden, cheer, please, charm, delight, divert, beguile, enliven, regale with. **2 occupy,** interest, entertain, divert, absorb, engross. *Ant.* bore; depress.

amusement *n.* **1 mirth,** laughter, fun, merriment, gaiety, hilarity, enjoyment, pleasure, delight. **2 entertainment,** diversion, interest, recreation, sport, pastime, hobby, entertainment, diverting.

amusing *adj.* **humorous,** funny, comical, witty, entertaining, hilarious, facetious, droll, jocular. *Ant.* boring; tedious; solemn.

analogous *adj.* **similar,** parallel, comparable, like, corresponding, related, kindred, matching, equivalent.

analysis *n.* **1 breakdown,** dissection, fractionation, decomposition, assay, examination, *fml.* anatomization. **2 study,** examination, investigation, inquiry, dissection, review, evaluation, interpretation.

analyze *v.* **1 break down,** dissect, separate out, fractionate, assay, decompose, examine, *fml.* anatomize. **2 study,** examine, investigate, inquire into, dissect, review, evaluate, interpret.

anarchy *n.* **nihilism,** lawlessness, misgovernment, misrule, revolution, riot, disorder, chaos, rebellion, mutiny, tumult, mayhem, insurrection, disorganization. *Ant.* law; order; government.

ancestor *n.* **forebear,** progenitor, forerunner, precursor, prototype. *Ant.* descendants; successor.

ancestry *n.* **lineage,** descent, extraction, parentage, origin, derivation, genealogy, pedigree, blood, stock, ancestors, antecedents, forefathers, forebears, progenitors, family tree.

anchor *n.* **1 mooring,** grapnel. **2 mainstay,** support, protection, stability, security.
▸ *v.* **1 secure by anchor,** secure, fasten, moor. **2 fasten,** attach, connect, bind, affix.

ancient *adj.* **1 earliest,** early, of long ago, primeval, prehistoric, primordial. **2 age-old,** time-worn, antique, long-lived, very old. **3 antiquated,** old-fashioned, out of date, outmoded, archaic, bygone, obsolete, passé, superannuated, atavistic. *Ant.* recent; modern; new.

ancillary *adj.* **auxiliary,** secondary, subsidiary, subordinate, accessory, contributory, supplementary, additional, extra, attendant.

anemic *adj.* **weak,** pale, wan, colorless, pallid, ashen, feeble, powerless, impotent, ineffective, ineffectual, enervated, *inf.* bloodless.

angelic *adj.* **1 seraphic,** cherubic, celestial, heavenly, ethereal, *fml.* empyrean. **2 virtuous,** innocent, pure, good, saintly, beautiful, adorable.

anger *n.* **annoyance,** rage, fury, indignation, temper, wrath, exasperation, irritation, vexation, ire, ill humor, irritability, outrage, pique, spleen, *lit.* choler.
▸ *v.* **annoy,** infuriate, enrage, exasperate, irritate, incense, madden, vex, outrage, provoke, nettle, rile, pique, gall. ***Ant.*** pacify; placate.

angle[1] *n.* **1 intersection,** inclination, projection, corner, bend, fork, nook, niche, recess, elbow. **2 slant,** spin, approach, viewpoint, standpoint, point of view, position, opinion.

angle[2] *v.* **fish,** cast, go fishing.

angry *adj.* **annoyed,** furious, infuriated, indignant, enraged, irate, wrathful, exasperated, irritated, irascible, heated, incensed, maddened, ill-humored, hot-tempered, outraged, vexed, provoked, *inf.* mad, hot under the collar, *fml.* choleric. ***Ant.*** calm; pleased.

anguish *n.* **agony,** suffering, torture, torment, pain, distress, misery, sorrow, grief, woe, pangs, throes.

angular *adj.* **1 sharp-cornered,** pointed, V-shaped, Y-shaped, forked, bifurcate. **2 bony,** gaunt, rawboned, rangy, scrawny, spare, skinny, lean.

animal *n.* **beast,** creature, brute, monster, barbarian, savage, fiend, *inf.* swine.
▸ *adj.* **1 animalistic,** zooid, zooidal. **2 carnal,** sensual, fleshly, bodily, physical, brutish, bestial.

animate *v.* **give life to,** enliven, liven up, cheer up, gladden, vitalize, encourage, hearten, inspire, excite, fire, rouse, stir, stimulate, incite, energize, *inf.* pep up.
▸ *adj.* **living,** alive, live, breathing.

animated *adj.* **lively,** energetic, active, vigorous, excited, enthusiastic, spirited, fiery, passionate, dynamic, forceful, vital, fervent, vivacious, buoyant. ***Ant.*** apathetic; inactive; sluggish.

animation *n.* **liveliness,** energy, vigor, excitement, enthusiasm, fieriness, dynamism, passion, forcefulness, vitality, fervor, vivacity, buoyancy, verve, zest, sparkle, *inf.* zing.

annex *v.* **1 add,** attach, join, connect, append, adjoin, affix.

2 take over, occupy, seize, conquer, appropriate, expropriate.
▸ *n.* **extension,** wing, ell.

annihilate *v.* **destroy,** wipe out, exterminate, decimate, eliminate, liquidate, abolish, obliterate, eradicate, extinguish, erase. *Ant.* create; build; establish.

annotate *v.* **gloss,** comment on, explain, interpret, elucidate, explicate.

annotation *n.* **note,** comment, gloss, commentary, footnote, explanation, interpretation, observation, elucidation, explication.

announce *v.* **1 make known/public,** give out, declare, intimate, proclaim, report, disclose, reveal, divulge, publicize, broadcast, publish, advertise, promulgate. **2 give the name of,** name, herald, usher in. **3 signal,** indicate, signify, give notice of, warn, foretell, herald, betoken, augur, portend.

announcement *n.* **declaration,** intimation, proclamation, report, disclosure, statement, bulletin, communiqué, message, information.

announcer *n.* **commentator,** newscaster, broadcaster, reporter, anchor, master of ceremonies, emcee, herald.

annoy *v.* **irritate,** exasperate, vex, ruffle, rile, irk, provoke, displease, anger, madden, rub one the wrong way, get on one's nerves, bother, disturb, pester, worry, harass, trouble, plague, harry, *inf.* get to, bug.

annoyance *n.* **1 irritation,** exasperation, displeasure, anger, vexation, ire. **2 nuisance,** pest, bother, trial, irritant, *inf.* pain, pain in the neck/butt/ass, hassle.

annul *v.* **nullify,** declare null and void, quash, cancel, invalidate, rescind, revoke, repeal, abrogate, void, negate.

anoint *v.* **1 oil,** apply ointment, spread over, smear, rub, embrocate. **2 consecrate,** sanctify, bless, ordain, hallow.

anomalous *adj.* **abnormal,** atypical, irregular, deviant, deviating, aberrant, exceptional, rare, unusual, eccentric, odd, bizarre, peculiar, inconsistent. *Ant.* normal; regular.

anonymous *adj.* **unnamed,** nameless, unidentified, unknown, unspecified, undesignated, unacknowledged, uncredited, unsigned, incognito.

answer *n.* **1 reply,** response, acknowledgment, rejoinder, retort, riposte, reaction, *inf.* comeback. **2 solution,** explanation, resolution.

3 defense, plea, refutation, rebuttal, vindication. **Ant.** question; query; puzzle.

▸ *v.* **1 reply to,** respond to, acknowledge, come back to, react to, riposte. **2 meet,** satisfy, fulfill, fill, measure up to, serve. **3 pay,** suffer, be punished, make amends, make reparation, atone. **4 vouch for,** be responsible for, be accountable for, be liable for, take the blame for, *inf.* take the rap for.

answerable *adj.* **responsible,** accountable, liable.

antagonism *n.* **hostility,** opposition, animosity, antipathy, enmity, rivalry, competition, dissension, friction, conflict.

antagonize *v.* **arouse hostility/enmity in,** alienate, put against, estrange, *fml.* disaffect.

anthem *n.* **1 hymn,** psalm, song of praise, chorale, chant, canticle. **2 song of praise,** paean, state song.

anthology *n.* **collection,** compendium, treasury, compilation, miscellany, selection, *lit.* garland, *fml.* collectanea, ana, analects.

anticipate *v.* **1 expect,** foresee, predict, forecast, count on, look for, prepare for, await, contemplate, look forward to, await, look toward. **2 forestall,** intercept, prevent, nullify, *inf.*

beat one to it, beat to the draw on. **3 antedate,** predate, come/go before, be earlier than.

anticipation *n.* **expectation,** prediction, preparation, awaiting, contemplation, expectancy, hope, hopefulness.

anticlimax *n.* **letdown,** disappointment, comedown, disillusionment.

antics *pl. n.* **pranks,** capers, larks, tricks, romps, frolics, high jinks, horseplay.

antidote *n.* **1 antitoxin. 2 cure,** remedy, corrective, countermeasure, counteragent.

antipathy *n.* **aversion,** hostility, dislike, enmity, opposition, antagonism, animosity, hatred, abhorrence, loathing, repugnance, animus. **Ant.** liking; friendship; rapport.

antiquated *adj.* **out of date,** old-fashioned, outmoded, passé, archaic, obsolete, antediluvian.

antique *adj.* **1 antiquarian,** old, vintage. **2 age-old,** timeworn, early, earliest, prehistoric, primeval, primordial. **3 old-fashioned,** passé.

▸ *n.* **heirloom,** relic, curio, collectible, collector's item.

antiseptic *adj.* **1 disinfectant,** germicidal, bactericidal. **2 sterile,** germ-free, uncontaminated, unpolluted, aseptic, sanitary,

hygienic. **3 clinical,** characterless, undistinguished, unexciting.
▸ *n.* **disinfectant,** germicide, bactericide.

antisocial *adj.* **1 disruptive,** disorderly, lawless, rebellious, asocial. **2 unsociable,** uncommunicative, reserved, unfriendly, withdrawn, retiring.

antithesis *n.* **opposite,** converse, reverse, inverse, other extreme, contrast, reversal.

anxiety *n.* **1 worry,** concern, uneasiness, apprehension, disquiet, nervousness, tenseness, misgiving, angst. **2 eagerness,** desire, longing, yearning, avidity.

anxious *adj.* **1 worried,** concerned, uneasy, apprehensive, fearful, nervous, disturbed, tense. **2 eager,** keen, longing, yearning, avid. *Ant.* carefree; unconcerned; nonchalant.

anyhow *adv.* **1 in any way,** anyway, in any manner, by any means. **2 in any case,** in any event, no matter what. **3 haphazardly,** carelessly, heedlessly, negligently.

apathetic *adj.* **uninterested,** unmoved, unconcerned, unfeeling, unemotional, emotionless, unresponsive, indifferent, impassive, passive, listless, lethargic, languid, phlegmatic, torpid.

apathy *n.* **lack of interest/concern/ feeling/emotion,** unconcern, unresponsiveness, indifference, impassivity, passivity, dispassion, dispassionateness, listlessness, lethargy, languor, torpor. *Ant.* enthusiasm; emotion; passion.

aperture *n.* **opening,** gap, hole, orifice, window, crack, slit, space, chink, fissure, perforation, breach, eye, interstice.

apex *n.* **top,** summit, peak, pinnacle, tip, crest, vertex, acme, zenith, apogee.

apocryphal *adj.* **unverified,** unauthenticated, unsubstantiated, spurious, debatable, questionable, dubious, doubtful, mythical, fictitious, legendary, false, untrue, phony.

apologetic *adj.* **sorry,** regretful, contrite, remorseful, penitent, repentant, rueful. *Ant.* unrepentant; impenitent.

apologize *v.* **say one is sorry,** make an apology, express regret, ask forgiveness, ask for pardon, beg pardon, *inf.* eat humble pie.

apology *n.* **1 expression of regret,** regrets. **2 defense,** vindication, justification, argument, apologia, plea, excuse.

apostle *n.* **1 missionary,** evangelical, evangelist, preacher, teacher, reformer, spreader of the faith/word, *fml.* proselytizer.

2 advocate, supporter, crusader, campaigner, proponent, propagandist, pioneer.

appall *v.* **shock,** dismay, horrify, outrage, astound, alarm.

appalling *adj.* **shocking,** horrifying, frightful, outrageous, terrible, awful, dreadful, ghastly, hideous, harrowing, dire.

apparatus *n.* **1 equipment,** gear, tackle, mechanism, outfit, plant, appliance, machine, device, contraption, instruments, tools. **2 structure,** system, organization, network, setup, hierarchy.

apparel *n.* **clothing,** dress, attire, outfit, wear, costume, garb, habit, clothes, garments, robes, vestments, *inf.* gear, togs, duds.

apparent *adj.* **1 clear,** plain, obvious, evident, discernible, perceivable, perceptible, manifest, patent. **2 seeming,** ostensible, outward, superficial, specious, quasi.

apparition *n.* **1 ghost,** specter, phantom, spirit, *inf.* spook. **2 appearance,** manifestation, materialization, emergence, visitation.

appeal *n.* **1 request,** call, plea, entreaty, petition, supplication, solicitation, *fml.* imploration. **2 reconsideration,** reexamination, review, another opinion. **3 attraction,** attractiveness, allure, charm, interest, fascination, temptation, enticement.

▸ *v.* phrases: **appeal for ask for,** request, put in a plea for, entreat, beg/beseech/plead for, implore, solicit, petition for. **appeal to 1 apply for an appeal,** seek reconsideration/reexamination/review/another opinion from. **2 attract,** charm, interest, engage, fascinate, tempt, entice, allure, invite.

appear *v.* **1 come into view/sight,** emerge, come forth, arrive, turn/show/crop up, materialize, surface, loom, come into being/existence, come out, become available, come on the market, be published/produced. **2 attend,** be present, turn up, *inf.* show up, show. **3 seem,** look, have the appearance/air of being, give the impression of being. **4 perform,** play, act, take part, be on stage, come on. *Ant.* disappear; vanish.

appearance *n.* **1 coming into view,** emergence, arrival, advent, materialization, surfacing, looming. **2 attendance,** presence, turning up. **3 look,** air, expression, impression, manner, demeanor, bearing, aspect, *lit.* mien. **4 semblance,** guise, show, pretense, image, outward appearance, front, impression.

appease *v.* **1 placate,** pacify, make peace with, conciliate, calm, tranquilize, soothe, quiet down, mollify, soften, propitiate. **2 satisfy,** assuage, take the edge off, blunt, relieve, quench, diminish.

appendage *n.* **1 addition,** attachment, adjunct, addendum, appurtenance, accessory. **2 extremity,** protuberance, projection, member, limb, tail.

appendix *n.* **supplement,** addendum, postscript, addition, extension, adjunct, codicil.

appetite *n.* **hunger,** taste, palate, desire, relish, thirst, need, liking, inclination, passion, longing, craving, yearning, hankering, zest, gusto, propensity, proclivity.

appetizing *adj.* **mouthwatering,** tasty, succulent, delicious, palatable, tempting, inviting, enticing, appealing, alluring.

applaud *v.* **1 clap,** cheer, whistle, *inf.* give someone a big hand. **2 praise,** express admiration/ approval for, admire, compliment on, commend, acclaim, extol, laud. *Ant.* hiss; condemn; censure.

applause *n.* **1 clapping,** handclapping, cheering, whistling, standing ovation, cheers, whistles, encores, bravos, curtain calls. **2 praise,** admiration, approval, approbation, commendation, acclaim, acclamation, compliments, accolades, plaudits, *fml.* extolment, laudation.

appliance *n.* **1 device,** gadget, convenience, apparatus, implement, machine, instrument, tool, mechanism. **2 application,** use.

applicable *adj.* **1 relevant,** appropriate, pertinent, apposite, apropos. **2 fitting,** suitable, useful. *Ant.* inapplicable; irrelevant.

applicant *n.* **candidate,** interviewee, competitor, inquirer, claimant, suppliant, supplicant, petitioner, suitor, postulant.

apply *v.* **1 use,** put to use, employ, utilize, administer, exercise, put into practice, bring into effect/play, bring to bear. **2 be relevant/significant/pertinent,** be apt/apposite/germane, have a bearing on. **3 put on,** rub in, cover with, spread, smear.

appoint *v.* **1 name,** designate, nominate, select, choose, elect, install as. **2 set,** fix, arrange, choose, establish, settle, determine, assign, designate, allot.

appointment *n.* **1 meeting,** engagement, date, interview, arrangement, rendezvous, assignation, *lit.* tryst. **2 job,** post, position, situation, place, office, station. **3 naming,** nomination, selection. **4 setting,** arrangement, establishment.

appreciable *adj.* **considerable,** substantial, significant, sizable, visible, goodly.

appreciate *v.* **1 be appreciative of,** be thankful/grateful for, be indebted/beholden for. **2 value,** hold in high regard, hold in esteem, prize, cherish, treasure, rate highly, respect, think highly of, think much of. **3 recognize,** acknowledge, realize, know, be aware of, be conscious/cognizant of, understand, comprehend, perceive, discern. **4 increase,** gain, grow, rise, mount, inflate, escalate. **Ant.** disparage; ignore; depreciate.

appreciative *adj.* **grateful,** thankful, indebted, obliged, beholden, enthusiastic, responsive, supportive, encouraging, sympathetic, sensitive.

apprehensive *adj.* **anxious,** alarmed, worried, uneasy, nervous, frightened, fearful, mistrustful, concerned.

apprentice *n.* **trainee,** learner, beginner, probationer, pupil, student, cub, greenhorn, tyro, novice, neophyte, *inf.* rookie.

approach *v.* **1 come/go/draw near/nearer/close/closer,** move/edge near/nearer, draw nigh, catch up, gain on, near, advance, push forward, reach, arrive. **2 talk/speak to,** make conversation with, engage in conversation with, greet, address, salute, hail, apply/appeal to, broach the matter to, make advances/overtures to, make a proposal to, sound out, proposition, solicit. **3 set about,** tackle, begin, start, commence, embark on, make a start on, undertake. **4 come near/close to,** approximate, be comparable/ similar to, compare with. **Ant.** leave; avoid.

▸ *n.* **1 nearing,** advance, advent, arrival. **2 driveway,** drive, access road, road, avenue, street, passageway. **3 application,** appeal, proposal, proposition, advances, overtures. **4 approximation,** likeness, semblance. **5 method,** procedure, technique, style, way, manner, mode, modus operandi, means.

appropriate *adj.* **suitable,** fitting, befitting, proper, seemly, right, apt, relevant, pertinent, apposite, applicable, congruous, opportune, felicitous, germane, *fml.* appurtenant. **Ant.** inappropriate; unsuitable; irrelevant.

▸ *v.* **1 take possession of,** take over, seize, commandeer,

expropriate, annex, arrogate.
2 set apart/aside, assign, allot,
allocate, earmark, devote,
apportion. **3 embezzle,**
misappropriate, steal, pilfer, filch,
pocket, purloin, *inf.* pinch, swipe,
fml. peculate.

approval *n.* **1 favor,** liking,
approbation, acceptance,
admiration, appreciation, regard,
esteem, respect, commendation,
applause, acclaim, acclamation,
praise. **2 acceptance,** agreement,
consent, assent, sanction,
endorsement, blessing,
permission, leave, confirmation,
ratification, authorization,
mandate, license, validation,
acquiescence, concurrence, *inf.*
the go-ahead, the green light, the
OK.

approve *v.* **accept,** pass, agree to,
sanction, consent/assent to, ratify,
authorize, validate, accede to,
acquiesce in, concur in, warrant,
inf. give the go-ahead to, give the
OK to, give the green light to, buy.
Ant. condemn; disapprove; reject.

approximate *adj.* **rough,**
estimated, near, close, inexact.
▶ *v.* **come close/near to,** approach,
border on, verge on, resemble, be
similar to.

approximately *adv.* **roughly,**
about, just about, around, circa,
or so, more or less, in the

neighborhood of, in the region of,
nearly, close to, near to, almost.

apt *adj.* **1 suitable,** fitting,
appropriate, applicable, apposite,
felicitous, apropos. **2 inclined,**
given, likely, liable, disposed,
prone, ready, subject. **3 quick to
learn,** quick, bright, sharp, clever,
smart, intelligent, able, gifted,
talented, adept, competent,
astute. **Ant.** inappropriate;
unlikely; slow.

aptitude *n.* **talent,** gift, flair, bent,
skill, knack, ability, proficiency,
quickness, competence,
capability, potential, capacity,
faculty.

arbitrary *adj.* **1 discretionary,**
discretional, personal, subjective,
random, chance, whimsical,
capricious, erratic, inconsistent,
unreasoned, unreasonable,
unsupported, irrational.
2 despotic, tyrannical, tyrannous,
absolute, autocratic, dictatorial,
imperious, domineering, high-
handed. **Ant.** objective; rational;
reasoned.

arbitrate *v.* **adjudicate,** judge,
referee, umpire, adjudge, sit in
judgment, pass judgment, settle,
decide, determine.

arbitration *n.* **adjudication,**
judgment, settlement, decision,
determination.

arbitrator *n.* **adjudicator,** judge, referee, umpire, arbiter.

arc *n.* **curve,** bow, arch, bend, crescent, half-moon, semicircle, circular section/line, curvature.

arch[1] *n.* **archway,** vault, span, arc, bow, curve, semicircle, curvature, convexity.

▸ *v.* **curve,** bow, bend, arc, *fml.* embow.

arch[2] *adj.* **playful,** mischievous, roguish, saucy, artful, sly, knowing, frolicsome.

archetype *n.* **prototype,** original, pattern, model, standard, exemplar, mold, paradigm, ideal.

architect *n.* **1 designer,** planner, building consultant, draftsman. **2 author,** engineer, creator, originator, planner, deviser, instigator, founder, inventor, contriver, prime mover.

ardent *adj.* **passionate,** avid, impassioned, fervent, fervid, zealous, eager, earnest, enthusiastic, emotional, vehement, intense, fierce, fiery, profound, consuming.

arduous *adj.* **taxing,** difficult, hard, onerous, heavy, laborious, burdensome, exhausting, wearying, fatiguing, tiring, strenuous, grueling, punishing, vigorous, tough, formidable, Herculean. ***Ant.*** easy; effortless.

area *n.* **1 region,** district, zone, sector, territory, tract, stretch, quarter, locality, neighborhood, domain, realm, sphere. **2 extent,** size, expanse, scope, compass, range, measurements. **3 field,** sphere, discipline, realm, department, sector, province, domain, territory.

argue *v.* **1 disagree,** quarrel, squabble, bicker, fight, dispute, feud, debate, discuss, controvert. **2 assert,** declare, maintain, insist, hold, claim, contend. **3 persuade,** convince, prevail upon. **4 point to,** indicate, demonstrate, show, suggest, imply, exhibit, denote, be evidence of, display, evince.

argument *n.* **1 disagreement,** quarrel, squabble, fight, difference of opinion, dispute, clash, altercation, controversy, feud, *inf.* tiff, falling out. **2 assertion,** declaration, claim, plea, contention. **3 line of reasoning,** reasoning, logic, case, defense, evidence, argumentation, polemic, reasons, grounds. **4 theme,** topic, subject matter, gist, outline, plot, story line, summary, synopsis, abstract, précis.

argumentative *adj.* **quarrelsome,** belligerent, disputatious, contentious, combative, litigious, *fml.* dissentient.

arid *adj.* **1 dry,** dried up, desert, waterless, moistureless, parched, baked, scorched, dehydrated, desiccated, barren. **2 uninspiring,** unstimulating, dull, dreary, drab, dry, colorless, flat, boring, uninteresting, monotonous, lifeless, tedious, vapid, jejune. *Ant.* wet; fertile; interesting.

arise *v.* **1 appear,** come to light, make an appearance, crop/turn up, spring up, emerge, occur, ensue, set in, come into being/existence, begin. **2 result,** be caused (by), proceed, follow, stem, originate, emanate, ensue. **3 rise,** stand up, get to one's feet, get up. **4 rise,** ascend, go up, mount, climb, fly, soar.

aristocracy *n.* **nobility,** peerage, gentry, upper class, privileged/ruling class, elite, high society, *inf.* upper crust, blue bloods, *lit.* haut monde.

aristocratic *adj.* **1 noble,** titled, blue-blooded, high-born, upper-class, patrician, elite. **2 well-bred,** dignified, courtly, refined, elegant, stylish, gracious, fine, polite, haughty, proud. *Ant.* plebeian; vulgar.

arm[1] *v.* **1 provide,** supply, equip, furnish, issue. **2 prepare,** forearm, make ready, brace, steel, fortify, gird one's loins.

arm[2] *n.* **1 limb,** upper limb, forelimb, member, appendage. **2 inlet,** estuary, channel, branch, strait, sound. **3 branch,** offshoot, section, department, division, sector, detachment, extension. **4 power,** force, authority, strength, might, potency.

armaments *pl. n.* **arms,** weapons, firearms, munitions, weaponry, ordnance, matériel.

armistice *n.* **truce,** ceasefire, peace, suspension of hostilities.

armory *n.* **arms depot,** ordnance depot, arsenal, magazine, ammunition dump.

army *n.* **1 armed/military force,** land force, soldiery, infantry, troops, soldiers, land forces, military. **2 horde,** pack, host, multitude, mob, crowd, swarm, throng, array.

aroma *n.* **smell,** scent, odor, bouquet, fragrance, perfume, redolence.

arouse *v.* **1 rouse,** awaken, waken, wake, wake up. **2 cause,** induce, stir up, inspire, call forth, kindle, provoke, foster, whip up, sow the seeds of. **3 rouse,** incite, excite, provoke, goad, prompt, spur on, urge, encourage, egg on, animate, inflame, build a fire under. **4 excite,** stimulate, *inf.* turn on.

arrange *v.* **1 put in order,** order, set out, group, sort, organize, tidy, position, dispose, marshal, range, align, line up, rank, file, classify, categorize, array, systematize. **2 settle on,** decide, determine, agree, come to an agreement, settle on, come to terms about, plan, schedule, devise, contrive. **3 make preparations,** prepare, plan, organize. **4 score,** adapt, orchestrate, harmonize. *Ant.* disarrange; disturb; cancel.

arrangement *n.* **1 order,** ordering, grouping, organization, positioning, system, disposition, marshalling, ranging, alignment, filing, classification, categorization, array.
2 preparation, plan, provision, agreement, contract, compact.
3 score, adaptation, orchestration, instrumentation, harmonization.

array *n.* **1 collection,** arrangement, assembling, assemblage, lineup, formation, ordering, disposition, muster, amassing, show, display, agglomeration, aggregation.
2 attire, apparel, clothing, dress, garb, finery, garments.
▸ *v.* **1 assemble,** arrange, draw up, group, order, line up, place, position, dispose, muster, amass, agglomerate, aggregate. **2 attire,** clothe, dress, fit out, garb, deck, robe, apparel, *fml.* accouter.

arrest *v.* **1 apprehend,** take into custody, take prisoner, detain, seize, capture, catch, lay hold of, haul in, *inf.* run in, nab, pinch, collar, bust, nail, pick up. **2 stop,** halt, end, bring to a standstill, check, block, hinder, delay, interrupt, prevent, obstruct, inhibit, slow down, retard, nip in the bud, stay. **3 attract,** capture, catch, catch hold of, grip, engage, absorb, occupy, rivet, engross.
▸ *n.* **1 apprehension,** taking into custody, detention, seizure, capture, *inf.* running in.
2 stopping, stoppage, halt, ending, end, check, blocking, hindrance, delay, interruption, prevention, obstruction, retardation.

arresting *adj.* **striking,** impressive, remarkable, extraordinary, unusual, noticeable, outstanding, conspicuous, stunning.

arrival *n.* **1 coming,** advent, appearance, entrance, entry, occurrence, approach.
2 newcomer, visitor, visitant, guest, immigrant.

arrive *v.* **1 come,** appear, put in an appearance, come on the scene, enter, get here/there, happen, occur, present itself, turn/show up, *inf.* blow in. **2 succeed,** make good, reach the top, prosper, flourish, get ahead, become famous, achieve recognition, *inf.* make it, make the grade, get somewhere. **Ant.** depart; leave.

arrogant *adj.* **haughty,** proud, self-important, conceited, egotistic, snobbish, pompous, supercilious, overbearing, overweening, high-handed, condescending, disdainful, imperious, lordly, presumptuous, pretentious, swaggering, blustering, bumptious, insolent, *inf.* stuck-up, uppity, high and mighty. **Ant.** modest; diffident.

art *n.* **1 painting,** drawing, design, visual arts. **2 skill,** craft, aptitude, talent, flair, gift, knack, facility, artistry, mastery, dexterity, expertness, skillfulness, adroitness, cleverness, ingenuity, virtuosity. **3 artfulness,** cunning, deceit, deception, wiliness, slyness, craft, craftiness, guile, trickery, duplicity, artifice, wiles.

artful *adj.* **cunning,** deceitful, wily, sly, crafty, duplicitous, scheming, designing, shrewd, politic, ingenious.

article *n.* **1 object,** thing, item, commodity, *inf.* thingamajig, thingamabob, what-d'ya-call-it, whatchamacallit. **2 item,** piece, story, feature, report, account, write-up. **3 clause,** section, point, paragraph, division, part, passage.

articulate *adj.* **1 eloquent,** fluent, well-spoken, communicative, coherent, lucid, expressive, silver-tongued, vocal. **2 eloquent,** clear, fluent, intelligible, comprehensible, understandable, lucid, coherent. **Ant.** inarticulate; hesitant; unintelligible.

▶ *v.* **1 enunciate,** pronounce, voice, say, utter, express, vocalize.
2 joint, hinge, connect, link, couple.

artifice *n.* **trick,** stratagem, ruse, dodge, subterfuge, machination, maneuver, tactic, device, contrivance, trickery, strategy, cunning, deceit, deception, craftiness, artfulness, wiliness, slyness, duplicity, guile, chicanery.

artificial *adj.* **1 man-made,** manufactured, synthetic, imitation, simulated, pseudo, ersatz, plastic, mock, sham, fake, bogus, counterfeit, *inf.* phony. **2 feigned,** false, affected, unnatural, assumed, pretended, insincere, contrived, forced, labored, strained, hollow, spurious, meretricious, *inf.* phony. **Ant.** natural; genuine; sincere.

artist *n.* **painter,** drawer, sculptor, old master, craftsman, craftswoman, expert, adept, genius, past master, maestro.

artistic *adj.* **1 creative,** talented,

gifted, accomplished, imaginative, sensitive, cultivated. **2 decorative,** beautiful, attractive, lovely, tasteful, graceful, stylish, elegant, exquisite, aesthetic, ornamental. **3 temperamental,** unconventional, bohemian, nonconformist.

artistry *n.* **art,** skill, ability, talent, genius, brilliance, expertness, flair, gift, creativity, proficiency, virtuosity, craftsmanship, workmanship.

ascend *v.* **climb,** go/move up, mount, scale, rise, levitate, fly up, soar, slope upward.

ascertain *v.* **find out,** get to know, ferret out, establish, discover, learn, determine, settle, identify, decide, verify, make certain, confirm, *inf.* pin down.

ascribe *v.* **attribute,** assign, accredit, credit, give credit to, put/set down to, chalk up to, impute, charge with, lay on, blame.

ashamed *adj.* **1 humiliated,** conscience-stricken, sorry, mortified, abashed, crestfallen, shamefaced, remorseful, discomfited, embarrassed, distressed, sheepish, red-faced, blushing, with one's tail between one's legs. **2 reluctant,** unwilling, hesitant, restrained. **Ant.** proud; shameless; pleased.

asinine *adj.* **stupid,** silly, idiotic, foolish, brainless, nonsensical, senseless, halfwitted, fatuous, inane, imbecilic, moronic, *inf.* daft, dopey, balmy, batty, nutty, dumb, gormless.

ask *v.* **1 inquire,** question, put a question to, query, interrogate, quiz, cross-examine, catechize, *inf.* grill, pump, give the third degree to. **2 request,** demand, appeal to, apply to, petition, call upon, entreat, beg, implore, beseech, plead, supplicate. **3 invite,** bid, summon. **Ant.** answer; reply.

asleep *adj./adv.* **1 sleeping,** fast/sound asleep, in a deep sleep, slumbering, napping, catnapping, dozing, resting, reposing, dormant, comatose, *inf.* snoozing, dead to the world, out like a light, *lit.* in the arms of Morpheus. **2 numb,** without feeling, deadened, benumbed. **Ant.** awake.

aspect *n.* **1 feature,** facet, side, angle, slant, viewpoint, standpoint, light. **2 appearance,** look, expression, air, countenance, demeanor, bearing, features, *fml.* mien. **3 direction,** situation, position, location, exposure, outlook. **4 outlook,** view, scene, prospect.

asphyxiate *v.* **choke,** suffocate, smother, stifle, throttle, strangle, strangulate.

aspiration *n.* **desire,** longing,

yearning, hankering, wish, ambition, hope, aim, objective, goal, object, dream, eagerness, enthusiasm.

aspire *v.* **desire,** long to/for, yearn to/for, hanker after, be ambitious for, hope to/for, wish to/for, dream of, hunger for, aim to/for, seek, pursue.

aspiring *adj.* **would-be,** expectant, hopeful, ambitious, enterprising, optimistic, eager, striving, wishful.

assail *v.* **1 attack,** assault, set about, lay into, beset, fall/set upon, accost, mug, charge, *inf.* jump. **2 bombard,** berate, belabor, lash, abuse, criticize, harangue, revile, lambaste, fulminate against, *inf.* sail/light/tear into.

assassin *n.* **murderer,** killer, slayer, executioner, liquidator, *inf.* hit man, contract man.

assassinate *v.* **murder,** kill, slay, execute, liquidate, eliminate, *inf.* hit.

assault *n.* **attack,** onslaught, onset, charge, offensive, act of aggression, storming, violent act, physical/verbal attack, molesting, molestation, threat, threatening.
▸ *v.* **1 attack,** make an onslaught/onset on, charge, undertake an offensive against, storm. **2 attack,** strike, hit, *inf.* lay into. **3 attack,** mug, molest, rape.

assemble *v.* **1 get together,** bring/put together, gather, collect, round up, marshal, muster, summon, congregate, accumulate, amass, rally, convoke. **2 gather,** collect, come together, foregather, meet, congregate, convene, flock together. **3 put together,** piece/fit together, build, fabricate, construct, erect, manufacture, set up, connect, join. *Ant.* disperse; demolish.

assembly *n.* **1 gathering,** meeting, group, body of people, crowd, throng, congregation, convention. **2 putting/fitting together,** building, fabrication, construction, erection, manufacture.

assent *n.* **agreement,** concurrence, acceptance, approval, consent, acquiescence, compliance, approbation, permission, sanction, accord, accordance, accession. *Ant.* dissent; refusal.

assert *v.* **1 declare,** state, announce, maintain, pronounce, proclaim, contend, aver, swear, avow, attest, affirm, allege, claim, postulate. **2 uphold,** press/push for, insist upon, stand up for, defend, vindicate.

assertive *adj.* **positive,** confident, self-assured, dogmatic, aggressive, self-assertive, strong-willed, forceful, dominant, domineering, *inf.* pushy. *Ant.* retiring; bashful; timid.

assess *v.* **1 evaluate,** judge, gauge, rate, estimate, appraise, determine, weigh up, compute. **2 fix,** evaluate, levy, impose, demand, rate.

asset *n.* **advantage,** benefit, blessing, strong point, strength, boon, aid, help. *Ant.* liability; handicap.

assiduous *adj.* **diligent,** industrious, hardworking, studious, persevering, persistent, laborious, unflagging, indefatigable, zealous, sedulous.

assign *v.* **1 allocate,** allot, distribute, give out, dispense, apportion, consign. **2 appoint,** select, install, designate, nominate, name, delegate, commission. **3 fix,** appoint, decide on, determine, set aside/apart, stipulate, appropriate. **4 ascribe,** put down, attribute, accredit, chalk up. **5 transfer,** convey, consign.

assignation *n.* **rendezvous,** tryst, date, appointment, meeting.

assignment *n.* **1 task,** job, duty, commission, charge, mission, responsibility, obligation. **2 allocation,** allotment, dispensation, apportionment,

consignment. **3 appointment,** selection, installation, nomination. **4 ascribing.** **5 transfer,** conveyance, consignment.

assimilate *v.* **1 absorb,** take in, incorporate, digest, ingest. **2 adapt,** adjust, accustom, acclimatize, accommodate, become like/similar, blend in, fit, homogenize.

assist *v.* **1 help,** aid, lend a hand, succor, support, cooperate/ collaborate with, abet, work with, play a part, help out, support, back, second. **2 make easier,** facilitate, expedite. *Ant.* hinder; impede.

assistance *n.* **help,** aid, succor, support, reinforcement, cooperation, collaboration, a helping hand.

assistant *n.* **1 subordinate,** deputy, auxiliary, second in command, *inf.* right-hand man/woman, man/girl Friday, henchman. **2 helper,** colleague, associate, partner, confederate, accomplice, collaborator, accessory, abettor.

associate *v.* **1 link,** connect, relate, think of together, couple. **2 mix,** keep company, mingle, socialize, hobnob, fraternize, *inf.* run around, hang out, pal around. **3 combine,** join, connect, attach, affiliate, band together, ally, syndicate, incorporate, conjoin.

assorted *adj.* **mixed,** varied, variegated, miscellaneous, diverse, diversified, motley, sundry, heterogeneous. *Ant.* homogeneous; similar; identical.

assortment *n.* **mixture,** variety, miscellany, selection, medley, mélange, diversity, jumble, mishmash, hodgepodge, potpourri.

assume *v.* **1 suppose,** take for granted, presuppose, presume, imagine, think, believe, fancy, expect, accept, suspect, surmise, understand, gather, guess. **2 feign,** pretend, simulate, put on. **3 adopt,** take on, acquire, come to have. **4 undertake,** enter upon, begin, set about, take on/up, embark on, take upon oneself, accept, shoulder. **5 seize,** take, take over, appropriate, usurp, preempt, commandeer.

assumption *n.* **1 supposition,** presupposition, presumption, premise, belief, expectation, conjecture, surmise, guess, theory, hypothesis, suspicion, postulation. **2 adoption,** taking on. **3 seizure,** appropriation, usurping. **4 arrogance,** presumption, conceit, impertinence.

assurance *n.* **1 self-assurance,**

self-confidence, confidence, self-reliance, nerve, poise, positiveness. **2 word of honor,** word, guarantee, promise, pledge, vow, oath, affirmation. **3 certainty,** guarantee.

assure *v.* **1 declare to,** affirm to, give one's word to, guarantee, promise, swear to, certify to, pledge to, vow to, attest to. **2 convince,** persuade, reassure, prove to. **3 ensure,** make certain, make sure, secure, guarantee, seal, clinch, confirm.

assured *adj.* **1 self-assured,** self-confident, confident, self-reliant, poised, positive. **2 certain,** sure, guaranteed, secure, reliable, dependable.

astonish *v.* **amaze,** astound, dumbfound, stagger, surprise, stun, take aback, confound, take one's breath away, *inf.* flabbergast, floor.

astonishing *adj.* **amazing,** astounding, staggering, surprising, breathtaking, striking, impressive, bewildering, stunning.

astound *v.* **amaze,** astonish, dumbfound, stagger, surprise.

astray *adv./adj.* **1 off course,** off the right track, adrift, lost. **2 into wrongdoing/error/sin,** to the bad.

astute *adj.* **shrewd,** sharp, acute,

quick, quick-witted, clever,
cunning, artful, ingenious,
perceptive, discerning, crafty,
wily, calculating, perspicacious,
sagacious. *Ant.* stupid; dull.

asylum *n.* **1 refuge,** sanctuary,
shelter, safety, safekeeping,
protection, haven, retreat, harbor,
port in a storm. **2 mental hospital,**
psychiatric hospital, institution,
derog. madhouse, nuthouse, loony
bin, funny farm.

asymmetrical *adj.*
disproportionate,
misproportioned, irregular,
uneven, distorted, malformed,
formless.

atheist *n.* **nonbeliever,**
disbeliever, unbeliever, heretic,
skeptic, heathen, freethinker,
nihilist, infidel.

athletic *adj.* **1 muscular,**
powerful, robust, able-bodied,
sturdy, strong, strapping,
vigorous, hardy, stalwart, well-
built, brawny, thickset,
Herculean. **2 sports,** sporting.

atmosphere *n.* **1 air,** aerosphere,
aerospace, sky, heavens.
2 environment, milieu, medium,
background, setting, air,
ambience, aura, climate, mood,
feeling, character, tone, tenor,
spirit, quality, flavor,
surroundings.

atom *n.* **iota,** jot, bit, whit,
particle, scrap, shred, trace,
speck, spot, dot, crumb, fragment,
grain, morsel, mite.

atone *v.* **make amends/reparation,**
compensate, pay the penalty, pay
for, recompense, expiate, do
penance.

atrocious *adj.* **1 brutal,** barbaric,
barbarous, savage, vicious,
wicked, cruel, ruthless, merciless,
villainous, murderous, heinous,
nefarious, monstrous, inhuman,
infernal, fiendish, diabolical,
flagrant, outrageous. **2 very bad,**
unpleasant, appalling, dreadful,
terrible, shocking.

atrocity *n.* **1 act of brutality/**
barbarity/savagery, crime, offense,
injury, brutality, cruelty,
barbarity. **2 abomination,**
enormity, outrage, horror, evil,
monstrosity, violation.

atrophy *v.* **waste,** waste away,
wither, shrivel up, shrink, dry up,
decay, wilt, decline, deteriorate,
degenerate.

attach *v.* **1 fasten,** fix, affix, join,
connect, couple, link, secure, tie,
stick, adhere, pin, hitch, bond,
add, append, annex, subjoin.
2 ascribe, assign, attribute,
accredit, apply, put, place, lay.
3 seize, confiscate, appropriate,
Law distrain. **4 assign,** second,
allot, allocate, detail, appoint.
Ant. detach; separate.

attached *adj.* **married,** engaged, having a partner, spoken for, *inf.* going steady.

attack *v.* **1 assault,** set/fall upon, strike at, rush, storm, charge, pounce upon, beset, besiege, beleaguer, strike, begin hostilities, affect, infect, *inf.* lay into, let one have it. **2 criticize,** censure, berate, reprove, rebuke, impugn, harangue, find fault with, blame, revile, fulminate against, vilify, *inf.* knock, slam. **3 set about,** get/go to work on, get started on, undertake, embark on. *Ant.* defend; protect; praise.

▸ *n.* **1 assault,** onslaught, offensive, onset, strike, storming, charge, foray, rush, incursion, inroad. **2 criticism,** censure, berating, rebuke, reproval, impugnment, blame, revilement, vilification. **3 start,** beginning, commencement, undertaking, onslaught. **4 fit,** bout, seizure, spasm, convulsion, paroxysm, stroke. *Ant.* defense.

attacker *n.* **assailant,** aggressor, assaulter, striker, mugger.

attain *v.* **achieve,** accomplish, obtain, gain, procure, secure, get, grasp, win, earn, acquire, reach, arrive at, realize, fulfill, succeed in, bring off, be successful.

attempt *v.* **try,** strive, aim, venture, endeavor, seek, undertake, set out, do one's best, take it upon oneself, essay, tackle, have a go/shot at, essay, *inf.* have a crack at give it a whirl.

▸ *n.* **effort,** try, endeavor, venture, trial, experiment, essay, *inf.* crack, go, shot.

attend *v.* **1 be present,** be at, be here/there, appear, put in an appearance, turn up, visit, frequent, haunt, *inf.* show up, show. **2 look after,** take care of, care for, tend, nurse, mind, minister to. **3 accompany,** escort, guard, chaperon, squire, convoy.

attendant *n.* **1 assistant,** helper, auxiliary, steward, waiter, servant, menial. **2 companion,** escort, aide, guard, custodian, guide, usher.

▸ *adj.* **accompanying,** concomitant, related, accessory, resultant, consequent.

attention *n.* **1 concentration,** attentiveness, intentness, notice, observation, heed, heedfulness, regard, contemplation, deliberation, scrutiny, thought, thinking, studying. **2 notice,** awareness, observation, consciousness, heed, recognition, regard. **3 care,** treatment, ministration, therapy. **4 civility,** politeness, courtesy, respect, gallantry, urbanity, deference, compliments.

attentive *adj.* **1 alert,** aware,

awake, watchful, wide awake, observant, noticing, concentrating, heeding, heedful, mindful, vigilant, on guard, *inf.* all ears, *fml.* on the qui vive.
2 considerate, thoughtful, kind, polite, courteous, gracious, conscientious, civil, obliging, accommodating, gallant, chivalrous. *Ant.* inattentive; heedless; discourteous.

attire *n.* **clothing,** dress, wear, outfit, apparel, garb, ensemble, costume, array, habit, wardrobe, clothes, garments, habiliments, accouterments, *inf.* gear, togs, threads, glad rags, duds.
▸ *v.* **dress,** clothe, dress up, garb, robe, array, deck out, costume, *inf.* doll up.

attitude *n.* **1 point of view,** viewpoint, opinion, frame of mind, outlook, perspective, reaction, stance, position, approach, thoughts, ideas.
2 position, stance, pose, stand, bearing, deportment, carriage.

attract *v.* **1 draw,** pull, magnetize.
2 allure, entice, tempt, interest, fascinate, charm, engage, enchant, captivate, bewitch, seduce, inveigle.

attractive *adj.* **1 appealing,** agreeable, pleasing, inviting, tempting, interesting. **2 good-looking,** striking, beautiful, handsome, pretty, stunning, gorgeous, prepossessing, fetching, comely, captivating, charming, fascinating, interesting, appealing, enchanting, alluring. *Ant.* uninviting; ugly; unattractive.

attribute *n.* **1 quality,** feature, characteristic, property, mark, trait, distinction, idiosyncrasy.
2 symbol, indicator, mark, sign, trade mark, status symbol.
▸ *v.* **ascribe,** assign, accredit, put down, chalk up.

attrition *n.* **1 abrasion,** friction, rubbing, chafing, corroding, corrosion, erosion, eating away, grinding, scraping, wearing away, excoriation, detrition. **2 wearing down,** weakening, debilitation, enfeebling, enervation, sapping, attenuation.

attune *v.* **tune,** regulate, modulate, harmonize.

audacious *adj.* **1 bold,** daring, fearless, intrepid, brave, courageous, valiant, adventurous, plucky, daredevil, reckless, *inf.* gutsy, spunky. **2 impudent,** impertinent, insolent, presumptuous, forward, rude, brazen, shameless, saucy, defiant.

audacity *n.* **1 boldness,** daring, fearlessness, intrepidity, bravery, courage, valor, pluck, recklessness, *inf.* guts, spunk.

2 impudence, impertinence, insolence, presumption, forwardness, rudeness, brazenness, shamelessness, defiance.

audible *adj.* **heard,** hearable, clear, distinct, perceptible, discernible. ***Ant.*** inaudible; faint; indistinct.

audience *n.* **1 listeners,** spectators, viewers, onlookers, assembly, gathering, crowd, assemblage, house, turnout, congregation, gallery. **2 public,** market, following, fans, devotees, aficionados. **3 interview,** meeting, hearing, consultation, discussion, reception.

audit *n.* **inspection,** examination, scrutiny, investigation, review, check.
  ▸ *v.* **inspect,** examine, go over/through, scrutinize, investigate, review, check.

augment *v.* **1 increase,** make larger/bigger/greater, boost, build up, enlarge, add to, expand, extend, amplify, raise, enhance, heighten, multiply, magnify, elevate, swell, inflate, escalate, intensify. **2 increase,** grow, build up, enlarge, expand, extend, rise, multiply, swell, inflate, escalate. ***Ant.*** decrease; diminish.

augur *v.* **be a sign of,** foretell, forecast, predict, prophesy, bode, foreshadow, promise, presage, portend, herald, betoken.
  ▸ *n.* **seer,** soothsayer, prophet, oracle.

august *adj.* **dignified,** solemn, majestic, stately, magnificent, noble, regal, imposing, impressive, exalted, lofty, grand, high-ranking, illustrious, distinguished, awe-inspiring.

auspicious *adj.* **propitious,** favorable, promising, bright, optimistic, hopeful, encouraging, opportune, timely, lucky, fortunate, providential, felicitous, rosy.

austere *adj.* **1 harsh,** stern, severe, strict, unfeeling, hard, rigorous, stringent, grim, cold, distant, formal, stiff, aloof, forbidding, grave, solemn, serious, unsmiling, unyielding, unbending, unrelenting, inflexible. **2 strict,** self-denying, self-abnegating, ascetic, Spartan, abstemious, abstinent, moral, upright, celibate, chaste, puritanical. **3 plain,** simple, severe, unadorned, unornamented, unembellished, stark, subdued, somber. ***Ant.*** genial; immoderate; elaborate.

authentic *adj.* **1 genuine,** true, bona fide, rightful, legitimate, lawful, legal, valid, *inf.* the real McCoy, kosher. **2 reliable,**

dependable, trustworthy, true, truthful, honest, faithful, credible, *inf.* straight from the horse's mouth. *Ant.* fake; counterfeit; unreliable.

authenticate *v.* **1 validate,** ratify, confirm, certify, seal, endorse, guarantee, warrant, underwrite. **2 verify,** substantiate, support, prove, evidence.

author *n.* **1 writer,** composer, novelist, dramatist, playwright, screenwriter, poet, essayist, biographer, librettist, lyricist, songwriter, journalist, columnist, reporter. **2 cause,** creator, originator, initiator, founder, planner, prime mover, designer.

authoritarian *n.* **disciplinarian,** autocrat, despot, dictator, tyrant, absolutist.

▸ *adj.* **disciplinarian,** harsh, strict, autocratic, despotic, dictatorial, tyrannical, domineering, dogmatic, imperious, absolute, draconian.

authoritative *adj.* **1 official,** approved, authorized, sanctioned, validated, authentic, genuine. **2 sound,** dependable, reliable, trustworthy, authentic, valid, certified, attested, definitive, factual, accurate, scholarly. **3 self-assured,** confident, assertive, imposing, masterful, dogmatic, peremptory, arrogant, commanding, dominating, domineering, imperious, overbearing, authoritarian.

authority *n.* **1 authorization,** right, power, might, sanction, influence, force, control, charge, prerogative, jurisdiction, rule, command, dominion, sovereignty, ascendancy, supremacy, *inf.* say-so. **2 expert,** specialist, professional, master, scholar, pundit, *inf.* walking encyclopedia. **3 source,** reference, documentation, bibliography, citation, quotation, quote, excerpt, passage. **4 permission,** authorization, sanction, license, warrant, *inf.* say-so. **5 testimony,** evidence, witness, attestation, sworn statement, declaration, word, avowal, deposition, profession.

authorize *v.* **1 give authority to,** commission, empower, entitle, enable, accredit, license, certify, validate. **2 give authority/ permission for,** permit, allow, approve, give one's assent to, agree to, sanction, ratify, warrant, countenance, accede to, *inf.* give the green light to, give the go-ahead for.

automatic *adj.* **1 automated,** mechanized, mechanical, push-button, robotic, self-activating, self-regulating, self-directing, self-propelling. **2 instinctive,**

spontaneous, involuntary, unconscious, reflex, natural, mechanical. **3 inevitable,** routine, certain, assured, unavoidable, necessary.

autonomy *n.* **independence,** self-determination, autarchy, self-sufficiency, individualism.

available *adj.* **unoccupied,** free, untaken, vacant, usable, employable, ready, accessible, obtainable, at hand, convenient.

avarice *n.* **greed,** acquisitiveness, covetousness, materialism, selfishness, self-interest, meanness, miserliness.

average *n.* **mean,** median, midpoint, center, norm, standard, yardstick, rule.
▸ *adj.* **1 ordinary,** normal, typical, everyday, common, widespread, prevalent. **2 mediocre,** moderate, unexceptional, second-rate, banal, pedestrian. ***Ant.*** outstanding; exceptional.

aversion *n.* **dislike of,** antipathy for, distaste for, abhorrence of, hatred of, loathing of, detestation of, hostility toward; reluctance toward, unwillingness for, disinclination toward. ***Ant.*** liking; inclination.

avid *adj.* **keen,** eager, enthusiastic, partial to, fond of, fervent, zealous, passionate about, *inf.* crazy about, mad about. ***Ant.*** apathetic; indifferent.

avoid *v.* **shun,** keep away from, eschew, steer clear of, evade, hide from, elude, shirk, dodge, abstain from, refrain from, hold back from. ***Ant.*** confront; face.

aware *adj.* **awake,** watchful, vigilant, alert, cautious, paying attention. ***Ant.*** unaware; ignorant; oblivious.

awe *n.* **amazement,** wonder, astonishment, stupefaction, reverence, honor, veneration, dread, fear.

awful *adj.* **1 nasty,** unpleasant, distressing, troublesome, horrible, serious, severe, ugly, unattractive, foul, disgusting. **2 awe-inspiring,** awesome, venerable, demanding respect, admirable, impressive, authoritative, daunting.

awkward *adj.* **1 inconvenient,** difficult, problematic, unhelpful, annoying, obstructive, vexatious, perverse. **2 clumsy,** ungainly, inelegant, inept, gauche, lumbering, out of proportion, unwieldy. ***Ant.*** convenient; adroit.

Bb

babble *v.* **1 jabber,** chatter, mutter, mumble, prate, drivel, cackle, *inf.* run on. **2 blab,** blurt out, reveal, divulge, let slip. **3 murmur,** whisper, gurgle.
▸ *n.* **jabbering,** gibberish, chatter, muttering, mumbling, clamor.

baby *n.* **1 infant,** newborn, child, babe, tiny tot. **2 junior,** youngest, subordinate.
▸ *v.* **pamper,** spoil, indulge, pet, humor, coddle, mollycoddle, overindulge, spoonfeed.

babyish *adj.* **childish,** immature, infantile, juvenile, puerile, adolescent, jejune, pathetic, inane, namby-pamby.

back *n.* **1 spine,** backbone, spinal column, posterior, *Med.* dorsum. **2 rear,** rear end, far end, end, reverse, reverse side, other side, hind part, posterior, tail end, backside, hindquarters, stern. *Ant.* front.
▸ *adj.* **1 rear,** hind, end, hindmost, posterior, aft. **2 past,** previous, earlier, former, bygone, expired, elapsed, obsolete. *Ant.* front; foremost; future.

backer *n.* **1 sponsor,** patron, financier, benefactor, subsidizer, underwriter, well-wisher, *inf.* angel. **2 supporter,** advocate, promoter, upholder, champion, seconder, abettor.

background *n.* **1 distance,** rear, horizon. **2 setting,** backcloth, backdrop, scene, stage. **3 upbringing,** rearing, education, history, environment, class, culture, experience, family circumstances, circumstances, qualifications, credentials. **4 conditions,** circumstances, environment, milieu, framework, factors, influences. *Ant.* foreground; front.

backing *n.* **1 support,** approval, commendation, help, assistance, aid, helping hand, encouragement, cooperation, championship, promotion, advocacy, endorsement. **2 sponsorship,** financing, finance, grant, subsidy, funds. **3 security,** surety, collateral, assurance, insurance, guarantee, warranty. **4 accompaniment,** backup, harmony, obbligato.

backlash *n.* **reaction,** counteraction, repercussion, recoil, kickback, rebound, boomerang, retroaction, retaliation.

backward *adj.* **1 toward the back/rear,** rearward,after, reverse. **2 slow,** behind, behindhand, underdeveloped, undeveloped, retarded, unprogressive, dull, sluggish, subnormal, unsophisticated. **3 bashful,** shy, retiring, diffident, hesitant, shrinking, timid, demure, reluctant. ***Ant.*** forward; advanced; bold.

bad *adj.* **1 poor,** unsatisfactory, inadequate, deficient, imperfect, defective, inferior, substandard, faulty, unacceptable, useless, worthless, inept, ineffectual, *inf.* lousy, crummy. **2 harmful,** hurtful, damaging, dangerous, injurious, detrimental, destructive, ruinous, deleterious, unhealthy, unwholesome, poisonous. **3 immoral,** wicked, wrong, evil, sinful, corrupt, base, reprobate, depraved, dishonest, dishonorable, crooked. **4 naughty,** mischievous, disobedient, unruly, wayward, refractory. **5 disagreeable,** unpleasant, unwelcome, uncomfortable, nasty, terrible, dreadful, adverse, grim, gloomy, unfortunate, unfavorable, unlucky, distressing. **6 adverse,** difficult, unfavorable, unfortunate, unsuitable,

inappropriate, inapt. **7 serious,** severe, grave, disastrous, terrible, critical, acute. **8 rotten,** decayed, moldy, putrid, tainted, spoiled, contaminated, putrescent, putrefacient. **9 ill,** unwell, sick, poorly, indisposed, ailing, weak, feeble, diseased, *inf.* under the weather, below par. **10 sorry,** apologetic, regretful, conscience-stricken, contrite, remorseful, guilty, penitent, rueful, sad, upset. **11 worthless,** invalid, counterfeit, false, spurious, fraudulent, fake, *inf.* bogus, phony. ***Ant.*** good; beneficial; virtuous; pleasant.

badge *n.* **1 crest,** emblem, insignia, device, shield, escutcheon, brand. **2 mark,** sign, symbol, indication, indicator, signal, characteristic, trademark.

baffle *v.* **1 puzzle,** perplex, mystify, nonplus, stump, flummox, confound, dumbfound, bamboozle, bewilder, confuse, amaze, stagger, stun. **2 thwart,** frustrate, foil, check, block, hinder, obstruct, bar, prevent, deflect, divert.

bag *n.* **receptacle,** handbag, pocketbook, purse, shoulder bag, case, suitcase, grip, flight bag, satchel, duffel bag, briefcase, attaché case, backpack, knapsack, rucksack, haversack.

▸ *v.* **1 catch,** capture, shoot, kill, trap, snare, land. **2 sag,** hang loosely.

baggage *n.* **luggage,** gear, equipment, pack, belongings, things, suitcases, bags, effects, paraphernalia, trappings, accoutrements.

bait *n.* **1 lure,** decoy, troll, plug, fly, chum. **2 attraction,** lure, incentive, snare, temptation, allurement, enticement, incitement, inducement.

▸ *v.* **torment,** persecute, badger, plague, harry, harass, hound, provoke, tease, annoy, irritate, *inf.* hassle, needle, give a hard time to.

balance *n.* **1 scale,** scales, weighing machine. **2 equilibrium,** evenness, symmetry, parity, equity, equipoise, correspondence, uniformity, equivalence. **3 steadiness,** stability. **4 composure,** poise, equanimity, aplomb, stability, assurance, confidence, self-possession, coolness, levelheadedness, sang-froid. **5 counterbalance,** countercheck, counterweight, stabilizer, compensation, recompense, ballast. **6 remainder,** rest, residue, difference, surplus, excess. *Ant.* difference; instability; uncertainty.

▸ *v.* **1 steady,** stabilize, poise. **2 counterbalance,** counterweigh, counteract, offset, equalize, neutralize, compensate for, make up for, counterpoise. **3 correspond,** match, be level/parallel. **4 weigh,** compare, evaluate, consider, deliberate, assess, appraise, estimate, review.

bald *adj.* **1 hairless,** baldheaded, depilated. **2 barren,** treeless, bare, uncovered, stark, exposed, bleak, unsheltered. **3 blunt,** direct, forthright, straight, straightforward, downright, outright, plain, simple, unadorned, unvarnished, unembellished, stark, severe, austere. *Ant.* hairy; fertile; embellished.

ball[1] *n.* **1 sphere,** globe, orb, globule, spheroid. **2 projectile,** shot, grapeshot, bullet, pellet, slug.

ball[2] *n.* **1 dance,** formal dance, social gathering, *inf.* prom, hop. **2 great time,** fun.

ballot *n.* **vote,** poll, election, referendum, plebiscite, voting, polling.

ban *v.* **prohibit,** forbid, veto, disallow, bar, debar, outlaw, proscribe, suppress, interdict, reject, restrict, banish. *Ant.* allow; sanction.

▸ *n.* **prohibition,** veto, bar,

embargo, boycott, proscription, interdict, interdiction, suppression, stoppage, restriction, taboo, censorship, banishment. *Ant.* permission; sanction.

banal *adj.* **hackneyed,** trite, clichéd, commonplace, platitudinous, humdrum, stock, stereotyped, pedestrian, unoriginal, unimaginative, stale, uninspired, prosaic, dull, everyday, ordinary, tired, inane, fatuous, jejune, *inf.* old hat. *Ant.* original; imaginative; fresh.

band[1] *n.* **1 bond,** binding, cord, strap, tie, connection, link, chain, thong, fetter, manacle, shackle, ligature, ring, hoop. **2 belt,** cord, braid, sash, girdle, ribbon, fillet, cincture, waistband, headband, hatband, wristband, sweatband. **3 strip,** stripe, streak, line, bar, striation.

band[2] *n.* **1 group,** troop, company, gang, mob, pack, bunch, body, gathering, crowd, horde, throng, assembly, assemblage, association, society, club, clique, set, coterie. **2 musical group,** group, pop group, combo, ensemble, orchestra.

bandit *n.* **robber,** brigand, outlaw, desperado, banditto, hijacker, plunderer, marauder, gangster, criminal, crook, thief, gunman, highwayman, pirate, racketeer.

bandy *adj.* **bandy-legged,** bowed, bowlegged, curved, crooked, bent, misshapen.
▸ *v.* **1 exchange,** swap, trade, interchange, barter, reciprocate. **2 circulate,** spread, pass, toss about, disseminate.

bang *n.* **1 explosive noise,** report, burst, boom, clash, clang, peal, clap, pop, slam, thud, thump. **2 blow,** bump, hit, slap, punch, knock, stroke, smack, whack, rap, cuff, box, buffet, *inf.* wallop, bash, sock.
▸ *v.* **1 hit,** strike, beat, thump, hammer, knock, rap, pound, thud, pummel, whack, *inf.* bash. **2 slam,** crash. **3 explode,** burst, blow up, detonate, pop, resound, echo.

banish *v.* **1 exile,** deport, expel, eject, drive away, expatriate, cast out, outlaw, transport, oust, evict, throw out, exclude, proscribe, excommunicate. **2 dismiss,** drive/send away, dispel, oust, cast/shut out, get rid of, ban, bar, exclude, eliminate, dislodge. *Ant.* admit; accept; welcome.

bank[1] *n.* **1 slope,** rise, incline, gradient, mound, hillock, knoll. **2 edge,** side, shore, brink, margin, embankment.

bank[2] *v.* **tilt,** slope, slant, incline, pitch.

bankrupt *adj.* **insolvent,** failed,

ruined, penurious, impecunious, financially embarrassed, distressed, in the red, *inf.* on the rocks, broke, hard up. **Ant.** solvent.

▸ *v.* **impoverish,** beggar, wipe out, break, ruin, *inf.* bust.

banner *n.* **1 flag,** standard, pennant, pennon, colors, sign. **2 banner line,** headline, streamer, screamer.

▸ *adj.* **excellent,** red-letter, outstanding, notable, exceptional, leading.

banquet *n.* **dinner,** dinner party, feast, meal, party, repast, treat, revel.

banter *n.* **repartee,** badinage, teasing, joking, jesting, jocularity, raillery, wordplay, mockery, ridicule, *inf.* kidding, ribbing, joshing.

▸ *v.* **tease,** joke, jest, mock, ridicule, make fun of, twit, *inf.* kid, rib, rag, josh.

bar *n.* **1 rod,** pole, stake, stick, shaft, rail, spar, crosspiece. **2 block,** brick, cake, wedge, lump. **3 obstacle,** barrier. **4 band,** strip, line, belt, streak, stripe. **5 sandbar,** shoal, shallow, reef, sandbank, ridge, ledge, shelf. **6 tavern,** saloon, pub, lounge.

▸ *v.* **1 bolt,** lock, fasten, padlock, secure, latch. **2 debar,** prohibit, preclude, forbid, ban, exclude,

keep out, block, impede, obstruct, hinder, restrain, check, stop, defer. **Ant.** unlock; admit; accept.

barbarian *n.* **1 savage,** brute, wild man/woman, troglodyte, monster. **2 ruffian,** lout, vandal, hooligan, boor, ignoramus, philistine, yahoo.

▸ *adj.* **1 savage,** uncivilized, primitive, brutish, wild, heathen. **2 loutish,** hooligan, boorish, uncivilized, wild, rough, coarse, gross, uncouth, vulgar, philistine.

barbaric *adj.* **1 savage,** uncivilized, primitive. **2 brutal,** savage, cruel, vicious, fierce, ferocious, bestial, barbarous, murderous, inhuman, ruthless, remorseless.

bare *adj.* **1 naked,** stark naked, nude, uncovered, exposed, unclothed, undressed, unclad, stripped, denuded. **2 empty,** vacant, unfurnished, unadorned, uncovered, stark, austere, unembellished. **3 bleak,** unsheltered, unprotected, unshielded, desolate, barren, treeless, without vegetation. **4 simple,** plain, bald, basic, essential, straightforward, stark, unvarnished, unembellished, cold, hard, sheer, literal. **5 mere,** basic, meager, scanty, inadequate. **Ant.** clothed; embellished.

▸ *v.* **reveal,** uncover, expose, lay

bare, unveil, disclose, show, divulge, unmask, bring to light.

barely *adv.* **hardly,** scarcely, only just, just, by the skin of one's teeth. *Ant.* fully.

bargain *n.* **1 agreement,** contract, pact, transaction, deal, treaty, negotiation, arrangement, compact, covenant, concordat, understanding, pledge, promise, engagement. **2 discount,** reduction, good buy, sales article, *inf.* steal, giveaway.
▸ *v.* **haggle,** barter, deal, trade, traffic.

barrage *n.* **1 gunfire,** bombardment, shelling, battery, cannonade, volley, broadside, salvo, fusillade, wall/curtain of fire. **2 deluge,** stream, storm, torrent, onslaught, flood, avalanche, hail, burst, mass, abundance, superabundance, plethora, profusion.

barrel *n.* **cask,** keg, butt, vat, tun, tub, tank, hogshead.

barren *adj.* **1 infertile,** sterile, childless. **2 infertile,** unproductive, uncultivable, unfruitful, arid, desert, waste, desolate. **3 uninteresting,** boring, dull, uninspiring, stale, prosaic, futile, worthless, useless, valueless, unrewarding, purposeless, vapid, lackluster. *Ant.* fertile; fruitful; productive.

barricade *n.* **barrier,** obstacle, blockade, bar, fence, obstruction, roadblock, bulwark, stockade, rampart, palisade.
▸ *v.* **block,** blockade, obstruct, bar, shut off/in, fence in, defend, fortify.

barrier *n.* **1 barricade,** bar, fence, railing, obstacle, blockade, roadblock. **2 obstacle,** hindrance, impediment, drawback, check, hurdle, restriction, stumbling block, handicap, difficulty, restraint.

barter *n.* **trading,** exchange, swapping, bargaining, haggling, trafficking.
▸ *v.* **1 trade,** trade off, exchange, swap. **2 bargain,** haggle.

base *n.* **1 foundation,** support, prop, stay, stand, pedestal, rest, bottom, bed, foot, substructure, plinth. **2 basis,** core, essence, component, essential, fundamental, root, heart, principal, source, origin. **3 headquarters,** center, camp, site, station, settlement, post, starting point. *Ant.* top; apex.
▸ *v.* **1 found,** build, construct, form, establish, ground, rest, root, fasten, hinge, derive. **2 locate,** station, situate, post, place, install.

bashful *adj.* **shy,** reserved, diffident, retiring, modest, self-conscious, coy, demure, reticent, self-effacing, hesitant, shrinking, backward, timid, timorous, abashed, blushing, embarrassed, shamefaced, sheepish. *Ant.* bold; confident; forward.

basic *adj.* **1 fundamental,** elementary, rudimentary, primary, radical, key, central, essential, vital, necessary, indispensable, intrinsic, underlying. **2 bottom,** lowest-level, lowest, starting, ground, without commission. **3 plain,** simple, spartan, sparse, stark, unadorned, without frills, no-frills. *Ant.* secondary; supplementary; fancy.

basin *n.* **1 container,** receptacle, vessel, bowl, dish, pan. **2 bed,** channel.

basis *n.* **1 support,** foundation, base, footing, reasoning, grounds. **2 starting point,** premise, fundamental point/principle, principal constituent, main ingredient, groundwork, core, essence. **3 footing,** procedure, condition, status, position.

bask *v.* **1 lie,** laze, lounge, relax, loll, sunbathe, sun/warm oneself. **2 luxuriate,** revel, wallow, enjoy, delight, take pleasure, rejoice, relish, savor, indulge oneself.

bastard *n.* **1 illegitimate child,** love child. **2 scoundrel,** cad, blackguard, villain, rascal.

▸ *adj.* **1 illegitimate. 2 adulterated,** impure, hybrid, alloyed, inferior, imperfect, spurious, counterfeit, artificial, sham, false, fake.

batch *n.* **group,** quantity, lot, bunch, accumulation, mass, cluster, set, collection, assemblage, pack, crowd, aggregate, conglomeration.

bathe *v.* **1 have/take a bath,** wash, soak, shower. **2 clean,** cleanse, wash, soak, steep, immerse, wet, moisten, rinse, suffuse. **3 swim,** take a dip. **4 envelope,** suffuse.

baton *n.* **stick,** bar, wand, rod, staff, club, truncheon, mace.

batter *v.* **1 hit,** strike, beat, bash, assault, wallop, thump, thrash, lash, pound, deliver/rain blows on, pummel, buffet, abuse, *inf.* whack. **2 damage,** injure, hurt, harm, bruise, wound, crush, shatter, smash, destroy, demolish, ruin, impair, mar, spoil.

battle *n.* **1 war,** armed conflict, conflict, fight, clash, contest, struggle, skirmish, engagement, encounter, confrontation, collision, meeting, campaign, crusade, tussle, scuffle, scrap, melee, fighting, warfare, combat, action, hostilities. **2 clash,** conflict, contest, competition, tournament, struggle, disagreement, argument, dispute, controversy, debate, dissension, altercation, strife. *Ant.* truce; peace.

▸ *v.* **1 fight,** struggle, strive, combat, contend, war, feud. **2 fight,** struggle, labor, push. **3 fight,** war, feud, argue, quarrel, disagree, bicker, wrangle, cross swords, lock horns.

battlefield *n.* **battleground,** front, battlefront, battle lines, field of operations, field of battle, combat zone, theater/arena of war, war zone.

bawdy *adj.* **pornographic,** obscene, vulgar, indecent, blue, racy, titillating, crude, coarse, rude, gross, ribald, lewd, dirty, filthy, smutty, off-color, naughty, suggestive, indelicate, unseemly, indecorous, salacious, erotic, prurient, lascivious, licentious, risqué, scatological, *inf.* raunchy. *Ant.* decent; seemly; clean.

bawl *v.* **1 cry,** sob, weep, wail, blubber, snivel, squall. **2 shout,** call/cry out, yell, roar, bellow, screech, scream, howl, whoop, vociferate, *inf.* holler.

bay[1] *n.* **cove,** inlet, indentation, natural harbor, gulf, basin, sound, arm.

bay[2] *n.* **alcove,** recess, niche, opening, nook.

bazaar *n.* **1 market,** marketplace, mart, exchange. **2 fête,** fair, sale.

be *v.* **1 exist,** live, be alive, have life/being, breathe. **2 be situated,** be located, dwell, reside. **3 take place,** occur, come about, come to pass, arise, crop up, transpire. **4 remain,** stay, last, continue, survive, endure, persist, prevail, obtain. **5 attend.**

beach *n.* **seaside,** coast, seashore, shore, water's edge, coastline, sands, sand, strand.

beached *adj.* **aground,** ashore, grounded, high and dry, marooned, stranded, wrecked, abandoned.

bead *n.* **1 ball,** pellet, pill, globule, spheroid, oval. **2 drop,** droplet, bubble, blob, dot, glob, dewdrop, teardrop.

beam *n.* **1 timber,** joist, rafter, girder, spar, support, lath. **2 ray,** shaft, stream, streak, flash, gleam, glow, glimmer, glint, radiation, emission. **3 smile,** grin.

▸ *v.* **1 emit,** radiate, shine. **2 broadcast,** transmit, direct, aim. **3 smile,** grin.

bear *v.* **1 carry,** bring, transport, move, convey, take, fetch, haul, *inf.* tote. **2 spread,** transmit, carry. **3 carry,** display, exhibit, show, be marked with. **4 yield,** produce, give forth, give, provide, supply, generate. **5 give birth to,** breed, bring forth, beget, engender. **6 carry,** sustain, support, shoulder, uphold. **7 stand,**

endorse, tolerate, put up with, abide, stomach, permit, allow, admit, brook. **8 suffer,** endure, undergo, tolerate, put up with, experience, go through, support, weather. **9 have,** hold, harbor, possess, entertain, cherish.
10 veer, curve, go, move, turn, fork, diverge, deviate, bend. *Ant.* abandon; give up (see give).

bearable *adj.* **endurable,** tolerable, supportable, sufferable, sustainable, admissible, passable, manageable. *Ant.* unbearable; intolerable; insufferable.

bearing *n.* **1 deportment,** posture, carriage, gait, attitude, behavior, manner, demeanor, air, aspect, mien. **2 course,** direction.
3 relevance, pertinence, connection. **4 orientation,** location, position, situation, whereabouts, track, way.

beast *n.* **1 animal,** creature, brute, mammal, quadruped. **2 brute,** monster, savage, swine, pig, ogre, fiend, sadist, barbarian.

beat *v.* **1 bang,** hit, strike, pound.
2 hit, strike, batter, thump, wallop, hammer, punch, knock, thrash, pound, pummel, slap, smack, flay, whip, lash, chastise, thwack, cuff, bruise, buffet, box, cudgel, club, maul, pelt, drub, *inf.* belt, bash, whack, clout, slug, tan, bop, lay into, knock about, rough

up. **3 throb,** pound, thump, pulsate, pulse, palpitate, vibrate, tremble. **4 flap,** flutter, quiver, tremble, vibrate. **5 mix,** blend, whip, whisk, stir. **6 strike,** dash, break against, lap, wash.
7 hammer, forge, form, shape, work, stamp, fashion, model.
8 tread, tramp, trample, wear, track, groove. **9 defeat,** conquer, vanquish, trounce, rout, overpower, overcome, overwhelm, overthrow, subdue, quash, *inf.* lick. **10 outdo,** surpass, exceed, eclipse, transcend, top, outstrip.
▸ *n.* **1 bang,** banging, stroke, striking, blow, hit, punch, pound, pummel, slap, smack, thwack.
2 throb, throbbing, pounding, pulsating, pulsing, beating, thumping, palpitating, vibrating, vibration. **3 rhythm,** stress, meter, time, measure, accent, cadence.
4 round, circuit, course, route, way, path, orbit.

beautiful *adj.* **ravishing,** gorgeous, stunning, alluring, lovely, attractive, pretty, handsome, good-looking, pleasing, comely, charming, delightful, glamorous, appealing, fair, fine, becoming, seemly, winsome, graceful, elegant, exquisite. *Ant.* ugly; hideous.

beautify *v.* **1 adorn,** embellish,

enhance, decorate, ornament, garnish, gild, smarten, prettify, glamorize. **2 apply makeup/ cosmetics,** prettify, glamorize, primp, preen, *inf.* do/doll oneself up.

beauty *n.* **1 loveliness,** attractiveness, prettiness, handsomeness, allure, allurement, charm, glamour, grace, artistry, symmetry, *fml.* pulchritude. **2 belle,** charmer, enchantress, seductress, femme fatale, Venus, goddess, *inf.* good-looker, looker, lovely, stunner, knockout, dish. **3 attraction,** good thing, advantage, benefit, asset, strong point, boon, blessing.

because *conjunction* **since,** as, in view of the fact that, owing to the fact that, seeing that.

beckon *v.* **1 signal,** gesture, make a gesture, gesticulate, motion, wave, nod, call, summon, bid. **2 draw,** pull, call, invite, attract, tempt, entice, allure, coax, persuade, induce.

become *v.* **1 come to be,** turn out to be, grow, grow into, mature into, evolve into, pass into, change into, turn into, alter into, transform into, be transformed into, be converted into, metamorphose into. **2 suit,** flatter, look good on, set off, enhance, embellish, ornament, grace. **3 befit,** behoove, suit, be suitable/fitting to.

becoming *adj.* **1 flattering,** comely, attractive, lovely, pretty, handsome, stylish, elegant, chic, tasteful. **2 suitable,** fitting, appropriate, apt, proper, right, decent, seemly, worthy, decorous, graceful. ***Ant.*** unbecoming; inappropriate; improper.

bed *n.* **1 divan,** bunk, cot, berth, couch, hammock, litter, stretcher, double bed, single bed, four-poster, bunk bed, water bed, crib, cradle, bassinet, *inf.* sack. **2 plot,** area, lot, patch, space, border, strip, row. **3 base,** basis, foundation, bottom, support, substructure, substratum, groundwork.
▸ *v.* **1 embed,** set, fix into, insert, inlay, implant, bury, base, establish, found. **2 go to bed with,** have sex with, sleep with, spend the night with. **3 plant.**

bedraggled *adj.* **messy,** disheveled, muddy, muddied, wet, dirty, sodden, soaking, soaking wet, soaked, drenched, saturated, dripping, soggy, splashed, soiled, stained, disordered, untidy, unkempt.

beef *n.* **1 brawn,** muscle, muscularity, heftiness, burliness, bulk, physique, strength, powerfulness, robustness.

2 complaint, grumbling, grumble, criticism, objection, protestation, grievance, *inf.* griping, gripe, grousing, nitpicking.

befall *v.* **happen,** occur, take place, chance, crop up, arise, come about, come to pass, transpire, materialize, ensue, follow, result, fall, supervene.

before *adv.* **1 previously,** earlier, formerly, hitherto, in the past. **2 ahead,** in front, in advance, in the lead.
▸ *prep.* **1 prior to,** previous to, earlier than. **2 in front of,** ahead of, in advance of. **3 in the presence of,** in the sight of. **4 in preference to,** rather/sooner than. *Ant.* after; behind.

befriend *v.* **make friends with,** make a friend of, look after, protect, keep an eye on, help, assist, aid, support, back, stand by, side with, encourage, sustain, uphold, succor, advise.

beg *v.* **1 ask for money,** solicit money, seek charity/alms, cadge, scrounge, *inf.* sponge, bum, mooch. **2 ask for,** request, seek, look for, desire, crave, solicit, plead for, beseech, entreat, importune, plead with.

beggar *n.* **tramp,** vagrant, mendicant, cadger, vagabond, pauper, down-and-out, derelict, *inf.* scrounger, sponger, bum, moocher, bag lady, hobo.
▸ *v.* **impoverish,** make poor, reduce to poverty, bankrupt, pauperize.

begin *v.* **start,** commence, set about, embark on, initiate, set in motion, institute, inaugurate, go ahead, get going, *inf.* fire away, kick off, get the show on the road, get to it, start the ball rolling, take the plunge, arise, come into existence/being, happen, occur, spring up, crop up, emerge, dawn, appear, originate . *Ant.* finish; end; stop.

beginner *n.* **novice,** trainee, learner, apprentice, student, pupil, recruit, raw recruit, tyro, fledgling, neophyte, initiate, novitiate, tenderfoot, *inf.* greenhorn, rookie. *Ant.* expert; veteran.

beginning *n.* **1 start,** starting point, commencement, onset, outset, dawn, birth, inception, conception, emergence, rise, *inf.* kickoff. **2 start,** commencement, first part, opening, prelude, preface, introduction. **3 origin,** source, starting point, fountainhead, spring, mainspring, embryo, germ, roots, seeds.

begrudge *v.* **1 grudge,** envy, resent, hold against, be jealous of. **2 grudge,** resent, give unwillingly, be dissatisfied with.

beguile *v.* **1 charm,** attract, delight, please, enchant, bewitch, seduce. **2 entertain,** amuse, occupy, absorb, engage, distract, divert, engross. **3 pass,** while away, spend.

behave *v.* **act,** perform, conduct oneself, acquit oneself, comport oneself, function, operate.

behavior *n.* **conduct,** way of acting, response, comportment, deportment, bearing, actions, manners, ways, action, performance, functioning, operation, reaction.

being *n.* **1 existence,** living, life, animation, actuality, life blood, vital force, entity. **2 spirit,** soul, nature, essence, substance, entity. **3 creature,** person, human being, human, individual, mortal, living thing, man, woman, animal. *Ant.* nothingness; oblivion.

belated *adj.* **late,** overdue, behindhand, behind time, delayed, tardy, unpunctual.

belief *n.* **1 opinion,** feeling, impression, view, viewpoint, conviction, judgment, thinking, way of thinking, theory, notion. **2 faith,** credence, freedom from doubt, trust, reliance, confidence. **3 doctrine,** teaching, creed, dogma, ideology, principles, tenet, canon, credence, credo. *Ant.* disbelief; doubt; skepticism.

believe *v.* **1 trust. 2 regard/accept as true,** accept, credit, be convinced by, trust, *inf.* swallow, fall for, buy. **3 think,** be of the opinion that, understand, suppose, assume, presume, surmise, reckon, guess, postulate/ theorize that. *Ant.* disbelieve; doubt.

believer *n.* **follower,** adherent, supporter, disciple, upholder. *Ant.* disbeliever; skeptic; agnostic.

belittle *v.* **disparage,** decry, deprecate, undervalue, underrate, underestimate, minimize, denigrate, make light of, slight, detract from, downgrade, play down, depreciate, derogate, scoff at, sneer at. *Ant.* praise; exaggerate; magnify.

belligerent *adj.* **1 aggressive,** antagonistic, militant, pugnacious, quarrelsome, argumentative, disputatious, combative, quick-tempered, hot-tempered, irascible. **2 at war,** warring, battling, contending, militant, martial, warlike, warmongering. *Ant.* friendly; peaceable; peaceful.

belong *v.* **1 have a place/home,** be classified, be categorized. **2 fit in,** be suited to, have a rightful place, be part of, *inf.* go, click.

belongings *pl. n.* **possessions,** personal possessions/effects, effects, goods, accouterments, appurtenances, property, paraphernalia, *inf.* gear, things, stuff, junk.

beloved *adj.* **dear,** dearest, darling, precious, cherished, sweet, treasured, prized, worshiped, idolized, loved, liked, adored, admired, respected, valued, esteemed, revered.
 ▸ *n.* **sweetheart,** fiancé, fiancée, boyfriend, girlfriend, love, lover, betrothed, *fml.* paramour, inamorato, inamorata.

belt *n.* **1 girdle,** sash, cummerbund, waistband, band. **2 band,** conveyor belt, fan belt. **3 zone,** region, area, district, tract, stretch, extent. **4 strip,** band, stripe, bar, line, stria. **5 blow,** punch, smack, bang, thump, *inf.* clout, bash, wallop.
 ▸ *v.* **1 encircle,** gird, encompass, bind, tie, fasten. **2 strap,** flog, whip, lash, cane, thrash, scourge, flail, strike, hit, beat, punch, smack, thrash, thump, bang, batter, pound, pummel, *inf.* bash, sock.

bemused *adj.* **confused,** bewildered, puzzled, perplexed, dazed, stunned, muddled, overwhelmed, disconcerted, discomfited, astonished, astounded, stupefied, preoccupied, absentminded, engrossed.

bend *v.* **1 curve,** crook, flex, twist, bow, arch, warp, contort, turn, swerve, veer, incline, diverge, deviate, deflect, coil, spiral, loop. **2 curve,** turn, twist, swerve, veer, incline, diverge, deviate, deflect, coil, spiral, loop. **3 stoop,** crouch, lean down/over, bow, hunch. **4 mold,** shape, direct, force, influence, compel, persuade, subdue, sway, subjugate. **5 direct,** point, aim, turn, train, steer, set. *Ant.* straighten.
 ▸ *n.* **curve,** turn, corner, twist, angle, arc, swerve, incline, divergence, crook, deviation, deflection, coiling, spiral, loop, hook, dogleg, hairpin turn, zigzag.

beneath *adv.* **below,** underneath. *Ant.* above; over.
 ▸ *prep.* **1 below,** under, underneath, lower than. **2 below,** lower than, inferior to, secondary to, subservient to. **3 below,** unworthy of, undignified for, unbefitting, unbecoming.

benefactor *n.* **helper,** patron, backer, sponsor, supporter, promoter, contributor, subscriber, subsidizer, donor, philanthropist, sympathizer, well-wisher, *inf.* angel, friend.

beneficial *adj.* **advantageous,** favorable, propitious, promising, helpful, accommodating, obliging, useful, serviceable, valuable, profitable, rewarding, gainful. *Ant.* disadvantageous; detrimental.

beneficiary *n.* **heir,** inheritor, recipient, receiver, legatee, payee, assignee.

benefit *n.* **1 advantage,** good, gain, profit, help, aid, assistance, interest, welfare, well-being, betterment, asset, avail, use, service. **2 advantage,** blessing, boon, good, usefulness, perquisites, perks, fringe benefits. **3 social security,** insurance, disability, unemployment (insurance), workers'/workmen's compensation, pension, welfare, *inf.* workers'/workmen's comp. *Ant.* disadvantage; detriment.
▸ *v.* **1 do good to,** be of service to, profit, serve, be of advantage to, help, aid, assist, contribute to, better, improve, advance, further. **2 profit,** gain, reap benefits, make money, *inf.* cash in, make a killing. *Ant.* damage; injure.

benevolent *adj.* **1 kind,** kindly, kindhearted, friendly, amiable, benign, generous, magnanimous, warmhearted, considerate, thoughtful, well-meaning, altruistic, humane, compassionate, caring, sympathetic, obliging, helpful, humanitarian, philanthropic, bountiful, liberal, bounteous, beneficent. **2 charitable,** nonprofit. *Ant.* malevolent; unkind; unsympathetic.

benign *adj.* **1 kind,** kindly, friendly, amiable, genial, gracious, cordial, generous, benevolent, gentle, sympathetic, obliging, accommodating, liberal. **2 healthy,** health-giving, wholesome, salubrious, temperate, pleasant, mild, balmy, agreeable, refreshing. **3 nonmalignant,** harmless, innocent, curable, remediable, treatable. *Ant.* unfriendly; hostile; unfavorable; malignant.

bent *adj.* **1 curved,** crooked, twisted, bowed, angled, warped, contorted, arched, stooped, hunched. **2 bowed,** arched, curved, stooped, hunched. *Ant.* straight; upright.
▸ *n.* **inclination,** predisposition, disposition, leaning, tendency, penchant, bias, predilection, proclivity, propensity, talent, gift, flair, ability, knack, aptitude, facility, skill, capability, capacity, forte, genius.

bequeath *v.* **1 leave,** will, cede, endow on, bestow on, consign, commit, entrust, grant, transfer. **2 hand down,** pass down/on, impart, transmit.

bequest *n.* **legacy,** inheritance, endowment, estate, heritage, bestowal, bequeathal, gift, settlement.

bereavement *n.* **1 loss,** deprivation, dispossession. **2 death,** loss, passing, demise.

berserk *adj.* **frenzied,** mad, insane, crazed, crazy, hysterical, maniacal, manic, raving, wild, enraged, raging, uncontrollable, amok, unrestrainable, *inf.* out of one's mind, hyper, ape.

berth *n.* **1 bed,** bunk, sleeping accommodations, billet, hammock, cot. **2 anchorage,** mooring, dock. **3 job,** post, position, situation, place, employment, appointment, living.
▸ *v.* **moor,** dock, anchor, land, tie up.

beseech *v.* **beg,** implore, entreat, ask, plead with, pray, petition, call upon, appeal to, supplicate, invoke, adjure, crave.

besiege *v.* **1 lay siege to,** beleaguer, blockade, surround, encircle, encompass. **2 surround,** enclose, encircle, beleaguer, beset, shut in, hem in, fence in, hedge in. **3 harass,** assail, worry, plague, beset.

best *adj.* **1 foremost,** finest, leading, top, chief, principal, highest, worthiest, supreme, superlative, unsurpassed, unexcelled, excellent, first-class, first-rate, outstanding, preeminent, *inf.* ace. **2 right,** correct, most fitting, most suitable, most desirable, apt, advantageous. *Ant.* worst.
▸ *adv.* **1 superlatively,** unsurpassedly, excellently, outstandingly. **2 greatly,** extremely. **3 most sensibly,** most wisely, most suitably, most fittingly, most advantageously.

bestial *adj.* **1 brutish,** savage, brutal, inhuman, beastly, barbarous, barbaric, abominable, atrocious, cruel, primitive, wild, heathen. **2 depraved,** vile, sordid, degenerate, degraded, gross, carnal, lustful, lecherous, prurient, lascivious, lewd, crude. **3 beastlike,** animal.

bestow *v.* **give,** present, confer on, grant, donate, endow with, hand over, allot, assign, consign, apportion, distribute, bequeath, impart, accord, award, honor with, entrust with, commit.

bet *v.* **1 wager,** gamble, stake, pledge, risk, venture, hazard, chance, speculate. **2 be certain/sure,** state confidently, predict.
▸ *n.* **1 wager,** gamble, speculation, venture, game of chance, lottery, sweepstake. **2 wager,** stake, ante, pledge. **3 prediction,** forecast,

opinion, belief, feeling, view, theory. **4 choice,** option, alternative, selection, possibility, course of action.

betray v. **1 inform on/against,** be disloyal/unfaithful to, treat treacherously, break faith with, break one's promise to, *inf.* tell on, double-cross, stab in the back, sell down the river, sell out, blow the whistle on, squeal on. **2 reveal,** disclose, divulge, give away, let slip, blurt out, blab, lay bare, bring to light, uncover, expose, exhibit, manifest, unmask. **3 abandon,** desert, forsake, walk out on, jilt. **Ant.** stand by (see stand); conceal.

better adj. **1 finer,** of higher quality, greater, superior, worthier, fitter. **2 more fitting,** more suitable, more appropriate, more desirable, more advantageous, more useful, more valuable. **3 healthier,** fitter, less ill, stronger, well, cured, recovered, recovering, progressing, improving, *inf.* mending, on the mend.
  ▸ adv. **1 in a better way,** in a superior/finer way. **2 more,** to a greater degree. **3 more sensibly,** more wisely, more suitably, more fittingly, more advantageously.

beware v. **be careful/wary,** be cautious, be on one's guard, take

heed, watch out, look out, watch/look out for, be on the lookout/alert for. **Ant.** ignore.

bewilder v. **confuse,** mix up, muddle, puzzle, perplex, baffle, mystify, nonplus, disconcert, confound, bemuse, daze, stupefy, befuddle, obfuscate, *inf.* stump, bamboozle.

bewitch v. **1 put a spell on,** cast a spell over, enchant, entrance, curse, *inf.* hex. **2 charm,** enchant, beguile, captivate, entrance, fascinate, enthrall, delight, allure, enrapture, spellbind, hypnotize, mesmerize, transfix.

bias n. **1 slant,** cross, diagonal, skew, angle, oblique, slope. **2 tendency,** inclination, leaning, bent, partiality, penchant, predisposition, propensity, proclivity, proneness, predilection, prejudice, bigotry, intolerance, narrow-mindedness, one-sidedness. **Ant.** objectivity; fairness; impartiality.
  ▸ v. **prejudice,** influence, sway, predispose, distort, bend, twist, warp, weight.

biased adj. **prejudiced,** partial, one-sided, influenced, slanted, weighted, swayed, distorted, predisposed. **Ant.** unbiased; impartial; fair.

bid v. **1 offer,** tender, proffer, propose, submit, put forward, advance. **2 command,** order, instruct, ask, tell, call for, direct, demand, enjoin, charge, summon, require, invite. **3 wish,** greet, tell, call, say.

▸ *n.* **1 offer,** proposition, proffer, proposal, submission, tender, advance, ante, price, sum, amount. **2 attempt,** effort.

big *adj.* **1 large,** sizable, great, huge, enormous, immense, vast, massive, extensive, substantial, spacious, colossal, gigantic, mammoth, prodigious, tall, bulky, burly, hulking, muscular, beefy, brawny, strapping, thickset, heavy, solid, corpulent, fat, obese, stout, gargantuan, elephantine. **2 large,** tall, bulky, burly, hulking, huge, enormous, muscular, beefy, brawny, strapping, thickset, heavy, solid, corpulent, fat, obese, stout, gargantuan, elephantine. **3 grown-up,** adult, grown, mature, elder. **4 important,** significant, serious, momentous, salient, weighty, paramount. **5 important,** influential, powerful, prominent, outstanding, leading, well-known, principal, foremost, noteworthy, notable, eminent, distinguished. **6 arrogant,** pretentious, ambitious, inflated, pompous, proud, haughty, conceited, boastful, bragging, bombastic. **7 generous,** kindly, kindhearted,

benevolent, magnanimous, unselfish, altruistic, philanthropic, beneficent, humane. *Ant.* small; little; minor.

bigot *n.* fanatic, zealot, sectarian, dogmatist, chauvinist, jingoist, racist, sexist.

bigoted *adj.* **prejudiced,** intolerant, fanatical, narrow-minded, illiberal, biased, partial, one-sided, dogmatic, warped, twisted, jaundiced, chauvinistic, jingoistic, racist, sexist. *Ant.* tolerant; liberal.

bill[1] *n.* **1 account,** invoice, statement, list of charges, reckoning, tally, score, check, *inf.* tab. **2 poster,** advertisement, flyer, notice, announcement, leaflet, circular, handout, handbill, brochure, placard, bulletin, *inf.* ad. **3 program,** playbill, list, listing, agenda, card, schedule, timetable, syllabus, roster, calendar, catalog, inventory. **4 proposal,** measure, projected/proposed law, piece of legislation.

billow *n.* **wave,** surge, swell, tide, rush, deluge, flood, breaker, roller.

▸ *v.* **puff up,** swell, fill out, balloon, belly, surge, roll.

bind *v.* **1 tie,** tie up, fasten, secure, attach, rope, strap, truss, lash, tether, fetter, chain, hitch, wrap. **2 bandage,** dress, tape, wrap, cover, swathe. **3 stick,** glue, cement, paste. **4 edge,** trim, hem, border, finish. **5 compel,** obligate, oblige, constrain, force, impel, engage, require, prescribe. **6 constrain,** restrain, restrict, hamper, hinder, inhibit, yoke. **Ant.** loosen; separate.

▸ *n.* **quandary,** dilemma, predicament, difficulty, spot, tight spot.

binding *adj.* **irrevocable,** unalterable, compulsory, obligatory, imperative, mandatory, necessary, conclusive.

birth *n.* **1 childbirth,** delivery, parturition, nativity. **2 origin,** beginnings, start, source, emergence, commencement, fountainhead, genesis. **3 origin,** descent, ancestry, lineage, line, extraction, derivation, family, parentage, house, blood, breeding, genealogy, pedigree, heritage, patrimony, stock, race, strain, background. **Ant.** death; demise.

bisect *v.* **halve,** split, cleave, separate, bifurcate, dichotomize.

bit *n.* **1 small piece,** piece, section, part, segment, chunk, lump, hunk, portion, particle, fragment, atom, flake, sliver, chip, crumb, grain, speck, scrap, shred, trace, morsel, iota, jot, whit, modicum, shard, hint, tinge, suggestion.

2 little, little while, short time, moment, minute, second, instant, short spell, short period, flash, blink of an eye, *inf.* jiffy, two shakes of a lamb's tail.

bite *v.* **1 chew,** nibble at, gnaw at, sink one's teeth into, nip, snap at, tear at, wound. **2 sting,** prick, wound. **3 clamp,** grip, hold on to. **4 take effect,** work, have results. **5 take the bait,** be lured, be enticed, be tempted, be allured. **6 annoy,** irritate, bother, displease, peeve, provoke, vex, *inf.* bug, get at, needle.

▸ *n.* **1 nip,** snap. **2 sting,** prick, puncture, wound, lesion, itch, smarting. **3 mouthful,** piece, morsel, bit. **4 snack,** refreshment. **5 sharpness,** spiciness, piquancy, pungency, edge, *inf.* kick, punch.

biting *adj.* **1 sharp,** freezing, cold, bitterly cold, harsh, nipping, stinging, piercing, penetrating. **2 sharp,** bitter, cutting, caustic, sarcastic, scathing, trenchant, mordant, stinging, withering, incisive, acid.

bitter *adj.* **1 acid,** pungent, acrid, tart, sour, biting, harsh, unsweetened, vinegary, acetous, acerbic. **2 resentful,** embittered, rancorous, acrimonious, piqued, ill-disposed, indignant, sullen, crabbed, sour, morose, begrudging, petulant, peevish.

3 painful, distressing, distressful, harrowing, heartbreaking, heart-rending, agonizing, unhappy, sad, poignant, grievous, tragic, galling, vexatious. **4 biting,** sharp, intensely cold, freezing, harsh, stinging, piercing, penetrating, fierce. **5 virulent,** acrimonious, hostile, antagonistic, spiteful, vicious, rancorous, vindictive, malicious, malevolent, venomous. **Ant.** sweet; pleasant; happy.

bizarre *adj.* **strange,** weird, peculiar, odd, unusual, uncommon, curious, abnormal, extraordinary, queer, freakish, offbeat, outlandish, unconventional, fantastic, outré, eccentric, grotesque, ludicrous, comical, ridiculous, droll, deviant, aberrant, *inf.* oddball, wacky, way-out, off-the-wall. **Ant.** ordinary; normal.

black *adj.* **1 dark,** pitch-black, pitch-dark, pitch, jet-black, jet, ebony, raven, sable, inky, coal-black, dusky, swarthy, blackish. **2 African-American,** Negro, Negroid, colored, dark-skinned. **3 dark,** starless, moonless, unlit, unlighted, unilluminated, gloomy, dusky, dim, overcast, threatening, *lit.* crepuscular. **4 dirty,** grubby, filthy, grimy, unclean, muddy, sooty, soiled, stained, dingy. **5 sad,** melancholy, depressing, dismal, distressing, gloomy, hopeless, somber, doleful, mournful, lugubrious, funereal, pessimistic, ominous, foreboding. **6 angry,** threatening, menacing, hostile, furious, aggressive, belligerent, resentful, sullen. **7 evil,** wicked, sinful, bad, vile, villainous, criminal, iniquitous, nefarious, heinous, foul, ignoble, base, corrupt, depraved, devilish, diabolic. **8 cynical,** sick, macabre. **Ant.** white; clear; light; cheerful.

blacken *v.* **1 darken,** besmudge. **2 defame,** speak ill/evil of, slander, libel, denigrate, disparage, slur, sully, decry, run down, vilify, malign, defile, impugn, smear, besmirch, tarnish, taint, stain, dishonor, drag through the mud, calumniate, traduce.

blame *v.* **accuse,** condemn, find fault with, criticize, censure, reprimand, reproach, reprove, upbraid, scold, chide, berate, take to task. **Ant.** forgive; absolve; praise.

▸ *n.* **1 responsibility,** guilt, accountability, liability, onus, culpability, fault, *inf.* rap. **2 censure,** criticism, incrimination, accusation, condemnation, reprimanding, reproach, recrimination, reproof,

castigation, complaint,
indictment, berating. **Ant.**
innocence; absolution; praise.

blameless *adj.* **innocent,** not to
blame, guiltless, above reproach/
suspicion, in the clear, without
fault, virtuous, moral, upright,
irreproachable, unimpeachable,
unoffending, sinless. **Ant.** guilty;
blameworthy.

bland *adj.* **1 tasteless,** flavorless,
mild, insipid. **2 dull,** middle-of-
the-road, mediocre, nondescript,
humdrum, boring, uninteresting,
monotonous, unexciting, tedious,
uninspiring, weak, vapid. **Ant.**
spicy; interesting; stimulating.

blank *adj.* **1 void,** empty, unfilled,
unmarked, unwritten, clear, bare,
clean, plain, spotless, white,
vacant. **2 expressionless,** empty,
vacant, deadpan, impassive,
poker-faced, vacuous, lifeless,
uninterested, emotionless,
indifferent, uncomprehending.
3 uncomprehending, without
ideas, at a loss, confused, puzzled,
perplexed, bewildered,
disconcerted, nonplussed,
muddled, dumbfounded, *inf.*
floored. **4 outright,** absolute,
unqualified, utter, complete,
thorough. **Ant.** full; expressive.
▸ *n.* **space,** gap, emptiness, void,
vacuum, vacancy, vacuity,
nothingness.

blasphemous *adj.* **profane,**
sacrilegious, irreligious,
irreverent, impious, ungodly,
godless, unholy.

blasphemy *n.* **1 profanity,**
sacrilege, irreligiousness,
irreverence, impiety,
impiousness, profaneness,
ungodliness, unholiness,
desecration, execration. **2 cursing,**
swearing, execration, curses,
oaths, profanities.

blast *n.* **1 gust,** rush, draft, blow,
gale, squall, storm. **2 blare,**
blaring, trumpeting, clamor,
bellowing, boom, roar, clang,
screech, wail, toot, honk, peal.
3 explosion, detonation,
discharge, blow-up, blowing-up,
eruption. **4 outburst,** attack,
reprimand, rebuke, criticism,
castigation, reproof.
▸ *v.* **1 sound loudly,** trumpet, blare,
boom, roar, screech. **2 blow,**
demolish, shatter, explode, break
up. **3 blight,** kill, destroy, wither,
shrivel, crush, dash, blight, wreck,
ruin, spoil, mar, annihilate,
disappoint, frustrate. **4 attack,**
reprimand, rebuke, criticize,
upbraid, berate, castigate,
reprove, rail at, flay. **5 shoot,** fire,
blaze away, discharge.

blatant *adj.* **flagrant,** glaring,
obtrusive, obvious, overt,
manifest, conspicuous,

prominent, pronounced, bare-faced, naked, sheer, outright, out-and-out, unmitigated, brazen, shameless. *Ant.* inconspicuous; subtle.

blaze *n.* **1 fire,** conflagration, holocaust, flames. **2 beam,** flash, flare, glare, streak, glitter, brightness, radiance, brilliance. **3 outburst,** burst, eruption, flare-up, explosion, outbreak, storm, torrent, blast, rush.
▸ *v.* **1 burn,** be ablaze, flame, burst into flames, catch fire. **2 shine,** beam, flash, flare, glare, glitter. **3 flare up,** blow up, explode, seethe, fume, boil, smolder, *inf.* see red, work oneself up, get steamed up.

bleach *v.* **lighten,** blanch, fade, wash out.

bleak *adj.* **1 bare,** barren, desolate, exposed, unsheltered, open, windswept, windy, chilly, cold, waste, arid, desert. **2 dreary,** dismal, dark, gloomy, drab, somber, wretched, depressing, grim, miserable, cheerless, joyless, uninviting, discouraging, disheartening, unpromising, hopeless. *Ant.* sheltered; cozy; cheerful.

bleary *adj.* **1 blurred,** blurry, tired, watery. **2 indistinct,** dim, unclear, hazy, foggy, fogged, fuzzy, clouded, misty, murky.

blemish *n.* **1 mark,** blotch, spot, patch, bruise, scar, speck, speckle, imperfection, discoloration, disfigurement, birthmark, nevus, pimple, *inf.* zit. **2 defect,** flaw, blot, taint, stain, smirch, dishonor, disgrace. *Ant.* improvement; enhancement.
▸ *v.* **1 damage,** mar, spoil, flaw, mark, spot, speckle, blotch, disfigure, discolor, deface. **2 sully,** tarnish, blot, taint, stain, besmirch, injure, damage, impair, flaw.

blend *v.* **1 mix,** combine, intermix, admix, mingle, commingle, amalgamate, coalesce, unite, merge, compound, alloy, fuse, synthesize, homogenize. **2 harmonize,** go with, complement, fit, suit.
▸ *n.* **mixture,** mix, combination, admixture, mingling, commingling, amalgamation, amalgam, uniting, union, merging, compound, alloy, fusion, composite, concoction, synthesis, homogenization.

bless *v.* **1 consecrate,** sanctify, hallow, dedicate. **2 glorify,** praise, laud, exalt, magnify, extol. **3 endow,** bestow, favor, provide, grace. **4 sanction,** approve, give approval for, be in favor of, endorse, support, give consent, smile upon. **Ant.** curse; damn; blight.

blessed adj. **1 consecrated,** sanctified, hallowed, sacred, holy, divine, venerated, revered, beatified, glorified, exalted. **2 fortunate,** lucky, favored, endowed. **3 happy,** joyful, joyous, blissful, glad, cheerful, blithe, contented.

blessing n. **1 benediction,** dedication, thanksgiving, consecration, invocation, commendation, grace. **2 approval,** approbation, sanction, endorsement, support, backing, permission, leave, consent, assent, concurrence, good wishes. **3 advantage,** benefit, help, boon, godsend, favor, gift, luck, good fortune, gain, profit, bounty. **Ant.** curse; disadvantage; blight.

blight n. **1 disease,** canker, infestation, pestilence, fungus, mildew. **2 affliction,** plague, scourge, bane, woe, curse, misfortune, calamity, trouble, tribulation, evil, corruption, pollution, contamination. **Ant.** blessing; favor.
▸ v. **kill,** destroy, wither, shrivel, blast, mildew, crush, dash, blast, wreck, ruin.

blind adj. **1 unsighted,** sightless, visually impaired, visionless, unseeing, stone-blind, inf. visually challenged. **2 imperceptive,** slow, slow-witted, dim-witted, obtuse, dense, thick. **3 unreasoned,** uncritical, unthinking, mindless, injudicious, undiscerning, indiscriminate, prejudiced, biased. **4 rash,** impetuous, hasty, reckless, uncontrolled, uncontrollable, unrestrained, wild, frantic, violent, furious, irrational. **5 concealed,** hidden, obscured, out of sight. **6 dead-end,** without exit, exitless, blocked, closed, barred, impassable. **Ant.** sighted; perceptive; mindful.
▸ v. **1 dazzle. 2 deprive of judgment/reason/sense,** deceive, delude, beguile, hoodwink.

bliss n. **1 ecstasy,** joy, elation, rapture, euphoria, happiness, delight, gladness, pleasure, heaven, paradise, seventh heaven, Utopia, halcyon days. **2 blessedness,** rapture, heavenly joy, divine happiness, beatitude. **Ant.** misery; hell.

blob n. **globule,** glob, drop, droplet, bead, ball, bubble, pellet, pill, dollop, lump, smidgen, spot, dab, splash, daub, blotch, blot, smudge, smear, mark, inf. smidge.

block n. **1 bar,** cake, brick, chunk, hunk, lump, cube, ingot, wedge, mass, piece, wad. **2 building,** complex. **3 group,** batch, band,

cluster, set, section, quantity.
4 blockage, obstruction, stoppage.
▸ *v.* **1 clog,** stop up, choke, plug,
close, obstruct. **2 hinder,** obstruct,
impede, halt, stop, bar, check,
arrest, deter, thwart, frustrate,
stand in the way of. *Ant.* clear;
facilitate.

blockage *n.* **1 obstruction,**
stoppage, block, occlusion,
impediment. **2 obstructing,**
blocking, stopping up, occluding.

blood *n.* **1 lifeblood,** vital fluid, *lit.*
ichor. **2 ancestry,** lineage, line,
family, birth, extraction, descent,
origin, genealogy, heritage, stock,
race, pedigree, kinship,
consanguinity. **3 relations,** kin,
kindred, relationship, kinship.

blood-curdling *adj.* **spine-
chilling,** chilling, terrifying, hair-
raising, horrifying, horrific,
horrendous, frightening, fearful,
appalling, scary.

bloodshed *n.* **killing,** slaughter,
slaying, carnage, butchery,
massacre, murder, blood-letting,
blood bath, gore, pogrom,
decimation.

bloodthirsty *adj.* **murderous,**
homicidal, savage, vicious,
ruthless, barbarous, barbaric,
brutal, bloody, sadistic,
slaughterous, warlike, bellicose,
fml. sanguinary.

bloody *adj.* **1 bleeding,** blood-
stained, blood-soaked, blood-
marked, blood-spattered, *fml.*
sanguinary. **2 bloodthirsty,**
murderous, homicidal, savage,
vicious, slaughterous, *fml.*
sanguinary.

bloom *n.* **1 flower,** blossom,
floweret, flowering, blossoming,
efflorescence. **2 freshness,** glow,
luster, sheen, radiance, flush,
perfection, blush.
▸ *v.* **1 flower,** blossom, open, open
out, bud, burgeon. **2 flourish,**
thrive, be in good health, get on
well, prosper, succeed, progress.
Ant. wither; fade; fail.

blot *n.* **1 spot,** blotch, smudge,
patch, dot, mark, speck, smear.
2 stain, blemish, taint, flaw, fault,
defect, tarnishing, imperfection,
disgrace.
▸ *v.* **1 spot,** blotch, smudge, dot,
mark, speckle, smear, bespatter.
2 stain, sully, tarnish, taint,
besmirch, blacken.

blow[1] *v.* **1 puff,** flurry, bluster,
blast. **2 move,** wave, flap, flutter,
waft, stream, drift, whirl,
undulate. **3 move,** toss, sweep,
whisk, drive, buffet, whirl,
transport, convey. **4 breathe out,**
puff out, exhale, emit, expel.
5 sound, play, toot, blare, blast.
6 squander, fritter away, spend
freely. **7 spoil,** ruin, bungle, make

a mess of, muff, *inf.* botch, screw up.

blow2 *n.* **1 hit,** knock, bang, punch, thump, smack, whack, thwack, buffet, stroke, rap; *inf.* bash, belt, clout, sock, wallop, battering, bat. **2 shock,** upset, calamity, catastrophe, disaster, misfortune, setback, disappointment, jolt, reversal.

blueprint *n.* **plan,** design, prototype, draft, outline, sketch, pattern, layout, representation.

bluff1 *v.* **1 pretend,** fake, feign, put on, lie. **2 deceive,** delude, mislead, trick, hoodwink, hoax, take in, humbug, bamboozle, *inf.* put one over on.
  ▸ *n.* **deception,** deceit, pretense, sham, subterfuge, fake, show, false show, idle boast, feint, delusion, hoax, fraud.

bluff2 *adj.* **1 frank,** open, candid, outspoken, blunt, direct, plainspoken, straightforward, downright, hearty. **2 steep,** sheer, vertical, precipitous, abrupt, sudden, perpendicular.

bluff3 *n.* **cliff,** headland, ridge, promontory, peak, crag, bank, slope, height, escarpment, scarp.

blunder *n.* **mistake,** error, inaccuracy, fault, slip, oversight, faux pas, gaffe, *inf.* slipup, boo-boo.
  ▸ *v.* **make a mistake,** err,

mismanage, botch, bungle, make a mess of, *inf.* slip up, screw up, blow it.

blunt *adj.* **1 unsharpened,** dull, dulled, edgeless. **2 frank,** candid, outspoken, plainspoken, straightforward, direct, bluff, to the point, brusque, abrupt, curt, short, *inf.* up-front. *Ant.* sharp; keen; subtle.
  ▸ *v.* **1 dull. 2 dull,** take the edge off, deaden, dampen, numb, weaken, impair, appease. *Ant.* sharpen.

blur *v.* **1 make indistinct,** make vague, obscure, dim, bedim, make hazy, befog, fog, cloud, becloud, mask, veil. **2 smear,** besmear, smudge, spot, blotch, besmirch. **3 dull,** numb, dim, deaden.
  ▸ *n.* **1 haze,** haziness, indistinctness, obscureness, obscurity, dimness, fogginess, cloudiness. **2 smear,** smudge, spot, blotch.

blurred *adj.* **hazy,** indistinct, faint, fuzzy, blurry, misty, foggy, unclear, vague, lacking definition, out of focus, nebulous. *Ant.* clear; distinct; sharp.

blush *v.* **redden,** go pink/red, turn red/crimson/scarlet, flush, be red-faced, burn up.
  ▸ *n.* **flush,** reddening, color, rosiness, pinkness, ruddiness.

bluster *v.* **1 blow,** blast, gust, storm, roar. **2 rant,** bully, domineer, harangue, threaten, boast, brag, swagger, throw one's weight about, be overbearing, lord it.

▸ *n.* **1 noise,** roar, tumult, blasting, gusting, storming. **2 ranting,** bravado, domineering, bombast, boasting, bragging, swaggering, braggadocio, empty threats.

blustery *adj.* **stormy,** gusty, gusting, windy, squally, wild, tempestuous.

board *n.* **1 plank,** beam, panel, slat. **2 food,** sustenance, meals, daily meals, provisions, victuals, *inf.* grub, nosh. **3 committee,** council, panel, directorate, advisory group, panel of trustees.

▸ *v.* **1 lodge,** live, room, be quartered, be housed. **2 take in,** put up, accommodate, house, feed. **3 get on,** enter, go/get on board, go/get aboard, embark.

boast *v.* **1 brag,** crow, exaggerate, overstate, swagger, blow one's own trumpet, sing one's own praises, congratulate oneself, pat oneself on the back, *inf.* talk big, blow hard. **2 possess,** have, own, enjoy, pride oneself/itself on. *Ant.* deprecate; belittle.

▸ *n.* **1 brag,** overstatement, self-praise, bluster, bragging, crowing, blustering. **2 pride,** pride and joy, treasure, gem, pearl, valued object, source of satisfaction.

boastful *adj.* **bragging,** crowing, swaggering, cocky, conceited, arrogant, vain, egotistical, overbearing, blustering, overweening, *fml.* vainglorious, *inf.* swanky, big-headed, swellheaded. *Ant.* modest; unassuming.

bob *v.* **1 move up and down,** float, bounce, quiver, wobble. **2 nod,** jerk, twitch, duck.

bodily *adj.* **physical,** corporeal, corporal, carnal, fleshly.

▸ *adv.* **as a body/group/mass,** in a mass, as a whole, together, as one, collectively, en masse, wholly, completely, entirely, totally.

body *n.* **1 frame,** form, figure, shape, build, physique, framework, skeleton, trunk, torso. **2 dead body,** corpse, cadaver, carcass, remains, *inf.* stiff. **3 person,** individual, being, human being, human, creature, mortal. **4 main part,** principal part, hub, core. **5 mass,** expanse, extent, aggregate. **6 majority,** preponderance, bulk, mass. **7 group,** party, band, association, company, confederation, bloc, congress, corporation, society. **8 substance,** firmness, solidity, density, shape, structure.

bog *n.* **marsh,** marshland, swamp, mire, quagmire, morass, slough, fen.

bogus *adj.* **fraudulent,** counterfeit, fake, spurious, false, forged, sham, artificial, mock, make-believe, quasi, pseudo, *inf.* phony. ***Ant.*** genuine; authentic.

boil *v.* **1 bubble,** simmer, cook, seethe, heat, stew, churn, froth, foam, fizz, effervesce. **2 rage,** fume, seethe, rant, rave, storm, fulminate, bluster, explode, flare up, *inf.* blow one's top, fly off the handle, go off the deep end, hit the roof, go up the wall, blow a fuse.
▸ *n.* carbuncle, furuncle, abscess, pustule, pimple.

boisterous *adj.* **1 lively,** active, bouncy, frisky, exuberant, spirited, noisy, loud, rowdy, unruly, wild, unrestrained, romping, rollicking, disorderly, rambunctious. **2 blustery,** gusting, gusty, breezy, stormy, squally, rough, turbulent, raging, wild. ***Ant.*** calm; quiet.

bold *adj.* **1 daring,** intrepid, audacious, courageous, brave, valiant, fearless, gallant, heroic, adventurous, enterprising, confident, undaunted, valorous. **2 brazen,** shameless, forward, brash, impudent, audacious, saucy, pert, immodest, unabashed, *inf.* brassy. **3 striking,** vivid, bright, eye-catching, conspicuous, distinct, pronounced, prominent, well-marked, showy, flashy. ***Ant.*** timid; retiring; pale.

bolster *n.* **pillow,** cushion, pad, support.
▸ *v.* **strengthen,** reinforce, support, boost, give a boost to, prop up, buoy up, shore up, hold up, maintain, buttress, aid, assist, help, revitalize, invigorate.

bolt *n.* **1 bar,** catch, latch, lock, fastener, hasp. **2 rivet,** pin, peg. **3 flash,** shaft, streak, burst, discharge, flare.
▸ *v.* **1 bar,** lock, fasten, latch. **2 rivet,** pin, clamp, fasten, batten. **3 dash,** dart, run, sprint, hurtle, rush, bound, hurry, flee, fly, spring, leap, abscond, escape, make a break/run for it, *inf.* tear from. **4 gulp,** gobble, devour, wolf, guzzle.

bombard *v.* **1 bomb,** shell, torpedo, pound, blitz, strafe, pepper, cannonade, fusillade, fire at, attack, assault, raid. **2 assail,** attack, besiege, beset, bother, subject to, hound, belabor.

bombardment *n.* **1 bombing,** shelling, strafing, torpedoing, blitz, blitzkrieg, air raid, strafe, cannonade, fusillade, attack, assault. **2 assailing,** attack, besieging, barraging.

bonanza *n.* **windfall,** godsend, stroke/run of luck, boon, bonus.

bond *n.* **1 tie,** link, binding, connection, attachment, union, ligature, nexus. **2 agreement,** contract, pact, transaction, bargain, deal, covenant, compact, pledge, promise, treaty, concordat.

▸ *v.* **join,** connect, fasten, stick, unite, attach, bind, glue, gum, fuse, weld.

bondage *n.* **slavery,** enslavement, captivity, servitude, serfdom, oppression.

bonus *n.* **1 extra,** plus, gain, benefit, boon, perquisite, dividend, premium. **2 gratuity,** tip, gift, perk, honorarium, reward, bounty, commission. *Ant.* disadvantage; penalty.

bony *adj.* **angular,** rawboned, gaunt, scraggy, scrawny, skinny, thin, emaciated, skeletal, cadaverous.

book *n.* **volume,** tome, work, publication, title, opus, treatise, manual, booklet, pad, loose-leaf notebook, notebook, ledger, log.

▸ *v.* **reserve,** make reservations for, arrange in advance, engage, charter, program, schedule, line up.

bookish *adj.* **studious,** scholarly, academic, literary, intellectual, brainy, highbrow, erudite, learned, pedantic, pedagogic.

boom *v.* **1 resound,** sound loudly, explode, bang, blast, blare, roar, bellow, rumble, reverberate, thunder, roar, bellow, shout. **2 burgeon,** flourish, thrive, prosper, progress, do well, succeed, grow, develop, expand, increase, swell, intensify, mushroom.

▸ *n.* **1 resounding,** loud noise, explosion, banging, bang, blasting, blast, blare, roaring, roar, bellow, rumble, reverberation, thundering, thunder. **2 increase,** upturn, upsurge, upswing, advance, growth, spurt, progress, development, expansion, improvement, boost, success. *Ant.* decline; slump.

boorish *adj.* **rough,** rude, coarse, ill-bred, ill-mannered, uncouth, churlish, gruff, uncivilized, unsophisticated, unrefined, crude, vulgar, gross, brutish, bearish, barbaric. *Ant.* refined; cultivated; sophisticated.

boost *v.* **1 lift,** raise, hoist, push, thrust, shove, heave, elevate, help, assist. **2 raise,** increase, improve, encourage, heighten, help, promote, foster, inspire, uplift. **3 increase,** expand, raise, add to, improve, amplify, enlarge, inflate, promote, advance, develop, further, foster, facilitate, help, assist, *inf.* jack up, hike up.

4 promote, advertise, publicize, praise, write up, *inf.* plug, give a plug to. ***Ant.*** decrease; hinder.
▶ *n.* **1 lift up,** push, thrust, shove, heave. **2 uplift,** shot in the arm, encouragement, help, inspiration, stimulus. **3 increase,** expansion, rise, improvement, advance.

boot *v.* **kick,** punt.

booth *n.* **1 stall,** stand, kiosk. **2 cubicle,** compartment, enclosure.

booty *n.* **spoil,** loot, plunder, pillage, prize, haul, spoils, profits, pickings, takings, winnings, *inf.* swag, the goods.

border *n.* **1 edge,** verge, perimeter, boundary, margin, brink, skirt, fringes, bounds, limits, confines. **2 frontier,** boundary, divide.
▶ *v.* **1 edge,** skirt, bound. **2 adjoin,** abut (on), be adjacent to, be next to, neighbor, touch, join, connect. **3 edge,** fringe, hem, trim, bind, decorate.

bore[1] *v.* **pierce,** perforate, puncture, penetrate, drill, tap, tunnel, burrow, mine, dig out, gouge out, sink.

bore[2] *v.* **weary,** be tedious to, tire, fatigue, send to sleep, exhaust, wear out; bore to tears, bore to death, bore out of one's mind. ***Ant.*** interest; amuse; entertain.
▶ *n.* **tiresome person/thing,** tedious person/thing, nuisance, bother, pest; *inf.* drag, pain, pain in the neck.

boring *adj.* **tedious,** dull, monotonous, humdrum, repetitious, unvaried, uninteresting, unexciting, flat, dry as dust, weary, wearisome, tiring, tiresome. ***Ant.*** interesting; amusing; entertaining.

borrow *v.* **1 ask/receive the loan of,** *inf.* cadge, mooch, scrounge, sponge, beg, bum. **2 appropriate,** commandeer, use as one's own, copy, plagiarize, pirate, take, adopt, purloin, steal, grab, filch, pinch, help oneself to, abstract, imitate, simulate, adopt, take in, take over, acquire, embrace. ***Ant.*** lend; loan.

boss *n.* **head,** chief, manager, director, chief executive, administrator, leader, superintendent, supervisor, foreman, overseer, employer, master, owner, *inf.* honcho, bossman, top dog.

bossy *adj.* **domineering,** dominating, overbearing, dictatorial, authoritarian, despotic, imperious, high-handed, autocratic.

botch *v.* **bungle,** make a mess of, spoil, mar, muff, mismanage, mangle, fumble, *inf.* mess up, foul up, screw up, blow, louse up.

bother *v.* **1 disturb,** trouble, worry, pester, harass, annoy, upset, irritate, vex, inconvenience, provoke, plague, torment, nag, molest, *inf.* hassle, give someone a hard time, get in someone's hair. **2 concern oneself,** occupy/busy oneself, take the time, make the effort, trouble oneself, go to the/any trouble, inconvenience oneself, worry oneself. **3 upset,** trouble, worry, concern, distress, perturb, disconcert.
▸ *n.* **1 trouble,** effort, inconvenience, exertion, strain, pains. **2 nuisance,** pest, annoyance, irritation, inconvenience, difficulty, problem, vexation.

bottle *n.* **container,** flask, carafe, decanter, pitcher, flagon, demijohn, magnum.

bottleneck *n.* **constriction,** narrowing, obstruction, congestion, block, blockage, jam, traffic jam, gridlock, holdup.

bottom *n.* **1 foot,** lowest part/point, base. **2 base,** foundation, basis, support, pedestal, substructure, substratum, groundwork, underpinning. **3 underside,** lower side, underneath, undersurface, belly. **4 floor,** bed, depths. **5 lowest level/position,** least important/ successful part, least honorable/ valuable part. **6 hindquarters,** buttocks, rear end, rear, seat, tail, posterior, rump, *inf.* backside, behind, derrière, butt, ass, keister, tush. **7 origin,** cause, root, source, starting point, core, center, heart, base. **8 basis,** foundation, reality, essence, nitty-gritty, substance, essentials. *Ant.* top; apex; surface.
▸ *adj.* **lowest,** last, undermost, ground. *Ant.* top; upper; highest.

bottomless *adj.* **1 deep,** immeasurable, fathomless, unfathomable, unfathomed. **2 boundless,** inexhaustible, infinite, unlimited, immeasurable, endless, limitless.

bounce *v.* **1 rebound,** spring back, bob, recoil, ricochet. **2 leap,** bound, jump, spring, bob, skip, prance, romp, caper, hurtle. **3 throw out,** eject, remove, expel, oust, get rid of, evict, *inf.* kick out, boot out.
▸ *n.* **1 spring,** springiness, rebound, recoil, resilience, elasticity, give. **2 vitality,** vigor, energy, vivacity, liveliness, life, animation, spiritedness, spirit, dynamism, *inf.* go, get-up-and-go, pep, oomph, pizzazz, zing, zip. **3 leap,** bound, jump, spring, bob, skip.

bound[1] *adj.* **tied,** tied up, secured,

roped, tethered, fettered, fastened, secured, fixed, fastened, secured, fixed

bound2 *n.* **leap,** jump, spring, bounce, hop, vault, hurdle; skip, bob, dance, prance, romp, caper, frolic, gambol.

▸ *v.* **leap,** jump, spring, bounce, hop, vault, hurdle, skip, bob, dance, prance, romp, caper, frolic, gambol.

boundary *n.* **1 border,** frontier, partition, dividing/bounding line. **2 bounds,** border, periphery, perimeter, confines, limits, extremities, margins, edges. **3 dividing line,** borderline, demarcation line. **4 bounds,** limits, outer limits, confines, extremities, barriers.

boundless *adj.* **limitless,** without limit, unlimited, illimitable, unbounded, endless, unending, never-ending, without end, inexhaustible, infinite, interminable, unceasing, everlasting, untold, immeasurable, measureless, incalculable, immense, vast, great. ***Ant.*** limited; restricted.

bountiful *adj.* **1 generous,** magnanimous, liberal, kind, giving, open-handed, unstinting, unsparing, munificent, benevolent, beneficent, philanthropic. **2 ample,** abundant, bumper, superabundant, plentiful, copious, lavish, prolific, profuse, bounteous, luxuriant, plenteous. ***Ant.*** mean; inhospitable; meager.

bounty *n.* **reward,** recompense, remuneration, gratuity, tip, premium, bonus.

bouquet *n.* **1 bunch/spray of flowers,** spray, posy, wreath, garland, nosegay, boutonnière, chaplet, corsage. **2 aroma,** smell, fragrance, perfume, scent, redolence, savor, odor, odoriferousness. **3 compliment,** commendation, tribute, eulogy, praise, congratulations.

bout *n.* **1 spell,** period, time, stretch, stint, turn, fit, run, session, round, season. **2 attack,** case, fit, spell, paroxysm. **3 match,** contest, round, competition, encounter, fight, struggle, set-to.

bow1 *v.* **1 incline the head/body,** make obeisance, nod, curtsy, genuflect, bend the knee, salaam, prostrate oneself. **2 bend,** stoop, curve, arch, crook. **3 give in,** give way, yield, submit, surrender, succumb, capitulate, defer, acquiesce, kowtow.

▸ *n.* **inclination of the head/body,** obeisance, nod, curtsy, salaam; genuflection, prostration.

bow2 *n.* **prow,** front, fore-part, fore end, stem, head.

bowl *n.* **1 dish,** basin, vessel, container. **2 hollow part,** hollow, depression, crater, hole, valley.
▸ *v.* **roll,** throw, spin, send, deliver.

box[1] *n.* **1 container,** receptacle, crate, case, carton, pack, package, chest, trunk, bin, casket. **2 compartment,** cubicle, enclosure.
▸ *v.* **package,** pack, wrap, bundle up.

box[2] *n.* **thump,** cuff, slap, punch.
▸ *v.* **1 fight,** spar, grapple. **2 strike,** hit, thump, cuff, slap, punch, knock, wallop, batter, pummel, thwack, buffet; *inf.* belt, sock, clout, whack, slug, slam, whop.

boxer *n.* **fighter,** pugilist, prizefighter, sparring partner.

boy *n.* **youth,** lad, youngster, young person, kid, junior, stripling, whippersnapper.
▸ *interj.* **wow,** gosh, gee, God, Lord, holy cow, jeepers, goodness.

boycott *v.* **ostracize,** spurn, avoid, eschew, shun, reject, blackball, blacklist, ban, bar, embargo, prohibit, debar, outlaw, proscribe. *Ant.* welcome; support; promote.

brace *n.* **1 clamp,** vice, fastener, coupling. **2 support,** prop, beam, strut, stay, truss, reinforcement, buttress, shoring-up, stanchion. **3 two,** couple, pair, duo. **4 bracket,** parenthesis.
▸ *v.* **support,** strengthen, reinforce, fortify, shore up, prop up, hold up, buttress, steady, secure, stabilize, make fast, prepare, steady, strengthen, fortify, tense.

brag *v.* **boast,** crow, show off, bluster, blow one's own trumpet, sing one's own praises, pat oneself on the back, *inf.* talk big, blow hard, lay it on thick.

brain *n.* **1 cerebral matter,** *fml.* encephalon. **2 mind,** intellect, brainpower, intelligence, wit, head, power of reasoning, *inf.* gray matter. **3 genius,** intellectual, intellect, thinker, mind, scholar, mastermind, sage, pundit, *inf.* highbrow, egghead, Einstein.

brainy *adj.* **clever,** intelligent, bright, brilliant, smart, gifted. *Ant.* stupid; dull.

branch *n.* **1 bough,** limb, stem, twig, shoot, sprig, arm. **2 offshoot,** prong. **3 division,** subdivision, section, subsection, department, part, wing, office. **4 subdivision,** subsidiary, tributary, feeder.
▸ *v.* **fork,** divide, subdivide, furcate, bifurcate, divaricate, separate, diverge.

brand *n.* **1 make,** kind, type, sort, variety, line, label, trade name, trademark, registered trademark, kind, type, sort, variety, style, stamp, cast, tag, marker, earmark.

2 stigma, stain, blot, taint, slur.
▸ *v.* **1 burn,** burn in, scorch, sear, stamp, mark. **2 stamp,** imprint, print, engrave, impress, fix.
3 stigmatize, mark, disgrace, discredit, denounce, besmirch, taint.

brandish *v.* **wave,** flourish, wield, raise, swing, shake, wag, display, flaunt, show off.

brash *adj.* **1 bold,** self-confident, self-assertive, audacious, aggressive, brazen, forward, cocky, impudent, insolent, impertinent, rude. **2 hasty,** rash, impetuous, impulsive, reckless, precipitate, careless, heedless, incautious. **3 loud,** showy, garish, gaudy, ostentatious, vulgar, tasteless, tawdry. *Ant.* reserved; cautious; quiet.

bravado *n.* **show of courage/ confidence,** swagger, swaggering, boldness, audacity, blustering, boasting, boastfulness, bragging, bombast, swashbuckling, *lit.* braggadocio.

brave *adj.* **1 courageous,** valiant, intrepid, fearless, plucky, game, gallant, heroic, bold, daring, audacious, resolute, undaunted, dauntless, lionhearted, valorous, *inf.* gutsy, spunky. **2 splendid,** spectacular, fine, grand, handsome, ostentatious, showy. *Ant.* cowardly; fearful; timid.

▸ *n.* **warrior,** soldier, fighter, fighting man.

bravery *n.* **courage,** courageousness, valor, intrepidity, fearlessness, pluck, pluckiness, gameness, gallantry, heroism, boldness, daring, audacity, resolution, fortitude, grit, mettle, spirit, dauntlessness, *inf.* guts, spunk.

brawl *n.* **fight,** affray, fracas, wrangle, melee, rumpus, scuffle, altercation, squabble, clash, quarrel, argument, disagreement, free-for-all, tussle, brouhaha, commotion, uproar, donnybrook, fisticuffs, *inf.* scrap, ruckus.
▸ *v.* **fight,** wrangle, wrestle, scuffle, tussle, clash, battle, quarrel, argue, *inf.* scrap.

brawny *adj.* **muscular,** burly, hefty, powerfully built, strong, robust, sturdy, powerful, strapping, husky, bulky, stalwart, mighty, sinewy, well-knit. *Ant.* scrawny; puny; weak.

brazen *adj.* **bold,** audacious, defiant, forward, brash, presumptuous, impudent, insolent, impertinent, brassy, pert, saucy, shameless, immodest, unashamed, unabashed, *inf.* pushy. *Ant.* reserved; modest; shy.

breach *n.* **1 break,** rupture, split, crack, fissure, fracture, rent, rift, cleft, opening, gap, hole, aperture, chasm, gulf. **2 breaking,** contravention, violation, infringement, transgression, neglect, infraction. **3 breaking-off,** estrangement, separation, severance, parting, parting of the ways, division, rift, schism, disunion, alienation, disaffection, variance, difference, dissension, falling-out, quarrel, discord.

▸ *v.* **1 break/burst through,** rupture, split, make a gap in, open up. **2 break,** contravene, violate, infringe, defy, disobey, flaunt, transgress against, infract.

break *v.* **1 smash,** shatter, crack, fracture, split, burst, fragment, splinter, shiver, crash, snap, rend, tear, divide, sever, separate, part, demolish, disintegrate, sever, separate, pierce, puncture, perforate, penetrate, open up, *inf.* go kaput. **2 contravene,** violate, infringe, breach, commit a breach of, defy, disobey, flaunt, transgress against, *fml.* infract. **3 take a break,** stop, pause, discontinue, rest, *inf.* knock off, take five. **4 interrupt,** suspend, discontinue, cut, disturb, interfere with. **5 overcome,** overpower, overwhelm, subdue, defeat, cow, suppress, extinguish, weaken, impair, undermine, dispirit, demoralize, incapacitate, cripple, enfeeble, ruin, crush, bring to one's knees, humble, degrade, reduce to nothing, bankrupt, make bankrupt. **6 train,** tame. **7 be overcome,** crack, collapse, give in, yield, cave in, crumple, go to pieces. **8 tell,** announce, impart, reveal, divulge, disclose, let out, make public, proclaim. **9 beat,** surpass, outdo, better, exceed, outstrip, top, *inf.* cap. **10 decipher,** decode, unravel, solve, figure out. **11 begin,** come into being, come forth, emerge, erupt, burst out, appear, occur. **12 change,** alter, vary, shift, metamorphose. **13 cushion,** soften, lessen, diminish, moderate. **14 crash,** hurl, dash, beat. *Ant.* repair; mend; join; abide; obey.

▸ *n.* **1 crack,** hole, gap, opening, gash, chink, fracture, split, fissure, tear, rent, rupture, rift, chasm, cleft. **2 interval,** stop, pause, halt, rest, respite, lull, interlude, intermission, recess, vacation, time off, interruption, discontinuation, suspension, hiatus, coffee break, *inf.* breather, breathing spell, letup, time out, down time. **3 change,** alteration, variation. **4 rift,** breach, split, rupture, discontinuation, schism, chasm, alienation, disaffection. **5 lucky break,** stroke of luck, advantage, gain, opportunity, chance, opening.

breakdown *n.* **1 stopping,** stoppage, seizing up, failure, malfunctioning, *inf.* conking out. **2 failure,** collapse, foundering, falling through, *inf.* fizzling out. **3 collapse,** nervous breakdown, loss of control, going to pieces, disintegration, caving in, *inf.* crack-up. **4 separation,** division, segregation, itemization, analysis, dissection, categorization, classification.

breakthrough *n.* **advance,** step forward, leap, quantum leap, discovery, find, development, improvement, progress.

breast *n.* **1 bust,** bosom, chest, front, *inf.* boob, tit, knocker, jug. **2 heart,** soul, being, core, seat of the emotions/affections, feelings.

breath *n.* **1 gulp of air,** inhalation, inspiration, exhalation, expiration, pant, gasp, wheeze, breathing, respiration. **2 breath of life,** life, life force, animation, vital force. **3 breeze,** puff, gust, waft, zephyr. **4 hint,** suggestion, whiff, undertone, trace, touch, whisper, suspicion. **5 break,** interval, pause, lull, rest, respite, breathing space, *inf.* breather.

breathe *v.* **1 respire,** inhale, inspire, exhale, expire, puff, pant, gasp, wheeze, gulp. **2 be alive,** live, have life. **3 infuse,** instill, inject, impart, transfuse.

4 whisper, murmur, sigh, say, utter, voice, articulate, express. **5 express,** suggest, indicate, manifest, intimate, betoken, augur.

breathless *adj.* **1 out of breath,** wheezing, panting, puffing, gasping, choking, gulping, winded. **2 agog,** all agog, avid, eager, excited, on edge, on tenterhooks, in suspense, open-mouthed, anxious.

breathtaking *adj.* **spectacular,** impressive, magnificent, awesome, awe-inspiring, astounding, astonishing, amazing, thrilling, stunning, exciting.

breed *v.* **1 reproduce,** procreate, multiply, give birth, bring forth young, beget, propagate. **2 raise,** rear, nurture, bring up, develop, educate, train. **3 cause,** bring about, give rise to, create, produce, generate, arouse, stir up, induce, originate, occasion, make for.

▸ *n.* **1 family,** variety, type, kind, class, strain, stock, line, stock, race, lineage, extraction, pedigree. **2 kind,** type, variety, class, brand, strain.

breeze *n.* **1 gentle wind,** breath of wind, puff of air, zephyr, gust, flurry, waft, current of air, draft, sea breeze, land breeze, onshore breeze, offshore breeze. **2 cinch,** snap, no-brainer.

▸ *v.* **stroll,** sally, sail, sweep, glide, drift, flit.

breezy *adj.* **1 windy,** blustery, gusty, squally, airy. **2 jaunty,** cheerful, cheery, lighthearted, carefree, blithe, free and easy, easygoing, casual, airy, sprightly, lively, spirited, buoyant, sparkling, animated, vivacious, frisky, sunny, *inf.* bright-eyed and bushy-tailed.

brevity *n.* **shortness,** briefness, conciseness, succinctness, compactness, terseness, economy of language, pithiness, crispness, concision, condensation, pointedness, curtness, compendiousness,transitoriness, transience, impermanence, ephemerality. *Ant.* verbosity; length.

brew *v.* **1 make,** ferment. **2 infuse,** steep, prepare. **3 gather,** gather force, form, loom, threaten, impend. **4 plot,** scheme, hatch, plan, devise, invent, concoct, stir up, foment, *inf.* cook up.

▸ *n.* **drink,** beverage, liquor, ale, beer, tea, infusion, preparation, witches' brew.

bribe *n.* **inducement,** enticement, lure, subornation, carrot, *inf.* graft, hush money, protection money, boodle, kickback, payola.

▸ *v.* **buy off,** corrupt, give an inducement to, suborn, *inf.* grease/oil the palm of, get at, pay off.

bridge *n.* **1 arch,** span, overpass, viaduct. **2 bond,** link, tie, connection, cord, binding.

▸ *v.* **1 span,** cross, cross over, go over, pass over, traverse, extend across, reach across, arch over. **2 overcome,** reconcile, bridge the gap between. *Ant.* divide; separate.

brief *adj.* **1 short,** concise, succinct, to the point, compact, terse, economic, pithy, crisp, condensed, compressed, pointed, curt, thumbnail, epigrammatic, sparing, compendious, scanty, skimpy. **2 short,** short-lived, fleeting, momentary, passing, fading, transitory, transient, temporary, impermanent, ephemeral, evanescent. **3 short,** abrupt, curt, sharp, brusque, blunt. *Ant.* long; lengthy; long-drawn-out.

▸ *n.* **1 outline,** summary, abstract, résumé, synopsis, précis, sketch, digest, epitome. **2 argument,** case, proof, defense, evidence, demonstration.

briefly *adv.* **1 concisely,** succinctly, to the point, tersely, economically, sparingly, in brief, in a few words, in a nutshell.

2 fleetingly, momentarily, transitorily, transiently, temporarily, ephemerally.

bright *adj.* **1 shining,** brilliant, vivid, intense, blazing, dazzling, beaming, sparkling, flashing, glittering, scintillating, gleaming, glowing, twinkling, glistening, shimmering, illuminated, luminous, lustrous, radiant, effulgent, incandescent, phosphorescent, bold, rich. **2 clear,** cloudless, unclouded, fair, sunny, pleasant, clement. **3 clever,** intelligent, sharp, quick-witted, quick, smart, brainy, brilliant, astute, acute, ingenious, inventive, resourceful, proficient, accomplished. **4 happy,** genial, cheerful, jolly, joyful, gay, merry, lighthearted, vivacious, lively, buoyant. **5 promising,** optimistic, hopeful, favorable, propitious, auspicious, providential, encouraging, lucky, fortunate, good, excellent, golden. *Ant.* dull; dark; stupid.

brighten *v.* **1 make bright/ brighter,** light up, lighten, illuminate, illumine, irradiate. **2 cheer up,** perk up, gladden, enliven, buoy up, animate, *inf.* buck up, pep up.

brilliant *adj.* **1 bright,** shining, vivid, intense, blinding, radiant, beaming, gleaming, dazzling, luminous, lustrous, scintillating, resplendent, *lit.* effulgent, coruscating. **2 bright,** clever, intelligent, smart, brainy, intellectual, gifted, talented, accomplished, educated, scholarly, learned, erudite, cerebral, precocious. **3 clever,** intelligent, smart, astute, masterly, resourceful, inventive, discerning. **4 magnificent,** splendid, superb, impressive, remarkable, exceptional, glorious, illustrious. *Ant.* dim; stupid.

brim *n.* **1 rim,** lip, brink, edge. **2 visor,** shield, shade.
▸ *v.* **be full/filled,** overflow, run/ well over.

bring *v.* **1 come conveying/ carrying,** carry, bear, take, fetch, convey, transport, deliver, lead, guide, conduct, usher, escort. **2 cause,** create, produce, result in, wreak, effect, contribute to, engender, occasion. **3 put forward,** prefer, propose, initiate, institute. **4 make,** fetch, yield, net, gross, return, produce, command.

brink *n.* **edge,** verge, margin, rim, extremity, limit, border, boundary, fringe, skirt, threshold, point.

brisk *adj.* **1 quick,** rapid, fast, swift, speedy, energetic, lively, vigorous, agile, nimble, spry, sprightly, spirited. **2 bracing,**

crisp, keen, biting, invigorating, refreshing, exhilarating, energizing, *inf.* nippy. **3 no-nonsense,** brusque, abrupt, sharp, curt, crisp, snappy. **4 rapid,** busy, bustling, active, hectic. *Ant.* sluggish; quiet.

bristle *n.* **hair,** stubble, whiskers, prickle, spine, quill, thorn, barb.
▸ *v.* **1 stiffen,** rise, stand up, stand on end. **2 bridle,** get angry/infuriated, become indignant, be irritated/defensive, rear up, draw oneself up. **3 swarm,** teem, crawl, *inf.* be thick, be alive.

brittle *adj.* **1 breakable,** splintery, shatterable, hard, crisp, fragile, frail, delicate, frangible, weak, unstable. **2 harsh,** hard, sharp, strident, grating, rasping.

broach *v.* **introduce,** bring up, raise, mention, open, put forward, propound, propose, suggest, submit.

broad *adj.* **1 wide,** large, extensive, vast, spacious, expansive, sweeping, boundless. **2 wide,** wide-ranging, broad-ranging, general, comprehensive, inclusive, encyclopedic, all-embracing, universal, unlimited. **3 general,** nonspecific, unspecific, vague, loose. **4 clear,** obvious, direct, plain, explicit, straightforward, clear-cut,

unmistakable, undisguised, unconcealed. **5 full,** complete, total, clear, open. **6 broad-minded,** liberal, open-minded, tolerant, unprejudiced, unbiased, fair, just, free-thinking, progressive. **7 coarse,** vulgar, gross, unrefined, indelicate, indecent, improper, blue. *Ant.* narrow; limited; detailed.

broadcast *v.* **1 transmit,** relay, beam, send out, put on the air, radio, televise, telecast. **2 make public,** announce, report, publicize, publish, advertise, proclaim, air, spread, circulate, pass around, disseminate, promulgate, blazon. **3 scatter,** sow, disperse, strew.
▸ *n.* **program,** radio/television show, show, transmission, telecast.

broaden *v.* **1 widen,** fill out. **2 widen,** expand, enlarge, extend, increase, augment, supplement, add to, amplify, fill out, develop, open up, swell.

broad-minded *adj.* **open-minded,** liberal, tolerant, forbearing, indulgent, impartial, unprejudiced, unbiased, unbigoted, undogmatic, catholic, flexible, dispassionate, just, fair, progressive, free-thinking.

brochure *n.* **booklet,** leaflet, pamphlet, folder, handbill, handout, circular, notice, advertisement, flyer.

broke *adj.* **penniless,** moneyless, bankrupt, insolvent, poverty-stricken, impoverished, impecunious, penurious, indigent, destitute, ruined, without a penny to one's name, stone-broke, flat broke, *inf.* cleaned out, strapped for cash, bust.

brokenhearted *adj.* **heartbroken,** grief-stricken, desolate, despairing, devastated, inconsolable, prostrated, miserable, wretched, sorrowing, mourning, forlorn, woeful, crestfallen.

brood *n.* **young,** offspring, progeny, family, hatch, clutch, nest, litter, children, youngsters, *inf.* kids.
▸ *v.* **1 worry,** fret, agonize, think, ponder, meditate, muse, mull, dwell (on/upon), ruminate. **2 hatch,** incubate, cover young.

brook[1] *n.* **stream,** streamlet, creek, rivulet, rill, brooklet, runnel, branch, run.

brook[2] *v.* **tolerate,** stand, bear, allow.

browbeat *v.* **bully,** force, coerce, compel, badger, dragoon, intimidate, tyrannize, hector, terrorize, *inf.* bulldoze.

brown *adj.* **1 dark brown,** chocolate, cocoa, umber, reddish-brown, auburn, copper, copper-colored, bronze, henna, mahogany, walnut, rust, brick, terra-cotta, puce, yellowish-brown, tan, tawny, ginger, cinnamon, hazel, gold, light brown, fawn, beige, ecru, brunette, bay, chestnut, sorrel, roan. **2 tanned,** sunburned, sunburnt, browned, bronze, bronzed.
▸ *v.* **sear,** seal, fry, grill, sauté.

browse *v.* **1 scan,** skim, glance/look through, thumb/leaf/flip through, look around, have a look, window-shop. **2 graze,** feed, eat, nibble, pasture.

bruise *v.* **1 discolor,** blacken, mark, blemish, contuse, injure, hurt, damage, mark, discolor, spoil. **2 hurt,** upset, offend, insult, wound, displease, peeve, vex, distress.
▸ *n.* **black-and-blue mark,** skin discoloration, blackening, mark, blemish, contusion, injury, swelling.

brunt *n.* **full force,** force, impact, shock, burden, thrust, violence, pressure, strain, stress, repercussions, consequences.

brush *n.* **1 broom,** besom, whisk broom. **2 touch,** stroke, *inf.* swipe. **3 encounter,** clash, conflict, confrontation, skirmish, tussle, fight, battle, engagement, *inf.* scrap, set-to. **4 brushwood,** undergrowth, scrub, thicket, copse, bushes.

▸ *v.* **1 sweep,** groom, clean, buff. **2 touch,** caress, kiss, glance, contact, stroke, sweep, scrape.

brusque *adj.* **abrupt,** curt, blunt, short, sharp, terse, caustic, gruff, bluff, hasty, outspoken, plainspoken, discourteous, impolite, rude, churlish. *Ant.* polite; courteous.

brutal *adj.* **1 savage,** cruel, bloodthirsty, vicious, ruthless, callous, heartless, merciless, pitiless, remorseless, uncivilized, inhuman, barbarous. **2 bestial,** brutish, beastly, animal, coarse, carnal, sensual. *Ant.* gentle; humane; civilized.

brute *n.* **1 beast,** wild beast, wild animal, animal, creature. **2 beast,** monster, animal, swine, savage, sadist, barbarian, devil, fiend, ogre, lout, oaf, boor, churl, dolt.

bubble *n.* **1 globule,** glob, bead, blister, drop, droplet, vesicle, air cavity. **2 illusion,** delusion, fantasy, dream, chimera.

▸ *v.* **1 fizz,** effervesce, sparkle, foam, froth, spume. **2 boil,** simmer, seethe, percolate. **3 overflow,** brim over, be filled.

bubbly *adj.* **1 fizzy,** effervescent, carbonated, sparkling, foamy, frothy, sudsy. **2 bubbling,** vivacious, effervescent, sparkling, animated, ebullient, scintillating, bouncy, buoyant, excited, elated, lively, merry, happy.

bucket *n.* pail, scuttle, can.

buckle *n.* **1 clasp,** clip, catch, fastener, fastening, hasp. **2 kink,** warp, curve, distortion, wrinkle, bulge.

▸ *v.* **1 fasten,** hook, secure, clasp, catch, clip. **2 warp,** bulge, crumple, cave in.

bud *n.* shoot, sprout, flowerlet, floret.

▸ *v.* **sprout,** send out shoots, form/ develop buds, germinate, burgeon.

budge *v.* **1 move,** shift, stir, go, proceed. **2 change one's mind,** give way, give in, yield, acquiesce. **3 influence,** sway, convince, persuade, bend.

budget *n.* **1 financial plan/ estimate/statement/blueprint. 2 allowance,** allocation, allotment, quota, ration.

▸ *v.* **1 plan,** schedule, allocate, ration, apportion. **2 plan,** allow, save, set aside money, set aside.

buff[1] *adj.* **beige,** straw-colored, sandy-colored, yellowish, yellowish-brown.

buff[2] *v.* polish, burnish, rub up, rub, smooth, shine.

buffer *n.* **cushion,** bulwark, guard, safeguard, shield, screen, intermediary.

buffet *n.* **1 smorgasbord,** *inf.* spread. **2 sideboard,** cabinet, china cabinet/cupboard.

buffoon *n.* **1 fool,** clown, jester, comic, comedian, wit, wag, merry andrew. **2 fool,** dolt, idiot, nincompoop, *inf.* chump, numskull, dope, twit, nitwit, halfwit.

bug *n.* **1 insect,** beetle, fly, flea, mite, *inf.* creepy-crawly. **2 bacterium,** germ, virus, microorganism, infection. **3 craze,** fad, mania, obsession, passion, fixation. **4 fault,** flaw, defect, imperfection, failing, error, obstruction, *inf.* glitch, gremlin. **5 listening device,** wiretap, tap. ▶ *v.* **1 tap,** wiretap, listen in on, eavesdrop on. **2 annoy,** irritate, exasperate, anger, irk, vex, infuriate, inflame, provoke, try one's patience, get one's hackles up, *inf.* get one's back up, get on one's nerves, get in one's hair, be a thorn in one's flesh/side.

build *v.* **1 construct,** erect, put up, assemble, set up, raise, make, manufacture, fabricate, form. **2 found,** base, establish, set up, originate, institute, start, begin, inaugurate, initiate, develop. *Ant.* demolish; dismantle; destroy.

▶ *n.* **body,** frame, physique, figure, form, structure, shape.

building *n.* **structure,** construction, edifice, erection.

buildup *n.* **1 expansion,** increase, growth, enlargement, escalation, development, accumulation. **2 accumulation,** stockpile, accretion, mass, heap, store, stack, pile. **3 promotion,** publicity, advertising, *inf.* hype, plugging, plug, ballyhoo.

bulge *n.* **swelling,** bump, lump, protuberance, protrusion, prominence, projection. ▶ *v.* **swell,** swell out, puff up/out, stick out, bag, balloon, balloon up/out, project, protrude, jut out, distend, expand, dilate, enlarge, bloat.

bulk *n.* **1 size,** volume, bulkiness, quantity, weight, extent, mass, substance, magnitude, massiveness, hugeness, largeness, bigness, ampleness, amplitude, dimensions. **2 majority,** greater part/number, preponderance, major/main/better part, mass, body, lion's share.

bulky *adj.* **large,** big, substantial, huge, enormous, massive, vast, immense, voluminous, colossal, hulking, heavy, weighty, ponderous, stout, thickset, plump, fat, chubby, portly, tubby, obese, awkward, unwieldy, cumbersome, unmanageable. *Ant.* small; slim; manageable.

bulldoze *v.* **1 demolish,** flatten, level, raze. **2 force,** push, drive, shove, propel. **3 bully,** browbeat, coerce, intimidate, cow, bludgeon, dragoon, steamroll, steamroller, railroad, *inf.* strong-arm.

bulletin *n.* **1 news report,** report, statement, announcement, news flash, flash, account, message, communication, communiqué, dispatch, notification.
2 newspaper, newsletter, pamphlet, leaflet, broadsheet, listings.

bullish *adj.* **1 rising,** advancing, up, improving, confident.
2 optimistic, hopeful, confident, positive, assured, cheerful, sanguine.

bully *n.* **browbeater,** intimidator, coercer, oppressor, persecutor, tyrant, tormentor, tough, ruffian, thug, hooligan, rowdy, *inf.* hood.
▸ *v.* **browbeat,** intimidate, coerce, oppress, domineer, persecute, cow, tyrannize, pressurize, pressure, bulldoze, *inf.* push around, strong-arm.

bulwark *n.* **1 rampart,** fortification, buttress, bastion, embankment, breastwork, redoubt, wall, dam. **2 support,** mainstay, defense, guard, safeguard, defender, protector.

bumbling *adj.* **clumsy,** blundering, awkward, bungling, incompetent, inept, inefficient, stumbling, lumbering, foolish.

bump *v.* **1 hit,** bang, strike, knock, crash into, collide with, hurt, injure, damage, *inf.* slam. **2 hit,** bang, strike, knock, hurt, injure, damage. **3 bounce,** jolt, jerk, rattle, shake, jounce. **4 displace,** supplant, dismiss, remove, eject, oust.
▸ *n.* **1 thud,** thump, bang, crash, jolt, smash, knock, rap, impact. **2 jolt,** crash, smash, bang, thud, thump, knock, rap, impact. **3 lump,** swelling, injury, contusion, nodule, node, tumescence, intumescence, protuberance. **4 bulge,** hump, lump, knob, knot, protuberance.

bumpkin *n.* **country bumpkin,** yokel, clodhopper, oaf, boor, lout, peasant, rustic, *inf.* hillbilly, hick, hayseed, rube.

bumptious *adj.* **self-important,** conceited, arrogant, self-assertive, full of oneself, overbearing, puffed up, self-opinionated, cocky, presumptuous, pompous, forward, *inf.* pushy.

bumpy *adj.* **1 uneven,** rough, potholed, rutted, pitted, lumpy, knobby. **2 choppy,** jolting, jolty, jerky, jarring, bouncy, rough. *Ant.* even; smooth.

bunch *n.* **1 bouquet,** spray, posy, sheaf, nosegay, corsage. **2 cluster,** assemblage, collection, batch, pile, stack, heap, bundle, mass, quantity, accumulation, agglomeration, group, collection, gathering, band, gang, cluster, party, crowd, flock, swarm, troop, mob, multitude, *inf.* passel.
▸ *v.* **cluster,** huddle, gather, group, bundle, pack, herd, crowd, flock, mass, cram.

bundle *n.* **1 collection,** batch, pile, stack, heap, bunch, mass, quantity, accumulation, agglomeration. **2 package,** pack, bale, parcel, packet, bunch, bale, truss, faggot.
▸ *v.* **1 tie,** tie up/together, package, wrap, bind, fasten together, bale, truss. **2 hurry,** hustle, rush, push, shove, thrust, throw. **3 clothe,** wrap, cover.

bungle *v.* **botch,** muff, spoil, make a mess of, mess up, mishandle, mismanage, fudge, mar, ruin, *inf.* louse up, screw up, foul up.

bungling *adj.* **clumsy,** incompetent, inept, unskillful, inexpert, blundering, maladroit, *inf.* ham-handed.

buoy *n.* **1 marker,** navigation mark, guide, beacon, signal. **2 lifebuoy,** lifebelt, life jacket, life preserver, *inf.* Mae West.

buoyant *adj.* **1 floatable,** floating, afloat, light. **2 cheerful,** cheery, lighthearted, bouncy, carefree, joyful, vivacious, animated, lively, high-spirited, sparkling, sprightly, blithe, jaunty, breezy, happy, merry, *inf.* peppy, zingy, zippy. ***Ant.*** leaden; depressed.

burden *n.* **1 load,** cargo, weight, freight. **2 responsibility,** onus, charge, duty, obligation, tax, trouble, care, worry, anxiety, tribulation, difficulty, strain, stress, weight, encumbrance, millstone, albatross, trials, tribulations.
▸ *v.* **1 load,** lade, weight, charge, weigh down, encumber, hamper. **2 oppress,** trouble, worry, distress, bother, afflict, torment, strain, stress, tax, overwhelm.

bureau *n.* **1 agency,** office, service, department, division, branch. **2 dresser,** chest of drawers, highboy.

bureaucracy *n.* **1 civil service,** central administration, directorate, government officials. **2 red tape,** officialdom, formalities, rules and regulations.

burglar *n.* **housebreaker,** cat burglar, thief, sneak thief, robber, crook, pilferer, filcher, picklock, *inf.* second-story man.

burglary *n.* **housebreaking,** breaking and entering, breaking in, forced entry, theft, robbery, larceny, pilfering, filching, break-in.

burial *n.* **1 burying,** interment, entombment, inhumation, sepulture. **2 funeral,** sepulture, obsequies, exequies.

burly *adj.* **thickset,** brawny, powerfully built, well-built, muscular, strapping, big, hulking, hefty, beefy, bulky, sturdy, stocky, stout. *Ant.* scrawny; puny; slight.

burn *v.* **1 be on fire,** be afire, be ablaze, blaze, go up, smoke, flame, be aflame, flare, flash, flicker, glow. **2 set on fire,** set alight, ignite, put a match to, light, kindle, incinerate, reduce to ashes, scorch, singe, sear, char. **3 be hot,** be warm, feel hot, be feverish, be fevered, *inf.* be on fire. **4 smart,** sting, tingle, be sore, hurt, throb, bite, prickle, irritate, pain. **5 be aroused,** be emotional, simmer, smolder, seethe. **6 long,** yearn, desire, hunger after, lust, itch, pant, wish, want. **7 use,** use up, consume, expend, eat up, exhaust.

burning *adj.* **1 blazing,** aflaming, flaring, raging, ignited, glowing, flickering, smoldering, scorching, singeing, searing, charring. **2 hot,** warm, *inf.* scorching, roasting, boiling, baking. **3 smarting,** stinging, biting, prickling, irritating, caustic, searing, corroding, corrosive, painful. **4 intense,** fervent, fervid, ardent, passionate, eager. **5 important,** crucial, significant, urgent, pressing, compelling, critical, vital, essential, acute, pivotal, climacteric.

burnish *v.* **polish,** shine, brighten, rub, buff, buff up, smooth.

burrow *n.* **tunnel,** hole, hollow, excavation, lair, den, retreat.
▸ *v.* **1 dig,** tunnel, excavate, hollow out, gouge out, scoop out. **2 go under,** hide, shelter, conceal oneself.

burst *v.* **1 split,** split open, break open, rupture, crack, fracture, fragment, shatter, shiver, fly open, tear apart, rend asunder. **2 blow up,** explode, detonate, fulminate. **3 break out,** burst forth, pour forth, gush out, surge out, rush out. **4 barge,** push/shove one's way. **5 break out,** erupt.

bury *v.* **1 inter,** lay to rest, consign to the grave, entomb, inhume, sepulcher. **2 conceal,** hide, put out of sight, submerge, sink, secrete, enshroud. **3 drive in,** embed, implant, sink, submerge. **4 absorb oneself,** immerse oneself, engross oneself, engage oneself, interest oneself. *Ant.* exhume; unearth; expose.

bush *n.* **1 shrub,** woody plant. **2 brush,** scrub land, scrub, the wild, backwoods, wilderness.

bushy *adj.* **thick,** shaggy, fuzzy, fluffy, luxuriant, unruly, rough.

business *n.* **1 occupation,** line, profession, career, trade, work, employment, job, pursuit, vocation, métier. **2 trade,** trading, commerce, trafficking, buying and selling, merchandizing, bargaining, dealings, transactions, proceedings. **3 firm,** company, concern, enterprise, organization, corporation, establishment, store, shop, venture, industry. **4 concern,** affair, responsibility, duty, function, task, assignment, obligation, problem. **5 matter,** subject, topic, point of discussion, theme, issue, question, problem, thesis. **6 affair,** matter, thing, case, set of circumstances, issue.

businesslike *adj.* **1 professional,** efficient, methodical, systematic, orderly, organized, well-ordered, practical, pragmatic, thorough, painstaking, meticulous, correct. **2 workaday,** routine, prosaic, down-to-earth, conventional, unimaginative.

bust¹ *n.* **chest,** breasts, bosom, torso, *inf.* boobs, tits, knockers, rack.

bust² *v.* **1 break,** fracture, burst, rupture, crack. **2 bankrupt,** ruin, impoverish, pauperize, break. **3 arrest,** capture, catch, seize, *inf.* collar, nab.

bustle *v.* **hurry,** rush, dash, scuttle, scurry, hasten, scamper, scramble, flutter, fuss, *inf.* tear.
▸ *n.* **activity,** flurry, stir, briskness, commotion, tumult, excitement, agitation, fuss, *inf.* to-do.

busy *adj.* **1 occupied,** engaged, working, at work, on duty, in a meeting, otherwise engaged, involved in, absorbed in, engrossed in, preoccupied with, working at, laboring at, toiling at, slaving at. **2 active,** energetic, strenuous, full, hectic, exacting, bustling, industrious, lively, tireless, restless, *inf.* on the go. **3 ornate,** overelaborate, overdetailed, overdecorated, cluttered, fussy. ***Ant.*** unoccupied; inactive; quiet; idle.
▸ *v.* **occupy,** engage, employ, absorb, immerse, engross, involve, interest.

busybody *n.* **meddler,** interferer, snooper, snoop, mischief-maker, troublemaker, gossip, scandalmonger, muckraker.

butt¹ *n.* **1 handle,** shaft, hilt, haft. **2 stub,** end, remnant, *inf.* roach. **3 bottom,** buttocks, keister, tush.

butt² *n.* **scapegoat,** dupe, target, victim, laughingstock, object, subject.

butt[3] *v.* **1 push,** thrust, shove, ram, bump, buffet, prod, poke, jab, knock, bunt. **2 abut,** join, meet, conjoin.

buttocks *n.* **bottom,** posterior, rump, hindquarters, *inf.* behind, backside, butt, can, ass, keister, tush.

buttonhole *v.* **accost,** waylay, take aside, importune, detain, grab, catch, talk at.

buttress *n.* **1 prop,** support, abutment, strut, reinforcement, stanchion, pier. **2 mainstay,** upholder, sustainer, cornerstone, pillar.
▸ *v.* **strengthen,** reinforce, prop up, support, shore up, underpin, brace, uphold, defend, back up.

buxom *adj.* **plump,** large-bosomed, big-bosomed, full-bosomed, shapely, *inf.* busty.

buy *v.* **1 purchase,** make a purchase of, pay for, invest in, procure. **2 bribe,** suborn, corrupt, *inf.* fix, rig. *Ant.* sell.
▸ *n.* **purchase,** acquisition, deal, bargain.

buzz *n.* **1 buzzing,** hum, humming, murmur, drone, whir, whirring, hiss, sibilation, whisper, ring, ringing, purr, purring. **2 rumor,** gossip, talk, scuttlebutt, news, report, whisper, scandal, hearsay, word around town/here, word going around.
▸ *v.* **1 hum,** murmur, drone, whir, hiss, whisper, sibilate, ring, reverberate, purr. **2 gossip,** chatter, tattle, spread rumors. **3 bustle,** rush, dash, hurry.

bygone *adj.* past, departed, dead, former, one-time, previous, forgotten, lost, of old, olden, ancient, antiquated, of yore, obsolete, extinct, out of date, outmoded, passé

bypass *n.* **detour,** circuitous route, roundabout way, alternative route.
▸ *v.* **1 make a detour around,** go around, pass around. **2 get around,** circumvent, find a way around, avoid, evade, ignore, pass over, miss out, circumvent, go over the head of. **3 ignore,** pass over, miss out, circumvent, avoid, go over the head of.

bystander *n.* **onlooker,** looker-on, observer, eyewitness, witness, spectator, watcher, viewer, beholder, gaper, passerby, *inf.* rubberneck.

Cc

cabin *n.* **1 log cabin,** hut, chalet, cottage, shack, shanty, shed. **2 stateroom,** room, sleeping quarters, berth, compartment.

cable *n.* **1 rope,** cord, wire, line, cordage. **2 cablegram,** telegram, telegraph, wire.
 ▸ *v.* **telegraph,** wire, radio.

cache *n.* **1 hiding place,** hide-out, secret place, hole. **2 hoard,** store, collection, fund, supply, hidden treasure, treasure, loot, *inf.* stash.

cacophony *n.* **discord,** dissonance, discordance, jarring, stridency, grating, rasping, caterwauling.

cadaverous *adj.* **corpselike,** deathlike, gaunt, haggard, drawn, emaciated, skeletal, thin, hollow-eyed, ashen, pale, wan, ghostly.

cadence *n.* **1 rhythm,** beat, pulse, measure, meter, tempo, swing, lilt, cadency. **2 intonation,** inflection, accent, modulation.

cage *n.* **enclosure,** pen, corral, pound, lockup, coop, birdcage, aviary.
 ▸ *v.* **confine,** shut in, impound, pen, corral, lock up, incarcerate, imprison, coop, coop up.

cajole *v.* **wheedle,** coax, beguile, flatter, seduce, lure, entice, tempt, inveigle, maneuver, humor, *inf.* sweet-talk, soft-soap, butter up.

cake *n.* **1 cupcake,** sponge cake, angel food cake, chocolate cake, layer cake, fruitcake, cheesecake, gingerbread, shortcake, bun, pastry. **2 block,** bar, slab, lump, mass, cube, loaf, chunk.
 ▸ *v.* **1 solidify,** harden, thicken, dry, bake, coagulate, consolidate. **2 cover,** coat, encrust, plaster.

calamitous *adj.* **disastrous,** catastrophic, cataclysmic, devastating, ruinous, dire, tragic, fatal, wretched, woeful.

calamity *n.* **disaster,** catastrophe, tragedy, misfortune, cataclysm, devastation, scourge, misadventure, mischance, mishap, ruin, tribulation, woe.

calculate *v.* **1 work out,** compute, estimate, count up, figure out, evaluate, enumerate, determine, gauge, judge, measure, weigh, reckon, rate. **2 design,** plan, aim, intend. **3 rely,** depend, count, bank.

calculated *adj.* **considered,** planned, premeditated, deliberate, intentional, intended, purposeful. **Ant.** unintentional; spontaneous.

calculating *adj.* **scheming,** designing, contriving, devious, shrewd, manipulative, sharp, sly, crafty, Machiavellian. **Ant.** ingenuous; guileless.

caliber *n.* **1 bore,** diameter. **2 quality,** worth, distinction, stature, excellence, merit, ability, talent, capability, competence, capacity, endowments, gifts, strengths, scope.

call *v.* **1 cry,** cry out, shout, exclaim, yell, scream, shriek, roar. **2 awaken,** waken, arouse, rouse. **3 call up,** phone, telephone, give one a ring, *inf.* give one a buzz. **4 pay a call,** pay a visit, pay a brief visit, stop by, *inf.* drop in, pop in. **5 call together,** convene, summon, order, convoke, assemble, announce, declare, proclaim, decree. **6 send for,** ask for, summon, contact, order, bid, fetch. **7 name,** christen, designate, dub, entitle, denominate, label, term. **8 consider,** think, regard, judge, estimate. **9 appoint,** elect, ordain.
▸ *n.* **1 cry,** shout, exclamation, yell, scream, shriek, roar, song, chirp, chirping, tweet. **2 signal,** hail, whoop. **3 telephone call,** ring, *inf.* buzz. **4 visit,** brief visit.

5 summons, invitation, request, plea, bidding, order, command, appeal, notice. **6 need,** occasion, reason, cause, justification, grounds, excuse. **7 demand,** request, requirement, need, want, requisition. **8 attraction,** lure, allurement, fascination, appeal, bewitchment.

calling *n.* **vocation,** occupation, career, profession, business, work, employment, job, trade, craft, line, line of work, pursuit, métier, walk of life, province, field.

callous *adj.* **1 hard,** hardened, tough, harsh, cold, insensitive, unfeeling, cold-hearted, hard-hearted, heartless, hard-bitten, cruel, obdurate, inured, uncaring, unsympathetic, unresponsive, indifferent, soulless. **2 hard,** hardened, thickened, leathery. **Ant.** kind; compassionate.

callow *adj.* **immature,** inexperienced, uninitiated, naïve, unsophisticated, innocent, undeveloped, adolescent. **Ant.** experienced; sophisticated.

calm *adj.* **1 still,** windless, mild, tranquil, balmy, halcyon, quiet, peaceful, pacific, undisturbed, restful, smooth, motionless, placid, waveless, unagitated, storm-free. **2 composed,** collected, cool, cool-headed, controlled, self-controlled, self-possessed, quiet, tranquil, unruffled, relaxed, serene, unexcited, unexcitable, unflappable, undisturbed, unagitated, imperturbable, unemotional, unmoved, equable, stoical, *inf.* together. *Ant.* stormy; excited; frantic.

▸ *n.* **1 stillness,** tranquillity, serenity, quietness, quietude, peace, peacefulness, harmony, restfulness, repose. **2 composure,** coolness, self-control, tranquillity, serenity, equanimity, unflappability, imperturbability, equability, poise, sang-froid, *inf.* cool. *Ant.* turmoil; upheaval.

calumny *n.* **slander,** calumniation, defamation, libel, misrepresentation, false accusation, denigration, vilification, aspersions, mud-slinging, backbiting, detraction, disparagement, deprecation, evil-speaking, insult, abuse, vituperation, obloquy, revilement, smear campaign.

camouflage *n.* **disguise,** protective coloring, mask, screen, cloak, cover, cover-up, false front, front, façade, masquerade, blind, concealment, subterfuge.

▸ *v.* **disguise,** hide, conceal, mask, screen, veil, cloak, cover, cover up, obscure.

camp[1] *n.* **1 encampment,** camping ground, campsite, tents, bivouac, cantonment. **2 faction,** party, group, clique, coterie, set, sect, cabal.

campaign *n.* **1 war,** battle, expedition, offensive, attack, crusade. **2 course of action,** operation, promotion, strategy, set of tactics, drive, push, crusade, movement, maneuver, battle plan.

▸ *v.* **fight,** battle, work, push, crusade, strive, struggle, agitate.

cancel *v.* **1 call off,** stop, discontinue, give up, withdraw from, countermand, revoke, rescind, annul, declare void, declare null and void, nullify, quash, invalidate, set aside, retract, negate, repudiate, abrogate, repeal, abolish. **2 annul,** declare void, declare null and void, nullify, quash, invalidate, set aside, retract, negate, revoke, rescind, repudiate, abrogate, repeal, abolish. **3 delete,** cross out, erase, strike out, rub out, blot out, expunge, eliminate, obliterate, eradicate, efface.

4 counterbalance, balance, offset, compensate, make up for, counteract, neutralize, redeem. *Ant.* confirm.

cancer *n.* **1 tumor,** malignant tumor, malignancy, growth, malignant growth. **2 canker,** blight, evil, corruption, sickness, disease, pestilence, scourge, plague.

candid *adj.* **1 frank,** open, honest, truthful, sincere, forthright, direct, plainspoken, outspoken, blunt, unequivocal, bluff, brusque, *inf.* straight from the shoulder. **2 unposed,** spontaneous, impromptu, extemporary, uncontrived, informal, unstudied. ***Ant.*** secretive; guarded; equivocal.

candidate *n.* **1 applicant,** job applicant, office seeker, contender, nominee, contestant, aspirant, possibility, *inf.* runner. **2 entrant,** examinee.

candor *n.* **frankness,** openness, honesty, truthfulness, sincerity, forthrightness, directness, plainspokenness, outspokenness, unequivocalness, bluntness, bluffness, brusqueness.

canny *adj.* **1 careful,** cautious, prudent, thrifty. **2 shrewd,** sharp, astute, discerning, penetrating, perspicacious, clever, sensible, wise, judicious, sagacious, circumspect. ***Ant.*** careless; foolish.

canopy *n.* **awning,** shade, sunshade, cover, covering, tarpaulin.

canvass *v.* **1 solicit votes,** seek votes, campaign, electioneer, drum up support, persuade, convince. **2 investigate,** find out about, inquire into, look into, examine, scrutinize, explore, study, analyze, evaluate, survey, scan, poll. **3 discuss,** debate, air, ventilate, argue, dispute.

canyon *n.* **ravine,** gully, valley, gorge, chasm, gulf, abyss.

capability *n.* **1 ability,** capacity, potential, aptitude, faculty, facility, power, competence, efficiency, effectiveness, proficiency, accomplishment, talent, adeptness, skill, skillfulness, experience, cleverness, intelligence, smartness, gifts, flair, knack, forte, strong point. **2 talent,** gifts, skill, aptitude, flair, knack, forte, strong point.

capable *adj.* **able,** competent, adequate, efficient, effective, proficient, accomplished, talented, gifted, adept, skillful, masterly, experienced, practiced, qualified, clever, intelligent, smart. ***Ant.*** incapable; incompetent.

capacity *n.* **1 space,** room, size, largeness, ampleness, amplitude, scope, magnitude, dimensions, proportions, extent. **2 ability,** capability, aptitude, potential, faculty, facility, power, competence, competency, proficiency, accomplishment, cleverness, intelligence, brains, head. **3 position,** post, job, office, function, role, appointment.

cape *n.* **cloak,** mantle, shawl, wrap, poncho, pelisse.

caper *v.* **frolic,** frisk, romp, skip, gambol, cavort, prance, dance, leap, hop, jump, bound, spring, bounce.
▸ *n.* **1 frolics,** frisking, romping, skipping, gambols, gamboling, cavorting, prancing, dancing, leap. **2 prank,** trick, practical joke, antic, lark, jest, jesting, high jinks, mischief, escapade, stunt, game, sport, fun, *inf.* shenanigans.

capital *adj.* **1 principal,** chief, main, major, prime, paramount, foremost, predominant, overruling, leading, cardinal, central, key. **2 grave,** vital, important, serious, crucial, fatal. **3 splendid,** excellent, first-rate, first-class, superb, fine, outstanding, *inf.* super, top-notch.
▸ *n.* **1 first city,** seat of government, center of administration. **2 capital letter,** uppercase letter, uncial, uncial letter, *inf.* cap. **3 money,** finance, finances, funds, cash, hard cash, wherewithal, means, assets, liquid assets, wealth, resources, reserves, principal.

capitulate *v.* **surrender,** yield, submit, give in, give up, come to terms, succumb, accede, back down, cave in, relent, acquiesce, *inf.* throw in the towel.

caprice *n.* **whim,** whimsy, vagary, fancy, notion, fad, freak, humor, impulse, quirk, changeableness, fickleness, volatility, inconstancy.

capricious *adj.* **changeable,** unpredictable, fickle, variable, inconstant, unstable, mercurial, volatile, impulsive, erratic, fanciful, faddish, freakish, irregular, fitful, whimsical, wayward, quirky. *Ant.* stable; consistent; constant.

capsize *v.* **overturn,** turn over, upset, upend, knock over, tip over, invert, keel over.

capsule *n.* **1 pill,** tablet, lozenge. **2 seed case,** pod, pericarp. **3 spacecraft,** probe.

captain *n.* **1 commander,** master, skipper, *inf.* old man. **2 leader,** head, skipper, chief, boss, principal, *inf.* honcho. **3 chief,** head, leader, boss, principal, *inf.* honcho.

caption *n.* **heading,** title, wording, head, legend, inscription.

captious *adj.* **carping,** criticizing, critical, faultfinding, quibbling, *inf.* nitpicking.

captivate *v.* **charm,** delight, enchant, bewitch, fascinate, beguile, enthrall, entrance, enrapture, attract, allure, lure, win, infatuate, seduce, ravish, ensnare, dazzle, hypnotize, mesmerize.

captive *n.* **prisoner,** prisoner of war, hostage, slave, bondsman, convict, jailbird, detainee, *inf.* con.
▸ *adj.* **imprisoned,** incarcerated, locked up, caged, interned, confined, penned up, detained, restrained, in captivity, in bondage.

captivity *n.* **imprisonment,** custody, detention, confinement, internment, incarceration, restraint, constraint, committal, bondage, slavery, servitude, enslavement, subjection. *Ant.* freedom; liberty.

capture *v.* **catch,** arrest, apprehend, take prisoner, take captive, take into custody, seize, take, lay hold of, trap, *inf.* nab, collar, pinch, nail, bag. *Ant.* free; liberate.
▸ *n.* **1 arrest,** apprehension, imprisonment, seizure, trapping, *inf.* nabbing, collaring, pinching. **2 prize,** trophy, gain, booty, pickings, pillage.

car *n.* **1 vehicle,** motor vehicle, automobile, motorcar, *inf.* wheels, heap, crate, jalopy, limo, auto. **2 coach,** dining car, sleeping car, Pullman, cable car.

carcass *n.* **1 corpse,** dead body, body, remains, *Med.* cadaver, *inf.* stiff. **2 body,** person, self, oneself. **3 frame,** framework, skeleton, shell, hulk.

cardinal *adj.* **1 main,** chief, capital, principal, important, greatest, highest, vital, key, central, major, essential, foremost, leading, prime, paramount, preeminent, fundamental, basic, primary. **2 red,** scarlet, crimson, vermilion.
▸ *n.* **cardinal bishop,** cardinal priest, high priest, archpriest.

care *n.* **1 worry,** anxiety, trouble, disquiet, unease, distress, sorrow, anguish, grief, sadness, affliction, woe, hardship, tribulation, responsibility, stress, pressure, strain, burdens. **2 concern,** regard, attention, interest, solicitude, looking after, sympathy.
3 carefulness, attention, thought, regard, heed, forethought, mindfulness, conscientiousness, painstakingness, pains, accuracy, precision, meticulousness, punctiliousness, fastidiousness.
4 attention, caution, heedfulness, alertness, watchfulness, vigilance, wariness, awareness, circumspection, prudence.
5 charge, protection, custody, keeping, safekeeping, control, management, supervision,

guardianship, wardship. *Ant.* happiness; neglect; carelessness; inattention.

▶ *v.* **be concerned,** be interested, interest oneself, have regard, worry, trouble, bother, mind, *inf.* give a damn, give a hoot, give a rap.

career *n.* **1 occupation,** profession, vocation, calling, employment, job, métier. **2 course,** progress, progression, procedure, passage, path. **3 rush,** onrush, run, race, bolt, dash, gallop, impetus.

carefree *adj.* **lighthearted,** happy-go-lucky, cheerful, cheery, happy, merry, jolly, buoyant, breezy, easygoing, jaunty, frisky, blithe, airy, nonchalant, unworried, untroubled, insouciant, *inf.* upbeat. *Ant.* anxious; worried; miserable.

careful *adj.* **1 cautious,** heedful, alert, aware, attentive, watchful, vigilant, wary, on guard, chary, circumspect, prudent, mindful. **2 mindful,** heedful, protective, solicitous, thoughtful, attentive, concerned. **3 attentive,** conscientious, painstaking, meticulous, accurate, precise, scrupulous, punctilious, fastidious. **4 cautious,** thrifty, economical, economic. *Ant.* careless; inattentive; extravagant.

careless *adj.* **1 inattentive,** thoughtless, unthinking, forgetful, absentminded, negligent, irresponsible, slipshod, lax, slack, negligent, remiss, slipshod, untidy, slovenly, slatternly, *inf.* sloppy, messy. **2 hasty,** cursory, perfunctory, inaccurate, disorganized, slapdash, slipshod, *inf.* sloppy. **3 unthinking,** thoughtless, insensitive, indiscreet, unguarded. **4 carefree,** lighthearted, happy-go-lucky, cheerful, merry, buoyant, blithe, nonchalant. **5 unstudied,** artless, casual, nonchalant, informal. *Ant.* careful; meticulous.

caress *n.* **touch,** stroke, fondle, fondling, pat, embrace, cuddle, hug, nuzzle, kiss.

▶ *v.* **cuddle,** fondle, pet, pat, embrace, hug, nuzzle, kiss.

caretaker *n.* **superintendent,** janitor, warden, porter, custodian, keeper, watchman, steward, curator.

cargo *n.* **freight,** freightage, load, lading, haul, consignment, contents, goods, merchandise, baggage, shipment, shipload, boatload, truckload.

caricature *n.* **cartoon,** parody, burlesque, mimicry, travesty, distortion, satire, farce, lampoon, *inf.* send-up, takeoff, spoof.

▸ *v.* **parody,** mimic, mock, ridicule, distort, satirize, lampoon, burlesque, *inf.* send up, take off.

carnage *n.* **slaughter,** wholesale slaughter, butchery, massacre, mass murder, mass destruction, indiscriminate bloodshed, blood bath, holocaust, pogrom, *inf.* shambles.

carnal *adj.* **sexual,** sensual, fleshly, erotic, lustful, lascivious, libidinous, lecherous, lewd, prurient, salacious, coarse, gross, lubricious.

carnival *n.* **1 fiesta,** festival, fête, gala, jamboree, holiday, revelry, merrymaking, festivity, celebration, Mardi Gras. **2 fair,** sideshows, circus.

carouse *v.* **go on a spree,** go on a binge, binge, party, paint the town red, overindulge, live it up, go on a bender.

carp *v.* **complain,** faultfind, find fault, criticize, cavil, pick on, quibble, censure, reproach, nag, *inf.* nitpick. **Ant.** applaud; praise.

carpenter *n.* **joiner,** cabinetmaker, woodworker.

carriage *n.* **1 coach,** cab, coach-and-four, stagecoach, hackney, hansom, gig, chaise, phaeton, surrey. **2 posture,** bearing, stance, deportment, comportment, attitude, manner, presence, air, guise, demeanor, mien, behavior,

conduct. **3 transport,** transportation, freight, freightage, conveyance, delivery, carrying.

carry *v.* **1 transport,** convey, transfer, move, take, bring, bear, lug, haul, shift, fetch, conduct, pass on, transmit, relay. **2 support,** sustain, bear, shoulder. **3 win,** capture, gain, secure, effect, accomplish. **4 sell,** stock, offer, have for sale, retail. **5 communicate,** give, release, publish, broadcast. **6 influence,** affect, have an effect on, motivate, stimulate, urge, spur on, impel, drive. **7 bear oneself,** hold oneself, comport oneself, deport oneself, conduct oneself.

cart *n.* **handcart,** wheelbarrow, pushcart.

▸ *v.* **1 transport,** convey, haul, transfer, move, shift. **2 lug,** tote, carry.

carton *n.* **box,** package, cardboard box, container, case.

cartoon *n.* **1 comic strip,** animated movie, animation. **2 caricature,** parody, lampoon, satire, burlesque, *inf.* takeoff, send-up, spoof.

cartridge *n.* **case,** container, cylinder, capsule, cassette, magazine.

carve *v.* **sculpt,** sculpture, cut, chisel, hew, whittle, chip, form, shape, fashion, mold, engrave, etch, notch, cut in, incise, slice, cut up.

cascade *n.* **waterfall,** falls, fountain, shower, cataract, torrent, flood, deluge, outpouring, avalanche.
▸ *v.* **tumble,** descend, pour, gush, surge, spill, overflow.

case[1] *n.* **1 container,** box, receptacle, holder, canister, crate, box, carton, coffer, casket.
2 casing, covering, sheath, sheathing, wrapper, wrapping, cover, envelope, housing, jacket, capsule, folder. **3 cabinet,** cupboard.

case[2] *n.* **1 position,** situation, circumstances, instance, occurrence, happening, occasion, conditions, plight, predicament, event, contingency, phenomenon.
2 instance, occurrence, occasion, example, illustration, specimen.
3 lawsuit, suit, action, trial, proceedings, legal proceedings, legal process, legal cause, legal dispute. **4 statement,** plea, claim, alibi, postulation, explanation, exposition, thesis, testing, presentation. **5 patient,** sick person, invalid, sufferer, victim.

cash *n.* **1 money,** ready money, coinage, notes, bank notes, currency, *fml.* specie, legal tender.
2 money, finance, wherewithal, resources, funds, capital, investment capital, *inf.* dough, bread, cabbage.
▸ *v.* **exchange,** change, turn into cash/money.

cashier *n.* **bank teller,** teller, banker, treasurer, bursar, purser, accountant, controller, comptroller, money man.
▸ *v.* **dismiss,** discharge, expel, drum out, throw out, cast out, discard, get rid of, *inf.* sack, give the boot to, boot out, can.

cask *n.* **barrel,** keg, tun, vat, vessel, hogshead.

cast *v.* **1 throw,** toss, fling, pitch, hurl, sling, heave, shy, lob, launch, let fly, shoot, direct, turn, throw, send out. **2 shed,** discard, slough off, peel off, throw off, get rid of, let fall, let drop. **3 emit,** give off, send out, shed, radiate, diffuse, spread out, form, create.
4 throw, bestow, impart, confer, give, grant. **5 register,** record, enter, vote. **6 shape,** fashion, form, mold, model, sculpt.
7 choose, select, pick, name, assign, appoint, allot.
▸ *n.* **1 throw,** toss, fling, pitch, hurl, lob. **2 sort,** kind, style, type, stamp, nature. **3 figure,** shape, mold, form. **4 squint,** twist, defect.

caste *n.* **class,** social class, order, social order, grade, grading, station, place, standing, position, status.

castle *n.* **stronghold,** fortress, keep, hold, citadel, palace, chateau.

casual *adj.* **1 chance,** accidental, unintentional, unexpected, unforeseen, unanticipated, fortuitous, serendipitous. **2 offhand,** random, impromptu, spontaneous, unpremeditated, unthinking. **3 part-time,** temporary, irregular. **4 cursory,** perfunctory, superficial, desultory, hasty, hurried. **5 indifferent,** apathetic, uncaring, uninterested, unconcerned, lackadaisical, blasé, nonchalant, lukewarm, insouciant. **6 informal,** not formal, unceremonious, relaxed, leisure, *inf.* sporty. **7 slight,** superficial, shallow. **Ant.** intentional; thorough; formal.

casualty *n.* **1 fatality,** dead/wounded/injured person, victim. **2 victim,** sufferer, loser, loss.

cat *n.* **1 feline,** domestic cat, *inf.* pussy, pussy cat, puss, tabby, tomcat, tom, tortoiseshell, Siamese, Burmese, kitten, mouser, alley cat. **2 big cat,** lion, tiger, leopard, lynx.

catapult *v.* **launch/propel rapidly,** hurtle, shoot, fling.

cataract *n.* **1 cascade,** waterfall, falls, rapids, torrent, downpour. **2 opacity,** opaqueness.

catastrophe *n.* **disaster,** calamity, tragedy, blow, adversity, trouble, trials, mishap, misfortune, mischance, misadventure, failure, reverses, affliction, distress.

catch *v.* **1 grasp,** snatch, grab, seize, grip, clutch, clench, pluck, receive, acquire, take possession of, intercept. **2 capture,** seize, take captive, apprehend, take, arrest, lay hold of, trap, snare, *inf.* nab, collar. **3 understand,** follow, grasp, comprehend, make out, take in, fathom, discern, perceive, apprehend, *inf.* get, get the drift of, get the hang of. **4 surprise,** discover, come across, startle, detect. **5 contract,** get, become infected with, develop, succumb to, suffer from, *inf.* come down with. **6 capture,** attract, draw, captivate, bewitch. **7 capture,** reproduce, represent, photograph, draw, paint. **Ant.** drop; release; lose.
▸ *n.* **1 bolt,** lock, fastener, fastening, clasp, hasp, hook, clip, latch. **2 snag,** disadvantage, drawback, stumbling block, hitch, fly in the ointment, trap, trick, snare, *inf.* catch-22. **3 bag,** haul, net, take, yield. **4 eligible man/woman/person,** marriage prospect, suitable husband/wife/spouse.

catching *adj.* **1 contagious,**

infectious, communicable, transmittable, transmissible.
2 attractive, appealing, winning, captivating, charming, fetching, taking, fascinating, enchanting, bewitching, alluring.

catchy *adj.* **memorable,** popular, appealing, captivating, haunting, melodious, singable.

categorical *adj.* **unqualified,** unconditional, unequivocal, explicit, unambiguous, unreserved, absolute, direct, downright, emphatic, positive, express, conclusive. *Ant.* qualified; equivocal; tentative.

category *n.* **class,** classification, group, grouping, head, heading, list, listing, designation, type, sort, kind, variety, grade, grading, order, rank, status, division, section, department.

cater *v.* **feed,** provision.

catholic *adj.* **1 general,** universal, widespread, global, worldwide, comprehensive, all-encompassing, all-embracing, all-inclusive.
2 wide, broad, broad-based, eclectic, liberal, open-minded, tolerant, unbigoted, unsectarian, ecumenical. **3 Roman Catholic,** *inf.* RC. *Ant.* limited; narrow.

cattle *pl. n.* **bovines,** steer, oxen, stock, livestock.

cause *n.* **1 origin,** root, source, beginning, genesis, occasion, mainspring, originator, author, creator, producer, agent, prime mover, maker. **2 reason,** grounds, justification, call, basis, motive, motivation. **3 principle,** ideal, belief, conviction, tenet, object, aim, objective, purpose, raison d'être. **4 case,** point of view, contention. *Ant.* effect; result.
▸ *v.* **be the cause of,** make happen, bring about, give rise to, begin, create, produce, originate, occasion, generate, effect, engender, lead to, result in, precipitate, provoke.

caustic *adj.* **1 corrosive,** corroding, mordant, burning, acrid, destructive. **2 sarcastic,** cutting, biting, mordant, stinging, sharp, scathing, trenchant, virulent, acrimonious, astringent.

caution *n.* **1 alertness,** care, carefulness, attention, wariness, attentiveness, heed, heedfulness, watchfulness, vigilance, guardedness, circumspection, discretion, forethought, prudence, mindfulness. **2 comic,** comedian, wit, humorist, wag, clown, joker, jester.
▸ *v.* **warn,** advise, counsel, urge, admonish.

cautious *adj.* **careful,** wary, watchful, shrewd, prudent, circumspect, discreet, guarded, chary, alert, heedful, attentive, vigilant, mindful, *inf.* cagey. **Ant.** incautious; careless; reckless.

cavalier *n.* **1 horseman,** horse soldier, mounted soldier, equestrian, knight. **2 escort,** beau, gallant, gentleman, courtier.
▶ *adj.* **offhand,** condescending, haughty, arrogant, lofty, lordly, disdainful, supercilious, patronizing, scornful, contemptuous, discourteous, insolent.

cave *n.* **cavern,** grotto, hollow, cavity, underground chamber, tunnel, cellar, dugout, den.

cavity *n.* **hole,** hollow, crater, pit, orifice, aperture, gap, dent.

cease *v.* **stop,** discontinue, desist, desist from, end, finish, leave off, quit, conclude, terminate, suspend, halt, bring to an end, break off, come to a stop, come to an end, let up, die away, abate, terminate. **Ant.** start; begin; commence.

ceaseless *adj.* **incessant,** unceasing, unending, endless, never-ending, interminable, nonstop, constant, continuous, continual, uninterrupted, eternal, perpetual, unremitting, persistent.

celebrate *v.* **1 commemorate,** observe, honor, mark, keep, drink to, toast, rejoice, enjoy oneself, party, paint the town, *inf.* go on a spree, go out on the town, whoop it up. **2 proclaim,** make known, herald, announce, publicize, broadcast, advertise. **3 praise,** laud, extol, glorify, exalt, eulogize, reverence. **4 perform,** solemnize, ceremonialize.

celebrated *adj.* **famous,** famed, notable, noted, renowned, well-known, popular, prominent, distinguished, great, eminent, preeminent, outstanding, illustrious, acclaimed, revered, glorious, legendary, lionized. **Ant.** unknown; obscure; unsung.

celebration *n.*
1 commemoration, observance, honoring, keeping, remembrance, performance, solemnization.
2 party, carousal, festival, fête, carnival, gala, festivity, merrymaking, revelry, *inf.* spree, binge, bash.

celebrity *n.* **1 VIP,** famous person, dignitary, big name, name, personality, star, superstar, lion, notable, luminary, personage, *inf.* bigwig, big shot, big wheel. **2 fame,** renown, notability, popularity, reputation, honor, prominence, prestige, distinction, eminence, preeminence, glory, illustriousness, stardom. **Ant.** nonentity; obscurity.

celestial *adj.* **1 heavenly,** divine,

godly, godlike, ethereal, sublime, paradisiacal, elysian, spiritual, immortal, angelic, seraphic, cherubic. **2 heavenly,** astronomical, extraterrestrial, stellar.

celibacy *n.* **chastity,** singleness, abstinence, self-denial, self-restraint, continence, abnegation, asceticism, virginity, bachelorhood, spinsterhood, monkhood, nunhood, monasticism, *inf.* single blessedness. *Ant.* marriage; promiscuity.

cell *n.* **1 cubicle,** room, apartment, compartment, chamber, stall, enclosure, dungeon, lockup, compartment, cavity, hole. **2 faction,** caucus, nucleus, clique, coterie, group, party, unit.

cement *n.* **adhesive,** bonding, binder, glue, superglue, gum, paste.
  ▸ *v.* **bind,** bond, stick, join, unite, attach, cohere, combine, affix, glue, gum, paste, solder, weld.

cemetery *n.* **graveyard,** burial ground, burial place, churchyard.

censor *v.* **cut,** delete, delete from, blue-pencil, expurgate, bowdlerize.
  ▸ *n.* **examiner,** inspector, expurgator, bowdlerizer.

censorious *adj.* **faultfinding,** critical, disapproving, condemnatory, reproachful, censuring.

censure *v.* **criticize,** condemn, blame, castigate, denounce, disapprove of, berate, upbraid, reprove, reproach, rebuke, reprimand, scold, chide, reprehend. *Ant.* praise; approve; commend.
  ▸ *n.* **criticism,** condemnation, blame, castigation, denunciation, disapproval, berating, upbraiding, reproval, reproof, reproach, rebuke, reprimand, scolding, chiding, reprehension.

center *n.* **middle,** middle point, midpoint, nucleus, heart, core, hub, focus, focal point. *Ant.* edge; periphery; outskirts.
  ▸ *v.* **concentrate,** focus, pivot, converge, close in.

centered *adj.* **confident,** serene, well balanced, self-possessed.

central *adj.* **1 middle,** mid, median, mean, inner, interior. **2 main,** chief, principal, foremost, fundamental, basic, key, essential, primary, pivotal, focal, core, cardinal. *Ant.* outer; subordinate; minor.

centralize *v.* **concentrate,** center, concenter, consolidate, amalgamate, condense, compact, unify, incorporate, streamline, focus, rationalize.

ceremonial *adj.* **formal,** ritual,

ritualistic, stately, solemn, dignified, celebratory, sacramental, liturgical.
▸ *n.* **ceremony,** rite, ritual, formality, custom, solemnity, sacrament, liturgy.

ceremonious *adj.* **1 ceremonial,** formal, ritual. **2 formal,** punctilious, precise, scrupulous, stately, courtly, courteous, civil, deferential, stiff, rigid, affected, *inf.* just-so.

ceremony *n.* **1 rite,** service, formality, observance, function, custom, sacrament, show. **2 formalities,** niceties, pomp, protocol, decorum, etiquette, propriety, conventionality, attention to detail, *inf.* fuss.

certain *adj.* **1 sure,** positive, confident, convinced, assured, unwavering, unshaken, secure, satisfied, persuaded. **2 sure,** assured, destined, fated, inevitable, reliable, inescapable, bound to happen, inexorable, *inf.* in the bag. **3 sure,** definite, unquestionable, beyond question, indubitable, undeniable, irrefutable, incontrovertible, incontestable, obvious, evident, plain, clear, conclusive. **4 sure,** definite, assured, unfailing, unquestionable, undisputed, dependable, reliable, trustworthy, sound, foolproof, *inf.* sure-fire.

5 definite, decided, settled, fixed, established, determined.
6 particular, specific, individual, special, especial, precise.
7 indeterminate, moderate, minimum. *Ant.* uncertain; unsure; indefinite.

certainly *adv.* **1 surely,** definitely, assuredly, undoubtedly, undeniably, obviously, plainly, clearly. **2 yes,** of course, by all means.

certainty *n.* **1 sureness,** assuredness, positiveness, confidence, conviction, reliability, validity, conclusiveness, authoritativeness, truth, fact, factualness. **2 inevitability,** indubitability, inescapability, fact, *inf.* sure thing, cinch. *Ant.* uncertainty; doubt.

certificate *n.* **certification,** document, authorization, credentials, testimonial, warrant, license, voucher, diploma.

certify *v.* **1 testify to,** attest, corroborate, substantiate, verify, confirm, endorse, validate, vouch for, guarantee, authenticate, document, bear witness to, ratify, warrant, certified dead verified as, confirmed as, officially declared.
2 give a certificate/diploma, recognize, accredit, license, authorize, qualify.

cessation *n.* **end,** termination, finish, conclusion, pause, break, respite, letup, ceasing, stopping, halting, ending, finishing.

chain *n.* **1 series,** succession, string, sequence, train, progression, course, set, cycle, line, row, concatenation. **2 group,** firm, company.
▸ *v.* **fasten,** secure, tie, bind, tether, shackle, fetter, manacle, hitch, moor, handcuff, confine, restrain, trammel, gird, imprison.

chair *n.* **1 seat,** stool, bench, pew, stall, throne. **2 professorship,** professorate. **3 chairperson,** chairman, chairwoman, president, spokesperson, spokesman, spokeswoman, MC, master/mistress of ceremonies.
▸ *v.* **preside over,** lead, direct, manage, control, oversee, supervise.

chalky *adj.* **white,** pale, wan, pallid, ashen, pasty, waxen, blanched, bleached, colorless.

challenge *n.* **1 summons,** call, invitation, bidding. **2 difficult task/venture,** hazard, risk, obstacle.
▸ *v.* **1 dare,** summon, invite, bid, throw down the gauntlet to. **2 question,** call into question, dispute, protest against, take exception to, object to, disagree with, demur against, be a dissenter of. **3 test,** tax, stimulate, arouse, inspire, excite, spur on.

chamber *n.* **1 room,** apartment, compartment, cubicle, hall, bedroom, bedchamber, boudoir. **2 compartment,** cavity, hollow, cell. **3 legislative body,** legislature, assembly, council, house.

champion *n.* **1 winner,** title-holder, victor, conqueror, hero. **2 defender,** protector, upholder, supporter, advocate, backer, patron, *inf.* angel. **3 knight,** paladin, hero, warrior.
▸ *v.* **defend,** protect, uphold, support, stand up for, fight for, speak for, advocate, back, promote, espouse.

chance *n.* **1 accident,** coincidence, fortuity, serendipity, fate, destiny, fortune, luck, providence. **2 prospect,** possibility, probability, likelihood, likeliness, conceivability, odds. **3 opportunity,** opening, occasion, turn, time, *inf.* shot. **4 risk,** gamble, hazard, venture, speculation, long shot. ***Ant.*** design; certainty.
▸ *v.* **1 happen,** occur, take place, come about, come to pass, befall, turn up, crop up. **2 risk,** hazard, gamble, venture, speculate, take a chance that, try one's luck, take a leap in the dark.

chancy *adj.* **risky,** uncertain,

hazardous, speculative, perilous, dangerous, *inf.* dicey, iffy.

change *v.* **1 alter,** modify, transform, convert, vary, remodel, recast, restyle, reconstruct, reorder, reorganize, metamorphose, transmute, permutate, permute. **2 alter,** be transformed, move on, evolve, metamorphose, fluctuate, diversify, *inf.* do an about-face, do a U-turn. **3 exchange,** interchange, substitute, switch, replace, trade, barter, *inf.* swap. **Ant.** retain; stay.
▸ *n.* **1 difference,** alteration, modification, transformation, conversion, variation, remodeling, reconstruction, reorganization, transition, innovation, metamorphosis, transfiguration, vicissitude, transmutation, mutation, permutation, *inf.* about-turn, U-turn. **2 exchange,** interchange, substitution, switch, trade, bartering, *inf.* swap. **3 diversion,** variation, variety, *inf.* break.
4 coins, coinage, cash, silver, petty cash. **Ant.** endurance; stability.

changeable *adj.* **1 changing,** variable, varying, changeful, chameleonlike, chameleonic, protean, shifting, vacillating, volatile, mercurial, capricious, fluctuating, fluctuant, fluid, kaleidoscopic, fitful, wavering, unstable, unsteady, unsettled, irregular, erratic, unreliable, inconstant, fickle, mutable, unpredictable, many-faceted, checkered, vicissitudinous.
2 alterable, modifiable, convertible, mutable, permutable. **Ant.** unchangeable; constant; invariable.

channel *n.* **1 passage,** strait, neck, narrows, waterway, watercourse. **2 bed,** floor, bottom, depths. **3 gutter,** groove, furrow, conduit, duct, culvert, ditch.
4 course, way, direction, path, route, approach. **5 means,** medium, agency, vehicle, route.
6 band, frequency.
▸ *v.* **1 furrow,** groove, flute, hollow out, cut. **2 transmit,** convey, transport, conduct, direct, guide.

chant *n.* **song,** singing, chorus, melody, ditty, carol, psalm.
▸ *v.* **sing,** recite, intone, *lit.* cantillate.

chaos *n.* **disorder,** confusion, pandemonium, bedlam, tumult, upset, upheaval, disorganization, uproar, disruption, disarray, anarchy, lawlessness, riot. **Ant.** order; tranquillity.

chaotic *adj.* **in chaos,** disordered, confused, tumultuous, upset, disorganized, jumbled, topsy-turvy, askew, awry, disrupted, in disarray, anarchic, lawless, orderless. **Ant.** orderly; ordered.

character *n.* **1 personality,** nature, disposition, temperament, temper, essential quality, ethos, individuality, complexion, constitution, makeup, cast, attributes, bent, genius. **2 moral strength/fiber,** strength, honor, integrity, rectitude, uprightness, fortitude, backbone. **3 reputation,** name, standing, position, status. **4 eccentric,** oddity, original, individual, *inf.* oddball, queer fish, card, weirdo. **5 person,** individual, human being, fellow, *inf.* guy, sort, type, customer. **6 persona,** person, portrayal, representation, role, part. **7 letter,** sign, mark, symbol, type, cipher, hieroglyph, figure, device, rune, logo, emblem.

characteristic *n.* **quality,** essential quality, attribute, feature, trait, property, mannerism, mark, trade mark, idiosyncrasy, peculiarity, quirk.
▸ *adj.* **typical,** distinguishing, distinctive, particular, special, individual, specific, peculiar, idiosyncratic, singular, representative, symbolic, symptomatic, diagnostic. **Ant.** uncharacteristic; untypical; unusual.

characterize *v.* **1 typify,** distinguish, identify, specify, signalize, indicate, denote, designate, mark, stamp, brand, label. **2 portray,** depict, present, represent, describe.

charade *n.* **pretense,** travesty, fake, farce, parody, pantomime.

charge *v.* **1 ask in payment,** ask, fix a charge/price, expect, impose, levy. **2 debit,** put down to, bill. **3 accuse,** indict, arraign, impeach, impute, blame, incriminate. **4 attack,** storm, assault, rush, open fire on, fall on, *inf.* lay into, tear into. **5 entrust,** tax, weigh, weigh down, load, burden, encumber, hamper, saddle. **6 fill,** fill up, load, load up, pack, plug, fill, load, imbue, suffuse, pervade, permeate, infuse, instill. **Ant.** absolve; acquit.
▸ *n.* **1 cost,** price, fee, amount, rate, payment, expense, expenditure, outlay, dues, levy, toll. **2 accusation,** allegation, indictment, arraignment, impeachment, citation, imputation, blame, incrimination. **3 attack,** storming, assault, onrush, onslaught, onset, sortie, incursion. **4 responsibility,** care, custody, guardianship, trust, protection, safekeeping, surveillance, duty, task, job, responsibility, office, obligation,

assignment, business, burden.
5 ward, protégé, dependent,
minor. **6 instruction,** direction,
order, command, dictate,
injunction, exhortation, mandate.

charitable *adj.* **philanthropic,**
giving, benevolent, generous,
liberal, open-handed, kind,
magnanimous, beneficent,
bountiful, bounteous, munificent,
big-hearted, humane, tolerant,
broad-minded, understanding,
sympathetic, compassionate,
lenient, indulgent, forgiving,
kindly, favorable, gracious. *Ant.*
uncharitable; unkind.

charity *n.* **1 financial assistance,**
donations, contributions,
handouts, gifts, funding,
endowments, financial relief,
philanthropy, benefaction.
2 goodwill, compassion,
humanity, humanitarianism,
kindliness, love, sympathy,
tolerance, indulgence, altruism,
thoughtfulness, generosity,
liberality, benevolence.

charm *n.* **1 attractiveness,**
attraction, appeal, allure,
allurement, fascination,
captivation, pleasingness,
desirability, engagingness,
delightfulness, beauty, wiles,
blandishments. **2 spell,** magic
formula, magic word,
abracadabra, sorcery, magic.

3 trinket, ornament, bauble,
souvenir, good-luck charm, token,
amulet, talisman, fetish.
▸ *v.* **delight,** please, attract, win,
win over, captivate, allure, lure,
draw, fascinate, bewitch, beguile,
enchant, enrapture, enamor,
seduce, cajole, hypnotize,
mesmerize. *Ant.* repel; alienate.

chart *n.* **graph,** table, map,
diagram, plan, blueprint, guide,
scheme, tabulation.
▸ *v.* **tabulate,** map, map out, plot,
graph, delineate, diagram, sketch,
chart a course of, draft, follow,
record, register, note.

chase *v.* **give chase to,** pursue,
run after, follow, hunt, hound,
track, trail, tail.
▸ *n.* **pursuit,** hunt, trail, hunting.

chasm *n.* **1 gorge,** abyss, canyon,
ravine, pit, crater, crevasse, hole,
hollow, opening, gap, fissure,
crevice, cleft, rift, rent. **2 schism,**
breach, gulf, rift, separation,
alienation.

chaste *adj.* **1 virgin,** virginal,
vestal, celibate, abstinent, self-
restrained, unmarried. **2 virtuous,**
good, innocent, pure, decent,
moral, decorous, modest,
wholesome, righteous, upright,
uncorrupted, incorrupt,
uncontaminated, undefiled,
unsullied. **3 simple,** plain,
unadorned, unembellished,

unaffected, unpretentious, austere, restrained. *Ant.* promiscuous; immoral.

chastity *n.* **1 chasteness,** virginity, celibacy, abstinence, self-restraint, self-denial, continence, singleness, unmarried state, virtue, immaculateness. **2 virtue,** goodness, innocence, purity, decency, morality, decorum, modesty, wholesomeness, righteousness. **3** simplicity, plainness, unpretentiousness, austerity. *Ant.* promiscuity; immorality.

chat *v.* **talk,** gossip, chatter, have a conversation, converse, prattle, jabber, prate, *inf.* have a confab, jaw, chew the fat with, rap.
▶ *n.* **talk,** gossip, conversation, chatter, heart-to-heart, tête-à-tête; *inf.* confab.

chatty *adj.* **1 talkative,** gossipy, gossiping, garrulous, loquacious, voluble, glib, effusive, gushing. **2 informal,** conversational, colloquial, gossipy, familiar, friendly, lively. *Ant.* taciturn; formal.

chauvinism *n.* jingoism, partisanship, excessive loyalty, prejudice, bias.

cheap *adj.* **1 inexpensive,** low-priced, low-cost, economical, reasonable, moderately priced, bargain, economy, sale, reduced, marked-down, slashed, discounted, *inf.* bargain-basement. **2 poor-quality,** inferior, shoddy, common, trashy, tawdry, paltry, worthless, second-rate, gimcrack, *inf.* tacky. **3 despicable,** contemptible, low, base, unpleasant, mean, sordid, vulgar. **4 mean,** stingy, parsimonious, tight-fisted, niggardly, money-grubbing, penny-pinching, frugal, sparing. *Ant.* expensive; high-class; admirable.

cheapen *v.* **1 lower,** reduce, cut, mark down, slash, discount, depreciate. **2 degrade,** debase, demean, devalue, lower, belittle, denigrate, discredit, depreciate, derogate.

cheat *v.* **1 deceive,** trick, swindle, defraud, dupe, hoodwink, double-cross, gull, exploit, take advantage of, victimize, *inf.* con, bamboozle, finagle, bilk, rip off, fleece, take for a ride. **2 avoid,** elude, evade, dodge, escape, steer clear of, shun, eschew. **3 be unfaithful,** commit adultery, *inf.* two-time.
▶ *n.* **1 cheater,** swindler, fraud, confidence man/woman, trickster, deceiver, double-crosser, crook, rogue, shark, charlatan, *inf.* con man. **2 swindle,** fraud, deception, deceit, trick, trickery, imposture, artifice, *inf.* con.

check *v.* **1 examine,** inspect, look at, look over, scrutinize, test, monitor, investigate, probe, study, *inf.* give the once-over to. **2 confirm,** make sure, verify, corroborate, validate, substantiate. **3 stop,** arrest, halt, bring to a standstill, slow down, brake, bar, obstruct, impede, block, retard, curb, delay, restrain, suppress, repress, contain, control, bridle, inhibit, *inf.* nip in the bud. **4 correspond,** agree, tally, dovetail, harmonize. *Ant.* neglect; ignore; start; release.
▸ *n.* **1 examination,** inspection, scrutiny, scrutinization, test, monitoring, investigation, probe, inquiry, study, *inf.* once-over. **2 confirmation,** verification, corroboration. **3 stop,** stopping, stoppage, arrest, halt, slowing-down, braking, obstruction, retardation, delay, restraint, constraint, control, deterrent, hindrance, impediment, obstruction, inhibition, limitation, curb. **4 bill,** account, invoice, reckoning, tally, *inf.* tab.

cheek *n.* **1 jowl,** chop, gill. **2 impudence,** audacity, temerity, brazenness, effrontery, nerve, impertinence, insolence, *inf.* gall.

cheeky *adj.* **impudent,** audacious, impertinent, insolent, forward, pert, disrespectful, fresh, insulting, *inf.* saucy, sassy.

cheep *v.* **chirp,** chirrup, twitter, tweet, warble, trill, chatter.

cheer *v.* **1 hail,** acclaim, hurrah, hurray, applaud, shout at, clap for. **2 raise the spirits of,** brighten, buoy up, perk up, enliven, animate, elate, exhilarate, hearten, uplift, give a lift to, gladden, encourage, incite, stimulate, arouse, comfort, solace, console, inspirit, *inf.* buck up. *Ant.* deride; discourage; sadden.
▸ *n.* **1 acclaim,** acclamation, hurrah, hurray, applause, ovation, plaudit, hailing, shout, shouting, clapping. **2 cheerfulness,** gladness, happiness, merriment, mirth, gaiety, joy, pleasure, blitheness, jubilation, high spirits, animation, buoyancy, lightheartedness, glee, optimism, hopefulness, merrymaking, rejoicing, revelry, festivity. **3 fare,** food, provisions, foodstuffs, drink, *inf.* eats.

cheerful *adj.* **1 happy,** bright, merry, glad, gladsome, gay, sunny, joyful, jolly, blithe, animated, buoyant, lighthearted, sparkling, gleeful, carefree, happy-go-lucky, breezy, cheery, sprightly, jaunty, smiling, laughing, bright-eyed and bushy-tailed, optimistic, hopeful,

positive, in good spirits, sunny, cheering, pleasant, agreeable, friendly, *inf.* peppy, chipper.
2 willing, obliging, cooperative, compliant, complying, acquiescent, agreeing, assenting. *Ant.* sad; cheerless; dull; unwilling.

cheerless *adj.* **gloomy,** dreary, miserable, dull, depressing, dismal, bleak, drab, grim, austere, desolate, dark, dingy, somber, uninviting, comfortless, forlorn. *Ant.* cheerful; happy; bright.

cheery *adj.* **cheerful,** happy, merry, glad, in good spirits.

cherish *v.* **1 care for,** treasure, prize, hold dear, love, dote on, adore, idolize, revere, indulge, look after, tend, protect, preserve, shelter, support, nurture, foster. **2 have,** entertain, harbor, cling to, foster, nurture. *Ant.* abandon; neglect.

chest *n.* **1 thorax,** breast, sternum. **2 box,** crate, case, trunk, container, coffer, casket.

chew *v.* **masticate,** munch, chomp, crunch, bite, gnaw, grind.

chic *adj.* **stylish,** fashionable, smart, elegant, modish, voguish, *inf.* trendy, dressy, snazzy. *Ant.* unfashionable; inelegant.

chief *n.* **1 head,** headman, leader, chieftain, ruler, overlord, lord and master, commander, sachem.

2 head, principal, leader, director, chairman, chairperson, chief executive, manager, superintendent, master, foreman, *inf.* boss, bossman, kingpin, top dog, big cheese, Mr. Big.
▸ *adj.* **supreme,** head, foremost, principal, highest, leading, grand, superior, premier, directing, governing, main, principal, most important, uppermost, primary, prime, cardinal, central, key, vital, essential, predominant, preeminent. *Ant.* minor; subordinate.

chiefly *adv.* **mainly,** in the main, principally, primarily, predominantly, especially, particularly, essentially, mostly, for the most part, on the whole, above all.

child *n.* **1 youngster,** young person, young one, little one, boy, girl, baby, babe, infant, toddler, tot, tiny tot, adolescent, youth, juvenile, minor, *derog.* brat, *inf.* kid, nipper, shaver. **2 offspring,** progeny, issue, descendant, scion, son, daughter.

childbirth *n.* **labor,** parturition, delivery, accouchement, *archaic* confinement, lying-in, travail.

childhood *n.* **youth,** infancy, babyhood, preteens, minority, immaturity, boyhood, girlhood.

childish *adj.* **1 immature,**

childlike

infantile, juvenile, puerile, silly, foolish, irresponsible, jejune. **2 children's,** childlike, youthful, boyish, girlish. **Ant.** adult; mature.

childlike *adj.* **1 children's,** youthful. **2 ingenuous,** innocent, artless, guileless, simple, naïve, trusting, trustful, credulous, gullible.

chill *n.* **1 chilliness,** coldness, coolness, iciness, crispness, rawness, sharpness, nip, bite, frigidity, *fml.* gelidity. **2 cold,** flu, influenza, respiratory infection, virus. **3 chilliness,** coldness, coolness, aloofness, distance, unresponsiveness, lack of sympathy, frigidity, lack of welcome, hostility, unfriendliness. **4 dread,** fear, gloom, cloud, depression, damper. **Ant.** warmth; heat.
▶ *adj.* **1 chilly,** cold, cool, icy, raw, biting. **2 chilly,** cold, cool, aloof, distant, frigid, unresponsive, hostile. **Ant.** warm; hot.

chilly *adj.* **1 cold,** cool, icy, crisp, brisk, fresh, raw, sharp, biting, penetrating, freezing, frigid, chill, frozen, shivery, *inf.* nippy. **2 cold,** cool, aloof, distant, unresponsive, unsympathetic, frigid, unwelcoming, hostile, unfriendly. **Ant.** warm; passionate.

chime *v.* **ring,** peal, toll, sound, ding, dong, clang, boom, tinkle, resound, reverberate, strike.

china *n.* **1 porcelain,** faience, ceramics, pottery. **2 dishes,** tableware, dinner/tea service.

chink *n.* **crack,** fissure, crevice, cleft, cut, rift, split, slit, gap, opening, aperture, cavity, cranny.

chip *n.* **1 shaving,** paring, shard, flake, shred, sliver, splinter, fragment, snippet, scrap. **2 nick,** crack, notch, flaw. **3 counter,** token, disk.
▶ *v.* **1 nick,** crack, damage, break off, fragment, crumble. **2 break off,** crack, fragment, crumble. **3 whittle,** chisel, hew.

chivalrous *adj.* **1 gallant,** gentlemanly, courteous, gracious, mannerly, well-mannered, polite, thoughtful, protective, courtly. **2 knightly,** courtly, bold, courageous, brave, valiant, heroic, daring, intrepid, honorable, high-minded, just, fair, loyal, constant, true, gallant, magnanimous, protective. **Ant.** rude; boorish; unmannerly; cowardly.

choice *n.* **1 choosing,** selection, picking, option, preference, election, adoption. **2 alternative,** option, possibility, solution, answer, way out. **3 selection,** range, variety, supply, store, array, display. **4 selection,** appointment, appointee, nominee, candidate.

▸ *adj.* **1 best,** select, superior, first-class, first-rate, excellent, prime, prize, special, rare, exclusive.
2 well-chosen, select, handpicked, appropriate, apposite, apt.

choke *v.* **1 strangle,** strangulate, throttle, asphyxiate, suffocate, smother, stifle, overpower, gag, gasp, retch, struggle for air.
2 clog, block, obstruct, occlude, plug, dam up, congest.

choose *v.* **1 select,** pick, pick out, handpick, take, opt for, settle on, decide on, fix on, single out, adopt, designate, elect, espouse.
2 prefer, like, wish, want, desire, fancy, favor. *Ant.* reject; decline.

choosy *adj.* **fussy,** finicky, persnickety, fastidious, particular, exacting, discriminating.

chop *v.* **chop up,** cut up, cube, dice, fragment, crumble.

choppy *adj.* **rough,** wavy, bumpy, turbulent, blustery, stormy, tempestuous.

chorus *n.* **1 choir,** ensemble, choral group, choristers, singers, vocalists, dance troupe/company, corps de ballet. **2 refrain,** strain, response.

christen *v.* **1 baptize,** give a name to, name, sprinkle, immerse.
2 name, call, dub, style, term, designate, denominate. **3 begin using,** break in.

chronic *adj.* **1 persistent,** long-lasting, long-standing, constant, continual, continuous, incessant, lingering, unabating, deep-rooted, deep-seated, ingrained.
2 inveterate, confirmed, habitual, hardened. *Ant.* acute; temporary; mild.

chronicle *n.* **register,** record, annals, calendar, diary, journal, log, account, archive, history, story.
▸ *v.* **record,** put on record, set down, document, register, report, enter, note, relate, tell about.

chronological *adj.* **sequential,** consecutive, progressive, serial, ordered, historical, in order of time, in sequence.

chubby *adj.* **plump,** tubby, rotund, stout, portly, round, dumpy, fat, fleshy, flabby, paunchy. *Ant.* skinny; slender.

chunk *n.* **lump,** hunk, block, slab, mass, square, wedge, dollop, piece, portion, part.

church *n.* **place of worship,** the house of God, the Lord's house, cathedral, minster, chapel, temple, tabernacle, mosque, synagogue.

churlish *adj.* **boorish,** oafish, loutish, ill-mannered, unmannerly, rude, impolite, discourteous, uncivil, surly, sullen, ill-tempered, curt, brusque, rough. *Ant.* mannerly; polite.

churn *v.* **1 beat,** whip up, agitate, disturb, stir up, shake up.
2 seethe, foam, froth, boil, swirl, toss, convulse.

cinema *n.* **films,** pictures, movies, motion pictures, *inf.* big screen, silver screen.

circle *n.* **1 ring,** disk, loop, circumference, ball, globe, sphere, orb. **2 area of activity,** field of interest, scene, sphere, domain, province, realm, range, region, circuit, orbit, compass. **3 group,** set, company, crowd, ring, coterie, clique, assembly, fellowship, class.
▸ *v.* **1 move round,** rotate, revolve, circulate, wheel, whirl, gyrate, pivot, swivel. **2 surround,** encircle, ring, enclose, envelop, hedge in, hem in, gird, belt, circumscribe, go around, orbit, circumnavigate.

circuit *n.* **1 lap,** turn, beat, ambit, cycle, loop, compass, circumference. **2 border,** boundary, bounds, compass, limits, circumference. **3 tour,** journey, trip, excursion.

circuitous *adj.* **roundabout,** winding, meandering, tortuous, twisting, rambling, indirect, maze-like, labyrinthine.

circular *adj.* **round,** ring-shaped, Fannular, spherical, spheroidal, globular.

circulate *v.* **1 spread,** spread around, disseminate, propagate, distribute, transmit, give out, issue, make known, make public, broadcast, publicize, advertise, publish, promulgate, pronounce.
2 flow, move round, go round, rotate, revolve, whirl, gyrate.

circumference *n.* **perimeter,** periphery, border, boundary, bounds, limits, confines, outline, circuit, compass, extremity, edge, rim, verge, fringe, skirt.

circumspect *adj.* **wary,** cautious, careful, chary, watchful, alert, attentive, guarded, canny, vigilant, observant, suspicious, apprehensive, leery, prudent, judicious, politic, discerning, sagacious.

circumstances *pl. n.* **1 situation,** state of affairs, conditions, position, event, occurrence, background, state, times, financial position, plight, predicament, lot, fortune, means, resources, lifestyle, station.
2 state, situation, conditions, times, financial position, plight, predicament, lot, fortune, means, resources, lifestyle, station.

circumstantial *adj.* **1 based on circumstances,** indirect, incidental, evidential, deduced, presumed, inferential, conjectural. **2 detailed,** precise, particular, exact, accurate, minute, explicit, pointed, to the point.

citadel *n.* **fortress,** fort, fortification, stronghold, keep, castle, tower, bastion.

citation *n.* **1 quotation,** quote, extract, excerpt, reference, illustration, allusion, passage, source. **2 commendation,** award, honor, mention. **3 summons,** subpoena, arraignment.

cite *v.* **1 quote,** mention, name, enumerate, evidence, refer to, allude to, exemplify, excerpt, extract. **2 commend,** recommend, pay tribute to, mention. **3 summon,** subpoena, arraign, serve with a writ.

citizen *n.* **resident,** inhabitant, dweller, denizen, townsman, townswoman, taxpayer, voter, constituent, subject.

city *n.* **metropolis,** metropolitan area,municipality, town, metro area, conurbation, *inf.* concrete jungle.

civil *adj.* **1 interior,** internal, domestic, at home. **2 civic,** municipal, public, community, local. **3 civilian,** lay, nonmilitary, nonreligious, secular. **4 polite,** courteous, well-mannered, mannerly, well-bred, gentlemanly, ladylike, refined, urbane, polished, cultured, cultivated, civilized, cordial, genial, pleasant, affable, amiable. *Ant.* military; religious; rude; uncivil.

civility *n.* **1 courtesy,** courteousness, politeness, good manners, mannerliness, graciousness, cordiality, geniality, pleasantness, affability, amiability, urbanity, gallantry. **2 polite act,** courtesy, etiquette, protocol, propriety, decorum.

civilization *n.* **1 development,** advancement, progress, enlightenment, culture, cultivation, edification, refinement, sophistication. **2 society,** community, nation, country, people, way of life. **3 civilizing,** enlightenment, socialization, humanizing, edification, education, improvement.

civilize *v.* **enlighten,** socialize, humanize, edify, cultivate, educate, instruct, improve, culture, refine, polish, sophisticate.

civilized *adj.* **1 developed,** modern, socialized, educated, cultured, cultivated, sophisticated, enlightened, urbane. **2 cultured,** cultivated, sophisticated, educated, enlightened, urbane. *Ant.* uncivilized; barbarous; unsophisticated.

claim *v.* **1 lay claim to,** ask as one's right, establish rights to, ask for, demand, request, requisition, require. **2 profess,** maintain, assert, declare, protest, avow, aver, allege, postulate, affirm, hold. **3 take,** cause, result in, involve.
▸ *n.* **1 demand,** request, application, petition, call. **2 right,** rights, title, prerogative, privilege, heritage, inheritance, legacy. **3 profession,** assertion, declaration, protestation, avowal, allegation, postulation, affirmation.

clamber *v.* **scramble,** climb, scale, ascend, mount, shin, shinny, scrabble, claw one's way.

clammy *adj.* **moist,** damp, humid, sweaty, sticky.

clamor *n.* **1 uproar,** noise, din, racket, shout, shouting, yelling, blaring, commotion, brouhaha, hubbub, hullabaloo, outcry, vociferation. **2 demand,** call, petition, request, urging, protest, complaint, insistence, exigency. *Ant.* quiet; serenity.

clamp *n.* **vice,** press, brace, clasp, fastener, hasp.
▸ *v.* **grip,** hold, fix, clench, press, squeeze, secure, make fast, brace.

clandestine *adj.* **secret,** undercover, surreptitious, cloak-and-dagger, back-alley, furtive, concealed, hidden, underhand. *Ant.* open; aboveboard.

clarify *v.* **1 make clear,** clear up, resolve, make plain, explain, elucidate, illuminate, throw light on, make simple, simplify. **2 purify,** refine. *Ant.* confuse; muddy.

clash *v.* **1 strike,** bang, clang, crash, clatter, clank, clink, rattle, jangle. **2 be in conflict,** war, fight, contend, do battle, come to blows, feud, grapple, wrangle, quarrel, cross swords, lock horns. **3 coincide,** co-occur, conflict. **4 be discordant,** do not match, lack harmony, jar, be incompatible, *inf.* scream. *Ant.* agree; harmonize.
▸ *n.* **1 striking,** bang, clang, crash, clatter, clank. **2 conflict,** collision, confrontation, brush, warring, fighting, contending, feud, grappling, wrangling, quarreling, discordance, discord, lack of harmony, incompatibility, jarring. **3 coincidence,** co-occurrence, concurrence, conflict. *Ant.* harmony; accord.

clasp *n.* **1 catch,** fastener, fastening, clip, hook, hook and eye, snap fastener, buckle, hasp. **2 pin,** brooch. **3 embrace,** hug, cuddle, hold, grip, grasp.

class *n.* **1 social order,** social division, stratum, rank, level,

status, sphere, grade, group, grouping, set, classification, caste. **2 category,** classification, division, section, group, set, grade, kind, sort, type, collection, denomination, order, species, genre, genus. **3 study group,** school group, seminar, tutorial, course, year, grade. **4 quality,** excellence, distinction, stylishness, elegance, chic.
▸ *v.* **classify,** categorize, group, grade, arrange, order, sort, codify, file, index, pigeonhole.

classic *adj.* **1 first-rate,** first-class, excellent, brilliant, finest, outstanding, exemplary, masterly, consummate. **2 typical,** standard, model, guiding, archetypal, stock, true-to-form, paradigmatic, prototypical. **3 simple,** traditional, timeless, ageless, long-lasting, enduring, abiding, time-honored, long-standing, long-established.
▸ *n.* **1 great work,** established work, standard work, masterpiece. **2 masterpiece,** excellent example.

classical *adj.* **1 Greek,** Grecian, Hellenic, Attic, Greco-Roman, Roman, Latin. **2 orchestral,** symphonic. **3 simple,** plain, restrained, pure, understated, harmonious, well-proportioned, balanced, symmetrical, elegant, aesthetic.

classification *n.* **classifying,** categorizing, categorization, grouping, grading, arrangement, codifying, codification, taxonomy.

classify *v.* **categorize,** class, group, grade, arrange, order, sort, type, rank, rate, designate, codify, catalog, tabulate, file, index, assign, pigeonhole, brand.

clause *n.* **section,** paragraph, article, note, item, point, passage, part, heading, condition, provision, proviso, stipulation.

claw *n.* **nail,** talon, pincer, nipper, chela.
▸ *v.* **scratch,** tear, lacerate, scrape, graze, rip, dig into, maul.

clean *adj.* **1 unsoiled,** spotless, unstained, unspotted, unsullied, unblemished, immaculate, speckless, hygienic, sanitary, washed, cleansed, laundered, scrubbed, pure, clear, natural, unpolluted, unadulterated, uncontaminated, untainted, unmixed. **2 good,** upright, honorable, respectable, virtuous, righteous, moral, reputable, upstanding, exemplary, innocent, guiltless, pure, decent, chaste, undefiled, guilt-free, crime-free. **3 unused,** unmarked, blank, vacant, void. **4 streamlined,** smooth, well-defined, definite, clean-cut, regular, symmetrical, simple, elegant, graceful,

uncluttered, trim, shapely.
5 complete, thorough, total, entire, conclusive, decisive, final. *Ant.* dirty; filthy; immoral.
▸ *adv.* **completely,** entirely, totally, fully, wholly, thoroughly, altogether, quite, utterly, absolutely.

cleanse *v.* **1 clean,** make clean, clean up, wash, bathe, rinse, disinfect. **2 purify,** purge, absolve.

clear *adj.* **1 bright,** cloudless, unclouded, fair, fine, light, undimmed, sunny, sunshiny.
2 transparent, limpid, translucent, crystalline, diaphanous, see-through. **3 obvious,** evident, plain, apparent, sure, definite, unmistakable, manifest, indisputable, patent, incontrovertible, irrefutable, palpable, beyond doubt, beyond question. **4 understandable,** comprehensible, intelligible, plain, explicit, lucid, coherent, distinct. **5 astute,** keen, sharp, quick, perceptive, discerning, perspicacious, penetrating.
6 open, empty, free, unobstructed, unimpeded, unhindered, unlimited. **7 untroubled,** undisturbed, peaceful, at peace, tranquil, serene, calm, innocent, guiltless, guilt-free, clean, sinless, stainless. *Ant.* cloudy; opaque; vague; ambiguous.

▸ *adv.* **1 clearly,** distinctly, plainly, audibly. **2 completely,** entirely, thoroughly, fully, wholly, clear.

clearance *n.* **1 clearing,** removal, evacuation, eviction, emptying, depopulation, unpeopling, withdrawal, decanting. **2 clearing,** space, gap, allowance, margin, headroom, leeway, room to spare. **3 authorization,** consent, permission, sanction, go-ahead, leave, endorsement, *inf.* green light, OK.

clear-cut *adj.* **definite,** specific, precise, explicit, unambiguous, unequivocal.

clearly *adv.* **obviously,** undoubtedly, without doubt, indubitably, plainly, undeniably, decidedly, surely, certainly, incontrovertibly, irrefutably, incontestably, patently.

cleave[1] *v.* **split,** split open, open, crack, lay open, divide, hew, hack, chop/slice up, sever, rend, rive, cut, plow, drive, bulldoze.

cleft *n.* **split,** crack, gap, fissure, crevice, rift, break, fracture.

clemency *n.* **mercy,** leniency, compassion, humanity, pity, sympathy, kindness, magnanimity, fairness, temperance, moderation, indulgence.

clench *v.* **1 close,** shut, seal,

fasten. **2 grip,** grasp, clutch, hold, seize.

clerical *adj.* **1 secretarial,** office, writing, typing, filing, bookkeeping. **2 ecclesiastical,** churchly, priestly, pastoral, sacerdotal, apostolic, canonical.

clever *adj.* **1 intelligent,** bright, sharp-witted, quick-witted, talented, gifted, smart, capable, able, competent, apt, knowledgeable, educated, sagacious, shrewd, astute, adroit, canny, cunning, ingenious, artful, wily, inventive, *inf.* brainy. **2 dexterous,** skillful, adroit, nimble, deft, handy. *Ant.* dull; stupid; awkward.

click *n.* **clink,** clack, chink, snap, tick.
▸ *v.* **1 clink,** clack, chink, snap, tick. **2 become clear,** fall into place, come home to one, make sense. **3 get along,** take to each other, hit it off, be compatible, be on the same wavelength, feel a rapport. **4 make a hit,** prove popular, be successful, be a success, succeed, go down well.

client *n.* **customer,** patron, regular, habitué, buyer, purchaser, shopper, consumer, user, patient.

cliff *n.* **precipice,** rock face, face, crag, bluff, escarpment, scarp, overhang, promontory, tor.

climate *n.* **1 weather pattern,** weather, temperature. **2 clime,** country, place, region, area, zone. **3 atmosphere,** mood, temper, spirit, feeling, feel, ambience, aura, ethos.

climax *n.* **1 culmination,** height, peak, pinnacle, high point, summit, top, highlight, acme, zenith, apex, apogee, crowning point. **2 sexual climax,** orgasm. *Ant.* nadir; anticlimax.
▸ *v.* **1 culminate,** peak, come to a head, result, end. **2 have an orgasm,** *inf.* come.

climb *v.* **1 go,** ascend, mount, scale, clamber. **2 go up,** rise, increase, shoot up, soar. **3 slope upward,** incline, bank. **4 make progress,** get ahead, advance, work one's way up, make strides. *Ant.* descend.

clinch *v.* **1 settle,** secure, seal, set the seal on, complete, confirm, conclude, assure, cap, close, wind up, *inf.* sew up. **2 fasten,** make fast, secure, fix, clamp, bolt, rivet, pinion. **3 hug,** embrace, cuddle, squeeze, clutch, grasp, grapple.

cling *v.* **stick,** adhere, hold, grip, clasp, clutch.

clinic *n.* **medical center,** health center, infirmary, sick bay, first-aid station.

clip *v.* **1 cut,** crop, snip, trim, shear, prune. **2 hit,** strike, box, cuff, smack, wallop, thump, punch, knock, *inf.* clout, whack, clobber. **3 speed,** go fast, race, gallop, rush, dash, zoom, whip, go like lightning.

clique *n.* **coterie,** circle, crowd, in-crowd, set, gang, group, clan, faction, pack, band, ring, fraternity, society, mob.

cloak *n.* **1 cape,** mantle, wrap, shawl, pelisse, coat. **2 cover,** screen, blind, mask, mantle, veil, shroud, shield, front, camouflage, pretext.

▸ *v.* **hide,** conceal, cover, cover up, screen, mask, veil, shroud, shield, cloud, camouflage, obscure, disguise. *Ant.* reveal; expose.

clog *n.* **sabot,** wooden shoe, wooden-soled shoe.

▸ *v.* **clog up,** block, obstruct, dam, congest, jam, occlude, stop up, dam up, hinder, impede, hamper, shackle, burden.

close¹ *v.* **1 shut,** slam, fasten, secure, lock, bolt, bar, latch, padlock. **2 stop up,** plug, seal, clog, choke, obstruct, occlude. **3 bring/come to an end,** end, conclude, finish, terminate, wind up, adjourn, discontinue, complete, settle, clinch, seal, establish, fix. **4 narrow,** lessen, grow smaller, dwindle, reduce. **5 come together,** join, connect, come into contact, unite, clutch one another, grip, clench, grapple, couple. *Ant.* open; clear; start.

▸ *n.* **end,** finish, conclusion, termination, cessation, completion, culmination, finale, wind-up.

close² *adj.* **1 near,** adjacent, in close proximity, adjoining, neighboring, abutting; birthdays close together, near, occurring/falling near. **2 near,** similar, like, alike, comparable, parallel, corresponding, akin. **3 intimate,** dear, bosom, close-knit, inseparable, loving, devoted, attached, confidential; *inf.* chummy. **4 dense,** condensed, compact, crowded, packed, solid, tight, cramped, congested, crushed, squeezed. **5 evenly matched,** well-matched, hard-fought, sharply contested, neck-and-neck, nose-to-nose; *inf.* fifty-fifty. **6 accurate,** true, faithful, literal, exact, precise, conscientious. **7 careful,** concentrated, attentive, assiduous, alert, vigilant, intent, dogged, painstaking, detailed, minute, intense, keen, thorough, rigorous, searching. **8 strict,** stringent, rigorous, thorough, tight. **9 humid,** muggy, airless, stuffy, heavy, oppressive, stifling, suffocating, musty, unventilated. **10 quiet,** reticent, uncommunicative, reserved, private, unforthcoming, secretive, evasive. **11 mean,** miserly, stingy, niggardly, parsimonious, penny-pinching, tight-fisted, tight. *Ant.* far; distant; remote; fresh.

closet *n.* cupboard, wardrobe, cabinet, locker, storage room.

▸ *adj.* **secret,** unrevealed, undisclosed, hidden, concealed, furtive.

clot *n.* **glob,** lump, gob, clump, mass, obstruction, thrombus.

▸ *v.* **coagulate,** set, congeal, jell, thicken, cake, curdle.

cloth *n.* **fabric,** material, stuff, textiles, dry goods, soft goods.

clothe *v.* **1 dress,** attire, rig, rig out, turn out, apparel, fit out, outfit, robe, garb, array, deck out, drape, *inf.* doll up. **2 cover,** wrap, cloak, envelop, swathe. *Ant.* undress; uncover.

clothes *pl. n.* **garments,** articles of clothing/dress, clothing, attire, outfits, *inf.* duds, rags.

cloud *n.* **1 rain cloud,** storm cloud, thundercloud, billow, cirrus, cumulus, altostratus, altocumulus, cumulonimbus, haze, cloudbank, mackerel sky. **2 pall,** shroud, mantle, cloak, screen, cover, shadow, threat, gloom, darkness. **3 swarm,** flock, mass, multitude, host, horde, throng.

cloudy *adj.* **1 overcast,** hazy, dark, gray, somber, leaden, heavy, gloomy, dim, lowering, sunless, starless. **2 blurred,** vague, indistinct, hazy, indefinite, nebulous, obscure, confused, muddled. **3 opaque,** nontransparent, murky, muddy, milky, emulsified, opalescent, turbid. *Ant.* bright; clear.

clown *n.* **1 jester,** fool, buffoon, zany, harlequin, joker, comedian, comic, humorist, funnyman, wag, wit, prankster. **2 fool,** idiot, dolt, nitwit, halfwit, *inf.* jerk, dope.

▸ *v.* **fool,** act foolishly, jest, joke.

club *n.* **1 cudgel,** bludgeon, stick, staff, truncheon, bat, baton, blackjack. **2 society,** group, association, organization, circle, set, clique, coterie, affiliation, league, union, federation, company, fraternity, brotherhood, sorority.

▸ *v.* **hit,** strike, beat, batter, bash, cudgel, bludgeon, truncheon, *inf.* clout, clobber.

clue *n.* **hint,** indication, sign, evidence, information, intimation, pointer, guide, lead, tip, tip-off, inkling.

clump *n.* **group,** cluster, bunch, collection, assembly, assemblage, mass, lump, clod, glob, agglutination.

▸ *v.* **1 group,** cluster, bunch,

collect, assemble, congregate, mass, lump, bundle, pack.
2 clomp, stamp, stump, stomp, thump, thud, bang, tramp, lumber, plod, trudge, stumble.

clumsy *adj.* **1 awkward,** uncoordinated, ungainly, blundering, bungling, bumbling, inept, maladroit, inexpert, unhandy, unskillful, like a bull in a china shop, *inf.* ham-handed, butter-fingered. **2 awkward,** unwieldy, hulking, heavy, solid, unmaneuverable. **3 awkward,** gauche, graceless, tactless, unpolished, crude, uncouth, crass. *Ant.* adroit; graceful.

cluster *n.* **1 bunch,** clump, collection, knot, group, *Tech.* raceme, panicle. **2 gathering,** group, collection, bunch, band, company, knot, body, assemblage, congregation.
▸ *v.* **gather,** collect, assemble, congregate, group, come together, flock together.

clutch *v.* **1 grip,** grasp, clasp, cling to, hang on to, clench. **2 reach for,** snatch at, grab, make a grab for, seize, catch at, claw at.
▸ *n.* **set,** setting, hatch, hatching, nest, incubation.

clutches *pl. n.* **hands,** power, control, hold, grip, grasp, claws, tyranny, possession, keeping, custody.

clutter *n.* **mess,** muddle, disorder, chaos, disarray, state of confusion, untidiness, heap, litter, *inf.* junk, stuff.
▸ *v.* **litter,** make untidy, make a mess of, mess up, be strewn about, be scattered about.

coach[1] *n.* **1 bus,** omnibus. **2 stagecoach,** carriage, gig, surrey.

coagulate *v.* **congeal,** clot, gel, thicken, curdle.

coalesce *v.* **unite,** join together, combine, merge, amalgamate, integrate, affiliate, blend, fuse, *lit.* commingle.

coalition *n.* **union,** alliance, affiliation, league, association, federation, confederacy, bloc, compact, amalgamation, merger, conjunction, combination, fusion.

coarse *adj.* **1 rough,** bristly, scratchy, prickly, hairy, shaggy. **2 heavy,** rough, rugged, craggy, unrefined. **3 crude,** unrefined, unprocessed, unpurified. **4 rude,** ill-mannered, uncivil, rough, boorish, loutish, churlish, uncouth, crass. **5 bawdy,** earthy, blue, ribald, vulgar, smutty, obscene, indelicate, indecent, offensive, lewd, pornographic, prurient, *inf.* raunchy. *Ant.* fine; refined; decent.

coast *n.* **coastline,** shore, seashore, shoreline, seacoast, beach, strand, seaboard, water's edge.

▶ *v.* **freewheel,** cruise, taxi, drift, glide, sail.

coat *n.* **1 overcoat,** topcoat, jacket, fur. **2 fur,** hair, wool, fleece, hide, pelt, skin. **3 layer,** covering, overlay, coating, film.

cocky *adj.* **arrogant,** conceited, egotistical, swellheaded, vain, cocksure, swaggering, brash.

code *n.* **1 cipher,** secret writing, coded message, cryptograph. **2 ethics,** morals, principles, maxims, morality, convention, etiquette, custom. **3 laws,** rules, regulations, system, canon.

coerce *v.* **compel,** force, pressure, pressurize, drive, impel, constrain, oblige, *inf.* twist one's arm, lean on, put the screws on, strong-arm.

coffer *n.* **strongbox,** moneybox, money chest, safe, chest, casket, box.

cogent *adj.* **convincing,** forceful, forcible, effective, conclusive, persuasive, compelling, powerful, strong, potent, weighty, influential, authoritative, telling. ***Ant.*** weak; unconvincing; ineffective.

coherent *adj.* **logical,** rational, reasoned, lucid, articulate, systematic, orderly, organized, consistent, comprehensible, intelligible. ***Ant.*** incoherent; muddled.

cohort *n.* **troop,** brigade, legion, squad, squadron, column, group, company, body, band, class.

coil *v.* **wind,** spiral, loop, curl, twist, twine, entwine, snake, wreathe, convolute.

coin *n.* **coins,** coinage, change, specie, silver, copper, gold.

▶ *v.* **invent,** create, make up, devise, conceive, originate, think up, dream up, formulate, fabricate.

coincide *v.* **1 be concurrent,** co-occur, happen together, coexist, concur, synchronize. **2 accord,** agree, correspond, concur, match, square, tally, harmonize.

coincidence *n.* **accident,** chance, a fluke, luck, fortuity, serendipity.

coincidental *adj.* **1 accidental,** chance, unplanned, unintentional, casual, lucky, fortuitous, serendipitous, *inf.* fluky. **2 simultaneous,** concurrent, synchronous, coexistent.

cold *adj.* **1 chilly,** chill, cool, freezing, bitter, raw, icy, frigid, wintry, frosty, arctic, inclement, sunless, windy, glacial, polar, *inf.* nippy. **2 chilly,** chilled, cool, freezing, frozen, frozen stiff, frozen/chilled to the bone/marrow, shivery, numbed, benumbed. **3 frigid,** unresponsive, unfeeling, unemotional, phlegmatic, unexcitable, passionless, spiritless, unmoved, indifferent, lukewarm, apathetic, dispassionate, aloof, distant, reserved, remote, standoffish, insensitive, unsympathetic, uncaring, heartless, callous, cold-hearted, unfriendly, inhospitable. **4 dead,** gone, extinguished, finished, defunct. *Ant.* hot; warm; passionate.

cold-blooded *adj.* **savage,** inhuman, barbarous, barbaric, heartless, ruthless, pitiless, merciless.

collaborate *v.* **1 cooperate,** work together/jointly, join forces, join, unite, combine. **2 conspire,** fraternize, collude.

collaborator *n.* **1 coworker,** associate, colleague, partner, confederate. **2 conspirator,** fraternizer, traitor, quisling, turncoat, colluder.

collapse *v.* **1 fall in,** cave in, give way, come apart, fall to pieces, crumple. **2 faint,** pass out, lose consciousness, fall unconscious, keel over, fall prostrate, swoon. **3 break down,** fall through, fail, disintegrate, fold, founder, fall flat, miscarry, come to nothing, *inf.* flop. **4 break down,** go to pieces, *inf.* crack up.

▸ *n.* **1 cave-in,** giving way. **2 fainting,** faint, passing out, loss of consciousness, swooning, swoon. **3 breakdown,** failure, disintegration, unsuccessfulness, foundering, *inf.* flop. **4 breakdown,** nervous breakdown, attack, seizure, prostration, *inf.* crack-up.

collate *v.* **arrange,** put in order, order, sort, categorize.

colleague *n.* **associate,** partner, teammate, workmate, fellow worker, coworker, collaborator, confederate, comrade.

collect *v.* **1 gather,** accumulate, assemble, amass, pile up, stockpile, save, store, hoard, heap up, aggregate. **2 gather,** assemble, congregate, converge, cluster, flock together, mass, convene, rally. **3 gather,** solicit, raise, secure, obtain, acquire. **4 gather/ collect one's wits,** muster, summon, assemble, rally. *Ant.* disperse; distribute.

collected *adj.* **cool,** calm, serene, poised, controlled, composed, unperturbed, unruffled, unshaken. *Ant.* excited; hysterical.

collection *n.* **1 accumulation,** pile, stockpile, store, supply, stock, hoard, heap, mass, aggregation. **2 gathering,** assembly, assemblage, crowd, body, group, cluster, company, number, throng, congregation, flock, convocation. **3 set,** series, array, assortment. **4 anthology,** corpus, compilation, ana, miscellanea, collected works, analects, analecta. **5 subscription,** donation, contribution, gift, alms. **6 offering,** offertory, tithe.

collective *adj.* **joint,** united, combined, shared, common, concerted, cooperative, corporate, collaborative, cumulative, aggregate.

college *n.* **1 school,** educational establishment/institution, technical college, community college, university. **2 association,** fellowship, society, academy, union.

collide *v.* **1 crash,** crash head on, come into collision, smash, bump, bang. **2 conflict,** be in conflict, clash, differ, disagree, be at variance.

collision *n.* **1 crash,** accident, smash, pile-up, impact. **2 conflict,** clash, difference, disagreement, variance, opposition, confrontation, encounter, skirmish.

colloquial *adj.* **conversational,** informal, everyday, casual, familiar, chatty, idiomatic, vernacular.

collusion *n.* **connivance,** complicity, collaboration, intrigue, plotting, *inf.* cahoots.

colonize *v.* **settle,** people, populate, pioneer, open up, found.

colony *n.* **1 settlement,** territory, province, dominion, protectorate, dependency, possession, satellite state. **2 community,** section, ghetto, district, quarter, group, association, commune, settlement.

color *n.* **1 hue,** shade, tint, tone, tinge, pinkness, rosiness, redness, ruddiness, blush, flush, glow, bloom. **2 skin color,** skin coloring, skin tone, complexion, coloring, pigmentation. **3 vividness,** life, animation, richness. **4 outward appearance,** false show, guise, show, front, façade, cloak, mask, semblance, pretense, pretext.
▸ *v.* **1 tint,** paint, dye, stain, tinge. **2 blush,** flush, redden, go red, burn. **3 influence,** affect, prejudice, distort, slant, taint, pervert, warp. **4 exaggerate,** overstate, overdraw, embroider, varnish, misrepresent, falsify, disguise, garble.

colorful *adj.* **1 bright-colored,** deep-colored, bright, brilliant, intense, vivid, rich, vibrant, multicolored, many-colored, motley, variegated, psychedelic, *inf.* jazzy. **2 vivid,** graphic, interesting, lively, animated, rich. **Ant.** colorless; drab; dull.

colorless *adj.* **1 uncolored,** achromatic, achromic, white, bleached, faded. **2 pale,** wan, anemic, washed-out, ashen, sickly. **3 uninteresting,** dull, boring, tame, lifeless, dreary, lackluster, characterless, insipid, vapid, vacuous.

colossal *adj.* **huge,** gigantic, immense, enormous, massive, vast, gargantuan, mammoth, prodigious, mountainous, elephantine, Herculean, monumental, titanic. ***Ant.*** tiny; microscopic.

column *n.* **1 pillar,** support, upright, post, shaft, pilaster, obelisk. **2 line,** file, row, rank, string, procession, train, progression, cavalcade. **3 newspaper article/piece/item,** editorial, leader, gossip column.

comb *n.* **1 hair comb,** fine-tooth comb, currycomb. **2 coxcomb,** crest, tuft, plume.
▶ *v.* **1 groom,** untangle, curry, arrange. **2 dress,** card, tease, hackle, heckle. **3 search,** scour, ransack, go over with a fine-tooth comb, rake, hunt, sift, rummage.

combat *n.* **battle,** fight, conflict, clash, skirmish, encounter, engagement, single combat, hand-to-hand combat, fighting, hostilities.
▶ *v.* **fight,** do battle, wage war, clash, enter into conflict, take up arms (against), grapple, combat the enemy, fight with/against, battle against, oppose, strive against, make a stand against, resist, withstand, defy.

combative *adj.* **pugnacious,** belligerent, aggressive, militant, bellicose, warlike, quarrelsome, argumentative, contentious, antagonistic, truculent.

combination *n.* **1 cooperation,** association, union, alliance, partnership, coalition, league, consortium, syndication, federation. **2 mixture,** mix, blend, amalgam, amalgamation, compound, alloy, composite.

combine *v.* **1 join forces,** get together, unite, team up, cooperate, associate, ally, pool resources, amalgamate, merge, integrate. **2 join,** put together, unite, pool, merge, integrate, fuse, marry, unify, synthesize. **3 mix,** blend, admix, amalgamate, bind, bond, compound, alloy, homogenize. ***Ant.*** separate; part.

combustible *adj.* **inflammable,** flammable, incendiary, explosive, *fml.* conflagratory. ***Ant.*** incombustible.

come *v.* **1 arrive,** appear, put in an appearance, turn up, enter, materialize, *inf.* show up, blow in. **2 occur,** fall, take place, happen, transpire, come about, come to pass. **3 reach,** extend, stretch. **4 be available,** be made, be produced, be offered. **5 act,** play, play the part of, behave like, imitate. **6 climax,** achieve orgasm. *Ant.* go; leave.

comedian *n.* **1 comic,** stand-up comic, funny man, funny woman, comedienne, comedy actor/actress, humorist. **2 comic,** joker, wit, wag, jester, clown, *inf.* card, laugh.

comedy *n.* **1 light entertainment,** humorous play, farce, musical comedy, situation comedy, comedy of errors, burlesque, pantomime, slapstick, satire, vaudeville, comic opera, *inf.* sitcom. **2 humor,** fun, funniness, wit, wittiness, hilarity, levity, facetiousness. *Ant.* tragedy; gravity.

comfort *n.* **1 freedom from hardship,** serenity, repose, tranquillity, contentment, content, well-being, coziness, plenty, sufficiency, luxury, opulence. **2 consolation,** solace, condolence, sympathy, commiseration, help, support, succor, relief, aid, alleviation, cheer, gladdening. *Ant.* discomfort; grief; aggravation.
▶ *v.* **1 bring comfort to,** console, solace, give condolences to, give

sympathy to, help, support, succor, reassure, soothe, assuage, cheer, gladden. **2 ease,** soothe, refresh, revive, hearten, cheer, invigorate, strengthen. *Ant.* distress; depress.

comfortable *adj.* **1 homey,** cozy, snug. **2 well-fitting,** loose-fitting, roomy. **3 pleasant,** adequate, free from hardship, well-off, well-to-do, affluent, luxurious, opulent. **4 at ease,** at one's ease, relaxed, serene, tranquil, contented, cozy. *Ant.* uncomfortable; tight; tense.

comic *adj.* **funny,** humorous, amusing, entertaining, diverting, droll, jocular, joking, facetious, comical, witty, farcical, hilarious, zany, sidesplitting, priceless, waggish, whimsical. *Ant.* serious; grave.
▶ *n.* **1 stand-up comic,** comedian, funny man/woman, humorist. **2 comedian,** joker, wag.

command *v.* **1 order,** give orders to, direct, charge, instruct, bid, enjoin, adjure, summon, prescribe, require. **2 be in command of,** have charge of, control, have control of, rule, govern, direct, preside over, head, lead, manage, supervise, superintend.
▶ *n.* **1 order,** decree, dictate, edict, instruction, directive, direction, bidding, injunction, behest,

mandate, fiat, precept, commandment, enjoining.
2 charge, control, authority, power, mastery, ascendancy, government, direction, management, administration, supervision, dominion, sway, domination.

commander *n.* **leader,** head, director, chief, boss, captain, commander-in-chief, C in C, commanding officer, CO, *inf.* top dog, kingpin, big cheese.

commemorate *v.* **celebrate,** pay tribute to, pay homage to, remember, honor, salute, mark, memorialize.

commence *v.* **begin,** start, make a beginning/start, go ahead, be off, embark, set sail, set the ball rolling, get something off the ground, open, enter/embark upon, inaugurate, initiate, originate, *inf.* get the show on the road. *Ant.* finish; end; conclude.

commend *v.* **1 praise,** applaud, speak highly of, approve, acclaim, extol, laud, eulogize.
2 recommend, approve, endorse, advocate. **3 entrust,** trust, deliver, commit, hand over, give, consign, assign. *Ant.* criticize; disapprove.

commendable *adj.*
praiseworthy, admirable, laudable, estimable, meritorious, creditable, reputable, worthy,

deserving. *Ant.* deplorable; lamentable.

comment *v.* **1 remark,** speak, make remarks, make a comment on, express an opinion on, say something about. **2 say,** remark, state, observe, interpose. **3 write notes,** annotate, explain, interpret, elucidate, clarify, shed light on.
▸ *n.* **1 remark,** opinion, observation, view, statement, criticism. **2 annotation,** note, footnote, gloss, marginalia, explanation, interpretation, elucidation, exposition.

commentary *n.* **1 narration,** description, account, review, analysis. **2 annotation,** notes, interpretation, analysis, exegesis, critique.

commerce *n.* **1 business,** trade, buying and selling, merchandising, dealing, financial transaction, marketing, traffic.
2 social relations, socializing, communication, dealings, traffic, intercourse.

commercial *adj.* **1 business,** trade, marketing, merchandising, sales, mercantile. **2 profitable,** profit-making, business, profit-oriented, money-oriented, mercantile, materialistic, mercenary.

commission *n.* **1 percentage,**

brokerage, share, fee, compensation, *inf.* cut. **2 task,** employment, piece of work, work, duty, charge, mission, responsibility. **3 authority,** sanction, warrant, license. **4 committee,** board, board of commissioners, council, advisory body, delegation. **5 committing,** committal, execution, perpetration, performance. ▸ *v.* **1 employ,** engage, contract, appoint, book, authorize. **2 order,** put in an order for, place an order for, contract for, pay for, authorize. **3 authorize,** empower, accredit, sanction, invest.

commit *v.* **1 perform,** carry out, execute, enact, perpetrate, effect, do. **2 entrust,** trust, deliver, hand over, give, consign, assign. **3 pledge,** promise, engage, bind, covenant, obligate, dedicate. **4 imprison,** jail, confine, lock up, put into custody, put away. **5 hospitalize,** institutionalize, confine.

commitment *n.* **1 undertaking,** obligation, responsibility, duty, liability, tie, task, engagement. **2 dedication,** devotion, loyalty, allegiance, adherence. **3 pledge,** promise, vow, assurance, covenant.

common *adj.* **1 ordinary,** average, normal, typical, unexceptional, run-of-the-mill, plain, simple, undistinguished, workaday, commonplace, mediocre, pedestrian, hackneyed, trite, humdrum,usual, everyday, daily, regular, frequent, customary, habitual, routine, standard, repeated, recurrent, familiar, stock, conventional, traditional. **2 widespread,** general, universal, popular, accepted, prevalent, prevailing. **3 communal,** collective, community, public, popular. **4 low,** vulgar, coarse, uncouth, inferior, plebeian. *Ant.* uncommon; special; rare.

commotion *n.* disturbance, racket, uproar, rumpus, tumult, clamor, riot, hubbub, hullabaloo, brouhaha, furor, disorder, confusion, upheaval, disruption, agitation, excitement, fuss, disquiet, ferment, to-do, bustle, hustle and bustle.

communal *adj.* **common,** collective, shared, joint, general, public, community, cooperative, communalist. *Ant.* individual; exclusive.

communicable *adj.* **infectious,** contagious, catching, transmittable, transmissible, transferable.

communicate *v.* **1 transmit,** pass on, transfer, impart, convey, relay, spread, disseminate, make known, publish, broadcast, announce, report, divulge, disclose, unfold, proclaim, get one's ideas/message across, interface, be articulate, be fluent, be eloquent. **2 be in touch,** be in contact, have dealings, interface. **3 transmit,** pass on, transfer, spread, infect with.

communication *n.*
1 information transmission/ transfer, transmission, dissemination, contact, getting in touch, radio/telephone link, connection, interface, social intercourse. **2 message,** letter, report, statement, dispatch, news, information, data, intelligence, word.

communicative *adj.* **expansive,** forthcoming, talkative, loquacious, voluble, chatty, conversational, informative, frank, open, candid. *Ant.* uncommunicative; taciturn; reserved.

communion *n.* **1 rapport,** empathy, sympathy, accord, affinity, fellowship, togetherness, harmony, closeness, agreement, sharing, concord, unity, fusion, communication. **2 Eucharist,** Holy Communion, Sacrament.

commute *v.* **1 travel to and from,** travel back and forth, shuttle.
2 lessen, reduce, shorten, curtail, mitigate, modify. **3 exchange,** change, interchange, substitute, trade, barter, switch.

compact *adj.* **1 dense,** packed close, pressed together, close, firm, solid, compressed, condensed. **2 small,** economy-sized. **3 concise,** succinct, terse, brief, condensed, pithy, to the point, epigrammatic, compendious. *Ant.* loose; large; lengthy; rambling.
▸ *v.* **pack down,** press down, compress, press together, condense, tamp.

companion *n.* **1 partner,** escort, consort, friend, crony, comrade, colleague, associate, ally, confederate, *inf.* buddy, pal.
2 attendant, aide, chaperon, duenna, squire. **3 fellow,** mate, twin, match, counterpart, complement. **4 guide,** handbook, manual, reference book.

companionship *n.* **friendship,** fellowship, company, society, togetherness, social intercourse, comradeship, camaraderie, association, brotherhood, sisterhood, intimacy, rapport.

company *n.* **1 companionship,** friendship, fellowship.
2 assembly, assemblage, gathering, meeting, audience, group, crowd, throng, congregation, convention.

3 group, band, party, body, association, society, fellowship, troupe, collection, circle, league, crew, guild. **4 business,** firm, concern, corporation, house, establishment, conglomerate, *inf.* outfit. **5 subdivision,** unit, detachment. **6 guest(s),** visitor(s), caller(s).

comparable *adj.* **equivalent,** commensurable, corresponding, proportional, proportionate, similar, like, parallel, analogous, related. *Ant.* dissimilar; unlike.

compare *v.* **1 contrast,** juxtapose, collate, differentiate. **2 liken,** equate, analogize.

comparison *n.* **1 contrast,** juxtaposition, collation, differentiation. **2 comparability,** analogy, resemblance, likeness, similarity, correlation.

compassionate *adj.* **softhearted,** tender, gentle, merciful, lenient, understanding, sympathetic, pitying, humanitarian, humane, kindly, kindhearted, charitable, benevolent. *Ant.* cruel; unkind; unsympathetic.

compatible *adj.* **1 well-suited,** suited, like-minded, of the same mind, in agreement, in tune, in harmony, reconcilable, having affinity/rapport, accordant. **2 consistent,** in keeping, reconcilable, consonant, congruous, congruent. *Ant.* incompatible; inconsistent.

compel *v.* **1 force,** make, coerce, drive, pressure, pressurize, dragoon, constrain, impel, oblige, necessitate, urge, *inf.* bulldoze, railroad, twist one's arm, strong-arm, put the screws on. **2 force,** enforce, exact, insist upon, necessitate, extort.

compelling *adj.* **1 fascinating,** gripping, enthralling, irresistible, hypnotic, mesmeric. **2 cogent,** convincing, forceful, powerful, weighty, telling, conclusive, irrefutable. *Ant.* boring; weak.

compensate *v.* **1 make amends,** make restitution, make reparation, make up for, atone, expiate. **2 recompense,** repay, reimburse, requite, indemnify.

compensation *n.* **1 recompense,** repayment, reimbursement, requital, indemnification, indemnity, damages. **2 amends,** restitution, redress, atonement, expiation.

compete *v.* **1 take part,** enter, participate, be a contestant, *inf.* throw one's hat in the ring, be in the running. **2 contend,** vie, strive, struggle, fight, pit oneself (against).

competent *adj.* **1 capable,** able, proficient, qualified, efficient,

adept, accomplished, skillful.
2 adequate, appropriate, suitable, pertinent, apposite, fit, fitted, qualified. **Ant.** incompetent; inept.

competition *n.* **1 contest,** match, game, tournament, event, meet, quiz. **2 rivalry,** vying, contest, opposition, struggle, contention, strife. **3 field,** opposition, challengers, opponents, rivals.

competitive *adj.* **1 competition-oriented,** ambitious, combative, aggressive. **2 aggressive,** dog-eat-dog, cutthroat.

competitor *n.* **1 contestant,** contender, challenger, participant, candidate, entrant. **2 rival,** opponent, adversary, antagonist, opposition. **Ant.** ally; colleague.

compile *v.* **gather,** collect, accumulate, amass, assemble, put together, collate, marshal, organize, systematize, anthologize.

complain *v.* **1 lodge a complaint,** criticize, find fault, carp, make a fuss, *inf.* kick up a fuss. **2 grumble,** grouse, gripe, moan, grouch, whine, lament, bewail, *inf.* bellyache, beef, bitch.

complaint *n.* **1 criticism,** grievance, charge, accusation, protest, remonstrance, statement of dissatisfaction, faultfinding, *Law* plaint. **2 grumbling,** grousing.

3 illness, disease, ailment, disorder, sickness, affliction, malady.

complement *n.* **1 companion,** addition, supplement, accessory, final/finishing touch. **2 amount,** allowance, total, aggregate, load, capacity, quota.
▶ *v.* **complete,** round/set off, add to, go well with, be the perfect companion/addition to, add the final/finishing touch to, supplement.

complementary *adj.* **complemental,** completing, finishing, perfecting, culminative, consummative.

complete *adj.* **1 entire,** whole, full, total, intact, unbroken, undivided, uncut, unshortened, unabridged, plenary. **2 completed,** finished, ended, concluded, accomplished, finalized.
3 absolute, out-and-out, thoroughgoing, thorough, utter, total, perfect, consummate, unqualified, dyed-in-the-wool. **Ant.** incomplete; partial.
▶ *v.* **1 finish,** end, conclude, finalize, realize, accomplish, achieve, fulfill, execute, effect, discharge, settle, clinch, do, *inf.* wrap up, polish off. **2 finish off,** round off, make perfect, perfect, crown, cap, add the final/finishing touch to. **Ant.** begin; commence.

completely adv. **totally,** utterly, absolutely, thoroughly, quite, wholly, altogether.

complex adj. **1 complicated,** difficult, involved, intricate, convoluted, knotty, perplexing, puzzling, cryptic, enigmatic. **2 composite,** compound, compounded, multiple, manifold, multiplex, heterogeneous. **Ant.** simple; easy; elementary.
▸ n. **1 structure,** scheme, composite, conglomerate, aggregation, network, system, organization, synthesis. **2 obsession,** phobia, fixation, preoccupation, idée fixe.

complicate v. **make difficult,** make involved/intricate, confuse, muddle, jumble, snarl up, entangle.

complicated adj. **difficult,** involved, intricate, complex, convoluted, perplexing, puzzling, enigmatic, cryptic, entangled, Byzantine. **Ant.** easy; simple; straightforward.

complication n. **1 difficulty,** problem, drawback, snag, obstacle, aggravation. **2 difficulty,** intricacy, complexity, confusion, muddle.

compliment n. **flattering remark/ comment,** bouquet. **Ant.** insult; criticism.
▸ v. **congratulate,** felicitate, speak highly of, praise, sing the praises of, pay tribute/homage to, salute, admire, flatter, commend, honor, acclaim, laud, eulogize. **Ant.** insult; criticize; condemn.

complimentary adj. **1 congratulatory,** admiring, appreciative, approving, flattering, commendatory, laudatory, eulogizing, panegyrical. **2 free of charge,** given free, gratis, inf. on the house.

component n. **part,** piece, section, constituent, element, unit, module, item.
▸ adj. **constituent,** composing, integral, sectional, fractional.

compose v. **1 write,** make up, create, think up, devise, concoct, invent, compile, contrive, formulate, fashion, produce. **2 put together,** arrange, put in order, align, organize, assemble, collate, systematize. **3 make up,** form, constitute, comprise. **4 calm,** calm down, quiet, collect, control, soothe, still, tranquilize, quell, pacify, assuage.

composed adj. **calm,** cool, collected, cool and collected, serene, tranquil, relaxed, poised, at ease, unruffled, self-controlled, untroubled, undisturbed, unperturbed, unworried, confident, self-possessed, levelheaded, *inf.* together. **Ant.** excited; overwrought.

composition *n.* **1 structure,** constitution, makeup, conformation, configuration, organization, arrangement, layout, character, proportions, harmony, balance, symmetry. **2 compound,** amalgam, blend, mixture, mix, admixture. **3 writing,** making-up, creation, concoction, invention, compilation. **4 work of art,** creation, literary/musical/artistic work, poem, novel, opus, arrangement, symphony, picture, essay, theme, piece of writing.

compound *n.* **amalgam,** blend, mixture, admixture, complex, combination, fusion, alloy, conglomerate, synthesis, medley, hybrid.
▸ *adj.* composite, complex, conglomerate, blended, not simple, fused. **Ant.** simple.

comprehend *v.* **understand,** grasp, take in, assimilate, fathom, perceive, discern, apprehend, conceive, imagine.

comprehensible *adj.* **intelligible,** understandable, graspable, fathomable, discernible, conceivable, plain, clear, explicit, coherent, lucid.

comprehensive *adj.* **inclusive,** all-inclusive, all-embracing, complete, full, encyclopedic, exhaustive, thorough, extensive, broad, widespread, far-reaching, blanket, universal, catholic. **Ant.** partial; limited.

compress *v.* **1 pack down,** press down, press together, squeeze together, squash, crush, condense, compact, cram, tamp, constrict. **2 abbreviate,** shorten, abridge, contract, reduce. **Ant.** expand; spread.

comprise *v.* **1 consist of,** contain, include, be composed of, take in, embrace, encompass. **2 make up,** form, constitute, compose.

compromise *v.* **1 come to terms,** come to an understanding, make a deal, make concessions, find a happy medium, find the middle ground, strike a balance, meet halfway, give and take, take part in a trade-off. **2 discredit,** dishonor, bring shame to, bring into disrepute, shame, embarrass, endanger, jeopardize, imperil. **3 prejudice,** damage, injure, endanger, weaken.
▸ *n.* **understanding,** deal, happy medium, middle course, balance, trade-off, settlement by concession, set of terms, middle ground, give and take, adjustment.

compulsion *n.* **1 obligation,** force, duress, constraint, coercion, pressure, oppression, enforcement. **2 urge,** need, desire, motivation, necessity, preoccupation, obsession.

compulsive *adj.* **1 fascinating,** gripping, irresistible, compelling. **2 obsessive,** uncontrollable, irresistible, compelling, driving, overwhelming, urgent, besetting. **3 addictive,** obsessional, obsessive, uncontrollable, out of control, ungovernable. **4 addicted,** addictive, obsessive, obsessional, dependent, *inf.* hooked.

compulsory *adj.* **obligatory,** mandatory, required, binding, forced, necessary, essential, de rigueur. ***Ant.*** optional; elective.

compunction *n.* **remorse,** regret, pangs of conscience, guilt, contrition, contriteness, penitence, repentance, scruples.

compute *v.* **calculate,** reckon, count, add up, total, figure out, work out, enumerate, sum, tally, cast up, measure, rate.

comrade *n.* **companion,** friend, colleague, partner, associate, coworker, fellow worker, mate, teammate, ally, confederate, compatriot, *inf.* pal, buddy.

con *v.* **swindle,** deceive, cheat, hoodwink, mislead, delude, bamboozle.
▸ *n.* **confidence trick,** swindle, deception, fraud, cheating, racket,

con man, confidence man, swindler, deceiver, cheater, *inf.* rip-off, scam, gyp.

conceal *v.* **hide,** cover, keep out of sight, keep hidden, screen, obscure, disguise, camouflage, mask, secrete, shelter, bury, tuck away, keep secret, keep dark, hush up, cover up, dissemble, *inf.* keep the lid on. ***Ant.*** reveal; expose.

concealed *adj.* **hidden,** obscured, unseen, invisible, screened, secreted, tucked away.

concede *v.* **1 acknowledge,** admit, accept, own, allow, grant, accede, confess, recognize. **2 give up,** yield, surrender, relinquish, cede, hand over. ***Ant.*** deny; dispute; retain.

conceited *adj.* **proud,** arrogant, vain, self-important, cocky, haughty, supercilious, overweening, narcissistic, immodest, egotistical, puffed up, self-satisfied, complacent, boastful, swaggering, vainglorious, *inf.* bigheaded, swellheaded, stuck-up. ***Ant.*** humble; modest.

conceivable *adj.* **credible,** believable, imaginable, thinkable, possible, understandable, comprehensible.

conceive *v.* **1 become pregnant,** become impregnated, become fertilized. **2 think up,** draw up, form, formulate, produce, develop, project, devise, contrive, conjure up, envisage. **3 imagine,** think, believe, realize, appreciate, suppose, understand, comprehend, perceive, grasp, apprehend, envisage, visualize, fancy.

concentrate _v._ **1 focus,** center, converge, centralize, consolidate, bring to bear, congregate, cluster. **2 collect,** gather, congregate, accumulate, amass, cluster, rally, huddle. **3 condense,** boil down, reduce, compress, distill. _**Ant.**_ diffuse; disperse; dissipate.

concentrated _adj._ **1 intensive,** intense, consolidated, rigorous, vigorous, _inf._ all-out. **2 strong,** thick, condensed.

concern _v._ **1 be the business of,** affect, be relevant to, involve, apply to, pertain to, have a bearing on, bear on, be of interest to, touch. **2 be about,** deal with, be connected with, relate to, have to do with, appertain to. **3 interest/involve oneself (in),** be interested/involved (in), take/have a hand (in), busy oneself (with), devote one's time (to), be busy (with). **4 worry,** disturb, trouble, bother, perturb, make anxious, cause disquiet to, distress.
  ▸ _n._ **1 business,** affair, interest, matter of interest, involvement, responsibility, charge, duty, job, task, occupation, mission, department, field, subject, discipline. **2 interest,** importance, relevance, bearing, applicability. **3 worry,** disturbance, anxiety, disquiet, perturbation, distress, apprehension. **4 care,** caringness, solicitude, attentiveness, attention, consideration, regard. **5 business,** firm, company, enterprise, organization, corporation, establishment, house. _**Ant.**_ disinterest; indifference.

concerned _adj._ **1 interested,** involved, implicated. **2 worried,** disturbed, anxious, upset, uneasy, troubled, perturbed, distressed, bothered, apprehensive. **3 caring,** attentive, solicitous, responsible, considerate. _**Ant.**_ disinterested; indifferent.

concerning _prep._ **about,** on the subject of, relating to, relevant to, regarding, as regards, with regard to, with reference to, referring to, with respect to, respecting, as to, touching on, in the matter of, re, apropos of.

concerted _adj._ **jointly planned,** combined, cooperative, joint, coordinated, united, collaborative, synchronized, interactive, synergetic. _**Ant.**_ separate.

conciliate *v.* **placate,** appease, pacify, propitiate, mollify, assuage, calm down, soothe, humor, reconcile, disarm, win over, restore harmony to.

concise *adj.* **succinct,** compact, terse, brief, short, condensed, compressed, crisp, pithy, to the point, epigrammatic, compendious, summary, synoptic. *Ant.* lengthy; discursive; wordy.

conclude *v.* **1 end,** finish, close, bring/come/draw to an end, halt, cease, terminate, discontinue, *inf.* wind up. **2 negotiate,** come to terms on, reach terms on, bring about, pull off, clinch, work out, accomplish, fix, effect, establish, engineer, settle, decide, determine, resolve. **3 come to the conclusion,** deduce, infer, decide, gather, reckon, judge, assume, presume, suppose, conjecture, surmise. *Ant.* start; commence; extend.

conclusion *n.* **1 end,** finish, close, halting, cessation, termination, discontinuance, *inf.* wind-up. **2 negotiation,** clinching, accomplishment, establishment, settling, resolution. **3 outcome,** result, upshot, issue, culmination, consequence. **4 deduction,** inference, decision, opinion, judgment, verdict, conviction, assumption, presumption. *Ant.*

beginning; opening; commencement; start.

conclusive *adj.* **decisive,** clinching, definitive, definite, final, ultimate, categorical, incontestable, irrefutable, convincing, cogent.

concoct *v.* **1 prepare,** put together, make, cook, muster, mix, blend, brew, *inf.* rustle up. **2 devise,** invent, make up, think up, dream up, fabricate, form, formulate, hatch, plot, forge, scheme, design, fashion, *inf.* cook up.

concrete *adj.* **1 actual,** real, factual, definite, genuine, substantial, material, tangible, unimaginary, specific. **2 solid,** solidified, firm, consolidated, compact, dense, condensed, compressed, coalesced, petrified, calcified. *Ant.* abstract; unreal.

concur *v.* **1 agree,** be in accord, accord, be in harmony, acquiesce, assent, be in assent, be of the same mind, be in concord. **2 coincide,** happen/occur together, be simultaneous, coexist, synchronize. **3 cooperate,** combine, unite, collaborate, join forces, act together, work together, pool resources. *Ant.* disagree.

concurrent *adj.* **1 simultaneous,** parallel, coexisting, coexistent, coincident, contemporaneous, synchronous, side-by-side. **2 converging,** convergent, meeting, joining, uniting, intersecting. **3 agreeing,** in agreement, in accord, in harmony, harmonious, assenting, in assent, of the same mind, like-minded, as one, at one, in rapport, compatible, consentient. **4 cooperative,** combined, united, joint, collaborative.

condemn v. **1 censure,** denounce, deprecate, disapprove of, criticize, berate, upbraid, reprove, reproach, blame, reprehend, reprobate. **2 sentence,** pass sentence on, convict, declare guilty, prove one's guilt, accuse, incriminate, indict, inculpate, implicate, doom, damn, force, compel, coerce, impel. **3 declare unfit,** forbid the use of, proscribe, ban, bar. *Ant.* praise; acquit.

condense v. **1 concentrate,** thicken, boil down, reduce, solidify, coagulate. **2 liquefy,** liquidize, deliquesce, precipitate. **3 shorten,** abridge, abbreviate, cut, compress, contract, compact, curtail, summarize, epitomize, encapsulate. *Ant.* dilute; lengthen; expand.

condescend v. **1 lower oneself,** deign, stoop, descend, unbend, humble/demean oneself, vouchsafe, *inf.* come down from one's high horse. **2 treat condescendingly,** patronize, talk down to, look down one's nose at.

condescending *adj.* **patronizing,** disdainful, supercilious, superior, snobbish, lofty, lordly, *inf.* snooty, snotty, uppity.

condition *n.* **1 state,** state of existence, circumstance, situation, predicament, state of affairs, position, plight, predicament, quandary. **2 shape,** form, order, fitness, physical fitness, health, state of health, fettle, kilter, trim, working order. **3 qualification,** requirement, necessity, essential, demand, prerequisite, stipulation, terms, restriction, rule, provision, proviso, contingency, stipulation, limitation, modification, term, limit. **4 disease,** disorder, illness, complaint, problem, ailment, weakness, infirmity, malady.
▶ v. **1 make healthy,** improve, tone, tone up, prepare, make ready. **2 train,** teach, educate, coach, tutor, accustom, adapt, habituate, inure. **3 influence,** affect, govern, determine.

conditional *adj.* **1 dependent on,** contingent on, subject to, based upon. **2 qualified,** having conditions, with reservations, restrictive, provisional, provisory, stipulatory. **Ant.** unconditional; absolute.

condone *v.* **overlook,** disregard, let pass, turn a blind eye to, wink at, excuse, pardon, forgive, make allowances for, forget. **Ant.** condemn; punish.

conducive *adj.* **contributing,** contributory, helpful, instrumental, useful, favorable, advantageous.

conduct *n.* **1 behavior,** way of behaving, comportment, bearing, deportment, actions, ways, habits, practices, manners. **2 direction,** running, management, administration, organization, control, guidance, supervision, leadership.
▸ *v.* **1 behave,** act, comport, deport, acquit. **2 direct,** run, be in charge of, manage, administer, organize, handle, be in control of, control, govern, regulate, supervise, lead, preside over. **3 show,** guide, lead, escort, accompany, take.

confer *v.* **1 bestow,** present, grant, award, give, give out, hand out, accord. **2 have discussions,** discuss, talk, consult, converse, exchange views, discourse, parley.

conference *n.* **meeting,** congress, convention, seminar, symposium, colloquium, forum, convocation, discussion, consultation, conversation, deliberation, debate, communication, dialogue.

confess *v.* **1 admit,** acknowledge, make a clean breast of, own up to, declare, make known, disclose, reveal, divulge, blurt out, expose, admit guilt, plead guilty, accept blame/responsibility, *inf.* tell all, spill the beans, get something off one's chest. **2 admit,** acknowledge, concede, grant, allow, own, say, declare, affirm, profess, assert. **Ant.** conceal; deny.

confide *v.* **1 disclose,** reveal, divulge, impart, tell, intimate, confess, admit, open one's heart to, unburden oneself to, tell one's all to. **2 entrust,** consign, hand over, make over, turn over, give over, commit, commend, assign.

confidence *n.* **1 self-confidence,** self-assurance, assurance, self-reliance, self-possession, aplomb, poise, nerve, firmness, courage, boldness, mettle, fortitude. **2 trust,** reliance, faith, dependence, belief, credence. **3 secret,** private affair, confidentiality, intimacy. **Ant.** doubt; uncertainty; distrust.

confidential *adj.* **1 secret,** private, classified, nonpublic, off-the-record, restricted, personal, intimate, privy, *inf.* hush-hush.

2 close, bosom, dear, intimate, familiar, trusted, trustworthy, trusty, faithful, reliable, dependable.

confine *v.* **1 enclose,** shut up, shut, cage, keep, coop up, pen, box up, lock up, imprison, intern, hold captive, incarcerate, impound. **2 restrict,** limit. ***Ant.*** release; free.

confirm *v.* **1 bear out,** verify, corroborate, prove, endorse, validate, authenticate, substantiate, give credence to, evidence. **2 reassert,** assert, give assurance, assure, affirm, pledge, promise, guarantee. **3 ratify,** endorse, approve, sanction, underwrite, authorize, warrant, accredit. **4 strengthen,** make firmer, reinforce, fortify. ***Ant.*** deny; contradict.

confiscate *v.* **seize,** impound, take possession of, appropriate, commandeer, expropriate, sequestrate, sequester, arrogate.

conflict *n.* **1 battle,** fight, war, warfare, clash, engagement, encounter, hostilities, contest, combat, collision, struggle, strife, tussle, scuffle, fracas, scrap, *inf.* set-to. **2 disagreement,** dissension, hostility, feud, discord, friction, strife, antagonism, antipathy, ill will, bad blood, contention, clash, variance, divided loyalties,

opposition, friction, schism. ***Ant.*** harmony; agreement; peace.
▸ *v.* **clash,** differ, disagree, be at variance, be in opposition, be at odds, be incompatible, collide, contend, contest, fight, combat, struggle, strive.

conform *v.* **follow convention,** be conventional, comply, obey the rules, adapt, adjust, follow the crowd, run with the pack, go with the flow. ***Ant.*** rebel; contradict; differ.

conformity *n.* **1 conventionality,** traditionalism, orthodoxy. **2 compliance,** obedience, observance, adaptation, adjustment, accommodation. **3 likeness,** similarity, resemblance, correspondence, agreement, harmony, accord, affinity, compatibility, congruity, consonance.

confront *v.* **1 face,** face up to, stand up to, resist, defy, oppose, challenge, attack, assault, accost, waylay, tackle, come to grips with, meet head on. **2 bring face to face,** show, present. **3 face,** be in one's way, threat, trouble, harass, annoy, molest. ***Ant.*** avoid; dodge.

confuse *v.* **1 bewilder,** bemuse, perplex, baffle, puzzle, confound, mystify, nonplus, befog. **2 muddle,** mix up, throw into disorder,

disorder, disarrange, tangle up, *inf.* snarl up. **3 mistake,** mix up. ***Ant.*** enlighten; clarify; differentiate.

confused *adj.* **1 unclear,** blurred, indistinct, hazy, foggy, obscure. **2 muddled,** jumbled, untidy, disordered, disorderly, disarranged, out of order, chaotic, disorganized, upset, topsy-turvy. **3 muddled,** addled, befuddled, bewildered, dazed, disoriented, disorientated, at sea, unbalanced, unhinged, demented, *inf.* discombobulated. ***Ant.*** clear; orderly; perceptive.

confusion *n.* **1 bewilderment,** perplexity, bafflement, puzzlement, mystification, disorientation, befuddlement. **2 untidiness,** disorder, chaos, shambles, disorderliness, disarrangement, disorganization, disorganization, bustle, commotion, upheaval, turmoil. ***Ant.*** enlightenment; order; organization.

congeal *v.* **solidify,** harden, coagulate, thicken, set, concentrate, cake.

congenial *adj.* **genial,** agreeable, friendly, pleasant, kindly, pleasing, amiable, nice, companionable, good-natured, sympathetic, compatible, like-minded, kindred, suitable, well-suited, fit, favorable. ***Ant.*** unfriendly; disagreeable; unpleasant.

congenital *adj.* **1 inborn,** inbred, innate, inherent, constitutional, inherited, hereditary. **2 inveterate,** dyed-in-the-wool, out-and-out, thoroughgoing, thorough, utter, complete, established, rooted, ingrained, fixed, settled, set.

congested *adj.* **crowded,** overcrowded, packed, jammed, blocked, obstructed, overflowing, teeming, clogged, choked, plugged, stopped up, gorged.

congratulate *v.* **wish joy to,** felicitate, compliment, offer good wishes to.

congregate *v.* **gather,** assemble, group, flock together, convene, meet, amass, crowd, cluster, throng, rendezvous. ***Ant.*** disperse; scatter.

conjecture *v.* **guess,** surmise, speculate, infer, imagine, fancy, suspect, assume, suppose, believe, think, presume, presuppose, theorize, hypothesize.
▸ *n.* **guess,** guesstimate, inference, fancy, notion, suspicion, presumption, presupposition, theory, hypothesis, guessing, surmise, surmising, imagination, speculation, theorizing.

connect *v.* **join,** attach, fasten, affix, couple, clamp, secure, rivet, fuse, solder, weld, link, unite, bridge. *Ant.* disconnect; sever; separate.

connection *n.* **1 attachment,** fastening, coupling, clamp, clasp, joint. **2 link,** relationship, relation, relatedness, association, bond, tie-in, correspondence, parallel, analogy. **3 context,** reference, frame of reference, relation. **4 contact,** friend, acquaintance, ally, associate, sponsor.

connive *v.* **conspire,** collaborate, collude, be in collusion, intrigue, plot, scheme, be a party to, be an accessory to.

connotation *n.* **undertone,** undermeaning, nuance, hint, intimation, suggestion, implication, allusion, insinuation, reference.

conquer *v.* **1 defeat,** beat, overpower, overthrow, vanquish, subdue, rout, trounce, subjugate, triumph over, crush, quell, overcome, get the better of, master, surmount, rise above, prevail over. **2 seize,** take possession of, occupy, invade, annex, appropriate, overrun, win. *Ant.* surrender; yield.

conquest *n.* **1 conquering,** victory, defeat, beating, overpowering, overthrow, vanquishment, rout, trouncing, subjugation, triumph, mastery, crushing, discomfiture. **2 seizing,** possession, occupation, invasion, annexation, appropriation, overrunning, subjection. **3 captivation,** enchantment, bewitching, seduction, enticement, enthrallment. **4 captive,** catch, acquisition, prize, admirer, fan, adherent, follower, supporter, worshiper, *inf.* pushover.

conscience *n.* **sense of right and wrong,** moral sense, still small voice, morals, scruples, principles, ethics.

conscientious *adj.* **1 diligent,** careful, attentive, thorough, meticulous, punctilious, painstaking, hard-working, dedicated, thorough, precise, accurate, detailed. **2 careful,** thorough, meticulous, precise, accurate, detailed. *Ant.* careless; inattentive; lax; slapdash.

conscious *adj.* **1 deliberate,** calculated, premeditated, on purpose, reasoned, knowing, studied, willed, volitional. **2 awake,** aware, sentient, responsive, alert. *Ant.* unconscious; unaware.

consecrate *v.* **1 sanctify,** bless, make holy, hallow, dedicate to God. **2 dedicate,** devote, pledge, commit, vow, set apart.

consecutive *adj.* **successive,** succeeding, following, in sequence, sequential, serial, in turn, progressive, step-by-step, continuous, uninterrupted, unbroken, chronological, seriate.

consensus *n.* **agreement,** consent, common consent, unanimity, harmony, concord, unity, concurrence.

consent ▸ *v.* **agree** go along, acquiesce, accede, concede, yield, give in, submit, comply, concur. ▸ *n.* **agreement,** assent, acceptance, approval, permission, sanction, acquiescence, compliance, concurrence, *inf.* go-ahead, OK, green light. **Ant.** refusal; dissent.

consequence *n.* **1 result,** effect, upshot, outcome, issue, event, end, aftermath, repercussion, reverberation. **2 importance,** note, significance, import, moment, weight, substance, portent, distinction, standing, status, prominence, prestige, eminence, repute, mark, esteem, rank. **Ant.** cause; impetus.

consequent *adj.* **resulting,** resultant, ensuing, following, subsequent, successive, sequential.

conservation *n.* **preservation,** protection, safeguarding, safekeeping, guarding, saving, care, charge, custody, husbandry, supervision, upkeep, maintenance.

conservative *adj.* **1 right-wing,** reactionary, traditionalist. **2 conventional,** traditional, reactionary, orthodox, cautious, prudent, careful, moderate, middle-of-the-road, temperate, stable, unchanging, old-fashioned, unprogressive, sober. **3 conserving,** preservative, protective, saving. **Ant.** radical; progressive.

conserve *v.* **preserve,** save, keep, protect, take care of, hoard, store up, husband, use sparingly, reserve, nurse. **Ant.** squander; waste.

consider *v.* **1 think about,** weigh, give thought to, examine, study, mull over, ponder, contemplate, deliberate over, cogitate about, chew over, meditate over, ruminate over, turn over in one's mind. **2 take into consideration,** take into account, make allowances for, respect, bear in mind, have regard to, reckon with, remember. **3 think,** believe, regard as, deem, hold to be, judge, rate. **4 contemplate,** look at, observe, regard, survey, view, scrutinize, scan, examine, inspect. **Ant.** ignore; neglect; disregard.

considerable *adj.* **1 sizable,** substantial, appreciable, goodly, tolerable, fair, reasonable, tidy, ample, plentiful, abundant, marked, noticeable, comfortable, decent, great, large, lavish. **2 much,** a lot of, a great deal of, great, a fair amount of. **3 distinguished,** noteworthy, noted, important, significant, influential, illustrious, renowned. *Ant.* little; negligible; paltry; insignificant.

considerate *adj.* **thoughtful,** attentive, concerned, solicitous, mindful, heedful, kind, kindly, unselfish, compassionate, sympathetic, patient, charitable, generous, obliging, accommodating. *Ant.* thoughtless; selfish.

consign *v.* **1 hand over,** give over, deliver, assign, entrust, commend, remit, bequeath. **2 dismiss,** assign, deliver, commit, reduce, dispossess. **3 send,** dispatch, transmit, convey, mail.

consignment *n.* **1 handing over,** assignment, entrusting, commendation. **2 sending,** dispatch, conveyance. **3 delivery,** batch, load, shipment.

consist *v.* **be composed of,** be made up of, be formed of, comprise, contain, include, incorporate, embody, involve.

consistent *adj.* **1 steady,** dependable, constant, uniform, unchanging, undeviating, true to type. **2 compatible,** congruous, agreeing, accordant, consonant. *Ant.* inconsistent; irregular; incompatible.

consolation *n.* **comfort,** solace, sympathy, compassion, pity, commiseration, relief, help, support, cheer, encouragement, soothing, easement, succor, assuagement, alleviation.

consolidate *v.* **1 strengthen,** secure, make stable, stabilize, reinforce, fortify, cement. **2 combine,** unite, merge, amalgamate, join, affiliate, fuse, federate.

consort *n.* **spouse,** partner, companion, escort, husband, wife. ▸ *v.* **associate,** keep company, hang around, go around, mix, spend time, fraternize, have dealings.

conspicuous *adj.* **1 easily seen,** clear, visible, obvious, evident, apparent, noticeable, observable, recognizable, discernible, perceptible, distinguishable, manifest, vivid. **2 striking,** glaring, obtrusive, blatant, flagrant, showy, garish, bold, ostentatious. **3 distinguished,** outstanding, prominent, eminent, well-known, notable, famous, renowned, celebrated, illustrious. **Ant.** inconspicuous; unobtrusive; obscure.

conspiracy n. **1 plot**, scheme, stratagem, plan, machination, cabal, inf. frame-up. **2 plotting**, collusion, intrigue, connivance, collaboration, machination, treason.

conspirator n. **conspirer**, plotter, schemer, intriguer, colluder, collaborator, confederate, cabalist, traitor.

conspire v. **form a conspiracy**, plot, hatch a plot, scheme, intrigue, collude, collaborate, cabal, machinate, act together, work together, combine, join, unite, join forces, cooperate, coact, gang up (on), inf. be in cahoots with.

constant adj. **1 uniform**, even, regular, stable, steady, fixed, invariable, unvarying, unchanging, immutable.
2 continuous, unbroken, uninterrupted, continual, never-ending, endless, unending, nonstop, incessant, unceasing, ceaseless, perpetual, persistent, interminable, unremitting, sustained, relentless, unrelenting.
3 faithful, devoted, loyal, staunch, dependable, true, trustworthy, trusty. **4 firm**, steadfast, steady, resolute, determined, persevering,

tenacious, dogged, unwavering, unflagging, unshaken. **Ant.** inconstant; variable; fickle.

consternation n. **surprise**, amazement, astonishment, dismay, bewilderment, perturbation, mystification, confusion, anxiety, distress, alarm, panic, fear, fright, dread, horror, trepidation, shock, terror, awe.

construct v. **1 build**, erect, put up, set up, raise, elevate, establish, assemble, manufacture, fabricate, make. **2 form**, formulate, put together, create, devise, design, invent, compose, fashion, mold, model, shape, frame, forge, engineer, fabricate, manufacture. **Ant.** destroy; demolish.

construction n. **1 building**, erection, elevation, establishment, assembly, manufacture, fabrication.
2 structure, building, edifice, assembly, framework.
3 interpretation, reading, meaning, explanation, inference, explication.

constructive adj. **useful**, helpful, productive, practical, positive, valuable. **Ant.** destructive; negative.

consult v. **1 ask**, seek advice/ information from, call in, turn to, take counsel from, look up in, check (in), refer to. **2 confer,** discuss, talk, talk over, exchange views, deliberate, parley, powwow, palaver, *inf.* talk turkey. **3 consider,** take into consideration/account, have regard to, respect, have an eye to.

consume *v.* **1 eat,** eat up, drink, drink up, devour, ingest, swallow, gobble, gobble up, guzzle, snack on, *inf.* tuck into, scoff, down, put away, polish off, graze on. **2 absorb,** preoccupy, engross, eat up, devour, obsess, grip, monopolize, enthrall. **3 destroy,** demolish, lay waste, wipe out, annihilate, devastate, raze, gut, ravage. **4 use,** use up, utilize, expend, deplete, exhaust, waste, squander, drain, dissipate, fritter away.

contact *n.* **1 touch,** touching, proximity, exposure, contiguity, junction, union, tangency. **2 touch,** communication, connection, correspondence, association. **3 connection,** acquaintance.

▶ *v.* **get/be in touch with,** get hold/ahold of, communicate with, be in communication with, write to, write, notify, phone, call, speak to, reach.

contagious *adj.* **catching,** communicable, transmittable, transmissible, transferable, spreadable, infectious, epidemic, pandemic.

contain *v.* **1 hold,** have capacity for, carry, accommodate, seat. **2 include,** comprise, embrace, take in, incorporate, involve. **3 keep back,** hold in, restrain, control, keep under control, keep in check, suppress, repress, curb, stifle.

container *n.* **receptacle,** vessel, holder, repository, semi-trailer.

contaminate *v.* **make impure,** pollute, adulterate, defile, debase, corrupt, taint, infect, foul, spoil, soil, sully, tarnish, stain, befoul, vitiate, radioactivate.

contemplate *v.* **1 look at,** view, regard, examine, inspect, observe, survey, scrutinize, scan, stare at, gaze at, eye, think about, meditate over, consider, ponder, reflect over, mull over, muse on, dwell on, deliberate over, cogitate over, ruminate over, turn over in one's mind, give thought to, have in mind/view, envisage, intend, plan, propose, aim at, foresee. **2 think about,** give thought to, consider, have in mind/view, envisage, intend, plan, propose, aim at, foresee.

contemplative *adj.* **thoughtful,** pensive, reflective, meditative, musing, ruminative, introspective, intent, rapt, deep/

lost in thought, *inf.* in a brown study.

contemporary *adj.*
1 contemporaneous, coexisting, coexistent, concurrent, synchronous. **2 modern,** present-day, present, current, present-time, up-to-date, up-to-the-minute, fashionable, in fashion, latest, recent, ultramodern, newfangled, à la mode, *inf.* with it. ***Ant.*** old-fashioned; out of date.
▸ *n.* **peer,** compeer, fellow.

contempt *n.* **1 scorn,** disdain, disrespect, condescension, derision, mockery, disgust, loathing, abhorrence. **2 disregard,** disrespect, slighting, neglect. ***Ant.*** admiration; respect.

contemptible *adj.* **despicable,** detestable, ignominious, lamentable, pitiful, low, mean, shameful, abject, unworthy, worthless, base, vile, shabby, cheap, sordid, degenerate. ***Ant.*** admirable; honorable.

contemptuous *adj.* **scornful,** disdainful, disrespectful, insulting, insolent, derisory, derisive, mocking, sneering, jeering, condescending, supercilious, arrogant, high and mighty.

contend *v.* **1 compete,** oppose, challenge, vie, contest, clash, strive, struggle, tussle, grapple, wrestle, scuffle, skirmish, battle, combat, fight, war, wage war, join battle, cross swords. **2 state,** declare, assert, maintain, hold, claim, profess, allege, affirm, aver, pronounce.

content[1] *n.* **1 component parts/elements. 2 subject matter,** subject, material, substance, matter, theme, ideas, gist.
3 amount, proportion, quantity.
4 volume, capacity, size.

content[2] *adj.* **contented,** satisfied, pleased, happy, cheerful, glad, gratified, fulfilled, at ease, at peace, comfortable, serene, tranquil, unworried, untroubled, complacent. ***Ant.*** discontented; dissatisfied; unhappy.
▸ *v.* **1 make content,** satisfy, be pleased/happy/glad, be fulfilled, be gratified. **2 pacify,** placate, soothe, appease, mollify.

contented *adj.* **content,** satisfied, pleased.

contentment *n.* **content,** contentedness, satisfaction, pleasure, happiness, cheerfulness, gladness, gratification, fulfillment, ease, comfort, peace, equanimity, serenity, tranquillity, repletion, complacency.

contest *n.* **competition,** match, game, event, tournament, meet, trial, struggle, conflict, battle, fight, combat, tussle, skirmish.

▸ *v.* **challenge,** question, call into question, oppose, doubt, dispute, object to, litigate, argue, debate, quarrel over, contend.

contestant *n.* **competitor,** entrant, candidate, participant, player, contender, rival, opponent, adversary, antagonist, aspirant.

context *n.* **1 circumstances,** conditions, situation, state of affairs, background, environment. **2 text,** frame of reference, contextual relationship, subject, theme, topic.

contingency *n.* **chance event,** event, eventuality, incident, happening, occurrence, juncture, accident, chance, possibility, fortuity, emergency, uncertainty.

continual *adj.* **1 frequent,** repeated, constant, regular, persistent, habitual, recurrent, repetitive, oft-repeated. **2** continuous, perpetual, endless, constant, interminable. **Ant.** intermittent; irregular.

continue *v.* **1 go on,** extend, keep on, carry on, maintain course, drag on, last, remain, stay, endure, survive, live on, persist, subsist, abide, maintain, sustain, retain, prolong, protract, perpetuate, preserve, keep at, not stop, persist in, persevere in,

prolong, pursue, *inf.* stick with/at. **2 resume,** renew, recommence, start again, carry on with, return to, take up, go on, proceed, pick up where one has left off. **3 go on,** carry on, resume, recommence, proceed, pick up where one has left off. **Ant.** stop; discontinue; give up (see give).

continuous *adj.* **uninterrupted,** unbroken, consecutive, constant, without stopping, nonstop, perpetual, ceaseless, incessant, unceasing, unremitting, endless, everlasting, interminable, undivided. **Ant.** intermittent; sporadic.

contour *n.* **outline,** silhouette, profile, figure, shape, form, lines, curves.

contract *n.* **agreement,** compact, covenant, pact, settlement, arrangement, understanding, transaction, bargain, deal, treaty, concordat, convention, bond, commitment, entente.

▸ *v.* **1 shrink,** reduce, shrivel. **2 narrow,** tighten, tense, draw in, constrict. **3 shorten,** abbreviate, abridge, lessen, compress, condense, curtail, concentrate, summarize, synopsize. **4 arrange,** agree, reach an arrangement, establish, come to terms, negotiate, bargain, strike a bargain, close/clinch a deal, close,

engage, settle, covenant. **5 catch,**
get, come down with, develop,
become infected with. **6 incur,**
acquire, fall into. *Ant.* expand;
distend; lengthen.

contradict *v.* **1 say the opposite
of,** oppose, challenge, counter, be
at variance with, deny, dispute,
refute, rebut, controvert, impugn,
confute. **2 be at variance with,**
disagree with, be in conflict with,
clash with, contravene, run
counter to, be inconsistent with,
dissent from, negate. *Ant.* agree;
confirm; verify.

contradictory *adj.* **1 opposing,**
opposite, dissenting, contrary,
dissident, at variance, at odds.
2 contradicting, disagreeing,
conflicting, clashing, contrasting,
incompatible, irreconcilable,
inconsistent, incongruous,
contravening, negating,
antithetical.

contraption *n.* **device,** machine,
mechanism, gadget, contrivance,
apparatus, invention, appliance,
inf. thingamajig, thingamabob,
whatsit, whatchamacallit, doodad,
gizmo.

contrary *adj.* **1 opposite,**
opposing, contradictory, clashing,
conflicting, contrasting,
incompatible, irreconcilable,
inconsistent, incongruous,
antithetical. **2 willful,** obstinate,

stubborn, headstrong, pigheaded,
unaccommodating, intractable,
recalcitrant, intransigent,
refractory, cantankerous. *Ant.*
compatible; accommodating.
▸ *n.* **opposite,** antithesis, reverse,
contrariety.

contrast *n.* **1 difference,**
dissimilarity, distinction,
disparity, dissimilitude,
differentiation, distinguishment,
comparison. **2 opposite,**
antithesis. *Ant.* similarity;
sameness.
▸ *v.* **1 compare,** juxtapose, set side
by side, distinguish, differentiate,
discriminate. **2 form a contrast,**
contradict, be at variance, be
contrary, diverge, differ.

contribute *v.* **1 give,** donate,
hand out, present, grant, endow,
bestow, accord, confer, provide,
supply, furnish, *inf.* chip in, pitch
in. **2 be conducive to,** lead to, be
instrumental in, have a hand in,
bear a part in, add to, help,
promote, advance.

contribution *n.* **1 donation,** gift,
offering, present, grant, bestowal,
allowance, subsidy, endowment.
2 article, piece, story, item.
3 input, participation, *inf.* two
cents' worth.

contrite *adj.* **penitent,** repentant,
remorseful, regretful, sorry,
chastened, conscience-stricken,

guilt-ridden, in sackcloth and ashes, wearing a hair shirt.

control *v.* **1 be in control of,** be in charge of, head, manage, direct, preside over, conduct, be in authority over, command, rule, govern, lead, supervise, superintend, oversee, dominate, master, reign over, be in the driver's seat of, be in the saddle of, *inf.* be the boss of. **2 keep in check,** restrain, curb, contain, hold back, restrict, limit, regulate, constrain, subdue, bridle, guide, monitor, steer, pilot.
▸ *n.* **1 charge,** management, authority, power, command, direction, rule, government, jurisdiction, supervision, superintendence, guidance, dominance, mastery, reign, supremacy. **2 self-control,** self-restraint, restraint, hold, check, curb, constraint, limitation, restriction, regulation. **3 standard of comparison,** standard, check. **4 headquarters,** base, center of operations, command post.

controversial *adj.* **open to discussion/question,** disputed, disputable, debatable, under discussion, at issue, contentious, contended, controvertible.

controversy *n.* **dispute,** argument, debate, disagreement, dissension, contention,

altercation, wrangle, wrangling, quarreling, squabbling, bickering, polemic. *Ant.* accord; harmony.

convene *v.* **1 call,** call together, summon, convoke, round up, rally. **2 assemble,** gather, collect, congregate, meet, muster.

convenient *adj.* **1 accessible,** handy, at hand, close at hand, within reach, nearby, just around the corner, at one's fingertips, available. **2 suitable,** suited, appropriate, fit, fitting, favorable, advantageous, opportune, timely, well-timed, expedient, useful, serviceable. *Ant.* inconvenient; inaccessible; unsuitable.

convention *n.* **1 conference,** congress, gathering, meeting, assembly, convocation, council of delegates/representatives, synod, conclave. **2 conventionality,** etiquette, formality, protocol, propriety, code, custom, tradition, usage, practice. **3 agreement,** contract, pact, treaty, bargain, deal, compact, concordat.

conventional *adj.* **1 accepted,** expected, customary, usual, standard, regular, normal, ordinary, correct, decorous, proper, orthodox, traditional, prevailing, prevalent, conformist, conservative, formal, ritual, *inf.* square, straight, straitlaced. **2 run-of-the-mill,** commonplace, common, ordinary, everyday, common garden variety, prosaic, routine, stereotyped, pedestrian, hackneyed, unoriginal, clichéd, trite, platitudinous, bourgeois. *Ant.* unconventional; unorthodox; original.

converge *v.* **1 meet,** intersect, join, merge, unite, come together, become one, coincide, concur. **2 approach,** move toward, come closer to, close in on, center on, focus on. *Ant.* divide; separate; diverge.

conversant *adj.* **acquainted with,** familiar with, knowledgeable about, well-versed in, informed about, well-informed about, apprised of, au fait with, experienced in, proficient in, practiced in, skilled in, *inf.* (well) up on.

conversation *n.* **talk,** discussion, chat, dialogue, discourse, communication, conference, gossip, colloquy, intercourse, exchange, powwow, tête-à-tête; *inf.* confab, rap session.

convert *v.* **1 change,** transform, metamorphose, transfigure, transmute, *inf.* transmogrify. **2 change (into),** make (into), adapt, transform (into). **3 alter,** adapt, modify, reshape, refashion, remodel, restyle, remake, reconstruct, rebuild, reorganize.

4 reform, regenerate, convince, cause to change beliefs, bring to God, baptize, proselytize, cause to be reborn. **5 change,** turn into, exchange for, substitute by, switch from.

convey *v.* **1 transport,** carry, bring, fetch, bear, move, shift, transfer, cart, lug, conduct, transmit, channel, guide. **2 transmit,** pass on, hand on, send, dispatch, communicate, make known, impart, relate, announce, tell, reveal, disclose. **3 give the rights to,** transfer, transmit, grant, cede, devolve, lease, bequeath, will, *Law* demise.

convict *v.* **declare/find/ pronounce/judge guilty,** sentence, condemn.
> *n.* **prisoner,** criminal, offender, lawbreaker, felon, *inf.* crook, con, jailbird.

conviction *n.* **1 declaration/ pronouncement of guilt,** sentence, judgment, condemnation. **2 confidence,** assurance, belief, certainty, certitude, persuasion, firmness, trust, earnestness. **3 belief,** opinion, view, thought, idea, persuasion. **4 principle,** belief, faith, creed.

convince *v.* **1 make one certain,** prove to, satisfy, assure, reassure. **2 persuade,** prevail upon, sway, bring around, win over.

convincing *adj.* **1 cogent,** powerful, persuasive, plausible, incontrovertible, conclusive, credible. **2 impressive,** decisive, conclusive.

convivial *adj.* **genial,** cordial, sociable, friendly, affable, amiable, congenial, agreeable, jolly, cheerful. *Ant.* unfriendly; unsociable.

convoy *n.* **1 group,** company, assemblage, line, fleet, cortege, caravan. **2 escort,** protection, guard, bodyguard, defense, shield, guidance.
▶ *v.* **escort,** accompany, attend, protect, guard, defend, guide, shepherd, flank, chaperon.

cook *v.* **1 prepare,** put together, improvise, bake, roast, grill, stew, steam, braise, sauté, fry, deep-fry. **2 falsify,** forge, alter. **3 happen,** occur, take place.

cool *adj.* **1 fresh,** refreshing, coldish, chilly, chilled, chilling, nippy, unheated, sunless, windy, breezy, drafty. **2 calm,** composed, collected, self-possessed, self-controlled, levelheaded, unexcited, unperturbed, unmoved, unruffled, unemotional, relaxed, placid, quiet, serene, *inf.* together. **3 aloof,** distant, reserved, standoffish, unfriendly, offhand, unwelcoming, uncommunicative, chilly, impassive, undemonstrative, unresponsive, unenthusiastic, indifferent, unconcerned, uninterested. **4 bold,** audacious, brazen, presumptuous, overconfident, impudent, insolent, impertinent, forward, shameless. **5 calculated,** premeditated, planned, deliberate, intentional, purposeful, dispassionate, cold, cold-blooded. **6 sophisticated,** suave, stylish, urbane, cosmopolitan, elegant, *inf.* streetwise, in. **7 great,** superb, excellent, very good, splendid, *inf.* awesome, far-out. *Ant.* warm; excited; passionate.
▶ *v.* **1 chill,** refrigerate, freeze. **2 lessen,** abate, moderate, temper, diminish, reduce, dampen, quiet, soothe, assuage, allay, mollify, settle, cool off. *Ant.* warm; intensify.

cooperate *v.* **work together,** act/pull together, join forces, unite, act jointly, combine, collaborate, pool resources, conspire, connive, concur, coordinate, coact, be of assistance, assist, help, lend a hand, contribute, aid, abet, participate, go along, *inf.* pitch in, play ball.

cooperative *adj.* **1 joint,** united, shared, unified, combined, concerted, collected, coordinated, collaborative, coactive. **2 of assistance,** assisting, helpful, helping, obliging, accommodating, aiding, contributing, participating, responsive.

coordinate *v.* **1 arrange,** organize, order, integrate, synchronize, correlate, harmonize, systematize. **2 cooperate,** unite, combine, collaborate, coact, interrelate.

cope *v.* **manage,** succeed, survive, carry on, get through, get on, get along, get by, subsist, make the grade, come through, hold one's own, *inf.* make out.

copious *adj.* **abundant,** superabundant, plentiful, ample, profuse, full, extensive, generous, lavish, rich, liberal, bounteous, bountiful, exuberant, luxuriant, overflowing, abounding. ***Ant.*** scarce; sparse; paltry.

copy *n.* **1 transcript,** facsimile, duplicate, duplication, carbon, carbon copy, photocopy, *Trademark* Xerox, Photostat. **2 imitation,** reproduction, replica, replication, likeness, counterfeit, forgery, fake, sham. **3 specimen,** example, sample, issue.
▸ *v.* **1 duplicate,** photocopy, transcribe, *Trademark* Xerox, Photostat. **2 reproduce,** replicate,

forge, counterfeit. **3 imitate,** mimic, emulate, follow, echo, mirror, simulate, ape, parrot.

cordon *n.* **1 barrier,** line, chain, ring, picket line. **2 braid,** cord, ribbon, sash, decoration.

core *n.* **center,** heart, nucleus, nub, kernel, crux, heart of the matter, essence, quintessence, substance, gist, pith, *inf.* nitty-gritty.

corner *n.* **1 angle,** bend, curve, crook, turn, projecting angle, intersection, junction, fork, convergence, juncture. **2 nook,** cranny, niche, recess, crevice, cavity, hole, secret place, hideaway, hide-out, part, region, area, district, section, quarter, *inf.* neck of the woods. **3 predicament,** plight, tight spot, *inf.* pickle. **4 control,** position of control, dominance, monopoly.
▸ *v.* **1 drive into a corner,** run to earth, block off, trap, bring to bay. **2 gain control/dominance of,** control, dominate, monopolize, *inf.* hog.

corpse *n.* **dead body,** body, cadaver, carcass, skeleton, remains, *inf.* stiff.

correct *adj.* **1 right,** accurate, true, actual, exact, precise, unerring, close, faithful, strict, faultless, flawless, *inf.* OK, okay, on the mark, on the beam. **2 proper,** suitable, fit, fitting,

befitting, appropriate, apt, seemly, conventional, approved, accepted, standard, usual, customary, *inf.* OK, okay. *Ant.* incorrect; wrong; improper.
▶ *v.* **1 make/set right,** rectify, right, amend, emend, remedy, redress, cure, improve, better, ameliorate, repair. **2 edit. 3 rectify,** counteract, offset, counterbalance, compensate for, make up for, neutralize. **4 adjust,** regulate, fix, set, standardize, normalize, make conform. **5 scold,** rebuke, chide, reprimand, reprove, admonish, lecture, berate, discipline, punish, chastise.

correspond *v.* **1 agree,** be in agreement, accord, concur, coincide, conform, match, fit together, square, tally, dovetail, correlate. **2 be analogous,** be similar, be comparable, be equivalent, be akin. **3 exchange letters,** write, communicate, keep in touch/contact. *Ant.* differ; vary.

correspondence *n.*
1 agreement, accordance, accord, concurrence, coincidence, conformity, harmony, matching. **2 analogy,** similarity, resemblance, comparability, correlation, relation. **3 mail,** communication, letters, notes, messages, E-mail, letter-writing, writing.

corroborate *v.* **confirm,** verify, bear out, authenticate, validate, certify, endorse, ratify, substantiate, back up, uphold, support, attest to, sustain, evidence. *Ant.* disprove; contradict.

corrode *v.* **1 eat away,** wear away, erode, gnaw, abrade, destroy, consume, rust, oxidize. **2 wear away,** waste away, rust, disintegrate, crumble, fragment, be destroyed.

corrugated *adj.* **furrowed,** grooved, ridged, fluted, wavy, channeled, folded, crinkled, puckered, creased, wrinkled, crumpled, striate.

corrupt *adj.* **1 dishonest,** bribable, crooked, fraudulent, dishonorable, unscrupulous, untrustworthy, venal, *inf.* shady. **2 immoral,** depraved, wicked, evil, sinful, degenerate, reprobate, perverted, dissolute, debauched, decadent, abandoned, lascivious, lewd, lecherous. **3 rotten,** polluted, putrid, decayed, putrescent, tainted, infected, contaminated. **4 adulterated,** impure, alloyed, contaminated, tainted. *Ant.* honest; ethical; moral; pure.
▶ *v.* **1 bribe,** suborn, buy, buy off, induce, lure, entice, *inf.* pay off,

grease the palm of. **2 deprave,** pervert, warp, make degenerate, debauch. **3 make rotten,** pollute, putrefy, taint, infect, contaminate, blight, mar. **4 adulterate,** alloy, contaminate, taint, defile, debase. **5 alter,** tamper with, falsify, doctor, damage. *Ant.* purify; sanctify.

cosmic *adj.* **1 universal,** worldwide. **2 space,** celestial. **3 vast,** huge, immense, enormous, immeasurable, measureless, infinite, limitless.

cosmopolitan *adj.* **1 international,** multiethnic, universal, global, worldwide. **2 liberal,** broad-minded, unprejudiced, sophisticated, urbane, worldly, worldly-wise, well-traveled, jet-setting, globe-trotting, unprovincial, cultivated, cultured. *Ant.* provincial; parochial; unsophisticated.

cost *v.* **1 be priced at,** sell for, be valued at, fetch, come to, amount to, *inf.* set one back. **2 involve,** result in, lead to, involve the loss/ expense/sacrifice of, necessitate. **3 do a disservice to,** harm, hurt, injure, damage.
▸ *n.* **1 price,** asking price, selling price, charge, amount, value, valuation, quotation, rate, worth, payment, expenditure, expense, outlay, *inf.* damage. **2 sacrifice,**

expense, loss, penalty, suffering, harm, hurt, injury, damage, deprivation, detriment.

costly *adj.* **1 expensive,** high-cost, high-priced, valuable, exorbitant, extortionate, extravagant, *inf.* steep. **2 ruinous,** catastrophic, disastrous, sacrificial, damaging, harmful, deleterious. *Ant.* cheap; inexpensive.

counsel *n.* **1 advice,** guidance, direction, recommendation, information, opinion, suggestion, warning, admonition, caution. **2 consultation,** discussion, conference, deliberation, dialogue. **3 lawyer,** attorney, advocate.
▸ *v.* **advise,** give guidance/ direction, guide, direct, recommend, give one's opinion/ suggestions, warn, admonish, caution.

count *v.* **1 add up,** total, sum up, calculate, compute, enumerate, tally, keep a count of, count off, keep a tally of. **2 include,** take into account/consideration, number among, embrace, embody. **3 consider,** think, regard, look upon, hold, judge, rate, deem, esteem. **4 matter,** enter into consideration, be of account, be of consequence, have effect, signify, carry weight, weigh, mean anything, amount to anything, make a difference, rate, *inf.* carry (any) weight/clout.

▶ *n.* **counting,** enumeration, calculation, computation, tally, tallying, poll, total, sum/grand total, amount, full amount, aggregate, whole, tally, reckoning.

countenance *n.* **1 face,** features, facial expression, expression, look, appearance, aspect, air, complexion, visage, physiognomy, *lit.* mien. **2 support,** backing, encouragement, endorsement, assistance, aid, approval, sanction, approbation, favor, acceptance, adoption, advocacy.

▶ *v.* **1 tolerate,** approve, put up with, permit, allow, endure, brook, *inf.* stand for. **2 encourage,** support, back, help, aid, assist, champion, abet, take the side of, sanction, condone, endorse, warrant.

counter *n.* **1 countertop,** bar, work surface, table, checkout. **2 token,** disk, chip, piece, man, marker.

▶ *adv.* phrase: **counter to against,** in opposition to, contrary to, at variance with, in defiance of, against the tide of, contrarily to, contrariwise to, conversely to.

▶ *adj.* phrase: **counter to opposing,** opposed to, opposite to, contrary to, adverse to, conflicting with,

contradictory to, contrasting, obverse to.

counteract *v.* **1 act against,** act counter to, hinder, oppose, thwart, frustrate, foil, impede, check, restrain, resist, withstand, defeat. **2 counterbalance,** offset, neutralize, annul, negate, invalidate, countervail, counterpoise.

counterbalance *v.* **balance,** equalize, compensate for, make up for, neutralize, offset, set off, undo, countervail, counterpoise.

counterfeit *adj.* **fake,** faked, copied, forged, imitation, feigned, simulated, fraudulent, sham, spurious, bogus, ersatz, *inf.* phony, pseudo. **Ant.** genuine; authentic.

▶ *n.* **fake,** copy, forgery, reproduction, imitation, fraud, sham, *inf.* phony.

▶ *v.* **fake,** copy, forge, reproduce, imitate, feign, falsify, sham.

counterpart *n.* **equivalent,** equal, opposite number, parallel, complement, match, twin, mate, fellow, analog, correlative, copy, duplicate.

countless *adj.* **innumerable,** incalculable, immeasurable, endless, limitless, without end/ limit, boundless, infinite, inexhaustible, untold, legion, myriad, no end to.

country *n.* **1 nation,** state,

sovereign state, kingdom, realm, people, community, commonwealth. **2 native land,** homeland, fatherland, motherland, mother country, land of one's birth, one's roots. **3 terrain,** land, territory, region, area, district, part, neighborhood, parts, *inf.* neck of the woods. **4 people,** nation, public, population, populace, community, citizenry, inhabitants, residents, citizens, electors, voters. **5 countryside,** rural area/district, farmland, great outdoors, *derog.* backwoods, sticks, wilds, wilderness, middle of nowhere, *inf.* boondocks, boonies.

▸ *adj.* **rural,** agrarian, agricultural, rustic, provincial, pastoral, Arcadian, bucolic, *lit.* sylvan.

coupon *n.* **1 voucher,** ticket, slip, certificate, stub. **2 form,** entry/application form.

courage *n.* **bravery,** valor, gallantry, heroism, fearlessness, intrepidity, lionheartedness, stoutheartedness, pluck, nerve, boldness, daring, audacity, dauntlessness, mettle, fortitude, firmness, resolution, tenacity, determination, *inf.* spunk, guts, grit, moxie. **Ant.** cowardice; fear.

courageous *adj.* **brave,** valiant, valorous, gallant, heroic, fearless,

intrepid, lionhearted, plucky, bold, daring, audacious, dauntless, firm, resolute, tenacious, determined, indomitable. **Ant.** cowardly; timid.

course *n.* **1 progression,** progress, advance, advancement, rise, march, furtherance, proceeding, development, unfolding, flow, movement, continuity, sequence, order, succession. **2 route,** way, track, direction, tack, path, line, lane, road, passage, channel, trail, trajectory, orbit, circuit, ambit. **3 method,** way, line (of action), process, procedure, manner, mode of behavior/conduct, plan, system, policy, program, regimen. **4 duration,** passing, passage, lapse, period, term, span, spell, sweep. **5 course of study,** set of lectures, curriculum, program, schedule, classes, lectures, studies. **6 sequence,** series, system, regimen. **7 racecourse,** track, circuit, ground.

▸ *v.* **flow,** move, run, rush, surge, gush, race, hurry, speed, charge, dash.

court *n.* **1 court of law,** bench, bar, court of justice, justiciary, tribunal. **2 royal household,** retinue, entourage, train, suite, cortege, attendants, palace, castle, manor, hall, chateau. **3 assembly,**

reception. **4 attention,** homage, deference, suit, wooing, courtship, respects. **5 courtyard,** quadrangle, square, cloister, atrium, esplanade, patio, piazza, plaza, *inf.* quad.

▸ *v.* **1 pay court to,** woo, pursue, chase, run after, pay suit to, go out, go out, go with each other, go steady, date. **2 curry favor with,** try to win over, pander to, fawn over, *inf.* soft-soap, butter up. **3 seek,** solicit, ask for, crave. **4 invite,** risk, provoke, lead to, cause, bring on, elicit.

courteous *adj.* **polite,** well-mannered, mannerly, civil, chivalrous, gallant, gracious, kind, considerate, pleasant, tactful, diplomatic, politic, cordial, genial, affable, respectful, deferential, well-bred, polished, refined, civilized, urbane. **Ant.** discourteous; rude.

courtier *n.* **attendant,** follower, lady-in-waiting, page, squire.

cove *n.* **bay,** inlet, creek, sound, anchorage.

cover *v.* **1 place over,** place under cover, protect, shield, shelter, conceal, hide, house, secrete, bury. **2 overlay,** overspread, blanket, carpet, overlie, extend over, coat, layer, pave, submerge. **3 clothe,** attire, outfit, garb, robe, wrap, accouter, sheathe. **4 protect,** defend, guard, shield, safeguard. **5 include,** deal with, contain, take in, comprise, involve, provide for, embrace, embody, incorporate, subsume, refer to, consider, examine, review, survey, take stock of. **6 report (on),** write up, describe, tell of, give an account of, give details of, investigate. **7 be enough for,** offset, balance, counterbalance, compensate for, make up for. **8 insure,** provide for, indemnify, protect. **9 travel,** travel/pass over, traverse, cross, range/tramp over. **Ant.** uncover; expose; exclude.

▸ *n.* **1 covering,** protection, shield, shelter, concealment, housing, refuge, sanctuary, haven, hiding place. **2 lid,** top, cap, covering. **3 covering,** layer, coat, coating, film, blanket, overlay, carpet, mantle, canopy, crust. **4 cover-up,** disguise, front, camouflage, pretense, façade, pretext, false front, screen, smokescreen, mask, cloak, veil, window dressing. **5 protection,** defense, guard, shield. **6 relief,** replacement, stand-in, substitute. **7 jacket,** dust jacket, boards. **8 envelope,** wrapper, package, wrapping, packaging. **9 undergrowth,** woods, shrubbery, thicket, copse.

covert *adj.* **secret,** concealed, hidden, surreptitious, furtive, stealthy, private, underground. *Ant.* overt; open.

covet *v.* **desire,** want, wish for, long/yearn for, crave, hanker/lust after, thirst for, hunger after, set one's heart on, aspire to, aim after.

cowardly *adj.* **lily-livered,** faint-hearted, chickenhearted, craven, base, spineless, timorous, timid, fearful, shrinking, pusillanimous, dastardly, afraid of one's (own) shadow, *inf.* chicken, yellow, weak-kneed, gutless, yellow-bellied. *Ant.* brave; courageous.

cower *v.* **cringe,** shrink, flinch, draw back, recoil, crouch, wince, blench, quail, quake, tremble, quiver, grovel.

coy *adj.* **arch,** coquettish, flirtatious, kittenish, skittish, shy, modest, bashful, reticent, diffident, retiring, backward, self-effacing, shrinking, withdrawn, timid, demure, prudish, unconfident, lacking confidence, unsure. *Ant.* bold; brazen; impudent.

cozy *adj.* **snug,** comfortable, warm, homelike, homey, sheltered, secure, safe, at ease, *inf.* comfy, snug as a bug. *Ant.* uncomfortable.

crack *v.* **1 chip,** fracture, fragment, break, split, splinter, snap, cleave. **2 ring out,** go bang,

pop, snap, crackle, boom, explode, detonate. **3 hit,** bang, bump, strike, knock, smack, whack, thump, *inf.* wallop, clout, clip. **4 give way,** break down, collapse, go to pieces, lose control, yield, succumb, founder, *inf.* fall/come apart at the seams. **5 solve,** work out, get the answer to, find the solution to, fathom, decipher.
▸ *n.* **1 chip,** fracture, break, split, crevice, fissure, chink, gap, cavity, breach, rift, rupture, cleft, slit, cranny, interstice. **2 bang,** report, shot, pop, snap, crackle, boom, explosion, detonation. **3 blow,** hit, bang, bump, strike, knock, smack, whack, thump, *inf.* wallop, clout, clip. **4 attempt,** try, shot, opportunity, *inf.* go, stab. **5 joke,** funny remark, quip, witticism, wisecrack, gag, jibe, satirical remark, insult, *inf.* dig.

cradle *n.* **1 crib,** bassinet, bed, cot. **2 birthplace,** fount, fountainhead, source, place of origin, wellspring, beginning, breeding place, nursery, origins, beginnings.
▸ *v.* **hold,** rock, nestle, shelter, support.

craft *n.* **1 skill,** skillfulness, expertise, expertness, ability, mastery, artistry, art, technique, workmanship, aptitude, dexterity, talent, flair, knack, cleverness,

genius, *inf.* know-how.
2 craftiness, cunning, artfulness, artifice, scheming, guile, subterfuge, stratagem, slyness, wiliness, shrewdness, trickery, duplicity, deceit, wiles, ruses.
3 occupation, trade, vocation, calling, pursuit, business, line, work, employment. **4 vessel,** ship, boat, aircraft, plane, spacecraft.

crafty *adj.* **cunning,** artful, scheming, designing, calculating, wily, sly, devious, guileful, tricky, shrewd, astute, canny, sharp, duplicitous, deceitful, subtle, insidious, treacherous, crooked, fraudulent, underhand, underhanded. *Ant.* naïve; honest; ingenuous.

crag *n.* **cliff,** bluff, escarpment, scarp, ridge, peak, pinnacle, tor.

cram *v.* **1 stuff,** push, shove, force, pack in, ram down, press, squeeze, jam, crush, compress, compact, condense, overfill, fill, fill up, fill to overflowing, stuff to the gills, fill to the brim, overcrowd. **2 study,** revise, grind, grind away.

cramped *adj.* **1 narrow,** small, restricted, limited, confined, uncomfortable, closed in, hemmed in, tight, crowded, overfull, packed, squeezed, jammed in, congested. **2 close,** tightly packed, small, squeezed, crabbed, illegible, unreadable, indecipherable.

crash *v.* **1 smash,** batter, dash, shatter, break, disintegrate, shiver, splinter, fracture, fragment, smash, wreck. **2 clash,** clang, clank, clatter, bang, smash, boom, thunder, explode. **3 fall,** topple, tumble, pitch, plunge, hurtle, lurch. **4 collapse,** fail, fold, fold up, go under, smash, founder, be ruined, cave in, *inf.* go broke/bust, come a cropper.
5 gatecrash, come uninvited to, intrude, sneak/slip into, invade, *inf.* horn in on.
▸ *n.* **1 clash,** clank, clang, clatter, bang, smash, clangor, racket, din, boom, thunder, explosion.
2 accident, smash, smash-up, collision, pile-up. **3 collapse,** failure, bankruptcy, fold, smash, fall, ruin, ruination, downfall, depression, debacle.

crate *n.* **1 box,** case, packing case, chest, container, receptacle. **2 car,** jalopy, *inf.* junker.

crater *n.* **hole,** hollow, depression, dip, cavity, chasm.

craze *n.* **fad,** vogue, trend, fashion, enthusiasm, passion, infatuation, obsession, mania, fixation, fancy, novelty, whim, fascination, preoccupation, rage, *inf.* thing, the latest.

crazy *adj.* **1 crazed,** of unsound

mind, insane, mad, mad as a hatter, mad as a March hare, lunatic, idiotic, wild, unbalanced, demented, deranged, berserk, unhinged, touched, maniacal, delirious, out of one's mind/head, *inf.* cracked, daft, bats, batty, loony, loopy, screwy, flaky, nuts, nutty, nutty as a fruit cake, cuckoo, bonkers, mental, not all there, out to lunch, off one's rocker, around the bend. **2 absurd,** idiotic, stupid, silly, ridiculous, foolish, peculiar, odd, strange, queer, weird, eccentric, bizarre, fantastic, outrageous, wild, fatuous, inane, puerile, impracticable, senseless, unworkable, foolhardy, unrealistic, unwise, imprudent, ill-conceived, preposterous, *inf.* screwy, screwball, harebrained, cockeyed, half-baked. *Ant.* sane; lucid; rational.

cream *n.* **1 lotion,** emulsion, emollient, paste, cosmetic, ointment, salve, unguent, liniment. **2 best/choice part,** flower, elite, pick, prime, quintessence, crème de la crème.
▸ *adj.* **cream-colored,** off-white, whitish, yellowish-white, buff.

crease *n.* **ridge,** furrow, groove, corrugation, fold, line, pleat, tuck, wrinkle, line, crinkle, pucker, crow's foot.

▸ *v.* **crumple,** wrinkle, crinkle, rumple, pucker, put a crease/fold in, corrugate, pleat, tuck.

create *v.* **1 generate,** originate, invent, initiate, engender, produce, design, devise, make, frame, fabricate, build, construct, erect, develop, shape, form, mold, forge, concoct, hatch. **2 produce,** make, result in, cause, be the cause of, bring about, give rise to, lead to. *Ant.* demolish; destroy.

creative *adj.* **inventive,** imaginative, original, artistic, inspired, visionary, talented, gifted, resourceful, ingenious, clever, productive, fertile.

creator *n.* **1 God,** the Almighty. **2 author,** inventor, originator, initiator, maker, designer, producer, architect, prime mover, begetter, generator.

creature *n.* **1 living thing/entity,** being. **2 animal,** beast, *inf.* critter. **3 person,** human being, human, individual, character, fellow, soul, mortal, *inf.* body.

credentials *pl. n.* **testimonial,** proof of identity/ qualifications, certificate, diploma, document, warrant, license, permit, card, voucher, passport, letter of introduction/ recommendation, missive, deed, title, references, attestation, documentation.

credible *adj.* **1 believable,** conceivable, imaginable, plausible, tenable. **2 acceptable,** trustworthy, reliable, dependable. *Ant.* incredible; unbelievable; untrustworthy.

credit *v.* **believe,** accept, put confidence in, trust, have faith in, rely on, depend on, *inf.* fall for, swallow, buy. *Ant.* disbelieve; discredit.

▸ *n.* **1 praise,** acclaim, approval, commendation, acknowledgment, tribute, kudos, glory, recognition, regard, esteem, respect, merit, veneration, laudation, thanks. **2 name,** reputation, repute, character, prestige, influence, standing, status, regard, esteem, estimation, acceptability, credibility, *inf.* clout. **3 source of honor/pride,** feather in the cap, asset, boast, glory, flower, gem. **4 belief,** believability, credence, faith, trust, reliability, reliance, confidence.

creditable *adj.* **praiseworthy,** commendable, laudable, meritorious, admirable, exemplary, worthy, up to the mark, respectable, reputable, estimable, honorable, deserving.

credulous *adj.* **overtrusting,** overtrustful, gullible, naïve, green, dupable, deceivable, unsuspicious, unskeptical, uncritical, *inf.* wet behind the ears. *Ant.* incredulous; skeptical.

creed *n.* **set of principles,** system/ statement of beliefs, profession of faith, teaching, doctrine, canon, dogma, tenet, catechism, beliefs, principles, rules, articles of faith, maxims.

creek *n.* **stream,** brook, rivulet, small river, channel, inlet, bay, cove, *inf.* crick.

creep *v.* **1 crawl,** go on all fours, move on hands and knees, inch, slither, squirm, wriggle, writhe, worm one's way, insinuate. **2 move stealthily,** steal, sneak, tiptoe, approach unnoticed, slink, skulk.

▸ *n.* **bore,** *inf.* dweeb, nerd, jerk.

creepy *adj.* **horrifying,** horrific, horrible, frightening, terrifying, hair-raising, awful, disturbing, eerie, sinister, weird, nightmarish, macabre, menacing, ominous, threatening, disgusting, repellent, repulsive, revolting, *inf.* scary.

crest *n.* **1 cockscomb,** comb, tuft, plume, topknot, tassel, mane, panache, *Tech.* caruncle. **2 summit,** top, pinnacle, peak, crown, apex, ridge, heights. **3 regalia,** insignia, badge, emblem, device, coat of arms, *Heraldry* bearing, charge.

crestfallen *adj.* **downcast,**

dejected, depressed, glum, downhearted, disheartened, discouraged, dispirited, despondent, disappointed, disconsolate, in the doldrums, down in the dumps.

crevice *n.* **fissure,** cleft, chink, crack, cranny, split, rift, slit, gash, rent, fracture, opening, gap, hole, interstice.

crick *n.* **1 pain,** cramp, twinge, spasm, pang, stiffness. **2 creek,** stream, brook, rivulet, small river, channel.

crime *n.* **1 offense,** unlawful/illegal act, misdemeanor, misdeed, wrong, felony, violation, transgression, trespass, fault, injury, lawbreaking, delinquency, wrongdoing, villainy, malefaction, illegality, misconduct, corruption, wickedness, evil, *Law* malfeasance, tort. **2 sin,** immoral act, evil, evil action, wrong, wrongdoing, vice, iniquity.

criminal *adj.* **1 unlawful,** illegal, lawbreaking, illicit, lawless, felonious, indictable, delinquent, culpable, wrong, villainous, corrupt, evil, wicked, iniquitous, nefarious, *Law* malfeasant, *inf.* crooked, bent. **2 deplorable,** scandalous, preposterous, shameful, reprehensible, senseless, foolish, ridiculous,

sinful, immoral. ***Ant.*** lawful; law-abiding; commendable.

▸ *n.* **lawbreaker,** offender, wrongdoer, felon, delinquent, miscreant, malefactor, culprit, villain, gangster, bandit, transgressor, sinner, trespasser, *Law* malfeasant, *inf.* crook, con.

cringe *v.* **1 cower,** shrink, draw back, quail, flinch, recoil, start, shy, blench, dodge, duck, crouch, wince, tremble, quiver, shake. **2 kowtow,** grovel, *inf.* crawl, creep.

cripple *v.* **1 make lame,** disable, incapacitate, debilitate, impair, damage, hamstring, maim, weaken, enfeeble, paralyze. **2 damage,** injure, ruin, destroy, weaken, impair, hamstring, hamper, impede, cramp, spoil, bring to a standstill, paralyze, enfeeble, vitiate.

crisis *n.* **1 turning point,** critical/decisive point, crux, climax, culmination, height, moment of truth, zero hour, Rubicon, *inf.* crunch. **2 emergency,** disaster, catastrophe, calamity, extremity, predicament, plight, mess, trouble, difficulty, dilemma, quandary, exigency, dire straits, *inf.* fix, pickle, scrape.

crisp *adj.* **1 brittle,** crispy, crumbly, crunchy, breakable. **2 firm,** fresh, unwilted, unwithered. **3 brisk,** bracing, fresh, refreshing, invigorating, dry, cool, chilly. **4 brief,** terse, succinct, concise, short, incisive, clear, pithy. **5 brisk,** vigorous, decisive, brusque, curt, abrupt. **6 clean-cut,** neat, smart, spruce, trim, well-groomed, *inf.* snappy. *Ant.* soft; flaccid; wordy.

criterion *n.* **measure,** gauge, scale, yardstick, standard, norm, benchmark, touchstone, barometer, model, exemplar, classic example, rule, law, principle, canon.

critic *n.* **1 reviewer,** commentator, pundit, arbiter, evaluator, analyst, judge, expounder. **2 faultfinder,** attacker, censurer, detractor, backbiter, reviler, vilifier, *inf.* nitpicker.

critical *adj.* **1 crucial,** deciding, decisive, climacteric, pivotal, important, momentous, high-priority, serious, vital, urgent, pressing, compelling, essential, exigent. **2 dangerous,** grave, serious, risky, perilous, hazardous, touch-and-go, uncertain, precarious, *inf.* chancy. **3 faultfinding,** captious, censorious, carping, quibbling, disapproving, disparaging, judgmental, hypercritical, overcritical, *inf.* nitpicking. **4 evaluative,** analytic, interpretative, expository, commentative, explanatory, explicative, elucidative, annotative. *Ant.* unimportant; safe; complimentary.

criticism *n.* **1 faultfinding,** censure, reproof, condemnation, disapproval, disparagement, captiousness, carping, *inf.* nitpicking, flak, bad press, bad notices, knocking, panning, slamming. **2 evaluation,** comment, commentary, assessment, appreciation, appraisal, analysis, interpretation, explanation, explication, elucidation, annotation. **3 review,** notice, commentary, evaluation, critique, analysis, appraisal, *inf.* write-up.

criticize *v.* **find fault with,** censure, denounce, blame, condemn, pick holes in, disapprove of, disparage, carp at, cavil at, excoriate, *inf.* nitpick, throw brickbats, give flak to, knock, pan, slam.

crockery *n.* **dishes,** earthenware, pottery, china, stoneware, porcelain.

crook *n.* **1 criminal,** villain, rogue, lawbreaker, thief, robber, swindler, cheat, racketeer, *inf.* shark, con man. **2 bend,** curve, curvature, angle, bow.
▸ *v.* **bend,** curve, angle, flex, hook, bow.

crooked *adj.* **1 bent,** curved, twisted, contorted, warped, irregular, angled, bowed, hooked, flexed, winding, twisting, zigzag, meandering, deviating, sinuous, tortuous, serpentine, deformed, misshapen, out of shape, disfigured, crippled. **2 not straight,** tilted, at an angle, angled, slanted, aslant, slanting, sloping, askew, awry, to one side, off-center, lopsided, uneven, unsymmetrical, asymmetric. **3 criminal,** dishonest, corrupt, dishonorable, unscrupulous, unprincipled, fraudulent, illegal, unlawful, nefarious, crafty, deceitful, shifty, underhand, underhanded, questionable, dubious, *inf.* shady. **Ant.** straight; honest.

crop *n.* **1 year's growth,** harvest, yield, produce, vintage, gathering, reaping, gleaning, garnering, garner, fruits. **2 batch,** lot, collection, assortment, selection, supply. **3 craw,** gullet, maw, throat.
▸ *v.* **cut,** cut short, clip, trim, snip, shear, lop, curtail, reduce, prune.

cross *n.* **1 crucifix,** rood. **2 trouble,** worry, burden, trial, disaster, tribulation, affliction, misfortune, adversity, misery, woe, pain, suffering, calamity, catastrophe. **3 crossbreed,** hybrid, hybridization, mixture, amalgam, blend, combination, mongrel, cur.
▸ *v.* **1 go across,** span, extend/ stretch across, pass over, bridge, ford, cut across, traverse. **2 intersect,** meet, join, converge, crisscross, interweave, intertwine, zigzag. **3 oppose,** resist, thwart, frustrate, foil, obstruct, impede, hinder, hamper, block, check, deny, contradict. **4 crossbreed,** interbreed, cross-fertilize, cross-pollinate, intercross, hybridize, mix, intermix, blend.

crossing *n.* **junction,** crossroads, intersection, crosswalk.

crouch *v.* **squat,** bend, bend down, hunker, stoop, hunch over, cower, cringe.

crowd *n.* **1 throng,** horde, mob, rabble, large number, mass, multitude, host, army, herd, flock, drove, swarm, troupe, pack, flood, collection, company, gathering, assembly, assemblage, array, congregation, convention, concourse. **2 majority,** multitude, common people, populace, general public, mob, rank and file, hoi polloi, proletariat, riff-raff, masses. **3 group,** set, lot, gang, bunch, circle, fraternity, clique, coterie. **4 gate,** house, turnout, audience, attendance, spectators, listeners, viewers.

▸ v. **1 gather,** cluster, congregate, flock, swarm, throng, huddle, concentrate, throng, pack, fill, overfill, congest, pack, squeeze, cram, jam, stuff, pile. **2 push,** push one's way, shove, thrust forward, elbow, squeeze, pile, pack. **3 pressure,** pressurize, harass, badger, pester, hound, nag, torment, plague, *inf.* hassle.

crowded *adj.* **full,** overfull, busy, overflowing, packed, jam-packed, crushed, cramped, congested, teeming, swarming, thronged, populous, mobbed, *inf.* full to bursting.

crown *n.* **1 diadem,** coronet, coronal, tiara, chaplet, circlet, wreath. **2 laurel wreath,** victor's garland, prize, trophy, honor, distinction, glory, kudos, laurels. **3 monarchy,** monarch, sovereignty, sovereign, ruler, king, queen, emperor, empress, royalty, *inf.* royals. **4 top,** crest, summit, apex, head, tip, pinnacle. **5 climax,** height, culmination, pinnacle, zenith, acme, ultimate, flower.

▸ v. **1 invest,** inaugurate, induct, install. **2 cap,** round off, be the culmination/climax of, put the finishing touch/touches to, consummate, top off, complete, perfect, conclude. **3 top,** surmount, overtop. **4 hit over the head,** strike, cuff, punch, buffet, *inf.* wallop, bash.

crucial *adj.* **decisive,** critical, determining, pivotal, central, testing, trying, searching, high-priority, essential, momentous, vital, urgent, pressing, compelling.

crude *adj.* **1 raw,** unrefined, natural, coarse, unprocessed, unmilled, unpolished. **2 rudimentary,** primitive, rough, rough-and-ready, rough-hewn, makeshift, unfinished, unpolished, unformed, undeveloped, rude. **3 coarse,** vulgar, rude, uncouth, indelicate, earthy, indecent, dirty, bawdy, smutty, obscene, offensive, lewd, ribald, boorish, crass, tasteless, *inf.* blue, raunchy. *Ant.* refined; sophisticated; delicate.

cruel *adj.* **1 savage,** brutal, inhuman, barbaric, barbarous, bloodthirsty, vicious, ferocious, fierce, evil, fiendish, callous, cold-blooded, sadistic, ruthless, merciless, pitiless, unrelenting, remorseless, unfeeling, heartless, inhumane, severe, harsh, stern, stony-hearted, hard-hearted. **2 unkind,** painful, distressing, harrowing, harsh, grim, heartless. *Ant.* kind; merciful; compassionate.

cruelty *n.* **1 savageness,**

savagery, brutality, inhumanity, barbarism, barbarousness, viciousness, ferocity, fierceness, evil, fiendishness, callousness, sadism, ruthlessness, pitilessness, relentlessness, severity, harshness, inclemency. **2 unkindness,** painfulness, harshness, grimness, heartlessness, pain, resulting distress. *Ant.* compassion; kindness.

cruise *v.* **1 sail,** voyage, journey. **2 coast,** travel steadily, drift.
▸ *n.* **sea/boat trip,** voyage, sail.

crumb *n.* **bit,** fragment, morsel, particle, grain, atom, speck, scrap, shred, sliver, snippet, mite.

crumble *v.* **1 break up,** crush, pulverize, pound, grind, powder, granulate, fragment.
2 disintegrate, fall to pieces, fall apart, collapse, break down/up, tumble down, decay, deteriorate, degenerate, fall into decay, go to rack and ruin, decompose, rot, rot away, molder, perish, vanish, fade away, come to dust.

crumple *v.* **1 crush,** crease, rumple, wrinkle, crinkle.
2 collapse, fail, cave in, fall apart, give way, go to pieces, topple, shrivel. *Ant.* iron; straighten; survive.

crunch *v.* **1 chew noisily,** bite, munch, champ, chomp, gnaw,

masticate. **2 crush,** grind, pulverize, pound, smash.
▸ *n.* **1 shortage, (period of) reduction,** deficit, deficiency, scarcity, shortfall, lack. **2 crux,** crisis, critical point, test, moment of truth/decision.

crusade *n.* **1 campaign,** holy war. **2 campaign,** drive, push, struggle, cause, movement.
▸ *v.* **campaign,** fight, work, do battle, take up arms, take up a cause.

crush *v.* **1 squash,** squeeze, mash, press, press down, compress, bruise. **2 crease,** crumple, rumple, wrinkle, crinkle. **3 break up,** smash, shatter, pound, pulverize, grind, crumble, crunch. **4 put down,** quell, quash, suppress, subdue, overcome, overwhelm, overpower, stamp out, defeat, conquer, vanquish, extinguish. **5 mortify,** humiliate, abash, quash, shame, chagrin, *inf.* put down. **6 embrace,** enfold, hug, squeeze, hold/press tight, clutch.

crust *n.* **outside,** casing, shell, husk, covering, cover, coating, caking, topping, layer, film, skin, blanket, mantle, incrustation, concretion, scab.

crusty *adj.* **1 crisp,** crispy, brittle, hard, well-baked, well-done. **2 brusque,** surly, curt, gruff, cross, crabbed, crabby, grouchy, bad-tempered, short-tempered, irritable, irascible, ill-humored, ill-natured, snappish, touchy, testy, snarling, cantankerous, choleric, splenetic, captious. **3 coated,** caked, covered, incrusted, scabby

cry v. **1 shed tears,** weep, sob, wail, snivel, blubber, whimper, whine, bawl, howl. **2 call out,** exclaim, yell, scream, screech, bawl, shout, bellow, howl. *Ant.* laugh; whisper.
▸ n. **call,** exclamation, scream, screech, yell, shout, bellow, howl.

crypt n. **tomb,** vault, burial chamber, sepulcher.

cuddle v. **hug,** embrace, enfold, clasp, pet, fondle, snuggle, nestle, curl up, *inf.* neck, smooch.

cudgel n. **club,** bludgeon, stick, baton, truncheon, bat, blackjack.
▸ v. **bludgeon,** club, beat/strike with a stick, truncheon.

cue n. **1 catchword,** keyword, prompt, prompt-word, prompting, reminder. **2 signal,** sign, indication, hint, suggestion, intimation.

culminate v. **come to a climax,** peak, reach a pinnacle, come to a crescendo, come to an end, end, close, finish, conclude, terminate, come to a head, *inf.* wind up.

culpable adj. **at fault,** in the wrong, guilty, answerable, blameworthy, blamable, to blame, censurable, reproachable, reprovable, reprehensible, sinful. *Ant.* blameless; innocent.

culprit n. **person responsible,** guilty party, wrongdoer, evildoer, lawbreaker, criminal, miscreant, delinquent, reprobate, transgressor, felon, sinner, malefactor, *inf.* baddie, bad guy.

cult n. **1 sect,** religion, denomination, body, affiliation, faith, belief, persuasion, following, party, faction, clique. **2 craze,** fashion, fad, admiration, devotion, obsession, homage, worship, reverence, veneration, idolization.

cultivate v. **1 till,** farm, work, plow, dig, prepare, fertilize, plant, raise, tend, bring on, produce. **2 culture,** educate, train, civilize, enlighten, enrich, improve, better, develop, refine, polish, ameliorate, elevate. **3 seek the friendship/company of,** run after, make advances to, ingratiate oneself with, curry favor with, woo, court, associate/consort with, *inf.* butter up, suck up to. **4 pursue,** devote oneself to, foster, promote, advance, further, forward, encourage, support, back, aid, help, assist, abet.

cultivated adj. **cultured,**

educated, civilized, enlightened, refined, polished, sophisticated, discerning, discriminating, urbane.

cultural *adj.* **1 artistic,** educational, educative, enlightening, enriching, broadening, developmental, edifying, civilizing, elevating. **2 lifestyle,** ethnic, folk, racial.

culture *n.* **1 cultivation,** education, enlightenment, accomplishment, edification, erudition, refinement, polish, sophistication, urbanity, discernment, discrimination, good taste, taste, breeding, politeness, gentility, savoir faire. **2 the arts. 3 civilization,** way of life, lifestyle, customs, habits, ways, mores. **4 cultivation,** farming, agriculture, husbandry, agronomy.

cultured *adj.* **cultivated,** artistic, educated, enlightened, learned, knowledgeable, intellectual, highbrow, scholarly, well-informed, well-read, erudite, accomplished, well-versed, refined, genteel, polished, sophisticated, urbane. *Ant.* ignorant; unrefined; unsophisticated.

cunning *adj.* **1 crafty,** devious, deceitful, wily, sly, shifty, artful, foxy, tricky, guileful, shrewd,

astute, sharp, knowing, subtle, Machiavellian. **2 clever,** ingenious, resourceful, inventive, imaginative, skillful, deft, adroit, subtle, dexterous. *Ant.* honest; guileless; ingenuous.

▸ *n.* **1 craftiness,** deviousness, deceitfulness, deceit, wiliness, slyness, artfulness, foxiness, trickery, trickiness, guile, shrewdness, astuteness, sharpness, subtlety. **2 cleverness,** ingenuity, resourcefulness, inventiveness, imaginativeness, skill, skillfulness, deftness, adroitness, subtlety, finesse, dexterity, ability, capability. *Ant.* openness; simplicity.

cup *n.* **1 teacup,** coffee cup, mug, demitasse. **2 trophy,** award, prize. **3 cupful,** measuring cup.

curator *n.* **keeper,** custodian, conservator, guardian, caretaker, steward.

curb *v.* **restrain,** check, keep in check, control, constrain, contain, hold back, bite back, repress, suppress, moderate, dampen, put a brake on, impede, retard, subdue, bridle.

▸ *n.* **restraint,** check, control, constraint, deterrent, curtailment, limitation, limit, damper, brake, rein, suppressant, hindrance, retardant.

curdle *v.* **turn,** turn sour, congeal,

coagulate, clot, solidify, thicken, condense.

cure *n.* **remedy,** curative, medicine, cure-all, panacea, restorative, corrective, antidote, nostrum, treatment, therapy, healing, alleviation.

▶ *v.* **1 heal,** restore, restore to health, make well/better, rehabilitate, treat, remedy, doctor, put/set right, fix, repair. **2 preserve,** smoke, salt, dry, pickle.

curiosity *n.* **1 inquisitiveness,** spirit of inquiry, interest, investigativeness, researching, querying, asking questions, questioning, prying, snooping, *inf.* nosiness. **2 eccentric,** individual, oddity, character, card, freak, original, *inf.* weirdo, oddball. **3 novelty,** oddity, phenomenon, rarity, wonder, marvel, sight, spectacle.

curious *adj.* **1 inquisitive,** inquiring, interested, investigating, searching, researching, querying, questioning, interrogative, puzzled, burning with curiosity. **2 inquisitive,** prying, snooping, meddling, meddlesome, interfering, intrusive, *inf.* nosy, snoopy. **3 strange,** unusual, rare, odd, peculiar, out of the ordinary, unexpected, extraordinary, remarkable, singular, novel, queer, bizarre, unconventional, unorthodox, phenomenal, weird, freakish, marvelous, wonderful, prodigious, exotic, mysterious, puzzling, quaint, unique, *inf.* far out. *Ant.* uninterested; indifferent; ordinary.

curl *v.* **1 spiral,** coil, twist, twist and turn, wind, curve, bend, loop, twirl, wreathe, meander, snake, corkscrew. **2 bend,** twist, curve, coil, crisp. **3 crimp,** crinkle, kink, frizz, coil, wave.

▶ *n.* **kink,** ringlet, coil, wave, curlicue, corkscrew, spiral, twist, whorl, helix.

curly *adj.* **1 curling,** curled, crimped, crinkly, kinked, wavy, waved, frizzy, permed, fuzzy, corkscrew. **2 spiraled,** spiraling, coiling, coiled, curving, winding, corkscrew.

current *adj.* **1 present,** present-day, contemporary, ongoing, extant, existing, popular, modern, fashionable, in fashion/vogue, up-to-date, up-to-the-minute, *inf.* trendy, now, in. **2 prevalent,** prevailing, accepted, in circulation, circulating, going around, making the rounds, talked of, common, general, popular, widespread, rife, on everyone's lips. *Ant.* out of date; obsolete.

▸ *n.* **1 steady flow,** draft, updraft, downdraft, wind, thermal, stream, tide, channel. **2 course,** flow, progress, progression, tide, trend, drift, tendency, tenor.

curse *n.* **1 malediction,** evil eye, execration, imprecation, anathema, damnation, excommunication, *inf.* jinx. **2 oath,** swearword, expletive, profanity, obscenity, swearing, blasphemy, bad/foul language, *inf.* cussword. **3 evil,** affliction, burden, cross, bane, misfortune, misery, trouble, blight, harm, disaster, calamity, ordeal, tribulation, scourge, plague, torment. **Ant.** benediction; blessing.

▸ *v.* **1 put a curse on,** accurse, put the evil eye on, execrate, imprecate, anathematize, damn, excommunicate, *inf.* put a jinx on, jinx. **2 utter oaths,** swear, use bad/foul language, blaspheme, take God's/the Lord's name in vain, be foul-mouthed, *inf.* cuss. **3 blight,** afflict, trouble, beset, harm, burden, plague, torment, destroy, ruin, scourge.

cursory *adj.* **hasty,** rapid, hurried, quick, superficial, perfunctory, desultory, ephemeral, fleeting, passing, transient. **Ant.** thorough; leisurely.

curt *adj.* **terse,** abrupt, brusque, blunt, short-spoken, short, snappy, snappish, sharp, crisp, tart, gruff, offhand, summary, rude, impolite, unceremonious, ungracious, uncivil, brief, concise, succinct, compact, pithy. **Ant.** polite; suave; verbose.

curtail *v.* **reduce,** cut short, cut, cut down/back, decrease, lessen, diminish, retrench, slim down, tighten up, pare down, trim, dock, lop, truncate, shorten, abridge, abbreviate, contract, compress, shrink. **Ant.** increase; lengthen; expand.

curtain *n.* **1 drape,** drapery, window hanging, screen, blind. **2 screen,** cover, shield, cloak, veil.

curve *n.* **arc,** bend, arch, turn, bow, loop, hook, half moon, crescent, winding, camber, curvature.

▸ *v.* **bend,** arc, arch, bow, turn, inflect, swerve, twist, wind, hook, loop, spiral, coil.

curved *adj.* **bent,** arched, rounded, bowed, twisted, crooked, humped, sinuous.

cushion *n.* **pillow,** throw pillow, bolster, pad, hassock, mat, beanbag.

▸ *v.* **1 pillow,** bolster, cradle, support, prop up. **2 soften,** lessen, diminish, mitigate, allay, deaden, muffle, stifle. **3 protect,** shield, buttress.

custody *n.* **1 guardianship,** wardship, trusteeship, charge, care, keeping, keep, safekeeping, protection, guidance, supervision, superintendence, surveillance, control, tutelage, aegis, auspices. **2 imprisonment,** detention, confinement, incarceration, restraint, constraint, duress.

custom *n.* **1 habit,** practice, routine, way, wont, policy, rule. **2 practice,** convention, ritual, procedure, ceremony, form, formality, usage, observance, way, fashion, mode, style.

customary *adj.* **accustomed,** usual, regular, common, habitual, traditional, routine, fixed, set, established, everyday, familiar, confirmed, normal, ordinary, favorite, popular, stock, well-worn. *Ant.* unusual; exceptional; rare.

customer *n.* **patron,** client, buyer, purchaser, shopper, consumer, clientele, *inf.* regular.

cut *v.* **1 gash,** slash, lacerate, slit, nick, notch, pierce, penetrate, wound, lance, incise, score, cut up, chop, sever, divide, cleave, carve, slice. **2 shape,** fashion, form, mold, chisel, carve, sculpt, sculpture, chip away, whittle. **3 carve,** engrave, incise, score. **4 trim,** clip, snip, crop, prune, dock, shear, shave, pare, mow. **5 detach,** gather, harvest, reap. **6 reduce,** curtail, curb, retrench, cut back/down on, decrease, lessen, lower, diminish, contract, ease up on, prune, slash, slim down, slenderize, economize on. **7 shorten,** abridge, condense, abbreviate, contract, compact, summarize, epitomize, delete, edit out, blue-pencil, excise. **8 hurt,** offend, wound, distress, grieve, pain, sting, trouble, discomfort. **9 shun,** ignore, snub, spurn, give the cold shoulder to, look right through, turn one's back on, slight, scorn, insult. **10 intersect,** bisect, cross. **11 stop,** come to a stop, halt, turn off, switch off, stop working, malfunction. **12 record,** make a recording on, put on disk/tape, make a tape of, tape-record. ▸ *n.* **1 gash,** slash, laceration, incision, slit. **2 section,** piece. **3 trim,** clip, crop. **4 cutback,** decrease, reduction, lessening, curtailment, retrenchment, contraction. **5 fashion,** style. **6 loss,** temporary interruption. **7 share,** portion, proportion.

cutting *adj.* **1 biting,** bitter, piercing, raw, keen, penetrating, stinging, sharp, chill, chilling, icy. **2 hurtful,** wounding, caustic, acid, barbed, acrimonious, trenchant, mordant, scathing, acerbic, sarcastic, sardonic, spiteful, vicious, malicious.

▸ *n.* **root,** stem, slip, scion.

cycle *n.* **1 recurrent period,** rotation, round, revolution. **2 series,** sequence, succession, run. **3 bicycle,** bike, tandem, tricycle, trike, motorcycle, unicycle.

cynical *adj.* **pessimistic,** skeptical, scoffing, doubting, unbelieving, disbelieving, distrustful, suspicious, misanthropic, critical, sardonic. ***Ant.*** optimistic; credulous; trustful.

Dd

dab *v.* **pat,** press, touch, blot, smudge, besmear, bedaub.
▸ *n.* **pat,** press, touch, blot, smudge, touch, bit, speck, spot, trace, drop, dash, tinge, suggestion, hint, modicum.

dabble *v.* **dip,** splash, paddle, wet, moisten, dampen, sprinkle, spray, spatter, slosh.

dabbler *n.* **dilettante,** amateur, nonprofessional, layman, laywoman, tinkerer, putterer, trifler, dallier.

daily *adj.* **1 of/occurring each day,** everyday, diurnal, quotidian, circadian. **2 everyday,** day-to-day, routine, ordinary, common, commonplace, usual, regular, habitual, customary.
▸ *adv.* **every day,** once a day, day after day, day by day, per diem.

dainty *adj.* **1 petite,** neat, delicate, exquisite, refined, tasteful, fine, elegant, graceful, trim, pretty.
2 tasty, delicious, appetizing, choice, delectable, palatable, flavorsome, savory, toothsome, luscious, juicy, succulent.
3 particular, discriminating, fastidious, fussy, choosy, finicky, refined, nice, scrupulous, meticulous. *Ant.* clumsy; nasty; uncouth.

dally *v.* **dawdle,** delay, loiter, linger, tarry, waste/kill time, take one's time, while away time, trifle, toy, flirt, tinker, *inf.* dilly-dally, fool. *Ant.* hurry; hasten.

dam *n.* **barricade,** barrier, barrage, wall, embankment, obstruction, hindrance.

damage *v.* **do damage to,** harm, injure, hurt, impair, abuse, spoil, mar, deface, defile, vandalize, wreck, destroy, ruin, play havoc with, devastate, do mischief to, tamper with, mutilate. *Ant.* repair; improve.
▸ *n.* **1 harm,** injury, hurt, impairment, abuse, defilement, defacement, detriment, vandalism, destruction, ruin, havoc, devastation, mischief, outrage, accident, loss, suffering.
2 cost, expense, charge, bill, account, total.

damn *v.* **1 curse,** doom, execrate, imprecate, excommunicate, anathematize, proscribe, interdict. **2 condemn,** censure, criticize, castigate, denounce, berate, reprimand, reprove,

abuse, inveigh against, excoriate.
3 criticize, attack, flay, *inf.* pan,
slam, knock, blast, take to pieces,
take apart. *Ant.* bless; acclaim;
praise.
▸ *n.* **jot,** whit, iota, hoot, two
hoots, *inf.* darn, tinker's damn.
damning *adj.* **incriminating,**
condemnatory, condemning,
damnatory, implicating,
implicatory, accusatorial.
damp *adj.* **1 wettish,** moist, dank,
soggy, dewy. **2 wettish,** rainy,
drizzly, humid, clammy, muggy,
misty, foggy, vaporous. *Ant.* dry;
arid.
dance *v.* **move/sway to music,**
execute dance steps, twirl,
pirouette, caper, skip, prance,
hop, frolic, gambol, jump, jig,
romp, bounce, whirl, spin, *inf.*
shake a leg, hoof it, cut the rug,
trip the light fantastic.
▸ *n.* **1 ball,** *inf.* hop. **2 dancing,**
ballroom dance, folk dance, tap
dance, modern dance, ballet,
eurythmics.
dandy *n.* **fop,** popinjay, beau,
blade, man about town, sharp
dresser.
danger *n.* **1 risk,** peril, hazard,
jeopardy, endangerment,
imperilment, precariousness,
insecurity, instability, *lit.* Scylla
and Charybdis. **2 menace,** threat,
peril, risk. *Ant.* safety; security.

dangerous *adj.* **1 risky,** perilous,
hazardous, chancy, precarious,
uncertain, insecure, unsound,
unsafe, exposed, defenseless, *inf.*
hairy. **2 menacing,** threatening,
alarming, ominous, nasty, ugly,
treacherous. *Ant.* safe; harmless.
dangle *v.* **1 hang,** hang down,
swing, sway, trail, droop. **2 swing,**
sway, wave, brandish, flourish,
flaunt. **3 hold out,** entice someone
with, lure someone with, tempt
someone with.
dank *adj.* **damp,** wet, moist,
humid, clammy, chilly.
dappled *adj.* **spotted,** marked,
mottled, flecked, blotched,
blotchy, variegated, parti-colored,
pied, piebald, brindled, pinto.
dare *v.* **1 have the courage,** take
the risk, be brave enough, have
the nerve, risk, hazard, venture.
2 challenge, provoke, goad, taunt.
3 defy, brave, face, meet, meet
head on, confront, stand up to.
▸ *n.* **challenge,** provocation, goad,
taunt, ultimatum.
daring *adj.* **bold,** adventurous,
brave, courageous, valiant,
audacious, intrepid, fearless,
undaunted, dauntless,
unshrinking, rash, reckless,
madcap, foolhardy, wild,
daredevil, desperate. *Ant.*
cowardly; cautious.

▸ *n.* **boldness,** adventurousness, bravery, courage, courageousness, valor, audacity, nerve, pluck, grit, intrepidity, fearlessness, rashness, recklessness, temerity, foolhardiness, wildness, desperation, *inf.* guts, spunk.

dark *adj.* **1 black,** pitch-black, pitch-dark, inky, jet-black, unlit, unlighted, ill-lighted, poorly lit, dim, dingy, indistinct, shadowy, shady, murky, foggy, misty, cloudy, overcast, sunless. **2 dark-haired,** brunette, dark brown, jet-black, sable, ebony. **3** dark-skinned, swarthy, sallow, olive-skinned, dusky, black, ebony. **4 dismal,** gloomy, somber, cheerless, bleak, joyless, drab, dreary, depressed, dejected, melancholy, grim, grave, funereal, morose, mournful, doleful. **5 angry,** moody, brooding, sullen, dour, glum, morose, sulky, frowning, scowling, glowering, forbidding, threatening, ominous. **6 evil,** wicked, sinful, villainous, iniquitous, vile, base, foul, horrible, atrocious, abominable, nefarious, barbaric, barbarous, sinister, damnable, fiendish, infernal, satanic, hellish. **7 unenlightened,** ignorant, uneducated, unschooled, uncultivated, uncultured. **8 concealed,** hidden, veiled,

secret, mysterious, mystic, esoteric, occult. *Ant.* light; fair; cheerful.

▸ *n.* **1 darkness,** blackness, absence of light, gloom, gloominess, dimness, murk, murkiness, shadowiness, shade. **2 night,** nighttime, nightfall, dead of night, evening, twilight. **3 a state of ignorance/ unenlightenment.**

darken *v.* **1 blacken,** cloud over, dim, grow dim, shade. **2 make dark/darker,** tan, blacken, black, make opaque. **3 blacken,** grow angry/annoyed, grow/become gloomy, become depressed/ dispirited, grow troubled, sadden. *Ant.* lighten; brighten.

darling *n.* **dear,** dearest, dear one, love, sweetheart, beloved, sweet, honey, charmer, pet, favorite, pet, apple of one's eye, toast, *inf.* fair-haired boy, sweetie.

▸ *adj.* **1 dear,** dearest, loved, beloved, adored, cherished, treasured, precious, prized, valued. **2 adorable,** sweet, lovely, attractive, charming, winsome, enchanting, engaging, captivating, bewitching, alluring, *inf.* cute.

dart *n.* **1 arrow,** barb. **2 dash,** rush, run, bolt, bound, spring, leap, start.

▸ *v.* **1 dash,** rush, bolt, fly, flash,

sprint, tear, run, bound, shoot, spring, leap, start, *inf.* scoot.
2 throw, cast, shoot, send, fling, toss, flash, hurl, sling, propel, project.

dash *n.* **1 rush,** bolt, run, race, flight, dart, sprint, sortie, spurt, *inf.* scoot. **2 splash,** sprinkle, spattering. **3 little,** bit, drop, pinch, sprinkling, grain, touch, trace, tinge, smack, suspicion, suggestion. **4 style,** élan, verve, vigor, spirit, vivacity, liveliness, flair, panache, flourish, *inf.* pizzazz.
▸ *v.* **1 rush,** hurry, hasten, bolt, run, race, fly, dart, sprint, tear, speed, *inf.* scoot. **2 strike,** beat, break, crash, smash, batter, splinter, shatter. **3 smash,** crash, throw, hurl, fling, slam, sling, cast, pitch, catapult. **4 shatter,** destroy, ruin, blight, spoil, frustrate, thwart, check.
5 depress, dispirit, deject, cast down, lower, sadden, dishearten, discourage, daunt, abash, dampen.

dashing *adj.* **1 debonair,** stylish, spirited, lively, buoyant, energetic, animated, dynamic, gallant, bold, daring, plucky, dazzling, swashbuckling, *inf.* peppy. **2 smart,** jaunty, sporty, stylish, elegant, fashionable, chic, dazzling, showy, flamboyant.

data *pl. n.* **basic facts,** facts, figures, statistics, details, information, material, input.

date *n.* **1 day,** point in time.
2 time, age, period, era, century, decade, year, stage.
3 appointment, engagement, meeting, rendezvous, assignation, tryst. **4 partner,** escort, girlfriend, boyfriend, beau, *inf.* steady.
▸ *v.* **1 originate in,** come from, belong to, exist from, bear the date of. **2 assign a date to,** put a date to, determine the date of, fix the period of. **3 go out/around with,** go with, take out, *inf.* go steady with.

dated *adj.* **out of date,** outdated, old-fashioned, outmoded, antiquated, passé, *inf.* old hat. **Ant.** fashionable; up-to-date.

daunt *v.* **intimidate,** frighten, scare, alarm, overawe, dismay, disconcert, unnerve, take aback, abash, cow, discourage, dishearten, dispirit, deter, put off. **Ant.** encourage; hearten.

dawdle *v.* **go/walk slowly,** move at a snail's pace, loiter, take one's time, dally, linger, delay, lag/trail behind, kill/waste time, fritter time away, idle, *inf.* dilly-dally. **Ant.** hurry; hasten.

dawn *n.* **1 daybreak,** break of day, sunrise, first light, early morning, crack of dawn, sunup, *lit.* aurora.

2 dawning, beginning, birth, start, rise, emergence, commencement, origin, inception, genesis, outset, onset, advent, appearance, arrival, unfolding, development. **Ant.** dusk; end.

▸ *v.* **1 begin,** break, lighten, brighten, gleam. **2 begin,** be born, come into being/existence, start, rise, emerge, commence, originate, appear, arrive, unfold, develop.

day *n.* **1 daytime,** daylight, daylight hours, broad daylight. **2 twenty-four hours,** full day, working day, solar day. **3 period,** time, age, era, epoch, generation. **4 prime,** heyday, full flowering, useful/productive lifetime, peak, zenith, ascendancy. **5 date,** set time, time, particular day, appointed day.

daze *v.* **1 stun,** stupefy, shock, confuse, bewilder, befuddle, muddle, addle, numb, benumb, paralyze. **2 stun,** shock, amaze, astonish, astound, dumbfound, stagger, startle, surprise, dismay, disconcert, take aback, bewilder, perplex, nonplus, *inf.* flabbergast, floor, take one's breath away.

▸ *n.* **stupor,** state of shock, trancelike state, confused state, confusion, bewilderment, distraction, numbness.

dazzle *v.* **1 blind temporarily,** deprive of sight, bedazzle, daze, overpower. **2 overpower,** overwhelm, overawe, awe, stagger, fascinate, hypnotize, strike dumb, dumbfound, strike, impress, amaze, astonish, *inf.* bowl over, take one's breath away.

▸ *n.* **brightness,** brilliance, gleam, flash, splendor, magnificence, glitter, sparkle, glory, *inf.* razzle-dazzle, razzmatazz, pizzazz.

dead *adj.* **1 deceased,** late, defunct, departed, lifeless, extinct, perished, gone, no more, passed on/away. **2 inanimate,** lifeless, *fml.* exanimate. **3 obsolete,** outmoded, outdated, extinct, lapsed, passed, passé, discontinued, disused, fallen into disuse, stagnant, inactive, invalid, ineffective, inoperative, nonfunctional, barren, sterile. **4 unresponsive,** insensitive, indifferent, apathetic, dispassionate, unsympathetic, emotionless, unemotional, unfeeling, lukewarm, cold, frigid, wooden, inert. **5 numb,** numbed, benumbed, unfeeling, paralyzed. **6 extinguished,** finished, terminated, quenched, quashed, quelled, suppressed, smothered, stifled. **7 dull,** boring, uninteresting, tedious, tiresome, wearisome, uneventful,

humdrum, flat, stale, insipid, vapid. **8 complete,** absolute, total, entire, outright, utter, downright, out-and-out, thorough, unqualified, unmitigated.
9 abrupt, sudden, quick, rapid, swift, hurried, instantaneous, unexpected, unforeseen.
10 accurate, exact, precise, unerring, unfailing, sure, correct, direct. **11 tired,** tired out, exhausted, worn out, fatigued, spent, *inf.* dead beat, played out, pooped. ***Ant.*** live; alive; living; lively.
▸ *adv.* **completely,** absolutely, totally, entirely, exactly, utterly, thoroughly, categorically, without qualification.

deaden *v.* **1 blunt,** dull, muffle, weaken, diminish, reduce, subdue, suppress, moderate, soothe, assuage, abate, mitigate, alleviate, smother, stifle, damp, damp down, numb, mute.
2 render/make insensitive, desensitize, numb, benumb, anesthetize, impair, incapacitate, paralyze.

deadlock *n.* **1 stalemate,** impasse, standstill, halt, stop, stoppage, cessation, standoff.
2 tie, draw, dead heat.

deadly *adj.* **1 fatal, lethal,** mortal, death-dealing, dangerous, destructive, harmful, pernicious, noxious, malignant, venomous, toxic, poisonous, virulent.
2 mortal, hated, hostile, murderous, fierce, implacable, remorseless, unrelenting, grim, savage, *inf.* at each other's throats.
3 intense, great, marked, extreme, excessive, immoderate, inordinate. **4 boring,** dull, tedious, uninteresting, dry, monotonous, wearisome, humdrum, lackluster.
▸ *adv.* **completely,** absolutely.

deafening *adj.* **very loud,** earsplitting, ear-piercing, overpowering, overwhelming, booming, thunderous, resounding, reverberating, ringing, dinning.

deal *v.* **1 attend to,** see to, take care of, cope with, handle, manage, sort out, tackle, take measures. **2 be about,** have to do with, concern, concern itself with, discuss, consider, treat of. **3 act,** behave, conduct oneself. **4 trade,** traffic, do business, buy and sell, be concerned/engaged, negotiate, bargain. **5 distribute,** give out, share out, divide out, hand out, dole out, mete out, allocate, dispense, allot, assign, apportion, bestow. **6 deliver,** administer, give, direct, aim.
▸ *n.* **1 amount,** quantity, degree.
2 arrangement, transaction, agreement, negotiation, bargain,

contract, pact, understanding, compact, concordat. **3 treatment,** handling, usage, procedure.

dealer *n.* **1 trader,** salesman, saleswoman, salesperson, tradesman, merchant, marketer, retailer, wholesaler, vendor, trafficker, peddler. **2 agent,** broker.

dear *adj.* **1 beloved,** loved, darling, adored, cherished, close, intimate, esteemed, respected, precious, treasured, valued, prized, cherished, favorite, favored, sweet, endearing, lovable, attractive, winning, enchanting, winsome, angelic. **2 sweet,** darling, endearing, lovable, attractive, winning, enchanting, winsome, angelic. **3 expensive,** costly, highly priced, high-priced, overpriced, exorbitant, valuable, *inf.* pricey, steep. **Ant.** worthless; disagreeable; cheap.
  ▶ *n.* **love,** beloved, darling, loved one, sweetheart, sweet, honey, pet, precious, treasure, angel.

dearth *n.* **lack,** scarcity, scarceness, want, deficiency, shortage, shortness, insufficiency, paucity, sparseness, meagerness, scantiness, rareness, exiguity. **Ant.** abundance; surfeit.

debacle *n.* **fiasco,** failure, downfall, collapse, disintegration, disaster, catastrophe, tumult, turmoil, havoc, ruin, ruination, devastation, defeat, rout, overthrow.

debase *v.* **1 degrade,** devalue, demean, drag down, disgrace, dishonor, shame, bring shame to, discredit, lower/reduce the status of, cheapen, humble, humiliate. **2 alloy,** adulterate, depreciate, dilute, contaminate, pollute, taint, corrupt, bastardize, vitiate.

debatable *adj.* **arguable,** disputable, questionable, open to question, controversial, contentious, doubtful, open to doubt, dubious, uncertain, unsure, unsettled, undecided, borderline, moot.

debate *n.* **1 discussion,** argument, dispute, disputation, difference of opinion, wrangle, altercation, controversy, contention, war of words, polemic. **2 consideration,** deliberation, reflection, contemplation, musing, meditation, cogitation.
  ▶ *v.* **1 discuss,** argue, argue the pros and cons of, dispute, wrangle, bandy words, contend, contest, altercate, controvert, *inf.* kick around. **2 consider,** think over, deliberate, reflect, contemplate, muse, meditate, cogitate.

debauched *adj.* **dissipated,** dissolute, degenerate, corrupt, immoral, abandoned, profligate, intemperate, licentious, promiscuous, wanton.

debris *n.* **rubble,** wreckage, detritus, rubbish, litter, remains, ruins, fragments.

debt *n.* **1 money owed,** bill, balance due, account, score, tally, dues, arrears, debits.
2 indebtedness, obligation, liability, arrears, *inf.* the red.

decamp *v.* **1 make off,** run off/away, flee, take off, abscond, escape, cut and run, *inf.* skedaddle, hightail it, hotfoot it, vamoose, skip. **2 break camp,** move on.

decay *v.* **1 rot,** go bad, decompose, putrefy, spoil, perish, corrode. **2 degenerate,** deteriorate, decline, fail, wane, ebb, dwindle, crumble, disintegrate, fall to pieces, sink, collapse, molder, shrivel, wither, die, waste/wear away, atrophy. *Ant.* thrive; flourish; prosper.
▸ *n.* **1 rotting,** going bad, decomposition, putrefaction, putrescence, putridity, spoilage, perishing, corrosion. **2 rot,** decomposition, caries, gangrene, mortification. **3 degeneration,** deterioration, decline, failure, waning, ebb, crumbling,

disintegration, collapse, withering, death, atrophy.

deceit *n.* **1 deceitfulness,** deception, duplicity, double-dealing, fraud, fraudulence, cheating, trickery, duping, chicanery, underhandedness, cunning, craftiness, craft, wiliness, guile, pretense, artifice, treachery, *inf.* hanky-panky.
2 deception, trick, stratagem, ruse, dodge, subterfuge, fraud, cheat, swindle, sham, imposture, hoax, pretense, fake, misrepresentation, wile, artifice, Trojan horse. *Ant.* honesty; candor; sincerity.

deceitful *adj.* **lying,** untruthful, dishonest, mendacious, insincere, false, untrustworthy, two-faced, underhand, underhanded, crafty, cunning, sly, guileful, hypocritical, perfidious, deceptive, duplicitous, misleading, double-dealing, fraudulent, cheating, crooked, counterfeit, sham, bogus, dissembling, treacherous, illusory, spurious, specious, *inf.* sneaky, tricky. *Ant.* honest; open; sincere.

deceive *v.* **take in,** mislead, delude, fool, pull the wool over one's eyes, misguide, lead on, trick, hoodwink, hoax, dupe, swindle, outwit, bamboozle, seduce, ensnare, entrap, beguile, double-cross, cozen, gull, betray, *inf.* con, pull a fast one on, pull one's leg, take one for a ride, two-time, cheat on.

decelerate *v.* **slow down**, reduce speed, brake, put the brakes on, ease up.

decent *adj.* **1 decorous**, seemly, modest, proper, nice, tasteful, polite, respectable, pure, correct, dignified, delicate, appropriate, fitting, fit, suitable, becoming. **2 obliging**, helpful, accommodating, generous, kind, thoughtful, courteous, civil, honest, honorable, trustworthy, dependable, worthy, respectable, upright. **3 acceptable**, adequate, sufficient, ample, average, competent. *Ant.* indecent; unsuitable; dishonest.

deception *n.* **deceit**, deceitfulness, double-dealing, duplicity, fraud, fraudulence, cheating, chicanery, trickery, underhandedness, cunning, pretense, artifice, trick, stratagem, ruse, dodge, subterfuge, cheat, swindle, sham, pretense.

deceptive *adj.* **1 deceiving**, misleading, false, illusory, delusive, fallacious, ambiguous, specious, spurious, mock, pseudo. **2 deceitful**, duplicitous, fraudulent, cheating, underhand, underhanded, cunning, crafty, crooked, counterfeit, sham, bogus, *inf.* sneaky, tricky. *Ant.* authentic; true; honest.

decide *v.* **1 come to a decision**, reach/make a decision, make up one's mind, resolve, come to a conclusion, commit oneself, choose. **2 settle**, resolve, bring to a conclusion, determine, work out, clinch, *inf.* sew up. **3 judge**, adjudge, adjudicate, arbitrate, umpire, referee, make a judgment on, pass/pronounce judgment, give a verdict, make a ruling. *Ant.* hesitate; waver.

decided *adj.* **1 distinct**, clear, clear-cut, definite, certain, marked, pronounced, obvious, express, unmistakable, absolute, emphatic, categorical, unambiguous, undeniable, unequivocal, indisputable, undisputed, unquestionable. **2 determined**, resolute, firm, strong-minded, dogged, purposeful, unhesitating, unwavering, unswerving, unfaltering, incisive, forceful, emphatic. **3 settled**, resolved, concluded, determined, brought to a conclusion, clinched, *inf.* sewn up. *Ant.* doubtful; indecisive.

decision *n.* **1 resolution,**

conclusion, determination, settling, settlement. **2 judgment,** ruling, pronouncement, verdict, adjudgment, adjudication, arbitration, findings.
3 decisiveness, determination, resolution, resoluteness, resolve, firmness, strong-mindedness, doggedness, strength of mind/will, firmness of purpose, purpose, purposefulness.

decisive *adj.* **1 determined,** resolute, firm, dogged, purposeful, unhesitating, unwavering, unswerving, unfaltering, incisive, forceful, emphatic. **2 deciding,** determining, determinate, definitive, conclusive, final, settling, critical, crucial, momentous, emphatic, absolute, categorical, significant, influential, important, definite, positive. ***Ant.*** hesitant; indecisive; irresolute; insignificant.

declaration *n.* **1 announcement,** statement, proclamation, notification, pronouncement, publishing, broadcasting, promulgation, edict, manifesto. **2 statement,** assertion, maintaining, insistence, protestation, averment, affirmation, contention, profession, claim, allegation, avowal, swearing,

acknowledgment, revelation, disclosure, manifestation, confirmation, proof, testimony, validation, certification, attestation.

declare *v.* **1 announce,** make known, proclaim, pronounce, publish, broadcast, promulgate, trumpet, blazon. **2 state,** assert, maintain, aver, affirm, contend, profess, claim, allege, avow, swear, show, make known, reveal, disclose, manifest, confirm, prove, testify to, validate, certify, attest. ***Ant.*** deny; suppress; conceal.

decline *v.* **1 turn down,** give the thumbs down to, rebuff, repudiate, forgo, refuse, say no, send one's regrets, lessen, decrease, diminish, wane, dwindle, fade, ebb, fall/taper off, abate, flag. **2 deteriorate,** degenerate, decay, fail, fall, wither, weaken, fade away, wane, ebb, sink. **3 descend,** slope/slant down, dip, sink. ***Ant.*** accept; flourish; increase.

▸ *n.* **1 lessening,** decrease, downturn, downswing, diminishing, diminution, waning, dwindling, fading, ebb, falling off, abatement, flagging, slump, plunge, nosedive. **2 deterioration,** degeneration, decay, failure, fall, withering, enfeeblement, wane, ebb, atrophy. **3 slope,** declivity, dip. **Ant.** growth; improvement.

decompose *v.* **decay,** rot, go bad, putrefy, fester, break up, fall apart, disintegrate, crumble, separate, break down, divide, disintegrate, dissect, analyze, atomize, dissolve.

decor *n.* **decoration,** furnishing, furbishing, color scheme, ornamentation.

decorate *v.* **1 adorn,** ornament, trim, embellish, garnish, festoon, garland, beautify, prettify, enhance, grace, enrich. **2 paint,** wallpaper, paper, renovate, refurbish, furbish, *inf.* do up, spruce up. **3 cite,** honor, confer an award on, give a medal to, pin a medal on.

decoration *n.* **1 adornment,** ornamentation, trimming, embellishment, garnishing, beautification, prettification, enhancement. **2 furnishing,** color scheme. **3 ornament,** trinket, bauble, knickknack, doodad, gewgaw, trimming, tinsel, trimming, frill, folderol, frippery, flourish, scroll, arabesque, curlicue. **4 award,** medal, badge, star, ribbon, laurel, wreath, colors, insignia.

decorative *adj.* **ornamental,** fancy, adorning, embellishing, garnishing, beautifying, prettifying, enhancing, nonfunctional.

decorous *adj.* **1 proper,** seemly, decent, becoming, befitting, tasteful, in good taste, correct, appropriate, suitable, fitting, apt, apposite, polite, well-mannered, mannerly, well-behaved, genteel, refined, well-bred, dignified, respectable. **2 modest,** demure, reserved, sedate, staid. **Ant.** indecorous; unseemly; immodest.

decorum *n.* **1 decorousness,** propriety, properness, seemliness, decency, good taste, correctness, appropriateness, politeness, courtesy, refinement, breeding, deportment, dignity, respectability. **2 etiquette,** protocol, punctilio .

decoy *n.* **lure,** bait, enticement, inducement, temptation, attraction, allurement, ensnarement, entrapment, snare, trap, pitfall.

decrease *v.* **1 lessen,** grow less, diminish, reduce, drop, fall off, decline, dwindle, contract, shrink, lower, cut down/back, cut down/back on, curtail, contract. **2 die down,** abate, subside, let up, slacken, ebb, wane, taper off, peter out. **Ant.** increase.

▸ *n.* **1 lessening,** lowering, reduction, drop, decline, falling off, downturn, cutback, curtailment, diminution, contraction, shrinkage. **2 dying down,** abatement, subsidence, letting up, letup, slackening, ebb, wane. **Ant.** increase.

decree *n.* **1 edict,** order, law, statute, act, ordinance, regulation, rule, injunction, enactment, command, mandate, proclamation, dictum, precept, manifesto. **2 ruling,** verdict, judgment, decision, findings.
▸ *v.* **ordain,** rule, order, command, dictate, lay down, prescribe, pronounce, proclaim, enact, adjudge, enjoin, direct, decide, determine.

decrepit *adj.* **1 feeble,** enfeebled, infirm, weak, weakened, weakly, frail, wasted, debilitated, disabled, incapacitated, crippled, doddering, tottering, aged, old, elderly, senile, effete, emasculated. **2 dilapidated,** rickety, broken-down, tumbledown, ramshackle, rundown, worn-out, battered, decayed, deteriorated, antiquated, the worse for wear, on its last legs. **Ant.** strong; fit.

dedicate *v.* **1 devote,** give, give over, commit, pledge, surrender. **2 inscribe,** address, name, assign, offer. **3 bless,** make holy, consecrate, sanctify, hallow.

dedicated *adj.* **devoted,** committed, wholehearted, single-minded, enthusiastic, zealous, sworn, pledged. **Ant.** indifferent; apathetic.

deduce *v.* **conclude,** come to the conclusion, infer, reason, gather, glean, come to understand, understand, assume, presume.

deduct *v.* **subtract,** take away, take off, withdraw, abstract, remove, discount, *inf.* knock off. **Ant.** add.

deduction *n.* **1 conclusion,** inference, reasoning, assumption, presumption, corollary, results, findings. **2 subtraction,** taking off, withdrawal, removal.

deed *n.* **1 act,** action, feat, exploit, performance, achievement, accomplishment, undertaking, enterprise. **2 fact,** reality, truth. **3 signed document,** contract, legal agreement, indenture, instrument, title deed, deed of covenant.

deep *adj.* **1 extending far down/in,** cavernous, yawning, profound, bottomless, immeasurable, fathomless, unfathomable. **2 low,** low-pitched, full-toned, bass, rich, powerful, resonant, sonorous, rumbling, booming, resounding. **3 dark,** intense, vivid, rich, strong. **4 profound,** extreme, intense, very great, great, grave, deep-seated, deep-rooted. **5 clever,** intellectual,

learned, wise, sagacious, sage, discerning, penetrating, perspicacious. **6 intense,** heartfelt, deep-felt, fervent, ardent, impassioned, deep-seated, deep-rooted. **7 obscure,** unclear, abstruse, mysterious, hidden, secret, unfathomable, recondite, esoteric, enigmatic, arcane. **8 absorbed,** engrossed, preoccupied, rapt, immersed, lost, intent, engaged. *Ant.* high; shallow; light; superficial.
▸ *adv.* **1 far down,** far in. **2 far,** long, late.

deface *v.* **spoil,** disfigure, mar, blemish, deform, ruin, sully, tarnish, damage, vandalize, injure. *Ant.* beautify; decorate.

defame *v.* **slander,** libel, cast aspersions on, asperse, blacken the name/character of, malign, smear, run down, speak evil of, backbite, vilify, traduce, besmirch, defile, stigmatize, disparage, denigrate, discredit, decry, insult, *inf.* do a hatchet job on, sling/throw mud at, drag through the mud, bad-mouth.

defeat *v.* **1 beat,** conquer, win a victory over, get the better of, vanquish, rout, trounce, thrash, overcome, overpower, overthrow, overwhelm, crush, quash, quell, subjugate, subdue, repulse, *inf.* wipe the floor with, clobber, zap.

2 baffle, puzzle, perplex, confound, frustrate. **3 hinder,** prevent, ruin, thwart, frustrate, foil, balk, hamper, obstruct, impede, discomfit, *inf.* put the kibosh on, nip in the bud. **4 reject,** overthrow, throw out, outvote. *Ant.* lose; surrender; advance.
▸ *n.* **1 conquest,** vanquishment, rout, beating, trouncing, thrashing, debacle, reverse, overpowering, overthrow, subjugation. **2 downfall,** breakdown, collapse, failure, ruin, abortion, miscarriage, undoing, reverse, disappointment, setback, discomfiture, rejection, overthrow. *Ant.* victory; success; triumph.

defect *n.* **1 fault,** flaw, imperfection, deficiency, weakness, weak spot/point, shortcoming, failing, snag, kink, deformity, blemish, crack, break, tear, scratch, spot, mistake, error, *inf.* bug. **2 deficiency,** shortage, shortfall, inadequacy, insufficiency, shortcoming, lack, want, omission, weakness, failing, fault, flaw, absence. *Ant.* perfection; flawlessness.
▸ *v.* **1 go over to the enemy,** desert, turn traitor, change sides/allegiances, desert one's side/cause, shift ground, break faith, apostatize. **2 desert,**

abandon, forsake, renounce, repudiate, secede from, rebel against, revolt against, *inf.* rat on. *Ant.* join; support.

defective *adj.* **1 faulty,** flawed, imperfect, weak, deficient, deformed, incomplete, malfunctioning, in disrepair, cracked, torn, scratched. **2 lacking,** wanting, deficient, inadequate, insufficient, short, low, scant. **3 having learning difficulties,** impaired, retarded, abnormal, subnormal. *Ant.* perfect; intact; normal.

defend *v.* **1 protect,** guard, safeguard, watch over, keep from harm, preserve, secure, shield, shelter, screen, fortify, garrison, fight for. **2 vindicate,** justify, argue/speak for, speak on behalf of, give an apologia for, make a case for, plead for, explain, give reasons for, give the rationale behind, exonerate. **3 support,** back, stand by, stand/stick up for, argue for, champion, endorse, uphold, sustain, bolster. *Ant.* attack; criticize.

defendant *n.* **accused,** prisoner at the bar, appellant, litigant, respondent.

defense *n.* **1 protection,** shield, safeguard, guard, security, cover, shelter, screen, fortification, resistance, deterrent. **2 barricade,** fortification, rampart, bulwark, buttress, fortress, keep, bastion. **3 armaments,** weapons. **4 vindication,** justification, apologia, apology, argument, plea, explanation, explication, excuse, extenuation, exoneration. **5 denial,** rebuttal, plea, pleading, testimony, declaration, case, excuse, alibi.

defenseless *adj.* **1 helpless,** vulnerable, weak, powerless, impotent. **2 undefended,** unprotected, unguarded, unfortified, unarmed, vulnerable, open to attack, wide open, exposed, endangered.

defer[1] *v.* **postpone,** put off, adjourn, delay, hold over, shelve, put on ice, pigeonhole, suspend, table, stay, hold in abeyance, prorogue.

defer[2] *v.* **yield,** submit, bow, give way, give in, surrender, accede, capitulate, acquiesce.

deference *n.* **1 respect,** regard, consideration, attentiveness, attention, thoughtfulness, esteem, courteousness, courtesy, politeness, civility, dutifulness, reverence, veneration, homage. **2 yielding,** submission, surrender, capitulation, accession, acquiescence, complaisance, obeisance. *Ant.* disrespect; discourtesy.

defiant *adj.* **1 resistant,** noncompliant, disobedient, recalcitrant, rebellious, insubordinate, mutinous, refractory, contemptuous, scornful, indifferent, insolent. **2 challenging,** provocative, bold, audacious, aggressive, truculent. *Ant.* submissive; yielding.

deficiency *n.* **1 lack,** want, shortage, dearth, insufficiency, inadequacy, scarcity, deficit, scantiness, paucity, absence. **2 defect,** fault, flaw, imperfection, weakness, weak point/spot, failing, shortcoming, snag.

defile *v.* **1 pollute,** foul, befoul, dirty, soil, corrupt, contaminate, taint, infect, tarnish, sully, pervert, vitiate. **2 defame,** sully, blacken, cast aspersions on, cast a slur on, denigrate, besmirch, stigmatize. **3 desecrate,** profane, treat sacrilegiously, make impure, contaminate, vitiate. **4 ravish,** rape, deflower, violate. *Ant.* purify.

define *v.* **1 spell out,** describe, explain, expound, interpret, elucidate, clarify, determine, set out, outline, detail, specify, designate. **2 mark out,** fix, establish, settle, demarcate, bound, delimit, delineate, circumscribe, outline, delineate, silhouette.

definite *adj.* **1 specific,** particular, precise, exact, defined, well-defined, clear, clear-cut, explicit, express, determined, fixed, established, confirmed. **2 certain,** sure, positive, guaranteed, settled, decided, assured, conclusive, final. **3 fixed,** marked, demarcated, delimited, circumscribed. *Ant.* indefinite; uncertain; indeterminate.

definitely *adv.* **certainly,** surely, for sure, without doubt/question, beyond any doubt, undoubtedly, indubitably, positively, absolutely, undeniably, unmistakably, plainly, clearly, obviously, categorically, decidedly, unequivocally, easily, far and away, without fail.

definition *n.* **1 meaning,** statement of meaning, description, explanation, exposition, expounding, interpretation, elucidation, clarification. **2 marking out,** fixing, settling, establishment, determination, demarcation, bounding, delimiting, delimitation, delineation, circumscribing. **3 precision,** sharpness, distinctness, clearness, clarity, contrast, visibility, focus, resolution.

definitive *adj.* **1 conclusive,** final, ultimate, decisive, unconditional,

unqualified, absolute, categorical.
2 authoritative, most reliable,
most complete, exhaustive.

deflect *v.* **turn aside/away,** turn,
alter course, change
course/direction, diverge, deviate,
veer, swerve, slew, drift, bend,
twist, curve, shy, ricochet, glance
off, divaricate, divert, switch,
avert, sidetrack.

deformed *adj.* **1 misshapen,**
malformed, distorted, contorted,
twisted, crooked, curved, gnarled,
crippled, maimed, humpbacked,
hunchbacked, disfigured, ugly,
unsightly, damaged, marred,
mutilated, mangled. **2 twisted,**
warped, perverted, corrupted,
depraved, vile, gross.

defraud *v.* **cheat,** swindle, rob,
fleece, sting, dupe, rook, bilk,
trick, fool, take in, hoodwink,
mislead, delude, deceive, beguile,
outwit, *lit.* cozen, *inf.* gyp, con, rip
off, take for a ride, pull a fast one
on, put one over on.

deft *adj.* **dexterous,** adroit, handy,
nimble, nimble-fingered, agile,
skillful, skilled, proficient, adept,
able, clever, expert, experienced.
Ant. clumsy; awkward; maladroit.

defy *v.* **1 disobey,** disregard,
ignore, slight, flout, fly in the face
of, thumb one's nose at, spurn,
scoff at, deride, scorn. **2 resist,**

withstand, brave, stand up to,
confront, face, meet head-on,
square up to, beard, defeat,
repulse, repel, thwart, frustrate,
foil. **3 challenge,** dare, throw
down the gauntlet to. ***Ant.*** obey;
surrender.

degenerate *adj.* **degenerated,**
deteriorated, debased, declined,
degraded, corrupt, decadent,
immoral, depraved, dissolute,
debauched, abandoned,
profligate, wicked, vile, sinful,
vice-ridden, disreputable,
despicable, base, sordid, low,
mean, ignoble.
 ▸ *v.* **deteriorate,** decline, worsen,
decay, rot, fail, fall off, sink, slip,
slide, go downhill, regress,
retrogress, lapse, *inf.* go to pot, go
to the dogs, hit the skids. ***Ant.***
improve.

degrade *v.* **debase,** discredit,
cheapen, belittle, demean,
deprecate, deflate, devalue, lower,
reduce, shame, disgrace,
dishonor, humble, humiliate,
mortify, abase, vitiate, corrupt,
pervert, defile, sully, debauch.
Ant. dignify; upgrade; promote;
improve.

degree *n.* **1 stage,** level, grade,
step, gradation, rung, point,
mark, measure, notch, limit.
2 extent, measure, magnitude,
level, amount, quality, intensity,

strength, proportion, ratio.
3 rank, class, standing, status, station, position, grade, level, order, condition, estate.

deign *v.* **condescend,** stoop, lower oneself, think/see fit, deem worthy, consent.

deity *n.* **God,** god, goddess, divine being, celestial being, supreme being, divinity, godhead.

dejected *adj.* **depressed,** dispirited, discouraged, disheartened, downhearted, crestfallen, cast down, downcast, down, disappointed, unhappy, sad, miserable, blue, wretched, despondent, woebegone, forlorn, sorrowful, disconsolate, doleful, glum, gloomy, melancholy, morose, low in spirits, low-spirited, long-faced, *inf.* down in the mouth/dumps. *Ant.* cheerful; lighthearted; happy.

delay *v.* **1 postpone,** put off, adjourn, defer, hold over, shelve, suspend, table, stay, hold in abeyance, put on hold, put on ice, put on the back burner. **2 hold up/back,** detain, slow up, set back, hinder, obstruct, hamper, impede, bog down, check, hold in check, restrain, halt, stop, arrest. **3 linger,** loiter, hold back, dawdle, dally, dilly-dally, lag/fall behind, not keep pace, procrastinate, stall, tarry. *Ant.* advance; accelerate.

▸ *n.* **1 postponement,** adjournment, deferment, suspension, tabling, stay. **2 holdup,** wait, setback, detainment, detention, hindrance, obstruction, impediment, check, stoppage, halt, interruption. **3 wait,** waiting period, interval, lull, interlude, intermission. **4 lingering,** loitering, dawdling, dallying, dilly-dallying, lagging/falling behind, procrastination, stalling, tarrying.

delegate *n.* **representative,** deputy, agent, spokesman, spokeswoman, spokesperson, ambassador, envoy, legate, messenger, go-between, proxy, emissary, commissary.

▸ *v.* **1 pass on,** hand over, transfer, give, commit, entrust, assign, relegate, consign. **2 appoint,** designate, nominate, name, authorize, deputize, commission, mandate, empower, choose, select, elect, ordain.

delegation *n.* **1 deputation,** legation, contingent, mission, commission, embassy, delegates, envoys. **2 transference,** committal, entrustment, assignment, relegation, consignment. **3 appointment,** designation, nomination, authorization, commissioning, selection, election.

delete *v.* **cross/strike out,** rub out, cut out, erase, cancel, blue-pencil, edit out, remove, take out, expunge, eradicate, obliterate, efface, wipe/blot out, *inf.* scratch, kill. *Ant.* add; insert.

deliberate *adj.* **1 intentional,** planned, considered, calculated, designed, studied, studious, painstaking, conscious, purposeful, willful, premeditated, preplanned, prearranged, preconceived, predetermined, aforethought. **2 careful,** unhurried, cautious, thoughtful, steady, regular, measured, unwavering, unhesitating, unfaltering, determined, resolute, ponderous, laborious. *Ant.* accidental; unintentional; hasty.
▸ *v.* **think,** ponder, muse, meditate, reflect, cogitate, ruminate, brood, excogitate, think over, consider, reflect on, mull over, review, weigh up, evaluate, discuss, debate, confer, consult.

deliberately *adv.* **1 intentionally,** on purpose, purposefully, by design, knowingly, wittingly, consciously, premeditatedly, calculatedly, in cold blood. **2 carefully,** unhurriedly, cautiously, steadily, measuredly, unwaveringly, unhesitatingly, determinedly, ponderously.

delicate *adj.* **1 fine,** exquisite, fragile, slender, slight, elegant, graceful, dainty, flimsy, silky, gauzy, gossamer, wispy. **2 frail,** sickly, weak, debilitated, infirm, ailing, in poor health, unwell. **3 pastel,** pale, muted, subtle, soft, subdued, understated, faint. **4 difficult,** tricky, sensitive, ticklish, critical, precarious, touchy, *inf.* sticky, dicey. **5 careful,** considerate, sensitive, tactful, discreet, diplomatic, politic, kid-glove. **6 discriminating,** discerning, refined, perceptive, critical, fastidious, finicky, persnickety, squeamish. **7 sensitive,** precise, accurate, exact. **8 deft,** skilled, skillful, expert.

delicious *adj.* **1 tasty,** appetizing, mouthwatering, delectable, choice, savory, flavorsome, flavorful, luscious, palatable, toothsome, ambrosial, ambrosian, *inf.* scrumptious, yummy. **2 delightful,** enchanting, exquisite, enjoyable, pleasurable, entertaining, amusing, diverting, pleasant, agreeable, charming, nice. *Ant.* revolting; disgusting; nasty.

delight *n.* **pleasure,** joy, happiness, gladness, gratification, bliss, rapture, ecstasy, elation, jubilation, excitement, entertainment, amusement, transports. **Ant.** revulsion; disgust.

▸ v. **1 please,** gladden, cheer, gratify, thrill, excite, transport, enchant, captivate, entrance, charm, entertain, amuse, divert, *inf.* send. **2 take/find pleasure,** indulge, glory. **Ant.** dismay; displease; disgust.

delighted *adj.* **pleased,** joyful, happy, glad, gratified, overjoyed, blissful, enraptured, ecstatic, jubilant, thrilled, transported, excited, enchanted, captivated, entranced, charmed, entertained, amused, diverted, *inf.* sent.

delightful *adj.* **pleasant,** pleasing, agreeable, enjoyable, amusing, entertaining, diverting, pleasurable, pleasure-giving, gratifying, delectable, joyful, exciting, thrilling, rapturous, enchanting, captivating, fascinating, entrancing, ravishing, charming, attractive, beautiful, pretty, engaging, winning. **Ant.** unpleasant; disagreeable.

delinquent *n.* **offender,** wrongdoer, culprit, lawbreaker, criminal, hooligan, vandal, ruffian, hoodlum, miscreant, malefactor, transgressor, juvenile delinquent, young offender.

▸ *adj.* **1 mischievous,** culpable, transgressing, offending, criminal. **2 negligent,** neglectful, remiss, careless, slack, derelict.

delirious *adj.* **1 raving,** incoherent, babbling, light-headed, irrational, deranged, demented, unhinged, mad, insane, crazy, out of one's mind. **2 ecstatic,** euphoric, beside oneself, carried away, transported, hysterical, frenzied, wild with excitement, distracted, frantic, out of one's wits, feverish. **Ant.** rational; coherent; depressed.

deliver *v.* **1 distribute,** carry, bring, take, transport, convey, send, dispatch, remit. **2 hand over,** turn over, transfer, commit, grant, make over, give up, yield, surrender, relinquish, cede, resign, set free, free, liberate, release, save, rescue, set loose, loose, extricate, discharge, ransom, emancipate, redeem. **3 utter,** give voice to, voice, speak, give, give forth, express, pronounce, enunciate, proclaim, announce, declare, read, recite, broadcast, promulgate. **4 direct,** aim, give, deal, administer, launch, inflict, throw, strike, hurl, pitch, discharge. **5 come up with,** achieve, attain, provide, supply, produce. **Ant.** collect; receive.

delivery *n.* **1 distribution,** carriage, transporting, transport, conveyance, dispatch.

2 consignment, load, batch.
3 manner of speaking, enunciation, articulation, intonation, elocution, utterance, presentation. **4 labor,** childbirth, parturition. **5 deliverance,** liberation, release, rescue, escape. **6 directing,** aiming, launching, throwing, pitching.

deluge *n.* **1 flood,** spate, inundation, overflowing, flash flood, cataclysm, downpour, torrent, torrential rain, cloudburst. **2 flood,** rush, spate, torrent, avalanche, barrage, outpouring.
▸ *v.* **1 flood,** inundate, swamp, engulf, submerge, drown, soak, drench, douse. **2 inundate,** flood, overrun, overwhelm, engulf, swamp, overload.

delusion *n.* **false impression,** false belief, misconception, misapprehension, misunderstanding, misbelief, mistake, self-deception, deception, error, fallacy, illusion, fancy, phantasm, fool's paradise, deluding, misleading, deception, fooling, tricking, duping.

demand *v.* **1 ask/call for,** request, press for, insist on, urge, clamor for, make a claim for, lay claim to, claim, require, need, necessitate, call for, take, involve, want, cry out for. **2 ask,** inquire, question, interrogate, challenge.
3 expect, insist on, exact, impose, order, requisition.
▸ *n.* **1 request,** entreaty, claim, requisition, insistence, pressure, clamor. **2 inquiry,** question, interrogation, challenge.
3 requirement, need, necessity, want, claim, imposition, exigency.

demanding *adj.* **1 nagging,** harassing, clamorous, importunate, insistent, imperious. **2 challenging,** taxing, exacting, exigent, tough, hard, difficult, tiring, wearing, exhausting. ***Ant.*** easygoing; easy; effortless.

demean *v.* **lower,** degrade, debase, devalue, demote, humble, abase, belittle, deprecate.

demeanor *n.* **behavior,** conduct, bearing, air, appearance, mien, deportment, carriage, comportment.

demolish *v.* **1 knock down,** pull/tear down, bring down, flatten, raze, level, bulldoze, dismantle, break up, pulverize, destroy, put an end to, ruin, wreck, undo. **2 defeat,** conquer, vanquish, overthrow, overturn, quell, quash, suppress, destroy, annihilate, wipe out, finish off.
3 eat up, consume, devour, gobble up, put away. ***Ant.*** build; construct; create.

demonstrable *adj.* **provable,**

verifiable, attestable, confirmable, evincible.

demonstrate *v.* **1 show,** indicate, determine, prove, validate, confirm, verify, establish, display, exhibit, express, manifest, evince, evidence, illustrate, describe, explain, expound on. **2 protest,** march, parade, rally, sit in, picket.

demonstration *n.* **1 indication,** substantiation, confirmation, affirmation, verification, validation, indication, expression, manifestation, evincement, evidence, illustration, description, explanation, exposition. **2 protest,** protest march, march, parade, rally, mass rally/lobby, sit-in, picket.

demonstrative *adj.* **1 emotional,** unreserved, unrestrained, expressive, open, effusive, expansive, gushing, affectionate, loving, warm. **2 indicative,** illustrative, evincive, expository. **3 conclusive,** convincing, telling, material, incontrovertible, irrefutable. **Ant.** undemonstrative; unemotional; reserved.

demoralize *v.* **1 discourage,** dishearten, cast down, dispirit, deject, depress, daunt, crush, sap, shake, undermine, devitalize, cripple, paralyze, weaken, enervate. **2 corrupt,** deprave,

debauch, pervert, debase, contaminate, defile, vitiate. **Ant.** encourage; hearten.

demure *adj.* **1 modest,** unassuming, decorous, meek, reserved, quiet, shy, bashful, retiring, diffident, reticent, timid, timorous, shrinking, serious, grave, sedate, staid. **2 overmodest,** coy, prim, priggish, prissy, prudish, goody-goody, straitlaced, puritanical. **Ant.** brazen; shameless.

denial *n.* **1 contradiction,** repudiation, disclaimer, retraction, abjuration, disaffirmation, negation, dissent. **2 refusal,** rejection, dismissal, rebuff, repulse, declination, veto, turndown, *inf.* thumbs down. **3 renunciation,** renouncement, disowning, repudiation, disavowal. **Ant.** confession; acceptance.

denigrate *v.* **disparage,** belittle, diminish, deprecate, detract from, decry, blacken one's character, defame, slander, libel, cast aspersions on, malign, vilify, calumniate, besmirch, run down, abuse, revile, bad-mouth. **Ant.** extol; laud; acclaim.

denomination *n.* **1 creed,** faith, religious belief, church, sect, religious group, persuasion, communion, order, fraternity,

brotherhood, sisterhood, school.
2 value, unit, grade, size.
3 classification, class, category, grouping, group, type. **4 name,** title, term, designation, appellation, epithet, style, label, tag, *inf.* handle, moniker.

denote *v.* **1 indicate,** be a sign/mark of, signify, betoken, symbolize, represent, stand for, typify. **2 mean,** convey, designate, suggest, bring to mind, intimate, refer to, allude to, imply, connote.

denounce *v.* **1 condemn,** criticize, attack, censure, castigate, decry, rail/inveigh/fulminate against, declaim against, arraign, denunciate, revile. **2 accuse,** inform against, incriminate, implicate, inculpate, charge, file charges, indict, impeach, take to court, turn in, *inf.* rat on.

dense *adj.* **1 close-packed,** tightly packed, crowded, thickset, closely set, jammed together, crammed, compressed, compacted. **2 of high density,** heavy, concentrated, condensed. **3 thick,** concentrated, opaque, impenetrable. **4 stupid,** thick, slow-witted, slow, dull-witted, blockish, obtuse, *inf.* dim. *Ant.* sparse; thin; light; clever.

deny *v.* **1 declare untrue,** contradict, negate, nullify, dissent from, disagree with, repudiate, refute, controvert, disclaim, retract, take back, back-pedal, abjure, disaffirm, gainsay. **2 refuse,** reject, turn down, dismiss, repulse, decline, veto, *inf.* give the thumbs down to, give the red light to. **3 renounce,** disown, turn one's back on, repudiate, discard, disavow. *Ant.* admit; accept.

depart *v.* **1 leave,** go, go away/off, take one's leave, take oneself off, withdraw, set off/out, start out, get going, get under way, quit, make an exit, exit, break camp, decamp, retreat, retire, *inf.* make tracks, shove off, split, cut out, vamoose, hightail it. **2 deviate,** diverge, differ, vary, digress, veer, branch off, fork, swerve, turn aside. *Ant.* arrive; stay.

departed *adj.* **dead,** deceased, late, gone, passed away/on, expired.

department *n.* **1 section,** division, subdivision, unit, branch, segment, compartment, office, bureau, agency. **2 area,** area of responsibility, responsibility, area of interest, specialty, line, province, sphere, sphere of activity, domain, realm, jurisdiction, authority, function.

departure *n.* **1 leaving,** leave-taking, going, going away/off, withdrawal, setting off/out, starting out, exit, exodus, decamping, retreat. **2 deviation,** divergence, variation, digression, veering, branching off, swerving. **3 change of direction,** change, difference of emphasis, shift, innovation, branching out, novelty. *Ant.* arrival; return.

depend *v.* **1 be dependent on,** turn/hinge on, hang on, rest on, be contingent upon, be subject to, be controlled/determined by, be based on, revolve around, be influenced by, be resultant from, be subordinate to. **2 rely on,** place reliance on, count/bank on, lean on, cling to, reckon/calculate on, trust in, put one's faith in, have confidence in, swear by, be sure of, be supported/sustained by.

dependable *adj.* **reliable,** trustworthy, faithful, responsible, steady, stable, sure, unfailing, true, steadfast. *Ant.* unreliable; untrustworthy.

dependent *adj.* **1 depending on,** conditional on, contingent on, determined by, subject to. **2 reliant,** helpless, weak, defenseless, vulnerable, immature. **3 subsidiary,** subject, subservient.
▸ *n.* **minor,** child, charge, protégé; minion, parasite, hanger-on, henchman.

depict *v.* **portray,** represent, draw, paint, sketch, illustrate, delineate, outline, reproduce, render, limn, chart, map out, describe, set forth/out, detail, relate, narrate, recount, record, chronicle.

deplete *v.* **exhaust,** use up, consume, expend, spend, drain, empty, milk, evacuate, bankrupt, impoverish, reduce, decrease, diminish, lessen, lower, attenuate. *Ant.* augment; increase.

deplorable *adj.* **1 disgraceful,** shameful, dishonorable, blameworthy, disreputable, scandalous, reprehensible, despicable, abominable, base, sordid, vile, contemptible. **2 lamentable,** regrettable, unfortunate, wretched, dire, miserable, pitiable, pathetic, unhappy, sad, tragic, disastrous, distressing, grievous, calamitous. *Ant.* honorable; admirable; fortunate.

deplore *v.* **1 be scandalized/ shocked by,** be offended by, disapprove of, condemn, censure, deprecate, denounce, decry, abhor. **2 regret,** lament, mourn, rue, bemoan, grieve/sorrow over, bewail, pine for, shed tears for, weep over.

deploy *v.* **1 arrange,** position, dispose, spread out, extend, redistribute, station. **2 use,**

utilize, set out/up, bring into play, have recourse to.

deport *v.* **1 banish,** expel, exile, evict, transport, oust, expatriate, extradite. **2 behave,** conduct oneself, act, acquit oneself, comport oneself, bear/carry/hold oneself.

depose *v.* **remove from office,** remove, unseat, dethrone, oust, displace, dismiss, discharge, cashier, strip of rank, demote, *inf.* sack, fire, give the boot to.

deposit *v.* **1 put,** lay, set, set/put/lay down, drop, let fall, let settle, set down, precipitate, dump. **2 bank,** entrust, consign, save, store, hoard, stow, put away, lay in, squirrel away.
▸ *n.* **1 precipitate,** sediment, sublimate, accumulation, deposition, dregs, lees, silt, alluvium. **2 bed,** vein, lode, mine, layer. **3 down/part payment,** installment, security, retainer.

depot *n.* **1 terminal,** terminus, bus/railroad station, garage. **2 storehouse,** warehouse, repository, depository, magazine, cache, arsenal.

deprave *v.* **corrupt,** debauch, lead astray, pervert, seduce, debase, degrade, make degenerate, defile, pollute, contaminate, vitiate, brutalize, abuse.

depraved *adj.* **corrupt,** corrupted, immoral, unprincipled, reprobate, debauched, dissolute, abandoned, perverted, degenerate, profligate, debased, degraded, wicked, sinful, vile, base, iniquitous, criminal, vicious, brutal, lewd, licentious, lascivious, lecherous, prurient, obscene, indecent, libertine. *Ant.* upright; virtuous; pure.

depreciate *v.* **1 decline,** fall, devalue, reduce, mark down, cheapen, cut, slash. **2 belittle,** disparage, denigrate, decry, deprecate, make light of, discredit, underrate, undervalue, underestimate, deflate, detract from, derogate, diminish, minimize, run down, disdain, ridicule, deride, sneer at, mock, defame, traduce. *Ant.* appreciate; praise; overrate.

depress *v.* **1 make sad/unhappy,** sadden, deject, cast down, make gloomy/despondent, dispirit, dishearten, discourage, dampen the spirits of, daunt, desolate, make desolate, weigh down, oppress. **2 slow down/up,** weaken, lower, reduce, sap, enervate, debilitate, devitalize, impair, enfeeble, exhaust, drain.
3 reduce, lower, cut, cheapen, put/keep down, slash, depreciate, devalue, diminish, downgrade.
4 push down, press down, lower.
Ant. cheer; encourage; raise.

depressed *adj.* **1 sad,** saddened, unhappy, gloomy, blue, glum, dejected, downhearted, cast down, downcast, down, crestfallen, despondent, dispirited, low, low in spirits, low-spirited, melancholy, disheartened, discouraged, fed up, daunted, desolate, moody, morose, pessimistic, weighed down, oppressed, *inf.* down in the dumps. **2 sunken,** hollow, concave, indented, dented, pushed in, recessed, set back. **3 weak,** weakened, slow, enervated, debilitated, devitalized, impaired. **4 reduced,** lowered, cut, cheapened, slashed, devalued, marked-down, discounted. **5 poverty-stricken,** poor, destitute, disadvantaged, deprived, needy, distressed, rundown, down-at-the-heels. *Ant.* cheerful; strong; prosperous.

depression *n.* **1 clinical depression,** endogenous depression, reactive depression, melancholia. **2 sadness,** unhappiness, despair, gloom, glumness, dejection, downheartedness, despondency, dispiritedness, melancholy, discouragement, desolation, dolefulness, moodiness, moroseness, pessimism, hopelessness, low spirits, blues, *inf.* the dumps. **3 hollow,** indentation, dent, cavity, concavity, dip, valley, pit, hole, bowl, sink, sinkhole, excavation. **4 slump,** recession, decline, slowdown, standstill, paralysis, inactivity, stagnation, hard/bad times.

deprive *v.* **dispossess,** strip, expropriate, divest, wrest, rob.

deprived *adj.* **poor,** destitute, disadvantaged, needy, in need, in want, lacking, distressed, forlorn. *Ant.* fortunate; wealthy.

deputy *n.* **substitute,** stand-in, representative, second in command, assistant, surrogate, proxy, delegate, agent, spokesperson, ambassador, lieutenant, legate, commissioner, envoy, go-between, mediator, vice president.
 ▸ *adj.* **assistant,** substitute, stand-in, representative, surrogate, proxy, subordinate.

derelict *adj.* **1 abandoned,** forsaken, deserted, discarded, rejected, cast off, relinquished, ownerless. **2 dilapidated,** ramshackle, tumbledown, rundown, broken-down, in disrepair, crumbling, falling to pieces, rickety, neglected. **3 negligent,** neglectful, remiss, lax, careless, sloppy, slipshod, slack, irresponsible, delinquent.

▸ *n.* **vagrant,** tramp, beggar, bum, hobo, outcast, pariah, ne'er-do-well, good-for-nothing, wastrel.

deride *v.* **mock,** ridicule, jeer at, scoff at, sneer at, make fun of, poke fun at, laugh at, scorn, pooh-pooh, lampoon, satirize, taunt, insult, torment, rag, tease, chaff, disdain, disparage, denigrate, slight, detract from, vilify, *fml.* contemn.

derogatory *adj.* **disparaging,** denigratory, belittling, diminishing, slighting, deprecatory, depreciatory, depreciative, detracting, deflating, discrediting, dishonoring, unfavorable, disapproving, uncomplimentary, unflattering, insulting, offensive, damaging, injurious, defamatory, vilifying. *Ant.* complimentary; flattering; laudatory.

descend *v.* **1 go down,** come down, move down, climb down, pass down, drop, fall, sink, subside, plummet, plunge, tumble, slump. **2 get down,** get off, alight, dismount, disembark, detrain, deplane. **3 go down,** slope, incline, dip, slant. **4 condescend,** stoop, lower/abase oneself. **5 degenerate,** deteriorate, decline, sink, go downhill, *inf.* go to pot, go to the dogs. **6 attack,** assault, assail, pounce, raid, swoop, charge, come in force, arrive in hordes. **7 be a descendant of,** derive/originate from, issue/spring from. **8 be handed/passed down,** pass by heredity, be transferred by inheritance. *Ant.* ascend; climb.

descent *n.* **1 going down,** coming down, drop, fall, sinking, subsiding, plummeting, plunge. **2 getting down/off,** alighting. **3 slope,** incline, dip, drop, gradient, declivity, declination, slant. **4 degeneracy,** deterioration, decline, debasement, degradation, sinking, decadence. **5 attack,** assault, assailing, raid, charge, onslaught, incursion, foray, sortie. **6 ancestry,** parentage, lineage, extraction, genealogy, heredity, succession, stock, line, pedigree, blood, strain, origins.

describe *v.* **1 give a description/account of,** give details of, detail, tell, narrate, put into words, express, recount, relate, report, set out, chronicle, define, explain, elucidate, illustrate. **2 designate,** pronounce, style, label, characterize, portray, depict. **3 draw,** delineate, mark out, outline, trace, sketch.

description *n.* **1 account,** detailed statement, report, setting out, chronicle, narration, recounting, relation, commentary, explanation, elucidation, illustration, details. **2 designation,** pronouncement, styling, labeling, characterization, portrayal, depiction. **3 drawing,** delineation, outline, tracing. **4 kind,** sort, variety, type, brand, breed, category, class, designation, genre, ilk, mold.

descriptive *adj.* **detailed,** explanatory, elucidatory, graphic, vivid, striking, expressive, illustrative, pictorial, depictive, picturesque, circumstantial.

desecrate *v.* **violate,** defile, profane, treat sacrilegiously, blaspheme, pollute, contaminate, infect, befoul, debase, degrade, dishonor, vitiate.

desert[1] *n.* **1 wasteland,** waste, wilderness, barrenness, solitude, wilds, Sahara. **2 uninteresting place/period,** unproductive place/period, wasteland.

desert[2] *v.* **abandon,** forsake, give up, cast off, leave, turn one's back on, leave high and dry, leave in the lurch, throw over, betray, jilt, strand, leave stranded, maroon, neglect, shun, relinquish, renounce, abscond, defect, run away, make off, decamp, flee, fly, bolt, turn tail, go AWOL, depart, quit, escape, renege, apostatize, *inf.* walk/run out on. **Ant.**

maintain; stay; stand by (see stand).

deserted *adj.* **1 abandoned,** forsaken, cast off, betrayed, jilted, stranded, marooned, neglected, shunned, relinquished, renounced, forlorn, bereft. **2 abandoned,** forsaken, neglected, empty, vacant, uninhabited, unoccupied, untenanted, tenantless, unfrequented, secluded, isolated, desolate, lonely, solitary, godforsaken. **Ant.** crowded; populous.

deserter *n.* **absconder,** defector, runaway, fugitive, truant, escapee, derelict, renegade, turncoat, traitor, betrayer, apostate, derelict, *inf.* rat.

deserve *v.* **merit,** be worthy of, warrant, rate, justify, earn, be entitled to, have a right to, have a claim on, be qualified for.

deserving *adj.* **worthy,** meritorious, commendable, praiseworthy, laudable, admirable, estimable, creditable, virtuous, righteous, upright, good.

design *v.* **1 plan,** draw, draw plans of, sketch, outline, map out, plot, block out, delineate, draft, depict. **2 create,** invent, originate, think up, conceive, fashion, fabricate, hatch, innovate, *inf.* dream up. **3 intend,** aim, devise, contrive, plan, tailor, mean, destine.

▸ *n.* **1 plan,** blueprint, drawing, sketch, outline, map, plot, diagram, delineation, draft, depiction, scheme, model.
2 pattern, motif, style, arrangement, composition, makeup, constitution, configuration, organization, construction, shape, figure.
3 plan, enterprise, undertaking, scheme, plot, intrigue, expedient, stratagem, device, artifice.
4 intention, aim, purpose, plan, objective, goal, end, target, point, hope, desire, wish, dream, aspiration, ambition.

designer *n.* **1 creator,** inventor, deviser, fashioner, originator, author, producer, architect, artificer. **2 couturier,** fashion designer, creator, fashioner.

desire *v.* **1 wish for,** want, long/yearn for, crave, set one's heart on, hanker after, have a fancy for, fancy, be bent on, covet, aspire to, *inf.* have a yen for. **2 lust after,** burn for, *inf.* lech after, have the hots for. **3 request,** ask for, want.
▸ *n.* **1 wish,** want, fancy, inclination, preference, wanting, longing, yearning, craving, eagerness, enthusiasm, hankering, predilection, aspiration, proclivity, predisposition. **2 sexual attraction,** lust, lustfulness, sexual appetite, passion, carnal passion, concupiscence, libido, sensuality, sexuality, lasciviousness, lechery, salaciousness, libidinousness, prurience, *inf.* the hots.

desolate *adj.* **1 bare,** barren, bleak, dismal, desert, waste, wild.
2 deserted, uninhabited, unoccupied, depopulated, forsaken, abandoned, unpeopled, untenanted, unfrequented, unvisited, solitary, lonely, isolated. **3 sad,** unhappy, miserable, brokenhearted, wretched, downcast, cast down, dejected, downhearted, melancholy, gloomy, despondent, depressed, disconsolate, forlorn, cheerless, distressed, grieving, bereft. ***Ant.*** fertile; populous; joyful.

despair *n.* **hopelessness,** dejection, depression, desperation, disheartenment, discouragement, despondency, disconsolateness, defeatism, pessimism, resignedness, melancholy, gloom, melancholia, misery, wretchedness, distress, anguish. ***Ant.*** hope; joy.
▸ *v.* **lose hope,** give up hope, give up, lose heart, be discouraged, be despondent, be pessimistic, resign oneself, throw in the towel.

desperate *adj.* **1 reckless,** rash,

hasty, impetuous, foolhardy, audacious, daring, bold, madcap, wild, violent, frantic, mad, frenzied, lawless, risky, hazardous, daring, precipitate, harebrained, wild, imprudent, incautious, injudicious, indiscreet, ill-conceived. **2 urgent,** pressing, compelling, acute, critical, crucial, drastic, serious, grave, dire, extreme, great. **3 in great need of,** urgently requiring, in want of, lacking. **4 grave,** very bad, appalling, outrageous, intolerable, deplorable, lamentable. **5 despairing,** hopeless, wretched. **6 last-ditch,** last-resort, do-or-die.

despise *v.* **scorn,** look down on, spurn, shun, disdain, slight, undervalue, deride, scoff/jeer at, sneer at, mock, revile, hate, detest, loathe, abhor, abominate, execrate, *fml.* contemn.

despondent *adj.* **hopeless,** downcast, cast down, down, low, disheartened, discouraged, disconsolate, low-spirited, dispirited, downhearted, in despair, despairing, defeatist, blue, melancholy, gloomy, glum, morose, doleful, woebegone, miserable, wretched, distressed, sorrowful, sad. **Ant.** hopeful; cheerful; happy.

despotic *adj.* **absolute,** autocratic, dictatorial, tyrannical, oppressive, totalitarian, domineering, imperious, arrogant, high-handed, authoritarian, arbitrary, unconstitutional.

destination *n.* **journey's end,** landing place, point of disembarkation, terminus, end of the line, end, station, stop, stopping place, port of call.

destined *adj.* **1 bound for,** en route for, heading for/toward, directed/routed to, scheduled for. **2 designed,** intended, meant, set, set apart, designated, appointed, allotted, fated, ordained, preordained, foreordained, predestined, predetermined, doomed, foredoomed, certain, sure, bound, written in the cards.

destiny *n.* **fate,** fortune, lot, portion, cup, due, future, doom, divine decree, predestination, luck, chance, karma, kismet, the stars.

destitute *adj.* **1 poverty-stricken,** indigent, impoverished, penurious, impecunious, penniless, insolvent, beggarly, down-and-out, poor, needy, hard up, badly off, on the breadline, hard-pressed, distressed, pauperized, *inf.* up against it. **2 devoid of,** without, bereft of, deficient in, lacking, wanting, deprived of, empty, drained. **Ant.** prosperous; wealthy; rich.

destroy v. **1 demolish,** knock down, pull down, tear down, level, raze, fell, dismantle, wreck, smash, shatter, crash, blow up, blow to bits, explode, annihilate, wipe out, bomb, torpedo, ruin, spoil, devastate, lay waste, ravage, wreak havoc on, ransack, defeat, beat, conquer, vanquish, trounce, rout, drub, *inf.* lick, thrash. **2 terminate,** quash, quell, crush, stifle, subdue, squash, extinguish, extirpate, kill, kill off, slaughter, put to sleep, exterminate, slay, murder, assassinate, wipe out, massacre, liquidate, decimate. **Ant.** build; construct; create.

destruction n. **1 demolition,** knocking down, pulling down, tearing down, leveling, razing, dismantling, wrecking, smashing, blowing up, wiping out, annihilation, ruination, spoiling, devastation, laying waste, desolation, ransacking, ravaging, ruin, havoc, defeat, beating, conquest, vanquishing, trouncing, rout. **2 termination,** quashing, quelling, crushing, stifling, subduing, squashing, extinguishing, extirpation, extinction, killing, slaughter, slaying, murder, assassination, massacre.

destructive adj. **1 ruinous,** devastating, disastrous, catastrophic, calamitous, cataclysmic, ravaging, fatal, deadly, dangerous, lethal, damaging, pernicious, noxious, injurious, harmful, detrimental, deleterious, disadvantageous, hurtful, mischievous. **2 nonconstructive,** negative, unfavorable, adverse, antagonistic, hostile, unfriendly, contrary, discrediting, invalidating, derogatory, denigrating, disparaging, disapproving, discouraging, undermining.

desultory adj. **halfhearted,** haphazard, random, aimless, rambling, erratic, irregular, unmethodical, unsystematic, chaotic, inconsistent, inconstant, fitful, capricious. **Ant.** thorough; methodical; systematic.

detach v. **1 unfasten,** disconnect, unhitch, remove, separate, uncouple, loosen, free, sever, tear off, disengage, disjoin, disunite. **2 separate,** move off, dissociate, segregate, isolate, cut off, disconnect, divide. **Ant.** attach; join.

detached adj. **1 standing alone,** separate, unconnected, not attached. **2 unfastened,** disconnected, unhitched,

separate, loosened, free, severed.
3 dispassionate, aloof, indifferent, unconcerned, reserved, unemotional, impersonal, cool, remote.
4 objective, disinterested, unbiased, unprejudiced, impartial, nonpartisan, neutral, fair. *Ant.* passionate; biased; involved.

detail *n.* **1 item,** particular, fact, point, factor, element, circumstance, aspect, feature, respect, attribute, part, unit, component, member, accessory.
2 unimportant point, insignificant item, trivial fact. **3 detachment,** task force, patrol.
▸ *v.* **1 specify,** set forth, set out, list, enumerate, tabulate, catalog, spell out, delineate, relate, recount, narrate, recite, rehearse, describe, cite, point out, indicate, portray, depict, itemize, particularize, individualize.
2 appoint, assign, allocate, delegate, select, choose, name, nominate, elect, charge, commission, send.

detailed *adj.* **1 itemized,** particularized, full, comprehensive, thorough, exhaustive, all-inclusive, circumstantial, precise, exact, specific, particular, meticulous.
2 complex, involved, elaborate, complicated, intricate, convoluted, entangled.

detain *v.* **1 hold/keep back,** hold up, delay, keep, slow up/down, hinder, impede, check, retard, inhibit, stay. **2 put/keep in custody,** confine, imprison, lock up, incarcerate, impound, intern, restrain, hold.

detect *v.* **1 notice,** note, discern, perceive, make out, observe, spot, become aware of, recognize, distinguish, identify, catch, decry, sense, see, smell. **2 discover,** find out, turn up, uncover, bring to light, expose, unearth, reveal, unmask, unveil.

detective *n.* **investigator,** private investigator, FBI agent, police officer, *inf.* sleuth, tec, dick, private eye, private dick, tail, shadow, cop, gumshoe, G-man.

detention *n.* **1 holdup,** delay, slowing up, hindrance, impediment, check, retardation.
2 custody, confinement, imprisonment, incarceration, internment, restraint, detainment, duress, quarantine, arrest, punishment.

deter *v.* **put off,** prevent, stop, discourage, dissuade, talk out of, check, restrain, caution, frighten, intimidate, daunt, scare off, warn against, hold back, prohibit, hinder, impede, obstruct, block, inhibit. **Ant.** encourage; persuade.

deteriorate v. **1 get worse,** worsen, decline, degenerate, sink, slip, go downhill, slide, lapse, fail, fall, drop, ebb, wane, retrograde, retrogress, slump, depreciate, disintegrate, become dilapidated, crumble, fall apart, fall to pieces, fall down, break up, decay, decompose, go bad, *inf.* go to pot, go to hell, go to the dogs. **2 corrupt,** debase, defile, impair. **Ant.** improve; ameliorate.

determination n. **1 firmness,** firmness of purpose, resoluteness, steadfastness, tenacity, single-mindedness, resolve, drive, push, thrust, fortitude, dedication, backbone, stamina, mettle, strong will, persistence, perseverance, conviction, doggedness, stubbornness, obduracy, intransigence. **2 decision,** conclusion, judgment, verdict, opinion, decree, solution, result, arbitration, settlement, diagnosis, prognosis.

determine v. **1 settle,** fix, decide, agree on, establish, judge, arbitrate, decree, ordain, resolve, conclude, end, terminate, finish. **2 find out,** discover, learn, establish, calculate, work out, ascertain, check, verify, certify. **3 make up one's mind,** decide, resolve, choose, elect. **4 affect,** influence, act/work on, condition, regulate, decide, control, direct, rule, dictate, govern, form, shape, modify.

determined adj. **1 firm,** resolute, steadfast, tenacious, purposeful, single-minded, dedicated, strong-willed, mettlesome, plucky, persistent, persevering, dogged, unflinching, unwavering, stubborn, obdurate, intransigent, indomitable, inflexible. **2 bent,** intent, set. **Ant.** irresolute; hesitant.

deterrent n. **curb,** disincentive, discouragement, check, restraint, obstacle, hindrance, impediment, obstruction, block, barrier, inhibition. **Ant.** incitement; incentive.

detest v. **loathe,** abhor, hate, despise, abominate, execrate, feel aversion/hostility/animosity toward, feel disgust/distaste for, recoil/shrink from, feel repugnance toward. **Ant.** love; adore.

detestable adj. **loathsome,** abhorrent, hateful, odious, despicable, contemptible, abominable, reprehensible, execrable, distasteful, disgusting, repugnant, *inf.* beastly.

detract v. **distract,** divert, turn

away, deflect, avert, shift. *Ant.* increase; enhance; augment.

detrimental *adj.* **injurious,** harmful, damaging, hurtful, deleterious, destructive, pernicious, disadvantageous, adverse, unfavorable, inimical, prejudicial. *Ant.* advantageous; beneficial; favorable.

devastate *v.* **1 lay waste,** leave desolate, destroy, ruin, demolish, wreck, raze, level, annihilate, ravage, ransack, sack, despoil, spoil. **2 overcome,** overwhelm, shock, traumatize, take aback, confound, bewilder, nonplus, disconcert, discompose, discomfit, perturb, chagrin, *inf.* floor.

develop *v.* **1 grow,** evolve, mature, expand, enlarge, spread, advance, progress, prosper, flourish, make headway. **2 begin,** commence, start, set in motion, originate, invent, form, establish, institute, fashion, generate. **3 generate,** breed, propagate, rear, cultivate. **4 begin to have,** acquire, contract, pick up. **5 elaborate (on),** unfold, work out, enlarge on, expand (on), broaden, amplify, add to, augment, magnify, supplement, reinforce. **6 begin,** start, come about, follow, happen, result, ensue, break out. *Ant.* deteriorate; degenerate.

development *n.* **1 growth,** evolution, maturing, expansion, spread, progress, headway. **2 originating,** invention, forming, establishment, institution, generation. **3 generation,** breeding, propagation, rearing, cultivation. **4 elaboration,** unfolding, enlarging, expansion, augmentation. **5 event,** turn of events, occurrence, happening, circumstance, incident, situation, issue, outcome, upshot. **6 complex,** estate, structure, conglomeration.

deviate *v.* **diverge,** turn aside, step aside, depart from, digress, deflect, differ, vary, change, veer, swerve, bend, drift, stray, tack.

device *n.* **1 appliance,** gadget, implement, utensil, tool, piece of equipment/apparatus, apparatus, instrument, machine, contrivance, contraption, invention, *inf.* gizmo. **2 design,** plan, plot, scheme, ploy, project, stratagem, trick, artifice, ruse, dodge, stunt, gambit, shift, subterfuge, blind, maneuver, expedient, machination, strategy, improvisation, intrigue, conspiracy, fraud, wile, deception, imposture, sleight, humbug. **3 emblem,** symbol, insignia, crest, coat of arms, seal, badge, token, motif, design, mark, figure, motto, slogan, legend, logo, colophon, trademark.

devilish adj. **1 diabolic,** diabolical, demonic, demoniacal, fiendish, satanic, infernal, hellish.
2 wicked, evil, abominable, atrocious, detestable, villainous, sinister, accursed, damnable.

devious adj. **1 underhand,** underhanded, cunning, crafty, sly, wily, artful, guileful, scheming, designing, calculating, dishonest, deceitful, double-dealing, treacherous, misleading, subtle, insidious, surreptitious, furtive, secretive, inf. crooked.
2 indirect, roundabout, deviating, circuitous, tortuous, rambling, wandering, erratic, digressive, excursive. **Ant.** honest; candid; direct.

devise v. **concoct,** contrive, work out, plan, form, formulate, plot, scheme, project, invent, originate, create, compose, construct, frame, think/dream up, conceive, imagine, fabricate, hatch, put together, arrange, prepare, order.

devoted adj. **1 loyal,** faithful, true, true blue, staunch, steadfast, constant, committed, dedicated, devout, fond, loving, admiring, affectionate, caring, attentive, warm, ardent. **2 assigned,** allotted, set aside, dedicated.
3 dedicated, consecrated, blessed, sanctified, hallowed. **Ant.** disloyal; unfaithful; indifferent.

devotee n. **enthusiast,** fan, admirer, addict, follower, adherent, disciple, supporter, champion, advocate, votary, fanatic, zealot, inf. buff, freak.

devotion n. **1 loyalty,** faithfulness, fidelity, trueness, staunchness, steadfastness, constancy, commitment, adherence, allegiance, dedication, devoutness, fondness, love, admiration, affection, attentiveness, care, caring, warmness, closeness.
2 devoutness, piety, religiousness, spirituality, godliness, holiness, sanctity, saintliness. **3 ardor,** idolization, love, fondness, affection, infatuation, passion, fervor, admiration, eagerness, yearning. **Ant.** disloyalty; indifference; hatred.

devour v. **1 eat greedily/hungrily,** eat up, consume, swallow up, gulp down, gobble up, bolt, wolf down, guzzle, stuff down, cram in, gorge oneself on, feast on, inf. tuck into, pack away, dispatch, polish off, stuff one's face with, pig out on. **2 consume,** engulf, envelop, destroy, devastate, lay waste, demolish, wipe out, ruin, wreck, annihilate. **3 be absorbed in,** be engrossed in, take in, drink in/up, feast on, revel in, delight in, enjoy, relish, appreciate. **4 consume,** swallow up, engulf, swamp, overcome, overwhelm.

devout *adj.* **1 pious,** religious, reverent, churchgoing, godly, saintly, holy, prayerful, orthodox, pure, righteous. **2 sincere,** genuine, deep, profound, heartfelt, earnest, fervent, fervid, intense, ardent, vehement, passionate, zealous. *Ant.* impious; irreverent; insincere.

dexterity *n.* **1 manual dexterity,** deftness, adroitness, nimbleness of fingers, nimbleness, agility, skillfulness, skill, knack, adeptness, handiness, facility, proficiency, expertise, talent, artistry, craft, mastery, finesse, effortlessness, felicity. **2 mental dexterity/agility,** cleverness, shrewdness, smartness, astuteness, cunning, craft, sagacity, sharp-wittedness, acuteness, ingenuity, resourcefulness, inventiveness.

diagnose *v.* **identify,** determine, distinguish, recognize, detect, pinpoint, pronounce.

diagonal *adj.* **crossing,** crossways, crosswise, slanting, slanted, sloping, oblique, angled, cornerways, cornerwise.

diagram *n.* **line drawing,** drawing, sketch, draft, illustration, picture, representation, outline, delineation.

dialect *n.* **regional language,** language variety, vernacular, patois, nonstandard language, regionalism, localism, provincialism, *inf.* local lingo.

dialogue *n.* **1 conversation,** talk, tête-à-tête, chat, chitchat, gossip, communication, debate, argument, exchange of views, discourse, discussion, conference, converse, colloquy, interlocution, duologue, confabulation, parley, palaver, *inf.* powwow, confab, rap session. **2 spoken part,** script, lines.

diary *n.* **1 appointment/ engagement book,** personal organizer. **2 day-by-day account,** daily record, journal, chronicle, log, logbook, history, annals.

dictate *v.* **1 read out/out loud,** read aloud, speak, say, utter, recite. **2 prescribe,** lay down, impose, set down, order, command, decree, ordain, direct, pronounce, enjoin, promulgate. **3 give orders,** order about, lay down the law, impose one's will, boss about, domineer, *inf.* call the shots, throw one's weight around. ▸ *n.* **1 order,** command, decree, edict, ordinance, dictum, direction, bidding, charge, behest, pronouncement, mandate, requirement, enjoining, injunction, ultimatum, promulgation. **2 code,** guiding principle, law, rule, precept, dictum, axiom, maxim.

dictator *n.* **absolute ruler,** despot, autocrat, tyrant, oppressor.

dictatorial *adj.* **1 absolute,** unlimited, unrestricted, arbitrary, omnipotent, all-powerful, autocratic, totalitarian, authoritarian, despotic, tyrannical, autarchic. **2 tyrannical,** despotic, oppressive, iron-handed, imperious, overbearing, domineering, peremptory, high-handed, authoritarian, dogmatic, high and mighty, *inf.* bossy. **Ant.** democratic; liberal; limited; submissive.

diction *n.* **1 enunciation,** articulation, elocution, pronunciation, speech, intonation, inflection, delivery, fluency, rhetoric. **2 style,** language, phraseology, phrasing, wording, usage, vocabulary, terminology, expression, idiom.

dictum *n.* **1 utterance,** pronouncement, direction, injunction, assertion, statement, dictate, command, order, decree, edict. **2 saying,** maxim, axiom, proverb, adage, aphorism, saw, truism, platitude, cliché.

die *v.* **1 pass away,** pass on, lose one's life, depart this life, expire, decease, breathe one's last, meet one's end, lay down one's life, be no more, perish, go to one's last resting place, *inf.* give up the ghost, kick the bucket, push up the daisies, bite the dust, snuff it, croak, turn up one's toes, cash in one's chips, buy the farm. **2 come to an end,** end, vanish, disappear, pass, fade, fall away, dwindle, melt away, dissolve, subside, decline, sink, lapse, ebb, wane, wilt, wither, evanesce. **3 stop,** halt, fail, break down, peter out, fizzle out, run down, fade away, lose power. **4 collapse with,** be overcome with, be overwhelmed/overpowered by, succumb to. **5 be eager,** be desperate, long. **Ant.** live; exist; start.

diehard *adj.* **ultraconservative,** conservative, reactionary, dyed in the wool, intransigent, inflexible, immovable, unchanging, uncompromising, unyielding, indomitable, adamant, rigid.

differ *v.* **1 be different,** be unlike, be dissimilar, be distinguishable, vary, diverge. **2 disagree,** fail to agree, dissent, be at variance, be in dispute/opposition, oppose, take issue, conflict, clash, quarrel, argue, wrangle, quibble, squabble, altercate.

difference *n.* **1 dissimilarity,** unlikeness, dissimilitude, contrast, distinction, distinctness, differentiation, variance, variation, divergence, deviation, contrariety, antithesis, contradiction, contradistinction, nonconformity, disparity, imbalance, incongruity.
2 distinction, peculiarity, oddity, idiosyncrasy, singularity, eccentricity, individuality.
3 difference of opinion, disagreement, dispute, disputation, argument, debate, misunderstanding, quarrel, row, wrangle, set-to, tiff, altercation, contretemps, clash, controversy, feud, vendetta. **4 balance,** remainder, rest, residue, residuum, excess. *Ant.* similarity; likeness; affinity.

different *adj.* **1 unlike,** dissimilar, nonidentical, contrasting, diverse, divergent, deviating, disparate, incompatible, inconsistent, opposed, at variance, at odds, clashing, conflicting, discrepant, changed, altered, modified, transformed, metamorphosed, separate, other, not the same, nonidentical, distinct, individual, discrete. **2 various,** several, many, numerous, some, sundry, certain, assorted, varied, miscellaneous, diverse, manifold, multifarious, motley, variegated. **3 unusual,** out of the ordinary, uncommon, distinctive, rare, unique, novel, special, singular, remarkable, extraordinary, noteworthy, unconventional, atypical, odd, strange, bizarre, *inf.* something else. *Ant.* similar; alike; same; ordinary.

difficult *adj.* **1 hard,** strenuous, arduous, laborious, demanding, formidable, tough, onerous, burdensome, exhausting, tiring, wearisome, backbreaking, painful, oppressive, *inf.* no picnic.
2 hard, complicated, complex, involved, intricate, puzzling, problematic, baffling, perplexing, knotty, thorny, ticklish, delicate, obscure, abstract, abstruse, recondite, enigmatic, profound, deep. **3 troublesome,** tiresome, demanding, unmanageable, intractable, perverse, recalcitrant, obstreperous, refractory, fractious, unaccommodating, uncooperative, uncompliant, unamenable. **4 hard to please/satisfy,** fussy, particular, fastidious, perfectionist, critical, hypercritical, finicky.
5 inconvenient, ill-timed, disadvantageous, unfavorable.
6 hard, straitened, hard-pressed, bad, tough, grim, dark. *Ant.* easy; simple; accommodating.

difficulty *n.* **1 difficultness,** hardness, strenousness, arduousness, laboriousness, toughness, struggling, awkwardness, labor, strain, struggle. **2 difficultness,** hardness, complicatedness, complexity, intricacy, perplexity, knottiness, delicacy, obscurity, abstruseness. **3 complication,** problem, snag, hitch, hindrance, obstacle, pitfall, hurdle, impediment, obstruction, barrier. **4 protest,** objection, complaint, gripe, demur, cavil. **5 predicament,** quandary, dilemma, plight, distress, embarrassment, trouble, hot/deep water, straits, *inf.* fix, jam, spot, scrape. **6 hardship,** trial, tribulation, ordeal, exigency. **Ant.** ease.

diffident *adj.* **shy,** bashful, modest, sheepish, unconfident, unassertive, timid, timorous, apprehensive, fearful, shrinking, reserved, withdrawn, hesitant, reluctant, doubtful, unsure, insecure, distrustful, suspicious, unobtrusive, self-effacing, unassuming, humble, meek. **Ant.** bold; assertive.

diffuse *adj.* **1 diffused,** spread out, scattered, dispersed, not concentrated. **2 verbose,** wordy, prolix, long-winded, copious, profuse, discursive, rambling, wandering, meandering, digressive, circuitous, roundabout, circumlocutory, waffling, loose, vague. **Ant.** concentrated; concise; succinct.
▸ *v.* **spread around,** send out, scatter, disperse, disseminate, dissipate, dispel, distribute, dispense, circulate, propagate, broadcast, promulgate, effuse.

dig *v.* **1 break up soil/ground,** work, break up, loosen up, turn over, spade, delve, till, cultivate, harrow, plow, dig out, excavate, quarry, hollow out, scoop out, gouge, tunnel, burrow, mine, channel, unearth, dig up. **2 poke,** prod, jab, thrust, drive, push, punch. **3 delve,** search, probe, investigate, research. **4 like,** love, enjoy, appreciate. **5 understand,** comprehend, follow, grasp, make out, *inf.* get.
▸ *n.* **1 poke,** prod, jab, thrust, push, punch. **2 cutting remark,** gibe, jeer, taunt, sneer, insult, slur, quip, insinuation, *inf.* wisecrack, crack.

digest *v.* **1 assimilate,** absorb, break down, dissolve, macerate. **2 assimilate,** absorb, take in, understand, comprehend, grasp, master, consider, think about, contemplate, mull over, weigh up, reflect on, ponder, meditate on, study. **3 shorten,** reduce, condense, abridge, compress, compact, summarize, précis.

▶ *n.* **summary,** synopsis, abstract, précis, résumé, outline, abridgment, epitome, review, compendium.

dignified *adj.* **stately,** noble, solemn, grave, formal, decorous, reserved, ceremonious, courtly, majestic, august, lofty, exalted, regal, lordly, imposing, impressive, grand.

dignitary *n.* **public figure,** notable, notability, worthy, personage, luminary, VIP, pillar of society, leading light, celebrity, big name, somebody, star, lion, *inf.* bigwig, top brass, big gun, big shot, big wheel, celeb.

dignity *n.* **1 stateliness,** nobleness, nobility, solemnity, gravity, formality, decorum, propriety, reserve, ceremoniousness, courtliness, majesty, augustness, loftiness, exaltedness, regalness, regality, lordliness, impressiveness, grandeur. **2 worthiness,** honorability, nobility, excellence, respectability, worth, merit, virtue. **3 high rank,** high standing, high station, status, elevation, eminence, honor, glory, greatness, importance. **4 pride,** self-esteem, self-conceit, self-regard, self-importance, self-

respect. **Ant.** informality; dishonor; degradation.

digress *v.* **get off the subject,** stray from the point, deviate/deflect from the topic, go off on a tangent, diverge, turn aside, depart, drift, ramble, wander, meander.

dilapidated *adj.* **rundown,** broken-down, tumbledown, ramshackle, in ruins, ruined, falling to pieces, falling apart, in disrepair, shabby, battered, rickety, shaky, crumbling, decayed, decaying, decrepit, worn-out, neglected, uncared-for.

dilate *v.* **1 enlarge,** widen, expand. **2 expand,** expound, expatiate, elaborate. **Ant.** narrow; contract.

dilemma *n.* **difficult choice,** devil and the deep blue sea, Catch-22, vicious circle, quandary, predicament, plight, difficulty, tight corner/spot, problem, puzzle, mess, muddle, trouble, perplexity, confusion, embarrassment.

diligent *adj.* **assiduous,** industrious, conscientious, hardworking, painstaking, meticulous, thorough, careful, attentive, heedful, intent, earnest, studious, constant, persevering, sedulous, persistent, tenacious, zealous, active, busy, untiring, tireless, indefatigable, dogged, plodding, slogging, laborious. *Ant.* lazy; careless; indifferent.

dilute *v.* **weaken,** thin, thin out, water down, cut, adulterate, attenuate, reduce, diminish, decrease, lessen, mitigate, temper. *Ant.* concentrate; thicken; intensify.

dim *adj.* **1 faint,** weak, feeble, pale, dull, dingy, lusterless, muted, dark, darkish, gray, overcast, leaden, gloomy, somber, dusky, lowering, cloudy, hazy, misty, foggy, crepuscular, tenebrous, dark, darkened, badly lit, poorly lit, dismal. **2 vague,** ill-defined, indistinct, unclear, shadowy, blurred, blurry, fuzzy, imperceptible, nebulous, obscured, bleared, bleary, obfuscated, indistinct, hazy, confused, shadowy, imperfect, obscure, remote. **3 stupid,** thick, dense, slow-witted, slow, dull, doltish, limited, obtuse, *inf.* dumb, slow on the uptake. **4 gloomy,** somber, unpromising, unfavorable, discouraging, disheartening, depressing, dispiriting. *Ant.* bright; distinct; clever.
▸ *v.* **turn down,** lower, grow dim, fade, grow faint/feeble, dull, pale, blur, grow dark, darken, cloud over, grow leaden, become blurred/confused. *Ant.* brighten.

dimension *n.* **1 measured extent,** extent, length, width, breadth, depth, area, size, volume, capacity, bulk, proportions. **2 aspect,** side, feature, facet, element.

diminish *v.* **1 lessen,** grow less, decrease, reduce, shrink, contract, abate, grow weak/weaker, lower, decrease, reduce, curtail, cut, contract, narrow, constrict, truncate, retrench, subside, ebb, recede, wane, dwindle, slacken, die/fall away, fade, decline, die/peter out. **2 belittle,** disparage, denigrate, depreciate, deprecate, derogate, devalue, demean, detract from, cheapen, defame, vilify. *Ant.* increase; grow; boost.

diminutive *adj.* **small,** little, tiny, petite, slight, elfin, minute, miniature, mini, small-scale, compact, microscopic, midget, undersized, dwarfish, pygmy, Lilliputian, *inf.* wee, baby. *Ant.* enormous; gigantic.

din *n.* **loud noise,** uproar, row, racket, commotion, hullabaloo, hubbub, tumult, clangor, outcry, brouhaha, crash, clatter, clash, shouting, yelling, clamor, noise, pandemonium, bedlam, babel. *Ant.* silence; hush.

dingy *adj.* **dark,** dull, dim, gloomy, drab, dismal, dreary, cheerless, dusky, somber, murky, hazy, smoggy, smoky, sooty, dirty, discolored, grimy, soiled, faded, shabby, worn, seedy, rundown, tacky. **Ant.** bright; well-lit; clean.

dip *v.* **1 immerse,** submerge, plunge, duck, dunk, lower, sink, souse, douse, soak, drench, steep, bathe, rinse. **2 sink,** set, go/drop down, descend, fade, disappear, subside. **3 fall,** go down, drop, drop/fall off, decrease, decline, slump. **4 slope down,** slope, descend, go down, fall, sink, decline, slant down, droop, sag. **5 scoop up,** scoop, spoon, ladle. **Ant.** rise; ascend.

▸ *n.* **1 immersion,** plunge, ducking, dunking, sousing, dousing, soaking, drenching. **2 swim,** dive, plunge. **3 fall,** falling-off, drop, dropping-off, decrease, decline, lowering, slump. **4 slope,** incline, decline, slant, descent, hollow, concavity, depression, basin.

diplomacy *n.* **1 statesmanship,** statecraft, international relations/politics, negotiations. **2 tactfulness,** subtlety, discretion, judiciousness, prudence, delicacy, sensitivity, finesse, savoir faire, politeness, cleverness, artfulness, cunning, tact, care, skill.

diplomatic *adj.* **1 ambassadorial,** consular, foreign office. **2 tactful,** subtle, discreet, judicious, prudent, careful, delicate, sensitive, polite, politic, clever, skillful, artful. **Ant.** indiscreet; tactless.

dire *adj.* **1 terrible,** dreadful, appalling, frightful, awful, horrible, atrocious, grim, cruel, grievous, disastrous, ruinous, miserable, wretched, woeful, calamitous, catastrophic, cataclysmic, distressing, harrowing, alarming, unspeakable, shocking, outrageous. **2 ominous,** sinister, portentous, gloomy, gloom-and-doom, grim, dreadful, dismal, unpropitious, inauspicious, unfavorable, pessimistic. **3 urgent,** desperate, drastic, pressing, crying, vital, grave, critical, crucial, extreme, compelling, exigent. **Ant.** wonderful; delightful.

direct *v.* **1 administer,** manage, be in charge/control/command of, lead, run, command, control, govern, conduct, handle, preside over, rule, supervise, superintend, oversee, guide, mastermind, regulate, orchestrate, engineer, dispose, dominate, domineer, order, give orders to, instruct, charge, bid, dictate, adjure, enjoin, *inf.* be the boss of, run the show, call the shots. **2 give directions to,** show/point/indicate

the way, guide, steer, lead, conduct, accompany, usher, escort, navigate, pilot.
▸ *adj.* **1 straight,** undeviating, unswerving, uncircuitous, shortest. **2 straight through,** through, nonstop, unbroken, uninterrupted. **3 immediate,** firsthand, personal, face-to-face, head-on, noninterventional. **4 frank,** blunt, straightforward, straight, straight to the point, explicit, clear, plain, unequivocal, unambiguous, honest, candid, open, sincere, plainspoken, outspoken, forthright, downright, point blank, matter-of-fact, categorical. **5 exact,** absolute, complete, downright, thorough, diametrical. **6 exact,** precise, word for word, verbatim, accurate, correct. *Ant.* indirect; evasive; ambiguous.

directive *n.* **direction,** command, order, instruction, charge, bidding, injunction, ruling, regulation, dictate, decree, edict, notice, ordinance, enjoinment, prescription, mandate, fiat.

director *n.* **administrator,** controller, manager, executive, chairman, chairwoman, chairperson, chair, head, chief, principal, leader, governor, president, superintendent, supervisor, overseer, organizer, producer, *inf.* boss, kingpin, top dog, honcho.

dirge *n.* **elegy,** lament, funeral song/chant, burial hymn, dead march, requiem, keen, threnody.

dirt *n.* **1 grime,** dust, soot, smut, muck, mud, filth, mire, sludge, slime, ooze, waste, dross, pollution, smudge, stain, tarnish, *inf.* crud, yuck, grunge. **2 earth,** soil, loam, clay, silt. **3 obscenity,** indecency, smut, sordidness, coarseness, bawdiness, ribaldry, salaciousness, lewdness, pornography, *inf.* sleaze, sleaziness. **4 scandal,** gossip, talk, rumor, slander, libel, revelations.

dirty *adj.* **1 unclean,** soiled, grimy, begrimed, grubby, messy, dusty, sooty, mucky, muddy, filthy, bedraggled, slimy, polluted, sullied, foul, stained, spotted, smudged, tarnished, defiled, nasty, *inf.* cruddy, yucky, grungy. **2 blue,** obscene, indecent, vulgar, smutty, coarse, bawdy, suggestive, ribald, salacious, risqué, prurient, lewd, lascivious, licentious, pornographic, off color, *inf.* sleazy. **3 nasty,** unpleasant, mean, base, low, vile, contemptible, despicable, cowardly, ignominious, sordid, beggarly, squalid. **4 unsporting,** unfair, dishonorable, unscrupulous, dishonest, crooked, illegal,

deceitful, fraudulent, double-dealing, corrupt, treacherous.
5 malevolent, smoldering, resentful, bitter, angry, indignant, annoyed, peeved, offended.
6 unpleasant, nasty, foul, stormy, squally, gusty, rainy, misty, gloomy, murky, overcast. **7 nasty,** unkind, scandalous, defamatory, slanderous, libelous. **Ant.** clean; honorable; pleasant.

▸ *v.* **soil,** stain, muddy, begrime, blacken, mess up, spatter, smudge, smear, spot, splash, spoil, sully, pollute, foul, defile, besmirch.

disability *n.* **1 impairment,** disablement, infirmity, defect, handicap, disorder, affliction, ailment, complaint, illness, malady. **2 incapacity,** infirmity, unfitness, weakness, powerlessness, impotence, incapability, inability, incompetence, ineptitude, disqualification.

disable *v.* **1 incapacitate,** impair, damage, put out of action, debilitate, indispose, weaken, enfeeble, make unfit, render infirm, cripple, lame, handicap, immobilize, hamstring, paralyze, prostrate. **2 render inoperative,** make ineffective, paralyze, make harmless.

disadvantage *n.* **1 drawback,** snag, downside, weak spot/point, weakness, flaw, defect, fault, handicap, trouble, liability, nuisance, hindrance, obstacle, impediment, *inf.* minus, fly in the ointment. **2 deprivation,** privation, hardship, lack, burden. **3 disservice,** detriment, prejudice, harm, damage, loss, injury, hurt, mischief. **Ant.** advantage; benefit; gain.

disaffected *adj.* **alienated,** estranged, unfriendly, disunited, dissatisfied, disgruntled, discontented, disloyal, rebellious, mutinous, seditious, up in arms, hostile, antagonistic.

disagree *v.* **1 differ,** fail to agree, dissent, stand opposed, be in dispute/contention, be at variance/odds, diverge, disaccord. **2 differ,** be dissimilar, be unlike, be different, vary, conflict, clash, contrast, diverge, not correspond, not accord, be discordant. **3 quarrel,** argue, bicker, wrangle, squabble, spar, dispute, debate, take issue with, altercate, *inf.* fall out, have words.

disagreeable *adj.* **1 unpleasant,** displeasing, nasty, horrible, dreadful, hateful, detestable, abominable, odious, objectionable, offensive, obnoxious, repugnant, repulsive, repellent, revolting, disgusting, distasteful, nauseating, unsavory, unpalatable. **2 bad-tempered,** ill-natured, unfriendly, unpleasant, difficult, nasty, cross, irritable, rude, surly, discourteous, impolite, churlish, peevish, brusque, abrupt, disobliging, contrary.

disallow *v.* **reject,** say no to, refuse, dismiss, rebuff, repel, repulse, repudiate, ban, bar, debar, forbid, prohibit, veto, embargo, proscribe, negative, cancel, disclaim, disown, abjure, disavow.

disappear *v.* **1 pass from sight,** cease to be visible, vanish from sight, vanish, be lost to view/sight, recede, recede from view, fade, fade/melt away, withdraw, depart, retire, go, pass, flee, retreat, ebb, wane, dematerialize, evanesce, evaporate, *inf.* vamoose. **2 die out,** die, cease to be/exist, be no more, come to an end, end, vanish, pass away, expire, perish, become extinct, fade, melt away, leave no trace, pass into oblivion. *Ant.* appear; emerge.

disappoint *v.* **1 let down,** fail, dishearten, depress, dispirit, upset, sadden, dash the hopes of, chagrin, dismay, disgruntle, disenchant, disillusion, dissatisfy, vex. **2 thwart,** frustrate, foil, defeat, baffle, hinder, obstruct, hamper, impede, interfere with. *Ant.* cheer; delight; fulfill.

disappointed *adj.* **1 upset,** saddened, let down, disheartened, downhearted, cast down, downcast, depressed, dispirited, despondent, distressed, chagrined, disgruntled, disenchanted, disillusioned, discontented, dissatisfied, vexed. **2 thwarted,** frustrated, foiled, defeated, failed, baffled.

disapproval *n.* **disapprobation,** disfavor, displeasure, dislike, dissatisfaction, criticism, censure, blame, condemnation, denunciation, objection, exception, reproach, rebuke, reproof, remonstration, disparagement, deprecation.

disapprove *v.* **1 have/express a poor opinion of,** dislike, find unacceptable, be against, be dissatisfied/displeased with, deplore, criticize, frown on, take a dim view of, look askance at, censure, blame, condemn, denounce, object to, take exception to, reproach, rebuke, reprove, remonstrate against, disparage, deprecate, *inf.* look down one's nose at. **2 turn down,** reject, veto, disallow, set aside, *inf.* give the thumbs down to.

disarray *n.* **disorder,** confusion, upset, disorderliness, disorganization, discomposure, unsettledness, disunity, indiscipline, unruliness, untidiness, chaos, dishevelment, mess, muddle, clutter, jumble, mix-up, tangle, shambles.

disaster *n.* **1 catastrophe,** calamity, cataclysm, tragedy, act of God, accident, mishap, misadventure, mischance, stroke of ill-luck, setback, reverse/ reversal of fortune, reversal, heavy blow, shock, buffet, adversity, trouble, misfortune, ruin, ruination. **2 failure,** fiasco, *inf.* flop, bomb, dud, washout. **Ant.** blessing; godsend; success.

disastrous *adj.* **catastrophic,** calamitous, cataclysmic, tragic, adverse, devastating, ravaging, dire, terrible, shocking, appalling, dreadful, black, harmful, injurious, detrimental, ruinous, unfortunate, unlucky, hapless, ill-fated, ill-starred.

disbelieve *v.* **not believe,** not credit, give no credence to, be incredulous, be unconvinced, discredit, discount, not accept, reject, repudiate, distrust, mistrust, question, challenge, scoff at.

discard *v.* **throw away/out,** get rid of, dispose of, toss out, jettison, scrap, dispense with, cast aside, reject, repudiate, abandon, relinquish, forsake, drop, have done with, shed, *inf.* dump, ditch. **Ant.** keep; retain.

discern *v.* **see,** notice, observe, perceive, make out, distinguish, detect, descry, recognize, determine, differentiate. **Ant.** overlook; miss.

discernible *adj.* **visible,** noticeable, observable, perceptible, perceivable, distinguishable, detectable, recognizable, apparent, obvious, clear, manifest, conspicuous, patent.

discerning *adj.* **discriminating,** astute, shrewd, ingenious, clever, intelligent, perceptive, sharp, quick, perspicacious, penetrating, critical, percipient, judicious, sensitive, subtle, prudent, sound, wise, aware, knowing, sagacious, sapient.

discharge *v.* **1 set free,** free, let go, release, liberate, acquit, clear, absolve, pardon, exonerate, reprieve, exculpate, emancipate, manumit. **2 dismiss,** remove, get rid of, discard, eject, oust, expel, cashier, *inf.* sack, fire, ax, send packing, give the ax/sack/boot to, boot out. **3 fire,** shoot, let/set off, explode, detonate. **4 exude,** ooze, excrete, give off, leak, dispense, emit, send out, send/pour forth, eject, release, gush, void. **5 carry**

out, perform, do, accomplish, achieve, fulfill, execute, observe, abide by. **6 unload,** disburden, remove, unburden, off-load, relieve. **7 pay,** settle, clear, honor, meet, liquidate, satisfy, *inf.* square. ***Ant.*** imprison; engage; neglect.

▸ *n.* **1 release,** liberation, acquittal, clearance, absolution, pardon, exoneration, reprieve, exculpation, manumission. **2 dismissal,** removal, ejection, ousting, expulsion, cashiering, *inf.* firing, axing, sacking. **3 discharging,** firing, shooting, shot, explosion, detonation, blast, burst, pop, report, volley, salvo, fusillade. **4 exuding,** oozing, excretion, emission, ejection, release, emptying, voiding, voidance. **5 excretion,** exudate, emission, flow, secretion, ooze, suppuration, pus, seepage. **6 carrying out,** performing, doing, accomplishment, achievement, fulfillment, execution, observance, performance. **7 payment,** settlement, clearance, honoring, meeting.

disciple *n.* **apostle,** follower, pupil, student, believer, adherent, devotee, votary, upholder, supporter, advocate, proponent, satellite, partisan.

disciplinarian *n.* **martinet,** authoritarian, taskmaster, tyrant, despot.

discipline *n.* **1 training,** drilling, exercise, regimen, routine, method, instruction, coaching, teaching, indoctrination, inculcation, systematization. **2 control,** self-control, self-restraint, strictness, orderliness, regulation, direction, government, restriction, limitation, restraint, check, curb. **3 punishment,** chastisement, castigation, correction, penalty, reprimand, rebuke, reproof. **4 field of study,** field, branch of knowledge, course of study, course, area, subject, specialist subject, speciality, specialty.

▸ *v.* **1 train,** drill, break in, exercise, instruct, coach, teach, educate, tutor, prepare, ground, indoctrinate, inculcate, inure, toughen. **2 control,** restrain, regulate, govern, restrict, limit, check, curb. **3 punish,** chastise, castigate, correct, penalize, reprimand, rebuke, reprove.

disclaim *v.* **deny,** renounce, repudiate, reject, refuse, decline, disown, cast off, discard, abandon, wash one's hands of, turn one's back on, abjure, forswear, disavow, disaffirm.

disclose *v.* **1 make known,** reveal, divulge, tell, impart, communicate, make public, broadcast, publish, release, unveil, leak, let slip, blurt out, blab, admit, confess, avow, *inf.* spill the beans about, let the cat out of the bag about, blow the lid off, squeal about. **2 reveal,** show, exhibit, expose, uncover, lay bare, unveil, bring to light. *Ant.* conceal; hide.

discolor *v.* **stain,** soil, mark, streak, spot, tarnish, fade, bleach, wash out.

discomfort *n.* **1 ache,** pain, soreness, twinge, hurt, irritation, pang, throb, smart, malaise. **2 unease,** trouble, unpleasantness, hardship, distress. **3 embarrassment,** anxiety, disconcertment, unease, uneasiness, discomfiture, discomposure, disquietude. **4 inconvenience,** difficulty, trouble, bother, nuisance, vexation, drawback, disadvantage, problem, trial, tribulation. ▸ *v.* **make uncomfortable/uneasy,** embarrass, disconcert, upset, ruffle, discompose, discomfit.

disconcert *v.* **1 unsettle,** shake, disturb, perturb, daunt, take aback, abash, nonplus, confuse, bewilder, fluster, ruffle, upset, agitate, worry, embarrass, discomfit, discompose, perplex, confound, distract, throw off

balance, put off one's stroke, *inf.* throw, faze, rattle. **2 thwart,** frustrate, foil, obstruct, hinder, hamper, upset, undo.

disconnect *v.* **1 undo,** cut off, sever, uncouple, disengage, detach, unhook, unhitch, unlink, disjoin, disunite, separate, divide, part, split up, dissociate, disentangle. **2 discontinue,** interrupt, suspend, halt, stop. *Ant.* connect; engage; tie; bind.

disconnected *adj.*
1 unconnected, separate, separated, unattached, dissociated. **2 disjointed,** garbled, confused, jumbled, mixed-up, incoherent, unintelligible, rambling, wandering, disordered, illogical, irrational, uncoordinated.

discontented *adj.* **dissatisfied,** fed up, restless, impatient, fretful, complaining, displeased, disgruntled, querulous, unhappy, miserable, wretched, envious, regretful, disaffected, exasperated, irritated, chagrined, annoyed, peeved, piqued, *vulg.* pissed off, p.o.'d. *Ant.* content; satisfied; pleased.

discord *n.* **1 disagreement,** difference of opinion, dissension, dispute, argument, conflict, friction, contention, strife, opposition, hostility, wrangling, clashing, quarreling, falling-out, war, division, incompatibility, variance, disunity, rupture. **2 lack of harmony,** disharmony, dissonance, cacophony, harshness, jarring, jangling, din, racket. *Ant.* accord; concord; harmony.

discordant *adj.* **1 disagreeing,** differing, contradictory, contrary, dissenting, disputatious, conflicting, at variance, at odds, contentious, opposing, hostile, clashing, divergent, incompatible, incongruous. **2 inharmonious,** harsh, strident, shrill, grating, jarring, jangling, dissonant, cacophonous. *Ant.* compatible; harmonious; dulcet.

discount *v.* **1 disregard,** ignore, pass over, overlook, pay no attention to, take no notice of, brush off, gloss over. **2 deduct,** take off, rebate, *inf.* knock off. **3 reduce,** lower, lessen, mark down, reduce, put on sale, *inf.* knock down. *Ant.* note; increase; mark up (see mark).
▸ *n.* **1 markdown,** deduction, price cut, cut, rebate, concession. **2 cut price,** reduction.

discourage *v.* **1 dishearten,** dispirit, deject, cast down, depress, demoralize, disappoint, daunt, put off, intimidate, cow, unnerve. **2 put off,** dissuade, deter, talk out of, advise against, urge against, caution against, restrain, inhibit, divert from, sidetrack from. **3 oppose,** disapprove of, repress, deprecate, put a damper on, throw cold water on. **4 prevent,** check, curb, hinder, obstruct, suppress, inhibit. *Ant.* encourage; persuade.

discouragement *n.*
1 dispiritedness, downheartedness, dejection, depression, demoralization, disappointment, despondency, hopelessness, lack of confidence, pessimism, despair, gloom, melancholy, low spirits.
2 opposition, disapproval, repression, deprecation.
3 deterrent, hindrance, obstacle, impediment, barrier, curb, check, damper, restraint, constraint, restriction, disincentive, setback, rebuff, *inf.* put-down.

discourse *n.* **1 conversation,** talk, dialogue, communication, discussion, conference, colloquy, converse, verbal exchange, chat, chitchat, confabulation, *inf.* confab. **2 address,** speech, lecture, oration, sermon, homily, essay, treatise, dissertation, paper, study.
▸ *v.* **1 converse,** talk, discuss, debate, confer, speak, chat, *inf.* have a confab, chew the fat, rap.

2 give an address/talk, deliver a speech/lecture, lecture, sermonize, preach, hold forth, write at length, *inf.* spout.

discover *v.* **1 find,** come across/upon, stumble upon, chance upon, light upon, locate, bring to light, uncover, unearth, turn up, *inf.* dig up. **2 find out,** come to know, learn, realize, detect, determine, ascertain, recognize, see, spot, notice, perceive, reveal, disclose, *inf.* get wise to the fact. **3 invent,** originate, devise, pioneer, design, contrive, conceive of. **4 explore,** pioneer. *Ant.* conceal; hide.

discoverer *n.* founder, explorer, pioneer, inventor, originator, deviser, designer, initiator.

discovery *n.* **1 finding,** locating, location, uncovering. **2 finding out,** learning, realization, detection, determination, recognition, revelation, disclosure. **3 invention,** origination, devising, pioneering, introduction. **4 find,** invention, breakthrough, innovation, lucky strike, bonanza, findings. **5 exploration,** pioneering, research.

discredit *v.* **1 detract from,** bring into disrepute, defame, slur, slander, cast aspersions on, vilify, disparage, deprecate, denigrate, devalue, devaluate, degrade, belittle, decry, dishonor, disgrace, censure. **2 disprove,** invalidate, refute, dispute, challenge, destroy the credibility of, shake one's faith in, reject, deny. **3 disbelieve,** give no credence to, discount, doubt, distrust, mistrust.

▶ *n.* **1 disrepute,** ill repute, infamy, disgrace, dishonor, shame, humiliation, ignominy, stigma, harm, damage, censure, blame, reproach, scandal, odium. **2 disbelief,** lack of credence, incredulity, question, doubt, distrust, mistrust, skepticism, suspicion.

discreet *adj.* careful, cautious, prudent, judicious, circumspect, wary, guarded, chary, tactful, reserved, diplomatic, considerate, politic, strategic, wise, sensible, sagacious. *Ant.* indiscreet; rash; tactless.

discrepancy *n.* inconsistency, variance, variation, disparity, deviation, divergence, incongruity, difference, disagreement, dissimilarity, contrariety, conflict, discordance, gap.

discretionary *adj.* optional, elective, open, open to choice, nonmandatory, unrestricted, voluntary, volitional.

discriminate *v.* **1 distinguish,**

make/draw a distinction, differentiate, tell the difference, make a difference, discern, separate, separate the men from the boys, separate the wheat from the chaff, segregate. **2 be biased/prejudiced against/toward,** treat differently, disfavor/favor, be intolerant of.

discriminating *adj.*
1 discerning, perceptive, astute, shrewd, selective, particular, fastidious, critical, keen, tasteful, refined, sensitive, cultivated, cultured, artistic, aesthetic.
2 distinguishing, differentiating, prejudiced.

discrimination *n.*
1 discernment, perception, penetration, perspicacity, acumen, astuteness, shrewdness, selectivity, fastidiousness, judgment, keenness, taste, refinement, sensitivity, insight, subtlety, cultivation, culture, artistry, aestheticism. **2 prejudice,** bias, unfairness, inequity, intolerance, bigotry, narrow-mindedness, favoritism, segregation, positive discrimination.

discuss *v.* **talk over,** talk/chat about, converse about, confer about, debate, exchange views on/about, deliberate, consider, go into, thrash out, examine, review, study, scrutinize, analyze, weigh up, sift, ventilate, argue, dispute, *inf.* kick around.

discussion *n.* **talk,** conversation, dialogue, chat, conference, debate, discourse, exchange of views, symposium, seminar, consultation, deliberation, parley, examination, review, study, scrutiny, analysis, ventilation, argument, dispute, *inf.* confab.

disdainful *adj.* **scornful,** contemptuous, sneering, derisive, slighting, disparaging, arrogant, proud, supercilious, haughty, superior, lordly, pompous, snobbish, insolent, aloof, indifferent, *inf.* high and mighty, hoity-toity.

disease *n.* **illness,** sickness, disorder, complaint, malady, ailment, affliction, condition, indisposition, infirmity, disability, abnormality, infection, contagion, pestilence, plague, canker, blight. *Ant.* health.

diseased *adj.* **unhealthy,** ill, ailing, sick, sickly, unwell, unsound, unwholesome, infirm, infected, abnormal, blighted, rotten, cankerous.

disembark *v.* **land,** arrive, get off, step off, alight, go ashore, deplane, detrain, *inf.* pile out.

disfigure *v.* **deface,** deform, mutilate, blemish, flaw, scar, make ugly, uglify, spoil, mar, damage, injure, maim, vandalize, ruin. *Ant.* adorn; enhance.

disgrace *n.* **1 shame,** humiliation, dishonor, scandal, degradation, ignominy, infamy, discredit, debasement, vitiation. **2 disfavor,** discredit, disrepute, loss of face, disrespect, disapproval, disapprobation, disesteem, contempt. **3 blot,** stain, blemish, black mark, scandal, smear, smirch, stigma, slur, dishonor, aspersion, defamation. *Ant.* respect; approval.

▸ *v.* **1 bring disgrace to,** bring shame upon, shame, humiliate, bring dishonor to, dishonor, discredit, degrade, debase, sully, besmirch, taint, stain, slur, stigmatize, brand, drag through the mud. **2 discredit,** reproach, censure, blame, dishonor, disfavor, humiliate, mortify, disparage, demean, denigrate, belittle. *Ant.* honor; esteem; favor.

disgraceful *adj.* **1 scandalous,** shocking, outrageous, shameful, shameless, dishonorable, disreputable, degrading, ignominious, blameworthy, culpable, contemptible, despicable, reprehensible, improper, unseemly, unworthy. **2 very bad,** appalling, dreadful, terrible, shocking, intolerable, unworthy.

disgruntled *adj.* **discontented,** dissatisfied, displeased, unhappy, disappointed, annoyed, exasperated, vexed, irritated, peeved, put out, resentful, sulky, sullen, petulant, grumpy, churlish, testy, *inf.* ticked off, fed up; *vulgar* pissed off, p.o.'d.

disguise *v.* **1 camouflage,** dress up, be under cover, be incognito, cover up, conceal, hide, mask, screen, shroud, veil, cloak. **2 cover up,** misrepresent, falsify, give a false picture of, fake, fudge, feign, dissemble, gloss over, varnish. *Ant.* reveal; display.

disgust *v.* **1 sicken,** nauseate, turn one's stomach, revolt, repel, cause aversion, *inf.* turn off. **2 offend,** outrage, shock, appall, scandalize, displease, dissatisfy, annoy, anger.

▸ *n.* **1 revulsion,** repugnance, repulsion, aversion, nausea, distaste, abhorrence, loathing, detestation. **2 offense,** outrage, shock, disapproval, displeasure, dissatisfaction, annoyance, anger. *Ant.* pleasure; admiration; approval.

dish *n.* **1 container,** receptacle, bowl, plate, platter, salver. **2 food,** fare, recipe, menu item, plat du jour. **3 dish antenna,** satellite dish, microwave dish.

dishearten *v.* **discourage,** cast down, dispirit, make dispirited/dejected, depress, crush, make crestfallen/downhearted, dash, dampen, put a damper on, daunt, disappoint, deter, sadden, weigh down.

disheveled *adj.* **untidy,** tousled, rumpled, bedraggled, disordered, disarranged, messy, in a mess, unkempt, uncombed, slovenly, slatternly, blowzy, frowzy, *inf.* mussed. **Ant.** tidy; neat.

dishonest *adj.* **fraudulent,** cheating, untrustworthy, false, untruthful, dishonorable, unscrupulous, unprincipled, corrupt, swindling, deceitful, deceiving, deceptive, lying, crafty, cunning, designing, mendacious, double-dealing, underhand, underhanded, treacherous, perfidious, unfair, unjust, disreputable, rascally, roguish, knavish, *inf.* crooked, shady. **Ant.** honest; upright.

dishonor *n.* **1 disgrace,** shame, humiliation, scandal, discredit, degradation, ignominy, infamy, disrepute, ill repute, loss of face, disfavor, debasement, abasement, odium. **2 indignity,** insult, affront, offense, abuse, outrage, slight,

discourtesy. **3 disgrace,** blot, blemish, stigma.

▸ *v.* **1 disgrace,** bring dishonor/shame to, shame, humiliate, discredit, degrade, debase, sully, stain, stigmatize. **2 insult,** affront, abuse, slight, offend. **3 rape,** violate, ravish, defile, seduce, deflower.

dishonorable *adj.* **1 disgraceful,** shameful, shameless, shaming, disreputable, degrading, debasing, ignominious, ignoble, blameworthy, contemptible, despicable, reprehensible, base. **2 unprincipled,** blackguardly, unscrupulous, corrupt, untrustworthy, treacherous, perfidious, traitorous, disreputable, discreditable, *inf.* shady.

disillusion *v.* **disabuse,** disenchant, open the eyes of, shatter the illusions of, undeceive, set straight, enlighten, disappoint, make sadder and wiser.

disinclined *adj.* **reluctant,** unenthusiastic, not in the mood, hesitant, unwilling, loath, averse, antipathetic, resistant, opposed, recalcitrant.

disinfect *v.* **sterilize,** sanitize, clean, cleanse, purify, fumigate, decontaminate.

disingenuous *adj.* **insincere,**

feigned, deceitful, underhand, underhanded, duplicitous, double-dealing, two-faced, false, lying, untruthful, artful, cunning, crafty, wily, sly, shifty, scheming, calculating, designing, insidious.

disintegrate *v.* **fall apart,** fall to pieces, break up, break apart, shatter, splinter, crumble, decompose, decay, rot, molder, erode, dissolve, go to wrack and ruin.

disinterested *adj.* **1 unbiased,** unprejudiced, impartial, detached, objective, uninvolved, dispassionate, impersonal, open-minded, neutral, outside, fair, just, equitable, evenhanded, unselfish. **2 uninterested,** unconcerned, uninvolved, unresponsive, indifferent, bored, apathetic, blasé. *Ant.* biased; partial; interested.

disjointed *n.* **1 incoherent,** unconnected, disconnected, without unity, ununified, discontinuous, rambling, wandering, disorganized, confused, disordered, fitful, spasmodic, aimless, directionless. **2 dislocated,** displaced, dismembered, disconnected, severed, separated, disarticulated, torn apart, disunited.

dislike *v.* **have no liking for,** have an aversion to, regard with distaste/animosity, feel hostility toward, be unable to tolerate/stomach, hold in disfavor, disfavor, have no taste for, object to, hate, detest, loathe, abominate, abhor, despise, scorn, shun, have a grudge against.

▸ *n.* **aversion,** disapproval, disapprobation, distaste, animosity, hostility, antipathy, antagonism, disinclination, disfavor, disesteem, hate, detestation, loathing, disgust, repugnance, enmity, abhorrence.

dislocate *v.* **1 put out of joint,** put out of place, displace, disjoint, disconnect, disengage. **2 disrupt,** disturb, throw into disorder/disarray/confusion, confuse, disorganize, mess up, disorder, disarrange, turn topsy-turvy.

disloyal *adj.* **unfaithful,** faithless, false, false-hearted, untrue, inconstant, untrustworthy, treacherous, perfidious, traitorous, disaffected, subversive, seditious, unpatriotic, renegade, apostate, dissident, two-faced, double-dealing, deceitful.

disloyalty *n.* **unfaithfulness,** infidelity, faithlessness, breach of trust, breaking of faith, falseness, false-heartedness, falsity, inconstancy, untrustworthiness, treachery, perfidy, treason, disaffection, subversion, sedition, apostasy, dissidence, double-dealing.

dismal *adj.* **1 gloomy,** sad, unhappy, miserable, wretched, despondent, disconsolate, sorrowful, solemn, blue, melancholy, morose, woebegone, forlorn, lugubrious. **2 gloomy,** dreary, bleak, drab, dull, dark, dingy, cheerless, desolate, depressing, grim, funereal, comfortless, inhospitable, uninviting. **3 bad,** poor, inept, bungling, disgraceful. *Ant.* cheerful; bright.

dismantle *v.* **take apart,** take to pieces, disassemble, pull apart, tear down, demolish, fell, destroy. *Ant.* assemble.

dismay *v.* **disconcert,** take aback, startle, surprise, shock, disturb, perturb, upset, jolt, unsettle, unnerve, alarm, frighten, scare, discourage, put off, dishearten, dispirit, cast down, depress, disappoint, daunt, abash. *Ant.* encourage; hearten.

dismiss *v.* **1 give notice to,** discharge, expel, cashier, remove, oust, eject, lay off, *inf.* sack, fire, give one one's marching orders, send packing, give the boot/heave-ho to, boot out. **2 disband,** disperse, dissolve, discharge, send away, let go, release, free. **3 put**

away, banish, think no more of, put out of one's mind, set/lay aside, abandon, have done with, reject, drop, disregard, repudiate, spurn, *inf.* pooh-pooh. *Ant.* engage; retain.

disobedient *adj.* **insubordinate,** unruly, wayward, undisciplined, rebellious, defiant, mutinous, recalcitrant, intractable, willful, refractory, disorderly, delinquent, noncompliant, perverse, naughty, mischievous, contrary.

disobey *v.* **defy,** not comply with, disregard, flout, contravene, infringe, overstep, resist, rebel against, fly in the face of, transgress, violate.

disobliging *adj.* **unhelpful,** uncooperative, unaccommodating, unfriendly, unsympathetic, discourteous, uncivil.

disorder *n.* **1 untidiness,** mess, chaos, muddle, clutter, jumble, confusion, disorderliness, disarray, disorganization, *inf.* shambles. **2 disturbance,** disruption, tumult, riot, breach of the peace, fracas, rumpus, brouhaha, melee, unrest. **3 disease,** ailment, complaint, affliction, malady, sickness, illness. *Ant.* neatness; organization; order.

disorderly *adj.* **1 untidy,** messy,

chaotic, cluttered, jumbled, muddled, out of order, out of place, in disarray, disorganized, confused, deranged, upside-down, at sixes and sevens, unsystematic, irregular. **2 unruly,** boisterous, rough, rowdy, disobedient, undisciplined, lawless, wild, unmanageable, uncontrollable, ungovernable, refractory, rebellious, mutinous, turbulent, tumultuous, rioting.

disorganized adj. **1 disorderly,** chaotic, jumbled, muddled, out of order, in disarray, confused, haphazard, random, unsystematic, irregular.
2 unorganized, unmethodical, unsystematic, haphazard, muddled, careless, inf. hit-or-miss.

disown v. **repudiate,** renounce, reject, cast off, abandon, forsake, turn one's back on, disclaim, deny, disallow, abnegate, disavow, disinherit.

disparage v. **1 belittle,** slight, decry, depreciate, devalue, devaluate, downgrade, demean, detract from, discredit, deprecate, denigrate, derogate, deflate, minimize, undervalue, underestimate, underrate, make light of, play down, disdain, dismiss, ridicule, deride, mock, scorn, lampoon. **2 defame,** run down, slander, libel, malign, speak ill/evil of, cast aspersions on, impugn, calumniate, vilify, traduce, inf. do a hatchet job on, bad-mouth, trash. **Ant.** praise; overrate.

disparity n. **discrepancy,** inequality, unevenness, inconsistency, imbalance, incongruity, difference, dissimilarity, contrast, gap.

dispassionate adj.
1 unemotional, emotionless, unmoved, unexcited, unexcitable, unflappable, unperturbed, nonchalant, unruffled, cool, collected, cool and collected, calm, composed, self-possessed, levelheaded, self-controlled, temperate, sober, placid, equable, tranquil, serene, inf. laid-back, together. **2 detached,** impartial, objective, disinterested, indifferent, uninvolved, impersonal, unbiased, unprejudiced, neutral, fair, just, equitable, evenhanded, square dealing, open-minded.

dispatch v. **1 send,** send off, mail, forward, transmit, consign, remit, convey. **2 finish,** dispose of, conclude, settle, discharge, execute, perform, expedite, push through, accelerate, hasten, speed up, hurry on, inf. make short work of. **3 kill,** put to death, slay, do to death, put an end to, finish off, take the life of, slaughter, murder, assassinate, execute, *inf.* bump off, do in, knock off, eliminate, erase.

▸ *n.* **1 promptness,** promptitude, speed, alacrity, quickness, haste, hurry, swiftness, rapidity, expedition, expeditiousness. **2 communication,** communiqué, bulletin, report, account, document, missive, letter, epistle, message, item, piece, article, news, instruction. ***Ant.*** slowness; hesitancy.

dispense *v.* **1 distribute,** hand out, deal out, dole out, share out, divide out, parcel out, allocate, allot, apportion, assign, bestow, confer, supply, disburse.
2 administer, discharge, carry out, execute, implement, apply, enforce, effectuate, operate, direct. **3 make up,** prepare, mix, supply. **4 grant a dispensation to,** exempt, excuse, except, release, relieve, reprieve, absolve, *inf.* let off.

disperse *v.* **1 break up,** disband, separate, go separate ways, scatter, dissolve, leave, vanish, melt away, dissipate, dispel, drive away, banish. **2 scatter,** scatter to the winds, disseminate, distribute, sow, sprinkle, spread, diffuse, strew, bestrew. **3 put into circulation,** circulate, broadcast, publish, publicize, spread, diffuse. ***Ant.*** gather; assemble; collect.

displace *v.* **1 put out of place/order,** disarrange, move, shift, relocate, transpose, derange, disorder, throw into disorder, dislocate, transfer, resettle, unsettle, disturb. **2 remove,** dismiss, discharge, depose, dislodge, eject, expel, force out, discard, cashier, *inf.* sack, fire. **3 replace,** take the place of, take over from, supplant, oust, supersede, succeed, *inf.* crowd out.

display *v.* **1 put on show,** show, exhibit, put on view, expose to view, present, unveil, set forth, arrange, dispose, array, demonstrate, advertise, publicize, show off, flaunt, parade, flourish, boast, vaunt, *inf.* flash. **2 show,** evince, manifest, betray, show evidence of, reveal, disclose. ***Ant.*** conceal; hide.

▸ *n.* **1 show,** exhibition, exhibit, presentation, demonstration, spectacle, array, parade, pageant, pomp, flourish, ostentation. **2 showing,** evincement, manifestation, betrayal, evidence, revelation, disclosure.

displease *v.* **dissatisfy,** put out, annoy, irritate, anger, irk, vex, provoke, offend, pique, peeve, gall, nettle, incense, exasperate, upset, perturb, disturb, discompose, disgust, *inf.* aggravate.

dispose *v.* **1 arrange,** order, place, put, position, array, range, line up, set up, organize, marshal, group, rank, categorize, systematize, adjust, fix, regulate. **2 incline,** make willing, predispose, make, move, prompt, lead, induce, tempt, actuate, motivate, bias, influence, condition, direct. **Ant.** keep; retain.

disposed *adj.* **inclined,** willing, of a mind to, in the mood to, ready, prepared, given, prone, liable, apt.

disprove *v.* **prove false,** invalidate, refute, negate, rebut, confute, deny, contradict, controvert, discredit, expose.

dispute *v.* **1 debate,** discuss, argue, disagree, have an altercation, altercate, clash, quarrel, wrangle, bicker, squabble. **2 question,** call into question, challenge, contest, deny, doubt, contradict, object to, oppose, controvert, impugn, gainsay. **Ant.** agree; confirm.
▸ *n.* **1 debate,** discussion, argument, controversy, contention, disagreement, altercation, dissension, conflict, friction, strife, discord, litigation. **2 argument,** row, altercation,

clash, quarrel, wrangle, squabble, feud, disturbance, fracas, brawl. **Ant.** agreement; accord.

disqualify *v.* **declare ineligible,** rule out, preclude, debar, reject, prohibit, disentitle.

disquiet *n.* **disquietude,** inquietude, uneasiness, unease, unrest, anxiety, anxiousness, angst, nervousness, agitation, perturbation, upset, worry, concern, distress, trouble, alarm, fear, fretfulness, restlessness, dread, foreboding.
▸ *v.* **make uneasy/anxious/ nervous,** agitate, perturb, upset, disturb, unsettle, discompose, ruffle, worry, concern, distress, trouble, bother, alarm, frighten, make fretful/restless, vex.

disregard *v.* **1 ignore,** take no notice/account of, pay no attention/heed to, discount, set aside, neglect, forget, never mind, overlook, turn a blind eye to, pass over, gloss over, brush aside, laugh off, make light of, *inf.* play down. **2 slight,** disparage, denigrate, disdain, despise, shun, cold shoulder, insult, affront, *inf.* turn one's nose up at.
▸ *n.* **1 lack of notice/attention/ heed,** inattention, heedlessness, carelessness, neglect, negligence, indifference. **2 scorn,** contempt,

disparagement, denigration, disdain, disrespect, disesteem.

disrepair *n.* dilapidation, deterioration, decay, collapse, shabbiness, ruin, ruination, decrepitude.

disreputable *adj.* **1 of bad reputation,** infamous, dishonorable, dishonest, unprincipled, villainous, notorious, ignominious, corrupt, unworthy, base, low, mean, questionable, unsavory, unscrupulous, rascally, contemptible, reprehensible, despicable, discreditable, disgraceful, shameful, shocking, outrageous, scandalous, *inf.* crooked, shady. **2 shabby,** slovenly, down-at-the-heels, seedy, dilapidated, threadbare, untidy, disheveled, bedraggled, *inf.* scruffy.

disrespectful *adj.* discourteous, uncivil, impolite, unmannerly, ill-mannered, rude, irreverent, inconsiderate, insolent, impudent, impertinent, scornful, contemptuous, insulting. **Ant.** respectful; courteous.

disrupt *v.* **throw into disorder/disarray,** disorder, disorganize, cause confusion/turmoil in, disarrange, disturb, upset, interrupt, suspend, discontinue, interfere with, obstruct, impede, hamper, *inf.* throw a monkey wrench in/into (the works of).

dissatisfaction *n.* discontent, discontentment, disapproval, disapprobation, disappointment, frustration, unhappiness, regret, chagrin, dismay, vexation, annoyance, irritation, anger, exasperation, resentment, disquiet, restlessness, malaise.

dissatisfied *adj.* discontented, displeased, disgruntled, disapproving, unsatisfied, disappointed, unfulfilled, frustrated, unhappy, regretful, vexed, angry, resentful, restless.

disseminate *v.* **spread,** circulate, broadcast, publish, publicize, proclaim, promulgate, propagate, dissipate, scatter, distribute, disperse, diffuse.

dissident *adj.* dissentient, dissenting, disagreeing, differing, nonconformist, apostate, schismatic, heterodox.
▸ *n.* **dissenter,** rebel, objector, protester, nonconformist, apostate, heretic.

dissimilar *adj.* **unlike,** unalike, different, varying, variant, disparate, unrelated, divergent, deviating, diverse, various, contrasting, mismatched, distinct.

dissipate *v.* **1 disperse,** scatter,

drive away, dispel, dissolve, break up, disappear, vanish, melt away, melt into thin air, evaporate. **2 squander,** fritter, misspend, lavish, waste, exhaust, drain, deplete, spend, expend, burn up, use up, consume, run through. *Ant.* assemble; conserve.

dissipated *adj.* **dissolute,** debauched, intemperate, profligate, abandoned, rakish, licentious, promiscuous, drunken, self-indulgent, wild, unrestrained, wanton, depraved, degenerate, corrupt.

dissociate *v.* **separate,** set apart, segregate, isolate, detach, disconnect, sever, divorce, disband, break up, dissolve, disperse, scatter, dismiss.

dissolve *v.* **1 go into solution,** liquefy, melt, deliquesce. **2 disappear,** vanish, melt away, evaporate, dwindle, disperse, dissipate, disintegrate, crumble, decompose, perish, die, evanesce. **3 bring to an end,** end, terminate, break up, discontinue, wind up, disband, dismiss, suspend, ruin, split up, separate, sever, disunite, disjoin, disperse, scatter, go their separate ways. **4 break into,** collapse into, be overcome with.

dissuade *v.* **persuade/advise against,** persuade/advise/urge not to, put off, stop, talk out of, discourage/deter from, divert, turn aside from, disincline from.

distance *n.* **1 space,** interval, span, gap, separation, stretch, extent, length, width, depth. **2 remoteness,** farness. **3 aloofness,** reserve, remoteness, reticence, coolness, coldness, frigidity, stiffness, formality, restraint, unresponsiveness. ▸ *v.* **1 place far off,** set apart, separate, dissociate, remove. **2 outdistance,** outstrip, outrun, leave behind, pass, outdo, surpass.

distant *adj.* **1 far,** faraway, far off, remote, out of the way, outlying, abroad, far-flung. **2 far-off,** long ago. **3 away,** off, apart, separated, dispersed, scattered. **4 not close,** remote, indirect, slight. **5 vague,** faint, indistinct, obscure, uncertain. **6 aloof,** reserved, remote, uncommunicative, unapproachable, standoffish, withdrawn, reticent, restrained, cool, cold, frigid, stiff, formal, ceremonious, unresponsive, unfriendly, haughty, condescending. *Ant.* near; recent; friendly; approachable.

distasteful *adj.* **1 unpleasant,** disagreeable, displeasing, undesirable, uninviting, objectionable, offensive, obnoxious, unsavory, disgusting, revolting, repugnant, abhorrent,

loathsome, detestable.
2 unpalatable, unsavory,
unappetizing, disgusting,
sickening, nauseating, nauseous.
distinct *adj.* **1 clear,** clear-cut,
well-defined, sharp, marked,
decided, definite, unmistakable,
recognizable, obvious, plain, plain
as day, evident, apparent,
manifest, patent, palpable,
unambiguous, unequivocal.
2 separate, individual, different,
unconnected, unassociated,
detached, discrete, dissimilar,
unalike, disparate. *Ant.* indistinct;
indefinite; vague.
distinction *n.* **1 differentiation,**
contradistinction, discrimination,
division, separation, dividing line,
contrast. **2 difference,**
dissimilarity, dissimilitude,
contrast, differential, subtlety,
nicety, nuance. **3 feature,**
characteristic, mark,
individuality, peculiarity. **4 honor,**
credit, excellence, merit. **5 note,**
consequence, importance,
account, significance, greatness,
prestige, prominence, eminence,
repute, reputation, renown, fame,
mark, celebrity, honor, merit,
worth, excellence, glory, name,
rank, quality, superiority.
distinctive *adj.* **distinguishing,**
characteristic, typical, individual,
particular, peculiar, special,

different, uncommon, unusual,
remarkable, singular,
extraordinary, noteworthy,
original, idiosyncratic. *Ant.*
ordinary; run-of-the-mill.
distinguish *v.* **1 tell apart,**
differentiate, discriminate,
determine, tell the difference
between, decide between. **2 make
distinctive,** set apart, separate,
single out, mark off, characterize,
individualize, designate,
categorize, classify. **3 make out,**
see, discern, perceive, observe,
notice, detect, recognize, identify,
pick out. **4 make famous,** bring
fame/honor to, bestow honor on,
ennoble, dignify, glorify, win
acclaim for, lionize, immortalize.
distinguished *adj.* **famous,**
famed, eminent, renowned,
prominent, well-known, noted,
notable, esteemed, acclaimed,
illustrious, celebrated, respected,
legendary. *Ant.* unknown;
obscure.
distort *v.* **1 twist,** warp, contort,
bend, buckle, deform, misshape,
disfigure, mangle, wrench, wring,
wrest. **2 misrepresent,** pervert,
twist, falsify, garble, slant, bias,
color, tamper with, alter, change,
torture.
distract *v.* **1 deflect,** divert,
sidetrack, turn aside, draw away.
2 amuse, entertain, divert,

beguile, absorb, engage, occupy.
3 confuse, bewilder, perplex, puzzle, disturb, fluster, agitate, disconcert, discompose, confound, annoy, trouble, harass, worry, torment, *inf.* hassle. **4 make frantic,** drive/make mad, madden, drive insane, make crazy, derange, throw into a frenzy. ***Ant.*** focus; concentrate.

distracted *adj.* **1 confused,** bewildered, bemused, perplexed, agitated, flustered, troubled, harassed, worried, *inf.* hassled. **2 grief-stricken,** distraught, frantic, frenzied, raving, wild, hysterical, overwrought, mad, maddened, insane, crazed, deranged, out of one's mind.

distraction *n.* **1 diversion,** interruption, disturbance, interference, obstruction. **2 amusement,** entertainment, diversion, pastime, recreation, hobby, game, occupation. **3 confusion,** bewilderment, befuddlement, perplexity, disturbance, agitation, perturbation, harassment. **4 frenzy,** hysteria, mental distress, madness, insanity, craziness, mania, derangement, delirium.

distress *n.* **1 anguish,** suffering, pain, agony, ache, affliction, torment, torture, misery, wretchedness, discomfort, heartache, heartbreak, sorrow, grief, woe, sadness, desolation, trouble, worry, anxiety, perturbation, uneasiness, angst, tribulations, cries, wails. **2 hardship,** adversity, misfortune, trouble, calamity, need, want, poverty, lack, privation, destitution, indigence, impoverishment, penury, difficulties, dire straits. ***Ant.*** tranquillity; serenity.
▸ *v.* **1 cause anguish/suffering,** pain, upset, make miserable/ wretched, grieve, sadden, trouble, worry, bother, arouse anxiety in, perturb, disturb, vex, harrow, torment. **2 dent,** scratch, antique, simulate age/wear in. ***Ant.*** please; gladden.

distribute *v.* **1 give out,** hand out, allocate, allot, issue, dispense, administer, apportion, assign, deal out, share out, divide out, dole out, measure out, mete out, parcel out, dispose, circulate, pass out/around, hand out, deliver, convey, transmit. **2 disseminate,** disperse, diffuse, scatter, spread, strew, sow. **3 place,** position, arrange, organize, dispose, group, class, classify, categorize, file, assort, compart, locate.

district *n.* **1 area,** region, place, locality, neighborhood, quarter, sector, vicinity, territory, domain.

2 administrative division, county, ward, parish, community, constituency, department, canton.

distrust *v.* **mistrust,** be suspicious of, be wary/chary of, be skeptical of, have doubts about, doubt, have misgivings about, wonder about, question, suspect, disbelieve, discredit, *inf.* be leery of. **Ant.** trust.

▸ *n.* **mistrust,** lack of trust, no confidence, lack of faith, suspicion, wariness, chariness, skepticism, doubt, doubtfulness, dubiety, misgiving, questioning, qualms, disbelief, unbelief, incredulity, incredulousness, discredit, *inf.* leeriness.

disturb *v.* **1 interrupt,** butt in on, distract, bother, trouble, pester, intrude on, interfere with, hinder, plague, harass, molest, *inf.* hassle. **2 disarrange,** muddle, disorganize, disorder, confuse, derange, unsettle. **3 concern,** perturb, trouble, worry, upset, agitate, fluster, discomfit, disconcert, alarm, frighten, startle, dismay, distress, discompose, unsettle, ruffle, shake, confuse, bewilder, perplex, confound, excite. **4 agitate,** churn up, convulse, roil.
5 inconvenience, put out, put to trouble. **Ant.** calm; ease.

disturbed *adj.* **upset,** troubled, unbalanced, disordered, maladjusted, neurotic, psychotic, *inf.* screwed up.

disused *adj.* **unused,** neglected, abandoned, discontinued, obsolete.

ditch *n.* **trench,** channel, watercourse, dike, canal, drain, gutter, gully, moat, furrow, rut.
▸ *v.* **1 dig,** trench, excavate, gouge, hollow out, drain. **2 abandon,** throw out, discard, drop, scrap, jettison, get rid of, dispose of, *inf.* dump. **3 evade,** escape, elude, shake off, defeat, frustrate, balk.

dive *v.* **1 plunge,** plummet, jump, leap, bound, spring, nosedive, fall, descend, submerge, drop, swoop, dip, bellyflop. **2 leap,** jump, lunge, rush, dart, dash, duck, dodge.
▸ *n.* **1 plunge,** plummet, jump, leap, spring, nosedive, fall, drop, swoop, bellyflop. **2 leap,** jump, lunge, rush, dart, dash, duck, dodge. **3** *inf.* **joint,** dump.

diverge *v.* **1 separate,** divide, subdivide, split, part, disunite, fork, branch off, radiate, spread out, bifurcate, divaricate. **2 differ,** disagree, be at variance/odds, conflict, clash. **3 deviate,** digress, depart, veer, stray, drift, turn aside, wander. **Ant.** join; converge; agree; stay.

diverse *adj.* **various,** miscellaneous, assorted, mixed, diversified, variegated, varied, varying, heterogeneous, different, differing, distinct, unlike, dissimilar, distinctive, contrasting, conflicting. *Ant.* identical; similar; like.

diversify *v.* **1 vary,** variegate, modify, assort, mix, alter, change, transform. **2 expand,** spread.

diversion *n.* **1 redirection,** turning aside, deflection, digression, deviation, divergence. **2 amusement,** entertainment, pastime, distraction, recreation, fun, relaxation, game, play, sport, hobby, pleasure, delight, enjoyment, beguilement, enchantment. *Ant.* routine.

divert *v.* **1 turn aside,** deflect, draw away, avert, switch/change the course of, redirect. **2 distract,** detract, sidetrack, lead away, turn aside, deflect. **3 amuse,** entertain, distract, delight, give pleasure to, beguile, enchant, interest, occupy, absorb, engross, recreate. *Ant.* bore; weary.

diverting *adj.* **amusing,** entertaining, humorous, fun, enjoyable, pleasurable, recreational, beguiling, interesting, absorbing.

divide *v.* **1 cut up,** sever, split, shear, bisect, halve, quarter, cleave, rend, sunder, rive, separate, part, segregate, partition, detach, disconnect, disjoin. **2 diverge,** branch, fork, split in two, divaricate. **3 share,** allocate, allot, apportion, portion out, distribute, dispense, deal out, hand out, dole out, measure out, parcel out, *inf.* divvy (up/out). **4 estrange,** alienate, break up, separate, spilt up, disunite, disaffect, set/pit against one another, cause disagreement between, sow dissension between, set at variance/odds, come between. **5 classify,** sort, arrange, order, group, grade, rank, categorize, dispose, separate, segregate. *Ant.* join; unite; combine.

divine[1] *adj.* **1 godly,** godlike, heavenly, celestial, holy, angelic, seraphic, spiritual, saintly. **2 religious,** holy, sacred, sanctified, consecrated, spiritual. **3 supernatural,** superhuman, mystical, exalted, beatific, blissful, ethereal, transcendental, transcendent. **4 lovely,** beautiful, charming, perfect, excellent, superlative, wonderful, glorious, marvelous, admirable, *inf.* super, stunning. *Ant.* mortal; hellish; mundane; ugly.

▶ *n.* **theologian,** clergyman, churchman, churchwoman, cleric, ecclesiastic, minister, priest, pastor, parson, reverend.

divine[2] *v.* **1 guess,** surmise, conjecture, speculate, suspect, suppose, assume, presume, deduce, infer, theorize, hypothesize. **2 intuit,** discern, perceive, understand, grasp, apprehend, comprehend. **3 foretell,** predict, foresee, forecast, presage, augur, portend, prognosticate, forebode. **4 dowse.**

divinity *n.* **1 divine nature,** divineness, deity, godhead, godliness, holiness, sanctity. **2 deity,** god, goddess, genius, spirit, guardian, angel.

division *n.* **1 dividing,** cutting up, severance, splitting, bisection, cleaving, parting, separation, segregation, partitioning, disconnection, detachment. **2 sharing,** allocation, allotment, apportionment, distribution. **3 dividing line,** divide, boundary, boundary line, border, partition, line of demarcation. **4 section,** part, portion, piece, bit, segment, slice, fragment, chunk, component, share, compartment, category, class, group, grade, family. **5 branch,** department, section, sector, arm. **6 disagreement,** difference of opinion, feud, breach, rupture, split, dissension, conflict, discord, variance, disunion, estrangement, alienation.

divorce *n.* **1 dissolution,** disunion, breakup, split-up, annulment, official separation, separation, severance, breach, rupture. **2 separation,** severance, division, split, partition.
▶ *v.* **1 annul/dissolve a marriage,** split up, break up, separate, part. **2 separate,** disconnect, divide, dissociate, detach, disunite, sever, disjoin, split. *Ant.* marry; connect; join.

dizzy *adj.* **1 light-headed,** faint, vertiginous, weak in the knees, shaky, wobbly, off-balance, reeling, staggering, *inf.* woozy. **2 dazed,** bewildered, confused, muddled, bemused, befuddled, puzzled, perplexed, *inf.* woozy. **3 giddy,** scatterbrained, featherbrained, flighty, foolish, silly, light-headed, fickle, capricious, inconstant.

do *v.* **1 act,** behave, conduct oneself, comport oneself. **2 perform,** carry out, undertake, discharge, execute, accomplish, implement, achieve, complete, finish, conclude, bring about, effect, effectuate, realize, produce, engineer. **3 be enough,** be sufficient, be adequate, suffice, be satisfactory, be of use, fill/fit the bill, answer/serve the purpose, meet the needs, pass muster, measure up. **4 make,** prepare, get

ready, fix, produce, see to, arrange, organize, be responsible for, be in charge of, look after, take on. **5 create,** make, produce, originate, form, fashion, design, fabricate, manufacture. **6 put on,** perform, act, present, produce, give. **7 render,** afford, give, bestow, grant, pay. **8 solve,** resolve, work out, figure out, decipher. **9 work at,** be employed at, have as a job/profession/occupation, earn a living at. **10 get on/along,** progress, fare, make out, manage, continue. **11 translate,** put, render, adapt, transform. **12 travel at,** go/proceed at, be driven at. **13 travel,** journey, cover, traverse. **14 sightsee,** look at, visit, tour.
▸ *n.* **party,** function, affair, event, occasion, fête, soirée, *inf.* bash, blowout.

docile *adj.* **manageable,** controllable, tractable, malleable, amenable, accommodating, compliant, pliant, obedient, biddable, dutiful, submissive, yielding, ductile. ***Ant.*** disobedient; willful; intractable.

dock[1] *n.* **pier,** quay, wharf, jetty, marina, waterfront, drydock.

dock[2] *v.* **1 cut,** cut short, shorten, crop, lop, truncate. **2 deduct,** subtract, remove, take off, reduce, decrease, lessen, diminish.

doctor *n.* **medical practitioner,** physician, surgeon, MD, medical man/woman/person, general practitioner, GP, medicine man, healer, shaman, *inf.* doc, sawbones, *derog.* quack, witch doctor.
▸ *v.* **1 treat,** prescribe for, attend to, minister to, care for, cure, heal. **2 patch up,** repair, fix, mend, botch. **3 adulterate,** contaminate, dilute, water down, weaken, mix, cut, lace, *inf.* spike. **4 tamper with,** interfere with, alter, change, falsify, disguise, fudge, pervert, misrepresent.

doctrine *n.* **creed,** credo, dogma, belief, conviction, teaching, tenet, principle, precept, maxim, articles of faith, canons.

document *n.* **official paper,** legal paper, paper, form, certificate, record, report, deed, voucher, instrument, charter, paperwork, documentation.
▸ *v.* **1 prove,** back up, support, give weight to, corroborate, substantiate, authenticate, verify, validate, certify. **2 report,** record, detail, tabulate, chart, register, cite, instance.

documentary *adj.*
1 documented, recorded, registered, tabulated, charted, written. **2 factual,** nonfictional, real-life, true to life, realistic.

dodge *v.* **1 dart,** duck, dive, swerve, sidestep, veer. **2 evade,** elude, escape, fend off, avoid, stay/steer clear of, deceive, trick, *inf.* give the slip to. **3 avoid,** evade, shirk, shun, stay/steer clear of.
▸ *n.* **1 dart,** duck, dive, swerve, jump. **2 ruse,** ploy, scheme, stratagem, subterfuge, trick, wile, deception, maneuver, device, machination, contrivance, artifice, expedient.

dog *n.* **1 canine,** hound, mongrel, cur, bitch, sire, pup, puppy, whelp, *inf.* doggy, doggie, fido, pooch, mutt. **2 scoundrel,** blackguard, beast, cad, rogue, villain, cur, knave, heel, bastard.
▸ *v.* **pursue,** follow, track, trail, shadow, hound, plague, trouble, haunt, *inf* tail.

dogged *adj.* **determined,** resolute, obstinate, stubborn, tenacious, relentless, intent, single-minded, unshakable, unflagging, indefatigable, tireless, unfaltering, unwavering, persistent, persevering, pertinacious, unyielding, obdurate, firm, steadfast, steady, staunch. *Ant.* hesitant; halfhearted.

dogmatic *adj.* **1 doctrinal,** doctrinaire, canonical, authoritative, ex cathedra. **2 assertive,** insistent, emphatic, categorical, downright, authoritarian, opinionated, peremptory, domineering, imperious, arrogant, overbearing, dictatorial, intolerant, biased, prejudiced, *inf.* pushy.

doleful *adj.* **mournful,** sorrowful, sad, dejected, disconsolate, depressed, gloomy, melancholy, blue, miserable, wretched, *inf.* down in the mouth/dumps. *Ant.* cheerful; joyful; happy.

domestic *adj.* **1 home,** family, household, domiciliary, residential, private. **2 domesticated,** housewifely, stay-at-home, home-loving. **3 domesticated,** tame, pet, house-trained, housebroken, trained, not wild. **4 home,** internal, native, indigenous, homegrown, home-bred, aboriginal . *Ant.* public; wild; foreign.
▸ *n.* **domestic help,** help, maid, domestic servant, servant, au pair, hired help.

domesticate *v.* **1 tame,** house-train, housebreak, train, break in, gentle. **2 naturalize,** acclimatize, habituate, accustom, familiarize, assimilate.

dominant *adj.* **1 ruling,** governing, controlling, commanding, ascendant, presiding, supreme, authoritative, most influential, superior, most

assertive, domineering.
2 predominant, most important, chief, main, principal, leading, primary, paramount, preeminent, outstanding, prominent, prevailing. **Ant.** submissive; subservient.

dominate *v.* **1 rule,** govern, control, exercise control over, command, direct, preside over, have ascendancy/mastery over, master, domineer, tyrannize, intimidate, have the upper hand over, ride roughshod over, have under one's thumb, be in the driver's seat, be in the saddle, wear the pants, *inf.* boss, call the shots. **2 predominate,** be paramount, be preeminent, prevail, be conspicuous, be most obvious, be most important. **3 overlook,** tower above, stand over, project/jut over, hang/loom over, bestride.

domineering *adj.* **overbearing,** imperious, authoritarian, high-handed, autocratic, peremptory, arrogant, haughty, dictatorial, masterful, forceful, coercive, tyrannical, despotic, oppressive, subjugating, iron-fisted, iron-handed, *inf.* bossy, pushy. **Ant.** meek; servile.

donate *v.* **give,** contribute, make a contribution of, subscribe, make a gift of, gift, present, pledge, put oneself down for, bestow, *inf.* chip in, kick in.

donation *n.* **contribution,** subscription, gift, present, grant, offering, gratuity, alms, charity, benefaction, largesse.

donor *n.* **giver,** contributor, donator, grantor, benefactor, benefactress, supporter, backer, philanthropist, *inf.* angel.

doom *n.* **1 grim/terrible fate,** ruin, ruination, rack and ruin, downfall, destruction, catastrophe, disaster, extinction, annihilation, death, termination, quietus. **2 condemnation,** guilty verdict, sentence, judgment, pronouncement, decree, damnation. **3 the Last Judgment,** Judgment Day, doomsday, Armageddon, end of the world.
▸ *v.* **1 fate,** destine, predestine, ordain, preordain, foreordain, consign, condemn. **2 condemn,** sentence, judge, pronounce, decree, damn.

doomed *adj.* **ill-fated,** star-crossed, foredoomed, unlucky, damned, bedeviled, ruined, crushed.

door *n.* **1 doorway,** portal, entrance, entry, exit, barrier. **2 entrance,** entry, access, opening, entrée, gateway, way, path, road, ingress.

dormant *adj.* **sleeping,** asleep,

slumbering, inactive, inert, latent, fallow, quiescent, inoperative, hibernating, comatose, stagnant, sluggish, lethargic, torpid, passive, motionless, immobile. **Ant.** awake; active.

dose *n.* **amount,** quantity, measure, portion, draft.

dot *n.* **spot,** speck, fleck, point, mark, dab, particle, atom, iota, jot, mote, mite, period, decimal point.
▸ *v.* **1 spot,** fleck, bespeckle, mark, dab, stud, bestud, stipple, pock, freckle, sprinkle, scatter, pepper. **2 mark with a dot,** add a dot to, punctuate.

double *adj.* **1 duplicate,** twin, paired, in pairs, dual, coupled, twofold, binal, binate. **2 doubled,** twice as much/many as usual, twofold, large. **3 doubled,** twofold, folded, folded in two, two-ply. **4 dual,** ambiguous, double-edged, two-edged, ambivalent, equivocal. **5 dual,** deceitful, false, dishonest, hypocritical, insincere, double-dealing, two-faced, treacherous, perfidious, Janus-faced. **Ant.** single.
▸ *adv.* **1 two together,** two at a time, in twos, by twos, two by two. **2 twice,** twice over, twice the amount.

double-cross *v.* **betray,** cheat, defraud, trick, hoodwink, mislead, deceive, swindle, *inf.* two-time, take for a ride.

doubt *v.* **1 suspect,** distrust, mistrust, have misgivings about, feel uneasy/apprehensive about, call in question, query, question. **2 have doubts,** be dubious, hesitate to believe, feel uncertain, be undecided, lack conviction, query, question, challenge. **Ant.** trust; believe.
▸ *n.* **1 distrust,** mistrust, lack of confidence/faith, skepticism, uneasiness, apprehension, reservations, misgivings, suspicions, qualms. **2 dubiousness,** lack of certainty, uncertainty, indecision, lack of conviction, incredulity, queries, questions. **3 uncertainty,** indecision, hesitation, hesitancy, wavering, vacillation, irresolution, lack of conviction. **Ant.** trust; confidence; certainty.

doubtful *adj.* **1 in doubt,** uncertain, unsure, unconfirmed, unsettled, improbable, unlikely. **2 suspicious,** distrustful, mistrustful, skeptical, having reservations/misgivings, apprehensive, uneasy, questioning, unsure, incredulous. **3 uncertain,** dubious, open to question, questionable, debatable, disputable, not definite, inconclusive, unresolved,

unconfirmed, unsettled.
4 dubious, unclear, ambiguous, equivocal, obscure, vague, nebulous. **5 uncertain,** indecisive, hesitating, irresolute, wavering, vacillating. *Ant.* certain; sure; clear.

dour *adj.* **unsmiling,** sullen, morose, sour, gruff, churlish, uncommunicative, unfriendly, forbidding, grim, stern, severe, austere, harsh, dismal, dreary, gloomy. *Ant.* cheerful; friendly; sociable.

dowdy *adj.* **frumpish,** frumpy, drab, dull, old-fashioned, unfashionable, inelegant, shabby, untidy, dingy, frowzy, *inf.* tacky. *Ant.* chic; fashionable.

downcast *adj.* **disheartened,** dispirited, downhearted, dejected, depressed, discouraged, daunted, dismayed, disappointed, disconsolate, crestfallen, despondent, sad, unhappy, miserable, wretched, down, low, blue, gloomy, glum, melancholy, sorrowful, doleful, mournful. *Ant.* cheerful; upbeat.

downright *adj.* **1 complete,** total, absolute, out and out, outright, utter, sheer, thorough, thoroughgoing, categorical, unmitigated, unqualified, unconditional, positive, simple, wholesale, all out, arrant, rank.
2 frank, forthright, straightforward, open, candid, plainspoken, matter-of-fact, outspoken, blunt, brusque.
▸ *adv.* **completely,** totally, absolutely, utterly, thoroughly, profoundly, categorically, positively.

downward *adj.* **going down,** moving down, descending, sliding down, earthbound.

drab *adj.* **1 dull,** dull-colored, colorless, mousy, gray, grayish, dingy, dreary, dismal, cheerless, gloomy, somber, depressing.
2 uninteresting, boring, tedious, dry, dreary, lifeless, lackluster, uninspired. *Ant.* bright; gaudy; cheerful; interesting.

draft *n.* **1 preliminary version,** rough sketch, outline, plan, skeleton, abstract. **2 plan,** sketch, drawing, line drawing, diagram, blueprint, delineation. **3 money order,** check, bill of exchange.
4 conscription, call-up, selective service.
▸ *v.* **1 outline, plan,** draw (up), frame, sketch (out), design, delineate. **2 recruit,** conscript, call up, induct.

drag *v.* **1 haul,** pull, draw, tug, yank, trail, tow, lug. **2 go/move slowly,** creep/limp along, crawl, go at a snail's pace. **3 go on too long,** go on and on, become tedious.

▸ *n.* **nuisance,** source of annoyance, pest, trouble, bother, bore, *inf.* pain in the neck.

drain *v.* **1 draw off,** extract, withdraw, remove, pump off, milk, bleed, tap, empty, void, evacuate, flow out, ooze, trickle, seep out, leak, discharge, exude, effuse. **2 use up,** exhaust, deplete, consume, expend, empty, sap, strain, tax, bleed. **3 drink up,** finish, gulp down, swallow, quaff, *inf.* down.

▸ *n.* **1 channel,** conduit, culvert, duct, gutter, sewer, trench, ditch, dike, pipe, outlet. **2 exhaustion,** depletion, consumption, expenditure, outflow, sapping, strain, tax.

dramatic *adj.* **1 theatrical,** stage, thespian. **2 exciting,** sensational, spectacular, startling, unexpected, thrilling, tense, suspenseful, electrifying, stirring, affecting. **3 striking,** impressive, vivid, spectacular, breathtaking, moving, affecting, emotive, graphic, effective, powerful. **4 theatrical,** artificial, exaggerated, overdone, stagy, histrionic.

dramatist *n.* **playwright,** scriptwriter, screenwriter, tragedy writer, comedy writer, *fml.* dramaturgist, dramaturge.

dramatize *v.* **1 turn/adapt into a play,** make a screenplay/stage play of, put into dramatic form. **2 exaggerate,** make a drama/performance of, overdo, overstate, *inf.* lay it on thick, ham it up.

drape *v.* **1 cover,** envelope, blanket, overlay, cloak, veil, shroud, decorate, adorn, array, deck, festoon. **2 hang,** arrange, let fall in folds, lean, dangle, droop.

drastic *adj.* **extreme,** severe, desperate, dire, radical, harsh, sharp, forceful, rigorous, draconian. *Ant.* mild; moderate.

draw *v.* **1 pull,** haul, tow, trail, tug, yank. **2 move,** go, come, proceed, approach. **3 pull out,** take out, bring out, extract, withdraw, produce, unsheathe. **4 shut,** close, pull together. **5 attract,** allure, lure, entice, invite, engage, interest, win, catch the eye of, capture, captivate, fascinate, tempt, seduce. **6 breathe in,** inhale, suck in, inspire, respire. **7 take,** take in, receive, be in receipt of, get, procure, obtain, earn. **8 deduce,** infer, conclude, derive, gather, glean. **9 drain,** siphon off, pump off, tap, milk, bleed, filtrate. **10 choose,** pick, select, opt for, make a choice of, decide on, single out. **11 sketch,** portray, depict, delineate, represent, trace, map out, mark out, chart, paint, design.

▶ *n.* **1 attraction,** lure, allure, pull, enticement, magnetism. **2 tie,** dead heat, stalemate.

drawback *n.* **disadvantage,** snag, catch, problem, difficulty, trouble, flaw, stumbling block, hitch, handicap, hindrance, obstacle, impediment, hurdle, obstruction, barrier, curb, check, discouragement, deterrent, damper, inconvenience, nuisance, detriment, fault, weak spot, weakness, imperfection, defect, *inf.* fly in the ointment. **Ant.** advantage; benefit.

drawing *n.* **1 sketch,** picture, illustration, representation, portrayal, delineation, depiction, composition, study, diagram, outline. **2 raffle,** sweepstakes, lottery.

dread *v.* **fear,** be afraid of, be terrified by, worry about, be anxious about, have forebodings about, tremble/shudder about, cringe/shrink from, quail/cower/flinch from, *inf.* have cold feet about, be in a blue funk about.

▶ *n.* **fear,** fearfulness, fright, alarm, terror, apprehension, trepidation, horror, anxiety, concern, foreboding, dismay, perturbation, trembling, shuddering, flinching, *inf.* blue funk, heebie-jeebies.

dreadful *adj.* **1 terrible,** frightful, horrible, grim, awful, dire, frightening, terrifying, alarming, distressing, shocking, appalling, harrowing, ghastly, fearful, hideous, horrendous, gruesome, tragic, calamitous, grievous. **2 nasty,** unpleasant, disagreeable, frightful, shocking, very bad, distasteful, repugnant, odious. **3 shocking,** outrageous, inordinate, great, tremendous. **Ant.** pleasant; agreeable.

dream *n.* **1 nightmare,** vision, fantasy, hallucination. **2 ambition,** aspiration, goal, design, plan, aim, hope, yearning, desire, wish, notion, daydream, fantasy, castles in the air. **3 beauty,** vision of loveliness, vision, delight, pleasure to behold, joy, marvel. **4 daydream,** reverie, state of unreality, trance, daze, fog, stupor.

▶ *v.* **1 have dreams/nightmares.** **2 hallucinate,** have a vision, imagine things, fantasize. **3 daydream,** be in a trance/reverie, be lost in thought, muse, be preoccupied. **4 think,** consider, visualize, conceive, suppose.

dreamy *adj.* **1 visionary,** fanciful, fantasizing, romantic, idealistic, impractical, unrealistic, theorizing, daydreaming, quixotic. **2 daydreaming,** thoughtful, lost in thought, pensive, speculative, preoccupied, absentminded, in a brown study, with one's head in the clouds. **3 dreamlike,** vague, dim, hazy, shadowy, misty, faint, indistinct, unclear. **4 romantic,** relaxing, soothing, calming, lulling, gentle, tranquil, peaceful. **5 wonderful,** marvelous, terrific, fabulous, gorgeous, heavenly, *inf.* to die for. *Ant.* practical; down-to-earth.

dreary *adj.* **1 gloomy,** dismal, bleak, somber, dull, dark, overcast, depressing. **2 dull,** drab, uninteresting, flat, dry, colorless, lifeless, tedious, wearisome, boring, humdrum, routine, monotonous, uneventful, run-of-the-mill, prosaic, commonplace, unvaried, repetitive. **3 gloomy,** glum, sad, miserable, wretched, downcast, dejected, depressed, despondent, doleful, mournful, melancholic. *Ant.* bright; interesting; cheerful.

drench *v.* **soak,** saturate, permeate, drown, inundate, flood, steep, douse, souse, wet, slosh.

dress *n.* **1 gown,** garment, robe. **2 clothes,** garments, clothing, attire, apparel, costume, outfit, ensemble, garb, *inf.* gear, get-up, togs, duds. **3 covering,** outer covering, plumage, feathers, pelt.
 ▶ *v.* **1 clothe,** attire, garb, fit out, turn out, array, apparel, robe, put on clothes, don clothes, slip into clothes, change, wear formal clothes, put on evening dress. **2 prepare,** get ready, clean, stuff. **3 cover,** bandage, bind up. *Ant.* undress; strip.

dribble *v.* **1 drip,** trickle, fall in drops, drop, leak, ooze, exude, seep. **2 drool,** slaver, slobber.
 ▶ *n.* **trickle,** drip, small stream.

drift *v.* **1 be carried along/away,** be borne, be wafted, float, go with the current, coast. **2 wander aimlessly,** wander, roam, rove, meander, coast, stray. **3 pile up,** bank up, accumulate, gather, amass.
 ▶ *n.* **1 movement,** deviation, digression, variation. **2 gist,** essence, meaning, substance, core, significance, import, purport, tenor, vein, implication, direction, course, tendency, trend. **3 pile,** heap, bank, mound, mass, accumulation.

drill *v.* **1 train,** instruct, coach, teach, ground, inculcate, discipline, exercise, rehearse, put one through one's paces. **2 bore,** pierce, puncture, penetrate, perforate.

▸ *n.* **1 training,** instruction, coaching, teaching, grounding, indoctrination. **2 exercises,** physical exercises, strict training, workout. **3 procedure,** routine, practice. **4 auger,** bit.

drink *v.* **1 swallow,** gulp down, drain, quaff, imbibe, partake of, swill, guzzle, sip, *inf.* swig. **2 tipple,** indulge, *inf.* hit the bottle, bend one's elbow, booze.

▸ *n.* **1 beverage,** drinkable/potable liquid, liquid refreshment, thirst-quencher. **2 alcohol,** liquor, spirits, *inf.* booze, hard stuff, hooch. **3 swallow,** gulp, sip, swill, *inf.* swig, slug.

drip *v.* **drop,** dribble, trickle, splash, sprinkle, plop, leak, ooze, exude, filter, percolate.

▸ *n.* **1 drop,** dribble, trickle, splash, plop, leak. **2 ineffective person,** weakling, ninny, milksop, *inf.* nerd, dweeb.

drive *v.* **1 operate,** steer, handle, guide, direct, manage. **2 travel. 3 chauffeur,** run, give one a lift. **4 urge,** press, push, impel, propel, herd, round up. **5 force,** compel, constrain, impel, oblige, coerce, make, pressure, goad, spur, prod. **6 work,** overwork, tax, overtax, overburden. **7 hammer,** ram, bang, sink, plunge, thrust, stab.

▸ *n.* **1 run,** trip, jaunt, outing, journey, excursion, tour, turn, *inf.* spin, joyride. **2 driveway,** road, roadway, avenue. **3 effort,** push, campaign, publicity campaign, crusade, surge. **4 energy,** vigor, verve, ambition, push, enterprise, motivation, initiative, action, aggressiveness, *inf.* get-up-and-go, zip, pizzazz, punch.

drop *n.* **1 droplet,** globule, bead, bubble, blob, spheroid, oval. **2 little,** bit, dash, spot, dribble, splash, sprinkle, trickle, taste, trace, pinch, dab, speck, particle, modicum, *inf.* smidgen, smidge, tad. **3 decline,** decrease, reduction, cut, cutback, lowering, falling-off, downturn, depreciation, devaluation, slump. **4 descent,** incline, declivity, slope, plunge, drop-off, abyss, chasm, precipice, cliff.

▸ *v.* **1 fall in drops,** fall, drip, dribble, trickle, plop, leak. **2 fall,** descend, plunge, plummet, dive, tumble, let fall/go. **3 fall/sink down,** collapse, faint, swoon, drop/fall dead. **4 fall,** decrease, lessen, diminish, depreciate, go into decline, dwindle, sink, slacken off, plunge, plummet. **5 give up,** discontinue, end, stop, cease, terminate, finish with, withdraw/retire from, quit, abandon, forgo, relinquish, dispense with. **6 desert,** abandon, forsake, leave, throw over, jilt, discard, reject, repudiate, renounce, disown, *inf.* ditch, chuck, run out on, leave flat. **7 omit,** leave out, eliminate, elide, contract, slur. *Ant.* lift; rise; retain.

drown *v.* **1 flood,** submerge, immerse, inundate, deluge, swamp, engulf, drench. **2 drown out,** make inaudible, muffle, be louder than, deaden, stifle, overpower, overwhelm, overcome, engulf, swallow up. **3 suppress,** deaden, stifle, quash, quench, extinguish, obliterate, wipe out, get rid of.

drowsy *adj.* **1 sleepy,** half asleep, tired, weary, heavy-eyed, yawning, lethargic, sluggish, somnolent, dazed, drugged, *inf.* dopey. **2 sleepy,** sleep-inducing, soporific, lulling, soothing, dreamy, somniferous. *Ant.* alert; lively.

drug *n.* **1 medical drug,** medicine, medication, medicament, remedy, cure, cure-all, panacea, *lit.* physic. **2 addictive drug,** narcotic, opiate, *inf.* dope.
▸ *v.* **anesthetize,** give an anesthetic to, knock out, make/render unconscious, make/render insensible, stupefy, befuddle, *inf.* dope (up).

drum *v.* **1 tap,** beat, rap, knock, strike. **2 drive home,** instill, hammer, inculcate.

drunk *adj.* **drunken,** blind drunk, dead drunk, intoxicated, inebriated, inebriate, under the influence, tipsy, soused, *inf.* tight, woozy, pie-eyed, three sheets to the wind, under the table, out of it, plastered, smashed, sloshed, stoned, well-oiled, blotto, blitzed, lit up, stewed, pickled, tanked (up), bombed. *Ant.* sober.
▸ *n.* **drunkard,** inebriate, heavy/hard drinker, sot, toper, tippler, alcoholic, dipsomaniac, problem drinker, *inf.* boozer, lush, alky, wino, elbow-bender.

dry *adj.* **1 arid,** dried up/out, parched, scorched, dehydrated, desiccated, waterless, unwatered, moistureless, rainless, torrid, thirsty, droughty, barren, unproductive, sterile. **2 withered,** shriveled, wilted, dehydrated, desiccated, wizened, sapless, juiceless, dried out, hard, hardened, stale. **3 dull,** uninteresting, boring, tedious, tiresome, wearisome, dreary, monotonous, flat, unimaginative, commonplace, prosaic, run-of-the-mill, humdrum, vapid. **4 subtle,** low-key, deadpan, laconic, sly, sharp, ironic, sarcastic, satirical, cynical, droll, waggish. **5 unemotional,** indifferent, cool, cold, aloof, remote, impersonal. **6 prohibitionist,** teetotal,

teetotaling, alcohol-free. **Ant.** wet;
fresh; interesting.

▸ *v.* **1 make dry,** dry out/up, parch,
scorch, dehydrate, desiccate,
dehumidify, sear. **2 dry up,**
wither, shrivel, wilt, dehydrate,
desiccate, wizen, mummify.
3 dehydrate, preserve, cure. **4 dry
off,** mop up, blot up, towel, drain.

dub *v.* **1 call,** name, christen,
designate, term, entitle, style,
label, denominate, nominate, tag,
nickname. **2 knight.**

dubious *adj.* **1 doubtful,**
uncertain, unsure, hesitant,
undecided, wavering, vacillating,
irresolute, on the horns of a
dilemma, skeptical, suspicious, *inf.*
iffy. **2 doubtful,** undecided,
unsure, unsettled, undetermined,
indefinite, unresolved, up in the
air, open, equivocal, debatable,
questionable. **3 equivocal,**
ambiguous, indeterminate,
indefinite, unclear, vague,
imprecise, hazy, puzzling,
enigmatic, cryptic.
4 questionable, suspicious,
suspect, under suspicion,
untrustworthy, unreliable,
undependable, *inf.* shady, fishy.
Ant. certain; sure; definite.

duck *v.* **1 bend,** bow down, bob
down, stoop, crouch, squat,
hunch down, hunker down,
lower, drop. **2 immerse,**

submerge, plunge, dip, souse,
douse, dunk. **3 dodge,** evade,
sidestep, avoid, steer clear of,
elude, escape, shirk, shun.

duct *n.* **pipe,** tube, conduit,
channel, passage, canal, culvert.

due *adj.* **1 owing,** owed, payable,
outstanding. **2 deserved by,**
merited by, earned by, justified
by, appropriate to, fit for, fitting
to, suitable for, right for.
3 proper, right and proper,
correct, rightful, fitting,
appropriate, apt, adequate,
sufficient, enough, ample,
satisfactory, requisite, apposite.
4 scheduled, expected, required,
awaited, anticipated.

▸ *n.* **rights,** deserts, *inf.*
comeuppance.

▸ *adv.* **directly,** straight, without
deviating, undeviatingly, dead,
exactly.

dull *adj.* **1 dull-witted,** slow, slow-
witted, unintelligent, stupid,
dense, doltish, stolid, vacuous, *inf.*
dim, dim-witted, thick, dumb,
birdbrained. **2 insensitive,**
unfeeling, unemotional,
indifferent, unsympathetic,
unresponsive, apathetic, blank,
uncaring, passionless, callous.
3 inactive, inert, slow, slow-
moving, sleepy, drowsy, idle,
sluggish, stagnant, lethargic,
listless, languid, heavy, apathetic,

torpid, phlegmatic, vegetative.
4 dull as dishwater, uninteresting, boring, tedious, tiresome, wearisome, dry, monotonous, flat, bland, unimaginative, commonplace, prosaic, run-of-the-mill, humdrum, uneventful, vapid. **5 overcast,** cloudy, gloomy, dark, dim, dismal, dreary, bleak, somber, leaden, murky, sunless.
6 drab, dreary, somber, dark, subdued, muted, toned-down, lackluster, lusterless, colorless, faded, washed-out. **7 muffled,** muted, indistinct, feeble. **8 blunt,** blunted, not sharp, unkeen, unsharpened, dulled, edgeless. *Ant.* clever; active; interesting; bright.
▸ *v.* **1 take the edge off,** blunt, lessen, decrease, diminish, reduce, deaden, mute, tone down, allay, ease, soothe, assuage, alleviate, palliate. **2 numb,** benumb, stupefy, drug, sedate, tranquilize. **3 fade,** bleach, wash out. **4 darken,** dim, bedim, obscure. **5 dispirit,** dishearten, depress, deject, sadden, discourage, cast down, dampen, put a damper on, cast a pall over.
dumbfound *v.* **astound,** astonish, amaze, startle, surprise, stun, take aback, stagger, overwhelm, confound, shock, confuse, bewilder, baffle, nonplus, perplex, disconcert, *inf.* flabbergast, throw, shake, throw for a loop.
dummy *n.* **1 model,** mannequin, manikin, figure, lay figure.
2 representation, reproduction, sample, copy, imitation, counterfeit, sham, substitute.
3 idiot, fool, dolt, dunce, blockhead, numskull, oaf, nincompoop, ninny, ass, dullard, *inf.* clod, nitwit, dimwit, dope, chump, bonehead, jerk, airhead, schmuck.
dump *v.* **1 place,** put, put down, lay down, deposit, drop, let fall, throw down, fling down, discharge, empty out, pour out, tip out, unload, jettison.
2 dispose of, get rid of, throw away/out, scrap, jettison.
3 abandon, desert, leave, leave in the lurch, forsake, walk out on.
▸ *n.* **1 landfill,** junkyard, scrapyard, transfer station. **2 hovel,** shack, slum, shanty, pigsty, *inf.* hole, joint.
dunce *n.* **dolt,** blockhead, dunderhead, thickhead, numskull, nincompoop, ninny, simpleton, halfwit, idiot, moron, ass, ignoramus, dullard, *inf.* dimwit, dummy, bonehead, deadhead.
duplicate *adj.* **identical,** twin, matching, matched, paired, corresponding, twofold.

▶ *n.* **1 copy,** replica, facsimile, reproduction, exact/close likeness, twin, double, clone, match, mate, fellow, counterpart, *inf.* look-alike, spitting image, ringer, dead ringer. **2 copy,** carbon copy, carbon, photocopy, facsimile, fax, *Trademark* Photostat, Xerox, Xerox copy.

duplicity *n.* **deceitfulness,** double-dealing, trickery, guile, chicanery, artifice, dishonesty, knavery, two-facedness. *Ant.* honesty; candor.

durable *adj.* **lasting,** long-lasting, enduring, persisting, persistent, abiding, continuing, constant, stable, fast, firm, fixed, permanent, unfading, changeless, unchanging, invariable, dependable, reliable, hard-wearing, strong, sturdy, sound, tough, resistant, substantial, imperishable. *Ant.* ephemeral; flimsy.

dusk *n.* **twilight,** evening, sunset, sundown, nightfall, *dial.* eventide.

dust *n.* **1 dirt,** soot, soil, soil. **2 fuss,** commotion, disturbance, uproar, fracas, rumpus, racket. ▶ *v.* **1 wipe,** brush, clean, mop. **2 sprinkle,** dredge, sift, scatter, powder, spray, cover, spread, strew.

dusty *adj.* **1 dust-covered,** undusted, dirty, grubby, grimy, unclean, sooty. **2 powdery,** chalky, crumbly, friable. **3 grayish,** muted, dull, pale.

dutiful *adj.* **respectful,** filial, deferential, reverent, reverential, conscientious, devoted, considerate, thoughtful, obedient, compliant, pliant, docile, submissive. *Ant.* disrespectful; remiss.

duty *n.* **1 responsibility,** obligation, obedience, allegiance, loyalty, faithfulness, fidelity, respect, deference, reverence, homage. **2 task,** job, chore, assignment, commission, mission, function, office, charge, part, role, requirement, responsibility, obligation, work, burden, onus. **3 tax,** levy, tariff, excise, toll, fee, impost, customs, dues.

dwarf *v.* **1 stunt,** arrest/check growth, atrophy. **2 tower above/over,** overshadow, stand head and shoulders over, dominate. **3 overshadow,** diminish, minimize.

dwell *v.* **reside,** live, be domiciled, lodge, stay, abide.

dwindle *v.* **1 become/grow less,** become/grow smaller, decrease, lessen, diminish, shrink, contract, fade, wane. **2 decline,** fail, sink, ebb, wane, degenerate, deteriorate, decay, wither, rot,

disappear, vanish, die out, *inf.*
peter out. ***Ant.*** increase; grow;
flourish.

dye *n.* **colorant,** color, coloring
agent, coloring, pigment, tint,
stain, wash.

▸ *v.* **color,** tint.

dynamic *adj.* **energetic,** active,
lively, alive, spirited, vital,
vigorous, strong, forceful,
powerful, potent, effective,
effectual, high-powered,
magnetic, aggressive, go-ahead,
driving, electric, *inf.* go-getting,
zippy, peppy. ***Ant.*** listless;
lackadaisical.

Ee

eager *adj.* **1 keen,** enthusiastic, impatient, avid, fervent, earnest, diligent, zealous, passionate, wholehearted, ambitious, enterprising, *inf.* bright-eyed and bushy-tailed. **2 agog,** anxious, intent, longing, yearning, itching, wishing, desirous, hopeful, thirsty, hungry, greedy, *inf.* hot. **Ant.** indifferent; uninterested; apathetic.

early *adv.* **1 at dawn,** at the crack/break of dawn, at daybreak. **2 ahead of time,** too soon, beforehand, before the usual/appointed time, prematurely, in good time, ahead of schedule. ▸ *adj.* **1 advanced,** premature, untimely. **2 prompt,** without delay, quick, speedy, rapid, fast, expeditious, timely. **3 primitive,** primeval, primordial, prehistoric. **Ant.** late; belated; overdue.

earn *v.* **1 make,** get, receive, obtain, draw, clear, collect, bring in, take home, pull in, pocket, gross, net. **2 gain,** win, rate, merit, attain, achieve, secure, obtain, deserve, be entitled to, be worthy of, have a right to, warrant.

earnest *adj.* **1 serious,** solemn, grave, intense, staid, studious, thoughtful, committed, dedicated, assiduous, keen, diligent, zealous, steady, hard-working. **2 sincere,** fervent, fervid, ardent, passionate, warm, intense, heartfelt, wholehearted, profound, enthusiastic, zealous, urgent. **Ant.** frivolous; flippant; insincere.

earnings *pl. n.* **income,** salary, wage, pay, take-home pay, remuneration, emolument, fee, stipend, honorarium, revenue, yield, profit, gain, return, wages.

earth *n.* **1 globe,** world, planet, sphere, orb. **2 soil,** loam, clay, dirt, sod, clod, turf, ground. **3 ground,** dry ground, land, terra firma.

earthly *adj.* **1 terrestrial,** telluric, tellurian. **2 worldly,** temporal, secular, mortal, human, mundane, material, nonspiritual, materialistic, carnal, fleshly, physical, corporeal, gross, sensual, base, sordid, vile, profane. **3 possible,** conceivable, imaginable. **Ant.** heavenly; spiritual.

earthy *adj.* **1 soil-like,** dirtlike.

2 down-to-earth, unsophisticated, unrefined, simple, plain, unpretentious, natural, uninhibited, rough, robust.
3 bawdy, crude, coarse, rough, ribald, blue, indecent, indecorous.

ease *n.* **1 facility,** simplicity, effortlessness, deftness, adroitness, dexterity, proficiency, mastery. **2 naturalness,** casualness, informality, unceremoniousness, relaxedness, amiability, affability, unconcern, composure, aplomb, nonchalance, insouciance, urbanity, suaveness. **3 peace,** peacefulness, calmness, tranquillity, composure, serenity, repose, restfulness, quiet, contentment, security, comfort.
4 comfort, contentment, content, enjoyment, affluence, wealth, prosperity, prosperousness, luxury, opulence, bed of roses. *Ant.* difficulty; trouble.
▸ *v.* **1 mitigate,** lessen, reduce, lighten, diminish, moderate, abate, ameliorate, relieve, assuage, allay, soothe, soften, palliate, mollify, appease, grow less, grow quiet, slacken off.
2 comfort, give solace to, solace, console, soothe, calm, quieten, pacify. **3 make easy/easier,** facilitate, expedite, speed up, assist, help, aid, advance, further, forward, smooth/clear the way for, simplify. **4 guide,** maneuver, inch, edge, steer, slide, slip, squeeze. *Ant.* aggravate; increase; hinder.

easy *adj.* **1 not difficult,** simple, effortless, uncomplicated, straightforward, undemanding, painless, trouble-free, facile, idiot-proof. **2 compliant,** exploitable, susceptible, accommodating, obliging, amenable, docile, gullible, manageable, maneuverable, tractable, pliant, yielding, trusting, acquiescent.
3 natural, casual, informal, unceremonious, unreserved, unconstrained, unforced, easygoing, amiable, affable, unconcerned, composed, carefree, nonchalant, insouciant, urbane, suave, *inf.* laid-back. **4 at ease,** trouble-free, untroubled, unworried, at peace, calm, tranquil, composed, serene, quiet, contented, secure, relaxed, comfortable. **5 even,** steady, regular, comfortable, moderate, unexacting, undemanding, leisured, unhurried. *Ant.* difficult; demanding; formal; uneasy.

easygoing *adj.* **even-tempered,** placid, happy-go-lucky, serene, relaxed, carefree, nonchalant, insouciant, tolerant, undemanding, amiable, patient, understanding, imperturbable, *inf.* laid-back, together. **Ant.** intolerant; tense.

eat *v.* **1 consume,** devour, swallow, chew, munch, gulp down, bolt, wolf, ingest, *inf.* put away, scoff (up/down). **2 have a meal,** take food, feed, partake of food, breakfast, lunch, dine, *inf.* snack, graze. **3 erode,** corrode, wear, dissolve, rot, decay, destroy.

eavesdrop *v.* **listen in,** snoop, spy, monitor, tap, wiretap, overhear, *inf.* bug.

ebb *v.* **1 go out,** flow back, retreat, draw back, fall back, fall away, recede, abate, subside, retrocede. **2 decline,** die/fade away, die out, lessen, wane, decrease, diminish, flag, dwindle, peter out, sink, weaken, deteriorate, decay, degenerate.
▸ *n.* **1 going out,** flowing back, retreat, retreating, drawing back, receding, abating, subsiding, retrocession. **2 decline,** dying/fading away, lessening, waning, decrease, flagging, diminution, dwindling, petering out, sinking, deterioration, decay, degeneration.

ebullience *n.* **exuberance,** effervescence, buoyancy, exhilaration, elation, euphoria, high-spiritedness, jubilation, animation, sparkle, vivacity, enthusiasm, zest, irrepressibility, high spirits.

eccentric *adj.* **odd,** queer, strange, peculiar, weird, bizarre, outlandish, freakish, uncommon, irregular, abnormal, aberrant, anomalous, nonconformist, unconventional, singular, idiosyncratic, capricious, whimsical, quirky, *inf.* way-out, offbeat, nutty, screwy. **Ant.** ordinary; conventional.
▸ *n.* **oddity,** freak, character, case, *inf.* oddball, weirdo, nut, screwball.

echo *n.* **1 reverberation,** reverberating, resounding, ringing, repeating. **2 copy,** imitation, reproduction, clone, duplicate, repeat, reflection, mirror image, parallel, parody. **3 suggestion,** hint, trace, allusion, memory, reminder, remembrance, evocation, intimation, overtones, reminiscences.
▸ *v.* **1 reverberate,** resound, reflect, ring, repeat. **2 copy,** imitate, reproduce, repeat, reiterate, parrot, reflect, mirror, parallel, parody.

eclipse *v.* **1 blot out,** block, cover, obscure, conceal, cast a shadow over, darken, shade, veil, shroud. **2 outshine,** overshadow, dwarf, put in the shade, surpass, excel, exceed, outstrip, transcend, outrival.

▸ *n.* **1 blotting out,** blocking, covering, obscuring, concealing, veiling, shrouding, occultation. **2 decline,** fall, failure, deterioration, degeneration, weakening, ebb, waning. **3 outshining,** overshadowing, dwarfing, surpassing, excelling, outstripping, transcending.

economical *adj.* **1 economizing,** thrifty, sparing, careful, prudent, frugal, scrimping, mean, niggardly, stingy, parsimonious, conservationist, *inf.* penny-pinching. **2 cheap,** inexpensive, reasonable, low-cost, low-price, low-budget, budget. *Ant.* extravagant; wasteful; expensive.

economize *v.* **cut back,** retrench, budget, cut expenditure, be economical, be sparing/frugal, reduce/decrease waste/wastage, scrimp, save, scrimp and save, *inf.* cut corners, tighten one's belt, pinch pennies. *Ant.* squander.

economy *n.* **1 wealth,** resources, financial state, financial management. **2 thriftiness,** sparingness, carefulness, prudence, frugalness, scrimping, meanness, niggardliness, stinginess, parsimony, parsimoniousness, thrift, care,

restraint, frugality, husbandry, conservation, *inf.* penny-pinching.

ecstasy *n.* **bliss,** rapture, elation, euphoria, joy, joyousness, jubilation, exultation, cloud nine, seventh heaven, rhapsodies. *Ant.* misery; anguish; torment.

ecstatic *adj.* **blissful,** enraptured, rapturous, joyful, joyous, overjoyed, jumping for joy, jubilant, exultant, elated, rhapsodic, delirious, on cloud nine, in seventh heaven. *Ant.* miserable; depressed.

eddy *n.* **whirlpool,** vortex, maelstrom, swirling, swirl, countercurrent.

▸ *v.* **swirl,** swirl around, whirl.

edge *n.* **1 border,** side, boundary, rim, margin, fringe, outer limit, extremity, verge, brink, lip, contour, perimeter, periphery, parameter, ambit. **2 sting,** bite, sharpness, severity, pointedness, acerbity, causticity, acidity, acrimony, virulence, trenchancy, pungency. **3 advantage,** upper hand, lead, head start, dominance, superiority.

▸ *v.* **1 put an edge on,** sharpen, hone, whet, strop, file. **2 trim,** bind, hem, border, fringe. **3 inch,** ease, elbow, worm, work, sidle, sidestep, gravitate, sidle, creep, steal.

edgy *adj.* **on edge,** nervous, tense,

ill at ease, anxious, on tenterhooks, keyed up, restive, apprehensive, uneasy, irritable, irascible, touchy, tetchy, *inf.* nervy, twitchy, uptight, wired. **Ant.** tranquil; calm; relaxed.

edit *v.* **1 copyedit,** revise, correct, blue-pencil, emend, polish, check, modify, rewrite, rephrase, prepare/adapt/assemble for publication, redact, *inf.* clean up. **2 be the editor of,** run, direct, be in charge of, be chief of, head, head up.

edition *n.* **issue,** number, printing, version, impression, publication, issue.

educate *v.* **instruct,** teach, school, tutor, coach, train, drill, prime, inform, indoctrinate, inculcate, enlighten, edify, cultivate, develop, improve, prepare, rear, nurture, foster.

educated *adj.* **literate,** schooled, well-read, informed, knowledgeable, enlightened, lettered, erudite, cultivated, cultured, refined, *inf.* highbrow. **Ant.** illiterate; ignorant.

education *n.* **1 schooling,** teaching, instruction, tuition, coaching, training, tutelage, drilling, disciplining, priming, informing, indoctrination, inculcation, enlightenment, edification, cultivation, development, improvement, preparation, rearing, nurturing, fostering. **2 literacy,** schooling, scholarship, knowledge, enlightenment, cultivation, culture, refinement, letters.

eerie *adj.* **uncanny,** unearthly, ghostly, spectral, mysterious, strange, unnatural, frightening, fearful, scaring, chilling, spine-chilling, blood-curdling, *inf.* spooky, scary, creepy.

effect *n.* **1 result,** net result, outcome, upshot, consequence, conclusion, aftermath, issue, results, fruits. **2 force,** enforcement, operation, implementation, execution, action. **3 effectiveness,** success, influence, efficacy, effectuality, weight, power, cogency. **4 sense,** meaning, drift, tenor, significance, import, purport, essence. **Ant.** cause.
▸ *v.* **effectuate,** bring about, carry out, cause, make, produce, create, give rise to, perform, achieve, accomplish, complete, fulfill, implement, execute, actuate, initiate.

effective *adj.* **1 successful,** productive, competent, capable, able, efficient, efficacious, effectual, useful, adequate, active, energetic. **2 striking,** impressive, exciting, attractive. **3 powerful,**

forceful, forcible, cogent, compelling, potent, telling, persuasive, convincing, moving. **4 valid,** in force, in operation, operative, active, effectual. *Ant.* ineffective; incompetent; weak.

effeminate *adj.* **womanish,** unmanly, effete, milksoppish, *inf.* wimpish, pansy-like, sissy. *Ant.* virile; manly.

efficient *adj.* **capable,** able, competent, effective, productive, skillful, expert, proficient, adept, deft, organized, workmanlike, businesslike, organized, well-organized, well-run, well-ordered, streamlined, laborsaving. *Ant.* inefficient; inept; disorganized.

effigy *n.* **likeness,** image, model, dummy.

effort *n.* **1 exertion,** force, power, energy, work, muscle, application, labor, striving, endeavor, toil, struggle, strain, stress, *lit.* travail, *inf.* elbow grease. **2 attempt,** try, endeavor, *inf.* shot, go, crack, stab. **3 achievement,** accomplishment, attainment, result, creation, production, opus, feat, deed.

effrontery *n.* **impertinence,** insolence, boldness, audacity, arrogance, impudence, cheek, temerity, presumption, gall, brashness, *inf.* nerve, brass.

effusive *adj.* **gushing,** unrestrained, unreserved, extravagant, fulsome, demonstrative, lavish, enthusiastic, rhapsodic, lyrical, exuberant, ebullient, expansive, wordy, verbose, long-winded, profuse.

eject *v.* **1 emit,** discharge, exude, excrete, expel, cast out, release, spew out, disgorge, spout, vomit, ejaculate, propel, thrust out, throw out. **2 throw out,** turn out, put out, cast out, remove, evict, expel, oust, put out in the street, dispossess, banish, deport, exile, *inf.* kick out, boot out, bounce. **3 sack,** dismiss, discharge, oust, dislodge, get rid of, send packing, *inf.* fire, axe, hand someone his/her pink slip, kick out, boot out, give the boot to.

elaborate *adj.* **1 complicated,** detailed, complex, involved, intricate, studied, painstaking, careful. **2 detailed,** complex, ornate, fancy, showy, ostentatious, extravagant. *Ant.* simple; plain.
▶ *v.* **1 expand on,** enlarge on, amplify, flesh out, detail, expatiate on. **2 develop,** work out, improve, refine, polish, perfect, embellish, enhance, ornament, embroider. *Ant.* simplify; streamline.

elastic *adj.* **stretchy,** stretchable,

springy, flexible, pliant, pliable, supple, yielding, rubbery, plastic, rebounding, recoiling, resilient, adaptable, fluid, adjustable. **Ant.** rigid; inflexible.

elderly *adj.* **aging,** aged, old, oldish, advanced in years, gray-haired, ancient, superannuated, past one's prime, *inf.* over the hill, long in the tooth. **Ant.** young; youthful.

▸ *pl. n.* **seniors,** senior citizens, old folks. **Ant.** young; youth.

elect *v.* **vote for,** cast one's vote for, choose by ballot, choose, pick, select, appoint, opt for, decide on, designate, determine.

election *n.* **1 ballot,** poll, general election, local election. **2 voting,** choosing, picking, selection, choice, appointment, vote, ballot.

electric *adj.* **1 galvanic,** voltaic. **2 tense,** charged, exciting, dynamic, thrilling, startling, stimulating, rousing, stirring, moving, jolting, shocking, galvanizing.

electrify *v.* **excite,** thrill, startle, shock, arouse, rouse, move, stimulate, stir, animate, fire, charge, invigorate, jolt, galvanize.

elegant *adj.* **stylish,** graceful, tasteful, artistic, fashionable, cultured, beautiful, lovely, charming, exquisite, polished, cultivated, refined, aesthetic, suave, debonair, modish, dignified, luxurious, sumptuous, opulent. **Ant.** inelegant; unfashionable; gauche.

element *n.* **1 basis,** ingredient, factor, feature, detail, trace, component, constituent, part, section, portion, piece, segment, member, unit, module, subdivision. **2 environment,** habitat, medium, milieu, sphere, field, domain, realm, circle, resort, haunt.

elementary *adj.* **1 easy,** simple, straightforward, uncomplicated, rudimentary, facile, simplistic. **2 basic,** fundamental, rudimentary, primary, preparatory, introductory. **Ant.** complicated; advanced; senior.

elevate *v.* **1 raise,** lift, hoist, hike up, raise up/aloft. **2 promote,** give promotion, upgrade, improve the position/status of, advance, give advancement, exalt, prefer, aggrandize, *inf.* kick upstairs. **3 cheer,** gladden, brighten, perk up, give a lift/boost to, lighten, cheer up, animate, exhilarate, elate, boost, buoy up, uplift. **Ant.** lower; demote; depress.

elevated *adj.* **1 raised,** lifted up, hoisted, high up, aloft, upraised, uplifted. **2 high,** higher, high/higher up, great, grand, lofty, dignified, noble, exalted, magnificent, sublime, inflated, pompous, bombastic. **3 cheerful,** cheered up, glad, joyful, happy, overjoyed, gleeful, excited, animated, elated, exhilarated, in high spirits, blithe.

elf *n.* **fairy,** pixie, sprite, dwarf, gnome, goblin, hobgoblin, imp, brownie, leprechaun, puck, troll, banshee.

elicit *v.* **obtain,** bring out, draw out, extract, extort, exact, wrest, evoke, derive, call forth, educe.

elite *n.* **1 best,** pick, cream, crème de la crème, elect, meritocracy. **2 aristocracy,** nobility, gentry, establishment, high society, jet set, beautiful people, upper crust. *Ant.* riff-raff; rabble.

eloquent *adj.* **1 expressive,** well-spoken, articulate, fluent, graceful, silver-tongued, smooth-tongued, well-expressed, vivid, effective, graphic, pithy, persuasive, glib, forceful. **2 expressive,** significant, meaningful, suggestive, revealing, telling, pregnant. *Ant.* inarticulate; tongue-tied.

elude *v.* **avoid,** get away from, dodge, evade, escape, lose, duck, shake off, give the slip to, throw off the scent, flee, circumvent, *inf.* ditch.

elusive *adj.* **1 difficult to catch/ find,** evasive, slippery, shifty, cagey. **2 indefinable,** subtle, unanalyzable, intangible, impalpable, fleeting, transient, transitory, fugitive. **3 ambiguous,** baffling, puzzling, misleading, evasive, equivocal, deceitful, deceptive, fallacious, fraudulent, elusory.

emaciated *adj.* **wasted,** gaunt, skeletal, anorexic, scrawny, cadaverous, shriveled, shrunken, withered, haggard, drawn, pinched, wizened, attenuated, atrophied.

emancipate *v.* **1 free,** set free, liberate, release, let loose, deliver, discharge, unchain, unfetter, unshackle, untie, unyoke, manumit. **2 enfranchise.**

emasculate *v.* **1 castrate,** neuter, geld, spay, desex, unman. **2 weaken,** debilitate, make feeble/ feebler, enfeeble, enervate, impoverish.

embargo *n.* **ban,** bar, prohibition, stoppage, interdict, proscription, restriction, restraint, blockage, check, barrier, impediment, obstruction, hindrance.
 ▶ *v.* **ban,** bar, prohibit, stop, interdict, debar, proscribe, restrict, restrain, block, check, impede, obstruct, hinder.

embarrass v. disconcert, discomfit, discompose, confuse, nonplus, distress, chagrin, shame, humiliate, abash, mortify.

embed v. imbed, insert, implant, plant, set/fix in, root, drive in, hammer in, ram in, sink.

embellish v. decorate, adorn, ornament, dress, dress up, beautify, enhance, trim, garnish, gild, varnish, embroider, enrich, deck, bedeck, festoon, emblazon, bespangle, elaborate, exaggerate.

embezzle v. steal, rob, thieve, pilfer, appropriate, misappropriate, purloin, filch, abstract, put one's hand in the till, peculate, defalcate, inf. rip off.

emblazon v. 1 decorate, adorn, ornament, embellish, illuminate, color, paint. 2 proclaim, publicize, publish, trumpet, glorify, extol, praise, laud.

emblem n. crest, badge, symbol, device, representation, token, image, figure, mark, sign, insignia.

embody v. 1 incorporate, combine, bring together, comprise, collect, include, contain, constitute, take in, consolidate, encompass, assimilate, integrate, concentrate, organize, systematize. 2 personify, represent, symbolize, stand for, typify, exemplify, incorporate, realize, manifest, express, incarnate.

embrace v. 1 take/hold in one's arms, hold, hug, cuddle, clasp, squeeze, clutch, seize, grab, nuzzle, enfold, enclasp, encircle, inf. neck with. 2 welcome, accept, receive enthusiastically/ wholeheartedly, take up, adopt, fml. espouse. 3 cover, include, take in, deal with, involve, take into account, contain, comprise, incorporate, encompass, embody, subsume, comprehend, enfold. *Ant.* reject; exclude.
▶ n. **hug**, bear hug, cuddle, squeeze, clasp, hold, clutch, clinch, nuzzle.

emerge v. 1 come out, come into view, appear, come up, become visible, surface, spring up, crop up, materialize, arise, proceed, issue, come forth, emanate. 2 come out, come to light, get around, become known/apparent, transpire, come to the fore. *Ant.* enter; disappear; fade.

emergency n. urgent situation, crisis, danger, accident, difficulty, plight, predicament, quandary, dilemma, crunch, scrape, extremity, exigency, necessity, unforeseen circumstances, dire/ desperate straits, inf. pickle.
▶ adj. **urgent**, reserve, backup,

substitute, alternative, spare,
extra.

eminence *n.* **1 importance,**
greatness, prestige, reputation,
fame, distinction, renown,
preeminence, celebrity,
prominence, illustriousness,
notability, rank, standing, station,
note, dignity. **2 elevation,** rise,
rising/raised ground, height.

eminent *adj.* **important,** great,
distinguished, well-known,
celebrated, famous, renowned,
noted, prominent, esteemed,
noteworthy, preeminent,
superior, outstanding, high-
ranking, exalted, revered,
elevated, august, paramount. ***Ant.***
unimportant; unknown.

emit *v.* **1 discharge,** pour out, give
out/off, issue, send forth, throw
out, ooze, leak, excrete, secrete,
eject, emanate, radiate, exhale,
ejaculate, exude. **2 utter,** express,
voice, pronounce, declare,
articulate, vocalize.

emotional *adj.* **1 feeling,**
passionate, hot-blooded, warm,
responsive, demonstrative,
tender, loving, sentimental,
ardent, fervent, sensitive,
excitable, temperamental,
melodramatic. **2 moving,**
touching, affecting, poignant,
emotive, pathetic, tear-jerking,
heart-rending, soul-stirring,

impassioned. ***Ant.*** unemotional;
apathetic; cold.

emotive *adj.* **sensitive,** delicate,
controversial, touchy, awkward.

emphasis *n.* **1 stress,** accent,
accentuation, weight.
2 importance, stress, attention,
priority, weight, urgency, force,
accent, accentuation, insistence,
significance, prominence,
underlining, intensity, import,
mark, power, moment,
preeminence, underscoring.

emphasize *v.* **1 stress,**
accentuate, accent, underline, call
attention to, highlight, point up,
spotlight, play up, feature,
intensify, strengthen, heighten,
deepen, underscore. **2 put/lay
stress on,** give an emphasis to,
stress, accent, accentuate,
underline, call attention to,
highlight, give prominence to,
point up, spotlight, play up,
feature, intensify, strengthen,
heighten, deepen, underscore.
Ant. understate; play down (see
play); minimize.

emphatic *adj.* **1 marked,**
pronounced, decided, positive,
definite, unmistakable,
important, significant, strong,
striking, powerful, resounding,
telling, momentous, certain,
determined, direct, forceful,
earnest, energetic, vigorous,

categorical, unequivocal.
2 definite, decided, certain, determined, absolute, direct, forceful, forcible, earnest, energetic, vigorous, categorical, unequivocal. **Ant.** insignificant; hesitant; tentative.

employ *v.* **1 hire,** engage, take on, sign up, put on the payroll, enroll, commission, enlist, retain, indenture, apprentice. **2 occupy,** engage, keep busy. **3 occupy,** take up, use up, put to use, make use of, fill, spend. **4 use,** apply, make use of, exercise, exert, utilize, ply, bring to bear.

employee *n.* **worker,** blue-collar worker, white-collar worker, workman, member of staff, wage-earner, hand, hired hand, assistant, laborer, hireling. **Ant.** employer; boss.

employer *n.* **boss,** manager, owner, proprietor, patron, contractor, director, head man/woman, top man/woman, firm, organization. **Ant.** employee; hireling; underling.

empower *v.* **1 authorize,** license, certify, accredit, qualify, sanction, warrant, commission, delegate. **2 allow,** enable, give power/means/strength to, equip.

empty *adj.* **1 containing nothing,** without contents, unfilled, vacant, hollow, void, unoccupied, uninhabited, desolate, bare, unadorned, barren, blank, clear.
2 meaningless, futile, ineffective, ineffectual, useless, worthless, idle, insubstantial, fruitless, aimless, purposeless, hollow, barren, senseless, unsatisfactory, silly, banal, inane, frivolous, trivial, worthless, valueless, profitless. **Ant.** full; occupied; meaningful; worthwhile.
▸ *v.* **1 vacate,** clear, evacuate, void, unload, unburden. **2 drain,** pour out, exhaust, use up, deplete, sap.
3 flow out, pour out, drain, discharge, issue, emit, exude, ooze.

enable *v.* **allow,** permit, authorize, entitle, qualify, fit, license, sanction, warrant, accredit, validate, commission, delegate, legalize, empower, equip, prepare, facilitate.

enchant *v.* **bewitch,** make spellbound, fascinate, charm, captivate, entrance, enthrall, beguile, hypnotize, mesmerize, enrapture, delight, enamor.

enchanting *adj.* **bewitching,** charming, delightful, attractive, appealing, captivating, irresistible, fascinating, engaging, endearing, entrancing, alluring, winsome, ravishing.

enclose *v.* **1 surround,** circle, ring, close in, shut in, fence/wall/

hedge in, hem in, confine, encompass, encircle, circumscribe, encase, *fml.* gird. **2 include,** send with, put in, insert.

enclosure *n.* **1 arena,** compound, ring, yard, pen, pound, fold, paddock, stockade, sty, corral, court. **2 inclusion,** insertion. **3 insertion,** thing enclosed.

encompass *v.* **1 surround,** enclose, ring, encircle, close in, shut in, fence/wall/hedge in, hem in, confine. **2 include,** cover, embrace, take in, contain, envelop, deal with, comprise, incorporate, embody.

encounter *v.* **1 meet,** meet by chance, run into, run across, come upon, stumble across, chance/happen upon, *inf.* bump into. **2 be faced with,** confront, contend with, tussle with. **3 accost,** confront, fight, do battle with, clash with, come into conflict with, engage with, struggle with, contend with, combat, skirmish with, tussle with.
 ▶ *n.* **1 meeting,** chance meeting. **2 fight,** battle, clash, conflict, contest, dispute, combat, collision, confrontation, engagement, skirmish, scuffle, tussle, brawl, *inf.* run-in, set-to, brush.

encourage *v.* **1 cheer,** rally, stimulate, motivate, inspire, stir, incite, animate, hearten, invigorate, embolden, inspirit, urge, persuade, egg on, prompt, influence, exhort, sway, spur, goad, *inf.* buck up. **2 help,** assist, aid, support, back, advocate, abet, boost, favor, promote, further, advance, forward, foster, strengthen. *Ant.* discourage; dissuade; hinder.

encroach *v.* **trespass,** intrude, invade, infringe, impinge, infiltrate, overrun, usurp, appropriate, tread on someone's toes, *inf.* muscle in on, invade someone's space.

encumber *v.* **1 hinder,** hamper, obstruct, impede, inconvenience, handicap, retard, check, cramp, constrain, restrain. **2 block up,** fill up, stuff, clog, congest. **3 burden,** load, weigh down, tax, overtax, saddle, trammel, stress, strain.

encyclopedic *adj.* **comprehensive,** complete, wide-ranging, all-inclusive, thorough, exhaustive, all-embracing, universal, all-encompassing, vast, compendious.

end *n.* **1 edge,** border, boundary, extremity, limit, margin, furthermost part, point, tip, extent. **2 ending,** finish, close, conclusion, termination, completion, resolution, climax, finale, culmination, denouement, epilogue, *inf.* wind-up. **3 remnant,** remainder, fragment, vestige, leftovers. **4 aim,** goal, purpose, intention, intent, objective, object, design, motive, aspiration, raison d'être. **5 death,** dying, demise, doom, extinction, annihilation, extermination, ruin, ruination, destruction, dissolution, death-blow, coup de grâce, finishing stroke, curtains. **6 result,** consequence, outcome, upshot, issue. *Ant.* beginning; start; birth.

▸ *v.* **come to an end,** finish, close, stop, cease, conclude, terminate, discontinue, break off, fade away, peter out, complete, dissolve, resolve, destroy, annihilate, extinguish, *inf.* wind up. *Ant.* begin; start.

endanger *v.* **threaten,** put in danger, expose to danger, put at risk, expose, risk, jeopardize, imperil, hazard, compromise. *Ant.* secure; protect.

endearing *adj.* **charming,** attractive, adorable, lovable, sweet, engaging, winning, captivating, enchanting, winsome.

endearment *n.* **1 sweet talk,** sweet nothings, soft words, blandishments. **2 love,** affection, fondness, liking, attachment.

endeavor *v.* **try,** attempt, strive, work at, try one's hand at, do one's best, venture, aspire, undertake, struggle, labor, essay, *inf.* have a go/shot/stab at.
▸ *n.* **try,** attempt, trial, effort, striving, venture, undertaking, aspiration, enterprise, struggle, laboring, essay, *inf.* go, crack, shot, stab.

endless *adj.* **1 unending,** unlimited, infinite, limitless, boundless, continual, constant, unfading, everlasting, unceasing, interminable, incessant, measureless, untold, incalculable. **2 continuous,** uninterrupted, unbroken, whole, entire, never-ending, nonstop, interminable, monotonous, unremitting, boring. *Ant.* finite; limited; transient.

endorse *v.* **1 countersign,** sign, autograph, underwrite, superscribe, validate. **2 approve,** support, back, favor, recommend, advocate, champion, subscribe to, uphold, authorize, ratify, sanction, warrant, affirm, confirm, vouch for, corroborate.

endow *v.* **1 provide,** give, present, gift, confer, bestow, enrich, supply, furnish, award, invest. **2 bequeath money for,** bestow, will, donate money for, leave money for, make over to, settle on, pay for, finance, fund. *Ant.* divest.

endurance *n.* **1 lasting power,** durability, stability, permanence, continuance, continuity, changelessness, immutability, longevity, everlastingness, immortality. **2 toleration,** sufferance, fortitude, forbearance, perseverance, acceptance, patience, resignation. **3 stamina,** staying power, fortitude, perseverance, tenacity, *inf.* guts.

endure *v.* **1 last,** live on, continue, persist, remain, stay, hold on, survive, wear well, *lit.* abide, bide, tarry. **2 put up with,** stand, bear, tolerate, suffer, abide, submit to, countenance, brook, *inf.* stomach, swallow. **3 experience,** undergo, go through, meet, encounter, bear, tolerate, cope with, suffer, brave, withstand, sustain, weather. *Ant.* die; fade.

enemy *n.* **foe,** opponent, rival, adversary, antagonist, hostile party, opposition, competition. *Ant.* ally; friend.

energetic *adj.* **1 active,** lively, vigorous, strenuous, brisk, dynamic, spirited, animated, vital, vibrant, sprightly, tireless, indefatigable, peppy, zippy, bright-eyed and bushy-tailed. **2 forceful,** forcible, determined, emphatic, aggressive, high-powered, driving, effective, effectual, powerful, potent. *Ant.* lazy; inactive; weak.

energy *n.* **vigor,** strength, stamina, forcefulness, power, might, potency, drive, push, exertion, enterprise, enthusiasm, animation, life, liveliness, pep, vivacity, vitality, spirit, spiritedness, fire, zest, verve, dash, élan, sparkle, buoyancy, effervescence, exuberance, ardor, zeal, passion, *inf.* vim, zip, zing. *Ant.* lethargy; weakness.

enfold *v.* **enclose,** envelop, encircle, shroud, clasp, embrace, hug, hold, wrap.

enforce *v.* **1 apply,** carry out, administer, implement, bring to bear, impose, discharge, fulfill, execute, prosecute, put through. **2 force,** compel, insist on, require, necessitate, oblige, urge, exact, coerce, pressure, pressurize, dragoon, bulldoze, constrain, extort.

engage *v.* **1 employ,** hire, take on, appoint, enlist, enroll, commission. **2 rent,** hire, book, reserve, charter, lease, prearrange, bespeak. **3 occupy,** fill, employ, hold, grip, secure, preoccupy, absorb, engross. **4 catch,** attract, draw, gain, win, capture, captivate, arrest. **5 enter into,** become involved in, undertake, occupy oneself with, embark on, set about, take part in, join in, participate in, partake in/of, launch into, throw oneself into, tackle. **6 contract,** promise, agree, guarantee, undertake, pledge, oblige, obligate, vouch, vow, commit oneself, bind oneself, covenant. **7 join battle,** do battle with, fight with, wage war with, attack, enter into combat, clash with, encounter, take on, set to, skirmish with, grapple with, wrest with, take the field. **8 fit together,** join together, join, interconnect, mesh, intermesh. *Ant.* dismiss; discharge; give up (see give).

engender *v.* **1 cause,** produce, create, give rise to, bring about, lead to, arouse, rouse, excite, provoke, incite, induce, instigate, generate, hatch, effect, occasion, effectuate, foment. **2 give birth to,** father, breed, create, conceive, procreate, reproduce, bring forth, propagate, spawn, sire, beget.

engine *n.* **1 motor,** mechanism, machine. **2 instrument,** implement, machinery, apparatus, means.

engineer *n.* **1 planner,** designer, builder, architect, inventor, originator, deviser, contriver. **2 operator,** controller, handler, director, driver.

▸ *v.* **bring about,** cause, plan, plot, scheme, contrive, devise, maneuver, manipulate, orchestrate, mastermind, originate, manage, control, superintend, direct, conduct, handle, concoct.

engrave *v.* **carve,** etch, inscribe, cut, chisel, imprint, impress, print, mark, fix, set, imprint, stamp, brand, impress, embed, ingrain.

enhance *v.* **1 add to,** increase, heighten, stress, emphasize, strengthen, improve, augment, boost, intensify, reinforce, magnify, amplify, enrich, complement. **2 raise,** lift, increase, escalate, elevate, augment, swell, aggrandize, *inf.* jack up, hike.

enjoy *v.* **1 like,** love, delight in, appreciate, rejoice in, relish, revel in, savor, luxuriate in, *inf.* fancy. **2 have,** possess, own, benefit from, avail oneself of, be blessed/favored with. *Ant.* dislike; hate.

enjoyable *adj.* **entertaining,** amusing, delightful, nice, pleasant, lovely, fine, good, great, agreeable, pleasurable, delicious, delectable, diverting, satisfying, gratifying. *Ant.* unpleasant; disagreeable; hateful.

enlarge *v.* **1 make larger/bigger,** expand, extend, add to, stretch, amplify, augment, supplement, magnify, multiply, widen, broaden, lengthen, elongate, deepen, thicken, distend, dilate, swell, blow up, inflate, bloat, bulge. **2 elaborate,** expound. ***Ant.*** reduce; diminish; lessen.

enlighten *v.* **inform,** make aware, instruct, teach, educate, tutor, indoctrinate, illuminate, apprise, edify, civilize, cultivate, counsel, advise. ***Ant.*** confuse; muddle.

enlist *v.* **1 enroll,** sign up, recruit, hire, employ, register, take on, engage, obtain, procure, secure, gather, muster. **2 join,** join up, enroll/register in, sign on/up for, enter into, volunteer for.

enliven *v.* **brighten up,** cheer up, wake up, give a lift/boost to, buoy up, hearten, gladden, excite, stimulate, rouse, refresh, exhilarate, invigorate, revitalize, vitalize, light a fire under, *inf.* perk up, spice up, jazz up.

enormous *adj.* **huge,** immense, massive, vast, gigantic, colossal, astronomic, mammoth, mountainous, gargantuan, prodigious, tremendous, stupendous, excessive, titanic, Herculean, Brobdingnagian, *inf.* jumbo. ***Ant.*** minute; tiny.

enough *adj.* **sufficient,** adequate, ample, abundant. ***Ant.*** insufficient; inadequate.

▸ *n.* **sufficient/adequate amount,** sufficiency, adequacy, ample supply, abundance, amplitude, plenty, full measure, *inf.* plenitude.

enrage *v.* **annoy,** anger, infuriate, irritate, madden, exasperate, provoke, incense, irk, agitate, inflame, incite, make one's hackles rise, make one's blood boil, *inf.* get one's back/dander up. ***Ant.*** pacify; appease.

enrapture *v.* **delight,** thrill, charm, captivate, fascinate, enchant, bewitch, entrance, enthrall, beguile, transport, ravish, *inf.* blow one's mind, turn on.

ensue *v.* **follow,** come next/after, result, occur, happen, turn up, arise, come to pass, transpire, befall, proceed, succeed, issue, derive, stem, supervene.

ensure *v.* **1 make certain,** make sure, guarantee, secure, effect, warrant, certify, confirm. **2 make safe,** protect, guard, safeguard, secure.

entail *v.* **involve,** require, call for, necessitate, demand, impose, cause, bring about, produce, result in, lead to, give rise to, occasion.

enter *v.* **1 come in/into,** go in/into, pass into, move into, flow into, penetrate, pierce, puncture. **2 join,**

enroll in, enlist in, sign up for, take up, commit oneself to. **3 take part in,** participate in. **4 record,** register, put down, set/take down, note, mark down, catalog, document, list, log, file, index. **5 put forward,** offer, present, proffer, submit, register, tender. **6 begin,** start, commence, embark on, engage in, undertake, venture on. **7 participate in,** engage in, join in. *Ant.* leave; depart; withdraw.

enterprise *n.* **1 venture,** undertaking, project, operation, endeavor, effort, task, plan, scheme, campaign. **2 resourcefulness,** resource, initiative, drive, gumption, imagination, imaginativeness, spirit, spiritedness, enthusiasm, zest, dash, ambition, energy, vigor, vitality, boldness, daring, spirit of adventure, audacity, courage, intrepidity, *inf.* get-up-and-go, go, push, oomph, zip, vim. **3 business,** industry, firm, company, corporation, establishment, house.

enterprising *adj.* **resourceful,** go-ahead, entrepreneurial, imaginative, spirited, enthusiastic, eager, keen, zealous, ambitious, energetic, active, vigorous, vital, bold, daring, adventurous, audacious, courageous, intrepid, *inf.* peppy, pushy, up-and-coming. *Ant.* unimaginative; unadventurous.

entertain *v.* **1 amuse,** divert, delight, please, charm, cheer, beguile, interest, engage, occupy. **2 have company,** throw a party. **3 play host/hostess to,** wine and dine, treat, welcome, fête. **4 harbor,** nurture, foster, cherish, hold, have, possess, hide, conceal. **5 consider,** take into consideration, think about/over, contemplate, weigh, ponder, muse over, cogitate, bear in mind. *Ant.* bore; depress; reject.

entertainment *n.* **1 amusement,** fun, enjoyment, diversion, recreation, distraction, pastime, hobby, leisure activity/pursuit, sport. **2 show,** performance, concert, play, cabaret, presentation, spectacle, pageant.

enthralling *adj.* **spellbinding,** captivating, enchanting, fascinating, bewitching, gripping, riveting, charming, delightful, intriguing, mesmerizing, hypnotic.

enthusiasm *n.* **eagerness,** keenness, ardor, fervor, warmth, passion, zeal, zest, vehemence, fire, excitement, exuberance, ebullience, avidity, wholeheartedness, commitment, devotion, devotedness, fanaticism. *Ant.* indifference; apathy.

enthusiast *n.* **fan,** supporter, follower, devotee, lover, admirer, fanatic, zealot, aficionado, *inf.* buff, freak.

enthusiastic *adj.* **eager,** keen, ardent, fervent, warm, passionate, zealous, vehement, excited, exuberant, ebullient, spirited, avid, hearty, wholehearted, committed, devoted, fanatical, earnest. *Ant.* apathetic; uninterested; indifferent.

entice *v.* **lure,** tempt, seduce, inveigle, lead astray/on, beguile, coax, cajole, wheedle, decoy, bait.

entire *adj.* **1 whole,** complete, total, full, continuous, unbroken. **2 absolute,** total, outright, unqualified, thorough, unreserved, unmitigated, unmodified, unrestricted. **3 sound,** intact, undamaged, unmarked, unharmed, perfect, unbroken, unimpaired, unblemished, unflawed, unspoiled. *Ant.* partial; incomplete; qualified.

entirely *adv.* **absolutely,** completely, totally, fully, wholly, altogether, utterly, in every respect, unreservedly, without reservation, without exception, thoroughly, perfectly, solely, exclusively. *Ant.* partly; partially; slightly.

entitle *v.* **1 qualify,** make eligible, authorize, sanction, allow, permit, enable, empower, warrant, accredit, enfranchise, capacitate. **2 call,** name.

entity *n.* **1 body,** being, person, creature, individual, organism, object, article, thing, real thing, substance, quantity, existence. **2 being,** inner being, existence, life, substance, essence, essential nature, quintessence.

entourage *n.* **retinue,** escort, attendant, company, cortege, train, suite, bodyguard, attendants, companions, members of court, followers, camp followers, associates, *inf.* groupies.

entrails *pl. n.* **intestines,** internal organs, bowels, vital organs, viscera, *inf.* guts, insides, innards.

entrance[1] *v.* **hold spellbound,** captivate, enchant, bewitch, beguile, enthrall, enrapture, ravish, charm, delight, put under a spell, put in a trance, hypnotize, mesmerize.

entrance[2] *n.* **1 entry,** access, approach, door, doorway, gate, gateway, drive, driveway, foyer, lobby, portal, threshold. **2 entry,** appearance, arrival, introduction, ingress. **3 entry,** admission, admittance, access, ingress, entrée. *Ant.* exit; departure.

entrant *n.* **competitor,** contestant, participant, player, candidate, applicant, rival, opponent.

entreat *v.* **beg,** implore, beseech, plead with, appeal to, petition, solicit, pray, crave, exhort, enjoin, importune, supplicate.

entrenched *adj.* **deep-seated,** deep-rooted, rooted, well-established, fixed, set firm, firm, ingrained, unshakable, irremovable, indelible, dyed-in-the-wool.

envelop *v.* **enfold,** cover, wrap, enwrap, cloak, blanket, surround, engulf, encircle, encompass, conceal, hide, obscure.

envelope *n.* **wrapping,** wrap, cover, covering, casing, case, jacket, shell, sheath.

enviable *adj.* **desirable,** worth having, covetable, tempting, excellent, fortunate, lucky, favored.

envious *adj.* **jealous,** covetous, desirous, green with envy, green, green-eyed, grudging, begrudging, resentful, jaundiced.

environment *n.* **surroundings,** conditions, circumstances, habitat, territory, ecology, domain, milieu, medium, element, situation, location, locale, background, setting, scene, context, ambience, atmosphere, mood.

envisage *v.* **foresee,** predict, imagine, visualize, picture, anticipate, envision, imagine, contemplate, conceive of, accept.

envy *n.* **1 enviousness,** covetousness, jealousy, desire, resentment, resentfulness, discontent, spite. **2 object of envy.** ▸ *v.* **covet,** begrudge, grudge.

ephemeral *adj.* **fleeting,** short-lived, transitory, momentary, transient, brief, short, temporary, passing, impermanent, evanescent.

epidemic *n.* **1 outbreak,** plague, scourge. **2 outbreak,** wave, upsurge, upswing, increase. ▸ *adj.* **rife,** rampant, wide-ranging, widespread, sweeping.

episode *n.* **1 installment,** part, section, chapter, passage, scene. **2 incident,** occurrence, event, happening, experience, adventure, occasion, matter, affair, business, interlude, circumstance.

epitome *n.* **1 personification,** embodiment, essence, quintessence, archetype, representation, model, typification, type, example, exemplar, prototype. **2 summary,** précis, résumé, outline, synopsis, abstract, digest, abridgment, abbreviation, condensation, compendium.

epoch *n.* **era**, age, period, time, date.

equal *adj.* **1 the same**, one and the same, identical, alike, like, comparable, commensurate. **2 the same as**, identical to, equivalent to, commensurate with, proportionate to, tantamount to, on a par with. **3 even**, matched, balanced, balanced, level, proportioned, *inf.* fifty-fifty, neck and neck. **4 the same**, identical, like, uniform, unbiased, impartial, nonpartisan, fair, just, evenhanded, egalitarian. **5 even**, constant, uniform, steady, stable, level, unchanging, unvarying, unfluctuating. *Ant.* unequal; different; uneven.
▶ *n.* **equivalent**, peer, compeer, coequal, mate, twin, alter ego, counterpart, match, parallel.

equality *n.* **sameness**, identicalness, identity, equitability, parity, likeness, similarity, uniformity, evenness, levelness, balance, correspondence, parallelism, comparability, fairness, justness, impartiality, egalitarianism, equal opportunity. *Ant.* inequality; difference; unevenness.

equanimity *n.* **composure**, presence of mind, self-possession, self-control, levelheadedness, even-temperedness, equilibrium, poise, aplomb, sang-froid, calmness, calm, coolness, coolheadedness, serenity, placidity, tranquillity, imperturbability, unexcitability, *inf.* cool, unflappability.

equilibrium *n.* **1 balance**, stability, steadiness, evenness, symmetry, equipoise, counterpoise. **2 equanimity**, composure, calmness, coolness, sang-froid, tranquillity, collectedness, serenity, poise, self-possession, imperturbability, steadiness, stability, *inf.* cool, unflappability.

equip *v.* **fit out**, rig out, prepare, supply, stock, arm, array, attire, dress, outfit, suit, endow.

equitable *adj.* **fair**, fair-minded, just, evenhanded, right, rightful, proper, reasonable, honest, impartial, unbiased, unprejudiced, nondiscriminatory, disinterested, dispassionate, open-minded. *Ant.* inequitable; unfair; unjust.

equivalent *adj.* **equal**, the same, much the same, identical, similar, like, alike, interchangeable, comparable, corresponding, correspondent, commensurate, matching, on a par, tantamount, synonymous. *Ant.* different; dissimilar.
▶ *n.* **equal**, counterpart, parallel,

alternative, match, double, twin, peer.

equivocal *adj.* **1 ambiguous,** ambivalent, two-edged, indefinite, vague, obscure, unclear, uncertain, hazy, indeterminate, roundabout, oblique, circuitous, misleading, evasive, duplicitous, paradoxical, doubtful, dubious, questionable, suspicious, suspect. **2 doubtful,** dubious, questionable, suspicious, suspect. **Ant.** unequivocal; definite.

era *n.* **age,** epoch, eon, period, time, generation, stage, cycle, season, times, days.

eradicate *v.* **get rid of,** root out, uproot, remove, extirpate, wipe out, weed out, eliminate, do away with, abolish, stamp out, annihilate, extinguish, excise, erase, obliterate, efface, expunge, destroy, kill.

erase *v.* **remove,** rub out, wipe out, wipe off, blot out, scrape off, obliterate, efface, expunge, excise, cross out, strike out, delete, cancel, blue-pencil.

erect *v.* **1 build,** construct, put up, assemble, put together, raise, elevate, mount, set up. **2 establish,** form, set up, found, institute, initiate, create, organize. **Ant.** demolish; dismantle; destroy.
  ▸ *adj.* **1 upright,** straight, vertical, raised, elevated. **2 hard,** rigid, stiff, firm. **Ant.** bent; horizontal; flaccid.

erode *v.* **wear,** wear away/down, eat, eat away at, corrode, abrade, gnaw, gnaw away at, grind down, excoriate, consume, devour, spoil, disintegrate, deteriorate, destroy.

erotic *adj.* **titillating,** stimulating, exciting, arousing, erogenous, aphrodisiac, seductive, sensual, carnal, amatory, salacious, suggestive, pornographic, *inf.* sexy, steamy.

err *v.* **1 be in error,** be wrong, be incorrect, be inaccurate, make a mistake, be mistaken, blunder, misjudge, miscalculate, misunderstand, misapprehend, misconstrue, get things/it wrong, bark up the wrong tree, be wide of the mark, *inf.* slip up, make a booboo. **2 do wrong,** go wrong, go astray, sin, behave badly, misbehave, transgress, trespass, fall from grace, lapse, degenerate.

errand *n.* **message,** task, job, commission, chore, assignment, undertaking, charge, mission.

erratic *adj.* **1 inconsistent,** variable, varying, irregular, unstable, unreliable, unpredictable, capricious, whimsical, fitful, wayward, abnormal, eccentric, aberrant, deviant. **2 wandering,**

meandering, wavering, directionless. **Ant.** consistent; predictable.

error *n.* **1 mistake,** inaccuracy, miscalculation, blunder, fault, flaw, oversight, misprint, erratum, misinterpretation, misreading, fallacy, misconception, delusion, erroneousness, oversight, misjudgment, *inf.* slipup, booboo, boner. **2 wrongdoing,** mischief, mischievousness, misbehavior, misconduct, lawlessness, criminality, delinquency, sin, sinfulness, evil, evildoing.

erupt *v.* **1 belch,** gush, vent, spew, boil over, become active, flare up, eject, eruct, eructate. **2 break out,** flare up, blow up, explode, go off, burst forth, pop up, emerge.

escalate *v.* **1 mushroom,** increase, be stepped up, heighten, intensify, accelerate. **2 go up,** mount, soar, climb, spiral, *inf.* be jacked/hiked up, go through the roof/ceiling. **Ant.** decrease; diminish; lessen.

escapade *n.* adventure, stunt, prank, trick, caper, romp, frolic, fling, spree, antics, *inf.* lark, fooling around, shenanigans.

escape *v.* **1 get away,** run away, run off, break out, break free, make a break for it, flee, make one's getaway, bolt, abscond,

decamp, fly, slip away, steal away, *inf.* vamoose, skedaddle, hightail it, fly the coop, take a powder. **2 avoid,** evade, dodge, elude, sidestep, circumvent, shake off, give the slip to, keep out of the way of, shun, steer clear of, shirk, *inf.* duck. **3 leak,** seep, pour out/ forth, gush, spurt, issue, flow, discharge, emanate, drain.
▸ *n.* **1 running away,** breakout, flight, getaway, bolting, absconding, decamping, fleeing. **2 avoidance,** evasion, dodging, eluding, elusion, circumvention, *inf.* ducking. **3 leak,** leakage, seepage, gush, spurt, issue, flow, discharge, outflow, outpouring, emanation, efflux. **4 escapism,** fantasy, fantasizing, woolgathering.

escort *n.* **1 entourage,** retinue, train, cortège, attendant company, protection, bodyguard, defense, convoy, contingent, attendant, guide, chaperon, guard, protector, safeguard, defender. **2 partner,** companion, beau, attendant, gigolo, call girl, prostitute, *inf.* date.
▸ *v.* **1 accompany,** guide, conduct, lead, usher, shepherd, guard, protect, safeguard, defend, convoy. **2 accompany,** take out, go out with.

esoteric *adj.* **abstruse,** obscure,

cryptic, recondite, arcane, abstract, inscrutable, mysterious, hidden, secret, private, mystic, magical, occult, cabalistic.

essence *n.* **1 quintessence,** substance, sum and substance, nature, crux, heart, soul, life, lifeblood, kernel, marrow, pith, quiddity, esse, reality. **2 extract,** concentrate, concentration, distillate, tincture, elixir, abstraction, scent, perfume.

essential *adj.* **1 necessary,** indispensable, vital, crucial, requisite, important, needed. **2 basic,** fundamental, inherent, intrinsic, innate, elemental, characteristic, indigenous, principal, cardinal. **3 absolute,** complete, perfect, ideal, quintessential. *Ant.* nonessential; dispensable; secondary.
▸ *n.* **necessity,** prerequisite, requisite, basic, fundamental, sine qua non, rudiment, *inf.* must.

establish *v.* **1 set up,** form, found, institute, start, begin, bring into being, create, inaugurate, organize, build, construct, install, plant. **2 prove,** show to be true, show, demonstrate, attest to, certify, confirm, verify, evidence, substantiate, corroborate, validate, authenticate, ratify. *Ant.* demolish; destroy; disprove.

established *adj.* **accepted,** official, conventional, traditional, proven, settled, fixed, entrenched, dyed-in-the-wool, inveterate.

establishment *n.* **1 setting up,** formation, founding, foundation, inception, creation, inauguration, organization, building, construction, installation. **2 firm,** business, place of business, company, store, shop, office, factory, emporium, concern, organization, enterprise, corporation.

estate *n.* **1 property,** piece of land, landholding, manor, domain, lands. **2 assets,** resources, effects, possessions, belongings, wealth, fortune, property. **3 social/political group,** level, order, stratum, grade, class, rank, standing, status, caste. **4 state,** condition, situation, circumstance, lot, position.

esteem *n.* **estimation,** good opinion, regard, respect, admiration, honor, reverence, deference, veneration, appreciation, approval, approbation, favor, credit. *Ant.* scorn; contempt.
▸ *v.* **1 regard,** respect, value, admire, honor, look up to, think highly of, revere, venerate, appreciate, approve of, favor, like, love, cherish, prize, treasure.

2 consider, regard as, think, deem, hold, view as, judge, adjudge, rate, reckon, account, believe, *lit.* opine. *Ant.* disdain; scorn.

estimate *v.* **1 calculate,** assess, compute, gauge, reckon, evaluate, judge, appraise, guess, *inf.* guesstimate. **2 consider,** believe, regard as, judge, rate, reckon, guess, conjecture, surmise, *lit.* opine.
▸ *n.* **1 cost,** price, costing, valuation, evaluation, assessment, appraisal. **2 estimation,** calculation, educated/rough guess, *inf.* guesstimate.

estimation *n.* **1 opinion,** judgment, consideration, mind, thinking, way of thinking, view, point of view, viewpoint, conviction, feeling. **2 esteem,** favorable opinion, regard, respect, admiration, deference, reverence, veneration, appreciation, approval, approbation, favor.

estrangement *n.* **alienation,** parting, separation, divorce, breakup, split, breach, severance, disunity, division, hostility, antagonism, antipathy, embitteredness, disaffection.

estuary *n.* **inlet,** river mouth, cove, bay, creek, arm of the sea.

eternal *adj.* **1 everlasting,** without end, endless, never-ending, immortal, infinite, enduring, deathless, permanent, immutable, indestructible, imperishable. **2 endless,** never-ending, without end, ceaseless, incessant, nonstop, constant, continuous, continual, unbroken, without respite, interminable, unremitting, relentless, persistent, perpetual. *Ant.* transient; intermittent.

eternity *n.* **1 immortality,** everlasting life, afterlife, the hereafter, world without end,heaven, paradise, nirvana. **2 long time,** age, seemingly forever, the duration, ages, ages and ages.

ethical *adj.* **moral,** honorable, upright, righteous, good, virtuous, high-minded, decent, principled, honest, just, fair, right, correct, proper, fitting, seemly, decorous. *Ant.* unethical; immoral; unprincipled.

euphoric *adj.* **elated,** joyful, jubilant, ecstatic, enraptured, rapturous, blissful, exhilarated, exalted, high-spirited, gleeful, excited, buoyant, intoxicated, merry, on cloud nine, in seventh heaven, *inf.* on a high.

evacuate *v.* **1 leave,** vacate, abandon, move out of, quit, withdraw from, retreat from, flee, depart from, retire from, decamp from, desert, forsake, empty, clear, *inf.* pull out of. **2 excrete,** expel, eject, discharge, eliminate, void, purge, empty out, drain, defecate.

evade *v.* **1 avoid,** dodge, escape from, elude, sidestep, circumvent, shake off, give the slip to, keep out of the way of, keep one's distance from, steer clear of, shun, shirk, *inf.* duck. **2 avoid,** quibble about, be equivocal/evasive about, dodge, hedge, fence, fend off, parry, skirt around, fudge, not give a straight answer to, *inf.* duck, cop out of. *Ant.* face; confront.

evaluate *v.* **assess,** put a value/price on, appraise, size up, weigh up, gauge, judge, rate, rank, estimate, calculate, reckon, measure, determine.

evaporate *v.* **1 vaporize,** dry, dry up, dry out, dehydrate, desiccate. **2 vanish,** fade, disappear, melt away, dissolve, disperse, dissipate, dematerialize, evanesce.

evasive *adj.* **1 avoiding,** dodging, escaping, eluding, sidestepping, shunning, shirking. **2 equivocal,** indirect, roundabout, circuitous, oblique, cunning, artful, casuistic, *inf.* cagey. *Ant.* frank; direct.

even *adj.* **1 level,** flat, plane, smooth, uniform, flush, true. **2 uniform,** constant, steady, stable, consistent, unvarying, unchanging, unwavering, unfluctuating, regular. **3 equal,** the same, much the same, identical, like, alike, similar, to the same degree, comparable, commensurate, corresponding, parallel, on a par, on an equal footing, evenly matched, *inf.* even steven. **4 all square,** drawn, tied (up), neck and neck, *inf.* even steven. **5 even-tempered,** equable, placid, serene, well-balanced, composed, calm, tranquil, cool, unperturbable, unexcitable, unruffled, unflappable, peaceful. *Ant.* uneven; bumpy; unequal; variable.

▸ *adv.* **1 yet,** still, more so, all the more, all the greater, to a greater extent. **2 unexpectedly,** paradoxically, surprisingly.

evening *n.* **1 late afternoon,** night, close of day, twilight, dusk, nightfall, sunset, sundown, *lit.* eve, even, eventide. **2 close,** end, declining years, last/latter part, epilogue. *Ant.* dawn; sunup.

event *n.* **1 occasion,** affair, business, matter, happening, occurrence, episode, experience, circumstance, fact, eventuality, phenomenon. **2 competition,** contest, game, tournament, round, bout, race. **3 end,** conclusion, outcome, result, upshot, consequence, issue, termination, effect, aftermath.

eventful *adj.* **busy,** event-filled, action-packed, full, lively, active, important, noteworthy, memorable, notable, remarkable, outstanding, fateful, momentous, significant, crucial, critical, historic, consequential, decisive. *Ant.* uneventful; dull; insignificant.

eventual *adj.* **final,** end, closing, concluding, last, ultimate, later, resulting, ensuing, consequent, subsequent.

eventually *adv.* **in the end,** at the end of the day, ultimately, in the long run, finally, when all is said and done, one day, some day, sooner or later, sometime.

everlasting *adj.* **never-ending,** endless, without end, eternal, perpetual, undying, immortal, deathless, indestructible, abiding, enduring, infinite, boundless, timeless, interminable, nonstop, incessant, ceaseless, constant, continual, continuous, unremitting, relentless, uninterrupted, recurrent, monotonous, tedious, wearisome, tiresome, boring. *Ant.* transient; occasional.

evermore *adv.* **forever,** always, for all time, until the end of time, until death, until death do us part, endlessly, without end, ceaselessly, unceasingly, constantly.

evict *v.* **turn out,** put out, throw out, throw out on the streets, throw out on one's ear, eject, expel, oust, remove, dispossess, dislodge, drum out, show the door to, *inf.* chuck out, kick out, boot out, heave out, give the heave-ho to, bounce, give the bum's rush to.

evidence *n.* **1 proof,** confirmation, verification, substantiation, corroboration, affirmation, authentication, support, grounds. **2 testimony,** sworn statement, attestation, deposition, declaration, allegation, affidavit. **3 sign,** indication, mark, manifestation, token, signs.
▸ *v.* **indicate,** show, be evidence of, reveal, display, exhibit, manifest, denote, evince, signify, testify to.

evident *adj.* **obvious,** clear, apparent, plain, plain as daylight, plain as the nose on your face, unmistakable, noticeable, conspicuous, perceptible, visible, discernible, transparent, manifest, patent, palpable, tangible, indisputable, undoubted, incontrovertible, incontestable. *Ant.* obscure; dubious.

evil *adj.* **1 wicked,** bad, wrong, morally wrong, immoral, sinful, vile, base, corrupt, iniquitous, depraved, heinous, villainous, nefarious, reprobate, sinister, atrocious, vicious, malicious, malevolent, demonic, devilish, diabolic. **2 bad,** harmful, hurtful, injurious, destructive, detrimental, deleterious, mischievous, pernicious, malignant, venomous, noxious. **3 unlucky,** unfortunate, unfavorable, adverse, unhappy, disastrous, catastrophic, ruinous, calamitous, unpropitious, inauspicious, dire, woeful. ***Ant.*** virtuous; good; pleasant.
▸ *n.* **1 wickedness,** bad, badness, wrong, wrongdoing, sin, sinfulness, immorality, vice, iniquity, vileness, baseness, corruption, depravity, villainy, atrocity, malevolence, devilishness. **2 harm,** pain, hurt, misery, sorrow, suffering, disaster, misfortune, catastrophe, ruin, calamity, affliction, woe, ills. ***Ant.*** virtue; goodness; benefit.

evoke *v.* **cause,** bring about, bring forth, induce, arouse, excite, awaken, give rise to, stir up, kindle, stimulate, elicit, educe, summon (up), call forth, conjure up, invoke, raise, recall.

evolution *n.* **evolvement,** development, unfolding, unrolling, growth, progress, progression, working out, expansion, natural selection, Darwinism.

evolve *v.* **develop,** unfold, unroll, grow, progress, open out, work out, mature, expand, elaborate, disclose.

exacerbate *v.* **aggravate,** worsen, intensify, add fuel to the fire, put salt on the wound.

exact *adj.* **1 precise,** accurate, correct, unerring, faithful, close, true, just, literal, strict, *inf.* on the mark. **2 precise,** careful, meticulous, painstaking, methodical, punctilious, conscientious, rigorous, scrupulous, exacting. ***Ant.*** inexact; inaccurate; careless.
▸ *v.* **1 demand,** require, insist on, compel, command, call for, impose, request. **2 demand,** extort, extract, force, wring, wrest, squeeze, *inf.* bleed.

exacting *adj.* **1 demanding,** difficult, hard, arduous, tough, laborious, tiring, taxing, troublesome, stringent, onerous. **2 demanding,** strict, stern, firm, rigorous.

exaggerate *v.* **overstate,** overemphasize, overstress, overestimate, overvalue, magnify, amplify, aggrandize, embellish, embroider, overdraw, make a mountain out of a molehill, hyperbolize, *inf.* lay it on thick. *Ant.* understate; play down (see play); minimize.

exalted *adj.* **1 high,** high-ranking, lofty, grand, eminent, prestigious, elevated, august. **2 high-minded,** lofty, elevated, noble, intellectual, ideal, sublime, inflated, pretentious.

examination *n.* **1 study,** inspection, scrutiny, investigation, analysis, review, research, observation, exploration, consideration, appraisal. **2 checkup,** inspection, assessment, observation, scrutiny. **3 questioning,** interrogation, cross-examination, cross-questioning, third degree. **4 exam,** test.

examine *v.* **1 look at,** look into, study, inspect, survey, scrutinize, investigate, analyze, review, scan, observe, research, sift, explore, probe, check out, consider, appraise, weigh, weigh up. **2 look at,** inspect, check over, give a checkup to, assess, observe, scrutinize. **3 put/address questions to,** question, test, quiz, interrogate, cross-examine, cross-question, give the third degree to, *inf.* grill, pump.

example *n.* **1 sample,** specimen, instance, representative case, case in point, illustration. **2 model,** pattern, precedent, paradigm, standard, criterion, ideal, paragon. **3 warning,** caution, lesson, admonition.

exasperate *v.* **anger,** annoy, infuriate, irritate, incense, madden, enrage, provoke, irk, vex, gall, pique, try the patience of, get on the nerves of, make one's blood boil, *inf.* bug, needle, get to, rile.

excavate *v.* **dig,** dig out, hollow out, scoop out, gouge, cut out, quarry, mine, unearth, dig up, uncover, reveal.

exceed *v.* **1 go beyond,** pass, top, surpass, better, pass, beat, outdo, outstrip, outshine, transcend, cap, overshadow, eclipse. **2 go beyond,** overstep.

exceedingly *adv.* **extremely,** exceptionally, extraordinarily, tremendously, enormously, vastly, greatly, highly, hugely, supremely, inordinately, surpassingly, superlatively, especially, unusually, very.

excellence *n.* **merit,** eminence, preeminence, distinction, greatness, fineness, quality, superiority, supremacy, transcendence, value, worth, skill. *Ant.* inferiority.

excellent *adj.* **first-rate,** first-class, great, fine, distinguished, superior, superb, outstanding, marvelous, brilliant, noted, notable, eminent, preeminent, supreme, superlative, admirable, worthy, sterling, prime, select, *inf.* A-1, top-notch, tip-top. **Ant.** poor; inferior.

except *prep.* **excepting,** excluding, but, besides, barring, bar, other than, omitting, with the omission/exclusion of, exclusive of, saving, save.
▸ *v.* **exclude,** leave out, omit, rule out, pass over, bar.

exception *n.* **1 exclusion,** omission, noninclusion. **2 special case,** departure, deviation, anomaly, irregularity, inconsistency, quirk, peculiarity, oddity, freak.

exceptional *adj.* **1 unusual,** uncommon, abnormal, out of the ordinary, atypical, rare, odd, anomalous, singular, peculiar, inconsistent, deviant, divergent, aberrant. **2 excellent,** extraordinary, remarkable, outstanding, special, especial, phenomenal, prodigious. **Ant.** usual; normal; average.

excerpt *n.* **extract,** citation, quotation, quote, passage, selection, part, section, fragment, piece, portion.

excess *n.* **1 surplus,** surfeit, overabundance, superabundance, superfluity, plethora, glut, overkill, oversufficiency, too much, more than enough, enough and to spare. **2 remainder,** residue, overload, overflow, leftovers. **3 immoderation,** lack of restraint, overindulgence, prodigality, intemperance, debauchery, dissipation, dissoluteness. **Ant.** dearth; shortage; moderation.
▸ *adj.* **extra,** additional, too much, surplus, superfluous, spare, redundant.

excessive *adj.* **too much,** superfluous, immoderate, extravagant, lavish, superabundant, unreasonable, undue, uncalled-for, extreme, inordinate, unwarranted, unnecessary, needless, disproportionate, exorbitant, enormous, outrageous, intemperate, unconscionable.

exchange *v.* **trade,** swap, barter, interchange, reciprocate, bandy.
▸ *n.* **1 interchange,** trade, trade-off, swapping, barter, give and take, bandying, traffic, reciprocity, tit for tat, dealings. **2 stock exchange,** stock market, market.

excise *v.* **1 cut out,** cut off, remove, eradicate, extirpate, *Tech.* resect. **2 remove,** delete, cut out, cut, cross/strike out, erase, blue-

pencil, expunge, eliminate, expurgate, bowdlerize.
▸ *n.* **duty,** tariff, toll, levy, customs.

excitable *adj.* **temperamental,** emotional, highly strung, nervous, edgy, mercurial, volatile, tempestuous, hot-tempered, quick-tempered, hot-headed, passionate, fiery, irascible, testy, moody, choleric.

excite *v.* **1 stimulate,** rouse, arouse, animate, move, thrill, inflame, titillate, *inf.* turn on, wind up. **2 cause,** bring about, rouse, arouse, awaken, incite, provoke, stimulate, kindle, evoke, stir up, elicit, instigate, foment.

excited *adj.* **stimulated,** aroused, animated, thrilled, agitated, overwrought, feverish, wild, *inf.* high, wound up, turned on. **Ant.** indifferent; apathetic.

excitement *n.* **1 agitation,** animation, emotion, anticipation, exhilaration, elation, enthusiasm, feverishness, ferment, tumult. **2 adventure,** thrill, pleasure, stimulation, *inf.* kick. **3 arousal,** awakening, stimulation, evocation, kindling.

exciting *adj.* **thrilling,** stirring, stimulating, exhilarating, intoxicating, rousing, electrifying, invigorating, moving, inspiring, titillating, provocative,
sensational, *inf.* sexy. **Ant.** boring; uninteresting; flat.

exclaim *v.* **call,** cry, call/cry out, shout, yell, roar, bellow, shriek, ejaculate, utter, proclaim, *fml.* vociferate.

exclamation *n.* **call,** cry, shout, yell, roar, bellow, shriek, ejaculation, interjection, utterance, expletive.

exclude *v.* **1 debar,** bar, keep out, shut out, prohibit, forbid, prevent, disallow, refuse, ban, blackball, veto, stand in the way of, proscribe, interdict, throw out, turn out, eject, remove, evict, expel, oust, ban, *inf.* bounce, kick/boot out. **2 eliminate,** rule out, preclude, count out, reject, set aside, except, repudiate, omit, pass over, leave out, ignore. **3 be exclusive of,** omit, leave out. **Ant.** include; accept; admit.

exclusive *adj.* **1 select,** selective, choice, restrictive, restricted, closed, private, limited, discriminating, cliquish, clannish, snobbish, fashionable, chic, elegant, luxurious, high-class, aristocratic, *inf.* posh, ritzy, classy, up-scale. **2 complete,** undivided, full, absolute, entire, whole, total, all of, unshared. **3 sole,** only, unique, individual, single. **4 excluding,** omitting, excepting, barring. **5 incompatible,** inimical, antithetical. *Ant.* open; partial; inclusive.

excommunicate *v.* **exclude,** expel, cast out, banish, eject, remove, bar, debar, proscribe, interdict, repudiate, *fml.* anathematize, unchurch.

excrement *n.* **waste matter,** ordure, dung, manure, excreta, feces, stools, droppings.

excrete *v.* **pass,** void, discharge, eject, evacuate, expel, eliminate, exude, emit, egest, defecate, urinate.

excruciating *adj.* **agonizing,** racking, torturous, insufferable, unbearable, severe, intense, extreme, harrowing, searing, piercing, acute, *fml.* exquisite.

excusable *adj.* **forgivable,** pardonable, defensible, justifiable, understandable, condonable, venial. *Ant.* inexcusable; unforgivable.

excuse *v.* **1 forgive,** pardon, exonerate, absolve, acquit, make allowances for, bear with, tolerate, indulge, *fml.* exculpate. **2 forgive,** pardon, condone, justify, defend, vindicate, mitigate, explain. **3 let off,** exempt, spare, absolve, release, relieve, free, liberate. *Ant.* punish; condemn; oblige.
▸ *n.* **1 defense,** justification, reason, explanation, apology,

vindication, mitigation, grounds, mitigating circumstances. **2 pretext,** ostensible reason, pretense, front, cover-up, subterfuge, fabrication, evasion, escape, *inf.* cop-out.

execute *v.* **1 put to death,** kill, hang, send to the gallows, behead, guillotine, decapitate, electrocute, shoot, crucify, *inf.* string up, fry. **2 carry out,** accomplish, perform, implement, effect, bring off, achieve, complete, fulfill, enact, enforce, put into effect, do, discharge, prosecute, engineer, administer, attain, realize, render.

exemplary *adj.* **ideal,** model, perfect, excellent, admirable, commendable, faultless, laudable, praiseworthy, meritorious, honorable, typical, representative, illustrative, characteristic, epitomic.

exemplify *v.* **1 typify,** epitomize, represent, personify, embody, illustrate. **2 illustrate,** give an example/instance of, demonstrate, instance, depict.

exempt
▸ *adj.* **free from,** excused from, immune to, not subject/liable to, absolved/excepted from, spared, released from, discharged from, dismissed from.

exercise *n.* **1 activity,** exertion,

effort, action, work, movement, training, physical training, drill, drilling, discipline, workout, warm-up, limbering-up, gymnastics, sports, aerobics, calisthenics. **2 employment,** use, application, utilization, implementation, practice, operation, exertion, discharge, accomplishment. **3 problem,** task, piece of work, practice.
▸ *v.* **1 do exercises,** work out, train, exert oneself, drill.
2 employ, use, make use of, utilize, apply, implement, practice, exert.

exert *v.* **1 exercise,** employ, use, make use of, utilize, apply, wield, bring into play, bring to bear, set in motion, expend, spend. **2 apply oneself,** put oneself out, make an effort, spare no effort, try hard, do one's best, give one's all, strive, endeavor, struggle, labor, toil, strain, work, push, drive, go all out, *inf.* put one's back into it.

exhaust *v.* **1 tire,** tire out, wear out, fatigue, drain, weary, sap, enervate, tax, overtax, debilitate, prostrate, enfeeble, disable, *inf.* take it out of, poop out, fag out, knock out, burn out. **2 use up,** consume, finish, deplete, expend, spend, run through, dissipate, waste, squander, fritter away, *inf.* blow. **3 empty,** drain, void,

evacuate, deplete. **Ant.** invigorate; replenish.

exhausting *adj.* tiring, fatiguing, wearying, wearing, grueling, punishing, strenuous, arduous, backbreaking, taxing, laborious, enervating, sapping, debilitating.

exhaustion *n.* **1 fatigue,** tiredness, weakness, debility, collapse, weariness, faintness, prostration, enervation, lassitude. **2 using up,** consumption, depletion, dissipation.

exhaustive *adj.* all-inclusive, comprehensive, intensive, all-out, in-depth, total, all-embracing, encyclopedic, thorough, complete, full, thoroughgoing, extensive, profound, far-reaching, sweeping. **Ant.** perfunctory; sketchy.

exhibit *v.* **1 display,** show, demonstrate, set out/forth, present, model, expose, air, unveil, array, flaunt, parade.
2 show, express, indicate, reveal, display, demonstrate, make clear/plain, betray, give away, disclose, manifest, evince, evidence. **Ant.** conceal; hide.
▸ *n.* **display,** show, showing, demonstration, presentation, exhibition, viewing.

exhibition *n.* **1 display,** show, fair, demonstration, presentation, exhibit, exposition, spectacle.

2 display, show, expression, indication, revelation, demonstration, betrayal, disclosure, manifestation.

exhilarate *v.* **make happy/ cheerful,** cheer up, enliven, elate, gladden, delight, brighten, excite, thrill, animate, invigorate, lift, stimulate, raise the spirits of, revitalize, exalt, inspirit, *inf.* perk/pep up.

exhilaration *n.* elation, joy, happiness, gladness, delight, excitement, gaiety, merriment, mirth, hilarity, glee, animation, vivacity, invigoration, stimulation, revitalization, exaltation, high spirits.

exhort *v.* **urge,** persuade, press, encourage, sway, prompt, advise, counsel, incite, goad, stimulate, push, beseech, entreat, bid, enjoin, admonish, warn.

exile *v.* **banish,** expatriate, deport, expel, drive out, eject, oust, proscribe, outlaw, bar, ban, ostracize, uproot, separate, excommunicate.
　▸ *n.* **1 banishment,** expatriation, deportation, expulsion, uprooting, separation.
2 expatriate, deportee, displaced person, refugee, outlaw, outcast, pariah.

exist *v.* **1 be,** live, subsist, breathe, draw breath, be extant. **2 live,** survive, subsist, occur, remain, continue, last, endure, prevail.
3 survive, live, stay alive, eke out a living, subsist. *Ant.* die; fade.

exit *n.* **1 door,** gate, door out, passage out, outlet, egress.
2 departure, leaving, withdrawal, retirement, going, retreat, leave-taking, flight, exodus, farewell, adieu. *Ant.* entrance; entry; arrival.

exonerate *v.* **1 absolve,** acquit, clear, discharge, vindicate, exculpate, declare innocent, dismiss, let off, excuse, pardon, justify. **2 excuse,** exempt, except, release, relieve, free, let off, liberate, discharge. *Ant.* charge; implicate; incriminate.

exorbitant *adj.* **excessive,** extortionate, extreme, unreasonable, immoderate, inordinate, outrageous, preposterous, monstrous, unwarranted, undue, unconscionable. *Ant.* cheap; moderate.

exotic *adj.* **1 foreign,** nonnative, tropical, imported, introduced, novel, alien, external, extraneous, extrinsic. **2 striking,** outrageous, colorful, extraordinary, extravagant, sensational, unusual, remarkable, astonishing, strange, outlandish, bizarre, peculiar, impressive, glamorous, fascinating, mysterious, curious, different, unfamiliar. **3 erotic,** go-go, striptease, titillating, risqué, sexy.

expand *v.* **1 enlarge,** increase, swell, inflate, magnify, amplify, distend, lengthen, stretch, extend, multiply. **2 increase,** magnify, amplify, add to, extend, multiply. **3 elaborate on,** add detail to, amplify, embellish, enlarge on, flesh out, develop, expound. *Ant.* contract; condense.

expanse *n.* **area,** stretch, region, tract, breadth, extent, sweep, space, plain, field, extension, vastness.

expansive *adj.* **1 expandable,** expanding, extendable, extending, extensive, wide. **2 extensive,** wide-ranging, broad, wide, widespread, all-embracing, comprehensive, thorough, universal.

expect *v.* **1 think,** believe, assume, suppose, imagine, presume, conjecture, calculate, surmise, reckon. **2 anticipate,** await, envisage, look for, look forward to, watch for, hope for, contemplate, bargain for, have in prospect, predict, forecast. **3 insist on,** require, demand, exact, count on, call for, rely on, look for, wish, want, hope for.

expectant *adj.* **anticipating,** anticipatory, expecting, awaiting, eager, hopeful, in suspense, ready, watchful, anxious, on tenterhooks.

expectation *n.* **1 anticipation,** expectancy, readiness, hope. **2 assumption,** belief, supposition, presumption, assurance, conjecture, surmise, reckoning, calculation, confidence.

expecting *adj.* **pregnant,** *inf.* in a family way.

expedient *adj.* **convenient,** advantageous, useful, beneficial, profitable, gainful, practical, pragmatic, desirable, suitable, advisable, appropriate, apt, fit, effective, helpful, politic, judicious, timely, opportune, propitious.
▸ *n.* **means,** measure, method, resource, scheme, plan, plot, stratagem, maneuver, machination, agency, trick, ruse, artifice, device, tool, contrivance, invention, shift, stopgap.

expel *v.* **1 banish,** exile, evict, oust, drive out, throw out, cast out, deport, proscribe, outlaw, bar, ban, debar, blackball, drum out, reject, dismiss, ostracize, *inf.* kick/boot out, give the bum's rush to, send packing. **2 discharge,** eject, eliminate, excrete, evacuate, belch, void, spew out. *Ant.* admit; welcome.

expend _v._ **1 spend,** lay out, pay out, disburse, lavish, squander, waste, fritter, dissipate, _inf._ fork out, shell out, dish out. **2 use up,** consume, exhaust, deplete, drain, sap, empty, finish off.

expendable _adj._ **dispensable,** replaceable, nonessential, inessential, unimportant.

expense _n._ **cost,** price, charge, outlay, fee, amount, rate, figure, quotation, spending, outlay, laying out, paying out, disbursement, lavishing, squandering, sacrifice.

expensive _adj._ **costly,** high-priced, dear, exorbitant, overpriced, lavish, extravagant, _inf._ steep. **Ant.** cheap; economical.

experience _n._ **1 event,** incident, occurrence, happening, affair, episode, adventure, encounter, circumstance, case, test, trial, ordeal. **2 skill,** practical knowledge, practice, training, learning, understanding, wisdom, maturity, _inf._ know-how. **Ant.** inexperience; naïveté.
▸ _v._ **undergo,** encounter, meet, feel, know, become familiar with, face, participate in, live/go through, sustain, suffer.

experienced _adj._ **1 practiced,** accomplished, skillful, proficient, seasoned, trained, expert, adept, competent, capable, knowledgeable, qualified, well-versed, professional, mature, master, veteran. **2 worldly-wise,** sophisticated, knowing, mature, worldly, initiated, _inf._ having been around. **Ant.** novice; untrained; naïve.

experiment _n._ **1 test,** investigation, trial, trial run, tryout, examination, observation, inquiry, questioning, pilot study, demonstration, venture. **2 research,** experimentation, observation, trial and error, tryout, analysis, testing.
▸ _v._ **conduct experiments,** test, investigate, examine, explore, observe.

experimental _adj._ **trial,** test, trial and error, exploratory, empirical, investigational, observational, pilot, tentative, speculative, preliminary, probationary, under review, on the drawing board.

expert _n._ **authority,** past master, specialist, professional, adept, pundit, maestro, virtuoso, wizard, connoisseur, _inf._ old hand, ace, buff, pro.
▸ _adj._ **skillful,** experienced, practiced, qualified, knowledgeable, specialist, professional, proficient, adept, master, masterly, brilliant, accomplished, able, deft, dexterous, adroit, apt, capable,

competent, clever, well-versed, au fait, *inf.* ace, crack, top-notch. ***Ant.*** inexpert; amateur.

expire *v.* **1 be no longer valid,** run out, finish, end, come to an end, terminate, conclude, discontinue, stop, cease, lapse. **2 die,** pass away/on, decease, depart this life, perish, breathe one's last, meet one's Maker, give up the ghost, go to the great beyond, cross the great divide, *inf.* kick the bucket.

explain *v.* **1 give an explanation of,** describe, define, make clear/plain/intelligible, spell out, interpret, unfold, clarify, throw light on, clear up, decipher, decode, elucidate, expound, explicate, delineate, demonstrate, teach, illustrate, expose, resolve, solve. **2 account for,** justify, vindicate, mitigate.

explanation *n.* **1 description,** definition, interpretation, clarification, deciphering, decoding, elucidation, expounding, explication, demonstration, illustration, exposure, resolution, solution. **2 account,** justification, reason, excuse, defense, vindication, mitigation, apologia.

explanatory *adj.* **by way of explanation,** descriptive, illustrative, interpretive, demonstrative, illuminative, elucidative, elucidatory, explicative, expository.

expletive *n.* **swearword,** oath, curse, obscenity, epithet, exclamation, *inf.* dirty word, four-letter word, cussword.

explicit *adj.* **1 clearly expressed,** easily understandable, detailed, clear, crystal-clear, direct, plain, obvious, precise, exact, straightforward, definite, distinct, categorical, specific, positive, unequivocal, unambiguous. **2 outspoken,** unrestrained, unreserved, uninhibited, open, candid, frank, forthright, direct, plainspoken, full-frontal. ***Ant.*** vague; implicit; indirect.

explode *v.* **1 blow up,** detonate, burst, fly apart, fly into pieces, go off, erupt, *inf.* go bang. **2 detonate,** set off, let off, fire off. **3 give vent to,** blow up, rage, rant and rave, storm, *inf.* fly off the handle, hit the roof, blow one's cool/top, blow a fuse, flip one's lid, freak out. **4 disprove,** invalidate, refute, repudiate, discredit, debunk, belie. **5 increase,** mushroom, escalate, burgeon, rocket, accelerate, heighten.

exploit *n.* **feat,** deed, adventure, stunt, achievement, accomplishment, attainment.
▶ *v.* **1 make use of,** put to use, utilize, use, turn/put to good use,

turn to account, profit from/by, capitalize on, *inf.* cash in on, milk. **2 make use of,** take advantage of, abuse, impose upon, play upon, misuse, *inf.* walk all over, walk over, take for a ride.

explore *v.* **1 travel,** traverse, tour, range over, survey, take a look at, inspect, scout, reconnoiter, prospect. **2 investigate,** look into, inquire into, consider, examine, research, survey, scrutinize, study, review, take stock of.

explosion *n.* **1 bang,** blast, boom, rumble, crash, crack, report, thunder, roll, clap, detonation, discharge, eruption. **2 outburst,** flare-up, fit, outbreak, paroxysm, eruption. **3 increase,** mushrooming, escalation, burgeoning, rocketing, acceleration, heightening.

explosive *adj.* **1 inflammable,** volatile, eruptive, unstable. **2 fiery,** angry, touchy, stormy, violent, vehement, volatile, volcanic. **3 tense,** charged, critical, serious, inflammable, volcanic, dangerous, perilous, hazardous, ugly.

exponent *n.* **1 advocate,** supporter, upholder, backer, defender, champion, spokesperson, promoter, propagandist, proponent. **2 interpreter,** commentator,

expounder, explainer, expositor, elucidator, illustrator, demonstrator, practitioner, performer, player, interpreter, presenter.

expose *v.* **1 uncover,** lay bare, bare, leave unprotected, strip, reveal, denude. **2 lay open to,** make subject to, subject to, endanger, risk, hazard. **3 reveal,** uncover, show, display, make obvious, exhibit, disclose, manifest, unveil. **4 bring to light,** disclose, uncover, reveal, make known, let out, divulge, unearth, unmask, detect, betray, smoke out, *inf.* spill the beans on, blow the whistle on. **5 introduce to,** present with. *Ant.* cover; protect; conceal.

express *v.* **1 put into words,** state, voice, give voice to, enunciate, communicate, utter, pronounce, articulate, verbalize, give vent to, word, proclaim, assert, point out, speak, say. **2 show,** indicate, demonstrate, convey, communicate, intimate, denote, exhibit, illustrate, manifest, make manifest, reveal, evince, evidence, symbolize, embody. **3 press out,** squeeze, extract, force out.

▸ *adj.* **1 rapid,** swift, fast, quick, speedy, prompt, high-speed, brisk, expeditious, direct, nonstop. **2 explicit,** clear, plain,

distinct, unambiguous, precise, specific, well-defined, unmistakable, unequivocal, pointed, exact, outright.
3 particular, sole, purposeful, special, especial, specific, singular.

expression *n.* **1 statement,** voicing, uttering, utterance, pronouncement, articulation, verbalization, venting, wording, proclamation, assertion. **2 indication,** demonstration, show, conveyance, communication, intimation, exhibition, illustration, manifestation, revelation, embodiment. **3 word,** phrase, term, choice of words, wording, language, phrasing, phraseology, speech, diction, idiom, style, delivery, intonation, execution, *fml.* locution. **4 look,** appearance, air, countenance, aspect, *fml.* mien. **5 feeling,** emotion, passion, intensity, poignancy, artistry, depth, spirit, vividness, ardor, power, force, imagination.

expressionless *adj.* **dull,** dry, boring, wooden, undemonstrative, apathetic, unimpassioned, weak, devoid of feeling/emotion, blank, deadpan, *inf.* poker-faced, inscrutable, emotionless, vacuous.

expressive *adj.* **1 emotional,** eloquent, telling, demonstrative, suggestive, vivid, passionate, intense, poignant, moving, striking, evocative, sympathetic, artistic, vivid, graphic, ardent, powerful, imaginative. **2 showing,** indicative, demonstrating, demonstrative, suggesting, revealing, underlining. *Ant.* expressionless; inexpressive; unemotional.

expressly *adv.* **1 absolutely,** explicitly, clearly, plainly, distinctly, precisely, specifically, unequivocally. **2 purposefully,** particularly, solely, specially, especially, specifically, singularly.

extend *v.* **1 expand,** increase, enlarge, lengthen, widen, broaden, stretch, stretch out, draw out, elongate, reach out, spread out, straighten out, unroll, unfurl. **2 widen,** increase, add to, expand, broaden, enlarge, augment, amplify, supplement, enhance, develop. **3 prolong,** increase, lengthen, stretch out, protract, drag out. **4 offer,** give, grant, proffer, present, confer, hold out, advance, impart, put forth, reach out. **5 continue,** stretch, stretch out, carry on, run on, last, unroll, unfurl, unfold, range. *Ant.* decrease; contract; narrow; curtail.

extensive *adj.* **1 large,** large-scale, sizable, substantial, spacious, considerable, capacious, commodious, vast, immense. **2 comprehensive,** thorough, complete, broad, wide, wide-ranging, all-inclusive, all-embracing, universal, boundless, catholic. **Ant.** small; limited.

extent *n.* **length,** area, expanse, stretch, range, scope, coverage, breadth, degree, comprehensiveness, thoroughness, completeness, all-inclusiveness.

exterior *n.* **outside,** outside surface, outer/external surface, outward appearance/aspect, façade, covering, shell. **Ant.** interior; inside.

▸ *adj.* **outer,** outside, outermost, outward, external, surface, superficial. **Ant.** inner; inside.

exterminate *v.* **kill,** destroy, eradicate, annihilate, eliminate, abolish, extirpate, *inf.* bump off.

extinguish *v.* **1 put out,** blow out, quench, smother, douse, snuff out, stifle, choke. **2 destroy,** kill, end, remove, annihilate, wipe out, eliminate, abolish, eradicate, erase, expunge, exterminate, extirpate, obscure, suppress. **Ant.** light; kindle.

extol *v.* **praise,** praise to the skies, sing the praises of, applaud, acclaim, pay tribute to, laud, exalt, commend, congratulate, celebrate, compliment, glorify, magnify. **Ant.** condemn; criticize.

extra *adj.* **1 more,** additional, further, supplementary, supplemental, added, auxiliary, ancillary, subsidiary, other, accessory. **2 spare,** surplus, leftover, excess, superfluous, redundant, reserve, unused.

▸ *adv.* **1 especially,** exceptionally, extremely, unusually, particularly, extraordinarily, uncommonly, remarkably, *inf.* with all the stops out. **2 in addition,** as well, besides, over and above, on top, to boot.

extract *v.* **1 draw out,** pull out, remove, take out, pluck out, wrench out, tear out, uproot, withdraw, extirpate. **2 extort,** force, exact, elicit, coerce, wrest, wring, squeeze. **3 squeeze,** press, express, distill, separate, take out. **4 abstract,** select, choose, reproduce, copy, quote, cite, cull. **5 deduce,** educe, derive, elicit, develop.

▸ *n.* **1 concentrate,** essence, distillate, juice, solution, decoction. **2 excerpt,** passage, abstract, citation, selection, quotation, cutting, clipping, fragment.

extraordinary *adj.* **1 exceptional,** unusual, uncommon, rare,

unique, singular, signal, peculiar, unprecedented, outstanding, striking, remarkable, phenomenal, marvelous, wonderful, *inf.* fabulous.
2 amazing, surprising, strange, unusual, remarkable, astounding, curious. **3 odd,** weird, strange, curious, bizarre, unconventional. *Ant.* ordinary; commonplace.

extravagant *adj.* **1 spendthrift,** squandering, thriftless, profligate, prodigal, improvident, wasteful, lavish, reckless, imprudent, excessive. **2 excessive,** exaggerated, unrestrained, unreserved, outrageous, immoderate, preposterous, absurd, irrational, reckless, wild. **3 exorbitant,** excessive, extortionate, unreasonable, immoderate, inordinate, expensive, costly, overpriced, *inf.* steep. *Ant.* thrifty; restrained; cheap.

extreme *adj.* **1 utmost,** uttermost, maximum, supreme, greatest, great, acute, intense, severe, highest, high, ultimate, exceptional, extraordinary. **2 harsh,** severe, draconian, stringent, stern, strict, drastic, unrelenting, relentless, unbending, unyielding, uncompromising, unmitigated, radical, overzealous.

3 immoderate, intemperate, fanatical, exaggerated, excessive, overzealous, outrageous, inordinate, unreasonable. **4 outermost,** farthest, most remote, remotest, most distant, outlying, far-off, faraway, ultimate, last, endmost, final, terminal. *Ant.* moderate; mild; near.

▸ *n.* **1 highest/greatest degree,** maximum, height, ultimate, zenith, pinnacle, climax, acme, apex. **2 opposite,** pole, contrary.

extremely *adv.* **very,** exceedingly, exceptionally, intensely, greatly, acutely, utterly, excessively, inordinately, extraordinarily, markedly, uncommonly, severely, *inf.* awfully, terribly.

extrovert *n.* **socializer,** mixer, mingler, life of the party.

exuberant *adj.* **1 elated,** animated, exhilarated, lively, high-spirited, spirited, buoyant, cheerful, sparkling, full of life, effervescent, vivacious, excited, ebullient, exultant, enthusiastic, irrepressible, energetic, vigorous, zestful, *inf.* bouncy, upbeat. **2 effusive,** lavish, fulsome, exaggerated, unreserved, unrestrained, unlimited, wholehearted, generous, excessive, superfluous, prodigal. **3 profuse,** luxuriant, lush, thriving, abundant, superabundant, prolific, teeming, lavish, copious, rich, plentiful, abounding, overflowing, rank. *Ant.* depressed; restrained; meager.

exultant *adj.* **exulting,** rejoicing, overjoyed, joyful, jubilant, elated, triumphant, delighted, ecstatic, gleeful, enraptured, transported.

eyeful *n.* **1 look,** good look, stare, gaze, view, *inf.* gander, load.

2 vision, dream, beauty, dazzler, *inf.* stunner, good-looker, knockout, sight for sore eyes.

eyesore *n.* **blemish,** blot, scar, blight, disfigurement, defacement, defect, monstrosity, carbuncle, atrocity, disgrace, ugliness, *inf.* sight.

eyewitness *n.* **witness,** observer, onlooker, bystander, spectator, watcher, viewer, beholder, passerby.

Ff

fabric *n.* **1 cloth,** material, textile, stuff, web. **2 framework,** frame, structure, makeup, constitution, essence.

fabricate *v.* **1 assemble,** construct, build, erect, put together, make, form, frame, fashion, shape, manufacture, produce. **2 make up,** invent, think up, concoct, hatch, trump up, devise, formulate, forge, falsify, fake, counterfeit.

fabulous *adj.* **1 incredible,** unbelievable, inconceivable, unimaginable, astounding, amazing, astonishing, breathtaking, prodigious, phenomenal, remarkable, extraordinary, tremendous, *inf.* legendary. **2 marvelous,** wonderful, great, superb, spectacular, *inf.* fab, fantastic, super, super-duper, out of this world. **3 mythical,** imaginary, legendary, fantastical, fictitious, fictional, made-up, invented, unreal, hypothetical, apocryphal.

face *n.* **1 countenance,** visage, physiognomy, features, *inf.* mug, kisser. **2 expression,** look, air, demeanor, aspect. **3 scowl,** grimace, frown, pout, moue. **4 front,** frontage, façade. **5 facet,** side, plane, surface. **6 outward appearance,** appearance, aspect, air. **7 appearance,** façade, display, show, exterior, guise, mask, veneer, camouflage, pretense. **8 prestige,** standing, status, dignity, honor, respect, image. **9 audacity,** effrontery, impudence, impertinence, cheek, boldness, presumption, temerity, *inf.* nerve, gall.
▸ *v.* **1 look toward,** look onto, overlook, be opposite to. **2 confront,** present itself, meet, be in the way of, stand in the way of. **3 encounter,** meet, come across, be confronted by, come up against, experience, face up to, come to terms with, accept, confront, meet head-on, cope with, deal with, come to grips with, dare, brave, defy, oppose, resist, withstand. **4 cover,** line. **5 dress,** finish, polish, smooth, level, coat, cover, surface, clad, veneer.

facet *n.* **1 aspect,** angle, side, slant, feature, characteristic, factor, element, point, part, phase. **2 side,** plane, surface, face.

facetious *adj.* **jocular,** flippant, playful, frivolous, lighthearted, nonserious, funny, amusing, humorous, comical, comic, joking, jesting, witty, droll, whimsical, tongue-in-cheek, waggish, jocose. ***Ant.*** serious; grave.

facile *adj.* **easy,** simple, uncomplicated, unchallenging.

facility *n.* **1 ease,** effortlessness, smoothness. **2 ease,** smoothness, fluency, eloquence, articulateness, slickness, glibness. **3 skill,** skillfulness, dexterity, adroitness, adeptness, deftness, aptitude, ability, gift, talent, expertise, expertness, knack, proficiency, bent, readiness. **4 establishment,** structure, building, buildings, complex, system, plant, resource, equipment.

fact *n.* **1 actuality,** reality, certainty, factuality, certitude, truth, naked truth, gospel. **2 detail,** particular, point, item, piece of information/data, factor, feature, element, component, circumstance, specific. **3 happening,** occurrence, incident, event, act, deed. ***Ant.*** untruth; falsehood; fiction.

faction *n.* **1 sector,** section, group, side, party, band, set, ring, division, contingent, lobby, camp, bloc, clique, coalition, confederacy, coterie, caucus, cabal, junta, splinter group, pressure group, minority (group), *inf.* gang, crew. **2 infighting,** dissension, discord, strife, contention, conflict, friction, argument, difference of opinion, disagreement, controversy, quarreling, division, divisiveness, clashing, disharmony, disunity, variance, rupture, tumult, turbulence, upheaval, dissidence, rebellion, insurrection, sedition, mutiny, schism.

factor *n.* **element,** part, component, ingredient, constituent, point, detail, item, facet, aspect, feature, characteristic, consideration, influence, circumstance, thing, determinant.

factual *adj.* **fact-based,** realistic, real, true to life, circumstantial, true, truthful, accurate, authentic, genuine, sure, veritable, exact, precise, strict, honest, faithful, literal, matter-of-fact, verbatim, word for word, unbiased, objective, unprejudiced, unvarnished, unadorned, unadulterated, unexaggerated. ***Ant.*** untrue; fictitious; unreal.

fad *n.* **craze,** mania, rage,

enthusiasm, fancy, passing fancy, whim, vogue, fashion, trend, mode.

fade *v.* **1 lose color,** grow pale, pale, become washed out, dull, dim, grow dull/dim, lose luster, bleach, whiten, discolor, decolorize, dim. **2 wither,** wilt, die, droop, shrivel, decay. **3 grow less,** dim, die away, dwindle, grow faint, fail, wane, disappear, vanish, die, decline, dissolve, peter out, melt away, evanesce. **4** die out, diminish, decline, fail, deteriorate, degenerate. *Ant.* thrive; increase.

fail *v.* **1 fall through,** fall flat, break down, abort, miscarry, be defeated, suffer defeat, be in vain, be frustrated, collapse, founder, misfire, meet with disaster, come to grief, come to nothing/naught, fizzle out, miss the mark, run aground, go astray, *inf.* flop, come a cropper, bite the dust. **2 not pass,** be found wanting/deficient/defective, not make the grade, not pass muster, be rejected, *inf.* flunk. **3 be unable,** neglect, forget. **4 let down,** neglect, desert, forsake, abandon, disappoint. **5 be insufficient,** be inadequate, be deficient, be wanting, be lacking, fall short. **6 fade,** grow less, dim, die away, dwindle, wane, disappear, vanish, peter out, dissolve. **7 break down,** stop working, cease to function, *inf.* conk out. **8 grow weak/weaker,** become feeble, lose strength, flag, become ill, sink. **9 decline,** go into decline, fade, diminish, dwindle, wane, ebb, deteriorate, sink, collapse, pass, decay, crumble, degenerate. **10 collapse,** crash, smash, go under, go to the wall, go bankrupt, become insolvent, go into receivership, cease trading, be closed, close down, *inf.* fold, flop, go bust/broke. *Ant.* succeed; increase; thrive.

failing *n.* **fault,** shortcoming, weakness, weak spot, imperfection, defect, flaw, blemish, frailty, foible, drawback. *Ant.* strength; forte; asset.

failure *n.* **1 nonsuccess,** nonfulfillment, abortion, miscarriage, defeat, frustration, collapse, foundering, misfiring, fizzling out. **2 vain attempt,** abortion, defeat, fiasco, debacle, botch, blunder, *inf.* flop, washout. **3 incompetent,** loser, nonachiever, ne'er-do-well, disappointment, *inf.* flop, dud, washout. **4 omission,** neglect, negligence, remissness, nonobservance, nonperformance, dereliction, delinquency. **5 insufficiency,** inadequacy, deficiency, lack, dearth, scarcity, shortfall. **6 fading,** lessening, dimming, waning, vanishing. **7 breaking down,** nonfunction, *inf.* conking out. **8 failing,** decline, fading, dwindling, waning, sinking, deterioration, collapse, breakdown, loss, decay, crumbling, degeneration. **9 collapse,** crashing, going under, bankruptcy, ruin, ruination, *inf.* folding, flop. **Ant.** success; triumph.

faint *adj.* **1 indistinct,** unclear, dim, obscure, pale, faded, bleached. **2 indistinct,** scarcely audible/perceptible/visible, vague, low, soft, muted, muffled, stifled, subdued, weak, feeble, whispered. **3 slight,** small, remote, vague, minimal. **4 weak,** feeble, unenthusiastic, halfhearted, low-key. **5 giddy,** dizzy, light-headed, weak-headed, weak, *inf.* woozy. **Ant.** clear; loud; great; strong.
▸ *v.* **lose consciousness,** black out, pass out, collapse, *inf.* keel over, conk out, *lit.* swoon.

fair[1] *adj.* **1 just,** impartial, unbiased, unprejudiced, objective, evenhanded, dispassionate, disinterested, detached, equitable, aboveboard, lawful, legal, legitimate, proper, square, *inf.* on the level. **2 fair-minded,** just, impartial, unbiased, unprejudiced, open-minded, honest, upright, honorable, trustworthy, aboveboard. **3 fine,** dry, bright, clear, sunny, cloudless, unclouded. **4 favorable,** advantageous, helpful, beneficial. **5 blond/blonde,** yellow, flaxen, light brown, strawberry blond, fair-haired, light-haired, flaxen-haired, tow-headed. **6 pale,** light-colored, white, cream-colored, creamy, peaches and cream, chalky. **7 beautiful,** pretty, lovely, attractive, good-looking, comely, *lit.* beauteous. **8 reasonable,** passable, tolerable, satisfactory, respectable, decent, all right, pretty good, not bad, moderate, so-so, average, fair-to-middling, ample, adequate, sufficient. **Ant.** unfair; dark; ugly.

fair[2] *n.* **exhibition,** display, show, exhibit, exposition, *inf.* expo.

fairly *adv.* **1 justly,** equitably, impartially, without prejudice, objectively, evenhandedly, properly, lawfully, legally, legitimately. **2 quite,** reasonably, passably, tolerably, satisfactorily, moderately, rather, somewhat, adequately, *inf.* pretty. **3 positively,** really, absolutely, decidedly, veritably.

faith *n.* **1 trust,** belief, confidence, conviction, credence, credit, reliance, dependence, optimism, hopefulness. **2 religion,** church, persuasion, belief, creed, teaching, dogma, doctrine, sect, denomination. **3 loyalty,** allegiance, faithfulness, fidelity, fealty, constancy, devotion, obedience, commitment. *Ant.* disbelief; distrust; disloyalty.

faithful *adj.* **1 loyal,** constant, devoted, dependable, reliable, true, true-blue, trusty, trustworthy, staunch, unswerving, unwavering, steadfast, obedient, dutiful, dedicated, committed. **2 accurate,** true, exact, precise, close, strict, without error, unerring. *Ant.* disloyal; unfaithful; treacherous; imprecise.

fake *adj.* **1 counterfeit,** forged, sham, imitation, fraudulent, false, bogus, spurious, pseudo, *inf.* phony. **2 sham,** imitation, artificial, synthetic, mock, simulated, reproduction, ersatz. **3 affected,** put-on, assumed, feigned, pseudo, insincere, *inf.* phony. *Ant.* genuine; authentic; sincere.

▸ *n.* **1 counterfeit,** forgery, copy, sham, imitation, fraud, reproduction, hoax, *inf.* phony. **2 charlatan,** impostor, mountebank, quack, *inf.* phony.

fall *v.* **1 descend,** drop, drop down, sink, gravitate, cascade, plop, plummet. **2 fall down,** fall over, trip, trip over, stumble, slip, slide, tumble, topple over, keel over, go head over heels, collapse, fall in a heap, take a spill. **3 fall away,** slope, slope down, incline/slant downward. **4 sink,** sink lower, subside, recede, abate, settle. **5 fall off,** drop off, go down, decline, decrease, grow less, diminish, dwindle, depreciate, plummet, slump. **6 die,** fade, fail, decline, deteriorate, flag, wane, ebb, degenerate, go downhill, *inf.* go to the dogs. **7 die,** be killed/slain, be lost, drop dead, perish, meet one's end. **8 surrender,** yield, submit, give in, give up, give way, capitulate, succumb, resign oneself, be overthrown by, be taken by, be defeated by, be conquered by, lose one's position to, pass into the hands of. **9 take place,** occur, happen, come about, come to pass. **10 become,** grow, pass into. **11 sin,** do wrong, transgress, err, go astray, yield to temptation, commit an offense, lapse, fall from grace, backslide, trespass. *Ant.* rise; thrive; survive.

▸ *n.* **1 trip,** tumble, spill, stumble, slipping, slip, slide, topple, nosedive, collapse. **2 drop,** dropping off, decline, decrease, cut, lessening, lowering, dip, diminishing, dwindling, reduction, depreciation, plummeting, slump, deterioration. **3 death,** demise, downfall, ruin, collapse, failure, decline, deterioration, wane, ebb, degeneration, destruction, overthrow. **4 surrender,** yielding, submission, giving in, capitulation, succumbing, resignation, defeat. **5 slope,** downward slope/slant/incline, declivity, descent, downgrade. **6 sin,** wrongdoing, transgression, error, yielding to temptation, offense, lapse, fall from grace, backsliding, original sin, the Fall.

fallacy *n.* **mistaken belief,** misbelief, misconception, false notion, misapprehension, misjudgment, miscalculation, error, mistake, untruth, inconsistency, illusion, delusion, deceit, deception, sophism, sophistry.

false *adj.* **1 untrue,** incorrect, wrong, erroneous, faulty, invalid, unfounded, untruthful, fictitious, concocted, fabricated, invented, inaccurate, inexact, imprecise, flawed, unreal, counterfeit, forged, fraudulent, spurious, misleading. **2 false-hearted,** unfaithful, faithless, treacherous, disloyal, traitorous, perfidious, two-faced, double-dealing, untrustworthy, untrue, deceitful,

deceiving, deceptive, dishonorable, dishonest, duplicitous, hypocritical, unreliable, unsound, untruthful, lying, mendacious. **3 fake,** artificial, imitation, synthetic, simulated, sham, mock, bogus, ersatz, spurious, counterfeit, feigned, forged, make-believe, pseudo, *inf.* phony. *Ant.* true; loyal; faithful; genuine.

falsehood *n.* **1 lie,** fib, untruth, false statement, falsification, perjury, fabrication, invention, piece of fiction, fiction, story, fairy story/tale, exaggeration. **2 deceit,** deception, deceitfulness, two-facedness, double-dealing, prevarication, equivocation, mendacity, untruthfulness, perjury, perfidy, treachery, treason. *Ant.* truth; verity.

falsify *v.* **1 alter,** counterfeit, forge, fake, doctor, tamper with, distort, adulterate, pervert. **2 disprove,** show to be false, prove unsound, refute, confute, rebut, contradict, oppose, misrepresent, garble, misstate, misquote.

falter *v.* **1 hesitate,** waver, oscillate, fluctuate, delay, vacillate, be undecided, blow hot and cold, shilly-shally, hem and haw, drag one's feet, sit on the fence. **2 stammer,** stutter, stumble, speak haltingly.

fame *n.* **renown**, celebrity, eminence, notability, note, distinction, mark, prominence, esteem, importance, greatness, account, preeminence, glory, honor, illustriousness, stardom, reputation, repute, notoriety, infamy. *Ant.* obscurity; disgrace; disrepute.

familiar *adj.* **1 well-known**, known, recognized, customary, accustomed, common, everyday, ordinary, commonplace, frequent, habitual, usual, repeated, routine, stock, mundane, run-of-the-mill, conventional, household. **2 informal**, casual, relaxed, comfortable, easy, free, free and easy, at ease, at home, friendly, unceremonious, unrestrained, unconstrained, unreserved, open, natural, simple. **3 close**, intimate, dear, near, confidential, bosom, friendly, neighborly, sociable, amicable, *inf.* pally, chummy, buddy-buddy, thick as thieves. **4 overfamiliar**, presumptuous, disrespectful, forward, bold, impudent, impertinent, intrusive, *inf.* pushy. *Ant.* unfamiliar; strange; formal.

family *n.* **1 household**, clan, tribe, nuclear family, extended family. **2 children**, offspring, little ones, progeny, descendants, issue, scions, brood, *inf.* kids. **3 relatives**, relations, people, kin, next of kin, kinsfolk, kinsmen, one's own flesh and blood, folk. **4 ancestry**, extraction, parentage, birth, pedigree, genealogy, background, family tree, descent, lineage, line, bloodline, blood, race, strain, stock, breed, dynasty, house, forebears, forefathers, antecedents, roots. **5 group**, taxonomic group.

famine *n.* **scarcity**, lack, dearth, want, deficiency, shortage, insufficiency, paucity, drought, starvation, hunger.

famished *adj.* **starving**, starving to death, starved, ravenous, hungry, undernourished.

famous *adj.* **well-known**, renowned, celebrated, famed, prominent, noted, notable, great, eminent, preeminent, distinguished, esteemed, respected, venerable, illustrious, acclaimed, honored, exalted, glorious, remarkable, signal, popular, legendary, lionized, much-publicized. *Ant.* unknown; obscure.

fanatic *n.* **zealot**, extremist, radical, activist, militant, sectarian, bigot, partisan, devotee, addict, enthusiast, visionary.

fanatical *adj.* **1 extremist**, extreme, zealous, radical, activist, militant, sectarian, bigoted, dogmatic, prejudiced, intolerant, narrow-minded, partisan, rabid. **2 enthusiastic,** eager, fervent, passionate, overenthusiastic, obsessive, immoderate, frenzied, frenetic, *inf.* wild, gung-ho.

fanciful *adj.* **1 imaginary,** fancied, fantastic, romantic, mythical, fabulous, legendary, unreal, illusory, visionary, made-up, make-believe, fairy-tale, extravagant. **2 imaginative,** inventive, impractical, whimsical, capricious, visionary, chimerical. **3 imaginative,** creative, curious, extravagant, fantastic, bizarre, strange, eccentric.

fancy *n.* **1 caprice,** whimsy, sudden impulse, vagary, eccentricity, peculiarity, whim, quirk, notion, kink. **2 desire,** urge, wish, want, yearning, longing, inclination, bent, hankering, impulse, fondness, liking, love, partiality, preference, predilection, taste, penchant, *inf.* yen, itch. **3 imagination,** imaginative power, creativity, conception, images, mental images, visualizations. **4 idea,** vague idea, guess, thought, notion, supposition, opinion.
▸ *v.* **1 guess,** think, believe, suppose, surmise, suspect, conjecture, reckon. **2 would like,** wish for, want, desire, long for, yearn for, crave, hanker after, *inf.* have a yen for. **3 find attractive,** be attracted to, be captivated by, be infatuated with, take to, desire, lust after, burn for, *inf.* have taken a shine to, have a crush on, be wild/mad about, go for.

fantastic *adj.* **1 fanciful,** imaginary, romantic, unreal, illusory, make-believe, irrational, extravagant, wild, mad, absurd, incredible, strange, eccentric, whimsical, capricious. **2 strange,** weird, queer, peculiar, outlandish, eccentric, bizarre, grotesque, freakish, whimsical, fanciful, quaint, imaginative, exotic, unreal, extravagant, elaborate, ornate, intricate, rococo, baroque, phantasmagoric. **3 tremendous,** enormous, huge, very great, terrific, impressive, overwhelming. **4 marvelous,** wonderful, sensational, superb, excellent, brilliant, great, first-class, top-notch, *inf.* cool, awesome. ***Ant.*** real; ordinary; poor.

fantasy *n.* **1 fancy,** imagination, creativity, invention, originality, vision, myth, romance. **2 fancy,** speculation, daydreaming, reverie, flight of fancy, fanciful notion, dream, daydream, pipedream.

far *adv.* **1 a long way,** a great distance, any great distance, a good way, afar. **2 to a great extent/degree,** very much, much, by much, by a great amount, considerably, by a long way, markedly, immeasurably, decidedly, by far.
▸ *adj.* **faraway,** far-off, distant, remote, out of the way, far-flung, far-removed, outlying, inaccessible, back of beyond, godforsaken. *Ant.* near; neighboring.

farcical *adj.* **1 ridiculous,** ludicrous, absurd, laughable, risible, preposterous, facetious, silly, foolish, nonsensical, asinine. **2 comic,** slapstick, humorous, amusing.

farewell *interj.* **goodbye,** so long, adieu, ciao, adios, auf Wiedersehen, au revoir; *inf.* see you, see you later, toodle-oo.
▸ *n.* **goodbye,** adieu, leave-taking, parting, send-off, departure, departing, going away.

far-fetched *adj.* **improbable,** unlikely, remote, implausible, incredible, scarcely credible, unbelievable, difficult to believe, dubious, doubtful, unconvincing, strained, labored, strange, fantastic, fanciful, unrealistic, *inf.* hard to swallow/take.

fascinate *v.* **captivate,** enchant, beguile, bewitch, enthrall, infatuate, enrapture, entrance, hold spellbound, transfix, rivet, mesmerize, hypnotize, allure, lure, tempt, entice, draw, tantalize, charm, attract, intrigue, delight, absorb, engross. *Ant.* bore; repel; turn off (see turn).

fashion *n.* **1 style,** vogue, trend, latest thing, mode, craze, rage, fad, convention, custom, practice. **2 clothes,** clothes industry, clothes design, couture, *inf.* rag trade. **3 manner,** way, style, method, mode, system, approach. **4 kind,** type, sort, make, design, description.
▸ *v.* **make,** construct, build, manufacture, create, devise, shape, form, mold, forge.

fashionable *adj.* **1 in fashion,** stylish, up-to-date, up-to-the-minute, modern, voguish, in vogue, modish, popular, all the rage, trendsetting, latest, smart, chic, elegant, natty, *inf.* trendy, with it, ritzy. **2 high-class,** *inf.* classy, swank. *Ant.* unfashionable; old-fashioned; dated.

fast *adj.* **1 quick,** rapid, swift, speedy, brisk, fleet-footed, hasty, hurried, accelerated, express, flying. **2 loyal,** devoted, faithful, firm, steadfast, staunch, constant, lasting, unchanging, unwavering, enduring. **3 fastened,** closed, shut,

secured, secure, firmly fixed.
4 promiscuous, licentious,
dissolute, loose, wanton. **5 wild,**
dissipated, dissolute, debauched,
promiscuous, intemperate,
immoderate, rakish, unrestrained,
reckless, profligate, self-
indulgent, extravagant. *Ant.* slow;
disloyal; virtuous.

▸ *adv.* **1 quickly,** rapidly, swiftly,
speedily, briskly, hastily, with all
haste, in haste, hurriedly, in a
hurry, post-haste, expeditiously,
with dispatch, like the wind, like
a shot/flash, hell-bent, hell-bent
for leather, like a bat out of hell,
inf. lickety-split. **2 firmly,** tightly,
securely, immovably, fixedly.
3 sound, deeply, completely.
4 wildly, dissipatedly,
intemperately, rakishly,
recklessly.

fasten *v.* **1 attach,** fix, affix, clip,
pin, tack. **2 bolt,** lock, secure,
make secure/fast, chain, seal, join,
connect, couple, unite, link,
attach, tie, bind, tether, hitch,
anchor. **3 direct,** aim, point, focus,
fix, rivet, concentrate, zero in.
4 become closed, close, button,
zip. **5 take hold of,** seize, catch/
grab hold of, grab, snatch. *Ant.*
unfasten; open; unlock.

fastidious *adj.* **hard to please,**
critical, overcritical, hypercritical,
fussy, finicky, overparticular, *inf.*
choosy, picky, persnickety. *Ant.*
easygoing; sloppy.

fat *adj.* **1 plump,** stout, overweight,
obese, heavy, large, solid,
corpulent, chubby, tubby, portly,
rotund, pudgy, flabby, gross,
potbellied, paunchy, *inf.* beefy,
roly-poly, elephantine. **2 fatty,**
greasy, oily, oleaginous, adipose,
unctuous, sebaceous. **3 fertile,**
productive, fruitful, rich, lush,
flourishing, thriving.
4 substantial, large, sizable,
major, important, significant,
considerable, profitable,
remunerative, lucrative. **5 thick,**
big, substantial, broad, extended.
Ant. thin; lean; minor.

▸ *n.* **1 fatty tissue,** fat cells,
adipose tissue. **2 excessive
weight,** fatness, plumpness,
stoutness, obesity, chubbiness,
tubbiness, flabbiness, corpulence,
bulk, *inf.* flab, blubber, beef. **3 oil,**
cooking oil, animal/vegetable fat,
lard, suet, butter, margarine,
oleomargarine, *inf.* oleo.

fatal *adj.* **1 causing death,** mortal,
deadly, lethal, death-dealing,
killing, terminal, final, incurable.
2 ruinous, destructive, disastrous,
catastrophic, calamitous,
cataclysmic. **3 fateful,** critical,
crucial, decisive, determining,
pivotal, momentous, important.
Ant. harmless; beneficial.

fatalism *n.* **stoicism,** resignation, passive acceptance, acceptance, predeterminism, predestinarianism, necessitarianism.

fatality *n.* **1 dead person,** death, casualty, mortality, loss, dead. **2 deadliness,** lethality.

fate *n.* **1 destiny,** providence, God's will, kismet, predestination, predetermination, chance, one's lot in life, the stars. **2 future,** outcome, upshot, end. **3 death,** end, destruction, ruin, doom, catastrophe, downfall, disaster, collapse, defeat.

father *n.* **1 begetter,** paterfamilias, patriarch, *inf.* dad, daddy, pop, pops, poppa, pa, old man. **2 forefather,** ancestor, forebear, progenitor, primogenitor, predecessor, forerunner, precursor. **3 founder,** originator, initiator, prime mover, architect, inventor, creator, maker, author. **4 leader,** elder, patriarch, senator. **5 priest,** pastor, padre, parson, clergyman, abbé.
▸ *v.* **1 sire,** beget, procreate, engender, bring into being, give life to. **2 found,** establish, institute, originate, initiate, invent, create, generate, conceive.

fathom *v.* **1 sound,** plumb, measure, estimate, gauge, probe. **2 understand,** comprehend, grasp, perceive, penetrate, divine, search out, get to the bottom of, ferret out.

fatigue *v.* **tire,** tire out, overtire, weary, exhaust, wear out, drain, prostrate, enervate, *inf.* take it out of, do in, poop out.
▸ *n.* **tiredness,** overtiredness, weariness, exhaustion, prostration, lassitude, debility, enervation, lethargy, listlessness. *Ant.* energy; vigor.

fatuous *adj.* **silly,** foolish, stupid, inane, pointless, senseless, nonsensical, childish, puerile, idiotic, brainless, mindless, vacuous, asinine, moronic, witless, ridiculous, ludicrous, laughable, risible.

fault *n.* **1 defect,** flaw, imperfection, blemish, snag, failing, shortcoming, weakness, weak point, infirmity, lack, deficiency. **2 error,** mistake, inaccuracy, blunder, oversight, *inf.* slipup, booboo. **3 misdeed,** wrongdoing, offense, misdemeanor, misconduct, sin, vice, lapse, indiscretion, peccadillo, transgression, trespass. **4 culpability,** blameworthiness, responsibility, accountability, answerability. *Ant.* merit; strength; asset.
▸ *v.* **1 find fault with,** criticize, complain about, quibble about,

find lacking, censure, impugn, pick holes in. **2 hold responsible/ accountable/blameworthy/ culpable,** hold to blame, call to account.

faultless *adj.* **1 without fault,** perfect, flawless, without blemish, unblemished, impeccable, accurate, correct, exemplary, model. **2 innocent,** without guilt, guiltless, blameless, above reproach, irreproachable, sinless, pure, unsullied. ***Ant.*** imperfect; guilty.

faulty *adj.* **1 broken,** not working, malfunctioning, out of order, damaged, defective, unsound, *inf.* on the blink, kaput. **2 defective,** flawed, unsound, illogical, wrong, inaccurate, incorrect, erroneous, imprecise, fallacious, impaired, weak, invalid. ***Ant.*** perfect; working; correct.

favor *n.* **1 good turn,** service, kind act, good deed, kindness, courtesy, benefit. **2 approval,** approbation, esteem, goodwill, kindness, benevolence, friendliness. **3 favoritism,** bias, partiality, prejudice, partisanship. **4 patronage,** backing, support, aid, assistance. **5 trinket,** toy, treat, noisemaker, balloon. ***Ant.*** disfavor; disapproval; disservice.
▸ *v.* **1 advocate,** approve of, recommend, support, back,

endorse, sanction. **2 prefer,** go in for, go for, choose, opt for, select, pick, single out, fancy, like, incline toward. **3 indulge,** pamper, spoil. **4 be to the advantage of,** be advantageous to, benefit, help, assist, aid, advance, abet. **5 oblige,** serve, accommodate, satisfy, please. ***Ant.*** oppose; dislike; hinder.

favorable *adj.* **1 good,** approving, commendatory, praising, well-disposed, enthusiastic. **2 in one's favor,** advantageous, beneficial, on one's side, helpful, good, hopeful, promising, fair, auspicious, propitious, opportune, timely, encouraging, conducive, convenient, suitable, fit, appropriate. **3 affirmative,** in the affirmative, positive, encouraging. **4 good,** pleasing, agreeable, successful, positive. ***Ant.*** unfavorable; critical; disadvantageous.

favorite *adj.* **best-loved,** most-liked, pet, favored, dearest, preferred, chosen, choice, treasured, ideal.
▸ *n.* **1 preference,** first choice, choice, pick, pet, beloved, darling, idol, jewel, jewel in the crown, blue-eyed boy, apple of one's eye, teacher's pet. **2 expected/probable winner,** front runner. ***Ant.*** bête noire; aversion.

fear *n.* **1 fright,** fearfulness, terror, alarm, panic, trepidation, apprehensiveness, dread, nervousness, fear and trembling, timidity, disquiet, trembling, quaking, quivering, consternation, dismay, shivers, butterflies, tremors, phobia, aversion, dread, bugbear, nightmare, horror, terror.
2 anxiety, worry, unease, uneasiness, apprehension, nervousness, agitation, concern, disquiet, disquietude, foreboding, misgiving, doubt, suspicion, angst.
3 awe, wonder, amazement, reverence, veneration.
4 likelihood, probability, possibility, chance, prospect.
▸ *v.* **1 be afraid/fearful/ apprehensive of,** be scared of, dread, live in fear/dread of, have a horror/dread of, have a phobia about, shudder at. **2 stand in awe of,** revere, reverence, venerate.
3 be afraid, suspect, have a suspicion, expect, anticipate, foresee, have a foreboding.

fearful *adj.* **1 afraid,** frightened, scared, terrified, alarmed, apprehensive, uneasy, nervous, tense, panicky, timid, timorous, faint-hearted, intimidated, hesitant, disquieted, trembling, quaking, quivering, shrinking, cowering, cowardly, pusillanimous, *inf.* jittery, jumpy.
2 terrible, dreadful, appalling, frightful, ghastly, horrific, horrible, horrendous, shocking, awful, atrocious, hideous, monstrous, dire, grim, unspeakable, gruesome, distressing, harrowing, alarming.
3 awesome, awe-inspiring, imposing, impressive. ***Ant.*** intrepid; bold.

fearless *adj.* **unafraid,** brave, courageous, valiant, intrepid, valorous, gallant, plucky, lionhearted, stouthearted, heroic, bold, daring, confident, audacious, indomitable, undaunted, unflinching, unshrinking, *inf.* game, gutsy, spunky. ***Ant.*** cowardly; craven.

fearsome *adj.* **frightening,** alarming, unnerving, daunting, horrifying, horrendous, dismaying, awe-inspiring, awesome.

feasible *adj.* **practicable,** possible, likely, workable, doable, achievable, attainable, accomplishable, realizable, reasonable, viable, realistic, within reason, useful, suitable, expedient. ***Ant.*** impractical; impossible.

feast *n.* **1 banquet,** repast, orgy, revels, festivities, *inf.* blowout, spread, bash. **2 celebration,**

festival, religious festival, feast day, saint's day, holy day, holiday, fête, festivity. **3 pleasure,** gratification, delight, treat, joy. *Ant.* fast; famine.

▸ *v.* **hold a banquet for,** wine and dine, regale, entertain, treat.

feat *n.* **deed,** act, action, exploit, performance, accomplishment, achievement, attainment, move, stunt.

feather *n.* **plume,** quill, pinion.

feature *n.* **1 aspect,** characteristic, facet, side, point, attribute, quality, property, trait, mark, hallmark, trademark, peculiarity, idiosyncrasy. **2 attraction,** highlight, focal point, focus, draw. **3 main item/article,** article, piece, item, report, story, column.

▸ *v.* **1 present,** promote, star, spotlight, highlight, emphasize, play up, accentuate. **2 play a part,** have a place.

federation *n.* **confederation,** confederacy, federacy, league, alliance, coalition, union, syndicate, association, amalgamation, combination, combine, entente, society, fraternity.

feeble *adj.* **1 weak,** weakly, weakened, frail, infirm, delicate, slight, sickly, puny, failing, ailing, helpless, powerless, debilitated, decrepit, doddering, tottering, enervated, enfeebled, effete. **2 ineffective,** ineffectual, unsuccessful, inadequate, unconvincing, futile, poor, weak, tame, paltry, slight, inefficient, incompetent, inadequate, indecisive, wishy-washy. **3 dim,** indistinct, faint, unclear, vague, inaudible. *Ant.* strong; robust; effective; forceful.

feed *v.* **1 nurture,** suckle, breast-feed, bottle-feed, nourish, sustain, cater for, provide for, wine and dine. **2 eat,** take nourishment, partake of food, consume, devour food, graze, browse, live on, exist on, subsist on. **3 gratify,** bolster, strengthen, augment, add to, encourage, minister to, add fuel to. **4 supply,** provide, give, furnish.

▸ *n.* **1 food,** fodder, provender, forage, pasturage, silage. **2 feast,** meal, dinner, repast, banquet, *inf.* spread.

feel *v.* **1 touch,** stroke, caress, fondle, finger, thumb, handle, manipulate, paw, maul. **2 notice,** observe, perceive, be sensible of, have a sensation of. **3 experience,** know, have, undergo, go through, bear, endure, suffer. **4 grope,** fumble, poke, explore. **5 sense,** try, try out, test, sound out. **6 think,** believe, consider it right, consider, be of the opinion, hold, judge, deem, have a feeling, sense, get the impression, feel in one's bones, have a hunch, have a funny feeling, just know. **7 seem,** appear, strike one as.

▶ *n.* **1 touch,** sense of touch, tactile sense. **2 texture,** surface, finish. **3 atmosphere,** ambience, aura, mood, air, impression, *inf.* vibrations, vibes. **4 knack,** aptitude, flair, talent, gift, art, faculty.

feeling *n.* **1 feel,** touch, sense of touch, tactile sense. **2 awareness,** consciousness, sensation, sense, perception. **3 idea,** vague idea, funny feeling, impression, suspicion, sneaking suspicion, notion, inkling, hunch, apprehension, presentiment, premonition, foreboding. **4 emotion,** affection, fondness, warmth, love, sentiment, passion, ardor, fervor, intensity, heat, fire, vehemence. **5 sympathy,** pity, compassion, understanding, concern, sensitivity, tender-heartedness, grief, commiseration, condolence, empathy. **6 instinct,** opinion, intuition, impression, point of view, thought, way of thinking, theory, hunch. **7 feel,** atmosphere, ambience, aura, mood, air, impression, *inf.* vibrations, vibes.

▶ *adj.* **1 sensitive,** warm, tender, caring, soft-hearted, sympathetic, compassionate, responsive, sentient, sensible, emotional, demonstrative. **2 emotional,** passionate, impassioned, ardent, intense, fervent, fervid.

felicitous *adj.* **1 apt,** well-chosen, well-expressed, well-put, fitting, suitable, appropriate, apposite, pertinent, germane, to the point. **2 happy,** joyful, harmonious, fortunate, lucky, successful, prosperous.

fell *v.* **cut down,** hew, level, raze, raze to the ground, demolish, knock down, strike down, flatten, ground, floor, prostrate, overthrow, kill.

fellow *n.* **man,** male, boy, person, individual, *inf.* chap, guy, character, customer.

feminine *adj.* **1 delicate,** gentle, tender, graceful, womanly, ladylike, girlish, refined, modest. **2 effeminate,** womanish, effete, unmanly, unmasculine, weak, *inf.* sissy, sissyish, limp-wristed. ***Ant.*** masculine; mannish; manly.

fence *n.* **1 enclosure,** barrier, railing, rail, wall, hedge, barricade, rampart, stockade, palisade. **2 receiver,** dealer.

▶ *v.* **1 enclose,** surround, circumscribe, encircle, encompass. **2 hedge,** be evasive, beat around the bush, dodge the issue, prevaricate, equivocate, fudge the issue, shilly-shally, vacillate.

ferment *n.* **1 fermentation agent,** yeast, mold, bacteria, leaven, leavening. **2 stir,** fever, furor, frenzy, brouhaha, confusion, fuss, stew, hubbub, racket, imbroglio, tumult, commotion, uproar, turmoil, agitation, disruption, turbulence.
▸ *v.* **1 undergo fermentation,** foam, froth, bubble, effervesce, seethe, boil, rise, work. **2 excite,** agitate, inflame, incite, cause, provoke, arouse, stir up, foment. **3 cause,** incite, excite, provoke, arouse, stir up, foment. **4 seethe,** smolder, boil, be agitated.

ferocious *adj.* **1 fierce,** savage, wild, feral, untamed, predatory, rapacious, ruthless, brutal, brutish, cruel, pitiless, merciless, vicious, violent, inexorable, barbarous, barbaric, inhuman, bloodthirsty, murderous. **2 fierce,** intense, extreme, acute. **Ant.** tame; gentle; mild.

ferry *n.* **ferryboat,** shuttle.
▸ *v.* **run,** shuttle, carry, transport, convey, run, ship, shuttle, chauffeur.

fertile *adj.* **1 fruitful,** productive, fecund, rich. **2 potent,** virile, fecund, reproductive, propagative.

3 inventive, creative, original, ingenious, resourceful, visionary, constructive, productive. **Ant.** infertile; barren.

fertilize *v.* **1 feed,** enrich, mulch, compost, dress, top-dress.
2 impregnate, inseminate, fecundate, make pregnant.
3 pollinate, make fruitful, fructify.

fertilizer *n.* **plant food,** manure, dung, compost, dressing, top dressing.

fervent *adj.* **passionate,** ardent, impassioned, intense, vehement, heartfelt, fervid, emotional, emotive, warm, devout, sincere, eager, earnest, zealous, enthusiastic, excited, animated, spirited. **Ant.** apathetic; cold; unemotional.

fervor *n.* **fervency,** passion, ardor, impassionedness, intensity, vehemence, fervidness, emotion, warmth, devoutness, sincerity, eagerness, earnestness, zeal, enthusiasm, excitement, animation, spirit. **Ant.** apathy; indifference.

fester *v.* **1 suppurate,** matter, come to a head, gather, maturate, run, discharge. **2 rot,** decay, go bad, go off, decompose, disintegrate. **3 rankle,** chafe, gnaw.

festival *n.* **1 saint's day,** holy day, feast day, holiday, anniversary, commemoration, rite, ritual, day of observance. **2 fair,** gala, fête, carnival, celebrations, festivities.

festive *adj.* **joyous,** joyful, happy, jolly, merry, gay, jovial, lighthearted, cheerful, cheery, jubilant, convivial, good-time, gleeful, mirthful, uproarious, rollicking, backslapping, celebratory, gala, holiday, carnival, sportive, festal.

festoon *n.* **garland,** wreath, chaplet, lei, swag.

▸ *v.* **garland,** wreathe, hang, drape, decorate, adorn, ornament, array, deck, bedeck, swathe, beribbon.

fetch *v.* **1 go and get,** get, go for, bring, carry, deliver, convey, transport, escort, conduct, lead, usher in. **2 sell for,** go for, bring in, realize, yield, earn, cost.

fetching *adj.* **attractive,** charming, enchanting, sweet, winsome, taking, captivating, fascinating, alluring.

feud *n.* **vendetta,** rivalry, hostility, enmity, conflict, strife, discord, bad blood, animosity, antagonism, unfriendliness, grudge, estrangement, schism, quarrel, argument, bickering, falling-out.

fever *n.* **1 feverishness,** *inf.* temperature, temp. **2 ferment,** frenzy, furor, turmoil, agitation, excitement, restlessness, unrest, passion, intensity.

feverish *adj.* **1 fevered,** febrile, burning, hot, flushed, red-faced, red. **2 frenzied,** frenetic, agitated, excited, restless, nervous, worked up, overwrought, frantic, distracted, flustered, impatient, *inf.* in a tizzy.

few *adj.* **not many,** hardly any, scarcely any, one or two, a handful of, a sprinkling of, a couple of, few and far between, infrequent, sporadic, irregular, scarce, rare, negligible, scant, hard to find. ***Ant.*** many; frequent; plentiful.

▸ *n.* **a small number,** one or two, a handful, a sprinkling.

fiasco *n.* **failure,** disaster, catastrophe, mess, ruination, debacle, *inf.* flop, washout.

fiber *n.* **1 thread,** strand, tendril, filament, fibril. **2 material,** substance, cloth, stuff. **3 character,** nature, makeup, spirit, disposition, temperament.

fickle *adj.* **capricious,** changeable, variable, unpredictable, volatile, mercurial, inconstant, unstable, vacillating, unsteady, unfaithful, faithless, irresolute, flighty, giddy, erratic, fitful, irregular, mutable. ***Ant.*** constant; stable.

fiction *n.* **1 storytelling,** romance, fable, fantasy, legend.

2 fabrication, invention, concoction, lie, fib, untruth, falsehood, fairy tale/story, tall story, improvisation, prevarication, *inf.* cock-and-bull story, whopper, fish story. *Ant.* fact; truth.

fictional *adj.* **fictitious,** made up, invented, imaginary, unreal, nonexistent. *Ant.* real; actual.

fictitious *adj.* **1 fictional,** made up, imaginary. **2 false,** untrue, bogus, sham, counterfeit, fake, fabricated, assumed, invented, made up, concocted, spurious, improvised, imagined, imaginary, apocryphal. *Ant.* factual; real; genuine.

fidelity *n.* **1 faithfulness,** loyalty, devotedness, devotion, allegiance, commitment, constancy, true-heartedness, trustworthiness, dependability, reliability, staunchness, obedience. **2 accuracy,** exactness, exactitude, precision, preciseness, strictness, closeness, faithfulness, correspondence, conformity, authenticity. *Ant.* disloyalty; treachery; perfidy.

fidget *v.* **1 move restlessly,** wriggle, squirm, twitch, jiggle, *inf.* have ants in one's pants. **2 fiddle,** play, fuss.

fidgety *adj.* **restless,** restive, on edge, jumpy, uneasy, nervous, nervy, twitchy, *inf.* jittery, like a cat on a hot tin roof.

field *n.* **1 pasture,** meadow, grassland, *lit.* lea, greensward. **2 area,** area of activity, sphere, regime, discipline, province, department, line, speciality, métier. **3 range,** scope, purview, limits, confines. **4 applicants,** candidates, entrants, competitors, runners, possibles, possibilities, competition.
▸ *v.* **1 catch,** stop, retrieve, return, throw back. **2 deal with,** handle, cope with, answer, respond/react to, reply to.

fiend *n.* **1 devil,** demon, evil spirit. **2 brute,** savage, beast, barbarian, monster, ogre, sadist, blackguard. **3 addict,** abuser, user.

fiendish *adj.* **1 wicked,** cruel, brutal, brutish, savage, barbaric, barbarous, inhuman, murderous, vicious, bloodthirsty, ferocious, ruthless, heartless, pitiless, merciless, black-hearted, unfeeling, malevolent, malicious, villainous, odious, base, malignant, devilish, diabolical, hellish, demonic, satanic, ungodly. **2 cunning,** clever, ingenious. **3 difficult,** complex, complicated, intricate.

fierce *adj.* **1 ferocious,** savage, wild, vicious, feral, untamed, bloodthirsty, dangerous, cruel, brutal, murderous, slaughterous, menacing, threatening, terrible, grim. **2 intense,** ardent, passionate, impassioned, fervent, fervid, fiery, uncontrolled. **3 violent,** strong, stormy, blustery, gusty, boisterous, tempestuous, raging, furious, turbulent, tumultuous, cyclonic, typhonic. **4 very bad,** severe, intense, grave, awful, dreadful. **5 competitive,** keen, intense, strong, relentless, cutthroat. *Ant.* tame; gentle; mild.

fight *v.* **1 battle,** do battle, war, wage/make war, go to war, make war, attack, mount an attack, take up arms, combat, engage, meet, come to blows, exchange blows, close, clash, skirmish, struggle, contend, grapple, wrestle, scuffle, tussle, collide, spar, joust, tilt. **2 come to blows,** exchange blows, attack/assault each other, hit/punch each other, box, brawl, *inf.* scrap. **3 feud,** quarrel, argue, bicker, squabble, wrangle, dispute, be at odds, disagree, battle, altercate, *inf.* fall out. **4 contest,** take a stand against, oppose, dispute, object to, withstand, resist, defy, strive/struggle against, take issue with. **5 wage,** carry on, conduct, engage in, wage, prosecute.
▸ *n.* **1 battle,** engagement, action, clash, conflict, combat, contest,

encounter, skirmish, scuffle, tussle, brush, exchange. **2 brawl,** affray, fracas, melee, sparring match, exchange, free-for-all, struggle, disturbance, fisticuffs, *inf.* set-to, scrap. **3 quarrel,** disagreement, difference of opinion, dispute, argument, altercation, feud. **4 spirit,** will to win, gameness, pluck, aggression, belligerence, militancy, resistance, power to resist.

figurative *adj.* **nonliteral,** metaphorical, allegorical, representative, emblematic, symbolic.

figure *n.* **1 number,** whole number, numeral, digit, integer, cipher, numerical symbol. **2 cost,** price, amount, value, total, sum, aggregate. **3 shape,** form, outline, silhouette. **4 body,** physique, build, frame, torso, proportions, *inf.* vital statistics, chassis. **5 diagram,** illustration, picture, drawing, sketch, chart, plan, map. **6 human representation,** likeness, image of a person. **7 symbol,** emblem, sign, representative. **8 pattern,** design, motif, device, depiction. **9 dignitary,** notable, notability, personage, somebody, worthy, celebrity, leader, force, personality, presence, character, *inf.* big shot, bigwig.
▸ *v.* **1 calculate,** work out,

compute, tally, reckon. **2 appear,** feature, be featured/mentioned, play a part/role. **3 think,** consider, conclude. **4 be likely/probable,** be understandable, make sense.

file[1] *n.* **1 folder,** box, portfolio, document case, filing cabinet, card file, computer file, data file. **2 dossier,** folder, information, documents, records, data, particulars, case notes. **3 line,** column, row, string, chain, queue. ▸ *v.* **1 categorize,** classify, organize, put in place, put in order, pigeon-hole, put on record, record, enter, store. **2 apply,** put in, register, sign up. **3 walk/march in a line,** march, parade, troop, pass in formation.

file[2] *v.* **smooth,** shape, buff, rub, rub down, polish, burnish, furbish, refine, scrape, abrade, rasp, sandpaper, pumice.

fill *v.* **1 crowd,** overcrowd, congest, cram, pervade. **2 stock,** pack, load, supply, furnish, provide, replenish, restock, refill. **3 satisfy,** stuff, cram, satiate, sate, surfeit, glut. **4 pervade,** spread throughout, permeate, suffuse, imbue, charge, saturate. **5 stop,** stop up, block up, plug (up), seal, close, clog. **6 occupy,** hold, take up. **7 carry out,** execute, perform, complete, fulfill. *Ant.* empty; vacate.

film *n.* **1 layer,** coat, coating, covering, cover, dusting, sheet, blanket, skin, tissue, membrane. **2 haze,** mist, cloud, blur, veil, murkiness. **3 movie,** motion picture, picture, *inf.* video, flick. ▸ *v.* **1 photograph,** record, take pictures of, shoot, make a film of, videotape. **2 become blurred,** blur, cloud over, mist over, dull, blear.

filter *n.* **strainer,** purifier, cleaner, gauze, netting, cheesecloth. ▸ *v.* **1 strain,** sieve, sift, filtrate, clarify, purify, clear, refine. **2 trickle,** ooze, seep, leak, dribble, percolate, flow out, drain, exude, escape, leach.

filth *n.* **1 dirt,** muck, grime, mud, mire, sludge, slime, squalor, foul matter, excrement, dung, manure, sewage, rubbish, refuse, garbage, trash, pollution, contamination, defilement, decay, putrefaction, putrescence, filthiness, uncleanness, foulness, nastiness, *inf.* crud. **2 pornography,** obscenity, indecency, smut, corruption, vulgarity, vileness, *inf.* porn, hard porn, raunchiness.

filthy *adj.* **1 dirty,** mucky, muddy, murky, slimy, squalid, unclean, foul, nasty, feculent, polluted, contaminated, rotten, decaying, smelly, fetid, putrid. **2 unwashed,** unclean, dirty, dirt-encrusted, grubby, muddy, mucky, black, blackened. **3 low-down,** despicable, contemptible, base, mean, vile, nasty, sordid. **4 pornographic,** obscene, indecent, smutty, corrupt, coarse, bawdy, vulgar, lewd, licentious, vile, depraved, foul, dirty, impure, *inf.* blue, raunchy. **Ant.** spotless; clean; pure.

final *adj.* **1 last,** closing, concluding, finishing, end, ending, terminating, terminal, ultimate, eventual, endmost. **2 absolute,** conclusive, irrevocable, unalterable, irrefutable, incontrovertible, indisputable, unappealable, decisive, definitive, definite, settled, determinate. **Ant.** first; introductory.

finale *n.* **end,** finish, close, conclusion, climax, culmination, denouement, last act, final scene, final curtain, epilogue, *inf.* wind-up.

finalize *v.* **complete,** conclude, settle, decide, agree on, work out, tie up, wrap up, put the finishing touches to, *inf.* sew up, clinch.

finance *n.* **1 financial affairs,** money/fiscal matters, economics, money management, commerce, business, investment, banking, accounting. **2 funds,** assets, resources, money, capital, cash, wealth, wherewithal, revenue, stock, financial condition/state. ▸ *v.* **pay for,** fund, back, subsidize, underwrite, capitalize, guarantee, provide capital/security for, furnish credit for.

financial *adj.* **money,** monetary, pecuniary, fiscal, economic, budgetary.

find *v.* **1 come across,** chance upon, light upon, happen upon, stumble on, discover, come up with, hit upon, turn up, bring to light, uncover, unearth, ferret out, locate, lay one's hands on, encounter. **2 get back,** recover, retrieve, regain, repossess, recoup. **3 get,** obtain, acquire, procure, gain, earn, achieve, attain, win. **4 discover,** become aware, realize, learn, conclude, detect, observe, notice, note, perceive. **5 consider,** regard as, think, judge, deem, gauge, rate. **6 reach,** attain, arrive at, gain, achieve. **Ant.** lose; mislay. ▸ *n.* **asset,** acquisition, lucky discovery, catch, bargain, good buy, godsend, boon, windfall.

finding *n.* **decision,** verdict, conclusion, pronouncement, judgment, decree, order, recommendation.

fine *adj.* **1 all right,** satisfactory, acceptable, agreeable, convenient, suitable, good, *inf.* OK. **2 all right,** in good health, quite well, *inf.* OK.

3 excellent, first-class, first-rate, great, exceptional, outstanding, admirable, quality, superior, splendid, magnificent, beautiful, exquisite, choice, select, prime, supreme, rare, *inf.* A-1, splendiferous, top-notch. **4 fair,** dry, bright, clear, cloudless, sunny, balmy, clement. **5 fragile,** delicate, frail, dainty, slight.
6 sheer, light, lightweight, chiffony, diaphanous, filmy, gossamer, gossamery, gauzelike, gauzy, cobwebby, transparent, translucent, airy, ethereal, thin, flimsy. **7 fine-grained,** powdery, powdered, ground, crushed, pulverized. **8 expensive,** elegant, stylish, smart, chic, fashionable, modish, high-fashion, lavish.
9 refined, pure, solid, unadulterated, unalloyed, unpolluted, one hundred percent.
10 subtle, fine-drawn, tenuous, hairsplitting, precise, minute, elusive, abstruse.
11 discriminating, discerning, tasteful, fastidious, critical, sensitive, refined, intelligent.
12 keen, acute, sharp, quick, perspicacious, clever, intelligent, brilliant, finely honed/tuned.
13 good-looking, attractive, handsome, lovely, pretty, striking.
Ant. poor; dull; coarse.
▸ *n.* **penalty,** financial penalty,

punishment, forfeit, forfeiture, damages.
finish *v.* **1 complete,** accomplish, execute, discharge, carry out, deal with, do, get done, fulfill, achieve, attain, end, conclude, close, bring to a conclusion/end/close, finalize, stop, cease, terminate, round off, put the finishing touches to, *inf.* wind up, wrap up, sew up, polish off, knock off. **2 stop,** cease, discontinue, give up, have done with, suspend. **3 use,** use up, consume, eat, devour, drink, exhaust, empty, deplete, drain, expend, dispatch, dispose of.
4 overcome, defeat, overpower, conquer, overwhelm, get the better of, best, worst, rout, bring down, put an end to, do away with, dispose of, get rid of, destroy, annihilate, kill, exterminate, liquidate, drive to the wall, *inf.* wipe out, do in.
5 perfect, polish, refine, put the final/finishing touches to, crown, put a finish on, varnish, lacquer, stain, coat, veneer, wax, gild, glaze, give a shine to, polish, burnish, smooth off. ***Ant.*** start; begin.
▸ *n.* **1 completion,** accomplishment, execution, fulfillment, achievement, consummation, end, conclusion, close, closing, cessation, final act,

finale, denouement, last stages, *inf.* winding up. **2 defeat,** overpowering, destruction, rout, bringing down, end, annihilation, death, extermination, liquidation, ruination, *inf.* ruin, curtains.
3 cultivation, culture, refinement, polish, style, sophistication, suaveness, urbanity, education.
4 surface, texture, grain, veneer, coating, lacquer, glaze, luster, gloss, polish, shine, patina, smoothness.

finite *adj.* **bounded,** limited, subject to limitations, restricted, delimited, demarcated, terminable.

fire *n.* **1 blaze,** conflagration, inferno, holocaust, flames.
2 gunfire, sniping, flak, bombardment, shelling, volley, barrage, fusillade, salvo. **3 energy,** spirit, life, liveliness, animation, vigor, verve, vivacity, sparkle, scintillation, dash, vim, gusto, élan, enthusiasm, fervor, eagerness, impetuosity, force, potency, driving power, vehemence, ardor, passion, intensity, zeal, ardor, inspiration, imagination, creativity, inventiveness, flair, *inf.* pep.
▸ *v.* **1 set fire to,** set on fire, set alight, set ablaze, put a match to, light, ignite, kindle. **2 shoot,** let off, discharge, trigger, set off.

3 launch, hurl, discharge, eject.
4 explode, detonate, touch off.
5 arouse, rouse, stir up, excite, enliven, inflame, put/breathe life into, animate, inspire, motivate, stimulate, incite, galvanize, electrify, impassion. **6 dismiss,** discharge, give someone his/her marching orders, get rid of, show someone the door, oust, depose, cashier, *inf.* sack, ax.

firebrand *n.* **troublemaker,** agitator, rabble-rouser, demagogue.

fireproof *adj.* **nonflammable,** incombustible, unburnable, fire-resistant, flame-resistant, flame-retardant, flameproof.

firm[1] *adj.* **1 hard,** hardened, stiff, rigid, inflexible, inelastic, unyielding, resistant, solid, solidified, compacted, compressed, condensed, dense, close-grained, congealed, frozen, set, jelled. **2 fixed,** fast, secure, secured, stable, set, established, tight, immovable, irremovable, unshakable, stationary, motionless, taut, anchored, rooted, embedded, riveted, braced, cemented, nailed, tied.
3 fixed, settled, decided, definite, established, unalterable, unchangeable. **4 strong,** vigorous, sturdy. **5 constant,** unchanging, enduring, abiding, durable, deep-

rooted, long-standing, long-lasting, steady, stable, staunch.
6 resolute, determined, decided, resolved, unfaltering, unwavering, unflinching, unswerving, unyielding, unbending, inflexible, obdurate, obstinate, stubborn, hard-line, strict, intransigent, unmalleable. **Ant.** soft; flabby; unstable; indefinite.

firm[2] *n.* **company,** business, concern, house, establishment, organization, corporation, conglomerate, partnership, cooperative, *inf.* outfit.

first *adj.* **1 earliest,** initial, opening, introductory, original, premier, primitive, primeval, primordial, pristine. **2 primary,** beginning, basic, fundamental, key, rudimentary, cardinal.
3 leading, foremost, principal, highest, ruling, chief, head, main, major, greatest, preeminent, supreme. **Ant.** last; subsidiary; lowly.
▸ *adv.* **1 at first,** to begin with, at the beginning/start, at the outset, initially. **2 before anything/all else,** first and foremost. **3 in the first place,** firstly. **4 sooner,** rather, in preference, more willingly.

fish *v.* **1 go fishing,** angle, cast.
2 look, search, hunt, grope, delve, cast about.

fishy *adj.* **1 fishlike,** piscatorial, piscine. **2 questionable,** dubious, doubtful, suspect, suspicious, odd, queer, peculiar, strange, not quite right, *inf.* funny, shady, not kosher.

fit[1] *adj.* **1 well,** healthy, in good health, in shape, in good shape/trim/condition, in trim, strong, robust, hale and hearty, sturdy, hardy, stalwart, vigorous. **2 able,** capable, competent, adequate, good enough, satisfactory, ready, prepared, qualified, trained, equipped, eligible, worthy, *inf.* up to scratch. **3 fitting,** proper, due, seemly, decorous, decent, right, correct, apt, appropriate, suitable, convenient, apposite, relevant, pertinent. **Ant.** unhealthy; unfit; inappropriate.

fit[2] *v.* **1 agree with,** concur with, correspond with, match, dovetail with, tally with, suit, go with, be congruent with, conform to, be consonant with. **2 join,** connect, put together. **3 put in place/position,** position, lay, fix, insert, arrange, adjust, shape. **4 adjust,** adapt, modify, alter, regulate, accommodate. **5 make suitable,** qualify, prepare, make ready, prime, condition, train. **6 fit out,** equip, provide, supply, furnish.

fix *v.* **1 fasten,** secure, make fast, attach, connect, join, couple, stick, glue, cement, pin, nail, screw, bolt, clamp, bind, tie, pinion. **2 plant,** implant, install, anchor, embed, establish, position, station, situate. **3 decide on,** settle, set, agree on, arrive at, arrange, determine, establish, define, name, specify. **4 repair,** mend, see to, patch up, put right, put to rights, restore, remedy, rectify, adjust. **5 direct,** focus, level at, rivet. **6 arrange,** put in order, adjust, dress. **7 prepare,** make, make ready, put together, cook. **8 get even with,** revenge oneself on, get one's revenge on, wreak vengeance on, take retribution on, give someone his/her just deserts, punish, deal with, *inf.* get back at, pay someone back, cook someone's goose. **9 rig,** manipulate, maneuver, arrange fraudulently, *inf.* fiddle with. **10 bribe,** influence, influence unduly. ***Ant.*** break; cancel; change.

▸ *n.* **predicament,** plight, quandary, dilemma, difficulty, spot of trouble, bit of bother, muddle, mess, corner, ticklish/tricky situation, tight spot, *inf.* pickle, jam, hole, spot, scrape, bind.

fixation *n.* **obsession,** preoccupation, complex, compulsion, mania, idée fixe, phobia, *inf.* hang-up, thing.

fizz *v.* **bubble,** effervesce, sparkle, froth, foam, hiss, sputter, fizzle, sibilate.

flag[1] *n.* **standard,** ensign, banner, pennant, burgee, streamer, bunting, colors.

▸ *v.* **indicate,** mark, mark out, label, tab.

flag[2] *v.* **1 tire,** become fatigued, grow tired/weary, weaken, grow weak, lose one's strength. **2 fade,** fail, decline, wane, ebb, diminish, decrease, taper off.

flagrant *adj.* **glaring,** obvious, blatant, egregious, outrageous, scandalous, shocking, disgraceful, shameless, dreadful, terrible, gross, notorious, heinous, atrocious, monstrous, wicked, iniquitous, villainous. ***Ant.*** unobtrusive; slight.

flair *n.* **1 ability,** aptitude, capability, facility, skill, talent, gift, knack, bent, feel, genius. **2 style,** panache, elegance, dash, élan, taste, good taste, discernment, discrimination.

flap *v.* **move up and down,** flutter, sway, beat, thresh, thrash, wave, agitate, vibrate, wag, waggle, shake, swing, oscillate, flail.

▸ *n.* **1 flutter,** beat, fluttering, beating, waving, shaking, flailing. **2 fold,** overlap, overhang, covering, tab, apron.

flash *v.* **1 light up,** shine out, flare,

blaze, glare, beam, gleam, glint, sparkle, flicker, shimmer, twinkle, glimmer, glisten, scintillate, coruscate. **2 dart,** dash, tear, shoot, zoom, streak, fly, rush, bolt, race, bound, speed, *inf.* scoot. **3 show off,** flaunt, flourish, display, exhibit.

▸ *n.* **1 blaze,** burst, glare, flare, shaft, ray, streak, gleam, glint, sparkle, flicker, shimmer, twinkle, glimmer. **2 instant,** moment, second, split second, minute, trice, twinkling, twinkling of an eye, twinkle, wink of an eye, two shakes, two shakes of a lamb's tail, *inf.* jiffy, bat of an eye. **3 sudden show,** outburst, burst, outbreak, brief display/ exhibition.

flat *adj.* **1 level,** horizontal, leveled, even, smooth, unbroken, plane. **2 stretched out,** spread-eagle, prone, supine, prostrate, recumbent. **3 shallow,** not deep. **4 flat-chested,** small-breasted. **5 deflated,** collapsed, blown out, burst, punctured, ruptured. **6 outright,** direct, out-and-out, downright, straight, plain, explicit, absolute, definite, positive, firm, final, conclusive, complete, utter, categorical, unqualified, unconditional, unquestionable, unequivocal. **7 monotonous,** boring, dull,

tedious, uninteresting, lifeless, lackluster, dead, vapid, bland, insipid, prosaic. **8 depressed,** dejected, dispirited, low, down, without energy, enervated. **9 slow,** inactive, sluggish, slack, not busy. *Ant.* uneven; vertical; exciting.

▸ *adv.* **outright,** directly, straight, plainly, explicitly, absolutely, definitely, conclusively, categorically.

flatten *v.* **1 level,** make even, even out, smooth, smooth out/off, plane. **2 compress,** trample, press down, crush, squash, compact. **3 demolish,** tear down, knock down, raze, raze to the ground. **4 knock down,** knock to the ground, floor, knock off one's feet, fell, prostrate. **5 crush,** quash, squash, deflate, snub, humiliate, *inf.* put down.

flatter *v.* **1 compliment,** praise, sing the praises of, praise to excess, praise to the skies, eulogize, puff up, blandish, fawn upon, cajole, humor, *inf.* sweet-talk, soft-soap, butter up, lay it on thick to/for, play up to. **2 suit,** become, set off, show to advantage, enhance, *inf.* do something for.

flattering *adj.* **1 complimentary,** fulsome, adulatory, praising, blandishing, laudatory, ingratiating, cajoling, *inf.* sweet-talking, soft-soaping. **2 becoming,** enhancing. **Ant.** unflattering; condemnatory; unbecoming.

flattery *n.* **praise,** adulation, overpraise, false praise, eulogy, puffery, fawning, cajolery, compliments, blandishments, *inf.* sweet talk, soft soap, buttering-up.

flaunt *v.* **show off,** parade, display ostentatiously, exhibit, draw attention to, make a show of, wave, dangle, brandish.

flavor *n.* **1 taste,** savor, tang, relish. **2 flavoring,** seasoning, tastiness, tang, relish, piquancy, spiciness, zest, *inf.* zing. **3 spirit,** essence, soul, nature, character, quality, feel, feeling, ambience, tone, style, stamp, property. ▸ *v.* **1 add flavor/flavoring to,** season, add seasoning/herbs/spices to, spice, add piquancy to. **2 season,** lace, imbue, infuse.

flaw *n.* **1 fault,** defect, imperfection, blemish, failing, foible, shortcoming, weakness, weak spot. **2 defect,** crack, chip, fracture, break, crevice, fissure, rent, split, tear. **Ant.** asset; strength.

flawless *adj.* **1 faultless,** perfect, impeccable. **2 perfect,** blemish-free, unflawed, unimpaired, unmarred. **3 perfect,** whole, intact, sound, unbroken, undamaged. **Ant.** imperfect; defective.

flee *v.* **1 run,** run away, run off, bolt, rush, speed, take flight, take to flight, make off, fly, abscond, retreat, beat a retreat, beat a hasty retreat, run for it, make a run for it, take off, take to one's heels, decamp, escape, make one's escape/getaway, do a disappearing act, vanish, *inf.* cut and run, make oneself scarce, beat it, skedaddle, split, scram. **2 run away from,** leave hastily/abruptly, fly, escape from, *inf.* skip.

fleeting *adj.* **rapid,** swift, brief, short-lived, short, momentary, transient, transitory, ephemeral, fugitive, evanescent, fugacious, vanishing, flying, passing, flitting, here today and gone tomorrow, temporary, impermanent. **Ant.** permanent; enduring.

flesh *n.* **1 muscle,** tissue, muscle tissue, brawn. **2 fat,** fatness, obesity, corpulence. **3 substance,** pith, matter, body. **4 body,** human body, human nature, physical nature, physicality, corporeality, carnality, animality, sensuality, sensualism. **5 mankind,** man, humankind, people, human race/species, humanity, Homo sapiens, animate life, the living, human beings, living creatures.

flexible *adj.* **1 bendable,** pliant, pliable, elastic, springy, plastic, moldable. **2 supple,** agile, limber, lithe, lissome, double-jointed. **3 adaptable,** adjustable, open-ended, open, open to change, changeable, variable. **4 tractable,** malleable, compliant, manageable, amenable, biddable, docile, submissive, yielding. *Ant.* rigid; stiff; inflexible; set.

flick *v.* **strike,** hit, rap, tap, touch, click, flip, tap, swish, wag, waggle.

flight *n.* **1 flying,** soaring, mounting. **2 squadron,** flock, skein, bevy, covey, migration. **3 swarm,** cloud. **4 aviation,** flying, air transport, aerial navigation, aeronautics. **5 airline trip,** journey, shuttle, *inf.* plane trip. **6 flight of stairs,** staircase, set of steps/stairs.

flimsy *adj.* **1 insubstantial,** unsubstantial, slight, makeshift, jerry-built, gimcrack, rickety, ramshackle, shaky, fragile, frail. **2 thin,** light, lightweight, delicate, sheer, filmy, diaphanous, transparent, translucent, see-through, gossamer, gauzy. **3 feeble,** weak, poor, inadequate, thin, transparent, unconvincing, implausible, unsatisfactory, paltry, trifling, trivial, shallow. *Ant.* sturdy; thick; solid.

flinch *v.* **draw back,** pull back, start back, recoil, withdraw, shrink back, shy away, cringe, cower, crouch, quail, wince, blench.

fling *v.* **throw,** toss, hurl, cast, pitch, sling, heave, fire, shy, launch, propel, catapult, send flying, let fly, *inf.* lob, chuck.
▶ *n.* **1 throw,** toss, hurl, cast, pitch, shot, heave, *inf.* lob, chuck. **2 binge,** spree, good time, bit of fun, night on the town. **3 try,** attempt, go, shot, stab, venture, *inf.* crack, whirl.

flippant *adj.* **frivolous,** superficial, shallow, glib, thoughtless, carefree, irresponsible, insouciant, offhand, disrespectful, impertinent, impudent, irreverent, saucy, *inf.* flip. *Ant.* serious; responsible.

flirtatious *adj.* **coquettish,** provocative, teasing, amorous, philandering, dallying.

float *v.* **1 stay afloat,** be buoyant, be buoyed up. **2 bob,** glide, sail, drift. **3 move aimlessly,** drift, wander, meander, *inf.* bum (around). *Ant.* sink; submerge.

flock *v.* **collect,** gather, foregather, come together, assemble, group, bunch, congregate, converge, crowd, herd, troop, throng, swarm, mill, huddle.
▶ *n.* **1 fold,** drove, herd. **2 flight,** bevy, skein, gaggle. **3 crowd,** gathering, assembly, company,

collection, congregation, group, throng, mass, host, multitude, troop, herd, convoy.

flog *v.* **whip,** horsewhip, lash, flay, flagellate, birch, scourge, belt, cane, strap, thrash, beat, whack, wallop, chastise, trounce, *inf.* lambaste, tan the hide of.

flood *n.* **1 deluge,** inundation, torrent, spate, overflow, flash flood. **2 downpour,** torrent, cloudburst. **3 profusion,** overabundance, superabundance, plethora, superfluity, glut, *inf.* tons, heaps. **4 outpouring,** rush, stream, flow.
▶ *v.* **1 overflow,** break the banks, brim over, swell, surge, pour forth. **2 inundate,** deluge, pour over, immerse, submerge, swamp, drown, engulf. **3 pour,** flow, surge. **4 overfill,** oversupply, saturate, glut, overwhelm.

floor *n.* **story,** level, tier, deck.
▶ *v.* **1 knock down,** ground, fell, prostrate. **2 defeat,** beat, baffle, stump, perplex, puzzle, nonplus, confound, dumbfound, confuse, discomfit, disconcert, *inf.* throw.

flop *v.* **1 collapse,** slump, drop, fall, tumble. **2 dangle,** droop, sag, hang limply. **3 fail,** fall flat, founder, close, be unsuccessful, be a disaster, miss the mark, go over/down like a lead balloon, *inf.* bomb. ***Ant.*** succeed; flourish.

▶ *n.* **failure,** fiasco, loser, disaster, debacle, *inf.* no-go, washout, dud, lemon, bomb, bust.

florid *adj.* **1 ruddy,** red-faced, red, reddish, high-colored, flushed, blushing, rubicund. **2 ornate,** flamboyant, overelaborate, embellished, busy, baroque. **3** high-flown, flowery, verbose, overelaborate, grandiloquent, purple. ***Ant.*** pale; plain.

flounder *v.* **1 thrash,** struggle, stumble, blunder, fumble, grope. **2 struggle,** be confused, be in the dark, be out of one's element. **3 stumble,** falter, blunder, muddle, bungle.

flourish *v.* **1 brandish,** wave, twirl, wield, swing, hold aloft, display, exhibit, flaunt, parade, vaunt, *inf.* show off. **2 thrive,** grow, grow/do well, develop, burgeon, bloom, blossom, bear fruit, burst forth. **3 be well,** be in good health, be strong, be vigorous, bloom, thrive, get on/ahead, get on well, prosper, be successful, succeed, make progress/headway, *inf.* be in the pink, be fine and dandy, go great guns. ***Ant.*** fail; wither; decline.

flout *v.* **defy,** scorn, disdain, show contempt for, spurn, scoff at, mock, laugh at, deride, ridicule, sneer at, jeer at, gibe at, insult, poke fun at, make a fool of. ***Ant.*** obey; observe.

flow *v.* **1 move,** go along, course, run, circulate, proceed, glide, stream, ripple, swirl, surge, sweep, roll, rush, whirl, drift, slide, trickle, gurgle, babble. **2 gush,** stream, well, spurt, spout, squirt, spew, jet, spill, leak, seep, ooze, drip. **3 arise,** issue, spring, originate, derive, emanate, emerge, pour, proceed.
▶ *n.* **1 course,** current, drift, stream, spate, tide. **2 gush,** stream, welling, spurting, spouting, outpouring, outflow. **3 flood,** deluge, outpouring, outflow, abundance, superabundance, plethora, excess, effusion, succession, train.

flower *n.* **1 bloom,** blossom, floweret, floret, annual, perennial. **2 prime,** peak, zenith, acme, flowering, height, heyday, springtime, salad days. **3 finest,** best, pick, choice, elite, cream, crème de la crème.

fluctuate *v.* **1 rise and fall,** go up and down, seesaw, yo-yo, be unstable, be unsteady, vary, shift, change, alter, swing, oscillate, undulate, ebb and flow. **2 waver,** vacillate, hesitate, change one's mind, alternate, veer, shilly-shally, hem and haw, teeter, totter, seesaw, yo-yo, blow hot and cold.

fluent *adj.* **1 articulate,** eloquent, smooth-spoken, silver-tongued, voluble. **2 smooth,** flowing, fluid, graceful, effortless, natural, easy, elegant, smooth-sounding, mellifluous, euphonious. **3 having a command of,** articulate in. *Ant.* hesitant; inarticulate.

fluff *n.* **1 down,** fuzz, lint, dust, dustball, fuzzball, downiness, soft fur. **2 mistake,** error, bungle, forgetfulness, *inf.* foul-up, screw-up. **3 drivel,** piffle, meaninglessness, frivolousness, superficiality.
▶ *v.* **1 forget,** deliver badly, bungle, muddle up, make a mess of, miss, *inf.* mess up, foul up, screw up. **2 miss,** bungle.

fluid *n.* liquid, gas, solution.
▶ *adj.* **1 gaseous,** gassy, liquid, liquefied, melted, molten, uncongealed, running, flowing. **2 fluent,** smooth, smooth-flowing, flowing, graceful, elegant, effortless, easy, natural. **3 flexible,** open to change, adaptable, adjustable, not fixed, not settled, variable, mutable. **4 subject/likely to change,** unstable, unsteady, ever-shifting, fluctuating, mobile, mercurial. *Ant.* solid; firm; stilted.

flush *v.* **1 blush,** turn red, redden, crimson, color, burn up, flame up, glow, suffuse with color. **2 wash out,** rinse (out), clean, cleanse. **3 eject,** expel.

▸ *n.* **1 blush. 2 bloom,** glow, freshness, radiance, vigor.

fluster *v.* **make nervous,** agitate, ruffle, unsettle, upset, bother, put on edge, discompose, panic, perturb, disconcert, confuse, throw off balance, confound, nonplus, *inf.* hassle, rattle, faze, throw into a tizzy.

▸ *n.* **nervous state,** state of agitation, flurry, bustle, flutter, panic, upset, discomposure, agitation, perturbation, confusion, turmoil, commotion, *inf.* dither, state, tizzy.

flutter *v.* **1 flap,** beat, quiver, agitate, vibrate, ruffle. **2 flicker,** bat. **3 flit,** hover, flitter. **4 flap,** wave, flop, ripple, quiver, shiver, tremble. **5 beat rapidly,** pulsate, palpitate.

▸ *n.* **1 flapping,** beating, quivering. **2 flickering,** batting. **3 flapping,** waving, flopping, rippling. **4 fluster,** flurry, bustle, panic, *inf.* dither, state, tizzy.

fly *v.* **1 flutter,** flit, hover, soar, wing, wing its way, take wing, take to the air, mount. **2 go by airplane,** travel/go by air, *inf.* jet. **3 pilot,** operate, control, maneuver. **4 display,** show, wave. **5 flap,** wave, flutter, toss. **6 go quickly,** pass swiftly, slip past, race, rush/tear past. **7 race,** dash, shoot, rush, tear, bolt, zoom, scoot, dart, speed, hasten, hurry, scamper, career, go like the wind, *inf.* be off like a shot. **8 flee,** run, run away, bolt, take flight, make off, abscond, beat a retreat, run for it, take to one's heels, decamp, make one's escape, *inf.* cut and run, skedaddle.

foam *n.* **froth,** bubbles, fizz, effervescence, head, spume, lather, suds.

▸ *v.* **froth,** froth up, cream, bubble, fizz, effervesce, spume, lather.

focus *n.* **1 focal point,** center, central point, center of attention, core, hub, pivot, magnet, cynosure. **2 focal point,** point of convergence.

▸ *v.* **1 turn,** converge, bring into focus, bring to a focus. **2 concentrate,** fix, bring to bear, center, pinpoint, rivet, *inf.* zero/ zoom in on.

foe *n.* **enemy,** opponent, adversary, rival, antagonist, combatant.

fog *n.* **1 mist,** mistiness, smog, murk, murkiness, haze, *inf.* pea soup. **2 haze,** daze, stupor, trance, bewilderment, confusion, perplexity, bafflement, vagueness, stupefaction, disorientation.

▸ *v.* **1 mist over,** become misty, cloud over, steam up. **2 befuddle,** becloud, bedim, bewilder, confuse, muddle, perplex, baffle, blind, darken, obscure, daze, stupefy, obfuscate.

foggy *adj.* **1 misty,** smoggy, dark, dim, gray, overcast, murky, hazy, gloomy, *inf.* soupy. **2 vague,** indistinct, dim, hazy, shadowy, cloudy, clouded, dark, obscure, unclear, befuddled, confused, bewildered, muddled, dazed, stupefied.

foible *n.* **weakness,** weak point, failing, shortcoming, flaw, blemish, defect, frailty, infirmity, quirk, idiosyncrasy. *Ant.* strength; asset.

foil *n.* **contrast,** striking difference, antithesis, complement.

▸ *v.* **thwart,** frustrate, put a stop to, stop, baffle, defeat, check, checkmate, circumvent, counter, disappoint, impede, obstruct, hamper, hinder, cripple, nip in the bud, *inf.* mess up, screw up.

fold¹ *n.* **1 enclosure,** pen, sheepfold. **2 congregation,** assembly, body, church membership, brethren, parishioners, churchgoers, *inf.* flock.

fold² *n.* **1 folded portion,** double thickness, overlap, layer, pleat, turn, gather, crease, knife pleat; dog-ear. **2 wrinkle,** pucker, furrow, crinkle; crow's foot.

▸ *v.* **1 double,** double over, double up, crease, turn under, turn up, bend, overlap, tuck, gather, pleat, crimp, crumple, dog-ear. **2 enfold,** wrap, wrap up, enclose, envelop, clasp, embrace, hug, squeeze. **3 fail,** collapse, go out of business, close, shut down, go bankrupt, crash; *inf.* go bust, go under, flop.

folk *n.* **1 people,** citizenry, populace, population, general public, public, race, clan, tribe, ethnic group. **2 relatives,** relations, family, kinsfolk, kinsmen, kin, kindred, flesh and blood.

▸ *adj.* **popular,** traditional.

follow *v.* **1 go behind/after,** come behind/after, walk behind, tread on the heels of, succeed, replace, take the place of, step into the shoes of, supersede, supplant, go with, escort, accompany, trail, *inf.* tag. **2 chase,** pursue, run after, trail, shadow, hunt, stalk, track, dog, hound, course, *inf.* tail. **3 obey,** observe, comply with, conform to, heed, pay attention to, note, have regard to, mind, be guided by, accept, yield to. **4 result,** arise, develop, ensue, emanate, issue, proceed, spring, flow, supervene. **5 understand,** comprehend, take in, grasp, fathom, get, catch on to, appreciate, keep up with, see, *inf.* latch on to. **6 copy,** imitate, emulate, pattern oneself on, adopt the style of, style oneself on. **7 be a follower of,** be a fan/admirer/devotee of, be devoted to, be interested in, cultivate an interest in, be a supporter of, support, keep abreast of, keep up to date with. *Ant.* lead; precede; flout.

following *adj.* **1 next,** ensuing, succeeding, subsequent, successive. **2 resulting,** ensuing, consequent, consequential. *Ant.* preceding; foregoing.
▸ *n.* **body of support,** backing, clientele, public, audience, circle, coterie, retinue, train, supporters, backers, admirers, fans, adherents, devotees, advocates, patrons.

foment *v.* **instigate,** incite, provoke, agitate, excite, stir up, arouse, encourage, urge, actuate, initiate.

fond *adj.* **1 adoring,** devoted, loving, affectionate, caring, warm, tender, amorous, doting, indulgent, uxorious. **2 deep,** cherished, heartfelt. *Ant.* hostile; indifferent.

fondle *v.* **caress,** stroke, touch, pat, pet, cuddle, hug, nuzzle.

food *n.* **1 nourishment,** sustenance, nutriment, subsistence, aliment, fare, diet, menu, table, bread, daily bread, board, provender, cooking, cuisine, foodstuffs, refreshments, edibles, meals, provisions, rations, stores, viands, victuals/vittles, commons, comestibles, solids, *inf.* eats, eatables, nosh, grub, chow. **2 fodder,** feed, provender, forage. **3 stimulus,** mental nourishment, something to think about.

fool *n.* **1 idiot,** ass, nitwit, halfwit, numskull, nincompoop, ninny, blockhead, dunce, dunderhead, dolt, ignoramus, dullard, illiterate, moron, simpleton, jackass, loon, *inf.* dope, clod, chump, bonehead, fathead, birdbrain, twit, twerp, nerd, airhead. **2 dupe,** butt, laughingstock, pushover, easy mark, *inf.* stooge, sucker, sap, fall guy. **3 jester,** clown, buffoon, comic, jokester, zany, merry andrew, harlequin.
▸ *v.* **1 deceive,** trick, play a trick on, hoax, make a fool of, dupe, take in, mislead, hoodwink, bluff, delude, beguile, bamboozle, cozen, gull, *inf.* con, kid, put one over on. **2 pretend,** make believe, feign, put on an act, act, fake, counterfeit, *inf.* kid.

foolish *adj.* **1 silly,** absurd, senseless, nonsensical, unintelligent, inane, pointless, fatuous, ridiculous, laughable, derisible, risible, imprudent, incautious, irresponsible, injudicious, indiscreet, unwise, unreasonable, ill-advised, ill-considered, impolitic, *inf.* damfool, damfoolish, crackbrained, nutty, for the birds. **2 stupid,** silly, idiotic, simple, unintelligent, halfwitted, brainless, doltish, dull, dull-witted, dense, ignorant, illiterate, moronic, witless, weak-minded, mad, crazy, *inf.* dumb, dopey, daft, balmy, batty, dippy, cuckoo, screwy, wacky. **Ant.** sensible; wise; sound.

foolproof *adj.* **infallible,** never-failing, unfailing, certain, sure, guaranteed, safe, dependable, trustworthy.

forbid *v.* **prohibit,** ban, bar, debar, outlaw, veto, proscribe, disallow, interdict, preclude, exclude, rule out, stop, declare taboo. **Ant.** allow; authorize; permit.

forbidden *adj.* **prohibited,** out of bounds, banned, debarred, outlawed, vetoed, proscribed, interdicted, taboo, verboten.

forbidding *adj.* **1 stern,** harsh, grim, hard, tough, hostile, unfriendly, disagreeable, nasty, mean, abhorrent, repellent. **2 frightening,** threatening, ominous, menacing, sinister, daunting, foreboding.

force *n.* **1 strength,** power, potency, vigor, energy, might, muscle, stamina, effort, exertion, impact, pressure, life, vitality, stimulus, dynamism, *inf.* punch. **2 compulsion,** coercion, duress, pressure, pressurization, constraint, enforcement, violence, *inf.* arm twisting. **3 persuasiveness,** cogency, validity, weight, effectiveness, efficacy, efficaciousness, influence, power, strength, vehemence, significance, *inf.* bite, punch. **4 agency,** effect, influence. **5 vehemence,** intensity, vigor, drive, fierceness, feeling, passion, vividness. **6 body of people,** corps, detachment, unit, squad, squadron, battalion, division, patrol, regiment, army.
▸ *v.* **1 exert/use force on,** compel, coerce, make, use duress on, bring pressure to bear on, pressurize, pressure, constrain, impel, drive, oblige, necessitate, urge by force, *inf.* put the squeeze/bite on, use strong-arm tactics on. **2 force open,** break open, burst open, blast, prize open, crack. **3 drive,** propel, push, thrust, shove, press. **4 wrest,** extract, wring, extort, drag.

forceful *adj.* **vigorous,** powerful, potent, strong, weighty, dynamic, energetic, assertive, effective, cogent, telling, persuasive, convincing, compelling, moving, impressive, valid. *Ant.* weak; feeble.

forecast *v.* **predict,** foretell, foresee, prophesy, forewarn, prognosticate, augur, divine, guess, hazard a guess, conjecture, speculate, estimate, calculate.
▸ *n.* **prediction,** prophecy, forewarning, prognostication, augury, guess, conjecture, speculation, prognosis, projection, *inf.* guesstimate.

foregoing *adj.* **preceding,** precedent, prior, previous, former, above, aforesaid, aforementioned, antecedent, anterior.

foreign *adj.* **1 overseas,** alien, nonnative, distant, remote. **2 strange,** unfamiliar, unknown, exotic, outlandish, odd, peculiar, curious. **3 irrelevant,** not pertinent, unrelated, unconnected, inappropriate, inapposite, extraneous, extrinsic, outside. *Ant.* home; native; familiar; relevant.

foreigner *n.* **nonnative,** alien, immigrant, newcomer, stranger, outsider.

foremost *adj.* **leading,** principal, premier, prime, top, first, primary, front, advanced, paramount, chief, main, most important, supreme, highest, preeminent.

forerunner *n.* **predecessor,** precursor, ancestor, antecedent, forefather, herald, harbinger, usher, advance guard.

foreshadow *v.* **forebode,** bode, presage, augur, portend, omen, foretoken, betoken, foreshow, indicate, signify, mean, point to, suggest, signal, prefigure, promise.

foresight *n.* **forethought,** discernment, farsightedness, circumspection, prudence, presence of mind, judiciousness, discrimination, perspicacity, care, caution, precaution, readiness, preparedness, anticipation, provision, prescience.

forest *n.* **woods,** wood, woodland, tree plantation, plantation, trees.

forestall *v.* **preempt,** intercept, anticipate, be beforehand, get ahead of, thwart, frustrate, stave off, ward off, fend off, avert, prevent, hinder, impede, obstruct, sidetrack.

foretell *v.* **1 predict,** forecast, foresee, prophesy, forewarn, prognosticate, augur, divine. **2 forebode,** augur, presage, portend, foreshadow, foreshow, foretoken, betoken, prefigure, point to, indicate.

forethought *n.* **foresight,** farsightedness, circumspection, prudence, judiciousness, care, precaution, anticipation, provision.

forever *adv.* **1 always,** ever, evermore, for all time, till the end of time, till the cows come home, till hell freezes over, till doomsday, eternally, undyingly, perpetually, in perpetuity, *inf.* for keeps, for good. **2 all the time,** incessantly, continually, constantly, perpetually, endlessly, unremittingly, interminably, everlastingly.

forfeit *n.* **forfeiture,** fine, penalty, damages, loss, relinquishment.
▸ *v.* **relinquish,** hand over, give up, surrender, renounce, be stripped/ deprived of.

forge *v.* **1 hammer out,** beat into shape, shape, form, fashion, mold, found, cast, make, manufacture, frame, construct, create. **2 invent,** make up, devise, coin, fabricate, put together. **3 copy,** copy fraudulently, imitate, fake, falsify, counterfeit.

forgery *n.* **1 fraudulent copying/ imitation,** falsification, faking, counterfeiting, coining. **2 fake,** counterfeit, sham, fraud, imitation, reproduction, *inf.* phony.

forget *v.* **1 fail to remember/recall,** fail to think of, let slip, *inf.* draw a blank on. **2 cease to remember,** put out of one's mind, disregard,

ignore, let bygones be bygones. **3 leave behind,** go/come without, overlook, miss. **Ant.** remember; recollect.

forgetful *adj.* **1 apt to forget,** absentminded, amnesic, amnesiac, abstracted, vague. **2 neglectful,** negligent, heedless, careless, unmindful, inattentive, oblivious, lax, remiss, disregardful.

forgive *v.* **pardon,** excuse, exonerate, absolve, acquit, let off, let bygones be bygones, bear no malice, harbor no grudge, bury the hatchet, *inf.* let someone off the hook. **Ant.** blame; condemn; convict.

forgiveness *n.* **pardon,** amnesty, exoneration, absolution, acquittal, remission, absence of malice/grudges, mercy.

forgiving *adj.* **lenient,** merciful, compassionate, magnanimous, humane, clement, mild, softhearted, forbearing, tolerant, placable.

fork *v.* **branch,** branch off, diverge, bifurcate, divaricate, divide, split, separate, go in different directions, go separate ways.

forlorn *adj.* **1 unhappy,** sad, miserable, wretched, pathetic, woebegone, lonely, disconsolate, desolate, cheerless, pitiable, pitiful, uncared-for. **2 abandoned,**

forsaken, deserted, forgotten, neglected. **3 hopeless,** desperate, despairing, in despair. *Ant.* happy; hopeful.

form *v.* **1 make,** fashion, shape, model, mold, forge, found, construct, build, assemble, put together, set up, erect, create, produce, concoct, devise.
2 formulate, devise, think up, plan, draw up, frame, forge, hatch, develop, organize, set up, bring about, devise, establish, found, organize, institute, inaugurate, *inf.* dream up. **3 take shape,** materialize, appear, show up, become visible, come into being/existence. **4 acquire,** develop, get, pick up, contract, grow into, *inf.* get into. **5 arrange,** draw up, line up, assemble, organize, order, rank. **6 make,** make up, comprise, constitute, compose, serve as, be a component/element/part of.
7 develop, train, teach, instruct, educate, school, drill, discipline.
▸ *n.* **1 shape,** configuration, formation, conformation, structure, construction, arrangement, disposition, outward form/appearance, exterior. **2 body,** physique, figure, shape, build, frame, anatomy, silhouette, contour. **3 shape,** appearance, manifestation, semblance, guise, character, description. **4 type,** kind, sort, variety, species, genus, genre, stamp. **5 structure,** framework, format, organization, planning, order, orderliness, symmetry, proportion. **6 mold,** cast, shape, matrix, pattern. **7 fitness,** condition, good condition, health, shape, trim, fettle. **8 manners,** behavior, conduct, etiquette, convention, protocol. **9 manner,** method, mode, style, system, formula, set formula, procedure, correct/usual way, convention, custom, ritual, protocol, etiquette, rules. **10 document,** application form, application, sheet of paper, paper.

formal *adj.* **1 official,** set, fixed, conventional, standard, regular, customary, approved, prescribed, pro forma, legal, lawful, ceremonial, ritual. **2 ceremonial,** ceremonious, ritualistic, elaborate. **3 reserved,** aloof, remote, correct, proper, conventional, precise, exact, punctilious, stiff, unbending, inflexible, standoffish, prim, stuffy, straitlaced. **4 symmetrical,** regular, orderly, arranged, methodical. *Ant.* informal; casual; unofficial.

formation *n.* **1 configuration,** format, structure, organization, order, arrangement, pattern, design, disposition, grouping, layout, composition, makeup, constitution. **2 manufacture,** making, construction, building, erecting, fashioning, shaping, setting up, establishment, founding, institution, creation, inauguration, genesis, development, evolution, emergence.

former *adj.* **1 ex-,** previous, prior, preceding, precedent, foregoing, earlier, one-time, erstwhile, antecedent, late, sometime. **2 earlier,** past, long past, bygone, long ago, long departed, long gone, old, ancient, of yore. **3 first-mentioned,** first.

formidable *adj.* **1 intimidating,** redoubtable, daunting, alarming, frightening, terrifying, petrifying, horrifying, dreadful, awesome, fearsome, menacing, threatening, dangerous, *inf.* scary. **2 arduous,** onerous, difficult, tough, colossal, mammoth, challenging, overwhelming, staggering, huge, tremendous, *inf.* mind-boggling, mind-blowing. **3 strong,** powerful, mighty, impressive, terrific, tremendous, great, redoubtable, indomitable, invincible. *Ant.* pleasant; easy; weak.

formula *n.* **1 symbols,** expression, code. **2 recipe,** list of ingredients,

contents, ingredients, prescription, rubric, blueprint, method, procedure, convention, ritual, modus operandi, principles, rules, precepts.

formulate *v.* **1 define,** articulate, set down, frame, give form to, specify, particularize, itemize, detail, designate, systematize, indicate. **2 draw up,** work out, map out, plan, prepare, compose, devise, think up, conceive, create, invent, originate, coin, design.

forsake *v.* **1 desert,** abandon, leave, leave in the lurch, quit, jilt, cast off, discard, repudiate, reject, disown. **2 give up,** renounce, relinquish, forgo, turn one's back on, repudiate, have done with, discard, set aside. *Ant.* keep; retain.

forthcoming *adj.* **1 future,** coming, approaching, expected, prospective, imminent, impending. **2 made available,** available, ready, at hand, accessible, obtainable, at one's disposal, *inf.* on tap. **3 communicative,** informative, talkative, expansive, voluble, chatty, conversational, loquacious, open, unreserved. *Ant.* past; reticent.

forthright *adj.* **direct,** frank, candid, blunt, outspoken, plain-speaking, plainspoken,

straightforward, open, honest.
Ant. secretive; reticent; dishonest.

fortify *v.* **1 build defenses around,** garrison, embattle, guard, cover, protect, secure, strengthen, reinforce, shore up, brace, buttress. **2 strengthen,** invigorate, energize, revive, embolden, give courage to, encourage, cheer, hearten, buoy up, reassure, make confident, brace, sustain.

fortitude *n.* **strength,** strength of mind, moral strength, firmness of purpose, backbone, grit, mettle, courage, nerve, pluck, bravery, fearlessness, valor, intrepidity, stoutheartedness, endurance, patience, forbearance, tenacity, pertinacity, perseverance, resolution, resoluteness, determination.

fortunate *adj.* **1 lucky,** in luck, favored, blessed, born with a silver spoon in one's mouth, born under a lucky star, having a charmed life, happy, felicitous, prosperous, well-off, successful, flourishing, *inf.* sitting pretty. **2 advantageous,** favorable, helpful, providential, auspicious, propitious, promising, encouraging, opportune, felicitous, profitable, fortuitous, timely, well-timed, convenient.

fortune *n.* **1 wealth,** treasure, affluence, opulence, opulency, prosperity, substance, property, riches, assets, means, possessions, estates. **2 huge amount,** mint, king's ransom, *inf.* packet, bundle, pile. **3 chance,** accident, coincidence, contingency, happy chance, fortuity, serendipity, luck, providence. **4 destiny,** fate, lot, cup, portion, kismet, stars. **5 Lady Luck,** Dame Fortune, fate.

fortune-teller *n.* **seer,** soothsayer, prophet, prophetess, augur, diviner, sibyl, oracle, clairvoyant, psychic, prognosticator, astrologer, palm reader, phrenologist, *inf.* stargazer.

forward *adj.* **1 onward,** advancing, progressing, progressive. **2 advanced,** well-advanced, early, premature, precocious. **3 front,** at the front/fore, fore, frontal, foremost, head, leading, advance. **4 bold,** brash, brazen, audacious, presumptuous, presuming, assuming, familiar, overfamiliar, overassertive, overconfident, overweening, aggressive, pert, impudent, impertinent, insolent, unabashed, *inf.* pushy, cocky, fresh. **Ant.** backward; late; shy.
▸ *adv.* **1 toward the front,** frontward, onward, on, ahead, forth. **2 out,** forth, into view, into the open, into public notice, into prominence.

foster v. **1 encourage,** promote, further, stimulate, boost, advance, forward, cultivate, foment, help, aid, assist, support, uphold, back, give backing to, facilitate. **2 bring up,** rear, raise, care for, take care of, mother, parent. **3 cherish,** harbor, entertain, nurse, nourish, nurture, hold, sustain.

foul adj. **1 disgusting,** revolting, repulsive, nauseating, sickening, loathsome, abominable, odious, offensive, nasty, foul-smelling, evil-smelling, ill-smelling, stinking, fetid, rank, mephitic. **2 contaminated,** polluted, adulterated, infected, tainted, defiled, impure, filthy, dirty, unclean, rotten, rotting, decayed, decomposed, putrid, putrescent, putrefactive, carious. **3 foul-mouthed,** blasphemous, profane, obscene, vulgar, gross, coarse, filthy, dirty, indecent, indelicate, suggestive, smutty, blue, off-color, low, lewd, ribald, salacious, scatological, offensive, abusive. **4 horrible,** detestable, abhorrent, loathsome, hateful, despicable, contemptible, abominable, offensive, odious, disgusting, revolting, dishonorable, disgraceful, base, low, mean, sordid, vile, wicked, vicious, heinous, execrable, iniquitous, nefarious, notorious, infamous, scandalous, egregious. **5 unfair,** unjust, dishonorable, dishonest, underhand, underhanded, unsportsmanlike, unsporting, unscrupulous, unprincipled, immoral, crooked, fraudulent, dirty, inf. shady. **6 dirty,** filthy, unwashed, soiled, grimy, grubby, stained, dirt-encrusted, muddied. **7 nasty,** disagreeable, bad, rough, wild, stormy, rainy, wet, blustery, foggy, murky, gloomy. **Ant.** attractive; fragrant; pure; fair.
▸ n. **violation, infraction,** breach, illegality.

found v. **1 establish,** set up, institute, originate, initiate, bring into being, create, start, inaugurate, constitute, endow, organize, develop. **2 lay the foundations of,** build, construct, erect, put up, elevate. **3 base,** ground, construct, build, rest.

foundation n. **1 base,** bottom, bedrock, substructure, substratum, understructure, underpinning. **2 basis,** groundwork, principles, fundamentals, rudiments. **3 founding,** establishing, setting up, institution, initiation, inauguration, constitution, endowment. **4 endowed institution,** institution.

founder n. **builder,** constructor, maker, establisher, institutor,

initiator, beginner, inventor, discoverer, framer, designer, architect, creator, author, originator, organizer, developer, generator, prime mover, father, patriarch.
▸ *v.* **1 sink,** go to the bottom, go down, be lost at sea, capsize, be swamped, *inf.* go to Davy Jones's locker. **2 fail,** fall through, break down, go wrong/awry, misfire, come to grief/nothing, miscarry, abort, flounder, collapse, *inf.* flatline, flop, bomb. **3 stumble,** trip, stagger, lurch, fall, topple, sprawl, go lame, collapse.

fountain *n.* **1 water fountain,** jet, spray, spout, spurt, well, fount. **2 spring,** stream, source, well, fountainhead, source, rise, well-spring, beginning, commencement, origin, cause, birth, genesis, root, mainspring, derivation, inception, inspiration. **3 fount,** fountainhead, source, rise, well-spring, well, beginning, commencement, origin, cause, birth, genesis, root, mainspring, derivation, inception, inspiration.

fractious *adj.* **1 cross,** irritable, fretful, bad-tempered, crabbed, peevish, petulant, ill-humored, ill-natured, querulous, testy, snappish, touchy, irascible, sulky, sullen, morose. **2 unruly,** rebellious, insubordinate, stubborn, obstinate, contrary, refractory, recalcitrant, unmanageable, intractable.

fracture *n.* **breaking,** breakage, splitting, cleavage, rupture, break, crack, split, fissure, cleft, rift, slit, rent, chink, crevice, gap, opening, aperture.
▸ *v.* **break,** crack, split, splinter, rupture.

fragile *adj.* **easily broken,** breakable, brittle, frangible, smashable, splintery, flimsy, frail, insubstantial, delicate, dainty, fine. *Ant.* durable; tough; strong.

fragment *n.* **1 piece,** part, particle, chip, shard, sliver, splinter, smithereens. **2 scrap,** bit, snip, snippet, wisp, tatter. **3 remnant,** remainder, fraction, remains, shreds.

fragrance *n.* **1 scent,** perfume, bouquet, aroma, smell, sweet smell, redolence, balm, balminess. **2 scent,** perfume, toilet water, cologne, eau de cologne.

fragrant *adj.* **scented,** perfumed, aromatic, sweet-smelling, redolent, balmy, odorous, odoriferous. *Ant.* smelly; foul.

frail *adj.* **1 fragile,** easily broken, breakable, frangible, delicate. **2 infirm,** weak, delicate, slight, slender, puny, unsound, ill, ailing, unwell, sickly. **3 weak,** easily led/tempted, susceptible, impressionable, vulnerable, fallible. **Ant.** tough; robust; strong.

frame *n.* **1 framework,** substructure, structure, shell, casing, support, skeleton, scaffolding, foundation, body, chassis. **2 body,** physique, build, figure, shape, size, skeleton, carcass. **3 mount,** mounting, setting. **4 order,** organization, scheme, system, plan, fabric, form, constitution. **5 state,** condition, mood, humor, temper, spirit, attitude.
▸ *v.* **1 assemble,** put together, put/set up, build, construct, erect, elevate, make, fabricate, manufacture, fashion, mold, shape, forge. **2 put together,** formulate, draw up, plan, draft, map/plot/sketch out, shape, compose, form, devise, create, establish, conceive, think up, hatch, *inf.* dream up, cook up. **3 enclose,** encase, surround. **4 incriminate,** fabricate charges/evidence against, *inf.* set up.

framework *n.* **1 frame,** structure, shell, skeleton. **2 order,** organization, scheme, system, plan, fabric, form, constitution.

frank *adj.* **1 candid,** direct, forthright, plain, plainspoken, straight, straight from the shoulder, downright, explicit, outspoken, blunt, bluff, open, sincere, honest, truthful, undissembling, guileless, artless. **2 open,** obvious, transparent, patent, manifest, undisguised, unconcealed, unmistakable, evident, noticeable, visible. **Ant.** reticent; evasive; insincere.

frantic *adj.* **panic-stricken,** panic-struck, panicky, beside oneself, at one's wits' end, frenzied, wild, hysterical, frenetic, berserk, distraught, overwrought, worked up, distracted, agitated, distressed, out of control, unhinged, mad, crazy, out of one's mind, maniacal.

fraud *n.* **1 fraudulence,** cheating, swindling, trickery, deceit, double-dealing, duplicity, treachery, chicanery, skullduggery, imposture, embezzlement, crookedness, *inf.* monkey business. **2 ruse,** trick, hoax, deception, subterfuge, stratagem, wile, artifice, swindle, *inf.* con, rip-off. **3 impostor,** fake, sham, cheat, cheater, swindler, double-dealer, trickster, pretender, charlatan, *inf.* phony, quack, con man. **4 fake,** sham, counterfeit, forgery, *inf.* phony.

fraudulent *adj.* **dishonest,** cheating, swindling, criminal, deceitful, double-dealing, duplicitous, dishonorable, unscrupulous, *inf.* crooked, shady.

fraught *adj.* **anxious,** overwrought, distraught, worked up, distracted, agitated, distressed.

fray *v.* **1 unravel,** ravel, wear, wear thin, wear out/away, become threadbare, become tattered/ragged. **2 strain,** tax, overtax, irritate, put on edge, make edgy/tense.

freak *n.* **1 aberration,** abnormality, irregularity, oddity, monster, monstrosity, malformation, mutant, rara avis, anomaly, quirk, twist of fate, chance, *inf.* fluke.
2 oddity, peculiar person, *inf.* queer fish, oddball, weirdo, way-out person, nutcase, nut.
3 enthusiast, fan, fanatic, addict, aficionado, devotee, *inf.* buff, fiend, nut.
▸ *adj.* **abnormal,** unusual, atypical, aberrant, exceptional, unaccountable, unpredictable, unforeseeable, bizarre, queer, odd, unparalleled, *inf.* fluky.

free *adj.* **1 complimentary,** gratis, without charge, at no cost, *inf.* for free, on the house. **2 unoccupied,** available, not at work, not busy, not tied up, idle, at leisure, with time on one's hands, with time to spare. **3 empty,** vacant, available, spare, unoccupied, untaken, uninhabited, tenantless.

4 independent, self-governing, self-governed, self-ruling, self-directing, sovereign, autonomous, democratic, emancipated, enfranchised, manumitted. **5 at liberty,** at large, loose, on the loose, unconfined, unbound, untied, unchained, unshackled, unfettered, unrestrained, wild.
6 able, allowed, permitted, unrestricted. **7 unobstructed,** unimpeded, unhampered, clear, unblocked. **8 not fixed,** unattached, unfastened, loose.
9 generous, lavish, liberal, openhanded, unstinting, giving, munificent, bountiful, bounteous, charitable, extravagant, prodigal.
10 free and easy, easygoing, natural, open, frank, relaxed, casual, informal, unceremonious, unforced, spontaneous, uninhibited, artless, ingenuous, *inf.* laid-back. ***Ant.*** occupied; busy; dependent; captive.
▸ *v.* **1 set free,** release, let go, set at liberty, liberate, set/let/turn loose, untie, unchain, unfetter, unshackle, uncage, unleash, deliver. **2 rescue,** release, get loose, extricate, disentangle, disengage, disencumber.
3 exempt, make exempt, except, excuse, relieve.

freedom *n.* **1 independence,** self-government, sovereignty, autonomy, democracy, emancipation, manumission, enfranchisement, home rule. **2 liberty,** release, deliverance, nonconfinement. **3 exemption,** immunity, impunity. **4 right,** privilege, prerogative. **5 scope,** latitude, elbow room, wide margin, flexibility, facility, free rein, license. **6 naturalness,** openness, lack of reserve/ inhibition, casualness, informality, lack of ceremony, spontaneity, artlessness, ingenuousness. *Ant.* dependence; captivity.

freeze *v.* **1 ice over/up,** glaciate, solidify, harden. **2 get chilled,** get chilled to the bone/marrow, go numb with cold, turn blue with cold, shiver, shiver with cold. **3 deep-freeze. 4 stop dead,** stop in one's tracks, stop, stand still, go rigid, become motionless. **5 fix,** hold, peg, suspend.

freezing *adj.* **1 bitterly cold,** chill, chilling, frosty, glacial, arctic, wintry, raw, biting, piercing, penetrating, cutting, stinging, numbing, Siberian. **2 chilled through,** chilled to the bone/ marrow, numb with cold, frostbitten.

freight *n.* **1 transportation,** conveyance, freightage, carriage, portage, haulage. **2 cargo,** load, lading, consignment, merchandise, goods.

frenzy *n.* **derangement,** madness, mania, insanity, wild excitement, wildness, hysteria, distraction, agitation, fit, seizure, paroxysm, spasm, bout, outburst.

frequent *adj.* **1 recurrent,** repeated, persistent, continuing, many, numerous, several. **2 regular,** habitual, customary, common, usual, familiar, everyday, continual, constant, incessant. *Ant.* infrequent; few; rare.

▸ *v.* **visit,** visit often, attend, haunt, patronize, *inf.* hang out at.

fresh *adj.* **1 garden-fresh,** newly harvested, crisp, unwilted, unfaded, not stale. **2 raw,** natural, unprocessed, unpreserved, undried, uncured, crude. **3 new,** brand-new, recent, latest, up-to-date, modern, modernistic, ultramodern, newfangled, different, innovative, original, novel, unusual, unconventional, unorthodox. **4 energetic,** vigorous, invigorated, vital, lively, vibrant, spry, sprightly, bright, alert, bouncing, refreshed, rested, restored, revived, like a new person, fresh as a daisy, *inf.* full of vim/beans, raring to go, bright-eyed and bushy-tailed, chipper. **5 healthy-looking,** healthy, clear, bright, youthful-looking, wholesome, glowing, fair, rosy, pink, reddish, ruddy. **6 bright,** clean, spick-and-span, unfaded. **7 more,** other, additional, further, extra, supplementary, auxiliary. **8 bright,** clear, cool, crispy, crisp, sparkling, pure, unpolluted, clean, refreshing. **9 cool,** chilly, brisk, bracing, invigorating. **10 young,** youthful, new, newly arrived, untrained, inexperienced, untried, raw, callow, green, immature, artless, ingenuous, naïve, *inf.* wet behind the ears. **11 familiar,** overfamiliar, presumptuous, forward, bold, audacious, brazen, impudent, impertinent, insolent, disrespectful, *inf.* cocky. **Ant.** stale; tired; dull.

fret *v.* **worry,** agonize, anguish, fuss, make a fuss, complain, grumble, whine, *inf.* feel peeved.

friction *n.* **1 rubbing,** abrading, abrasion, attrition, chafing, gnawing, grating, rasping, scraping, excoriation. **2 dissension,** dissent, disagreement, discord, strife, conflict, clashing, contention, dispute, disputation, arguing, argument, quarreling, bickering, squabbling, wrangling, fighting, hostility, rivalry, animosity, antagonism, resentment, bad feeling, ill feeling, bad blood, disharmony.

friend *n.* **1 companion,** crony, comrade, playmate, soul mate, intimate, confidante, confidant, familiar, alter ego, ally, associate, *inf.* pal, chum, buddy. **2 patron,** backer, supporter, benefactor, well-wisher, *inf.* angel. **Ant.** enemy; foe.

friendless *adj.* **companionless,** alone, all alone, by oneself, lone, lonely, lonesome, with no one to turn to, solitary, with no ties, unattached, single, forlorn, unpopular, unbefriended.

friendliness *n.* **affability,** amiability, warmth, geniality, affection, companionability, cordiality, conviviality, sociability, comradeship, neighborliness, approachability, communicativeness, good-naturedness, amenability, benevolence.

friendly *adj.* **1 affable,** amiable, warm, genial, agreeable, affectionate, companionable, cordial, convivial, sociable, hospitable, comradely, neighborly, outgoing, approachable, accessible, communicative, open, unreserved, easygoing, good-natured, kindly, benign, amenable, well-disposed, sympathetic, benevolent, *inf.* chummy, buddy-buddy. **2 amicable,** congenial, cordial, close, intimate, familiar, peaceable, peaceful, conciliatory, nonhostile. **3 helpful,** favorable, advantageous, benevolent, well-disposed. ***Ant.*** unfriendly; unsociable; hostile.

friendship *n.* **companionship,** intimacy, amity, mutual affection, affinity, rapport, mutual understanding, harmony, comradeship, fellowship, attachment, alliance, friendliness, affability, amiability, warmth, geniality, cordiality, neighborliness, good-naturedness, kindliness.

fright *n.* **1 fear,** fear and trembling, terror, alarm, horror, dread, fearfulness, apprehension, trepidation, consternation, dismay, perturbation, disquiet, panic, nervousness, jitteriness. **2 scare,** shock, shivers, *inf.* jitters, the heebie-jeebies. **3 ugly/horrible/ grotesque sight,** eyesore, *inf.* mess, sight.

frighten *v.* **scare,** alarm, startle, terrify, terrorize, petrify, give a shock to, shock, appall, panic, unnerve, intimidate, cow, daunt, dismay, make one's blood run cold, *inf.* scare the living daylights out of, scare stiff, scare out of

one's wits, make one's hair stand on end, make someone jump out of his/her skin, spook. ***Ant.*** reassure; comfort; encourage.

frightful *adj.* **1 dreadful,** terrible, horrible, horrid, hideous, ghastly, grisly, gruesome, macabre, grim, dire, abhorrent, revolting, repulsive, loathsome, odious, fearful, fearsome, terrifying, alarming, shocking, harrowing, appalling, daunting, unnerving, awful, nasty. **2 unpleasant,** disagreeable, dreadful, horrible, terrible, awful, appalling, ghastly, insufferable, unbearable, annoying, irritating.

frigid *adj.* **1 very cold,** bitterly cold, bitter, freezing, frozen, icy, frosty, chilly, wintry, arctic, glacial, Siberian, polar, arctic. **2 cold,** icy, austere, distant, aloof, remote, unapproachable, forbidding, stiff, formal, unbending, cool, unfeeling, unemotional, unfriendly, hostile, unenthusiastic. **3 unaroused,** unresponsive.

fringe *n.* **1 border,** trimming, frill, edging, tassels. **2 outer edge,** edge, borderline, perimeter, periphery, margin, rim, limits, borders, outskirts, verges. ▸ *adj.* **experimental,** unconventional, unorthodox.

frisky *adj.* **lively,** bouncy, active,

frolicsome, coltish, playful, romping, rollicking, spirited, in high spirits, high-spirited, exuberant, joyful.

frivolity *n.* **1 lightheartedness,** levity, gaiety, fun, silliness, foolishness. **2 frivolousness,** giddiness, flightiness, dizziness, flippancy, silliness, zaniness, empty-headedness.
3 frivolousness, flippancy, superficiality, shallowness.

frivolous *adj.* **1 lacking seriousness,** nonserious, lacking in sense, senseless, flippant, giddy, flighty, dizzy, silly, foolish, facetious, zany, lighthearted, merry, superficial, shallow, empty-headed, featherbrained, *inf.* flip. **2 flippant,** ill-considered, superficial, shallow, inane, facetious, *inf.* flip. **3 impractical,** flimsy, frothy. **4 trivial,** trifling, minor, petty, insignificant, unimportant, paltry, niggling, peripheral.

frolic *v.* **frisk,** gambol, cavort, caper, skip.
▶ *n.* **1 game,** romp, lark, antic, caper, escapade, prank, revel, spree. **2 fun,** fun and games, gaiety, merriment, mirth, amusement, laughter, jollity, *inf.* skylarking, high jinks.

front *n.* **1 fore,** forepart, foremost part, forefront, foreground, anterior, frontage, face, facing, façade. **2 front line,** vanguard, van, first line, firing line. **3 beginning,** head, top, lead. **4 look,** appearance, face, exterior, air, manner, expression, show, countenance, demeanor, bearing, mien, aspect. **5 cover,** cover-up, blind, façade, disguise, pretext, mask. *Ant.* back; rear.
▶ *adj.* **first,** foremost, leading, lead.

frontier *n.* **border,** boundary, bound, limit, edge, rim.

frosty *adj.* **1 freezing,** frozen, rimy, frigid, glacial, arctic, icy, wintry, bitterly cold, bitter, cold, *inf.* nippy. **2 cold,** cool, icy, glacial, frigid, unfriendly, unwelcoming, unenthusiastic.

froth *n.* **foam,** spume, fizz, effervescence, scum, lather, head, bubbles, suds.
▶ *v.* **foam,** spume, cream, bubble, fizz, effervesce, lather.

frown *v.* **1 scowl,** glower, glare, look daggers at, *inf.* give a dirty look to. **2 knit one's brows.**
3 disapprove of, dislike, discourage, look askance at, not take kindly to, not think much of, take a dim view of.

frugal *adj.* **1 thrifty,** sparing, economical, saving, careful, prudent, provident, unwasteful, abstemious, scrimping, niggardly, penny-pinching, miserly, parsimonious, stingy. **2 meager,** scanty, paltry, insufficient. **Ant.** extravagant; spendthrift; lavish.

fruitful *adj.* **1 fruit-bearing,** fruiting. **2 fertile,** fecund, potent, progenitive. **3 useful,** worthwhile, productive, well-spent, profitable, advantageous, beneficial, rewarding, gainful, successful, effective. **Ant.** barren; futile; fruitless.

fruition *n.* **fulfillment,** realization, materialization, actualization, achievement, attainment, success, completion, consummation, perfection, maturity, maturation, ripening.

fruitless *adj.* **futile,** vain, in vain, useless, abortive, to no avail, worthless, pointless, to no effect, idle, ineffectual, ineffective, inefficacious, unproductive, unrewarding, profitless, unsuccessful, unavailing. **Ant.** productive; profitable; fruitful.

frustrate *v.* **1 defeat,** thwart, check, block, counter, foil, balk, disappoint, forestall, baffle, stymie, stop, spoil, cripple, nullify, obstruct, impede, hamper, hinder, circumvent. **2 discourage,** dishearten, dispirit, depress, dissatisfy, make discontented, anger, annoy, vex, irk, irritate, embitter. **Ant.** facilitate; encourage.

fudge *v.* **1 evade,** dodge, skirt, avoid. **2 falsify,** fake, *inf.* cook. **3 equivocate,** hedge, hem and haw, shuffle.

fuel *n.* **1 coal,** wood, oil, gasoline, gas, diesel oil, kerosene. **2 nourishment,** food, sustenance, fodder. **3 incitement,** provocation, goading, stimulus, incentive, encouragement, ammunition. ▸ *v.* **1 fire,** stoke up, charge, power. **2 fan,** inflame, incite, provoke, goad, stimulate, encourage.

fugitive *n.* **escapee,** runaway, deserter, refugee. ▸ *adj.* **1 escaping,** runaway, fleeing, deserting, *inf.* AWOL, on the run. **2 transient,** transitory, fleeting, ephemeral, evanescent, elusive, momentary, short-lived, short, brief, passing, impermanent.

fulfill *v.* **1 carry out,** accomplish, achieve, execute, perform, discharge, implement, complete, bring to completion, finish, conclude, effect, effectuate, perfect. **2 satisfy,** realize, attain, consummate. **3 fill,** answer, meet, obey, comply with, satisfy, conform to, observe. **Ant.** fail; neglect.

full *adj.* **1 filled,** filled up, filled to the brim/capacity, brimful, brimming, crowded, packed, crammed, chock-full, *inf.* jam-packed, wall-to-wall. **2 occupied,** taken, in use. **3 filled,** loaded, well-stocked. **4 replete,** satisfied, sated, gorged, glutted, cloyed. **5 complete,** entire, whole, comprehensive, thorough, exhaustive, detailed, all-inclusive, all-encompassing, extensive, unabridged. **6 abundant,** plentiful, copious, ample, sufficient, broad-ranging, satisfying, complete. **7 well-rounded,** rounded, plump, buxom, shapely, curvaceous, voluptuous, *inf.* busty. **8 loose-fitting,** baggy, voluminous, capacious. **9 rich,** deep, resonant, loud, strong. *Ant.* empty; incomplete; limited.

fully *adv.* **1 completely,** entirely, wholly, totally, thoroughly, in all respects, utterly, amply, sufficiently, satisfactorily, enough. **2 quite,** at least, without exaggeration.

fumble *v.* **1 grope,** feel about/around, fish (around), search blindly, feel/grope one's way, stumble, blunder, flounder. **2 bungle,** botch, mismanage, mishandle, muff, spoil, *inf.* make a mess/hash of, fluff, screw up, foul up, flub. **3 fail to catch,** miss, drop, mishandle, misfield, bobble.

fume *v.* **be enraged,** seethe, boil, be livid, rage, rant and rave, be furious, be incensed, flare up, *inf.*

be up in arms, get hot under the collar, fly off the handle, be at the boiling point, foam at the mouth, get all steamed up, raise the roof, flip one's lid/wig, blow one's top.

fumes *pl. n.* **1 vapor,** gas, smoke, exhalation, exhaust, pollution. **2 smell,** stink, reek, stench.

fun *n.* **1 amusement,** entertainment, relaxation, recreation, enjoyment, pleasure, diversion, distraction, play, good time, merrymaking, merriment, gaiety, mirth, laughter, hilarity, glee, gladness, cheerfulness, joy, zest, high spirits, *inf.* living it up. **2 joking,** jest, teasing, banter, badinage. *Ant.* work; misery.
▸ *adj.* **1 amusing,** entertaining, enjoyable, diverting, pleasurable. **2 amusing,** witty, entertaining, lively, convivial.

function *n.* **1 role,** capacity, responsibility, duty, task, chore, job, post, situation, office, occupation, employment, business, charge, concern, province, part, activity, operation, line, mission, raison d'être, *inf.* thing, bag. **2 use,** purpose, task. **3 social event/occasion,** affair, gathering, reception, party, *inf.* do.
▸ *v.* **work,** go, run, be in working/running order, operate.

functional *adj.* **1 practical,** useful,

serviceable, utilitarian, utility, working, workaday. **2 working,** in working order, going, running, operative, in operation, in commission.

fund *n.* **1 reserve,** pool, collection, kitty, endowment, foundation, grant, investment, capital, savings. **2 stock,** store, accumulation, mass, mine, reservoir, supply, storehouse, treasury, treasure-house, hoard, repository.
▶ *v.* **finance,** back, pay for, capitalize, provide finance/capital for, subsidize, stake, endow, support, float.

fundamental *adj.* **basic,** basal, foundational, rudimentary, elemental, underlying, primary, cardinal, initial, original, prime, first, principal, chief, key, central, structural, organic, constitutional, inherent, intrinsic, vital, essential, important, indispensable, necessary.

fundamentally *adj.* **basically,** at heart, deep down, essentially, intrinsically.

funds *pl. n.* **money,** ready money, cash, hard cash, capital, the wherewithal, means, assets, resources, savings, *inf.* dough, bread.

funny *adj.* **1 amusing,** comic, comical, humorous, hilarious, entertaining, diverting, laughable, hysterical, riotous, sidesplitting, droll, absurd, rich, ridiculous, ludicrous, risible, farcical, silly, slapstick, witty, waggish, jocular. **2 strange,** peculiar, odd, queer, weird, bizarre, curious, mysterious, suspicious, dubious, *inf.* shady. *Ant.* serious; sad; normal.

furious *adj.* **1 enraged,** raging, infuriated, fuming, boiling, incensed, inflamed, frenzied, very angry, indignant, mad, raving mad, maddened, wrathful, beside oneself, in high dudgeon, *inf.* livid, hot under the collar, up in arms, foaming at the mouth. **2 violent,** fierce, wild, intense, vehement, unrestrained, tumultuous, turbulent, tempestuous, stormy, boisterous.

furnish *v.* **fit out,** outfit, supply, equip, provide, provision, give, grant, present, offer, bestow on, endow.

furniture *n.* **furnishings,** effects, tables and chairs, *inf.* stuff, things.

furor *n.* **1 commotion,** uproar, disturbance, hullabaloo, turmoil, tempest, tumult, brouhaha, stir, excitement, to-do, outburst, outcry. **2 rage,** madness, frenzy, fit.

furrow *n.* **1 groove,** trench, channel, rut, trough, hollow, ditch, seam. **2 crease,** line, wrinkle, corrugation, crinkle, crow's foot.

further *adj.* **1 additional,** more, extra, supplementary, other, new, fresh. **2 more distant/advanced/ remote,** remoter, further away/off, farther.

▸ *adv.* **1 furthermore,** moreover, what's more, also. **2 farther.**

furthest *adj.* farthest, furthermost, most distant, most remote, outermost, outmost, extreme, uttermost, ultimate.

furtive *adj.* **secret,** secretive, stealthy, surreptitious, sneaky, sneaking, skulking, slinking, clandestine, hidden, covert, cloaked, conspiratorial, sly, underhand, underhanded, under the table, wily. ***Ant.*** open; aboveboard.

fury *n.* **1 great anger,** rage, ire, wrath, madness, passion, frenzy, furor. **2 fierceness,** ferocity, violence, turbulence, tempestuousness, severity, intensity, vehemence, force, great force, power, potency. **3 virago,** hellcat, termagant, spitfire, vixen, shrew, hag.

fuse *v.* **1 combine,** amalgamate, put together, unite, blend, intermix, intermingle, merge, meld, coalesce, compound, agglutinate, join, integrate, weld,

solder. **2 melt,** melt down, smelt, dissolve, liquefy. ***Ant.*** separate; disconnect.

fuss *n.* **1 fluster,** flurry, bustle, to-do, ado, agitation, excitement, bother, stir, commotion, confusion, tumult, uproar, upset, worry, overanxiety, *inf.* tempest in a teacup, much ado about nothing, flap, tizzy, stew. **2 row,** altercation, squabble, argument, quarrel, dispute, upset, trouble, bother, unrest. **3 complaint,** objection.

▸ *v.* **1 bustle,** bustle about, dash about, worry, be agitated/worried, make a big deal, make a mountain out of a molehill, *inf.* get worked up over nothing, be in a tizzy, be in a stew. **2 kick up a fuss,** make a fuss, complain, raise an objection, *inf.* grouse, gripe. **3 be upset,** fret, cry, be cross.

fussy *adj.* **particular,** overparticular, finicky, persnickety, fastidious, hard to please, difficult, exacting, demanding, discriminating, selective, dainty, *inf.* choosy, picky, nitpicking.

futile *adj.* **1 vain,** in vain, to no avail, unavailing, useless, ineffectual, ineffective, inefficacious, unsuccessful, fruitless, abortive, unproductive, impotent, barren, unprofitable, hollow. **2 trivial,** unimportant, petty, trifling, valueless, worthless, inconsequential, idle. *Ant.* useful; fruitful; significant.

future *n.* **1 time to come,** hereafter, coming times. **2 prospects,** expectations, anticipation, outlook.

fuzzy *adj.* **1 frizzy,** downy, down-covered, woolly, linty. **2 out of focus,** unfocused, blurred, blurry, bleary, misty, indistinct, unclear, distorted, ill-defined, indefinite. **3 confused,** muddled, fuddled, befuddled, foggy, misty, shadowy, blurred.

Gg

gadget *n.* **appliance,** apparatus, instrument, implement, tool, contrivance, device, mechanism, invention, thing, *inf.* contraption, widget, gizmo.

gaffe *n.* **mistake,** blunder, slip, indiscretion, faux pas, *inf.* blooper, goof, boner, booboo.

gag *n.* **joke,** jest, witticism, quip, funny remark, hoax, prank, *inf.* wisecrack, crack.
▶ *v.* **1 stop up,** block, plug, clog, stifle, smother, muffle. **2 silence,** muzzle, curb, check, restrain, suppress, repress. **3 choke,** retch, gasp, struggle for breath, convulse, almost vomit.

gaiety *n.* **1 cheerfulness,** lightheartedness, merriment, glee, blitheness, gladness, happiness, high spirits, good spirits, delight, pleasure, joy, joyfulness, joyousness, exuberance, elation, mirth, joviality, liveliness, vivacity, animation, effervescence, buoyancy, sprightliness, exultation, joie de vivre. **2 fun,** festivity, merrymaking, revelry, revels, celebration. **3 colorfulness,** brightness, brilliance, sparkle, glitter, gaudiness, showiness, show, garishness. *Ant.* gloom; misery.

gain *v.* **1 obtain,** get, acquire, procure, secure, attain, build up, achieve, arrive at, win, capture, net, pick up, reap, gather. **2 earn,** bring in, make, get, clear, gross, net, realize, produce. *Ant.* lose; forfeit.
▶ *n.* **1 profit,** earnings, income, advantage, benefit, reward, emolument, yield, return, winnings, proceeds, dividend, interest. **2 increase,** augmentation, addition, rise, increment, accretion, accumulation. **3 advance,** advancement, progress, headway, improvement, step forward. **4 acquisition,** acquirement, achievement. *Ant.* loss; decrease.

gainful *adj.* **profitable,** remunerative, paying, financially rewarding, rewarding, lucrative, moneymaking, productive, beneficial, advantageous, worthwhile, useful.

gait *n.* **walk,** step, stride, pace, tread, manner of walking, bearing, carriage.

gale *n.* **1 storm,** tempest, squall, hurricane, tornado, cyclone, typhoon, mistral, sirocco.
2 outburst, peal, ring, shriek, shout, roar, scream, howl, fit, eruption.

gallant *adj.* **1 brave,** courageous, valiant, valorous, bold, plucky, daring, fearless, intrepid, manly, manful, dashing, heroic, heroical, lionhearted, stouthearted, doughty, mettlesome, great-spirited, honorable, noble.
2 chivalrous, gentlemanly, courtly, courteous, mannerly, polite, attentive, gracious, considerate, thoughtful, obliging, deferential. **3 fine,** great, dignified, stately, noble, splendid, elegant, magnificent, majestic, imposing, glorious, regal, august. *Ant.* cowardly; discourteous; rude.
▸ *n.* **man about town,** man of fashion, man of the world, ladies' man, lady-killer, dandy, fop, beau, suitor, wooer, admirer, lover, boyfriend, paramour.

galvanize *v.* **electrify,** shock, startle, jolt, stir, excite, rouse, arouse, awaken, spur, prod, urge, stimulate, invigorate, fire, animate, vitalize, energize, exhilarate, thrill, inspire.

gamble *v.* **1 bet,** wager, place a bet, lay a wager/bet, game, try one's luck, *inf.* play the ponies.

2 take a chance, take a risk, leave things to chance, speculate, venture, buy a pig in a poke, *inf.* stick one's neck out, go out on a limb.
▸ *n.* **risk,** hazard, chance, lottery, speculation, venture, uncertainty, pig in a poke.

game *n.* **1 pastime,** diversion, entertainment, amusement, recreation, play, sport, distraction. **2 joke,** practical joke, prank, jest, trick, hoax. **3 match,** contest, tournament, meeting, sports/sporting event, athletic event, round, bout. **4 business,** line, occupation, trade, profession, industry, enterprise, activity, calling. **5 scheme,** trick, plot, ploy, stratagem, strategy, cunning plan, tactics, artifice, device, maneuver. **6 wild animals,** wild fowl, quarry, prey, big game.
▸ *v.* **gamble,** bet, wager.

gang *n.* **group,** band, crowd, company, gathering, pack, horde, mob, herd, clique, circle, social set, coterie, lot, ring, club, fraternity, sorority, crew, squad, team, troop, shift, detachment, posse, troupe.

gangster *n.* **gang member,** racketeer, bandit, brigand, robber, ruffian, thug, hoodlum, tough, desperado, Mafioso, terrorist, *inf.* crook, mobster, hood.

gap *n.* **1 opening,** cavity, hole, aperture, space, breach, orifice, break, fracture, rift, rent, fissure, cleft, chink, crack, crevice, cranny, divide, discontinuity, interstice. **2 pause,** intermission, interval, interlude, break, recess. **3 omission,** blank, hole, void. **4 breach,** difference, divergence, disparity.

gape *v.* **1 stare,** stare in wonder, gaze, ogle, *inf.* gawk, rubberneck. **2 open wide,** become open wide, open up, yawn, part, crack, split.

garb *n.* **1 clothes,** clothing, garments, dress, attire, style, fashion, look, apparel, costume, outfit, wear, habit, uniform, array, habiliment, vestments, livery, trappings, *inf.* gear, get-up, togs, duds. **2 outward appearance,** appearance, guise, outward form, exterior, aspect, semblance, look. ► *v.* **clothe,** dress, attire, array, robe, cover, outfit.

garbage *n.* **1 trash,** waste, rubbish, refuse, debris, litter, junk, discarded matter, swill, detritus, scraps, leftovers, remains, slops. **2 nonsense,** rubbish, twaddle, drivel, foolishness, balderdash, *inf.* hogwash, poppycock, rot, crap, baloney, piffle.

garble *v.* **mix up,** get mixed up, jumble, confuse, change around, distort, twist, twist around, warp, slant, mutilate, tamper with, doctor, falsify, pervert, corrupt, adulterate, misstate, misquote, misreport, misrender, misrepresent, mistranslate, misinterpret, misunderstand.

garish *adj.* **flashy,** loud, showy, gaudy, glaring, flaunting, bold-colored, glittering, tinselly, brassy, tawdry, raffish, tasteless, in bad taste, vulgar, cheap, flashy. *Ant.* drab; sober; tasteful.

garner *v.* **gather,** collect, accumulate, heap, pile up, amass, assemble, stack up, store, lay by, put/stow away, hoard, stockpile, deposit, husband, reserve, save, preserve, save for a rainy day.

garrison *n.* **1 armed force,** military detachment/unit, platoon, brigade, squadron, troops, militia, soldiers. **2 fort,** fortress, fortification, stronghold, blockhouse, citadel, camp, encampment, command post, base, station, barracks. ► *v.* **1 defend,** guard, protect, preserve, fortify, man, occupy, supply with troops. **2 station,** post, put on duty, assign, position, billet, send in.

garrulous *adj.* **talkative,** chatty, chattering, gossiping, loquacious, voluble, verbose, long-winded, babbling, prattling, prating, blathering, jabbering, gushing, effusive, wordy, rambling, prolix, diffuse, *inf.* mouthy, gabby. **Ant.** taciturn; reticent.

gash *n.* **cut,** slash, wound, tear, laceration, gouge, incision, slit, split, nick, cleft.
▸ *v.* **cut,** slash, wound, tear, lacerate, gouge, incise, slit, split, rend, nick, cleave.

gasp *v.* **pant,** puff, blow, catch one's breath, draw in one's breath, gulp, choke, fight for breath, wheeze, huff and puff.
▸ *n.* (sudden/short) breath/ inhalation, pant, puff, gulp, choke.

gate *n.* **1 barrier,** door, portal. **2 gateway,** doorway, access, entrance, exit, egress, opening, passage.

gather *v.* **1 come together,** collect, assemble, congregate, meet, group, cluster together, crowd, mass, flock together, convene, converge, call together, summon, get together, convene, round up, muster, marshal. **2 get/put together,** collect, accumulate, amass, assemble, garner, store, stockpile, heap up, pile up, stack up, hoard, *inf.* stash away. **3 attract,** draw, draw together/in, pull, pull in, collect, pick up. **4 understand,** be given to understand, believe, be led to believe, hear, learn, infer, draw the inference, deduce, conclude, come to the conclusion, assume, surmise. **5 embrace,** clasp, enfold, hold, hug, cuddle. **6 harvest,** collect, pick, pluck, cull, garner, crop, reap, glean. **7 increase,** grow, rise, build, expand, enlarge, swell, extend, wax, intensify, deepen, heighten, thicken. **8 ruffle,** shirr, pleat, pucker, tuck, fold. **Ant.** scatter; disperse; separate.

gathering *n.* **1 assembly,** assemblage, collection, company, congregation, group, party, band, knot, crowd, flock, throng, mass, mob, horde, meeting, meet, convention, conclave, rally, turnout, congress, convocation, concourse, muster, *inf.* get-together. **2 collection,** accumulation, assemblage, aggregation, aggregate, mass, store, stock, stockpile, heap, pile, cluster, agglomeration, conglomeration, concentration, collecting, assembly, assembling, garnering. **3 collecting,** accumulation, assembly, assembling, garnering.

gauche *adj.* **awkward,** clumsy, gawky, ungainly, bumbling, lumbering, maladroit, socially inept, lacking in social graces, inelegant, graceless, unpolished, unsophisticated, uncultured, uncultivated. **Ant.** sophisticated; elegant; adroit.

gaudy *adj.* **bold-colored,** garish, loud, glaring, bright, brilliant, flashy, showy, ostentatious, tawdry, raffish, tasteless, in bad taste, vulgar, cheap. **Ant.** drab; sober; tasteful.

gauge *v.* **1 measure,** calculate, compute, determine, count, weigh, check, ascertain. **2 evaluate,** appraise, assess, place a value on, estimate, guess, judge, adjudge, rate, reckon, determine, *inf.* guesstimate.
▸ *n.* **1 measure,** basis, standard, guide, guideline, touchstone, yardstick, benchmark, criterion, rule, norm, example, model, pattern, exemplar, sample, test, indicator. **2 extent,** degree, scope, area, size, measure, capacity, magnitude, depth, height, width, thickness, span, bore.

gaunt *adj.* **1 haggard,** drawn, cadaverous, skeletal, emaciated, skin and bones, skinny, spindly, stalky, spare, bony, angular, lank, lean, rawboned, pinched, hollow-cheeked, starved-looking, scrawny, scraggy, shriveled, wasted, withered, *inf.* looking like death warmed over. **2 bleak,** barren, bare, desolate, dreary, dismal, forlorn, grim, stern, harsh, forbidding. **Ant.** obese; fat; lush.

gay *adj.* **1 merry,** jolly, lighthearted, cheerful, mirthful, jovial, glad, happy, bright, in good spirits, in high spirits, joyful, elated, exuberant, animated, lively, sprightly, vivacious, buoyant, effervescent, playful, frolicsome. **2 merry,** festive, amusing, enjoyable, entertaining, convivial, hilarious. **3 bright,** brightly colored, vivid, brilliant, many-colored, multicolored, flamboyant, gaudy. **4 homosexual,** lesbian, *derog. inf.* queer, limp-wristed, butch. **Ant.** gloomy; dull; drab.
▸ *n.* **homosexual,** lesbian, *derog. inf.* queer, homo, dyke, fag.

gaze *v.* **stare,** look fixedly, gape, stand agog, watch in wonder, ogle, eye, take a good look, contemplate, *inf.* gawk, rubberneck, give the once-over.
▸ *n.* **stare,** fixed look, intent look, gape.

gear *n.* **1 cog,** cogwheel. **2 gears,** mechanism, machinery, works. **3 clothes,** clothing, garments, dress, attire, apparel, garb, outfit, wear, costume, array, vestments, *inf.* get-up, togs, duds.

genealogy *n.* **pedigree,** family tree, ancestry, line, lineage, descent, parentage, birth, derivation, extraction, family, dynasty, house, race, strain, stock, breed, bloodline, heritage, history, roots.

general *adj.* **1 usual,** customary, common, ordinary, normal, standard, regular, typical, conventional, everyday, habitual, run-of-the-mill. **2 common,** extensive, widespread, broad, wide, accepted, prevalent, prevailing, universal, popular, public, generic. **3 across-the-board,** blanket, universal, sweeping, broad, broad-ranging, comprehensive, all-inclusive, encyclopedic, indiscriminate, catholic. **4 mixed,** assorted, miscellaneous, variegated, diversified, composite, heterogeneous. **5 nondetailed,** undetailed, broad, loose, approximate, nonspecific, unspecific, vague, ill-defined, indefinite, inexact, imprecise, rough. **6 panoramic,** sweeping, extended, bird's-eye. ***Ant.*** unusual; specific; detailed.

generally *adv.* **1 in general,** usually, as a rule, normally, ordinarily, almost always, customarily, habitually, typically, regularly, for the most part, mainly, by and large, on average, on the whole, in most cases. **2 commonly,** widely, extensively,

comprehensively, universally. **3 in a general sense,** without detail, loosely, approximately, broadly, in nonspecific terms. **4 mostly,** for the most part, mainly, in the main, largely, chiefly, predominantly, on the whole. ***Ant.*** unusually; particularly; rarely.

generate *v.* **1 bring into being,** cause to exist, produce. **2 beget,** procreate, engender, sire, father, breed, spawn, produce, propagate. **3 cause,** give rise to, create, produce, initiate, originate, occasion, sow the seeds of, arouse, whip up, propagate.

generosity *n.* **1 liberality,** kindness, magnanimity, benevolence, beneficence, bounteousness, bounty, munificence, hospitality, charity, openhandedness, lavishness. **2 nobility,** nobleness, magnanimity, loftiness, high-mindedness, honorableness, honor, goodness, unselfishness, altruism.

generous *adj.* **1 liberal,** kind, magnanimous, benevolent, beneficent, bountiful, bounteous, munificent, hospitable, charitable, openhanded, lavish, ungrudging, unstinting. **2 noble,** magnanimous, lofty, high-minded, honorable, good, unselfish, altruistic, unprejudiced, disinterested. **3 liberal,** abundant, plentiful, lavish, ample, copious, rich, superabundant, overflowing. *Ant.* stingy; selfish; meager.

genial *adj.* **amiable,** affable, good-humored, good-natured, warm, warm-natured, pleasant, agreeable, cordial, well-disposed, amenable, cheerful, cheery, friendly, congenial, amicable, sociable, convivial, kind, kindly, benign, happy, sunny, jovial, easygoing, sympathetic. *Ant.* unfriendly; unkind; morose.

genius *n.* **1 brilliant person,** virtuoso, prodigy, master, mastermind, maestro, gifted child, intellectual, intellect, expert, *inf.* brains, mental giant, Einstein. **2 brilliance,** intellect, cleverness, brains. **3 gift,** talent, flair, bent, knack, aptitude, forte, faculty, ability, capability, capacity, endowment, propensity, inclination. *Ant.* dolt; dunce; stupidity.

genteel *adj.* **1 well-born,** aristocratic, noble, blue-blooded, patrician, well-bred, respectable, refined, ladylike, gentlemanly. **2 polite,** well-mannered, mannerly, courteous, civil, decorous, gracious, courtly, polished, cultivated, stylish, elegant. **3 overpolite,** mannered,

affected, ultrarefined. *Ant.* plebeian; rude; coarse.

gentle *adj.* **1 kind,** kindly, tender, benign, humane, lenient, merciful, clement, compassionate, tender-hearted, sweet-tempered, placid, serene, mild, soft, quiet, still, tranquil, peaceful, pacific, reposeful, meek, dovelike. **2 mild,** moderate, light, temperate, balmy, soft, zephyrlike. **3 soft,** light, smooth, soothing. **4 tame,** placid, docile, manageable, tractable, meek, easily handled, trained, schooled, broken. **5 gradual,** slight, easy, imperceptible. **6 genteel,** aristocratic, noble, well-born, well-bred, blue-blooded, patrician, upper-class, high-born, respectable, refined, cultured, elegant, polished, polite, ladylike, gentlemanly. *Ant.* cruel; harsh; rough; fierce.

genuine *adj.* **1 real,** authentic, true, pure, actual, bona fide, veritable, sound, sterling, legitimate, lawful, legal, valid, original, unadulterated, unalloyed, *inf.* the real McCoy, honest-to-goodness, kosher. **2 sincere,** truthful, honest, frank, candid, open, undeceitful, natural, unaffected, artless, ingenuous, *inf.* up-front. *Ant.* fake; bogus; insincere.

germ *n.* **1 microbe,**
microorganism, bacillus,
bacterium, virus, *inf.* bug.
2 beginning, start,
commencement, inception, seed,
embryo, bud, root, rudiment,
origin, source, fountain,
fountainhead.

gesture *n.* **1 sign,** signal, motion,
motioning, wave, indication,
gesticulation. **2 action,** deed, act.
▸ *v.* **gesticulate,** make a sign,
signal, motion, wave, indicate.

get *v.* **1 acquire,** obtain, come by,
come into possession of, procure,
secure, buy, purchase. **2 receive,**
be sent, be given. **3 go for,** fetch,
bring, collect, carry, transport,
convey. **4 gain,** acquire, achieve,
attain, reach, win, find, *inf.* bag.
5 earn, be paid, bring in, make,
clear, gross, net, pocket, *inf.* pull
in, take home. **6 capture,** seize,
grab, lay hold of, grasp, collar,
take captive, arrest, apprehend,
take, trap, entrap, *inf.* nab, bag.
7 catch, become infected by,
contract, be smitten by, come
down with, be afflicted by.
8 telephone, call, phone, radio,
reach, contact, get in touch with.
9 hear, catch, take in, perceive,
understand, grasp, comprehend,
see, fathom, follow, make head or
tail of, *inf.* catch on to, get the
hang of. **10 arrive,** reach, come,

inf. make it. **11 persuade,** induce,
coax, wheedle into, talk into,
prevail upon, influence, sway,
convince, win over. **12 manage,**
succeed, arrange, contrive.
13 become, grow, come to be,
turn, turn into, wax. **14 prepare,**
make preparations for, get ready,
cook, *inf.* fix. **15 affect,** have an
effect on, move, touch, stir,
arouse, stimulate, excite, grip,
impress, leave an impression on,
inf. send, turn on. **16 avenge
oneself on,** take vengeance on,
get even with, pay someone back,
give tit for tat to, settle the score
with, demand an eye for an eye
and a tooth for a tooth with, *inf.*
get back at. **17 baffle,** puzzle,
stump, mystify, confound,
nonplus.

getaway *n.* **escape,** flight,
breakout, break, decampment.

ghastly *adj.* **1 terrible,** horrible,
frightful, dreadful, awful, horrid,
horrendous, hideous, shocking,
grim, grisly, gruesome, gory,
terrifying, frightening. **2 ill,**
unwell, sick, *inf.* awful, terrible,
dreadful. **3 bad,** ashamed,
shameful, *inf.* awful, terrible,
dreadful. **4 very bad,** serious,
grave, critical, unforgivable, *inf.*
awful, terrible, dreadful. **5 odious,**
loathsome, nasty, foul,
contemptible, low, mean, base,

inf. horrible, dreadful, abominable, appalling.

6 deathlike, deathly pale, pale, pallid, wan, ashen, colorless, white, white as a sheet, haggard, drawn, ghostlike, ghostly, spectral, cadaverous. *Ant.* pleasant; charming; healthy.

ghost *n.* **1 specter,** apparition, phantom, spirit, phantasm, *inf.* spook. **2 suggestion,** hint, trace, glimmer, semblance, shadow, impression, faint appearance.

ghostly *adj.* **ghostlike,** spectral, phantomlike, phantom, phantasmal, phantasmic, unearthly, supernatural, otherworldly, insubstantial, illusory, shadowy, eerie, weird, uncanny, *inf.* spooky.

giant *n.* **colossus,** Titan, Goliath, behemoth, leviathan, superhuman.

▸ *adj.* **gigantic,** enormous, colossal, huge, immense, vast, mammoth, monumental, monstrous, gargantuan, titanic, elephantine, prodigious, stupendous, very large, *inf.* jumbo, humongous, industrial-size.

giddy *adj.* **1 dizzy,** light-headed, faint, reeling, unsteady, *inf.* woozy. **2 flighty,** silly, frivolous, skittish, irresponsible, flippant, whimsical, capricious, featherbrained, scatterbrained,

fickle, erratic, changeable, inconstant, irresolute, mercurial, volatile, unsteady, unstable, unbalanced, impulsive, reckless, wild, careless, thoughtless, heedless, carefree, insouciant.

gift *n.* **1 present,** offering, bounty, largesse, donation, contribution, boon, grant, bonus, gratuity, benefaction, bequest, legacy, inheritance, endowment. **2 giving,** presentation, bestowal, conferment, donation, contribution, grant, endowment. **3 talent,** flair, aptitude, facility, knack, bent, turn, aptness, ability, faculty, capacity, capability, attribute, skill, expertise, genius, mind for.

gifted *adj.* **talented,** brilliant, intelligent, clever, bright, smart, sharp, ingenious, able, accomplished, capable, masterly, skilled, adroit, proficient, expert. *Ant.* stupid; unskilled; inept.

gigantic *adj.* giant, enormous, colossal, huge, immense, vast, mammoth, gargantuan. *Ant.* diminutive; tiny.

giggle *v.* **titter,** snigger, snicker, chuckle, chortle, laugh, cackle, *inf.* tee-hee, ha-ha.

gingerly *adv.* **cautiously,** with caution, warily, charily, cannily, carefully, attentively, heedfully, vigilantly, watchfully, guardedly, prudently, circumspectly, judiciously, suspiciously, hesitantly, reluctantly, timidly, timorously.

girl *n.* **1 female child,** daughter, miss, lass, young woman, young lady, young unmarried woman, *derog. inf.* babe, chick. **2 girlfriend,** sweetheart, fiancée, lover, ladylove, mistress, inamorata.

girth *n.* **circumference,** size, bulk, measure, perimeter.

gist *n.* **substance,** essence, quintessence, drift, sense, general sense, significance, idea, import, core, nucleus, nub, kernel, pith, marrow, burden, crux, important point.

give *v.* **1 hand,** present, donate, bestow, contribute, confer, hand over, turn over, award, grant, accord, leave, will, bequeath, make over, entrust, consign, vouchsafe. **2 show,** display, demonstrate, set forth, indicate, manifest, evidence. **3 allow,** permit, grant, accord, offer. **4 administer,** deliver, deal. **5 provide,** supply, furnish, proffer, offer. **6 cause,** be a source of, make, create. **7 impart,** communicate, announce, transmit, convey, transfer, send, purvey. **8 produce,** yield, afford, result in. **9 perform,** execute, make, do. **10 let out,** utter, issue, emit. **11 give up,** sacrifice, relinquish, devote. **12 surrender,** concede, yield, give up, cede. **13 lead,** make, cause, force. **14 give way,** collapse, break, break down, fall apart, come apart, bend, buckle. phrases: **give away 1** betray, **inform on;** *informal* rat on, blow the whistle on, sell down the river, rat out, finger. **2** reveal, **disclose,** divulge, let slip, leak, let out. **3** donate, **make a gift of,** confer, contribute, will, bequeath; distribute; sacrifice; get rid of, dispose of, relent, throw in the towel/sponge. **give in** capitulate, **concede defeat,** admit defeat, give up, surrender, yield, submit, back down, give way, defer, relent, throw in the towel. **give off** emit, **produce,** send out, throw out; discharge, release, exude, vent. **give out 1** run out, **be used up,** be consumed, be exhausted, be depleted; fail, flag; dry up. **2** distribute, **issue,** hand out, pass around, dispense; dole out, dish out, mete out; allocate, allot. **give up. 1** See give in (above). **2** stop, **cease,** discontinue, desist from, abstain from, cut out, renounce, forgo; resign from, stand down from; *informal* quit, kick, swear off, leave off, pack in, lay off. *Ant.* accept; receive; take.

glad *adj.* **1 happy,** pleased, pleased as Punch, well-pleased, delighted, gratified, thrilled, overjoyed, elated, satisfied, contented, grateful, *inf.* tickled pink. **2 willing,** more than willing, eager, ready, prepared, happy, pleased, delighted. **3 happy,** joyful, delightful, welcome, cheering, cheerful, pleasing, gratifying. **4 merry,** gay, jolly, cheerful, cheery, joyful, joyous, gleeful, mirthful, happy, animated. *Ant.* unhappy; sad; reluctant.

gladden *v.* **make happy,** delight, cheer, cheer up, hearten, brighten up, raise the spirits of, please, elate, buoy up, give a lift to, *inf.* buck up.

glamorous *adj.* **1 alluring,** dazzling, glittering, well-dressed, smart, elegant, beautiful, lovely, attractive, charming, fascinating, exciting, beguiling, bewitching, enchanting, entrancing, irresistible, tantalizing, *inf.* glitzy, ritzy. **2 exciting,** fascinating, stimulating, thrilling, high-profile, dazzling, glossy, glittering, *inf.* ritzy, glitzy. *Ant.* dowdy; dull; boring.

glamour *n.* **1 beauty,** loveliness, attractiveness, allure, attraction, elegance, charm, fascination, *inf.* glitz, pizzazz. **2 allure,** attraction, charm, fascination, excitement, enchantment, captivation, magic, spell.

glance *v.* **1 glimpse,** peek, peep, *inf.* sneak a look. **2 skim,** leaf, flip, thumb, scan. **3 flash,** gleam, glitter, glisten, glint, glimmer, shimmer, flicker, sparkle, twinkle, reflect. **4 ricochet,** rebound, be deflected, bounce, graze, skim, touch, brush. *Ant.* study; scrutinize.
  ▸ *n.* **1 brief look,** quick look, rapid look, glimpse, peek, peep, *inf.* gander, once-over. **2 flash,** gleam, glitter, glittering, glint, glimmer, shimmer, flicker, sparkle, twinkle, reflection.

glare *v.* **1 glower,** scowl, frown, give someone a dirty look, look daggers. **2 blaze,** flare, flame, beam, dazzle.
  ▸ *n.* **1 glower,** scowl, frown, dirty look. **2 blaze,** flare, flame, harsh beam, dazzle.

glaring *adj.* **1 blazing,** dazzling. **2 conspicuous,** obvious, overt, manifest, patent, visible, unconcealed, flagrant, blatant, egregious, outrageous, gross. *Ant.* dim; inconspicuous.

glass *n.* **1 tumbler,** goblet, wineglass, chalice, beaker. **2 magnifying glass,** monocle, (plutal) binoculars.

glassy *adj.* **1 glasslike,** shiny,

glossy, highly polished, smooth, mirrorlike, clear, crystal-clear, transparent, translucent, limpid. **2 slippery,** icy, ice-covered. **3 expressionless,** glazed, blank, empty, vacant, vacuous, deadpan, fixed, unmoving, motionless, lifeless.

glaze *v.* **1 enamel,** lacquer, varnish, coat, polish, burnish, gloss. **2 coat,** cover, ice, frost.
▸ *n.* **1 enamel,** lacquer, gloss, luster, finish. **2 coating,** icing, frosting.

gleam *n.* **1 beam,** flash, glow, shaft, ray, flare, glint. **2 glow,** luster, gloss, shine, sheen, brightness, brilliance, flash. **3 glimmer,** flicker, ray, trace, suggestion, hint, inkling, grain.
▸ *v.* **shine,** radiate, flash, glow, flare, glint, glisten, glitter, beam, shimmer, glimmer, glance, sparkle, twinkle, scintillate.

glee *n.* **merriment,** gaiety, mirth, mirthfulness, delight, joy, joyfulness, joyousness, gladness, happiness, pleasure, jollity, hilarity, jocularity, joviality, exhilaration, high spirits, blitheness, cheerfulness, exaltation, elation, exuberance, verve, liveliness, triumph.

glib *adj.* **slick,** smooth, smooth-talking, smooth-spoken, fast-talking, plausible, fluent, suave, talkative, voluble, loquacious, unctuous, *inf.* sweet-talking, having the gift of gab. *Ant.* tongue-tied; inarticulate.

glimpse *n.* **glance,** brief look, quick look, peek, peep.
▸ *v.* **catch a glimpse of,** catch sight of, spot, spy, espy.

glint *v.* **shine,** sparkle, flash, twinkle, glitter, glimmer, blink, wink, shimmer, glisten, dazzle, gleam, scintillate.
▸ *n.* **sparkle,** flash, twinkle, glitter, glimmer, blink, gleam.

glisten *v.* **shine,** shimmer, sparkle, twinkle, flicker, blink, wink, glint, glance, gleam, flash, scintillate.

glitter *v.* **sparkle,** twinkle, flicker, blink, wink, shimmer, glimmer, glint, gleam, flash, scintillate, coruscate.
▸ *n.* **1 sparkle,** twinkle, flicker, blink, winking. **2 showiness,** flashiness, ostentation, glamour, pageantry, fanfare, splendor, *inf.* razzle-dazzle, glitz, ritziness, pizzazz.

gloat *v.* **relish,** take pleasure in, delight in, revel in, rejoice in, glory in, exult in, triumph over, crow about, *inf.* rub it in.

global *adj.* **1 worldwide,** world, universal, international, planetary. **2 general,** comprehensive, all-inclusive, all-encompassing, all-out, encyclopedic, exhaustive, thorough, total, across-the-board, without exception.

globule *n.* **bead,** ball, drop, droplet, pearl, particle.

gloom *n.* **1 gloominess,** dimness, darkness, dark, blackness, murkiness, murk, shadowiness, shadow, shade, shadiness, cloud, cloudiness, dullness, obscurity, dusk, twilight. **2 low spirits,** melancholy, sadness, unhappiness, sorrow, grief, woe, despondency, misery, dejection, downheartedness, dispiritedness, glumness, desolation, depression, the blues, despair, pessimism, hopelessness. ***Ant.*** light; gaiety; cheer.

gloomy *adj.* **1 dark,** cloudy, overcast, sunless, dull, dim, shadowy, dismal, dreary, black, unlit, murky, shadowy, somber, dingy. **2 bad,** black, sad, saddening, distressing, somber, melancholy, depressing, dispiriting, disheartening, disappointing, cheerless, comfortless, pessimistic, hopeless. **3 in low spirits,** melancholy, sad, unhappy, sorrowful, woebegone, despondent, disconsolate, miserable, dejected, downcast, downhearted, dispirited, glum, desolate, depressed, blue, despairing, pessimistic, morose, *inf.* down in the mouth. ***Ant.*** bright; happy; cheerful.

glorious *adj.* **1 illustrious,** noble, celebrated, famous, famed, renowned, distinguished, honored, eminent, excellent, magnificent, majestic, splendid, supreme, sublime, triumphant, victorious. **2 beautiful,** bright, brilliant, sunny, perfect. **3 splendid,** marvelous, wonderful, delightful, enjoyable, pleasurable, excellent, fine, *inf.* terrific, great, fab. ***Ant.*** unknown; dull; miserable.

glory *n.* **1 worship,** adoration, exaltation, extolment, honor, reverence, veneration, thanksgiving. **2 renown,** fame, prestige, honor, distinction, illustriousness, acclaim, credit, accolade, recognition, laudation, extolment, *inf.* kudos. **3 splendor,** resplendence, magnificence, grandeur, majesty, pomp, pageantry, beauty. ***Ant.*** blasphemy; shame; disgrace; ugliness.

gloss *n.* **1 shine,** sheen, luster, gleam, brightness, brilliance, sparkle, shimmer, polish, burnish. **2 façade,** front, camouflage, disguise, mask, false appearance, semblance, show, deceptive show, veneer, surface.

glossy *adj.* **shining,** shiny, glassy, gleaming, bright, brilliant, sparkling, shimmering, polished, burnished, glazed, sleek, smooth, silky, silken. *Ant.* dull; lusterless.

glow *n.* **1 gleam,** glimmer, incandescence, luminosity, phosphorescence. **2 brightness,** vividness, brilliance, colorfulness, richness, radiance, splendor. **3 blush,** flush, rosiness, pinkness, redness, crimson, scarlet, reddening, bloom. **4 warmth,** happiness, contentment, satisfaction. **5 passion,** ardor, fervor, vehemence, intensity, earnestness, impetuosity.
▸ *v.* **1 shed a glow,** gleam, glimmer, shine. **2 burn without flames,** smolder. **3 blush,** flush, redden, color. **4 radiate,** thrill, tingle.

glower *v.* **scowl,** stare angrily, glare, frown, give someone dirty looks, look daggers. *Ant.* smile; grin.
▸ *n.* **scowl,** angry stare, glare, frown, dirty look.

glowing *adj.* **1 aglow,** smoldering, incandescent, candescent, luminous, phosphorescent. **2 rosy,** pink, reddish, red, ruddy, florid. **3 bright,** vivid, brilliant, colorful, rich, radiant. **4 complimentary,** highly favorable, enthusiastic, ecstatic, rhapsodic, eulogistic, laudatory, acclamatory, adulatory, *inf.* rave.

glue *n.* **adhesive,** fixative, gum, paste, cement, mucilage, epoxy (resin).
▸ *v.* **stick,** gum, paste, affix, fix, cement.

glum *adj.* **in low spirits,** gloomy, melancholy, sad, despondent, miserable, dejected, downcast, downhearted, dispirited, depressed; *inf.* down in the mouth. *Ant.* cheerful; merry.

glut *n.* **surplus,** excess, surfeit, superfluity, overabundance, superabundance, oversupply, overprofusion, saturation. *Ant.* dearth; scarcity.
▸ *v.* **1 saturate,** overload, oversupply, flood, inundate, deluge. **2 cram full,** stuff, gorge, satiate, overfeed, fill up. **3 clog,** choke up, obstruct, stop up, dam up.

glutinous *adj.* **gluelike,** sticky, gummy, adhesive, viscid, mucilaginous, viscous, pasty, tacky, mucous.

gluttonous *adj.* **greedy,** gormandizing, insatiable, voracious, *inf.* piggish, hoggish.

gnaw *v.* **chew,** munch, crunch, masticate, bite.

go *v.* **1 move,** proceed, progress, pass, walk, travel, journey, repair.

2 go away, leave, depart, withdraw, set off, set out, decamp, *inf.* beat it, scram. **3 work,** be in working order, function, operate, be operative, run, perform. **4 become,** grow, get, come to be, wax. **5 make/emit a sound,** sound, sound out, resound. **6 extend,** stretch, reach, spread, give access, lead. **7 belong,** have a place, fit in, be located, be situated, be found, lie, stand. **8 stop,** cease, disappear, vanish, be no more, fade away, melt away. **9 be finished,** be spent, be used up, be exhausted, be consumed. **10 die,** be dead, pass away, decease, expire, perish, *inf.* give up the ghost, kick the bucket. **11 be discarded,** be thrown away, be disposed of, be dismissed, be laid off, *inf.* be fired, be axed, get the ax. **12 be assigned,** be allotted, be applied, be devoted, be awarded, be granted/given, be ceded. **13 turn out,** work out, fare, progress, develop, result, end, end up, eventuate. **14 go together,** go with each other, match, harmonize, blend, suit each other, be suited, complement each other, be in accord, accord, be compatible. **15 serve,** contribute, help, incline, tend. **16 break,** give way, collapse, fall down, cave in, crumble, disintegrate, fall to pieces.

▶ *n.* **1 try,** attempt, effort, bid, essay, endeavor, *inf.* shot, stab, crack, whirl, whack. **2 energy,** vigor, dynamism, force, verve, vim, vitality, spirit, animation, vivacity, drive, push, determination, enterprise, *inf.* get-up-and-go, pep, oomph.

goad *n.* **1 spiked stick,** stick, spike, prod, staff, crook, pole, rod. **2 stimulus,** incentive, incitement, instigation, inducement, stimulation, impetus, motivation, pressure, spur, prick, jolt, poke.

go-ahead *n.* **permission,** assent, consent, authorization, sanction, leave, warranty, confirmation, *inf.* green light, OK, okay, thumbs up.

goal *n.* **aim,** objective, object, end, purpose, target, ambition, design, intention, intent, aspiration, ideal.

go-between *n.* **intermediary,** mediator, middleman, medium, agent, broker, dealer, factor, liaison, contact, contact person, pander, panderer.

godforsaken *adj.* **desolate,** dismal, dreary, bleak, wretched, miserable, gloomy, deserted, abandoned, forlorn, neglected, remote, backward.

godless *adj.* **1 atheistic,** agnostic,

skeptical, faithless. **2 heathen,** pagan, ungodly, impious, irreligious, unrighteous, unprincipled, sinful, wicked, evil, depraved.

godsend *n.* **boon,** blessing, benediction, stroke of luck, bit/ piece of good fortune, windfall, bonanza.

good *adj.* **1 virtuous,** moral, ethical, righteous, right-minded, right-thinking, honorable, honest, upright, high-minded, noble, worthy, admirable, estimable, exemplary. **2 well-behaved,** obedient, well-mannered, manageable, tractable, reliable, dependable, trustworthy. **3 satisfactory,** acceptable, good enough, passable, tolerable, adequate, fine, excellent, right, correct, proper, fitting, suitable, appropriate, decorous, seemly, *inf.* great, OK, okay, hunky-dory. **4 competent,** capable, able, accomplished, efficient, skillful, adept, proficient, dexterous, expert, excellent, first-class, first-rate, *inf.* A-1, tip-top, top-notch. **5 fine,** healthy, sound, robust, strong, vigorous. **6 enjoyable,** pleasant, agreeable, pleasing, pleasurable, amusing, cheerful, convivial, congenial, sociable, satisfying, gratifying, to one's liking. **7 kind,** kindly, kindhearted, good-hearted, friendly, obliging, well-disposed, charitable, gracious, sympathetic, benevolent, benign, altruistic. **8 convenient,** fitting, suitable, favorable, advantageous, fortunate, lucky, propitious, auspicious. **9 wholesome,** health-giving, healthful, nutritional, beneficial, salubrious, salutary, fit to eat, eatable, edible, untainted, fresh, delicious, tasty, appetizing, *inf.* scrumptious, yummy. **10 valid,** genuine, authentic, legitimate, sound, bona fide. **11 full,** entire, whole, complete, solid, not less than. **12 considerable,** substantial, goodly, sizable, large, sufficient, ample, *inf.* tidy. **13 close,** intimate, bosom, fast, dear, valued, treasured. **14 best,** finest, newest, nicest, smartest, special, party, Sunday. **15 fine,** fair, mild, clear, bright, cloudless, sunshiny, sunny, calm, balmy, tranquil, clement, halcyon. ***Ant.*** bad; inadequate; poor.

▸ *n.* **1 benefit,** advantage, behalf, gain, profit, interest, well-being, welfare, usefulness, avail, service. **2 virtue,** goodness, morality, ethics, righteousness, rightness, rectitude, honor, honesty, uprightness, integrity, probity, worth, merit.

goodbye *interj.* **farewell,** au revoir,

adieu, *inf.* bye, cheers, see you later, see you, so long, toodle-oo, ciao, bye-bye, ta-ta, sayonara, adios.

good-humored *adj.* **amiable,** affable, easygoing, genial, cheerful, cheery, happy, pleasant, good-tempered.

good-looking *adj.* **attractive,** handsome, pretty, lovely, beautiful, personable, comely, fair.

goodly *adj.* **considerable,** substantial, sizable, significant, large, great, ample, sufficient, *inf.* tidy.

good-natured *adj.* **kind,** kindly, kindhearted, warmhearted, generous, benevolent, charitable, friendly, helpful, accommodating, amiable, tolerant.

goods *pl. n.* **belongings,** possessions, property, effects, gear, things, paraphernalia, chattels, appurtenances, trappings, accouterments, *inf.* stuff.

gorge *n.* **chasm,** canyon, ravine, abyss, defile, pass, cleft, crevice, rift, fissure.
 ▸ *v.* **bolt,** gobble, guzzle, gulp down, wolf (down), devour, stuff down, gormandize, *inf.* shovel in.

gorgeous *adj.* **1 magnificent,** splendid, superb, grand, resplendent, stately, impressive, imposing, sumptuous, luxurious, elegant, opulent, dazzling, brilliant, glittering, breathtaking. **2 wonderful,** marvelous, first-rate, delightful, enjoyable, entertaining, excellent, *inf.* glorious, terrific. **3 attractive,** beautiful, lovely, good-looking, sexy, *inf.* stunning. *Ant.* dull; miserable; ugly.

gory *adj.* **1 bloody,** bloodthirsty, violent, murderous, brutal, savage, horror-filled, horrific, *inf.* blood-and-guts. **2 bloody,** blood-stained, blood-soaked.

gossip *n.* **1 rumors,** scandal, idle talk, hearsay, smear campaign, *inf.* mudslinging, dirt, low-down. **2 gossipmonger,** scandalmonger, busybody, blabbermouth, tattletale.
 ▸ *v.* **spread rumors,** talk, blab, tattle.

govern *v.* **1 rule,** reign over, be in power over, exercise control over, hold sway over, preside over, administer, lead, be in charge of, control, command, direct, order, guide, manage, conduct, oversee, supervise, superintend, steer, pilot. **2 control,** restrain, keep in check, check, curb, hold back, keep back, bridle, rein in, subdue, constrain, contain, arrest. **3 determine,** decide, sway, rule, influence, have an influence on, be a factor in.

government *n.* **1 administration,** regime, congress, parliament, ministry, council, executive, the powers that be. **2 rule,** administration, leadership, command, direction, control, guidance, management, conduct, supervision, superintendence. **3 control,** restraint, checking, curbing, bridling, constraint, discipline.

gown *n.* **dress,** evening gown, ball gown.

grab *v.* **1 grasp,** clutch, grip, clasp, lay hold of, catch hold of, take hold of, fasten upon. **2 seize,** snatch, pluck, snap up, appropriate, capture, *inf.* bag, nab.
▸ *n.* **clutch,** grasp, firm hold, hug, embrace.

grace *n.* **1 gracefulness,** suppleness, fluidity, smoothness, ease, elegance, agility, *inf.* poetry in motion. **2 elegance,** refinement, finesse, culture, cultivation, polish, suaveness, good taste, taste, tastefulness, charm, attractiveness, beauty, loveliness, comeliness. **3 manners,** mannerliness, courtesy, courteousness, decency, consideration, tact, tactfulness, breeding, decorum, propriety, etiquette. **4 favor,** goodwill,

preferment, generosity, kindness, kindliness, benefaction, beneficence, indulgence. **5 mercy,** mercifulness, compassion, pardon, reprieve, forgiveness, leniency, lenity, clemency, indulgence, charity, quarter. **6 delay,** postponement, deferment, deferral. **7 blessing,** benediction, thanks, thanksgiving, prayer.
▸ *v.* **1 adorn,** decorate, ornament, embellish, enhance, beautify, prettify, set off, deck, enrich, garnish. **2 dignify,** distinguish, add distinction to, honor, favor, glorify, elevate.

graceful *adj.* **1 supple,** fluid, flowing, smooth, easy, elegant, agile, nimble. **2 elegant,** refined, cultured, cultivated, polished, suave, having good taste, charming, appealing, attractive, beautiful, lovely, comely. **Ant.** inelegant; ungainly.

gracious *adj.* **1 kind,** kindly, kindhearted, warmhearted, benevolent, friendly, amiable, affable, pleasant, cordial, courteous, considerate, polite, civil, chivalrous, well-mannered, charitable, indulgent, obliging, accommodating, beneficent, benign, merciful, compassionate, gentle, mild, lenient, humane, clement. **2 elegant,** tasteful, comfortable, luxurious. *Ant.* discourteous; ungracious; inelegant; cruel.

grade *n.* **1 level,** stage, echelon, rank, standing, station, position, order, class, year. **2 category,** class, classification, type, brand. **3 stage,** step, rung, notch. **4 gradient,** slope, incline, hill, rise, bank, acclivity, declivity.
▸ *v.* **classify,** class, categorize, sort, group, order, brand, size, rank, evaluate, rate, value, range, graduate.

gradient *n.* **slope,** incline, hill, rise, rising ground, bank, acclivity, declivity, grade.

gradual *adj.* **1 step-by-step,** degree-by-degree, progressive, successive, continuous, systematic, regular, steady, even, moderate, slow, measured, unhurried. **2 gentle,** not steep, moderate. *Ant.* sudden; abrupt.

gradually *adv.* **bit by bit,** little by little, by degrees, step by step, inch by inch, piece by piece, drop by drop, slowly, progressively, successively, continuously, constantly, regularly, at a regular pace, steadily, evenly, moderately.

graduate *v.* **1 take an academic degree,** receive one's degree/diploma, become a graduate. **2 mark off,** measure off, divide into degrees, grade, calibrate.

3 move up, progress, advance, gain promotion, be promoted.

graft[1] *n.* **1 shoot,** bud, scion, slip, new growth, sprout, splice. **2 transplant,** implantation, implant.
▸ *v.* **insert,** affix, slip, join, transplant, implant.

graft[2] *n.* **bribery,** illegal means, unlawful practices, underhand/underhanded means, payola; *inf.* palm-greasing.

grain *n.* **1 cereal,** cereal crops, corn, wheat, barley, rye, oats. **2 kernel,** seed, grist. **3 particle,** granule, bit, piece, scrap, crumb, fragment, morsel, mote, speck, mite, molecule, atom. **4 iota,** trace, hint, suggestion, suspicion, scintilla. **5 texture,** surface, fabric, weave, nap, fiber, pattern. **6 disposition,** character, nature, makeup, humor, temperament, temper, inclination.

grand *adj.* **1 impressive,** magnificent, imposing, splendid, striking, superb, palatial, stately, large, monumental, majestic. **2 splendid,** luxurious, sumptuous, lavish, magnificent, glorious, opulent, princely. **3 great,** noble, aristocratic, distinguished, august, illustrious, eminent, esteemed, elevated, exalted, celebrated, preeminent, prominent, leading, notable, renowned, famous.

4 ostentatious, showy, pretentious, lordly, ambitious, imperious. **5 complete,** comprehensive, total, all-inclusive, inclusive, exhaustive, final. **6 principal,** main, chief, leading, head, supreme. **7 very good,** excellent, wonderful, marvelous, splendid, first-class, first-rate, outstanding, fine, enjoyable, admirable, *inf.* superb, terrific, great, super, smashing. *Ant.* inferior; unimpressive; lowly.

grandiose *adj.* **1 ambitious,** overambitious, extravagant, high-flown, high-sounding, pompous, pretentious, flamboyant. **2 grand,** impressive, magnificent, imposing, splendid, striking, superb, stately, majestic. *Ant.* modest; humble.

grant *v.* **1 permit,** allow, accord. **2 bestow on,** confer on, give to, impart to, award with, present with, donate to, contribute to, provide with, endow with, furnish with, supply with, allocate to, allot to, assign to. **3 admit to,** acknowledge to, concede to, go along with, yield to. **4 transfer,** convey, transmit, pass on, hand over, assign, bequeath. ▸ *n.* **award,** endowment, donation, contribution, allowance, subsidy, allocation, allotment, gift, present.

granule *n.* **grain,** particle, crumb, fragment, bit, scrap, mite, molecule, atom, iota, jot.

graphic *adj.* **1 vivid,** striking, expressive, descriptive, illustrative, lively, forcible, detailed, well-defined, well-delineated, well-drawn, telling, effective, cogent, clear, lucid, explicit. **2 diagrammatic,** representational, pictorial, illustrative, drawn, delineative. *Ant.* vague; fuzzy.

grapple *v.* **wrestle,** fight, struggle, tussle, clash, close, engage, combat, battle, brawl.

grasp *v.* **1 grip,** clutch, clasp, hold, clench, latch on to, take/lay hold of, catch, seize, grab, snatch. **2 understand,** comprehend, follow, see, take in, realize, perceive, apprehend, *inf.* get, get the picture, get the drift, catch on. ▸ *n.* **1 grip,** hold, clutch, clasp, clench, clutches, power, control, command, mastery, dominion, rule. **2 capacity,** reach, scope, limits, range, compass. **3 understanding,** comprehension, perception, apprehension, awareness, grip, realization, knowledge, ken, mastery.

grate *v.* **1 shred,** rub into pieces, pulverize, mince, grind, granulate. **2 rasp,** scrape, jar, scratch, grind, creak, rub.

grateful *adj.* **1 thankful,** filled with gratitude, indebted, obliged, obligated, under obligation, beholden, appreciative.
2 pleasant, agreeable, pleasing, pleasurable, satisfying, gratifying, cheering, refreshing, welcome, acceptable, nice. *Ant.* ungrateful; unappreciative.

gratify *v.* **1 please,** give pleasure to, make happy, make content, delight, make someone feel good, gladden, satisfy, warm the cockles of the heart, thrill. **2 fulfill,** indulge, humor, comply with, pander to, cater to, pacify, appease, give in to.

gratuitous *adj.* **1 free,** gratis, complimentary, voluntary, unpaid, unrewarded, unasked-for, free of charge, without charge, for nothing, at no cost, without payment, on the house, *inf.* for free. **2 unjustified,** unprovoked, groundless, ungrounded, causeless, without cause, without reason, unfounded, baseless, uncalled-for, unwarranted, unmerited, needless, unnecessary, superfluous.

gratuity *n.* **tip,** perquisite, fringe benefit, bonus, gift, present, donation, reward, recompense, largesse, lagniappe, *inf.* perk.

grave *n.* **burying place,** burial ground, tomb, sepulcher, vault, burial chamber, mausoleum, crypt, last/final resting place.
▸ *adj.* **1 solemn,** earnest, serious, sober, somber, severe, unsmiling, long-faced, stone-faced, grim-faced, grim, gloomy, preoccupied, thoughtful, pensive, subdued, muted, quiet, sedate, dignified, staid, dour. **2 serious,** important, all-important, significant, momentous, weighty, urgent, pressing, of great consequence, vital, crucial, critical, acute, pivotal, life-and-death, exigent, perilous, hazardous, dangerous, threatening, menacing. *Ant.* carefree; frivolous; trivial.

graveyard *n.* **cemetery,** burial ground, churchyard, memorial park, *inf.* boneyard, potter's field.

gravitate *v.* **1 sink,** fall, drop, descend, precipitate, be precipitated, settle. **2 move toward,** head toward, be drawn to, be pulled toward, be attracted to, drift toward, lean toward, incline toward.

gravity *n.* **1 solemnity,** earnestness, seriousness, sobriety, somberness, severity, grimness, thoughtfulness, pensiveness, sedateness, dignity, staidness, dourness. **2 seriousness,** importance, significance, momentousness, moment, weightiness, consequence, vitalness, crucialness, criticalness, acuteness, exigence, perilousness, peril, hazard, danger.

graze[1] *v.* **feed,** browse, ruminate.

greasy *adj.* **1 fatty,** fat, oily, buttery, adipose, sebaceous. **2 slippery,** slippy, slimy. **3 unctuous,** oily, slimy, smooth-tongued, smooth, glib, suave, slick, fawning, ingratiating, groveling, sycophantic, toadying, flattering, gushing, *inf.* smarmy.

great *adj.* **1 large,** big, extensive, vast, immense, unlimited, boundless, spacious, huge, enormous, gigantic, colossal, mammoth, monstrous, prodigious, tremendous, stupendous. **2 considerable,** substantial, pronounced, exceptional, inordinate, sizable. **3 major,** main, most important, leading, chief, principal, capital, paramount, primary. **4 grand,** impressive, magnificent, imposing, splendid, majestic, glorious, sumptuous. **5 prominent,** eminent, preeminent, distinguished, august, illustrious, celebrated, noted, notable, noteworthy, famous, famed, renowned, leading, top, high, high-ranking, noble. **6 gifted,** talented, outstanding, remarkable, exceptional, first-rate, incomparable. **7 expert,**

skillful, skilled, able, masterly, adept, adroit, proficient, good, *inf.* crack, ace, A-1. **8 enthusiastic,** eager, keen, zealous, devoted, active. **9 enjoyable,** excellent, marvelous, wonderful, first-class, first-rate, admirable, fine, very good, *inf.* terrific, tremendous, fantastic, fabulous, fab. **10 absolute,** utter, out-and-out, downright, thoroughgoing, total, complete, perfect, positive, arrant, unmitigated, unqualified, consummate, egregious. ***Ant.*** small; unimportant; ordinary.

greatly *adv.* **very much,** much, by a considerable amount, considerably, to a great extent, extremely, exceedingly, enormously, vastly, immensely, tremendously, hugely, markedly, mightily, remarkably, abundantly.

greedy *adj.* **1 avaricious,** acquisitive, grasping, rapacious, grabbing, covetous, hoarding, miserly, niggardly, tight-fisted, close-fisted, parsimonious, *inf.* money-grubbing. **2 avid,** eager, hungry, desirous, craving, longing, enthusiastic, anxious, impatient. ***Ant.*** generous; altruistic; apathetic.

greet *v.* **say hello to,** address, salute, hail, nod to, wave to, raise one's hat to, acknowledge the presence of, accost, receive, meet, welcome.

greeting *n.* **hello,** salute, salutation, address, nod, wave, acknowledgment, message, tidings.

greetings *pl. n.* **good wishes,** best wishes, regards, kind regards, congratulations, compliments, respects.

grief *n.* **sorrow,** mourning, mournfulness, bereavement, lamentation, misery, sadness, anguish, pain, distress, agony, affliction, suffering, heartache, heartbreak, brokenheartedness, heaviness of heart, trouble, woe, tribulation, trial, desolation, despondency, dejection, despair, remorse, regret. *Ant.* joy; delight; celebration.

grievance *n.* **1 complaint,** charge, protest, moan, ax to grind, bone to pick, *lit.* plaint, *inf.* grouse, gripe, beef. **2 wrong,** injustice, unjust act, unfairness, injury, damage, hardship, offense, affront, insult.

grieve *v.* **1 mourn,** lament, be sorrowful, sorrow, be sad, weep and wail, cry, sob, suffer, ache, be in anguish, be distressed, eat one's heart out, bewail, bemoan. **2 hurt,** wound, pain, sadden, break someone's heart, upset, distress, cause suffering to, crush. **3 bewail,** bemoan, regret, rue, deplore, take to heart. *Ant.* rejoice; cheer.

grim *adj.* **1 stern,** forbidding, formidable, fierce, ferocious, threatening, menacing, harsh, somber, cross, churlish, crabbed, morose, surly, sour, ill-tempered, implacable, cruel, ruthless, merciless. **2 resolute,** determined, firm, decided, obstinate, adamant, unyielding, unwavering, unfaltering, unshakable, obdurate, inflexible, unrelenting, relentless. **3 dreadful,** dire, ghastly, horrible, horrendous, horrid, terrible, awful, appalling, frightful, shocking, unspeakable, harrowing, grisly, gruesome, hideous, macabre. *Ant.* gentle; amiable; pleasant.

grimy *adj.* **begrimed,** dirty, dirt-encrusted, grubby, soiled, stained, smutty, sooty, dusty, muddy, muddied, filthy, *inf.* mucky, grungy, yucky, cruddy.

grind *v.* **1 crush,** pound, pulverize, mill, powder, granulate, grate, crumble, mash, smash. **2 sharpen,** file, whet, smooth, polish, sand. **3 gnash,** grit, grate, scrape, rasp. **4 labor,** toil, slog, slave, drudge, plod, sweat, *inf.* plug.

▶ *n.* **drudgery,** chore, slog, travail, toil, hard work, labor, slavery, forced labor, exertion, *inf.* drag, sweat.

grip *n.* **1 hold,** grasp, clutch, clasp, clench, handshake, handclasp, hug, embrace, *inf.* clinch. **2 grasp,** understanding, comprehension, perception, awareness, apprehension. **3 clutches,** control, domination, dominion, command, power, mastery, influence, hold, possession, rule. **4 bag,** carryall, overnight bag, travel bag, duffel bag, valise.
▶ *v.* **1 grasp,** clutch, clasp, clench, hold, latch on to, grab, seize, catch, catch at. **2 absorb,** engross, rivet, spellbind, entrance, fascinate, enthrall, hold, catch, compel, mesmerize.

grisly *adj.* **gruesome,** ghastly, frightful, horrid, horrifying, horrible, horrendous, grim, awful, dreadful, terrible, fearful, hideous, disgusting, repulsive, repugnant, revolting, repellent, macabre, spine-chilling, sickening, shocking, appalling, abominable, loathsome, abhorrent, odious. *Ant.* pleasant; attractive.

grit *n.* **1 granules,** sand, abrasive particles, gravel, pebbles, dust, dirt. **2 pluck,** mettle, mettlesomeness, backbone, spirit, strength of character, nerve, gameness, courage, bravery, valor, fortitude, stamina, toughness, hardiness, determination, resolution, doggedness, tenacity, perseverance, endurance, *inf.* gumption, guts, spunk.
▶ *v.* **grate,** grind, gnash, scrape, rasp, clamp, clench.

groan *n.* **1 moan,** cry, sigh, murmur, whimper. **2 complaint,** grumble, whine, whining, objection, protest, grievance, moan, *inf.* grouse, gripe, beefing, bellyaching, bitching. **3 creak,** grating, squeak, screech.
▶ *v.* **1 moan,** cry, call out, sigh, murmur, whimper. **2 complain,** grumble, whine, object, moan, lament, *inf.* grouse, gripe, beef, bellyache, bitch. **3 creak,** grate, squeak, screech.

groove *n.* **1 furrow,** channel, trench, trough, canal, gouge, hollow, indentation, rut, gutter, cutting, cut, score, rabbet. **2 rut,** routine, habit, treadmill, *inf.* daily grind.

grope *v.* **feel,** fumble, move blindly, fish, search, hunt, look.

gross *adj.* **1 obese,** massive, immense, huge, colossal, corpulent, overweight, bloated, bulky, hulking, fat, big, large, cumbersome, unwieldy. **2 coarse,** crude, vulgar, obscene, rude, ribald, lewd, bawdy, dirty, filthy, earthy, smutty, blue, risqué, indecent, indelicate, improper, impure, unseemly, offensive,

sensual, sexual, pornographic.
3 boorish, loutish, oafish, coarse, crass, vulgar, ignorant, unrefined, unsophisticated, uncultured, uncultivated, undiscriminating, tasteless, insensitive, unfeeling, imperceptive, callous. **4 flagrant,** blatant, glaring, outrageous, shocking, serious, egregious, manifest, obvious, plain, apparent. **5 total,** whole, entire, aggregate, before deductions, before taxes. ***Ant.*** slender; pure; refined; net.
▸ *v.* **earn,** make, bring in, take (in), *inf.* rake in.

grotesque *adj.* **1 bizarre,** weird, outlandish, freakish, strange, odd, peculiar, unnatural, fantastic, fanciful, whimsical, ridiculous, ludicrous, absurd, incongruous, preposterous, extravagant.
2 misshapen, distorted, twisted, deformed, malformed, misproportioned.

ground *n.* **1 earth,** terra firma, floor, *inf.* deck. **2 earth,** soil, dirt, land, terrain, clay, loam, turf, sod.
▸ *v.* **base,** found, establish, set, settle.

groundless *adj.* **without basis,** baseless, without foundation, unfounded, unsupported, imaginary, illusory, false, unsubstantiated, unwarranted, unjustified, unjustifiable,

uncalled-for, unprovoked, without cause/reason/justification, unreasonable, irrational, illogical, empty, idle, chimerical.

grounds *pl. n.* **1 surroundings,** land, property, estate, acres, lawns, gardens, park, area, domain, holding, territory.
2 stadium, field, arena, ballpark, park. **3 reason,** cause, basis, base, foundation, call, justification, rationale, argument, premise, occasion, factor, excuse, pretext, motive, inducement. **4 dregs,** lees, deposit, sediment, precipitate.

group *n.* **1 category,** classification, class, set, lot, batch, family, species, genus, bracket. **2 band,** company, party, body, gathering, congregation, assembly, collection, cluster, crowd, flock, pack, troop, gang, batch, *inf.* bunch. **3 clique,** coterie, faction, circle, set. **4 society,** association, league, guild, circle, club, work party. **5 clump,** cluster.
▸ *v.* **1 classify,** class, categorize, sort, grade, rank, bracket.
2 assemble, collect, gather together, arrange, organize, marshal, line up. **3 collect,** gather, assemble, cluster. **4 get together,** band together, associate, consort.

grouse *v.* **complain,** grumble, moan, groan, protest, *inf.* gripe, bellyache, beef, bitch, grouch.

grovel v. **abase oneself,** humble oneself, kowtow, bow and scrape, kneel before, fall on one's knees, prostrate oneself, fawn, fawn upon, curry favor, curry favor with, flatter, *inf.* crawl, butter someone up, be all over someone, suck up to, lick someone's boots, bootlick, throw oneself at someone's feet.

grow v. **1 get taller,** get bigger, get larger, stretch, heighten, lengthen, enlarge, extend, expand, spread, thicken, widen, fill out, swell, increase, multiply. **2 shoot up,** spring up, develop, sprout, burgeon, bud, germinate, flourish, thrive. **3 arise,** originate, stem, spring, issue. **4 flourish,** thrive, prosper, succeed, progress, make progress, make headway, advance, improve, expand. **5 become,** come to be, get to be, get, turn, wax. **6 cultivate,** produce, farm, propagate, raise. *Ant.* shrink; decrease; fail.

grown-up n. **adult,** grown man, man, grown woman, woman, mature man, mature woman. ▸ *adj.* **adult,** mature, of age, fully grown, full-grown, fully developed.

growth n. **1 augmentation,** increase, proliferation, multiplication, enlargement, expansion, extension, development, evolution, aggrandizement, magnification, amplification, growing, deepening, heightening, widening, thickening, broadening, swelling. **2 development,** maturation, germination, shooting up, springing up, burgeoning, sprouting, blooming, vegetation. **3 expansion,** rise, progress, success, advance, advancement, improvement, headway. **4 tumor,** lump, excrescence, intumescence, tumefaction. *Ant.* decrease; decline; failure.

grubby *adj.* **dirty,** unwashed, grimy, filthy, messy, soiled, smutty, scruffy, shabby, untidy, unkempt, slovenly, squalid, *inf.* grungy, cruddy. *Ant.* clean; spotless.

grudge n. **resentment,** spite, malice, bitterness, ill-will, pique, umbrage, grievance, hard feelings, rancor, malevolence, venom, hate, hatred, dislike, aversion, animosity, antipathy, antagonism, enmity. ▸ *v.* **1 begrudge,** give unwillingly, give reluctantly, give stintingly. **2 resent,** mind, begrudge, envy, be jealous of.

grueling *adj.* **exhausting,** tiring, fatiguing, wearying, taxing, demanding, trying, arduous, laborious, backbreaking, strenuous, punishing, crushing, draining, difficult, hard, harsh, severe, stiff, grinding, brutal.

gruesome *adj.* **grisly,** ghastly, frightful, horrid, horrible, horrifying, horrendous, awful, grim, dreadful, terrible, fearful, hideous, disgusting, repulsive, repugnant, revolting, repellent, macabre, spine-chilling, sickening, shocking, appalling, abominable, loathsome, abhorrent, odious.

grumble *v.* **1 complain,** moan, groan, protest, object, find fault with, carp, whine, *inf.* grouse, gripe, bellyache, beef, bitch, grouch. **2 rumble,** gurgle, murmur, growl, mutter, roar. ▸ *n.* **1 complaint,** moan, groan, protest, grievance, objection, whine, *inf.* grouse, gripe, bellyaching, beefing, beef, bitching, grouching. **2 rumble,** gurgle, murmur, growl, muttering, roar.

grumpy *adj.* **bad-tempered,** surly, churlish, crotchety, crabby, crusty, bearish, ill-natured, *inf.* grouchy.

guarantee *n.* **1 warranty,** warrant, contract, covenant, bond, guaranty. **2 pledge,** promise, assurance, word, word of honor, oath, bond. **3 collateral,**
security, surety, earnest, guaranty. **4 guarantor,** warrantor, underwriter, voucher, sponsor, supporter, backer, *Law* bondsman. ▸ *v.* **1 underwrite,** sponsor, vouch for, support, back. **2 promise,** pledge, give assurances, assure, insure, give one's word, swear, swear to the fact.

guard *v.* **1 stand guard over,** protect, watch over, cover, patrol, police, defend, shield, safeguard, preserve, save, conserve, secure, screen, shelter. **2 keep under surveillance,** keep watch over, mind, supervise, restrain. ▸ *n.* **1 protector,** defender, guardian, guarder, bodyguard, custodian, sentinel, sentry, watchman, night watchman, scout, lookout, watch, picket. **2 jailer,** keeper, *inf.* screw. **3 escort,** convoy, patrol. **4 watch,** watchfulness, vigilance, caution, attention, care, wariness. **5 safety guard,** safety device, safeguard, protective device, shield, screen, fence, fender, bumper, buffer, cushion, pad.

guarded *adj.* **careful,** cautious, circumspect, wary, chary, reluctant, noncommittal, reticent, restrained, reserved, discreet, prudent, *inf.* cagey.

guess *v.* **1 conjecture,** surmise, estimate, reckon, fathom,

hypothesize, postulate, predict, speculate, *inf.* guesstimate.
2 conjecture, surmise, reckon, hazard a guess, suppose, believe, think, imagine, judge, consider, feel, suspect, dare say, fancy, deem.
▸ *n.* **conjecture,** surmise, estimate, guesswork, hypothesis, theory, reckoning, judgment, supposition, feeling, assumption, inference, prediction, speculation, notion, *inf.* guesstimate.

guest *n.* **visitor,** caller, company, boarder, lodger, roomer, patron, customer. *Ant.* host; landlady, landlord.

guidance *n.* **1 direction,** leadership, auspices, management, control, handling, conduct, government, charge, rule, teaching, instruction.
2 counseling, counsel, advice, direction, recommendation, suggestion, tip, hint, pointer, intelligence, information, instruction.

guide *v.* **1 lead,** lead the way to, conduct, show, usher, shepherd, direct, show the way to, pilot, steer, escort, accompany, convoy, attend. **2 control,** direct, steer, manage, command, be in charge of, govern, rule, preside over, superintend, supervise, handle, regulate, manipulate, maneuver.

3 counsel, advise, direct, inform, give information/intelligence to, instruct.
▸ *n.* **1 leader,** conductor, director, courier, pilot, usher, escort, attendant, convoy, chaperon.
2 counselor, adviser, mentor, confidant, tutor, teacher, guru, therapist. **3 marker,** indicator, pointer, mark, landmark, guiding light, sign, signal, beacon, lodestar, signpost, key, clue.
4 model, pattern, example, exemplar, standard, criterion, touchstone, measure, benchmark, yardstick, gauge, norm, archetype, prototype, paradigm, ideal, precedent, guiding principle. **5 guidebook,** tourist guide, travelogue, directory, handbook, manual, instructions, key, catalog.

guile *n.* **cunning,** duplicity, craftiness, craft, artfulness, art, artifice, wiliness, wiles, foxiness, slyness, deception, deceit, underhandedness, double-dealing, trickery, trickiness, treachery, chicanery, skullduggery, fraud. *Ant.* honesty; candor.

guilty *adj.* **1 to blame,** blameworthy, blamable, culpable, at fault, responsible, censurable, criminal, convicted, reproachable, condemnable, erring, errant, wrong, delinquent, offending, sinful, wicked, evil, unlawful, illegal, illicit, reprehensible, felonious, iniquitous. **2 conscience-stricken,** remorseful, ashamed, shamefaced, regretful, contrite, compunctious, repentant, penitent, rueful, sheepish. **Ant.** innocent; blameless; unrepentant.

guise *n.* **1 external appearance,** likeness, costume, clothes, outfit, dress, habit, style. **2 pretense,** disguise, show, external appearance, outward form, screen, cover, blind.

gulf *n.* **1 bay,** inlet, bight. **2 chasm,** abyss, hollow, pit, hole, opening, rift, cleft, fissure, split, crevice, gully, canyon, gorge, ravine, division, gap, separation.

gullible *adj.* **credulous,** trustful, overtrustful, easily deceived, easily taken in, unsuspecting, unsuspicious, ingenuous, naïve, innocent, simple, inexperienced, green, foolish, silly, wet behind the ears. **Ant.** cynical; suspicious.

gulp *v.* **1 swallow,** quaff, swill, *inf.* swig, knock back. **2 bolt,** wolf (down), gobble, guzzle, devour.
▸ *n.* **swallow,** mouthful, draft, *inf.* swig, slurp.

gunman *n.* **holdup man,** armed robber, sniper, gunfighter, shootist, gangster, terrorist, assassin, murderer, liquidator,

bandit, *inf.* gunslinger, hitman, hired gun, hood, mobster.

gurgle *v.* **bubble,** ripple, murmur, babble, burble, tinkle, lap, splash, chuckle, laugh.
▸ *n.* **bubbling,** ripple, babble, tinkle, chuckle, laughing, laughter.

gush *v.* **1 stream,** rush forth, spout, spurt, surge, jet, well out, pour forth, burst forth, cascade, flood, flow, run, issue, emanate. **2 be effusive,** enthuse, wax enthusiastic/lyrical, effervesce, bubble over, get carried away, fuss, babble, prattle, jabber, blather, chatter.
▸ *n.* **stream,** outpouring, spurt, jet, spout, burst, rush, surge, cascade, flood, torrent, spate, freshet.

gusto *n.* **relish,** zest, enthusiasm, zeal, fervor, verve, enjoyment, delight, exhilaration, pleasure, appreciation, liking, fondness, appetite, savor, taste. **Ant.** apathy; indifference; distaste.

gut *n.* **stomach,** belly, abdomen, bowels, colon, solar plexus, *inf.* insides, innards.
▸ *v.* **1 eviscerate,** disembowel, draw, dress, clean. **2 ransack,** strip, empty, plunder, loot, rob, rifle, ravage, sack, clear out, destroy, devastate, lay waste (to).

guts *pl. n.* **1 intestines,** entrails, vital organs, vital parts, viscera, *inf.* insides, innards. **2 courage,** bravery, valor, backbone, nerve, fortitude, pluck, mettle, mettlesomeness, gameness, spirit, boldness, audacity, daring, hardiness, toughness, forcefulness, stamina, willpower, tenacity, *inf.* grit, gumption, spunk.

gutter *n.* **drain,** sewer, sluice, culvert, conduit, pipe, duct, channel, trough, trench, ditch, furrow.

guttural *adj.* **throaty,** husky, gruff, gravelly, croaking, harsh, rasping, deep, low, rough, thick.

gyrate *v.* **rotate,** revolve, wheel around, turn around, circle, whirl, pirouette, twirl, swirl, spin, swivel.

Hh

habit *n.* **1 custom,** practice, procedure, wont, way, routine, matter of course, style, pattern, convention, policy, mode, rule. **2 addiction,** dependence, weakness, fixation, obsession. **3 costume,** dress, garb, attire, apparel, clothes, clothing, garments, livery, uniform, *inf.* gear, togs, duds.

habitable *adj.* **inhabitable,** fit to live/reside in, fit to occupy, tenantable.

habitual *adj.* **1 customary,** accustomed, regular, usual, normal, set, fixed, established, routine, wonted, common, ordinary, familiar, traditional. **2 persistent,** constant, continual, recurrent, repeated, perpetual, nonstop, continuous, frequent. **3 by habit,** confirmed, addicted, chronic, inveterate, hardened, ingrained. **Ant.** unaccustomed; infrequent; occasional.

hackneyed *adj.* **hack,** banal, trite, overused, overworked, tired, worn-out, time-worn, stale, stereotyped, clichéd, platitudinous, unoriginal, unimaginative, commonplace, common, pedestrian, prosaic, run-of-the-mill, stock, conventional, *inf.* played-out, corny, old-hat. **Ant.** fresh; original.

haggard *adj.* **drawn,** gaunt, pinched, hollow-cheeked, hollow-eyed, ghastly, ghostlike, deathlike, wan, pallid, cadaverous, peaked, drained, careworn, emaciated, wasted, thin. **Ant.** sleek; plump; hale.

hail *v.* **1 salute,** greet, say hello to, nod to, wave to, smile at, lift one's hat to, acknowledge. **2 signal,** make a sign to, flag, flag down, wave down, call, shout to. **3 acclaim,** applaud, cheer, praise, sound the praises of, laud, extol, pay tribute to, pay homage to, exalt, glorify. **4 come from,** be a native of, be born in, originate in, have one's roots in.

hair *n.* **1 head of hair,** locks, tresses, *inf.* mane, mop. **2 coat,** fur, pelt, hide, wool, fleece, mane.

hairy *adj.* **hair-covered,** hirsute, woolly, shaggy, bushy, furry, fleecy, fuzzy, bearded, unshaven, bewhiskered, stubbly, *Tech.* pilose, pileous.

halfhearted *adj.* **lukewarm,**

unenthusiastic, apathetic, indifferent, uninterested, unconcerned, cool, listless, lackluster, dispassionate, unemotional, cursory, perfunctory, superficial, passive, neutral.

hallmark *n.* **1 assay mark,** stamp of authenticity, authentication seal, endorsement of authentication. **2 mark,** trademark, stamp, sign, sure sign, telltale sign, badge, device, symbol, indicator, indication, index.

hallucinate *v.* **see visions,** have a vision, fantasize, imagine things, dream, be delirious, *inf.* see things, trip.

hallucination *n.* **illusion,** figment of the imagination, imagining, vision, mirage, false conception, fantasy, apparition, dream, delirium, phantasmagoria, trip.

halt *v.* **1 stop,** come to a stop, come to a standstill, pull up, wait, finish, cease, break off, call it a day, desist, discontinue, rest, come to an end, be at an end, draw to a close, run its course, *inf.* knock off. **2 bring to a halt/stop,** arrest, check, block, curb, stem, terminate, end, put an end to, put a stop to, bring an end to, crush, nip in the bud, frustrate, balk,

obstruct, impede, hold back. **Ant.** go; begin; further.

hammer *n.* **maul,** sledgehammer, sledge, mallet, gavel.
▸ *v.* **1 beat,** shape, form, mold, forge, fashion, make, fabricate. **2 beat,** batter, pound, pummel, hit, strike, slap, cudgel, bludgeon, club, trounce, defeat, bring someone to their knees, beat, thrash, worst, drub, *inf.* wallop, clobber. **3 drum,** drive, drub.

hamper *v.* **hinder,** obstruct, impede, hold back, inhibit, retard, slow down, hold up, restrain, block, check, frustrate, balk, thwart, foil, curb, interfere with, cramp, restrict, bridle, handicap, stymie, hamstring, shackle, fetter, encumber, cumber, trammel, *inf.* throw a monkey wrench in the works. **Ant.** aid; expedite; facilitate.
▸ *n.* **laundry hamper,** laundry basket, basket, picnic basket.

hand *n.* **1 palm,** fist, *inf.* paw, mitt, dukes. **2 pointer,** indicator, needle. **3 help,** assistance, aid, support, succor, relief. **4 worker,** workman, work person, employee, operative, hired hand, hired man, hired person, hired help, laborer, artisan, crewman. **5 writing,** handwriting, penmanship, script, calligraphy. **6 ability,** skill, art, artistry, craftsmanship.

7 applause, round of applause, clapping of hands, clap, ovation.
▸ *v.* **give,** pass, pass over, hand over, deliver, present.

handicap *n.* **1 disability,** disadvantage, abnormality, impairment. **2 disadvantage,** impediment, hindrance, obstruction, obstacle, encumbrance, check, block, curb, trammel, barrier, stumbling block, constraint, restriction, limitation, drawback, shortcoming. *Ant.* advantage; benefit.
▸ *v.* **put at a disadvantage,** disadvantage, impede, hinder, impair, hamper, obstruct, check, block, encumber, curb, trammel, bridle, hold back, constrain, restrict, limit.

handiwork *n.* **1 handicraft,** craft, craftsmanship. **2 action,** achievement, work, doing, creation, design, product, production, result.

handle *n.* **shaft,** grip, handgrip, hilt, haft, knob, stock.
▸ *v.* **1 touch,** feel, finger, hold, grasp, grip, pick up, caress, stroke, fondle, poke, maul, *inf.* paw. **2 cope with,** deal with, treat, manage, control. **3 be in charge of,** control, manage, administer, direct, guide, conduct, supervise, take care of. **4 drive,** steer, operate, maneuver. **5 deal with,** treat, discuss. **6 deal in,** traffic in, trade in, market, sell, stock, carry.

handsome *adj.* **1 good-looking,** attractive, *inf.* gorgeous, easy on the eyes, foxy, to die for. **2 good-looking,** attractive, personable, elegant, fine, well-formed, well-proportioned, stately, dignified. **3 generous,** magnanimous, liberal, lavish, bounteous, considerable, sizable, large, ample, abundant, plentiful. *Ant.* ugly; plain; meager.

handy *adj.* **1 at hand,** available, within reach, accessible, near, nearby, close, at one's fingertips, convenient, *inf.* on tap. **2 useful,** helpful, practicable, practical, serviceable, functional, expedient, easy-to-use, neat, convenient. **3 dexterous,** deft, nimble-fingered, adroit, adept, proficient, skillful, skilled, expert, clever/good with one's hands. *Ant.* inconvenient; useless; inept.

hang *v.* **1 hang down,** be suspended, dangle, swing, sway, be pendent, suspend, put up, put on a hook. **2 send to the gallows,** gibbet, execute, lynch, *inf.* string up. **3 stick on,** attach, fix, fasten on, append, paste, glue, cement. **4 decorate,** adorn, ornament, deck, drape, cover, furnish.

5 hover, float, be poised, flutter, flit, drift, remain static.

hang-up *n.* **1 preoccupation,** fixation, obsession, bee in one's bonnet, idée fixe, *inf.* issue, thing. **2 mental block,** psychological block, block, inhibition, difficulty, problem, *inf.* thing.

haphazard *adj.* **unplanned,** random, unsystematic, unorganized, unmethodical, orderless, aimless, indiscriminate, undirected, irregular, slapdash, thrown together, careless, casual, hit-or-miss. ***Ant.*** methodical; systematic.

hapless *adj.* **unlucky,** luckless, out of luck, unfortunate, ill-starred, forlorn, wretched, woebegone, unhappy, *inf.* down on one's luck.

happen *v.* **take place,** occur, come about, come to pass, present itself, arise, materialize, appear, come into being, chance, arrive, transpire, crop up, develop, supervene, eventuate, *inf.* come off.

happening *n.* **occurrence,** event, incident, occasion, affair, circumstance, action, case, phenomenon, eventuality, episode, experience, adventure, scene, proceedings, chance.

happiness *n.* **cheerfulness,** cheeriness, merriness, gaiety, good spirits, high spirits, lightheartedness, joy, joyfulness, joviality, glee, blitheness, carefreeness, enjoyment, gladness, delight, exuberance, elation, ecstasy, bliss, blissfulness, euphoria.

happy *adj.* **1 cheerful,** cheery, merry, gay, in good spirits, in high spirits, lighthearted, joyful, joyous, jovial, gleeful, buoyant, blithe, blithesome, carefree, untroubled, smiling, glad, delighted, exuberant, elated, ecstatic, blissful, euphoric, overjoyed, thrilled, in seventh heaven, floating/walking on air, *inf.* on cloud nine, on top of the world. **2 glad,** pleased, delighted, contented, satisfied, gratified, thrilled. **3 lucky,** fortunate, favorable, advantageous, beneficial, helpful, opportune, timely, convenient, propitious, auspicious. **4 apt,** appropriate, fitting, fit, good, right, proper, seemly. ***Ant.*** sad; displeased; unfortunate.

harangue *n.* **lecture,** tirade, diatribe, speech, talk, sermon, exhortation, declamation, oration, address, homily, *inf.* spiel.

harass *v.* **1 bother,** pester, annoy, exasperate, worry, fret, disturb, agitate, provoke, badger, hound, torment, plague, persecute, harry, tease, bait, nag, molest, bedevil, *inf.* hassle, give someone a hard time, drive someone up the wall. **2 harry,** attack repeatedly, raid, beleaguer, press hard, oppress.

harassed *adj.* **distraught,** under pressure, stressed, under stress, strained, worried, careworn, troubled, vexed, agitated, fretting, *inf.* hassled.

harbor *n.* **1 port,** anchorage, haven, marina. **2 place of safety,** refuge, shelter, haven, sanctuary, retreat, asylum, sanctum, covert.
▸ *v.* **1 give shelter to,** shelter, house, lodge, put up, take in, billet, provide refuge for, shield, protect, conceal, hide, secrete. **2 nurture,** maintain, hold on to, cherish, cling to, retain, entertain, brood over.

hard *adj.* **1 firm,** solid, solidified, compact, compacted, condensed, close-packed, compressed, dense, rigid, stiff, unyielding, resistant, unmalleable, inflexible, unpliable, tough, strong, stony, rocklike. **2 arduous,** strenuous, heavy, tiring, fatiguing, exhausting, backbreaking, laborious, rigorous, exacting, formidable, tough, difficult, uphill, toilsome, Herculean. **3 difficult,** complicated, complex, involved, intricate, puzzling, perplexing, baffling, knotty,

thorny, bewildering, enigmatic, insoluble, insolvable, unfathomable, incomprehensible. **4 harsh,** hard-hearted, severe, stern, cold, cold-hearted, unfeeling, unsympathetic, grim, ruthless, oppressive, tyrannical, pitiless, merciless, unrelenting, unsparing, lacking compassion, callous, cruel, vicious, implacable, obdurate, unyielding, unjust, unfair. **5 difficult,** grim, harsh, unpleasant, disagreeable, uncomfortable, intolerable, unendurable, unbearable, insupportable, distressing, painful, disastrous, calamitous. **6 forceful,** violent, heavy, strong, powerful, sharp, fierce, harsh. **7 hardworking,** energetic, industrious, diligent, assiduous, conscientious, sedulous, keen, enthusiastic, zealous, earnest, persevering, persistent, unflagging, untiring, indefatigable. **8 angry,** acrimonious, bitter, antagonistic, hostile, resentful, rancorous. **9 actual,** definite, undeniable, indisputable, verifiable, plain, cold, bare, bold, harsh, unvarnished, unembellished. **10 alcoholic,** strong, potent. **11 potent,** hard-core, addictive, habit-forming, harmful, noxious, injurious. ***Ant.*** soft; easy; gentle.

▸ *adv.* **1 strenuously,** energetically, powerfully, heavily, with all one's might, with might and main, heartily, vigorously, with vigor, forcefully, with force, forcibly, with great effort, fiercely, intensely. **2 energetically,** industriously, diligently, assiduously, conscientiously, enthusiastically, sedulously, with application, earnestly, with perseverance, persistently, indefatigably, *inf.* like a slave. **3 with difficulty,** with effort, laboriously, after a struggle, painfully. **4 badly,** intensely, violently, forcefully, harshly, distressingly, painfully, agonizingly. **5 heavily,** steadily, *inf.* cats and dogs, buckets. **6 keenly,** sharply, carefully, closely, painstakingly.

harden *v.* **1 become hard,** solidify, set, stiffen, bake, anneal, cake, freeze, congeal, clot, coagulate. **2 toughen,** deaden, numb, benumb. **3 make tough,** toughen, case-harden, make unfeeling, brutalize, make callous. **4 accustom,** habituate, acclimatize, inure. **5 strengthen,** fortify, reinforce, buttress, brace, gird.

hard-hitting *adj.* **tough,** uncompromising, unsparing, strongly worded, vigorous, pulling no punches, straight-talking, blunt, frank, critical.

hardly *adv.* **scarcely,** barely, only just, just, almost not, with difficulty, with effort.

hardship *n.* **adversity,** deprivation, privation, want, need, destitution, poverty, austerity, desolation, misfortune, distress, suffering, affliction, pain, misery, wretchedness, tribulation, trials, trials and tribulation, burdens, calamity, catastrophe, disaster, ruin, ruination, oppression, persecution, torment, torture, travail. ***Ant.*** prosperity; ease; comfort.

hardy *adj.* **1 healthy,** fit, strong, robust, sturdy, tough, rugged, vigorous, lusty, stalwart, hale and hearty, fit as a fiddle, in fine fettle, in good kilter, in good condition. **2 brave,** courageous, valiant, bold, valorous, intrepid, fearless, heroic, stouthearted, daring, plucky, mettlesome. ***Ant.*** delicate; weak; cowardly.

harm *n.* **1 hurt,** injury, pain, suffering, trauma, adversity, disservice, abuse, damage, mischief, detriment, defacement, defilement, impairment, destruction, loss, ruin, havoc. **2 badness,** evil, wrongdoing, wrong, wickedness, vice, iniquity,

sin, sinfulness, immorality, nefariousness. *Ant.* good; benefit.
▸ *v.* **hurt,** injure, wound, abuse, maltreat, ill-treat, ill-use, molest, do violence to, damage, do mischief to, deface, defile, impair, spoil, mar, blemish, destroy.

harmful *adj.* **1 hurtful,** injurious, wounding, abusive, detrimental, deleterious, disadvantageous, destructive, dangerous, pernicious, noxious, baneful, toxic. **2 bad,** evil, malign, wicked, corrupting, subversive. *Ant.* harmless; beneficial; good.

harmless *adj.* **1 innocuous,** innoxious, safe, nondangerous, nontoxic, nonirritant, mild.
2 innocuous, inoffensive, unoffending, innocent, blameless, gentle.

harmonious *adj.* **1 melodious,** tuneful, musical, harmonizing, sweet-sounding, mellifluous, dulcet, euphonious, symphonious, rhythmic, consonant. **2 peaceful,** peaceable, friendly, amicable, cordial, amiable, agreeable, congenial, united, in harmony, in rapport, in tune, attuned, in accord, compatible, sympathetic.
3 compatible, congruous, coordinated, concordant, well-matched, matching. *Ant.* discordant; hostile; incongruous.

harmonize *v.* **1 go/fit together,** be compatible, blend, mix well, be congruous, be consonant, be well-coordinated, match. **2 be in accord,** agree, be in assent, correspond, coincide, tally, be in unison, be congruent, be of one mind. **3 reconcile,** patch up, make peaceful, negotiate peace between, heal the breach, pour oil on troubled waters.

harmony *n.* **1 agreement,** assent, accord, accordance, concordance, concurrence, cooperation, unanimity, unity, unison, oneness, amity, amicability, goodwill, affinity, rapport, sympathy, like-mindedness, friendship, fellowship, comradeship, peace, peacefulness.
2 compatibility, congruity, consonance, concord, coordination, blending, balance, symmetry, suitability.
3 tunefulness, melodiousness, mellifluousness, euphony, euphoniousness. *Ant.* disagreement; incongruity; dissonance.

harrowing *adj.* **distressing,** agonizing, excruciating, traumatic, heartbreaking, heart-rending, painful, racking, afflicting, chilling, disturbing, vexing, alarming, perturbing, unnerving, horrifying, terrifying.

harsh *adj.* **1 grating,** jarring, grinding, rasping, strident, jangling, raucous, ear-piercing, discordant, dissonant, unharmonious, rough, coarse, guttural, hoarse, croaking, raucous, strident, gravelly, gruff. **2 gaudy,** garish, glaring, bold, loud, flashy, showy, crass, crude, vulgar. **3 grim,** severe, desolate, stark, austere, barren, rough, bleak, bitter, wild, inhospitable, comfortless, spartan. **4 severe,** hard, bitter, bitterly cold, freezing, arctic, Siberian. **5 abrupt,** brusque, blunt, curt, gruff, short, surly, concise, impolite, discourteous, uncivil, ungracious. **6 cruel,** brutal, savage, barbarous, hard-hearted, despotic, tyrannical, ruthless, uncompassionate, unfeeling, merciless, pitiless, relentless, unrelenting, inhuman. **7 stern,** severe, grim, stringent, austere, uncompromising, inflexible, punitive, draconian. *Ant.* mellifluous; soft; gentle; lenient.

harvest *n.* **1 reaping,** ingathering. **2 crop,** yield, vintage. **3 store,** supply, stock, stockpile, hoard, cache, accumulation. **4 product,** fruits, return, effect, result, consequence.
▶ *v.* **1 gather in,** gather, reap, glean, pick, pluck, collect, amass, accumulate, hoard, garner. **2 acquire,** gain, obtain, get, derive, procure, secure, net.

hassle *n.* **1 inconvenience,** trouble, bother, annoyance, nuisance, trials and tribulation, harassment, badgering, difficulty, problem, struggle. **2 fight,** quarrel, squabble, argument, disagreement, dispute, altercation, tussle.
▶ *v.* **annoy,** badger, harass, hound, pester, bother, trouble, worry, torment, plague, *inf.* give someone a hard time.

haste *n.* **1 speed,** swiftness, rapidity, rapidness, quickness, fastness, alacrity, promptness, dispatch, expeditiousness, expedition, celerity, fleetness, briskness, immediateness, urgency. **2 hastiness,** hurriedness, hurry, rushing, hustling, impetuosity, recklessness, rashness, foolhardiness, impulsiveness, heedlessness, carelessness. *Ant.* delay; care.

hasty *adj.* **1 swift,** rapid, quick, fast, speedy, hurried, hurrying, running, prompt, expeditious, fleet, brisk, urgent. **2 quick,** short, rapid, brief, rushed, short-lived, fleeting, transitory, cursory, perfunctory, superficial, slight. **3 hurried,** rushed, impetuous, reckless, rash, foolhardy, precipitate, impulsive, headlong, heedless, thoughtless, careless, ill-conceived. **4 hot-headed,** quick-tempered, irascible, irritable, impatient, fiery, excitable, volatile, choleric, snappish, snappy, brusque. *Ant.* slow; leisurely; cautious.

hatch *v.* **1 incubate,** brood, sit on, cover. **2 bring forth. 3 devise,** concoct, contrive, plan, scheme, design, invent, formulate, originate, conceive, dream up, think up, *inf.* cook up.

hate *v.* **1 loathe,** detest, abhor, dislike, abominate, despise, have an aversion to, feel hostile toward, be unable to abide/bear/stand, view with dislike, be sick of, be tired of, shudder at the thought of, be repelled by, recoil from. **2 be reluctant,** be loath, be unwilling, feel disinclined, be sorry, dislike, not have the heart. *Ant.* love; like; relish.

hateful *adj.* **loathsome,** detestable, abhorrent, abominable, despicable, odious, revolting, repugnant, repellent, disgusting, obnoxious, offensive, insufferable, horrible, unpleasant, nasty, disagreeable, foul, vile, heinous. *Ant.* admirable; lovable.

hatred *n.* **hate,** loathing, detestation, abhorrence, dislike, abomination, aversion, hostility, ill will, enmity, animosity, antagonism, antipathy, revulsion, repugnance, odium, rancor.

haughty *adj.* **proud,** arrogant, conceited, self-important, egotistical, vain, swellheaded, overweening, overbearing, presumptuous, supercilious, condescending, lofty, patronizing, snobbish, scornful, imperious, lordly, high-handed, *inf.* on one's high horse, snooty, high and mighty, stuck-up, hoity-toity, uppity. *Ant.* modest; humble.

haul *v.* **1 drag,** draw, pull, tug, heave, trail, lug, tow. **2 transport,** convey, move, carry, convoy, ship.

haunt *v.* **1 walk,** roam, visit, *inf.* spook. **2 frequent,** be a regular client of, visit regularly, spend all one's time in, *inf.* hang out in, hang around/about. **3 obsess,** prey on the mind of, prey on, torment, plague, beset, harry, disturb, trouble, worry, oppress, burden, weigh on, recur to, come back to, stay with.
▶ *n.* **stamping ground,** frequented place, favorite spot, resort, rendezvous, meeting place, *inf.* hangout.

have *v.* **1 own,** possess, keep, keep for one's use, use, hold, retain, occupy. **2 get,** be given, receive, accept, obtain, acquire, procure, secure, gain. **3 contain,** include, comprise, embrace, embody, incorporate. **4 experience,** undergo, go through, encounter, meet, find, be subjected to, submit to, suffer from, endure, tolerate, put up with, enjoy. **5 feel,** entertain, have/keep/bear in mind, harbor, foster, nurse, cherish. **6 show,** display, exhibit, demonstrate, manifest, express. **7 make,** cause to, require to, force to, coerce to, induce to, prevail upon to, talk into, persuade to. **8 ask to,** request that, bid to, tell to, order to, command to, direct to, enjoin to. **9 permit,** allow, put up with, tolerate, stand, brook, support, endure, abide. **10 give birth to,** bear, deliver, be delivered of, bring into the world, bring forth, beget. **11 fool,** trick, take in, dupe, outwit, deceive, cheat, swindle. **12 have sexual intercourse with,** have sex with, make love to/with, copulate with, *inf.* bed, lay.

haven *n.* **1 harbor,** port, anchorage, moorage, cove, bay. **2 refuge,** shelter, sanctuary, asylum, retreat, inner sanctum, sanctum sanctorum, covert.

havoc *n.* **1 devastation,** destruction, damage, ruination, ruin, rack and ruin, waste, wreckage, desolation, extermination, disaster, catastrophe, cataclysm. **2 chaos,** disorder, confusion, disruption, disorganization, mayhem, *inf.* shambles.

hazard *n.* **danger,** peril, risk, jeopardy, threat, menace.
  ▸ *v.* **1 venture,** put forward, proffer, offer, submit, advance, volunteer. **2 risk,** endanger, imperil, put in jeopardy.

hazardous *adj.* **1 dangerous,** danger-filled, risky, perilous, fraught with danger/risk/peril, precarious, unsafe, insecure, threatening, menacing, *inf.* dicey, hairy. **2 open to chance,** chancy, risky, uncertain, unpredictable, precarious, speculative. ***Ant.*** safe; sure.

hazy *adj.* **1 misty,** foggy, cloudy, smoggy, overcast. **2 vague,** indefinite, blurred, fuzzy, faint, confused, muddled, unclear, obscure, dim, indistinct, ill-defined. ***Ant.*** clear; distinct.

head *n.* **1 skull,** cranium, *inf.* pate, nut, noodle, noggin, bean. **2 mind,** intellect, intelligence, brain, brains, mentality, wit, wits, wisdom, sense, reasoning, rationality, understanding, aptitude, ability, capacity, flair, talent, faculty, *inf.* gray matter. **3 leader,** chief, commander, director, chairman, chair, chairperson, manager, superintendent, controller, administrator, supervisor, captain, principal, governor, president, premier, prime minister. **4 top,** command, control, controls, charge, leadership, directorship. **5 top,** summit, peak, crest, crown, tip, brow, apex, vertex. **6 front,** fore, forefront, van, vanguard. **7 climax,** culmination, crisis, critical point, turning point, crossroads. **8 froth,** foam, lather, suds. **9 headland,** promontory, point, cape. **10 heading,** category, class, classification. **11 toilet,** lavatory, bathroom, latrine, *inf.* john, can. ▸ *adj.* **chief,** leading, main, principal, first, prime, premier, foremost, topmost, supreme, cardinal.

headlong *adv.* **1 head first,** on one's head, head foremost, head on, diving, plunging. **2 hastily,** in haste, hurriedly, impetuously, impulsively, unrestrainedly, impatiently, without thinking, rashly, recklessly, wildly, prematurely, precipitately, carelessly, heedlessly.

headquarters *pl. n.* **HQ,** main office, head office, main branch, center of operations, home base, command post.

heal *v.* **1 cure,** make/get well, make/get better, remedy, treat, mend, restore, regenerate, be cured, mend, be on the mend, be restored, improve. **2 conciliate,** reconcile, patch up, settle, set right, put right, make good, harmonize. **3 alleviate,** appease, mitigate, ameliorate, assuage, allay, palliate, soften.

health *n.* **1 healthiness,** fitness, well-being, good condition, good trim, good shape, fine fettle, soundness, robustness, strength, vigor, salubrity. **2 state of health,** constitution, physical state, physical health, physical shape, condition, form, tone.

healthy *adj.* **1 in good health,** fit, physically fit, in good condition/ trim/shape, in fine fettle, in fine/top form, robust, strong, vigorous, hardy, flourishing, hale and hearty, hale, hearty, *inf.* in the pink. **2 health-giving,** salubrious, invigorating, bracing, stimulating, refreshing, tonic, healthful, good for one, nutritious, nourishing, wholesome, beneficial. *Ant.* unhealthy; ill.

heap *n.* **pile,** stack, mass, mound, mountain, stockpile, accumulation, collection, lot, assemblage, aggregation, agglomeration, conglomeration, hoard, store, stock, supply.

hear *v.* **1 catch,** take in, overhear,

inf. get. **2 be informed,** be told, be made aware, receive information, find out, discover, learn, gather, pick up, be given to understand, hear tell, get wind. **3 try,** judge, pass judgment on, adjudicate, examine, investigate, inquire into, consider.

hearing *n.* **1 inquiry,** trial, inquest, investigation, inquisition, review, examination interview, audience. **2 earshot,** hearing distance/range, reach, carrying range, range of one's voice, auditory range.

heart *n.* **1** *inf.* **ticker. 2 passion,** love, affection, emotions, feelings, tender feelings, tenderness, warm emotions, compassion, sympathy, empathy, humanity, fellow feeling, concern, pathos, goodwill, humanitarianism, benevolence, kindness, kindliness, brotherly love. **3 tender feelings,** tenderness, warm emotions, compassion, sympathy, empathy, responsiveness to others, humanity, fellow feeling, concern for others, pathos, goodwill, humanitarianism, benevolence, kindness, kindliness, brotherly love. **4 courage,** bravery, valor, intrepidity, fearlessness, heroism, stoutheartedness, boldness, pluck, mettle, backbone, nerve,

fortitude, purpose, resolution, determination, *inf.* guts, spunk, gumption. **5 center,** central part, core, nucleus, middle, kernel, essential part, hub, quintessence, essence, crux, marrow, pith, substance, sum and substance.

heartache *n.* **sorrow,** grief, sadness, anguish, pain, hurt, agony, suffering, misery, wretchedness, despair, desolation, despondency, woe, *lit.* dolor.

heartbreaking *adj.* **heart-rending,** sad, pitiful, poignant, tragic, painful, agonizing, distressing, affecting, grievous, bitter, cruel, harsh, harrowing, tear-jerking, excruciating.

hearten *v.* **cheer,** cheer up, raise the spirits of, invigorate, revitalize, energize, animate, revivify, exhilarate, uplift, elate, comfort, encourage, buoy up, pep up, *inf.* buck up, give a shot in the arm to. **Ant.** discourage; depress; dishearten.

heartfelt *adj.* **deeply felt,** deep, profound, wholehearted, sincere, honest, devout, genuine, unfeigned, earnest, ardent, fervent, passionate, kindly, warm, cordial, enthusiastic, eager.

heartless *adj.* **unfeeling,** unsympathetic, uncompassionate, unkind, uncaring, unmoved, untouched, cold, cold-hearted, cold-blooded, hard-hearted, cruel, harsh, stern, hard, brutal, merciless, pitiless, ruthless. *Ant.* compassionate; kind; merciful.

heat *n.* **1 hotness,** warmth, warmness, torridness, sultriness, torridness, torridity, swelter, heatwave, hot spell, *inf.* dog days. **2 high temperature,** fever, feverishness, febrility. **3 warmth,** passion, vehemence, intensity, ardor, fervor, fervency, fervidness, zeal, eagerness, enthusiasm, animation, earnestness, excitement, agitation. *Ant.* cold; apathy.

heated *adj.* **1 passionate,** vehement, fierce, angry, furious, stormy, tempestuous, frenzied, raging, intense, impassioned, violent. **2 excited,** roused, animated, inflamed, angry, furious, enraged.

heathen *n.* **1 unbeliever,** infidel, pagan, idolater/idolatress, atheist, disbeliever, agnostic, skeptic, heretic. **2 barbarian,** savage.
▸ *adj.* **1 heathenish,** infidel, pagan, godless, irreligious, idolatrous, atheistic, agnostic, heretical. **2 barbarian,** barbarous, savage, uncivilized, brutish.

heave *v.* **1 lift,** haul, pull, tug, raise, hoist, upheave. **2 throw,** cast, toss, fling, hurl, let fly, pitch, send, *inf.* sling, chuck. **3 give,**

utter, let out, pant, gasp, blow, puff, breathe, sigh, sob. **4 vomit,** be sick, spew, retch, gag, *inf.* throw up.

heaven *n.* **1 Kingdom of God,** paradise, next life, life to come, next world, the hereafter, Zion, nirvana, Valhalla, Elysium, Elysian Fields, empyrean, happy hunting ground. **2 ecstasy,** bliss, sheer bliss, rapture, supreme happiness, supreme joy, perfect contentment, seventh heaven, paradise, Eden, Utopia, dreamland. **3 sky,** skies, firmament, ether, empyrean, aerosphere, vault of heaven, *inf.* (wild) blue yonder.

heavenly *adj.* **1 cosmic,** extraterrestrial, unearthly, extramundane, not of this world, otherworldly, celestial, paradisiacal, empyrean, empyreal, Elysian. **2 celestial,** divine, angelic, seraphic, cherubic, blessed, blest, beatific, beatified, holy, godlike, immortal, superhuman, paradisiacal. **3 delightful,** pleasurable, enjoyable, marvelous, gratifying, wonderful, blissful, rapturous, sublime, *inf.* glorious, divine. **4 beautiful,** exquisite, perfect, superb, ravishing, alluring, enchanting, entrancing, ideal, *inf.* divine. *Ant.* hellish; dreadful; ugly.

heavy *adj.* **1 weighty,** bulky, hefty, big, large, substantial, massive, enormous, mighty, colossal, ponderous, unwieldy, cumbersome, burdensome, awkward, unmanageable. **2 onerous,** burdensome, difficult, oppressive, unbearable, intolerable, hard, difficult, arduous, laborious, demanding, exacting, irksome, troublesome, trying. **3 hard,** forceful, strong, severe, grievous, harsh, intense, sharp, stinging, penetrating, overwhelming. **4 large,** bulky, hulking, stout, overweight, fat, obese, corpulent, portly, tubby, paunchy, lumbering. **5 dense,** thick, solid. **6 muddy,** sticky, considerable, boggy, clayey, clogged. **7 large,** considerable, abundant, copious, profuse, superabundant. **8 severe,** intense, serious, grave. **9 serious,** grave, deep, somber, profound. **10 difficult,** dull, tedious, boring, uninteresting, dry, wearisome, dry as dust. **11 sleepy,** drowsy, sluggish, inactive, indolent, inept, idle, apathetic, listless, torpid. **12 sad,** sorrowful, downcast, dejected, disconsolate, disheartened, despondent, downhearted, depressed, crestfallen, disappointed, grieving, gloomy, melancholy.

13 burdened, encumbered, weighted down, laden, loaded, oppressed. **14 rough,** wild, stormy, tempestuous, turbulent, squally, boisterous, violent. **15 filling,** indigestible, dense, sickening. *Ant.* light; slight; happy.

heavy-handed *adj.* **1 clumsy,** awkward, maladroit, bungling, blundering, unhandy, inept, unskillful, inexpert, graceless, ungraceful, like a bull in a china shop, *inf.* ham-handed, ham-fisted. **2 insensitive,** tactless, thoughtless, inept. **3 harsh,** hard, stern, severe, oppressive, domineering, overbearing, tyrannical, despotic, autocratic, ruthless, merciless.

hectic *adj.* **very busy,** very active, frantic, frenetic, frenzied, bustling, flustering, flurried, fast and furious, turbulent, tumultuous, confused, exciting, excited, wild. *Ant.* quiet; calm; leisurely.

hedge *n.* **1 row of bushes/shrubs,** hedgerow, natural fence, barrier, screen, protection, windbreak. **2 safeguard,** guard, protection, shield, cover, insurance.
▸ *v.* **1 equivocate,** prevaricate, be vague/ambivalent/noncommittal, dodge the question/issue, sidestep the issue, hem and haw, beat

around the bush, pussyfoot around, temporize, quibble, *inf.* duck the question. **2 safeguard,** guard, protect, cover, shield, insure.

heed *n.* **heedfulness,** attention, attentiveness, notice, note, regard, mindfulness, mind, respect, consideration, thought, care, caution, watchfulness, wariness, chariness.
▸ *v.* **pay heed to,** be heedful of, pay attention to, attend to, take notice of, take note of, notice, note, bear in mind, be mindful of, mind, mark, consider, take into account/consideration, be guided by, follow, obey, adhere to, observe, take to heart, be on guard for, be alert to, be cautious of, watch out for.

heedful *adj.* **attentive,** careful, mindful, cautious, prudent, circumspect, wary, chary, observant, watchful, vigilant, alert, on guard, on the alert, on one's toes, on the qui vive.

heedless *adj.* **unheeding,** inattentive, careless, incautious, unmindful, disregardful, regardless, unnoticing, unthinking, thoughtless, improvident, unwary, oblivious, unobservant, unwatchful, unvigilant, negligent, neglectful, rash, reckless, foolhardy,

precipitate. *Ant.* heedful; attentive; mindful.

heft *n.* heaviness, weight, mass; *inf.* meat.
▸ *v.* **lift,** lift up, raise, raise up, hoist, hike up, heave, throw up, boost, boost up.

hefty *adj.* **1 heavy,** bulky, hulking, big, large, stout, massive, huge, muscular, brawny, strapping, solidly built, powerfully built, sturdy, rugged, stalwart, beefy. **2 hard,** forceful, heavy, powerful, vigorous, mighty. **3 heavy,** weighty, big, large, massive, tremendous, immense, bulky, awkward, unwieldy, cumbersome, ponderous. **4 substantial,** high, sizable, expensive, huge, colossal. *Ant.* slight; light; small.

height *n.* **1 highness,** altitude, loftiness, elevation. **2 tallness,** highness, stature. **3 top,** mountaintop, hilltop, summit, crest, crown, pinnacle, peak, apex, vertex, apogee. **4 culmination,** crowning point, high point, peak, zenith, climax, consummation, perfection, apex. **5 utmost degree,** uttermost, ultimate, acme, ne plus ultra, very limit, limit, extremity, maximum, ceiling.

heighten *v.* **1 make higher,** raise, lift, elevate. **2 magnify,** ennoble, exalt, enhance. **3 make greater,** intensify, raise, increase, add to, augment, build up, boost, strengthen, amplify, magnify, aggravate, enhance, improve.

heinous *adj.* **atrocious,** abominable, abhorrent, odious, detestable, loathsome, hateful, execrable, wicked, monstrous, horrible, ghastly, shocking, flagrant, contemptible, reprehensible, despicable.

hellish *adj.* **1 diabolical,** demonic, demoniac, demoniacal, devilish, fiendish, satanic, infernal. **2 brutal,** brutish, barbarous, barbaric, savage, murderous, bloodthirsty, cruel, wicked, inhuman, ferocious, vicious, ruthless, relentless, detestable, abominable, accursed, execrable, nefarious. **3 unpleasant,** nasty, disagreeable, *inf.* horrible, horrid, awful.

help *v.* **1 assist,** aid, lend a helping hand to, lend a hand to, guide, be of service to, be useful to, succor, befriend, contribute to, support, back, promote, boost, give a boost to, uphold. **2 soothe,** relieve, ameliorate, alleviate, mitigate, assuage, remedy, cure, heal, improve, ease, facilitate, restore. **3 serve,** be of assistance/help to, give help to.
 ▸ *n.* **1 assistance,** aid, helping hand, service, use, guidance, benefit, advantage, avail, support, backing, succor. **2 relief,** amelioration, alleviation, mitigation, assuagement, remedy, cure, healing, improvement, ease, restorative, corrective, balm, salve. **3 helper,** assistant, employee, worker, hired help, maid, servant, staff.

helper *n.* **1 assistant,** worker, volunteer. **2 assistant,** subsidiary, aide, adjutant, deputy, second, second-in-command, auxiliary, right-hand man/woman, henchman, girl/man Friday, *inf.* sidekick. **3 colleague,** associate, co-worker, helpmate, partner, ally, collaborator.

helpful *adj.* **1 useful,** of use, of service, beneficial, advantageous, valuable, profitable, instrumental, constructive, practical, productive. **2 supportive,** friendly, kind, obliging, accommodating, cooperative, sympathetic, considerate, caring, neighborly, charitable, benevolent. *Ant.* useless; futile.

helping *n.* **serving,** portion, ration, piece, plateful, bowlful, spoonful.

helpless *adj.* **1 weak,** feeble, disabled, impotent, incapable, infirm, debilitated, powerless, dependent, unfit, invalid, bedridden, paralyzed, *inf.* laid-up. **2 defenseless,** unprotected, vulnerable, exposed, abandoned, forlorn, destitute, desolate. *Ant.* fit; capable.

hem *n.* **border,** edge, edging, trim, trimming, fringe, frill, flounce, valance.

▸ *v.* **1 put a hem on,** bind, edge, trim, fringe. **2 border,** edge, skirt, surround, encircle, circle, enclose, encompass.

herd *n.* **1 drove,** collection, assemblage, flock, pack, cluster. **2 shepherd,** cowherd, cattle-man, cowman, herdsman, herder, drover. **3 crowd,** horde, multitude, mob, mass, host, throng, swarm, press. **4 masses,** mob, populace, rabble, riff-raff, hoi polloi, peasants, *inf.* great unwashed.

▸ *v.* **1 drive,** round up, shepherd, guide, lead, force, urge, goad. **2 assemble,** gather, collect, congregate, flock, rally, muster, huddle, get together. **3 look after,** take care of, watch, stand guard over, guard, tend.

hereditary *adj.* **1 genetic,** congenital, innate, inborn, inherent, inbred, family, transmissible, transferable. **2 inherited,** handed down, obtained by inheritance, bequeathed, willed, transferred, transmitted, family, ancestral.

heresy *n.* **apostasy,** dissent, dissension, dissidence, unbelief, skepticism, agnosticism, atheism, nonconformity, unorthodoxy, separatism, sectarianism, freethinking, heterodoxy, revisionism, idolatry, paganism.

heretic *n.* **apostate,** dissenter, dissident, unbeliever, skeptic, agnostic, atheist, nonconformist, separatist, sectarian, freethinker, renegade, revisionist, idolater, pagan, heathen.

heretical *adj.* **dissident,** skeptical, agnostic, atheistical, nonconformist, separatist, sectarian, freethinking, heterodox, unorthodox, renegade, revisionist, idolatrous, pagan.

heritage *n.* **1 history,** tradition, background. **2 ancestry,** lineage, descent, extraction, family, dynasty, bloodline, heredity, birth. **3 inheritance,** legacy, bequest, endowment, estate, patrimony, portion, birthright, lot.

hermit *n.* **recluse,** solitary, anchorite/anchoress, eremite, ascetic.

heroic *adj.* **1 brave,** courageous, valiant, valorous, intrepid, fearless, gallant, stouthearted, lionhearted, bold, daring, undaunted, dauntless, doughty, manly, virile, chivalrous. **2 classic,** classical, Homeric, mythological, legendary, fabulous.

3 epic, epical, Homeric, grandiloquent, high-flown, high-sounding, extravagant, grandiose, bombastic, rhetorical, pretentious, elevated. *Ant.* cowardly; timid; simple.

heroism *n.* **bravery,** courage, courageousness, valor, valiance, intrepidity, fearlessness, gallantry, stoutheartedness, lionheartedness, boldness, daring, dauntlessness, doughtiness, manliness, virility, mettle, spirit, fortitude, chivalry.

hesitant *adj.* **1 hesitating,** uncertain, unsure, doubtful, dubious, skeptical, irresolute, indecisive, vacillating, wavering, oscillating, shilly-shallying, hanging back, stalling, delaying, disinclined, unwilling, halfhearted, lacking confidence, diffident, timid, shy. **2 reluctant,** unwilling, disinclined, diffident, having scruples/misgivings/qualms. *Ant.* determined; firm; confident.

hesitate *v.* **1 pause,** delay, hang back, wait, be uncertain, be unsure, be doubtful, be indecisive, vacillate, oscillate, waver, shilly-shally, dally, stall, temporize, *inf.* dilly-dally. **2 be reluctant,** be unwilling, be disinclined, shrink (from), hang back (from), think twice (about), balk (at), have

misgivings/qualms (about), be diffident (about). **3 stammer,** stumble, stutter, falter, hem and haw, fumble for words, be halting, halt.

hew *v.* **carve,** sculpt, sculpture, shape, fashion, form, model, whittle, chip, chisel, rough-hew.

hidden *adj.* **1 concealed,** unrevealed, secret, unseen, out of sight, not visible, not in view, covered, masked, shrouded. **2 secret,** concealed, obscure, indistinct, indefinite, unclear, vague, cryptic, mysterious, covert, under wraps, abstruse, arcane, recondite, clandestine, ulterior, unfathomable, inexplicable, occult, mystical.

hide *v.* **1 go into hiding,** conceal oneself, take cover, lie low, keep out of sight, secrete oneself, go underground, cover one's tracks, secrete, conceal, store away, stow away, stash, lock up, *inf.* hole up. **2 secrete,** conceal, put in a hiding place, store away, stow away, stash, lock up. **3 obscure,** cloud, darken, block, eclipse, obstruct. **4 keep secret,** conceal, keep dark, withhold, suppress, hush up, mask, veil, shroud, camouflage, disguise, *inf.* keep mum, keep under one's hat. *Ant.* reveal; disclose.

▸ *n.* **skin,** pelt, coat, fur, fleece.

hideous *adj.* **1 ugly,** unsightly, grotesque, monstrous, repulsive, repellent, revolting, gruesome, disgusting, grim, ghastly, macabre. **2 horrible,** horrific, horrendous, horrifying, frightful, shocking, dreadful, outrageous, monstrous, appalling, terrible, terrifying, heinous, abominable, foul, vile, odious, loathsome, contemptible, execrable. *Ant.* beautiful; pleasant.

hierarchy *n.* **ranking,** grading, social order, class system, pecking order.

high *adj.* **1 tall,** lofty, elevated, soaring, towering, steep. **2 high-ranking,** leading, top, ruling, powerful, important, principal, chief, main, prominent, eminent, influential, distinguished, notable, exalted, illustrious. **3 high-minded,** noble, virtuous, moral, lofty. **4 intense,** extreme, strong, forceful, vigorous, powerful, potent, sharp, violent. **5 expensive,** dear, top, excessive, stiff, inflated, exorbitant, extortionate, high-priced, costly, *inf.* steep. **6 good,** favorable, approving, admiring, flattering. **7 overexcited,** excited, boisterous, in high spirits, high-spirited, ebullient, bouncy, elated, ecstatic, euphoric, exhilarated, joyful, merry, happy, cheerful, jolly, *inf.*

high as a kite. **8 drugged,** intoxicated, inebriated, delirious, hallucinating, *inf.* stoned, turned on, tripping, hyped up, freaked out, spaced out. **9 high-pitched,** acute, high-frequency, soprano, treble, piping, shrill, sharp-toned, piercing, penetrating. *Ant.* low; lowly; deep.
▸ *adv.* **far up,** way up, at a great height, at altitude, aloft.

highbrow *n.* **intellectual,** scholar, savant, mastermind, genius, *inf.* egghead, brain, bookworm.
▸ *adj.* **intellectual,** scholarly, bookish, cultured, cultivated, educated, sophisticated, *inf.* brainy.

high-handed *adj.* **arbitrary,** autocratic, dictatorial, despotic, tyrannical, domineering, oppressive, peremptory, imperious, overbearing, arrogant, haughty, lordly, *inf.* bossy.

hike *v.* **1 walk,** march, tramp, trek, trudge, plod, ramble, wander, backpack, *inf.* hoof it. **2 pull up,** lift. **3 increase,** raise. **4 snap.**
▸ *n.* **walk,** march, tramp, trek, ramble, trudge.

hill *n.* **1 elevation,** heights, high land, hillock, hilltop, knoll, hummock, mound, rising ground, tor, mount, ridge. **2 slope,** rise, incline, gradient, acclivity.

3 mountain, heap, pile, mound, stack, drift.

hinder *v.* **hamper,** impede, hold back, interfere with, delay, hold up, slow down, retard, obstruct, inhibit, handicap, hamstring, block, interrupt, check, trammel, forestall, curb, balk, thwart, frustrate, foil, baffle, stymie, stop, bring to a halt, arrest, abort, defer, prevent, debar. *Ant.* aid; facilitate; expedite.

hindrance *n.* **impediment,** obstacle, interference, obstruction, handicap, block, restraint, interruption, check, bar, barrier, drawback, snag, difficulty, stumbling block, encumbrance, curb, stoppage, trammel, deterrent, prevention, debarment. *Ant.* aid; help; advantage.

hint *n.* **1 inkling,** clue, suggestion, innuendo, tip-off, insinuation, implication, indication, mention, allusion, intimation, whisper, a word to the wise, tip, pointer, advice, help, suggestion, *inf.* wrinkle. **2 suspicion,** suggestion, trace, touch, dash, soupçon, speck, sprinkling, tinge, whiff, breath, taste, scent.
 ▶ *v.* **give a clue,** suggest, give someone a tip-off, insinuate, imply, indicate, mention, allude to the fact, intimate, signal.

hire *v.* **appoint,** sign on, take on, engage, employ, secure the services of, enlist.

historic *adj.* **famous,** famed, notable, celebrated, renowned, momentous, significant, important, consequential, red-letter, memorable, remarkable, outstanding, extraordinary.

historical *adj.* **1 factual,** recorded, documented, chronicled, archival, authentic, actual, attested, verified, confirmed. **2 old,** past, former, prior, bygone, ancient, *lit.* of yore.

history *n.* **1 annals,** chronicles, records, public records, account, study, story, tale, saga, narrative, recital, reports, memoirs, biography, autobiography. **2 life story,** background, antecedents, experiences, adventures, fortunes. **3 the past,** former times, bygone days, yesterday, the old days, the good old days, days of old, time gone by, antiquity, *lit.* days of yore, olden days/times, yesteryear.

hit *v.* **1 strike,** slap, smack, buffet, punch, box, cuff, beat, thump, batter, pound, pummel, thrash, hammer, bang, knock, swat, *inf.* whack, wallop, bash, belt, clout, clip, clobber, sock, swipe. **2 run into,** bang into, smash into, crash into, knock into, bump into,

collide with, meet head-on.
3 affect, have an effect on, make an impression on, influence, make an impact on, leave a mark on, impinge on, move, touch, overwhelm, devastate, damage, hurt. **4 achieve,** accomplish, reach, attain, arrive at, gain, secure, touch, strike.
▶ *n.* **1 blow,** slap, smack, punch, beating, thump, thumping, battering, attack, onset, *inf.* whack, wallop, bashing, belting, clout, clobbering, swipe. **2 winner,** success.

hoard *n.* **store,** stockpile, supply, reserve, reservoir, fund, cache, accumulation, heap, pile, mass, aggregation, conglomeration, treasure house, treasure trove, *inf.* stash.
▶ *v.* **store,** store up, stock up, stockpile, put by, put away, lay by, lay in, set aside, pile up, stack up, stow away, husband, save, buy up, accumulate, amass, heap up, collect, gather, garner, squirrel away, *inf.* stash away.

hoarse *adj.* **croaking,** croaky, throaty, harsh, rough, gruff, husky, gravelly, grating, rasping, guttural, raucous, discordant, cracked. *Ant.* mellow; smooth; soft.

hoax *n.* **practical joke,** joke, jest, prank, trick, ruse, deception, fraud, imposture, cheat, swindle, *inf.* con, fast one, spoof, scam.
▶ *v.* **play a practical joke on,** play a joke/jest on, play a prank on, trick, fool, deceive, bluff, hoodwink, delude, dupe, take in, cheat, swindle, defraud, pull the wool over someone's eyes, gull, *inf.* con, pull a fast one on, take someone for a ride, put one over on someone, spoof, *lit.* cozen.

hobble *v.* **walk with difficulty,** limp, walk with a limp, walk lamely, walk haltingly, falter, move unsteadily, shuffle, totter, stagger, reel.

hold *v.* **1 clasp,** clutch, grasp, grip, seize, clench, cling to, *lit.* cleave to. **2 embrace,** hug, enfold, clasp, cradle, fondle. **3 have,** possess, own, retain, keep. **4 cherish,** harbor, treasure, retain. **5 bear,** carry, take, support, hold up, keep up, sustain, prop up, buttress, brace, suspend. **6 detain,** confine, hold in custody, impound, constrain, keep under constraint, lock up, imprison, put behind bars, incarcerate. **7 hold back,** restrain, impede, check, bar, curb, stop, retard, delay, prevent. **8 keep,** maintain, occupy, engage, involve, absorb, engross, immerse, monopolize, arrest, catch, spellbind, fascinate, rivet. **9 be in,** occupy, fill, maintain, continue in, enjoy, boast. **10 contain,** have a capacity for, accommodate, take, comprise. **11 maintain,** think, believe, consider, regard, deem, judge, assume, presume, reckon, suppose, esteem. **12 go on,** carry on, remain, continue, stay, persist, last, endure, keep up, persevere. **13 stand,** apply, be in force, be in operation, operate, remain valid, remain, exist, be the case. **14 make,** think, consider, regard as, view, treat as. **15 call,** convene, assemble, conduct, run, preside over, officiate at. *Ant.* give up (see give); hand over (see hand); release.

▸ *n.* **1 grasp,** grip, clutch, clasp. **2 grip,** power, control, dominion, authority, ascendancy. **3 influence,** mastery, dominance, sway, *inf.* pull, clout. **4 pause,** delay, postponement, deferment.

holder *n.* **1 owner,** possessor, bearer, proprietor, keeper, custodian, purchaser, incumbent, occupant. **2 container,** case, casing, receptacle, stand, cover, covering, housing, sheath.

hole *n.* **1 opening,** aperture, orifice, gap, space, breach, break, fissure, crack, rift, puncture, perforation, cut, incision, split, gash, rent, slit, vent, notch. **2 excavation,** pit, crater, shaft, mine, dugout, cave, cavern, pothole, cavity, chamber, hollow, scoop, pocket, depression, dent, dint, dip. **3 burrow,** lair, den, covert, nest, retreat, shelter, recess. **4 slum,** hovel, *inf.* dump, dive, joint. **5 dungeon,** prison, cell. **6 flaw,** fault, defect, loophole, inconsistency, discrepancy, error, fallacy. **7 predicament,** mess, plight, difficulty, trouble, corner, tight corner, spot, tight spot, quandary, dilemma, muddle, tangle, imbroglio, *inf.* fix, jam, scrape, pickle, hot water.

▸ *v.* **make a hole in,** puncture, perforate, pierce, spike, stab, lacerate, gash, split, rent.

holiness *n.* **sanctity,** sanctitude, saintliness, sacredness, divineness, divinity, godliness, blessedness, spirituality, religiousness, piety, righteousness, goodness, virtue, virtuousness, purity.

holocaust *n.* **fire,** inferno, conflagration, destruction, devastation, demolition, ravaging, annihilation, massacre, mass murder, carnage, slaughter, butchery, extermination, genocide, ethnic cleansing.

holy *adj.* **1 God-fearing,** godly, pious, pietistic, devout, spiritual, religious, righteous, good, virtuous, moral, saintly, saintlike, sinless. **2 blessed,** blest, sanctified, consecrated, hallowed, sacred, sacrosanct, dedicated, venerated, divine, religious. *Ant.* sacrilegious; impious.

home *n.* **1 house,** abode, domicile, residence, dwelling, dwelling place, habitation. **2 home town,** birthplace, homeland, native land, fatherland, motherland, mother country, country of origin. **3 family,** family background, family circle, household. **4 house,** apartment, condominium, bungalow, cottage, *inf.* condo, digs, pad. **5 residential home,** institution, shelter, refuge, hostel, hospice, retirement home, nursing home, rest home, children's home, *inf.* old folk's home. **6 abode,** habitat, environment, range, stamping ground, haunt, domain.

▸ *adj.* **1 domestic,** internal, interior, local, national, native. **2 homegrown,** homemade, homespun.

homeless *adj.* **down-and-out,** destitute, derelict, dispossessed, (out) on the streets, without a roof over one's head, vagrant, evicted.

homely *adj.* **1 plain,** plain-featured, plain-looking, unattractive, ugly, *inf.* not much to look at, short on looks. **2 homelike,** comfortable, cozy, snug, welcoming, informal, relaxed. **3 plain,** simple, modest, unsophisticated, natural, everyday, ordinary, unaffected, unassuming, unpretentious. *Ant.* elegant; grand; elaborate; beautiful.

homicide *n.* **1 murder,** manslaughter, killing, slaying, slaughter, assassination, patricide, matricide, fratricide, infanticide. **2 murderer,** killer, slayer, assassin, patricide, matricide, fratricide, infanticide, *inf.* hit man.

homily *n.* **sermon,** preaching, lecture, discourse, lesson, talk, speech, address, oration.

homosexual *adj.* **gay,** homoerotic, homophile, lesbian, *inf. derog.* butch, queer.

▸ *n.* **gay,** homophile, lesbian, *inf. derog.* queer, queen, faggot, fag, butch, dyke.

honest *adj.* **1 upright,** honorable, moral, ethical, principled, righteous, right-minded, virtuous, good, worthy, decent, law-abiding, high-minded, upstanding, just, fair, incorruptible, truthful, true, veracious, trustworthy, trusty, reliable, conscientious, scrupulous, reputable, dependable, loyal, faithful. **2 truthful,** sincere, candid, frank, direct, forthright, straightforward, open, genuine, plain-speaking, matter-of-fact, outspoken, blunt, undisguised, unfeigned, unequivocal. **3 real,** true, genuine, authentic, actual, aboveboard, bona fide, proper, straight, fair and square, *inf.* on the level, honest-to-goodness. **4 fair,** just, equitable, evenhanded, impartial, objective, balanced, unprejudiced, disinterested, unbiased. *Ant.* dishonest; insincere; unfair.

honestly *adv.* **1 fairly,** by fair means, by just means, lawfully, legally, legitimately, honorably, decently, ethically, morally, without corruption, *inf.* on the level. **2 to be honest,** truthfully, speaking frankly, in all sincerity, candidly, frankly, openly, plainly, in plain language, to someone's face, straight out, *inf.* straight up, Scouts' honor.

honor *n.* **1 honesty,** uprightness, integrity, ethics, morals, high principles, righteousness, rectitude, virtue, goodness, decency, probity, worthiness, worth, fairness, justness, justice, truthfulness, trustworthiness, reliability, dependability, faithfulness, fidelity. **2 fame,** renown, glory, prestige, illustriousness, noble reputation, esteem, distinction, notability, credit. **3 reputation,** good name, name. **4 chastity,** virginity, virtue, purity, innocence, modesty.

5 acclaim, acclamation, applause, accolades, tributes, homage, praise, compliments, lauding, eulogy, paeans, adoration, reverence, veneration, adulation, exaltation, glorification. **6 privilege,** source of pleasure/ pride/satisfaction, pleasure, joy. *Ant.* dishonor; disgrace; condemnation.

▸ *v.* **1 hold in honor,** have a high regard for, hold in esteem, esteem, respect, admire, defer to, reverence, revere, venerate, worship, idolize, value, prize. **2 acclaim,** applaud, give accolades to, pay homage to, pay tribute to, lionize, praise, cheer, compliment, laud, eulogize. **3 fulfill,** discharge, carry out, observe, keep, be true to, be faithful to, live up to. **4 cash,** pay out money for, clear, accept, take, pass.

honorable *adj.* **1 honest,** upright, ethical, moral, principled, high-principled, upstanding, righteous, right-minded, virtuous, good, decent, worthy, fair, just, true, truthful, trustworthy, trusty, reliable, dependable, faithful. **2 famous,** renowned, glorious, prestigious, distinguished, esteemed, notable, noted, great, eminent, noble, illustrious, creditable. **3 worthy,** respected, respectable, reputable, decent, venerable.

honorary *adj.* **nominal,** in name/ title only, titular, unofficial, ex officio, complimentary, unpaid.

hook *n.* **1 peg. 2 hook and eye,** fastener, catch, clasp, clip, link. **3 crook,** angle, loop, curve, bend, bow, arc, dogleg, horseshoe bend, oxbow, hairpin turn.
▸ *v.* **1 fasten,** secure, fix, close the clasp. **2 snare,** ensnare, trap, entrap.

hooligan *n.* **ruffian,** thug, rowdy, delinquent, vandal, mugger, hoodlum, *inf.* tough, hood.

hoop *n.* **ring,** band, circle, circlet, loop, wheel, girdle.

hope *n.* **hopefulness,** expectation, expectancy, anticipation, desire, longing, wish, wishing, craving, yearning, aspiration, ambition, dream, belief, assurance, assumption, confidence, conviction, faith, trust, optimism. *Ant.* despair; pessimism.
▸ *v.* **be hopeful of,** expect, anticipate, look forward to, await, contemplate, foresee, desire, long, wish, crave, yearn, aspire, be ambitious, dream, believe, feel assured, assume, have confidence, be convinced, rely on, count on, trust in.

hopeful *adj.* **1 full of hope,** expectant, anticipating, anticipative, looking forward to, optimistic, confident, assured, buoyant, sanguine. **2 promising,** encouraging, heartening, gladdening, optimistic, reassuring, auspicious, favorable, propitious, cheerful, bright, pleasant, rosy. *Ant.* hopeless; pessimistic; discouraging.

hopefully *adv.* **1 with hope,** expectantly, with anticipation, optimistically, confidently, with assurance, buoyantly, sanguinely. **2 it is to be hoped that,** with luck, all going well, if all goes well, if everything turns out all right, probably, conceivably, feasibly.

hopeless *adj.* **1 without hope,** despairing, in despair, desperate, pessimistic, defeatist, dejected, downhearted, despondent, demoralized, disconsolate, downcast, wretched, woebegone, forlorn, suicidal. **2 beyond hope,** despaired of, lost, beyond remedy, irremediable, beyond recovery, past cure, incurable, beyond repair, irreparable, irreversible, serious, grave, fatal, deadly. **3 impossible,** impracticable, futile, useless, vain, pointless, worthless, forlorn, no-win, unattainable, unachievable. **4 poor,** incompetent, ineffective, ineffectual, inadequate, inferior, *inf.* no good, useless, worthless.

Ant. hopeful; optimistic; accomplished.

horde *n.* **crowd,** mob, throng, mass, multitude, host, army, pack, gang, troop, drove, crew, band, flock, swarm, gathering, assemblage.

horrible *adj.* **1 dreadful,** awful, horrid, terrible, horrifying, terrifying, frightful, fearful, horrendous, shocking, appalling, hideous, grim, ghastly, harrowing, gruesome, disgusting, revolting, repulsive, loathsome, abhorrent, detestable, hateful, abominable. **2 nasty,** disagreeable, unpleasant, mean, unkind, obnoxious, odious, *inf.* horrid, awful, dreadful, terrible, beastly, ghastly, frightful, fearful, horrendous, shocking, appalling, hideous, revolting, abominable. ***Ant.*** pleasant; agreeable.

horrify *v.* **1 terrify,** terrorize, intimidate, frighten, frighten out of one's wits, alarm, scare, scare to death, startle, panic, throw into a panic, make someone's blood run cold, *inf.* make someone's hair stand on end, make someone's hair curl, scare stiff, scare the living daylights out of. **2 shock,** appall, outrage, scandalize, disgust, revolt, repel, nauseate, sicken, offend, dismay, *inf.* turn off.

horror *n.* **1 terror,** fear, fear and trembling, fearfulness, fright, alarm, dread, awe, panic, trepidation, apprehensiveness, uneasiness, nervousness, dismay, consternation. **2 abhorrence,** abomination, loathing, hate, detestation, repulsion, revulsion, disgust, distaste, aversion, hostility, antipathy, animosity.

horse *n.* **mount,** steed, pony, racehorse, draft horse, packhorse, bay, sorrel, pinto, piebald, Arabian, Clydesdale, palomino, foal, colt, stallion, mare, *inf.* nag, dobbin, filly.

horseplay *n.* **clowning,** fooling, fooling around, tomfoolery, buffoonery, pranks, practical jokes, antics, capers, high jinks, rough-and-tumble, romping, *inf.* roughhousing, shenanigans, monkey business.

hospitable *adj.* **welcoming,** sociable, convivial, generous, liberal, bountiful, openhanded, congenial, friendly, neighborly, warm, warmhearted, cordial, kind, kindly, kindhearted, amicable, well-disposed, amenable, helpful. ***Ant.*** inhospitable; unfriendly.

hospital *n.* **medical center,** clinic, infirmary, sanatorium, asylum.

host[1] *n.* **1 proprietor,** proprietress, landlord, landlady, manager,

innkeeper, hotelkeeper, hotelier.
2 party-giver, entertainer.
3 presenter, master of
ceremonies, MC, anchorman,
anchorwoman, *inf.* emcee. **Ant.**
guest; attendee.
▸ *v.* **1 be the host/hostess of,** give.
2 present, introduce; *inf.* emcee.
host[2] *n.* **multitude,** crowd, throng,
horde, mob, army, legion, herd,
pack, flock, swarm, troop, band,
mass, assemblage, assembly,
array, myriad.
hostage *n.* **pawn,** security, surety,
pledge, captive, prisoner.
hostile *adj.* **1 antagonistic,**
opposed, averse, opposite, ill-
disposed, against, inimical, *inf.*
anti. **2 adverse,** unfavorable,
unpropitious, disadvantageous,
inauspicious. **3 belligerent,**
bellicose, aggressive, warlike,
warring, militant, antagonistic,
unfriendly, unkind,
unsympathetic, malevolent,
malicious, spiteful, wrathful,
angry. **Ant.** friendly; favorable;
peaceful.
hostility *n.* **1 antagonism,**
opposition, aversion, animosity,
ill will, enmity. **2 belligerence,**
bellicosity, aggression,
warlikeness, militancy,
antagonism, unfriendliness,
unkindness, malevolence, malice,
spite, wrath, anger.

hot *adj.* **1 heated,** boiling, boiling
hot, piping, piping hot, scalding,
red-hot, sizzling, steaming,
scorching, roasting, searing,
blazing hot, sweltering, parching,
blistering, baking, ovenlike,
torrid, sultry. **2 peppery,** spicy,
pungent, piquant, fiery, sharp,
biting. **3 feverish,** fevered, febrile,
flushed, red. **4 ardent,** eager,
enthusiastic, keen, fervent, fervid,
zealous, vehement, passionate,
animated, excited. **5 inflamed,**
furious, infuriated, seething,
raging, fuming, wrathful, angry,
indignant. **6 passionate,**
impassioned. **7 heated,** violent,
furious, fierce, ferocious, stormy,
tempestuous, savage. **8 new,** fresh,
recent, late, brand-new, just out,
just released, just issued.
9 popular, in vogue, in demand,
sought-after, well-liked, well-
loved. **10 close,** following closely,
near. **11 stolen,** illegally obtained,
smuggled, wanted. **Ant.** cold;
mild.
hotheaded *adj.* **hot-tempered,**
short-tempered, quick-tempered,
fiery, hasty, excitable, volatile,
rash, impetuous, impulsive,
reckless, foolhardy, wild, unruly.
house *n.* **1 abode,** residence,
domicile, home, habitation,
condominium, cottage, *inf.* condo.
2 family, clan, family tree, line,

lineage, dynasty, ancestry, ancestors, kindred, blood, race, strain, tribe. **3 firm,** business, company, concern, corporation, enterprise, organization, *inf.* outfit. **4 legislative body,** legislative assembly, congress, parliament, chamber. **5 audience,** gathering, assembly, congregation, listeners, spectators.
▸ *v.* **1 accommodate,** lodge, put up, take in, have room/space/capacity for, sleep, shelter, harbor. **2 cover,** sheathe, protect, shelter, guard, contain, keep.

household *n.* **family,** family circle, house, home, ménage.
▸ *adj.* **domestic,** family, ordinary, everyday, common, usual, run-of-the-mill.

hover *v.* **1 be suspended,** hang, fly, flutter, float, drift, be wafted. **2 waver,** vacillate, fluctuate, oscillate, alternate, seesaw.

however *adv.* **nevertheless,** be that as it may, nonetheless, notwithstanding, anyway, anyhow, regardless, despite that, still, yet, just the same, though.
▸ *conjunction* **whatever way,** regardless of how.

howl *v.* **1 bay,** yowl, yelp, yell, wail, bawl, scream, shriek, bellow, roar, shout, caterwaul, cry, weep, ululate, *inf.* holler.

2 laugh, roar with laughter, split one's sides.
▸ *n.* **bay,** yowl, yelp, yell, wail, bawl, bellow, roar, caterwauling, crying.

hub *n.* **1 pivot,** axis, nave. **2 center,** center of activity, middle, core, heart, nerve center, focus, focal point.

huddle *v.* **crowd,** press, throng, flock, pack, cram, herd, squeeze, bunch up, cluster, gather, congregate.
▸ *n.* **1 crowd,** throng, pack, cluster, gathering. **2 conference,** discussion, consultation, meeting, powwow, *inf.* confab.

hue *n.* **1 color,** tone, shade, tint, tinge, dye. **2 complexion,** cast, aspect, light.

hug *v.* **1 embrace,** cuddle, take in one's arms, hold close, enfold in one's arms, clasp/press to one's bosom, squeeze. **2 keep close to,** stay near to, follow closely, follow the course of. **3 cling to,** hold onto, cherish, harbor, nurse, keep close.
▸ *n.* **embrace,** cuddle, squeeze, hold, clasp, bear hug, *inf.* clinch.

huge *adj.* **enormous,** immense, great, massive, colossal, vast, prodigious, gigantic, giant, gargantuan, mammoth, monumental, monstrous, elephantine, extensive, bulky, mountainous, titanic, Herculean, *inf.* jumbo, humongous. **Ant.** tiny; diminutive.

hulk *n.* **1 wreck,** shipwreck, ruin, shell, skeleton, hull, frame. **2 oaf,** lout, *inf.* bull in a china shop, lummox, klutz.

hull *n.* **1 body,** framework, frame, skeleton, structure, casing, covering. **2 rind,** skin, peel, shell, husk, pod, shuck, capsule, integument, pericarp.
▸ *v.* **peel,** pare, skin, trim, shell, husk, shuck.

hum *v.* **1 drone,** murmur, vibrate, throb, thrum, buzz, whir, purr. **2 sing,** croon, whisper, mumble. **3 be busy,** be active, bustle, move quickly, vibrate, pulsate, buzz.
▸ *n.* **drone,** murmur, vibration, throb, thrum, buzz, whir, purr.

human *adj.* **1 anthropoid,** mortal. **2 mortal,** physical, bodily, fleshly, carnal, corporal. **3 kind,** kindly, considerate, understanding, sympathetic, compassionate, approachable, accessible, humane. **4 mortal,** flesh and blood, fallible, weak, frail, vulnerable, erring. **Ant.** animal; spiritual; inhuman.
▸ *n.* **human being,** mortal, member of the human race, individual, living soul, soul, man, woman, child, *inf.* body.

humane *adj.* **kind,** kindly, kindhearted, good, good-natured, compassionate, considerate, understanding, sympathetic, forgiving, merciful, lenient, forbearing, gentle, tender, mild, clement, benign, benevolent, charitable, generous, magnanimous, approachable, accessible. **Ant.** cruel; brutal; inhumane.

humble *adj.* **1 modest,** unassuming, self-effacing, unassertive, unpretentious, unostentatious, meek. **2 plain,** common, ordinary, simple, poor, of low birth, low-born, low-ranking, low, lowly, inferior, plebeian, proletarian, base, mean, unrefined, vulgar, unimportant, insignificant, inconsequential, undistinguished, ignoble. **3 servile,** submissive, obsequious, subservient, deferential, slavish, sycophantic. **Ant.** arrogant; proud.
▸ *v.* **1 humiliate,** mortify, shame, belittle, demean, deflate, depreciate, disparage. **2 crush,** trounce, rout, break, conquer, vanquish, defeat, utterly overwhelm, smash, bring to one's knees.

humdrum *adj.* **commonplace,** run-of-the-mill, routine, unvaried, unvarying, ordinary, everyday, mundane, uneventful, monotonous, repetitious, dull, uninteresting, banal, boring, tedious, tiresome, wearisome. *Ant.* remarkable; exciting.

humiliate *v.* **mortify,** humble, shame, bring low, put to shame, make ashamed, disgrace, embarrass, discomfit, chasten, subdue, abash, abase, debase, degrade, crush, make someone eat humble pie, take down a peg or two, *inf.* put down, make someone eat crow.

humiliation *n.* **mortification,** humbling, loss of pride, shame, disgrace, loss of face, dishonor, indignity, discredit, ignoring, embarrassment, discomfiture, affront, abasement, debasement, degradation, submission, humble pie, *inf.* put-down.

humility *n.* **1 lack of pride,** humbleness, modesty, modestness, meekness, self-effacement, unpretentiousness, unobtrusiveness, diffidence. **2 servility,** submissiveness, obsequiousness, subservience, deference, sycophancy. *Ant.* arrogance; pride.

humor *n.* **1 funny side,** funniness, comic side, comical aspect, comedy, laughableness, facetiousness, farce, jocularity, hilarity, ludicrousness, absurdness, absurdity, drollness. **2 comedy,** jokes, joking, jests, jesting, gags, wit, wittiness, witticisms, waggishness, pleasantries, buffoonery, *inf.* wisecracks. **3 mood,** temper, temperament, frame of mind, state of mind, disposition, spirits. *Ant.* gravity; solemnity.
▸ *v.* **1 indulge,** pamper, spoil, coddle, mollycoddle, mollify, soothe, placate, gratify, satisfy, pander to, go along with, accommodate. **2 adapt to,** make provision for, give in to, yield to, go along with, acquiesce in, indulge, pander to, tolerate, permit, allow, suffer.

humorous *adj.* **1 funny,** comic, comical, witty, jocular, amusing, laughable, hilarious, sidesplitting, rib-tickling, facetious, farcical, ridiculous, ludicrous, absurd, droll. **2 funny,** amusing, entertaining, witty, jocular, facetious, waggish, whimsical. *Ant.* serious; solemn.

hump *n.* **protuberance,** protrusion, projection, bulge, swelling, lump, bump, knob, hunch, mass.
▸ *v.* **1 hunch,** arch, curve, crook, curl up. **2 lug,** heave, carry, lift, shoulder, hoist.

hunch *n.* **1 hump,** protrusion, bulge. **2 feeling,** presentiment, premonition, intuition, sixth sense, suspicion, inkling, impression, idea.

▸ *v.* **hump,** arch, curve, crook, curl up.

hunger *n.* **1 hungriness,** emptiness, ravenousness, starvation, famine, voracity, greed, greediness. **2 craving,** longing, yearning, desire, want, need, thirst, appetite, pining, itch, lust, hankering, *inf.* yen.

▸ *v.* **be hungry,** feel hunger, be ravenous, be famished, be starving.

hungry *adj.* **empty,** hollow, ravenous, famished, famishing, starving, starved, half-starved, greedy, voracious. ***Ant.*** full; satiated.

hunt *v.* **1 chase,** give chase, pursue, stalk, track, trail, follow, shadow, hunt down, hound, *inf.* tail. **2 search,** look, look high and low, forage, fish, rummage.

▸ *n.* **1 chase,** pursuit, course, coursing, stalking, tracking, trailing, shadowing, *inf.* tailing. **2 search,** quest, rummage, foraging, ransacking.

hurdle *n.* **1 fence,** railing, rail, wall, hedge, bar, barrier, barricade. **2 barrier,** obstacle, hindrance, impediment, obstruction, stumbling block, snag, complication, difficulty, handicap.

hurl *v.* **throw,** fling, pitch, cast, toss, heave, fire, launch, let fly, propel, project, dart, catapult, *inf.* sling, chuck.

hurried *adj.* **1 quick,** fast, swift, rapid, speedy, hasty, breakneck, post-haste. **2 hasty,** quick, swift, rapid, rushed, cursory, superficial, perfunctory, offhand, passing, fleeting, transitory. ***Ant.*** slow; leisurely; thorough.

hurry *v.* **hurry up,** move quickly, be quick, make haste, hasten, speed, speed up, lose no time, press on, push on, run, dash, rush, *inf.* get a move on, step on it, get cracking, shake a leg, go hell for leather, fly, race, scurry, scamper, go like a bat out of hell, hightail it, hotfoot it. ***Ant.*** dawdle; delay.

▸ *n.* **1 speed,** quickness, fastness, swiftness, rapidity, haste, celerity, expedition, dispatch, promptitude. **2 haste,** urgency, rush, flurry, bustle, hubbub, turmoil, agitation, confusion, commotion.

hurt *v.* **1 be sore,** be painful, cause pain, ache, smart, nip, sting, throb, tingle, burn. **2 injure,** cause injury to, wound, cause pain to, bruise, cut, scratch, lacerate, maim, mutilate, damage, disable, incapacitate, debilitate, impair, harm, damage, spoil, mar, blight, blemish, impair. **3 upset,** sadden, cause sorrow, cause suffering, grieve, wound, distress, pain, cut to the quick, sting, cause anguish, offend, give offense, discompose. *Ant.* heal; cheer; soothe; improve.

▸ *n.* **1 pain,** soreness, ache, smarting, stinging, throbbing, suffering, pangs, discomfort. **2 sore,** wound, injury, bruise, cut, scratch, laceration, harm, damage, injury, detriment, blight, loss, disadvantage, mischief. **3 upset,** sadness, sorrow, suffering, grief, distress, pain, misery, anguish, affliction.

hurtful *adj.* **1 upsetting,** wounding, injurious, distressing, unkind, nasty, mean, malicious, spiteful, cutting, cruel, mischievous, offensive. **2 harmful,** damaging, injurious, detrimental, disadvantageous, deleterious, destructive, prejudicial, ruinous, inimical.

husband *n.* **spouse,** consort, partner, groom, bridegroom, *inf.* hubby, old man, the other half, *dial.* man.

▸ *v.* **conserve,** preserve, save, save for a rainy day, put aside, put by, reserve, store, hoard, budget.

hush *v.* **1 silence,** shush, *inf.* shut up. **2 fall silent,** become silent, *inf.* pipe down, shut up. **3 still,** quieten, calm, soothe, allay, assuage, pacify, mollify, compose.

▸ *n.* **quiet,** quietness, silence, stillness, still, soundlessness, peacefulness, peace, calm, tranquillity.

hustle *v.* **1 push,** shove, thrust, crowd, jostle, elbow, nudge, shoulder. **2 force,** coerce, impel, pressure, badger, pester, prompt, urge, goad, prod, spur, propel, egg on. **3 hurry,** be quick, hasten, make haste, move quickly, dash, rush, fly, *inf.* get a move on, step on it.

▸ *n.* **activity,** hurry, rushing, haste, flurry, bustle, hubbub, tumult, fuss.

hut *n.* **shed,** lean-to, shack, cabin, shanty, hovel.

hygiene *n.* **cleanliness,** public health, environmental health, sanitation, sanitary measures.

hygienic *adj.* **sanitary,** clean, germ-free, disinfected, sterilized, aseptic, sterile, unpolluted, uncontaminated, healthy, pure. *Ant.* dirty; filthy; insanitary.

hypnotic *adj.* **mesmerizing,** sleep-inducing, sleep-producing, soporific, somniferous, somnific, numbing, sedative, stupefactive.

hypnotize *v.* **1 put under,** put out, send into a trance, mesmerize, put to sleep. **2 fascinate,** bewitch, entrance, beguile, spellbind, magnetize.

hypocrisy *n.* **sanctimoniousness,** sanctimony, pietism, false goodness, insincerity, falseness, falsity, deceptiveness, deceit, deceitfulness, deception, dishonesty, duplicity, imposture, two-facedness, double-dealing, pretense, speciousness, phoniness. *Ant.* honesty; sincerity.

hypocritical *adj.* sanctimonious, pietistic, unctuous, insincere, false, fraudulent, deceitful, deceptive, dishonest, untruthful, lying, duplicitous, two-faced, double-dealing, untrustworthy, perfidious, specious, spurious, *inf.* phony.

hypothesis *n.* **1 theorem,** thesis, proposition, theory, postulate, axiom, premise. **2 supposition,** assumption, presumption, conjecture, speculation.

hypothetical *adj.* **supposed,** assumed, presumed, theoretical, conjectured, imagined, speculative, academic.

hysteria *n.* **hysterics,** frenzy, panic attack, madness, delirium.

hysterical *adj.* **1 frenzied,** in a frenzy, frantic, out of control, berserk, beside oneself, distracted, distraught, overwrought, agitated, in a panic, mad, crazed, delirious, out of one's mind/wits, raving. **2 very funny,** wildly amusing, hilarious, uproarious, sidesplitting, comical, farcical, screamingly funny. *Ant.* calm; composed; serious.

Ii

ice *n.* **1 frost,** rime, icicle, iceberg, glacier. **2 ice cubes,** crushed ice, *inf.* rocks. **3 coldness,** coolness, frigidity, stiffness, aloofness, distance, unresponsiveness, reserve, reticence, constraint, restraint.
▶ *v.* **1 cool,** chill, refrigerate. **2 cover with icing,** frost, add frosting to, glaze.

icy *adj.* **1 freezing,** frigid, chill, chilly, chilling, frosty, biting, bitter, raw, arctic, glacial, Siberian, polar, gelid. **2 frozen over,** ice-bound, frosty, rimy, glassy, like a sheet of glass, slippery. **3 cold,** cool, frigid, frosty, stiff, aloof, distant, unfriendly, unwelcoming, unresponsive, uncommunicative, reserved, reticent, constrained, restrained. *Ant.* boiling; hot; warm.

idea *n.* **1 concept,** conception, conceptualization, thought, image, abstraction, perception, notion. **2 thought,** theory, view, viewpoint, opinion, feeling, outlook, belief, judgment, conclusion. **3 thought,** understanding, belief, impression, feeling, notion, suspicion, fancy, inkling. **4 estimation,** approximation, guess, surmise, *inf.* guesstimate. **5 plan,** design, scheme, aim, intention, objective, object, purpose, end, goal, target. **6 notion,** vision, archetype, ideal example, exemplar, pattern.

ideal *n.* **epitome,** peak of perfection, paragon, nonpareil, archetype, prototype, model, pattern, exemplar, example, paradigm, criterion, yardstick.
▶ *adj.* **1 perfect,** consummate, supreme, absolute, complete, flawless, exemplary, classic, archetypal, model, quintessential. **2 abstract,** conceptual, intellectual, mental, philosophical, theoretical, hypothetical. **3 unattainable,** Utopian, unreal, impracticable, ivory-towered, imaginary, romantic, visionary, fanciful.

idealistic *adj.* **Utopian,** perfectionist, visionary, romantic, quixotic, unrealistic, impracticable, castle-building. *Ant.* practical; realistic; down-to-earth.

ideally *adv.* **in a perfect world,** all

things being equal, theoretically, hypothetically, in theory.

identical *adj.* **1 same,** very same, one and the same, selfsame. **2 alike,** like, very much the same, indistinguishable, corresponding, matching, twin. **Ant.** different; unlike.

identify *v.* **1 recognize,** single out, pick out, spot, point out, pinpoint, discern, distinguish, name, *inf.* put the finger on, finger. **2 establish,** find out, ascertain, diagnose, select, choose. **3 associate,** connect, think of in connection.

identity *n.* **1 name,** specification. **2 personality,** self, selfhood, ego, individuality, distinctiveness, singularity, uniqueness, differentness. **3 identification,** recognition, naming. **4 sameness,** selfsameness, indistinguishability, interchangeability, likeness, alikeness, similarity, closeness, accordance.

ideology *n.* **doctrine,** creed, credo, teaching, dogma, theory, thesis, tenets, beliefs, opinions.

idiocy *n.* **stupidity,** stupidness, foolishness, senselessness, inanity, absurdity, fatuity, fatuousness, asininity, lack of intelligence, lunacy, craziness, insanity, *inf.* dumbness, daftness. **Ant.** wisdom; sense.

idiom *n.* **1 turn of phrase,** phrase, expression, locution. **2 language,** mode of expression, phraseology, style, speech, talk, usage, parlance, vernacular, jargon, patois, *inf.* lingo.

idiosyncrasy *n.* **peculiarity,** individual/personal trait, singularity, oddity, eccentricity, mannerism, quirk, habit, characteristic, speciality, quality, feature.

idiot *n.* **blockhead,** nitwit, dunderhead, dolt, dunce, halfwit, fool, ass, boob, nincompoop, ninny, ignoramus, cretin, moron, *inf.* numskull, dimwit.

idiotic *adj.* **stupid,** foolish, senseless, inane, absurd, fatuous, asinine, unintelligent, halfwitted, harebrained, lunatic, crazy, insane, moronic, *inf.* dumb, daft.

idle *adj.* **1 lazy,** indolent, slothful, shiftless, sluggish, loafing, do-nothing, dronish. **2 not in operation,** not operating, inoperative, not working, inactive, out of action, unused, not in use, mothballed. **3 not working,** unemployed, out of work, jobless, out of a job, *inf.* on the dole. **4 unoccupied,** empty, vacant, unfilled. **5 groundless,** without grounds, baseless, foundationless, lacking foundation. **6 unimportant**, trivial, trifling, shallow, foolish, insignificant, superficial, without depth, inane, fatuous, senseless, meaningless, purposeless, unnecessary. **7 useless**, vain, worthless, futile, ineffective, ineffectual, inefficacious, unproductive, fruitless, pointless, meaningless. **8 frivolous**, trivial, trifling, shallow, insubstantial, worthless, nugatory. **Ant.** industrious; active; busy; meaningful.

▶ *v.* **1 while**, laze, loaf, lounge, loiter, dawdle, dally, fritter, putter, waste. **2 laze**, loaf, be inactive, mark time, shirk, slack, vegetate, *inf.* take it easy, rest on one's oars.

idol *n.* **1 icon**, god, false god, effigy, image, graven image, fetish, likeness. **2 hero**, heroine, favorite, darling, beloved, pet, apple of one's eye, blue-eyed boy/girl, star, superstar, *inf.* pinup.

idolize *v.* **1 worship**, bow down before, glorify, exalt, revere, deify. **2 hero-worship**, worship, adulate, adore, love, look up to, admire, dote upon, lionize, reverence, revere, venerate.

ignite *v.* **1 light**, set fire to, set on fire, set alight, fire, kindle, inflame, touch off, *inf.* set/put a match to. **2 catch fire**, catch, burst into flames, burn up, burn, flame up, kindle. **Ant.** extinguish; douse, dowse.

ignominious *adj.* **1 shameful**, dishonorable, disgraceful, humiliating, mortifying, discreditable, disreputable, undignified, infamous, ignoble, inglorious, scandalous, abject, sorry, base. **2 contemptible**, despicable, offensive, revolting, wicked, vile, base, low. **Ant.** honorable; glorious; admirable.

ignorance *n.* **1 unawareness**, unfamiliarity, unconsciousness, inexperience, greenness, innocence. **2 illiteracy**, lack of intelligence, unintelligence, stupidity, thickness, denseness, unenlightenment, benightedness. **Ant.** knowledge; education; enlightenment.

ignorant *adj.* **1 unaware of**, unfamiliar with, unconversant with, unacquainted with, unconscious of, uninformed about, unenlightened about, inexperienced in, blind to, uninitiated in, unschooled in, naïve about, innocent about, *inf.* in the dark about. **2 unscholarly**, uneducated, untaught, unschooled, untutored, untrained, illiterate, unlettered, unlearned, unread, uninformed, unknowledgeable, unintelligent, stupid, unenlightened, benighted, *inf.* thick, dense, dumb.

ignore *v.* **1 disregard,** pay no attention/heed to, take no notice of, brush aside, pass over, shrug off, push aside, shut one's eyes to, be oblivious to, turn a blind eye to, turn a deaf ear to. **2 slight,** spurn, cold-shoulder, look right through, turn one's back on, *inf.* give someone the brush-off, pass up. **3 set aside,** pay no attention to, take no account of, omit, leave out, overlook, neglect, *inf.* skip.

ill *adj.* **1 unwell,** ailing, poorly, sick, sickly, on the sick list, infirm, off-color, afflicted, indisposed, out of sorts, diseased, bedridden, weak, feeble, *inf.* under the weather, laid up, queasy. **2 hostile,** antagonistic, acrimonious, belligerent, bellicose, unfriendly, unkind, spiteful, rancorous, resentful, malicious, malevolent, bitter, fractious, irritable, irascible, cross, cantankerous, crabbed, surly, snappish, gruff, sullen. **3 adverse,** unfavorable, unadvantageous, unlucky, unfortunate, unpropitious, inauspicious, unpromising, ominous, infelicitous. **4 harmful,** detrimental, deleterious, hurtful, damaging, pernicious, destructive, ruinous. **5 bad,** infamous, low, wicked, nefarious,

vile, evil, foul, sinful, iniquitous, sinister, corrupt, depraved, degenerate. **6 rude,** unmannerly, impolite, objectionable, boorish. *Ant.* healthy; well; friendly; favorable.

▸ *n.* **1 harm,** hurt, injury, mischief, pain, trouble, unpleasantness, misfortune. **2 pain,** misfortune, suffering, misery, woe, affliction, damage, disaster, tribulation, troubles, problems, trials. **3 illness,** ill/poor health, ailment, disorder, complaint, sickness, disease, malady, infirmity, indisposition, infection, contagion.

ill-advised *adj.* **unwise,** ill-considered, imprudent, incautious, injudicious, ill-judged, impolitic, misguided, foolish, foolhardy, rash, hasty, shortsighted, uncircumspect, thoughtless, careless, reckless. *Ant.* wise; sensible.

illegal *adj.* **unlawful,** illegitimate, illicit, lawless, criminal, actionable, felonious, unlicensed, unauthorized, unsanctioned, unwarranted, unofficial, outlawed, banned, forbidden, barred, prohibited, interdicted, proscribed, contraband, black-market, under the counter, bootleg. *Ant.* legal; lawful.

illegible *adj.* **unreadable,** hard to

read, indecipherable, unintelligible, scrawled, scribbled, hieroglyphic, squiggly, crabbed, faint, obscure, *inf.* clear as mud. *Ant.* legible; readable.

illegitimate *adj.* **1 illegal,** unlawful, illicit, lawless, criminal, unlicensed, unauthorized, unsanctioned. **2 natural,** love, born out of wedlock, fatherless, bastard. **3 illogical,** unsound, spurious, incorrect, invalid. **4 irregular,** nonstandard, substandard, ungrammatical, dialectal, colloquial, informal. *Ant.* lawful; legal; legitimate.

ill-fated *adj.* **unlucky,** luckless, unfortunate, hapless, unhappy, doomed, blighted, star-crossed, ill-starred, ill-omened.

ill-judged *adj.* **ill-advised,** ill-considered, unwise, imprudent, injudicious, misguided, foolish, foolhardy, rash, hasty, shortsighted.

illness *n.* **ailment,** sickness, disorder, complaint, malady, disease, affliction, attack, disability, indisposition, infection, contagion, ill health, poor health. *Ant.* health; fitness.

illogical *adj.* **unsound,** unreasonable, unreasoned, irrational, faulty, spurious, fallacious, fallible, unproved, untenable, specious, unscientific, sophistic, casuistic, inconclusive, inconsistent, incorrect, invalid, wrong, absurd, preposterous, meaningless, senseless.

ill-treat *v.* **treat badly,** abuse, harm, injure, damage, handle roughly, mishandle, ill-use, maltreat, misuse, *inf.* knock about. *Ant.* pamper; cosset; spoil.

illuminating *adj.* **instructive,** informative, enlightening, explanatory, revealing, helpful.

illusion *n.* **1 false/deceptive appearance,** deception, faulty perception, misperception. **2 delusion,** misapprehension, misconception, deception, false/mistaken impression, fallacy, error, misjudgment, fancy. **3 hallucination,** figment of the imagination, phantom, specter, mirage, phantasm, fantasy, will-o'-the-wisp, ignis fatuus. *Ant.* reality; truth.

illustrate *v.* **1 adorn,** decorate, ornament, embellish. **2 exemplify,** demonstrate, point up, show, instance, make plain/clear, clarify, bring home, emphasize, interpret.

illustration *n.* **1 picture,** drawing, sketch, plate, figure, artwork, adornment, decoration, ornamentation, embellishment. **2 example,** typical case, case in point, instance, specimen, sample, exemplar, analogy, exemplification, demonstration, showing, clarification, emphasis, interpretation.

image *n.* **1 likeness,** representation, resemblance, effigy, figure, figurine, doll, statue, sculpture, bust, idol, icon, fetish, graven image, painting, picture, portrait. **2 reproduction,** reflection, picture, facsimile, photograph, snapshot, photo. **3 mental picture,** vision, concept, conception, idea, perception, impression, fancy, thought. **4 double,** replica, clone, copy, reproduction, counterpart, similitude, doppelgänger, *inf.* spitting image, chip off the old block, ringer, dead ringer. **5 emblem,** symbol, archetype, perfect example, embodiment, incarnation. **6 figure of speech,** conceit, figurative expression.

imaginary *adj.* **fanciful,** fancied, fantastic, unreal, nonexistent, illusory, illusive, visionary, dreamy, dreamlike, shadowy, unsubstantial, chimerical, figmental, notional, assumed, hypothetical, supposed, supposititious, fictitious, fictional, legendary, mythical, mythological, made-up, invented, hallucinatory, phantasmal, phantasmic, spectral, ghostly, ideal, idealistic, Utopian, romantic. *Ant.* real; actual.

imagination *n.* **1 creativity,** vision, inspiration, fancifulness, insight, inventiveness, originality, invention, innovation, resourcefulness, ingenuity, enterprise, cleverness, wit. **2 illusion,** fancy, figment of the imagination, vision, dream, chimera, shadow, phantom.

imaginative *adj.* **creative,** visionary, inspired, fanciful, inventive, original, innovative, resourceful, ingenious, enterprising, clever, whimsical. *Ant.* unimaginative; run-of-the-mill; pedestrian.

imagine *v.* **1 picture,** see in the mind's eye, visualize, envisage, envision, conjure up, dream about, dream up, fantasize about, conceptualize, think up, conceive, think of, plan, project, scheme. **2 assume,** presume, suppose, think, believe, be of the opinion that, take it, gather, fancy, judge, deem, infer, deduce, conjecture, surmise, guess, reckon, suspect, realize.

imbue *v.* **fill,** impregnate, inject, inculcate, instill, ingrain, inspire, permeate, charge.

imitate *v.* **1 copy,** emulate, follow the example of, take after, follow, follow suit, take a page from someone's book, tread in the steps of, walk in the footsteps of, echo. **2 mimic,** ape, impersonate, do an impression of, parody, mock, caricature, burlesque, travesty, *inf.* send up, take off, spoof, do, make like. **3 look like,** simulate, echo, mirror. **4 copy,** reproduce, replicate, duplicate, counterfeit, forge, fake.

imitation *n.* **1 emulation,** resemblance. **2 mimicking,** mimicry, aping, impersonation, impression, parody, mocking, mockery, caricature, burlesque, travesty, *inf.* send-up, take-off, spoof. **3 copy,** reproduction, counterfeit, forgery, fake.
▶ *adj.* **artificial,** synthetic, simulated, man-made, ersatz, mock, sham, fake, reproduction, repro, *inf.* pseudo, phony. ***Ant.*** real; genuine.

immature *adj.* **1 unripe,** undeveloped, unformed, imperfect, unfinished, incomplete, half-grown, crude, raw, green, unmellowed, unfledged, untimely.
2 adolescent, childish, babyish, infantile, juvenile, puerile, jejune, callow, inexperienced, green, unsophisticated, *inf.* wet behind the ears. ***Ant.*** ripe; mature.

immediate *adj.* **1 instant,** instantaneous, on the spot, prompt, swift, speedy, sudden, abrupt. **2 near,** nearest, next, next door, close, closest, adjacent, adjoining, abutting, contiguous, proximate. **3 direct,** primary.
4 recent. 5 present, current, existing, existent, actual, extant, urgent, pressing. **6 direct,** firsthand, hands-on, in service, in the field, on the job.

immediately *adv.* **1 right away,** right now, at once, instantly, instantaneously, now, this/that very second/minute, this/that instant, directly, promptly, forthwith, without delay, without hesitation, unhesitatingly, post-haste, tout de suite, *inf.* before you can/could say Jack Robinson, in the wink/twinkling of an eye, lickety-split, pronto. **2 right,** directly, closely, at close quarters. **3 directly,** firsthand, at first hand, without intermediary.

immense *adj.* **huge,** vast, massive, enormous, gigantic, colossal, giant, great, very large, extensive, infinite, immeasurable, illimitable, monumental, tremendous, prodigious, elephantine, monstrous, titanic, *inf.* mega. ***Ant.*** tiny; minute.

immerse *v.* **1 submerge,** plunge, dip, dunk, duck, sink, douse, souse, soak, drench, imbue, saturate. **2 baptize,** christen, purify, lustrate. **3 absorb,** engross, occupy, engage, preoccupy, involve, engulf, *inf.* lose.

immigrant *n.* **nonnative,** settler, incomer, newcomer, new arrival, migrant, naturalized citizen, expatriate.

imminent *adj.* **impending,** at hand, fast-approaching, close, near, approaching, coming, forthcoming, on the way, about to happen, upon us, in the offing, on the horizon, in the air, brewing, threatening, menacing, looming. *Ant.* distant; remote.

immobile *adj.* **immobilized,** without moving, unmoving, motionless, unable to move, immovable, still, static, at rest, stationary, at a standstill, stock-still, dormant, rooted, fixed to the spot, rigid, frozen, stiff, riveted, like a statue, as if turned to stone, immotile, immotive.

immobilize *v.* **bring to a standstill/halt,** halt, stop, put out of action, render inactive, inactivate, paralyze, make inoperative, freeze, transfix, disable, cripple.

immodest *adj.* **forward,** bold, brazen, impudent, unblushing, shameless, wanton, indecorous, improper, indecent, *inf.* fresh, cheeky.

immoral *adj.* **bad,** wrong, unprincipled, dishonest, unethical, wicked, evil, sinful, impure, iniquitous, corrupt, depraved, vile, base, degenerate, debauched, abandoned, dissolute, villainous, nefarious, miscreant, reprobate, perverted, indecent, lewd, licentious, pornographic, unchaste, of easy virtue, bawdy.

immortal *adj.* **1 never dying,** undying, deathless, eternal, ever-living, everlasting, never-ending, endless, imperishable, perdurable, timeless, indestructible, unfading, undecaying, perennial, evergreen, perpetual, lasting, enduring, constant, abiding, immutable, indissoluble, *lit.* sempiternal. **2 famous,** celebrated, remembered, commemorated, honored, lauded, glorified. *Ant.* mortal; ephemeral; transitory.
▸ *n.* **1 god,** goddess, Olympian. **2 great,** hero, genius, celebrity.

immortalize *v.* **commemorate,** memorialize, eternalize, eternize, perpetuate, exalt, laud, glorify.

immovable *adj.* **1 fast,** firm, fixed, secure, stable, rooted, riveted, moored, anchored, stuck, jammed, stiff, unbudgeable. **2 motionless,** unmoving, stationary, still, stock-still, at a standstill, dead still, statuelike. **3 adamant,** firm, steadfast, unwavering, unswerving, resolute, determined, tenacious, stubborn, dogged, obdurate, inflexible, unyielding, unbending, uncompromising, unshakable, inexorable.

immune *adj.* **not subject to,** not liable to, protected from, safe from, unsusceptible to, secure against, exempt from, clear of, free from, freed from, absolved from, released from, excused from, relieved of, spared from, excepted from, exempted from, unaffected by, resistant to, protected from/against, proof against. *Ant.* liable; susceptible; prone.

immunize *v.* inoculate, vaccinate, protect, shield, safeguard, *inf.* give a jab to.

impact *n.* **1 collision,** contact, crash, striking, clash, bumping, banging, jolt, thump, whack, thwack, slam, smack, slap. **2 influence,** effect, impression, results, consequences, repercussions. **3 force,** full force, shock, brunt, impetus, pressure.

impair *v.* **weaken,** lessen, decrease, reduce, blunt, diminish, deteriorate, enfeeble, debilitate, enervate, damage, mar, spoil, injure, harm, hinder, disable, cripple, impede, undermine, vitiate. *Ant.* improve; enhance.

impart *v.* **1 pass on,** convey, communicate, transmit, relate, tell, make known, report, disclose, reveal, divulge, proclaim, broadcast. **2 bestow,** confer, give, grant, lend, accord, afford, assign, offer, yield, contribute, dispense.

impartial *adj.* **unbiased,** unprejudiced, disinterested, detached, objective, neutral, equitable, evenhanded, fair, fair-minded, just, open-minded, without favoritism, free from discrimination, nonpartisan, with no ax to grind, without fear or favor.

impartiality *n.* **lack of bias/ prejudice,** disinterest, detachment, objectivity, neutrality, evenhandedness, fairness, justness, open-mindedness.

impassable *adj.* **1 unnavigable,** impenetrable, closed, blocked, obstructed, pathless, trackless. **2 insurmountable,** insuperable, unconquerable.

impatient *adj.* **1 restless,** restive, impetuous, eager, excitable, anxious, agitated, nervous, edgy. **2 abrupt,** brusque, terse, short, short-tempered, quick-tempered, curt, irritated, angry, testy, snappy, querulous, peevish, intolerant. **3 anxious,** eager, keen, avid, desirous, yearning, longing.

impede *v.* **hinder,** obstruct,

hamper, handicap, sabotage, block, check, bar, curb, hold back, hold up, delay, interfere with, disrupt, retard, slow, slow down, brake, restrain, thwart, frustrate, balk, stop, *inf.* throw a monkey wrench in the works. ***Ant.*** assist; advance; facilitate.

impediment *n.* **1 hindrance,** obstruction, obstacle, handicap, block, stumbling block, check, encumbrance, bar, barrier, curb, brake, restraint, drawback, difficulty, snag, setback. **2 stammer,** stutter, speech defect, hesitancy, faltering.

impel *v.* **1 urge,** press, exhort, force, oblige, constrain, necessitate, require, demand, make, apply pressure to, pressure, pressurize, spur, prod, goad, incite, prompt, persuade, inspire. **2 actuate,** set in motion, get going, get moving, propel.

impending *adj.* **imminent,** at hand, approaching, coming, forthcoming, close, near, nearing, on the way, about to happen, upon us, in the offing, on the horizon, in the air/wind, brewing, looming, threatening, menacing.

impenetrable *adj.* **1 impervious,** impermeable, solid, dense, thick, hard, closed, sealed, hermetically sealed, resistant, waterproof, tight. **2 impassable,** inaccessible, thick, dense, overgrown, jungly, pathless, trackless, untrodden. **3 incomprehensible,** unintelligible, indiscernible, baffling, puzzling, abstruse, obscure, hidden, inexplicable, unfathomable, recondite, inscrutable, enigmatic. **4 stupid,** senseless, obtuse, gross, prejudiced, bigoted, biased, narrow-minded.

imperceptible *adj.* **unnoticeable,** unobtrusive, unapparent, slight, small, gradual, subtle, faint, fine, inappreciable, inconsequential, tiny, minute, minuscule, microscopic, infinitesimal, undetectable, indistinguishable, indiscernible, invisible, indistinct, unclear, obscure, vague, indefinite, shadowy, inaudible, muffled, impalpable. ***Ant.*** obvious; noticeable.

imperceptibly *adv.* **unnoticeably,** unobtrusively, unseen, gradually, slowly, subtly, inappreciably, undetectably, infinitesimally, little by little, bit by bit.

imperfect *adj.* **1 faulty,** flawed, defective, blemished, damaged, impaired, broken. **2 incomplete,** not whole/entire, deficient, broken, partial. **3 deficient,** inadequate, insufficient, lacking, rudimentary, limited, patchy, sketchy. **4 undeveloped,** immature, premature.

imperfection *n.* **1 fault,** flaw, defect, deformity, blemish, crack, break, scratch, cut, tear, stain, spot. **2 incompleteness,** deficiency, partialness. **3 failing,** flaw, foible, deficiency, weakness, weak point, shortcoming, fallibility, frailty, infirmity, peccadillo.

imperious *adj.* **peremptory,** overbearing, overweening, domineering, high-handed, assertive, authoritative, commanding, lordly, masterful, dictatorial.

impersonal *adj.* **1 detached,** objective, disinterested, dispassionate, neutral, unbiased, unprejudiced, unswayed, fair, equitable, evenhanded. **2 cold,** cool, frigid, aloof, formal, stiff, rigid, wooden, starchy, stilted, stuffy, matter-of-fact, businesslike, bureaucratic. *Ant.* biased; friendly; warm.

impersonate *v.* **imitate,** mimic, personate, mock, ape, parody, caricature, burlesque, masquerade as, pose as, pass oneself off as, *inf.* take off, do.

impertinent *adj.* **1 insolent,** impudent, cheeky, rude, flippant, impolite, unmannerly, ill-mannered, uncivil, coarse, crude, uncouth, discourteous, disrespectful, bold, brazen, audacious, presumptuous, forward, pert, brash, shameless, *inf.* fresh, flip. **2 irrelevant,** inapplicable, inapposite, immaterial, unrelated, unconnected, not germane, beside the point. *Ant.* mannerly; polite; pertinent.

imperturbable *adj.* **self-possessed,** composed, collected, calm, cool, calm and collected, tranquil, serene, inexcitable, unflappable, even-tempered, easygoing, unperturbed, at ease, unruffled, untroubled, undismayed, unmoved, nonchalant. *Ant.* nervous; edgy; excitable.

impetuous *adj.* **1 hasty,** precipitate, headlong, impulsive, spontaneous, impromptu, spur-of-the-moment, unthinking, unplanned, ill-conceived, ill-considered, unreasoned, reckless, rash, foolhardy, heedless. **2 impulsive,** hasty, spontaneous, eager, enthusiastic, impatient, excitable, ardent, passionate, zealous, headstrong, rash, reckless, foolhardy, wild, uncontrolled. **3 violent,** forceful, powerful, vigorous, vehement, raging, rampant, unrestrained,

uncontrolled, unbridled. *Ant.*
cautious; wary.

impetus *n.* **1 momentum,**
propulsion, impelling force,
continuing motion, energy, force,
power. **2 stimulus,** instigation,
actuation, moving force,
motivation, incentive,
inducement, inspiration,
encouragement, influence, push,
urging, pressing, spur, goading,
goad.

implausible *adj.* **unlikely,**
improbable, incredible,
unbelievable, unimaginable,
inconceivable, debatable,
questionable, doubtful.

implement *n.* **1 tool,** utensil,
appliance, instrument, device,
apparatus, contrivance, gadget,
inf. gizmo. **2 agent,** medium,
channel, expedient, means.
▸ *v.* **fulfill,** carry out, execute,
perform, discharge, accomplish,
achieve, realize, put into effect/
action, bring about, effect,
enforce. *Ant.* impede; neglect.

implicate *v.* **1 incriminate,**
compromise, inculpate, accuse,
charge, blame, impeach, involve,
entangle. **2 involve,** concern,
include, associate, connect,
embroil, entangle, be a part of, tie
up with. *Ant.* absolve; dissociate.

implication *n.* **1 suggestion,**
inference, insinuation, innuendo,

hint, allusion, reference,
assumption, presumption.
2 incrimination, inculpation,
blame. **3 involvement,** concern,
association, connection,
entanglement.

implicit *adj.* **1 implied,** indirect,
inferred, deducible, unspoken,
unexpressed, undeclared,
unstated, tacit, understood,
hinted, suggested, inherent,
latent, taken for granted.
2 absolute, complete, entire,
total, wholehearted, perfect,
sheer, utter, unqualified,
unconditional, unreserved,
positive, unshaken, unshakable,
unhesitating, unquestioning,
firm, steadfast, constant. *Ant.*
direct; explicit; obvious; limited.

implore *v.* **beg,** entreat, plead
with, beseech, pray, ask, request,
solicit, supplicate, importune,
press, crave, plead for, appeal
to/for.

imply *v.* **1 insinuate,** say
indirectly, hint, suggest, infer,
intimate, give to understand,
signal, indicate. **2 involve,** entail,
presuppose, presume, assume.
3 signify, mean, indicate, denote,
connote, betoken, point to.

impolite *adj.* **unmannerly,** ill-
mannered, bad-mannered, rude,
discourteous, uncivil, ill-bred,
ungentlemanly, unladylike,

ungracious, ungallant,
disrespectful, inconsiderate,
boorish, churlish, loutish, rough,
crude, unrefined, indelicate,
indecorous, insolent, impudent,
impertinent.

important *adj.* **1 of import,**
consequential, significant, of
great import/consequence, far-
reaching, critical, crucial, pivotal,
momentous, of great moment,
serious, grave, urgent, substantial,
weighty, valuable, significant,
salient, chief, main, principal,
major, of concern, of interest,
relevant, of value, valuable,
necessary, essential. **2 prominent,**
eminent, preeminent, leading,
foremost, outstanding,
distinguished, esteemed, notable,
noteworthy, of note, of import,
influential, of influence,
powerful, power-wielding, high-
ranking, high-level, top-level,
prestigious. ***Ant.*** unimportant;
insignificant; minor.

importunate *adj.* **persistent,**
insistent, pertinacious, dogged,
earnest, unremitting, continuous,
pressing, urgent, demanding,
exigent, exacting, clamorous,
entreating, solicitous, suppliant,
imploratory, imprecatory.

importune *v.* **1 beg,** beseech,
entreat, implore, plead with,
appeal to, call upon, supplicate,

solicit, petition, harass, beset,
press, dun. **2 solicit,** make sexual
advances toward.

impose *v.* **1 enforce,** apply, exact,
levy, charge, put on, lay on, set,
establish, fix, decree, ordain,
institute, introduce, promulgate,
require, demand, dictate, *inf.*
saddle with. **2 force,** foist, inflict,
thrust, obtrude. **3 palm off,** foist,
pass off.

imposing *adj.* **impressive,**
striking, splendid, grand,
majestic, august, lofty, stately,
dignified. ***Ant.*** modest;
unimposing.

impossible *adj.* **1 not possible,**
beyond the bounds/realm of
possibility/reason, out of the
question, unthinkable,
unimaginable, inconceivable,
impracticable, unattainable,
unachievable, unobtainable,
beyond one, hopeless.
2 unbelievable, incredible, absurd,
ludicrous, ridiculous,
preposterous, outlandish,
outrageous. **3 unmanageable,**
intractable, recalcitrant, wayward,
objectionable, intolerable,
unbearable. **4 unbearable,**
intolerable, unendurable,
hopeless. ***Ant.*** possible; plausible;
tolerable.

impracticable *adj.* **not feasible,**
impossible, out of the question,

unworkable, unachievable, unattainable, unrealizable, unsuitable. *Ant.* possible; feasible.

impractical *adj.* **1 unworkable,** useless, ineffective, ineffectual, inefficacious, unrealistic, impossible, nonviable, inoperable, inoperative, unserviceable.
2 theoretical, abstract, academic, speculative. **3 unrealistic,** unbusinesslike, idealistic, romantic, starry-eyed, visionary, quixotic. *Ant.* practical; feasible; realistic.

imprecise *adj.* **1 inexact,** approximate, estimated, rough, inaccurate, incorrect. **2 vague,** loose, indefinite, inexplicit, hazy, blurred, indistinct, woolly, confused, ambiguous, equivocal.

impregnate *v.* **1 permeate,** suffuse, imbue, penetrate, pervade, fill, infuse, soak, steep, saturate, drench, inundate.
2 make pregnant, inseminate, *inf.* put in the family way, *vulg.* knock up. **3 fertilize,** fecundate.

impress *v.* **1 make an impression/ impact on**, move, sway, bend, influence, affect, affect deeply, stir, rouse, excite, inspire, galvanize, *inf.* grab. **2 emphasize,** stress, bring home, establish, fix deeply, instill, inculcate, urge.
3 stamp, imprint, print, mark, engrave, emboss. **4 make an**

impression on, draw attention to oneself to, show off to, show off in front of.

impression *n.* **1 effect,** influence, sway, impact, hold, power, control. **2 mark,** indentation, dent, hollow, outline, stamp, stamping, imprint, impress. **3 feeling,** vague feeling, sense, sensation, awareness, perception, notion, idea, thought, belief, opinion, conviction, fancy, suspicion, inkling, intuition, hunch, *inf.* funny feeling. **4 impersonation,** imitation, mimicry, parody, caricature, burlesque, travesty, *inf.* send-up, take-off.

impressionable *adj.* **susceptible,** suggestible, persuadable, receptive, responsive, sensitive, open, gullible, ingenuous, pliable, malleable, moldable.

impressive *adj.* **1 imposing,** magnificent, splendid. **2 moving,** affecting, touching, stirring, rousing, exciting, powerful, inspiring. *Ant.* ordinary; unexciting.

imprison *v.* **put in prison,** send to prison, jail, lock up, take into custody, put under lock and key, put away, incarcerate, intern, confine, detain, constrain, immure, *inf.* send up, send up the river. *Ant.* free; liberate; release.

imprisonment *n.* **custody,** incarceration, internment, confinement, detention, duress.

improbable *adj.* **unlikely,** highly unlikely, doubtful, dubious, questionable, implausible, far-fetched, unconvincing, unbelievable, incredible, ridiculous.

impromptu *adj.* **ad lib,** unrehearsed, unprepared, extempore, extemporized, extemporaneous, spontaneous, improvised, unscripted, unstudied, unpremeditated, *inf.* off the cuff.
‣ *adv.* **ad lib,** extempore, spontaneously, on the spur of the moment, *inf.* off the cuff, off the top of one's head.

improper *adj.* **1 unseemly,** indecorous, unbecoming, unfitting, unladylike, ungentlemanly, impolite, indiscreet, injudicious. **2 indecent,** risqué, off-color, indelicate, suggestive, blue, smutty, obscene, lewd, pornographic. **3 inaccurate,** incorrect, wrong, erroneous, false. **4 inappropriate,** unsuitable, unsuited, unfitting, inapt, inapplicable, incongruous.

improve *v.* **1 make better,** better, ameliorate, amend, mend, reform, rehabilitate, set/put right, correct, rectify, help, advance, upgrade, revamp, modernize, *inf.* give a face-lift to, gentrify. **2 get/grow better,** make headway, advance, come along, develop, progress, make progress, pick up, rally, perk up, *inf.* look up, take a turn for the better, get a new lease on life. **3 recover,** get better/well, recuperate, convalesce, gain strength, *inf.* be on the mend, turn the corner. *Ant.* worsen; deteriorate; impair; reduce.

improvident *adj.* **1 thriftless,** unthrifty, spendthrift, wasteful, prodigal, extravagant, squandering, unfrugal, uneconomical, shiftless. **2 incautious,** unobservant, unwatchful, unwary, unvigilant, unalert, heedless, careless, inattentive, *inf.* asleep on the job, asleep at the wheel. *Ant.* thrifty; cautious.

improvise *v.* **1 ad lib,** extemporize, *inf.* speak off the cuff, play it by ear, wing it. **2 throw/put together,** devise, contrive, concoct, rig, jury-rig.

impudent *adj.* **impertinent,** insolent, cheeky, bold, audacious, brazen, brazen-faced, pert, saucy, presumptuous, forward, bumptious, impolite, rude, disrespectful, ill-mannered, bad-mannered, unmannerly, ill-bred, shameless, immodest, *inf.* fresh, cocky. **Ant.** polite; respectful; modest.

impulse *n.* **1 impetus,** propulsion, impulsion, momentum, force, thrust, push, surge. **2 stimulus,** inspiration, stimulation, incitement, incentive, inducement, motivation, urge, drive, instinct, appetite, proclivity. **3 sudden desire/fancy, (the) spur of the moment,** notion, whim, caprice.

impulsive *adj.* **hasty,** impromptu, snap, spontaneous, extemporaneous, sudden, quick, precipitate, impetuous, ill-considered, unplanned, unpremeditated, thoughtless, rash, reckless, instinctive, intuitive, passionate, emotional, madcap, devil-may-care, foolhardy. **Ant.** deliberate; premeditated; cautious.

impure *adj.* **1 adulterated,** alloyed, mixed, admixed, combined, blended, debased. **2 contaminated,** polluted, tainted, infected, foul, dirty, filthy, unclean, feculent, sullied, defiled, unwholesome, poisoned. **3 unchaste,** unvirginal, immoral, loose, promiscuous, wanton, immodest, shameless, corrupt, dissolute, depraved, licentious, lascivious, prurient, lustful, lecherous, lewd. **4 lewd,** lustful, lecherous, obscene, dirty,

indecent, ribald, risqué, smutty, pornographic, improper, crude, vulgar, coarse, gross.

inaccessible *adj.* **unreachable,** out of reach, beyond reach, unapproachable, impenetrable, unattainable, out of the way, remote, godforsaken.

inaccurate *adj.* **incorrect,** wrong, erroneous, faulty, inexact, imprecise, fallacious, false, not true, not right, imperfect, flawed, defective, unsound, unreliable, wide of the mark, *inf.* full of holes.

inactive *adj.* **1 immobile,** motionless, inert, stationary, idle, inoperative, nonfunctioning, not working, out of service, unused, out of use, not in use, unoccupied, unemployed, mothballed. **2 idle,** inoperative, nonfunctioning, not working, out of service, unused, out of use, not in use, unoccupied, unemployed, inert, mothballed. **3 idle,** inert, slow, sluggish, indolent, lazy, lifeless, slothful, lethargic, stagnant, vegetating, dilatory, torpid. **4 dormant,** quiescent, latent, passive.

inadequate *adj.* **1 insufficient,** not enough, too little, too few, lacking, found wanting, deficient, short, in short supply, meager, scanty, scant, niggardly, scarce, sparse, skimpy, sketchy, incomplete. **2 incompetent,** incapable, unfit, ineffective, ineffectual, inefficient, inefficacious, unskillful, inexpert, unproficient, inapt, inept, *inf.* not up to scratch/snuff. **Ant.** adequate; sufficient; competent.

inadvertent *adj.* **1 accidental,** unintentional, chance, unpremeditated, unplanned, uncalculated, unconscious, unwitting, involuntary. **2 inattentive,** careless, negligent, thoughtless, heedless, unheeding, unmindful, unobservant. **Ant.** deliberate; intentional; careful.

inadvisable *adj.* **ill-advised,** unwise, injudicious, ill-judged, imprudent, impolitic, inexpedient, foolish.

inanimate *adj.* **1 lifeless,** without life, exanimate, dead, inert, insentient, insensate, extinct, defunct. **2 spiritless,** apathetic, lazy, inactive, phlegmatic, listless, lethargic, sluggish, torpid.

inappropriate *adj.* **unsuitable,** unfitting, unseemly, unbecoming, indecorous, improper, ungentlemanly, unladylike, ungenteel, inapposite, incongruous, out of place/ keeping, inexpedient, inadvisable, injudicious, infelicitous, untimely.

inarticulate *adj.* **1 unintelligible,** incomprehensible, incoherent, unclear, indistinct, blurred, muffled, mumbled, muttered. **2 nonfluent,** faltering, hesitating, halting, stumbling, stuttering, stammering. **3 unspoken,** unuttered, unexpressed, unvoiced, wordless, silent, mute, dumb, speechless, voiceless, soundless, taciturn, tongue-tied.

inattentive *adj.* **1 distracted,** preoccupied, absentminded, daydreaming, woolgathering, lost in thought, off in a world of one's own, lacking concentration/ application, with one's head in the clouds, *inf.* miles away. **2 neglectful,** negligent, remiss, forgetful, careless, thoughtless, heedless, disregarding, indifferent, unconcerned, inconsiderate.

inauspicious *adj.* **unpropitious,** unpromising, unlucky, unfortunate, infelicitous, unhappy, unfavorable, ill-omened, ominous, ill-fated, ill-starred, untoward, untimely.

incapable *adj.* **lacking ability,** incompetent, ineffective, ineffectual, inefficacious, inadequate, unfit, unqualified, inept, inapt, unable, useless, feeble, *inf.* not up to scratch/snuff.

inception *n.* **beginning,** commencement, start, starting point, outset, opening, debut, inauguration, initiation, institution, birth, dawn, origin, rise, *inf.* kickoff.

incessant *adj.* **ceaseless,** unceasing, nonstop, endless, unending, never-ending, everlasting, eternal, constant, continual, perpetual, continuous, uninterrupted, unbroken, ongoing, unremitting, persistent, recurrent. *Ant.* intermittent; interrupted.

incident *n.* **1 event,** happening, occurrence, episode, adventure, experience, proceeding, occasion, circumstance, fact, matter. **2 disturbance,** commotion, scene, fracas, contretemps, skirmish, clash, conflict, confrontation.

incidental *adj.* **1 accidental,** coincidental, by chance, chance, fortuitous, random. **2 minor,** trivial, trifling, petty, small, meager. *Ant.* deliberate; essential; major.

incise *v.* **1 cut,** cut into, make an incision in, slit, slit open, gash, slash, notch, nick, furrow. **2 engrave,** etch, sculpt, sculpture, carve.

incite *v.* **1 instigate,** provoke, foment, whip up, stir up, prompt. **2 egg on,** encourage, urge, goad, spur on, prod, stimulate, drive on, excite, arouse, agitate, inflame,

stir up, provoke. *Ant.* discourage; deter.

inclination *n.* **1 tendency,** leaning, propensity, proclivity, proneness, liableness, disposition, predisposition, subjectability, weakness, penchant, predilection, partiality, preference, affinity, attraction, fancy, liking, fondness, affection, love. **2 bow,** bowing, bend, bending, nod, lowering, stooping. **3 incline,** slope, slant, gradient, bank, ramp, lift, tilt, acclivity, rise, ascent, declivity, descent, drop, dip, sag, cant, bevel, angle. *Ant.* aversion; dislike; disinclination.

incline *v.* **1 curve,** bend, slope, slant, bank, cant, bevel, tilt, lean, tip, list, deviate. **2 predispose,** dispose, influence, bias, prejudice, sway, make willing, persuade, bend. **3 have a tendency,** be liable/likely. **4 bow,** bend, nod, lower, stoop, cast down.

include *v.* **1 contain,** hold, take in, admit, incorporate, embrace, encompass, comprise, embody, comprehend, subsume. **2 allow for,** add, insert, put in, enter, introduce, count in, take account of, build in, number, incorporate. *Ant.* exclude; omit.

incoherent *adj.* **unconnected,** disconnected, disjointed, disordered, confused, mixed-up, muddled, jumbled, scrambled, rambling, wandering, discursive, illogical, unintelligible, inarticulate, mumbled, muttered, stuttered, stammered.

income *n.* **salary,** pay, remuneration, revenue, earnings, wages, receipts, takings, profits, gains, proceeds, means.

incomparable *adj.* **beyond compare,** inimitable, unequaled, without equal, matchless, nonpareil, paramount, unrivaled, peerless, unparalleled, unsurpassed, transcendent, superior, superlative, supreme.

incompatible *adj.*
1 inharmonious, unsuited, mismatched, uncongenial, incongruous, like day and night, uncomplementary, conflicting, antagonistic, antipathetic, dissentient, disagreeing, discordant, like oil and water.
2 inharmonious, discordant, clashing, jarring, uncomplementary. *Ant.* compatible; harmonious; consistent.

incompetent *adj.* **1 unable,** incapable, unfitted, unfit, unsuitable, unqualified, inapt, inept, inefficient, ineffectual, ineffective, inadequate, deficient, insufficient, useless. **2 unskillful,** inexpert, inept, bungling,

botched, awkward, maladroit, clumsy, gauche, floundering.

incomplete *adj.* **unfinished,** unaccomplished, partial, undone, unexecuted, unperformed, undeveloped, deficient, lacking, wanting, defective, imperfect, broken, shortened, curtailed, abridged, expurgated, bowdlerized.

incomprehensible *adj.*
1 illegible, unintelligible, indecipherable, unreadable, complicated, complex, involved, intricate. **2 beyond comprehension,** unfathomable, impenetrable, profound, deep, inexplicable, puzzling, enigmatic, mysterious, abstruse, recondite, *inf.* over one's head, tough.

inconceivable *adj.*
unimaginable, unthinkable, incomprehensible, incredible, unbelievable, implausible, impossible, out of the question, preposterous, ridiculous, ludicrous.

inconclusive *adj.* **indefinite,** indecisive, indeterminate, undetermined, still open to question, open to doubt, vague, unestablished, unsettled, ambiguous, *inf.* up in the air.

incongruous *adj.* **out of place/ keeping,** strange, odd, absurd, unsuitable, inappropriate, incompatible, inharmonious, discordant, clashing, jarring. *Ant.* appropriate; consistent; suitable.

inconsequential *adj.* **insignificant,** negligible, inappreciable, unimportant, of minor importance, of little/no account, trivial, trifling, petty, *inf.* piddling.

inconsiderate *adj.* **thoughtless,** unthinking, unthoughtful, uncaring, heedless, unmindful, regardless, undiscerning, insensitive, unsolicitous, tactless, uncharitable, unkind, unbenevolent, ungracious, selfish, self-centered, egotistic.

inconsistent *adj.* **inconstant,** unstable, unsteady, changeable, variable, erratic, irregular, unpredictable, capricious, fickle, whimsical, mercurial, volatile.

inconspicuous *adj.*
1 unnoticeable, unobtrusive, indistinct, ordinary, plain, run-of-the-mill, unremarkable, undistinguished, unostentatious, unimposing, hidden, camouflaged. **2 unnoticeable,** unobtrusive, insignificant, quiet, retiring, in the background, *inf.* low-key.

inconvenience *n.* **1 trouble,** bother, disruption, disturbance, vexation, worry, annoyance, disadvantage, difficulty, embarrassment. **2 trouble,** bother, source of disruption/vexation/annoyance, nuisance, burden, hindrance, *inf.* pain, drag, bore.
3 awkwardness, unwieldiness, cumbersomeness, unhandiness.
▸ *v.* **disturb,** bother, trouble, worry, disrupt, put out, impose upon, burden, distract, annoy.

inconvenient *adj.* **awkward,** unsuitable, inappropriate, inopportune, inexpedient, disadvantageous, disturbing, troublesome, bothersome, tiresome, vexatious, annoying, embarrassing, ill-timed, untimely, unseasonable, unwieldy, cumbersome, unmanageable, unhandy, difficult.

incorporate *v.* **1 merge,** coalesce, fuse, blend, mix, amalgamate, combine, unite, integrate, unify, compact.
2 embody, include, comprise, embrace, absorb, subsume, assimilate.

incorrect *adj.* **1 not right,** wrong, inaccurate, erroneous, wide of the mark, mistaken, faulty, inexact, untrue, fallacious, nonfactual, flawed, *inf.* full of holes.
2 improper, lacking in propriety, unbecoming, unseemly, indecorous, unsuitable, inappropriate, unladylike, ungentlemanly.

incorrigible *adj.* **hardened,** incurable, inveterate, unreformable, irreformable, unreformative, irredeemable, hopeless, beyond hope/ redemption, impenitent, uncontrite, unrepentant.

incorruptible *adj.* **1 virtuous,** upright, high-principled, honorable, honest, moral, ethical, trustworthy, straight, unbribable, untemptable. **2 imperishable,** indestructible, nonbiodegradable, indissoluble, indissolvable, everlasting.

increase *v.* **1 grow,** expand, extend, multiply, intensify, heighten, mount, escalate, snowball, mushroom, swell, wax, add to, boost, enhance, build up, augment, extend, spread, raise, intensify, strengthen, magnify, proliferate, inflate, *inf.* step up. **2 add to,** boost, enhance, build up, augment, enlarge, expand, extend, spread, heighten, raise, intensify, strengthen, magnify, proliferate, inflate, *inf.* step up. *Ant.* decrease; reduce. ► *n.* **growth,** rise, enlargement, expansion, extension, increment, addition, development, intensification, heightening, escalation, snowballing, mushrooming, boost, augmentation, strengthening, magnification, inflation, *inf.* stepping-up, step-up.

incredible *adj.* **1 unbelievable,** beyond belief, far-fetched, inconceivable, unimaginable, unthinkable, impossible, implausible, highly unlikely, quite improbable, absurd, preposterous, questionable, dubious, doubtful, fictitious, mythical. **2 extraordinary,** supreme, great, wonderful, marvelous, tremendous, prodigious, astounding, amazing, astonishing, awe-inspiring, awesome, superhuman, *inf.* fabulous, fantastic.

incredulous *adj.* **disbelieving,** unbelieving, skeptical, cynical, distrusting, distrustful, mistrusting, mistrustful, doubtful, doubting, dubious, unconvinced, suspicious.

incriminate *v.* **charge,** accuse, indict, impeach, arraign, blame, implicate, inculpate, involve, inform against, blacken the name of, stigmatize, *inf.* finger, point the finger at, pin the blame on, rat on.

incumbent ► *n.* **officeholder,** official, functionary, occupier.

incur *v.* **bring upon oneself,** expose oneself to, lay oneself open to, provoke, be liable/subject to, contract, meet with, experience.

incurable *adj.* **1 beyond cure,** cureless, unhealable, terminal, fatal, untreatable, inoperable, irremediable. **2 inveterate,** dyed-in-the-wool, incorrigible, hopeless, beyond hope.

indecent *adj.* **1 suggestive,** indelicate, improper, impure, risqué, off-color, ribald, bawdy, foul, vulgar, gross, crude, dirty, smutty, coarse, obscene, blue, lewd, lascivious, licentious, salacious, pornographic, scatological, *inf.* raunchy. **2 improper,** unseemly, indecorous, unbecoming, unsuitable, inappropriate, unfitting, unbefitting, in bad taste, tasteless, unacceptable, offensive, outrageous. *Ant.* clean; inoffensive; proper; seemly.

indecisive *adj.* **1 irresolute,** vacillating, wavering, fluctuating, hesitant, tentative, faltering, ambivalent, doubtful, in two minds, shilly-shallying, undecided, indefinite, uncertain, unresolved, undetermined, sitting on the fence, *inf.* blowing hot and cold. **2 inconclusive,** open, indeterminate, undecided, unsettled, indefinite, unclear, *inf.* up in the air.

indefatigable *adj.* **tireless,** untiring, never-tiring, unwearied, unflagging, persistent, tenacious, dogged, assiduous, industrious, indomitable, relentless, unremitting.

indefensible *adj.* **1 inexcusable,** unjustifiable, unpardonable, unforgivable, inexpiable. **2 untenable,** unarguable, insupportable, unmaintainable, unwarrantable, flawed, faulty, specious, implausible. **3 defenseless,** vulnerable, exposed, pregnable, unfortified, unguarded, unprotected, unshielded, unarmed.

indefinite *adj.* **1 undecided,** unfixed, undetermined, unsettled, inconclusive, undefined, unknown, uncertain, unspecific, inexplicit, unexplicit, imprecise, inexact, vague, doubtful. **2 ill-defined,** indistinct, blurred, fuzzy, hazy, dim, vague, obscure. **3 vague,** unclear, imprecise, inexact, ambiguous, ambivalent, equivocal, confused, evasive, abstruse. **4 undecided,** indecisive, irresolute, vacillating, wavering, hesitant, tentative, uncertain. **5 indeterminate,** unspecified, unlimited, limitless, infinite, immeasurable, boundless.

indemnify *v.* **1 reimburse,** compensate, make restitution/ amends to, recompense, repay, pay, pay back, remunerate. **2 insure,** underwrite, guarantee, protect, secure, make secure, give security to, endorse.

independence *n.* **1 self-government,** self-rule, home rule, self-determination, sovereignty, autonomy, nonalignment, freedom, separation, autarchy. **2 self-sufficiency,** self-reliance. **3 individualism,** boldness, liberation, unconstraint, unrestraint.

independent *adj.* **1 self-governing,** self-ruling, self-legislating, self-determining, sovereign, autonomous, autonomic, free, absolute, nonaligned, autarchic. **2 separate,** individual, free-standing, self-contained, unconnected, unrelated, unattached, distinct. **3 self-sufficient,** self-supporting, self-reliant, *inf.* standing on one's own feet. **4 freethinking,** individualistic, unconventional, bold, liberated, unconstrained, unrestrained, unfettered, untrammeled. *Ant.* dependent; subservient.

indescribable *adj.* **undescribable,** inexpressible, undefinable, beyond words/description, surpassing description, incommunicable, ineffable, unutterable, incredible, extraordinary, remarkable, prodigious.

indestructible *adj.* **durable,** enduring, unbreakable, infrangible, imperishable, inextinguishable, undecaying, perennial, deathless, undying, immortal, endless, everlasting.

indeterminate *adj.* **1 undetermined,** unfixed, indefinite, unspecified, unstipulated, unknown, uncertain, unpredictable, uncounted, uncalculated. **2 vague,** hazy, unclear, obscure, ambiguous, ambivalent, equivocal, inconclusive, inexact, imprecise, inexplicit, ill-defined.

index *n.* **1 guide,** key, directory, catalog, table of contents, card file. **2 mark,** token, sign, symptom, indication, clue, hint. **3 pointer,** indicator, needle, hand.

indicate *v.* **1 point to,** show, evince, manifest, reveal, be a sign/symptom of, be symptomatic of, mark, signal, denote, bespeak, betoken, connote, suggest, imply. **2 point to/out,** designate, specify. **3 show,** demonstrate, exhibit, display, manifest, evince, express, make known, tell, state, reveal, disclose, register, record.

indication *n.* **1 sign,** symptom, mark, manifestation, signal, omen, augury, portent, warning, hint. **2 show,** demonstration, exhibition, display, manifestation,

evincement, revelation,
disclosure, register, record.

indicator *n.* **1 pointer,** needle,
marker, index, gauge, meter,
display. **2 index,** guide, mark,
sign, signal, signpost, symbol.

indifferent *adj.* **1 apathetic,**
unconcerned, careless, heedless,
regardless, uncaring,
uninterested, unimpressed, aloof,
detached, distant, cold, cool,
impassive, dispassionate,
unresponsive, passionless,
unemotional, emotionless,
unmoved, unexcited, unfeeling,
unsympathetic, uncompassionate,
callous. **2 mediocre,** middling,
moderate, medium, fair, not bad,
passable, adequate, barely
adequate, average, ordinary,
commonplace, undistinguished,
uninspired, *inf.* OK, okay, so-so.
3 unimportant, insignificant,
inconsequential, minor, trivial,
trifling, slight, petty, irrelevant,
immaterial. **4 impartial,**
disinterested, unbiased,
nondiscriminatory, neutral,
unprejudiced, nonpartisan,
uninvolved, objective,
dispassionate, detached, just,
equitable, evenhanded, fair, fair-
minded. *Ant.* enthusiastic;
brilliant; biased.

indigenous *adj.* **native,** original,
local, endemic, aboriginal.

indignant *adj.* **angry,** angered,
irate, incensed, furious,
infuriated, annoyed, wrathful,
enraged, exasperated, heated,
riled, in a temper, in high
dudgeon, provoked, piqued,
disgruntled, in a huff, *inf.* fuming,
livid, aggravated, mad, seeing red,
up in arms, peeved, huffy, miffed.

indirect *adj.* **1 roundabout,**
circuitous, deviant, divergent,
wandering, meandering, winding,
curving, tortuous, zigzag.
2 oblique, discursive, digressive,
long-drawn-out, rambling,
circumlocutory, periphrastic,
allusive. **3 backhanded,** left-
handed, devious, insidious,
deceitful, underhand,
surreptitious, *inf.* sneaky.
4 incidental, accidental,
unintended, secondary,
subordinate, ancillary, collateral,
contingent.

indiscreet *adj.* **1 unwise,**
imprudent, injudicious, impolitic,
ill-advised, ill-considered, ill-
judged, ill-gauged, foolish,
incautious, careless, unwary,
hasty, rash, reckless, impulsive,
precipitate, foolhardy, tactless,
untactful, insensitive,
undiplomatic. **2 immodest,**
indelicate, indecorous, unseemly,
indecent, shameless, brazen,
bold.

indiscriminate *adj.*

1 undiscriminating, unselective, unparticular, uncritical, undifferentiating, aimless, careless, haphazard, random, unsystematic, unmethodical, broad-based, wholesale, general, sweeping, *inf.* hit-or-miss.
2 jumbled, mixed, haphazard, motley, miscellaneous, diverse, varied, mongrel, confused, chaotic, thrown together, *inf.* higgledy-piggledy. **Ant.** selective; systematic.

indispensable *adj.* **essential,** of the essence, vital, crucial, imperative, key, necessary, requisite, required, needed, needful, important, of the utmost importance, urgent, pressing, high-priority, fundamental. **Ant.** dispensable; superfluous; nonessential.

indisputable *adj.* **incontestable,** incontrovertible, undeniable, irrefutable, unquestionable, indubitable, beyond dispute/ question/doubt, beyond the shadow of a doubt, unassailable, certain, sure, positive, definite, absolute, final, conclusive.

indistinct *adj.* **blurred,** fuzzy, out of focus, bleary, hazy, misty, shadowy, dim, obscure, indefinite, indistinguishable, barely perceptible, undefined, indecipherable, illegible, unreadable, unintelligible, pale, faded, muffled, low, muted, muttered, mumbled.

indistinguishable *adj.*

1 identical, alike, very similar, *inf.* like two peas in a pod.
2 indiscernible, imperceptible, hard to make out, indefinite, unnoticeable, obscure, camouflaged, invisible.

individual *adj.* **1 single,** separate, sole, lone, solitary, distinct, distinctive, particular, specific, peculiar, detached, isolated.
2 characteristic, distinctive, particular, peculiar, typical, personal, personalized, own, private, special, especial, singular, original, unique, exclusive, idiosyncratic. **Ant.** collective; ordinary.
▸ *n.* **1 person,** personage, human being, creature, mortal, living soul, body, character, type.
2 individualist, free spirit, nonconformist, original, eccentric, bohemian, maverick, egocentric, rara avis, rare bird, rarity, loner, lone wolf.

indolent *adj.* **lazy,** idle, slothful, do-nothing, sluggish, lethargic, slow, slow-moving, slack, shiftless, languid, lackadaisical, apathetic, listless, impassive, inactive, inert, torpid. **Ant.** industrious; active.

induce *v.* **1 persuade,** talk into, get, prevail upon, prompt, move, inspire, instigate, influence, exert influence on, press, urge, incite, encourage, impel, actuate, motivate, inveigle, coax, wheedle. **2 bring about,** bring on, cause, produce, effect, create, give rise to, generate, originate, engender, occasion, set in motion, develop, lead to. *Ant.* dissuade; hinder; deter.

inducement *n.* **1 incentive,** attraction, encouragement, bait, lure, reward, incitement, stimulus, influence, spur, goad, impetus, motive, provocation, *inf.* carrot, come-on. **2 persuasion,** prompting, urging, incitement, encouragement, inveigling.

indulge *v.* **1 give way to,** yield to, pander to, cater to, satisfy, gratify, fulfill, satiate, appease. **2 give oneself up to,** give rein to, give free rein to, wallow in, luxuriate in, revel in. **3 pamper,** spoil, coddle, mollycoddle, pander to, humor, go along with, baby, pet.

indulgent *adj.* **1 tolerant,** forbearing, compassionate, humane, kind, kindly, understanding, sympathetic, liberal, forgiving, lenient, merciful, clement. **2 permissive,** easygoing, compliant, fond, doting, pampering, spoiling, mollycoddling, cosseting, humoring. *Ant.* intolerant; stern; strict.

industrious *adj.* **hardworking,** diligent, assiduous, sedulous, conscientious, steady, laborious, busy, busy as a bee/beaver, active, bustling, energetic, on the go, vigorous, determined, dynamic, indefatigable, tireless, persistent, pertinacious, zealous, productive. *Ant.* idle; indolent; lazy.

industry *n.* **1 manufacturing,** production, fabrication, construction. **2 business,** trade, commercial enterprise, field, line, craft, métier. **3 industriousness,** diligence, assiduity, application, sedulousness, sedulity, conscientiousness, concentration, intentness, steadiness, laboriousness, busyness, activity, energy, vigor, effort, determination, dynamism, tirelessness, persistence, pertinacity, zeal, productiveness.

ineffective *adj.* **ineffectual,** vain, to no avail, unavailing, useless, worthless, unsuccessful, futile, fruitless, unproductive, profitless, abortive, inadequate, inefficient, inefficacious, powerless, impotent, idle, feeble, weak, incompetent, inept, lame, barren, sterile.

inelegant *adj.* **1 unrefined,** uncultured, uncultivated, unpolished, unsophisticated, unfinished, gauche, crude, uncouth, ill-bred, coarse, vulgar. **2 awkward,** clumsy, ungainly, ungraceful, graceless.

ineligible *adj.* **1 unqualified,** unfit, unequipped, unsuitable, unacceptable, undesirable, ruled out, legally disqualified, *Law* incompetent. **2 unmarriageable,** unsuitable, undesirable, unacceptable.

inept *adj.* **1 incompetent,** unadept, incapable, unskillful, unskilled, inexpert, clumsy, awkward, maladroit, heavy-handed. **2 inadequate,** bungling, awkward, maladroit, unproductive, unsuccessful, ineffectual, *inf.* ham-handed. **3 out of place,** badly timed, inapt, inappropriate, unsuitable, infelicitous. **4 absurd,** foolish, silly, stupid, inane, nonsensical, senseless, farcical, ridiculous, ludicrous, asinine, crazy, *inf.* screwy. *Ant.* competent; appropriate; sensible.

inequality *n.* **1 unequalness,** disparity, imparity, imbalance, lack of balance, unevenness, disproportion, discrepancy, nonconformity, variation, variability, difference, dissimilarity, contrast. **2 bias,** prejudice, discrimination, preferentiality.

inequitable *adj.* **unjust,** unfair, partial, prejudiced, biased, partisan, discriminatory, preferential, one-sided, intolerant, bigoted.

inert *adj.* **1 inactive,** unmoving, motionless, immobile, still, stock-still, stationary, static, lifeless, inanimate, unconscious, passive, out cold, comatose, dormant, dead. **2 inactive,** idle, indolent, slack, lazy, slothful, dull, sluggish, lethargic, stagnant, languid, lackadaisical, listless, torpid, otiose. *Ant.* active; energetic.

inertia *n.* **inertness,** inactivity, inaction, inactiveness, motionlessness, immobility, unemployment, stagnation, stasis, passivity, idleness, indolence, laziness, sloth, slothfulness, dullness, sluggishness, lethargy, languor, listlessness, torpor. *Ant.* action; activity; energy.

inescapable *adj.* **unavoidable,** inevitable, unpreventable, inexorable, assured, certain, bound/sure to happen, ineludible, ineluctable.

inestimable *adj.* **immeasurable,** measureless, incalculable, priceless, beyond price, precious, invaluable, worth its weight in gold, worth a king's ransom, unparalleled, supreme, superlative.

inevitable *adj.* **unavoidable,** unpreventable, inexorable, inescapable, fixed, settled, irrevocable, fated, destined, predestined, ordained, decreed, out of one's hands, assured, certain, sure, bound/sure to happen, for sure, necessary, ineluctable. *Ant.* avoidable; uncertain.

inexhaustible *adj.* **1 unlimited,** limitless, illimitable, infinite, boundless, endless, never-ending, unrestricted, bottomless, measureless, copious, abundant. **2 indefatigable,** tireless, untiring, unwearying, weariless, unfaltering, unfailing, unflagging, unwavering, unremitting, persevering, persistent, dogged.

inexpensive *adj.* **low-cost,** low-price, low-priced, reasonably priced, reasonable, economical, cheap, budget, reduced, sale-price, half-price, marked-down, discount, discounted, cut-rate, bargain, bargain-basement.

inexperienced *adj.* **lacking experience,** untrained, untutored, undrilled, unqualified, unpracticed, amateur, unskilled, uninitiated, uninformed, ignorant, unacquainted, unversed, naïve, unsophisticated,

unfledged, untried, unseasoned, new, callow, immature, fresh, green, raw, *inf.* wet behind the ears.

inexplicable *adj.* **unexplainable,** inexplainable, unaccountable, incomprehensible, beyond comprehension/understanding, unintelligible, unfathomable, baffling, puzzling, perplexing, mystifying, insoluble, bewildering, mysterious, strange, weird, abstruse, enigmatic, inscrutable.

infallible *adj.* **1 unfailing,** without failure, foolproof, dependable, trustworthy, reliable, sure, certain, *inf.* sure-fire. **2 error-free,** unerring, unfailing, faultless, flawless, impeccable, unimpeachable, perfect.

infamous *adj.* **1 notorious,** disreputable, ill-famed, of ill-repute, iniquitous, ignominious, dishonorable, discreditable, villainous, bad, wicked, vile, odious, nefarious. **2 abominable,** outrageous, shocking, monstrous, disgraceful, dishonorable, shameful, atrocious, heinous, detestable, loathsome, hateful, wicked, vile, base, iniquitous, criminal, odious, nefarious, scandalous, egregious, flagitious. *Ant.* honorable; reputable.

infant *n.* **baby,** babe, newborn,

little child, tot, little one, neonate.

▸ *adj.* **emergent,** developing, dawning, nascent.

infantile *adj.* **babyish,** childish, puerile, immature, juvenile.

infatuated *adj.* **in love,** head over heels in love, hopelessly in love, enamored, besotted, captivated, bewitched, beguiled, spellbound, fascinated, enraptured, carried away, obsessed, swept off one's feet, taken with, under the spell of, *inf.* smitten, sweet on, keen on, mad about, wild about, crazy about, nuts about, stuck on, turned on by.

infatuation *n.* **passing fancy,** fancy, passion, obsession, fixation, craze, mania, *inf.* puppy love, crush, thing.

infect *v.* **1 contaminate,** poison, ulcerate. **2 influence,** corrupt, pervert, debauch, debase, degrade, vitiate. **3 influence,** affect, imbue, infuse, excite, inspire, stimulate, animate.

infectious *adj.* **1 infective,** communicable, transmittable, transmissible, catching, spreading, contagious, germ-laden, contaminating, polluting, septic, toxic, noxious, virulent, poisonous. **2 catching,** spreading, contagious, communicable, irresistible, compelling.

infer *v.* **1 deduce,** reason, conclude, gather, understand, presume, conjecture, surmise, read between the lines, theorize, hypothesize, *inf.* figure, guesstimate. **2 indicate,** point to, signal, signify, demonstrate, show, bespeak, evidence. **3 imply,** insinuate, hint, suggest, intimate.

inferior *adj.* **1 lower,** lesser, subordinate, junior, secondary, subsidiary, ancillary, second-class, second-fiddle, minor, subservient, lowly, humble, servile, menial. **2 imperfect,** faulty, defective, substandard, low-quality, low-grade, shoddy, cheap, reject, gimcrack, second-rate, indifferent, mediocre, incompetent, poor, bad, awful. *Ant.* superior; senior; excellent.

▸ *n.* **subordinate,** junior, underling, menial.

infernal *adj.* **1 lower,** nether, hellish, Hadean, Stygian. **2 hellish,** diabolical, devilish, demonic, demoniac, fiendish, satanic, malevolent, malicious, heinous, vile, atrocious, execrable, unspeakable, outrageous. **3 damned,** damnable, accursed, cursed, pestilential, wretched.

infest *v.* **overrun,** spread through, take over, overspread, pervade, permeate, penetrate, infiltrate, invade, swarm over, crawl over, beset, pester, plague.

infidelity *n.* **1 unfaithfulness,** adultery, cuckoldry, affair, liaison, intrigue, amour, *inf.* fooling/ playing around, cheating, hanky-panky. **2 breach of trust,** faithlessness, unfaithfulness, treachery, perfidy, perfidiousness, disloyalty, falseness, traitorousness, treason, double-dealing, duplicity. *Ant.* fidelity; faithfulness.

infinite *adj.* **boundless,** unbounded, unlimited, limitless, without limit/end, extensive, vast, countless, without number, numberless, innumerable, immeasurable, incalculable, untold, uncountable, inestimable, indeterminable, vast, enormous, stupendous, prodigious, measureless, fathomless, bottomless, endless, unending, never-ending, inexhaustible, interminable, absolute, total.

infinity *n.* **boundlessness,** limitlessness, unlimitedness, endlessness, infinitude, infiniteness, infinite distance, space.

infirm *adj.* **1 feeble,** enfeebled, weak, frail, debilitated, decrepit, disabled, in poor/declining health, failing, ailing, doddering, tottering, lame, crippled, rickety, unsteady, shaky, wobbly, unsound, flimsy, tumbledown, jerry-built, on its last legs, decayed. **2 indecisive,** irresolute, wavering, vacillating, fluctuating, faltering. *Ant.* healthy; fit; stable.

inflame *v.* **incite,** excite, arouse, rouse, stir up, work up, whip up, agitate, fire, ignite, kindle, foment, impassion, provoke, stimulate, actuate, enrage, incense, infuriate, exasperate, anger, madden, provoke, rile, aggravate, intensify, make worse, exacerbate, fan, fuel.

inflate *v.* **1 blow up,** pump up, aerate, puff up, puff out, dilate, distend, swell. **2 increase,** extend, amplify, augment, expand, intensify, exaggerate, add to, boost, magnify, escalate, aggrandize. **3 increase,** boost, raise, escalate, step up. *Ant.* deflate; collapse; play down (see play); decrease.

inflexible *adj.* **1 nonflexible,** rigid, stiff, unbendable, unyielding, taut, hard, firm, inelastic, unmalleable. **2 unalterable,** unchangeable, immutable, unvarying, firm, fixed, hard and fast, unbendable, uncompromising, stringent, rigorous, inexorable. **3 adamant,** firm, immovable, unadaptable, dyed-in-the-wool, unaccommodating, uncompliant, stubborn, obdurate, obstinate, intractable, unbending, intolerant, relentless, merciless, pitiless, uncompromising, inexorable, steely, iron-willed.

inflict *v.* **administer,** deal out, mete out, serve out, deliver, apply, lay on, impose, levy, exact, wreak.

influence *n.* **effect,** impact, control, sway, ascendancy, power, mastery, agency, guidance, domination, rule, supremacy, leadership, direction, pressure, authority, prestige, standing, footing, good offices, connections, *inf.* clout, pull.
▸ *v.* **affect,** have an effect on, impact on, sway, bias, incline, motivate, actuate, determine, guide, control, change, alter, transform, bring pressure to bear on, persuade, induce, impel, incite, manipulate, prompt, *inf.* pull strings with, pull rank on.

influential *adj.* **1 powerful,** important, leading, authoritative, controlling, dominant, predominant, prestigious. **2 instrumental,** guiding, significant, important, persuasive, telling, meaningful. *Ant.* unimportant; impotent; insignificant.

influx *n.* **inrush,** rush, inflow, inundation, flood, invasion, intrusion, incursion, ingress, convergence.

inform *v.* **1 tell,** let know, apprise, advise, notify, announce to, impart to, relate to, communicate to, acquaint, brief, instruct, enlighten, make conversant, make knowledgeable, send word to, *inf.* put in the picture, fill in, clue in/up, spill the beans to, tip off, give the low-down to, give the inside story to. **2 characterize,** typify, pervade, permeate, suffuse, infuse, imbue, instill, shape, form, mold.

informal *adj.* **1 nonformal,** casual, unceremonious, unofficial, simple, unpretentious, everyday, relaxed, easy. **2 colloquial,** vernacular, nonliterary, simple, natural, everyday, unofficial, unpretentious, *inf.* slangy.

information *n.* **data,** facts, knowledge, intelligence, news, notice, word, advice, counsel, instruction, enlightenment, tidings, message, report, communiqué, communication, *inf.* info, low-down, dope, poop, inside story, dirt.

informative *adj.* **instructive,** illuminating, enlightening, edifying, educational, revealing, telling, communicative, chatty, newsy, gossipy.

informed *adj.* **knowledgeable,** well-briefed, well-posted, primed, well-versed, up-to-date, au courant, au fait.

informer *n.* **informant,** betrayer, traitor, Judas, *inf.* rat, squealer, stool pigeon, tattletale, whistleblower, canary, snitch.

infrequent *adj.* **few and far between,** rare, occasional, sporadic, irregular, uncommon, unusual, exceptional.

infringe *v.* **break,** disobey, violate, contravene, transgress, breach, infract, disregard, encroach, impinge, intrude, trespass.

ingenious *adj.* **clever,** shrewd, astute, smart, sharp, bright, brilliant, talented, masterly, resourceful, inventive, creative, original, subtle, crafty, wily, cunning, skillful, adroit, deft, capable, *inf.* on the ball. *Ant.* stupid; unimaginative.

ingenuous *adj.* **open,** sincere, honest, frank, candid, direct, forthright, artless, guileless, simple, naïve, innocent, genuine, undeceitful, undeceptive, undissembling, undissimulating, aboveboard, trustful, truthful, unsuspicious, *inf.* on the level. *Ant.* insincere; artful.

ingratiating *adj.* **sycophantic,** toadying, fawning, unctuous, obsequious, servile, overhumble, crawling, flattering, wheedling, cajoling, *inf.* bootlicking.

inhabit *v.* **live in,** dwell in, reside in, occupy, lodge in, make one's home in, settle in, settle, people, populate.

inhabitant *n.* **resident,** resider, dweller, occupant, occupier, habitant, settler.

inherent *adj.* **1 inborn,** inbred, innate, hereditary, inherited, in the blood/family, congenital, familial. **2 intrinsic,** immanent, innate, built-in, inseparable, essential, basic, fundamental, ingrained.

inherit *v.* **1 become/fall heir to,** be bequeathed, be left, be willed, come into/by. **2 succeed to,** accede to, assume, take over, be elevated to.

inheritance *n.* **legacy,** bequest, endowment, birthright, heritage, patrimony.

inhibit *v.* **hold back,** impede, hinder, hamper, interfere with, obstruct, curb, check, restrict, restrain, constrain, bridle, rein in, balk, frustrate, arrest, prevent, stop, forbid, prohibit, ban, bar, debar, interdict, proscribe.

inhibited *adj.* **shy,** reticent, self-conscious, reserved, constrained, repressed, embarrassed, tongue-tied, subdued, withdrawn, *inf.*

uptight. **Ant.** uninhibited; outgoing; easygoing.

inhibition n. **1 holding back,** impediment, hindrance, hampering, interference, obstruction, curb, check, restriction, restraint, constraint, bridling, balking, frustration, arrest, prevention, stopping.
2 shyness, reticence, reserve, self-consciousness, constraint, repression, embarrassment, subduedness, withdrawnness.

inhospitable adj.
1 unwelcoming, unsociable, unsocial, antisocial, unfriendly, uncivil, discourteous, ungracious, uncongenial, ungenerous, cool, cold, chilly, aloof, unkind, unsympathetic, ill-disposed, hostile, inimical, xenophobic.
2 uninviting, unwelcoming, barren, bleak, bare, uninhabitable, sterile, desolate, lonely, empty, forbidding, hostile, inimical.

initial adj. **first,** beginning, commencing, starting, opening, early, prime, primary, elementary, foundational, introductory, inaugural, inceptive, incipient, inchoate. **Ant.** final; terminal.
▸ v. **put one's initials on,** sign, undersign, countersign, endorse.

initiate v. **1 begin,** start off,

commence, open, institute, inaugurate, get under way, set in motion, lay the foundations of, launch, actuate, instigate, trigger, originate, pioneer, sow the seeds of, start the ball rolling for.
2 teach, instruct, coach, tutor, school, train, drill, prime, familiarize, indoctrinate, inculcate. **3 admit,** introduce, induct, install, instate, incorporate, ordain, invest, enlist, enroll, sign up. **Ant.** end; close.
▸ n. **beginner,** new boy/girl, newcomer, learner, trainee, apprentice, probationer, new/raw recruit, greenhorn, novice, tyro, novitiate, neophyte, inf. rookie.

initiative n. **1 first step,** first move, first blow, lead, gambit, opening move/gambit, beginning, start, commencement.
2 enterprise, inventiveness, resourcefulness, resource, originality, creativity, drive, dynamism, ambition, ambitiousness, verve, dash, leadership, inf. get-up-and-go, zing, push, pep, zip.

injunction n. **command,** instruction, order, ruling, direction, directive, dictum, dictate, mandate, ordainment, enjoinment, admonition, precept, ultimatum.

injure v. **1 hurt,** harm, damage,

wound, maim, cripple, lame, disable, mutilate, deform, mangle, impair, weaken, enfeeble, ruin, spoil, mar, blight, blemish, besmirch, tarnish, undermine. **2 ruin,** spoil, mar, damage, blight, blemish, besmirch, tarnish, undermine. **3 do an injury to,** wrong, do an injustice to, offend against, abuse, maltreat, defame, vilify, malign.

injurious *adj.* **harmful,** hurtful, damaging, deleterious, detrimental, disadvantageous, unfavorable, destructive, pernicious, ruinous, disastrous, calamitous, malignant. *Ant.* innocuous; advantageous; favorable.

injury *n.* **1 harm,** hurt, wounding, damage, impairment, affliction, wound, sore, bruise, cut, gash, laceration, abrasion, lesion, contusion, trauma. **2 injustice,** wrong, ill, offense, disservice, grievance, evil.

injustice *n.* **unjustness,** unfairness, inequitableness, inequity, bias, prejudice, favoritism, partiality, one-sidedness, discrimination, partisanship, wrong, injury, offense, evil, villainy, iniquity.

inkling *n.* **1 hint,** clue, intimation, suggestion, indication, whisper, suspicion, insinuation, innuendo.

2 idea, the vaguest idea, notion, glimmering, the slightest knowledge, *inf.* (the) foggiest idea, (the) foggiest.

innate *adj.* **1 inborn,** inbred, connate, congenital, hereditary, inherited, in the blood/family, inherent, intrinsic, ingrained, natural, native, indigenous. **2 essential,** basic, fundamental, quintessential, organic, radical, inherent, immanent. **3 instinctive,** intuitive, spontaneous, unlearned, untaught.

inner *adj.* **1 interior,** inside, central, middle, further in. **2 restricted,** privileged, confidential, intimate, private, exclusive, secret. **3 unapparent,** veiled, obscure, esoteric, hidden, secret, unrevealed. **4 private,** secret, deep, personal, innermost, intimate, hidden, spiritual, emotional, mental, psychological, psychic, subconscious, unconscious, innermost. *Ant.* outer; exterior; outside.

innocence *n.* **1 guiltlessness,** blamelessness, freedom from guilt/blame, inculpability, unimpeachability, irreproachability, clean hands. **2 harmlessness,** innocuousness, safety, lack of danger/malice, inoffensiveness. **3 virtuousness,** virtue, purity, lack of sin, sinlessness, morality, decency, righteousness, chastity, virginity, immaculateness, impeccability, spotlessness. **4** simpleness, ingenuousness, naïveté, lack of sophistication, artlessness, guilelessness, frankness, openness, credulity, inexperience, gullibility. **Ant.** guilt; sin; experience.

innocent *adj.* **1 not guilty,** guiltless, blameless, clear, in the clear, above suspicion, unblameworthy, inculpable, unimpeachable, irreproachable, clean-handed. **2 harmless,** innocuous, safe, noninjurious, unmalicious, unobjectionable, inoffensive, playful. **3 virtuous,** pure, sinless, moral, decent, righteous, upright, chaste, virginal, virgin, immaculate, impeccable, pristine, spotless, stainless, unblemished, unsullied, incorrupt, uncorrupted. **4 simple,** ingenuous, naïve, unsophisticated, artless, guileless, childlike, frank, open, unsuspicious, trustful, trusting, credulous, inexperienced, unworldly, green, gullible, *inf.* wet behind the ears. **Ant.** guilty; sinful; experienced; worldly.
▶ *n.* **child,** babe, babe in the woods/wood, babe in arms, ingenue, novice, greenhorn.

innocuous *adj.* **1 harmless,** unhurtful, uninjurious, safe, danger-free, nonpoisonous. **2 harmless,** inoffensive, unobjectionable, unexceptionable, unoffending, mild, peaceful, bland, commonplace, run-of-the-mill, insipid. **Ant.** harmful; dangerous; injurious.

innuendo *n.* insinuation, implication, suggestion, hint, overtone, allusion, inkling, imputation, aspersion.

innumerable *adj.* **very many,** numerous, countless, untold, incalculable, numberless, unnumbered, beyond number, infinite, myriad, *inf.* umpteen, masses, oodles. **Ant.** few; finite.

inquire *v.* **ask,** make inquiries (about), quiz, interrogate, *inf.* grill.

inquiry *n.* **1 investigation,** examination, exploration, sounding, probe, search, scrutiny, scrutinization, study, inspection, interrogation. **2 question,** query.

inquisitive *adj.* **inquiring,** questioning, probing, scrutinizing, curious, burning with curiosity, interested, overinterested, intrusive, meddlesome, prying, snooping, snoopy, peering, spying, *inf.* nosy. **Ant.** indifferent; apathetic; uninterested.

insane *adj.* **1 mad,** disordered, of unsound mind, deranged, demented, non compos mentis, out of one's mind, mad, mad as a hatter, raving mad, out of one's mind, unhinged, not all there, crazy, *inf.* bonkers, cracked, balmy, batty, bats, cuckoo, loony, loopy, nuts, nutty, screwy, bananas, off one's rocker, out of one's head, around the bend, off one's trolley, unhinged, crazed, crazy, non compos. **2 foolish,** mad, crazy, idiotic, stupid, senseless, nonsensical, irrational, impracticable, pointless, absurd, ridiculous, ludicrous, bizarre, fatuous, *inf.* daft.

inscrutable *adj.* **1 enigmatic,** unreadable, impenetrable, cryptic, deadpan, sphinxlike, *inf.* poker-faced. **2 mysterious,** inexplicable, unexplainable, incomprehensible unintelligible, puzzling, baffling, unfathomable, arcane. *Ant.* open; expressive; transparent.

insecure *adj.* **1 unconfident,** diffident, timid, uncertain, unsure, doubtful, hesitant, anxious, fearful, apprehensive, worried. **2 vulnerable,** open to attack, defenseless, unprotected, ill-protected, unguarded, unshielded, exposed, in danger, dangerous, perilous, hazardous.

3 loose, flimsy, frail, fragile, infirm, weak, unsubstantial, jerry-built, rickety, wobbly, shaky, unsteady, unstable, unsound, decrepit.

insensitive *adj.* **heartless,** unfeeling, callous, tactless, thick-skinned, uncaring, unconcerned, uncompassionate, unsympathetic.

insert *v.* **1 put in/into,** place in, press in, push in, stick in, thrust in, drive in, work in, slide in, slip in, tuck in, *inf.* pop in. **2 put in,** introduce, enter, interpolate, inset, interpose, interject, implant, infix. *Ant.* extract; withdraw.

▸ *n.* **insertion,** inset, supplement, circular, advertisement, *inf.* ad.

inside *n.* **interior,** contents.

▸ *adv.* **1 indoors,** in/into the house/building, within.
2 emotionally, intuitively, instinctively.

insidious *adj.* **stealthy,** subtle, surreptitious, sneaky, sneaking, cunning, crafty, designing, intriguing, Machiavellian, artful, guileful, sly, wily, tricky, slick, deceitful, deceptive, underhand, underhanded, double-dealing, duplicitous, dishonest, insincere, disingenuous, treacherous, perfidious, *inf.* crooked. *Ant.* straightforward; artless; honest.

insignificant *adj.* **unimportant,**

of little import, trivial, trifling, negligible, inconsequential, of no consequence/account, inconsiderable, not worth mentioning, nugatory, meager, paltry, scanty, petty, insubstantial, unsubstantial, flimsy, irrelevant, immaterial, *inf.* dinky.

insincere *adj.* **lacking sincerity,** not candid, not frank, disingenuous, dissembling, dissimulating, pretended, devious, hypocritical, deceitful, deceptive, duplicitous, dishonest, underhand, double-dealing, false, faithless, disloyal, treacherous, two-faced, lying, untruthful, mendacious, evasive, shifty, slippery.

insinuate *v.* **1 imply,** hint, whisper, suggest, indicate, convey the impression, intimate, mention. **2 infiltrate,** implant, instill, introduce, inculcate, infuse, inject.

insist *v.* **1 stand firm,** be firm, stand one's ground, make a stand, be resolute, be determined, be emphatic, not take no for an answer, brook no refusal, demand, require, command, importune, entreat, urge, exhort. **2 maintain,** assert, declare, hold, contend, pronounce, proclaim, aver, propound, avow, vow, swear, be emphatic, emphasize, stress, repeat, reiterate.

insistent *adj.* **1 emphatic,** determined, resolute, tenacious, importunate, persistent, unyielding, obstinate, dogged, unrelenting, inexorable. **2 persistent,** determined, dogged, incessant, urgent, pressing, compelling, high-pressure, pressurizing, coercive, demanding, exigent. **3 constant,** incessant, iterative, repeated, repetitive, recurrent.

insolence *n.* **impertinence,** impudence, cheek, cheekiness, ill-manneredness, rudeness, disrespect, incivility, insubordination, contempt, abuse, offensiveness, contumely, audacity, nerve, boldness, brazenness, brashness, pertness, forwardness, effrontery, insults, *inf.* gall, lip, chutzpah.

insolent *adj.* **impertinent,** impudent, cheeky, rude, ill-mannered, disrespectful, insubordinate, contemptuous, insulting, abusive, offensive, audacious, bold, brazen, brash, pert, forward, *inf.* fresh. ***Ant.*** polite; respectful; modest.

insoluble *adj.* **1 indissoluble,** indissolvable, undissolvable. **2 insolvable,** unsolvable, baffling, unfathomable, indecipherable, complicated, perplexing, intricate, involved, impenetrable, inscrutable, enigmatic, obscure, mystifying, inexplicable, incomprehensible, mysterious.

insolvent *adj.* **bankrupt,** indebted, in debt, liquidated, ruined, defaulting, in the hands of the receivers, penniless, impoverished, penurious, impecunious, *inf.* gone bust, gone to the wall, on the rocks, in the red, broke, hard up, strapped for cash.

inspect *v.* **examine,** check, go over, look over, survey, scrutinize, audit, study, pore over, view, scan, observe, investigate, assess, appraise, *inf.* give the once-over.

inspection *n.* **examination,** check, checkup, survey, scrutiny, view, scan, observation, investigation, probe, assessment, appraisal, *inf.* once-over, going-over, look-see.

inspector *n.* **examiner,** checker, scrutinizer, auditor, surveyor, scanner, observer, investigator, overseer, supervisor, assessor, appraiser, critic.

inspiration *n.* **stimulus,** stimulation, motivation, encouragement, influence, muse, goad, spur, incitement, arousal, rousing, stirring, creativity, originality, inventiveness, genius, insight, vision, bright idea, brilliant/timely thought, revelation, illumination, enlightenment.

inspire *v.* **stimulate,** motivate, encourage, influence, inspirit, animate, fire the imagination of, rouse, stir, spur, goad, energize, galvanize, arouse, excite, quicken, inflame, touch off, spark off, ignite, kindle, give rise to, produce, bring about, prompt, instigate. **Ant.** discourage; dispirit; extinguish.

instability *n.* **1 impermanence,** temporariness, transience, inconstancy, unsteadiness, uncertainty, precariousness, fluidity, fluctuation, unsoundness, shakiness, ricketiness, wobbliness, frailty, flimsiness, unsubstantiality, insecurity, unpredictability, unreliability, *inf.* chanciness. **2 insecurity,** precariousness, unpredictability, unreliability, uncertainty, *inf.* chanciness. **3 changeableness,** variability, capriciousness, volatility, flightiness, vacillation, wavering, fitfulness, oscillation.

install *v.* **1 put in,** insert, put in place, position, place, emplace, fix, locate, situate, station, lodge, ensconce, position, settle. **2 induct,** instate, institute, inaugurate, invest, ordain, introduce, initiate, establish. **Ant.** remove; extract.

installment *n.* **part,** portion, section, segment, chapter, division, episode.

instance *n.* **1 case,** case in point, example, illustration, exemplification, occasion, occurrence, stage, step. **2 behest,** instigation, urging, demand, insistence, request, prompting, solicitation, entreaty, importuning, pressure.
▸ *v.* **give,** cite, mention, name, specify, quote, adduce.

instant *n.* **1 moment,** minute, second, split second, trice, twinkling, twinkling of an eye, flash, *inf.* jiffy, jif, sec, two shakes of a lamb's tail. **2 moment,** time, present time, minute, very minute, particular/specific time, moment in time, juncture, point.
▸ *adj.* **1 instantaneous,** immediate, on-the-spot, prompt, rapid, sudden, abrupt. **2 prepared,** ready-mixed, precooked, fast.

instigate *v.* **1 bring about,** start, initiate, actuate, generate, incite, provoke, inspire, foment, kindle, stir up, whip up. **2 incite,** encourage, egg on, urge, prompt, goad, prod, induce, impel, constrain, press, persuade, prevail upon, sway, entice. **Ant.** halt; discourage.

instigator *n.* prime mover, inciter, motivator, agitator, fomenter, troublemaker, agent provocateur, ringleader, leader.

instill *v.* **1 add gradually,** introduce, infuse, inject. **2 infuse,** inculcate, implant, teach, drill, arouse, imbue, permeate, inculcate.

instinct *n.* intuition, sixth sense, talent, gift, ability, capacity, faculty, aptitude, knack, bent, trait, characteristic.

instinctive *adj.* **inborn,** inherent, innate, inbred, natural, intuitive, intuitional, involuntary, untaught, unlearned, automatic, reflex, mechanical, spontaneous, impulsive, unthinking, unpremeditated.

institute *v.* **1 begin,** start, commence, set in motion, put into operation, initiate. **2 found,** establish, start, launch, bring into being, bring about, constitute, set up, organize, develop, create, originate, pioneer. **Ant.** halt; end.
▸ *n.* **institution,** organization, foundation, society, association, league, guild, consortium, academy, school, college, conservatory, seminary, seat of learning.

institutional *adj.* **1 organized,** established, bureaucratic, accepted, orthodox, conventional, customary, formal, systematic, methodical, orderly, *inf.* establishment. **2 uniform,** same, unvarying, unvaried, unchanging, regimented, monotonous, bland, dull, insipid, *inf.* cafeteria. **3 cold,** cheerless, clinical, dreary, drab, unwelcoming, uninviting, impersonal, formal, forbidding.

instruct *v.* **1 tell,** direct, order, command, bid, charge, enjoin, demand, require. **2 teach,** educate, tutor, coach, train, school, drill, ground, prime, prepare, guide, inform, enlighten, edify, discipline. **3 inform,** tell, notify, acquaint, make known to, advise, apprise, brief.

instruction *n.* **1 teaching,** education, tutoring, tutelage, coaching, training, schooling, drilling, grounding, priming, preparation, guidance, information, enlightenment, edification, discipline, lessons, classes, lectures. **2 direction,** directive, briefing, order, command, charge, injunction, requirement, ruling, mandate.

instructive *adj.* **instructional,** informative, informational, educational, educative, enlightening, illuminating, useful, helpful, edifying, cultural, uplifting, academic, didactic, doctrinal.

instructor *n.* **teacher,** schoolteacher, schoolmaster, schoolmistress, educator, lecturer, professor, pedagogue, tutor, coach, trainer, adviser, counselor, guide, mentor, demonstrator.

instrument *n.* **1 implement,** tool, appliance, apparatus, mechanism, utensil, gadget, contrivance, device, aid, musical instrument, gauge, meter, *inf.* contraption. **2 agency,** agent, prime mover, catalyst, cause, factor, channel, medium, force, mechanism, instrumentality, vehicle, organ, means. **3 pawn,** puppet, tool, dupe, minion, flunky, *inf.* stooge.

instrumental *adj.* **helpful,** of help/assistance, useful, of use/service, contributory, active, involved, influential, significant, important.

insubordinate *adj.* **rebellious,** mutinous, insurgent, seditious, insurrectional, riotous, disobedient, noncompliant, defiant, refractory, recalcitrant, contumacious, undisciplined, ungovernable, uncontrollable, unmanageable, unruly, disorderly.

insufferable *adj.* **intolerable,** unbearable, unendurable, insupportable, too much to bear, impossible, too much, more than one can stand, more than flesh and blood can stand, enough to try the patience of Job, enough to test the patience of a saint, unspeakable, dreadful, excruciating, grim, outrageous.

insufficient *adj.* **inadequate,** deficient, in short supply, scarce, meager, scant, scanty, wanting, at a premium.

insular *adj.* **1 isolated,** detached, separate, segregated, solitary, insulated, self-sufficient. **2 narrow,** narrow-minded, illiberal, prejudiced, biased, bigoted, provincial, parochial, limited, restricted. *Ant.* liberal; open-minded; cosmopolitan.

insulate *v.* **1 isolate,** heatproof, soundproof, cover, wrap, encase, envelop, pad, cushion, seal. **2 segregate,** separate, isolate, detach, cut off, keep/set apart, sequester, exclude, protect, shield.

insult *v.* **offend,** give/cause offense to, affront, slight, hurt the feelings of, hurt, abuse, injure, wound, mortify, humiliate, disparage, discredit, depreciate, impugn, slur, revile. *Ant.* compliment; flatter.
▸ *n.* **affront,** slight, gibe, snub, barb, slur, abuse, disparagement, depreciation, impugnment, revilement, insolence, rudeness, contumely, aspersions, *inf.* dig.

insuperable *adj.*

insurmountable, impassable, overwhelming, invincible, unconquerable, unassailable.

insure *v.* **indemnify,** cover, underwrite, guarantee, warrant.

intact *adj.* **whole,** complete, entire, perfect, all in one piece, sound, untouched, unbroken, unsevered, undamaged, unscathed, uninjured, unharmed, unmutilated, inviolate, unviolated, undefiled, unblemished, unsullied, faultless, flawless. *Ant.* broken; damaged.

intangible *adj.* **1 impalpable,** untouchable, incorporeal, phantom, spectral, ghostly. **2 indefinable,** indescribable, vague, subtle, unclear, obscure, mysterious.

integral *adj.* **1 essential,** necessary, indispensable, requisite, basic, fundamental, inherent, intrinsic, innate, constituent, component. **2 entire,** complete, whole, total, full, intact, unified, integrated, undivided.

integrate *v.* **1 unite,** join, combine, amalgamate, consolidate, blend, incorporate, coalesce, fuse, merge, intermix, mingle, commingle, assimilate, homogenize, harmonize, mesh, concatenate. **2 desegregate,** open up.

integrity *n.* **1 uprightness,** honesty, rectitude, righteousness, virtue, probity, morality, honor, goodness, decency, truthfulness, fairness, sincerity, candor, principles, ethics. **2 unity,** unification, wholeness, entirety, completeness, totality, cohesion. *Ant.* dishonesty; fragmentation.

intellect *n.* **1 intelligence,** reason, understanding, comprehension, mind, brain, thought, sense, judgment. **2 intellectual,** genius, thinker, mastermind, *inf.* brain, mind, egghead, Einstein.

intellectual *adj.* **mental,** cerebral, academic, intelligent, academic, well-educated, well-read, erudite, learned, bookish, highbrow, scholarly, studious, rational, logical, clinical, unemotional, nonemotional. *Ant.* physical; illiterate; stupid.
▸ *n.* **intellect,** genius, thinker, mastermind, academic, academician, man/woman of letters, bluestocking, pundit, highbrow, bookworm, pedant, *inf.* egghead, walking encyclopedia.

intelligence *n.* **1 intellect,** mind, brain, brainpower, mental capacity/aptitude, reason, understanding, comprehension, acumen, wit, cleverness, brightness, brilliance, sharpness, quickness of mind, alertness, discernment, perception, perspicacity, penetration, sense, sagacity, brains, *inf.* gray matter. **2 information,** news, notification, notice, account, knowledge, advice, rumor, facts, data, reports, tidings, *inf.* low-down, poop, dope. **3 information collection,** espionage, surveillance, observation, spying.

intelligent *adj.* **1 clever,** bright, brilliant, sharp, quick, quick-witted, smart, apt, discerning, thinking, perceptive, perspicacious, penetrating, sensible, sagacious, well-informed, educated, enlightened, knowledgeable, *inf.* brainy. **2 rational,** reasoning, higher-order. *Ant.* stupid; slow.

intelligentsia *pl. n.* **intellectuals,** academics, literati, cognoscenti, illuminati, highbrows, pedants, the enlightened.

intelligible *adj.* **understandable,** comprehensible, clear, lucid, plain, explicit, unambiguous, legible, decipherable. *Ant.* unintelligible; incoherent; incomprehensible.

intemperate *adj.* **1 immoderate,** self-indulgent, excessive, inordinate, extreme, extravagant, unreasonable, outrageous, immoderate, drunken, drunk, intoxicated, inebriated, alcoholic, dissolute, dissipated, debauched, profligate, prodigal, loose, wild, wanton, licentious, libertine. **2 uncontrolled,** unrestrained, uncurbed, unbridled, ungoverned, tempestuous, violent.

intend v. **mean,** plan, have in mind/view, propose, aim, resolve, be resolved, be determined, expect, purpose, contemplate, think of, destine, scheme, devise.

intense adj. **1 acute,** fierce, severe, extreme, harsh, strong, powerful, potent, vigorous, great, profound, deep, concentrated, consuming. **2 earnest,** eager, ardent, keen, enthusiastic, zealous, excited, impassioned, passionate, fervent, fervid, burning, consuming, vehement, fanatical. **3 nervous,** nervy, tense, fraught, overwrought, highly strung, emotional. **Ant.** mild; calm.

intensify v. **heighten,** deepen, strengthen, increase, reinforce, magnify, enhance, fan, whet, aggravate, exacerbate, worsen, inflame, inf. add fuel to the flames, increase, extend, augment, boost, escalate, step up. **Ant.** decrease; diminish; relax.

intensive adj. **in-depth,** concentrated, exhaustive, all-out, thorough, thoroughgoing, total.

intent adj. **1 concentrated,** concentrating, fixed, steady, steadfast, absorbed, attentive, engrossed, occupied, preoccupied, rapt, enrapt, wrapped up, focused, observant, watchful, alert, earnest, committed, intense. **2 set on,** bent on, committed to, firm about, determined to, resolved to, inf. hell-bent on.
▶ n. **intention,** purpose, aim, objective, goal, end, plan.

intention n. **1 aim,** purpose, intent, goal, objective, end, end in view, target, aspiration, ambition, wish, plan, design, resolve, resolution, determination. **2 premeditation,** preconception, design, plan, calculation.

intentional adj. **intended,** deliberate, meant, done on purpose, willful, purposeful, purposed, planned, calculated, designed, premeditated, preconceived, predetermined, prearranged, preconcerted, considered, weighed up, studied. **Ant.** accidental; inadvertent.

inter v. **bury,** consign to the grave, entomb, lay to rest, inhume, inearth, sepulcher.

intercept v. **stop,** cut off, deflect, head off, seize, expropriate, commandeer, catch, check, arrest, block, obstruct, impede, deflect.

intercourse n. **1 dealings,** trade,

traffic, commerce, communication, intercommunication, association, connection, contact, correspondence, communion, congress. **2 sex,** sexual relations, coitus, coition, copulation, carnal knowledge, intimacy, lovemaking.

interest *n.* **1 attentiveness,** attention, undivided attention, absorption, engrossment, heed, regard, notice, scrutiny, curiosity, inquisitiveness. **2 curiosity,** attraction, appeal, fascination, charm, allure. **3 concern,** importance, import, consequence, moment, significance, note, relevance, seriousness, weight, gravity, priority, urgency. **4 leisure activity,** pastime, hobby, diversion, amusement, pursuit, relaxation, *inf.* thing, scene. **5 share,** stake, portion, claim, investment, involvement, participation, stock, equity. **6 involvement,** partiality, partisanship, preference, one-sidedness, favoritism, bias, prejudice, discrimination. **7 concern,** business, matter, care, affairs. **8 profit,** return, percentage, gain. **9 benefit,** advantage, good, profit, gain. *Ant.* boredom; tedium; impartiality.

▶ *v.* **1 attract/hold/engage the attention of,** attract, absorb, engross, fascinate, rivet, grip, captivate, amuse, intrigue, arouse curiosity in. **2 affect,** have an effect/bearing on, concern, involve.

interested *adj.* **1 attentive,** intent, absorbed, engrossed, curious, fascinated, riveted, gripped, captivated, intrigued. **2 concerned,** involved, implicated. **3 involved,** partial, partisan, one-sided, biased, prejudiced, discriminative, discriminating. *Ant.* apathetic; indifferent; disinterested.

interesting *adj.* **absorbing,** engrossing, fascinating, riveting, gripping, compelling, compulsive, spellbinding, captivating, appealing, engaging, amusing, entertaining, stimulating, thought-provoking, diverting, exciting, intriguing.

interim *adj.* **temporary,** provisional, pro tem, stopgap, caretaker, acting, intervening, makeshift, improvised.

▶ *n.* **meantime,** meanwhile, intervening time, interval, interregnum.

interior *adj.* **1 inner,** inside, internal, inward. **2 inland,** noncoastal, central, up-country, remote. **3 inner,** spiritual, mental, psychological, emotional, private, personal, intimate, secret, hidden.

▸ *n.* **1 inside,** inner part/side/ surface, center, middle, nucleus, core, heart. **2 center,** heartland, hinterland. ***Ant.*** exterior; outside.

interject *v.* **throw in,** insert, introduce, interpolate, interpose, insinuate, add, mingle, intersperse.

interlude *n.* interval, intermission, break, recess, pause, respite, rest, breathing space, halt, stop, stoppage, hiatus, delay, wait.

intermediary *n.* **mediator,** go-between, broker, agent, middleman, negotiator, arbitrator.

intermediate *adj.* **in-between,** halfway, in the middle, middle, mid, midway, medial, median, intermediary, intervening, interposed, transitional.

interminable *adj.* **1 (seemingly) endless,** never-ending, without end, everlasting, ceaseless, incessant. **2 (seemingly) endless,** never-ending, uninterrupted, monotonous, tedious, wearisome, boring, long-winded, wordy, loquacious, prolix, verbose, rambling.

intermittent *adj.* **fitful,** spasmodic, irregular, sporadic, occasional, periodic, cyclic, recurrent, recurring, broken, discontinuous, on again and off again, on and off. ***Ant.*** continuous; steady.

internal *adj.* **1 interior,** inside, inner, inward. **2 home,** domestic, civil, interior, in-house, in-company. **3 mental,** psychological, emotional, subjective, private, intimate.

international *adj.* **cosmopolitan,** global, universal, worldwide, intercontinental.

interpolate *v.* **insert,** interject, intercalate, interpose, introduce, insinuate, add, inject, put in, work in.

interpret *v.* **1 explain,** elucidate, expound, explicate, clarify, make clear, illuminate, shed light on, gloss, simplify, spell out. **2 understand,** understand by, construe, take, take to mean, read. **3 decode,** decipher, crack, solve, untangle, unravel. **4 translate,** transcribe, transliterate, paraphrase. **5 portray,** depict, present, perform, execute, enact.

interrogate *v.* **question,** put/pose questions to, inquire of, examine, cross-examine, cross-question, quiz, pump, grill, give the third degree to, probe, catechize, *inf.* put the screws to.

interrogation *n.* **questioning,** quizzing, investigation, examination, cross-examination, cross-questioning, pumping, grilling, third degree, probing, inquisition, catechization, inquiry, catechism.

interrogative *adj.* **questioning,** quizzing, quizzical, inquiring, curious, inquisitive, investigative, grilling, third-degree, inquisitorial, probing, catechistic.

interrupt *v.* **1 cut in (on),** break in (on), barge in (on), intrude (on), disturb, heckle, interfere (with), *inf.* butt in (on), chime in (on), horn in (on), muscle in (on). **2 suspend,** discontinue, break the continuity of, break, break off, hold up, delay, lay aside, leave off, postpone, stop, put a stop to, halt, bring to a halt/standstill, cease, end, cancel, sever. **3 break,** break up, punctuate. **4 obstruct,** impede, block, interfere with, cut off.

interruption *n.* **1 cutting in,** interference, disturbance, intrusion, obtrusion, *inf.* butting in. **2 suspension,** discontinuance, breaking off, delay, postponement, stopping, halt, cessation. **3 intermission,** interval, interlude, break, pause, recess, gap, hiatus.

intersect *v.* **1 cut across/through,** cut in two/half, divide, bisect. **2 cross,** crisscross, meet, connect.

intersection *n.* **1 crossing,** crisscrossing, meeting. **2 road junction,** junction, interchange, crossroads.

interval *n.* **1 interim,** interlude, time, period, meantime, meanwhile, wait, space, break, pause, lull, respite, breather, breathing space, gap, hiatus, delay. **2 distance,** space, gap, interspace.

intervene *v.* **1 occur,** befall, happen, arise, take place, ensue, supervene, succeed. **2 intercede,** mediate, arbitrate, negotiate, step in, involve oneself, come into, interpose, interfere, intrude.

interview *n.* **1 conference,** discussion, meeting, talk, dialogue, evaluation, examination. **2 audience,** question and answer session, exchange, dialogue, colloquy, interlocution. ▸ *v.* **talk to,** have a discussion/dialogue with, hold a meeting with, confer with, question, put questions to, sound out, examine, interrogate, cross-examine, evaluate.

interweave *v.* **1 weave,** intertwine, twine, twist, interlace, braid, plait. **2 intermingle,** mingle, interlink, intermix, mix, blend, fuse, interlock, knit, connect, associate, interconnect.

intimate *adj.* **1 close,** near, dear, nearest and dearest, cherished, bosom, familiar, confidential, warm, friendly, comradely, amicable, *inf.* thick, buddy-buddy. **2 informal,** warm, cozy, friendly, comfortable, snug, *inf.* comfy. **3 personal,** private, confidential, secret, privy, innermost, inmost, inner, inward, intrinsic, deep-seated, inherent. **4 experienced,** deep, in-depth, profound, detailed, thorough, exhaustive, personal, firsthand, direct, immediate. **5 sexual,** carnal, fornicatory, unchaste. *Ant.* distant; cold; formal; public.

▸ *n.* **close/best/bosom friend,** constant companion, confidant, confidante, close associate, mate, crony, alter ego, *inf.* chum, pal, buddy.

intimate2 *v.* **imply,** suggest, let it be known, hint, insinuate, give an inkling that, indicate, signal.

intimidate *v.* **frighten,** terrify, scare, alarm, terrorize, overawe, awe, cow, subdue, daunt, domineer, browbeat, bully, tyrannize, coerce, compel, bulldoze, pressure, pressurize, threaten, *inf.* push around, lean on, twist someone's arm.

intolerable *adj.* **unbearable,** unendurable, beyond endurance, insufferable, insupportable, impossible, painful, excruciating, agonizing.

intolerant *adj.* bigoted, illiberal, narrow-minded, narrow, parochial, provincial, insular, small-minded, prejudiced, biased, partial, partisan, one-sided, warped, twisted, fanatical; chauvinistic, jingoistic, racist, xenophobic, sexist, ageist, homophobic.

intonation *n.* **pitch,** tone, timbre, cadence, lilt, inflection, accentuation, emphasis, stress.

intoxicate *v.* **1 inebriate,** make drunk, befuddle, stupefy. **2 exhilarate,** elate, thrill, invigorate, animate, enliven, excite, arouse, inflame, enrapture.

intoxicated *adj.* **inebriated,** inebriate, drunk, drunken, dead drunk, under the influence, tipsy, befuddled, stupefied, staggering, *inf.* drunk as a skunk, three sheets to the wind, tight, pickled, soused, under the table, sloshed, plastered, stewed, well-oiled, loaded, stoned, bombed out of one's mind, lit up, tanked up, smashed. *Ant.* sober; abstemious.

intractable *adj.* **unmanageable,** ungovernable, uncontrollable, uncompliant, stubborn, obstinate, obdurate, perverse, disobedient, unsubmissive, indomitable, refractory, recalcitrant, insubordinate, rebellious, wild, unruly, rowdy. **Ant.** manageable; submissive; obedient.

intricate *adj.* **1 tangled,** entangled, raveled, twisted, knotty, convoluted, involute, mazelike, labyrinthine, winding, serpentine, circuitous, sinuous, roundabout, fancy, elaborate, ornate, Byzantine, rococo. **2 complex,** complicated, difficult, involved, perplexing, puzzling, thorny, mystifying, enigmatic, obscure. **Ant.** plain; simple; straightforward.

intrigue *v.* **1 interest,** absorb, arouse one's curiosity, attract, draw, pull, rivet one's attention, rivet, fascinate, charm, captivate, divert, pique, titillate. **2 plot,** conspire, scheme, connive, maneuver, machinate, devise. ▸ *n.* **plot,** conspiracy, collusion, conniving, cabal, scheme, ruse, stratagem, wile, dodge, artifice, maneuver, machination, trickery, double-dealing.

intrinsic *adj.* **inherent,** inborn, inbred, congenital, natural, native, indigenous, constitutional, built-in, ingrained, implanted, basic, fundamental, elemental, essential, true, genuine, real, authentic. **Ant.** extrinsic; extraneous.

introduce *v.* **1 present,** make known, acquaint, make acquainted, announce. **2 preface,** precede, lead into, commence, start off, begin. **3 bring in,** bring into being, originate, launch, inaugurate, institute, initiate, establish, found, set in motion, organize, develop, start, begin, commence, usher in, pioneer. **4 propose,** put forward, suggest, broach, advance, bring up, set forth, submit, air, ventilate. **5 insert,** inject, interject, interpose, interpolate, intercalate, add, bring, infuse, instill.

introduction *n.* **1 presentation,** announcement. **2 foreword,** preface, front matter, preamble, prologue, prelude, prolegomenon, proem, exordium, lead-in, *inf.* intro, prelims. **3 origination,** launch, inauguration, institution, establishment, development, start, commencement, pioneering. **4 baptism,** initiation, inauguration, debut, first acquaintanceship. **5 basics,** rudiments, fundamentals, groundwork. **6 insertion,** injection, interjection, interposition, interpolation, intercalation, addition, infusion.

introductory *adj.* **1 prefatory,** preliminary, precursory, lead-in, initiatory, opening, initial, starting, commencing. **2 preparatory,** elementary, basic, basal, rudimentary, fundamental, initiatory. *Ant.* final; closing; last.

introspective *adj.* **inward-looking**, inner-directed, introverted, self-analyzing, self-examining, subjective, contemplative, reflective, meditative, musing, pensive, brooding, preoccupied.

intrude *v.* **1 interrupt**, push/thrust oneself in, gatecrash, barge in, encroach, butt in, interfere, obtrude. **2 encroach on**, invade, impinge on, infringe on, trespass on, obtrude on, violate.

intruder *n.* **burglar**, housebreaker, thief, raider, invader, prowler, trespasser, gatecrasher, interloper, infiltrator.

intuition *n.* **instinct**, sixth sense, divination, presentiment, clairvoyance, second sight, extrasensory perception, ESP, feeling, feeling in one's bones, hunch, inkling, presentiment, foreboding.

inundate *v.* **1 flood**, deluge, overflow, overrun, swamp, submerge, engulf, drown, cover, saturate, soak. **2 overwhelm**, overpower, overburden, swamp, bog down, glut.

inure *v.* **harden**, toughen, indurate, season, temper, habituate, familiarize, accustom, naturalize, acclimatize.

invade *v.* **1 march into**, overrun, occupy, storm, take over, descend upon, make inroads on, attack, assail, assault, raid, plunder. **2 interrupt**, intrude on, obtrude on, encroach on, infringe on, trespass on, burst in on, violate. **3 assail**, permeate, pervade, fill, spread over.

invalid *adj.* **ill**, sick, ailing, unwell, infirm, bedridden, valetudinarian, disabled, frail, feeble, weak, debilitated, *inf.* poorly.
▸ *n.* **sufferer**, patient, convalescent.

invaluable *adj.* **priceless**, beyond price, inestimable, precious, costly, worth its weight in gold, worth a king's ransom.

invariable *adj.* **unchanging**, changeless, unchangeable, constant, unvarying, unvaried, invariant, unalterable, immutable, fixed, stable, set, steady, unwavering, static, uniform, regular, consistent.

invariably *adv.* **always**, every/each time, on every occasion, at all times, without fail/exception, regularly, consistently, repeatedly, habitually, unfailingly, infallibly, inevitably.

invasion *n.* **1 overrunning**, occupation, incursion, offensive, attack, assailing, assault, raid, foray, onslaught, plundering.

2 interruption, intrusion, obtrusion, encroachment, infringement, breach, infraction, trespass, violation.

inveigle *v.* **ensnare,** delude, persuade, talk into, cajole, wheedle, coax, sweet-talk, beguile, tempt, decoy, lure, allure, entice, seduce, deceive.

invent *v.* **1 originate,** create, innovate, discover, design, devise, contrive, formulate, think up, conceive, come up with, hit upon, compose, frame, coin. **2 make up,** fabricate, concoct, hatch, trump up, forge, *inf.* cook up.

invention *n.* **1 origination,** creation, innovation, discovery, design, devising, contriving, coining, coinage, contrivance, construction, coinage, *inf.* brainchild. **2 inventiveness,** originality, creativity, creativeness, imagination, artistry, inspiration, ingenuity, resourcefulness, genius, skill. **3 fabrication,** concoction, fiction, falsification, forgery, fake, deceit, myth, fantasy, romance, illusion, sham, lie, untruth, falsehood, fib, piece of fiction, figment of one's imagination, yarn, story, *inf.* tall story.

inventive *adj.* **original,** creative, innovational, imaginative, artistic, inspired, ingenious, resourceful, innovative, gifted, talented, skillful, clever. ***Ant.*** unimaginative; pedestrian.

inventor *n.* **originator,** creator, innovator, discoverer, author, architect, designer, deviser, developer, initiator, coiner, father, prime mover, maker, framer, producer.

inventory *n.* **1 list,** listing, checklist, catalog, record, register, tally, account, description, statement. **2 stock,** goods, merchandise.

inverse *adj.* **opposite,** converse, contrary, reverse, counter, reversed, inverted, transposed, retroverted.
▸ *n.* **opposite (side),** converse (side), obverse (side), other side, *inf.* flip side.

invert *v.* **1 turn upside down,** upturn, turn inside out, overturn, turn turtle, capsize, upset. **2 reverse,** interpose, retrovert.

invest *v.* **1 install,** induct, inaugurate, instate, ordain, initiate, swear in, consecrate, crown, enthrone. **2 clothe,** attire, dress, garb, robe, gown, drape, swathe, adorn, deck. **3 besiege,** lay siege to, beleaguer, beset, surround, enclose.

investigate *v.* **research,** probe, explore, inquire into, make inquiries about, go/look into, search, scrutinize, study, examine, inspect, consider, sift, analyze, *inf.* check out.

investigation *n.* **research,** probe, exploration, inquiry, fact-finding, search, scrutinization, scrutiny, study, survey, review, examination, inspection, consideration, sifting, analysis, inquest, hearing, questioning, inquisition.

inveterate *adj.* **1 confirmed,** habitual, inured, hardened, chronic, diehard, dyed-in-the-wool, long-standing, addicted, hard-core, incorrigible. **2 ingrained,** deep-seated, deep-rooted, deep-set, entrenched, long-established, ineradicable, incurable.

invidious *adj.* **1 discriminatory,** unfair, prejudicial, slighting, offensive, objectionable, deleterious, detrimental. **2 unpleasant,** awkward, unpopular, repugnant, hateful. *Ant.* fair; desirable.

invigorate *v.* **revitalize,** energize, fortify, strengthen, brace, refresh, rejuvenate, enliven, liven up, animate, exhilarate, pep up, perk up, stimulate, motivate, rouse, excite, wake up, galvanize, electrify.

invincible *adj.* **1 unconquerable,** undefeatable, unbeatable, unassailable, invulnerable, indestructible, impregnable, indomitable, unyielding, unflinching, dauntless. **2 insuperable,** insurmountable, overwhelming, overpowering. *Ant.* vulnerable; defenseless; weak.

inviolable *adj.* **inalienable,** untouchable, unalterable, sacrosanct, sacred, holy, hallowed.

invisible *adj.* **unseeable,** out of sight, undetectable, imperceivable, indiscernible, indistinguishable, unseen, unnoticed, unobserved, hidden, concealed, inconspicuous, unnoticeable, imperceptible.

invite *v.* **1 ask,** bid, summon. **2 ask for,** request, call for, solicit, look for, seek, appeal for, petition, summon. **3 cause,** bring on, bring upon oneself, draw, make happen, induce, provoke, welcome, encourage, foster, attract, draw, allure, entice, tempt, court, lead on.

inviting *adj.* **attractive,** appealing, pleasant, agreeable, delightful, engaging, tempting, enticing, alluring, winning, beguiling, fascinating, enchanting, entrancing, bewitching, captivating, intriguing, irresistible, ravishing, seductive.

Ant. repellent; repulsive; offensive.

invocation *n.* **call,** prayer, request, supplication, entreaty, solicitation, beseeching, imploring, importuning, petition, appeal.

invoke *v.* **1 call for,** call up, pray for, request, supplicate, entreat, solicit, beseech, beg, implore, importune, call on, petition, appeal/pray to. **2 apply,** implement, call into use, put into effect/use, resort to, use, have recourse to, initiate.

involuntary *adj.* **1 reflexive,** reflex, automatic, mechanical, unconditioned, spontaneous, instinctive, instinctual, unconscious, unthinking, unintentional, uncontrolled. **2 unwilling,** against one's will/ wishes, reluctant, unconsenting, grudging, disinclined, forced, coerced, coercive, compelled, compulsory, obligatory. *Ant.* voluntary; willing.

involve *v.* **1 entail,** imply, mean, denote, betoken, connote, require, necessitate, presuppose. **2 include,** count in, cover, embrace, take in, number, incorporate, encompass, comprise, contain, comprehend. **3 implicate,** incriminate, inculpate, associate, connect, concern. **4 interest,** be of interest to, absorb, engage, engage/hold/ rivet the attention of, rivet, grip, occupy, preoccupy, engross. **5 complicate,** perplex, confuse, mix up, confound, entangle, tangle, embroil, enmesh.

involved *adj.* **1 complicated,** difficult, intricate, complex, elaborate, confused, confusing, mixed up, jumbled, tangled, entangled, convoluted, knotty, tortuous, labyrinthine, Byzantine. **2 implicated,** incriminated, inculpated, associated, concerned, participating, taking part. *Ant.* simple; disinterested.

iota *n.* **bit,** mite, speck, atom, jot, whit, particle, fraction, morsel, grain, *inf.* smidgen, smidge.

ironic *adj.* **1 satirical,** mocking, scoffing, ridiculing, derisory, derisive, scornful, sneering, sardonic, wry, double-edged, sarcastic. **2 paradoxical,** incongruous.

irrational *adj.* **1 illogical,** unreasonable, groundless, invalid, unsound, implausible, absurd, ridiculous, silly, foolish, senseless, nonsensical, ludicrous, preposterous, crazy. **2 illogical,** unthinking, unintelligent, stupid, brainless, mindless, senseless, muddled, muddle-headed, confused, demented, insane, crazy, unstable.

irrefutable *adj.* **incontrovertible,** incontestable, indisputable, undeniable, unquestionable, beyond question, indubitable, beyond doubt, conclusive, decisive, definite, certain, sure, positive, definitive, fixed, final, *fml.* irrefragable, apodictic.

irregular *adj.* **1 asymmetric,** unsymmetrical, nonuniform, uneven, broken, jagged, ragged, serrated, crooked, curving, craggy, unlevel, rough, bumpy, lumpy, knotty, pitted. **2 uneven,** unsteady, shaky, fitful, variable, erratic, spasmodic, wavering, fluctuating, aperiodic.
3 inconsistent, erratic, sporadic, variable, inconstant, desultory, haphazard, intermittent, occasional, unpunctual, unsystematic, capricious, unmethodical. **4 disconnected,** sporadic, fragmentary, haphazard, patchy, intermittent, occasional, random, fluctuating, coming and going. **5 out of order,** contrary, perverse, against the rules, unofficial, unorthodox, unconventional, abnormal.
6 anomalous, aberrant, deviant, abnormal, unusual, uncommon, freak, extraordinary, exceptional, odd, peculiar, strange, eccentric, bizarre, queer. **7 guerrilla,** underground, resistance, mercenary.

irrelevant *adj.* **inapposite,** inapt, inapplicable, impertinent, nongermane, immaterial, unrelated, unconnected, inappropriate, extraneous, beside the point, not to the point, out of place, having nothing to do with it, neither here nor there.

irreparable *adj.* **beyond repair,** past mending, irreversible, irrevocable, irretrievable, irrecoverable, irremediable, incurable, ruinous.

irreplaceable *adj.* **priceless,** invaluable, inestimably precious, unique, worth its weight in gold, rare.

irrepressible *adj.*
1 unrestrainable, uncontainable, insuppressible, uncontrollable, unstoppable, unquenchable, unreserved, unchecked, unbridled. **2 bubbling over,** buoyant, effervescent, ebullient, vivacious, animated, spirited, lively.

irresistible *adj.* **1 overwhelming,** overpowering, compelling, insuppressible, irrepressible, forceful, potent, imperative, urgent. **2 unavoidable,** inevitable, inescapable, unpreventable, ineluctable, inexorable, relentless.

3 fascinating, alluring, enticing, seductive, captivating, enchanting, ravishing, tempting, tantalizing.

irresolute *adj.* **uncertain,** unsure, doubtful, dubious, undecided, indecisive, unresolved, undetermined, unsettled, vacillating, wavering, hesitant, hesitating, tentative, in two minds, oscillating.

irresponsible *adj.*
1 undependable, unreliable, untrustworthy, careless, reckless, rash, flighty, giddy, scatterbrained, erratic, harebrained, featherbrained, immature, *inf.* harum-scarum.
2 thoughtless, ill-considered, unwise, injudicious, careless, reckless, immature.

irreverent *adj.* **1 disrespectful,** unrespectful, impertinent, insolent, impudent, rude, cheeky, discourteous, impolite, uncivil, *inf.* flip. **2 impious,** irreligious, heretical, sacrilegious, ungodly, blasphemous, profane.

irrevocable *adj.* **unalterable,** unchangeable, irreversible, unreversible, fixed, settled, fated, immutable, predetermined, predestined.

irrigation *n.* **watering,** wetting, spraying, sprinkling, moistening, soaking, flooding, inundating.

irritable *adj.* **bad-tempered,** ill-tempered, ill-humored, irascible, cross, snappish, snappy, edgy, testy, touchy, crabbed, peevish, petulant, cantankerous, grumpy, grouchy, crusty, dyspeptic, choleric, splenetic. **Ant.** good-humored; cheerful; imperturbable.

irritate *v.* **1 annoy,** vex, provoke, irk, nettle, peeve, get on one's nerves, exasperate, infuriate, anger, enrage, incense, make one's hackles rise, ruffle, disturb, put out, bother, pester, try one's patience, *inf.* aggravate, rub the wrong way, get one's goat, get one's back up, drive up the wall, drive one bananas. **2 chafe,** fret, rub, pain, hurt, inflame, aggravate.

irritation *n.* **1 irritability,** annoyance, impatience, vexation, exasperation, indignation, crossness, ill-temper, anger, fury, rage, wrath, displeasure, ire, *inf.* aggravation. **2 source of annoyance,** annoyance, irritant, pest, nuisance, thorn in the/one's flesh/side, *inf.* pain in the neck/butt, pain.

isolate *v.* **set apart,** segregate, cut off, separate, detach, abstract, quarantine, keep in solitude, sequester, insulate.

isolated *adj.* **1 alone,** solitary,

lonely, separated, segregated, exiled, forsaken, forlorn.
2 remote, out of the way, off the beaten track, outlying, secluded, hidden, unfrequented, lonely, desolate, godforsaken. **3 single,** solitary, unique, random, unrelated, unusual, uncommon, exceptional, abnormal, atypical, untypical, anomalous, freak.

issue *n.* **1 matter,** matter in question, point at issue, question, subject, topic, affair, problem, bone of contention, controversy, argument. **2 result,** outcome, decision, upshot, end, conclusion, consequence, termination, effect, denouement. **3 edition,** number, printing, print run, impression, copy, installment, version.
4 issuing, issuance, publication, circulation, distribution, supplying, supply, dissemination, sending out, delivery. **5 offspring,** progeny, children, heirs, scions, descendants, *inf.* brood. **6 outflow,** effusion, discharge, debouchment, emanation.

▸ *v.* **1 put out,** give out, deal out, send out, distribute, circulate, release, disseminate, announce, proclaim, broadcast. **2 emit,** exude, discharge, emanate, gush, pour forth, seep, ooze. **3 emerge,** come out, come forth, appear, leave. **4 derive,** arise, stem, proceed, spring, originate, result, be a result/consequence of. *Ant.* withdraw; enter.

itch *v.* **tingle,** prickle, tickle, be irritated.

▸ *n.* **1 itchiness,** tingling, prickling, tickling, irritation, burning, *Med.* formication, paresthesia. **2 great desire,** longing, yearning, craving, hankering, ache, burning, hunger, thirst, lust, *inf.* yen.

item *n.* **1 article,** thing, piece of merchandise, goods. **2 point,** detail, matter, consideration, particular, feature, circumstance, aspect, component, element, ingredient. **3 entry,** record. **4 piece of news/information,** piece, story, bulletin, article, account, report, feature, dispatch. **5 couple,** partners.

Jj

jab *v.* **poke,** prod, dig (at/into), nudge, elbow, thrust (at/into), stab, bump, tap, punch, box, *inf.* sock.

▸ *n.* **poke,** prod, dig, nudge, stab, punch.

jacket *n.* **1 sports coat,** blazer, windbreaker, parka, anorak. **2 casing,** case, encasement, sheath, sheathing, envelope, cover, covering, wrapping, wrapper, wrap.

jaded *adj.* **1 satiated,** sated, allayed, surfeited, glutted, cloyed, gorged, dulled, blunted. **2 tired,** wearied, weary, fatigued, worn out, exhausted, spent, *inf.* played out, done, done in, bushed, pooped.

jagged *adj.* **serrated,** toothed, notched, indented, denticulate, pointed, spiked, barbed, uneven, rough, ridged, ragged, craggy, broken, cleft.

jam¹ *v.* **1 wedge,** sandwich, insert, force, ram, thrust, push, stick, press, cram, stuff, pack, crowd, squeeze, crush. **2 obstruct,** block, clog, close off, congest. **3 become stuck,** stick, stall, halt, stop.

▸ *n.* **1 traffic jam,** holdup, obstruction, congestion, bottleneck, stoppage, gridlock. **2 predicament,** plight, straits, trouble, quandary; *inf.* fix, pickle, hole, spot, tight spot, scrape.

jam² *n.* **preserve,** preserves, conserve, jelly, marmalade.

jar *n.* **glass container,** container, receptacle, vessel, carafe, flagon, flask, pitcher, jug, vase, urn.

▸ *v.* **1 jolt,** jerk, shake, vibrate. **2 clash,** conflict, be inharmonious, be in opposition, be at variance, be at odds, grate (on), jangle, irritate, disturb, upset, discompose, irk, annoy, nettle, vex.

jargon *n.* **1 cant,** slang, argot, idiom, usage, vernacular, dialect, patois, *inf.* lingo. **2 computerese,** legalese, bureaucratese, journalese, buzzword, gobbledygook, psychobabble.

jaundiced *adj.* **1 yellow,** yellowish, yellow-tinged, yellow-skinned, sallow. **2 cynical,** pessimistic, skeptical, distrustful, suspicious, misanthropic, bitter, resentful, jealous, envious, narrow-minded, bigoted, prejudiced. *Ant.* optimistic; naïve.

jaunt *n.* **trip,** outing, drive, excursion, expedition, airing, stroll.

jaunty *adj.* **1 sprightly,** bouncy, buoyant, lively, breezy, perky, frisky, merry, blithe, carefree, joyful. **2 smart,** stylish, spruce, trim, dapper, fancy, flashy, *inf.* natty. *Ant.* depressed; serious; sedate.

jazzy *adj.* **flashy,** fancy, stylish, smart, gaudy, *inf.* flash, snazzy.

jealous *adj.* **1 begrudging,** grudging, resentful, envious, green with envy, green-eyed, covetous, desirous. **2 suspicious,** distrustful, mistrustful, doubting, insecure, apprehensive of rivals, possessive. **3 protective,** vigilant, watchful, heedful, mindful, careful, solicitous, on guard, wary.

jeer *v.* **mock,** ridicule, deride, taunt, gibe, scorn, contemn, flout, cry down, tease, boo, hiss, scoff at, laugh at, sneer at, *inf.* knock. *Ant.* cheer; applaud.
▸ *n.* **mockery,** ridicule, derision, banter, scoffing, teasing, sneer, taunt, gibe, boo, hiss, catcall, abuse.

jeopardy *n.* **risk,** danger, endangerment, peril, hazard, precariousness, insecurity, vulnerability, threat, menace. *Ant.* safety; security.

jerk *v.* **1 pull,** yank, tug, wrench, tweak, pluck. **2 jolt,** lurch, bump, jump, bounce, jounce. **3 twitch,** shake, tremble, be in convulsion.
▸ *n.* **1 pull,** yank, tug, wrench, tweak. **2 jolt,** lurch, bump, start, jar. **3 fool,** idiot, rogue, scoundrel, *inf.* nerd, twit, dimwit, dope, creep, heel.

jerky *adj.* **1 spasmodic,** fitful, convulsive, twitchy, shaking, shaky, tremulous, uncontrolled. **2 jolting,** lurching, jumpy, bumpy, bouncy, jouncing, rough. *Ant.* smooth; fluid.

jester *n.* **1 joker,** comic, comedian, humorist, wag, wit, quipster, prankster, hoaxer. **2 fool,** court fool, clown, zany, buffoon, merry-andrew, harlequin.

jet *n.* **1 stream,** gush, spurt, spout, spray, rush, fountain, spring. **2 nozzle,** spout, nose, sprinkler, sprinkler head, spray, rose, atomizer. **3 jet airplane,** jet plane, jetliner, jumbo jet, turbojet, jet engine, ramjet.
▸ *v.* **1 shoot,** gush, spurt, spout, well, rush, spray, squirt, spew, stream, surge, flow, issue. **2 fly,** travel by plane, zoom.

jetty *n.* **pier,** wharf, quay, breakwater.

jewel *n.* **1 gem,** gemstone, precious stone, stone, bijou, *inf.* sparkler, rock, piece of jewelry, trinket, ornament. **2 choicest example,** pearl, flower, pride, pride and joy, cream, crème de la crème, plum, boast. **3 treasure,** one in a million, saint, paragon, *inf.* one of a kind.

jilt *v.* **reject,** cast aside, discard, throw over, drop, leave, forsake, *inf.* ditch, dump, give the brush-off, give the heave-ho, give the elbow.

jingle *v.* **clink,** chink, jangle, rattle, clank, tinkle, ding, go ding-dong, go ting-a-ling, ring, chime, tintinnabulate.
▸ *n.* **1 clink,** chink, tinkle, tinkling, ding, ding-dong, ting-a-ling, ringing, tintinnabulation, chime. **2 ditty,** chorus, refrain, short song, limerick, melody, tune, catchy tune.

job *n.* **1 work,** task, undertaking, chore, assignment, venture, enterprise, activity, business, affair. **2 occupation,** profession, trade, employment, vocation, calling, career, field of work, means of livelihood, métier, pursuit, position, post, situation, appointment. **3 duty,** task, chore, errand, responsibility, concern, function, role, charge, office, commission, capacity, contribution. **4 work,** product, batch, lot, consignment. **5 difficult task,** problem, trouble, bother,

hard time, trial, tribulation. **6 crime,** felony, burglary, break-in, theft.

jobless *adj.* **unemployed,** out of work, idle, inactive, unoccupied.

jocular *adj.* **humorous,** funny, witty, comic, comical, facetious, joking, jesting, playful, roguish, waggish, whimsical, droll, jocose, teasing, sportive, amusing, entertaining, diverting, hilarious, farcical, laughable. *Ant.* solemn; serious; earnest.

jog *v.* **1 go jogging,** run slowly, dogtrot, jog trot, trot, canter, lope. **2 nudge,** prod, poke, push, elbow, tap. **3 stimulate,** activate, stir, arouse, prompt. **4 bounce,** bob, joggle, jiggle, jounce, jolt, jerk, shake.

join *v.* **1 fasten,** attach, tie, bind, couple, connect, unite, link, splice, yoke, knit, glue, cement, fuse, weld, solder. **2 join forces (with),** amalgamate (with), merge (with), combine (with), unify (with), ally (with), league, federate (with), team up with, band together with, cooperate with, collaborate with, affiliate with. **3 enlist,** sign up, enroll, become a member of, enlist in, sign up for, enroll in. **4 join in,** participate in, take part in, partake in, contribute to, lend a hand with. **5 adjoin,** conjoin, abut on, border,

border on, touch, meet, verge on, reach to, extend to. **Ant.** detach; separate; leave.

joint *n.* **1 junction,** juncture, intersection, nexus, knot, seam, coupling. **2 club,** nightclub, bar. **3 place,** dwelling, house, establishment, *inf.* hole. **4 marijuana cigarette,** *inf.* reefer.
▸ *adj.* **common,** shared, joined, mutual, combined, collective, cooperative, allied, united, concerted, consolidated.

jointly *adv.* **together,** in combination, in conjunction, as one, mutually, in partnership, cooperatively, in cooperation, in league, in collusion, *inf.* in cahoots.

joke *n.* **1 jest,** witticism, quip, gag, yarn, pun, *inf.* wisecrack, crack, funny. **2 practical joke,** prank, trick, hoax. **3 laughingstock,** butt, target, fair game.
▸ *v.* **1 tell jokes,** crack jokes, jest, banter, quip, *inf.* wisecrack. **2 fool,** fool around, tease, pull someone's leg, *inf.* kid.

jolly *adj.* **merry,** gay, joyful, joyous, jovial, happy, glad, mirthful, gleeful, cheerful, cheery, carefree, buoyant, lively, bright, lighthearted, blithe, jocund, sprightly, elated, exuberant, exhilarated, jubilant, high-spirited, sportive, playful. **Ant.** miserable; lugubrious.

jolt *v.* **1 bump against,** knock against, bump into, bang into, collide with, jostle, push, shove, elbow, nudge, jar, bounce, jounce, start, jerk, lurch. **2 upset,** disturb, perturb, shake, shake up, shock, stun, disconcert, discompose, disquiet, startle, surprise, astonish, amaze, stagger.
▸ *n.* **1 bump,** knock, bang, hit, push, shove, nudge, jar, bounce, jounce, shake, jerk, lurch, start. **2 shock,** bombshell, blow, upset, setback, surprise, bolt from the blue, thunderbolt.

jostle *v.* **bump against,** knock against, bump into, bang into, collide with, jolt, push, shove, elbow, thrust, press, squeeze, force.

jot *n.* **iota,** whit, little bit, bit, scrap, fraction, atom, grain, particle, morsel, mite, speck, trace, trifle, smidgen, *inf.* tinge, smidge, tad.
▸ *v.* **write down,** note, note down, make a note of, take down, put down, mark down, list, make a list of, register, record, chronicle.

journal *n.* **1 diary,** daybook, notebook, commonplace book, log, logbook, chronicle, record, register. **2 periodical,** magazine, trade magazine, review,

publication, professional organ.
3 newspaper, paper, daily newspaper, daily, weekly newspaper, weekly, gazette.

journalist *n.* **reporter,** newspaperman/newspaperwoman, newsman/newswoman, newshound, pressman/presswoman, feature writer, columnist, correspondent, contributor, commentator, reviewer, editor, broadcaster, *inf.* stringer.

journey *n.* **trip,** expedition, excursion, travels, tour, trek, voyage, cruise, safari, peregrination, roaming, roving, globe-trotting, odyssey, pilgrimage, outing, jaunt.
▶ *v.* **go,** travel, go on a trip, go on an expedition, go on an excursion, tour, voyage, sail, cruise, fly, hike, trek, roam, rove, ramble, wander, meander, peregrinate, globe-trot.

jovial *adj.* **jolly,** jocular, jocose, jocund, happy, cheerful, cheery, glad, in good spirits, merry, gay, mirthful, blithe, buoyant, animated, convivial, sociable, cordial. *Ant.* miserable; morose.

joy *n.* **1 delight,** pleasure, gladness, enjoyment, gratification, happiness, rapture, glee, bliss, ecstasy, elation, rejoicing, exultation, jubilation, euphoria, ravishment, transport, felicity.
2 treasure, prize, gem, jewel, pride and joy, delight, pleasure, treat, thrill.

joyful *adj.* **1 overjoyed,** elated, beside oneself with joy, thrilled, delighted, pleased, gratified, happy, glad, blithe, gleeful, jubilant, ecstatic, exultant, euphoric, enraptured, in seventh heaven, on cloud nine, *inf.* tickled pink. **2 glad,** happy, good, pleasing, cheering, gratifying, heartwarming. **3 joyous,** happy, cheerful, merry, gay, festive, celebratory. *Ant.* depressed; miserable; sad.

judge *v.* **1 try,** hear evidence in, sit in judgment on/of, give a verdict in, pronounce a verdict in, pass sentence in, sentence in, decree.
2 adjudicate, adjudge, umpire, referee, arbitrate, mediate.
3 assess, appraise, evaluate, weigh up, size up, gauge, examine, review, criticize, diagnose, pass judgment on.
4 estimate, assess, reckon, guess, surmise, *inf.* guesstimate.
5 consider, believe, think, form the opinion, deduce, gather, conclude.
▶ *n.* **1 justice,** reviewer, magistrate, his/her honor. **2 appraiser,** assessor, evaluator, critic, expert.
3 adjudicator, umpire, referee, arbiter, arbitrator, mediator.

judgment *n.* **1 discernment,** acumen, shrewdness, common sense, good sense, sense, perception, perspicacity, percipience, penetration, discrimination, wisdom, judiciousness, prudence, sagacity, understanding, intelligence, powers of reasoning. **2 verdict,** decision, adjudication, ruling, finding, opinion, conclusion, decree, sentence. **3 opinion,** view, belief, conviction, estimation, evaluation, assessment, appraisal. **4 damnation,** doom, fate, punishment, retribution, sentence.

judicial *adj.* **1 judiciary,** juridical, judicatory, legal. **2 judgelike,** impartial, unbiased, critical, analytical, discriminating, discerning, perceptive.

judicious *adj.* **wise,** prudent, politic, sagacious, shrewd, astute, sensible, common-sense, sound, well-advised, well-considered, well-judged, considered, thoughtful, expedient, practical, discerning, discriminating, informed, intelligent, smart, clever, enlightened, logical, rational, discreet, careful, cautious, circumspect, diplomatic. *Ant.* injudicious; foolish; ill-advised.

jug *n.* **pitcher,** ewer, crock, carafe, decanter, jar, urn, vessel, receptacle, container.

juggle *v.* **change around,** alter, tamper with, falsify, fake, manipulate, maneuver, rig, massage, *inf.* fix, doctor, cook.

juice *n.* **extract,** sap, secretion, liquid, liquor, fluid, serum, fruit juice, meat juice.

juicy *adj.* **1 succulent,** moist, lush, sappy, watery, wet, flowing. **2 racy,** risqué, spicy, sensational, thrilling, fascinating, colorful, exciting, vivid. *Ant.* dry; unexciting.

jumble *v.* **disarrange,** disorganize, disorder, dishevel, muddle, confuse, tangle, shuffle, mix, mix up, mingle, put in disarray, make a shambles of, throw into chaos. ▶ *n.* **clutter,** muddle, confusion, litter, mess, hodgepodge, mishmash, confused heap, miscellany, motley collection, mixture, medley, gallimaufry.

jump *v.* **1 spring,** leap, bound, hop, bounce, skip, caper, gambol, frolic, frisk, cavort. **2 high-jump,** leap over, vault, pole-vault, hurdle, clear, sail over. **3 start,** flinch, jerk, recoil, twitch, quiver, shake, wince, *inf.* jump out of one's skin. **4 skip,** miss, omit, leave out, cut out, pass over, overlook, disregard, ignore. **5 rise,** go up, leap up, increase,

mount, escalate, surge, soar.
6 pounce on, set upon, fall on,
swoop down on, attack, assault,
inf. mug.
▸ *n.* **1 spring,** leap, vault, bound,
hop, bounce, skip. **2 hurdle,**
fence, rail, hedge, obstacle,
barrier, gate. **3 gap,** break, hiatus,
interruption, space, lacuna,
breach, interval. **4 start,** flinch,
jerk, twitch, quiver, shake, wince,
jolt, lurch, bump, jounce, jar.
5 rise, increase, upturn, upsurge,
escalation, hike, boost, advance,
elevation, augmentation.

jumpy *adj.* **nervous,** edgy, on
edge, jittery, agitated, fidgety,
anxious, uneasy, restive, tense,
alarmed, apprehensive, panicky.
Ant. calm; laid-back.

junction *n.* **1 joint,** juncture, link,
bond, connection, seam, joining,
coupling, linking, welding, union.
2 crossroads, crossing,
intersection, interchange.

juncture *n.* **point,** point in time,
time, stage, period, critical point,
crucial moment, moment of
truth, turning point, crisis, crux,
extremity.

junior *adj.* **1 younger.**
2 subordinate, lesser, lower,
minor, secondary, inferior.

junk *n.* **rubbish,** refuse, litter,
scrap, waste, garbage, trash,
debris, leavings, leftovers,
remnants, castoffs, rejects, odds
and ends, bric-à-brac.
▸ *v.* **throw out,** throw away,
discard, get rid of, dispose of,
scrap, *inf.* dump, deep-six.

just *adj.* **1 fair,** fair-minded,
equitable, evenhanded, impartial,
unbiased, objective, neutral,
disinterested, unprejudiced, open-
minded. **2 upright,** honorable,
upstanding, honest, righteous,
ethical, moral, virtuous,
principled, good, decent, straight,
truthful, sincere. **3 valid,** sound,
well-founded, well-grounded,
justified, justifiable, warrantable,
defensible, reasonable.
4 deserved, well-deserved,
merited, earned, rightful, due,
proper, fitting, appropriate, apt,
suitable, condign. **5 lawful,**
legitimate, legal, licit, rightful,
genuine, *inf.* kosher. **6 true,**
truthful, accurate, correct,
factual, exact, precise, close,
faithful, strict. *Ant.* unjust; biased;
dishonest; undeserved.
▸ *adv.* **1 only now,** a moment ago,
a second ago, a short time ago,
recently, lately, not long ago.
2 exactly, precisely, absolutely,
completely, totally, entirely,
perfectly. **3 only just,** barely,
scarcely, hardly, by a narrow
margin, by a hair's breadth, *inf.* by

the skin of one's teeth. **4 only,** merely, simply, but, nothing but, no more than. **5 really,** indeed, truly, actually, certainly.

justice *n.* **1 justness,** fairness, fair play, fair-mindedness, equitableness, equity, evenhandedness, impartiality, objectivity, neutrality, disinterestedness, open-mindedness. **2 justness,** uprightness, integrity, honor, honesty, righteousness, ethics, morals, virtue, principle, decency, propriety. **3 validity,** justification, soundness, reasonableness. **4 lawfulness,** legitimacy, legality, licitness. **5 amends,** recompense, redress, compensation, reparation, requital, retribution, penalty, punishment. **6 judge,** magistrate, sheriff. ***Ant.*** injustice; bias.

justifiable *adj.* **valid,** sound, well-founded, lawful, legitimate, legal, tenable, right, defensible, supportable, sustainable, warrantable, vindicable, reasonable, within reason, sensible, acceptable, plausible. ***Ant.*** unjustifiable; indefensible.

justify *v.* **1 give grounds/reasons for,** show just cause for, explain, rationalize, defend, stand up for, uphold, sustain. **2 substantiate,** prove, establish, verify, certify, vindicate, legalize, legitimize. **3 warrant,** substantiate, bear out, show to be reasonable, prove to be right, confirm.

jut *v.* **stick out,** project, protrude, poke out, bulge out, overhang, beetle.

juvenile *adj.* **1 young,** junior, minor. **2 childish,** puerile, infantile, jejune, immature, inexperienced, callow, green, unsophisticated, naïve, *inf.* wet behind the ears. ***Ant.*** adult; mature.

Kk

keen *adj.* **1 sharp,** sharp-edged, sharpened, fine-edged, razor-sharp. **2 sharp,** acute, discerning, perceptive, sensitive, discriminating, astute, quick-witted, sharp-witted, shrewd, penetrating, perspicacious, clever, bright, smart, intelligent, brilliant, wise, canny, sagacious, sapient, *inf.* brainy. **3 acerbic,** acid, biting, caustic, tart, pointed, mordant, trenchant, incisive, razorlike, razor-sharp, finely honed, cutting, stinging, scathing, sardonic, satirical. **4 willing,** eager, enthusiastic, avid, earnest, intent, diligent, assiduous, conscientious, zealous, fervent, fervid, impatient, longing, yearning, impatient, itching, *inf.* rarin'. **Ant.** blunt; dull; apathetic.

keep *v.* **1 carry on,** continue, maintain, persist, persevere. **2 hold on to,** keep hold of, retain, save up, accumulate, store, hoard, amass, pile up, collect, garner, *inf.* hang on to. **3 preserve,** conserve, keep alive, keep fresh. **4 sell,** stock, have in stock, carry, deal in, trade in. **5 look after,** keep in good order, tend, mind, maintain, keep up, manage, superintend, tend, care for, look after, mind, guard, safeguard, protect, watch over, shield, shelter, preserve, protect. **6 provide for,** support, maintain, sustain, subsidize, feed, nurture, provide board for. **7 hide,** conceal, keep dark, withhold, hush, hush up, not breathe a word of, suppress, censor. **8 abide by,** comply with, fulfill, carry out, effectuate, keep faith with, stand by, honor, obey, observe. **9 observe,** hold, celebrate, commemorate, respect, ritualize, solemnize, ceremonialize. **10 keep back,** hold back, hold up, delay, detain, retard, hinder, obstruct, impede, hamper, constrain, check, block, hamstring, prevent. **11 prevent,** stop, restrain, check, halt. **12 preserve,** protect, guard, safeguard, shield, shelter. **Ant.** give up (see give); discard; abandon.

▸ *n.* **1 maintenance,** support, board, room and board, subsistence, sustenance, food, nourishment, living, livelihood, upkeep. **2 donjon,** dungeon, tower, stronghold, citadel, fortress, fort, castle.

keeper *n.* **1 jailer,** warden, guard, custodian, sentry, *inf.* screw. **2 curator,** conservator, attendant, caretaker, steward, superintendent, overseer, administrator. **3 guardian,** escort, bodyguard, chaperon, chaperone, nursemaid, nurse.

keepsake *n.* **memento,** souvenir, remembrance, reminder, token of remembrance, relic, favor.

kernel *n.* **1 grain,** seed, germ, stone, nut. **2 nub,** nucleus, core, center, heart, marrow, pith, substance, essence, essential part, gist, quintessence, *inf.* nitty-gritty, nuts and bolts, brass tacks.

key *n.* **1 answer,** solution, explanation, guide, clue, cue, pointer, gloss, interpretation, explication, annotation, clarification, exposition, translation. **2 tone,** pitch, timbre, tonality.

kick *v.* **1 boot,** punt. **2 recoil,** spring back. **3 protest,** resist, oppose, rebel, spurn, object, complain, grumble, *inf.* gripe, grouse, beef, bitch. **4 give up,** stop, abandon, quit, leave off, desist from.

▸ *n.* **1 boot,** punt. **2 thrill,** excitement, stimulation, fun, pleasure, enjoyment, amusement, gratification, *inf.* buzz. **3 strength,** potency, tang, zip, alcoholic effect, *inf.* punch, zing. **4 vigor,** force, forcefulness, energy, vitality, vivacity, liveliness, verve, animation, enthusiasm, zest, zip, *inf.* punch, zing.

kill *v.* **1 take someone's life,** slay, murder, do away with, do to death, slaughter, butcher, massacre, assassinate, liquidate, wipe out, destroy, erase, eradicate, exterminate, eliminate, dispatch, put to death, execute, hang, behead, guillotine, *inf.* bump off, do in, knock off, off, ice, fry, rub out. **2 destroy,** put an end to, ruin, extinguish, scotch, quell. **3 pass,** spend, expend, while away, fill up, occupy, use up. **4 exhaust,** overtire, tire out, fatigue, wear out, fag out, debilitate, enervate, prostrate, tax, overtax, strain. **5 hurt,** cause pain, cause discomfort, be uncomfortable, be painful. **6 cancel,** delete, remove, erase, cut out, wipe out, eradicate, expunge, obliterate, *inf.* deep-six. **7 defeat,** veto, vote down, reject, overrule. **8 deaden,** muffle, dull, dampen, smother, stifle. **9 consume,** drink up, drain, empty, finish, *inf.* knock back. **10 overwhelm with laughter,** amuse greatly, make someone laugh, *inf.* have someone rolling in the aisles, make someone crack up.

killer *n.* **slayer,** murderer, slaughterer, butcher, assassin, liquidator, destroyer, exterminator, executioner, gunman, homicide, patricide, matricide, infanticide, fratricide, sororicide, regicide, *inf.* hit man.

killing *n.* **1 slaying,** murder, manslaughter, homicide, slaughter, butchery, massacre, bloodshed, carnage, liquidation, destruction, extermination, execution, patricide, matricide, infanticide. **2 financial success,** bonanza, fortune, windfall, gain, profit, piece of good luck, coup, *inf.* cleanup.
▸ *adj.* **1 deadly,** fatal, lethal, mortal, death-dealing, murderous, homicidal. **2 exhausting,** tiring, fatiguing, debilitating, enervating, prostrating, taxing, punishing. **3 hilarious,** uproarious, rib-tickling, comical, amusing, laughable, absurd, ludicrous, outrageous, *inf.* screamingly funny.

killjoy *n.* **spoilsport,** *inf.* wet blanket, party pooper.

kin *n.* **relatives,** relations, family, connections, folks, people, kindred, kith and kin, kinfolk, kinsfolk, kinsmen/kinswomen.

kind[1] *adj.* **kindhearted,** kindly, generous, charitable, giving, benevolent, bounteous, magnanimous, bighearted, warmhearted, altruistic, philanthropic, humanitarian, humane, tender-hearted, softhearted, gentle, mild, lenient, merciful, clement, pitying, forbearing, patient, tolerant, sympathetic, compassionate, understanding, considerate, helpful, thoughtful, good, nice, decent, pleasant, benign, friendly, genial, congenial, amiable, amicable, cordial, courteous, gracious, good-natured, warm, affectionate, loving, indulgent, obliging, accommodating, neighborly. ***Ant.*** unkind; mean; nasty.

kind[2] *n.* **1 sort,** type, variety, brand, class, category, genus, species, family, strain, species. **2 nature,** character, manner, aspect, disposition, humor, style, stamp, mold.

kindle *v.* **1 light,** set alight, set on fire, set fire to, ignite, start, torch. **2 stimulate,** rouse, arouse, excite, stir, awaken, inspire, inflame, incite, induce, provoke, actuate, activate, touch off.

kindred *n.* **kin,** relatives, relations, family, people.
▸ *adj.* **1 related,** connected, of the

same blood, of the same family, consanguineous, cognate. **2 like,** similar, resembling, corresponding, matching, congenial, allied.

kink *n.* **1 twist,** bend, coil, corkscrew, curl, twirl, knot, tangle, entanglement. **2 curl,** wave, crimp, frizz, crinkle. **3 crick,** spasm, twinge, tweak, stab of pain. **4 flaw,** defect, imperfection, hitch, snag, difficulty, complication. **5 quirk,** whim, whimsy, caprice, vagary, eccentricity, foible, idiosyncrasy, fetish, deviation.

kinky *adj.* **1 twisted,** bent, coiled, curled. **2 curly,** wavy, crimped, frizzy, frizzed, crinkled. **3 quirky,** peculiar, odd, strange, queer, bizarre, eccentric, idiosyncratic, weird, outlandish, unconventional, unorthodox, whimsical, capricious, fanciful, *inf.* way-out, far-out. **4 perverted,** warped, deviant, deviative, unnatural, abnormal, depraved, degenerate, lascivious, licentious, lewd, sadistic, masochistic.

kit *n.* **equipment,** apparatus, set, tools, implements, instruments, utensils, gear, tackle, supplies, paraphernalia, accouterments, effects, stuff, trappings, appurtenances, *inf.* things, the necessary.

knack *n.* **talent,** aptitude, aptness, gift, flair, bent, forte, ability, capability, capacity, expertise, expertness, skill, skillfulness, genius, facility, propensity, dexterity, adroitness, readiness, quickness, ingenuity, proficiency, competence, handiness. *Ant.* inability; blind spot.

knead *v.* **work,** manipulate, press, squeeze, massage, rub, form, shape.

kneel *v.* **get down on one's knees,** fall to one's knees, genuflect, bow, bow down, stoop, make obeisance, kowtow.

knife *n.* **blade,** cutting tool, dagger, dirk, machete, sword, stiletto, scalpel, *Trademark* Swiss Army knife, cleaver, paring knife, table knife, steak knife, penknife, pocket knife, bowie knife, jackknife, switchblade.
▸ *v.* **stab,** pierce, run through, impale, bayonet, transfix, cut, slash, lacerate, wound.

knit *v.* **1 loop,** weave, interweave, crochet. **2 wrinkle,** crease, furrow, gather, draw in, contract. **3 join,** link, bind, unite, draw (together), ally. **4 draw together,** heal, mend, become whole.

knob *n.* **1 doorknob,** handle, switch. **2 stud,** boss, protuberance, knot. **3 bump,** bulge, swelling, lump, knot, node, nodule, pustule, growth, tumor, protuberance, tumescence.

knock v. **1 tap,** rap, bang, pound, hammer. **2 strike,** hit, slap, smack, box, punch, cuff, buffet, thump, thwack, batter, pummel, *inf.* clip, clout, wallop. **3 criticize,** find fault with, take apart, take to pieces, pick holes in, run down, shoot down, carp at, cavil at, deprecate, belittle, disparage, minimize, censure, condemn, *inf.* slam, lambaste, pan.
▸ n. **1 tap,** rap, rat-tat, rat-tat-tat, bang. **2 slap,** smack, blow, punch, cuff, buffet, thump, thwack, *inf.* clip, clout, wallop. **3 collision,** crash, bang, bump, smash, thud, jolt. **4 criticism,** strictures, faultfinding, carping, caviling, deprecation, disparagement, censure, condemnation, *inf.* slamming, lambasting, panning.

knot n. **1 loop,** twist, bend, hitch, intertwinement, interlacement, ligature, joint. **2 lump,** knob, node, nodule, protuberance, knurl, knar, gnarl. **3 clump,** group, cluster, bunch, band, circle, ring, gathering, company, throng, crowd, flock, gang, assemblage, mob, pack.
▸ v. **tie,** loop, bind, secure, tether, lash, leash.

know v. **1 be aware of,** notice, perceive, realize, be conscious of, be cognizant of, sense, recognize, *inf.* latch on to. **2 understand,** comprehend, apprehend, be conversant with, be familiar with, be acquainted with, have memorized, have learned by heart, experience, undergo, go through. **3 have met,** be acquainted with, have dealings with, associate with, be friends with, socialize with, fraternize with, be intimate with, be close to, be on good terms with, *inf.* be thick with. **4 distinguish,** differentiate, tell, identify, make out, discern. *Ant.* ignore; misunderstand.

knowing adj. **1 astute,** shrewd, perceptive, meaningful, well-informed, significant, eloquent, expressive, aware, sophisticated, worldly, worldly-wise.
2 conscious, intentional, intended, deliberate, willful, purposeful, calculated, on purpose, by design. *Ant.* ingenuous; innocent; accidental.

knowledge n. **1 learning,** erudition, scholarship, letters, education, enlightenment, wisdom. **2 understanding,** grasp, comprehension, apprehension, cognition, adeptness, skill, expertise, proficiency, know-how, savoir faire. **3 acquaintanceship,**

familiarity, conversance.

4 information, facts, intelligence, data, news, reports, rumors. ***Ant.*** ignorance; illiteracy.

knowledgeable *adj.* **well-informed,** informed, educated, learned, erudite, scholarly, well-read, cultured, cultivated, enlightened.

known *adj.* **recognized,** acknowledged, admitted, declared, proclaimed, avowed, confessed, published, revealed. ***Ant.*** unknown; secret.

Ll

label *n.* **1 ID** tag, ticket, tab, sticker, marker, docket. **2 epithet,** name, nickname, title, sobriquet, designation, denomination, description, characterization. **3 brand,** brand name, trade name, trademark, proprietary name, logo.
▸ *v.* **1 tag,** tab, ticket, stamp, mark, put stickers on, docket. **2 describe,** designate, identify, classify, categorize, brand, call, name, term, dub.

labor *n.* **1 work,** employment, job, toil, exertion, effort, industry, industriousness, hard work, hard labor, travail, drudgery, sweat of one's brow, menial work, *inf.* grind, sweat. **2 task,** job, chore, undertaking, commission, assignment, charge, venture. **3 employees,** workers, workmen, workforce, working people, hands, laborers. **4 childbirth,** birth, parturition, delivery, birth contractions, contractions, labor pains, labor pangs, travail.
▸ *v.* **1 work,** toil, slave away, drudge, plod on/away, grind/sweat away, struggle, strive, exert oneself, overwork, travail, work like a slave, work one's fingers to the bone, work like a Trojan, *inf.* kill oneself, plug away. **2 belabor,** overemphasize, lay too much emphasis on, overdo, strain, overelaborate, dwell on, expound on, expand. **3 strive,** struggle, endeavor, work, make every effort, do one's best, do one's utmost. **4 roll,** pitch, heave, toss, turn.

labored *adj.* **1 difficult,** strained, forced, heavy, awkward. **2 contrived,** affected, studied, stiff, strained, stilted, forced, unnatural, artificial, overdone, overworked, heavy, ponderous, ornate, elaborate, overelaborate, intricate, convoluted, complex, laborious. ***Ant.*** easy; natural.

laborious *adj.* **1 hard,** heavy, difficult, arduous, strenuous, fatiguing, tiring, wearying, wearisome, tedious. **2 painstaking,** careful, meticulous, diligent, assiduous, industrious, hardworking, scrupulous, persevering, pertinacious, zealous. **3 labored,** strained, forced. ***Ant.*** easy; simple; effortless; natural.

labyrinth *n.* **1 maze,** warren,

network, circuitous course, winding, coil, convolution, twisting and turning, meander, meandering, entanglement.
2 entanglement, tangle, jungle, snarl, intricacy, confusion, perplexity, complication, puzzle, riddle, enigma, problem.

labyrinthine *adj.* **1 mazelike,** meandering, winding, wandering, twisting, circuitous, tangled.
2 intricate, complicated, complex, involved, tortuous, convoluted, tangled, entangled, confusing, puzzling, perplexing, mystifying, bewildering, baffling.

lacerate *v.* **1 tear,** gash, slash, cut, cut open, rip, rend, mangle, mutilate, hurt, wound, injure, maim. **2 hurt,** wound, distress, harrow, torture, torment, afflict, crucify.

lack *n.* **absence,** want, need, deprivation, deficiency, privation, dearth, insufficiency, shortage, shortness, scarcity, scarceness, paucity. *Ant.* abundance; excess; sufficiency.
▸ *v.* **be without,** have need of, need, stand in need of, require, want, feel the want of, be short of, be deficient in, miss.

laconic *adj.* **1 brief,** concise, terse, succinct, short, economical, elliptical, crisp, pithy, to the point, incisive, abrupt, blunt, curt. **2 of few words,** untalkative, uncommunicative, reticent, reserved, taciturn, quiet, silent. *Ant.* verbose; garrulous; long-winded.

laden *adj.* **loaded,** burdened, heavily laden, weighed down, weighted, fully charged, encumbered, hampered, oppressed, taxed.

lady *n.* **1 woman,** female.
2 noblewoman, gentlewoman, duchess, countess, peeress, viscountess, baroness.

ladylike *adj.* **genteel,** refined, well-bred, cultivated, polished, decorous, proper, correct, respectable, well-mannered, courteous, polite, civil, gracious.

lag *v.* **1 loiter,** linger, dally, straggle, dawdle, hang back, delay, move slowly, drag one's feet, *inf.* dilly-dally. **2 flag,** wane, ebb, fall off, diminish, decrease, ease up, let up, slacken, abate, fail, falter, grow faint.

laid-back *adj.* **relaxed,** at ease, easy, leisurely, unhurried, casual, easygoing, free and easy, informal, nonchalant, unexcitable, imperturbable, *inf.* unflappable. *Ant.* nervous; tense; edgy.

lair *n.* **1 den,** hole, earth, covert, burrow, nest, tunnel, dugout, hollow, cave, haunt. **2 retreat,**

hideaway, refuge, sanctuary, sanctum, sanctum sanctorum, study, den, *inf.* hide-out.

lake *n.* **pond,** tarn, pool, reservoir, lagoon, bayou.

lame *adj.* **1 limping,** hobbling, halting, crippled, game, disabled, incapacitated, defective. **2 weak,** feeble, thin, flimsy, unconvincing, unsatisfactory, inadequate, insufficient, deficient, defective, ineffectual.

lament *v.* **1 mourn,** grieve, sorrow, wail, moan, groan, weep, cry, sob, complain, keen, ululate, howl, beat one's breast. **2 complain about,** bemoan, bewail, deplore.
▸ *n.* **1 wail,** wailing, lamentation, moan, moaning, groan, weeping, crying, sob, sobbing, complaint, keening, ululation, howl. **2 dirge,** requiem, elegy, monody, threnody.

lamentable *adj.* **1 deplorable,** regrettable, tragic, terrible, wretched, woeful, sorrowful, distressing, grievous. **2 miserable,** pitiful, poor, meager, low, unsatisfactory, inadequate, *inf.* measly.

lamp *n.* **light,** lantern, table lamp, night-light, oil lamp, gas lamp, lightbulb, headlight, headlamp, taillight.

land *n.* **1 dry land,** ground, solid ground, earth, terra firma. **2 soil,** earth, loam, dirt. **3 farmland,** agricultural land, country, countryside, rural areas.
4 grounds, fields, open space, open area, expanse, stretch, tract, undeveloped land. **5 property,** grounds, acres, real estate, realty.
6 country, nation, fatherland, motherland, state, realm, province, territory, district, region, area, domain.
▸ *v.* **1 touch down,** alight, make a landing, come in to land, bring down, put down, make a landing.
2 berth, dock, reach the shore, go ashore, disembark, debark.
3 arrive, get, reach, find oneself, end up, turn up, *inf.* wind up.
4 get, acquire, obtain, procure, secure, gain, net, win, carry off.

landscape *n.* **countryside,** scene, scenery, outlook, view, aspect, prospect, vista, panorama, perspective.

landslide *n.* **1 avalanche,** rockfall. **2 decisive victory,** runaway victory, overwhelming majority.

language *n.* **1 speech,** speaking, talking, words, vocabulary, utterance, verbal expression, verbalization, vocalization, communication, conversation, converse, discourse, interchange.
2 tongue, speech, parlance, mother tongue, native tongue, *inf.*

lingo. **3 speech,** dialect, vernacular, regionalism, provincialism, localism, rhyming slang, patois, lingua franca, barbarism, vulgarism, colloquialism, informal language, slang, idiom, idiolect, jargon, patter, cant, legalese, medicalese, journalese, newspeak, bureaucratese, pidgin English, *inf.* lingo, gobbledygook. **4 vocabulary,** terminology, wording, phrasing, phraseology, style, diction, expression, manner of writing/speaking, rhetoric.

languid *adj.* **1 languishing,** listless, languorous, lackadaisical, spiritless, vigorless, lacking energy, lethargic, torpid, idle, inactive, inert, indolent, lazy, sluggish, slow-moving, unenthusiastic, apathetic, indifferent, weak, weakly, sickly, faint, feeble, frail, limp, flagging, drooping, fatigued, enervated, debilitated. **2 apathetic,** lukewarm, halfhearted, unenthusiastic, bored, passive. *Ant.* energetic; vigorous.

languish *v.* **1 droop,** flag, wilt, wither, fade, fail, weaken, decline, go into a decline, waste away, *inf.* go downhill. **2 waste away,** rot, decay, wither away, be abandoned, be neglected, be forgotten, be disregarded.

languor *n.* **1 listlessness,** lethargy, torpor, idleness, inactivity, inertia, indolence, laziness, sluggishness, sleepiness, drowsiness, somnolence, dreaminess, relaxation. **2 stillness,** tranquillity, calm, calmness, lull, silence, windlessness.

lank *adj.* **1 lifeless,** lusterless, limp, straggling, straight. **2 tall,** thin, lean, lanky, skinny, spindly, gangling, gangly, scrawny, scraggy, angular, bony, gaunt, rawboned, gawky, rangy, *inf.* weedy.

lap[1] *n.* **1 knee,** knees. **2 security,** secureness, safety, protection, refuge, comfort.

lap[2] *n.* **1 circuit,** circle, loop, orbit, round, compass, ambit. **2 round,** tour, section, stage, leg.

lap[3] *v.* **1 wrap,** wind, fold, twist. **2 wrap,** swathe, cover, envelop, enfold, encase, wind, swaddle.

lap[4] *v.* **1 wash,** splash, beat, swish, slap, slosh. **2 drink up,** drink, lick up, sip.

lapse *n.* **1 slip,** error, mistake, blunder, failing, fault, failure, omission, oversight, negligence, dereliction, *inf.* slipup. **2 interval,** gap, pause, intermission, interlude, lull, hiatus, break, passage. **3 decline,** downturn, fall, falling, falling-away, slipping,

drop, deterioration, worsening, degeneration, backsliding. **4 expiration,** invalidity, termination. **5 abandonment,** forsaking, relinquishment, defection, renunciation, repudiation, rejection, disavowal, denial, abjuration, apostasy.
▸ *v.* **1 decline,** fall, fall off, drop, deteriorate, worsen, degenerate, *inf.* go downhill, go to pot.
2 cease, end, stop, terminate.
3 become void, become invalid, expire, run out, terminate, become obsolete. **4 slide,** slip, drift, sink, subside, submerge.
5 elapse, pass, go by, go on, roll on, glide by, run its course.

larder *n.* **pantry,** storage room, storeroom, store.

large *adj.* **1 big,** great, sizable, substantial, goodly, tall, high, huge, immense, enormous, colossal, massive, mammoth, vast, prodigious, gigantic, giant, monumental, stupendous, gargantuan, man-size, king-size, giant-size, outsize, outsized, considerable, *inf.* jumbo, whopping. **2 big,** burly, heavy, bulky, thickset, powerfully built, heavyset, chunky, strapping, hulking, hefty, ample, fat, obese, corpulent. **3 abundant,** copious, plentiful, ample, liberal, generous. **4 wide,** wide-ranging, large-scale, broad, extensive, far-reaching, sweeping, comprehensive, exhaustive. *Ant.* small; slight; meager.

largely *adv.* **to a large extent,** to a great degree, chiefly, for the most part, mostly, mainly, in the main, principally, in great measure.

lascivious *adj.* **1 lewd,** lecherous, lustful, licentious, promiscuous, libidinous, prurient, salacious, lubricious, concupiscent, debauched, depraved, degenerate, dissolute, dissipated. **2 lewd,** blue, obscene, pornographic, smutty, gross, bawdy, risqué, suggestive, dirty, salacious, *inf.* raunchy.

lash *n.* **1 whip,** horsewhip, bullwhip, scourge, flagellum, cat-o'-nine-tails. **2 stroke,** stripe, blow, hit, strike, bang, thwack, thump, *inf.* swipe, wallop, whack.
▸ *v.* **1 whip,** horsewhip, scourge, birch, switch, flog, flail, flagellate, thrash, beat, strike, lace, batter, hammer, *inf.* wallop, whack.
2 buffet, pound, batter, beat against, dash against, smack against, strike, knock. **3 berate,** upbraid, castigate, scold, rebuke, chide, reprove, reproach, harangue, rant at, fulminate against, attack, censure, criticize, condemn, flay, *inf.* bawl out, lace into, lambaste. **4 flick,** wag, wave, whip, switch. **5 fasten,** bind, tie,

tether, hitch, attach, join, rope, strap, leash, make fast, secure.

last *adj.* **1 hindmost,** rearmost, at the end, at the back, final, aftermost. **2 final,** closing, concluding, ending, finishing, terminating, ultimate, terminal. **3 final,** only remaining, only one left. **4 least likely,** most unlikely, least suitable, least wanted, least favorite. **5 latest,** most recent. *Ant.* first; initial.

late *adj.* **1 unpunctual,** behind time, behind schedule, behind, behindhand, not on time, tardy, overdue, delayed, dilatory, slow. **2 deceased,** dead, departed, defunct, nonextant. **3 recent,** fresh, new, last-minute, up-to-date, up-to-the-minute. *Ant.* punctual; early.

▸ *adv.* **1 unpunctually,** behind time, behindhand, belatedly, tardily, at the last minute, at the tail end, dilatorily, slowly. **2 past the usual finishing/stopping/ closing time,** after hours. **3 late at night,** *inf.* in the wee small hours.

latent *adj.* **dormant,** quiescent, inactive, passive, hidden, unrevealed, concealed, unapparent, indiscernible, imperceptible, invisible, covert, undeveloped, unrealized, potential, possible. *Ant.* obvious; evident; conspicuous.

lateral *adj.* **sidewise,** sideways, sidelong, sideward, edgewise, edgeways, indirect, oblique, slanting, askance.

latitude *n.* **1 parallel,** meridian, grid line. **2 scope,** scope for initiative, freedom of action, freedom from restriction, freedom, unrestrictedness, liberty, free play, carte blanche, leeway, elbowroom, license, indulgence, laxity.

latter *adj.* **1 last-mentioned,** second-mentioned, second of the two, second. **2 later,** hindmost, closing, end, concluding, final. **3 recent,** latest, modern.

laudable *adj.* **praiseworthy,** commendable, admirable, worthy of admiration, meritorious, deserving, creditable, worthy, estimable, of note, noteworthy, exemplary, excellent. *Ant.* blameworthy; contemptible.

laugh *v.* **chuckle,** chortle, guffaw, giggle, titter, snigger, ha-ha, tee-hee, burst out laughing, roar/hoot with laughter, shake with laughter, be convulsed with laughter, split one's sides, be rolling in the aisles, be doubled up, *inf.* be in stitches, die laughing, crack up, break up.

▸ *n.* **1 chuckle,** chortle, guffaw, giggle, titter, snigger, roar/hoot of laughter, peal of laughter, belly laugh. **2 comedian,** comic, joker, humorist, wag, wit, entertainer, clown, *inf.* card, case, caution, hoot, scream.

laughter *n.* **1 laughing,** chuckling, chortling, guffawing, giggling, tittering, sniggering, *inf.* hooting. **2 amusement,** entertainment, humor, mirth, merriment, gaiety, hilarity, glee, lightheartedness, blitheness.

launch *v.* **1 set afloat,** float. **2 fire,** discharge, propel, project, send forth, throw, cast, hurl, let fly. **3 set in motion,** get going, begin, start, commence, embark upon, initiate, instigate, institute, inaugurate, establish, set up, organize, introduce, usher in, start the ball rolling. **4 burst into,** start, begin.

lavatory *n.* **toilet,** rest room, bathroom, public convenience, ladies' room, men's room, powder room, washroom, privy, latrine, *inf.* can, john, head, little girls' room, little boys' room.

lavish *adj.* **1 copious,** abundant, superabundant, plentiful, profuse, prolific, unlimited. **2 extravagant,** excessive, immoderate, wasteful, squandering, profligate, prodigal, thriftless, improvident, intemperate, unrestrained, dissolute, wild. **3 generous,** liberal, bountiful, openhanded, unstinting, free, munificent, overgenerous, extravagant. **4 luxuriant,** lush, gorgeous, sumptuous, costly, opulent, pretentious, showy. **Ant.** meager; frugal.

▸ *v.* **heap,** shower, pour, deluge, give freely, give generously, give unstintingly, bestow freely, waste, squander, dissipate.

law *n.* **1 constitution,** code, legal code, charter, rules and regulations, jurisprudence. **2 rule,** regulation, statute, enactment, act, decree, edict, command, order, ordinance, commandment, directive, pronouncement, covenant. **3 rule,** principle, precept, standard, criterion, formula, tenet, doctrine, canon. **4 generalization,** general truth, axiom, maxim, truism. **5 the legal profession,** the bar. **6 police,** authorities, officers of the law, *inf.* fuzz, cops, boys in blue.

law-abiding *adj.* **lawful,** righteous, honest, honorable, upright, upstanding, good, virtuous, orderly, peaceable, peacekeeping, peaceful, dutiful, duteous, obedient, compliant, complying.

lawful *adj.* **1 legal,** legitimate, licit, just, valid, permissible, allowable, rightful, proper, constitutional, legalized, sanctioned, authorized,

warranted, approved, recognized.
2 law-abiding, righteous,
honorable, orderly. ***Ant.*** unlawful;
illegal.

lawless *adj.* **1 without law and
order,** anarchic, disorderly,
ungoverned, unruly,
insurrectionary, insurgent,
revolutionary, rebellious,
insubordinate, riotous, mutinous,
seditious, terrorist. **2 unlawful,**
illegal, lawbreaking, illicit,
illegitimate, criminal, felonious,
miscreant, transgressing,
violating. ***Ant.*** law-abiding;
orderly; restrained.

lawyer *n.* **attorney,** legal adviser,
criminal lawyer, civil lawyer,
advocate, counsel, solicitor.

lax *adj.* **1 slack,** slipshod,
negligent, neglectful, remiss,
careless, heedless, unmindful,
inattentive, casual, easygoing,
lenient, permissive, indulgent,
overindulgent, complaisant,
overtolerant. **2 loose,** inexact,
inaccurate, imprecise, unrigorous,
vague, indefinite, nonspecific,
broad, general. ***Ant.***
conscientious; careful.

laxative *n.* **purgative,** cathartic,
senna, ipecacuanha, ipecac, castor
oil, cod liver oil, milk of
magnesia.

lay *v.* **1 put,** place, set, deposit,
plant, settle, posit. **2 position,** set
out, arrange, dispose. **3 put
forward,** bring forward, advance,
submit, present, prefer, offer,
lodge. **4 attribute,** assign, ascribe,
allocate, allot, impute. **5 wager,**
bet, gamble, stake, give odds,
hazard, risk, chance. **6 devise,**
arrange, contrive, make, prepare,
work out, hatch, concoct, design,
plan, plot. **7 impose,** inflict,
encumber, saddle, tax, charge,
burden, apply. **8 deposit,** produce,
bear, oviposit.

▸ *adj.* **1 laic,** laical, secular,
nonclerical, nonordained.
2 nonprofessional, amateur,
nonspecialist, dilettante.

layabout *n.* **good-for-nothing,**
ne'er-do-well, do-nothing, idler,
loafer, lounger, shirker, slacker,
drone, wastrel, fainéant, sluggard,
laggard, *inf.* gold brick, lazybones,
couch potato.

laze *v.* **idle,** do nothing, loaf,
lounge, lounge about, loll around,
waste time, fritter away time.

laziness *n.* **idleness,** indolence,
slothfulness, sloth, inactivity,
inertia, lethargy, languor,
remissness, laxity.

lazy *adj.* **idle,** indolent, slothful,
work-shy, inactive, inert, sluggish,
lethargic, languorous, listless,
torpid, slow-moving, remiss,
negligent, lax. ***Ant.*** active;
industrious; energetic.

lead *v.* **1 guide,** show someone the way, conduct, lead the way, usher, escort, steer, pilot. **2 cause,** induce, prompt, move, incline, dispose, predispose, persuade, sway, influence, prevail on, bring around. **3 be at the head of,** be at the front of, head, be in the lead, be in front, be out in front, be ahead, be first, come first, precede. **4 command,** direct, govern, rule, manage, be in charge of, regulate, preside over, head, supervise, superintend, oversee, *inf.* head up. **5 be at the front of,** be ahead of, outdistance, outrun, outstrip, leave behind, outdo, excel, exceed, surpass, outrival, outshine, eclipse, transcend. **6 have,** live, pass, spend, experience, undergo. *Ant.* follow; trail.

▸ *n.* **1 leading position/place,** first place, advance position, van, vanguard. **2 first position,** head place, forefront, primacy, preeminence, supremacy, advantage, edge, precedence. **3 margin,** gap, interval. **4 example,** model, pattern, standard of excellence. **5 leading role,** star/starring role, title role, principal part. **6 star,** principal character, male lead, female lead, leading man, leading lady, hero, heroine. **7 leash,** tether, rein, cord, rope, chain. **8 clue,** pointer, guide, hint, tip, suggestion, indication, intimation, tip-off.

▸ *adj.* **leading,** first, top, foremost, front, head, chief, principal, main, most important, premier, paramount, prime, primary. *Ant.* last; tail-end.

leader *n.* **1 ruler,** head, chief, commander, director, governor, principal, captain, skipper, manager, superintendent, supervisor, overseer, foreman, kingpin, *inf.* boss, number one, head honcho. **2 pacesetter,** trendsetter, front runner. **3 front runner,** innovator, pioneer, trailblazer, pathfinder, groundbreaker, originator.

leading *adj.* **1 chief,** main, most important, principal, foremost, supreme, paramount, dominant, superior, ruling, directing, guiding, controlling, greatest, best, outstanding, preeminent, top-rank, top-ranking, of the first rank, first-rate *inf.* number-one. **2 front,** first, in first place.

leaflet *n.* **pamphlet,** flyer, booklet, brochure, handbill, bill, circular.

league *n.* **1 alliance,** confederation, confederacy, federation, union, association, coalition, combine, consortium, affiliation, guild, corporation, conglomerate, cooperative, partnership, fellowship, syndicate, band, group. **2 pact,** compact, covenant, treaty, concordat, contract, agreement, settlement. **3 level,** class, category.

leak *n.* **1 hole,** opening, crack, crevice, chink, fissure, puncture, cut, gash, slit, rent, break, rift. **2 drip,** leaking, leakage, escape, seeping, seepage, oozing, percolation, discharge. **3 disclosure,** divulgence, revelation, uncovering.
▸ *v.* **1 escape,** drip, seep out/ through, ooze out, exude, discharge, issue, gush out, take on water. **2 disclose,** divulge, reveal, make known, make public, tell, impart, pass on, relate, give away, let slip, *inf.* spill the beans about, take the lid off, let the cat out of the bag.

lean *v.* **1 rest,** be supported, be propped up, recline, repose. **2 incline,** bend, slant, tilt, be at an angle, slope, bank, list, heel, careen.
▸ *adj.* **1 thin,** slender, slim, spare, lank, skinny, scrawny, scraggy, bony, gaunt, emaciated, skin and bones, rawboned, rangy, gangling. **2 nonfat,** low-fat, unfatty. **3 meager,** scanty, sparse, poor, inadequate, insufficient, unproductive, unfruitful, arid,

barren, bare, nonfertile. *Ant.* fat; abundant.

leaning *n.* **tendency,** inclination, bent, proclivity, propensity, penchant, predisposition, predilection, proneness, partiality, preference, bias, attraction, liking, fondness, taste.

leap *v.* **1 jump,** bound, bounce, hop, skip, romp, caper, spring, frolic, frisk, cavort, gambol, dance, jump up, jump over, high-jump, vault over, vault, spring over, bound over, hurdle, clear, cross over, sail over. **2 jump,** hurry, hasten, rush, hurtle. **3 increase rapidly,** soar, rocket, skyrocket, shoot up, escalate, mount.
▸ *n.* **1 jump,** vault, spring, bound, hop, skip. **2 rapid increase,** sudden rise, escalation, soaring, surge, upsurge, upswing.

learn *v.* **1 acquire a knowledge of,** gain an understanding of, acquire skill in, become competent in, grasp, master, take in, absorb, assimilate, pick up. **2 memorize,** commit to memory. **3 discover,** find out, detect, become aware, gather, hear, be informed, understand, ascertain, discern, perceive.

learned *adj.* **erudite,** scholarly, well-educated, knowledgeable, well-read, widely read, well-versed, well-informed, lettered, cultured, intellectual, academic, literary, bookish, studious, pedantic, sage, wise, *inf.* highbrow. *Ant.* ignorant; illiterate.

learner *n.* **beginner,** trainee, apprentice, pupil, student, novice, tyro, neophyte, initiate, greenhorn, *inf.* rookie.

lease *v.* **rent,** hire, charter, rent out, let, let out, hire, hire out, sublet, sublease.
▸ *n.* **rental agreement,** charter, contract.

leash *n.* **1 rein,** tether, rope, cord, chain. **2 rein,** curb, control, check, restraint, hold.
▸ *v.* **1 fasten,** hitch up, tether, tie up, secure. **2 curb,** control, keep under control, check, restrain, hold back, suppress.

leathery *adj.* **1 wrinkled,** wizened, weather-beaten, rough, rugged, coriaceous. **2 tough,** hard, hardened, coriaceous.

leave[1] *v.* **1 depart,** go away, go, withdraw, retire, take off, exit, take one's leave, make off, pull out, quit, be gone, decamp, disappear, say one's farewells/ goodbyes, *inf.* push off, shove off, cut, split, vamoose. **2 set off,** set sail. **3 abandon,** desert, forsake, discard, turn one's back on, leave in the lurch. **4 give up,** quit,

abandon. **5 leave behind,** forget, mislay. **6 assign,** allot, consign, hand over, give over, refer, commit, entrust, delegate. **7 bequeath,** will, endow, hand down, transfer, convey, *fml.* demise, devise. **8 leave behind,** cause, produce, generate, result in. *Ant.* come; arrive; stay.

leave[2] *n.* **1 permission,** consent, authorization, sanction, warrant, dispensation, concession, indulgence. **2 vacation,** break, time off, furlough, sabbatical, leave of absence. **3 leaving,** leave-taking, departure, parting, withdrawal, exit, farewell, goodbye, adieu.

lecherous *adj.* **lustful,** promiscuous, carnal, sensual, licentious, lascivious, lewd, salacious, libertine, libidinous, lubricious, concupiscent, debauched, dissolute, wanton, intemperate, dissipated, degenerate, depraved, *inf.* horny, raunchy.

lecture *n.* **1 talk,** speech, address, discourse, disquisition, lesson, sermon, homily, harangue. **2 scolding,** chiding, reprimand, rebuke, reproof, reproach, remonstration, upbraiding, berating, tirade, diatribe, *inf.* dressing-down, telling-off, talking-to.

▶ *v.* **1 give a lecture,** give a talk, talk, give a speech, make a speech, speak, give an address, discourse, expound, hold forth, give a sermon, sermonize, harangue, *inf.* spout, jaw. **2 scold,** chide, reprimand, rebuke, reprove, reproach, remonstrate with, upbraid, berate, castigate, haul over the coals, *inf.* lambaste, give a dressing-down to, give a talking-to to, tell off.

lecturer *n.* **1 speaker,** public speaker, speech-maker, orator, preacher. **2 university teacher,** college teacher, tutor, reader, instructor, academic, academician.

ledge *n.* **shelf,** sill, mantel, mantelpiece, mantelshelf, projection, protrusion, overhang, ridge, step.

leer *v.* phrase: **leer at ogle,** look lasciviously at, look suggestively at, give sly looks to, eye, wink at, watch, stare at, sneer at, smirk at, grin at, *inf.* give someone the once-over.

▶ *n.* **lascivious look,** lecherous glance, suggestive look, sly glance, wink, stare, sneer, smirk, grin, *inf.* the once-over.

left *adj.* **1 left-hand,** sinistral, sinister, sinistrous, port. **2 left-wing,** leftist, socialist, radical, progressive, liberal, communist, communistic. *Ant.* right; reactionary.

leg *n.* **1 lower limb,** limb, member, appendage, shank, *inf.* drumstick. **2 support,** upright, prop, brace, underpinning. **3 part,** portion, segment, section, bit, stretch, stage, lap.

legal *adj.* **1 lawful,** legitimate, licit, legalized, valid, right, proper, sound, permissible, permitted, allowable, allowed, aboveboard, admissible, acceptable, authorized, sanctioned, warranted, licensed, *inf.* legit. **2 judicial,** jurisdictive, forensic. *Ant.* illegal; unlawful; criminal.

legalize *v.* **make legal,** decriminalize, legitimize, legitimatize, legitimate, validate, ratify, permit, allow, admit, accept, authorize, sanction, warrant, license.

legend *n.* **1 myth,** saga, epic, folk tale, folk story, traditional story, tale, story, narrative, fable, romance. **2 famous person,** celebrity, star, superstar, luminary. **3 caption,** inscription, dedication, motto, device, key, code, cipher, explanation.

legendary *adj.* **1 mythical,** heroic, traditional, fabled, fictitious, fictional, storybook, romantic, fanciful, fantastical, fabulous.

2 celebrated, acclaimed, illustrious, famous, famed, renowned, well-known, popular, remembered, immortal. **Ant.** factual; historical; unknown.

legitimate *adj.* **1 legal,** lawful, licit, within the law, going by the rules, *inf.* legit. **2 lawful,** rightful, genuine, authentic, real, true, proper, correct, authorized, sanctioned, warranted, acknowledged, recognized, approved, *inf.* legit, kosher. **3 valid,** sound, admissible, acceptable, well-founded, justifiable, reasonable, plausible, credible, believable, reliable, logical, rational. **Ant.** illegal; illegitimate; invalid.

legitimize *v.* **legitimate,** legalize, pronounce lawful, declare legal, decriminalize, validate, permit, warrant, authorize, sanction, license, give the stamp of approval to.

leisure *n.* **free time,** spare time, spare moments, time to spare, idle hours, inactivity, time off, relaxation, recreation, freedom, holiday, vacation, breathing space, breathing spell, respite, *inf.* time to kill. **Ant.** work; occupation.

leisurely *adj.* **unhurried,** relaxed, easy, easygoing, gentle, comfortable, restful, slow, lazy, lingering, *inf.* laid-back. **Ant.** brisk; hurried; fast.

lend *v.* **1 loan,** give someone the loan of, let someone have the use of, advance. **2 impart,** add, give, bestow, confer, provide, supply, furnish, contribute, donate, grant. **Ant.** borrow; detract.

length *n.* **1 distance,** long dimension, extent, linear measure, span, reach. **2 period,** stretch, duration, term, span. **3 piece,** portion, section, measure, segment, swatch. **4 lengthiness,** extensiveness, protractedness, elongation, prolixity, prolixness, wordiness, verbosity, verboseness, long-windedness, tediousness, tedium.

lengthen *v.* **make/grow/get longer,** elongate, let down, draw out, stretch, prolong, increase, extend, expand, protract, stretch out. **Ant.** shorten; curtail; decrease.

lengthy *adj.* **long,** long-lasting, prolonged, extended, protracted, long-drawn-out, overlong, diffuse, discursive, verbose, wordy, prolix, long-winded, tedious. **Ant.** short; brief; concise.

lenient *adj.* **merciful,** clement, sparing, moderate, compassionate, humane, forbearing, tolerant, liberal, magnanimous, indulgent, kind, gentle, easygoing, mild. *Ant.* merciless; severe; harsh.

lessen *v.* **1 grow less,** abate, decrease, diminish, subside, moderate, slacken, die down, let up, ease off, ebb, wane. **2 relieve,** soothe, allay, assuage, alleviate, palliate, ease, dull, deaden, blunt, take the edge off. **3 diminish,** lower, reduce, minimize, degrade, discredit, devalue, belittle, humble. *Ant.* increase; magnify.

lesson *n.* **1 class,** period, exercise, schoolwork, homework, assignment, school task. **2 Bible passage,** Bible reading, scripture, text. **3 example,** warning, deterrent, message, moral, precept, knowledge, wisdom, enlightenment, experience, truths.

let *v.* **1 allow to,** permit to, give permission to, give leave to, authorize to, sanction to, grant to, warrant to, license to, give the go-ahead to, give the thumbs up to, *inf.* give the green light to. **2 cause,** make, enable.

letdown *n.* **disappointment,** disillusionment, nonsuccess, fiasco, anticlimax, *inf.* washout.

lethal *adj.* **fatal,** deadly, mortal, death-dealing, murderous, poisonous, toxic, dangerous, virulent, noxious, destructive, disastrous, calamitous, ruinous. *Ant.* harmless; safe.

lethargic *adj.* **sluggish,** inactive, slow, slothful, torpid, phlegmatic, listless, languid, apathetic, passive, weary, enervated, fatigued, sleepy, narcotic. *Ant.* active; energetic.

lethargy *n.* **sluggishness,** inertia, inactivity, slowness, sloth, idleness, torpor, torpidity, lifelessness, dullness, listlessness, languor, languidness, phlegm, apathy, passivity, weariness, lassitude, fatigue, sleepiness, drowsiness, somnolence, narcosis.

letter *n.* **character,** sign, symbol, message, communication, note, line, business letter, missive, epistle, dispatch, love letter, billet-doux, fan mail, thank-you note, reply, acknowledgment, *inf.* Dear John letter.

level *adj.* **1 flat,** smooth, even, uniform, plane, flush, horizontal. **2 even,** uniform, regular, consistent, constant, stable, steady, unchanging, unvarying, unfluctuating. **3 equal,** on a level, in a position of equality, close together, neck and neck, side by side, on a par, *inf.* even-steven. **4 on the same level,** on a level, at the same height, aligned, in line, balanced. *Ant.* uneven; bumpy; vertical; variable.

▸ *n.* **1 height,** highness, altitude, elevation, distance upward. **2 position,** rank, standing, status, station, degree, grade, stage, standard. **3 extent,** amount, quantity, measure, degree, volume, size. **4 layer,** stratum, bed. **5 floor,** story.

liable *adj.* **responsible,** legally responsible, accountable, answerable, chargeable, blameworthy, at fault, censurable. *Ant.* unaccountable; safe; unlikely.

liar *n.* **teller of lies,** teller of untruths, fibber, fibster, perjurer, falsifier, false witness, fabricator, equivocator, prevaricator, deceiver, spinner of yarns, *inf.* storyteller.

libel *n.* **defamation of character,** defamation, denigration, vilification, disparagement, derogation, aspersions, calumny, slander, false report, traducement, obloquy, abuse, slur, smear, smear campaign.
▸ *v.* **defame,** vilify, give someone a bad name, blacken someone's name, denigrate, disparage, derogate, cast aspersions on, calumniate, slander, traduce, abuse, revile, malign, slur, smear, fling mud at, drag someone through the mud, drag someone's name through the mud.

libelous *adj.* **defamatory,** denigratory, vilifying, disparaging, derogatory, aspersive, calumnious, calumniatory, slanderous, false, misrepresentative, traducing, abusive, reviling, malicious, maligning, scurrilous, slurring, smearing, muckraking.

liberal *adj.* **1 abundant,** copious, ample, plentiful, lavish, profuse, munificent, bountiful, rich, handsome, generous. **2 generous,** magnanimous, openhanded, unsparing, unstinting, ungrudging, lavish, munificent, bountiful, bounteous, beneficent, bighearted, kindhearted, kind, philanthropic, charitable, altruistic, unselfish. **3 tolerant,** unprejudiced, unbiased, unbigoted, impartial, nonpartisan, disinterested, broad-minded, enlightened, catholic, indulgent, permissive. **4 broad,** loose, flexible, nonrestrictive, free, general, nonliteral, not strict, not close, inexact, imprecise. **5 advanced,** forward-looking, progressive, reformist, radical, latitudinarian. **6 wide-ranging,** broad-based, general, humanistic. *Ant.* miserly; narrow-minded; conservative; reactionary.

liberate *v.* **set free,** free, release, let out, let go, discharge, set loose, unshackle, unfetter, unchain, deliver, rescue, emancipate, manumit, unyoke. *Ant.* confine; imprison.

liberty *n.* **1 freedom,** independence, autonomy, sovereignty, self-government, self-rule. **2 freedom,** liberation, release, discharge, deliverance, emancipation, manumission. **3 freedom,** free will, volition, latitude, option, choice, noncompulsion, noncoercion. **4 right,** prerogative, privilege, permission, sanction, authorization, license, carte blanche, dispensation, exemption. *Ant.* dependence; captivity; constraint.

license *n.* **1 permission,** leave, liberty, freedom, consent, authority, authorization, sanction, approval, warranty, certification, accreditation, entitlement, privilege, prerogative, right, dispensation, exemption. **2 freedom,** liberty, free will, latitude, choice, option, independence, self-determination. **3 permit,** certificate, credential, document, documentation, pass.
▸ *v.* **grant a license to,** give a license to, give a permit to, authorize, give authorization to, grant the right to, give permission to, permit, allow, entitle, give the freedom to, sanction, give one's approval to, empower, warrant, certify, accredit, charter, franchise. *Ant.* ban; forbid.

lid *n.* **cover,** top, cap, hat, cork, stopper, plug.

lie *n.* **untruth,** falsehood, barefaced lie, fib, white lie, little white lie, fabrication, made-up story, trumped-up story, invention, piece of fiction, fiction, falsification, falsity, fairy tale/story, cock-and-bull story, dissimulation, prevarication, departure from the truth, *inf.* tall tale, whopper. *Ant.* truth; fact.

life *n.* **1 existence,** being, animation, aliveness, viability. **2 living things,** beings, creatures, human/animal/plant life, fauna, flora, human activity. **3 person,** human being, being, individual, mortal, soul. **4 lifetime,** days, duration, course, life span, time on earth, existence, career, *inf.* one's born days. **5 the human condition,** the way of the world, the world, the times we live in, the usual state of affairs, the way it is, the way things go. **6 way of life,** way of living, manner of living, lifestyle, situation, position. **7 biography,** autobiography, life story, memoirs, history, career, diary, journal, confessions. **8 animation,**

vivacity, liveliness, vitality, verve, high spirits, sparkle, exuberance, buoyancy, effervescence, enthusiasm, energy, vigor, dynamism, *inf.* oomph, pizzazz, pep, zing. **9 life force,** vital spirit, spirit, vital spark, animating spirit, moving force, lifeblood, very essence, essence, heart, core, soul, élan vital. ***Ant.*** death; demise.

lifeless *adj.* **1 dead,** deceased, gone, cold, defunct, motionless, limp. **2 inanimate,** without life, inorganic, abiotic. **3 barren,** sterile, bare, desolate, stark, arid, unproductive, uncultivated, empty, uninhabited, unoccupied. **4 spiritless,** lacking vitality, unspirited, lackluster, apathetic, uninspired, colorless, dull, flat, stiff, wooden, tedious, uninspiring. ***Ant.*** alive; animate; lively.

lifelike *adj.* **true-to-life,** realistic, photographic, speaking, faithful, authentic, exact, vivid, graphic, natural.

lift *v.* **1 pick up,** uplift, hoist, upheave, raise, heft. **2 raise,** buoy up, boost, elevate. **3 rise,** disperse, dissipate, disappear, vanish, be dispelled. **4 raise,** remove, withdraw, revoke, rescind, cancel, annul, void, countermand, relax, end, stop, terminate. **5 raise,**

make louder, louden, amplify. **6 plagiarize,** pirate, copy, abstract. **7 steal,** thieve, rob, pilfer, purloin, filch, pocket, take, appropriate, *inf.* pinch, swipe. ***Ant.*** drop; lower.

▸ *n.* **1 hoist,** heave, push, thrust, shove, help, a helping hand. **2 boost,** pick-me-up, stimulus, *inf.* shot in the arm. **3 boost,** improvement, enhancement, upgrading, amelioration. **4 car ride,** ride, transportation.

light[1] *n.* **1 illumination,** luminescence, luminosity, shining, gleaming, brightness, brilliance, glowing, blaze, glare, incandescence, effulgence, refulgence, lambency, radiance, luster, sunlight, moonlight, starlight, lamplight, firelight, electric light, gaslight, ray of light, shaft of light, beam of light. **2 lamp,** flashlight, lantern, beacon, candle, taper, torch. **3 daylight,** daylight hours, daytime, day, hours of sunlight. **4 aspect,** angle, slant, approach, viewpoint, point of view. **5 enlightenment,** illumination, understanding, comprehension, awareness, knowledge, elucidation, explanation. **6 leading lights,** luminary, star, guiding light, expert, authority. ***Ant.*** dark; darkness; ignorance.

▸ *adj.* **1 full of light,** bright, well-lit, well-lighted, well-illuminated, sunny. **2 light-colored,** light-toned, pale, pale-colored, pastel, pastel-colored; whitish, faded, bleached. **3 light-colored,** fair, blond. ***Ant.*** dark; shaded.

▸ *v.* **1 set burning,** set fire to, set a match to, ignite, kindle. **2 illuminate,** brighten, lighten, irradiate, flood with light, floodlight; *lit.* illumine. **3 irradiate,** brighten, animate, make cheerful, cheer up, enliven.

light[2] *adj.* **1 nonheavy,** easy to carry, portable. **2 slight,** thin, slender, skinny, underweight, small, tiny. **3 lightweight,** thin, flimsy, insubstantial, delicate, floaty, gossamer. **4 gentle,** slight, delicate, soft, weak, faint, indistinct. **5 moderate,** easy, simple, undemanding, untaxing, unexacting, effortless, facile, *inf.* cushy. **6 nonserious,** readily understood, lighthearted, entertaining, diverting, recreative, pleasing, amusing, humorous, funny, frivolous, superficial, trivial, trifling. **7 nonsevere,** mild, moderate, slight. **8 unimportant,** insignificant, trivial, trifling, petty, inconsequential. **9 nonheavy,** nonrich, nonlarge, easily digested, small, modest, scanty, skimpy, frugal. **10 lighthearted,** carefree, cheerful, cheery, happy, gay, merry, blithe, sunny, untroubled. **11 nimble,** deft, agile, supple, lithe, spry, sprightly, graceful. **12 light-headed,** giddy, dizzy, vertiginous, faint, unsteady; *inf.* woozy. **13 frivolous,** giddy, flighty, fickle, erratic, mercurial, volatile, capricious. **14 unchaste,** loose, promiscuous, licentious, dissolute, dissipated, wanton. **15 nondense,** porous, crumbly, friable. ***Ant.*** heavy; weighty; serious; severe.

lighten[1] *v.* **1 become/make lighter,** grow/make brighter, brighten, light up, illuminate, shed light on, cast light on, irradiate. **2 emit lightning,** flash lightning, fulgurate. **3 whiten,** bleach, pale. ***Ant.*** darken; enshroud.

lighten[2] *v.* **1 make lighter,** lessen, reduce, ease. **2 lessen,** reduce, ease, alleviate, mitigate, allay, relieve, assuage, ameliorate. **3 brighten,** cheer up, gladden, hearten, buoy up, perk up, lift, uplift, enliven, elate, inspire, revive, restore. ***Ant.*** increase; intensify; depress.

lightly *adv.* **1 slightly,** thinly, softly, gently. **2 sparingly,** sparsely, slightly. **3 easily,** without severe punishment, leniently.

4 easily, nimbly, agilely, lithely, spryly, gracefully. **5 airily,** carelessly, heedlessly, uncaringly, indifferently, thoughtlessly, flippantly, frivolously, slightingly, *inf.* breezily.

like[1] *adj.* **similar,** much the same, more or less the same, not unlike, comparable, corresponding, resembling, analogous, parallel, equivalent, of a kind, identical, matching, akin. *Ant.* unlike; dissimilar; different.

▸ *prep.* **1 in the same way as,** in the manner of, in a similar way to, after the fashion of, along the lines of. **2 typical of,** characteristic of, in character with, in keeping with.

like[2] *v.* **1 be fond of,** have a liking/fondness for, be attracted to, be keen on, love, adore, have a soft spot for. **2 enjoy,** be keen on, find/take pleasure in, love, adore, find agreeable, delight in, relish, revel in, *inf.* get a kick from. **3 wish,** want, desire, prefer, sooner have, rather have. **4 feel about,** regard, think about, appreciate. *Ant.* dislike; hate.

likelihood *n.* **probability,** good chance, chance, prospect, good prospect, reasonable prospect, possibility, distinct possibility, strong possibility.

likely *adj.* **1 probable,** distinctly possible, to be expected, in the cards, odds-on, possible. **2 apt,** inclined, tending, disposed, liable, prone. **3 reasonable,** plausible, feasible, acceptable, believable, credible, tenable, conceivable. **4 unlikely,** implausible, unacceptable, unbelievable, incredible, untenable, inconceivable. **5 suitable,** appropriate, fit, fitting, acceptable, proper, right, qualified, relevant, reasonable. **6 likely-to-succeed,** promising, talented, gifted, *inf.* up-and-coming. *Ant.* unlikely; improbable; incredible.

▸ *adv.* **probably,** in all probability, no doubt, doubtlessly, *inf.* like as not.

likeness *n.* **1 alikeness,** resemblance, similarity, sameness, similitude, correspondence, analogy, parallelism. **2 guise,** semblance, appearance, outward form, form, shape, character. **3 picture,** drawing, sketch, painting, portrait, photograph, study, representation, image, bust, statue, statuette, sculpture, icon.

liking *n.* **fondness,** love, affection, desire, preference, partiality, penchant, bias, weakness, weak spot, soft spot, appreciation, taste, predilection, fancy, inclination, bent, leaning, affinity, proclivity, propensity, proneness, tendency. *Ant.* dislike; aversion; hatred.

limb *n.* **1 arm,** leg, wing, member, extremity, appendage. **2 branch,** bough. **3 branch,** section, member, offshoot.

limelight *n.* **focus of attention,** public attention, public notice, public eye, public recognition, publicity, glare of publicity, fame, renown, celebrity, stardom, notability, eminence, prominence, spotlight.

limit *n.* **1 boundary,** boundary line, bound, bounds, partition line, demarcation line, endpoint, cutoff point, termination, border, frontier, edge, perimeter, confines, periphery. **2 extremity,** utmost, greatest extent, ultimate, breaking point, endpoint, the bitter end. **3 maximum,** ceiling, limitation, restriction, curb, check, restraint.
▶ *v.* **1 place a limit on,** restrict, curb, check, keep within bounds, hold in check, restrain, confine, control, ration, reduce, constrain, hinder, impede, hamper, trammel. **2 demarcate,** define, delimit, delimitate, mark off, stake out, encircle, encompass, bound, circumscribe.

limitation *n.* **1 restriction,** curb, restraint, constraint, qualification, control, check, hindrance, impediment, obstacle, obstruction, bar, barrier, block, deterrent. **2 inability,** incapability, incapacity, defect, frailty, weakness. **3 weak point,** weakness, drawback, snag, defect.

limited *adj.* **1 restricted,** curbed, checked, controlled, restrained, constrained. **2 restricted,** scanty, sparse, cramped, basic, minimal, inadequate, little, narrow, insufficient. **3 unintelligent,** slow, slow-witted, not very bright, dull-witted, stupid, dense, unimaginative, stolid. *Ant.* unlimited; limitless; absolute; boundless.

limitless *adj.* **1 infinite,** endless, never-ending, interminable, immense, vast, extensive, measureless. **2 unlimited,** boundless, unbounded, illimitable, infinite, endless, never-ending, unceasing, interminable, inexhaustible, constant, perpetual.

limp *v.* **1 hobble,** shuffle. **2 move slowly,** crawl, drag.
▶ *n.* **lameness,** hobble, jerk, uneven gait, shuffle.

line *n.* **1 rule,** bar, score, underline, underscore, stroke, slash. **2 band,** stripe, strip, belt, seam. **3 furrow,** wrinkle, crease, crow's-foot, groove, scar.

4 outline, contour, configuration, shape, figure, delineation, silhouette, profile, cameo.
5 boundary, boundary line, limit, border, borderline, frontier, demarcation line, edge, margin, perimeter, periphery. **6 course,** route, track, channel, path, way, road, lane, trajectory. **7 direction,** course, drift, tack, tendency, trend, bias, tenor. **8 course of action,** course, procedure, technique, way, system, method, modus operandi, policy, practice, scheme, approach, avenue, position. **9 business,** field, area, trade, occupation, employment, profession, work, job, calling, career, pursuit, activity, province, specialty, forte, *inf.* game.
10 brand, kind, sort, type, variety.
11 row, column, series, sequence, succession, progression, queue, procession, column, file, string, chain, array. **12 formation,** position, disposition, front, front line, firing line. **13 lineage,** descent, ancestry, parentage, family, extraction, heritage, stock, strain, race, breed. **14 rope,** string, cord, cable, wire, thread, twine, strand, filament. **15 note,** letter, card, postcard, message, word, communication. **16 spiel,** story, patter, piece of fiction, fabrication.

linger *v.* **1 stay,** remain, wait around, hang around, delay, dawdle, loiter, dally, take one's time, tarry, *inf.* dilly-dally.
2 persist, continue, remain, stay, hang around, be protracted, endure. **3** (barely) stay alive, cling to life, survive, last, stay around, continue, hang on. *Ant.* leave; vanish; die.
link *n.* **1 ring,** loop, connection, connective, coupling, joint, knot.
2 component, constituent, element, part, piece, member, division. **3 connection,** relationship, relatedness, association, tie. **4 bond,** tie, attachment, connection, relationship, association, affiliation, mutual interest.
▸ *v.* **1 join,** connect, fasten together, attach, bind, unite, couple, yoke. **2 join,** connect, associate, relate, bracket. *Ant.* detach; separate.
lip *n.* **1 edge,** rim, brim, margin, border, verge, brink.
2 impertinence, impudence, insolence, rudeness, audacity, effrontery, cheek, *inf.* backtalk, sass.
liquid *n.* **fluid,** liquor, solution, juice, sap.
▸ *adj.* **1 fluid,** flowing, running, runny, watery, aqueous, liquefied, melted, molten, dissolved,

hydrous. **2 clear,** transparent, limpid, unclouded, bright, shining, brilliant, glowing, gleaming. **3 clear,** pure, smooth, flowing, fluent, fluid, mellifluent, mellifluous, dulcet, sweet, soft, melodious. **4 convertible,** negotiable. ***Ant.*** solid; cloudy.

liquidate *v.* **1 pay,** pay in full, pay off, settle, clear, discharge, square, make good, honor. **2 close down,** wind up, dissolve, break up, disband, terminate, annul. **3 convert to cash,** convert, cash in, sell off, sell up, realize. **4 kill,** murder, put to death, do away with, assassinate, put an end to, eliminate, get rid of, dispatch, finish off, destroy, annihilate, *inf.* do in, bump off, rub out, wipe out.

list *n.* **catalog,** inventory, record, register, roll, file, index, directory, listing, enumeration, table, tabulation, schedule, syllabus, calendar, program, series.
▸ *v.* **make a list of,** note down, write down, record, register, set down, enter, itemize, enumerate, catalog, file, tabulate, schedule, chronicle, classify, alphabetize.

listen *v.* **1 pay attention,** be attentive, concentrate on hearing, give ear, lend an ear, hang on someone's words, keep one's ears open, prick up one's ears, *inf.* be all ears. **2 pay attention,** take heed, heed, give heed, take notice, mind, obey, do as one is told. ***Ant.*** ignore; disregard.

listless *adj.* **languid,** lethargic, languishing, enervated, lackadaisical, spiritless, unenergetic, lifeless, inactive, inert, indolent, apathetic, passive, dull, heavy, sluggish, slothful, limp, languorous, torpid, supine, indifferent, uninterested, impassive. ***Ant.*** energetic; lively.

literal *adj.* **1 word-for-word,** verbatim, line-for-line, letter-for-letter, exact, precise, faithful, close, strict, undeviating, true, accurate. **2 true,** accurate, genuine, authentic, veritable, plain, simple, unexaggerated, unvarnished, unembellished, undistorted. **3 literal-minded,** down-to-earth, prosaic, factual, matter-of-fact, unimaginative, colorless, commonplace, tedious, boring, dull, uninspiring. ***Ant.*** loose; vague; inaccurate.

literary *adj.* **1 written,** published, printed, in print. **2 well-read,** widely read, educated, well-educated, scholarly, learned, intellectual, cultured, erudite, bookish, studious, lettered, *inf.* highbrow. **3 formal,** poetic.

literate *adj.* **1 able to read and write,** educated, schooled.

2 educated, well-educated, well-read, scholarly, learned, intellectual, erudite, cultured, cultivated, knowledgeable, well-informed. **3 well-written,** stylish, polished, articulate, lucid, eloquent.

literature *n.* **1 written works,** writings, printed works, published works, letters, belles lettres. **2 printed matter,** brochure, leaflet, pamphlet, flyer, circular, information, data, facts, *inf.* info.

lithe *adj.* **agile,** flexible, supple, limber, loose-limbed, pliant, pliable, lissome.

litigation *n.* **lawsuit,** legal case, case, legal dispute, legal contest, legal action, legal proceedings, suit.

litter *n.* **1 trash,** rubbish, debris, refuse, junk, odds and ends, fragments, detritus, flotsam. **2 disorder,** untidiness, clutter, jumble, confusion, mess, disarray, disorganization, disarrangement, *inf.* shambles. **3 brood,** young, offspring, progeny, family, issue. **4 stretcher,** cot, portable bed. **5 animal bedding,** bedding, straw, floor covering. ▸ *v.* **1 make untidy,** mess up, make a mess of, clutter up, throw into disorder, disarrange, *inf.* make a shambles of. **2 scatter,** strew, throw around.

little *adj.* **1 small,** short, slight, petite, tiny, wee, miniature, diminutive, minute, infinitesimal, microscopic, minuscule, dwarf, midget, pygmy, bantam, *inf.* teeny, teeny-weeny, pint-sized. **2 small,** young, junior. **3 unimportant,** insignificant, minor, trivial, trifling, petty, paltry, inconsequential, negligible, nugatory. **4 hardly any,** small, scant, meager, skimpy, sparse, insufficient, exiguous, *inf.* piddling. **5 mean,** narrow, narrow-minded, small-minded, base, cheap, shallow, petty, illiberal, provincial, parochial, insular. **Ant.** big; large; long; considerable. ▸ *adv.* **1 hardly,** barely, scarcely, not much, only slightly, only just, hardly ever, scarcely ever, scarcely, not much, rarely, seldom, infrequently. **2 hardly ever,** hardly, scarcely ever, rarely, seldom, infrequently.

liturgy *n.* **ritual,** worship, service, ceremony, rite, observance, celebration, office, sacrament.

live *v.* **1 be alive,** have life, be, have being, breathe, draw breath, exist, walk the earth. **2 survive,** last, endure, persist, abide, continue, stay around. **3 lead one's life,** behave, comport oneself. **4 keep alive,** survive, make a living, earn one's living, subsist, support oneself, maintain oneself, make ends meet, keep body and soul together. **5 dwell,** reside, have one's home, have one's residence, lodge, be settled, *inf.* hang one's hat. **6 enjoy life,** enjoy oneself, have fun, be happy, make the most of life, flourish, prosper, thrive.

▸ *adj.* **1 alive,** living, having life, breathing, animate, vital, existing, existent, *inf.* in the land of the living. **2 actual,** in the flesh, not imaginary, true-to-life, genuine, authentic. **3 nonrecorded,** in real time, unedited, with an audience. **4 glowing,** aglow, burning, alight, flaming, aflame, blazing, hot, smoldering. **5 charged,** connected, active, switched on. **6 unexploded,** explodable, explosive. **7 current,** topical, active, prevalent, important, of interest, lively, vital, pressing, burning, pertinent, controversial, debatable, unsettled. *Ant.* dead; inactive.

livelihood *n.* **1 living,** subsistence, means of support, income, keep, maintenance, sustenance, upkeep. **2 job,** work, employment, occupation, trade, profession, career.

lively *adj.* **1 full of life,** active, animated, energetic, alive, vigorous, alert, spirited, high-spirited, vivacious, enthusiastic, keen, cheerful, buoyant, sparkling, bouncy, perky, sprightly, spry, frisky, agile, nimble, *inf.* chipper, peppy. **2 brisk,** quick, rapid, swift, speedy, vigorous. **3 animated,** spirited, stimulating, heated, enthusiastic, forceful, interesting, eventful. **4 busy,** crowded, bustling, hectic, swarming, teeming, astir, buzzing, thronging. **5 vivid,** colorful, bright, striking, graphic, stimulating, exciting, effective, imaginative. *Ant.* listless; lifeless; slow; apathetic.

living *adj.* **1 alive,** live, having life, breathing, animate, vital, existing, existent, *inf.* in the land of the living. **2 current,** in use, extant, existing, existent, contemporary, operating, active, ongoing, continuing, surviving, persisting. **3 exact,** close, faithful, true-to-life, authentic, genuine. *Ant.* dead; extinct; obsolete.

▸ *n.* **1 livelihood,** subsistence, means of support, income, keep, maintenance, sustenance, upkeep. **2 job,** work, employment, occupation, trade, profession, career. **3 way of life,** lifestyle, life, conduct, behavior.

load *n.* **1 cargo,** freight, charge, burden, lading, contents, consignment, shipment,

truckload, shipload, busload.
2 burden, onus, weight,
responsibility, duty, charge,
obligation, tax, strain, trouble,
worry, encumbrance, affliction,
oppression, handicap, trial,
tribulation, cross, millstone,
albatross, incubus.
▸ *v.* **1 fill,** fill up, lade, pack, pile,
heap, stack, stuff, cram. **2 burden,**
weigh down, weight, saddle,
charge, tax, strain, encumber,
hamper, handicap, overburden,
overwhelm, oppress, trouble,
worry. **3 prime,** charge, fill.
4 weight, add weight to, bias, rig.
loaf *n.* **block,** cake, slab, brick,
lump, hunk.
▸ *v.* **laze,** lounge, do nothing, idle,
lie around, hang about, waste
time, fritter away time, take
things easy, twiddle one's
thumbs, sit on one's hands.
loan *n.* **advance,** credit, mortgage.
▸ *v.* **lend,** advance, give credit.
loath *adj.* **reluctant,** unwilling,
disinclined, not in the mood,
against, averse, opposed,
resisting. **Ant.** eager; enthusiastic.
loathe *v.* **hate,** detest, abhor,
despise, abominate, have an
aversion to, not be able to bear,
dislike, shrink from, recoil from,
feel repugnance toward, be
unable to stomach, execrate. **Ant.**
love; like.

loathing *n.* **hatred,** hate,
detestation, abhorrence, aversion,
abomination, repugnance,
disgust, revulsion, odium,
antipathy, dislike, ill will, enmity,
execration.
loathsome *adj.* **hateful,**
detestable, abhorrent, odious,
repugnant, disgusting, repulsive,
revolting, nauseating,
abominable, vile, nasty,
obnoxious, horrible, offensive,
disagreeable, despicable,
contemptible, reprehensible,
execrable, *inf.* horrid, yucky. **Ant.**
lovable; delightful.
local *adj.* **1 community,** district,
neighborhood, regional, city,
town, municipal, provincial,
village, parish. **2 nearby,** near, at
hand, close by, neighborhood.
3 confined, restricted, contained,
limited, circumscribed, delimited,
specific. **Ant.** national; general.
▸ *n.* **local person,** native,
inhabitant, resident, parishioner,
derog. inf. local yokel, homeboy.
locale *n.* **place,** site, spot,
position, location, venue, area,
neighborhood, locality, setting,
scene.
locality *n.* **1 vicinity,** surrounding
area, area, neighborhood, district,
region, environs, locale, *fml.* locus.
2 location, position, place,
whereabouts, bearings.

localize *v.* **confine,** restrict, contain, limit, circumscribe, delimit, delimitate.

locate *v.* **1 find,** find out, discover, identify, pinpoint, detect, uncover, track down, unearth, hit upon, come across, reveal, pin down, define. **2 situate,** site, position, place, put, build, establish, station, set, fix, settle.

location *n.* **1 position,** place, situation, whereabouts, bearings, site, spot, point, scene, setting, venue, locale, *fml.* locus. **2 position,** place, situation, site, spot, scene, setting, venue, locale.

lock *v.* **1 bolt,** fasten, bar, secure, make secure, padlock. **2 interlock,** engage, mesh, join, link, unite. **3 jam,** become immovable, become rigid. **4 clasp,** clench, entangle, entwine, embrace, hug, squeeze. *Ant.* unlock; open; separate.

locker *n.* **cupboard,** compartment, cabinet, cubicle, storeroom, storage room.

lodge *n.* **1 house,** cottage, cabin, chalet. **2 branch,** chapter, section, association, society, club, group, fraternity, sorority. **3 lair,** den, beaver-house, hole, retreat, haunt, shelter.
► *v.* **1 stay,** reside, dwell, room, sojourn, stop. **2 house,** provide accommodation for, accommodate, put up, billet, shelter, harbor, entertain. **3 register,** submit, put forward, place, file, lay, put on record, record. **4 become fixed,** become embedded, become implanted, stick, become caught, come to rest.

lofty *adj.* **1 towering,** soaring, tall, high, elevated, sky-high, skyscraping. **2 arrogant,** haughty, proud, self-important, conceited, overweening, disdainful, supercilious, condescending, patronizing, lordly, snobbish, scornful, contemptuous, insulting, cavalier, *inf.* high-and-mighty, stuck-up, snooty, uppity. **3 noble,** exalted, grand, sublime, imposing, esoteric. **4 eminent,** leading, noted, notable, well-known, distinguished, famous, renowned, illustrious, esteemed, celebrated, noble, aristocratic. *Ant.* low; modest; lowly.

log *n.* **1 block,** piece, chunk, billet, stump, trunk, branch, bole. **2 logbook,** record, register, journal, diary, daybook, chart, account, tally.
► *v.* **1 set down,** make a note of, note/write down, jot down, register, record, book down, file, chart, tabulate, catalog. **2 achieve,** attain, make, do, go, cover, travel, traverse.

logic *n.* **1 reasoning,** deduction, thought, dialectics, argumentation, ratiocination. **2 line of reasoning,** reasoning, argument, argumentation. **3 reason,** judgment, wisdom, sense, good sense, common sense, rationale, relevance, coherence, *inf.* horse sense.

logical *adj.* **1 reasoned,** well-reasoned, rational, sound, cogent, coherent, well-organized, clear, consistent, relevant, reasonable, sensible, intelligent, wise, judicious. **2 most likely,** likeliest, plausible, obvious. **3 reasoning,** thinking, straight-thinking, rational, consistent. *Ant.* illogical; irrational; unlikely.

loiter *v.* **1 hang around,** linger, wait, skulk, loaf, lounge, idle, waste time, *lit.* tarry. **2 dawdle,** take one's time, go at a snail's pace, dally, stroll, saunter, delay, loll, *inf.* dilly-dally.

lone *adj.* **by oneself,** alone, single, solitary, sole, unaccompanied, without companions, companionless, lonely.

lonely *adj.* **1 friendless,** companionless, lonesome, forlorn, forsaken, abandoned, rejected, isolated, outcast, sad, unhappy, despondent. **2 lone,** by oneself, alone, single, solitary, sole, companionless. **3 desolate,** barren, isolated, out-of-the-way, remote, secluded, off the beaten track, deserted, uninhabited, unfrequented, unpopulated, godforsaken, lone. *Ant.* popular; sociable; populous.

long *adj.* **1 in length,** lengthways, lengthwise. **2 lengthy,** extended, extensive, stretched out, spread out. **3 lengthy,** prolonged, protracted, extended, long-drawn-out, dragged out, seemingly endless, interminable, long-winded, verbose, prolix, tedious. *Ant.* short; brief.

longing *n.* **wish,** desire, wanting, yearning, craving, hunger, thirst, itch, covetousness, lust, hope, dream, aspiration, pining, fancy, urge, hankering, *inf.* yen.
  ▸ *adj.* **wishful,** desirous, yearning, craving, covetous, hopeful, wistful, avid.

look *v.* **1 see,** take a look, glance, fix one's gaze, focus, observe, view, regard, eye, take in, watch, examine, study, inspect, scan, scrutinize, survey, check, contemplate, consider, pay attention to, run the eyes over, peep, peek, glimpse, gaze, stare, gape, ogle, *inf.* take a gander, give someone/something the once-over, rubberneck, eyeball. **2 seem,** seem to be, appear, appear to be, give every appearance/indication of being, look to be, present as being, strike someone as being. **3 face,** front, front on.

▸ *n.* **1 sight,** glance, observation, view, examination, study, inspection, scan, survey, peep, peek, glimpse, gaze, stare, gape, ogle, *inf.* eyeful, gander, look-see, once-over. **2 expression,** face, countenance, features, mien. **3 appearance,** air, aspect, bearing, cast, demeanor, features, semblance, guise, façade, impression, effect. **4 fashion,** style, latest style, vogue, trend, fad, craze, rage.

loom *v.* **1 appear,** emerge, become visible, take shape, materialize, reveal itself, appear indistinctly, take on a threatening shape. **2 tower,** soar, rise, rise up, mount, overhang, hang over, dominate. **3 be imminent,** impend, be close, be ominously close, threaten, menace.

loop *n.* **coil,** hoop, noose, circle, ring, oval, spiral, curl, twirl, whorl, twist, convolution, bend, curve, kink, arc.

▸ *v.* **coil,** form a hoop with, form hoops with, make a circle with, make circles with, bend into spirals/whorls.

loophole *n.* **means of evasion/ avoidance,** means of escape, escape, escape clause, escape route, ambiguity, omission.

loose *adj.* **1 at large,** at liberty, free, on the loose, unconfined, untied, unchained, untethered, unsecured, unshackled, unfastened, unrestricted, unbound, freed, let go, liberated, released, set loose. **2 wobbly,** not secure, insecure, rickety, unsteady, movable. **3 untied,** unpinned, unbound, hanging free, flowing, floppy. **4 slack,** baggy, bagging, sagging, sloppy. **5 inexact,** imprecise, vague, indefinite, ill-defined, broad, general, nonspecific, diffuse, unrigorous, unmeticulous. **6 immoral,** disreputable, dissolute, corrupt, fast, promiscuous, debauched, dissipated, degenerate, wanton, whorish, unchaste, licentious, lascivious, lustful, libertine, abandoned, profligate, reprobate, careless, thoughtless, negligent, rash, heedless, unmindful. **7 relaxed,** informal, uninhibited, unreserved, frank, open, unceremonious, unconstrained. *Ant.* secure; tight; literal.

▸ *v.* **1 let loose,** set free, unloose, turn loose, set loose, untie, let go, release, free. **2 loosen,** relax, slacken, weaken, lessen, reduce, diminish, moderate, soften.

3 discharge, shoot, loose off, fire off, eject, catapult. **_Ant._** confine; tighten.

loosen _v._ **1 slacken,** slack, unstick, become loose, work loose, work free. **2 slacken,** let out, undo, unfasten, unhook. **3 loose,** relax, slacken, weaken, lessen, moderate. **_Ant._** tighten; fasten.

loot _n._ **booty,** spoils, spoil, plunder, haul, stolen goods, pillage, prize, _inf._ swag, the goods, hot goods, boodle.
▸ _v._ **plunder,** pillage, rob, burgle, steal from, ransack, sack, maraud, ravage, despoil, spoliate.

lop _v._ **cut,** cut back, slash, ax, remove, take off, trim, prune, dock, eliminate.

lose _v._ **1 mislay,** misplace, drop, forget. **2 be deprived of,** suffer the loss of. **3 leave behind,** outdistance, outstrip, outrun. **4 escape from,** evade, elude, dodge, give someone the slip, shake off, throw off, throw off the scent, duck, get rid of. **5 stray from,** wander from. **6 let pass,** miss, forfeit, neglect, _inf._ pass up, lose out on. **7 suffer defeat,** be defeated, be the loser, be worsted, get/have the worst of it, be beaten, be conquered, be vanquished, be trounced, come off second-best, fail, come to grief,

meet one's Waterloo, _inf._ lose out, come a cropper. **8 waste,** squander, dissipate, spend, expend, consume, deplete, exhaust, use up.

loser _n._ **runner-up,** also-ran, the defeated, the vanquished, failure, born loser, _inf._ flop, dud, washout, lemon.

loss _n._ **1 mislaying,** misplacement, dropping, forgetting. **2 losing,** deprivation, privation, forfeiture, bereavement, disappearance, waste, squandering, dissipation. **3 deprivation,** privation, detriment, disadvantage, damage, injury, impairment, harm, hurt, ruin, destruction, undoing, incapacitation, disablement. **4 casualty,** fatality, dead, death toll. **5 deficit,** debit, debt, lack of profit, deficiency, losing, depletion.

lost _adj._ **1 missing,** strayed, gone astray, mislaid, misplaced, vanished, disappeared, forgotten. **2 stray,** astray, off-course, off-track, disorientated, having lost one's bearings, adrift, going around in circles, at sea. **3 missed,** passed, forfeited, neglected, wasted, squandered, dissipated, frittered, gone by the board, _inf._ down the drain. **4 extinct,** dead, bygone, lost and gone, lost in time, past, vanished, forgotten,

unremembered, unrecalled, consigned to oblivion.
5 destroyed, ruined, wiped out, wrecked, finished, perished, demolished, obliterated, effaced, exterminated, eradicated, annihilated, extirpated.
6 damned, fallen, irredeemable, irreclaimable, irretrievable, past hope, hopeless, past praying for.
7 impervious, immune, closed, unreceptive, unaffected by, unmoved by, untouched by. **8 lost in thought,** abstracted, dreamy, distrait, absentminded, somewhere else, not there, not with us. **9 at a loss,** baffled, nonplussed.

lotion *n.* **cream,** salve, ointment, moisturizer, balm, emollient, lubricant, unguent, liniment, embrocation, pomade, hand lotion, body lotion.

lottery *n.* **1 draw,** raffle, sweepstake, game of chance, gamble, drawing of lots, lotto, bingo. **2 gamble,** game of chance, risk, hazard, venture.

loud *adj.* **1 blaring,** booming, noisy, deafening, resounding, reverberant, sonorous, stentorian, roaring, thunderous, tumultuous, clamorous, head-splitting, ear-splitting, ear-piercing, piercing, strident, harsh, raucous. **2 noisy,** rowdy, boisterous, rough, rollicking. **3 brash,** brazen, bold, loud-mouthed, vociferous, raucous, aggressive, coarse, crude, rough, crass, vulgar, brassy, *inf.* pushy. **4 vociferous,** clamorous, insistent, vehement, emphatic, urgent, importunate, demanding. **5 garish,** gaudy, flashy, bold, flamboyant, lurid, glaring, showy, obtrusive, vulgar, tawdry, tasteless, *inf.* camp, tacky. **Ant.** quiet; soft; gentle; restrained.

lounge *v.* **1 laze,** lie, lie around, recline, relax, take it easy, sprawl, loll, repose. **2 loaf,** idle, loiter, hang, linger, skulk, waste time, *inf.* hang out.
▸ *n.* **1 sitting room,** drawing room, living room, parlor. **2 sitting room,** cocktail lounge.

lousy *adj.* **1 bad,** poor, incompetent, inadequate, unsatisfactory, inferior, careless, second-rate, terrible, miserable, *inf.* rotten, no-good. **2 dirty,** low, mean, base, despicable, contemptible, low-down, hateful, detestable, loathsome, vile, wicked, vicious, *inf.* rotten.

lout *n.* **boor,** oaf, dolt, churl, bumpkin, yahoo, brute, rowdy, barbarian, *inf.* slob, clodhopper, clod, lummox.

lovable *adj.* **adorable,** dear, sweet, cute, charming, lovely, likable, attractive, delightful, captivating, enchanting, engaging, bewitching, pleasing, appealing, winsome, winning, taking, endearing, affectionate, warmhearted, cuddly. **Ant.** hateful; loathsome.

love *v.* **1 care for,** be in love with, be fond of, feel affection for, be attracted to, be attached to, hold dear, adore, think the world of, dote on, worship, idolize, treasure, prize, cherish, be devoted to, desire, want, be infatuated with, lust after, long for, yearn for, adulate, *inf.* fancy, have a crush on, have the hots for, be soft on. **2 like,** have a liking for, have a weakness for, be partial to, have a soft spot for, be addicted to, enjoy, find enjoyment in, relish, savor, appreciate, take pleasure in, delight in, *inf.* get a kick out of, have a thing about. **Ant.** hate; loathe; detest.
▸ *n.* **1 affection,** fondness, care, concern, attachment, regard, warmth, intimacy, devotion, adoration, passion, ardor, desire, lust, yearning, infatuation, adulation. **2 liking,** weakness, partiality, enjoyment, appreciation, relish, passion. **3 care,** caring, regard, solicitude, sympathy, warmth, friendliness, friendship, rapport, brotherhood, kindness, charity. **4 beloved,**

loved one, true love, love of one's life, dear, dearest, dear one, darling, sweetheart, sweet, sweet one, angel, lover, inamorato/inamorata. **5 love affair,** affair, romance, relationship, liaison.

lovely *adj.* **1 beautiful,** pretty, attractive, good-looking, glamorous, comely, handsome, sweet, fair, charming, adorable, enchanting, engaging, bewitching, winsome, seductive, ravishing. **2 delightful,** pleasant, nice, agreeable, pleasing, marvelous, wonderful, *inf.* terrific, fabulous, fab. **Ant.** ugly; horrible; disagreeable.

lover *n.* **1 boyfriend,** girlfriend, man friend, woman friend, mistress, ladylove, paramour, other man, other woman, beau, loved one, beloved, sweetheart, inamorato/inamorata. **2 admirer,** devotee, fan, enthusiast, aficionado, *inf.* buff, freak.

loving *adj.* **affectionate,** fond, devoted, caring, adoring, doting, solicitous, demonstrative, tender, warm, warmhearted, friendly, kind, sympathetic, charitable, cordial, amiable, amorous, ardent, passionate.

low *adj.* **1 short,** small, little, squat, stubby, stunted, truncated, dwarfish, knee-high. **2 low-lying,** ground-level, sea-level, flat, sunken, depressed, subsided, nether. **3 lowly,** humble, lowborn, lowbred, low-ranking, plebeian, peasant, poor, common, ordinary, simple, plain, unpretentious, inferior, subordinate, obscure. **4 sparse,** meager, scarce, scanty, scant, few, little, deficient, inadequate, paltry, measly, trifling, reduced, depleted, diminished. **5 soft,** quiet, muted, subdued, muffled, hushed, quietened, whispered, murmured, gentle, dulcet, indistinct, inaudible. **6 low-spirited,** down, depressed, dejected, despondent, disheartened, downhearted, downcast, gloomy, glum, unhappy, sad, miserable, blue, fed up, morose, moody, heavy-hearted, forlorn, *inf.* down in the mouth, down in the dumps. **7 low-grade,** inferior, substandard, below par, second-rate, deficient, defective, wanting, lacking, inadequate, mediocre, unacceptable, worthless. **8 lowly,** simple, plain, ordinary, commonplace, run-of-the-mill, modest, unambitious, unpretentious, unaspiring. **9 unfavorable,** poor, bad, adverse, hostile, negative. **10 mean,** nasty, foul, bad, wicked, evil, vile, vicious, despicable, contemptible, heinous, villainous, base,

dishonorable, unprincipled, dastardly, ignoble, sordid. **11 vulgar,** crude, coarse, obscene, indecent, gross, ribald, smutty, bawdy, pornographic, blue, rude, rough, unrefined, indelicate, improper, offensive. **12 cheap,** inexpensive, moderate, reasonable, modest, bargain-basement. *Ant.* high; cheerful; admirable.

▸ *v.* **moo,** bellow.

lower *adj.* **1 lesser,** lower-level, lower-grade, subordinate, junior, inferior, minor, secondary. **2 under,** underneath, nether. **3 cheaper,** reduced, decreased, lessened, cut, slashed, curtailed.

▸ *v.* **1 let down,** take down, haul down, drop, let fall, let sink. **2 modulate,** soften, quieten, hush, tone down, muffle, turn down, mute. **3 degrade,** debase, demean, downgrade, discredit, devalue, dishonor, disgrace, belittle, humble, humiliate, disparage. **4 reduce,** bring down, decrease, lessen, cut, slash, curtail. **5 abate,** die down, subside, let up, moderate, slacken, dwindle, lessen, ebb, fade away, wane, taper off, lull. *Ant.* raise; increase; boost.

lowly *adj.* **1 low,** humble, lowborn, low-ranking, plebeian, peasant, poor, common, ordinary, inferior, subordinate. **2 humble,** meek, submissive, dutiful, docile, mild, gentle, modest, unassuming. **3 low,** simple, plain, ordinary, commonplace, run-of-the-mill, modest, unambitious, unpretentious, unaspiring. *Ant.* noble; aristocratic; arrogant; high-flown.

loyal *adj.* **faithful,** true, true-hearted, tried and true, trusted, trustworthy, trusty, true-blue, steadfast, staunch, dependable, reliable, devoted, dutiful, patriotic, constant, unchanging, unwavering, unswerving, firm, stable. *Ant.* disloyal; treacherous.

loyalty *n.* **faithfulness,** fidelity, fealty, allegiance, trueness, true-heartedness, trustiness, trustworthiness, steadfastness, staunchness, dependability, reliability, devotion, duty, patriotism, constancy, stability. *Ant.* disloyalty; treachery.

lucid *adj.* **1 clear,** clear-cut, crystal-clear, comprehensible, intelligible, understandable, plain, simple, direct, straightforward, graphic, explicit, obvious, evident, apparent, distinct, transparent, overt, cogent. **2 sane,** rational, in one's right mind, in possession of one's faculties, of sound mind, compos mentis, sensible, clearheaded, *inf.*

all there, having all one's marbles. **3 clear,** crystal-clear, transparent, limpid, translucent, glassy, pellucid. **4 bright,** shining, gleaming, luminous, radiant, lustrous. *Ant.* confused; muddled; cloudy.

luck *n.* **1 fate,** fortune, destiny, predestination, the stars, chance, fortuity, accident, hazard, serendipity. **2 good luck,** good fortune, success, successfulness, prosperity, advantage, advantageousness, felicity, *inf.* lucky break.

lucky *adj.* **1 fortunate,** blessed with good luck, favored, born under a lucky star, charmed, successful, prosperous, happy, advantaged, born with a silver spoon in one's mouth. **2 fortunate,** fortuitous, providential, advantageous, timely, opportune, expedient, auspicious, propitious. *Ant.* unlucky; unfortunate; unfavorable.

lucrative *adj.* **profitable,** profit-making, moneymaking, paying, high-income, well-paid, high-paying, gainful, remunerative, productive, fat, fruitful, rewarding, worthwhile.

ludicrous *adj.* **absurd,** ridiculous, laughable, risible, derisible, comic, comical, farcical, silly, funny, humorous, droll, amusing, diverting, hilarious, crazy, zany, nonsensical, odd, outlandish, eccentric, incongruous, preposterous. *Ant.* sensible; serious; solemn.

lull *v.* **1 soothe,** quiet, silence, calm, hush, still, quell, assuage, allay, ease, alleviate, pacify, mitigate. **2 abate,** die down, subside, let up, moderate, slacken, lessen, dwindle, decrease, diminish, ebb, fade away, wane, taper off, lower.
▸ *n.* **1 pause,** respite, interval, break, hiatus, *inf.* letup. **2 calm,** calmness, stillness, quiet, quietness, tranquillity, silence, hush.

lumber *n.* **timber,** wood, boards, planks, planking, beams.

lumbering *adj.* **awkward,** clumsy, heavy-footed, blundering, bumbling, inept, maladroit, ungainly, like a bull in a china shop, ungraceful, hulking, ponderous, stolid, *inf.* clodhopping.

luminous *adj.* **1 lighted,** lit, illuminated, shining, bright, brilliant, radiant, dazzling, glowing, effulgent, luminescent, phosphorescent, vivid, resplendent. **2 lucid,** clear, crystal clear, comprehensible, intelligible, plain, simple, direct, straightforward, graphic, obvious, distinct, apparent.

lump *n.* **1 chunk,** wedge, hunk, piece, mass, cake, nugget, ball, dab, pat, clod, gob, wad, clump, mound. **2 bump,** swelling, bruise, bulge, protuberance, protrusion, growth, carbuncle, hump, tumor, tumescence, node.
▸ *v.* **put together,** combine, group, unite, pool, mix together, blend, merge, mass, fuse, conglomerate, coalesce, consolidate.

lunacy *n.* **1 insanity,** insaneness, madness, mental illness/ derangement, dementia, dementedness, loss of reason, unsoundness of mind, mania, frenzy, psychosis, *inf.* craziness. **2 madness,** insanity, foolishness, folly, foolhardiness, stupidity, idiocy, irrationality, illogicality, senselessness, absurdity, absurdness, silliness, inanity, ludicrousness, *inf.* craziness, daftness. *Ant.* sanity; sense; prudence.

lunatic *n.* **maniac,** madman, madwoman, imbecile, idiot, psychopath, *inf.* loony, nut, nutcase, head case, basket case, screwball, psycho.
▸ *adj.* **mad,** insane, foolish, stupid, foolhardy, idiotic, crack-brained, irrational, unreasonable, illogical, senseless, nonsensical, absurd,

silly, inane, asinine, ludicrous, imprudent, preposterous, *inf.* crazy, daft.

lunge *n.* **1 spring,** jump, leap, bound, dash, charge, pounce, dive. **2 stab,** jab, poke, thrust, swing, pass, cut, feint, *inf.* swipe.

▶ *v.* **1 spring,** jump, leap, bound, dash, charge, pounce, dive. **2 stab,** jab, poke, thrust.

lurch *v.* **1 stagger,** sway, reel, weave, stumble, totter. **2 list,** roll, pitch, toss, sway, veer, swerve.

lure *v.* **entice,** attract, induce, inveigle, decoy, draw, lead, allure, tempt, seduce, beguile, ensnare, magnetize, cajole.

▶ *n.* **enticement,** attraction, inducement, decoy, draw, allurement, temptation, bait, magnet, drawing card, carrot, *inf.* come-on.

lurid *adj.* **1 overbright,** brilliant, glaring, flaming, dazzling, glowing, intense, vivid, showy, gaudy, fiery, blood-red, burning. **2 sensational,** melodramatic, exaggerated, extravagant, graphic, explicit, unrestrained, shocking, startling, *inf.* full-frontal. **3 gruesome,** gory, grisly, macabre, repugnant, revolting, disgusting, ghastly. **4 pale,** pallid, ashen, colorless, chalk-white, white, wan, sallow, livid, ghostly, ghastly. **Ant.** muted; restrained; subtle.

lurk *v.* **skulk,** lie in wait, lie low, hide, conceal oneself, take cover, crouch, sneak, slink, prowl, steal, tiptoe.

luscious *adj.* **delicious,** juicy, sweet, succulent, mouthwatering, tasty, appetizing, delectable, palatable, toothsome, *inf.* scrumptious, yummy.

lush *adj.* **1 luxuriant,** abundant, profuse, exuberant, dense, thick, riotous, overgrown, prolific, rank, teeming, junglelike, flourishing, verdant, green. **2 juicy,** succulent, fleshy, pulpy, ripe, soft, tender, fresh. **3 luxurious,** sumptuous, grand, palatial, opulent, lavish, elaborate, extravagant, *inf.* plush, ritzy. **Ant.** barren; meager; dry.

▶ *n.* **alcoholic,** heavy/hard drinker, problem drinker, drinker, drunk, drunkard, toper, sot, dipsomaniac, *inf.* alky, boozer, tosspot.

lustful *adj.* **lecherous,** lascivious, lewd, libidinous, licentious, salacious, prurient, concupiscent, wanton, unchaste, hot-blooded, passionate, sensual, sexy, *inf.* horny.

lusty *adj.* **1 healthy,** strong, vigorous, robust, hale and hearty, hearty, energetic, lively, blooming, rugged, sturdy, tough, stalwart, brawny, hefty, husky, burly, solidly built, powerful, virile, red-blooded. **2 loud,** vigorous, hearty, powerful, forceful.

luxuriant *adj.* **1 lush,** abundant, profuse, exuberant, dense, thick, riotous, overgrown, prolific, teeming, verdant. **2 florid,** flowery, ornate, elaborate, fancy, adorned, decorated, embellished, embroidered, extravagant, flamboyant, ostentatious, showy, high-flown, baroque, rococo. *Ant.* barren; meager; plain.

luxurious *adj.* **1 opulent,** affluent, sumptuous, expensive, rich, costly, deluxe, lush, grand, splendid, magnificent, lavish, well-appointed, comfortable, extravagant, ornate, fancy, *inf.* plush, posh, ritzy, swanky. **2 self-indulgent,** sensual, pleasure-loving, comfort-seeking, epicurean, hedonistic, sybaritic. *Ant.* austere; spartan.

luxury *n.* **1 luxuriousness,** opulence, affluence, sumptuousness, richness, grandeur, splendor, magnificence, lavishness, lap of luxury, bed of roses. **2 boon,** benefit, advantage, delight, bliss, comfort. **3 extra,** nonessential, frill, extravagance, indulgence, treat, refinement.

lying *n.* **untruthfulness,** fabrication, fibbing, perjury, white lies, little white lies, falseness, falsity, dishonesty, mendacity, lack of veracity, storytelling, dissimulation, dissembling, prevarication, deceit, guile, crookedness, double-dealing.

▸ *adj.* **untruthful,** fabricating, false, dishonest, mendacious, dissimulating, dissembling, prevaricating, deceitful, guileful, crooked, double-dealing, two-faced. *Ant.* truthful; honest.

lyrical *adj.* **1 lyric,** songlike, musical, melodic, expressive, personal. **2 light,** silvery, clear, flowing, sweet.

Mm

macabre *adj.* **gruesome,** grisly, grim, gory, morbid, ghastly, hideous, horrific, horrible, horrifying, horrid, horrendous, terrifying, frightening, frightful, fearsome, shocking, dreadful, appalling, loathsome, repugnant, repulsive, sickening.

machine *n.* **1 appliance,** apparatus, instrument, tool, device, contraption, gadget, mechanism, engine, motor. **2 vehicle,** car, motorcycle, airplane, *inf.* bike, motorbike, plane. **3 robot,** automaton, mechanical man, puppet. **4 organization,** system, structure, agency, machinery, council, cabal, clique, *inf.* setup.

machismo *n.* **masculinity,** manliness, virility, toughness, chauvinism, male chauvinism, sexism.

mad *adj.* **1 stark (raving) mad,** insane, deranged, demented, of unsound mind, crazed, lunatic, non compos mentis, unbalanced, unhinged, unstable, distracted, manic, frenzied, raving, distraught, frantic, hysterical, delirious, psychotic, not quite right, mad as a hatter, mad as a March hare, foaming at the mouth, *inf.* crazy, out of one's mind, off one's nut, nuts, nutty, off one's rocker, round/around the bend, balmy, batty, bonkers, crackers, cuckoo, loopy, loony, bananas, loco, dippy, screwy, with a screw loose, out of one's tree, off one's trolley, off the wall, not all there, not right/OK/okay upstairs. **2 angry,** furious, infuriated, irate, raging, enraged, fuming, in a towering rage, incensed, wrathful, seeing red, cross, indignant, exasperated, irritated, berserk, out of control, beside oneself, *inf.* livid, wild. **3 insane,** foolish, stupid, lunatic, foolhardy, idiotic, crackbrained, irrational, unreasonable, illogical, senseless, nonsensical, absurd, impractical, silly, inane, asinine, ludicrous, wild, unwise, imprudent, preposterous, *inf.* crazy, daft. **4 wild,** unrestrained, uncontrolled, abandoned, excited, frenzied, frantic, frenetic, ebullient, energetic, boisterous.

madden *v.* **anger,** infuriate, send into a rage, enrage, incense, exasperate, irritate, inflame, annoy, provoke, upset, agitate, vex, irk, pique, gall, make one's hackles rise, raise one's hackles, make one's blood boil, make one see red, get one's back up, *inf.* aggravate, bug, make one livid.

madman *n.* **maniac,** lunatic, imbecile, psychopath, *inf.* loony, nut, nutter, nutcase, head case, basket case, screwball, psycho.

madness *n.* **1 insanity,** insaneness, dementia, mental illness/derangement, dementedness, instability of mind, unsoundness of mind, lunacy, distraction, mania, frenzy, psychosis, *inf.* craziness. **2 anger,** fury, rage, infuriation, irateness, wrath, ire, crossness, indignation, exasperation, irritation, *inf.* lividness, wildness. **3 insanity,** folly, foolishness, stupidity, lunacy, foolhardiness, idiocy, irrationality, unreasonableness, illogicality, senselessness, nonsense, nonsensicalness, absurdness, absurdity, silliness, inanity, ludicrousness, wildness, imprudence, preposterousness, *inf.* craziness, daftness.

magazine *n.* **periodical,** journal, publication, supplement, color supplement, *inf.* glossy, book.

magic *n.* **1 sorcery,** witchcraft, wizardry, enchantment, necromancy, the supernatural, occultism, the occult, black magic, voodoo, thaumaturgy. **2 sleight of hand,** legerdemain, conjuring, illusion, prestidigitation, deception, trickery, juggling, *inf.* hocus-pocus. **3 allure,** allurement, enchantment, entrancement, fascination, charm, glamour, magnetism, enticement.
▸ *adj.* **1 magical,** enchanting, entrancing, spellbinding, fascinating, captivating, charming, glamorous, magnetic, irresistible, hypnotic.
2 marvelous, wonderful, excellent, *inf.* brilliant, terrific, fabulous, fab.

magician *n.* **1 sorcerer,** sorceress, witch, wizard, warlock, enchanter, enchantress, spell-caster, necromancer, thaumaturge. **2 illusionist,** conjuror, legerdemainist, prestidigitator, juggler. **3 genius,** master, virtuoso, expert, marvel, wizard, maestro, *inf.* ace, whiz.

magnanimity *n.* **generosity,** charitableness, charity, benevolence, beneficence, openhandedness, bigheartedness, kindness, munificence, bountifulness, largesse, altruism, philanthropy, unselfishness, selflessness, self-sacrifice, mercy, leniency.

magnanimous *adj.* **generous,** generous to a fault, charitable, benevolent, beneficent, openhanded, bighearted, greathearted, kind, kindly, munificent, bountiful, liberal, altruistic, philanthropic, noble, unselfish, selfless, self-sacrificing, ungrudging, unstinting, forgiving, merciful, lenient, indulgent. *Ant.* mean; selfish; petty; vindictive.

magnificent *adj.* **1 splendid,** resplendent, grand, grandiose, impressive, imposing, striking, glorious, superb, majestic, august, noble, stately, exalted, awe-inspiring, royal, regal, kingly, princely, sumptuous, opulent, luxurious, lavish, rich, brilliant, radiant, elegant, gorgeous, *inf.* splendiferous, ritzy, posh.
2 excellent, masterly, skillful, virtuoso, splendid, impressive, fine, marvelous, wonderful, *inf.* terrific, glorious, superb, brilliant, out of this world. *Ant.* modest; poor.

magnify *v.* **1 increase,** augment, enlarge, extend, expand, amplify, intensify, heighten, deepen, broaden, widen, dilate, boost, enhance, aggrandize.
2 exaggerate, overstate, overdo, overemphasize, overplay, dramatize, color, embroider, embellish, enhance, inflate, make a mountain out of a molehill, draw the long bow, *inf.* make a big thing out of, blow up, blow up out of all proportion. *Ant.* reduce; understate; play down (see play).

magnitude *n.* **1 size,** extent, measure, proportions, dimensions, volume, weight, quantity, mass, bulk, amplitude, capacity. **2 size,** extent, greatness, largeness, bigness, immensity, vastness, hugeness, enormity, enormousness, expanse.
3 importance, significance, weight, moment, consequence, mark, notability, note, greatness, distinction, eminence, fame, renown. *Ant.* triviality; smallness.

mail[1] *n.* **1 letters,** packages, parcels, correspondence, communications, airmail, registered mail, electronic mail, E-mail. **2 postal system,** postal service, post office, post.
▸ *v.* **send by mail/post,** send, dispatch, post, airmail.

mail[2] *n.* **armor,** coat of mail, chain mail, chain armor, plate armor.

main *adj.* **1 head,** chief, principal, leading, foremost, most important, central, prime, premier, primary, supreme, predominant, preeminent, paramount, cardinal, crucial,

vital, critical, pivotal, urgent.
2 sheer, pure, utter, downright, mere, plain, brute, stark, absolute, out-and-out, direct. ***Ant.*** subsidiary; minor.
▸ *n.* **pipe,** channel, duct, conduit.

mainly *adv.* **for the most part,** mostly, in the main, on the whole, largely, by and large, to a large extent, to a great degree, predominantly, chiefly, principally, substantially, overall, in general, generally, usually, commonly, as a rule.

maintain *v.* **1 continue,** keep going, keep up, keep alive, keep in existence, carry on, preserve, conserve, prolong, perpetuate, sustain. **2 keep in good condition,** keep in repair, keep up, conserve, preserve, keep intact, care for, take good care of, look after.
3 support, provide for, keep, finance, feed, nurture, nourish, sustain. **4 insist on,** hold to, declare, assert, state, announce, affirm, aver, avow, profess, claim, allege, contend, asseverate.
5 uphold, defend, fight for, stand by, take up the cudgels for, argue for, champion, support, back, advocate. ***Ant.*** break off (see break); neglect; deny.

maintenance *n.* **1 continuation,** continuance, keeping up, carrying on, preservation, conservation, prolongation, perpetuation.
2 upkeep, repairs, preservation, conservation, care. **3 supporting,** keeping, upkeep, financing, feeding, nurture.

majestic *adj.* **regal,** royal, kingly, queenly, princely, imperial, noble, lordly, august, exalted, awesome, elevated, lofty, stately, dignified, distinguished, magnificent, grand, splendid, resplendent, glorious, impressive, imposing, marvelous, superb, proud.

major *adj.* **1 larger,** bigger, greater, main. **2 greatest,** best, most important, leading, foremost, chief, main, outstanding, first-rate, notable, eminent, preeminent, supreme.
3 important, significant, crucial, vital, great, weighty, paramount, utmost, prime. **4 serious,** radical, complicated. ***Ant.*** minor; unimportant; trivial.

majority *n.* **1 larger part/number,** greater part/number, most, more than half, bulk, mass, main body, preponderance, lion's share.
2 winning margin, winning difference, superiority of numbers/votes. **3 legal age,** coming-of-age, seniority, adulthood, manhood, womanhood, maturity, age of consent. ***Ant.*** minority; handful.

make *v.* **1 build,** construct, assemble, put together, put up, erect, manufacture, produce, fabricate, create, form, fashion, model, mold, shape, forge. **2 force (to),** compel (to), coerce (into), press (into), drive (into), pressure (into), oblige (to), require (to), prevail upon (to), impel (to), *inf.* railroad (into), put the heat on, put the screws on, use strong-arm tactics on. **3 cause,** create, give rise to, produce, bring about, generate, engender, occasion, effect. **4 perform,** execute, do, accomplish, carry out, effect, practice, engage in, prosecute. **5 create,** appoint, designate, name, nominate, select, elect, vote in, install, invest, ordain, assign. **6 compose,** put together, frame, formulate, prepare, write, direct. **7 gain,** acquire, obtain, get, realize, secure, win, earn, net, gross, clear, bring in, take home, pocket. **8 prepare,** get ready, make arrangements for, put together, concoct, cook, *inf.* whip up, fix. **9 draw up,** frame, form, formulate, enact, lay down, establish, institute, found, originate. **10 come to,** add up to, total, amount to. **11 estimate,** calculate, compute, gauge, reckon. **12 come to,** settle on, determine on, conclude, establish, seal. **13 give,** deliver, utter, give voice to, enunciate, recite, pronounce. **14 be,** act as, serve as, constitute, perform the function of, play the part of, represent, embody. **15 achieve,** attain, get into, gain access to, gain a place in. **16 catch,** arrive in time for, arrive at, reach, get to, succeed in attending. *Ant.* demolish; destroy.
▸ *n.* **1 brand,** label, trademark, sort, type, variety, style, mark, marque. **2 build,** form, frame, structure, construction, shape. **3 character,** nature, temperament, temper, disposition, humor.

make-believe *n.* **pretense,** fantasy, daydreaming, dreaming, imagination, romancing, fabrication, playacting, charade, masquerade.
▸ *adj.* **pretended,** feigned, made-up, fantasy, fantasized, dream, imagined, imaginary, unreal, fictitious, mock, sham, *inf.* pretend. *Ant.* real; actual.

maker *n.* **manufacturer,** builder, constructor, producer, creator, fabricator, author, architect, framer.

makeshift *adj.* **stopgap,** make-do, provisional, temporary, rough and ready, substitute, improvised, standby, jerry-built, thrown-together.

malice *n.* **malevolence,**

maliciousness, malignity, malignance, evil intentions, ill will, ill feeling, animosity, animus, hostility, enmity, bad blood, hatred, hate, spite, spitefulness, vindictiveness, rancor, bitterness, grudge, venom, spleen, harm, destruction, defamation, *inf.* bitchiness, cattiness.

malicious *adj.* **malevolent,** malign, malignant, evil, evil-intentioned, ill-natured, hostile, spiteful, baleful, vindictive, rancorous, bitter, venomous, pernicious, harmful, hurtful, destructive, defamatory, *inf.* bitchy, catty. **Ant.** benevolent; kindly; friendly.

malign *v.* **slander,** libel, defame, smear, run a smear campaign against, blacken someone's name/character, calumniate, vilify, speak ill of, spread lies about, accuse falsely, cast aspersions on, misrepresent, traduce, denigrate, disparage, slur, derogate, *inf.* bad-mouth, run down, drag through the mud. **Ant.** praise; extol.

malnutrition *n.* **undernourishment,** poor diet, starvation, famine, anorexia.

maltreat *v.* **treat badly,** ill-treat, ill-use, mistreat, misuse, abuse, handle/treat roughly, mishandle, manhandle, maul, bully, injure, harm, hurt, molest, *inf.* beat up, rough up, do over.

maltreatment *n.* **ill treatment,** ill use, mistreatment, abuse, rough handling, mishandling, manhandling, bullying, injury, harm.

manage *v.* **1 be in charge of,** run, be head of, head, direct, control, preside over, lead, govern, rule, command, superintend, supervise, oversee, administer, organize, conduct, handle, guide, be at the helm of, *inf.* head up. **2 succeed (in),** contrive, engineer, bring about/off, achieve, accomplish, effect, cope, deal with the situation, get along, carry on, survive, make do, be/fare all right, weather the storm, *inf.* make out, get by. **3 cope with,** deal with, handle, control, master, influence. **4 wield,** use, operate, work, ply, handle, manipulate, brandish, flourish. **Ant.** mismanage; fail.

manageable *adj.* **1 easy,** doable, practicable, possible, feasible, attainable, viable. **2 controllable,** governable, tamable, tractable, pliant, compliant, docile, accommodating, amenable, yielding, submissive. **3 handy,** easy, user-friendly. **Ant.** difficult; unmanageable; impracticable; intractable.

manifest

management *n.*
 1 administration, managers, employers, owners, proprietors, directors, board of directors, board, directorate, executives, *inf.* bosses, top brass. **2 administration,** running, charge, care, direction, leadership, control, governing, ruling, command, superintendence, supervision, overseeing, organization, conduct, handling, guidance.

mandatory *adj.* **obligatory,** compulsory, binding, required, requisite, essential, imperative, necessary. *Ant.* voluntary; optional; discretionary.

maneuver *n.* **1 movement,** deployment, operation, exercise. **2 skillful movement/move,** movement, move, clever stroke, stroke, skillful measure/handling. **3 trick,** stratagem, tactic, machination, manipulation, artifice, subterfuge, device, dodge, ploy, ruse, scheme, plan, plot, intrigue.
 ▶ *v.* **1 move,** work, negotiate, steer, guide, direct, manipulate. **2 manage,** manipulate, contrive, engineer, devise, plan, plot, *inf.* wangle. **3 scheme,** intrigue, plot, use trickery/artifice, machinate, pull strings.

mangle *v.* **1 mutilate,** hack, cut up, lacerate, maul, tear at, rend, butcher, disfigure, deform. **2 spoil,** ruin, mar, bungle, mess up, make a mess of, *inf.* murder.

mangy *adj.* **1 scabby,** scabious, scaly. **2 shabby,** scruffy, moth-eaten, worn, shoddy, dirty, squalid, filthy, seedy. **3 contemptible,** despicable, hateful, odious, nasty, mean, base, low.

manhandle *v.* **1 handle roughly,** push, pull, shove, maul, mistreat, ill-treat, abuse, injure, damage, beat, batter, *inf.* paw, knock about, beat up, rough up. **2 move/carry/ lift manually,** heave, haul, push, shove, pull, tug, maneuver.

mania *n.* **1 frenzy,** franticness, violence, wildness, hysteria, raving, derangement, dementia. **2 obsession,** compulsion, fixation, fetish, fascination, preoccupation, passion, enthusiasm, desire, urge, craving, craze, fad, *inf.* thing.

maniac *n.* **madman,** madwoman, mad person, deranged person, psychopath, lunatic, *inf.* loony, nutcase, nut, psycho, screwball.

manifest *v.* **1 display,** show, exhibit, demonstrate, present, evince, express, reveal, indicate, make plain, declare. **2 prove,** be evidence of, establish, show, evidence, substantiate,

corroborate, verify, confirm, settle. **Ant.** hide; mask; deny.
▸ *adj.* **obvious,** clear, plain, apparent, patent, noticeable, perceptible, visible, transparent, conspicuous, unmistakable, distinct, blatant, glaring.

manifestation *n.* **1 display,** show, exhibition, demonstration, presentation, exposition, illustration, exemplification, indication, declaration, expression, profession. **2 evidence,** proof, testimony, substantiation, sign, indication, mark, symbol, token, symptom.

manifold *adj.* **multifarious,** multiple, multifold, numerous, many, several, multitudinous, various, varied, diverse, assorted, sundry, copious, abundant.

manipulate *v.* **1 handle,** wield, ply, work, operate, use, employ, utilize, exercise. **2 influence,** control, use to one's advantage, exploit, maneuver, engineer, steer, direct, guide, pull the strings. **3 juggle,** massage, falsify, doctor, tamper with, fiddle with, tinker with, *inf.* cook.

manipulator *n.* **1 handler,** wielder, operator. **2 exploiter,** maneuverer, conniver, intriguer, puller of strings.

mankind *n.* **man,** Homo sapiens, the human race, the human species, humankind, human beings, humans, people.

manly *adj.* **1 manful,** brave, courageous, gallant, heroic, intrepid, valiant, valorous, bold, fearless, stout, stouthearted, dauntless, *inf.* macho, Ramboesque. **2 masculine,** all-male, virile, strong, robust, vigorous, muscular, powerful, well-built, strapping, sturdy, rugged, tough, *inf.* macho. **Ant.** cowardly; unmanly; effeminate.

manner *n.* **1 way,** means, method, system, approach, technique, procedure, process, methodology, routine, practice, fashion, mode, style, habit, custom. **2 look,** air, appearance, demeanor, aspect, mien, bearing, cast, deportment, behavior, conduct. **3 kind,** sort, type, variety, form, nature, breed, brand, stamp, class, category.

mannerism *n.* **habit,** characteristic, characteristic gesture, trait, idiosyncrasy, quirk, foible, peculiarity.

manufacture *v.* **1 make,** produce, mass-produce, build, construct, assemble, put together, create, fabricate, turn out, process, form, fashion, model, mold, shape, forge. **2 make up,** invent, fabricate, concoct, hatch, coin, trump up, dream up, think up, devise, formulate, frame, construct, *inf.* cook up.

▸ *n.* **making,** production, mass production, construction, assembly, creation, fabrication, processing.

manufacturer *n.* **maker,** producer, builder, constructor, creator, fabricator, industrialist, captain/baron of industry.

many *adj.* **numerous,** innumerable, a large/great number of, countless, scores of, myriad, great quantities of, multitudinous, multiple, copious, abundant, various, sundry, diverse, several, frequent, *inf.* a lot of, umpteen, lots of, masses of, scads of, heaps of, piles of, bags of, tons of, oodles of, an army of, zillions of.

▸ *n.* **many people,** many things, scores, large numbers, great quantities, a large number, a host, a horde, a crowd, a multitude, a mass, an accumulation, an abundance, a profusion, plenty, *inf.* lots, a lot, umpteen, armies, scads, heaps, piles, bags, tons, masses, oodles. *Ant.* few.

mar *v.* **spoil,** detract from, impair, damage, ruin, wreck, disfigure, blemish, scar, deface, harm, hurt, injure, deform, mutilate, maim, mangle, tarnish, taint, contaminate, pollute, sully, stain, blot, debase, vitiate, *inf.* foul up. *Ant.* improve; adorn.

marauder *n.* **raider,** plunderer, pillager, looter, ravager, robber, pirate, freebooter, buccaneer, corsair, rover, bandit, brigand, rustler, highwayman.

march *v.* **1 walk,** step, pace, tread, stride, footslog, tramp, hike, trudge, stalk, strut, parade, file. **2 move forward,** advance, progress, forge ahead, make headway, go on, continue on, roll on, develop, evolve.

▸ *n.* **1 route march,** walk, footslog, tramp, trek, hike, parade. **2 step,** pace, stride, gait. **3 demonstration,** parade, procession, rally. **4 advance,** progress, progression, passage, headway, continuance, development, evolution.

margin *n.* **1 edge,** side, verge, border, perimeter, boundary, limits, periphery, brink, brim. **2 border,** borderland, boundary, boundary line, frontier, bounding line, demarcation line. **3 leeway,** latitude, scope, room, room to maneuver, space, allowance, extra, surplus. **4 measure of difference,** degree of difference, difference, amount.

marginal *adj.* **1 border,** boundary, on the edge, peripheral. **2 slight,**

small, tiny, minute, low, minor, insignificant, minimal, negligible.

maritime *adj.* **1 naval,** marine, nautical, seafaring, seagoing. **2 coastal,** seaside, littoral.

mark *n.* **1 stain,** blemish, blot, smear, trace, spot, speck, dot, blotch, smudge, splotch, bruise, scratch, scar, dent, pit, pock, chip, notch, nick, line, score, cut, incision, gash. **2 marking,** blaze, spot, speckle, stripe, brand, earmark. **3 symbol,** sign, character, punctuation mark. **4 marker,** guide, pointer, landmark, direction post, signpost, milestone. **5 sign,** symbol, indication, symptom, feature, token, badge, emblem, evidence, proof, clue, hint. **6 cross,** X, scribble, signature, autograph, initials, imprint. **7 impression,** imprint, traces, vestiges, remains, effect, impact, influence. **8 characteristic,** feature, trait, attribute, quality, stamp, peculiarity. **9 target,** goal, aim, bull's-eye, objective, object, end, purpose, intent, intention. **10 standard,** required standard, norm, par, level, criterion, gauge, yardstick, rule, measure, scale.

▶ *v.* **1 stain,** smear, smudge, scratch, scar, dent, chip, notch, score, cut, gash. **2 put one's name on,** name, initial, put one's seal on, label, tag, stamp, flag, hallmark, watermark, brand, earmark. **3 name,** indicate, write down, tag, label, flag. **4 correct,** assess, evaluate, appraise, grade. **5 price,** put a price tag on. **6 see,** notice, observe, take note of, discern, spot, recognize, take heed of, pay heed to, heed, take notice of, pay attention to, attend to, note, mind, bear in mind, give a thought to, take into consideration, *inf.* get a load of. **7 characterize,** distinguish, identify, denote, brand, signalize. **8 celebrate,** commemorate, honor, observe, recognize, acknowledge, solemnize. **9 designate,** choose, select, nominate.

marked *adj.* **pronounced,** decided, striking, clear, glaring, blatant, unmistakable, remarkable, prominent, signal, conspicuous, noticeable, noted, distinct, pointed, salient, recognizable, identifiable, distinguishable, obvious, apparent, evident, manifest, open, patent, written all over one. *Ant.* imperceptible; inconspicuous.

maroon *v.* **abandon,** forsake, leave behind, leave, desert, strand, leave stranded, turn one's back on, leave isolated.

marriage *n.* **1 married state,**

matrimony, holy matrimony, wedlock, conjugal bond, union, match. **2 marriage ceremony,** wedding, wedding ceremony, nuptials. **3 alliance,** union, merger, unification, amalgamation, combination, affiliation, association, connection, coupling, *inf.* hookup.

marry *v.* **1 be married,** wed, be wed, become man and wife, become espoused, *inf.* tie the knot, walk down the aisle, take the plunge, get hitched, get yoked. **2 wed,** take to wife/husband, espouse. **3 join,** join together, unite, ally, merge, unify, amalgamate, combine, affiliate, associate, link, connect, fuse, weld, couple.

marsh *n.* **marshland,** bog, peatbog, swamp, swampland, morass, mire, quagmire, quag, slough, fen, bayou.

marshal *v.* **1 gather (together),** assemble, collect, muster, draw up, line up, align, set/put in order, arrange, deploy, dispose, rank. **2 usher,** guide, escort, conduct, lead, shepherd, take.

martial *adj.* **1 military,** soldierly, army, naval. **2 militant,** warlike, combative, belligerent, bellicose, aggressive, pugnacious.

marvel *v.* **be amazed by,** be filled with amazement at, be awed by, be full of wonder at, wonder at, stare at, gape at, goggle at, not believe one's eyes/ears at.
▸ *n.* **wonder,** wonderful thing, amazing thing, prodigy, sensation, spectacle, phenomenon, miracle, *inf.* something else, something to shout about, something to write home about, eye-opener.

marvelous *adj.* **1 amazing,** astounding, astonishing, awesome, breathtaking, sensational, remarkable, spectacular, stupendous, phenomenal, wondrous, prodigious, miraculous, extraordinary. **2 excellent,** splendid, wonderful, *inf.* magnificent, superb, glorious, super, great, boffo, smashing, fantastic, terrific, fabulous, awesome, mean, bad, wicked. **Ant.** ordinary; run-of-the-mill; dreadful.

masculine *adj.* **1 male,** manly, manlike, virile, of men, man's, men's, male-oriented, all-male, robust, vigorous, muscular, strapping, rugged, brave, courageous, gallant, heroic, valiant, bold, fearless, stouthearted, *inf.* macho, Ramboesque. **2 mannish,** manlike, unfeminine, unwomanly, Amazonian, *inf. derog.* butch. **Ant.** feminine; effeminate.

mash *v.* **crush,** pulp, purée, smash, squash, pound, beat.
▶ *n.* **pulp,** mush, paste, purée, slush, pap.

mask *n.* **1 false face,** domino. **2 swimming mask,** snorkel mask, gas mask, safety goggles, fencing mask, ski mask, surgical mask, visor. **3 disguise,** guise, concealment, cover, cover-up, cloak, camouflage, veil, screen, front, false front, façade, blind, semblance, false colors, pretense.
▶ *v.* **disguise,** hide, conceal, cover up, obscure, cloak, camouflage, veil, screen.

mass *n.* **1 concretion,** lump, block, chunk, hunk, piece. **2 concentration,** conglomeration, aggregation, amassment, assemblage, collection. **3 total,** totality, whole, entirety, aggregate. **4 size,** magnitude, bulk, dimension, capacity, greatness, bigness.
▶ *adj.* **wholesale,** universal, widespread, general, large-scale, extensive, pandemic, popular.

massacre *n.* **mass slaughter,** wholesale slaughter, slaughter, wholesale/indiscriminate killing, mass murder, mass homicide, mass slaying, mass execution, mass destruction, carnage, butchery, blood bath, annihilation, extermination, liquidation, decimation, pogrom, genocide, ethnic cleansing, holocaust.
▶ *v.* **slaughter,** butcher, slay, murder, kill, annihilate, exterminate, liquidate, decimate, eliminate, kill off, wipe out, mow down, cut down, cut to pieces.

massage *n.* **rub,** rubdown, rubbing, kneading, pummeling, palpation, manipulation, reflexology, acupressure, shiatsu, aromatherapy.
▶ *v.* **rub,** rub down, knead, pummel, palpate, manipulate.

master *n.* **1 lord and master,** lord, overlord, ruler, overseer, superintendent, director, manager, controller, governor, commander, captain, chief, head, headman, principal, owner, employer, *inf.* boss, top dog, big cheese, honcho. **2 captain,** skipper, commander. **3 schoolmaster,** headmaster, teacher, schoolteacher, tutor, instructor, pedagogue, preceptor. **4 expert,** adept, professional, authority, pundit, genius, master hand, maestro, virtuoso, prodigy, past master, grand master, wizard, *inf.* ace, pro, maven. **5 guru,** teacher, spiritual leader, guide, swami.
▶ *adj.* **1 masterly,** expert, adept, proficient, skilled, skillful, deft,

dexterous, practiced, experienced, *inf.* crack. **2 controlling,** ruling, directing, commanding, dominating. **3 chief,** main, principal, leading, prime, predominant, foremost, great, most important.

masterful *adj.* **1 dominating,** authoritative, powerful, controlling, domineering, tyrannical, despotic, dictatorial, overbearing, overweening, imperious, peremptory, high-handed, arrogant, haughty. **2 masterly,** expert, consummate, clever, adept, adroit, skillful, skilled, proficient, deft, dexterous, accomplished, polished, excellent, superlative, first-rate, fine, talented, gifted, *inf.* crack, ace. *Ant.* weak; inept.

masterly *adj.* **masterful,** expert, consummate, adept, skillful, deft, dexterous, accomplished, polished, excellent, superlative, first-rate, talented, gifted, *inf.* crack, ace.

mastermind *v.* **direct,** manage, plan, organize, arrange, engineer, conceive, devise, forge, originate, initiate, think up, come up with, have the bright idea of, *inf.* be the brains behind.
▶ *n.* **genius,** intellect, author, architect, engineer, director, planner, organizer, deviser, originator, manager, prime mover, *inf.* brain, brains.

masterpiece *n.* **magnum opus,** masterwork, chef-d'oeuvre, work of art, creation, pièce de résistance.

match *n.* **1 contest,** competition, game, tournament, bout, event, test, trial, meet. **2 equal,** equivalent, peer, counterpart, rival, competitor. **3 mate,** fellow, companion, twin, counterpart, pair, complement. **4 look-alike,** double, twin, duplicate, copy, replica, *inf.* spitting image, spit and image, ringer, dead ringer. **5 marriage,** union, partnership, pairing, alliance, affiliation, combination.
▶ *v.* **1 complement,** blend with, harmonize with, go with, coordinate with, correspond to, accord with. **2 be a pair,** be a set, be the same. **3 be equal to,** be a match for, measure up to, rival, vie with, compete with, compare with, parallel, be in the same category as, keep pace with, keep up with. **4 marry,** pair up, mate, couple, unite, join, combine, link, ally, *inf.* hitch up, yoke.

matching *adj.* **corresponding,** equivalent, complementing, parallel, analogous, complementary, harmonizing, blending, toning, coordinating, the same, paired, twin, coupled, double, duplicate, identical, like. *Ant.* unlike; different; dissimilar.

mate *n.* **1 husband,** wife, spouse, partner, companion, helpmate, lover, *inf.* significant other, other half, better half. **2 twin,** match, companion, one of a pair, other half, equivalent. **3 workmate,** fellow worker, coworker, associate, colleague, companion, compeer, shipmate, classmate, roommate, teammate.
▸ *v.* **1 breed,** copulate, couple. **2 bring together,** pair, couple, join.

material *n.* **1 matter,** substance, stuff, medium, constituent elements. **2 fabric,** cloth, stuff, textile. **3 data,** information, facts, facts and figures, evidence, details, notes, *inf.* info.
▸ *adj.* **1 corporeal,** physical, bodily, fleshly, tangible, substantial, concrete, nonspiritual, worldly, earthly, temporal. **2 important,** of consequence, consequential, momentous, weighty, vital, essential, indispensable, key, significant, meaningful.
3 relevant, applicable, pertinent, apposite, germane, apropos.

materialize *v.* **1 come into being,** happen, occur, come about, come to pass, take place, *inf.* shape up. **2 appear,** turn up, become visible, come into view, come into sight, show oneself/itself, present oneself/itself, reveal oneself/itself, come to light, emerge.

matrimonial *adj.* **marital,** marriage, wedding, conjugal, connubial, nuptial, spousal, married, wedded.

matter *n.* **1 material,** substance, stuff, medium. **2 content,** subject matter, text, argument, substance, sense, thesis. **3 affair,** business, proceeding, situation, circumstance, event, happening, occurrence, incident, episode, occasion, experience. **4 subject,** topic, issue, question, point, case, concern, theme. **5 importance,** consequence, significance, note, import, moment, weight. **6 trouble,** upset, distress, worry, problem, difficulty, complication.
▸ *v.* **be of importance,** be of consequence, make a difference, make any difference, be relevant, carry weight, count.

mature *adj.* **1 adult,** grown-up, grown, fully grown, full-grown, of age. **2 sensible,** responsible, wise, discriminating, shrewd, practical, sagacious. **3 ripe,** ripened, mellow, ready, seasoned. **4 complete,** finished, finalized, developed, prepared, ready. *Ant.* immature; childish; green.
▸ *v.* **1 grow up,** develop fully,

become adult, reach adulthood, be fully grown, be full-grown, come of age. **2 ripen,** become mellow, mellow, maturate.

maverick *n.* **nonconformist,** rebel, dissenter, dissident, individualist, bohemian, eccentric, *inf.* trendsetter.

maxim *n.* **aphorism,** proverb, adage, saw, saying, axiom, precept, epigram, gnome.

maximum *n.* **most,** utmost, uttermost, extremity, upper limit, height, ceiling, top, summit, peak, pinnacle, crest, apex, vertex, apogee, acme, zenith.
> *adj.* **highest,** greatest, biggest, largest, topmost, most, utmost, supreme, maximal. *Ant.* minimum; least.

mayhem *n.* **havoc,** disorder, confusion, chaos, bedlam, destruction, violence, trouble, disturbance, commotion, tumult, pandemonium.

meadow *n.* **field,** grassland, pasture, paddock, lea.

meager *adj.* **1 paltry,** sparse, scant, scanty, spare, inadequate, insufficient, insubstantial, exiguous, short, little, small, slight, slender, poor, puny, skimpy, scrimpy, miserly, niggardly, stingy, pathetic, *inf.* measly, as scarce as hens' teeth. **2 thin,** lean, emaciated, skinny, spare, scrawny, scraggy, bony, gaunt, starved, underfed. *Ant.* abundant; copious; obese.

mean[1] *v.* **1 indicate,** signify, betoken, express, convey, denote, designate, spell out, show, stand for, represent, symbolize, portend, connote, imply, purport, suggest, allude to, intimate, hint at, insinuate, drive at. **2 intend,** have in mind, have in view, contemplate, think of, purpose, plan, have plans, set out, aim, aspire, desire, want, wish. **3 intend,** make, design, destine, predestine, fate. **4 involve,** entail, lead to, result in, give rise to, bring about, cause, engender, produce. **5 have importance,** have significance, matter. **6 presage,** portend, foretell, augur, promise, foreshadow.

mean[2] *adj.* **1 nasty,** disagreeable, unpleasant, unfriendly, hurtful, unkind, offensive, obnoxious, cross, ill-natured, bad-tempered, irritable, surly, cantankerous, crotchety, crabbed, crabby, grumpy, *inf.* grouchy. **2 miserly,** niggardly, parsimonious, tight-fisted, close-fisted, penny-pinching, penurious, greedy, avaricious, ungenerous, illiberal, *inf.* stingy, tight, cheap. **3 base,** dishonorable, ignoble, disreputable, vile, sordid, foul,

nasty, despicable, contemptible, abominable, odious, hateful, horrible. **4 inferior,** poor, limited, restricted, meager, scant.
5 shabby, poor, wretched, dismal, miserable, squalid, sordid, seedy, mangy, broken-down, rundown, dilapidated, down-at-the-heels, *inf.* scruffy, grungy. **6 low,** lowly, lowborn, humble, modest, common, ordinary, base, proletarian, plebeian, obscure, undistinguished, ignoble. *Ant.* kind; pleasant; honorable; luxurious.

mean³ *n.* **midpoint,** middle, median, norm, average, middle course, middle ground, happy medium.

meander *v.* **1 wander,** roam, ramble, rove, stroll, amble, drift, *inf.* mosey. **2 wind,** zigzag, snake, curve, turn, bend.

meaning *n.* **1 signification,** sense, message, import, drift, gist, essence, substance, purport, connotation, denotation, implication, significance, thrust. **2 definition,** explanation, interpretation, elucidation, explication. **3 intention,** purpose, plan, aim, goal, end, object, objective, aspiration, desire, want, wish. **4 significance,** point, value, worth, consequence, account, implication, allusion, intimation, insinuation, eloquence, expression.
▸ *adj.* **meaningful,** significant, pointed, eloquent.

meaningful *adj.* **significant,** important, relevant, material, valid, worthwhile, serious, sincere, in earnest, pointed, suggestive, eloquent, expressive, pregnant. *Ant.* meaningless; unimportant; trivial.

meaningless *adj.* **1 senseless,** unintelligible, incomprehensible, incoherent, pointless, purposeless, motiveless, irrational, inane. **2 empty,** futile, pointless, aimless, valueless, worthless, trivial, insignificant, inconsequential.

means *pl. n.* **1 way,** method, expedient, process, mode, manner, agency, medium, instrument, channel, avenue, course. **2 money,** capital, wealth, riches, affluence, substance, fortune, property. **3 money,** resources, capital, finance, funds, wherewithal, *inf.* dough, bread.

meanwhile *adv.* **1 meantime,** in the meantime, for the time being, for now, for the moment, in the interim, in the interval. **2 at the same time,** simultaneously, concurrently, coincidentally.

measure *n.* **1 measurement,** size,

dimension, proportions, magnitude, amplitude, mass, bulk, volume, capacity, quantity, weight, extent, expanse, area, range. **2 system,** standard, units, scale. **3 rule,** ruler, tape measure, gauge, meter, scale, yardstick. **4 share,** portion, division, allotment, part, piece, quota, lot, ration, percentage. **5 quantity,** amount, certain amount, degree. **6 yardstick,** test, standard, touchstone, criterion, benchmark. **7 action,** act, course, course of action, deed, proceeding, procedure, step, means, expedient, maneuver. **8 statute,** act, bill, law, resolution. **9 meter,** cadence, rhythm.

▸ *v.* **1 calculate,** compute, estimate, quantify, weigh, size, evaluate, rate, assess, appraise, gauge, measure out, determine, judge, survey. **2 choose carefully,** select with care, consider, think carefully about, plan, calculate. **3 pit,** set, match, test, put into competition.

measured *adj.* **1 measured out,** calculated, computed, quantified. **2 regular,** steady, even, rhythmical, slow, dignified, stately, sedate, leisurely, unhurried. **3 carefully chosen,** selected with care, well-thought-out, studied, calculated, planned,

premeditated, considered, deliberate, reasoned.

mechanical *adj.* **1 automated,** automatic, machine-driven, motor-driven, power-driven. **2 automatic,** machinelike, unthinking, unconscious, unfeeling, unemotional, cold, involuntary, instinctive, routine, habitual, perfunctory, cursory, lackluster, lifeless, unanimated, dead, casual, careless, inattentive, negligent. *Ant.* manual; conscious; emotional.

mechanism *n.* **1 machine,** apparatus, appliance, tool, device, instrument, contraption, contrivance, gadget, structure, system. **2 motor,** workings, works, gears, components, *inf.* innards, guts. **3 process,** procedure, system, operation, method, technique, workings, means, medium, agency, channel.

meddle *v.* **interfere,** butt in, intrude, intervene, interlope, pry, nose, *inf.* stick one's nose in, horn in, snoop.

mediate *v.* **1 act as mediator,** act as (a) go-between, act as (a) middleman/intermediary, arbitrate, negotiate, conciliate, intervene, intercede, interpose, moderate, umpire, referee, act as peacemaker, reconcile differences, restore harmony, make peace, bring to terms, step in, settle, resolve, mend, clear up, patch up. **2 bring about,** effect, effectuate, make happen, negotiate.

mediator *n.* **arbitrator,** arbiter, negotiator, go-between, middleman, intermediary, peacemaker, intervenor, interceder, moderator, umpire, referee, judge, conciliator, reconciler.

medicinal *adj.* **medical,** therapeutic, curative, healing, remedial, restorative, health-giving, analeptic.

medicine *n.* **1 medication,** medicament, drug, remedy, cure, physic. **2 medical science,** practice of medicine, healing art.

mediocre *adj.* **1 indifferent,** average, middle-of-the-road, middling, ordinary, commonplace, pedestrian, run-of-the-mill, tolerable, passable, adequate, uninspired, undistinguished, unexceptional, *inf.* so-so, fair-to-middling, nothing to write home about, no great shakes. **2 inferior,** second-rate, second-class, low-grade, poor, shabby, minor.

meditate *v.* **think about,** consider, have in mind, intend, plan, project, design, devise, scheme, plot.

meditation *n.* **contemplation,** thought, musing, pondering, consideration, reflection, deliberation, rumination, brooding, mulling over, reverie, brown study, concentration.

medium *n.* **1 mean,** median, midpoint, middle, center point, average, norm, standard, middle course, middle ground, compromise, happy medium. **2 means of communication,** means/mode of expression, means, agency, channel, avenue, vehicle, organ, instrument, instrumentality. **3 habitat,** element, environment, surroundings, milieu, setting, conditions, atmosphere. **4 spiritualist,** spiritist, necromancer. ▸ *adj.* **1 middle,** mean, medial, median, midway, midpoint, intermediate. **2 average,** middling.

meek *adj.* **1 patient,** long-suffering, forbearing, resigned, gentle, peaceful, docile, modest, humble, unassuming, unpretentious. **2 submissive,** yielding, unresisting, compliant, acquiescent, deferential, weak, timid, frightened, spineless, spiritless, *inf.* weak-kneed. **Ant.** impatient; assertive; overbearing.

meet *v.* **1 encounter,** come face to

face with, make contact with, run into, run across, come across, come upon, chance upon, happen upon, light upon, *inf.* bump into. **2 come together,** abut, adjoin, join, link up, unite, connect, touch, converge, intersect. **3 gather,** assemble, come together, foregather, congregate, convene, convoke, muster, rally. **4 deal with,** handle, treat, cope with, approach, answer. **5 satisfy,** fulfill, measure up to, come up to, comply with. **6 carry out,** perform, execute, discharge, take care of. **7 pay,** settle, honor, square. **8 face,** encounter, undergo, experience, go through, bear, suffer, endure. **9 encounter,** confront, engage, engage in battle with, join battle with, clash with, fight with. *Ant.* avoid; separate; disperse.

meeting *n.* **1 encounter,** contact, assignation, rendezvous, tryst. **2 gathering,** assembly, conference, congregation, convention, convocation, conclave, *inf.* get-together. **3 abutment,** junction, conjunction, union, convergence, confluence, concourse, intersection.

melancholy *n.* **despondency,** dejection, depression, gloom, gloominess, misery, low spirits, doldrums, blues, woe, sadness, sorrow, unhappiness, pensiveness, defeatism, pessimism, melancholia, *inf.* dumps.

mellifluous *adj.* **sweet,** sweet-sounding, sweet-toned, dulcet, honeyed, mellow, soft, soothing, smooth, silvery, euphonious, musical.

mellow *adj.* **1 ripe,** mature, well-matured, soft, juicy, tender, luscious, sweet, full-flavored, flavorsome. **2 dulcet,** sweet, sweet-sounding, tuneful, euphonious, melodious, mellifluous, smooth, full, rich, well-rounded. **3 gentle,** easygoing, pleasant, kindly, kindhearted, amicable, amiable, good-natured, affable, gracious, genial, cheerful, relaxed. **4 tipsy,** *inf.* happy, merry. *Ant.* green; unripe; harsh; nasty.

melodious *adj.* **melodic,** musical, tuneful, harmonious, lyrical, dulcet, sweet, sweet-sounding, sweet-toned, silvery, silvery-toned, euphonious. *Ant.* discordant; harsh; grating.

melodramatic *adj.* **theatrical,** stagy, overdramatic, histrionic, oversensational, extravagant, overdone, overemotional, *inf.* camp, hammy.

melody *n.* **1 tune,** air, strain, music, refrain, theme, song. **2 melodiousness,** tunefulness, musicality, harmony, lyricism, sweetness, euphony.

melt *v.* **1 liquefy,** dissolve, deliquesce, thaw, unfreeze, defrost, soften, fuse. **2 disperse,** vanish, vanish into thin air, fade away, disappear, dissolve, evaporate, evanesce. **3 soften,** touch, disarm, mollify, assuage, move.

member *n.* **1 adherent,** associate, fellow, participant. **2 part of the body,** organ, limb, appendage, extremity, arm, leg. **3 element,** constituent, component, part, portion.

memorable *adj.* **unforgettable,** not to be forgotten, signal, momentous, significant, historic, notable, noteworthy, important, consequential, remarkable, outstanding, extraordinary, striking, impressive, distinctive, distinguished, famous, celebrated, illustrious, catchy, striking. *Ant.* run-of-the-mill; commonplace; forgettable.

memorial *n.* **1 monument,** statue, plaque, shrine, tombstone. **2 remembrance,** reminder, memento, souvenir.
▸ *adj.* **remembrance,** commemorative, commemorating, monumental.

memorize *v.* **commit to memory,** remember, retain, learn by heart, learn, learn word for word, learn by rote.

memory *n.* **1 remembrance,** recollection, powers of recall, recall, reminiscence, powers of retention, retention. **2 remembrance,** commemoration, honor, tribute. **3 memory bank,** storage bank, store, information store.

menace *n.* **1 threat,** ominousness, intimidation, warning, ill-omen, commination. **2 threat,** danger, peril, risk, hazard, jeopardy, source of apprehension/dread/fright/fear/terror. **3 nuisance,** pest, source of annoyance, annoyance, plague, torment, troublemaker, mischief-maker.
▸ *v.* **1 threaten,** intimidate, issue threats to, frighten, scare, alarm, terrify, bully, browbeat, cow, terrorize. **2 loom,** impend, lower, be in the air, be in the offing.

mend *v.* **1 repair,** fix, put back together, patch up, restore, rehabilitate, renew, renovate, make whole, make well, cure, heal. **2 sew,** stitch, darn, patch. **3 get better,** recover, recuperate, improve, be well, be cured, be all right. **4 put right,** set straight, rectify, put in order, correct, amend, emend, improve, make better, better, ameliorate, reform. *Ant.* break; tear; worsen.

menial *adj.* **lowly,** humble, low-grade, low-status, unskilled, routine, humdrum, boring, dull. *Ant.* noble; elevated; aristocratic; skilled.
▸ *n.* **servant,** domestic servant, domestic, drudge, maid, laborer, slave, underling, vassal, lackey, flunky, *inf.* gofer.

mentality *n.* **1 frame of mind,** way of thinking, way one's mind works, mind, psychology, mental attitude, outlook, character, disposition, makeup. **2 intellect,** intellectual capabilities, intelligence, IQ (= intelligence quotient), brainpower, brains, mind, comprehension, understanding, wit, rationality, powers of reasoning, *inf.* gray matter.

mention *v.* **1 allude to,** refer to, touch on, speak briefly of, hint at. **2 say,** state, name, cite, quote, call attention to, adduce. **3 tell,** speak about/of, utter, communicate, let someone know, disclose, divulge, reveal, intimate, whisper, breathe a word of, *inf.* let on about.
▸ *n.* **reference,** allusion, observation, remark, statement, announcement, indication, acknowledgment, citation, recognition.

mentor *n.* **guide,** adviser, counselor, therapist, guru, spiritual leader, confidant, teacher, tutor, coach, instructor.

mercenary *adj.* **1 money-oriented,** grasping, greedy, acquisitive, avaricious, covetous, bribable, venal, *inf.* money-grubbing. **2 hired,** paid, bought, professional, venal. *Ant.* altruistic; philanthropic; generous.
▸ *n.* **soldier of fortune,** condottiere.

merchandise *n.* **goods,** wares, stock, commodities, produce, vendibles.
▸ *v.* **1 market,** sell, retail, buy and sell, distribute, deal in, trade in, traffic in, do business in, vend. **2 promote,** advertize, publicize, push, *inf.* hype, plug.

merchant *n.* **trader,** dealer, trafficker, wholesaler, broker, seller, salesman, saleswoman, salesperson, vendor, retailer, store owner, storekeeper, shopkeeper, distributor.

merciful *adj.* **lenient,** clement, compassionate, pitying, forgiving, forbearing, sparing, humane, mild, softhearted, tender-hearted, kind, sympathetic, liberal, tolerant, generous, beneficent, benignant. *Ant.* merciless; cruel.

merciless *adj.* **unmerciful,** ruthless, relentless, inexorable, harsh, pitiless, uncompassionate, unforgiving, unsparing, unpitying, implacable, barbarous, inhumane, inhuman, hard-hearted, heartless, callous, cruel, unsympathetic, unfeeling, illiberal, intolerant, rigid, severe, stern. *Ant.* merciful; compassionate.

mercy *n.* **1 leniency,** clemency, compassion, compassionateness, pity, charity, forgiveness, forbearance, quarter, humanity, humaneness, mildness, softheartedness, tender-heartedness, kindness, sympathy, liberality, tolerance, generosity, beneficence. **2 boon,** favor, piece of luck, blessing, godsend. *Ant.* severity; cruelty; inhumanity.

mere *adj.* **nothing more than,** no better than, no more important than, just a, only a, pure and simple.

merge *v.* **join (together),** join forces, amalgamate, unite, combine, incorporate, coalesce, team up, blend, fuse, mingle, mix, intermix, homogenize. *Ant.* diverge; split; separate.

merit *n.* **1 excellence,** goodness, quality, high quality, worth, worthiness, value. **2 good point,** strong point, advantage, asset, plus. **3 what one deserves,** desert, just deserts, due, right, reward, recompense. *Ant.* inferiority; fault; disadvantage.
▸ *v.* **deserve,** be deserving of, earn, be worthy of, be worth, be entitled to, have a right to, have a claim to, warrant, rate, incur.

merriment *n.* **cheerfulness,** gaiety, high-spiritedness, high spirits, blitheness, buoyancy, carefreeness, levity, sportiveness, joy, joyfulness, joyousness, jolliness, jollity, rejoicing, jocundity, conviviality, festivity, merrymaking, revelry, mirth, mirthfulness, glee, gleefulness, laughter, hilarity, amusement, fun.

merry *adj.* **1 cheerful,** cheery, gay, in good spirits, high-spirited, blithe, blithesome, lighthearted, buoyant, carefree, frolicsome, sportive, joyful, joyous, rejoicing, jolly, jocund, convivial, festive, mirthful, gleeful, happy, glad, laughing. **2 comical,** comic, amusing, funny, humorous, facetious, hilarious. **3 tipsy,** mellow, *inf.* happy, tiddly. *Ant.* miserable; sad; gloomy.

mesh *n.* **1 network,** netting, net, tracery, web, lattice, latticework, lacework, trellis, reticulation, plexus. **2 net,** tangle, entanglement, web, snare, trap.
▸ *v.* **1 be engaged,** connect, interlock. **2 harmonize,** fit together, go together, coordinate, match, be on the same wavelength, dovetail.

mesmerize *v.* **1 hypnotize**, put into a trance, put under. **2 hold spellbound,** spellbind, entrance, enthrall, bewitch, captivate, enchant, fascinate, grip, magnetize, hypnotize.

mess *n.* **1 disorder,** untidiness, disarray, dirtiness, filthiness, clutter, litter, muddle, chaos, confusion, disorganization, turmoil. **2 plight,** predicament, tight spot, tight corner, difficulty, trouble, quandary, dilemma, muddle, mix-up, confusion, imbroglio, fine kettle of fish, *inf.* jam, fix, pickle, stew. **3 muddle,** botch, bungle, *inf.* hash, foul-up, screw-up. **4 dirt,** excrement, feces, excreta.
▶ *v.* **fiddle,** play, tinker, toy.

message *n.* **1 communication,** piece of information, news, word, tidings, note, memorandum, letter, missive, bulletin, communiqué, dispatch, *inf.* memo. **2 meaning,** import, idea, point, purport, intimation, theme, moral.

messenger *n.* **message-bearer,** message-carrier, courier, errand boy/girl, runner, envoy, emissary, agent, go-between, herald, harbinger, *inf.* gofer.

messy *adj.* **untidy,** disordered, dirty, filthy, grubby, slovenly, cluttered, littered, muddled, in a muddle, chaotic, confused, disorganized, in disarray, disarranged, disheveled, unkempt, *inf.* sloppy. *Ant.* tidy; clean; orderly.

metamorphosis *n.* **transformation,** transfiguration, change, alteration, conversion, changeover, mutation, transmutation, sea change, *inf.* transmogrification.

method *n.* **1 procedure,** technique, system, practice, modus operandi, process, approach, way, course of action, scheme, plan, rule, arrangement, form, style, manner, mode. **2 order,** orderliness, sense of order, organization, arrangement, structure, form, system, planning, plan, design, purpose, pattern, regularity.

methodical *adj.* **1 orderly,** well-ordered, organized, systematic, structured, logical, well-regulated, planned, efficient, businesslike. **2 organized,** systematic, efficient, businesslike, meticulous, punctilious. *Ant.* disorganized; chaotic; inefficient.

meticulous *adj.* **1 conscientious,** careful, ultracareful, scrupulous, punctilious, painstaking, demanding, exacting, thorough, perfectionist, fastidious, particular. **2 careful,** exact, precise, detailed, thorough, rigorous, painstaking. *Ant.* careless; sloppy; slapdash.

microscopic *adj.* invisible, scarcely perceptible, infinitesimal, minuscule, tiny, minute. *Ant.* massive; enormous; gigantic.

middle *adj.* **1 mid,** mean, medium, medial, median, midway, halfway, central, equidistant. **2 intermediate,** intermediary, intermedial.
▸ *n.* **1 mean,** median, midpoint, halfway point, center, dead center. **2 midst,** heart, center, thick. **3 midriff,** waist, waistline.

middling *adj.* **average,** medium, ordinary, fair, moderate, adequate, passable, tolerable, mediocre, indifferent, run-of-the-mill, unexceptional, unremarkable, *inf.* fair-to-middling, so-so.

might *n.* **force,** power, strength, mightiness, powerfulness, forcefulness, potency, toughness, robustness, sturdiness, muscularity, vigor, energy, stamina, stoutness.

mighty *adj.* **1 forceful,** powerful, strong, lusty, potent, tough, robust, sturdy, muscular, strapping, vigorous, energetic, stout. **2 huge,** massive, vast, enormous, colossal, giant, gigantic, prodigious, monumental, mountainous, towering, titanic. *Ant.* puny; feeble; tiny.

migrant *adj.* **migrating,** migratory, traveling, roving, roaming, wandering, drifting, nomadic, itinerant, peripatetic, vagrant, gypsy, transient, unsettled, on the move.
▸ *n.* **vagrant,** nomad, itinerant, traveler, gypsy, transient, rover, wanderer, drifter.

mild *adj.* **1 tender,** gentle, soft, softhearted, tender-hearted, sensitive, sympathetic, warm, warmhearted, compassionate, humane, forgiving, conciliatory, forbearing, merciful, lenient, clement, placid, meek, docile, calm, tranquil, serene, peaceful, peaceable, pacific, good-natured, amiable, affable, genial, easy, easygoing, mellow. **2 gentle,** soft, moderate, warm, balmy. **3 bland,** spiceless, nonspicy, insipid, tasteless. *Ant.* cruel; harsh; strong; spicy.

milieu *n.* **environment,** surroundings, background, setting, scene, location, sphere, element.

militant *adj.* **1 aggressive,** assertive, vigorous, active, ultra-active, combative, pugnacious, *inf.* pushy. **2 fighting,** warring, combating, contending, in conflict, clashing, embattled, in arms, belligerent, bellicose. **Ant.** retiring; pacific; peaceful.

▶ *n.* **1 activist,** partisan. **2 fighter,** fighting man/woman, soldier, warrior, combatant, belligerent, aggressor.

military *adj.* **army,** service, soldierly, soldierlike, armed, martial.

▶ *n.* **army,** forces, armed forces, services, militia, soldiery, navy, air force, marines.

milk *v.* **1 draw,** draw off, express, siphon, tap, drain, extract.
2 exploit, take advantage of, impose on, bleed, suck dry.

milky *adj.* **white,** milk-white, snow-white, whitish, creamy, pearly, nacreous, ivory, alabaster, off-white, clouded, cloudy.

mill *n.* **factory,** plant, foundry, works, workshop, shop.

▶ *v.* **grind,** pulverize, pound, crush, powder, crunch, granulate, comminute, triturate.

mimic *v.* **1 impersonate,** give an impersonation of, imitate, copy, ape, caricature, parody, *inf.* take off. **2 resemble,** look like, have/ take on the appearance of, echo, mirror, simulate.

▶ *n.* **mimicker,** impersonator, impressionist, imitator, parodist, copyist, parrot, ape.

mince *v.* **1 chop/cut into tiny**

pieces, grind, crumble, hash.
2 strike a pose, attitudinize, pose, posture, put on airs, be affected.
3 restrain, hold back, moderate, temper, soften, mitigate, refine, weaken.

mind *n.* **1 brain,** head, seat of intellect, psyche, ego, subconscious. **2 brainpower,** powers of thought, intellect, intellectual capabilities, mentality, intelligence, powers of reasoning, brain, brains, wits, understanding, comprehension, sense, ratiocination, *inf.* gray matter. **3 thoughts,** thinking, concentration, attention, application, absorption.
4 memory, recollection, remembrance. **5 opinion,** way of thinking, thoughts, outlook, view, viewpoint, point of view, belief, judgment, attitude, feeling, sentiment. **6 inclination,** desire, wish, urge, will, notion, fancy, intention, intent, aim, purpose, design. **7 mental balance,** sanity, senses, wits, reason, reasoning, judgment. **8 genius,** intellect, intellectual, thinker, *inf.* brain, egghead. **Ant.** body; disinclination.

▶ *v.* **1 be offended by,** take offense at, object to, care about, be bothered by, be upset by, be affronted by, resent, dislike,

disapprove of, look askance at.
2 take heed of, heed, pay heed to, be heedful of, pay attention to, attend to, concentrate on, listen to, note, take notice of, mark, observe, have regard for, respect, obey, follow, comply with, adhere to. **3 attend to,** pay attention to, concentrate on, apply oneself to, have regard for. **4 be careful of,** be cautious of, beware of, be on one's guard for, be wary of, be watchful of, watch out for, look out for, keep one's eyes open for, take care. **5 make sure,** be sure, ensure that, take care. **6 look after,** take care of, attend to, tend, have charge of, keep an eye on, watch.

mindful *adj.* **paying attention to,** heedful of, watchful of, careful of, wary of, chary of, regardful of, taking into account, cognizant of, aware of, conscious of, alert to, alive to, sensible of. *Ant.* heedless; oblivious.

mindless *adj.* **1 stupid,** foolish, brainless, senseless, witless, empty-headed, unintelligent, dull, slow-witted, obtuse, weak-minded, featherbrained, *inf.* birdbrained, dumb, dopey, moronic. **2 unthinking,** thoughtless, careless, ill-advised, negligent, neglectful, brutish, barbarous, barbaric, gratuitous.

3 mechanical, automatic, routine. *Ant.* intelligent; thoughtful; interesting.

mine *n.* **1 colliery,** pit, excavation, well, quarry, lode, vein, deposit, coal mine, gold mine, diamond mine. **2 source,** reservoir, quarry, repository, store, storehouse, abundant supply, wealth, mint, *inf.* gold mine. **3 explosive,** land mine, depth charge. **4 tunnel,** trench, sap.
▸ *v.* **1 excavate,** quarry for, dig for, dig up, extract, unearth. **2 dig a mine/tunnel/trench/sap under,** undermine, weaken.

mingle *v.* **1 mix,** blend, combine, compound, homogenize, merge, unite, join, amalgamate, fuse. **2 intermingle,** mix, intermix, coalesce, blend, fuse, merge, unite, commingle. **3 circulate,** socialize, hobnob, fraternize, associate with others, meet people. *Ant.* separate; part.

miniature *adj.* **small-scale,** scaled-down, mini, midget, baby, toy, pocket, dwarf, Lilliputian, reduced, diminished, small, tiny, wee, minute, minuscule, microscopic, *inf.* pint-sized. *Ant.* giant; gigantic; enormous.

minimal *adj.* **minimum,** least, least possible, smallest, littlest, slightest, nominal, token. *Ant.* maximum; most.

minimize *v.* **1 keep at/to a minimum,** reduce, decrease, curtail, cut back on, prune, slash. **2 reduce,** decrease, diminish, abbreviate, attenuate, shrink, miniaturize. **3 belittle,** make light of, decry, discount, play down, deprecate, depreciate, underestimate, underrate. *Ant.* maximize; increase; exaggerate.

minimum *n.* **lowest level,** bottom level, bottom, depth, nadir, least, lowest, slightest.
  ▸ *adj.* **minimal,** lowest, smallest, littlest, least, least possible, slightest. *Ant.* maximum; most.

minion *n.* **1 lackey,** flunky, henchman, toady, sycophant, flatterer, fawner, underling, hireling, servant, dependent, hanger-on, parasite, leech, *inf.* yes-man, bootlicker. **2 favorite,** pet, darling, jewel, apple of one's eye.

minor *adj.* **1 little-known,** unknown, lesser, insignificant, unimportant, inconsequential, inferior, lightweight, subordinate. **2 slight,** small, insignificant, unimportant, inconsequential, trivial, negligible, trifling. *Ant.* major; significant; considerable.

mint *n.* **fortune,** small fortune, vast sum of money, millions, king's ransom, *inf.* pile, stack, heap, packet, bundle.
  ▸ *adj.* **brand-new,** as new, unused, perfect, unblemished, undamaged, unmarred, untarnished, fresh, first-class, *inf.* spanking new.

minute *n.* **1 moment,** short time, second, instant, *inf.* jiffy, jiff. **2 moment,** instant, point, point in time, time, juncture.
  ▸ *adj.* **1 tiny,** minuscule, microscopic, miniature, diminutive, Lilliputian, little, small, *inf.* knee-high to a grasshopper. **2 infinitesimal,** negligible, trifling, trivial, paltry, petty, insignificant, inconsequential, unimportant, slight, minimal. **3 detailed,** exhaustive, meticulous, punctilious, painstaking, close, strict, exact, precise, accurate. *Ant.* gigantic; huge.

minutely *adv.* **in detail,** exhaustively, meticulously, punctiliously, painstakingly, closely, *inf.* with a fine-tooth comb.

miracle *n.* **wonder,** marvel, prodigy, phenomenon, act of thaumaturgy.

miraculous *adj.* **1 inexplicable,** unaccountable, preternatural, superhuman, supernatural, fantastic, magical, thaumaturgic, phenomenal, prodigious, wonderful, wondrous, remarkable. **2 amazing,** astounding, remarkable, extraordinary, incredible, unbelievable, *inf.* fantastic.

mire *n.* **1 marsh,** marshland, bog, peatbog, swamp, swampland, morass, quagmire, quag, slough, fen, bayou. **2 mud,** slime, dirt, filth, *inf.* muck.
➤ *v.* **1 sink,** sink down, bog down, stick in the mud. **2 entangle,** catch up, involve, bog down.

mirror *n.* **1 looking glass,** glass, reflector, reflecting surface, rear-view mirror. **2 reflection,** twin, double, exact likeness, image, replica, copy, clone, match, *inf.* spitting image, spit and image, dead ringer.
➤ *v.* **reflect,** imitate, emulate, simulate, copy, follow, mimic, echo, ape, parrot, impersonate.

mirth *n.* **gaiety,** merriment, high spirits, cheerfulness, cheeriness, hilarity, glee, laughter, jocularity, levity, buoyancy, blitheness, lightheartedness, joviality, joyousness, fun, enjoyment, amusement, pleasure, merrymaking, festivity, revelry, sport.

misapprehension *n.* **misunderstanding,** mistake, error, mix-up, misinterpretation, misconstruction, misreading, misjudgment, misconception, misbelief, miscalculation, wrong idea, false impression, delusion.

misappropriate *v.* **1 embezzle,** steal, thieve, swindle, pocket, peculate, help oneself to, *inf.* pinch, lift. **2 misuse,** misapply, misemploy, put to a wrong use.

misbehave *v.* **behave badly,** be bad, be naughty, be disobedient, get up to mischief, misconduct oneself, be guilty of misconduct, be bad-mannered, show bad/poor manners, be rude, fool around, *inf.* carry on, act up.

misbehavior *n.* **misconduct,** bad behavior, disorderly conduct, badness, naughtiness, disobedience, mischief, mischievousness, delinquency, misdeed, misdemeanor, bad/poor manners, rudeness, fooling around, *inf.* carrying on, acting up, shenanigans.

miscalculate *v.* **calculate wrongly,** make a mistake, go wrong, err, blunder, be wide of the mark, *inf.* slip up, make a booboo.

miscarry *v.* **1 have a miscarriage,** abort, have a spontaneous abortion, lose the baby. **2 go wrong,** go awry, go amiss, be unsuccessful, fail, misfire, abort, be abortive, founder, come to nothing, come to grief, meet with disaster, fall through, be ruined, fall flat, *inf.* bite the dust, go up in smoke.

miscellaneous *adj.* **varied,** assorted, mixed, diverse, sundry, variegated, diversified, motley, multifarious, jumbled, confused, indiscriminate, heterogeneous.

miscellany *n.* **assortment,** mixture, mélange, variety, collection, motley collection, medley, potpourri, conglomeration, jumble, confusion, mix, mishmash, hodgepodge, pastiche, patchwork, gallimaufry, olio, salmagundi, mixed bag.

mischief *n.* **1 mischievousness,** naughtiness, badness, bad behavior, misbehavior, misconduct, pranks, wrongdoing, delinquency, *inf.* monkey tricks, monkey business, shenanigans, goings-on. **2 impishness,** roguishness, rascality, devilment. **3 harm,** hurt, injury, impairment, damage, detriment, disruption, trouble.

mischievous *adj.* **1 full of mischief,** naughty, bad, badly behaved, misbehaving, disobedient, troublesome, vexatious, playful, frolicsome, rascally, roguish, delinquent. **2 playful,** teasing, impish, roguish, waggish, arch. **3 malicious,** spiteful, malignant, vicious, wicked, evil. **4 hurtful,** harmful, injurious, damaging, detrimental, deleterious, destructive, pernicious. *Ant.* good; well-behaved; harmless.

misconception *n.* **misapprehension,** misunderstanding, mistake, error, misinterpretation, the wrong idea, a false impression, delusion.

miserable *adj.* **1 unhappy,** sorrowful, dejected, depressed, downcast, downhearted, down, despondent, disconsolate, desolate, wretched, glum, gloomy, dismal, blue, melancholy, low-spirited, mournful, woeful, woebegone, sad, doleful, forlorn, crestfallen, *inf.* down in the mouth, down in the dumps. **2 wretched,** mean, poor, shabby, squalid, filthy, foul, sordid, seedy, dilapidated. **3 poverty-stricken,** needy, penniless, impoverished, beggarly, destitute, indigent, down-at-the-heels, out at the elbows. **4 contemptible,** despicable, base, mean, low, vile, sordid. **5 meager,** paltry, scanty, low, poor, niggardly, pathetic. **6 unpleasant,** disagreeable, displeasing, uncomfortable, wet, rainy, stormy. *Ant.* happy; cheerful; luxurious; respectable.

miserly *adj.* **mean,** niggardly, parsimonious, tight-fisted, close-fisted, penny-pinching, penurious, greedy, avaricious, ungenerous, illiberal, *inf.* stingy, tight, money-grubbing, cheap. *Ant.* generous; lavish; extravagant; spendthrift.

misery *n.* **1 distress,** wretchedness, hardship, suffering, affliction, anguish, torment, torture, agony, pain, discomfort, deprivation, poverty, grief, sorrow, heartbreak, heartbrokenness, despair, depression, dejection, desolation, gloom, melancholy, woe, sadness, unhappiness. **2 trouble,** misfortune, adversity, affliction, ordeal, pain, sorrow, burden, load, blow, trial, tribulation, woe, torment, catastrophe, calamity, disaster. **3 killjoy,** spoilsport, pessimist, prophet of doom, complainer, moaner, *inf.* sourpuss, grouch, wet blanket. *Ant.* comfort; pleasure; joy.

misfortune *n.* **bad luck,** ill fortune, ill/poor/hard luck, accident, misadventure, mischance, trouble, setback, reverse, reversal, adversity, mishap, stroke of bad luck, blow, failure, accident, disaster, tragedy, affliction, sorrow, misery, woe, trial, tribulation, catastrophe, calamity.

misgiving *n.* **qualm,** doubt, reservation, second thoughts, suspicion, distrust, anxiety, apprehension, unease, uncertainty, hesitation.

misguided *adj.* **mistaken,** deluded, erroneous, fallacious, wrong, unwarranted, uncalled-for, misplaced, ill-advised, unwise, injudicious, imprudent, foolish, misled, misdirected, misinformed, laboring under a delusion/misapprehension, ill-advised.

mishap *n.* **misfortune,** ill fortune, ill/bad/poor/hard luck, accident, misadventure, mischance, trouble, setback, reverse, adversity, misadventure, misfortune, stroke of bad luck, blow, disaster, trial, tribulation, catastrophe, calamity.

mislay *v.* **lose,** misplace, put in the wrong place, lose track of, miss, be unable to find, be unable to lay one's hands on, forget the whereabouts of, forget where one has put something. *Ant.* find; locate.

mislead *v.* **misinform,** misguide, misdirect, delude, take in, deceive, fool, hoodwink, lead astray, throw off the scent, send on a wild-goose chase, pull the wool over someone's eyes, *inf.* lead up the garden path, take for a ride.

misleading *adj.* **confusing,** deceptive, deceiving, delusive, evasive, equivocal, ambiguous, fallacious, spurious, illusory, casuistic, sophistical.

miss[1] *v.* **1 let go,** bungle, botch, muff, fail to achieve. **2 fail to catch/get,** be too late for. **3 fail to attend,** be too late for, absent oneself from, be absent from, play truant from, take French leave from, *inf.* skip. **4 fail to seize/ grasp,** let slip, let go, pass up, overlook, disregard. **5 fail to hear/ catch,** fail to take in, mishear, misunderstand. **6 regret the absence/loss of,** feel the loss of, feel nostalgic for, long to see, long for, pine for, yearn for, ache for. **7 avoid,** evade, escape, dodge, sidestep, steer clear of, give a wide berth to. *Ant.* catch; get; attend.
▶ *n.* **failure,** omission, slip, blunder, error, mistake, fiasco; *inf.* flop.

miss[2] *n.* **girl,** schoolgirl, young lady, lass; *lit.* maiden, maid, damsel.

misshapen *adj.* **out of shape,** deformed, malformed, ill-proportioned, misproportioned, twisted, distorted, contorted, warped, curved, crooked, wry, bent, hunchbacked.

missing *adj.* **lost,** mislaid, misplaced, nowhere to be found, absent, not present, gone, gone astray, unaccounted for.

mission *n.* **1 assignment,** commission, task, job, errand, work, chore, business, undertaking, operation, duty, charge, trust, goal, aim, purpose. **2 vocation,** calling, pursuit, quest, undertaking. **3 delegation,** deputation, committee, commission, task force, legation.

mistake *n.* **error,** fault, inaccuracy, slip, blunder, miscalculation, misunderstanding, oversight, gaffe, faux pas, solecism, misapprehension, misreading, *inf.* slipup, booboo.
▶ *v.* **get wrong,** misunderstand, misapprehend, misinterpret, misconstrue, misread.

mistakenly *adv.* **by mistake,** wrongly, in error, erroneously, incorrectly, falsely, fallaciously, misguidedly.

mistreat *v.* **maltreat,** treat badly, ill-treat, ill-use, misuse, abuse, handle/treat roughly, mishandle, harm, hurt, molest, manhandle, maul, bully, *inf.* beat up, rough up.

mistress *n.* **lover,** girlfriend, partner, ladylove, paramour, kept woman, concubine, inamorata.

mistrust *v.* **1 feel mistrustful of,** distrust, feel distrustful of, have doubts about, be suspicious of, suspect, have reservations about, have misgivings about, be wary of. **2 have no confidence in,** question, doubt, lack faith in.

misty *adj.* **1 hazy,** foggy, cloudy. **2 hazy,** blurred, fuzzy, dim, indistinct, vague, obscure, nebulous. *Ant.* clear; distinct.

misunderstand *v.* **misapprehend,** misinterpret, misconstrue, misread, get the wrong idea, receive a false impression, be barking up the wrong tree.

misunderstanding *n.* **1 misapprehension,** mistake, error, mix-up, misinterpretation, misconstruction, misreading, misjudgment, miscalculation, misconception, misbelief, wrong idea, delusion, false impression. **2 disagreement,** difference, difference of opinion, clash of views, dispute, quarrel, argument, tiff, squabble, conflict, *inf.* falling-out, spat, scrap.

misuse *v.* **1 put to wrong use,** misapply, misemploy, abuse, squander, waste, dissipate. **2 mistreat,** abuse, mishandle, manhandle, harm, vandalize. ▸ *n.* **1 wrong use,** misapplication, misemployment, abuse, squandering, waste, dissipation. **2 misusage,** malapropism, barbarism, catachresis. **3 maltreatment,** mistreatment, ill

use, abuse, rough handling, mishandling, manhandling.

mitigate *v.* **alleviate,** reduce, diminish, lessen, weaken, attenuate, allay, assuage, palliate, appease, soothe, relieve, ease, soften, temper, mollify, lighten, still, quieten, quiet, tone down, moderate, modify, extenuate, calm, lull, pacify, placate, tranquilize. *Ant.* aggravate; increase; intensify.

mix *v.* **1 admix,** blend, put together, combine, mingle, compound, homogenize, alloy, merge, unite, join, amalgamate, fuse, coalesce, interweave. **2 be compatible,** get along, be in harmony, be like-minded, be of the same mind, *inf.* be on the same wavelength. **3 socialize,** mingle, associate with others, meet people, associate, have dealings, fraternize, hobnob. *Ant.* separate; divide. ▸ *n.* **mixture,** blend, combination, compound, alloy, merger, union, amalgamation, fusion, coalition.

mixed *adj.* **1 assorted,** varied, miscellaneous, diverse, diversified, motley, heterogeneous. **2 hybrid,** crossbred, interbred, mongrel. **3 ambivalent,** equivocal, unsure, uncertain.

mixture *n.* **1 compound,** blend,

mix, brew, combination, concoction, alloy. **2 assortment,** variety, mélange, collection, miscellany, motley collection, medley, potpourri, conglomeration, jumble, mix, mishmash, hodgepodge, pastiche, mixed bag. **3 cross,** crossbreed, mongrel, hybrid.

moan *n.* **1 groan,** lament, lamentation, wail, whimper, whine, sigh, sough, murmur, whisper. **2 moans and groans,** complaint, complaining, whine, whining, carping, *inf.* grousing, gripe, griping, grouching, beef, beefing.
▸ *v.* **1 groan,** wail, whimper, whine, sigh, sough, murmur, whisper. **2 complain,** whine, carp, *inf.* grouse, gripe, grouch, beef.

mob *n.* **1 crowd,** horde, multitude, rabble, mass, body, throng, host, pack, press, gang, drove, herd, flock, gathering, assemblage, lot, group, set, troop, company. **2 common people,** masses, populace, multitude, commonality, proletariat, crowd, rabble, hoi polloi, canaille, *inf.* great unwashed.
▸ *v.* **1 crowd around/into,** swarm around, surround, besiege, jostle, cram full, fill to overflowing, fill, pack. **2 set upon,** attack, harass, fall upon, assault.

mobile *adj.* **1 able to move,** moving, walking, motile, ambulatory. **2 movable,** transportable, portable, traveling, peripatetic, locomotive. **3 moving,** on the move, flexible, adaptable, adjustable. *Ant.* immobile; expressionless; stationary.

mobilize *v.* **1 call up,** call to arms, muster, rally, marshal, assemble, organize, make ready, prepare, ready. **2 get ready,** prepare, ready oneself.

mock *v.* **1 ridicule,** jeer at, sneer at, deride, treat with contempt, treat contemptuously, scorn, make fun of, poke fun at, laugh at, tease, taunt, insult, flout, *inf.* rag, kid, rib. **2 imitate,** mimic, parody, ape, caricature, satirize, lampoon, burlesque, *inf.* take off, send up. **3 defy,** challenge, thwart, frustrate, foil, disappoint.
▸ *adj.* **imitation,** artificial, simulated, synthetic, ersatz, so-called, fake, sham, false, spurious, bogus, counterfeit, forged, pseudo, pretended, *inf.* pretend.

mockery *n.* **1 ridicule,** jeering, sneer, derision, contempt, scorn, disdain, teasing, taunting, gibe, insult, contumely, *inf.* ribbing. **2 laughingstock,** farce, parody, travesty, caricature, lampoon, burlesque, *inf.* takeoff, send-up, spoof. **3 travesty,** inanity, act of stupidity, futile act, joke, laugh.

mocking *adj.* **sneering,** derisive, derisory, contemptuous, scornful, disdainful, sardonic, insulting, satirical.

model *n.* **1 replica,** representation, mock-up, copy, dummy, imitation, facsimile, image, mannequin. **2 prototype,** protoplast, archetype, type, mold, original, pattern, design, paradigm, sample, example, exemplar. **3 style,** design, mode, form, mark, version, type, variety, kind, sort. **4 ideal,** paragon, perfect example, perfect specimen, exemplar, (the) epitome of something, (the) beau ideal, nonpareil, (the) crème de la crème. **5 sitter,** poser, subject. **6 mannequin.**

▸ *adj.* **prototypical,** prototypal, archetypal, illustrative, ideal, perfect.

moderate *adj.* **1 nonextreme,** middle-of-the-road, nonradical, nonreactionary. **2 nonexcessive,** reasonable, within reason, within due limits, fair, just. **3 not given to excesses,** restrained, controlled, temperate, sober, steady. **4 temperate,** calm, equable, mild. **5 average,** middle-of-the-road, middling, ordinary, fair, fairish, modest, tolerable, passable, adequate, indifferent, mediocre, run-of-the-mill, *inf.* so-so, fair-to-middling. **6 reasonable,** within reason, acceptable, average, fair, fairish, modest, lowish. *Ant.* immoderate; extreme; unreasonable.

▸ *v.* **1 die down,** abate, let up, calm down, lessen, decrease, diminish, slacken. **2 lessen,** decrease, diminish, mitigate, alleviate, allay, appease, assuage, ease, palliate, soothe, soften, calm, modulate, pacify. **3 curb,** check, keep in check, keep in control, temper, regulate, restrain, subdue, repress, tame. **4 arbitrate,** mediate, referee, judge, chair, take the chair of, preside over.

moderately *adv.* **1 quite,** rather, somewhat, fairly, reasonably, to a certain degree, to some extent, within reason, within limits. **2 fairly,** tolerably, passably.

modern *adj.* **1 contemporary,** present-day, present-time, present, current, twentieth-century, twenty-first-century, existing, existent. **2 up-to-date,** up-to-the-minute, fashionable, in fashion, in, in style, in vogue, voguish, modish, the latest, new, newfangled, fresh, modernistic, ultramodern, advanced, progressive, *inf.* trendy, with-it.

Ant. past; out of date; old-fashioned.

modernize *v.* **1 make modern,** update, bring up to date, bring into the twenty-first century, renovate, remodel, remake, redo, refresh, revamp, rejuvenate, *inf.* do over. **2 get up to date,** move with the times, *inf.* drag oneself into the twenty-first century, get on the ball, get with it.

modest *adj.* **1 self-effacing,** self-deprecating, humble, unpretentious, unassuming, free from vanity, keeping one's light under a bushel. **2 shy,** bashful, self-conscious, diffident, reserved, retiring, reticent, quiet, coy, embarrassed, blushing, timid, fearful, meek. **3 decorous,** decent, seemly, demure, proper, discreet, delicate, chaste, virtuous. **4 moderate,** fair, tolerable, passable, adequate, satisfactory, acceptable, unexceptional, small, limited. **5 unpretentious,** simple, plain, humble, inexpensive, low-cost. *Ant.* boastful; conceited; immodest; expensive.

modesty *n.* **1 humility,** self-effacement, unpretentiousness. **2 shyness,** bashfulness, self-consciousness, reserve, reticence, timidity, meekness. **3 decorum,** decorousness, seemliness, demureness, propriety, chasteness. **4 moderation,** fairness, passableness, adequacy, satisfactoriness, acceptability, smallness. **5 unpretentiousness,** simplicity, plainness, inexpensiveness.

modify *v.* **1 lessen,** reduce, decrease, diminish, lower, abate, soften, mitigate, restrict, limit, moderate, temper, blunt, dull, tone down, qualify. **2 alter,** make alterations to, change, adjust, make adjustments to, adapt, vary, revise, recast, reform, reshape, refashion, rework, remold, redo, revamp, reorganize, refine, transform.

moist *adj.* **1 wet,** wettish, damp, dampish, clammy, humid, dank, rainy, drizzly, drizzling, dewy, dripping, soggy. **2 succulent,** juicy, soft, spongy.

moisture *n.* **water,** liquid, wetness, wet, dampness, damp, humidity, dankness, wateriness, rain, dew, drizzle, perspiration, sweat.

moldy *adj.* **mildewed,** blighted, musty, fusty, decaying, rotting, rotten, bad, spoiled.

molest *v.* **1 pester,** annoy, nag, plague, torment, harass, badger, harry, persecute, bother, worry, trouble, needle, provoke, vex, agitate, disturb, upset, fluster, ruffle, irritate, exasperate, tease, *inf.* bug, hassle. **2 abuse,** sexually abuse, interfere with, sexually assault, rape, ravish, assault, attack, injure, hurt, harm, mistreat, maltreat, ill-treat, manhandle.

mollify *v.* **calm,** calm down, pacify, placate, appease, soothe, still, quiet, tranquilize.

moment *n.* **minute,** short time, second, instant, point, point in time, time, juncture, *inf.* jiffy, jiff.

momentary *adj.* **brief,** short, short-lived, fleeting, passing, transient, transitory, ephemeral, evanescent, fugitive, temporary, impermanent. ***Ant.*** lengthy; permanent.

momentous *adj.* **crucial,** critical, vital, decisive, pivotal, serious, grave, weighty, important, significant, consequential, of importance, of consequence, fateful, historic, *inf.* earthshaking, earth-shattering. ***Ant.*** unimportant; trivial; insignificant.

momentum *n.* **impetus,** impulse, propulsion, thrust, push, driving power/force, drive, power, energy, force.

money *n.* **1 cash,** hard cash, ready money, finance, capital, funds, banknotes, currency, coin, coinage, silver, copper, legal tender, specie, *inf.* wherewithal, dough, bread, loot, moolah, filthy lucre, green stuff. **2 affluence,** wealth, riches, prosperity.

monitor *n.* **1 detector,** scanner, recorder, security system, security camera, observer, watchdog, overseer, supervisor. **2 screen,** receiver, display device, cathode-ray tube, CRT.
▸ *v.* **observe,** scan, record, survey, follow, keep an eye on, keep track of, check, oversee, supervise.

monopolize *v.* **1 corner,** control, take over, have sole rights in. **2 dominate,** take over, not let anyone else take part in, not let anyone else get a word in edgewise.

monotonous *adj.* **1 unvarying,** lacking/without variety, unchanging, repetitious, all the same, uniform, routine, humdrum, run-of-the-mill, commonplace, mechanical, uninteresting, unexciting, prosaic, wearisome, dull, boring, tedious, tiresome. **2 flat,** unvarying, toneless, uninflected, droning, soporific. ***Ant.*** varied; interesting; exciting.

monster *n.* **1 fabulous creature,** mythical creature, ogre, giant, dragon, troll, bogeyman, werewolf, sea monster, behemoth. **2 fiend,** beast, brute, barbarian, savage, villain, ogre, devil, demon. **3 monstrosity,**

miscreation, malformation, freak, freak of nature, mutant, lusus naturae. **4 giant,** mammoth, colossus, titan, behemoth, leviathan.

▸ *adj.* **huge,** enormous, massive, vast, immense, colossal, gigantic, monstrous, stupendous, prodigious, tremendous, giant, mammoth, gargantuan, titanic, *inf.* jumbo, whopping, humongous.

monstrous *adj.* **1 miscreated,** malformed, unnatural, abnormal, grotesque, gruesome, repellent, freakish, mutant. **2 huge,** enormous, massive, vast, immense, colossal, gigantic, tremendous, giant. **3 outrageous,** shocking, disgraceful, scandalous, atrocious, heinous, evil, abominable, terrible, horrible, dreadful, hideous, foul, vile, nasty, ghastly, odious, loathsome, intolerable, contemptible, despicable, vicious, cruel, savage, brutish, bestial, barbaric, inhuman, fiendish, devilish, diabolical, satanic. *Ant.* normal; tiny; admirable.

monument *n.* **1 memorial,** statue, shrine, reliquary, sepulcher, mausoleum, cairn, pillar, column, obelisk, dolmen, megalith. **2 gravestone,** headstone, tombstone. **3 memorial,** commemoration, remembrance, reminder, testament, witness, token.

monumental *adj.* **1 great,** huge, enormous, immense, vast, exceptional, extraordinary, tremendous, stupendous, prodigious, staggering. **2 huge,** enormous, terrible, colossal, egregious, catastrophic, staggering, unforgivable, indefensible, *inf.* whopping. **3 massive,** impressive, striking, remarkable, magnificent, awe-inspiring, marvelous, majestic, stupendous, prodigious, historic, epoch-making, classic, memorable, unforgettable, enduring, permanent, immortal. **4 commemorative,** celebratory, in memory, recalling to mind.

mood *n.* **1 humor,** temper, disposition, frame of mind, state of mind, spirit, tenor, vein. **2 bad mood,** bad temper, fit of bad/ill temper, fit of irritability, fit of pique, low spirits, fit of melancholy, depression, (the) doldrums, *inf.* (the) dumps.

moody *adj.* **1 temperamental,** changeable, unpredictable, volatile, mercurial, unstable, unsteady, erratic, fitful, impulsive, capricious. **2 in a mood,** in a bad mood, bad-tempered, ill-tempered, ill-humored, short-tempered, irritable, irascible, crabbed, crabby, cantankerous, cross, crotchety, crusty, testy, touchy, petulant, in a pique, sullen, sulky, moping, gloomy, glum, depressed, dejected, despondent, melancholic, doleful, lugubrious, introspective, in a huff, huffy, *inf.* down in the dumps, down in the mouth. *Ant.* stable; amiable; happy.

moon *n.* **satellite,** *lit.* Luna, Selene, orb.
▶ *v.* **languish,** idle, mope, daydream, be in a reverie, be in a brown study.

moot *adj.* **debatable,** open to debate, open to discussion, questionable, open to question, open, doubtful, disputable, arguable, contestable, controversial, unresolved, undecided.

moral *adj.* **1 ethical,** good, virtuous, righteous, upright, upstanding, high-minded, principled, honorable, honest, just, decent, chaste, pure, blameless, right, proper, fit, decent, decorous. **2 psychological,** emotional, mental. *Ant.* immoral; bad; dishonorable.
▶ *n.* **lesson,** teaching, message, homily, meaning, significance, point.

morale *n.* **self-confidence,** confidence, heart, spirit, hope, hopefulness, optimism, determination, zeal.

morality *n.* **1 ethics,** rights and wrongs. **2 ethics,** goodness, virtue, righteousness, rectitude, uprightness, integrity, principles, honor, honesty, justness, decency, chasteness, chastity, purity, blamelessness. **3 morals,** moral code, moral standards, ethics, principles of right and wrong, standards/principles of behavior.

morbid *adj.* **1 gruesome,** grisly, macabre, hideous, dreadful, horrible, unwholesome. **2 gloomy,** glum, dejected, melancholy, lugubrious, funereal, pessimistic. **3 diseased,** infected, sickly, ailing. **4 malignant,** deadly, pathological.

more *adj.* **additional,** supplementary, further, added, extra, increased, spare, fresh, new.
▶ *adv.* **to a greater extent,** further, longer, some more.

moreover *adv.* **besides,** furthermore, further, more than that, what is more, in addition, also, as well, to boot.

moron *n.* **fool,** dolt, dunce, dullard, blockhead, dunderhead, ignoramus, numskull, nincompoop, *inf.* idiot, imbecile, nitwit, halfwit, dope, dimwit, dummy, schmuck.

morsel *n.* **mouthful,** bite, nibble, bit, crumb, grain, particle, fragment, piece, scrap, segment, soupçon, taste.

mortal *adj.* **1 temporal,** transient, ephemeral, passing, impermanent, perishable, human, earthly, worldly, corporeal, fleshly. **2 death-dealing,** deadly, fatal, lethal, killing, murderous, terminal, destructive. **3 deadly,** to the death, sworn, out-and-out, irreconcilable, bitter, implacable, unrelenting, remorseless. **4 terrible,** awful, intense, extreme, severe, grave, dire, very great, great, unbearable, agonizing. **5 conceivable,** imaginable, perceivable, possible.
▸ *n.* **human being,** human, earthling, person, man/woman, being, body, individual.

mortify *v.* **1 humiliate,** humble, cause to eat humble pie, bring low, disgrace, shame, dishonor, abash, fill with shame, put to shame, chasten, degrade, abase, deflate, crush, discomfit, embarrass, take down a peg or two. **2 hurt,** wound, affront, offend, annoy, displease, vex, embarrass. **3 subdue,** get under control, control, restrain, suppress, discipline, chasten.

4 become gangrenous, fester, necrose, putrefy.

mostly *adv.* **for the most part,** on the whole, in the main, largely, mainly, chiefly, predominantly, usually, generally, in general, as a (general) rule, as a rule, ordinarily, normally, commonly.

mother *n.* **materfamilias,** matriarch, earth mother, foster mother, biological mother, birth mother, adoptive mother, surrogate mother, *inf.* mom, mommy, ma, mama, mater, old lady.
▸ *adj.* **inborn,** innate, connate, native, natural.

motherly *adj.* **maternal,** protective, comforting, caring, loving, affectionate, fond, warm, tender, gentle, kind, kindly.

motion *n.* **1 motility,** mobility, locomotion, movement, moving, travel, traveling, going, progress, passing, passage, flow, action, activity, course. **2 movement,** gesture, gesticulation, signal, sign, wave, nod. **3 suggestion,** proposition, proposal, recommendation, submission.
▸ *v.* **gesture,** gesticulate, signal, sign, wave, nod.

motionless *adj.* **unmoving,** still, stock-still, at a standstill, stationary, immobile, immovable, static, at rest, halted, stopped, paralyzed, transfixed, frozen, inert, lifeless. **Ant.** moving; mobile; active.

motivate *v.* **move,** cause, lead, persuade, prompt, actuate, drive, impel, spur, induce, provoke, incite, inspire, give incentive to, stimulate, arouse, excite, stir, goad.

motive *n.* **motivation,** reason, rationale, justification, thinking, grounds, cause, basis, occasion, incentive, inducement, incitement, influence, lure, attraction, inspiration, persuasion, stimulus, spur, goad, pressure, *inf.* what makes one tick.

motley *adj.* **1 assorted,** varied, miscellaneous, mixed, diverse, diversified, variegated, heterogeneous. **2 many-colored,** multicolored, parti-colored, many-hued, variegated, kaleidoscopic, prismatic. **Ant.** homogeneous; uniform.

mottled *adj.* **blotched,** blotchy, splotchy, speckled, spotted, streaked, marbled, flecked, freckled, dappled, stippled, variegated, piebald, pied, brindled.

motto *n.* **1 maxim,** aphorism, adage, saying, saw, axiom, truism, precept, epigram, proverb, byword, gnome. **2 slogan,** catchword, cry.

mound *n.* **1 heap,** pile, stack, *inf.* mountain. **2 hillock,** hill, knoll, rise, hummock, embankment, bank, dune.
▸ *v.* **pile,** heap (up), stack (up), accumulate, amass, stockpile.

mount *v.* **1 ascend,** go up, climb up, clamber up, make one's way up, scale. **2 get on to,** get astride, get on the back of. **3 accumulate,** accrue, pile up, grow, multiply. **4 increase,** grow, escalate, intensify. **5 frame,** set. **6 stage,** put on, install, prepare, organize, arrange, set in motion, *inf.* get up. **Ant.** descend; alight; decrease.
▸ *n.* **1 horse,** steed. **2 setting,** fixture, frame, support, stand, base, backing, foil.

mountain *n.* **1 peak,** height, elevation, eminence, pinnacle, alp, *lit.* mount. **2 heap,** pile, mound, stack, abundance, *inf.* ton.

mountainous *adj.* **1 hilly,** high, highland, high-reaching, steep, lofty, towering, soaring, alpine, rocky. **2 huge,** enormous, immense, massive, vast, gigantic, mammoth, hulking, mighty, monumental, colossal, ponderous, prodigious. **Ant.** flat; level; puny.

mourn *v.* **grieve,** sorrow, keen, lament, wail, wear black. **Ant.** rejoice; exult.

mournful *adj.* **1 sad,** sorrowful, doleful, gloomy, somber, melancholy, lugubrious, funereal, elegaic. **2 sad,** doleful, dejected, depressed, downcast, disconsolate, melancholy, gloomy, miserable, lugubrious, woeful, unhappy, heavy-hearted, somber. *Ant.* joyful; happy; merry.

mouth *n.* **1 lips,** jaws, maw, muzzle, *inf.* trap, chops, kisser. **2 opening,** entrance, entry, inlet, door, doorway, gateway, portal, hatch, aperture, orifice, vent, cavity, crevice, rim, lips. **3 estuary,** outlet, embouchure. **4 empty talk,** idle talk, babble, claptrap, boasting, bragging, braggadocio, *inf.* hot air, gas. **5 impudence,** cheek, insolence, impertinence, rudeness, incivility, effrontery, audacity, *inf.* lip, back talk.

mouthful *n.* **bite,** swallow, spoonful, forkful, nibble, sip, sup, taste, drop, bit, piece, morsel, sample.

mouthpiece *n.* **1 spokesman,** spokeswoman, spokesperson, negotiator, intermediary, mediator, agent, representative. **2 organ,** journal, periodical, publication.

move *v.* **1 go,** walk, march, proceed, progress, advance, pass. **2 carry,** transport, transfer, transpose, change over, shift, switch. **3 take action,** act, do something, get moving. **4 relocate,** change houses, move away, leave, go away. **5 affect,** touch, impress, upset, disturb, disquiet, agitate, make an impression on, have an impact on, tug on someone's heartstrings. **6 provoke,** incite, actuate, rouse, excite, urge, incline, stimulate, motivate, influence, persuade, lead, prompt, cause, impel, induce. **7 activate,** get going, propel, drive, push, shift, motivate. **8 change,** budge, change someone's mind, *inf.* do an about-face, do a U-turn. **9 propose,** put forward, advocate, recommend, submit, urge, suggest. **10 sell,** be sold, move from the shelf, retail, be marketed. *Ant.* stand; stay; deter. ▸ *n.* **1 movement,** motion, moving, action, activity, gesture, gesticulation. **2 removal,** change of house/address/job, relocation, transfer. **3 action,** act, deed, measure, step, tack, maneuver, tactic, stratagem, ploy, ruse, trick. **4 turn,** opportunity, chance, *inf.* shot.

movement *n.* **1 moving,** carrying, transportation, transferral, shifting. **2 moving,** move, motion, action, activity, gesture, gesticulation. **3 progress,** progression, advance, passing, passage. **4 mechanism,** machinery, works, workings, action, wheels, *inf.* innards, guts. **5 group,** party, organization, faction, wing, coalition, front. **6 campaign,** crusade, drive. **7 part,** section, passage. **8 trend,** tendency, drift, swing, current, rise/fall, change, variation, fluctuation. **9 progress,** advance, improvement, step forward, breakthrough.

moving *adj.* **1 affecting,** touching, emotive, emotional, poignant, pathetic, stirring, arousing, upsetting, disturbing. **2 movable,** mobile, motile, unfixed. **3 driving,** dynamic, impelling, motivating, stimulating, inspirational. *Ant.* unemotional; immobile; inert.

mow *v.* **cut,** trim, crop, clip, scythe, shear.

muck *n.* **1 dung,** manure, ordure, excrement, guano, droppings, feces, dirt, grime, filth, mud, slime, sludge, scum, mire, *inf.* gunk, grunge. **2 dirt,** grime, filth, mud, slime, sludge, scum, mire, *inf.* gunk, grunge.

muddle *v.* **confuse,** get confused, disorient, bewilder, befuddle, daze, perplex, puzzle, baffle, nonplus, confound, mix up, jumble, jumble up, scramble, disarrange, disorganize, throw into disorder, get into a tangle, make a mess of, mess up.

▸ *n.* **1 chaos,** disorder, disarray, confusion, disorganization, jumble, mix-up, mess, clutter, tangle, state of confusion, disorientation, bewilderment, perplexity, puzzlement, bafflement. **2 state of confusion,** disorientation, bewilderment, perplexity, puzzlement, bafflement.

muddy *adj.* **1 mucky,** miry, oozy, slushy, slimy. **2 marshy,** boggy, swampy. **3 mud-caked,** dirty, filthy, grubby, grimy. **4 cloudy,** murky, smoky, dingy, dull, turbid, opaque, brownish-green. **5 confused,** jumbled, incoherent, unclear, muddied, woolly.

▸ *v.* **1 dirty,** begrime, soil. **2 make unclear,** cloud, confuse, mix up, jumble, scramble, get into a tangle.

muffle *v.* **deaden,** dull, dampen, stifle, smother, suppress, soften, hush, mute, silence.

mug *n.* **1 cup,** tankard, stein, glass, toby jug. **2 face,** countenance, visage, features, *inf.* puss, kisser, mush.

▸ *v.* **assault,** attack, beat up, knock down, rob, *inf.* rough up.

muggy *adj.* **close,** stuffy, sultry, oppressive, airless, humid, clammy, sticky. *Ant.* fresh; airy.

multiple *adj.* **several,** many,

numerous, various, collective, manifold.

multiply *v.* **breed,** reproduce, increase, grow, accumulate, augment, proliferate, spread.

multitude *n.* **crowd,** assembly, throng, host, horde, mass, mob, legion, army, common people, masses, populace, commonality, proletariat, crowd, rabble, hoi polloi, canaille, *inf.* great unwashed, a lot, lots.

munch *v.* **chew,** champ, chomp, masticate, crunch, eat.

mundane *adj.* **1 common,** ordinary, everyday, workaday, usual, prosaic, pedestrian, routine, customary, regular, normal, typical, commonplace, banal, hackneyed, trite, stale, platitudinous. **2 worldly,** earthly, terrestrial, secular, temporal, fleshly, carnal, sensual. *Ant.* extraordinary; imaginative; spiritual.

municipal *adj.* **civic,** civil, city, metropolitan, urban, town, borough, community, public.

murder *n.* **1 killing,** slaying, manslaughter, homicide, slaughter, assassination, butchery, carnage, massacre. **2 an ordeal,** a trial, a misery, agony, *inf.* hell, hell on earth.
 ▸ *v.* **1 kill,** slay, put to death, take the life of, shed the blood of, slaughter, assassinate, butcher, massacre, *inf.* bump off, do in, eliminate, hit, rub out, blow away. **2 mangle,** mutilate, ruin, make a mess of, spoil, mar, destroy. **3 trounce,** beat soundly, beat decisively, thrash, defeat utterly, give a drubbing to, *inf.* slaughter, hammer, make mincemeat of.

murderer *n.* **killer,** slayer, homicide, slaughterer, cutthroat, assassin, butcher, patricide, matricide, fratricide.

murderous *adj.* **1 fatal,** lethal, deadly, mortal, death-dealing, homicidal, savage, barbarous, brutal, bloodthirsty, bloody. **2 arduous,** difficult, strenuous, exhausting, formidable, harrowing, dangerous, *inf.* killing, hellish.

murky *adj.* **1 dark,** dim, gloomy. **2 foggy,** misty, cloudy, lowering, overcast, dull, gray, dismal, dreary, cheerless. **3 dirty,** muddy, dingy, dull, cloudy, turbid, opaque. **4 dark,** questionable, doubtful, obscure, enigmatic, nebulous, mysterious, hidden, secret. *Ant.* bright; clear; blameless.

murmur *n.* **1 babble,** burble, whisper, rustle, buzzing, drone, undertone, mutter, mumble, sigh, *inf.* whoosh. **2 mutter,** grumble,

moan, complaint, carping, whisper, *inf.* grouse, gripe, beef, bitch.
▸ *v.* **1 babble,** burble, whisper, rustle, buzz, drone, sigh, *inf.* whoosh. **2 whisper,** speak in an undertone, speak sotto voce, mutter, mumble. *Ant.* shout; yell.

muscular *adj.* **1 sinewy,** fibrous. **2 brawny,** strapping, powerfully built, solidly built, hefty, stalwart, sturdy, rugged, burly, *inf.* beefy, husky. **3 vigorous,** potent, powerful, strong, energetic, active, dynamic, aggressive, determined, resolute. *Ant.* weak; puny; feeble.

muse *v.* **1 think,** meditate, be lost in contemplation/thought, be in a brown study, reflect, deliberate, daydream, be in a reverie. **2 think over,** think about, consider, ponder, reflect on, contemplate, meditate on, deliberate about/on, mull over, ruminate over/on, weigh up, have one's mind on, examine, study, review.

musical *adj.* tuneful, melodic, melodious, harmonious, lyrical, sweet-sounding, mellifluous, dulcet, euphonious. *Ant.* discordant; harsh; grating.

muster *v.* **1 assemble,** bring together, call/gather together, call up, summon, rally, mobilize, round up, marshal, collect, convoke, meet, congregate, convene. **2 call up,** gather together, summon, rally, screw up.
▸ *n.* **assembly,** assemblage, rally, mobilization, call-up, roundup, convocation, meeting, congregation, convention.

musty *adj.* **1 moldy,** mildewed, mildewy, fusty, decaying, stale, stuffy, airless, damp, dank. **2 antiquated,** obsolete, ancient, antediluvian, out of date, outdated, old-fashioned, out-of-fashion, out-of-style, behind the times, passé, hoary, moth-eaten, worn-out, threadbare, hackneyed, trite, clichéd. *Ant.* fresh; modern.

mutation *n.* **1 change,** variation, alteration, modification, transformation, metamorphosis, evolution, transmutation, transfiguration. **2 mutant,** deviant, anomaly, freak.

mute *adj.* **1 silent,** speechless, wordless, unspeaking, taciturn, uncommunicative. **2 dumb,** voiceless, speechless, aphasic, aphonic. **3 silent,** wordless, unexpressed, unspoken. *Ant.* voluble; spoken.
▸ *v.* **1 deaden,** dull, dampen, muffle, stifle, smother, suppress, soften, quieten, soft-pedal, turn down. **2 soften,** subdue, tone down, make less intense.

muted *adj.* **soft,** softened, subdued, subtle, discreet, toned down, quiet, understated.

mutinous *adj.* **rebellious,** insurgent, insurrectionary, revolutionary, anarchistic, subversive, seditious, traitorous, insubordinate, disobedient, riotous, rioting, unruly, disorderly, restive, contumacious, refractory, out of control, uncontrollable, ungovernable, unmanageable.

mutiny *n.* **rebellion,** revolt, insurrection, insurgence, insurgency, uprising, rising, riot, revolution, resistance, disobedience, defiance, insubordination, protest, strike. ▸ *v.* **rebel,** revolt, riot, rise (up), resist/oppose authority, defy authority, be insubordinate, protest, strike.

mysterious *adj.* **1 enigmatic,** inscrutable, impenetrable, incomprehensible, inexplicable, unexplainable, unfathomable, unaccountable, insoluble, obscure, arcane, abstruse, cryptic, unknown, recondite, secret, preternatural, supernatural, uncanny, mystical, peculiar, strange, weird, curious, bizarre, undisclosed, mystifying, baffling, puzzling, perplexing, bewildering, confounding. **2 secretive,** reticent, noncommittal, discreet, evasive, furtive, surreptitious. *Ant.* obvious; straightforward; open.

mystery *n.* **1 enigma,** puzzle, secret, unsolved problem, problem, riddle, conundrum, question, question mark, closed book, unexplored ground, terra incognita. **2 secrecy,** concealment, obscurity, obscuration, vagueness, nebulousness, inscrutability, inexplicability.

mystify *v.* **confuse,** bewilder, confound, perplex, baffle, nonplus, puzzle, elude, escape, *inf.* stump, beat, bamboozle.

myth *n.* **1 legend,** saga, tale, story, fable, folk tale, allegory, parable, fairy tale/story, bestiary. **2 fantasy,** delusion, figment of the imagination, invention, fabrication, untruth, lie, *inf.* story, fairy tale/story, tall tale.

mythical *adj.* **1 legendary,** mythological, fabled, chimerical, imaginary, imagined, fabulous, fantastical, fairy-tale, storybook, fictitious, allegorical. **2 fantasy,** imagined, imaginary, pretended, make-believe, unreal, fictitious, invented, fabricated, made-up, untrue, *inf.* pretend. *Ant.* real; actual.

Nn

nadir *n.* **low point,** bottom, rock-bottom, the depths, all-time low, as low as one can go/get, zero, *inf.* the pits. ***Ant.*** zenith; acme; climax.

nag[1] *v.* **1 scold,** carp, pick on, harp on at, be on someone's back, henpeck, bully, upbraid, berate, criticize, find fault with, complain to, grumble to, *inf.* go on (and on) at. **2 badger,** pester, plague, torment, harry, goad, vex, harass, irritate, *inf.* hassle, drive up the wall.
▸ *n.* **shrew,** harpy, termagant, faultfinder, carper, caviler, complainer, grumbler.

nag[2] *n.* **horse,** racehorse, pony, dobbin; broken-down horse, hack; *inf.* bag of bones, plug.

naked *adj.* **1 stark naked,** nude, in the nude, bare, stripped, exposed, unclothed, undressed, uncovered, undraped, disrobed, au naturel, *inf.* without a stitch on, in one's birthday suit, in the raw, in the altogether, in the buff, naked as the day one was born, buck naked. **2 bare,** barren, stark, uncovered, denuded, stripped, treeless, grassless, unfurnished.

3 undisguised, unqualified, unadorned, stark, bald, unvarnished, unveiled, unmitigated, unexaggerated, plain, simple, open, patent, evident, apparent, obvious, manifest, overt, unmistakable, blatant, glaring, flagrant.
4 exposed, unprotected, unguarded, uncovered, unsheathed, unwrapped, defenseless, vulnerable, exposed, helpless, weak, powerless. ***Ant.*** clothed; embellished.

name *n.* **1 appellation,** designation, cognomen, denomination, sobriquet, title, style, label, tag, epithet, first/second name, Christian/given name, surname, family name, maiden name, nickname, pet name, stage name, pseudonym, alias, nom de guerre, nom de plume, *inf.* moniker, handle. **2 big name,** celebrity, luminary, star, dignitary, VIP, lion, *inf.* celeb, megastar, big shot, bigwig.
3 reputation, fame, renown, repute, note, distinction, eminence, prominence, prestige.
▸ *v.* **1 baptize,** christen, give a

name to, call, entitle, label, style, term, title, dub, denominate. **2 identify,** specify, mention, cite, give. **3 appoint,** choose, select, pick, nominate, designate.

nameless *adj.* **1 unnamed,** untitled, unlabeled, untagged, innominate, anonymous, unidentified, undesignated, unspecified. **2 unspeakable,** unutterable, inexpressible, unmentionable, indescribable, abominable, horrible, horrific.

nap[1] *v.* **take a nap,** catnap, doze, sleep lightly, rest, lie down, drowse, *inf.* drop off, nod off, snooze, catch forty winks, get some shut-eye, catch/get/take some Z's.
▸ *n.* **catnap,** doze, light sleep, rest; *inf.* snooze, forty winks, (some) shut-eye.

nap[2] *n.* **pile,** down, surface, shag, weave, grain, fiber.

narrate *v.* **tell,** relate, recount, recite, unfold, give an account of, give a report of, set forth, chronicle, describe, detail, portray, sketch out, rehearse, repeat.

narrator *n.* **1 recounter,** relater, reporter, describer, chronicler, annalist, storyteller, taleteller, teller of tales, raconteur, anecdotist, author, writer. **2 voice-over.**

narrow *adj.* **1 narrow-gauged,** slender, thin, slim, slight, spare, attenuated, tapering. **2 confined,** confining, constricted, tight, cramped, close, restricted, limited, incommodious, pinched, straitened, squeezed, meager, scant, scanty, spare, scrimped, exiguous. **3 limited,** restricted, select, exclusive. **4 literal,** exact, precise, close, faithful. **5 narrow-minded,** intolerant, illiberal, prejudiced, bigoted, parochial, provincial, insular, small-minded. *Ant.* wide; broad; broad-minded.

narrow-minded *adj.* **intolerant,** illiberal, unliberal, overconservative, conservative, hidebound, dyed-in-the-wool, reactionary, close-minded, unreasonable, prejudiced, bigoted, biased, discriminatory, warped, twisted, jaundiced, parochial, provincial, insular, small-minded, petty-minded, petty, mean-spirited, prudish, straitlaced.

nasty *adj.* **1 unpleasant,** disagreeable, distasteful, horrible, vile, foul, hateful, loathsome, revolting, disgusting, odious, obnoxious, repellent, repugnant, ugly, offensive, objectionable, noisome, squalid, dirty, filthy, impure, polluted, tainted, unpalatable, unsavory, unappetizing, evil-smelling, foul-smelling, smelly, stinking, rank, fetid, malodorous, mephitic, *inf.* yucky. **2 dangerous,** serious, critical, crucial, severe, alarming, threatening. **3 ill-tempered,** ill-natured, ill-humored, bad-tempered, cross, surly, unpleasant, disagreeable, vicious, spiteful, malicious, mean, *inf.* grouchy. **4 unpleasant,** disagreeable, foul, wet, rainy, stormy, foggy. **5 obscene,** pornographic, indecent, foul, vile, blue, off-color, smutty, bawdy, vulgar, ribald, risqué, lewd, lascivious, licentious. *Ant.* delightful; pleasant; agreeable.

nation *n.* **country,** land, state, kingdom, empire, realm, republic, confederation, union of states, commonwealth, people, race, tribe, society, community, population.

national *adj.* **1 state,** public, federal, governmental, civic, civil. **2 domestic,** internal, indigenous, native. **3 nationwide,** countrywide, state, coast-to-coast, widespread, overall, comprehensive, general.
▸ *n.* **citizen,** subject, native, resident, inhabitant.

native *adj.* **1 inborn,** inherent, innate, connate, built-in, intrinsic, instinctive, intuitive, natural, natural-born, congenital, hereditary, inherited, in the blood, in the family, inbred, ingrained. **2 indigenous,** original, homegrown, homemade, domestic, local. **3 mother,** vernacular. **4 original,** indigenous, aboriginal, autochthonous.
▸ *n.* **inhabitant,** dweller, resident, citizen, national, aborigine, autochthon.

natural *adj.* **1 usual,** normal, regular, common, ordinary, everyday, typical, routine, run-of-the-mill. **2 native,** native-born, inborn, inherent, innate, connate, built-in, intrinsic, instinctive, intuitive, natural, natural-born, congenital, hereditary, inherited, ingrained. **3 artless,** ingenuous, candid, open, frank, genuine, real, authentic, simple, unsophisticated, unaffected, unpretentious, spontaneous, relaxed, unstudied. **4 organic,** pure, unrefined, unpolished, unbleached, unmixed, whole, plain, real, chemical-free, additive-free. *Ant.* abnormal; unnatural; artificial; studied.

nature *n.* **1 character,** characteristic, essence, essential qualities/attributes/features/traits, constitution, makeup, complexion, stamp, personality, identity. **2 Mother Nature,** natural forces, creation, the environment, the earth, mother earth, the world, the universe, the cosmos, landscape, scenery. **3 kind,** sort, ilk, type, variety, description, category, class, classification, species, style. **4 temperament,** temper, personality, disposition, humor, mood, outlook.

naughty *adj.* **1 bad,** mischievous, badly behaved, misbehaving, disobedient, defiant, unruly, roguish, wayward, delinquent, undisciplined, unmanageable, ungovernable, fractious, refractory, perverse, errant, sinful, wicked, evil. **2 blue,** risqué, smutty, dirty, off-color, indecent, improper, vulgar, bawdy, ribald, lewd, licentious. *Ant.* good; well-behaved; obedient; decent.

nausea *n.* **1 sickness,** vomiting, retching, gagging, biliousness, queasiness, faintness, seasickness, carsickness, airsickness, motion sickness, morning sickness, *inf.* throwing-up. **2 disgust,** revulsion, repugnance, distaste, aversion, loathing, abhorrence, detestation, odium.

nauseous *adj.* **1 nauseating,** sickening, disgusting, revolting, repulsive, repellent, repugnant, offensive, loathsome, abhorrent, odious. **2 nauseated,** sick, sickly, queasy, green, unwell, indisposed, seasick, carsick, airsick, *inf.* green

around the gills, under the weather, out of sorts, below par.

nautical *adj.* **maritime,** naval, marine, seagoing, seafaring, yachting, boating, sailing.

navigable *adj.* **1 negotiable,** passable, traversable, clear, unobstructed. **2 steerable,** sailable, seaworthy, watertight.

near *adj.* **1 close,** close by, nearby, alongside, at close range/quarters, accessible, within reach, close/near at hand, at hand, handy, not far off/away, a stone's throw away, neighboring, adjacent, adjoining, bordering, contiguous, proximate, *inf.* within spitting distance. **2 close/near at hand,** approaching, coming, imminent, forthcoming, in the offing, impending, looming, proximate, immediate. **3 closely related,** related, connected, akin, allied, close, intimate, familiar, dear. **4 close,** narrow, by a hair's breadth, *inf.* by a whisker/hair. *Ant.* far; distant; remote.
▸ *adv.* **close,** nearby, close by, alongside, close/near at hand, at hand, within reach, within close range, within earshot, within sight, not far off/away, a stone's throw away, *inf.* within spitting distance.

nearly *adv.* **almost,** all but, as good as, virtually, next to, close to, well-nigh, about, just about, practically, roughly, approximately, not quite, *inf.* pretty nearly/much/well.

neat *adj.* **1 neat and tidy,** neat as a pin, tidy, orderly, well-ordered, straight, in good order, shipshape, in apple-pie order, spick and span, spruce, trim, smart, dapper, well-groomed, well-turned-out, dainty, fastidious, organized, well-organized, methodical, systematic, *inf.* natty. **2 elegant,** well-put, well-expressed, well-turned, clever, witty, pithy, apt, felicitous. **3 adroit,** skillful, expert, practiced, dexterous, deft, accurate, precise, nimble, agile, graceful, stylish, effortless, easy. **4 straight,** undiluted, unmixed, pure. **5 great,** terrific, wonderful, excellent, exceptional, first-class, first-rate. *Ant.* disorderly; untidy; clumsy.

necessary *adj.* **1 needed,** needful, essential, required, requisite, vital, indispensable, imperative, mandatory, obligatory, compulsory, de rigueur. **2 certain,** sure, inevitable, unavoidable, inescapable, inexorable, ineluctable, fated, preordained. *Ant.* unnecessary; nonessential; dispensable.

need *v.* **1 have need of,** require, necessitate, demand, call for, have occasion for, want, lack, be without. **2 miss,** desire, yearn for, long for, pine for, crave. **3 have,** be under an obligation, be obliged, be compelled, be under a compulsion.

▸ *n.* **1 requirement,** want, wish, demand, prerequisite, requisite, essential, desideratum. **2 want,** lack, shortage, requirement. **3 necessity,** call, force of circumstance, exigency, obligation. **4 neediness,** want, poverty, deprivation, privation, penury, destitution, indigence. **5 crisis,** emergency, urgency, distress, trouble, extremity, exigency.

needless *adj.* unnecessary, uncalled-for, gratuitous, undesired, unwanted, pointless, useless, dispensable, expendable, inessential. *Ant.* necessary; useful.

negative *adj.* **1 rejecting,** refusing, dissenting, contradictory, contradicting, contrary, opposing, opposite, opposed, denying, gainsaying. **2 unenthusiastic,** uninterested, lackadaisical, colorless, anemic, insipid, vapid, weak, spineless, purposeless, pessimistic, defeatist, gloomy, gloom-laden, cynical, jaundiced, critical, faultfinding, complaining, unhelpful, unconstructive, uncooperative.

Ant. positive; affirmative; enthusiastic; optimistic.

▶ *n.* **rejection,** refusal, dissension, opposite, denial, contradiction.

neglect *v.* **1 fail to look after,** fail to provide for, abandon, forsake, leave alone. **2 let slide,** skimp on, shirk, be remiss about, be lax about, pay little/no attention to, not attend to, leave undone, procrastinate about, omit, fail, forget, not remember.

3 disregard, ignore, pay no attention/heed to, overlook, disdain, scorn, slight, spurn, rebuff. *Ant.* care for (see care); attend to (see attend); heed.

▶ *n.* **1 negligence,** neglectfulness, lack of proper care and attention, remissness, carelessness, heedlessness, lack of concern, unconcern, slackness, laxity, laxness, failure to act, dereliction, default. **2 disregard,** ignoring, inattention to, heedlessness, indifference to, disdain, scorn, slight, spurning, rebuff. *Ant.* care; attention.

negligent *adj.* **neglectful,** remiss, lax, careless, inattentive, heedless, thoughtless, unmindful, uncaring, forgetful, disregardful, indifferent, offhand, cursory, slack, sloppy, slapdash, slipshod, procrastinating, dilatory. *Ant.* careful; attentive; conscientious.

negligible *adj.* **trivial,** trifling, insignificant, of no account, not worth bothering about, paltry, petty, tiny, minute, small, minor, inconsequential, inappreciable, imperceptible. *Ant.* significant; considerable.

negotiate *v.* **1 work out,** thrash out, arrange, reach an agreement on, agree on, settle, come to terms about, conclude, pull off, bring off, contract, complete, transact, execute, fulfill, orchestrate, engineer. **2 bargain,** drive a bargain, hold talks, confer, debate, discuss, discuss terms, discuss a settlement, consult together, parley, haggle, wheel and deal, dicker. **3 clear,** get over, get through, pass over, make it over, cross, get past, get around, surmount.

neighborhood *n.* **1 district,** area, region, locality, part, quarter, precinct, community, *inf.* stamping ground, neck of the woods, hood. **2 vicinity,** surrounding district, environs, proximity, purlieus.

neighboring *adj.* **adjacent,** adjoining, bordering, abutting, contiguous, next, nearby, nearest, closest, near, very near, close/near at hand, not far away, in the vicinity.

nervous *adj.* **easily frightened,**

timid, timorous, fearful, apprehensive, anxious, edgy, highly strung, tense, strained, excitable, jumpy, hysterical, on edge, anxious, agitated, worried, fretful, uneasy, disquieted, restless, impatient, excitable, on tenterhooks, fidgety, ruffled, flustered, perturbed, fearful, frightened, scared, with one's heart in one's mouth, quaking, trembling, shaking, shaking in one's shoes, shaky, *inf.* with butterflies in one's stomach, jittery, in a state, uptight, wired. ***Ant.*** bold; calm; laid-back.

nestle *v.* **snuggle**, curl up, huddle together, cuddle up, nuzzle.

net[1] *n.* **1 netting**, tulle, fishnet, meshwork, mesh, latticework, lattice, openwork, webbing, tracery, reticulum. **2 fishing net**, dragnet, drift net, seine, butterfly net, crab net, gill net, trawl. **3 trap**, booby trap, snare, mesh, pitfall, stratagem.

net[2] *adj.* **1 take-home**, after-tax, after-deductions, bottom-line, clear. **2 final**, ultimate, concluding, conclusive, closing, actual.

▸ *v.* **take home**, clear, earn, make, bring in, get, pocket, receive, gain, obtain, realize; *inf.* pull in.

nettle *v.* **irritate**, provoke, ruffle, try someone's patience, annoy, incense, exasperate, irk, vex, pique, bother, pester, harass, torment, plague, *inf.* aggravate, rile, peeve, rub the wrong way, get under someone's skin, get in someone's hair, get someone's goat, get to.

neurotic *adj.* **1 mentally ill**, mentally disturbed, mentally deranged, unstable, maladjusted, psychopathic, obsessive, phobic. **2 suffering from nerves**, overanxious, obsessive, phobic, fixated, compulsive, oversensitive, hysterical, irrational. ***Ant.*** stable; well-balanced; calm; laid-back.

neuter *adj.* **asexual**, sexless, unsexed.

▸ *v.* **castrate**, geld, emasculate, spay, *inf.* fix.

neutral *adj.* **1 impartial**, unbiased, unprejudiced, open-minded, nonpartisan, without favoritism, evenhanded, disinterested, nonaligned, dispassionate, objective, detached, uninvolved, uncommitted. **2 noncombatant**, noncombative, nonfighting, nonparticipating, nonaligned, unallied, uninvolved, noninterventionist. **3 indefinite**, indeterminate, unremarkable, ordinary, commonplace, average, run-of-the-mill, everyday, bland, uninteresting, colorless, insipid, dull. **4 beige**, ecru, gray, taupe, stone-colored, stone, pale, colorless, uncolored, achromatic, achromic. **Ant.** biased; partisan; combatant; colorful.

neutralize *v.* **1 counteract,** cancel, nullify, negate, annul, undo, invalidate, frustrate, be an antidote to. **2 offset,** counterbalance, counteract, compensate for, make up for, cancel out, negate.

new *adj.* **1 modern,** recent, advanced, state-of-the-art, present-day, contemporary, current, latest, up-to-date, up-to-the-minute, new-fashioned, modish, brand new, newly arrived, modernist, ultramodern, avant-garde, futuristic, newfangled, novel, original, fresh, unhackneyed, imaginative, creative, experimental, *inf.* way-out, far-out. **2 brand new,** unused, unworn, pristine, fresh, mint, in mint condition, virgin.
3 unfamiliar, unknown, strange, different, unaccustomed, untried.
4 additional, added, extra, supplementary, further, another.
5 refreshed, renewed, improved, restored, reinvigorated, regenerated, reborn, remodeled.
Ant. old; obsolete; secondhand.

newcomer *n.* **1 new arrival,** arrival, incomer, immigrant, settler, stranger, outsider, foreigner, alien, intruder, interloper, *inf.* johnny-come-lately.
2 beginner, novice, learner, trainee, probationer, new recruit, raw recruit, tyro, greenhorn, initiate, neophyte.

news *n.* **information,** facts, data, report, story, news item, news flash, account, statement, announcement, press release, communication, communiqué, message, bulletin, dispatch, disclosure, revelation, word, talk, the latest, gossip, rumor, scandal, exposé, *inf.* info, low-down, scuttlebutt, poop, dope.

newspaper *n.* **paper,** gazette, journal, tabloid, daily paper, daily, evening paper, weekly paper, weekly, scandal sheet, *inf.* rag.

next *adj.* **1 following,** succeeding, successive, subsequent, later, ensuing. **2 neighboring,** adjacent, adjoining, bordering, contiguous, closest, nearest, proximate.
▸ *adv.* **then,** later, at a later time, after, afterward, thereafter, subsequently, at a subsequent time, after this/that, after that time.

nice *adj.* **1 good,** pleasant, enjoyable, pleasurable, agreeable, delightful, amusing, satisfying, gratifying, marvelous, likable, charming, amiable, friendly, kindly, genial, gracious, sympathetic, understanding, compassionate, good. **2 polite,** courteous, civil, refined, cultivated, polished, genteel, elegant, seemly, decorous, proper, fitting, suitable, appropriate, respectable, good, virtuous. **3 fine,** ultrafine, subtle, minute, precise, exact, accurate, strict, close, careful, meticulous, rigorous. **4 fine,** dry, sunny, warm, pleasant, agreeable. **5 fastidious,** delicate, refined, dainty, particular, discriminating, overparticular, fussy, finicky, *inf.* persnickety. **6 good,** satisfactory, agreeable, acceptable, commendable, adequate, admirable. *Ant.* unpleasant; nasty; unrefined; rough.

nicety *n.* **1 finer point,** subtlety, nuance, detail. **2 precision,** accuracy, exactness, meticulousness, rigor.

niggardly *adj.* **1 mean,** miserly, stingy, tight-fisted, parsimonious, penny-pinching, avaricious. **2 meager,** paltry, skimpy, scanty, measly, inadequate, insubstantial, miserable, *inf.* piddling. *Ant.* generous; lavish; abundant.

nimble *adj.* **1 agile,** lithe, sprightly, spry, lively, quick, quick-moving, graceful, skillful, deft. **2 quick-thinking,** clever, bright, quick, quick-witted, alert. *Ant.* stiff; clumsy; dull.

nippy *adj.* **icy,** chilly, bitter, raw, piercing, stinging.

no *adv.* **no indeed,** absolutely not, under no circumstances, by no means, never, *inf.* not on your life, no way, nope, no siree. *Ant.* yes; affirmative.

noble *adj.* **1 aristocratic,** patrician, blue-blooded, highborn, titled, landed, born with a silver spoon in one's mouth. **2 noble-minded,** magnanimous, generous, self-sacrificing, honorable, virtuous, brave, righteous, honest, upright, true, loyal, principled, moral, decent, good. **3 lofty,** grand, exalted, elevated. **4 impressive,** magnificent, striking, awesome, stately, grand, dignified. *Ant.* humble; dishonorable; ignoble; base.

nod *v.* **1 incline,** bob, bow, dip, duck, signal, gesture, motion, sign, indicate. **2 doze off,** drop off, fall asleep, nap, slumber.

noise *n.* **sound,** loud sound, din, hubbub, clamor, racket, row, uproar, tumult, commotion, rumpus, pandemonium.

noisy *adj.* **rowdy,** clamorous, boisterous, obstreperous, loud, blaring, blasting, deafening, earsplitting. *Ant.* quiet; soft.

nomad *n.* itinerant, traveler, migrant, wanderer, roamer, rover, transient, vagabond, vagrant, tramp.

nominal *adj.* **1 in name (only)**, titular, formal, theoretical, self-styled, purported, supposed. **2 token**, symbolic, minimal, trivial, insignificant.

nominate *v.* **1 name**, propose, put forward, submit, present, recommend, *inf.* put up. **2 name**, designate, appoint, assign, select, choose.

nonchalant *adj.* **composed**, self-possessed, imperturbable, unexcitable, calm, cool, collected, cool as a cucumber, unconcerned, indifferent, unemotional, blasé, dispassionate, detached, apathetic, casual, offhand, carefree, insouciant, easygoing, careless, *inf.* laid-back. **Ant.** anxious; concerned; excited.

nonplus *v.* **take aback**, stun, dumbfound, confound, astound, astonish, amaze, surprise, disconcert, discomfit, dismay, make one halt in one's tracks, puzzle, perplex, baffle, mystify, stump, confuse, bewilder, embarrass, fluster, *inf.* faze, flummox, floor.

nonsense *n.* **1 rubbish**, balderdash, drivel, gibberish, twaddle, foolishness, folly, silliness, senselessness, stupidity, ridiculousness, ludicrousness, inanity, fatuity, joking, jesting, clowning, buffoonery, drollery, *inf.* tripe, gobbledygook, mumbo-jumbo, poppycock, claptrap, bilge, bull. **2 foolishness**, folly, silliness, senselessness, stupidity, ridiculousness, ludicrousness, inanity, fatuity, joking, jesting, clowning, buffoonery, drollery. **Ant.** sense; wisdom.

nonsensical *adj.* **1 meaningless**, incomprehensible, unintelligible, senseless, incongruous. **2 foolish**, absurd, silly, inane, senseless, stupid, ridiculous, ludicrous, preposterous, harebrained, irrational, idiotic, insane, *inf.* crazy, crackpot, nutty, wacky.

nonstop *adj.* **incessant**, unceasing, ceaseless, constant, continuous, continual, without interruption, unbroken, unfaltering, steady, unremitting, relentless, persistent, endless, never-ending, unending, interminable, *inf.* eternal.
▸ *adv.* **incessantly**, unceasingly, constantly, continuously, continually, steadily, unremittingly, relentlessly, persistently, endlessly.

nook *n.* **corner**, cranny, recess, alcove, niche, opening, cavity, crevice, gap, cubbyhole, inglenook, hideaway, retreat, refuge, shelter, den, *inf.* hide-out.

normal *adj.* **1 usual,** standard, average, common, ordinary, natural, general, commonplace, conventional, typical, regular, routine, run-of-the-mill, everyday, accustomed, habitual, prevailing, popular, accepted, acknowledged. **2 average,** medium, middling, standard, mean. **3 well-adjusted,** well-balanced, rational, compos mentis, sane. *Ant.* abnormal; unusual; irrational.

normally *adv.* **1 as usual,** ordinarily, naturally, conventionally, routinely, typically, regularly. **2 usually,** ordinarily, as a rule, as a general rule, generally, in general, mostly, commonly, habitually.

nose *n.* **1 proboscis,** bill, beak, snout, muzzle, trunk, *inf.* snoot, schnoz. **2 sense of smell,** olfactory sense. **3 instinct,** sixth sense, intuition, insight, perception.
▸ *v.* **1 nudge,** push, nuzzle. **2 pry,** search, peer, prowl, have a good look, *inf.* snoop. **3 ease,** inch, move, run.

nosy *adj.* **prying,** inquisitive, quizzing, probing, eavesdropping, curious, interfering, meddlesome, intrusive, *inf.* snooping, snoopy.

notable *adj.* **noteworthy,** remarkable, outstanding,

important, significant, momentous, memorable, unforgettable, pronounced, marked, striking, impressive, uncommon, unusual, particular, special, extraordinary, conspicuous, rare, signal, noted, of note, distinguished, eminent, preeminent, well-known, prominent, illustrious, great, famous, famed, renowned, celebrated, acclaimed. *Ant.* insignificant; unremarkable; unheard-of; obscure.
▸ *n.* **dignitary,** celebrity, luminary, star, superstar, lion, VIP, *inf.* celeb, megastar, big shot, big name, somebody.

note *n.* **1 record,** account, notation. **2 message,** memorandum, letter, epistle, missive, communication, thank-you note, *inf.* memo. **3 footnote,** annotation, commentary, gloss, marginalia, explanation, explication, exposition, exegesis. **4 notice,** attention, attentiveness, heed, observation, consideration, thought, regard, care, mindfulness. **5 distinction,** eminence, preeminence, illustriousness, greatness, prestige, fame, renown, reputation, acclaim, consequence. **6 tone,** intonation, inflection, sound, indication, hint, element.

▸ *v.* **1 write down,** put down, jot down, mark down, enter, mark, record, register. **2 mention,** make mention of, refer to, allude to, touch on, indicate, point out, make known, state. **3 take note of,** take notice of, see, observe, perceive, behold, detect, take in.

noted *adj.* **of note,** notable, distinguished, eminent, preeminent, well-known, prominent, illustrious, great, famous, famed, renowned, celebrated, acclaimed. ***Ant.*** unknown; unheard-of; obscure.

notice *n.* **1 attention,** attentiveness, heed, note, observation, cognizance, regard, consideration, interest, thought, mindfulness, watchfulness, vigilance. **2 information sheet,** bulletin, poster, handbill, bill, circular, leaflet, pamphlet, advertisement. **3 notification,** apprisal, announcement, intimation, information, intelligence, news, communication, advice, instruction, order, warning. **4 resignation,** dismissal, *inf.* marching orders, walking papers, pink slip, the sack, the boot. **5 review,** write-up, critique.
▸ *v.* **see,** note, take note of, observe, perceive, discern, detect, behold, descry, spot, distinguish,

make out, take heed of, heed, pay attention to, take notice of, mark, regard. ***Ant.*** overlook; ignore; disregard.

noticeable *adj.* **observable,** visible, discernible, perceptible, detectable, distinguishable, distinct, evident, obvious, apparent, manifest, patent, plain, clear, conspicuous, unmistakable, pronounced, striking, blatant. ***Ant.*** imperceptible; unobtrusive.

notify *v.* **inform,** tell, advise, acquaint, apprise, warn, alert, caution.

notion *n.* **1 idea,** belief, opinion, thought, impression, view, conviction, concept, conception, conceptualization, assumption, presumption, hypothesis, theory, postulation, abstraction, apprehension, understanding. **2 impulse,** inclination, fancy, whim, wish, desire, caprice.

notorious *adj.* **1 infamous,** of ill repute, having a bad reputation/ name, ill-famed, disreputable, dishonorable. **2 well-known,** infamous, prominent, scandalous, opprobrious, obloquial, legendary.

nourishing *adj.* **nutritious,** nutritive, wholesome, healthy, health-giving, healthful, beneficial, good for one. ***Ant.*** unhealthy; unwholesome.

nourishment *n.* **food,** nutriment,

nutrition, sustenance, subsistence, aliment, provisions, provender, meat, fare, viands, victuals, daily bread, *inf.* grub, chow, eats.

novel *adj.* **new,** fresh, different, original, unusual, uncommon, unfamiliar, rare, unique, singular, imaginative, unhackneyed, unconventional, creative, innovative, groundbreaking, trailblazing, modern, ultramodern, advanced, futuristic. *Ant.* old; run-of-the-mill; hackneyed; unimaginative.
▸ *n.* **book,** story, tale, narrative, work of fiction.

novice *n.* **1 beginner,** newcomer, apprentice, trainee, learner, probationer, student, pupil, (new) recruit, raw recruit, tyro, initiate, novitiate, neophyte, greenhorn, *inf.* rookie. **2 novitiate,** postulant, neophyte. *Ant.* veteran; expert; professional.

now *adv.* **1 just now,** right now, at present, at the present time, at this time, at the moment, at this moment in time, for the time being, currently, presently. **2 right away,** right now, immediately, at once, straight away, instantly, promptly, without delay. *Ant.* then; later.

noxious *adj.* **nocuous,** noisome, harmful, hurtful, injurious,

damaging, destructive, ruinous, pernicious, malignant, detrimental, deleterious, menacing, threatening, unwholesome, unhealthy, insalubrious, poisonous, toxic. *Ant.* innocuous; safe.

nuance *n.* **shade,** shading, gradation, subtlety, fine distinction, nicety, refinement, degree.

nucleus *n.* **core,** kernel, center, heart, nub, basis, pith, meat, marrow, focus, pivot.

nude *adj.* **in the nude,** naked, stark naked, bare, stripped, exposed, unclothed, undressed, uncovered, au naturel, *inf.* without a stitch on, in one's birthday suit, in the raw, in the altogether, in the buff, naked as the day one was born, buck naked.

nudge *v.* **poke,** jab, prod, dig, jog, elbow, bump, touch, push, shove.
▸ *n.* **poke,** jab, prod, dig, jog, dig in the ribs, elbow, bump, touch, push, shove.

nuisance *n.* **pest,** bother, plague, irritant, source of annoyance, annoyance, vexation, trouble, burden, weight, problem, difficulty, worry, affliction, trial, tribulation, bore, inconvenience, disadvantage, handicap, thorn in the side/flesh, *inf.* drag. *Ant.* help; blessing; advantage.

numb *adj.* **benumbed,** dead, without feeling, sensationless, deadened, insensible, insensate, torpid, dull, anesthetized, drugged, dazed, stunned, stupefied, in shock, paralyzed, immobilized, frozen, chilled. ***Ant.*** sensitive; responsive.

▸ *v.* **benumb,** deaden, dull, anesthetize, drug, daze, stun, stupefy, paralyze, immobilize, freeze, chill.

number *n.* **1 figure,** digit, numeral, cipher, character, symbol, unit, integer, whole number, cardinal number, ordinal number, Roman numeral, Arabic numeral. **2 total,** aggregate, score, tally, count, sum, summation. **3 quantity,** amount, group, collection, company, crowd. **4 edition,** issue, printing, imprint, copy.

▸ *v.* **1 enumerate,** count, add up, total, calculate, compute, reckon, tell, estimate, assess, take stock of. **2 assign a number to,** categorize by number, specify by number. **3 count,** include, reckon. **4 limit,** limit in number, restrict, fix.

numerous *adj.* **many,** very many, innumerable, myriad, multitudinous, several, quite a few, various, diverse, *inf.* a lot of, lots of. ***Ant.*** few; scant.

nurse *v.* **1 take care of,** care for, look after, tend, attend to, minister to, treat, doctor. **2 suckle,** breast-feed, feed, wet-nurse. **3 nurture,** encourage, promote, boost, further, advance, contribute to, assist, help. **4 harbor,** have, hold, entertain, foster, cherish, nourish. ***Ant.*** neglect; hinder.

nurture *v.* **1 feed,** nourish, provide for, care for, take care of, tend, attend to, bring up, rear. **2 educate,** school, train, tutor, coach. **3 encourage,** promote, foster, stimulate, develop, cultivate, boost, further, advance, forward, contribute to, be conducive to, assist, help, aid. ***Ant.*** neglect; hinder.

▸ *n.* **1 food,** nutrition, nutriment, sustenance, subsistence. **2 feeding,** tending, rearing. **3 education,** schooling, training, discipline. **4 encouragement,** promotion, fostering, development, cultivation, boosting, furtherance, advancement.

nutritious *adj.* **nourishing,** nutritive, wholesome, health-giving, healthy, healthful, beneficial, good for one. ***Ant.*** unhealthy; unwholesome.

nuzzle *v.* **1 nose,** nudge, prod, push. **2 snuggle,** cuddle, nestle, lie close to, curl up.

Oo

oaf *n.* **1 lout,** blunderer, bungler, boor, bumpkin, yokel, gorilla, bull in a china shop: *inf.* clodhopper, lummox, galoot. **2 fool,** dolt, blockhead, numskull, dunderhead, dunce, dullard, nincompoop, ninny, simpleton, boob, *inf.* idiot, moron, imbecile, sap, dummy, bonehead, nitwit, dimwit, halfwit, chump, clod, goon, schmuck.

oath *n.* **1 sworn statement,** vow, promise, pledge, avowal, affirmation, attestation, bond, word of honor, word. **2 curse,** swearword, expletive, blasphemy, profanity, imprecation, malediction, obscenity, bad/foul language, strong language, epithet, four-letter word, dirty word, bad word, naughty word, *inf.* cuss.

obedient *adj.* **dutiful,** duteous, law-abiding, rule-abiding, conforming, deferential, respectful, compliant, acquiescent, tractable, amenable, malleable, governable, under control, well-trained, yielding, submissive, docile, meek, subservient, obsequious, servile. ***Ant.*** disobedient; intractable; unruly.

obese *adj.* **overweight,** fat, plump, stout, ample, chubby, tubby, portly, rotund, corpulent, pudgy, paunchy, fleshy, big, heavy, on the heavy side, large, bulky, chunky, outsize, massive, gross. ***Ant.*** thin; skinny.

obey *v.* **1 abide by,** comply with, adhere to, observe, conform to, respect, acquiesce in, consent to, agree to, follow. **2 perform,** carry out, execute, put into effect, fulfill, act upon. **3 be dutiful to,** do as/what someone says, follow the orders of, carry out the orders of, heed, be regulated by, be governed by. ***Ant.*** disobey; ignore; defy.

object *n.* **1 thing,** something, anything, body, entity, phenomenon, article, item, device, gadget, *inf.* thingamajig, thingamabob, doodad, whatsit, what's-its-name, what-d'you-call-it, whatchamacallit, thingy. **2 subject,** subject matter, substance, issue, concern. **3 focus,** target, recipient, butt, victim. **4 objective,** aim, goal, target, end.

▸ v. **raise objections,** protest, lodge a protest, demur, beg to differ, be in opposition, remonstrate, expostulate, take exception, argue against, oppose, be in opposition to, remonstrate against, complain about. **Ant.** approve; accept.

objection n. **protest,** protestation, demurral, opposition, remonstration, remonstrance, expostulation, complaining about, dissatisfaction with, disapproval of, argument, counterargument, doubt, complaint, grievance, scruple, qualm. **Ant.** approval; acceptance.

objectionable adj. **offensive,** obnoxious, unpleasant, disagreeable, unacceptable, nasty, disgusting, repulsive, repellent, abhorrent, repugnant, revolting, loathsome, nauseating, hateful, detestable, reprehensible, deplorable, insufferable, intolerable, despicable, contemptible, odious, vile, obscene, foul, horrible, horrid, noxious. **Ant.** pleasant; agreeable; acceptable.

objective adj. **unbiased,** bias-free, unprejudiced, prejudice-free, impartial, neutral, uninvolved, nonpartisan, disinterested, detached, dispassionate, unswayed, evenhanded, equitable, fair, just, open-minded. **Ant.** biased; partial; subjective.

▸ n. **object,** aim, goal, target, end, end in view, ambition, aspiration, intent, intention, purpose, idea, point, desire, hope, design, plan, scheme, plot.

obligatory adj. **1 binding,** valid, legal, in force, effective. **2 compulsory,** enforced, prescriptive, mandatory, necessary, essential, required, requisite, imperative, de rigueur, unavoidable, unescapable. **Ant.** voluntary; optional.

oblige v. **1 put under an obligation,** leave someone no option, require, necessitate, obligate, compel, call for, force, constrain, press, pressure, pressurize, impel. **2 do someone a favor,** do someone a kindness, do someone a service, serve, accommodate, meet the wants/needs of, help accommodate, put oneself out for, indulge, gratify the wishes of, help, assist.

obliging adj. **helpful,** eager to help/please, accommodating, willing, complaisant, indulgent, friendly, kind, generous, considerate, cooperative, neighborly, agreeable, pleasant, good-natured, amiable, civil, courteous, polite. **Ant.** disobliging; obstructive; discourteous.

oblique *adj.* **1 slanting,** slanted, sloping, sloped, inclined, at an angle, angled, tilted, listing, diagonal, catercornered, *inf.* kitty-corner. **2 indirect,** implied, roundabout, circuitous, circumlocutory, ambagious, evasive, backhanded. *Ant.* straight; direct.
‣ *n.* **stroke,** solidus, slanting line, slant, slash, back slash.

obliterate *v.* **1 erase,** eradicate, efface, blot out, rub out, wipe out, expunge, sponge out, delete, cross out, strike out, blue-pencil, remove, cancel. **2 destroy,** exterminate, annihilate, wipe out, eliminate, eradicate, extirpate, decimate, liquidate, demolish. *Ant.* create; establish.

oblivious *adj.* **absentminded,** abstracted, distrait, preoccupied, absorbed, faraway. *Ant.* aware; conscious; attentive.

obscene *adj.* **1 indecent,** pornographic, blue, off-color, risqué, lewd, salacious, smutty, lecherous, lascivious, licentious, prurient, lubricious, ribald, scatological, scabrous, bawdy, suggestive, vulgar, dirty, filthy, foul, coarse, gross, vile, nasty, offensive, immoral, impure, immodest, shameless, unchaste, improper, unwholesome, erotic, carnal, sexy, *inf.* raunchy.

2 atrocious, heinous, vile, foul, outrageous, shocking, repugnant, repulsive, revolting, nauseating, sickening, wicked, evil, odious. *Ant.* decent; pure; proper.

obscenity *n.* **1 indecency,** lewdness, salaciousness, smuttiness, lechery, lasciviousness, licentiousness, prurience, lubricity, ribaldry, scatalogy, scabrousness, bawdiness, suggestiveness, vulgarity, dirt, dirtiness, filth, filthiness, foulness, coarseness, grossness, vileness, nastiness, immorality, impurity, immodesty, shamelessness, unchasteness, impropriety, unwholesomeness, eroticism, carnality, sexiness. **2 atrocity,** heinousness, vileness, foulness, repugnance, wickedness, evil. **3 curse,** oath, swearword, expletive, imprecation, blasphemy, bad/foul language, strong language, epithet, profanity, four-letter word, dirty word, bad word, naughty word, *inf.* cuss, cussword.

obscure *adj.* **1 unclear,** indeterminate, opaque, abstruse, recondite, unexplained, concealed, hidden, arcane, enigmatic, deep, cryptic, mysterious, puzzling, perplexing, confusing, intricate, involved, unfathomable, incomprehensible,

impenetrable, vague, indefinite, hazy, uncertain, doubtful, dubious, ambiguous, equivocal. **2 indistinct,** vague, shadowy, hazy, blurred, fuzzy, cloudy, dark, dim, black, unlit, murky, somber, gloomy, shady. **3 unknown,** unheard-of, out-of-the-way, off the beaten track, remote, hidden, secluded, godforsaken, little-known, unknown, unheard-of, undistinguished, insignificant, inconspicuous, minor, unimportant, unrenowned, unrecognized, unhonored, unsung, inglorious. **Ant.** clear; plain; distinct; famous.
▸ *v.* **1 confuse,** blur, muddle, complicate, make abstruse, obfuscate, garble, cloud, muddy, conceal, hide, veil. **2 hide,** conceal, cover, veil, screen, mask, cloak, shroud, block, block out, eclipse, adumbrate. **3 darken,** blacken, dim, bedim. **Ant.** clarify; reveal; brighten.

obsequious *adj.* **servile,** subservient, submissive, slavish, menial, abject, fawning, groveling, cringing, toadying, truckling, sycophantic, ingratiating, unctuous, oily, *inf.* bootlicking, Uriah Heepish. **Ant.** proud; arrogant.

observant *adj.* **1 alert,** sharp-eyed, sharp, eagle-eyed, attentive, vigilant, wide-awake, watchful, heedful, on the qui vive, on the lookout, on guard, mindful, intent, aware, conscious, with one's eyes peeled, *inf.* not missing a thing/trick, on the ball. **2 dutiful,** obedient, conforming, law-abiding, orthodox, practicing. **Ant.** inattentive; dreamy; unobservant; negligent.

observation *n.* **1 seeing,** noticing, watching, viewing, eyeing, witnessing, scrutiny, scrutinization, watch, monitoring, surveillance, inspection, attention, consideration, study, review, examination. **2 finding,** result, information, datum, remark, comment, note, annotation, report, description, opinion, thought, reflection. **3 remark,** comment, statement, utterance, pronouncement, declaration.

observe *v.* **1 see,** catch sight of, notice, note, perceive, discern, detect, espy, behold, watch, view, spot, witness, *inf.* get a load of. **2 keep under observation,** watch, keep watch on, look at, keep under surveillance, keep in sight, keep in view, spy upon, monitor, reconnoiter, scan, keep under scrutiny, scrutinize, inspect, study, review, examine, check, *inf.* keep an eye on, keep tabs on.

3 say, remark, comment, state, utter, enunciate, exclaim, announce, declare, pronounce.
4 keep, obey, adhere to, abide by, heed, follow, comply with, conform to, acquiesce in, consent to, accept, respect, defer to.
5 carry out, perform, execute, discharge, fulfill. **6 celebrate,** keep, recognize, commemorate, mark, remember, solemnize. *Ant.* overlook; ignore; disobey.

observer *n.* **watcher,** looker-on, onlooker, witness, eyewitness, spectator, bystander, beholder, viewer, commentator, reporter, sightseer, spotter, *inf.* rubberneck.

obsess *v.* **preoccupy,** haunt, monopolize, have a hold on, possess, consume, engross, have a grip on, grip, dominate, rule, control, be on one's mind, be uppermost in one's mind, prey on, plague, torment, hound, bedevil.

obsession *n.* **preoccupation,** fixation, idée fixe, ruling/ consuming passion, mania, enthusiasm, infatuation, compulsion, phobia, complex, fetish, craze, *inf.* bee in one's bonnet, hang-up, issue, thing. *Ant.* indifference; unconcern.

obsessive *adj.* **excessive,** overdone, consuming, compulsive, besetting, gripping, haunting.

obsolete *adj.* **no longer in use,** in disuse, disused, outworn, discarded, discontinued, extinct, bygone, outmoded, démodé, passé, antiquated, out of date, outdated, out, superannuated, old-fashioned, out of fashion, out of style, behind the times, old, dated, antique, archaic, ancient, antediluvian, time-worn, past its prime, having seen better days, *inf.* old hat. *Ant.* current; modern; up-to-date.

obstacle *n.* **bar,** barrier, obstruction, impediment, hindrance, hurdle, barricade, blockade, stumbling block, block, blockage, curb, check, stop, stoppage, deterrent, balk, snag, difficulty, catch, drawback, hitch, interference, interruption, fly in the ointment. *Ant.* help; advantage; encouragement.

obstinate *adj.* **stubborn,** stubborn as a mule, mulish, pigheaded, headstrong, willful, self-willed, strong-minded, perverse, refractory, recalcitrant, contumacious, unmanageable, firm, steadfast, unyielding, inflexible, unbending, immovable, intransigent, intractable, uncompromising, persistent, persevering, pertinacious, tenacious, dogged, single-minded, relentless, unrelenting. *Ant.* compliant; amenable; flexible; tractable.

obstruct *v.* **1 block,** barricade, bar, cut off, shut off, choke, clog (up), dam up. **2 hold up,** bring to a standstill, stop, halt, block, prohibit, hinder, impede, hamper, interfere with, interrupt, hold up, frustrate, thwart, balk, inhibit, curb, brake, bridle, hamstring, encumber, restrain, slow, retard, delay, arrest, check, restrict, limit. *Ant.* clear; advance; facilitate; help.

obtain *v.* **1 get,** get hold of, acquire, come by, procure, secure, gain, earn, take possession of, get one's hands on, seize, grab, pick up. **2 be in force,** be in use, be effective, exist, stand, prevail, hold, be the case, reign, rule, hold sway. *Ant.* lose; give up (see give); relinquish.

obtrusive *adj.* **1 noticeable,** conspicuous, obvious, unmistakable, blatant, flagrant, bold, audacious, intrusive. **2 forward,** interfering, meddling, prying, intrusive, officious, importunate, *inf.* pushy, nosy. *Ant.* unobtrusive; restrained; retiring.

obtuse *adj.* **stupid,** dull, dull-witted, slow-witted, slow, uncomprehending, unintelligent, imperceptive, bovine, stolid, insensitive, thick-skinned, *inf.*

dim, dense, thick, dim-witted, slow on the uptake, boneheaded, dumb, dopey. *Ant.* bright; clever.

obvious *adj.* **clear,** clear-cut, crystal-clear, plain, visible, noticeable, perceptible, discernible, detectable, recognizable, evident, apparent, manifest, distinct, palpable, patent, conspicuous, unconcealed, overt, pronounced, transparent, prominent, unmistakable, indisputable, undeniable, as plain as the nose on one's face, staring someone in the face, *inf.* sticking out like a sore thumb, sticking out a mile. *Ant.* imperceptible; inconspicuous; obscure.

occasion *n.* **1 time,** juncture, point, situation, instance, case, circumstance. **2 event,** incident, occurrence, happening, episode, affair, experience. **3 function,** party, affair, celebration, *inf.* get-together, do. **4 opportunity,** golden opportunity, chance, opening, contingency. **5 reason,** cause, grounds, justification, call, excuse, inducement.
▸ *v.* **cause,** give rise to, bring about, result in, lead to, prompt, provoke, produce, create, generate, engender, originate, effect.

occasional *adj.* **infrequent,** intermittent, irregular, sporadic, odd, rare, casual, incidental. *Ant.* regular; habitual.

occasionally *adv.* **now and then,** now and again, from time to time, sometimes, at times, every so often, once in a while, on occasion, periodically, at intervals, irregularly, sporadically, infrequently, intermittently, on and off, off and on.

occupation *n.* **1 job,** work, profession, business, employment, employ, career, calling, métier, vocation, trade, craft, line, field, province, area. **2 occupancy,** tenancy, tenure, residence, inhabitancy, habitation, possession, holding. **3 possession,** foreign rule, invasion, seizure, takeover, conquest, capture, overthrow, subjugation, subjection.

occupy *v.* **1 live in,** inhabit, reside in, dwell in, be the tenant of, tenant, have one's residence/ abode in, make one's home in, stay in. **2 fill,** fill up, take up, use up, utilize, cover. **3 hold,** be in, fill, have, *inf.* hold down. **4 engage,** employ, absorb, engross, preoccupy, immerse, interest, involve, entertain, divert, amuse, beguile. **5 take possession of,** invade, overrun, seize, take over, capture, garrison. *Ant.* leave; abandon; quit.

occur *v.* **1 happen,** take place, come about, come to pass, materialize, transpire, arise, crop up, turn up, befall, eventuate. **2 be found,** be met with, be, exist, have its being, appear, present itself, show itself, manifest itself, arise, spring up. **3 come to mind,** spring to mind, come to one, enter one's head, cross one's mind, strike one, hit one, dawn on, suggest itself.

occurrence *n.* **1 happening,** event, incident, circumstance, affair, episode, proceeding, adventure. **2 existence,** appearance, manifestation, materialization, springing up.

odd *adj.* **1 strange,** eccentric, queer, peculiar, idiosyncratic, unconventional, outlandish, droll, weird, bizarre, offbeat, freakish, whimsical, *inf.* wacky, freaky, kinky, off-the-wall. **2 unusual,** uncommon, irregular, strange, peculiar, funny, curious, queer, abnormal, atypical, different, out-of-the-ordinary, exceptional, rare, extraordinary, remarkable, singular, deviant, aberrant, freak, freakish, bizarre, weird. **3 occasional,** casual, temporary, part-time, seasonal, periodic, irregular, miscellaneous, various, varied, random, haphazard, chance, fortuitous, fragmentary, various, sundry. **4 unmatched,** unpaired, leftover, spare, remaining, surplus, superfluous, lone, single, solitary, sole. ***Ant.*** ordinary; usual; regular.

odious *adj.* **abhorrent,** repugnant, disgusting, repulsive, repellent, revolting, foul, vile, unpleasant, disagreeable, loathsome, detestable, hateful, despicable, contemptible, objectionable, offensive, horrible, horrid, abominable, heinous, atrocious, execrable. ***Ant.*** delightful; pleasant; agreeable.

odor *n.* **1 aroma,** smell, scent, perfume, fragrance, bouquet, redolence, essence, stench, stink. **2 atmosphere,** air, ambience, aura, spirit, quality, flavor, emanation.

offend *v.* **1 give offense to,** hurt the feelings of, wound, be an affront to, affront, upset, displease, annoy, anger, incense, exasperate, vex, pique, put out, gall, irritate, provoke, ruffle, disgruntle, rankle with, outrage, insult, slight, humiliate, *inf.* rile, rattle, put someone's back up, tread/step on someone's toes. **2 cause offense to,** be offensive to, displease, upset, be disagreeable to, put someone off, be distasteful to, repel, disgust, revolt, nauseate, *inf.* turn someone off. **3 commit a crime,** break the law, do wrong, sin, go astray, fall from grace, err, transgress. ***Ant.*** please; delight.

offender *n.* **wrongdoer,** culprit, criminal, lawbreaker, miscreant, delinquent, sinner, transgressor, malefactor.

offense *n.* **1 crime,** illegal act, breaking of the law, breach/violation/infraction of the law, wrongdoing, wrong, misdemeanor, act of misconduct, misdeed, peccadillo, sin, transgression, act of dereliction, shortcoming, fault, lapse, *Law* malfeasance. **2 affront,** injury, hurt, source of harm, outrage, atrocity, insult, injustice, indignity, slight, snub. **3 annoyance,** anger, indignation, exasperation, wrath, ire, displeasure, disapproval, dislike, animosity, resentment, pique, vexation, umbrage, antipathy, aversion, opposition, enmity. **4 attack,** assault, act of aggression, aggression, onslaught, offensive, thrust, charge, sortie, sally, invasion, incursion.

offensive *adj.* **1 hurtful,** wounding, abusive, affronting, displeasing, annoying, exasperating, vexing, galling, irritating, provocative, provoking, objectionable, outrageous,

insulting, humiliating, rude, discourteous, uncivil, impolite, unmannerly, impertinent, insolent, disrespectful.
2 disagreeable, unpleasant, nasty, foul, vile, objectionable, odious, abominable, detestable, loathsome, repugnant, disgusting, obnoxious, repulsive, repellent, nauseating, sickening, unpalatable, distasteful, unsavory, noisome, *inf.* horrid, yucky.
3 attacking, on the attack, assaulting, invading, invasive, aggressive, combative, martial, warlike, belligerent, bellicose, hostile, *inf.* on the warpath. ***Ant.*** complimentary; pleasant; defensive.
▸ *n.* **attack,** assault, onslaught, drive, invasion, push, thrust, charge, sortie, sally, act of war, incursion.
offer *v.* **1 put forward,** propose, advance, submit, propound, suggest, recommend, make a motion of, put to the motion, move. **2 volunteer one's services,** volunteer, offer one's service, offer assistance/help, be at someone's service, be at someone's disposal, make oneself available, show readiness/ willingness to help. **3 afford,** provide, supply, give, furnish, make available, present, give an

opportunity for, put up for sale, put on the market, ask for bids on/for, put in an offer of, bid, put in a bid of, offer to buy at. **4 offer up,** sacrifice. **5 arrive,** appear, happen, occur, come on the scene, present itself, show itself. **6 attempt,** try, essay, show, give. ***Ant.*** withdraw; refuse; withhold.
▸ *n.* **1 proposal,** proposition, suggestion, submission, approach, overture. **2 bid,** bidding price. **3 attempt,** endeavor, essay.
offering *n.* **1 contribution,** donation, subscription, gift, present, alms, charity, handout. **2 sacrifice,** oblation, immolation.
offhand *adj.* **casual,** unceremonious, cavalier, careless, indifferent, perfunctory, cursory, uninterested, unconcerned, blasé, curt, abrupt, terse, brusque, discourteous, uncivil, impolite, rude, *inf.* off, couldn't-care-less, take-it-or-leave-it. ***Ant.*** careful; thorough.
▸ *adv.* **1 casually,** unceremoniously, cavalierly, perfunctorily, cursorily, unconcernedly, curtly, abruptly, discourteously, rudely.
2 extempore, impromptu, ad lib, extemporaneously, without preparation, without consideration, without rehearsal, spontaneously, *inf.* off the cuff, off

the top of one's head, just like that.

office *n.* **1 place of business,** base, workplace, workroom, room. **2 post,** position, appointment, role, place, situation, station, work, employment, business, duty, function, responsibility, obligation, charge, tenure, job, task, chore, assignment, commission, routine.

official *adj.* **1 authorized,** accredited, approved, validated, authenticated, certified, endorsed, sanctioned, licensed, recognized, accepted, legitimate, legal, lawful, bona fide, proper, ex cathedra, *inf.* kosher. **2 formal,** ceremonial, solemn, conventional, ritualistic, pompous, *inf.* stuffed-shirt. **Ant.** unofficial; unauthorized; informal.
▸ *n.* **1 officer,** officeholder, office-bearer, administrator, executive. **2 officer,** representative, agent.

officiate *v.* **1 take charge,** be in charge, preside, take the chair. **2 be in charge of,** be responsible for, chair, preside over, manage, oversee, superintend, conduct, run, operate.

officious *adj.* **overzealous,** overbusy, bustling, interfering, intrusive, meddlesome, meddling, prying, inquisitive, importunate, forward, obtrusive, self-important, opinionated, dictatorial, domineering, *inf.* pushy, nosy.

offset *v.* **counterbalance,** counterpoise, counteract, countervail, balance, balance out, cancel out, neutralize, compensate for, make up for, make good, indemnify.

offshoot *n.* **1 side shoot,** shoot, sprout, branch, bough, limb, twig, sucker, tendril, runner, scion, spur. **2 descendant,** scion, relation, relative, kin. **3 branch,** subsidiary, adjunct, appendage. **4 result,** outcome, aftermath, consequence, upshot, product, by-product, spin-off, ramification.

offspring *n.* **child,** children, family, progeny, young, youngster(s), issue, descendant(s), heir(s), successor(s), spawn, *inf.* kid(s), young 'un(s). **Ant.** parent; ancestor; forebear.

often *adv.* **frequently,** many a time, on many occasions, repeatedly, again and again, time and again, time and time again, time after time, over and over, over and over again, day in (and) day out, *lit.* oft, oft-times, *inf.* a lot. **Ant.** seldom; rarely.

oily *adj.* **1 oil-containing,** oleaginous, greasy, fatty, buttery, swimming in oil/fat. **2 smooth,**

smooth-talking, honey-tongued, flattering, fulsome, glib, suave, urbane, unctuous, subservient, servile, oleaginous.

ointment *n.* **medicated cream/ lotion,** emollient, salve, balm, liniment, embrocation, unguent, gel.

old *adj.* **1 older,** mature, elderly, aged, advanced in years, up in years, getting on, gray-haired, grizzled, hoary, past one's prime, ancient, decrepit, senescent, senile, venerable, senior, *inf.* past it, over the hill, long in the tooth. **2 worn,** worn-out, cast-off, shabby, torn, tattered, ragged, old-fashioned, out of date, outmoded, démodé, dilapidated, broken-down, rundown, tumbledown, ramshackle, decaying, crumbling, disintegrating. **3 out of date,** outdated, old-fashioned, outmoded, passé, archaic, obsolete, extinct, antiquated, antediluvian, superannuated, *inf.* old hat. **4 of old,** olden, bygone, past, early, earlier, earliest, primeval, primordial, prehistoric. **5 age-old,** long-standing, long-lived, long-established, time-honored, enduring, lasting. **6 antique,** veteran, vintage. **7 mature,** wise, sensible, experienced, knowledgeable, well-versed, practiced, skilled, skillful,

adept. **8 ex-,** former, previous, one-time, sometime, erstwhile, *lit.* quondam. ***Ant.*** young; new; modern.

old-fashioned *adj.* **old,** former, out of fashion, outmoded, démodé unfashionable, out of style, out of date, outdated, dated, behind the times, past, bygone, passé, archaic, obsolescent, obsolete, ancient, antiquated, superannuated, antediluvian, old-fogeyish, old-fangled, *inf.* old hat, not with it. ***Ant.*** modern; up-to-date; fashionable.

omen *n.* **portent,** sign, token, foretoken, harbinger, premonition, forewarning, warning, foreshadowing, prediction, forecast, prophecy, augury, straw in the wind, writing on the wall, auspice, presage, presentiment, feeling, vague feeling, foreboding, misgiving, *inf.* funny feeling, feeling in one's bones.

ominous *adj.* **1 threatening,** menacing, minatory, black, dark, gloomy, heavy, sinister, bad, unpromising, unpropitious, pessimistic, inauspicious, unfavorable, unlucky, ill-fated. **2 oracular,** augural, divinatory, prophetic, premonitory, prognostic, sibyllic. ***Ant.*** promising; auspicious; propitious.

omission *n.* **1 leaving out,** exclusion, exception, noninclusion, deletion, erasure, elimination, expunction, oversight, gap, lacuna. **2 neglect,** neglectfulness, negligence, dereliction, forgetfulness, oversight, disregard, nonfulfillment, default, failure. *Ant.* addition; inclusion.

omit *v.* **1 leave out,** exclude, except, miss out, miss, fail to mention, pass over, drop, delete, erase, eliminate, expunge, rub out, cross out, *inf.* give something a miss. **2 forget,** neglect, fail, leave undone, overlook, skip. *Ant.* add; include.

omnipotent *adj.* **all-powerful,** almighty, supreme, preeminent, invincible.

onerous *adj.* **burdensome,** heavy, crushing, backbreaking, oppressive, weighty, arduous, strenuous, difficult, hard, formidable, laborious, exhausting, tiring, exigent, taxing, demanding, exacting, wearing, wearisome, fatiguing. *Ant.* easy; effortless.

ongoing *adj.* **1 in progress,** current, extant, progressing, advancing, successful, developing, evolving, growing. **2 continuous,** continual, uninterrupted, unbroken, nonstop, incessant, unending, constant.

onset *n.* **1 onslaught,** assault, attack, charge, onrush. **2 start,** beginning, commencement, inception, outbreak, *inf.* kickoff. *Ant.* retreat; end.

onslaught *n.* **assault,** attack, charge, onrush, onset, storming, sortie, sally, raid, foray, push, thrust, drive, blitz.

onus *n.* **burden,** weight, load, responsibility, liability, obligation, duty, charge, encumbrance, cross to bear, millstone around one's neck, albatross.

open *adj.* **1 unlocked,** unbolted, unlatched, unbarred, unfastened, unsecured, ajar, wide open, agape, gaping, yawning. **2 uncovered,** coverless, unlidded, topless, unsealed. **3 unenclosed,** unfenced, exposed, unsheltered, wide, wide open, extensive, broad, spacious, sweeping, airy, uncrowded, uncluttered, undeveloped. **4 unobstructed,** unblocked, clear, passable, navigable. **5 spread out,** unfolded, unfurled, unrolled, straightened out, extended, stretched out. **6 openwork,** full of holes, honeycombed, lacy, filigree, airy, cellular, porous, spongy. **7 frank,** candid, honest, forthright, direct,

blunt, plainspoken, downright.
8 public, general, nonexclusive, accessible, nonrestrictive, unrestricted, nondiscriminatory.
9 vacant, available, unfilled, unoccupied, free. **10 obvious,** clear, noticeable, visible, apparent, evident, manifest, overt, conspicuous, patent, unconcealed, unhidden, undisguised, blatant, flagrant.
11 available, on hand, obtainable, accessible. **12 open to debate,** open for discussion, yet to be decided, undecided, unresolved, unsettled, arguable, debatable, moot. **13 unbiased,** prejudice-free, unprejudiced, nonpartisan, impartial, nondiscriminatory, objective, disinterested, dispassionate, detached. **14 frank,** honest, artless, natural, simple, guileless, ingenuous, innocent. **Ant.** shut; closed; secretive; biased.
▸ *v.* **1 throw open,** unlock, unbolt, unlatch, unbar, unfasten.
2 unwrap, undo, untie, unseal.
3 uncork, broach, crack. **4 open up,** come apart, split, separate, rupture. **5 open for business,** open the/one's doors, begin business, set up shop, put up one's shingle, start, begin, commence, start the ball rolling, *inf.* kick off. **6 lay bare,** bare,

uncover, expose, exhibit, disclose, divulge, pour out. **Ant.** close; shut.
opening *n.* **1 gap,** aperture, space, hole, orifice, vent, slot, break, breach, crack, split, fissure, cleft, crevice, chink, interstice, rent, rupture. **2 vacancy,** position, job, opportunity, chance. **3 beginning,** start, commencement, outset, inception, launch, birth, dawn, *inf.* kickoff. **4 opening ceremony,** official opening, launch. **Ant.** closure; close; end; termination.
operate *v.* **1 work,** function, go, run, perform, act, be in action.
2 work, make go, run, use, utilize, employ, handle, manipulate, maneuver, ply, manage, be in charge of. **3 perform an operation,** perform surgery, *inf.* put under the knife. **Ant.** break down (see break); fail.
operational *adj.* operative, workable, in operation, working, in working order, functioning, functional, going, in use, usable, in action, ready for action. **Ant.** broken; out of order.
operative *adj.* **1 in operation,** in force, effective, valid.
2 operational, workable, working, functioning, functional, usable.
3 key, relevant, significant, crucial, vital, important, essential. **Ant.** invalid; out of order; irrelevant.

▸ *n.* **1 worker,** workman, machinist, operator, mechanic, factory hand/employee. **2 agent,** secret agent, undercover agent, spy, double agent, detective, private detective, private investigator, sleuth, *inf.* private eye, dick, gumshoe, *inf.* mole.

opinion *n.* **point of view,** view, viewpoint, belief, thought, thinking, way of thinking, standpoint, theory, judgment, estimation, feeling, sentiment, impression, notion, assumption, conception, conviction, persuasion, creed, dogma.

opponent *n.* **opposer,** the opposition, rival, adversary, fellow contestant, fellow competitor, enemy, foe, antagonist, contender, dissenter, disputant. *Ant.* ally; partner; colleague.

opportune *adj.* **advantageous,** favorable, auspicious, propitious, good, lucky, happy, timely, well-timed, fortunate, providential, felicitous, convenient, expedient, suitable, apt, fitting, relevant, applicable, pertinent. *Ant.* disadvantageous; unfavorable; inconvenient.

opportunity *n.* **lucky chance,** chance, good time, golden opportunity, favorable time/occasion/moment, right set of circumstances, appropriate time/moment, *inf.* break.

oppose *v.* **1 dislike,** disapprove of, be hostile to, take a stand against, be/stand against, stand up to, stand up and be counted against, take issue with, take on, contradict, counter, argue against, counterattack, confront, resist, withstand, defy, fight, put up a fight against, combat, fly in the face of. **2 compare,** contrast, juxtapose, offset, balance, counterbalance, set against, pit against, parallel. *Ant.* support; defend; promote.

opposite *adj.* **1 facing,** face-to-face with, *inf.* eyeball to eyeball with. **2 diametrically opposed,** opposing, differing, different, unlike, contrary, reverse, contradictory, conflicting, clashing, discordant, dissident, at variance, incompatible, irreconcilable, antipathetical, poles apart. *Ant.* same; identical; like.

▸ *n.* **reverse,** contrary, antithesis, converse, inverse, contradiction, the other extreme, the other side of the coin.

opposition *n.* **1 dislike,** disapproval, hostility, resistance, defiance. **2 opponent,** opposing side, other side, other team, rival, adversary, competition, antagonist, enemy, foe.

oppress *v.* **1 overwhelm,** overpower, subjugate, enslave, suppress, crush, subdue, quash, quell, bring someone to his/her knees, tyrannize, repress, abuse, maltreat, persecute, rule with a rod of iron, trample on, trample underfoot, ride roughshod over. **2 weigh down,** lie heavy on, weigh heavy on, burden, crush, depress, dispirit, dishearten, take the heart out of, discourage, sadden, make despondent, deject, desolate.

oppressed *adj.* **1 tyrannized,** subjugated, enslaved, crushed, subdued, repressed, persecuted, abused, maltreated, misused, browbeaten, downtrodden, disadvantaged, underprivileged. **2 weighed down,** depressed, dispirited, despondent, dejected, desolate.

oppression *n.* **1 overwhelming,** subjugation, subduing, tyranny, suppression, abuse, persecution, despotism, maltreatment, cruelty, brutality, injustice, ruthlessness, harshness, hardship, misery, suffering, wretchedness. **2 depression,** despondency, dejection, desolation.

oppressive *adj.* **1 tyrannical,** despotic, draconian, iron-fisted, high-handed, repressive, domineering, harsh, crushing, cruel, brutal, ruthless, relentless, merciless, pitiless, inexorable, unjust, undemocratic. **2 muggy,** close, airless, stuffy, stifling, suffocating, sultry, torrid. *Ant.* lenient; humane; fresh.

oppressor *n.* **tyrant,** despot, autocrat, subjugator, persecutor, bully, iron hand, slave driver, taskmaster, scourge, dictator, tormentor, torturer.

optimistic *adj.* **1 disposed to look on the bright side,** always expecting the best, inclined to look through rose-colored glasses, hopeful, full of hope, Pollyannaish, Panglossian. **2 positive,** sanguine, hopeful, confident, bullish, cheerful, buoyant, *inf.* upbeat. *Ant.* pessimistic; gloomy.

optimum *adj.* **1 most favorable,** best, most advantageous, most appropriate, ideal, perfect. **2 peak,** top, best, perfect, ideal, flawless, superlative, optimal, *inf.* tip-top, A-1.

option *n.* **1 choice,** freedom of choice, power to choose, right to choose. **2 choice,** alternative, other possibility, preference.

optional *adj.* **noncompulsory,** not required, voluntary, up to the individual, discretionary, at one's discretion, elective. *Ant.*

compulsory; obligatory;
mandatory.

opulent *adj.* **1 affluent,** wealthy,
rich, well-off, well-to-do,
moneyed, prosperous, *inf.* well-
heeled, rolling in it. **2 luxurious,**
sumptuous, lavishly appointed,
inf. plush, plushy, ritzy.
3 abundant, superabundant,
copious, plentiful, profuse,
prolific, luxuriant. ***Ant.*** penniless;
poor; sparse.

orbit *n.* **1 revolution,** circle, circuit,
cycle, rotation, circumgyration,
path, course, track, trajectory.
2 sphere, sphere of influence,
range, reach, scope, ambit, sweep,
domain.
  ▸ *v.* **revolve around,** circle around,
go/sail/fly around, encircle,
circumnavigate.

ordeal *n.* **trial,** test, tribulation,
painful/disturbing experience,
suffering, affliction, distress,
agony, anguish, torture, torment,
calamity, trouble, nightmare. ***Ant.***
bliss; pleasure.

order *n.* **1 orderliness,** neatness,
tidiness, trimness, harmony,
apple-pie order. **2 method,**
organization, system, plan,
uniformity, regularity, symmetry,
pattern. **3 condition,** state, shape,
situation. **4 arrangement,**
grouping, system, systemization,
organization, form, structure,
disposition, classification,
categorization, codification,
series, sequence, progression,
succession, layout, setup.
5 command, direction, directive,
instruction, behest, decree, edict,
injunction, law, rule, regulation,
mandate, ordinance, stipulation,
dictate, say-so. **6 law,** lawfulness,
law and order, discipline, control,
peace, calm, quiet, quietness,
peace and quiet, tranquillity.
7 request, call, requirement,
requisition, demand, booking,
reservation, commission,
notification, application. **8 rank,**
class, caste, grade, level, degree,
position, station, grouping,
grading, ranking, system, class
system, caste system, hierarchy,
pecking order, taxonomic group.
9 kind, sort, type, variety, genre,
nature. **10 brotherhood,**
sisterhood, community. **11 lodge,**
society, secret society, guild, club,
association, league, union,
fellowship, fraternity,
confraternity, sorority,
brotherhood, sisterhood, sodality.
12 procedure, correct procedure,
standard procedure, ruling. ***Ant.***
disorder; chaos; disarray.
  ▸ *v.* **1 command,** instruct, direct,
bid, enjoin, decree, ordain, rule,
legislate, enjoin, prescribe,
pronounce. **2 put in an order for,**

place an order for, request, call for, requisition, make one's requirements/demands known for, book, reserve, contract for, apply for, send away for. **3 put in order,** set in order, organize, systematize, methodize, arrange, dispose, lay out, marshal, group, classify, catalog, codify, tabulate, put/set to rights, sort out, tidy up, regulate.

orderly *adj.* **1 in order,** neat, tidy, trim, shipshape, shipshape and Bristol fashion, in Bristol fashion, in apple-pie order. **2 organized,** well-organized, well-regulated, methodical, systematic, systematized, efficient, businesslike. **3 well-behaved,** law-abiding, nonviolent, disciplined, quiet, peaceful, controlled, restrained. *Ant.* disorderly; untidy; unruly.

ordinary *adj.* **1 usual,** normal, standard, typical, stock, common, customary, habitual, accustomed, wonted, everyday, quotidian, regular, routine, established, settled, fixed, prevailing, humdrum, run-of-the-mill, conventional, average, commonplace, workaday, unremarkable, unexceptional, unmemorable, pedestrian, prosaic, unpretentious, modest, plain, simple, humble, prosaic,

uninteresting, dull, uninspired, unimaginative, hackneyed, stale, undistinguished, unexceptional, mediocre, indifferent, second-rate. **2 average,** run-of-the-mill, pedestrian, prosaic, uninteresting, dull, uninspired, unimaginative, hackneyed, stale, undistinguished, unexceptional, unremarkable, mediocre, indifferent, second-rate. *Ant.* unusual; extraordinary; unique.

organization *n.* **1 establishment,** development, assembly, arrangement, regulation, coordination, systematization, methodization, categorization, administration, running, management. **2 structure,** system, whole, unity, organism, setup. **3 company,** firm, concern, operation, corporation, institution, group, consortium, conglomerate, combine, syndicate, federation, confederation, association, body.

organize *v.* **establish,** set up, form, lay the foundations of, found, institute, create, originate, begin, start, develop, build, frame, construct, assemble, structure, shape, mold, put together, arrange, dispose, regulate, marshal, put in order, put straight, coordinate, systematize, methodize, standardize, collocate, group, sort, sort out, classify, categorize, catalog, codify, tabulate, be responsible for, be in charge of, take care of, administrate, run, manage, lick/knock into shape, see to. *Ant.* destroy; jumble; disarrange.

orifice *n.* **opening,** hole, vent, aperture, gap, space, breach, break, rent, slot, slit, cleft, cranny, fissure, crevice, rift, crack, chink.

origin *n.* **1 source,** derivation, root, roots, provenance, etymology, genesis, etiology. **2 source,** basis, base, wellspring, spring, wellhead, fountainhead, fountain, genesis, fons et origo. **3 birth,** dawn, dawning, beginning, start, commencement, emergence, inception, launch, creation, early stages, inauguration, foundation. **4 descent,** ancestry, pedigree, lineage, heritage, parentage, extraction, beginnings. *Ant.* end; death; demise.

original *adj.* **1 aboriginal,** indigenous, early, earliest, first, initial, primary, primordial, primal, primeval, primitive, autochthonal, autochthonous. **2 innovative,** innovatory, inventive, new, novel, fresh, creative, imaginative, resourceful, individual, ingenious, unusual, unconventional, unorthodox, unprecedented, groundbreaking. **3 genuine,** authentic, archetypal, prototypical, master. *Ant.* last; unoriginal; derivative.
▶ *n.* **1 original work/painting,** archetype, prototype, master. **2 standout,** paragon, nonpareil, exemplar, one of a kind, nonesuch, ne plus ultra, individualist, eccentric, nonconformist.

originate *v.* **1 arise,** rise, flow, emanate, issue, have its origin, stem, spring, result, derive, start, begin, commence. **2 give birth to,** be the father/mother of, set in motion, set up, invent, dream up, conceive, discover, initiate, create, formulate, inaugurate, pioneer, introduce, establish, found, evolve, develop, generate. *Ant.* terminate; destroy.

ornament *n.* **knickknack,** trinket, bauble, gewgaw, accessory, decoration, frill, whatnot, doodad, decoration, adornment, embellishment, trimming, garnish, garnishing, jewel, gem.

ornamental *adj.* **decorative,** decorated, ornate, ornamented, embellished, embroidered, fancy, fanciful.

ornate *adj.* **elaborate,** overelaborate, decorated,

embellished, adorned, ornamented, fancy, fussy, busy, ostentatious, showy, baroque, rococo, flowery, florid, flamboyant, labored, strained, stilted, pretentious, high-flown, high-sounding, grandiose, pompous, orotund, magniloquent, grandiloquent, oratorical, bombastic, *inf.* highfalutin, flashy. **Ant.** plain; austere; simple.

orthodox *adj.* **1 conformist,** doctrinal, of the faith, of the true faith, sound, conservative, correct, faithful, true, true-blue, devoted, strict, devout. **2 conventional,** accepted, approved, correct, proper, conformist, established, traditional, prevailing, customary, usual, regular, standard, comme il faut, de rigueur. **Ant.** unorthodox; nonconformist; unconventional.

ostensible *adj.* **outward,** apparent, seeming, professed, alleged, claimed, purported, pretended, feigned, specious, supposed.

ostentation *n.* **showiness,** show, conspicuousness, obtrusiveness, loudness, extravagance, flamboyance, gaudiness, flashiness, pretentiousness, affectation, flaunting, exhibitionism, vulgarity, bad taste, *inf.* showing off.

ostentatious *adj.* **showy,** conspicuous, obtrusive, loud, extravagant, flamboyant, gaudy, flashy, pretentious, affected, overdone, overelaborate, vulgar, kitsch. **Ant.** plain; unobtrusive; subdued.

ostracize *v.* **give someone the cold shoulder,** send to Coventry, exclude, shut out, bar, keep at arm's length, shun, spurn, avoid, boycott, repudiate, cast out, reject, blackball, blacklist, banish, exile, expel, excommunicate, debar, leave out in the cold. **Ant.** welcome; accept; fraternize.

other *adj.* **1 different,** unlike, variant, dissimilar, disparate, distinct, separate, alternative. **2 more,** additional, further, extra, supplementary.

outbreak *n.* **1 eruption,** flare-up, upsurge, outburst, sudden appearance, start, rash. **2 epidemic,** pandemic, plague.

outburst *n.* **burst,** explosion, eruption, outbreak, flare-up, access, attack, fit, spasm, paroxysm.

outcome *n.* **consequence,** result, end result, sequel, upshot, issue, product, conclusion, aftereffect, aftermath, wake, *inf.* payoff.

outdated *adj.* **out of date,** out of

style, out of fashion, old-fashioned, unfashionable, outmoded, dated, démodé, passé, behind the times, antiquated, archaic, *inf.* old hat, not with it. *Ant.* current; modern; fashionable.

outdo *v.* **surpass,** top, exceed, excel, get the better of, outstrip, outshine, eclipse, overshadow, transcend, outclass, outdistance, overcome, beat, defeat, outsmart, outmaneuver, *inf.* be a cut above, be head and shoulders above, run rings around, outfox.

outer *adj.* **1 outside,** outermost, outward, exterior, external, surface, superficial. **2 outlying,** distant, remote, faraway, peripheral, fringe, perimeter. *Ant.* inner; inside; interior.

outgoing *adj.* **1 extrovert,** extroverted, unreserved, demonstrative, affectionate, warm, friendly, genial, cordial, affable, hail-fellow-well-met, sociable, communicative, open, expansive, talkative, gregarious, approachable, easygoing, easy. **2 retiring,** departing, leaving, withdrawing. *Ant.* reserved; introverted; withdrawn; incoming.

outlandish *adj.* **strange,** unfamiliar, unknown, unheard-of, odd, unusual, extraordinary, peculiar, queer, curious, singular, eccentric, quaint, bizarre, grotesque, preposterous, fantastic, outré, weird, *inf.* freaky, wacky, far-out, off-the-wall. *Ant.* ordinary; commonplace; conventional.

outline *n.* **1 draft,** rough draft, rough, sketch, tracing, skeleton, framework, layout, diagram, plan, design, schema. **2 thumbnail sketch,** rough idea, quick rundown, abbreviated version, summary, synopsis, résumé, précis, main points, bones, bare bones. **3 contour,** silhouette, profile, lineaments, delineation, configuration, perimeter, circumference.
▸ *v.* **1 sketch,** delineate, trace, silhouette. **2 sketch out,** give a thumbnail sketch of, give a rough idea of, give a quick rundown on, summarize, précis.

outlook *n.* **1 view,** point of view, viewpoint, perspective, attitude, frame of mind, standpoint, slant, angle, interpretation, opinion. **2 view,** vista, prospect, panorama, aspect.

outlying *adj.* **outer,** outermost, out-of-the-way, remote, distant, faraway, far-flung, peripheral, isolated, inaccessible, off the beaten path/track, backwoods.

output *n.* **production,** product,

amount/quantity produced, productivity, yield, harvest, achievement, accomplishment.

outrage *n.* **1 atrocity,** act of violence, evil, act of wickedness, crime, horror, enormity, brutality, barbarism, inhumane act. **2 offense,** affront, insult, injury, abuse, indignity, scandal, desecration, violation. **3 anger,** fury, rage, indignation, wrath, annoyance, shock, resentment, horror, amazement.

▸ *v.* **anger,** infuriate, enrage, incense, make someone's blood boil, madden, annoy, shock, horrify, amaze, scandalize, offend, insult, affront, vex, distress.

outrageous *adj.* **1 intolerable,** insufferable, insupportable, unendurable, unbearable, impossible, exasperating, offensive, provocative, maddening, distressing. **2 atrocious,** heinous, abominable, wicked, vile, foul, monstrous, horrible, horrid, dreadful, terrible, horrendous, hideous, ghastly, unspeakable, gruesome. **3 immoderate,** excessive, exorbitant, unreasonable, preposterous, scandalous, shocking, *inf.* steep. **Ant.** acceptable; mild; moderate.

outside *adj.* **1 outer,** outermost,

outward, exterior, external. **2 outdoor,** out-of-doors. **3 unlikely,** improbable, slight, slender, slim, small, faint, negligible, marginal, remote, distant, vague. **Ant.** inside; inner; interior.

▸ *adv.* **outdoors,** out of doors, out of the house.

outsider *n.* **alien,** stranger, foreigner, outlander, immigrant, emigrant, émigré, incomer, newcomer, parvenu, arriviste, interloper, intruder, gatecrasher, outcast, misfit, odd man out.

outskirts *pl. n.* **vicinity,** neighborhood, environs, edges, outlying districts, fringes, margin, periphery, borders, boundary, suburbs, suburbia, purlieus.

outspoken *adj.* **candid,** frank, forthright, direct, straightforward, straight-from-the-shoulder, plain, plainspoken, explicit, blunt, brusque, unequivocal, unreserved, unceremonious. **Ant.** diplomatic; reticent; evasive.

outstanding *adj.* **1 preeminent,** eminent, well-known, notable, noteworthy, distinguished, important, famous, famed, renowned, celebrated, great, excellent, remarkable, exceptional, superlative. **2 striking,** impressive, eye-catching, arresting, memorable, remarkable. **3 unpaid,** unsettled, owing, due. **4 to be done,** unfinished, remaining, pending, ongoing. *Ant.* unexceptional; mediocre; complete.

outwardly *adv.* **1 externally,** on the outside. **2 on the surface,** superficially, on the face of it, to all appearances, to the eye, as far as one can see, to all intents and purposes, apparently, evidently.

outwit *v.* **get the better of,** outsmart, outmaneuver, trick, dupe, *inf.* outfox.

overall *adj.* **comprehensive,** universal, all-embracing, inclusive, all-inclusive, general, sweeping, complete, blanket, umbrella, global.
▸ *adv.* **on the whole,** in general, generally speaking.

overawe *v.* **intimidate,** daunt, disconcert, abash, dismay, frighten, alarm, scare, terrify, terrorize.

overcome *v.* **conquer,** defeat, vanquish, beat, be victorious over, gain a victory over, prevail over, get the better of, triumph over, best, worst, trounce, rout, gain mastery over, master, overpower, overwhelm, overthrow, subdue, subjugate, quell, quash, crush, *inf.* lick, clobber, whip, wipe (up) the floor with, blow out of the water, surmount, rise above.

▸ *adj.* **overwhelmed,** emotional, moved, affected, speechless, at a loss for words, *inf.* bowled over.

overdue *adj.* **1 late,** not on time, behind schedule, behindhand, delayed, belated, tardy, unpunctual. **2 unpaid,** owed, owing, outstanding, unsettled, in arrears.

overflow *v.* **1 flow over,** run over, spill over, brim over, well over, pour forth, stream forth, discharge, surge, debouch. **2 flood,** deluge, inundate, submerge, cover, swamp, engulf, drown, soak, drench, saturate.
▸ *n.* **excess,** overspill, spill, spillage, flood, flooding, inundation, surplus.

overhead *adv.* **above,** up above, high (up), up in the sky, on high, aloft.
▸ *n.* **expenses,** expenditure, outlay, disbursement, running cost(s), operating cost(s).

overlook *v.* **1 fail to notice/ observe/spot,** miss, leave, neglect to notice, leave unnoticed, *inf.* slip up on. **2 leave undone,** ignore, disregard, omit, neglect, forget, ignore, not take into consideration, take no notice of, let something pass, turn a blind eye to, wink at, blink at, excuse, pardon, forgive, condone, let someone off with, *inf.* let something ride. **3 deliberately ignore,** not take into consideration, disregard, take no notice of, let something pass, turn a blind eye to, wink at, blink at, excuse, pardon, forgive, condone, let someone off with, *inf.* let something ride. **4 look over,** look onto, front onto, open out over, have a view of, afford a view of, command a view of. *Ant.* spot; note; punish.

overpowering *adj.* **1 overwhelming,** burdensome, weighty, unbearable, unendurable, intolerable, shattering, *inf.* mind-blowing. **2 overstrong,** suffocating, stifling, nauseating. **3 compelling,** forceful, telling, irrefutable, undeniable, unquestionable, indisputable, incontestable, incontrovertible. *Ant.* mild; slight.

overriding *adj.* **most important,** predominant, principal, primary, paramount, chief, main, major, foremost, central, focal, pivotal, *inf.* number one. *Ant.* insignificant; irrelevant.

oversight *n.* **1 carelessness,** inattention, neglect, inadvertence, laxity, dereliction, omission, mistake, error, blunder, gaffe, fault, slip, lapse, *inf.* slipup, goof, booboo. **2 supervision,** surveillance, superintendence, charge, care, administration, management, direction, control, handling.

overt *adj.* **obvious,** noticeable, observable, visible, undisguised, unconcealed, apparent, plain, plainly seen, plain to see, manifest, patent, open, public, blatant, conspicuous. *Ant.* hidden; surreptitious; covert.

overtake *v.* **1 pass,** get/go past, go by, overhaul, leave behind, outdistance, outstrip, go faster than. **2 befall,** happen to, come upon, hit, strike, fall upon, overwhelm, engulf, take by surprise, surprise, catch unawares, catch unprepared, catch off guard.

overthrow *v.* **1 cause the downfall of,** remove from office, overturn, depose, oust, unseat, dethrone, disestablish, conquer, vanquish, defeat, beat, rout, trounce, best, worst, subjugate, crush, quash, quell, overcome, overwhelm, overpower. **2 throw over,** turn over, overturn, tip over, topple over, upset, capsize, knock over, upturn, upend, invert.
▸ *n.* **downfall,** deposition, ousting, defeat, vanquishing, rout, subjugation, crushing, overwhelming, overturning.

overtone *n.* **hidden meaning,** secondary meaning, implication, innuendo, hint, suggestion, insinuation, association, connotation, undercurrent, nuance, flavor, coloring.

overwhelm *v.* **1 overcome,** move, make emotional, daze, dumbfound, shake, take aback, leave speechless, stagger, *inf.* bowl over, knock for a loop, blow one's mind, flabbergast. **2 inundate,** flood, deluge, engulf, submerge, swamp, bury, overload, overburden, snow under. **3 overcome,** overpower, conquer, vanquish.

overwhelming *adj.*
1 uncontrollable, irrepressible, irresistible, overpowering.
2 profuse, enormous, immense, inordinate, massive, huge, stupendous, prodigious, staggering, shattering, vast, massive, great, large, *inf.* mind-boggling, mind-blowing.

owe *v.* **be in debt to,** be indebted to, be in arrears to, be under an obligation to, be obligated to, be beholden to.

own *adj.* **personal,** individual, particular, private.

Pp

pace *n.* **1 step,** stride. **2 gait,** walk, tread. **3 speed,** swiftness, fastness, quickness, rapidity, velocity, tempo, *inf.* clip. **4 rate of progress,** tempo, momentum, measure.

pacify *v.* **calm,** calm down, placate, conciliate, propitiate, appease, mollify, soothe, tranquilize, quieten.

pack *n.* **1 bundle,** parcel, bale, truss, *inf.* bindle. **2 bag,** backpack, rucksack, knapsack, haversack, duffel bag, kitbag. **3 packet,** container, package, carton. **4 herd,** drove, flock, troop. **5 gang,** crowd, mob, group, band, company, troop, set, clique, *inf.* crew, bunch. **6 great deal,** collection, parcel, assortment, mass, assemblage, bunch, *inf.* load, heap.
▸ *v.* **1 fill,** load, bundle, stuff, cram. put, place, store, stow. **2 package,** parcel, wrap, wrap up, box, bale, cover, protect. **3 fill,** crowd, throng, mob, cram, jam, press into, squeeze into, crowd, cram, jam, squeeze, press. **4 compact,** compress, press, tamp, ram. *Ant.* unpack.

packed *adj.* **full,** filled, filled to capacity, crowded, thronged, mobbed, crammed, jammed, packed like sardines, overfull, overloaded, brimful, chock-full, chockablock, *inf.* jam-packed.

pact *n.* **agreement,** treaty, deal, contract, settlement, bargain, compact, covenant, bond, concordat, entente, protocol.

pad *n.* **1 padding,** wadding, wad, stuffing, buffer. **2 cushion,** pillow, bolster. **3 gauze pad,** piece/wad of cotton wool, dressing, compress. **4 notepad,** writing pad, notebook, *inf.* memo pad. **5 paw,** foot, sole.
▸ *v.* **pack,** stuff, line, cushion, protect.

paddle *n.* **oar,** scull, sweep.
▸ *v.* **row,** pull, oar, scull, pole, punt.

paddock *n.* **field,** meadow, enclosure, yard, pen, pound, corral.

pagan *n.* **unbeliever,** nonbeliever, disbeliever, heathen, infidel, idolater, pantheist, atheist, polytheist.
▸ *adj.* **paganistic,** paganish, heathen, heathenish, heathenistic, infidel, idolatrous, pantheistic, atheistic, polytheistic. *Ant.* religious; godly.

pageantry *n.* **pageant**, display, spectacle, magnificence, pomp, splendor, grandeur, glamour, flourish, glitter, theatricality, show, showiness, *inf.* pizzazz.

pain *n.* **1 soreness**, hurt, ache, aching, throb, throbbing, smarting, twinge, pang, spasm, cramp, discomfort, irritation, tenderness. **2 suffering**, agony, affliction, torture, torment, hurt, sorrow, grief, heartache, brokenheartedness, sadness, unhappiness, distress, misery, wretchedness, anguish, woe. **3 nuisance**, pest, bother, vexation, source of irritation, worry, source of aggravation, *inf.* pain in the neck/butt, drag.
▸ *v.* **1 cause pain**, be painful, hurt, be sore, ache, throb, smart, twinge, cause discomfort, be tender. **2 hurt**, grieve, sadden, distress, make miserable/wretched, cause anguish to, afflict, torment, torture, worry, trouble, vex, embarrass.

pained *adj.* **hurt**, aggrieved, reproachful, offended, insulted, vexed, piqued, upset, unhappy, distressed, wounded, *inf.* miffed.

painful *adj.* **1 sore**, hurting, aching, throbbing, smarting, cramped, tender, inflamed, irritating, agonizing, excruciating. **2 disagreeable**, unpleasant, nasty, distressing, disquieting, disturbing, miserable, wretched, agonizing, harrowing, irksome, tedious, annoying, vexatious. **3 arduous**, laborious, strenuous, rigorous, demanding, exacting, trying, hard, tough, difficult. **Ant.** painless; pleasant; agreeable.

painless *adj.* **1 pain-free. 2 easy**, simple, trouble-free, effortless, *inf.* as easy as pie, as easy as falling off a log, as easy as ABC, a piece of cake, child's play, a cinch.

painstaking *adj.* **1 careful**, thorough, assiduous, conscientious, meticulous, punctilious, sedulous, scrupulous, searching, attentive, diligent, industrious, hardworking, persevering, pertinacious. **2 careful**, thorough, assiduous, attentive, diligent, industrious, hardworking, conscientious, meticulous, punctilious, sedulous, scrupulous, persevering, pertinacious. **Ant.** careless; negligent; slapdash.

painting *n.* **picture**, illustration, portrayal, depiction, delineation, representation, likeness, drawing, sketch, portrait, landscape, seascape, still life, oil painting, gouache, watercolor, *inf.* oil.

pair *n.* **1 twosome**, two, couple, duo, married couple, couple, man and wife, husband and wife,

partners, lovers. **2 brace,** couple.
3 matched set, matching set.
4 team, yoke, span, two horses.
palatable *adj.* **1 tasty,** appetizing,
pleasant-tasting, flavorful,
flavorsome, delicious, delectable,
mouthwatering, savory, luscious,
toothsome, *inf.* scrumptious,
yummy. **2 agreeable,** pleasant,
pleasing, pleasurable, nice,
attractive, acceptable, satisfactory.
Ant. unpalatable; tasteless;
insipid; unpleasant.

palatial *adj.* **luxurious,** deluxe,
imposing, splendid, grand,
magnificent, stately, majestic,
opulent, sumptuous, plush, *inf.*
plushy, posh. *Ant.* humble;
modest; cramped.

pale *adj.* **1 white,** whitish, white-
faced, colorless, anemic, wan,
drained, pallid, pasty, peaky,
ashen, ashy, waxen, green, as
white as a sheet/ghost, deathly
pale. **2 light,** light-colored, pastel,
muted, low-key, restrained, faded,
bleached, whitish, washed-out,
etoliated. **3 dim,** faint, weak,
feeble, thin. *Ant.* flushed; dark;
bright.
 ▸ *v.* **1 grow pale,** become pale,
go/turn white, blanch, lose color.
2 pale into insignificance, fade,
dim, diminish, lessen, decrease in
importance, lose significance.

pallid *adj.* **1 pale,** white, whitish,

white-faced, colorless, anemic,
wan, drained, pasty, peaked,
ashen, ashy, waxen, sickly,
ghostly, ghastly, lurid, green, as
white as a sheet/ghost, deathly
pale, like death, *inf.* like death
warmed over. **2 colorless,**
uninteresting, dull, boring,
tedious, unimaginative, lifeless,
uninspired, spiritless, bloodless,
bland, vapid. *Ant.* flushed; vivid.

palpable *adj.* **1 tangible,** feelable,
touchable, solid, concrete.
2 obvious, apparent, clear, plain,
evident, manifest, visible,
conspicuous, patent, blatant,
glaring, definite, unmistakable.
Ant. intangible; unobtrusive.

paltry *adj.* **1 small,** meager,
trifling, minor, insignificant,
trivial, derisory, *inf.* piddling.
2 mean, low, base, worthless,
despicable, contemptible,
miserable, wretched, sorry. *Ant.*
considerable; substantial;
impressive.

pamper *v.* **spoil,** cosset, indulge,
overindulge, humor, coddle,
mollycoddle, baby, wait on
someone hand and foot, cater to
someone's every whim,
featherbed.

pamphlet *n.* **leaflet,** booklet,
brochure, circular, flyer.

panache *n.* **dash,** flourish,

flamboyance, élan, style, verve, zest, brio, éclat, *inf.* pizzazz.

panic *n.* **alarm,** fright, fear, terror, horror, trepidation, nervousness, agitation, hysteria, perturbation, dismay, disquiet.

▸ *v.* **1 be alarmed,** take fright, be filled with fear, be scared, be terrified/horrified, be agitated, be hysterical, lose one's nerve, overreact, be perturbed, be filled with dismay, go to pieces, *inf.* lose one's cool, get/go into a tizzy, run around like a chicken with its head cut off. **2 alarm,** frighten, scare, terrify, petrify, startle, agitate, unnerve.

panoramic *adj.* **1 wide,** extensive, sweeping, bird's-eye. **2 wide,** wide-ranging, extensive, comprehensive.

pant *v.* **1 breathe heavily,** puff, huff and puff, blow, gasp, wheeze. **2 long,** yearn, pine, ache, hunger, thirst, burn, *inf.* have a yen.

▸ *n.* **puff,** gasp, wheeze.

paper *n.* **1 newspaper,** magazine, journal, gazette, tabloid, scandal sheet, daily, weekly, *inf.* rag. **2 legal paper,** document, certificate, record, deed, instrument, assignment. **3 essay,** assignment, article, work, dissertation, treatise, thesis, monograph, study, report,

analysis. **4 wallpaper,** wall covering, shelf paper.

▸ *v.* **wallpaper,** line, decorate.

parade *n.* **1 march,** procession, progression, cavalcade, spectacle, pageant, array. **2 display,** exhibition, show, spectacle, flaunting, ostentation, demonstration, *inf.* showing-off.

▸ *v.* **1 march,** go in columns, file by. **2 display,** exhibit, show, demonstrate, air, make a show of, flaunt, strut, swagger, *inf.* show off. **3 strut,** swagger.

paradox *n.* **contradiction,** self-contradiction, inconsistency, incongruity, anomaly, enigma, puzzle, absurdity, oxymoron.

paradoxical *adj.* **contradictory,** self-contradictory, inconsistent, incongruous, anomalous, enigmatic, puzzling, absurd.

parallel *adj.* **1 side by side,** equidistant, collateral. **2 similar,** like, resembling, analogous, comparable, equivalent, corresponding, matching, duplicate. **3 concurrent,** coexistent, coexisting. *Ant.* different; divergent.

▸ *n.* **1 analog,** counterpart, equivalent, correspondent, match, duplicate, equal. **2 similarity,** likeness, resemblance, analogy, correspondence, comparison, equivalence, symmetry.

paralysis *n.* **1 immobility,** powerlessness, numbness, palsy, incapacity, debilitation, *Med.* paresis. **2 immobilization,** breakdown, shutdown, stopping, stoppage, halt, standstill.

paralyze *v.* **immobilize,** render/ make powerless, numb, deaden, dull, obtund, incapacitate, debilitate, disable, cripple, bring to a halt, bring to a complete stop, bring to a grinding halt, bring to a standstill, freeze, put out of order/commission, unnerve, terrify, shock, stun.

parameter *n.* **limit,** value, variable, limitation, limiting factor, restriction, constant, specification, guidelines, framework.

parched *adj.* **1 dried up,** dried out, dry, baked, burned, scorched, seared, desiccated, dehydrated, withered, shriveled. **2 thirsty,** dehydrated, *inf.* dry. *Ant.* sodden; soaking.

pardon *n.* **1 forgiveness,** forbearance, indulgence, condonation, clemency, lenience, leniency, mercy. **2 reprieve,** release, acquittal, absolution, amnesty, exoneration, exculpation.
▶ *v.* **1 forgive,** excuse, condone, let off. **2 reprieve,** release, acquit,

absolve, exonerate, exculpate. *Ant.* blame; punish.

pardonable *adj.* **forgivable,** excusable, allowable, condonable, understandable, minor, slight, venial.

parentage *n.* **family,** birth, origins, extraction, ancestry, lineage, descent, heritage, pedigree.

parliament *n.* **legislature,** assembly, lawmaking body, congress, senate, chamber, house, convocation, diet.

parody *n.* **1 burlesque,** lampoon, satire, pastiche, caricature, mimicry, takeoff, *inf.* spoof, send-up. **2 travesty,** poor imitation, misrepresentation, perversion, corruption.
▶ *v.* **burlesque,** lampoon, satirize, caricature, mimic, take off, *inf.* send up.

parry *v.* **1 ward off,** fend off, stave off, turn aside, avert, deflect, block, rebuff, repel, repulse, hold at bay. **2 avoid,** dodge, evade, elude, steer clear of, sidestep, circumvent, fight shy of, *inf.* duck.

part *n.* **1 portion,** division, section, segment, bit, piece, fragment, scrap, slice, fraction, chunk, wedge. **2 component,** bit, constituent, element, module. **3 organ,** member, limb. **4 section,** area, region, sector, quarter,

territory, neighborhood.
5 volume, book, section, episode.
6 function, role, job, task, work,
chore, responsibility, capacity,
participation, duty, charge. **7 role,**
character, lines, words, script,
lyrics. ***Ant.*** whole; entirety.
▸ *v.* **1 divide (in two),** separate,
split (in two), break up, sever,
disjoin, cleave. **2 separate,** seek/
get a separation, split up, break
up, part company, go their (etc.)
separate ways, divorce, get
divorced, seek/get a divorce.
3 take one's departure, take one's
leave, leave, go, go away, say
goodbye/farewell/adieu, say one's
goodbyes, separate, *inf.* split, push
off, hit the road. ***Ant.*** gather; join;
marry; arrive.
partial *adj.* **1 part,** in part, limited,
incomplete, imperfect,
fragmentary. **2 biased,** prejudiced,
partisan, colored, one-sided,
discriminatory, preferential,
interested, unjust, unfair,
inequitable. ***Ant.*** complete;
whole; unbiased; impartial.
participate *v.* **take part,** join,
engage, play a part, contribute, be
associated, associate oneself, be
involved in, share, partake.
participation *n.* part,
contribution, association,
involvement, partaking.
particle *n.* **1 tiny bit,** tiny piece,

speck, spot, mote, atom,
molecule. **2 iota,** jot, whit, grain,
bit, scrap, shred, morsel, mite,
atom, hint, touch, trace,
suggestion.
particular *adj.* **1 specific,**
individual, single, distinct,
precise. **2 special,** especial,
singular, peculiar, exceptional,
unusual, uncommon, notable,
noteworthy, remarkable,
outstanding. **3 fastidious,**
discriminating, selective, fussy,
painstaking, meticulous,
punctilious, exacting, demanding,
critical, overparticular, finicky, *inf.*
persnickety, choosy, picky.
4 detailed, exact, precise, faithful,
close, thorough, blow-by-blow,
itemized, circumstantial,
painstaking, meticulous,
punctilious, minute. ***Ant.*** general;
ordinary; careless.
particularly *adv.* **1 especially,**
specially, singularly, peculiarly,
distinctly, markedly,
exceptionally, unusually,
uncommonly, notably,
remarkably, outstandingly,
surprisingly. **2 in particular,**
specifically, explicitly, expressly,
specially, especially.
partisan *n.* **1 supporter,**
adherent, devotee, backer,
champion, upholder, follower,
disciple, fan, votary. **2 guerrilla,**

resistance fighter, underground fighter.

▸ *adj.* **biased,** prejudiced, colored, one-sided, discriminatory, preferential, partial, interested, unjust, unfair, inequitable. ***Ant.*** impartial; unbiased.

partition *n.* **1 division,** dividing, subdivision, separation, segregation, splitting-up, breaking-up, breakup, severance. **2 divider,** dividing wall, separator, screen, barrier, wall, fence.

▸ *v.* **divide (up),** separate, segregate, split up, break up, sever, subdivide, separate, separate off, screen off, wall off, fence off.

partly *adv.* **in part,** partially, not wholly, not fully, half, somewhat, to a certain extent/degree, to some extent/degree, in some measure, fractionally, slightly.

partnership *n.* **1 association,** cooperation, collaboration, alliance, union, fellowship, companionship, consociation. **2 collaboration,** collusion, connivance, conspiracy. **3 company,** firm, corporation, cooperative, conglomerate, combine, syndicate.

party *n.* **1 social gathering,** social function, gathering, function, reception, celebration, festivity, soirée, orgy, bacchanal, *inf.* get-together, do, bash, shindig. **2 group,** band, company, body, squad, team, crew, contingent, detachment, unit, *inf.* bunch. **3 political party,** alliance, affiliation, association. **4 side,** grouping, faction, camp, set, caucus. **5 person,** individual, human being, somebody, someone, *inf.* character. **6** *Legal* **litigant,** plaintiff, defendant.

pass[1] *v.* **1 go,** move, proceed, progress, drive, run, travel, roll, flow, course. **2 go past,** move past, go ahead of, get ahead of, go by, overtake, outstrip, outdistance. **3 go over,** go across, get across, get through, cross, traverse. **4 hand over,** let someone have, give, transfer. **5 be passed on,** be left, be handed down, be transferred, be made over, be turned over, be signed over, go, devolve. **6 go by,** proceed, progress, advance, roll by, slip by, glide by, flow by, elapse. **7 spend,** occupy, fill, take up, use, employ, while away. **8 exceed,** surpass, transcend. **9 go,** go unheeded, go unnoticed, go unremarked, go undisputed, go uncensored. **10 get a passing grade (in),** get through, be successful in, succeed in, meet the requirements of, pass muster in, *inf.* come up to scratch in, come up to snuff in. **11 let**

through, declare acceptable/ adequate/satisfactory, declare successful, accept, approve. **12 vote for,** accept, approve, adopt, authorize, ratify, sanction, validate, legalize. **13 pronounce,** utter, express, deliver, declare. **14 happen,** occur, take place, come about, befall, supervene. **15 blow over,** run its course, ebb, die out, fade, fade away, evaporate, draw to a close, disappear, finish, end, terminate. **16 discharge,** excrete, eliminate, evacuate, expel, emit.
▸ *n.* **1 warrant,** permit, authorization, license, passport, visa, safe-conduct, exeat. **2 warrant,** permit, free ticket, free admission, complimentary ticket, reduced ticket; *inf.* freebie. **3 sexual advance,** advance, sexual overture, sexual approach/ suggestion; *inf.* proposition.

pass2 *n.* **narrow road,** gap, gorge, defile, col, canyon.

passable *adj.* **1 adequate,** all right, tolerable, fair, acceptable, satisfactory, mediocre, middling, ordinary, average, run-of-the-mill, moderately good, not too bad, unexceptional, indifferent, *inf.* so-so, OK, okay, nothing to write home about. **2 crossable,** traversable, navigable, unblocked, unobstructed, open, clear.

passage *n.* **1 passing,** progress, advance, process, flow, course, journey, voyage, transit, trek, crossing, trip, tour. **2 access,** entry, admission, leave to travel in, permission to pass through, safe-conduct, warrant, passport, visa. **3 change,** changeover, transformation, transition, conversion, shift, switch. **4 road,** route, path, way, track, trail, lane, channel, course, conduit. **5 passageway,** corridor, hall, hallway, entrance hall, entrance, vestibule, lobby. **6 extract,** excerpt, quotation, citation, section, verse. **7 acceptance,** approval, adoption, authorization, ratification, sanction, validation, enactment, legalization.

passerby *n.* **bystander,** onlooker, witness, spectator, *inf.* rubberneck, rubbernecker.

passion *n.* **1 intensity,** fervor, fervidness, ardor, zeal, vehemence, fire, emotion, feeling, zest, enthusiasm, eagerness, excitement, animation. **2 rage,** blind rage, fit of rage, fit of anger, fit of temper, temper, towering rage, outburst of anger, tantrum, fury, frenzy, paroxysm. **3 love,** sexual love, desire, sexual desire, lust, concupiscence, ardor, infatuation, adoration.

4 enthusiasm, fascination, keen interest, obsession, fixation, craze, mania. **5 idol,** hero/heroine, heart's desire, obsession, preoccupation.

passionate *adj.* **1 impassioned,** intense, fervent, fervid, ardent, zealous, vehement, fiery, emotional, heartfelt, zestful, enthusiastic, eager, excited, animated. **2 ardent,** aroused, desirous, hot, sexy, amorous, sensual, erotic, lustful, *inf.* turned-on. **3 enraged,** furious, angry, hot-tempered, frenzied, violent, wild, tempestuous. *Ant.* apathetic; frigid.

passive *adj.* **1 inactive,** nonactive, inert, nonparticipating, uninvolved. **2 unresisting,** nonresistant, unassertive, yielding, submissive, compliant, pliant, acquiescent, quiescent, resigned, obedient, tractable, malleable. **3 impassive,** emotionless, unmoved, unresponsive, undemonstrative, dispassionate, detached, distant, remote, aloof, indifferent. *Ant.* active; assertive; emotional.

past *adj.* **1 gone by,** gone, bygone, elapsed, over, over and done with, ended, former, long ago. **2 recent,** preceding, last, latter, foregone, former, previous, prior, foregoing, late, erstwhile, one-time, sometime, ex-. *Ant.* present; future.

pastel *adj.* **pale,** soft, delicate, muted, subdued, faint, low-key. *Ant.* dark; bright; rich; vivid.

pastime *n.* **hobby,** leisure activity, sport, game, recreation, diversion, amusement, entertainment, distraction, relaxation.

pastoral *adj.* **1 rural,** country, rustic, simple, idyllic, innocent, Arcadian, agricultural, bucolic, georgic. **2 ministerial,** vicarial, parsonical, priestly, rectorial, ecclesiastical, clerical.

pasture *n.* **pasturage,** pasture land, grassland, grass, field, grazing land, meadowland, meadow, *lit.* lea.

patch *n.* **1 piece of cloth,** piece of material. **2 cover,** covering, pad, shield. **3 plot,** area, piece, lot, tract, parcel. **4 period,** time, spell, stretch, interval, term.
▸ *v.* **cover,** mend, repair, sew, sew up, stitch, stitch up, fix.

patent *n.* **license,** copyright, registered trademark.
▸ *adj.* **1 obvious,** clear, plain, evident, apparent, manifest, transparent, conspicuous, blatant, glaringly obvious, unmistakable, unconcealed. **2 patented,** proprietary, licensed, branded, brand-name. *Ant.* unobtrusive; inconspicuous.

path *n.* **1 pathway,** footpath, track, trail, walk, walkway. **2 course,** route, circuit, track, orbit, trajectory. **3 course of action,** route, procedure, direction, approach, method, system, strategy. **4 way,** road, avenue, route.

pathetic *adj.* **1 pitiful,** pitiable, piteous, to be pitied, moving, touching, poignant, affecting, distressing, heartbreaking, heart-rending, sad, wretched, mournful, woeful. **2 pitiful,** lamentable, deplorable, miserable, wretched, feeble, woeful, sorry, poor, contemptible, inadequate, unsatisfactory, worthless. *Ant.* comical; cheerful; admirable; excellent.

pathological *adj.* **1 morbid,** diseased. **2 irrational,** compulsive, obsessive, unreasonable, illogical.

patience *n.* **1 calmness,** composure, even temper, even-temperedness, equanimity, equilibrium, serenity, tranquillity, restraint, self-restraint, imperturbability, inexcitability, tolerance, long-suffering, indulgence, forbearance, endurance, resignation, stoicism, fortitude, *inf.* unflappability, cool. **2 perseverance,** persistence, endurance, tenacity, assiduity, diligence, staying power, indefatigability, doggedness, singleness of purpose. *Ant.* impatience; agitation; exasperation.

patient *adj.* **uncomplaining,** serene, calm, composed, even-tempered, tranquil, restrained, imperturbable, unexcitable, tolerant, accommodating, long-suffering, forbearing, indulgent, resigned, stoical, *inf.* unflappable, cool.
▸ *n.* **sick person,** invalid, case, sufferer.

patriotic *adj.* **nationalist,** nationalistic, loyalist, loyal, chauvinistic, flag-waving, jingoistic.

patrol *v.* **make the rounds (of),** walk the beat (of), pound the beat (of), range, police, keep watch (on), guard, keep guard (on), keep a vigil (on), monitor.
▸ *n.* **1 patrolling,** round, sentry duty, beat-pounding, policing, watch, guard, vigil, monitoring. **2 patrolman/patrolwoman,** sentinel, sentry, garrison, guard, watchman, watch, night watchman, policeman/ policewoman.

patron *n.* **1 sponsor,** backer, benefactor/benefactress, promoter, friend, helper, supporter, upholder, champion, protector, *inf.* angel. **2 customer,** client, frequenter, shopper, buyer, purchaser, *inf.* regular.

patronize *v.* **1 look down on,** talk down to, condescend to, treat condescendingly, treat with condescension, treat like a child, treat as inferior, treat with disdain, treat scornfully/ contemptuously, be snobbish to. **2 be a customer of,** be a client of, frequent, shop at, buy from, do business with, deal with, trade with. **3 be a patron of,** sponsor, back, fund, finance, promote, help, aid, assist, support, encourage, champion, protect.

patronizing *adj.* **condescending,** supercilious, superior, haughty, lofty, lordly, disdainful, scornful, contemptuous, snobbish, *inf.* uppity, snooty.

pattern *n.* **1 design,** decoration, motif, marking, ornament, ornamentation, device, figure. **2 system,** order, arrangement, method, sequence. **3 design,** guide, blueprint, model, plan, template, stencil, instructions. **4 model,** ideal, exemplar, paradigm, example, archetype, prototype, paragon, criterion, standard, gauge, norm, guide, yardstick, touchstone, benchmark. **5 sample,** swatch, specimen.

▸ *v.* **model,** mold, style, form, shape.

pause *n.* **break,** halt, cessation, stoppage, interruption, lull, respite, stay, discontinuation, gap, interlude, intermission, interval, rest, delay, hesitation, *inf.* letup, breather.

▸ *v.* **stop,** halt, cease, discontinue, break, take a break, desist, rest, hold back, delay, hesitate, waver, *inf.* let up, take a breather. ***Ant.*** continue; proceed.

pay *v.* **1 make payment (to),** settle up (with), remunerate, reimburse, recompense, reward, indemnify, requite. **2 pay out,** spend, expend, lay out, part with, disburse, hand over, remit, render, *inf.* dish out, shell out, fork out, cough up. **3 pay off,** pay in full, settle, discharge, meet, clear, square, honor, liquidate, settle, foot, defray, square. **4 make money,** be profitable, make a profit, be remunerative, make a return. **5 pay out,** yield, return, produce, bring in, *inf.* rake in. **6 repay,** be advantageous to, be of advantage to, be of benefit to, be beneficial to, be profitable to, be worthwhile to. **7 give,** bestow, extend, offer, proffer, render. **8 pay back,** punish, avenge oneself on, get revenge on.

▸ *n.* **payment,** salary, wages,

earnings, fee, remuneration, recompense, reimbursement, reward, stipend, emoluments.

payment *n.* **1 pay,** salary, wages, earnings, fee, remuneration, recompense. **2 settlement,** discharge, clearance, squaring, liquidation. **3 installment,** premium, amount, remittance.

peace *n.* **1 peace and quiet,** peacefulness, tranquillity, restfulness, calm, calmness, quiet, quietness, stillness, still, serenity, composure, placidity, rest, repose, contentment. **2 peacefulness,** peaceableness, harmony, harmoniousness, accord, concord, amity, amicableness, goodwill, friendship, cordiality, nonaggression, nonviolence, cease-fire. **3 treaty,** truce, agreement, armistice, cessation of hostilities. **Ant.** noise; agitation; conflict; war.

peaceable *adj.* **unwarlike,** peace-loving, nonaggressive, nonbelligerent, nonviolent, noncombative, easygoing, placid, gentle, mild, good-natured, even-tempered, amiable, amicable, pacific, pacifist, pacifistic, dovelike, dovish, irenic, peaceful, strife-free, harmonious, friendly, cordial. **Ant.** aggressive; belligerent; warlike.

peaceful *adj.* **1 tranquil,** restful, quiet, calm, still, undisturbed, at peace, serene, composed, placid, at rest, in repose, reposeful, undisturbed, untroubled, unworried, anxiety-free, peaceable, on good terms, strife-free, harmonious, amicable, friendly, cordial, nonviolent, unwarlike. **2 peaceable,** at peace, on good terms, strife-free, harmonious, amicable, friendly, cordial, nonviolent, unwarlike. **Ant.** noisy; agitated; hostile; warring.

peacemaker *n.* **conciliator,** mediator, arbitrator, pacifier, appeaser, peacemonger.

peak *n.* **1 top,** summit, crest, pinnacle, mountain, hill, height, alp. **2 height,** high point, climax, culmination, zenith, acme, meridian, apogee, prime, heyday, ne plus ultra. **Ant.** bottom; nadir; trough.

▸ *v.* **reach its/their (etc.) height,** reach the highest point, culminate, reach the high point, reach a climax, reach the zenith.

peculiar *adj.* **1 strange,** odd, queer, funny, curious, unusual, abnormal, eccentric, unconventional, bizarre, weird, quaint, outlandish, out-of-the-way, grotesque, freakish, offbeat, droll, comical, *inf.* far-out, way-out. **2 characteristic,** distinctive, distinct, individual, individualistic, distinguishing, special, unique, idiosyncratic, conspicuous, notable, remarkable. **3 unwell,** poorly, ill, below par, strange, indisposed, *inf.* funny, under the weather. **Ant.** normal; ordinary.

peculiarity *n.* **1 peculiarness,** strangeness, oddness, queerness, curiousness, abnormality, eccentricity, unconventionality, bizarreness, weirdness, outlandishness, grotesqueness, freakishness, drollness. **2 characteristic,** feature, quality, property, trait, attribute, mark, stamp, hallmark. **3 abnormality,** eccentricity, oddity, idiosyncrasy, quirk, foible.

pedantic *adj.* **1 precise,** precisionist, exact, scrupulous, overscrupulous, punctilious, meticulous, perfectionist, formalist, dogmatic, literalist, literalistic, quibbling, hairsplitting, casuistic, casuistical, sophistic, sophistical, pettifogging, *inf.* nitpicking. **2 intellectual,** academic, scholastic, didactic, bookish, pedagogic, donnish, highbrow, pretentious, pompous, *inf.* egghead. **3 formal,** stilted, stiff, stuffy, unimaginative, uninspired, rhetorical, bombastic,

grandiloquent, high-flown, euphuistic, *inf.* highfalutin.

pedestal *n.* **base,** support, stand, foundation, pillar, column, plinth.

pedestrian *n.* **walker,** stroller, hiker. **Ant.** driver.
▸ *adj.* **1 on foot,** walking. **2 pedestrianized,** for pedestrians (only). **3 plodding,** unimaginative, uninspired, unexciting, dull, flat, prosaic, turgid, stodgy, mundane, humdrum, banal, run-of-the-mill, commonplace, ordinary, mediocre, *inf.* nothing to write home about. **Ant.** imaginative; inspired; exciting.

peek *v.* **take a look,** steal a glance, peep, glance, cast a brief look, look hurriedly, look, *inf.* sneak a look, take a gander, have a look-see.
▸ *n.* **peep,** glance, glimpse, look, *inf.* gander, look-see.

peephole *n.* **aperture,** opening, spyhole, slit, crack, crevice, fissure.

peer *v.* **look,** narrow one's eyes, screw up one's eyes, squint.

peer[2] *n.* **1 compeer,** associate, colleague, friend, fellow, equal, match, like, coequal, confrère. **2 noble,** nobleman, aristocrat, lord, titled man, patrician, duke, marquess, marquis, earl, viscount, baron.

peeve *v.* **irritate,** annoy, anger,

vex, provoke, upset, exasperate, irk, pique, nettle, get on someone's nerves, rub the wrong way, *inf.* aggravate, miff, rile, get under someone's skin, get in someone's hair.

penalize *v.* **1 punish,** discipline, castigate, correct. **2 handicap,** inflict a handicap on, disadvantage, put at a disadvantage. *Ant.* reward; recompense.

penalty *n.* **1 punishment,** punitive action, retribution, castigation, penance, fine, forfeit, sentence, mulct. **2 handicap,** disadvantage, drawback, snag, obstacle. *Ant.* reward; advantage.

penance *n.* **1 punishment,** penalty. **2 self-punishment,** atonement, reparation, amends, mortification.

penchant *n.* **liking,** fondness, preference, taste, partiality, soft spot, inclination, bent, proclivity, predilection, love, passion, desire, fancy, whim, weakness.

pending *prep.* **1 awaiting,** waiting for, until. **2 during,** throughout, in the course of, for the time/ duration of.
  ▸ *adj.* **1 undecided,** unsettled, unresolved, uncertain, awaiting action, undetermined, hanging fire, up in the air, *inf.* on the back burner. **2 imminent,** impending,

on the way, coming, approaching, forthcoming, near, nearing, close, close at hand, in the offing.

penetrate *v.* **1 pierce,** bore, perforate, stab, prick, gore, spike. **2 go into,** get in, enter, make one's way into/through, infiltrate. **3 permeate,** pervade, fill, imbue, suffuse, seep through, saturate. **4 be understood,** be comprehended, be taken in, be grasped, register. **5 get through to,** be understood/comprehended by, register on, make an impression on, have an impact on. **6 understand,** comprehend, apprehend, fathom, get to the bottom of, make out, solve, resolve, work out, figure out, unravel, decipher, *inf.* crack.

penitent *adj.* **repentant,** contrite, regretful, remorseful, sorry, apologetic, conscience-stricken, rueful, ashamed, abject, sorrowful. *Ant.* impenitent; unrepentant.

penniless *adj.* **without a penny,** without a penny to one's name, impecunious, penurious, impoverished, indigent, poor, as poor as a church mouse, poverty-stricken, destitute, bankrupt, in reduced circumstances, in straitened circumstances, hard up, *inf.* broke, stone-broke, flat broke, cleaned out, strapped for cash, strapped. *Ant.* wealthy; affluent.

pensive *adj.* **thoughtful,** thinking, reflective, contemplative, musing, meditative, pondering, cogitative, ruminative, absorbed, preoccupied, serious, solemn, dreamy, dreaming, wistful, melancholy, sad.

people *n.* **1 persons,** individuals, human beings, humans, mortals, living souls; men, women, and children. **2 race,** tribe, clan, nation, country, population, populace.

▸ *pl. n.* **common people,** ordinary people, ordinary citizens, general public, public, populace, electorate, masses, rank and file, commonalty, mob, multitude, hoi polloi, rabble, *inf.* plebs.

▸ *plural noun* **family,** relatives, relations, folk, kinsfolk, kin, kith and kin, *inf.* folks.

perceive *v.* **1 see,** catch sight of, spot, observe, glimpse, notice, make out, discern, behold, espy, detect, witness, remark. **2 discern,** appreciate, recognize, be cognizant of, be aware of, be conscious of, know, grasp, understand, comprehend, apprehend, figure out, see, sense.

perceptible *adj.* **perceivable,** discernible, noticeable, detectable, distinguishable, appreciable, visible, observable, distinct, clear, plain, evident, apparent, obvious, manifest, conspicuous, patent, palpable, tangible. *Ant.* imperceptible; inconspicuous.

perception *n.* **1 discernment,** appreciation, recognition, cognizance, awareness, consciousness, knowledge, grasp, understanding, comprehension, apprehension, notion, conception, idea, sense.
2 perspicacity, discernment, perceptiveness, understanding, discrimination, insight, intuition, feeling, sensitivity.

perceptive *adj.* **1 sharp-eyed,** sharp-sighted, keen-sighted, observant, alert, vigilant.
2 discerning, perspicacious, percipient, shrewd, understanding, discriminating, intuitive, responsive, sensitive, penetrating, astute, shrewd. *Ant.* heedless; obtuse; unobservant; dull.

perch *n.* **pole,** rod, branch, roost, rest.
▸ *v.* **sit,** rest, roost, settle, alight, land.

peremptory *adj.* **1 imperious,** high-handed, urgent, pressing, imperative, high-priority.
2 imperious, high-handed, overbearing, dogmatic, autocratic,

dictatorial, domineering, arbitrary, tyrannical, despotic, arrogant, overweening, supercilious, lordly.
3 incontrovertible, irreversible, binding, absolute, final, conclusive, decisive, definitive, categorical, irrefutable.

perfect *adj.* **1 complete,** full, whole, entire. **2 perfected,** completed, finished. **3 absolute,** complete, out-and-out, thorough, thoroughgoing, downright, utter, sheer, consummate, unmitigated, unqualified. **4 flawless,** faultless, unmarred, ideal, impeccable, consummate, immaculate, exemplary, superb, superlative, supreme, excellent, wonderful, model, exquisite,marvelous, *inf.* out of this world, terrific, fantastic, fabulous. **5 exact,** precise, accurate, faithful, correct, right, close, true, strict, *inf.* right-on. **6 ideal,** just right, right, appropriate, fitting, fit, suitable, apt. *Ant.* imperfect; faulty; defective.
▸ *v.* **make perfect,** render faultless/flawless, improve, better, polish, refine, elaborate, complete, consummate, put the finishing touches to.

perfection *n.* **1 perfecting,** improvement, betterment, polishing, refinement, completion, consummation. **2 perfectness,** flawlessness, faultlessness, consummation, impeccability, immaculateness, exemplariness, superbness. **3 a paragon,** the best, one in a million, ideal, the acme, the crown, the peak of perfection, *inf.* the tops, aces.

perfidious *adj.* **treacherous,** traitorous, treasonous, false, untrue, disloyal, faithless, unfaithful, deceitful, double-dealing, duplicitous, dishonest, two-faced.

perform *v.* **1 do,** carry out, execute, discharge, conduct, effect, bring about, bring off, accomplish, achieve, fulfill, complete. **2 act,** play, appear. **3 play,** execute. **4 function,** work, operate, run, go. *Ant.* neglect; omit.

performance *n.* **1 carrying out,** execution, discharge, conducting, effecting, accomplishment, achievement, fulfillment. **2 show,** production, entertainment, act, presentation, *inf.* gig. **3 acting,** playing, representation, staging.

performer *n.* **1 actor/actress,** player, entertainer, artist, artiste, thespian, trouper, musician, singer, dancer. **2 doer,** executor, worker, operator, architect, author.

perfume *n.* **1 scent,** fragrance, aroma, smell, bouquet, redolence. **2 scent,** fragrance, balm, essence, eau de toilette, toilet water, eau de cologne, cologne.

perfunctory *adj.* **cursory,** superficial, desultory, mechanical, automatic, routine, sketchy, brief, hasty, hurried, rapid, fleeting, quick, fast, offhand, casual, indifferent, careless, inattentive, negligent.

perhaps *adv.* **it may be that,** maybe, possibly, it is possible that, conceivably, feasibly, for all one knows, *lit.* peradventure.

peril *n.* **danger,** jeopardy, risk, hazard, menace, threat. ***Ant.*** safety; security.

perilous *adj.* **dangerous,** fraught with danger, menacing, risky, precarious, hazardous, chancy, threatening, unsafe. ***Ant.*** safe; secure.

perimeter *n.* **1 circumference. 2 boundary,** border, frontier, limits, outer limits, confines, edge, margin, fringe, periphery.

period *n.* **1 time,** space, spell, interval, term, stretch, span, while. **2 time,** days, age, era, epoch, eon. **3 finis,** end, finish, conclusion, stop, halt, and that's that. **4 menstruation,** menstrual flow, monthly flow, menses.

periodic *adj.* **periodical,** at fixed intervals, recurrent, recurring, repeated, cyclical, cyclic, regular, intermittent, occasional, infrequent, sporadic, every once in a while, every so often.

peripheral *adj.* **1 outer,** on the edge/outskirts, surrounding, neighboring. **2 minor,** lesser, secondary, subsidiary, ancillary, unimportant, superficial, irrelevant, beside the point. ***Ant.*** central; major; important; vital.

perish *v.* **1 die,** lose one's life, be killed, lay down one's life, meet one's death, breathe one's last, draw one's last breath, *inf.* bite the dust, kick the bucket. **2 come to an end,** die away, disappear, vanish, disintegrate, go under, be destroyed. **3 go bad,** go sour, rot, decay, decompose. ***Ant.*** live; survive.

perk[2] *n.* **perquisite,** fringe benefit.

permanent *adj.* **everlasting,** perpetual, eternal, enduring, perennial, lasting, abiding, constant, persistent, unending, endless, never-ending, immutable, unchangeable, inalterable, invariable, long-lasting, stable, fixed, established, sound, firm. ***Ant.*** temporary; fleeting; ephemeral.

permeate *v.* **spread through,** be disseminated through, pass through, pervade, fill, diffuse through, be diffused through, extend throughout, imbue, penetrate, infiltrate, percolate through, soak through, seep through, leak through, infiltrate, leach through, saturate.

permissible *adj.* **permitted,** allowable, admissible, acceptable, tolerated, authorized, sanctioned, legal, lawful, legitimate, licit, within bounds, *inf.* legit.

permission *n.* **authorization,** sanction, leave, license, dispensation, empowerment, allowance, consent, assent, acquiescence, go-ahead, thumbs up, agreement, approval, approbation, tolerance, sufferance, *inf.* green light.

permissive *adj.* **liberal,** tolerant, broad-minded, open-minded, easygoing, forbearing, latitudinarian, indulgent, lenient, unrestricted, overindulgent, lax, unprescriptive. *Ant.* intolerant; strict.

permit *v.* **1 give permission,** allow, let, authorize, give leave, sanction, grant, license, empower, enable, consent to, assent to, acquiesce in, give the go-ahead to, give the thumbs up to, agree to, approve of, tolerate, countenance, suffer, brook, *inf.* give the green light to. **2 allow,** make possible, enable. *Ant.* ban; forbid; refuse.

▸ *n.* **license,** authorization, warrant, sanction, pass, passport, visa.

perpetual *adj.* **1 everlasting,** eternal, never-ending, unending, endless, undying, perennial, permanent, perdurable, lasting, abiding, persisting, enduring, constant, unfailing, unchanging, unvarying, invariable.
2 incessant, unceasing, ceaseless, unending, endless, never-stopping, nonstop, continuous, uninterrupted, unbroken, unremitting, interminable, persistent, frequent, continual, recurrent, repeated, *inf.* eternal. *Ant.* transitory; temporary; intermittent.

perpetuate *v.* **1 keep alive,** keep going, keep up, preserve, conserve, sustain, maintain, continue. **2 memorialize,** commemorate, immortalize, eternalize.

perplex *v.* **puzzle,** baffle, mystify, stump, keep someone guessing, bewilder, confound, confuse, nonplus, disconcert, dismay, dumbfound, *inf.* bamboozle.

persecute *v.* **1 oppress,** tyrannize, abuse, mistreat, maltreat, ill-treat, molest, afflict, torment, torture, victimize, martyr. **2 harass,** pester, hound, badger, vex, bother, worry, annoy, *inf.* hassle.

persevere *v.* persist, go on, keep on, keep at, keep going, continue, carry on, struggle, work, hammer away, be tenacious, be persistent, be pertinacious, be resolute, be purposeful, be obstinate, be insistent, be intransigent, be patient, be diligent, be determined, stand one's ground, stand fast, not give up, *inf.* stick to one's guns, stick to it, plug away. *Ant.* give up (see give); stop; quit.

persist *v.* **1 persevere,** go on, keep on, keep going, continue, carry on, be resolute, stand one's ground, *inf.* plug away. **2 carry on,** keep on, keep up, continue, last, remain, linger, hold. *Ant.* give up (see give); stop; desist.

persistent *adj.* **1 persevering,** tenacious, pertinacious, determined, resolute, purposeful, obstinate, stubborn, insistent, intransigent, obdurate, intractable, patient, diligent. **2 constant,** continual, continuous, continuing, interminable, incessant, unceasing, endless, unremitting, unrelenting, relentless, chronic, frequent, repetitive, repetitious. *Ant.* irresolute; intermittent; occasional.

person *n.* **individual,** human being, human, creature, living soul, soul, mortal, *inf.* character.

personable *adj.* **pleasant,** agreeable, amiable, affable, likable, charming, nice, attractive, presentable, good-looking.

personal *adj.* **1 individual,** private, confidential, secret, one's own business, intimate. **2 personalized,** individual, idiosyncratic, characteristic, unique, peculiar. **3 in person,** individual, special. **4 insulting,** slighting, derogatory, disparaging, pejorative, offensive. *Ant.* public; general.

personality *n.* **1 nature,** disposition, character, temperament, temper, makeup, traits, psyche. **2 strength of personality,** force of personality, personal identity, character, charisma, magnetism, powers of attraction, charm. **3 public figure,** celebrity, VIP, famous name, household name, dignitary, notable, person of note, personage, luminary, worthy, *inf.* big shot, celeb.

personally *adv.* **1 in person,** oneself. **2 for my (etc.) part,** for my (etc.) own part, for myself (etc.), from my (etc.) own point of view, as far as I (etc.) am concerned.

personification *n.* **embodiment,** incarnation, epitome, quintessence, essence, symbol, representation, image, portrayal, likeness, semblance.

personnel *n.* **staff,** employees, workers, workforce, labor force, manpower, human resources.

perspective *n.* **1 outlook,** view, viewpoint, point of view, standpoint, vantage point, stand, stance, angle, slant, attitude, frame of mind. **2 view,** vista, bird's-eye view, prospect, scene, outlook, panorama, aspect, sweep.

persuade *v.* **prevail upon,** win over, talk into (doing something), bring around, induce, convince, influence, sway, prompt, coerce, inveigle, cajole, wheedle, *inf.* sweet-talk, soft-soap. *Ant.* dissuade; discourage; deter.

persuasive *adj.* **effective,** effectual, convincing, cogent, plausible, compelling, forceful, eloquent, weighty, influential, telling. *Ant.* ineffective; weak.

pertain *v.* **1 be connected with,** relate to, be relevant to, have relevance to, concern, apply to, be pertinent to, have reference to, have a bearing upon, be appropriate to, be suited to, befit, fit in with, appertain to. **2 belong to,** be a part of, be an adjunct of, go along with, be included in.

pertinent *adj.* **relevant,**

appropriate, suitable, fitting, fit, apt, apposite, to the point, applicable, material, germane, to the purpose, apropos, ad rem. *Ant.* irrelevant; inappropriate.

perturb *v.* **1 disturb,** make anxious, worry, alarm, trouble, upset, disquiet, discompose, disconcert, vex, bother, agitate, unsettle, fluster, ruffle, harass. **2 throw into confusion,** confuse, throw into disorder, disarrange, throw into disarray, muddle.

pervade *v.* **spread through,** be disseminated through, permeate, fill, pass through, extend throughout, suffuse, diffuse through, be diffused through, imbue, infuse, penetrate, infiltrate, percolate.

pervasive *adj.* **pervading,** permeating, prevalent, suffusive, extensive, ubiquitous, omnipresent, rife, widespread, universal.

perverse *adj.* **1 contrary,** wayward, troublesome, unruly, difficult, awkward, unreasonable, disobedient, unmanageable, uncontrollable, rebellious, willful, headstrong, capricious, stubborn, obstinate, obdurate, pertinacious, mulish, pigheaded, bullheaded, querulous, fractious, intractable, refractory, intransigent, contumacious. **2 contradictory,**

unreasonable, irrational, illogical, senseless, abnormal, deviant, excessive, undue, immoderate, inordinate, outrageous. *Ant.* accommodating; reasonable.

perversion *n.* **1 distortion,** misuse, misrepresentation, falsification, misinterpretation, misconstruction. **2 deviation,** aberration, abnormality, irregularity, unnaturalness, corruption, debauchery, depravity, vice, wickedness, *inf.* kinkiness.

pervert *v.* **1 turn aside,** divert, deflect, avert, subvert. **2 misapply,** misuse, distort, garble, warp, twist, misinterpret, misconstrue. **3 lead astray,** corrupt, warp, deprave, debauch, debase, degrade, vitiate.
▸ *n.* **deviant,** deviate, degenerate, debauchee, *inf.* sicko, weirdo.

perverted *adj.* **corrupt,** corrupted, depraved, debauched, debased, vitiated, deviant, abnormal, aberrant, warped, distorted, twisted, sick, unhealthy, immoral, evil, wicked, vile, *inf.* kinky.

pessimist *n.* **prophet of doom,** cynic, defeatist, fatalist, alarmist, doubter, doubting Thomas, *inf.* doomster.

pessimistic *adj.* **hopeless,** gloomy, gloom-ridden, cynical, defeatist, fatalistic, distrustful, alarmist, doubting, suspicious, bleak, resigned, depressed, dejected, despairing. *Ant.* optimistic; hopeful; cheerful.

pest *n.* **nuisance,** bother, source of annoyance/irritation, vexation, irritant, thorn in one's side, problem, trouble, worry, inconvenience, trial, tribulation, the bane of one's life, *inf.* pain, pain in the neck, aggravation.

pester *v.* **badger,** hound, irritate, annoy, bother, irk, nag, fret, worry, harass, get on someone's nerves, torment, plague, bedevil, harry, *inf.* get at, bug, hassle.

pet *n.* **favorite,** darling, idol, apple of one's eye, *inf.* blue-eyed boy/girl, fair-haired boy/girl.
▸ *adj.* **1 domesticated,** domestic, tame, tamed, housebroken. **2 favorite,** favored, cherished, prized, dear to one's heart, preferred, particular, special.

petition *n.* **1 protest document,** appeal, round robin. **2 entreaty,** supplication, plea, prayer, appeal, request, application, suit.
▸ *v.* **entreat,** beg, beseech, plead with, make a plea to, pray, appeal to, request, ask, apply to, call upon, press, adjure, present one's case to, sue.

petrify *v.* **1 terrify,** strike terror into, horrify, frighten, fill with fear, panic, alarm, scare out of one's wits, appall, paralyze, stun, stupefy, transfix. **2 turn to stone,** fossilize, calcify, ossify.

petulant *adj.* **querulous,** complaining, peevish, fretful, impatient, cross, irritable, moody, crabbed, crabby, snappish, crotchety, touchy, bad-tempered, ill-tempered, ill-humored, irascible, sulky, sullen. **Ant.** good-natured; easygoing; affable.

phantom *n.* **1 ghost,** apparition, specter, spirit, revenant, wraith, shadow, phantasm, *inf.* spook. **2 vision,** hallucination, illusion, figment of the imagination, chimera.

phenomenal *adj.* **extraordinary,** remarkable, exceptional, singular, uncommon, unheard-of, unique, unparalleled, unprecedented, amazing, astonishing, astounding, unusual, marvelous, prodigious, sensational, miraculous, *inf.* fantastic, fabulous, mind-boggling, mind-blowing. **Ant.** ordinary; usual; run-of-the-mill.

phenomenon *n.* **1 circumstance,** fact, experience, occurrence, happening, event, incident, episode. **2 marvel,** prodigy, rarity, wonder, sensation, miracle, nonpareil.

philanthropic *adj.* **humanitarian,** humane, public-spirited, socially concerned, solicitous, unselfish, selfless, altruistic, kindhearted, benevolent, beneficent, benignant, charitable, almsgiving, generous, kind, munificent, bountiful, bounteous, liberal, openhanded, giving, helping. **Ant.** selfish; stingy; miserly.

philistine *n.* **lowbrow,** ignoramus, boor, barbarian, vulgarian, yahoo, lout, clod, oaf.
▶ *adj.* **uncultured,** uncultivated, uneducated, unenlightened, unread, lowbrow, anti-intellectual, ignorant, bourgeois, boorish, barbaric, vulgar.

philosophical *adj.* **1 philosophic,** metaphysical. **2 thoughtful,** reflective, pensive, meditative, contemplative. **3 calm,** composed, cool, collected, self-possessed, serene, tranquil, stoical, impassive, phlegmatic, unperturbed, imperturbable, dispassionate, unruffled, patient, resigned, rational, logical, realistic, practical. **Ant.** active; practical; emotional; upset.

philosophy *n.* **1 thought,** thinking, reasoning, logic, wisdom, metaphysics, moral philosophy. **2 beliefs,** convictions, ideology, ideas, doctrine, tenets, values, principles, attitude, view, viewpoint, outlook. **3 philosophicalness,** calmness, calm, coolness, composure, equanimity, aplomb, self-possession, serenity, tranquillity, stoicism, impassivity, phlegm, imperturbability, dispassion, dispassionateness, patience, resignation, rationality, logic, realism, practicality, *inf.* cool.

phlegmatic *adj.* **1 calm,** cool, composed, serene, tranquil, placid, impassive, imperturbable, dispassionate, philosophical. **2 apathetic,** indifferent, uninterested, impassive, sluggish, lethargic, listless, languorous, dull, indolent, inert, inactive, stolid, placid, bovine. **Ant.** excitable; quick-tempered; enthusiastic; active.

phobia *n.* **aversion,** abnormal fear, irrational fear, obsessive fear, fear, dread, horror, terror, dislike, hatred, loathing, detestation, distaste, antipathy, revulsion, repulsion, *inf.* thing, hang-up.

phone *n.* **telephone,** mobile phone, car phone, cellular phone, pay phone, *inf.* horn, cell phone.
▶ *v.* **telephone,** call, make/place a call to, give someone a call, ring, ring up, give someone a ring, *inf.* give someone a buzz.

phony *adj.* **bogus,** sham, fake, fraudulent, pseudo, counterfeit, imitation, spurious, mock, ersatz, forged, feigned, simulated, make-believe, false, feigned, assumed, simulated, affected, contrived. **Ant.** authentic; genuine.
▶ *n.* **1 impostor,** pretender, sham, fraud, fake, faker, charlatan, mountebank, *inf.* quack. **2 counterfeit,** fake, forgery, imitation, sham.

photograph *n.* **photo,** snap, snapshot, picture, likeness, shot, print, slide, transparency.
▶ *v.* **take a photograph/photo of,** take a snapshot/snap of, snap, take a picture of, take a shot of, take a likeness of, shoot, capture on film.

photographic *adj.* **1 pictorial,** in photographs. **2 detailed,** graphic, exact, accurate, precise.

phrase *n.* **1 word group. 2 expression,** idiomatic expression, idiom, remark, saying, utterance, witticism, tag. **3 phrasing,** phraseology, manner, style, usage, choice of words, idiom, language, diction, parlance.
▶ *v.* **put into words,** put, word, express, formulate, couch, frame.

phraseology *n.* **1 style,** phrasing, usage, idiom, language, diction, parlance. **2 phrasing,** wording, words, choice of words, language, vocabulary, terminology.

physical *adj.* **1 bodily,**

nonmental, corporeal, corporal, somatic. **2 nonspiritual,** unspiritual, material, earthly, corporeal, carnal, fleshly, mortal. **3 material,** substantial, solid, concrete, tangible, palpable, visible, real. *Ant.* mental; spiritual.

physician *n.* **doctor,** doctor of medicine, medical practitioner, medical man/woman, general practitioner, GP, specialist, consultant, *inf.* doc, medic, medico, *derog.* quack.

physique *n.* **body,** body structure, build, shape, frame, form, figure.

pick *v.* **1 choose,** select, opt for, plump for, single out, handpick, decide upon, settle upon, fix upon, sift out, prefer, favor, elect. **2 harvest,** gather, collect, take in, pluck, pull, cull. **3 break into,** break open, force open, pry/prize open, crack, *inf.* jimmy.
▶ *n.* **1 choice,** selection, option, preference. **2 best,** choicest, prime, cream, flower, prize, elite, créme de la créme.

picture *n.* **1 painting,** drawing, sketch, oil painting, watercolor, print, canvas, delineation, portrait, portrayal, illustration, likeness, representation, similitude, semblance.
2 photograph, photo, snapshot, shot, snap, slide, print, still.

3 scene, view, image, impression, representation, vision, concept.
4 description, portrayal, account, report, narrative, narration, story, tale, recital. **5 personification,** embodiment, epitome, essence, perfect example, model, exemplar, archetype. **6 image,** living image, double, likeness, duplicate, replica, carbon copy, twin, *inf.* spitting image, spit and image, ringer, dead ringer.
7 movie, film, motion picture, *inf.* flick.
▶ *v.* **1 see in one's mind,** see in one's mind's eye, conjure up a picture of, conjure up an image of, imagine, call to mind, visualize, see, evoke. **2 paint,** draw, sketch, depict, delineate, portray, illustrate, reproduce, represent.

picturesque *adj.* **1 beautiful,** pretty, lovely, attractive, scenic, charming, quaint, pleasing, delightful. **2 vivid,** graphic, colorful, impressive, striking. *Ant.* ugly; drab; dull.

pie *n.* **pastry,** tart, quiche.

piece *n.* **1 part,** bit, section, segment, unit. **2 bit,** fragment, smithereens, shard, shred. **3 bit,** section, slice, chunk, lump, hunk, wedge. **4 length,** bit, remnant, scrap, snippet. **5 share,** slice, portion, allotment, allocation, quota, percentage, fraction, quantity. **6 example,** specimen, sample, instance, illustration, occurrence. **7 article,** item, story, report, essay, review, paper, column. **8 musical work,** work, composition, creation, opus. **9 work of art,** work, painting, canvas, composition, creation, opus.

▸ *v.* **put together,** assemble, join up, fit together, unite.

piecemeal *adv.* **piece by piece,** bit by bit, gradually, in stages, in steps, little by little, by degrees, in fits and starts.

pier *n.* **1 wharf,** dock, jetty, quay, landing stage, landing place, promenade. **2 support,** upright, pillar, post, column, pile, piling, buttress.

pierce *v.* **1 penetrate,** puncture, perforate, prick, stab, spike, enter, pass through, transfix, perforate, bore, drill. **2 wound,** hurt, pain, cut to the quick, affect, move, sting. **3 penetrate,** pass through, percolate, filter through, light up. **4 penetrate,** pervade, permeate, fill.

piercing *adj.* **1 penetrating,** sharp, keen, searching, alert, shrewd, perceptive, probing. **2 penetrating,** shrill, ear-piercing, earsplitting, high-pitched, loud. **3 perceptive,** percipient, perspicacious, discerning, quick-witted, sharp, sharp-witted, shrewd, keen, acute, astute. **4 penetrating,** sharp, stabbing, shooting, intense, severe, fierce, excruciating, agonizing, exquisite. **5 biting,** numbing, bitter, raw, keen, freezing, frigid, arctic.

piety *n.* **1 piousness,** religiousness, religion, holiness, godliness, devoutness, devotion to God, devotion, veneration, reverence, faith, religious duty, spirituality, sanctity, religious zeal. **2 obedience,** duty, dutifulness, respect, respectfulness, deference, veneration.

pile[1] *n.* **1 heap,** bundle, stack, mound, mass, accumulation, collection, assemblage, store, stockpile, hoard, load, mountain. **2 great deal,** quantity, abundance, mountain, *inf.* lot, lots, heap, ocean, stacks, oodles, tons. **3 fortune,** money, wealth, *inf.* mint, stacks of money, tidy sum.

▸ *v.* **1 heap,** fill, load, stock. **2 crowd,** charge, tumble, stream, flock, flood, pack, squeeze, crush, jam.

pile[2] *n.* **pillar,** column, support, post, foundation, piling, pier, buttress, upright.

pile[3] *n.* **1 soft surface,** surface, nap. **2 hair,** fur, down, wool, fluff.

pileup *n.* **crash,** multiple crash, collision, multiple collision, accident, traffic accident.

pill *n.* **1 tablet,** capsule, pellet, lozenge, bolus. **2 nuisance,** pest, bore, trial, *inf.* pain, pain in the neck, drag.

pillage *v.* **plunder,** rob, raid, loot, maraud, sack, ransack, ravage, lay waste, despoil, spoil, spoliate, depredate, rape.
▸ *n.* **pillaging,** plunder, plundering, robbery, robbing, raiding, looting, marauding, sacking, ransacking, ravaging, rapine, despoiling, laying waste, spoliation, depredation.

pillory *n.* **stocks.**
▸ *v.* **brand,** stigmatize, cast a slur on, denounce, show up, hold up to shame, hold up to ridicule, expose to ridicule, ridicule, heap scorn on.

pilot *n.* **1 airman/airwoman,** aviator, aviatrix, aeronaut, captain, commander, copilot, first/second officer, *inf.* flier. **2 navigator,** guide, steersman, helmsman. **3 guide,** leader, conductor, director.
▸ *v.* **1 fly,** drive, operate, control, handle, maneuver. **2 navigate,** guide, steer. **3 guide,** steer, conduct, direct, shepherd.

pimple *n.* **spot,** pustule, boil, swelling, papule, *inf.* blackhead, whitehead, zit.

pin *v.* **1 fasten,** join, attach, secure. **2 attach,** fasten, affix, fix, stick, tack, nail. **3 pinion,** hold, press, restrain, constrain, hold fast, immobilize.
▸ *n.* **1 straight pin,** dressmaker's/dressmaking pin, safety pin. **2 peg,** bolt, rivet, screw, dowel, post.

pinch *v.* **1 nip,** tweak, squeeze, compress. **2 hurt,** cause pain to, pain, crush, squeeze, cramp, confine. **3 scrimp,** skimp, stint, be sparing, be frugal, be economical, economize, be niggardly/tight-fisted, *inf.* be stingy, be tight. **4 steal,** thieve, rob, take, pilfer, filch, purloin, embezzle, misappropriate, *inf.* walk away/off with, swipe, lift. **5 arrest,** take into custody, apprehend, *inf.* pick up, pull in, run in, nab, collar, bust.
▸ *n.* **1 nip,** tweak, squeeze. **2 small quantity,** bit, touch, trace, soupçon, *inf.* smidgen, smidge, tad.

pinched *adj.* **drawn,** haggard, gaunt, worn, peaked, pale. *Ant.* healthy; glowing; chubby.

pinnacle *n.* **1 peak,** height, culmination, high point, acme, zenith, climax, crowning point, meridian, summit, apex, vertex, apogee. **2 peak,** summit, top, crest, mountain, hill. **3 turret,** spire, obelisk, pyramid, cone. **Ant.** nadir; trough.

pinpoint *v.* **identify,** discover, distinguish, locate, spot, home in on, put one's finger on.

pious *adj.* **1 religious,** holy, godly, spiritual, devout, devoted, dedicated, reverent, God-fearing, righteous, faithful, dutiful. **2 sanctimonious,** hypocritical, self-righteous, unctuous, pietistic, religiose, *inf.* holier-than-thou, goody-goody. **3 obedient,** dutiful, respectful, reverent, righteous. **Ant.** impious; irreligious.

pipe *n.* **1 tube,** cylinder, conduit, main, duct, channel, conveyor, pipeline, drainpipe. **2 brier,** meerschaum, clay pipe, tobacco pipe, corncob pipe, peace pipe, calumet, hookah. **3 whistle,** penny whistle, flute, recorder, fife, wind instrument.
▸ *v.* **1 convey,** channel, transmit, bring in, siphon. **2 play on a pipe,** play the pipes, tootle. **3 tweet,** cheep, chirp, chirrup, peep, twitter, sing, warble, whistle, squeak, shrill, squeal, squeak.

piquant *adj.* **1 spicy,** highly seasoned, flavorsome, peppery, tangy, pungent, sharp, tart, zesty, biting, stinging. **2 stimulating,** intriguing, interesting, fascinating, alluring, racy, salty, provocative. **3 lively,** sparkling, animated, spirited, sharp, clever, quick, racy, salty. **Ant.** bland; insipid; dull.

pirate *n.* **1 buccaneer,** rover, sea rover, sea robber, corsair, freebooter. **2 copyright infringer,** plagiarist, plagiarizer.
▸ *v.* **infringe the copyright of,** plagiarize, illegally reproduce, copy, poach, *inf.* crib, lift.

pit[1] *n.* **1 abyss,** chasm, crater, hole, cavity, excavation, quarry, mine. **2 depression,** hollow, dent, dint, indentation, dimple, pockmark, pock, mark.
▸ *v.* **depress,** dent, dint, dimple, mark, pockmark, scar.

pit[2] *n.* **stone,** pip, seed, kernel.

pitch *v.* **1 throw,** cast, fling, hurl, toss, heave, launch, *inf.* chuck, lob. **2 put up,** set up, erect, raise. **3 fall headlong,** fall, tumble, topple, plunge, dive. **4 lurch,** reel, sway, rock.
▸ *n.* **1 throw,** cast, fling, hurl, toss, heave; *inf.* chuck, lob. **2 level,** point, degree, height, extent, intensity. **3 angle,** slope, slant, tilt, cant, dip, inclination. **4 tone,** timbre, sound, tonality, modulation. **5 pitching,** lurch, roll, reeling, swaying, rocking, keeling, list. **6 spiel,** sales talk, patter; *inf.* line.

piteous *adj.* **pitiful,** to be pitied, pitiable, pathetic, distressing, affecting.

pitfall *n.* **trap,** snare, catch, stumbling block, hazard, peril, danger, difficulty.

pitiful *adj.* **1 to be pitied,** pitiable, piteous, pathetic, wretched, distressing, affecting, moving, sad, woeful, deplorable, heart-rending, heartbreaking, poignant, emotional, emotive.
2 contemptible, despicable, poor, sorry, miserable, inadequate, worthless, base, shabby, *inf.* pathetic.

pitiless *adj.* **merciless,** ruthless, relentless, cruel, severe, harsh, heartless, callous, brutal, inhuman, inhumane, cold-hearted, hard-hearted, unfeeling, uncaring, unsympathetic. ***Ant.*** merciful; compassionate; kindly.

pity *n.* **1 commiseration,** condolence, sympathy, compassion, fellow feeling, understanding, forbearance, distress, sadness, emotion, mercy, clemency, kindness, charity.
2 shame, crying shame, misfortune, unfortunate thing, sad thing, sin, *inf.* crime. ***Ant.*** indifference; cruelty; severity.
▸ *v.* **take pity on,** feel sorry for, weep for, grieve for, commiserate with, feel sympathy for, be sympathetic toward, sympathize with, have compassion for, be compassionate toward, feel for, show understanding toward, show forbearance toward, show mercy to, be merciful toward.

pivot *n.* **1 axis,** fulcrum, axle, swivel, spindle, central shaft.
2 central point, center, focal point, focus, hub, heart, raison d'être. **3 key person,** kingpin, key player, cornerstone, linchpin.
▸ *v.* **turn,** revolve, rotate, spin, swivel, twirl.

placate *v.* **calm,** calm down, pacify, soothe, appease, conciliate, propitiate, mollify, win over. ***Ant.*** agitate; anger.

place *n.* **1 location,** spot, scene, setting, position, site, situation, venue, area, region, whereabouts, locus, bit, part. **2 town,** city, village, hamlet, district, locality, neighborhood, quarter, country, state, area, region. **3 house,** apartment, residence, home, accommodation, abode, dwelling, domicile, property, *inf.* pad.
4 position, status, grade, rank, station, standing, footing, role, niche, post, job, appointment, situation, office. **5 seat,** position, space. **6 position,** correct position, space. **7 function,** job, role, task, duty, responsibility, charge, concern, affair, prerogative.

▸ *v.* **1 put,** put down, position, set down, lay down, deposit, rest, stand, install, establish, settle, station, situate. **2 order,** rank, grade, group, arrange, sort, class, classify, categorize, bracket. **3 put,** lay, set, invest, consign. **4 identify,** recognize, know, remember, put one's finger on, locate. **5 find employment for,** find a job for, find a home for, accommodate, find accommodation for, appoint, assign.

placid *adj.* **1 still,** calm, peaceful, at peace, pacific, tranquil, motionless, smooth, unruffled, undisturbed. **2 calm,** cool, cool-headed, collected, composed, self-possessed, serene, tranquil, equable, even-tempered, peaceable, easygoing, unmoved, undisturbed, unperturbed, imperturbable, unexcited, unexcitable, unruffled, unemotional. ***Ant.*** stormy; excited.

plagiarize *v.* **copy,** pirate, poach, borrow, reproduce, appropriate, *inf.* rip off, crib, lift.

plague *n.* **1 bubonic plague,** Black Death, contagious disease, contagion, disease, pestilence, sickness, epidemic, pandemic. **2 huge number,** multitude, host, swarm, influx, infestation. **3 affliction,** evil, scourge, curse, blight, bane, calamity, disaster, trial, tribulation, torment, visitation. **4 pest,** nuisance, thorn in one's side, problem, bother, source of annoyance/irritation, irritant, the bane of one's life/existence, *inf.* pain, pain in the neck, aggravation.

▸ *v.* **1 afflict,** cause suffering to, torture, torment, bedevil, trouble. **2 annoy,** irritate, bother, disturb, worry, pester, vex, harass, torment, tease, *inf.* hassle, bug.

plain *adj.* **1 clear,** clear as crystal, crystal-clear, obvious, evident, apparent, manifest, transparent, patent, unmistakable, clear-cut, visible, discernible, perceptible, distinct, noticeable, pronounced, marked, striking, conspicuous, simple, straightforward, uncomplicated, comprehensible, intelligible, understandable, lucid, unambiguous. **2 simple,** austere, stark, severe, basic, ordinary, unsophisticated, restrained, muted, basic, unadorned, undecorated, unembellished, unornamented, unpatterned, spartan. **3 unattractive,** ill-favored, ugly, unprepossessing, unlovely, homely. **4 simple,** straightforward, ordinary, average, typical, unpretentious, unassuming, unaffected, artless, guileless, sincere, honest, plain-speaking, plainspoken, frank, candid, blunt, outspoken, forthright, direct, downright. *Ant.* obscure; fancy; elaborate; attractive.

▸ *adv.* **downright,** utterly, completely, totally, thoroughly, positively, incontrovertibly, unquestionably, undeniably, simply.

plaintive *adj.* **mournful,** doleful, melancholy, sad, sorrowful, unhappy, disconsolate, wretched, woeful, grief-stricken, heartbroken, brokenhearted, pathetic, pitiful, piteous.

plan *n.* **1 plan of action,** scheme, system, procedure, method, program, schedule, project, way, means, strategy, tactics, formula. **2 idea,** scheme, proposal, project, intention, intent, aim, hope, aspiration, ambition. **3 drawing,** scale drawing, blueprint, layout, sketch, diagram, chart, map, illustration, representation, delineation.

▸ *v.* **1 arrange,** organize, line up, schedule, program. **2 devise,** design, plot, formulate, frame, outline, sketch out, draft, prepare, develop, shape, build, concoct, contrive, think out. **3 draw up a plan of,** design, make a drawing of, draw up a layout of, sketch out, make a chart of, map out, make a representation of. **4 make plans,** intend, aim, propose, mean, purpose, contemplate, envisage, foresee.

plane *n.* **1 flat surface,** level surface, the flat. **2 level,** stratum, stage, degree, position, rank, footing. **3 airplane,** aircraft, airliner, jet.

▸ *adj.* **flat,** level, horizontal, even, flush, smooth, regular, uniform.

plant *n.* **1 flower,** vegetable, herb, shrub, weed. **2 factory,** works, foundry, mill, workshop, shop, yard.

▸ *v.* **1 put in the ground,** implant, sow, scatter, transplant, bed (out), put in the ground, implant, set (out). **2 place,** position, set, situate, put, place, fix, establish, lodge, imbed, insert. **3 place secretly,** hide, conceal, secrete.

plaster *n.* **stucco,** plaster of Paris, gypsum.

▸ *v.* **cover thickly,** spread, coat, smear, overlay, bedaub.

plastic *adj.* **1 moldable,** shapable, ductile, fictile, pliant, pliable, supple, flexible, soft.
2 impressionable, responsive, receptive, malleable, moldable, ductile, pliable, supple, flexible, compliant, tractable, manageable, controllable, docile. **3 false,** artificial, synthetic, spurious, sham, bogus, assumed,

plate 628

superficial, specious, meretricious, pseudo, *inf.* phony. ***Ant.*** rigid; intractable; genuine.

plate *n.* **1 dish,** platter, dinner plate. **2 plateful,** helping, portion, serving. **3 illustration,** picture, photograph, print, lithograph. **4 sheet,** panel, slab.

platform *n.* **1 dais,** rostrum, podium, stage, stand. **2 plan,** plan of action, objectives, principles, tenets, program, policy, manifesto, party line.

platitude *n.* **cliché,** truism, hackneyed expression, commonplace, stock expression, trite phrase, banal phrase, banality, stereotyped phrase, bromide, inanity.

platter *n.* **serving plate,** salver, plate, dish, tray.

plausible *adj.* **tenable,** cogent, reasonable, believable, credible, convincing, persuasive, likely, probable, conceivable, imaginable.

play *v.* **1 amuse oneself,** entertain oneself, enjoy oneself, have fun, play games, frolic, frisk, gambol, romp, cavort, sport. **2 perform on. 3 play the part of,** act, act the part of, perform, portray, represent, execute. **4 perform,** carry out, execute, do, accomplish, discharge, fulfill. **5 take part in,** participate in, engage in, be

involved in. **6 play against,** compete against, contend against, oppose, take on, challenge, vie with, rival. **7 fiddle,** toy, fidget, fool around, *inf.* mess around. **8 trifle,** toy, dally, amuse oneself. **9 move lightly,** dance, flit, dart. ***Ant.*** work; toil.

▸ *n.* **1 amusement,** entertainment, recreation, diversion, leisure, enjoyment, fun, merrymaking, revelry. **2 drama,** stage play, stage show, radio play, television play, teleplay, comedy, tragedy, farce. **3 action,** activity, operation, agency, working, functioning, exercise, interaction, interplay. **4 movement,** freedom of movement, free motion, slack, *inf.* give. **5 scope,** range, latitude, liberty, license, freedom, indulgence, free rein. **6 fun,** jest, joking, sport, teasing.

player *n.* **1 competitor,** contestant, participant, team member, athlete, sportsman/sportswoman. **2 actor/actress,** performer, entertainer, artist, artiste, trouper, thespian. **3 performer,** musician, instrumentalist, artist, artiste, virtuoso.

playful *adj.* **1 fun-loving,** full of fun, high-spirited, frisky, skittish, coltish, frolicsome, sportive, mischievous, impish, puckish. **2 in fun,** in jest, joking, jesting, humorous, fun, facetious, waggish, tongue-in-cheek, arch, roguish. *Ant.* solemn; serious.

plea *n.* **1 appeal,** entreaty, imploration, supplication, petition, prayer, request, solicitation, suit, invocation. **2 answer,** statement, allegation, case, suit, action, claim. **3 excuse,** pretext, claim.

plead *v.* **put forward,** state, assert, argue, claim, allege.

pleasant *adj.* **1 pleasing,** pleasurable, agreeable, enjoyable, entertaining, amusing, delightful, satisfying, gratifying, nice, good, fine, welcome, acceptable, *inf.* lovely. **2 agreeable,** friendly, amiable, affable, genial, likable, nice, good-humored, charming, engaging, winning, delightful, *inf.* lovely. *Ant.* unpleasant; disagreeable.

please *v.* **1 give pleasure to,** gladden, delight, cheer up, charm, divert, entertain, amuse, tickle, satisfy, gratify, fulfill, content, suit, *inf.* tickle pink. **2 want,** wish, see fit, will, like, desire, be inclined, prefer, opt. *Ant.* displease; dissatisfy; annoy; bore.

pleased *adj.* **happy,** glad, cheerful, delighted, thrilled, elated, contented, satisfied, gratified, fulfilled, as pleased as Punch, *inf.* on cloud nine.

pleasure *n.* **1 happiness,** gladness, delight, joy, enjoyment, entertainment, amusemn, diversion, satisfaction, gratification, fulfillment, contentment, recreation. **2 wish,** desire, will, inclination, preference, choice, option, purpose. *Ant.* displeasure; sorrow; pain.

pledge *n.* **1 promise,** word, word of honor, vow, assurance, undertaking, oath, covenant, warrant. **2 security,** surety, guarantee, collateral, bond, earnest, deposit, pawn. **3 token,** symbol, sign, mark, testimony, proof, evidence.
▸ *v.* **1 promise,** give one's word, vow, give one's assurance, give an undertaking, undertake, take an oath, swear, swear an oath, vouch, engage, contract. **2 mortgage,** put up as collateral, guarantee, pawn.

plentiful *adj.* **abundant,** copious, ample, profuse, lavish, liberal, generous, large, huge, bumper, infinite. *Ant.* meager; sparse; scanty.

plenty *n.* **plentifulness,** plenteousness, affluence, prosperity, wealth, opulence, luxury, abundance, copiousness, fruitfulness, profusion.

plethora *n.* **overabundance,**

superabundance, excess, superfluity, surplus, surfeit, glut. *Ant.* dearth; lack.

pliable *adj.* **1 flexible,** bendable, bendy, pliant, elastic, supple, stretchable, ductile, plastic. **2 malleable,** yielding, compliant, docile, biddable, tractable, manageable, governable, controllable, amenable, adaptable, flexible, impressionable, persuadable. *Ant.* rigid; intractable; obdurate.

plot *n.* **1 conspiracy,** intrigue, secret plan, secret scheme, stratagem. **2 action,** theme, subject, story line, story, scenario, thread. **3 piece of ground,** patch, allotment, lot, parcel.
  ▸ *v.* **1 map out,** make a plan/drawing of, draw, draw a diagram of, draw the layout of, make a blueprint/chart of, sketch out, outline, mark, chart, map. **2 take part in a plot,** scheme, conspire, participate in a conspiracy, intrigue, form an intrigue.

ploy *n.* **dodge,** ruse, scheme, trick, stratagem, maneuver, move.

plummet *v.* **1 fall perpendicularly,** fall headlong, plunge, hurtle, nosedive, dive, drop. **2 fall steeply,** plunge, tumble, nosedive, take a nosedive, drop rapidly, go down.

plump *adj.* **chubby,** round, rounded, of ample proportions, rotund, buxom, stout, fat, fattish, obese, corpulent, fleshy, portly, tubby, dumpy, pudgy, roly-poly, *inf.* well-upholstered, beefy. *Ant.* thin; slender; skinny.
  ▸ *v.* **fall,** drop, flop, plunk, sink, collapse.

plunder *v.* **rob,** pillage, loot, raid, ransack, rifle, strip, fleece, ravage, lay waste, despoil, spoil, spoliate, depredate, harry, maraud, sack, rape, steal, thieve, purloin, filch, make off with, *inf.* walk away/off with.
  ▸ *n.* **1 plundering,** robbery, robbing, pillaging, looting, raiding, ransacking, despoiling, laying waste, harrying, marauding, rapine. **2 stolen goods,** loot, booty, spoils, prize, pillage, ill-gotten gains, *inf.* swag.

plunge *v.* **1 thrust,** stick, jab, push, drive. **2 dive,** nosedive, jump, plummet, drop, fall, fall headlong, swoop down, descend. **3 throw,** cast, pitch. **4 immerse,** sink, dip, douse. **5 charge,** lurch, rush, dash, hurtle, career. **6 fall steeply,** drop rapidly, go down, plummet, tumble, nosedive, take a nosedive.
  ▸ *n.* **1 dive,** nosedive, jump, fall, drop, swoop, descent, tumble. **2 charge,** lurch, rush, dash.

plush *adj.* **luxurious,** luxury, deluxe, sumptuous, lavish, gorgeous, opulent, rich, costly, *inf.* ritzy, classy. ***Ant.*** plain; austere; cheap.

pocket *n.* **1 pouch,** compartment, receptacle. **2 small area,** small region, small district, small zone.
‣ *adj.* **small,** little, miniature, compact, concise, abridged.

poet *n.* **versifier,** rhymer, rhymester, balladeer, lyricist, bard, minstrel, *derog.* poetaster, sonneteer, balladmonger.

poetic *adj.* **1 poetical,** metrical, rhythmical, lyrical, elegiac.
2 imaginative, creative, figurative, symbolic, flowery, aesthetic, artistic, tasteful, graceful, elegant, sensitive.

poignant *adj.* **moving,** affecting, touching, emotional, sentimental, heartfelt, sad, sorrowful, tearful, evocative, pitiful, piteous, pitiable.

point *n.* **1 sharp end,** tapered end, tip, top, extremity, prong, spike, tine. **2 promontory,** headland, head, foreland, cape, bluff.
3 place, position, location, situation, site, spot, area, locality.
4 extent, degree, stage, position, circumstance, condition. **5 point/ moment in time,** time, juncture, stage, period, moment, instant.
6 critical point, decisive point, crux, moment of truth, point of no return. **7 detail,** item,

particular. **8 main point,** central point, essential point, focal point, salient point, keynote, heart of the matter, essence, nub, core, pith, marrow, meat, crux, subject, subject under discussion, issue, topic, question, matter, item, part, element, constituent, component, ingredient.
9 meaning, significance, signification, import, essence, gist, substance, drift, thrust, burden, theme, tenor, vein.
10 aim, purpose, object, objective, goal, intention, reason for, use, utility. **11 characteristic,** trait, attribute, quality, feature, property, predisposition, streak, peculiarity, idiosyncrasy. **12 mark,** score.
‣ *v.* **direct,** aim, level, train.

pointed *adj.* **1 sharp,** cuspidate, acicular. **2 cutting,** trenchant, biting, incisive, penetrating, forceful, telling, significant.
3 obvious, evident, conspicuous, striking, emphasized, unmistakable.

pointless *adj.* **1 futile,** useless, in vain, unavailing, to no purpose/ avail, valueless, unproductive, senseless, absurd, foolish, nonsensical, stupid, silly.
2 meaningless, insignificant, vague, empty, worthless, irrelevant, senseless, fatuous,

foolish, nonsensical, stupid, silly, absurd, inane. **Ant.** useful; valuable; significant.

poise *n.* **1 composure,** equanimity, self-possession, aplomb, presence of mind, self-assurance, self-control, calmness, coolness, collectedness, serenity, dignity, imperturbability, suaveness, urbanity, elegance, *inf.* cool. **2 balance,** equilibrium, control, grace, gracefulness.
▸ *v.* **1 balance,** steady, position, support. **2 steady,** get into position, brace, get ready, prepare. **3 hang,** hang suspended, float, hover.

poised *adj.* **1 composed,** serene, self-possessed, self-assured, self-controlled, calm, cool, collected, dignified, imperturbable, unperturbed, unruffled, suave, urbane, elegant, *inf.* unflappable. **2 ready,** prepared, all set, standing by, waiting (and ready), waiting in the wings. **Ant.** perturbed; flustered.

poison *n.* **1 venom,** toxin. **2 blight,** bane, contagion, cancer, canker, malignancy, corruption, pollution.
▸ *v.* **1 contaminate,** pollute, blight, spoil, infect, defile, adulterate. **2 corrupt,** warp, pervert, deprave, defile, debauch.

poisonous *adj.* **1 venomous,** toxic, mephitic, noxious, deadly, fatal, lethal. **2 cancerous,** malignant, corrupting, polluting, harmful, injurious, noxious, pernicious, spiteful, malicious, rancorous, malevolent, vicious, vindictive, slanderous, libelous, defamatory. **Ant.** harmless; non-toxic; benign.

poke *v.* **jab,** prod, dig, elbow, nudge, butt, push, thrust, shove, stick.
▸ *n.* **jab,** prod, dig, nudge, elbow, butt, push, thrust, shove.

poky *adj.* **slow,** slow-moving, dawdling, unhurried, laggard.

pole *n.* **1 post,** upright, pillar, stanchion, standard, support, prop, rod, shaft, mast. **2 bar,** rod, stick.

police *n.* **police force,** the law, policemen, policewomen, police officers, constabulary, *inf.* the cops, the boys in blue, *derog* the fuzz, the pigs.
▸ *v.* **1 patrol,** make the rounds of, guard, keep guard over, keep watch on, protect. **2 keep in order,** control, keep under control, regulate, enforce, administer, oversee, monitor.

policy *n.* **plan,** scheme, program, schedule, code, system, approach, procedure, guideline, theory.

polish *v.* **wax,** buff, rub, burnish, shine.

polished *adj.* **1 waxed,** buffed, burnished, shining, shiny, glossy, gleaming, lustrous, glassy, slippery. **2 refined,** cultivated, civilized, well-bred, polite, well-mannered, genteel, courtly, urbane, suave, sophisticated. **3 expert,** accomplished, masterly, skillful, proficient, adept, impeccable, flawless, faultless, perfect, consummate, exquisite, outstanding, remarkable. *Ant.* dull; tarnished; rough; inexpert.

polite *adj.* **1 well-mannered,** mannerly, courteous, civil, respectful, deferential, well-behaved, well-bred, genteel, polished, tactful, diplomatic. **2 well-bred,** civilized, cultured, refined, polished, genteel, urbane, sophisticated, elegant, courtly. *Ant.* rude; impolite; unmannerly; uncouth.

politic *adj.* **wise,** prudent, sensible, advisable, judicious, well-judged, sagacious, expedient, shrewd, astute, discreet, tactful, diplomatic.

political *adj.* **1 governmental,** ministerial, public, civic, administrative, bureaucratic. **2 factional,** partisan, bipartisan, power, status.

poll *n.* **1 vote,** ballot, vote-casting, canvass, headcount, show of hands, straw vote/poll. **2 returns,** count, tally. **3 opinion poll,** survey, market research, sampling, *Trademark* Gallup poll.
▶ *v.* **1 register,** record, return, get, gain. **2 ballot,** canvass, question, interview, survey, sample.

pollute *v.* **1 contaminate,** adulterate, infect, taint, poison, befoul, foul, make dirty, make filthy. **2 corrupt,** poison, warp, pervert, deprave, defile, debauch. **3 besmirch,** sully, taint, blacken, tarnish, dishonor, debase, vitiate, desecrate. *Ant.* purify; clean; disinfect.

pomp *n.* **1 ceremony,** ceremoniousness, ritual, display, pageantry, pageant, show, spectacle, splendor, grandeur, magnificence, majesty, glory, brilliance, flourish, style. **2 ostentation,** exhibitionism, grandiosity, glitter, show, showiness, pomposity, vainglory, fanfaronade.

pompous *adj.* **1 self-important,** presumptuous, imperious, overbearing, grandiose, affected, pretentious, arrogant, vain, haughty, proud, conceited, egotistic, supercilious, condescending, patronizing, *inf.* uppity, uppish. **2 high-sounding,** high-flown, bombastic, turgid, grandiloquent, magniloquent, euphuistic, portentous, pedantic, stilted, fustian. *Ant.* modest; humble; self-effacing; unpretentious.

ponder *v.* **1 think about,** give thought to, consider, reflect on, mull over, contemplate, meditate on, deliberate about/on, dwell on, brood on/over, ruminate about/on/over, puzzle over, cogitate about/on, weigh up, review. **2 think,** consider, reflect, meditate, contemplate, deliberate, brood, ruminate, cogitate, cerebrate.

pontificate *v.* **hold forth,** expound, declaim, preach, lay down the law, sound off, dogmatize, sermonize, *inf.* preachify.

poor *adj.* **1 badly off,** poverty-stricken, penniless, hard up, needy, deprived, in need, needful, in want, indigent, impoverished, impecunious, destitute, penurious, beggared, in straitened circumstances, as poor as a church mouse, in the red, *inf.* broke, stone-broke, flat broke, on the rocks. **2 humble,** lowly, mean, modest, plain. **3 sparse,** scanty, meager, scarce, skimpy, reduced, paltry, miserable, exiguous, deficient, lacking, wanting, insufficient. **4 unproductive,** barren, unyielding, unfruitful, uncultivable, uncultivatable, bare, arid, sterile, infecund, unfecund. **5 wretched,** pitiable, pitiful, unfortunate, unlucky, luckless, unhappy, hapless, ill-fated, ill-starred. **6 miserable,** sad, sorry, spiritless, mean, low, base, disgraceful, despicable, contemptible, abject, pathetic. *Ant.* wealthy; rich; superior; satisfactory.

populace *n.* **1 (general) public,** people, population, common people, folk, masses, commonalty, mob, multitude, rabble, rank and file, hoi polloi, *inf.* proles, plebs. **2 population,** inhabitants, residents.

popular *adj.* **1 well-liked,** liked, favored, in favor, favorite, well-received, approved, admired, accepted, sought-after, in demand, desired, wanted, fashionable, in fashion, in vogue, in. **2 well-known,** famous, celebrated, renowned. **3 inexpensive,** budget, low-budget, low-priced, cheap, reasonably priced, reasonable, moderately priced, modestly priced. **4 middle-of-the-road,** middlebrow, lowbrow, accessible, simple, understandable, readily understood, easy to understand, readily comprehensible, *inf.* pop. **5 public,** general, civic. **6 current,** prevalent, prevailing, accepted, recognized, widespread, universal, general, common, customary, usual, standard, stock, conventional. *Ant.* unpopular; unknown; highbrow.

popularity *n.* **1 favor,** approval, approbation, admiration, acceptance. **2 demand,** fashionableness, vogue, trendiness. **3 currency,** prevalence, prevalency, recognition. **4 fame,** renown, acclaim, esteem, repute.

populate *v.* **inhabit,** dwell in, occupy, people.

population *n.* **1 inhabitants,** residents, community, people, citizenry, populace, society, folk. **2 census,** headcount.

populous *adj.* **densely populated,** heavily populated, thickly populated, crowded. *Ant.* empty; uninhabited; deserted.

pore *v.* phrase: **pore over 1 study closely,** read intently, peruse closely, be absorbed in, scrutinize, examine closely. **2 meditate on,** brood on/over, go over, ponder, reflect on, deliberate on, mull over, muse on, think about, contemplate.
▸ *n.* **opening,** orifice, hole, aperture, vent, outlet, *Tech.* spiracle, stoma.

pornographic *adj.* **obscene,** blue, salacious, lewd, prurient, erotic, indecent, dirty, smutty, filthy, *inf.* porn, porno. *Ant.* decent; pure.

porous *adj.* **absorbent,** permeable, penetrable, pervious, spongelike, spongy, honeycombed, holey. *Ant.* impermeable; impenetrable; impervious.

port *n.* **seaport,** harbor, harborage, haven, anchorage.

portable *adj.* **transportable,** movable, conveyable, easily carried, lightweight, compact, handy, manageable.

portend *v.* **be a sign of,** be a warning of, be an indication of, be a presage of, point to, be an omen of, herald, bode, augur, presage, forebode, foreshadow, foretell.

portion *n.* **1 helping,** serving, piece, quantity. **2 share,** division, quota, part, bit, piece, allocation, allotment, *inf.* cut. **3 lot,** fate, destiny, fortune, luck.
▸ *v.* **share,** divide, split, partition, carve up, parcel out, *inf.* divvy up.

portly *adj.* **stout,** plump, fat, corpulent, obese, tubby, ample, stocky.

portrait *n.* **1 painting,** picture, drawing, sketch, portrayal, representation, likeness, image, study, portraiture, canvas. **2 photograph,** photo, picture,

studio portrait, study, shot, snapshot, snap, still.
3 description, portrayal, depiction, account, story, chronicle, thumbnail sketch, vignette, profile.

portray *v.* **1 paint a picture of,** paint, draw a picture of, draw, sketch, depict, represent, delineate. **2 describe,** depict, characterize, paint a word picture of, paint in words, put into words. **3 play,** act the part of, play the part of, act, perform, represent, execute.

pose *v.* **1 sit,** model, take up a position. **2 arrange,** position, lay out, set out, dispose, place, put, locate, situate. **3 strike an attitude,** posture, put on an act, act, playact, attitudinize, put on airs, show off. **4 put forward,** put, submit, advance, propound, posit. **5 present,** set, create, cause, give rise to.
▸ *n.* **1 posture,** stance, position, attitude, bearing, carriage. **2 act,** playacting, pretense, façade, front, masquerade, posture, attitudinizing, affectation, airs.

poser *n.* **1 difficult question,** awkward problem, vexed question, enigma, dilemma, puzzle, mystery, conundrum, *inf.* brainteaser. **2 model,** sitter, subject.

posh *adj.* **luxurious,** luxury, deluxe, sumptuous, opulent, lavish, rich, grand, elegant, ornate, fancy, plush, *inf.* classy, ritzy, swanky.

position *n.* **1 situation,** location, site, place, spot, area, locality, locale, scene, setting, bearings, whereabouts. **2 posture,** stance, attitude, pose, bearing. **3 situation,** state, condition, circumstance, predicament, plight, pass. **4 advantageous position,** favorable position, primacy, the upper hand, the edge. **5 point of view,** viewpoint, opinion, way of thinking, outlook, attitude, stand, standpoint, stance. **6 post,** job, situation, appointment, role, office, place, capacity, duty. **7 place,** level, grade, grading, rank, status, standing. **8 rank,** status, stature, standing, social standing, prestige, influence, reputation, importance, consequence.
▸ *v.* **place,** locate, situate, put, arrange, set, settle, dispose, array.

positive *adj.* **1 clear,** clear-cut, definite, precise, categorical, direct, explicit, express, firm. **2 real,** actual, absolute, concrete, conclusive, unequivocal, incontrovertible, indisputable, undeniable, incontestable, unmistakable. **3 certain,** sure,

assured, confident, convinced.
4 affirmative. 5 constructive,
productive, helpful, practical,
useful, beneficial. **6 confident,**
optimistic, assured, assertive,
firm, forceful, determined,
resolute, emphatic, dogmatic.
7 good, favorable, effective,
promising, encouraging,
heartening. **8 utter,** complete,
absolute, perfect, out-and-out,
outright, thoroughgoing,
thorough, downright, sheer,
consummate, unmitigated, rank.
Ant. vague; uncertain; unsure;
negative.

possess *v.* **1 own,** be the owner
of, have, be the possessor of, be
the proud owner/possessor of,
count among one's possessions,
have to one's name, hold, be
blessed with, enjoy. **2 have,** be
endowed with, be gifted with.
3 seize, take into possession, take
possession of, take over, occupy.
4 influence, control, dominate,
have mastery over, bewitch,
enchant, put under a spell,
obsess, *inf.* get into someone.

possessions *pl. n.* **belongings,**
things, property, luggage,
baggage, bags and baggage,
personal effects, goods, goods and
chattels, accouterments,
paraphernalia, appendages,
assets, impedimenta.

possessive *adj.* **1 acquisitive,**
greedy, grasping, covetous,
selfish, *inf.* grabby.
2 overprotective, clinging,
controlling, dominating, jealous.

possibility *n.* **1 feasibility,**
practicability, attainability,
likelihood, potentiality,
conceivability, probability.
2 likelihood, prospect, chance,
hope, probability, risk, hazard.

possible *adj.* **1 feasible,** able to be
done, practicable, doable,
attainable, achievable, realizable,
within reach, *inf.* on. **2 likely,**
potential, conceivable,
imaginable, probable, credible,
tenable, odds-on. *Ant.* impossible;
impracticable; unlikely.

possibly *adv.* **1 perhaps,** maybe,
it may be, for all one knows, very
likely, *lit.* peradventure.
2 conceivably, by any means, by
any chance, at all.

post[1] *n.* **stake,** upright, pole, shaft,
prop, support, column, stanchion,
standard, stock, picket, pillar,
pale, palisade, baluster, newel.

post[2] *v.* **1 put up,** stick, stick up,
pin, pin up, tack, tack up, attach,
affix, hang, display. **2 announce,**
make known, advertise, publish,
publicize, circulate, broadcast.

post[3] *n.* **appointment,** assignment,
office, position, job, situation;
work, employment.

post[4] *v.* **station,** put, place, position, set, situate, locate.

post[5] *v.* **enter,** write in, fill in, record, register, note.

poster *n.* **1 placard,** bill, notice, flyer, public notice, advertisement, announcement, bulletin, *inf.* ad. **2** (large) picture, print, reproduction.

postpone *v.* **defer,** put off, put back, delay, hold over, adjourn, shelve, table, pigeonhole, *inf.* put on ice, put on the back burner. *Ant.* advance; bring forward.

postscript *n.* **1 PS,** subscript, afterthought. **2 subscript,** afterword, addendum, appendix, codicil, appendage, supplement.

posture *n.* **1 position,** pose, attitude. **2 carriage,** bearing, stance. **3 attitude,** position, point of view, viewpoint, opinion, way of thinking, outlook, stand, standpoint, stance, angle, slant.
▶ *v.* **pose,** strike an attitude, put on an act, act, playact, attitudinize, put on airs, show off.

potent *adj.* **powerful,** strong, effective, efficacious, forceful, vigorous, mighty, influential, authoritative, commanding, dominant, energetic, dynamic, cogent, compelling, convincing, persuasive, eloquent, impressive, telling, *lit.* puissant. *Ant.* weak; powerless; impotent.

potential *adj.* **1 budding,** embryonic, developing, promising, prospective, likely, possible, probable. **2 latent,** dormant, inherent, embryonic, developing, promising. **3 likely,** possible, probable.
▶ *n.* **1 promise,** capability, capacity, ability, aptitude, talent, flair. **2 possibilities,** promise, potentiality.

potion *n.* **drink,** beverage, brew, concoction, mixture, draft, elixir, philter.

pouch *n.* **bag,** purse, wallet, container.

pounce *v.* **swoop down,** drop down, descend.
▶ *n.* **swoop,** spring, lunge, leap, jump, bound, grab, attack.

pound[1] *v.* **1 crush,** beat, pulverize, smash, mash, grind, comminute, triturate. **2 beat,** batter, pummel, strike, belabor, hammer, pelt, thump. **3 tramp,** tread heavily on, trudge, walk heavily on, stomp along, clump along. **4 beat heavily,** pulsate, pulse, throb, thump, pump, palpitate, go pit-a-pat.

pound[2] *n.* **compound,** enclosure, pen, confine, yard.

pour *v.* **1 let flow,** decant, splash, spill. **2 gush,** rush, stream, flow, course, spout, jet, spurt. **3 rain heavily/hard,** come down in torrents/sheets, rain cats and dogs. **4 stream**, swarm, crowd, throng, flood.

poverty *n.* **1 pennilessness,** neediness, need, want, hardship, deprivation, indigence, impoverishment, impecuniousness, destitution, penury, privation, beggary, pauperism, straitened circumstances. **2 humbleness,** lowliness, meanness, modesty, plainness. **3 deficiency,** dearth, shortage, scarcity, paucity, insufficiency, lack, want, meagerness. **4 poorness,** barrenness, unfruitfulness, bareness, aridity, aridness, sterility, infecundity. ***Ant.*** wealth; luxury; abundance.

powder *n.* **dust,** fine grains, face powder, talcum powder, talc, dusting powder, baby powder, soap powder, baking powder.

powdery *adj.* **1 powderlike,** fine, dry, dusty, chalky, floury, friable, granulated, ground, crushed, pulverized. **2 powder-covered,** powdered.

power *n.* **1 ability,** capability, capacity, potential, potentiality, faculty, competence. **2 powerfulness,** strength, force, forcefulness, might, weight, vigor, energy, potency. **3 control,** authority, mastery, domination, dominance, rule, command, ascendancy, supremacy, dominion, sway, sovereignty, influence. **4 authority,** authorization, warrant, license, right, prerogative. **5 energy,** electrical power, nuclear power, solar power. **6 powerfulness,** potency, strength, force, forcefulness, eloquence, effectiveness, cogency, conviction, persuasiveness. ***Ant.*** inability; incapacity; weakness; impotence.

powerful *adj.* **1 strong,** sturdy, strapping, stout, stalwart, robust, vigorous, tough, mighty. **2 influential,** controlling, dominant, authoritative, commanding, forceful, strong, vigorous, potent, puissant. **3 forceful,** strong, effective, cogent, compelling, convincing, persuasive, eloquent, impressive, telling. **4 strong,** great, weighty, influential. ***Ant.*** powerless; weak; ineffective.

powerless *adj.* **1 impotent. 2 paralyzed,** disabled, incapacitated, debilitated, weak, feeble. **3 helpless,** unfit, impotent, ineffectual, inadequate. ***Ant.*** powerful; potent; strong.

practicable *adj.* **feasible,** possible, within the bounds of possibility, within the realm of possibility, viable, workable, doable, achievable, attainable, accomplishable. *Ant.* impracticable; impossible.

practical *adj.* **1 hands-on,** active, seasoned, applied, empirical, pragmatic, workaday, *inf.* nuts and bolts. **2 functional,** useful, utilitarian, sensible. **3 businesslike,** sensible, down-to-earth, pragmatic, realistic, matter-of-fact,utilitarian, expedient. **4 virtual,** effective, in effect, essential. *Ant.* theoretical; impractical.

practically *adv.* **1 almost,** nearly, very nearly, virtually, all but, in effect, *inf.* pretty nearly/well. **2 sensibly,** with common sense, realistically, reasonably, pragmatically.

practice *n.* **1 action,** operation, application, effect, exercise, use. **2 training,** preparation, study, exercise, drill, workout, rehearsal. **3 procedure,** method, system, usage, tradition, convention. **4 habit,** custom, routine, wont. **5 profession,** career, business, work, pursuit. **6 firm,** business.
▸ *v.* **1 carry out,** perform, do, execute, follow, pursue, observe. **2 work at,** go through, run through, go over, rehearse, polish, refine. **3 work at,** have a career in, pursue a career in, engage in, specialize in.

praise *v.* **1 applaud,** acclaim, cheer, compliment someone on, congratulate someone on, pay tribute to, extol, laud, sing the praises of. **2 worship,** glorify, honor, exalt, adore, laud, pay tribute to, give thanks to. *Ant.* criticize; condemn.
▸ *n.* **1 approval,** approbation, applause, acclaim, acclamation, cheers, compliments, congratulations, commendation, tributes, accolades, plaudits, eulogy, panegyric, encomium, extolment, laudation, ovation, bouquets. **2 worship,** glory, honor, devotion, exaltation, adoration, tribute, thanks.

praiseworthy *adj.* **commendable,** laudable, admirable, honorable, estimable, creditable, deserving, meritorious, worthy, excellent, exemplary, sterling, fine. *Ant.* disgraceful; dishonorable.

prance *v.* **1 leap,** spring, jump, skip, cavort, caper, frisk, gambol. **2 parade,** strut, swagger.

prank *n.* **trick,** practical joke, joke, hoax, caper, stunt, *inf.* lark.

pray *v.* **1 say one's prayers. 2 appeal to,** call upon, beseech, entreat, ask earnestly, request, implore, beg, petition, solicit, plead with, importune, supplicate, sue, invoke, crave, adjure.

prayer *n.* **1 devotion,** communion, litany, invocation, intercession. **2 appeal,** plea, beseeching, entreaty, petition, solicitation, supplication, suit, invocation, adjuration.

preach *v.* **1 give a sermon,** deliver a sermon, sermonize, spread the gospel, evangelize. **2 make known,** proclaim, teach, spread. **3 advocate,** recommend, advise, urge, exhort.

preacher *n.* **1 minister,** reverend, parson, clergyman, clergywoman, churchman, churchwoman, ecclesiastic, cleric, missionary, revivalist, evangelist, televangelist. **2 advocate,** adviser, urger, exhorter.

precarious *adj.* **1 uncertain,** unsure, unpredictable, undependable, unreliable, risky, hazardous, chancy, doubtful, dubious, unsettled, insecure, unstable, *inf.* dicey. **2 risky,** hazardous, insecure, unstable, shaky, tricky, perilous, dangerous, touch-and-go, *inf.* dicey, hairy. *Ant.* safe; secure.

precaution *n.* **1 preventive measure,** preventative measure, safety measure, safeguard, provision. **2 foresight,** foresightedness, forethought, farsightedness, anticipation, prudence, circumspection,

caution, care, attentiveness, chariness, wariness.

precede *v.* **1 go before,** be the predecessor of, come before, go/come ahead of, lead, usher in, antedate, antecede, lead to, lead up to, herald, pave the way for. **2 preface,** prefix, introduce, begin, open, launch. *Ant.* follow; succeed.

precedence *n.* **rank,** seniority, superiority, pre-eminence, eminence, supremacy, primacy, transcendence, ascendancy.

precedent *n.* **previous case,** prior case, previous instance, prior instance, pattern, model, example, exemplar, paradigm, criterion, yardstick, standard.

precious *adj.* **1 valuable,** high-priced, costly, expensive, dear, priceless, rare, choice, valued, cherished, prized, treasured, favorite, beloved, adored, revered, venerated. **2 affected,** artificial, chichi, overrefined, effete. *Ant.* worthless; cheap.

precipitate *v.* **1 hasten,** accelerate, expedite, speed up, push forward, bring on/about, trigger. **2 hurl headlong,** hurl, throw headlong, fling, thrust, heave, propel.
▸ *adj.* **1 hurried,** rapid, swift, speedy, headlong, abrupt, sudden, unexpected, breakneck, violent,

precipitous. **2 hasty,** hurried, rash, heedless, reckless, impetuous, impulsive, precipitous, harebrained.

precipitous *adj.* **1 steep,** sheer, perpendicular, abrupt, high. **2 precipitate,** hurried, abrupt. **3 precipitate,** hasty, impetuous.

precise *adj.* **1 exact,** literal, actual, close, faithful, strict, express, minute, accurate, correct. **2 exact,** very, actual, particular, specific, distinct. **3 careful,** exact, meticulous, scrupulous, conscientious, punctilious, particular, methodical, fastidious, finicky, rigid, strict, rigorous. ***Ant.*** loose; imprecise; inaccurate; careless.

preclude *v.* **1 prevent,** prohibit, debar, interdict, block, bar, hinder, impede. **2 make impossible,** rule out, eliminate.

precocious *adj.* **advanced,** (far) ahead, forward, gifted, talented, brilliant, bright, quick, intelligent, smart, adultlike.

preconception *n.* **preconceived idea/notion,** assumption, presupposition, presumption, prejudgment, prejudice, bias.

predatory *adj.* **1 predacious,** carnivorous, rapacious, raptorial. **2 plundering,** pillaging, marauding, ravaging, looting, robbing, thieving, rapacious.

3 exploitative, exploiting, imposing, greedy, acquisitive, rapacious, vulturine.

predecessor *n.* **1 precursor,** forerunner, antecedent. **2 ancestor,** forefather, forebear, progenitor, antecedent. ***Ant.*** successor; descendants.

predestine *v.* **preordain,** foreordain, predetermine, fate, destine, predestinate.

predicament *n.* **difficult situation,** problematic situation, corner, plight, tight corner, mess, emergency, crisis, dilemma, quandary, trouble, *inf.* jam, sticky situation, hole, fix, pickle, scrape, tight spot, spot.

predict *v.* **forecast,** foretell, prophesy, foresee, divine, prognosticate, forewarn, forebode, portend, presage, augur.

predictable *adj.* **foreseeable,** to be expected, expected, anticipated, probable, likely, certain, sure, *inf.* in the cards.

predilection *n.* **liking,** fondness, preference, love, partiality, taste, weakness, soft spot, fancy, inclination, leaning, bias, propensity, bent, proclivity, proneness, penchant, predisposition.

predominate *v.* **1 dominate,** be in control, rule, hold ascendancy, hold sway, have the upper hand, carry most weight. **2 be prevalent,** preponderate.

preeminent *adj.* **outstanding,** leading, foremost, chief, excellent, distinguished, prominent, eminent, important, famous, renowned, supreme, superior, unrivaled, unsurpassed, transcendent. *Ant.* unknown; undistinguished; obscure.

preface *n.* **introduction,** foreword, front matter, forward matter, preamble, prologue, prelude, proem, exordium, prolegomenon, *inf.* prelims, intro.
▸ *v.* **precede,** prefix, introduce, begin, open, launch.

prefer *v.* **1 like better/best,** favor, be more/most partial to, incline toward, choose, select, pick, opt for, go for, single out, *inf.* fancy.
2 would rather, would sooner, favor, choose, opt, elect, wish, want. **3 put forward,** proffer, present, offer, propose, tender, lodge, file, press. **4 promote,** upgrade, advance, move up, elevate, aggrandize.

preference *n.* **1 choice,** first choice, first option, liking, fancy, desire, wish, inclination, partiality, predilection, leaning, bias, bent. **2 choice,** selection, option, pick. **3 preferential treatment,** favored treatment, favor, precedence, priority, advantage.

preferential *adj.* **special,** better, advantageous, favored, privileged, partial, partisan.

pregnant *adj.* **1 having a baby/ child,** expectant, with child, enceinte, *inf.* expecting, in the family way, in a delicate condition, knocked up .
2 meaningful, significant, eloquent, expressive, suggestive, loaded, charged, pointed, telling.

prejudice *n.* **1 bias,** partiality, jaundiced eye, preconceived idea, preconceived notion, preconception, prejudgment, predetermination. **2 bias,** discrimination, partisanship, partiality, preference, one-sidedness, chauvinism, bigotry, narrow-mindedness, intolerance, unfairness, unjustness, racism, sexism, ageism, heterosexism.
3 detriment, disadvantage, damage, injury, harm, hurt, loss.
▸ *v.* **1 bias,** make partial, make partisan, color, poison, jaundice, influence, sway, predispose. **2 be prejudicial to,** be detrimental to, be deleterious to, be disadvantageous to, damage, injure, harm, hurt, mar, spoil, impair, undermine.

prejudicial *adj.* **detrimental,** deleterious, disadvantageous, unfavorable, damaging, injurious, harmful, hurtful, inimical.

preliminary *adj.* **1 introductory,** prefatory, prior, precursory, opening, initial, beginning, preparatory, initiatory. **2 prior,** precursory, qualifying, eliminating. **3 introductory,** early, exploratory, pilot, test, trial.
▶ *n.* **1 preliminary measure,** preliminary action, preparation, groundwork, first round, introduction, preamble, prelude, opening. **2 first round,** heat, trial, preliminary exam/examination.

prelude *n.* **1 precursor,** forerunner, curtain-raiser, harbinger, herald, preliminary, introduction, start, beginning. **2 introduction,** preface, prologue, preamble, proem, exordium, prolegomenon, *inf.* intro. **3 overture,** introductory movement, voluntary.

premature *adj.* **1 too soon,** too early, early, untimely. **2 too soon,** hasty, precipitate, impulsive, impetuous, rash. **3 incomplete,** undeveloped, immature, embryonic.

premeditated *adj.* **planned,** preplanned, prearranged, intentional, intended, deliberate, calculated, willful.

premier *n.* **head of government,** head of state, chief executive, president, prime minister, chancellor.
▶ *adj.* **leading,** foremost, chief, principal, head, top-ranking, top, prime, first, main.

premonition *n.* **1 foreboding,** presage, presentiment, intuition, feeling, hunch, suspicion, sneaking suspicion, misgiving, apprehension, fear, feeling in one's bones, funny feeling. **2 forewarning,** warning, sign, pre-indication, indication, omen, portent.

preoccupied *adj.* **lost in thought,** deep in thought, immersed in thought, in a brown study, absorbed, engrossed, pensive, absentminded, distracted, abstracted, distrait, oblivious, far away, rapt.

preparation *n.* **1 making ready,** preparing, arrangement, development, assembling, assembly, drawing up, production, construction, composing, composition, fashioning. **2 arrangement,** provision, preparatory measure, necessary step, groundwork, spadework. **3 coaching,** training, grooming, priming. **4 mixture,** compound, concoction, composition, tincture.

prepare *v.* **1 get ready,** make ready, arrange, develop, put together, assemble, draw up, produce, construct, compose, concoct, fashion, work up. **2 make preparations,** get ready, arrange things, make provision, get everything set, take the necessary steps, lay the groundwork, do the spadework, *inf.* gear oneself up, psych oneself up, gird up one's loins. **3 train,** get into shape, practice, exercise, warm up. **4 do preparation,** study, do homework. **5 coach,** train, groom, prime. **6 make ready,** brace, steel. **7 cook,** make, put together, assemble, *inf.* fix, throw together.

preposterous *adj.* **absurd,** ridiculous, foolish, ludicrous, farcical, asinine, senseless, unreasonable, irrational, outrageous, shocking, astonishing, unbelievable, incredible, unthinkable, *inf.* crazy, insane.

prerequisite *adj.* **necessary,** needed, required, called for, essential, requisite, vital, indispensable, imperative, obligatory, mandatory.
▶ *n.* **requirement,** requisite, necessity, essential, precondition, condition, sine qua non, *inf.* must.

prescribe *v.* **1 write a prescription for,** order, advise, direct. **2 advise,** recommend, commend, suggest. **3 lay down,** require, direct, stipulate, specify, impose, decree, order, command, ordain, enjoin.

presence *n.* **1 existence,** being. **2 attendance,** company, companionship. **3 company,** propinquity, proximity, neighborhood, vicinity, closeness, nearness. **4 magnetism,** aura, charisma, personality, attraction, poise, self-assurance, self-possession, self-confidence. **5 dignified bearing,** impressive carriage, dignified air/demeanor, dignity. **6 manifestation,** apparition, supernatural being, spirit, ghost, specter, wraith. *Ant.* absence; nonattendance.

present[1] *adj.* **1 existing,** existent, extant, present-day, current, contemporary. **2 in attendance,** here, there, near, nearby, available, at hand, ready. *Ant.* absent; missing.

present[2] *v.* **1 give,** hand over, confer, bestow, donate, award, grant, accord. **2 submit,** set forth, put forward, proffer, offer, tender, advance, give, send, tender. **3 introduce,** make known. **4 show,** put on show, exhibit, display, put on display, demonstrate, introduce, launch. **5 put on,** produce, perform, stage, mount.

present[3] *n.* **gift,** donation,

offering, contribution, gratuity, handout, giveaway, presentation, largesse, award, premium, bounty, boon, benefaction; *inf.* freebie.

presentable *adj.* **well-groomed,** smartly dressed, tidily dressed, tidy, spruce, of smart appearance, fit to be seen.

preserve *v.* **1 protect,** safeguard, care for, keep, defend, guard, secure, shelter, shield. **2 save,** keep, safeguard, maintain, perpetuate, keep up, keep alive, keep going, continue with, uphold, prolong, perpetuate. **3 keep up,** keep alive, keep going, maintain, continue with, uphold, prolong, perpetuate. **4 conserve,** keep, save, retain, put away, put aside, store, hoard. **5 cure,** smoke, dry, pickle, salt, marinate, kipper, freeze, freeze-dry, can, *inf.* put up, lay by. **Ant.** damage; neglect.
▸ *n.* **1 sanctuary,** reserve, reservation, game reserve. **2 area,** domain, field, sphere, realm, *inf.* thing.

preside *v.* **chair,** be in the chair, be chairman/chairwoman/chairperson, officiate.

press *v.* **1 press down,** depress, push down, force down, bear down on. **2 crush,** squeeze, compress, mash, reduce. **3 iron,** smooth out, put creases in, calender, mangle. **4 flatten,** make flat, smooth out. **5 clasp,** enfold, hold close, clutch, grasp, embrace, hug, cuddle, squeeze, crush. **6 squeeze,** give something a squeeze, pat, caress. **7 urge,** entreat, exhort, implore, put pressure on, use pressure on, pressurize, force, compel, coerce, constrain. **8 plead,** urge, push forward, advance insistently. **9 crowd,** surge, cluster, mill, flock, gather, swarm, throng. **10 harass,** besiege, attack, assail, beset, worry, torment.
▸ *n.* **1 newspapers,** papers, news media, journalism, the newspaper world, the media, the fourth estate, journalists, newspapermen, newspaperwomen, reporters, gentlemen/ladies of the press. **2 press coverage,** press reporting, newspaper articles, newspaper write-ups. **3 printing press. 4 printing firm,** publishing firm, publishing house. **5 crowd,** throng, multitude, mob, troop, horde, swarm, herd, flock, pack. **6 pressure,** strain, stress, urgency, demands, hurry, hustle, hustle and bustle, flurry.

pressing *adj.* **urgent,** vital, crucial, critical, demanding, important, high-priority, exigent, pivotal.

pressure *n.* **1 force,** weight, heaviness. **2 compression,** compressing, squeezing, crushing. **3 force,** compulsion, coercion, constraint, duress. **4 strain,** stress, tension, burden, load, weight, trouble, *inf.* hassle. **5 adversity,** difficulty, urgency, strain, stress, tension.
▶ *v.* **put pressure on,** use pressure on, press, force, compel, coerce, constrain, bulldoze, dragoon.

prestige *n.* **status,** standing, stature, importance, reputation, fame, renown, esteem, influence, authority, supremacy, eminence, superiority, predominance.

prestigious *adj.* **1 respected,** esteemed, eminent, distinguished, of high standing, well-known, celebrated, illustrious, renowned, famous. **2 conferring prestige,** important, prominent, impressive, high-ranking, influential, glamorous. *Ant.* unknown; obscure; minor; humble.

presume *v.* **1 assume,** take for granted, take it, suppose, presuppose, believe, think, imagine, judge, guess, surmise, conjecture, hypothesize, infer, deduce. **2 have the temerity,** have the audacity, be so bold as, make so bold as, have the effrontery, go so far as, dare, venture.

presumptuous *adj.* **presuming,** ultraconfident, overconfident, cocksure, (overly) self-confident, self-assured, arrogant, egotistical, conceited, overbold, bold, audacious, forward, insolent, impudent, bumptious, self-assertive, overbearing, overweening, haughty, *inf.* bigheaded, swellheaded, too big for one's britches/boots, pushy.

pretend *v.* **1 put on an act,** act, playact, dissemble, sham, feign, fake, fake it, dissimulate, make believe, put on a false front, posture, go through the motions, affect, profess, make out, fabricate, simulate, put on. **2 lay claim,** make a claim, aspire. **3 claim,** profess, purport.

pretender *n.* **claimant,** claimer, aspirant.

pretense *n.* **1 putting on an act,** acting, dissembling, shamming, faking, dissimulation, make-believe, invention, imagination, posturing, show, semblance, appearance, false front, guise, façade, masquerade, mask, veneer, cover, charade. **2 false show,** show, semblance, false appearance, appearance, false front, guise, façade, masquerade, mask, veneer, cover, charade. **3 pretext,** false excuse, guise, sham, ruse, wile, trickery, lie,

falsehood. **4 claim,** aspiration, purporting, profession.
5 pretentiousness, display, ostentation, affectation, showiness, flaunting, posturing. *Ant.* reality; fact.

pretentious *adj.* **affected,** ostentatious, showy, overambitious, pompous, artificial, mannered, high-flown, high-sounding, flowery, grandiose, elaborate, extravagant, flamboyant, grandiloquent, magniloquent, bombastic, orotund, flaunting, *inf.* highfalutin. *Ant.* plain; simple; natural; unaffected.

pretty *adj.* **1 attractive,** lovely, good-looking, nice-looking, comely, personable, prepossessing, appealing, charming, delightful, nice, engaging, pleasing, winning, winsome, cute, as pretty as a picture. **2 attractive,** lovely, appealing, pleasant, pleasing, charming, delightful, nice.
3 considerable, large, sizable, substantial, appreciable, fair, tolerable, goodly, *inf.* tidy. *Ant.* plain; ugly; unpleasant.
▸ *adv.* **1 moderately,** reasonably, fairly. **2 quite,** rather, somewhat, *inf.* kind of.

prevail *v.* **1 win,** win out, win through, triumph, be victorious, be the victor, carry the day, prove superior, conquer, overcome, gain mastery, gain ascendancy, take the crown, rule. **2 exist,** be in existence, obtain, occur, be prevalent, be current, be widespread, abound, hold sway, predominate, preponderate.

prevalent *adj.* **1 prevailing,** current, frequent, usual, common, general, widespread, pervasive, universal, set, established, accepted, popular, fashionable, in fashion, in style, in vogue. **2 common,** usual, endemic, widespread, universal, extensive, frequent, ubiquitous, rampant, rife. **3 prevailing,** dominant, predominant, predominating, preponderant, ruling, governing. *Ant.* uncommon; rare; unpopular.

prevaricate *v.* **lie,** hedge, fence, beat about the bush, be evasive, shilly-shally, hem and haw, dodge the issue, dodge, sidestep the issue, sidestep, equivocate, quibble, tergiversate.

prevent *v.* **1 stop,** put a stop to, halt, arrest, avert, nip in the bud, fend off, turn aside, stave off, ward off, block, check, hinder, impede, hamper, obstruct, balk, foil, thwart, frustrate, forestall, inhibit, hold back, restrain, prohibit, bar, deter. **2 stop,**

hinder, impede, hamper, obstruct, inhibit, hold back, restrain, prohibit, bar. *Ant.* cause; encourage.

previous *adj.* **1 former,** ex-, preceding, foregoing, past, sometime, onetime, quondam, erstwhile, antecedent, precursory. **2 preceding,** foregoing, earlier, prior, above, precursory, antecedent, anterior, former. *Ant.* following; next; consequent.

previously *adv.* **formerly,** earlier on, before, until now/then, hitherto, heretofore, once, at one time, in the past, in years gone by.

price *n.* **1 cost,** asking price, charge, fee, payment, rate, amount, figure, value, valuation, outlay, expense, expenditure, bill. **2 consequence,** result, cost, penalty, sacrifice, forfeit, forfeiture, punishment. **3 reward,** bounty, premium, recompense, compensation.
▶ *v.* **fix the price of,** set the price of, cost, value, rate, evaluate, assess, estimate, appraise, assay.

priceless *adj.* **1 beyond price,** without price, of incalculable value/worth, of inestimable value/worth, invaluable, precious, rare, incomparable, expensive, costly, rich, dear, irreplaceable, treasured, prized, cherished,

worth its weight in gold, worth a king's ransom. **2 hilarious,** extremely amusing, very funny, comic, riotous, sidesplitting, rib-tickling, absurd, ridiculous, comical *inf.* a scream, a hoot, a laugh riot. *Ant.* worthless; cheap.

prick *n.* **1 jag,** jab, stab, nick, wound, puncture, perforation, hole, pinhole. **2 prickle,** sting, smarting, tingle, tingling, pain. **3 pricking,** pang, twinge, gnawing. **4 spike,** thorn, barb, spine, prong, tine.
▶ *v.* **1 pierce,** puncture, perforate, penetrate, make a hole in, put a hole in, stab, nick, gash, slit, bore, jag, jab, stab, wound. **2 sting,** smart, tingle. **3 distress,** cause distress to, trouble, worry, gnaw at, cause pain to. **4 goad,** prod, urge, spur, prompt, incite, push, propel.

prickle *n.* **1 thorn,** needle, barb, spike, point, spine, spur. **2 prickling sensation,** tingle, tingling sensation, tingling, sting, stinging, smarting, itching, creeping sensation, goose bumps/ flesh/pimples, formication, paresthesia, pins and needles.
▶ *v.* **tingle,** sting, smart, itch, have a creeping sensation, have goose bumps/flesh/pimples, have pins and needles.

pride *n.* **1 self-esteem,** self-respect, ego, amour propre, self-worth, self-image, self-identity, feelings, sensibilities. **2 conceit,** vanity, arrogance, haughtiness, self-importance, self-conceit, self-love, self-glorification, egotism, presumption, hauteur, superciliousness, disdain, *inf.* bigheadedness, swellheadedness. **3 satisfaction,** gratification, pleasure, joy, delight. **4 pride and joy,** prize, jewel, jewel in the crown, flower, gem, treasure, glory. *Ant.* modesty; humility.

priest *n.* **clergyman,** minister, vicar, ecclesiastic, cleric, churchman, churchwoman, man/woman of the cloth, man/woman of God, father, padre.

prim *adj.* **proper,** demure, formal, precise, stuffy, starchy, straitlaced, prudish, prissy, priggish, puritanical. *Ant.* informal; carefree; laid-back.

primarily *adv.* **basically,** essentially, in essence, fundamentally, in the first place, first and foremost, chiefly, mainly, in the main, principally, mostly, for the most part, on the whole, predominantly, predominately.

primary *adj.* **1 prime,** chief, main, principal, leading, predominant, most important, paramount, basic, fundamental, elemental,

rudimentary, essential. **2 earliest,** original, initial, beginning, first, opening, introductory, first, prehistoric, primitive, primeval, primal, primordial, autochthonal. *Ant.* secondary; subordinate.

prime *adj.* **1 chief,** main, principal, leading, predominant, most important, major, paramount. **2 basic,** fundamental, elemental, rudimentary, essential, primary. **3 top-quality,** highest, top, best, first-class, high-grade, grade A, superior, choice, select, *inf.* A-1. **4 classic,** ideal, excellent, typical, standard. *Ant.* minor; inferior.

▸ *n.* **1 best part,** peak, pinnacle, best days, height, zenith, acme, culmination, apex, heyday, full flowering. **2 perfection,** peak, full flowering, blossoming.

primitive *adj.* **1 ancient,** earliest, primeval, primordial, primal, autochthonal. **2 crude,** simple, rudimentary, undeveloped, unrefined, rough, unsophisticated, rude. **3 uncivilized,** barbarian, barbaric, savage, wild. **4 simple,** natural, unsophisticated, naïve, undeveloped, childlike, untaught, untrained, untutored. *Ant.* modern; advanced; sophisticated.

principal *adj.* **1 chief,** leading, preeminent, foremost, most important, most influential, dominant, controlling, ruling, in charge. **2 chief,** main, major, most important, leading, key, primary, prime, paramount. **3 capital,** main, leading, major. *Ant.* minor; subordinate; subsidiary.

▸ *n.* **1 chief,** head, director, leader, manager, boss, ruler, controller, *inf.* honcho. **2 leading player,** leading performer, leading man/lady, lead, star. **3 capital,** capital sum, capital funds, working capital, financial resources.

principle *n.* **1 truth,** philosophy, idea, theory, basis, fundamental, essence, assumption. **2 rule,** golden rule, law, canon, tenet, code, maxim, axiom, dictum, postulate. **3 morals,** principles, ethics, integrity, uprightness, righteousness, probity, rectitude, sense of honor, honor, conscience, scruples.

print *v.* **1 set in print,** send to press, run off, put to bed. **2 publish,** issue. **3 imprint,** stamp, mark. **4 imprint,** impress, engrave, etch, stamp, mark.

▸ *n.* **1 type,** letters, lettering, typeface, newsprint. **2 copy,** reproduction, replica. **3 picture,** design, engraving, lithograph. **4 photograph,** photo, snap, snapshot. **5 chintz. 6 fingerprint,** footprint, mark, impression.

prior *adj.* **earlier,** previous, anterior. *Ant.* later; subsequent.

priority *n.* **1 precedence,** preference, urgency, highest place, top place. **2 precedence,** seniority, superiority, supremacy, paramountcy, prerogative.

prison *n.* **jail,** penitentiary, lockup, penal institution, place of detention, place of confinement, dungeon, *inf.* clink, cooler, slammer, stir, can, pen.

prisoner *n.* **1 convict,** jailbird, *inf.* con, lifer. **2 prisoner of war,** POW, hostage, captive, detainee, internee.

pristine *adj.* **unmarked,** unblemished, unspoiled, spotless, immaculate, clean, in mint condition, in perfect condition, fresh, virgin.

private *adj.* **1 personal,** individual, own, particular, especial, special, exclusive, intimate, secret. **2 confidential,** strictly confidential, not for publication, not to be made public, not to be disclosed, secret, unofficial, off-the-record, in camera, closet, privileged, *inf.* hush-hush. **3 secluded,** sequestered, quiet, secret, remote, out-of-the-way, withdrawn, retired. **4 nonpublic,** privately owned, off-limits. **5 undisturbed,** without disturbance,

uninterrupted, without interruption, alone, solitary.
6 reserved, retiring, self-contained, uncommunicative, noncommunicative, noncommittal, diffident, secretive. **7 nonofficial,** unofficial, nonpublic, personal. **8 nonstate,** private-enterprise, privatized, independent.

▶ *n.* **infantryman,** foot soldier, enlisted man, *inf.* GI, GI Joe.

privileged *adj.* **1 advantaged,** socially advantaged, favored, elite, indulgent, spoiled, protected, sheltered. **2 immune,** exempt, excepted. **3 confidential,** private, not for publication, off-the-record, secret, top-secret, *inf.* hush-hush.

prize[1] *n.* **1 winnings,** jackpot, stakes, purse. **2 trophy,** medal, award, accolade, reward, premium, honor, laurels. **3 goal,** aim, desire, hope. **4 spoils,** booty, plunder, loot, pillage, pickings, trophy.

▶ *adj.* **prizewinning,** award-winning, winning, champion, best, top, choice, select, first-class, first-rate, excellent, *inf.* top-notch, A-1.

▶ *v.* **value,** set a high value on, set great store by, treasure, cherish, hold dear, appreciate greatly, attach great importance to, esteem, hold in high regard.

prize[2] *v.* **pry,** lever, force, pull, *inf.* yank.

probable *adj.* **likely,** most likely, odds-on, expected, to be expected, anticipated, predictable, foreseeable, in the cards, credible, quite possible, possible. **Ant.** improbable; unlikely.

probably *adv.* **in all probability,** likely, most likely, in all likelihood, as likely as not, it is to be expected that, perhaps, maybe, it may be, possibly, *inf.* as like as not.

probe *n.* **investigation,** scrutiny, scrutinization, close inquiry, inquest, exploration, examination, study, research, analysis.

▶ *v.* **1 feel,** feel around, prod, poke, explore, check. **2 investigate,** conduct an investigation into, scrutinize, inquire into, conduct an inquiry into, carry out an inquest into, examine, subject to an examination, study, research, analyze.

problem *n.* **1 difficulty,** vexed question, complication, trouble, mess, predicament, plight, dilemma, quandary, *inf.* pickle, can of worms. **2 difficulty,** dispute, subject of dispute, point at issue, bone of contention. **3 question,** puzzle, poser, enigma, riddle, conundrum, *inf.* teaser, brainteaser. **4 bother,** nuisance, pest, vexation, *inf.* hassle, aggravation.

▸ *adj.* **difficult,** troublesome, delinquent, unmanageable, unruly, uncontrollable, intractable, recalcitrant, nuisance.

problematic *adj.*

1 problematical, difficult, troublesome, complicated, puzzling, knotty, thorny, ticklish, tricky. **2 doubtful,** open to doubt, uncertain, unsettled, questionable, open to question, debatable, arguable. *Ant.* simple; straightforward; certain.

procedure *n.* **1 course of action,** line of action, plan of action, policy, system, method, methodology, modus operandi, technique, means, practice, operation, strategy, way, routine, wont, custom. **2 action,** step, process, measure, move, operation, transaction.

proceed *v.* **1 make one's way,** go, go on, go forward, go ahead, advance, carry on, move on, press on, progress. **2 act,** take action, take steps, take measures, go ahead, move, make a start, progress, get under way. **3 arise,** originate, spring, stem, come, derive, result, follow, ensue, emanate, issue, flow.

proceedings *pl. n.* **1 activities,** events, action, process, business, affairs, doings, happenings. **2 legal proceedings,** legal action/case, case, lawsuit, litigation, trial. **3 minutes,** report, account, record, transactions.

proceeds *pl. n.* **takings,** profits, returns, receipts, gain, income, earnings.

process *n.* **1 operation,** action, activity, steps, stages. **2 method,** system, technique, means, practice, way, procedure. **3 development,** evolution, changes, stages, steps. **4 proceedings,** legal action, legal case, case, lawsuit, trial.

procession *n.* **parade,** march, column, file, train, cortege, cavalcade, motorcade, stream, steady stream, string, succession, series, sequence, run.

proclaim *v.* **1 announce,** declare, make known, give out, notify, circulate, advertise, publish, broadcast, promulgate, pronounce, blazon, trumpet, shout something from the rooftops. **2 pronounce,** announce, declare someone to be. **3 indicate,** show, reveal, testify.

procrastinate *v.* **delay,** postpone action, defer action, be dilatory, use delaying tactics, stall, temporize, play for time, play the waiting game, dally, dilly-dally, drag one's feet/heels.

prod *v.* **1 poke,** jab, dig, nudge, elbow, butt, push, shove, thrust. **2 urge,** encourage, rouse, move, motivate, stimulate, incite, spur on, impel, actuate, goad.
▸ *n.* **1 poke,** jab, dig, nudge, elbow, butt, push, shove, thrust. **2 goad,** stick, spike. **3 encouragement,** prompting, prompt, motivation, stimulus, incitement, spur, goad.

prodigious *adj.* **1 amazing,** astonishing, astounding, staggering, stupendous, marvelous, wonderful, phenomenal, miraculous, impressive, striking, startling, extraordinary, remarkable, exceptional, unusual, *inf.* fantastic, fabulous, flabbergasting. **2 enormous,** huge, colossal, gigantic, giant, mammoth, immense, massive, vast, monumental, tremendous, inordinate, monstrous, grotesque, abnormal, large, considerable, substantial, sizable, *inf.* vast, tremendous. **3 huge,** large, colossal, immense, massive, considerable, substantial, sizable, *inf.* vast, tremendous. ***Ant.*** ordinary; unexceptional; normal; tiny.

prodigy *n.* **1 genius,** child genius, gifted child, mastermind, *inf.*

Einstein. **2 wonder,** marvel, phenomenon, sensation, miracle. **3 classic example,** example, model, paragon, paradigm, epitome, exemplar, ideal.

produce *v.* **1 make,** manufacture, create, construct, build, fabricate, put together, assemble, turn out. **2 compose,** create, originate, prepare, develop, frame, fashion, turn out. **3 bring forward,** set forth, present, offer, proffer, advance, show, exhibit, demonstrate, disclose, reveal. **4 yield,** bear, give, bring forth, supply, provide, furnish. **5 give birth to,** bring forth, bear, breed, give life to, bring into the world, procreate. **6 cause,** give rise to, evoke, bring about, set off, occasion, generate, engender, induce, initiate, start, spark off. **7 mount,** stage, put on, present, direct.
▸ *n.* **crops,** fruit and vegetables, fruit, vegetables, greens.

product *n.* **1 commodity,** artifact, manufacture. **2 result,** outcome, effect, consequence, upshot, fruit, spin-off, legacy.

productive *adj.* **1 fertile,** fruitful, fecund, rich, high-yielding. **2 prolific,** energetic, vigorous, efficient. **3 profitable,** gainful, valuable, fruitful, useful, constructive, effective, worthwhile, beneficial, rewarding. **4 producing,** causing, resulting in. *Ant.* sterile; barren; unproductive.

profess *v.* **1 declare,** announce, proclaim, assert, state, utter, affirm, avow, aver. **2 claim,** lay claim to, allege, pretend, feign, make out, sham, fake, dissemble. **3 declare publicly,** make a public declaration of, avow, confess, confirm, declare one's allegiance to, acknowledge publicly.

profession *n.* **1 career,** calling, vocation, occupation, line of work, line of employment, position, situation, post, job, office, appointment, métier, sphere of work, line of work, area of work, walk of life, business. **2 declaration,** announcement, proclamation, assertion, statement, affirmation, avowal, averment, confession, public acknowledgment, testimony. **3 claim,** allegation, pretense, feigning, shamming, faking, dissembling.

professional *adj.* **1 white-collar. 2 skilled,** skillful, proficient, expert, adept, competent, efficient, experienced. **3 skillful,** expert, adept, masterly, excellent, fine, polished, finished. **4 nonamateur,** paid. **5 ethical,** fitting. *Ant.* inept; amateur; amateurish.

▶ *n.* **1 professional worker,** white-collar worker. **2 professional player,** nonamateur, paid player, *inf.* pro. **3 expert,** skilled person, master, past master, adept, authority, *inf.* pro.

proffer *v.* **offer,** tender, present, extend, give, submit, volunteer, suggest. *Ant.* refuse; withdraw.

profile *n.* **1 side-view,** outline. **2 silhouette,** outline, contour, lines, shape, form, figure. **3 short biography,** sketch, thumbnail sketch, portrait, vignette.

profit *n.* **1 takings,** proceeds, gain, yield, return, receipts, income, earnings, winnings. **2 gain,** benefit, advantage, good, value, use, avail. *Ant.* loss; disadvantage. ▶ *v.* **benefit,** be of benefit to, be of advantage to, be advantageous to, be of use/value to, be of service to, serve, do (someone) good, help, be helpful to, assist, aid, stand (someone) in good stead.

profitable *adj.* **1 profit-making,** moneymaking, commercial, gainful, remunerative, paying, lucrative, sound, solvent, in the black. **2 beneficial,** advantageous, rewarding, helpful, productive, useful, worthwhile, valuable.

profound *adj.* **1 discerning,** penetrating, thoughtful, philosophical, deep, weighty, serious, learned, erudite, wise, sagacious. **2 learned,** erudite, serious, deep, difficult, complex, abstract, abstruse, esoteric, impenetrable. **3 deep,** intense, keen, great, extreme, sincere, heartfelt. **4 deep,** pronounced, total, absolute, complete, utter. **5 far-reaching,** radical, extensive, exhaustive, thoroughgoing. *Ant.* shallow; superficial; slight.

profuse *adj.* **1 lavish,** liberal, unstinting, generous, fulsome, extravagant, inordinate, immoderate, excessive. **2 abundant,** copious, ample, plentiful, bountiful, luxuriant. *Ant.* meager; sparse.

program *n.* **1 agenda,** calendar, schedule, syllabus, list of events, order of the day. **2 playbill.** **3 production,** presentation, show, performance, broadcast. **4 syllabus,** prospectus, schedule, list, curriculum, literature. **5 schedule,** scheme, plan, plan of action, project. ▸ *v.* **1 schedule,** plan, line up, map out, arrange, prearrange, organize. **2 set,** fix, arrange.

progress *n.* **headway,** advance, going, passage, advancement, progression, improvement, betterment, upgrading, development, growth. ▸ *v.* **1 go forward,** move forward/ on, make one's way, advance, go on, continue, proceed, make progress, make headway, push forward, go/forge ahead, make strides, develop, get better, improve. **2 make progress,** get better, improve, recover, recuperate. *Ant.* return; regress; deteriorate.

progressive *adj.* **1 forward,** onward, advancing. **2 increasing,** growing, intensifying, accelerating, escalating. **3 modern,** advanced, forward-looking, forward-thinking, go-ahead, enlightened, enterprising, up-and-coming, innovative, avant-garde. **4 radical,** reforming, innovative, revolutionary, revisionist. *Ant.* conservative; reactionary.

prohibit *v.* **1 forbid,** ban, bar, disallow, proscribe, veto, interdict, outlaw. **2 prevent,** stop, rule out, preclude, make impossible, hinder, impede, hamper, obstruct, restrict, constrain. *Ant.* allow; authorize; facilitate.

prohibitive *adj.* **1 prohibitory,** forbidding, banning, barring, disallowing, proscriptive, restrictive, suppressive, vetoing, interdicting, outlawing. **2 exorbitant,** extortionate, excessive, preposterous, high-priced, sky-high, *inf.* steep.

project *n.* **scheme,** plan, program, enterprise, undertaking, venture, activity, operation, campaign.
▸ *v.* **1 plan,** propose, map out, devise, design, outline. **2 launch,** discharge, propel, hurl, throw, cast, fling, shoot. **3 jut,** jut out, protrude, extend, stick out, stand out, hang over, bulge out, beetle, obtrude. **4 extrapolate,** calculate, estimate, gauge, reckon, forecast, predict, predetermine.

proliferate *v.* **increase,** grow rapidly, multiply, extend, expand, burgeon, accelerate, escalate, rocket, snowball, mushroom. **Ant.** decrease; dwindle.

prolong *v.* **lengthen,** elongate, extend, stretch out, draw out, drag out, protract, spin out.

prominent *adj.* **1 protruding,** protuberant, protrusive, jutting, jutting out, projecting, standing out, sticking out, bulging. **2 easily seen,** conspicuous, noticeable, obvious, unmistakable, obtrusive, eye-catching, striking. **3 leading,** outstanding, chief, foremost, main, top, important, eminent, preeminent, distinguished, notable, noted, illustrious, celebrated, well-known, famous, renowned, acclaimed. **Ant.** inconspicuous; obscure.

promiscuous *adj.* **sexually indiscriminating,** dissolute, dissipated, fast, licentious, loose, profligate, abandoned, immoral, debauched, wanton, of easy virtue, unchaste. **Ant.** chaste; moral; pure.

promise *v.* **1 give one's word,** give one's assurance, swear, vow, take an oath, pledge, contract. **2 augur,** indicate, denote, signify, be a sign of, show signs of, hint at, suggest, betoken, presage.
▸ *n.* **1 word,** word of honor, assurance, guarantee, commitment, vow, oath, pledge, bond, contract, covenant. **2 indication,** hint, suggestion, sign. **3 talent,** potential, flair, ability, aptitude, capability, capacity.

promising *adj.* **1 encouraging,** hopeful, favorable, auspicious, propitious, optimistic, bright. **2 with potential,** talented, gifted, able, apt, *inf.* up-and-coming. **Ant.** unfavorable; unpromising.

promontory *n.* **headland,** point, cape, head, foreland, bluff, cliff, precipice, overhang, height, projection, prominence.

promote *v.* **1 upgrade,** elevate, advance, move up, prefer, aggrandize. **2 advance,** further, assist, aid, help, contribute to, foster, boost. **3 advocate,** recommend, urge, support, back, endorse, champion, sponsor, espouse. **4 advertise,** publicize, push, puff, puff up, beat the drum for, *inf.* plug, give a plug to, hype, hype up. *Ant.* demote; obstruct; impede.

promotion *n.* **1 upgrading,** move up, elevation, advancement, preferment, aggrandizement. **2 advancement,** furtherance, furthering, assistance, aid, help, contribution to, fostering, boosting. **3 advocacy,** recommendation, urging, support, backing, endorsement, championship, sponsoring, espousal. **4 advertising,** advertising campaign, publicity, publicizing, push, pushing, hard sell, *inf.* plug, plugging, hype, hyping.

prompt *adj.* **immediate,** instant, instantaneous, swift, rapid, speedy, quick, fast, expeditious, early, punctual, in good time, timely, ready, willing, eager. *Ant.* slow; late; tardy; unwilling.
 ▸ *v.* **1 cause,** make, encourage, move, induce, urge, incite, impel, spur on, motivate, stimulate, inspire, provoke, give rise to, call forth, occasion, elicit, evoke. **2 cause,** give rise to, induce, call forth, occasion, elicit, evoke, provoke. **3 remind,** jog someone's memory, refresh someone's memory, cue, give someone a cue,

help out. *Ant.* discourage; deter; restrain.

pronounce *v.* **1 enunciate,** articulate, say, utter, sound, voice, vocalize. **2 announce,** declare, proclaim, assert, affirm, rule, decree.

pronounced *adj.* **marked,** noticeable, obvious, evident, conspicuous, striking, unmistakable, decided, definite, clear, strong, positive, distinct. *Ant.* faint; inconspicuous; indefinite; vague.

pronunciation *n.* **enunciation,** articulation, saying, uttering, utterance, sounding, voicing, vocalization.

proof *n.* **1 evidence,** certification, verification, authentication, validation, confirmation, attestation, demonstration, substantiation, corroboration, confirmation, attestation, testimony. **2 galley proof,** galley, page proof, trial print.
 ▸ *adj.* **impervious,** impenetrable, resistant, repellent, waterproof, windproof, bulletproof, soundproof, childproof.

prop *n.* **1 support,** upright, brace, buttress, stay, bolster, stanchion, truss, column, post, rod, pole, shaft. **2 pillar,** mainstay, anchor, rock, backbone, supporter, upholder, sustainer.

▸ *v.* **lean,** rest, set, lay, stand, balance, steady.

propaganda *n.* **publicity,** promotion, advertising, advertisement, selected information, newspeak, agitprop, *inf.* hype.

propagate *v.* **1 grow,** breed, multiply, reproduce, proliferate, procreate. **2 spread,** communicate, circulate, disseminate, transmit, distribute, broadcast, publish, publicize, proclaim, promulgate.

propel *v.* **move,** set in motion, push forward, drive, thrust forward, force, impel.

propensity *n.* **tendency,** inclination, leaning, bent, bias, disposition, predisposition, proneness, proclivity, penchant, susceptibility, weakness.

proper *adj.* **1 right,** suitable, fitting, appropriate, apt, correct, precise, accepted, acceptable, established, orthodox, conventional, formal, comme il faut. **2 right,** correct, own, individual, particular, respective, special, specific. **3 seemly,** decorous, respectable, decent, refined, genteel, gentlemanly/ladylike, formal, conventional, orthodox, strict, punctilious, sedate. ***Ant.*** inappropriate; wrong; improper; unconventional.

property *n.* **1 possessions,** belongings, things, goods, effects, chattels, assets, resources. **2 real estate,** buildings, land, estates, acres. **3 quality,** attribute, characteristic, feature, power, peculiarity, idiosyncrasy, quirk.

prophecy *n.* **1 prediction,** forecast, prognostication, divination, augury. **2 prediction,** foretelling the future, forecasting the future, fortune-telling, second sight, prognostication, divination, augury, soothsaying.

prophesy *v.* **predict,** foretell, forecast, foresee, forewarn of, presage, prognosticate, divine, augur.

prophet *n.* **seer,** soothsayer, fortune-teller, diviner, clairvoyant, forecaster of the future, prognosticator, prophesier, oracle, augur, sibyl, Cassandra.

proportion *n.* **1 ratio,** distribution, relative amount/number, relationship. **2 portion,** part, segment, share, quota, division, percentage, fraction, measure, *inf.* cut. **3 balance,** symmetry, harmony, correspondence, congruity, agreement.

proportional *adj.* **proportionate,** in proportion to, corresponding, commensurate, equivalent, comparable.

proposal *n.* **1 putting forward,** advancing, offering, proffering, presentation, submitting.
2 scheme, plan, project, program, motion, bid, proposition, presentation, suggestion, recommendation, tender, terms.

propose *v.* **1 put forward,** advance, offer, proffer, present, submit, tender, propound, suggest, recommend, advocate.
2 intend, have the intention, mean, plan, have in mind, aim, purpose. **3 put forward,** put up, nominate, name, suggest, recommend. **4 offer marriage,** ask for someone's hand in marriage, pay suit, *inf.* pop the question.

proprieties *pl. n.* **etiquette,** social conventions, social graces, social niceties, protocol, civilities, formalities, rules of conduct, accepted behavior, good manners, good form, the done thing, punctilio.

proprietor *n.* **owner,** possessor, title-holder, deed-holder, landowner, landlord/landlady, host, innkeeper, hotelier, manager, restaurateur.

prosaic *adj.* **1 unimaginative,** uninspired, matter-of-fact, dull, dry, humdrum, mundane, pedestrian, lifeless, spiritless, stale, bland, vapid, banal, hackneyed, trite, insipid, monotonous, flat. **2 ordinary,** everyday, usual, common, routine, humdrum, commonplace, workaday, pedestrian, mundane, dull, tedious, boring, uninspiring, monotonous. *Ant.* imaginative; inspired; interesting.

prosecute *v.* **1 bring a charge against,** bring a criminal charge against, charge, prefer charges against, bring an action against, try, bring to trial, put on trial, sue, bring a suit against, interdict, arraign. **2 carry on,** conduct, direct, engage in, work at, proceed with, continue with.
3 accomplish, complete, finish, carry through, discharge, bring to an end.

prospect *n.* **1 likelihood,** likeliness, hope, expectation, anticipation, chance, chances, odds, probability, possibility.
2 thought, idea, contemplation, outlook. **3 view,** vista, outlook, perspective, panorama, scene, spectacle.
▸ *v.* **explore,** search, inspect, survey, examine, check out.

prospective *adj.* **1 future,** to-be, soon-to-be, intended, expected.
2 would-be, potential, possible,

likely, hoped-for, looked-for, awaited, anticipated.

prospects *pl. n.* **potential,** promise, possibilities, expectations, scope.

prosper *v.* **do well,** get on well, thrive, flourish, be successful, succeed, get ahead, progress, advance, get on in the world, make headway, make good, become rich, be in clover, *inf.* be on easy street, live the life of Riley. *Ant.* fail; collapse; crash.

prosperity *n.* **prosperousness,** success, good fortune, ease, plenty, affluence, wealth, riches, the good life, luxury, life of luxury.

prosperous *adj.* **thriving,** flourishing, successful, well-off, well-to-do, affluent, wealthy, rich, moneyed, opulent, in clover, *inf.* well-heeled, in the money, on easy street. *Ant.* poor; penniless; impecunious.

prostitute *n.* **call girl,** whore, woman of the streets, lady of the evening, streetwalker, loose woman, woman of ill repute, fallen woman, courtesan, fille de joie, *inf.* hooker, working girl, hustler.

prostrate *adj.* **1 prone,** lying down, flat, stretched out, horizontal, full-length, procumbent. **2 bowed low,** humbled. **3 overcome by/with,** overwhelmed by, overpowered by, brought to one's knees by, crushed by, helpless with, paralyzed by, laid low by/with, impotent with. **4 worn out,** exhausted, fatigued, tired out, dog-tired, spent, drained: *inf.* all in, done, fagged out, bushed, pooped. *Ant.* upright; vertical; thriving.

▸ *v.* **1 knock flat,** flatten, knock down, floor, level. **2 overcome,** overwhelm, overpower, bring to one's knees, crush, make helpless, paralyze, lay low, make powerless, make impotent. **3 wear out,** exhaust, tire out, fatigue, weary, drain, sap, *inf.* fag out, poop.

protect *v.* **1 keep safe,** save, safeguard, shield, preserve, defend, shelter, secure, guard, mount/stand guard on, secure, watch over, look after, take care of. **2 preserve,** shield, cover, cover up, conceal, mask. *Ant.* attack; harm; assault; expose.

protection *n.* **1 safekeeping,** safety, shield, preservation, defense, security, care, charge, keeping, protectorship. **2 safeguard,** shield, barrier, buffer, screen, cover.

protective *adj.* **1 protecting,** safeguarding, shielding, covering.

2 careful, watchful, vigilant, paternal/maternal, fatherly/motherly, overprotective, possessive, jealous, clinging.

protector *n.* **1 defender,** champion, bodyguard, guardian, knight in shining armor, guardian angel. **2 guard,** shield, pad, cushion.

protest *v.* **1 object to,** raise objections to, oppose, make/take a stand against, put up a fight against, take exception to, complain about, demur at, remonstrate about, make a fuss about, demonstrate against, *inf.* kick up a fuss about, gripe about, grouse about, beef about, bitch about. **2 declare,** announce, profess, proclaim, assert, affirm, argue, attest, testify to, maintain, insist on, aver, avow. **Ant.** accept; support.
  ▸ *n.* **1 objection,** opposition, exception, complaint, disapproval, disagreement, dissent, demurral, remonstration, fuss, outcry, demonstration, protestation. **2 protestation,** declaration, announcement, profession, assertion, affirmation, attestation, assurance, avowal, proclamation. **Ant.** support; approval.

protocol *n.* **etiquette,** rules of conduct, code of behavior, conventions, formalities, customs, propriety, proprieties, decorum, manners, courtesies, civilities, good form, politesse.

protract *v.* **prolong,** extend, stretch out, draw out, lengthen, make longer, drag out, spin out, keep something going, continue. **Ant.** curtail; shorten.

proud *adj.* **1 self-respecting,** dignified, independent. **2 arrogant,** conceited, vain, self-important, egotistical, boastful, haughty, disdainful, scornful, supercilious, snobbish, imperious, overbearing, lordly, presumptuous, overweening, high-handed, *inf.* high-and-mighty, stuck-up, uppity, snooty, highfalutin. **3 gratifying,** satisfying, happy, memorable, notable, red-letter, glorious, marvelous. **4 magnificent,** splendid, grand, noble, stately, imposing, majestic, august. **Ant.** ashamed; modest; humble; shameful.

prove *v.* **1 produce/submit proof,** produce/submit evidence, establish evidence, determine, demonstrate, show beyond (a/the shadow of a) doubt, substantiate, corroborate, verify, validate, authenticate, confirm. **2 analyze,** check, examine, put to the test, test, try out, put to trial. **3 be**

found, be shown, turn out. *Ant.*
disprove; invalidate.

proverb *n.* **saying,** adage, maxim,
saw, axiom, aphorism, gnome,
dictum, apothegm.

proverbial *adj.* **1 legendary,**
notorious, infamous, famous,
famed, renowned, well-known,
acknowledged, accepted,
traditional, time-honored.
2 axiomatic, epigrammatic,
aphoristic, apothegmatic, well-
known.

provide *v.* **1 supply,** furnish,
equip, accommodate, provision,
outfit, give, offer. **2 give,** bring,
afford, present, offer, accord,
yield, impart, lend. **3 stipulate,** lay
down, give as a condition,
require, state, specify. *Ant.*
deprive; refuse; withhold.

provident *adj.* **farsighted,**
prudent, judicious, shrewd,
circumspect, wise, sagacious,
cautious, careful, thrifty, canny,
economical, frugal.

provincial *adj.* **1 nonnational,**
regional, local, municipal, state,
county, district, topical.
2 uncultured, uncultivated,
unrefined, unpolished,
unsophisticated, parochial,
limited, small-minded, insular,
naïve, uninformed, inward-
looking, illiberal, narrow, narrow-
minded, inflexible, bigoted,

prejudiced, intolerant. *Ant.*
national; urban; sophisticated.
▸ *n.* **rustic,** yokel, peasant, *inf.*
country cousin, hick, hayseed.

provisional *adj.* **provisory,**
temporary, interim, stopgap,
transitional, to be confirmed,
conditional, tentative, contingent,
inf. pro tem. *Ant.* permanent;
definite.

provisions *pl. n.* **supplies,** food
supplies, stores, groceries, food,
food and drink, foodstuffs,
staples, rations, provender,
eatables, edibles, victuals,
comestibles, viands.

proviso *n.* **condition,** stipulation,
provision, clause, rider,
qualification, restriction,
reservation, limitation, strings.

provocative *adj.* **1 provoking,**
annoying, irritating, exasperating,
infuriating, maddening, vexing,
galling, affronting, insulting,
inflammatory, goading, *inf.*
aggravating. **2 sexually arousing,**
sexually exciting, alluring,
seductive, sexy, tempting,
suggestive, erotic, titillating.

provoke *v.* **1 annoy,** make angry,
anger, incense, enrage, irritate,
exasperate, infuriate, madden,
pique, nettle, vex, harass, irk,
gall, affront, insult, *inf.* rile,
needle, make someone's blood
boil, aggravate. **2 incite,** rouse,

stir, move, stimulate, motivate, excite, inflame, work/fire up, prompt, induce, spur, goad, prod, egg on. **3 evoke,** cause, give rise to, occasion, call forth, draw forth, elicit, induce, inspire, excite, kindle, produce, generate, engender, instigate, lead to, precipitate, promote, prompt. *Ant.* pacify; appease; deter.

prowess *n.* **1 skill,** skillfulness, expertise, expertness, facility, ability, capability, talent, genius, adroitness, adeptness, aptitude, dexterity, deftness, competence, proficiency, know-how, savoir faire. **2 courage,** bravery, gallantry, valor, heroism, intrepidity, fearlessness, mettle, pluck, pluckiness, gameness, nerve, boldness, daring, fortitude, steadfastness, stoutness, sturdiness, *inf.* grit, guts, spunk. *Ant.* inability; ineptitude; cowardice.

prowl *v.* **roam,** range, move stealthily, slink, skulk, steal, sneak, stalk, *inf.* snoop.

proxy *n.* **representative,** deputy, substitute, agent, delegate, surrogate.

prudent *adj.* **1 wise,** well-judged, judicious, sagacious, sage, shrewd, sensible, circumspect, farsighted, politic. **2 cautious,** careful, discreet, wary, vigilant, heedful.

3 provident, thrifty, economical, canny, sparing, frugal. *Ant.* unwise; imprudent; incautious; rash.

prudish *adj.* **puritan,** puritanical, priggish, prim, straitlaced, prissy, stuffy, starchy, Victorian, *inf.* goody-goody. *Ant.* permissive; liberal; broad-minded.

prune *v.* **1 trim,** thin, thin out, cut back, shape, cut, lop, chop, clip, snip, remove. **2 cut,** lop, chop, clip, snip, remove. **3 cut back on,** cut back, pare down, make cutbacks in, cut, trim, reduce, shorten, make reductions in, retrench, curtail.

pry *v.* **be inquisitive,** interfere, meddle, intrude, mind other people's business, be a busybody, *inf.* stick/poke one's nose in, snoop.

pseudonym *n.* **nom de plume,** pen name, stage name, professional name, assumed name, alias, allonym, false name, sobriquet, nickname, nom de guerre.

psychological *adj.* **1 mental,** cerebral, psychic, psychical. **2 in the mind,** all in the mind, psychosomatic, emotional, irrational, imaginary, subconscious, unconscious.

pub *n.* **bar,** tavern, barroom, taproom, *inf.* watering hole.

puberty *n.* **pubescence,** sexual maturity, adolescence, young adulthood, teenage years, teens.

public *adj.* **1 state,** national, civic, civil, social. **2 popular,** general, common, universal, widespread. **3 not private,** not exclusive, accessible to all, open to the public, of free access. **4 known,** widely known, acknowledged, overt, in circulation, published, publicized, plain, obvious. **5 in the public eye,** prominent, well-known, important, eminent, respected, influential, prestigious, famous, celebrated, illustrious. *Ant.* private; personal; secret.
▸ *n.* **1 people,** everyone, population, country, nation, community, citizens, populace, ordinary people, masses, commonalty, multitude, mob, hoi polloi, electorate, voters.
2 audience, spectators, readers, followers, following, fans, admirers, patrons, clientele.

publication *n.* **1 publishing,** production, issuing, issuance. **2 book,** newspaper, magazine, periodical, journal, daily, weekly, monthly, quarterly, booklet, brochure, leaflet, pamphlet, handbill. **3 publishing,** announcement, notification, reporting, declaration, communication, imparting, proclamation, disclosure, divulgence, broadcasting, publicizing, distribution, spreading, dissemination, promulgation, issuance.

publicize *v.* **1 make public,** make known, bring to public notice/attention, announce, publish, broadcast, distribute, disseminate, promulgate. **2 give publicity to,** promote, advertise, *inf.* hype, plug. *Ant.* conceal; withhold.

publish *v.* **1 produce,** issue, print, bring out. **2 make public,** make known, announce, notify, report, declare, communicate, impart, proclaim, disclose, divulge, broadcast, publicize, distribute, spread, disseminate, promulgate.

pucker *v.* **gather,** shirr, pleat, ruck, ruffle, wrinkle, crease, screw up, furrow, knit, crinkle, corrugate.

puerile *adj.* **childish,** immature, infantile, juvenile, adolescent, foolish, silly, inane, asinine. *Ant.* mature; sensible.

puff *n.* **gust,** blast, whiff, breath, flurry, draft.
▸ *v.* **breathe,** pant, blow, gasp, gulp.

pugnacious *adj.* **belligerent,** bellicose, combative, fighting, battling, aggressive, antagonistic, quarrelsome, argumentative, disputatious, hostile, threatening, irascible, ill-tempered, bad-tempered. ***Ant.*** peaceable; pacific; friendly.

pull *v.* **1 haul,** drag, draw, trail, tow, tug, jerk, *inf.*. **2 pull out,** draw out, take out, extract, remove, root out. **3 strain,** sprain, wrench, stretch, tear, dislocate, damage.
 ▸ *n.* **1 tug,** haul, yank, jerk. **2 tug,** force, forcefulness, power, exertion, effort. **3 attraction,** lure, enticement, drawing power, draw, magnetism, influence. **4 influence,** weight, leverage, muscle, *inf.* clout.

pulp *n.* **1 flesh,** marrow. **2 paste,** purée, mush, mash, pap, triturate. **3 pulp fiction,** rubbish, trash, trivia, drivel, pap.
 ▸ *adj.* **rubbishy,** trashy, sensational, lurid.

pulsate *v.* **beat,** throb, vibrate, pulse, palpitate, pound, thud, thump, drum.

pulse *n.* **beat,** rhythm, throb, throbbing, vibration, pulsation, pounding, thudding, thud, thumping, thump, drumming.
 ▸ *v.* **beat,** throb, vibrate, pulsate, palpitate, pound, thud, thump, drum.

pump *v.* **1 pump up,** blow up, inflate. **2 drive,** force, push, send. **3 question closely,** quiz, interrogate, cross-examine, give someone the third degree, *inf.* grill.

punch[1] *v.* **strike,** hit, knock, thump, thwack, box, jab, cuff, slug, smash, bash, slam, batter, pound, pummel, *inf.* sock, bop, wallop, whack, clout, plug.
 ▸ *n.* **1 blow,** hit, knock, thump, thwack, box, jab, cuff, slug, smash, bash, slam, *inf.* sock, bop, wallop, whack, clout, plug. **2 strength,** vigor, vigorousness, force, forcefulness, verve, drive, impact, bite, effectiveness, *inf.* oomph, pizzazz.

punch[2] *v.* **make a hole in,** put/punch holes in, perforate, puncture, pierce, prick, drill, bore, hole.

punctilious *adj.* **careful,** scrupulous, meticulous, conscientious, exact, precise, particular, strict, nice, finicky, fussy, *inf.* persnickety. ***Ant.*** careless; slapdash.

punctual *adj.* **on time,** on the dot, prompt, in good time, when expected, timely, well-timed, early. ***Ant.*** late; behindhand.

puncture *n.* **1 puncturing,** perforation, piercing, pricking, spiking, rupturing, cutting, nicking, slitting. **2 hole,** perforation, prick, rupture, cut, nick, slit, leak. **3 flat tire,** *inf.* flat.
 ▸ *v.* **1 make a hole in,** perforate,

pierce, bore, prick, spike,
penetrate, rupture, cut, nick, slit.
2 prick, deflate, flatten, reduce.

pungent *adj.* **1 sharp,** acrid, acid,
sour, biting, stinging, burning,
smarting, irritating, bitter, tart,
tangy, spicy, aromatic, piquant,
peppery, hot, fiery. **2 sharp,** acid,
sour, biting, bitter, tart, tangy,
spicy, highly flavored, aromatic,
piquant, peppery, hot, fiery.
3 caustic, acid, biting, cutting,
sharp, incisive, piercing,
penetrating, scathing, pointed,
acrimonious, trenchant, mordant,
stringent. **Ant.** bland; mild.

punish *v.* **mete out punishment to,**
discipline, subject to discipline,
take disciplinary action against,
teach someone a lesson, penalize,
castigate, chastise, smack, slap,
beat, cane, whip, flog, lash,
scourge, mistreat, abuse,
manhandle. **Ant.** pardon;
exonerate.

punishing *adj.* **arduous,**
demanding, taxing, strenuous,
hard, exhausting, fatiguing,
wearing, tiring, grueling, uphill,
backbreaking. **Ant.** easy;
effortless.

punitive *adj.* **1 punishing,**
penalizing, disciplinary,
corrective, castigating,
castigatory, chastising. **2 harsh,**
severe, stiff, taxing, cruel, savage.

puny *adj.* **1 weak,** weakly, frail,
feeble, undersized,
underdeveloped, stunted, small,
slight, little, dwarfish. **2 paltry,**
petty, trifling, trivial,
insignificant, inconsequential,
minor, meager, *inf.* piddling. **Ant.**
strong; sturdy; substantial.

pupil *n.* **student,** schoolboy,
schoolgirl, schoolchild, scholar,
disciple.

puppet *n.* **1 marionette,** hand
puppet, finger puppet. **2 tool,**
instrument, cat's-paw, pawn,
dupe, mouthpiece, *inf.* stooge, yes-
man.

purchase *v.* **1 buy,** pay for,
acquire, pick up, obtain, invest in,
put money into. **2 attain,** achieve,
gain, win. **Ant.** sell; market.
▸ *n.* **1 buy,** acquisition,
investment. **2 grip,** hold, foothold,
footing, toehold, support, grasp,
leverage, advantage.

pure *adj.* **1 unalloyed,** unmixed,
unadulterated, uncontaminated,
flawless, perfect, genuine, real,
true. **2 clean,** clear, fresh,
unpolluted, untainted,
unadulterated, uncontaminated,
uninfected, wholesome, natural.
3 virgin, virginal, chaste,
maidenly, virtuous, undefiled,
unsullied. **4 uncorrupted,**
noncorrupt, moral, righteous,
honorable, virtuous, honest,

upright, decent, good, worthy, noble, blameless, guiltless, pious, sinless, stainless, spotless, unsullied, unblemished, impeccable, immaculate. **5 sheer,** utter, absolute, downright, out-and-out, complete, total, perfect, unmitigated, unqualified. **6 theoretical,** abstract, conceptual. *Ant.* impure; dirty; adulterated; immoral.

purely *adv.* **entirely,** completely, totally, wholly, solely, only, simply, just, merely.

purge *v.* **1 cleanse,** clear, purify, make pure. **2 rid,** clear, empty, remove, clear out, expel, eject, dismiss, oust, depose, eradicate, root out, weed out. **3 clear,** absolve, pardon, forgive, exonerate, expiate.
▸ *n.* **1 purging,** cleansing, purification. **2 removal,** expulsion, ejection, dismissal, ousting, deposal, deposition, eradication, rooting out, weeding out.

purify *v.* **1 make pure,** clean, cleanse, decontaminate, depollute, filter, filtrate, freshen, deodorize, refine, disinfect, sterilize, sanitize, fumigate. **2 purge,** cleanse, clear, absolve. *Ant.* pollute; contaminate; corrupt.

puritanical *adj.* **puritan,** ascetic, austere, straitlaced, narrow-minded, rigid, stiff, prudish, prim, priggish, prissy, *inf.* goody-goody. *Ant.* permissive; liberal; broad-minded.

purpose *n.* **1 reason,** point, basis, motivation, cause, justification. **2 aim,** intention, object, objective, goal, end, target, ambition, aspiration, desire, wish, hope. **3 determination,** resoluteness, resolution, resolve, firmness, steadfastness, single-mindedness, persistence, perseverance, tenacity, doggedness. **4 benefit,** advantage, use, usefulness, value, gain, profit, avail, result, outcome, effect.
▸ *v.* **intend,** have the intention, mean, decide, resolve, determine, plan, aim, have a mind, propose, aspire.

purposeful *adj.* **determined,** resolute, resolved, firm, steadfast, single-minded, persistent, persevering, tenacious, dogged, unfaltering, unwavering. *Ant.* aimless; irresolute.

purposely *adv.* **on purpose,** intentionally, deliberately, by design, willfully, wittingly, knowingly, consciously.

pursue *v.* **1 go after,** run after, follow, chase, give chase to, hunt, stalk, track, trail, shadow, *inf.* tail. **2 follow,** go on with, proceed with, keep/carry on with, continue with, continue, persist in. **3 follow,** engage in, be engaged in, be occupied in, work at, practice, prosecute, conduct, ply, apply oneself to. **4 strive toward,** push toward, work toward, seek, search for, be intent on, aim at, have as a goal, have as an objective, aspire to. **5 chase after,** chase, run after, go after, play up to. *Ant.* flee; avoid; shun; eschew.

push *v.* **1 shove,** thrust, propel, drive, ram, jolt, butt, jostle, force, press, squeeze, jostle, elbow, shoulder. **2 press,** push down, press down, depress, exert pressure on. **3 encourage,** prompt, press, urge, egg on, spur on, prod, goad, incite, impel, dragoon, force, coerce, constrain, browbeat, strong-arm. **4 promote,** advertise, publicize, boost, *inf.* plug, hype. *Ant.* pull; deter; discourage.

▸ *n.* **1 shove,** thrust, ram, jolt, butt, jostle. **2 attack,** assault, advance, onslaught, onset, charge, sortie, sally. **3 drive,** force, ambition, enterprise, initiative, energy, vigor, vitality, spirit, verve, enthusiasm, go, vim, *inf.* get-up-and-go, gumption, pizzazz.

pushy *adj.* **pushing,** assertive, self-assertive, aggressive, forceful, forward, bold, brash, bumptious, presumptuous, cocksure, loud, obnoxious.

put *v.* **1** place, lay, lay down, set down, deposit, position, rest, stand, locate, situate, settle, emplace, install, posit. **2 translate,** transcribe, turn, render, construe, transliterate, interpret, word, express, phrase, frame, formulate, couch, say, utter, voice, speak, state, pronounce, proclaim. **3 set,** apply, employ, use, utilize, assign, allocate, devote. **4 commit,** consign, subject, condemn, sentence, convict, doom. **5 assess,** evaluate, value, estimate, calculate, reckon, guess, measure, establish, fix, place, set, *inf.* guesstimate. **6 place,** bet, wager, gamble, stake, risk, chance, hazard. **7 throw,** toss, fling, pitch, cast, hurl, heave, lob, let fly. **8 thrust,** drive, plunge, stick, push, force, lunge, knock, bang, smash, bash.

puzzle *v.* perplex, baffle, stump, beat, mystify, confuse, bewilder, nonplus, stagger, dumbfound, daze, confound, *inf.* flummox.

puzzling *adj.* difficult, hard, unclear, perplexing, knotty, baffling, enigmatic, abstruse, nonplussing, mystifying, bewildering, unfathomable, inexplicable, incomprehensible, beyond one, above one's head. *Ant.* clear; straightforward; comprehensible; lucid.

Qq

quail *v.* **flinch,** shrink, recoil, shy away, pull back, draw back, cower, cringe, shudder, shiver, tremble, shake, quake, blanch.

quake *v.* **shake,** tremble, quiver, shiver, shudder, rock, vibrate, pulsate, throb.

qualification *n.* **1 certification,** training, competence, competency, accomplishment, eligibility, acceptability, suitability, preparedness, fitness, proficiency, skillfulness, adeptness, capability, aptitude, skill, ability, attribute, endowment. **2 modification,** limitation, restriction, reservation, stipulation, allowance, adaptation, adjustment, condition, proviso, provision, caveat.

qualified *adj.* **1 certified,** certificated, trained, fitted, fit, equipped, prepared, competent, accomplished, proficient, skilled, skillful, adept, practiced, experienced, expert, capable, able. **2 modified,** limited, conditional, restricted, bounded, contingent, confined, circumscribed, reserved, guarded, equivocal, stipulated, adapted, adjusted.

qualify *v.* **1 be certified,** train, take instruction. **2 certify,** license, empower, authorize, allow, permit, sanction, warrant, fit, equip, prepare, arm, make ready, ground, train, educate, coach, teach, instruct. **3 modify,** limit, make conditional, restrict. **4 modify,** temper, soften, modulate, mitigate, reduce, lessen, diminish.

quality *n.* **1 degree of excellence,** standard, grade, level, make, sort, type, kind, variety. **2 excellence,** superiority, merit, worth, value, caliber, talent, talentedness, eminence, preeminence, distinction. **3 feature,** trait, attribute, characteristic, aspect, property, peculiarity. **4 character,** nature, constitution, makeup.

quantity *n.* **1 number,** amount, total, aggregate, sum, quota, weight. **2 size,** capacity, mass, volume, bulk, extent, length, area, time.

quarrel *n.* **argument,** fight, disagreement, difference of opinion, dispute, disputation, squabble, altercation, wrangle, tiff, row, misunderstanding, feud, vendetta, *inf.* falling-out, spat, scrap. *Ant.* reconciliation; agreement.

▸ *v.* **argue,** have a fight, fight, dispute, squabble, bicker, spar, wrangle, have a misunderstanding, *inf.* have a falling-out. *Ant.* agree; get on.

quarrelsome *adj.* **argumentative,** belligerent, disputatious, contentious, pugnacious, combative, ready for a fight, bellicose, litigious, hot-tempered, irascible, choleric, irritable. *Ant.* peaceable; dovish.

quarry *n.* **prey,** victim, prize.

quarter *n.* **1 district,** area, region, part, side, neighborhood, locality, zone, territory, province. **2 direction,** place, point, spot, location.

▸ *v.* **put up,** house, board, billet, accommodate, lodge, install.

quarters *pl. n.* **rooms,** chambers, barracks, lodging(s), accommodations, billet, residence, abode, dwelling, domicile, habitation, cantonment, *inf.* digs, pad.

quash *v.* **1 annul,** declare null and void, nullify, invalidate, void, cancel, overrule, override, overthrow, reject, set aside, reverse, revoke, rescind, repeal. **2 crush,** put down, squash, quell, subdue, suppress, repress, quench, extinguish, stamp out, put a stop to, end, terminate, defeat, destroy. *Ant.* validate; incite; provoke; support.

quaver *v.* **quiver,** vibrate, tremble, shake, waver.

queasy *adj.* **sick,** nauseated, nauseous, ill, indisposed, dizzy, sick to one's stomach.

queer *adj.* **1 odd,** strange, unusual, extraordinary, funny, curious, peculiar, weird, outlandish, singular, eccentric, unconventional, unorthodox, atypical, abnormal, irregular, anomalous, deviant, outré, offbeat, *inf.* off-the-wall. **2 homosexual,** gay, lesbian. **3 strange,** peculiar, suspicious, suspect, irregular, questionable, dubious, doubtful, *inf.* fishy, shady. **4 ill,** unwell, sick, queasy, faint, dizzy, giddy, light-headed. *Ant.* ordinary; conventional; normal; well.

quell *v.* **1 quash,** defeat, conquer, vanquish, overpower, overcome, overwhelm, rout, crush, suppress, subdue, extinguish, stamp out, put down. **2 allay,** lull, put at rest, quiet, silence, calm, soothe, appease, assuage, abate, deaden, dull, pacify, tranquilize, mitigate, palliate. *Ant.* agitate; excite; provoke.

quench *v.* **1 satisfy,** slake, sate, satiate. **2 extinguish,** put out, snuff out, blow out, douse. **3 suppress,** extinguish, stamp out, smother, stifle.

quest *n.* **1 search,** seeking, pursuit, chase, hunt. **2 goal,** aim, objective, purpose, quarry, prey. **3 adventure,** expedition, journey, voyage, exploration, crusade.

question *n.* **1 query,** inquiry, interrogation. **2 doubt,** dubiety, dubiousness, dispute, argument, debate, controversy, reservation. **3 issue,** point at issue, problem, matter, point, subject, topic, theme. *Ant.* answer; response; certainty.

▸ *v.* **1 ask questions of,** interrogate, cross-examine, cross-question, quiz, catechize, interview, sound out, examine, give the third degree to, *inf.* grill, pump. **2 call into question,** query, raise doubts about, throw doubt on, have suspicions about, express reservations about, challenge, raise objections to.

questionable *adj.* **open to question/doubt,** doubtful, dubious, uncertain, debatable, in dispute, arguable, controversial, controvertible. *Ant.* certain; indisputable.

queue *n.* **line,** row, column, file, chain, string, train, succession, sequence, series, concatenation.

quibble *v.* **1 raise petty objections,** cavil, carp, pettifog, split hairs, *inf.* nitpick. **2 be evasive,** equivocate, avoid the issue, prevaricate, hedge, fudge, be ambiguous, *inf.* beat about the bush.

quick *adj.* **1 fast,** rapid, speedy, swift, fleet, express. **2 prompt,** without delay, immediate, instantaneous, expeditious. **3 brief,** brisk, fleeting, momentary, hasty, hurried, cursory, perfunctory. **4 quick-witted,** sharp-witted, alert, intelligent. **5 quick-tempered,** irascible, irritable. *Ant.* slow; sluggish; long; dull.

quicken *v.* **1 speed up,** accelerate, expedite, hasten, hurry, hurry up, precipitate. **2 stimulate,** stir up, arouse, rouse, incite, instigate, whet, inspire, kindle, fan, refresh, strengthen, revive, revitalize, resuscitate, revivify.

quit *v.* **1 give up,** stop, cease, discontinue, drop, leave off, abandon, abstain from, desist from. **2 leave,** depart from, vacate, walk out on. **3 leave,** depart, go away, take off, *inf.* call it a day, call it quits, pack it in. *Ant.* start; begin; continue.

quite *adv.* **1 completely,** fully, entirely, totally, wholly, absolutely, in all respects. **2 fairly,** relatively, moderately, reasonably, to some extent/degree, to a certain extent, rather, somewhat. **3 truly,** really, definitely, absolutely, certainly, unequivocally.

quiver *v.* **tremble,** shiver, vibrate, quaver, quake, shudder, pulsate, convulse, palpitate.
▸ *n.* **tremble,** tremor, shiver, vibration, quaver, shudder, pulsation, convulsion, palpitation, throb, spasm, tic.

quota *n.* **share,** allowance, allocation, portion, ration, part, slice, measure, proportion, percentage, *inf.* cut.

quotation *n.* **1 citation,** reference, allusion, excerpt, extract, selection, passage, line, *inf.* quote. **2 estimate,** estimated price, cost, charge, figure, *inf.* quote.

quote *v.* **1 repeat,** iterate, recite, reproduce. **2 cite,** give, name, instance, mention, refer to, make reference to, allude to. **3 estimate,** price, set a price for.

Rr

rabble *n.* **1** (angry) mob, horde, swarm, (disorderly) crowd, throng. **2 common people,** populace, commonality, rank and file, peasantry, hoi polloi, riff-raff, masses, lower classes, dregs of society, *inf.* great unwashed. **Ant.** aristocracy; nobility.

race[1] *n.* **1 speed contest,** competition, chase, pursuit, relay. **2 contest,** competition, rivalry, contention. **3 channel,** waterway, watercourse, sluice, spillway, current.
▶ *v.* **1 run,** take part in a race, contend, compete. **2 run against,** compete against, be pitted against. **3 run,** sprint, dash, dart, bolt, make a dash/bolt for, speed, fly, tear, zoom, accelerate, career. **4 hurry,** hasten, make haste, rush, *inf.* get cracking, get a move on, step on it, shake a leg.

race[2] *n.* **1 racial division,** people, ethnic group. **2 racial type,** blood, bloodline, stock, line, lineage, breed, strain, stirps, extraction, ancestry, parentage. **3 group,** type, class, species.

racism *n.* **racialism,** racial discrimination, racial prejudice/bigotry, apartheid.

racist *n.* **racialist,** bigot, illiberal.
▶ *adj.* **racialist,** discriminatory, prejudiced, bigoted, intolerant, illiberal.

rack *n.* **frame,** framework, stand, form, trestle, structure, holder, shelf.
▶ *v.* **torture,** agonize, afflict, torment, persecute, plague, distress, rend, tear, harrow, crucify, convulse.

racket *n.* **1 noise,** din, row, commotion, disturbance, uproar, hubbub, hullabaloo, clamor, pandemonium, tumult, shouting, yelling. **2 criminal activity,** illegal scheme/enterprise, fraud, fraudulent scheme, swindle. **3 business,** line of business, line, occupation, profession, job, *inf.* game.

radiant *adj.* **1 irradiant,** shining, bright, illuminated, brilliant, luminous, luminescent, lustrous, lucent, effulgent, refulgent, incandescent, beaming, glowing, gleaming, glittering, sparkling, shimmering, glaring. **2 joyful,** elated, in raptures, ecstatic, blissfully happy, delighted, pleased, happy, glowing, *inf.* in seventh heaven, on cloud nine. **3 splendid,** resplendent, magnificent, dazzling, glowing, vivid, intense. ***Ant.*** dark; dull; gloomy.

radiate *v.* **1 send out/forth,** scatter, disperse, diffuse, spread, shed, give off/out, emit, emanate. **2 transmit,** emanate, show, exhibit, demonstrate, *inf.* be the picture of. **3 branch out,** spread out, diverge, divaricate, issue.

radical *adj.* **1 fundamental,** basic, rudimentary, elementary, elemental, constitutional. **2 thorough,** complete, total, entire, absolute, utter, comprehensive, exhaustive, sweeping, far-reaching, profound, drastic, stringent, violent. **3 extremist,** extreme, immoderate, revolutionary, rebel, rebellious, militant, fanatic, leftist, left-wing. ***Ant.*** minor; superficial; conservative.

raffle *n.* **lottery,** drawing, sweepstakes.

rage *n.* **1 fury,** anger, wrath, ire, high dudgeon, frenzy, madness, raving, fit of rage/fury, tantrum, paroxysm of rage/anger, rampage. **2 violence,** turbulence, tumult, fire and fury.
▶ *v.* **1 be furious,** be infuriated, be angry, seethe, be beside oneself, lose one's temper, boil over, rant, rave, rant and rave, storm, fume, fulminate, complain vociferously, inveigh, rail, *inf.* foam at the mouth, blow one's top, blow up, blow a fuse/gasket, hit the ceiling, flip one's lid, freak out. **2 be violent,** be at its height, be turbulent, be tempestuous.

ragged *adj.* **1 tattered,** in tatters, torn, rent, in holes, holey, worn to shreds, falling to pieces, threadbare, frayed, the worse for wear. **2 in rags,** shabby, unkempt, down and out, down-at-the-heel, poor, destitute, indigent. **3 jagged,** notched, serrated, sawtoothed, craggy, rugged, uneven, irregular. **4 rough,** crude, unpolished, unrefined, faulty, imperfect, irregular, uneven. **5 in disarray,** straggling, straggly, disorganized, fragmented.

raid *n.* **surprise attack,** assault, onset, onslaught, invasion, incursion, foray, charge, thrust, sortie, sally, search, *inf.* bust.
▶ *v.* **make a raid on,** attack, assault, invade, charge, assail, storm, rush, set upon, descend upon, swoop upon, plunder, pillage, loot, rifle, forage, ransack, search thoroughly, make a search of, *inf.* bust.

rain *n.* **rainfall,** precipitation,

raindrops, drizzle, shower, rainstorm, cloudburst, torrent, downpour, deluge, thunderstorm, shower, deluge, volley.
▸ *v.* **1 pour,** pour/come down, precipitate, shower, drizzle, rain hard, rain heavily, *inf.* rain cats and dogs, come down in buckets. **2 fall,** pour out/down, drop, shower. **3 lavish,** pour, give generously, bestow.

rainy *adj.* **wet,** showery, drizzly, damp.

raise *v.* **1 lift,** lift up, raise aloft, elevate, uplift, upthrust, hoist, heave up. **2 set up,** set upright, stand, upend, stand on end. **3 increase,** escalate, inflate, *inf.* step up, hike, jack up. **4 increase,** heighten, augment, amplify, intensify, *inf.* step up. **5 construct,** build, erect, put up. **6 get/gather together,** collect, assemble, muster, levy, accumulate, amass, scrape together. **7 put forward,** introduce, advance, bring up, broach, suggest, moot, present. **8 cause,** set going, bring into being, engender, create, set afoot, kindle, arouse, awaken, excite, summon up, provoke, activate, evoke, incite, stir up, foment, whip up, instigate. **9 bring up,** rear, nurture, educate. **10 breed,** rear, grow, farm, cultivate, propagate, till, produce.

11 promote, advance, upgrade, elevate, exalt. **12 cause to rise,** leaven, puff up. **13 end,** bring to an end, put an end to, terminate, abandon, lift. **14 remove,** get rid of, take away. **15 cause to appear,** call up, call forth, summon up, conjure up. *Ant.* lower; demolish; end.
▸ *n.* **gain,** (pay/wage) increase, growth, addition, appreciation, *inf.* boost.

rally *v.* **1 come/get together,** assemble, group (together), band together, convene, unite. **2 call/ bring together,** assemble, summon, round up, muster, marshal, mobilize. **3 regroup,** reassemble, re-form, reunite. **4 recover,** recuperate, revive, get better/well, improve, perk up, regain one's strength, pull through, take a turn for the better, turn the corner, be on the mend, get one's second wind. *Ant.* disperse; deteriorate.
▸ *n.* **1 mass meeting,** meeting, gathering, assembly, assemblage, convention, conference, congregation, convocation. **2 recovery,** recuperation, improvement, revival, rehabilitation, comeback, resurgence.

ram *v.* **1 force,** thrust, plunge, stab, push, sink, dig, stick, cram, jam, stuff, pack. **2 hit,** strike, crash into, collide with, impact, run into, smash into, smack into, bump (into), butt.

ramble v. **1 take a walk,** go for a walk, walk, hike, wander, stroll, saunter, amble, roam, range, rove, traipse, jaunt. **2 digress,** wander, speak/write discursively, go off on tangents, talk aimlessly, maunder, gibber, blather, babble, chatter, gabble, rattle on.
▸ n. **walk,** hike, wander, stroll, saunter, amble, roam, traipse, jaunt, trip, excursion, tour.

rambling adj. **1 digressive,** wandering, roundabout, circuitous, diffuse, periphrastic, disconnected, disjointed, maundering, long-winded, verbose, wordy, prolix.
2 sprawling, spreading, unsystematic. **3 straggling,** trailing, sprawling, spreading.

ramification n. **1 consequence,** aftermath, outcome, result, upshot, issue, sequel, complication, implication.
2 subdivision, offshoot, branch, outgrowth, limb, scion.

ramp n. **slope,** sloping surface, incline, inclined plane, gradient, acclivity, rise, access ramp.

rampage v. **rush/run wildly,** run riot, run amok, charge, tear.

▸ n. **uproar,** furor, mayhem, turmoil.

rampant adj. **1 uncontrolled,** out of control/hand, unrestrained, unchecked, unbridled, widespread, pandemic, epidemic, spreading like wildfire.
2 luxuriant, exuberant, rank, profuse, lavish. **3 rearing,** standing, upright, erect.
4 aggressive, vehement, violent, wild, fanatical.

random adj. **haphazard,** chance, accidental, fortuitous, serendipitous, adventitious, arbitrary, hit-or-miss, indiscriminate, sporadic, stray, spot, casual, unsystematic, unmethodical, orderless, disorganized, unarranged, unplanned, unpremeditated. **Ant.** deliberate; systematic; premeditated.

range n. **1 scope,** compass, radius, span, scale, gamut, reach, sweep, extent, area, field, orbit, province, domain, latitude, limits, bounds, confines. **2 row,** line, file, rank, string, chain, series, sequence, succession, tier.
3 mountain range, chain, sierra.
4 assortment, variety, kind, sort, type, class, rank, order, genus, species. **5 stove,** cooking stove, oven. **6 pasture,** pasturage, grass, grassland, grazing land.

▸ *v.* **1 extend,** stretch, reach, cover, go, run, pass, fluctuate between, vary between. **2 line up,** align, draw up, put/set in order, order, place, position, arrange, dispose, array, rank. **3 classify,** class, categorize, bracket, group, grade, catalog, file, pigeonhole. **4 roam,** rove, ramble, traverse, travel over, wander, meander, amble, stroll, stray, drift.

rank[1] *n.* **1 grade,** level, stratum, class, status, position, station, standing. **2 nobility,** aristocracy, high birth, eminence, distinction, influence, power, prestige, weight, importance. **3 grade,** position, gradation, point on the scale, mark, echelon, rung on the ladder. **4 array,** alignment, order, arrangement, organization.
▸ *v.* **1 be graded,** be placed, be positioned. **2 classify,** class, categorize, grade.

rank[2] *adj.* **1 lush,** luxuriant, abundant, dense, profuse, flourishing, exuberant, vigorous, productive, spreading, overgrown, jungly. **2 strong,** strong-smelling, pungent, acrid, malodorous, foul-smelling, evil-smelling, stinking, rancid, putrid, fetid, unpleasant, disagreeable, offensive, revolting, sickening, obnoxious, noxious, noisome, mephitic. **3 indecent,** immodest, indecorous, coarse, gross, vulgar, shocking, outrageous, lurid, crass, scurrilous, abusive, nasty, foul, filthy, vile, obscene, smutty, risqué, profane, pornographic. **4 utter,** complete, total, absolute, out and out, downright, thorough, thoroughgoing, sheer, unqualified, unmitigated, arrant, flagrant, blatant, glaring, gross, egregious.

rankle *v.* **fester,** cause resentment, cause annoyance, annoy, anger, irk, vex, peeve, irritate, rile, chafe, fret, gall, embitter, *inf.* get one's goat.

ransack *v.* **1 plunder,** pillage, raid, rob, loot, despoil, rifle, strip, fleece, sack, ravage, harry, maraud, devastate, depredate. **2 search,** rummage through, rake through, scour, look all over, go through, comb, explore, turn inside out, turn over.

rapid *adj.* **quick,** fast, swift, speedy, fleet, hurried, hasty, expeditious, express, brisk, lively, prompt, precipitate. ***Ant.*** slow; leisurely.

rapport *n.* **affinity,** bond, empathy, harmony, sympathy, understanding, close/special relationship, link.

rapture *n.* **joy,** ecstasy, elation, exaltation, exhilaration, bliss, euphoria, transport, rhapsody, ravishment, enchantment, delight, delectation, happiness, enthusiasm, *inf.* cloud nine, seventh heaven.

rare *adj.* **1 unusual,** uncommon, out of the ordinary, exceptional, atypical, singular, remarkable, phenomenal, strange, recherché, unique. **2 infrequent,** few and far between, scarce, sparse, sporadic, scattered. **3 outstanding,** superior, first-rate, special, choice, excellent, very fine, incomparable, unparalleled, peerless, matchless, *inf.* A-1, top-notch. **Ant.** common; frequent.

rascal *n.* **1 imp,** scamp, scalawag, mischief-maker, little devil. **2 scoundrel,** villain, rogue, blackguard, ne'er-do-well, good-for-nothing, wastrel, reprobate, cad, *inf.* creep, rat.

rash *adj.* **reckless,** impetuous, hasty, impulsive, madcap, overadventurous, adventurous, overbold, audacious, brash, daredevil, foolhardy, harum-scarum, devil-may-care, headstrong, hot-headed, incautious, careless, heedless, thoughtless, imprudent, incautious, unthinking, ill-advised, ill-considered, foolish, imprudent, injudicious, hare-brained, unwary, unguarded. **Ant.** careful; cautious; prudent.

▸ *n.* **1 skin eruption,** outbreak, breaking out, erythema, hives, heat rash, nettle rash, diaper rash. **2 outbreak,** spate, torrent, flood, wave, plague, epidemic, succession, series, run.

rate *n.* **1 percentage,** ratio, proportion, scale, degree, standard. **2 pay,** payment, fee, remuneration, price, cost, charge, rent, tariff, *inf.* damage. **3 pace,** stride, gait, motion, speed, tempo, velocity, measure.

▸ *v.* **1 adjudge,** judge, assess, appraise, evaluate, value, put a value on, measure, weigh up, grade, rank, classify, class, categorize. **2 regard as,** consider, count, deem, reckon, account, esteem. **3 be worthy of,** deserve, merit, be entitled to.

rather *adv.* **1 sooner,** preferably, by preference, from choice, more willingly, more readily. **2 more,** more truly. **3 correctly/strictly speaking,** to be exact/precise. **4 quite,** fairly, a bit, a little, slightly, somewhat, relatively, to some degree/extent, *inf.* sort of, kind of, pretty. **5 on the contrary,** instead, the truth is, actually, in reality.

ratify *v.* **confirm,** endorse, sign, countersign, corroborate, sanction, warrant, approve, authorize, authenticate, certify, validate, agree to, accept, consent to, uphold, bear out. **Ant.** reject; revoke.

ratio *n.* **proportion,** comparative size/extent, correlation, correspondence, percentage, fraction, quotient.

ration *n.* **allowance,** quota, allotment, portion, share, measure, part, lot, amount, helping, proportion, percentage, budget.

▸ *v.* **limit,** restrict, control, conserve, budget.

rational *adj.* **1 thinking,** cognitive, mental, cerebral, reasoning, logical, analytical, conceptual. **2 sensible,** reasonable, logical, sound, intelligent, wise, judicious, sagacious, prudent, circumspect, politic, astute, shrewd, perceptive, well-advised, well-grounded. **3 able to think/reason,** in sound mind, in one's right mind, compos mentis, lucid, coherent, well-balanced, sane, normal, *inf.* all there. **Ant.** irrational; illogical; insane.

rationalize *v.* **1 explain away,** account for, make excuses/ allowances for, make plausible, try to vindicate/justify. **2 reason out,** think through, elucidate, clarify, make consistent.

rattle *v.* **1 bang,** clatter, clang, clank, jangle, clink, knock, rap. **2 bounce,** bump, jiggle, jounce, shake, jolt, vibrate, jar. **3 reel off,** list/recite rapidly, run through. **4 go,** chatter, babble, gabble, prattle, jabber, gibber, blather, prate, *inf.* yak. **5 disconcert,** disturb, fluster, upset, shake, perturb, discompose, discomfit, discountenance, frighten, scare, *inf.* faze.

raucous *adj.* **strident,** shrill, screeching, piercing, ear-piercing, harsh, sharp, grating, rasping, scratching, discordant, dissonant, jarring. **Ant.** sweet; dulcet.

ravage *v.* **devastate,** lay waste, leave desolate, lay/leave in ruins, ruin, wreak havoc on, destroy, level, raze, demolish, wreck, shatter, damage, pillage, plunder, despoil, harry, maraud, ransack, sack, loot.

rave *v.* **1 talk wildly,** be delirious, babble, ramble. **2 rant and rave,** rage, deliver a tirade/harangue, storm, fulminate, explode in anger, lose one's temper, lose control, go into a frenzy, run amok, *inf.* fly off the handle, flip one's lid.

▸ *adj.* **rapturous,** ecstatic, enthusiastic, laudatory, praising, excellent, favorable.

ravenous *adj.* **1 very hungry,** starving, starved, famished. **2 greedy,** gluttonous, voracious, insatiable, insatiate, ravening, wolfish.

ravishing *adj.* **beautiful,** lovely, stunning, gorgeous, dazzling, radiant, enchanting, bewitching, charming.

raw *adj.* **1 uncooked,** fresh. **2 unrefined,** crude, green, coarse, unprocessed, unprepared, untreated, unfinished, unmanufactured. **3 inexperienced,** untrained, unskilled, untutored, unschooled, unpracticed, untried, untested, unseasoned, undisciplined, new, callow, immature, green, ignorant, naïve, unsophisticated, *inf.* wet behind the ears. **4 excoriated,** skinned, grazed, abraded, scratched, chafed, open, exposed, unhealed, sore, tender. **5 damp,** wet, cold, chilly, chilling, chill, freezing, bitter, biting, nippy, nipping, piercing, penetrating. **6 unrefined,** unpolished, unsophisticated, crude, rough, coarse. **7 realistic,** frank, candid, forthright, straightforward, blunt, outspoken, unembellished, unvarnished, naked, bare, brutal.

ray *n.* **beam,** shaft, streak, stream, gleam, glint, flash, glimmer, flicker, twinkle, spark, trace, hint, indication, suggestion.

raze *v.* **tear down,** pull down, take down, knock down, knock to pieces, fell, level, lay low, bulldoze, flatten, demolish, ruin, wreck.

reach *v.* **1 stretch,** stretch out, outstretch, extend, hold out, thrust out, stick out. **2 get as far as,** get to, arrive at, come to, set foot on, land at/on. **3 attain,** achieve, gain, accomplish, make, get to. **4 extend to,** go as far as, stretch to, neighbor, touch, border on, abut. **5 contact,** get in touch with, get hold of, get through to, communicate with.
▸ *n.* **1 grasp,** stretch, spread, extension, extent, span, distance. **2 scope,** range, compass, latitude, ambit, orbit, sphere, area, field, territory, authority, jurisdiction, sway, control, command.

react *v.* **1 respond,** change/behave in response to. **2 behave,** act, conduct oneself, proceed, operate, function, cope. **3 rebel against,** oppose, revolt against, rise up against.

reactionary *adj.* **ultraconservative,** conservative, obscurantist, diehard, rightist, right-wing. *Ant.* radical; progressive.

read *v.* **1 peruse,** study, scan, pore over, scrutinize, run one's eye over, look at, refer to, browse through, *inf.* wade through, dip into. **2 interpret,** construe, take to

mean, decipher, deduce, understand, comprehend.
3 register, record, display, show, indicate. **4 foresee,** foretell, predict, forecast, prophesy, divine.

▸ *n.* **perusal,** study, scan, scrutiny, browse, reference.

readable *adj.* **1 legible,** easy to read, decipherable, clear, intelligible, understandable, comprehensible. **2 enjoyable,** entertaining, interesting, gripping, enthralling, stimulating. *Ant.* illegible; boring; unreadable.

readily *adv.* **1 willingly,** without hesitation, gladly, happily, cheerfully, with pleasure, eagerly. **2 easily,** with ease, without difficulty, effortlessly.

ready *adj.* **1 prepared,** completed, finished, organized, equipped, all set, in a fit state, fit. **2 willing,** inclined, disposed, predisposed, apt, prone, given, agreeable, eager, keen, happy, glad, *inf.* game. **3 within reach,** available, on hand, present, near, near at hand, accessible, handy, convenient, on call, at one's fingertips, *inf.* on tap. **4 prompt,** quick, rapid, swift, speedy, punctual, timely. **5 alert,** resourceful, smart, sharp, astute, shrewd, keen, acute, perceptive, discerning, clever, intelligent, bright, apt, adroit, deft,

dexterous, skillful. **6 prepared,** eager, enthusiastic, anxious, keen, *inf.* psyched up, geared up. *Ant.* incomplete; unprepared; reluctant; inaccessible.

real *adj.* **1 actual,** existent, occurring, factual, unimaginary, nonfictitious. **2 authentic,** genuine, bona fide, veritable, valid, legal, licit. **3 sincere,** heartfelt, earnest, fervent, unfeigned, unpretended, unaffected, honest, truthful. *Ant.* unreal; imaginary; imitation; false.

realistic *adj.* **1 practical,** pragmatic, rational, down-to-earth, matter-of-fact, sensible, commonsensical, levelheaded, hardheaded, businesslike, hard-boiled, sober, unromantic, unsentimental, unidealistic, *inf.* with both feet on the ground, no-nonsense. **2 lifelike,** true-to-life, true, faithful, close, representational, graphic, naturalistic, authentic, genuine. *Ant.* unrealistic; idealistic; impractical; romantic.

reality *n.* **1 real world,** actuality, physical existence, corporeality, substantiality, materiality. **2 verisimilitude,** lifelikeness, authenticity, genuineness, validity. **3 fact,** actuality, truth, all honesty.

realize *v.* **1 understand (clearly),** grasp, take in, know, comprehend, apprehend, be aware, be conscious/cognizant of the fact, appreciate, recognize, perceive, discern, conceive, *inf.* get it. **2 fulfill,** achieve, accomplish, make happen, bring about, bring off, bring to fruition, consummate, effect, effectuate, perform, execute, actualize, reify. **3 make,** clear, acquire, gain, bring in, obtain, earn.

realm *n.* **1 kingdom,** country, land, state, province, empire, domain, monarchy, principality. **2 world,** field, sphere, area, department, region, province, orbit, zone.

reap *v.* **1 cut,** harvest, gather in, bring in, take in. **2 realize,** receive, obtain, get, acquire, secure, procure.

rear[1] *n.* **1 back,** back part, hind part, back end, stern. **2 rear end,** back end, end, tail, tail end. *Ant.* front; vanguard.

rear[2] *v.* **1 bring up,** raise, care for, nurture, parent, educate, train, instruct. **2 breed,** keep, tend, grow, cultivate. **3 raise,** lift up, hold up, hoist, elevate, upraise.

reason *n.* **1 grounds,** ground, cause, basis, motive, motivation, impetus, actuation, instigation, inducement. **2 explanation,** exposition, justification, argument, case, defense, vindication, apologia, rationalization, excuse, apology. **3 reasoning,** intellect, intelligence, intellectuality, mind, judgment, logic, rationality, thought, understanding, apprehension, comprehension, ratiocination, brains. **4 sanity,** mind, soundness of mind, senses. **5 reasonableness,** common sense, sense, good sense, practicality, practicability, shrewdness, wisdom, sagacity, moderation, propriety.
▸ *v.* **1 use reason,** think, think straight, use one's mind, use one's brain/head, analyze, cogitate, cerebrate, intellectualize, ratiocinate, *inf.* put on one's thinking cap. **2 deduce,** infer, conclude, work out, reckon, be of the opinion, think, surmise. **3 argue,** persuade, talk, urge, coax.

reasonable *adj.* **1 open to reason,** moderate, fair, just, equitable, impartial, dispassionate, unbiased, disinterested, aboveboard. **2 logical,** practical, rational, sensible, intelligent, wise, sound, judicious, advisable, well-thought-out, admissible, tenable, plausible. **3 moderate,**

inexpensive, low, modest, cheap, within one's means. **4** tolerable, passable, acceptable, average; *inf.* OK, okay. *Ant.* unreasonable; illogical.

reasoned *adj.* **logical**, rational, well-thought-out, clear, systematic, methodical, organized, well-expressed, well-presented.

reassure *v.* **put one's mind at rest,** put at ease, settle doubts, restore/give confidence to, encourage, hearten, buoy up, cheer up, inspirit. *Ant.* alarm; unnerve.

rebel *n.* **1 revolutionary,** revolutionist, insurrectionist, insurgent, revolter, mutineer, seditionist, agitator, freedom/resistance fighter, anarchist, traitor. **2 dissenter,** nonconformist, heretic, apostate, schismatic, recusant.
▸ *v.* **mutiny,** riot, revolt, rise up, rise up in arms, take to the streets. *Ant.* acquiesce; conform.

rebellion *n.* **1 revolt,** revolution, insurrection, insurgence, insurgency, uprising, rising, mutiny, riot, civil disobedience, resistance. **2 defiance,** disobedience, resistance, dissent, nonconformity, heresy, apostasy, schism, recusancy.

rebellious *adj.* **1 unruly,**
ungovernable, unmanageable, turbulent, disorderly, intractable, recalcitrant, incorrigible, contumacious. **2 rebelling,** revolutionary, insurrectionary, insurgent, mutinous, mutinying, rioting. **3 defiant,** disobedient, resistant, dissentient, nonconformist. *Ant.* obedient; subservient.

rebound *v.* **1 bounce,** bounce back, spring back, recoil, ricochet, boomerang. **2 misfire,** backfire, have an adverse effect, come back, redound.
▸ *n.* **1 bounce,** recoil, ricochet. **2 misfiring,** backfiring, kickback, repercussion.

rebuff *n.* **1 rejection,** refusal, spurning, repudiation, repulsion, cold shouldering, discouragement. **2 snub,** slight, repulse, cut, thumbs down, *inf.* brush-off, put-down, slap in the face.
▸ *v.* **reject,** refuse, decline, turn down, turn away, spurn, repudiate, repel, discourage, fend off, stave off, snub, slight, cold shoulder, cut, give the thumbs down to, *inf.* brush off, put down.

rebuke *v.* **reprimand,** scold, chide, admonish, reproach, reprove, remonstrate with, lecture, reprehend, censure, find fault with, berate, upbraid, castigate, take to task, *inf.* tell off, call on the carpet, lambaste, haul over the coals, chew out, bawl out. **Ant.** praise; applaud.

▸ *n.* **reprimand,** scolding, admonition, reproach, reproof, reproval, remonstration, lecture, censure, upbraiding, castigation, *inf.* tongue-lashing, lambasting, dressing-down, bawling out.

recalcitrant *adj.* **intractable,** refractory, unmanageable, ungovernable, disobedient, insubordinate, defiant, contrary, wayward, willful, headstrong, perverse, contumacious, rebellious, mutinous, obstinate, obdurate. **Ant.** amenable; docile; compliant.

recall *v.* **1 summon back,** call back, bring back. **2 call to mind,** remember, recollect, think of, call/bring to mind, call up, summon up, evoke, put one in mind of. **3 remember,** recollect, reminisce about, look back on/to, think back on/to, hark back to. **4 revoke,** retract, countermand, take back, withdraw, repeal, rescind, veto, overrule, override, invalidate, annul, nullify, cancel, recant.

▸ *n.* **1 memory,** recollection, remembrance. **2 revocation,** retracting, countermanding, withdrawal, repeal, rescinding,

vetoing, veto, invalidation, annulment, cancellation.

receive *v.* **1 be in receipt of,** accept delivery of, accept. **2 get,** obtain, acquire, come by, gain, take, gather, collect. **3 hear,** be told, find out about, learn about, gather, be informed of, be notified of, take, react to. **4 undergo,** experience, meet with, encounter, go through, sustain, be subjected to, bear, suffer. **5 hold,** contain, accommodate, admit, take. **6 welcome,** greet, entertain, be at home to. **Ant.** give; send; present.

recent *adj.* **1 new,** fresh, novel, latest, late, modern, contemporary, latter-day, current, up-to-date, up-to-the-minute. **2 occurring/appearing recently,** not long past. **Ant.** old; former.

recently *adv.* **newly,** freshly, lately, not long ago, of late.

receptacle *n.* **container,** holder, repository.

receptive *adj.* **open,** open to suggestions/ideas, flexible, willing, perceptive, sensitive, alert, bright, quick, keen.

recess *n.* **1 alcove,** niche, nook, corner, cavity, bay, oriel. **2 remote/secret/dark place,** interior, heart, retreat, refuge, sanctum, depths, *inf.* innards. **3 break,** respite, rest, interval, intermission, time off, vacation, holiday, closure, cessation of work/business, *inf.* breather, time out.

recession *n.* **1 economic decline,** downturn, depression, slump, hard times. **2 receding,** retreat, withdrawal, ebbing, subsiding, abatement.

recipe *n.* **1 directions,** instructions, guide, cooking procedure. **2 method,** technique, system, procedure, modus operandi, process, means, way, formula, prescription.

reciprocal *adj.* **1 return,** in return, returned, requited, retaliated. **2 mutual,** shared, common, reciprocative, reciprocatory, exchanged, give-and-take, complementary, corresponding, correlative.

reciprocate *v.* **1 return,** requite, feel/give in return, repay, give back. **2 respond,** respond in kind, return the favor/compliment, do the same. **3 interchange,** exchange, give and take/receive, swap, barter, trade, bandy.

recital *n.* **1 saying,** rendering, declaiming, reading, delivery, enumeration, detailing, itemizing, specification, account, report, recounting, telling, relation, description, narrative, record, story, tale, chronicle.

2 musical performance, performance, solo performance, concert, show.

recite *v.* **1 say,** repeat, read aloud, deliver, declaim, speak, render, read a passage. **2 enumerate,** detail, list, itemize, reel off, rattle off, specify, particularize, describe, recount, relate, narrate, recapitulate.

reckless *adj.* **rash,** careless, thoughtless, incautious, heedless, unheeding, inattentive, regardless, daredevil, devil-may-care, madcap, harum-scarum, wild, precipitate, headlong, hasty, irresponsible, harebrained, foolhardy, ill-advised, imprudent, unwise, indiscreet, mindless, negligent, temerarious. *Ant.* careful; cautious; prudent.

reckon *v.* **1 be of the opinion,** think, believe, suppose, assume, surmise, conjecture, imagine, fancy, guess. **2 regard as,** consider, judge, hold to be, think of as, look upon as, account, deem, rate, evaluate, gauge, count, estimate, appraise. **3 count,** calculate, add up, compute, total, tally, put a figure on, give a figure to.

reclaim *v.* **1 have returned,** get back, take back, regain, retrieve, recover. **2 retrieve,** regain, reinstate, save, rescue, salvage.

3 redeem, reform, regenerate, save, rescue.

recline *v.* **lie,** lie down, lean, be recumbent, rest, repose, loll, lounge, sprawl, stretch out, drape oneself.

recluse *n.* **hermit,** anchorite, ascetic, eremite, monk, nun, solitary, lone wolf, loner.

recognize *v.* **1 know,** know again, identify, place, spot, recall, recollect, remember, call to mind. **2 realize,** see, be aware/conscious of, perceive, discern, appreciate, understand, apprehend, acknowledge, accept, admit, concede, allow, grant, confess, own. **3 acknowledge,** accept, admit, concede, allow, grant, endorse, sanction, put the seal of approval on, approve, validate, ratify, uphold. **4 show appreciation of,** reward, honor, pay homage to, salute, applaud. *Ant.* forget; overlook; ignore.

recoil *v.* **1 draw back,** jump back, pull back, shrink, shy away, flinch, start, wince, cower, quail. **2 spring back,** fly back, kick (back), rebound, resile. **3 rebound,** come back, redound, misfire, backfire, go wrong, have an adverse effect, boomerang.
▶ *n.* **1 kickback,** kick. **2 rebound,** backlash, reaction, repercussions.

recollect *v.* **remember,** succeed in remembering, recall, call to mind, think of, summon up, place, *inf.* put one's finger on. *Ant.* forget; disremember.

recommend *v.* **1 advocate,** commend, put in a good word for, speak favorably of, look with favor on, endorse, approve, vouch for, suggest, offer, put forward, propose, advance. **2 advise,** counsel, guide, urge, exhort, enjoin. **3 make appealing/attractive/interesting,** endow with appeal/attraction/ interest, give an advantage to. *Ant.* reject; veto; disapprove.

recommendation *n.*
1 advocacy, commendation, endorsement. **2 advising,** counseling, urging.
3 commendation, endorsement, suggestion, tip, hint, proposal, good word, favorable mention, praise, words of approval, *inf.* plug. **4 advice,** counsel, guidance, exhortation, enjoinder. **5 good point,** advantage, favorable aspect, benefit, blessing, boon.

reconcile *v.* **1 make friendly gestures/overtures,** reunite, bring together, restore harmony between, make peace between, resolve differences between, bring to terms, pacify, appease, placate, propitiate, mollify. **2 come to accept,** accept, accommodate, get used, resign, submit, yield, make the best of, grin and bear it. **3 settle,** resolve, square, put to rights, mend, remedy, patch up, heal, cure, rectify. **4 harmonize,** make compatible, put in agreement, adjust, attune, make coincide, make congruent.

reconnaissance n. **preliminary survey,** survey, spying, exploration, scouting, probe, investigation, scrutiny, scan, inspection, observation.

reconnoiter v. **survey,** find out the lay of the land, see how the land lies, spy out, take stock of, explore, scout, investigate, scrutinize, scan, inspect, observe, *inf.* case, check out.

reconsider v. **think over,** rethink, review, reexamine, reevaluate, reassess, think better of, think again, think twice, have second thoughts, change one's mind.

reconstruct v. **1 rebuild,** remake, reassemble, refashion, recreate, remodel, revamp, renovate, recondition. **2 recreate,** reenact, piece together, build up. **3 reorganize,** rearrange, make over, redo, do over, overhaul, reestablish, reform.

record n. **1 official document,** register, log, logbook, file, official report/account, chronicle, diary, journal, documentation, documents, minutes, notes, annals, archives. **2 phonograph record,** long-playing record, disc, album, compact disc, single, recording, release, *inf.* platter, LP, CD. **3 employment/work history,** employment/work performance, career to date, past performance, curriculum vitae, life history, history, background, reputation, *inf.* track record. **4 police/criminal record,** history of crime, previous convictions, *inf.* rap sheet. **5 best** personal best. **6 memorial,** remembrance, souvenir, token, testimony, testimonial, witness, trace, documentation, evidence. **7 information,** data, reports, accounts.

▸ v. **1 put on record,** set down, write down, put in writing, take down, put down, enter, make a note of, document, minute, register, chronicle, file, put on file, docket, list, log, catalog, inscribe, transcribe. **2 register,** read, indicate, show, display. **3 make a record/recording of. 4 make,** produce, cut, tape, videotape.

recount v. **1 narrate,** tell, relate, unfold, repeat. **2 describe,** detail, enumerate, list, specify, itemize, cite, particularize, catalog.

recover v. **1 get back,** win back, regain, recoup, retrieve, reclaim, repossess, redeem, recuperate, recapture. **2 get better,** get back to normal, get well, recuperate, convalesce, heal, get back on one's feet, feel oneself again, improve, mend, pick up, rally, revive, pull through, bounce back, *inf.* perk up. **Ant.** lose; deteriorate.

recovery *n.* **1 recouping,** regaining, retrieval, reclamation, repossession, recapture. **2 return to normal/health,** recuperation, convalescence, healing, rallying, revival. **3 improvement,** betterment, amelioration, upturn, upswing.

recreation *n.* **1 relaxation,** refreshment, restoration, leisure, amusement, entertainment, distraction, diversion, pleasure, enjoyment, fun, play, sport, leisure activity, pastime, hobby. **2 leisure activity,** pastime, hobby, diversion, distraction. **Ant.** work; labor.

recrimination *n.* **counteraccusation,** countercharge, counterattack, retaliation, reprisal, retribution, vengeance, mutual accusations.

recruit *v.* **1 enlist,** enroll, sign up, draft, conscript, levy, engage, obtain, acquire, procure, take on, round up, muster. **2 form,** raise, gather/put together, muster, assemble. **3 replenish,** augment, increase, enlarge, add to, build up, strengthen, reinforce, fortify, shore up, *inf.* beef up. **4 recover,** recuperate, get better/well.
▸ *n.* **1 enlistee,** draftee, conscript. **2 new member,** new entrant, newcomer, initiate, beginner, learner, trainee, apprentice, novice, tyro, neophyte, proselyte, *inf.* rookie, greenhorn.

rectify *v.* **put/set right,** right, correct, amend, emend, remedy, repair, fix, make good, redress, reform, improve, better, ameliorate, adjust, square. **Ant.** damage; break.

rectitude *n.* **1 righteousness,** virtue, moral virtue, morality, honor, integrity, principle, probity, uprightness, good character, decency, honesty, upstandingness, scrupulousness, incomparability. **2 correctness,** accuracy, exactness, precision, soundness, verity. **Ant.** dishonor; dishonesty; inaccuracy.

recuperate *v.* **1 recover,** convalesce, recruit, get better, get back to normal, get well, regain one's strength/health, improve, mend, pick up, rally, revive, pull through, bounce back, *inf.* perk up. **2 recover,** recoup, get back, regain, retrieve, reclaim.

recur *v.* **reoccur,** happen/occur again, come back, return, reappear, be repeated, repeat itself, happen repeatedly.

recurrent *adj.* **recurring,** repeated, repetitive, reiterative, periodic, cyclical, regular, habitual, continual, frequent, intermittent, chronic. *Ant.* isolated; single; unique.

recycle *v.* **reuse,** reprocess, salvage, save.

redden *n.* **make/color red,** go red, blush, flush, color, color up, crimson.

redeem *v.* **1 reclaim,** get back, regain, recover, retrieve, repossess, recoup, buy back, repurchase. **2 exchange,** give in exchange, cash in, convert, turn in, trade in. **3 free/save/deliver from sin,** turn from sin, convert, purge/absolve of sin. **4 make up for,** compensate for, atone for, offset, redress, outweigh. **5 save/ free from blame,** vindicate, absolve, remove guilt from. **6 free,** set free, liberate, release, emancipate, ransom, rescue, save. **7 fulfill,** discharge, make good, carry out, execute, keep, hold to, adhere to, abide by, obey, be faithful to, meet, satisfy.

redolent *adj.* **1 evocative,** suggestive, reminiscent. **2 sweet-smelling,** fragrant, scented, perfumed, aromatic. **3 strong-smelling,** odorous, smelly, foul-smelling.

reduce *v.* **1 lessen,** lower, decrease, diminish, cut, curtail, contract, shorten, abbreviate, moderate, dilute, mitigate, alleviate, abate. **2 bring to,** bring to the point of, force to, drive to. **3 demote,** downgrade, lower, lower in rank/status, humble. **4 lower,** cut, mark down, slash, discount, put on sale. **5 get thinner,** slim, slim down, lose/ shed weight, go/be on a diet, diet, lose some inches, shed some pounds, slenderize. **6 conquer,** vanquish, overpower, subdue, subjugate, overcome, overrun. **7 bankrupt,** make penniless/poor, impoverish, ruin, break. *Ant.* increase; enlarge.

reduction *n.* **1 lessening,** lowering, decrease, diminution, cut, contraction, abbreviation, moderation, dilution, alleviation, abatement. **2 demotion,** downgrading, lowering, humbling. **3 discounting,** discount, deduction, cut, concession, allowance. **4 conquering,** vanquishing, overpowering, subjugation, overrunning. **5 smaller copy,** miniature, model.

redundant *adj.* **1 not required,** unnecessary, inessential, unwanted, de trop, surplus, supernumerary, excessive, in excess, extra, *inf.* needed like a hole in the head. **2 unnecessary,** inessential, padded, wordy, verbose, tautological, periphrastic, diffuse, pleonastic. *Ant.* essential; vital.

reel *v.* **1 stagger,** lurch, sway, stumble, totter, wobble, falter, waver, pitch, roll. **2 feel giddy/ dizzy,** feel confused, be shaken, be in shock, be upset. **3 go around (in circles),** whirl, spin, revolve, swirl, twirl, swim.

referee *n.* **umpire,** judge, adjudicator, arbitrator, arbiter, mediator, *inf.* ref.
▸ *v.* **umpire,** judge, adjudicate, arbitrate, mediate, intercede.

reference *n.* **1 mention,** allusion, citation, hint. **2 regard,** respect, relation, bearing, applicability, application, relevance, pertinence, connection, correlation. **3 source,** information source, citation, authority. **4 character reference,** testimonial, recommendation, good word, credentials.

refine *v.* **1 purify,** rarefy, clarify, clear, cleanse, strain, sift, filter, distill, process. **2 civilize,** make cultivated, polish, improve, make elegant. **3 improve,** perfect,

consummate, elaborate, hone, fine-tune, complete.

refined *adj.* **1 purified,** pure, rarefied, clarified, clear, filtered, distilled, processed. **2 cultivated,** cultured, polished, civilized, civil, gracious, stylish, elegant, sophisticated, urbane, courtly, well-mannered, well-bred, gentlemanly, ladylike, genteel. **3 discriminating,** discerning, tasteful, sophisticated, fastidious. *Ant.* crude; coarse; unrefined.

refinement *n.* **1 purification,** processing, distillation, filtration. **2 cultivation,** culture, taste, discrimination, polish, finish, civility, grace, graciousness, style, elegance, finesse, sophistication, urbanity, courtliness, good breeding, politeness, gentility, politesse, good manners. **3 revision,** improvement, enhancement, correction, amendment. **4 subtlety,** nicety, nuance, fine point.

reflect *v.* **1 throw back,** cast back, send back, give back, scatter, diffuse, bounce back, echo, re-echo. **2 mirror,** image. **3 indicate,** express, bespeak, communicate, show, display, demonstrate, exhibit, reveal, manifest, bear out, result from.

reflection *n.* **1 throwing back,** sending back, echoing, mirroring, diffusion, radiation. **2 image,** mirror image. **3 indication,** expression, display, demonstration, manifestation, result. **4 imputation,** slur, aspersion, source of discredit, derogation. **5 thought,** second thought, thinking, consideration, contemplation, deliberation, meditation, rumination, cogitation, cerebration. **6 thought,** opinion, view, idea, impression, comment, findings.

reform v. **1 improve,** make better, better, ameliorate, amend, mend, rectify, correct, rehabilitate, change, revise, revolutionize, reorganize, reconstruct, rebuild, refashion, remodel, remake, make over, revamp, renovate. **2 mend one's ways,** change for the better, turn over a new leaf, improve, *inf.* go straight, get back on the straight and narrow. *Ant.* worsen; backslide.

▸ *n.* **improvement,** betterment, amelioration, amendment, rectification, correction, rehabilitation, change, revision, reorganization, reconstruction, rebuilding, refashioning, remodeling, renovation.

refrain v. **desist,** abstain, hold back, forbear, forgo, do without, avoid, eschew, cease, stop, give up, leave off, quit, renounce.

refresh v. **1 freshen,** invigorate, revitalize, revive, brace, fortify, enliven, stimulate, energize, exhilarate, reanimate, resuscitate, revivify, rejuvenate, regenerate, breathe new life into, inspirit, *inf.* perk up. **2 stimulate,** prompt, prod, jog, activate, rouse, arouse.

refreshing *adj.* **1 freshening,** invigorating, revitalizing, reviving, bracing, stimulating, exhilarating, energizing. **2 fresh,** new, novel, original, different.

refuge n. **1 shelter,** safety, security, protection, asylum, sanctuary, place of safety, safe house, shelter, haven, retreat, harbor. **2 resort,** recourse, expedient, stopgap, tactic, stratagem, strategy.

refund v. **give back,** return, repay, pay back, reimburse, make good, restore, replace.

▸ *n.* **repayment,** reimbursement, rebate.

refuse[1] v. **turn down,** decline, say no to, reject, spurn, rebuff, repudiate, *inf.* pass up, be unwilling, balk at, demur at, avoid, resist, protest at, withhold, not grant. *Ant.* accept; consent; grant.

refuse[2] n. **rubbish,** garbage, trash, waste, debris, litter, dross, dregs, leavings, sweepings, flotsam, *inf.* junk.

regain *v.* **get back,** win back, recover, recoup, retrieve, reclaim, repossess, redeem, recuperate, take back, retake, recapture.

regal *adj.* **royal,** majestic, noble, proud, stately, magnificent, sumptuous, kingly, queenly, princely, fit for a king/queen/prince/princess.

regard *v.* **1 heed,** pay attention to, attend to, listen to, mind, take notice of, take into consideration/account. **2 look upon,** view, consider, contemplate, think of, weigh up, mull over, reflect on, deliberate on. **3 judge,** adjudge, rate, value, estimate, gauge, appraise, assess, account, deem, consider, look upon, hold.
4 watch, look at, gaze at, keep an eye on, stare at, observe, view, study, scrutinize, eye, mark, behold.
▸ *n.* **1 heed,** attention, notice, consideration, thought, mind.
2 respect, esteem, admiration, approval, approbation, appreciation, favor, deference, affection, love. **3 respect,** aspect, point, particular, detail, item, feature. **4 look,** gaze, stare, observation, scrutiny.

regarding *prep.* **with/in regard to,** as regards, as to, with reference to, on the subject/matter of, apropos, concerning, about, respecting.

regardless *adj.* phrase:
regardless of without regard to, disregarding, unmindful of, heedless of, without consideration of, indifferent to, negligent of.
▸ *adv.* **anyway,** anyhow, in any case, nevertheless, nonetheless, despite everything, for all that, no matter what. *Ant.* mindful; heedful.

regards *pl. n.* **best/good wishes,** greetings, salutations, respects, compliments, remembrances.

regenerate *v.* **1 renew,** breathe new life into, restore, invigorate, refresh, revitalize, revive, stimulate, energize, exhilarate, revivify, rejuvenate, uplift, inspirit. **2 breathe new life into,** change radically, improve, amend, reorganize, reconstruct, overhaul.

regiment *v.* **organize/order rigidly,** systematize, methodize, control strictly, discipline, keep a tight rein on, bring into line, rule with a rod of iron.

region *n.* **1 area,** province, territory, division, section, sector, zone, tract, part, quarter, locality. **2 part,** place, section, locality, site. **3 field,** sphere, orbit, ambit, realm, domain, world.

register *n.* **1 official list,** listing, roll, roster, index, directory, catalog. **2 record,** chronicle, diary, journal, log, annals, archives, files. **3 range,** compass, scope, scale, gamut, reach, sweep, spectrum.
▸ *v.* **1 record,** put on record, enter, set down, chronicle, enroll, inscribe, write down, put in writing, take down, note, list, catalog. **2 read,** record, indicate, show, display. **3 show,** express, display, exhibit, evince, betray, reveal, manifest, demonstrate, reflect. **4 make an impression,** get through, sink in, penetrate, have an effect.

regret *v.* **1 feel sorry/contrite about,** feel remorse about, wish undone, repent, rue. **2 feel sorry about,** lament, bemoan, be upset/disappointed about, mourn, grieve over, weep over, fret about, pine over, deplore.
▸ *n.* **1 sorrow,** remorse, contrition, repentance, pangs of conscience, compunction, ruefulness, self-reproach, penitence. **2 sorrow,** disappointment, lamentation, grief, mourning, pining.

regretful *adj.* **sorry,** apologetic, remorseful, contrite, repentant, conscience-stricken, rueful, penitent. *Ant.* impenitent; unrepentant.

regrettable *adj.* **deplorable,** reprehensible, disgraceful, blameworthy, unfortunate, unwelcome, distressing, ill-advised.

regular *adj.* **1 usual,** normal, customary, habitual, routine, typical, everyday, daily, unvarying, common, average, commonplace. **2 rhythmic,** periodic, steady, even, uniform, constant, unchanging. **3 even,** uniform, consistent, orderly, systematic, fixed. **4 level,** smooth, flat, uniform. **5 official,** established, fixed, stated, conventional, formal, proper, orthodox, approved, sanctioned, bona fide, standard, usual, traditional, classic, time-honored. **6 methodical,** systematic, well-organized, orderly, efficient, smooth-running, streamlined. **7 real,** thorough, absolute, utter, complete. *Ant.* irregular; unusual; erratic; uneven.

regulate *v.* **1 control,** direct, guide, govern, rule, manage, order, administer, handle, arrange, organize, conduct, run, supervise, oversee, superintend, monitor. **2 adjust,** balance, set, synchronize, modulate.

regulation *n.* **1 control,** direction, guidance, government, rule, management, administration,

organization, conducting, handling, supervision, monitoring. **2 adjustment,** balancing, synchronization, modulation. **3 rule,** ruling, order, directive, act, law, decree, statute, edict, ordinance, pronouncement, dictum, command, procedure, requirement, prescription, precept.
▸ *adj.* **official,** prescribed, mandatory, required, set, fixed, standard, normal, usual, customary.

rehearsal *n.* **practice,** practice session, trial performance, run-through, going-over.

rehearse *v.* **practice,** try out, run through, go over, have a practice session, prepare, try out, have a trial performance, go through one's paces, drill, train, prepare.

reign *v.* **1 be king/queen,** be monarch/sovereign, sit on the throne, occupy the throne, wear the crown, wield the scepter. **2 be in power,** govern, be in government, rule, be in command/charge/control, administer, hold sway, *inf.* be at the helm. **3 prevail,** predominate, obtain, hold sway, be supreme, be rife, be rampant.
▸ *n.* **1 monarchy,** sovereignty. **2 power,** government, rule, command, control, administration, charge, influence, sway, ascendancy, dominion, supremacy.

rein *n.* **check,** curb, restraint, constraint, restriction, limitation, control, bridle, brake.
▸ *v.* **check,** curb, restrain, constrain, hold back, restrict, control, bridle, put the brakes on, slow down.

reinforce *v.* **1 strengthen,** fortify, bolster up, shore up, buttress, prop up, brace, support, back up, uphold, stress, underline, emphasize. **2 augment,** increase, add to, supplement.

reiterate *v.* **repeat,** repeat/go over and over, say again, belabor, dwell on, harp on, hammer away at.

reject *v.* **1 refuse,** turn down, decline, say no to, give the thumbs down to, spurn, rebuff, repudiate, veto, deny, *inf.* pass up. **2 cast out,** cast aside, discard, jettison, renounce, abandon, forsake, scrap, exclude, eliminate. *Ant.* accept; approve.
▸ *n.* **1 discard,** castoff, irregular, second. **2 failure,** outcast, derelict, *inf.* dropout.

rejoice *v.* **1 be joyful,** be happy, be pleased, be glad, be delighted, be elated, be overjoyed, be jubilant, be euphoric, jump for joy, exult, glory, triumph, celebrate, revel, make merry,

feast. **2 take delight/pleasure in,**
find joy in. **Ant.** mourn; lament.

rejoinder *n.* **answer,** response,
reply, riposte, retort, *inf.*
comeback.

relapse *v.* **1 lapse,** regress,
retrogress, revert, backslide, fall
away, go backward, slip back,
degenerate, retrograde, recidivate.
2 have/suffer a relapse, get
ill/worse again, worsen, take a
turn for the worse, sicken,
deteriorate, sink.
▸ *n.* **1 lapse,** regression,
retrogression, reversion,
backsliding, recidivism.
2 recurrence, worsening, turn for
the worse, setback, deterioration.
Ant. improvement; recovery.

relate *v.* **1 recount,** tell, narrate,
describe, report, impart,
communicate, recite, rehearse,
present, detail, delineate,
chronicle, set forth. **2 connect,**
associate, link, correlate, ally,
couple, join.

related *adj.* **1 connected,**
interconnected, associated,
linked, correlated, allied,
affiliated, accompanying,
concomitant, akin. **2 connected,**
akin, kindred, agnate, cognate,
consanguineous. **Ant.**
unconnected; separate; unrelated.

relation *n.* **1 recounting,** telling,
narrating, narrative, description,
reporting, rehearsal, reciting.
2 connection, association, linking,
tie-in, correlation, alliance, bond,
interdependence. **3 applicability,**
application, relevance, reference,
pertinence, bearing. **4 relative,**
member of the family, kinsman,
kinswoman, connection, kin.

relationship *n.* **1 connection,**
association, link, correlation,
alliance, bond, tie-up, parallel,
correspondence, conjunction.
2 friendship, love affair, affair,
liaison. **3 family/blood ties,**
kinship.

relative *adj.* **1 comparative,**
comparable, respective,
correlative, parallel,
corresponding. **2 proportionate,** in
proportion/ratio, proportional,
related. **3 applicable,** relevant,
pertaining, pertinent, germane,
material, apposite, appropriate,
apropos, appurtenant.
▸ *n.* **relation,** member of the
family, kinsman, kinswoman,
connection, kin, parent, sibling,
grandparent, mother, father,
brother, sister, son, daughter,
stepmother, stepfather, stepchild,
stepbrother, stepsister, aunt,
uncle, niece, nephew, cousin,
grandfather, grandmother.

relax *v.* **1 loosen,** slacken,
weaken, untighten, lessen, let up,
reduce, diminish. **2 moderate,**

make less strict/formal, soften, ease. **3 lessen,** reduce, diminish, decrease, ease off, slacken off, let up on, abate. **4 loosen up,** ease up/off,calm, calm down, tranquilize, soothe, pacify, *inf.* unwind, take it easy, let it all hang out, hang loose. **5 be at leisure,** take time off, enjoy oneself, amuse oneself, entertain oneself, rest, *inf.* let one's hair down. **6 rest,** lounge, repose, take one's ease, idle, put one's feet up. *Ant.* tighten; increase; intensify; exercise.

relaxation *n.* **1 loosening,** slackening, weakening, untightening, letting-up. **2 moderation,** softening, easing. **3 lessening,** reduction, easing off, abatement. **4 loosening up,** calming, tranquilization, soothing, pacification. **5 leisure,** recreation, enjoyment, amusement, entertainment, fun, pleasure, rest.

relay *v.* **pass on,** hand on, communicate, send, transmit, broadcast, spread, circulate.

release *v.* **1 set free,** free, let go, set/turn loose, let out, liberate, deliver, emancipate, manumit, untie, undo, unloose, unbind, unchain, unfetter, unshackle, extricate. **2 let off,** let go, excuse, absolve, acquit, exonerate,

exempt. **3 make public,** make known, issue, break, announce, reveal, divulge, unveil, present, disclose, publish, broadcast, put out, circulate, disseminate, distribute, spread. *Ant.* imprison; engage; suppress.

▸ *n.* **1 freeing,** liberation, deliverance, emancipation, manumission, untying, unbinding, unchaining, extrication. **2 excusing,** absolution, acquittal, dispensation, exemption. **3 issuing,** breaking, announcement, divulging, publishing, publication, broadcasting, circulation. **4 announcement,** bulletin, publication, proclamation. **5 recording,** record, disc, compact disc, single, album, book, movie, motion picture, film, *inf.* CD, flick.

relent *v.* **1 soften,** become merciful/lenient, show mercy/pity, melt, capitulate, yield, give way, give in, come around, forbear, change one's mind, *inf.* do a U-turn. **2 let up,** ease, slacken, relax, abate, drop, fall off, die down, weaken.

relentless *adj.* **1 unrelenting,** ruthless, merciless, uncompassionate, pitiless, remorseless, unforgiving, implacable, inexorable, cruel, grim, harsh, hard, cold-hearted, fierce, strict, obdurate, unyielding, unflexible, unbending. **2 unrelenting,** unremitting, undeviating, persistent, unswerving, persevering, unflagging, punishing, unfaltering, unstoppable, incessant, unceasing, nonstop, unabated, unbroken. ***Ant.*** lenient; merciful.

relevant *adj.* **applicable,** pertinent, apposite, material, appurtenant, to the point/purpose, germane, admissible, appropriate, apt, fitting.

reliable *adj.* **dependable,** trustworthy, true, tried and true, faithful, devoted, steady, steadfast, constant, unfailing, infallible, certain, sure, responsible, well-founded, well-grounded, authentic, genuine, credible, sound, reputable, established, safe, stable. ***Ant.*** unreliable; untrustworthy; treacherous.

relic *n.* **1 ancient/historical object,** artifact, antique, heirloom. **2 vestige,** trace, survivor, remnant. **3 souvenir,** memento, keepsake, remembrance, reminder.

relief *n.* **1 relieving,** alleviating, mitigating, assuaging, allaying,

soothing, easing, dulling, lessening, reduction, alleviation, mitigation, assuagement, palliation, ease, appeasement, abatement. **2 aiding,** assisting, rescuing, saving. **3 aid,** help, assistance, succor. **4 respite,** remission, interruption, break, variation, diversion, lightening, brightening, *inf.* letup. **5 replacement,** substitute, stand-in, fill-in, alternate, understudy, *inf.* sub. **6 distinctness,** vividness, intensity, sharpness, focus, clarity, precision. **7 freedom,** release, liberation, deliverance, exemption, extrication, discharge.

relieve *v.* **1 alleviate,** mitigate, assuage, allay, soothe, soften, palliate, appease, ease, dull, abate, reduce, lessen, diminish. **2 aid,** help, assist, rescue, save, succor. **3 interrupt,** break up, vary, lighten, brighten. **4 take over from,** take the place of, stand in for, substitute for. **5 free,** release, liberate, deliver, exempt, extricate, discharge, unburden, disburden, disencumber. ***Ant.*** exacerbate; aggravate; worsen.

religious *adj.* **1 church,** holy, divine, theological, doctrinal, spiritual, sectarian. **2 churchgoing,** God-fearing, godly, pious, devout. **3 scrupulous,** conscientious, meticulous, zealous, strict, rigid, rigorous, exact, unfailing, unswerving, undeviating. *Ant.* irreligious; impious; ungodly.

relinquish *v.* **1 give up,** renounce, resign, abdicate, surrender, sign away, discontinue, stop, cease, drop, abstain from, forbear from, forgo, desist from. **2 depart from,** leave, quit, vacate, pull out of, abandon, forsake. **3 release,** let go, loosen, unloose. *Ant.* keep; retain; continue.

relish *n.* **1 enjoyment,** delight, pleasure, satisfaction, gratification, appreciation, liking, zest, gusto. **2 flavor,** taste, tang, piquancy, spiciness. *Ant.* dislike; distaste.
▸ *v.* **1 enjoy,** delight in, like, love, adore, appreciate, revel in, luxuriate in. **2 look forward to,** fancy, eagerly await/anticipate. *Ant.* detest; loathe.

reluctant *adj.* **unwilling,** disinclined, hesitant, unenthusiastic, grudging, loath, averse, slow. *Ant.* willing; eager; ready.

remain *v.* **1 be left,** be left over, stay behind, survive, last, abide, endure, prevail. **2 stay,** wait, linger, tarry, *inf.* stay put. **3 stay,** continue, persist in being. *Ant.* go; depart; leave.

remainder *n.* **remnant,** residue, residuum, balance, surplus, excess, superfluity, remains, remnants, relics, vestiges, leavings, dregs.

remains *pl. n.* **1 remnants,** leftovers, leavings, scraps, residue, debris, detritus. **2 relics,** reliquiae, fragments, shards. **3 corpse,** dead body, body, cadaver, carcass.

remark *v.* **mention,** say, state, declare, pronounce, assert, observe.
▸ *n.* **1 comment,** statement, utterance, declaration, pronouncement, observation, reference, opinion. **2 comment,** attention, mention, notice, observation, heed, acknowledgment, recognition.

remarkable *adj.* **1 out of the ordinary,** extraordinary, unusual, uncommon, conspicuous, singular, signal, rare, exceptional, outstanding, striking, impressive, considerable, notable, noteworthy, memorable, preeminent, significant, important, momentous, phenomenal, wonderful. **2 noteworthy,** notable, conspicuous, distinctive, unusual, uncommon, peculiar, special, curious, wonderful, unique, out of the ordinary. *Ant.* ordinary; commonplace; run-of-the-mill.

remedy *n.* **1 cure,** treatment, medicine, medication, medicament, therapy, antidote, restorative, nostrum, panacea. **2 corrective,** solution, redress, panacea.
▶ *v.* **1 cure,** heal, treat, counteract, control. **2 rectify,** solve, set to rights, put right, redress, fix, sort out.

remember *v.* **1 recall,** call to mind, recollect, think of. **2 keep/ bear in mind,** not forget. **3 recall,** recollect, reminisce, reminisce about, look/think back on, hark back to, summon up. **4 tip,** reward, recompense. **5 send greetings from,** send one's regards/compliments. *Ant.* forget; overlook.

remind *v.* **jog/refresh one's memory,** prompt.

reminiscent *adj.* **evocative,** suggestive, redolent.

remiss *adj.* **negligent,** neglectful, lax, slack, slipshod, careless, forgetful, inattentive, heedless, thoughtless, unthinking, unmindful, culpable, delinquent, *inf.* sloppy. *Ant.* careful; diligent; painstaking.

remission *n.* **1 cancellation,** revocation, repeal, rescinding. **2 reduction in sentence,** reduced sentence. **3 relaxation,** slackening, weakening, lessening, reduction, decrease, diminution, dwindling, cessation, stopping, halt. **4 easing,** moderation, abatement, lessening, decrease, dwindling, wane, waning, ebb, ebbing, subsidence. **5 sending,** dispatch, forwarding, transmission, posting, mailing. **6 referral,** passing on, transfer, direction. **7 postponement,** deferral, shelving, delay, suspension. **8 pardon,** absolution, exoneration, forgiveness, indulgence.

remit *v.* **1 cancel,** revoke, repeal, rescind, stop, halt. **2 relax,** slacken, weaken, lessen, reduce, decrease, diminish, cease, stop, halt, desist from. **3 ease,** moderate, abate, lessen, decrease, dwindle, wane, ebb, subside. **4 send,** dispatch, forward, transmit, post, mail. **5 refer,** pass on, hand on, send on, transfer, direct. **6 postpone,** defer, put off, shelve, delay, hold off, suspend, prorogue, reschedule. **7 pardon,** forgive, excuse, overlook, pass over.

remnant *n.* **1 remainder,** residue, balance, remains, vestiges. **2 piece,** fragment, scrap, cutoff.

remonstrate *v.* **1 take issue with,** argue with, dispute with, protest to, complain to, expostulate with. **2 argue against,** protest against, object to, complain about, take a stand against, oppose.

remorse *n.* **regret,** sorrow, sorriness, contriteness, compunction, penitence, repentance, bad/guilty conscience, guilt, shame, self-reproach, ruefulness, pangs of conscience.

remorseful *adj.* **sorry,** regretful, contrite, apologetic, penitent, repentant, guilt-ridden, conscience-stricken, ashamed, chastened, rueful.

remote *adj.* **1 distant,** far, far-off, faraway, far-removed, out-of-the-way, outlying, inaccessible, off the beaten track, isolated, secluded, lonely, godforsaken. **2 outside,** unlikely, improbable, implausible, negligible, insignificant, doubtful, dubious, inconsiderable, slight, slender, slim, small, poor. **3 aloof,** distant, detached, withdrawn, reserved, uncommunicative, unapproachable, standoffish, cool, haughty, uninvolved, indifferent, unconcerned. *Ant.* near; accessible; likely.

removal *n.* **1 taking away,** moving, shifting, conveying, conveyance, transfer, carrying away, transporting. **2 dismissal,** eviction, ejection, expulsion, ousting, dislodgment, deposition. **3 taking away,** withdrawal, deprivation, abolition. **4 deletion,** elimination, erasure, effacing, obliteration. **5 uprooting,** eradication, extirpation, destruction, extermination, annihilation. **6 cutting off,** amputation, excision. **7 move,** transfer, relocation. **8 disposal,** elimination, killing, murder, assassination, liquidation.

remove *v.* **1 take away,** carry away, move, shift, convey, transfer, transport. **2 get rid of,** dismiss, evict, eject, expel, cast out, oust, throw out, thrust out, dislodge, relegate, unseat, depose, displace, *inf.* sack, fire. **3 take off,** doff, pull off. **4 take away,** withdraw, do away with, abolish. **5 delete,** eliminate, erase, rub out, cross out, strike out, blue-pencil, efface, obliterate. **6 take out,** pull out, uproot, eradicate, extirpate, destroy, exterminate, annihilate. **7 cut off,** amputate, lop off, chop off, excise. **8 move,** transfer, relocate. **9 get rid of,** dispose of, do away with, eliminate, kill, murder, assassinate, liquidate, *inf.* bump off, do in. *Ant.* place; install; put on (see put).

remunerative *adj.* **profitable,** moneymaking, paying, lucrative, gainful, financially rewarding, rich.

render *v.* **1 make,** cause to

be/become, leave. **2 give,** contribute, make available, provide, supply, furnish, do, perform. **3 give,** exchange, trade, swap, return. **4 show,** display, exhibit, evince, manifest. **5 present,** send in, submit, tender, deliver, hand down. **6 paint,** portray, depict, represent. **7 act,** perform, play. **8 play,** execute, perform, interpret. **9 translate,** transcribe, construe, put, express. **10 give,** hand over, deliver, turn over, give up, yield, cede, surrender, relinquish. **11 give back,** return, restore.

rendezvous *n.* **1 appointment,** date, engagement, tryst, meeting, assignation. **2 meeting place,** venue, tryst.

▸ *v.* **meet,** come/gather together, gather, assemble.

renegade *n.* **defector,** deserter, turncoat, betrayer, traitor, dissenter, apostate, renouncer, recanter, revolutionary, rebel, mutineer.

renege *v.* **go back on one's word,** break one's promise, default, back out, pull out, *inf.* cop out, welsh.

renounce *v.* **1 give up,** relinquish, resign, abdicate, abnegate, surrender, sign away, waive, forgo. **2 repudiate,** disown, cast off, discard, reject, disinherit, wash one's hands of, spurn, shun.

3 give up, abstain from, desist from, swear off, eschew. **4 give up,** abandon, forsake, renege on, turn one's back on, abjure. *Ant.* claim; maintain; embrace.

renovate *v.* **modernize,** recondition, refurbish, rehabilitate, overhaul, restore, revamp, remodel, repair, redecorate, refit, *inf.* do up, fix up.

renown *n.* **fame,** repute, acclaim, celebrity, distinction, illustriousness, eminence, preeminence, prominence, mark, note, consequence, prestige.

renowned *adj.* **famous,** famed, well-known, of repute, acclaimed, celebrated, distinguished, illustrious, eminent, preeminent, prominent, noted, notable, of note, of consequence, prestigious. *Ant.* unknown; obscure; unsung.

rent[1] *n.* **rental,** tenant's payment, (hire) fee.

▸ *v.* **lease,** hire, charter.

rent[2] *n.* **tear,** rip, split, gash, slash, hole, perforation, break, crack, fracture, crevice, fissure, cleft.

repair[1] *v.* **1 mend,** fix, put right, restore, restore to working order, service, adjust, regulate, overhaul, darn, sew, patch. **2 make reparation for,** put right, make good, rectify, correct, redress, compensate for. *Ant.* break; tear; harm.

▸ *n.* **1 mending,** fixing, restoration, servicing, overhaul. **2 mend,** darn, patch. **3 condition,** state, form, fettle, kilter; *inf.* shape.

repay *v.* **1 pay/give back,** refund, reimburse, recompense, remunerate, square accounts with, settle up with, indemnify. **2 get back at,** hit back, retaliate against, get even with, settle the score with, avenge, revenge, make reprisal for.

repeal *v.* **revoke,** rescind, abrogate, annul, nullify, declare null and void, make void, void, invalidate, quash, set aside, cancel, countermand, retract, withdraw, recall, abjure, overrule, override, reverse. ***Ant.*** introduce; ratify.

▸ *n.* **revocation,** rescinding, rescission, abrogation, annulment, nullification, voiding, invalidation, quashing, setting aside, cancellation, countermanding, retraction, withdrawal, recall, abjuration, overruling, overriding, reversal.

repeat *v.* **1 say again,** restate, retell, iterate, recite, rehearse, recapitulate, echo, parrot, quote, duplicate, copy, reproduce, *inf.* recap. **2 do again,** redo, duplicate.

▸ *n.* **1 repetition,** restatement, retelling, iteration, recapitulation, echoing, parroting, duplication, copy, reproduction, *inf.* recap. **2 rerun,** replay, rebroadcast.

repeated *adj.* **recurrent,** frequent, continual, incessant, constant, endless.

repel *v.* **1 repulse,** drive back, push back, thrust back, force back, beat back, hold off, ward off, fend off, stave off, parry, keep at bay, keep at arm's length, foil, check, frustrate, put to flight. **2 repulse,** reject, decline, turn down, rebuff. **3 revolt,** disgust, sicken, nauseate, make one sick, turn one's stomach, be repugnant to, make one's flesh creep, put one off, offend, shock, *inf.* turn one off, give one the creeps/heebie-jeebies. ***Ant.*** welcome; attract; delight.

repellent *adj.* **repulsive,** revolting, disgusting, sickening, nauseating, distasteful, repugnant, abhorrent, offensive, obnoxious, loathsome, hateful, vile, nasty, shocking, despicable, reprehensible, contemptible, odious, abominable, horrible, horrid, foul, heinous, obscene.

repent *v.* **regret,** feel remorse for, rue, be penitent, be sorry, see the error of one's ways, be regretful, be contrite, feel remorse/remorseful, be conscience-stricken, reproach oneself, be ashamed, be guilt-ridden, *inf.* see the light.

repentant *adj.* penitent, sorrowful, apologetic, regretful, contrite, remorseful, conscience-stricken, rueful, ashamed, guilt-ridden.

repercussion *n.* **1 effect,** result, consequence, reverberation, backlash. **2 echo,** reverberation, reflection, recoil, rebound.

repetitive *adj.* **recurrent,** unchanging, unvaried, undiversified, monotonous, tedious, boring, mechanical, automatic.

replace *v.* **1 put back,** return, restore. **2 take the place of,** succeed, supersede, follow after, come after, supplant, substitute for, stand in for, act for, fill in for, cover for, understudy, *inf.* sub for. **3 give in place of,** give as a replacement for, give in return/exchange for.

replacement *n.* **successor,** substitute, stand-in, fill-in, understudy, proxy, surrogate, *inf.* sub.

replenish *v.* **1 refill,** top off, fill up, recharge, reload. **2 stock up,** fill up, make up, replace, renew.

replica *n.* **copy,** carbon copy, duplicate, facsimile, model, reproduction, imitation.

reply *v.* **1 answer,** respond, make/

give a response, write back, call/phone back. **2 answer,** respond, rejoin, retort, return, riposte, come back, counter. ***Ant.*** ask; question.

▸ *n.* **answer,** response, acknowledgment, rejoinder, retort, return, riposte, comeback.

report *n.* **1 account,** statement, record, exposition, delineation. **2 article,** piece, account, story, write-up, communication, communiqué, dispatch, bulletin. **3 formal statement,** record, register, chronicle. **4 reputation,** repute, regard, character, name. **5 bang,** boom, crack, crash, rumble, reverberation, noise, sound, echo.

▸ *v.* **1 bring word about,** announce, pass on, communicate, relay, relate, tell, recount, give an account of, set forth, document, narrate, describe, delineate, detail, divulge, disclose, circulate. **2 tell on,** inform on, accuse, make a charge/complaint against, *inf.* squeal on, rat on. **3 present oneself,** be present, appear, arrive, come, turn up, check in, *inf.* show up. **4 record,** document, minute, write up, chronicle, write down, take down.

reporter *n.* **journalist,** newsman, newswoman, pressman, correspondent, writer, broadcaster, announcer, presenter, news commentator, *inf.* newshound, hack.

reprehensible *adj.* **blameworthy,** blamable, reproachable, censurable, condemnable, reprovable, culpable, erring, errant, wrong, bad, shameful, disgraceful, discreditable, dishonorable, ignoble, objectionable, odious, opprobrious, unpardonable, indefensible, unjustifiable, inexcusable.

represent *v.* **1 stand for,** correspond to, be the counterpart of, equal, be equivalent to, symbolize, mean, betoken. **2 stand for,** symbolize, personify, epitomize, typify. **3 embody,** incorporate, typify, exemplify, be a sample/specimen of. **4 depict,** portray, delineate, illustrate, picture, denote, paint, draw, sketch, exhibit, show, display, evoke. **5 act as,** enact, portray, appear as, perform as. **6 act for,** appear for, speak for, be spokesperson for, be the representative of.

representation *n.* **1 depiction,** portrayal, portrait, delineation, illustration, picture, painting, drawing, sketch, image, model. **2 spokesman,** spokeswoman, spokesperson, representative, agent, deputy, ambassador, envoy, delegate, delegation, deputation. **3 statement,** account, report, declaration, allegation, argument, protestation, remonstrance, expostulation.

representative *adj.* **1 typical,** archetypal, exemplary, characteristic, indicative, illustrative. **2 emblematic,** symbolic, evocative. **3 elected,** elective, chosen, delegated, ambassadorial, authorized, accredited, official. *Ant.* atypical; unrepresentative; extraordinary.

▸ *n.* **1 example,** exemplification, exemplar, specimen, type, archetype, illustration, epitome, embodiment. **2 spokesman,** spokeswoman, spokesperson, agent, deputy, proxy. **3 traveling salesman,** agent, *inf.* rep. **4 delegate,** commissioner, ambassador, envoy. **5 congressman,** congresswoman, member of Congress, senator, member of the House/Senate, assemblyman, assemblywoman, councilman, councilwoman.

repress *v.* **1 subjugate,** conquer, vanquish, overpower, overcome, crush, master, dominate, domineer, bully, intimidate, oppress, tyrannize, put down, quell, quash, squash, subdue, suppress, extinguish, stamp out, stop, put an end to. **2 hold/keep back,** hold in, bite back, restrain, suppress, keep in check, check, inhibit, bottle up, silence, muffle, stifle, smother. *Ant.* encourage; support; release; express.

repressed *adj.* **1 subjugated,** oppressed, tyrannized.
2 restrained, suppressed, muffled, smothered. **3 inhibited,** withdrawn, restrained.

repression *n.* **1 suppression,** quashing, subduing, crushing, stamping out. **2 oppression,** subjugation, suppression, tyranny, despotism, authoritarianism. **3 restraint,** restraining, holding back, keeping back, suppression, keeping in check, control, keeping under control, stifling, bottling up.

repressive *adj.* **repressing,** tyrannical, despotic, dictatorial, authoritarian, dominating, oppressive, coercive, suppressive, harsh, severe, strict, cruel.

reprieve *v.* **1 grant a stay of execution to,** let off, pardon, *inf.* let off the hook. **2 give a respite (to),** save, rescue. *Ant.* charge; punish.
▸ *n.* **stay of execution,** pardon, *inf.* let-off.

reprimand *n.* **rebuke,** scolding, chiding, reproach, reproof, reproval, lecture, admonition, berating, upbraiding, castigation, tongue-lashing, *inf.* talking-to, telling-off, dressing-down, bawling-out.
▸ *v.* **rebuke,** scold, chide, reproach, reprove, lecture, admonish, berate, upbraid, castigate, take to task, rake/haul over the coals, blame, censure, check, *inf.* give a talking-to, tell off, give a dressing-down, bawl out.

reprisal *n.* **retaliation,** revenge, vengeance, retribution, redress, requital, recrimination, an eye for an eye, tit for tat.

reproach *v.* **criticize,** find fault with, censure, blame, admonish, condemn, reprehend, disparage, abuse, reprimand, scold, chide, reprove, berate, upbraid, castigate, take to task, rake/haul over the coals, *inf.* give a dressing-down to.
▸ *n.* **1 criticism,** faultfinding, censuring, admonition, condemnation, abuse, reprimand, scolding, reproof, reproval, upbraiding. **2 discredit,** disgrace, shame, source of shame, stigma, blemish, stain, slur, dishonor, disrepute, ignominy, scorn, contempt, opprobrium, odium, obloquy.

reproachful *adj.* **disapproving,** disappointed, critical, censorious, admonitory, condemnatory, disparaging, reproving, castigatory.

reproduce v. **1 copy,** make a copy of, duplicate, replicate, photocopy, Xerox, mimeograph, print, transcribe, clone. **2 repeat,** recreate, redo, remake, imitate, follow, emulate, echo, mirror, parallel, match, mimic, ape. **3 breed,** procreate, bear young, produce offspring, give birth, multiply, propagate, proliferate, spawn.

reproduction n. **1 copying,** duplicating, photocopying, Xeroxing, printing. **2 copy,** duplicate, replica, facsimile, imitation, print, fax, photocopy, mimeograph, *Trademark* Xerox. **3 breeding,** procreation, producing young, multiplying, propagation, proliferation.

repudiate v. **1 disown,** cast off, cut off, abandon, forsake, desert, discard, reject, renounce, disavow, abjure, turn one's back on, have nothing to do with, wash one's hands of. **2 deny,** contradict, gainsay, disclaim, disavow. **3 reject,** rescind, revoke, cancel, set aside, overrule, override, disregard, ignore, flout, spurn, dishonor, disobey. ***Ant.*** embrace; confirm; accept.

repugnant adj. **abhorrent,**

revolting, repulsive, repellent, disgusting, sickening, nauseating, disagreeable, distasteful, offensive, objectionable, obnoxious, loathsome, hateful, despicable, reprehensible, contemptible, abominable, horrible, horrid, foul, nasty, vile, ugly, odious, heinous. ***Ant.*** attractive; agreeable; pleasant.

repulsive adj. **abhorrent,** revolting, repellent, disgusting, sickening, nauseating, disagreeable, distasteful, offensive, objectionable, obnoxious, loathsome, hateful, despicable, reprehensible, contemptible, abominable, horrible, foul, nasty, vile, ugly, odious, heinous. ***Ant.*** attractive; agreeable; pleasant.

reputable adj. **of repute,** of good repute, respectable, respected, well-thought-of, esteemed, estimable, worthy, creditable, reliable, dependable, conscientious, trustworthy, honest, honorable, aboveboard, legitimate, upright, virtuous, good, excellent. ***Ant.*** disreputable; untrustworthy.

reputation n. **1 name,** estimation, character, repute, standing, position, status, station, rank, stature. **2 good name,** good character, good standing, respect, respectability, repute, esteem, fame, celebrity, renown.

request *n.* **1 asking,** entreaty, solicitation, petitioning, application, imploration, begging, pleading, behest, supplication, demand, summons, requisition. **2 entreaty,** appeal, petition, plea, behest, demand, call, suit.
▸ *v.* **ask for,** solicit, seek, apply for, put in for, call for, entreat, beseech, beg for, plead for, pray for, petition, implore, sue for, supplicate for, requisition, demand, desire.

require *v.* **1 need,** have need of, stand in need of, lack, be short of, be deficient in, want, wish, desire, crave, miss. **2 demand,** order, command, call for, insist on, ask for, request, instruct, oblige, enjoin, bid, compel. **3 call for,** demand, necessitate, involve, take.

required *adj.* **compulsory,** obligatory, mandatory, prescribed, recommended, set, essential, necessary, vital.

requirement *n.* **1 need,** want, lack, must, necessity, necessary/ essential item, demand. **2 prerequisite,** requisite, precondition, specification, qualification, sine qua non, stipulation.

requisite *adj.* **required,** prerequisite, needed, necessary, essential, indispensable, vital, called-for, demanded, obligatory, mandatory.
▸ *n.* **1 requirement,** need, want. **2 requirement,** prerequisite, precondition, specification, qualification, stipulation.

requisition *n.* **1 application,** order, claim, request, call, demand, summons. **2 commandeering,** appropriation, possession, occupation, seizure, confiscation.
▸ *v.* **1 apply for,** order, put in a claim for, request, call for, demand. **2 commandeer,** appropriate, take over, take possession of, occupy, seize, confiscate.

rescue *v.* **save,** come to the aid of, free, set free/loose, release, liberate, emancipate, get out, extricate, redeem, salvage, relieve. *Ant.* endanger; jeopardize; imprison.
▸ *n.* **rescuing,** saving, deliverance, delivery, freeing, release, liberation, emancipation, extrication, redemption, salvage, relief.

research *n.* **investigation,** experimentation, fact-finding, testing, exploration, analysis, examination, scrutiny, experiment, assessment, study,

review, inquiry, probe, inspection, tests.
▸ *v.* **do tests on,** investigate, inquire into, look into, probe, explore, analyze, study, examine, scrutinize, review, inspect, experiment with, assess.

resemblance *n.* **likeness,** alikeness, similarity, similitude, semblance, identicalness, sameness, uniformity, correspondence, comparability, comparison, parallelism, parity, analogy, affinity, closeness, nearness, agreement, congruity, concurrence, conformity.

resemble *v.* **be like,** look like, bear a resemblance to, be similar to, put one in mind of, remind one of, take after, echo, mirror, parrot, duplicate, parallel, *inf.* favor.

resent *v.* **feel aggrieved at,** take offense/umbrage at, take exception to, take amiss, be annoyed/angry at, begrudge, feel bitter about, dislike.

resentful *adj.* **aggrieved,** offended, indignant, irritated, displeased, annoyed, angry, irate, incensed, piqued, in high dudgeon, grudging, bitter, embittered, wounded, *inf.* huffy, in a huff, miffed, peeved.

resentment *n.* **offense,** indignation, irritation, displeasure, annoyance, anger, ire, pique, grudgingness, bitterness, animosity, hostility, hard feelings.

reservation *n.* **1 putting aside,** conservation, saving, retention, storing. **2 booking,** engaging, chartering. **3 advance booking,** booking, engagement, prearrangement, charter/hire arrangements. **4 qualification,** proviso, provision, condition, stipulation, limitation, qualm, scruple, hesitancy, doubt, demur. **5 reserve,** preserve, enclave, sanctuary, tract, area, territory.

reserve *v.* **1 put/set/lay aside,** put away, keep back, keep, withhold, conserve, save, retain, store, hoard, stockpile, *inf.* hang on to. **2 book,** engage, arrange for, prearrange for, bespeak, charter, hire. **3 put off,** postpone, defer, delay, withhold. **4 keep,** retain, secure, *inf.* hang on to.
▸ *n.* **1 store,** stock, supply, reservoir, pool, cache, fund, stockpile, accumulation, backlog, hoard. **2 reservation,** qualification, proviso, condition, limitation, stipulation, qualm, scruple. **3 self-restraint,** restraint, self-control, constraint, aloofness, detachment, distance, remoteness, formality, coolness, coldness, frigidity, reticence,

unapproachability, uncommunicativeness, unresponsiveness, shyness, diffidence, secretiveness, taciturnity, silence. **4 preserve,** reservation, sanctuary, park, tract, territory, area.

reserved *adj.* **1 conserved,** stored, stockpiled. **2 booked,** engaged, prearranged (for), taken, spoken for, chartered, hired. **3 self-restrained,** aloof, detached, remote, formal, unemotional, undemonstrative, cool, cold, frigid, reticent, unapproachable, uncommunicative, unsociable, unfriendly, unresponsive, unforthcoming, shy, retiring, diffident, secret, secretive, taciturn, silent. ***Ant.*** outgoing; communicative; sociable.

residence *n.* **1 house,** home, place, dwelling, domicile, habitation, quarters. **2 occupation,** occupancy, habitation, inhabitation, tenancy, stay, sojourn.

resident *n.* **inhabitant,** occupant, occupier, householder, dweller, resider, sojourner, tenant, local, denizen.
▸ *adj.* **1 live-in,** living-in. **2 inhabiting,** dwelling, neighborhood, local.

residue *n.* **residuum,** remainder, remnant, rest, surplus, extra, excess, balance, remains, leftovers, dregs, lees.

resign *v.* **1 give notice,** hand in one's notice, leave, quit. **2 renounce,** relinquish, give up, abdicate, surrender, cede. **3 reconcile.**

resilient *adj.* **1 elastic,** springy, rubbery, flexible, pliant, supple, pliable, plastic. **2 quick to recover,** quick to bounce back, difficult to keep down, irrepressible, tough, strong, hardy. ***Ant.*** inflexible; rigid.

resist *v.* **1 withstand,** be proof against, repel. **2 stop,** halt, prevent, check, stem, curb, obstruct, hinder, impede, block, thwart, frustrate, inhibit, restrain. **3 abstain from,** refrain from, keep from, forbear from, desist from, forgo, avoid. **4 fight,** battle against, stand up to, withstand, stand one's ground against, hold out against, defy, oppose, confront, struggle against, contend with.

resolute *adj.* **determined,** resolved, decided, firm, fixed, set, intent, steadfast, constant, earnest, staunch, bold, courageous, serious, purposeful, deliberate, inflexible, unyielding, unwavering, unfaltering, unhesitating, unswerving, unflinching, obstinate, obdurate, strong-willed, dogged, persevering, persistent, tenacious, relentless, unshakable, dedicated. *Ant.* irresolute; doubtful.

resolution *n.* **1 resolve,** determination, firmness, intentness, steadfastness, constancy, staunchness, boldness, courage, seriousness, purpose, purposefulness, obstinacy, obdurateness, obduracy, willpower, doggedness, perseverance, persistence, tenacity, staying power, dedication. **2 resolve,** decision, aim, intent, intention, purpose, object, plan, design, aspiration. **3 motion,** declaration, decree, verdict, judgment. **4 resolving,** solving, solution, answer, sorting out, working out, unraveling, disentanglement, cracking.

resolve *v.* **1 decide,** make up one's mind, determine, settle on, undertake. **2 solve,** answer, sort out, work out, clear up, fathom, unravel, disentangle, crack. **3 dispel,** remove, banish, clear up. **4 break down,** break up, separate, divide, disintegrate, reduce, dissolve, analyze, anatomize, dissect.
  ▸ *n.* **1 resolution,** decision, aim, intent, intention, purpose. **2 resolution,** determination, firmness of purpose, staunchness,

boldness, courage, purposefulness, obstinacy, perseverance, dedication.

resort *v.* phrase: **resort to fall back on,** turn to, have recourse to, look to, make use of, use, utilize, avail oneself of, bring into play/service, exercise.
  ▸ *n.* **1 vacation spot,** retreat, spa. **2 recourse,** source of help, expedient, measure, alternative, choice, possibility, hope.

resound *v.* **1 reverberate,** resonate, echo, ring. **2 be talked about,** be made known, spread, circulate, be proclaimed, be famed, be celebrated, be glorified.

resource *n.* **1 expedient,** resort, course, way, device, means. **2 reserve,** reservoir, store, stock, supply, pool, fund, stockpile, accumulation, hoard, assets, reserves, materials, wealth.

respect *n.* **1 esteem,** high regard, regard, high opinion, admiration, approbation, approval, appreciation, veneration, reverence, deference, honor, praise, homage, consideration, thoughtfulness, attentiveness, politeness, courtesy, civility. **2 heed,** regard, consideration, attention, notice. **3 aspect,** facet, feature, way, sense, characteristic, particular, point, detail, matter.

4 reference, relevance, regard, relation, connection, bearing.

▶ v. **1 esteem,** have a high opinion of, think highly of, admire, approve of, appreciate, venerate, revere, honor, praise, value, set store by. **2 show consideration/ regard for,** take into consideration, take cognizance of, observe, pay heed/attention to. **3 heed,** observe, comply with, follow, abide by, adhere to, obey.

respectable adj. **1 reputable,** of good repute, upright, honest, honorable, trustworthy, aboveboard, worthy, decent, good, virtuous, admirable, well-bred, proper, decorous. **2 reasonable,** fair, passable, tolerable, adequate, satisfactory, fairly good, considerable, ample, sizable, substantial, inf. not to be sneezed at, not bad. **Ant.** dishonorable; unworthy; small; paltry.

respective adj. **individual,** separate, personal, own, particular, specific, various.

respects pl. n. **greetings,** regards, best wishes, compliments, remembrances.

respite n. **1 rest,** break, breathing spell, interval, intermission, recess, lull, pause, hiatus, halt, relief, relaxation, inf. breather, letup. **2 remission,** reprieve, stay, stay of execution, suspension, postponement, adjournment, deferment, delay, moratorium.

respond v. **1 say in response,** answer, reply, rejoin, retort, return, riposte, come back, counter. **2 react,** act in response. **Ant.** ask; question.

response n. **1 answer,** reply, acknowledgment, rejoinder, retort, return, riposte, comeback. **2 reply,** reaction, feedback, inf. comeback.

responsibility n. **1 charge,** duty, onus, task, role, liability, accountability, answerability. **2 blame,** fault, guilt, culpability. **3 maturity,** reason, sanity, sense, common sense, soundness, stability, reliability, dependability, trustworthiness, competence, conscientiousness. **4 authority,** control, power.

responsible adj. **1 accountable,** answerable, to blame, blameworthy, at fault, guilty, culpable. **2 mature,** adult, levelheaded, rational, sane, reasonable, sensible, sound, stable, reliable, dependable, trustworthy, competent, conscientious, hardworking, industrious. **3 authoritative,** executive, decision-making, powerful, high, important. **Ant.** irresponsible; untrustworthy.

responsive *adj.* **quick to react,** reactive, receptive, forthcoming, sensitive, perceptive, sympathetic, susceptible, impressionable, open, alive, awake, aware, sharp. *Ant.* impassive; apathetic.

rest[1] *n.* **1 repose,** relaxation, leisure, ease, inactivity, respite, time off, breathing space, sleep, slumber, nap, doze, siesta, *inf.* breather, snooze, forty winks, lie-down. **2 break,** breathing space, interval, interlude, intermission, lull, pause, holiday, vacation, time off. **3 repose,** quiet, quietness, quietude, calm, calmness, tranquillity, peace, peacefulness, stillness, silence, hush. **4 stand,** base, holder, support, prop, shelf. ▶ *v.* **1 take a rest,** put one's feet up, relax, sit down, lie down, go to bed, sleep, take a nap, nap, catnap, doze, slumber; *inf.* take it easy, snooze. **2 support,** prop, steady, lay, place, position. **3 be supported by,** be propped up by, lie on, be laid on, recline on, stand on, sit on. **4 depend,** rely, hang, hinge, be based, be founded.

rest[2] *n.* **remainder,** residue, residuum, balance, remnant, surplus, excess, rump, those left, others, remains, leftovers.

rest[3] *v.* **remain,** stay, continue, be left.

restful *adj.* **1 calming,** relaxing, soothing, tranquilizing. **2 quiet,** calm, tranquil, relaxed, peaceful, placid, still, languid, undisturbed, unhurried, sleepy. *Ant.* stimulating; noisy.

restless *adj.* **1 sleepless,** wakeful, tossing and turning, fitful. **2 uneasy,** ill at ease, on edge, agitated, restive, fidgety, fidgeting. **3 moving,** in motion, on the move, changeable, changing. **4 unsettled,** roaming, roving, wandering, itinerant, traveling, nomadic, peripatetic. *Ant.* calm; composed.

restore *v.* **1 renovate,** repair, fix, mend, set to rights, recondition, rehabilitate, refurbish, rebuild, reconstruct, remodel, revamp, redecorate, touch up, *inf.* do up, fix up. **2 build up,** resuscitate, revitalize, refresh, revive, revivify. **3 return,** give back, hand back, send back. **4 put back,** return, replace, reinstate. **5 reestablish,** reinstitute, reinstate, reinstall, reinforce, reimpose.

restrain *v.* **1 control,** keep under control, hold in check, curb, keep within bounds, subdue. **2 control,** check, suppress, repress, contain, smother, stifle, bottle up, rein in, *inf.* keep the lid on. **3 prevent,** hold back, hinder, impede, obstruct, delay, inhibit. **4 tie up,**

bind, chain up, fetter, pinion, confine, lock up, imprison, detain, arrest.

restraint *n.* **1 constraint,** check, curb, barrier, block, hindrance, impediment, deterrent, inhibition. **2 self-restraint,** self-control, self-discipline, moderation, temperateness, prudence, judiciousness, self-possession, reserve, lack of emotion, coldness, formality, aloofness, detachment, reticence, uncommunicativeness. **3 confinement,** detention, imprisonment, incarceration, bondage, (a) straitjacket, bonds, chains, fetters, manacles.

restrict *v.* **1 hinder,** impede, hamper, retard, handicap, cramp. **2 limit,** set/impose limits on, keep within bounds, keep under control, regulate, control, moderate. **3 restrain,** confine, lock up, imprison, wall up, hem in.

restriction *n.* **1 constraint,** limitation, control, check, curb, regulation, condition, provision, proviso, stipulation, qualification, demarcation. **2 confinement,** crampedness, constraint. **3 hindrance,** impediment, handicap.

result *n.* **1 outcome,** consequence, issue, upshot, sequel, effect, reaction, repercussion, event, end, conclusion, termination, aftermath, product, by-product, fruits. **2 answer,** solution.

▸ *v.* **1 follow,** ensue, issue, develop, stem, arise, evolve, emerge, emanate, occur, happen, come about, eventuate. **2 end,** culminate, finish, terminate.

resume *v.* **1 take up,** carry on, continue, proceed, go on, recommence, restart, start/begin again, reopen, reinstitute. **2 take up again,** reoccupy, occupy again, take back, recover, assume again.

resurrect *v.* **1 raise from the dead,** restore to life, bring back to life. **2 revive,** breathe new life into, give new life to, bring back, restore, resuscitate, revitalize, reintroduce, reinstall, reestablish, *inf.* give the kiss of life to.

retain *v.* **1 keep,** keep possession/hold of, hold on/fast to, *inf.* hang on to. **2 keep,** maintain, continue, preserve, reserve. **3 keep/bear in mind,** memorize, remember, call to mind, recall, recollect. **4 hire,** employ, engage, commission, pay. *Ant.* give up (see give); discontinue; dismiss.

retaliate *v.* **return like for like,** give tit for tat, give as good as one gets, get one's own back, get back at, make reprisal(s), take/exact/wreak revenge, avenge oneself, exact retribution, reciprocate, get even with, even the score, settle a score.

retard *v.* **slow down,** slow up, hold back, set back, hold up, delay, hinder, hamper, obstruct, impede, decelerate, put a brake on, check, arrest, interfere with, interrupt, thwart, frustrate. *Ant.* accelerate; expedite.

reticent *adj.* **reserved,** restrained, diffident, uncommunicative, unforthcoming, secretive, tight-lipped, close-mouthed, quiet, taciturn, silent, *inf.* mum. *Ant.* outgoing; talkative.

retire *v.* **1 give up work,** stop working. **2 withdraw,** go away, go out, depart, exit, take oneself off, leave, absent oneself. **3 go to bed,** go to one's room, *inf.* turn in, call it a day, hit the hay/sack.
4 withdraw, pull back, fall back, pull out, give ground/way, retreat, decamp.

retiring *adj.* **shy,** diffident, bashful, self-effacing, shrinking, unassuming, unassertive, reserved, reticent, timid, timorous, nervous, modest, demure, coy, meek, humble. *Ant.* bold; brash.

retract *v.* **1 draw in,** pull in, pull back. **2 take back,** withdraw, revoke, repeal, rescind, annul, cancel, abrogate, disavow, abjure, renounce, recant, disclaim,

backtrack on, renege on, do an about-turn on.

retreat *v.* **1 withdraw,** pull back, fall back, back off, give way/ ground, decamp, depart, leave, flee, take flight, turn tail, beat a retreat, beat a hasty retreat. **2 go back,** recede, ebb.
▸ *n.* **1 withdrawal,** pulling back, decamping, departure, flight, evacuation. **2 refuge,** haven, shelter, den, sanctuary, sanctum sanctorum, hideaway, resort, asylum. **3 retirement,** seclusion, solitude, privacy, sanctuary.

retribution *n.* **punishment,** justice, nemesis, what is coming to one, reckoning, reprisal, requital, retaliation, revenge, vengeance, an eye for an eye, tit for tat, measure for measure, redress, reparation, recompense, restitution, just deserts.

retrieve *v.* **1 get back,** recover, regain, win back, recoup, redeem, reclaim, repossess, recapture, salvage, rescue. **2 fetch,** bring back. **3 set right,** set/put to rights, repair, mend, remedy, rectify, redress, make good.

retrograde *adj.* **1 backward,** retreating, retrogressive, reverse. **2 worsening,** deteriorating, declining, on the downgrade/ wane.

return *v.* **1 go back,** come back,

reappear, reoccur, come again, come around again. **2 rebound,** recoil, boomerang. **3 give back,** send back, take back, carry back, remit. **4 put back,** replace, restore, reinstate, reinstall. **5 reciprocate,** repay, requite, send/give in response to. **6 yield,** bring in, earn, make, net. **7 retort,** reply, answer, respond, come back, rejoin, riposte. **8 hit back,** send back, throw back. **9 bring in,** deliver, announce, submit. *Ant.* set off (see set); keep; retain.

▸ *n.* **1 homecoming,** reappearance, reoccurrence. **2 rebound,** recoil. **3 replacement,** restoration, reinstatement, reinstallment. **4 thing/item returned,** returned article, reject. **5 profit,** yield, gain, income, revenue, interest, benefit. **6 statement,** report, account, summary, form. **7 reciprocation,** repayment, response, exchange.

reveal *v.* **1 show,** display, exhibit, expose to view. **2 bring to light,** uncover, expose to view, lay bare, unearth, unveil, unmask. **3 disclose,** divulge, tell, let out, let on, let slip, give away, give out, leak, betray, make known/public, broadcast, publicize, publish, proclaim. *Ant.* conceal; hide.

revel *v.* **celebrate,** make merry,

have a party, party, carouse, roister, *inf.* live/whoop it up, go on a spree, have a fling, rave, paint the town red.

▸ *n.* **celebration,** party, festivity, merrymaking, carousal, carouse, bacchanal, *inf.* spree, bash, jag.

revelation *n.* **1 show,** display, exhibition, exposure. **2 bringing to light,** uncovering, unearthing. **3 disclosure,** divulgence, telling, leak, betrayal, broadcasting, publicizing, communication, publishing, proclamation. **4 disclosure,** divulgence, private/confidential information.

revelry *n.* **celebration,** festivities, merrymaking, mirth, carousal.

revenge *n.* **1 vengeance,** retaliation, retribution, reprisal, requital, redress, satisfaction, eye for an eye, tit for tat, measure for measure. **2 vengefulness,** vindictiveness, spite, spitefulness, malice, maliciousness, ill will, animosity, hostility, hate, hatred, venom, rancor, bitterness.

▸ *v.* **take revenge for,** avenge, make retaliation for, retaliate, exact retribution for, take reprisals for, requite, get redress/satisfaction for.

revenue *n.* **income,** return, yield, interest, gain, profits, returns, receipts, proceeds, takings, rewards.

reverberate *v.* resound, echo, ring, vibrate.

revere *v.* **look up to,** think highly of, admire, respect, esteem, defer to, honor, reverence, venerate, worship, pay homage to, adore, hold in awe, exalt, put on a pedestal, idolize. *Ant.* despise; scorn.

reverence *n.* **high esteem,** admiration, respect, deference, honor, veneration, worship, homage, adoration, devotion, awe, exaltation.
  ▸ *v.* **revere,** admire, respect, defer to, venerate, worship, adore, exalt, idolize.

reverent *adj.* reverential, admiring, respectful, deferential, worshiping, adoring, loving, devoted, awed, submissive, humble, meek.

reversal *n.* **1 turn-around,** turn-about, about-face, volte-face, change of heart, tergiversation, *inf.* U-turn. **2 change,** exchange, trading, trade-off, swapping. **3 overturn,** overthrow, revocation, repeal, rescinding, annulment, invalidation. **4 failure,** misfortune, adversity, vicissitude, reverse, upset, setback, check, defeat.

reverse *v.* **1 turn around,** put back to front, turn inside out, turn upside down, upend, upturn, invert. **2 move/direct backward,** back, back up. **3 change,** change around, exchange, trade, swap. **4 alter,** change, countermand, undo, set aside, upset, overturn, overthrow, revoke, repeal, rescind, annul, nullify, declare null and void, void, invalidate, quash.
  ▸ *adj.* **1 opposite,** contrary, converse, counter, inverse, contrasting, antithetical. **2 reversed,** backward, inverted, transposed, turned around.

review *n.* **1 survey,** study, analysis, examination, scrutiny, assessment, appraisal. **2 reconsideration,** reexamination, reassessment, reevaluation, reappraisal, revision, rethink, another look, fresh look. **3 inspection,** parade, display, procession. **4 criticism,** critique, notice, assessment, evaluation, study, judgment, rating. **5 journal,** periodical, magazine.
  ▸ *v.* **1 survey,** study, analyze, examine, scrutinize, assess, appraise. **2 reconsider,** rethink, reexamine, reevaluate, reassess, reappraise, revise. **3 remember,** recall, recollect, reflect on, look back on, call to mind, summon up, evoke. **4 inspect,** view, scrutinize. **5 criticize,** critique, evaluate, assess, appraise, judge, weigh up, discuss.

revise v. **1 emend,** amend, correct, alter, change, edit, rewrite, redraft, rework, update, revamp. **2 reconsider,** review, reassess, alter, change.

revival n. **resurrection,** rebirth, renaissance, restoration, resuscitation, reintroduction, reinstallation, reestablishment, *inf.* comeback.

revive v. **1 bring around,** resuscitate, give artificial respiration to, give/administer CPR to, save, restore to health, *inf.* give the kiss of life to. **2 come around,** recover consciousness, recover. **3 refresh,** restore, cheer up, comfort, enliven, revitalize. **4 breathe new life into,** give a new lease on life to, bring back, restore, resuscitate, resurrect, revitalize, reintroduce, reinstall, reestablish.

revoke v. **repeal,** rescind, abrogate, countermand, annul, nullify, declare null and void, make void, void, invalidate, quash, set aside, cancel, retract, withdraw, recall, abjure, overrule, override, reverse. **Ant.** enact; ratify.

revolt v. **1 rise up,** rise, take to the streets, take up arms, rebel, mutiny, show resistance (to). **2 repel,** disgust, sicken, nauseate, make sick, turn one's stomach, be repugnant to, make one's skin/ flesh crawl/creep, put one off, offend, shock, *inf.* turn one off, give one the creeps/heebie-jeebies.

revolting adj. **repulsive,** repellent, disgusting, sickening, nauseating, distasteful, repugnant, abhorrent, offensive, obnoxious, loathsome, hateful, foul, vile, nasty, shocking, abominable, despicable, reprehensible, contemptible, odious, heinous, obscene. **Ant.** attractive; pleasant; agreeable.

revolution n. **1 rebellion,** revolt, insurrection, uprising, rising, insurgence, mutiny, riot, coup, coup d'état. **2 drastic change,** radical alteration, complete shift, metamorphosis, upheaval, upset, transformation, innovation, reformation, cataclysm. **3 rotation,** single turn, whirl, round, spin. **4 orbital motion,** orbit.

revolutionary adj. **1 rebellious,** insurgent, insurrectionary, insurrectionist, mutinous, seditious, factious, insubordinate, subversive, extremist. **2 progressive,** radical, innovative, new, novel, avant-garde, experimental, different, drastic. ▸ n. **rebel,** insurgent, insurrectionist, mutineer.

revolve v. **1 go around,** turn around, rotate, spin, whirl.

2 circle, orbit, gyrate, whirl. **3 turn over,** think over, think about, deliberate, consider, reflect on, mull over, ponder, muse over, meditate, ruminate.

revulsion *n.* repulsion, disgust, nausea, distaste, aversion, repugnance, recoil, abhorrence, loathing, hate, hatred, detestation, contempt.

reward *n.* **1 recompense,** payment, remuneration, bonus, bounty, present, gift, tip, gratuity, prize, *inf.* cut. **2 punishment,** penalty, retribution, requital, retaliation, just deserts, deserts, *inf.* comeuppance.
▶ *v.* **recompense,** pay, remunerate, give a bounty/present to, tip.

rewarding *adj.* **satisfying,** worthwhile, fulfilling, enriching, edifying, beneficial, profitable, advantageous, productive, valuable.

rhetoric *n.* **1 oratory,** eloquence, power of speech, delivery. **2 bombast,** grandiloquence, magniloquence, hyperbole, pomposity, verbosity, long-windedness, wordiness, prolixity, turgidity, extravagant language, purple prose, fustian.

rhetorical *adj.* **1 extravagant,** pretentious, ostentatious, pompous, high-flown, flamboyant, showy, flowery, florid, oratorical, declamatory, bombastic, grandiloquent, magniloquent, hyperbolic, verbose, long-winded, wordy, prolix, turgid, periphrastic. **2 oratorical,** linguistic, verbal, stylistic.

rhythm *n.* **1 beat,** cadence, tempo, pulse, throb, lilt, flow, meter. **2 flow,** cadence, meter. **3 flow,** pattern, tempo, harmony.

ribald *adj.* **bawdy,** risqué, blue, smutty, broad, vulgar, coarse, earthy, off-color, rude, naughty, racy, suggestive, indecent, indelicate, offensive, filthy, gross, lewd, salacious, licentious, concupiscent.

rich *adj.* **1 wealthy,** affluent, well off, well-to-do, prosperous, moneyed, propertied, *inf.* well-heeled, filthy rich, loaded, made of money, rolling in it/money, flush, worth a bundle, on easy street. **2 opulent,** expensive, costly, precious, valuable, priceless, beyond price, lavish, luxurious, lush, sumptuous, palatial, splendid, superb, resplendent, elegant, fine, exquisite, magnificent, grand, gorgeous. **3 well-provided,** well-supplied, well-stocked, abounding, overflowing, replete, rife. **4 copious,** abundant, ample, plentiful, plenteous, bountiful.

5 fertile, productive, fecund, fruitful, lush. **6 creamy,** fatty, heavy, spicy, highly spiced, full-bodied. **7 strong,** deep, intense, vivid, brilliant, warm, vibrant. **8 full,** sonorous, resonant, deep, mellow, mellifluous, melodious. **9 preposterous,** outrageous, ridiculous, laughable, risible, amusing, comical, funny, humorous, hilarious, sidesplitting. **Ant.** poor; cheap; meager.

riches *pl. n.* **1 money,** gold, capital, property, treasure, assets, resources. **2 wealth,** affluence, opulence, prosperity.

richly *adv.* **1 expensively,** lavishly, luxuriously, sumptuously, palatially, splendidly, superbly, resplendently, magnificently. **2 fully,** in full measure, well, thoroughly, completely, amply, utterly.

rid *v.* **clear,** cleanse, purge, purify, free, make free, relieve, deliver, unburden.

riddle *n.* **puzzle,** poser, conundrum, brainteaser, problem, enigma, mystery.

ride *v.* **1 sit on,** mount, be mounted on, bestride, manage, control. **2 travel,** go, move, progress.
▸ *n.* **trip,** outing, journey, jaunt, *inf.* spin.

ridicule *n.* **derision,** mockery, laughter, scorn, jeering, gibing, teasing, taunting, chaff, banter, badinage, raillery, satire, sarcasm, irony, *inf.* kidding, ribbing, ragging.
▸ *v.* **deride,** mock, laugh at, scoff at, scorn, jeer at, gibe at, make/poke fun at, make a fool of, tease, taunt, chaff, banter, *inf.* kid, rib, rag, send up.

ridiculous *adj.* **1 absurd,** comical, funny, laughable, hilarious, humorous, droll, farcical, facetious, ludicrous, risible, derisory. **2 pointless,** senseless, foolish, inane, fatuous, nonsensical, mindless. **3 unreasonable,** illogical, unbelievable, incredible, outrageous, preposterous, shocking, monstrous. **Ant.** serious; sensible; reasonable.

rife *adj.* **1 prevalent,** predominant, widespread, common, general, extensive, ubiquitous, universal, global, rampant. **2 abounding,** overflowing, alive, swarming, teeming.

rifle *v.* **plunder,** pillage, loot, despoil, sack, ransack.

rift *n.* **1 fault,** split, break, breach, fissure, cleft, crevice, gap, crack, cranny, slit, chink, cavity, opening, space, hole, aperture. **2 breach,** division, estrangement, schism, split, alienation, quarrel, disagreement, fight, row, altercation, conflict, feud, *inf.* falling-out.

rig[1] *v.* **equip,** supply, outfit, furnish, provide, make ready.

rig[2] *v.* **falsify,** fake, tamper with, doctor, engineer, manipulate, juggle, arrange, massage, *inf.* fix.

right *adj.* **1 just,** fair, equitable, impartial, good, upright, righteous, virtuous, proper, moral, ethical, honorable, honest, principled, lawful, legal. **2 correct,** accurate, without error, unerring, exact, precise, valid, *inf.* on the mark. **3 rightful,** true, genuine, authentic, lawful, legal, legitimate, *inf.* legit. **4 suitable,** appropriate, fitting, fit, proper, desirable, preferable, ideal. **5 opportune,** favorable, convenient, suitable, appropriate, propitious. **6 sane,** sound, rational, lucid, sensible, reasonable, clear-thinking. **7 fine,** healthy, in good health, well, fit, normal, sound, unimpaired, up to par, *inf.* up to snuff, up to scratch, in the pink. **8 conservative,** reactionary. *Ant.* wrong; unjust; inaccurate.

▸ *adv.* **1 straight,** directly, in a straight line, as the crow flies. **2 immediately,** instantly, promptly, quickly, straightaway, without delay. **3 all the way,** completely, entirely, totally, wholly, altogether, utterly, quite. **4 exactly,** precisely, just, squarely, *inf.* smack-dab. **5 accurately,** correctly, properly, exactly, precisely. **6 justly,** fairly, properly, righteously, virtuously, honorably, honestly, morally, ethically. **7 well,** for the better/best, favorably, advantageously, to one's advantage, beneficially.

righteous *adj.* **1 good,** virtuous, upright, moral, ethical, law-abiding, honest, innocent, faultless, honorable, blameless, guiltless, pure, noble, God-fearing. **2 rightful,** justifiable, well-founded, defensible, admissible, allowable, reasonable. *Ant.* bad; dishonest; sinful.

rigid *adj.* **1 stiff,** hard, taut, inflexible, nonflexible, unbendable, unbending, unyielding, inelastic, nonpliant, unmalleable. **2 fixed,** set, firm, inflexible, unalterable, unchangeable, unvarying, invariable, hard and fast. **3 strict,** severe, stern, stringent, rigorous, austere, spartan, harsh, inflexible, intransigent, uncompromising. *Ant.* flexible; lenient.

rigorous *adj.* **1 strict,** severe, stern, stringent, austere, spartan, tough, hard, harsh, rigid, inflexible, intransigent, uncompromising, demanding, exacting. **2 meticulous,** punctilious, painstaking, thorough, laborious, scrupulous, conscientious, nice, exact, precise, accurate. **3 harsh,** severe, bad, bleak, extreme, inclement. ***Ant.*** gentle; mild; slapdash; lax.

rim *n.* **1 brim,** edge, lip, circumference. **2 edge,** border, verge, margin, brink, circumference.

rind *n.* **outer layer,** peel, skin, husk, crust, integument, epicarp.

ring[1] *n.* **1 band,** circlet, hoop, gold band, wedding ring, engagement ring, diamond ring, friendship ring, pinkie ring. **2 circle,** circlet, loop, circuit, halo, disk. **3 arena,** enclosure, area. **4 circle,** group, knot, gathering. **5 gang,** syndicate, cartel, mob, organization, confederacy, association, society, combine, alliance, league, fraternity, clique, cabal, junta.

▶ *v.* **circle,** encircle, circumscribe, encompass, loop, gird, enclose, surround, hem in, fence in, seal off.

ring[2] *v.* **1 toll,** sound. **2 resound,** reverberate, resonate, echo, re-echo.

▶ *n.* **1 ringing,** toll, tolling, peal, pealing, knell, chime, clang, tinkle. **2 call,** telephone call; *inf.* phone call, buzz.

rinse *v.* **wash,** wash out, wash lightly, clean.

riot *n.* **1 rebellion,** revolt, uprising, insurrection, insurgence, street fight, commotion, disturbance, uproar, tumult, melee, row, scuffle, fracas, fray, brawl, free-for-all. **2 lavish display,** splash, extravagance, flourish, show, exhibition.

▶ *v.* **rebel,** revolt, mutiny, take to the streets, run riot, rampage, go on the rampage, run wild/amok, go berserk, fight, brawl.

riotous *adj.* **1 rebellious,** mutinous, unruly, disorderly, uncontrollable, ungovernable, unmanageable, insubordinate, rowdy, wild, violent, brawling, lawless, anarchic. **2 loud,** noisy, boisterous, uproarious, rollicking, orgiastic. **3 hilarious,** uproarious, sidesplitting, too funny for words.

ripe *adj.* **1 mature,** fully developed, full-grown, ready to eat, ready, mellow, seasoned, tempered. **2 ready,** all ready/set, developed, prepared, arranged, complete, finished. **3 advanced,** far on, old. **4 ready,** fit, suitable, right. **5 suitable,** convenient, opportune, favorable, advantageous, auspicious. ***Ant.*** immature; unripe; green.

ripen *v.* **1 grow/make ripe,** mature, come/bring to maturity, (make) mellow, season. **2 develop,** be in preparation, come to fruition.

riposte *n.* **retort,** rejoinder, answer, reply, response, return, sally, *inf.* comeback.

▶ *v.* **retort,** rejoin, answer, reply, respond, return, come back.

rise *v.* **1 arise,** come/go/move up, ascend, climb. **2 tower,** soar, loom, rear up. **3 go up,** get higher, increase, soar, rocket, escalate. **4 go up,** get higher/better, improve, advance. **5 get higher,** grow, increase, become louder, swell, intensify. **6 stand up,** get to one's feet, get up, jump up, leap up, spring up, become erect. **7 arise,** get up, get out of bed, wake up, *inf.* rise and shine, surface. **8 climb,** make progress, advance, get on, make/work one's way, be promoted. **9 come to life,** come back from the dead, be resurrected. **10 swell,** expand, enlarge. **11 rebel,** revolt, mutiny, stage an insurrection, take up arms, mount the barricades. **12 originate,** begin, start, commence, issue, spring (up), flow, emanate. **13 become more cheerful,** grow buoyant, become optimistic/hopeful. **14 slope/slant upward,** go uphill, climb, mount,

get steeper. *Ant.* set; fall; decrease; sit.

▶ *n.* **1 rising,** ascent. **2 increase,** escalation, upsurge, upswing. **3 improvement,** amelioration, advance, upturn. **4 climb,** progress, progression, advancement, promotion, aggrandizement. **5 incline,** elevation, upward slope, acclivity, rising ground, hillock, hill.

risk *n.* **1 chance,** possibility. **2 chance,** hazard, uncertainty, speculation, venture.

▶ *v.* **1 put at risk,** endanger, imperil, jeopardize, gamble, hazard, chance, venture. **2 take the risk of,** chance, venture, *inf.* grin and bear.

risky *adj.* **dangerous,** fraught with danger, hazardous, perilous, unsafe, precarious, touch-and-go, tricky, uncertain, *inf.* chancy, dicey. *Ant.* safe; secure.

rite *n.* **ritual,** ceremony, ceremonial, observance, service, sacrament, celebration, performance, act, practice, tradition, convention, formality, procedure, usage.

rival *n.* **1 opponent,** opposition, adversary, antagonist, contestant, competitor, challenger, vier, contender. **2 equal,** match, equivalent, fellow, peer.

▶ *v.* **compete with,** vie with, match,

equal, emulate, measure up to, compare with, bear comparison with, parallel.

rivalry *n.* **opposition,** competition, competitiveness, vying, contention, conflict.

road *n.* **1 street,** avenue, roadway, boulevard, thoroughfare, highway, turnpike, expressway, parkway, freeway. **2 way,** route, direction.

roam *v.* **wander (around/through),** rove, ramble, meander, drift, range, travel, walk, tramp, traverse, trek, peregrinate.

roar *v.* **1 bellow,** yell, bawl, shout, howl, thunder, shriek, scream, cry, bay. **2 roar/howl with laughter,** laugh heartily, guffaw, *inf.* split one's sides, roll in the aisles.
▸ *n.* **1 bellow,** growl, yell, bawl, shout, howl, rumble, shriek, scream, cry. **2 guffaw,** howl, hoot.

rob *v.* **1 steal from,** burgle, burglarize, hold up, break into, mug, *inf.* . **2 defraud,** swindle, cheat, mulct, dispossess, *inf.* diddle, bilk, do out of. **3 deprive.**

robber *n.* **burglar,** thief, mugger, stealer, pilferer, housebreaker, looter, raider, bandit, brigand, pirate, highwayman.

robbery *n.* **1 burglary,** theft, thievery, stealing, housebreaking, larceny, pilfering, filching, embezzlement, misappropriation,

swindling, fraud, mugging, holdup, break-in, *inf.* rip-off. **2 mugging,** holdup, break-in, raid, *inf.* rip-off.

robe *n.* **1 vestment,** habit, costume, gown. **2 bathrobe,** dressing gown, housecoat, kimono, peignoir.

robust *adj.* **1 healthy,** strong, vigorous, hale and hearty, energetic, muscular, powerful, powerfully built, tough, rugged, sturdy, stalwart, strapping, brawny, burly. **2 earthy,** crude, coarse, rough, raw, unsubtle, indecorous, unrefined. **3 sensible,** common-sense, no-nonsense, down-to-earth, practical, realistic, pragmatic, hardheaded. ***Ant.*** weak; feeble; frail.

rock[1] *n.* **1 boulder,** stone, bedrock, ledge. **2 foundation,** cornerstone, support, prop, mainstay. **3 bulwark,** anchor, tower of strength, protection, security.

rock[2] *v.* **1 move to and fro,** swing, sway, roll, lurch, pitch, reel, wobble, undulate, oscillate. **2 stun,** shock, stagger, astound, astonish, amaze, dumbfound, surprise, shake, take aback, bewilder.

rocky *adj.* **1 rock-strewn,** craggy, stony, pebbly, rough. **2 unsteady,** unstable, shaky, tottering, teetering, wobbly, wobbling.

3 unsteady, unstable, uncertain, unsure; *inf.* iffy.

rod *n.* **1 bar,** stick, pole, baton, staff. **2 cane,** stick, birch, switch, wand.

rogue *n.* **1 villain,** scoundrel, rascal, reprobate, swindler, fraudster, cheat, deceiver, charlatan, mountebank, sharper, wretch, cad, blackguard, ne'er-do-well, wastrel, good-for-nothing, *inf.* con man, crook, bad guy. **2 scamp,** imp, rascal, little devil, mischief-maker.

role *n.* **1 part,** character, representation, portrayal. **2 capacity,** function, position, place, situation, job, post, task.

roll *v.* **1 go around,** turn, turn around, rotate, revolve, spin, whirl, wheel. **2 furl,** coil, fold. **3 pass,** go, flow, travel. **4 flatten,** level, smooth, even, press down, crush. **5 toss,** rock, pitch, lurch, sway, reel. **6 billow,** toss, tumble.
▸ *n.* **1 turn,** rotation, revolution, spin, whirl. **2 spool,** reel, bobbin, cylinder. **3 bun,** hard roll, crescent roll, croissant, dinner roll. **4 register,** list, file, index, roster, directory, catalog. **5 boom,** reverberation, thunder, rumble. **6 undulation,** billowing, swell, tossing, pitching, rocking.

romance *n.* **1 fantasy,** fancy, whimsy, fabrication, glamour, mystery, legend. **2 love affair,** affair, liaison, attachment, intrigue, courtship, amour. **3 love story,** romantic fiction, melodrama, *inf.* tearjerker. **4 fabrication,** invention, trumped-up story, piece of fiction, fairy tale, flight of fancy, exaggeration, *inf.* tall tale/story.
▸ *v.* **court,** woo, go out with, *inf.* go steady with, date.

romantic *adj.* **1 unrealistic,** idealistic, visionary, Utopian, starry-eyed, optimistic, hopeful. **2 loving,** amorous, passionate, fond, tender, sentimental, *inf.* mushy. **3 fascinating,** mysterious, glamorous, exotic, exciting. **4 fantastic,** fanciful, imaginative, extravagant, exaggerated, fictitious, improbable, unlikely, implausible. *Ant.* practical; realistic.
▸ *n.* **romanticist,** dreamer, visionary, idealist, Utopian.

room *n.* **1 space,** area, territory, expanse, extent, volume, elbowroom. **2 scope,** capacity, margin, leeway, latitude, occasion, opportunity. **3 bedroom,** apartment, office.
▸ *v.* **board,** stay, dwell, reside.

roomy *adj.* **spacious,** commodious, capacious, voluminous, ample, generous, sizable, large, broad, wide, extensive. *Ant.* narrow; tiny; cramped.

root *n.* **1 radicle,** radix, rhizome, tuber, tap root. **2 source,** origin, fountainhead, starting point, basis, foundation, fundamental, seat, nucleus, kernel, nub, cause, reason, rationale, occasion, motivation, beginnings.
▸ *v.* **1 take root,** grow roots, become established, set. **2 fix,** establish, embed, implant, entrench.

rope *n.* **cord,** cable, line, hawser.
▸ *v.* **bind,** tie, fasten, lash, tether, pinion.

roster *n.* **list,** listing, rota, roll, register, schedule, agenda, calendar, directory, index, table.

rot *v.* **1 decompose,** decay, crumble, disintegrate, corrode, perish, go bad, spoil, go sour, molder, putrefy, fester.
2 degenerate, deteriorate, decline, break down, waste away, wither away.
▸ *n.* **1 decomposition,** decay, disintegration, corrosion, putrefaction, mold, blight.
2 degeneracy, deterioration, decline, dissoluteness. **3 rubbish,** nonsense, stuff and nonsense, bunkum, claptrap, twaddle, drivel, moonshine, *inf.* bosh, bunk, tommyrot, gobbledygook, hogwash, poppycock, bull.

rotary *adj.* **rotating,** rotational, revolving, turning, gyrating, gyratory, spinning, whirling.

rotate *v.* **1 go around,** move around, turn, turn around, revolve, spin, whirl, swivel, reel, wheel, gyrate. **2 alternate,** take turns, work/act in sequence.

rotten *adj.* **1 bad,** moldy, moldering, spoiled, tainted, sour, rancid, rank, decaying, decomposed, putrid, putrescent, festering, fetid, stinking, decomposing, decaying, crumbling, disintegrating, corroding, perishing, carious, *inf.* off. **2 corrupt,** dishonorable, dishonest, untrustworthy, immoral, unprincipled, unscrupulous, villainous, bad, wicked, evil, sinful, iniquitous, vicious, debauched, degenerate, dissolute, dissipated, perverted, wanton, *inf.* crooked, bent.
3 nasty, foul, mean, bad, dirty, filthy, contemptible, despicable, base, scurrilous. **4 miserable,** unpleasant, disagreeable, disappointing, regrettable, unfortunate, unlucky. **5 ill-considered,** ill thought out, ill-advised, injudicious. **6 poor,** inadequate, inferior, substandard, unsatisfactory, unacceptable, *inf.* lousy, crummy. **7 ill,** sick, unwell, unhealthy, below par, *inf.* under

the weather, poorly, lousy, yucky. *Ant.* fresh; nice; pleasant; good.

rough *adj.* **1 uneven,** irregular, bumpy, broken, stony, rugged, jaggy, craggy, lumpy, nodulous. **2 shaggy,** hairy, bushy, fuzzy, bristly, hirsute. **3 boisterous,** rowdy, disorderly, wild, violent, savage. **4 turbulent,** tumultuous, choppy. **5 inclement,** stormy, squally, wild, tempestuous, wintry. **6 coarse,** crude, uncouth, vulgar, unrefined, uncultured, loutish, boorish, churlish, brutish, ill-bred, ill-mannered, unmannerly, impolite, discourteous, uncivil, brusque, blunt, curt. **7 curt,** sharp, harsh, stern, unfeeling, insensitive. **8 harsh,** severe, hard, tough, difficult, unpleasant, disagreeable, nasty, cruel. **9 unfortunate,** undeserved. **10 harsh,** hard, stern, unrelenting, merciless, unfeeling, unfair, unjust. **11 crude,** raw, unpolished, undressed, uncut, rough-hewn, unrefined, unprocessed. **12 husky,** gruff, hoarse, harsh, discordant, inharmonious, cacophonous, grating, jarring, strident, raucous. **13 rough-and-ready,** hasty, quick, sketchy, cursory, crude, incomplete, rudimentary, basic, unpolished, unrefined.

14 approximate, inexact, imprecise, vague, hazy. *Ant.* smooth; gentle; refined; precise.
▸ *n.* **ruffian,** thug, bully, *inf.* tough, tough guy, roughneck, bruiser.

round *adj.* **1 circular,** ring-shaped, hooplike, annular, discoid, disklike, cylindrical, spherical, spheroidal, ball-shaped, globelike, globular, globate, globose, orblike, orbicular, orbiculate, bulb-shaped, balloonlike, convex, curved. **2 complete,** entire, whole, full, undivided, unbroken. **3 well-rounded,** ample, rotund, chubby, buxom, roly-poly, tubby, portly, stout, corpulent, pudgy, fat, obese. **4 rounded off,** approximate, rough, *inf.* ballpark. **5 sonorous,** resonant, rich, full, mellow, flowing, orotund.
▸ *n.* **1 circle,** circlet, ring, hoop, band, disk, cylinder, sphere, ball, globe, orb. **2 succession,** sequence, series, cycle. **3 bullet,** cartridge, shell. **4 stage,** level, division, lap, heat, game.

roundabout *adj.* **1 indirect,** circuitous, meandering, winding, tortuous. **2 indirect,** circuitous, discursive, oblique, circumlocutory, periphrastic.

rouse *v.* **1 wake,** wake up, call, get up, awaken, get out of bed, rise. **2 wake up,** awaken, get up, get out of bed, rise. **3 stir up,** bestir, excite, incite, egg on, induce, impel, inflame, agitate, whip up, galvanize, stimulate. **4 anger,** annoy, infuriate, incense, exasperate, work up. **5 stir up,** kindle, touch off, provoke, induce, evoke, call up, conjure up.

rout *n.* **1 disorderly retreat,** retreat, flight, headlong flight. **2 crushing defeat,** defeat, drubbing, trouncing, conquest, subjugation, overthrow, beating, thrashing, *inf.* licking, pasting.
▸ *v.* **1 put to rout/flight,** drive off, dispel, scatter. **2 defeat,** drub, trounce, worst, conquer, subjugate, overthrow, crush, beat, thrash, *inf.* lick, give a pasting to.

route *n.* **course,** way, itinerary, road, path.

routine *n.* **1 pattern,** procedure, practice, custom, habit, wont, program, schedule, formula, method, system, order, way. **2 act,** performance, piece, line, *inf.* spiel.
▸ *adj.* **1 usual,** normal, everyday, workaday, common, ordinary, typical, customary, habitual, wonted, scheduled, conventional, standard. **2 boring,** tedious, tiresome, monotonous, humdrum, run-of-the-mill, hackneyed, predictable, unexciting, uninspiring. ***Ant.*** unusual; exciting.

row[1] *n.* **line,** column, queue, procession, chain, string, sequence, series, tier, rank, bank.

row[2] *n.* **argument,** dispute, disagreement, controversy, quarrel, squabble, tiff, fight, conflict, altercation, brawl, affray, wrangle, scuffle, free-for-all, fracas, melee, *inf.* falling-out, set-to, scrap.

rowdy *adj.* **unruly,** disorderly, noisy, boisterous, loud, obstreperous, wild, rough, unrestrained, lawless. ***Ant.*** peaceful; quiet; law-abiding.
▸ *n.* **ruffian,** thug, hooligan, troublemaker, brawler, *inf.* tough, rough.

royal *adj.* **1 kingly,** queenly, kinglike, queenlike, princely, regal, monarchical, sovereign. **2 majestic,** magnificent, impressive, glorious, splendid, imposing, grand, superb. **3 excellent,** fine, first-rate, first-class, marvelous, wonderful. **4 extreme,** unmitigated, absolute, relentless, outright, sheer.

rub *v.* **1 massage,** knead, embrocate, stroke, caress, fondle, pat. **2 polish,** buff up, burnish.
▸ *n.* **1 massage,** kneading, embrocation, stroke, caress, pat. **2 polish,** buffing, burnishing. **3 difficulty,** problem, trouble, drawback, snag, hitch, hindrance,

obstacle, obstruction, impediment.

rubbish *n.* **1 garbage,** trash, waste, refuse, litter, junk, debris, detritus, dross, rubble, scrap, flotsam and jetsam, sweepings, leavings, dregs, odds and ends. **2 nonsense,** stuff and nonsense, drivel, gibberish, balderdash, bunkum, twaddle, *inf.* rot, bunk, gobbledygook, bosh, piffle, hogwash.

rude *adj.* **1 ill-mannered,** bad-mannered, mannerless, impolite, discourteous, impertinent, insolent, impudent, uncivil, disrespectful, churlish, curt, brusque, blunt, offhand, short, offensive. **2 primitive,** crude, rudimentary, rough, rough-hewn, simple. **3 simple,** artless, uncivilized, uneducated, untutored, ignorant, illiterate, uncultured, unrefined, rough, coarse, uncouth, oafish, loutish. **4 vulgar,** coarse, indelicate, smutty, dirty, naughty, risqué, blue, ribald, bawdy, licentious. **5 sudden,** abrupt, sharp, violent, startling, harsh, unpleasant, disagreeable, nasty. ***Ant.*** polite; sophisticated.

rudimentary *adj.* **1 elementary,** basic, fundamental, introductory, early. **2 primitive,** crude, rough, simple. **3 undeveloped,** immature, incomplete, vestigial. ***Ant.*** advanced; sophisticated.

rudiments *pl. n.* **basics,** fundamentals, beginnings, elements, essentials, foundation, *inf.* nuts and bolts.

rueful *adj.* **regretful,** apologetic, sorry, remorseful, contrite, repentant, penitent, conscience-stricken, self-reproachful, woebegone, woeful, plaintive.

ruffle *v.* **1 disarrange,** discompose, disorder, derange, rumple, dishevel, tousle, tangle, mess up, *inf.* muss up. **2 annoy,** irritate, irk, vex, nettle, rile, anger, exasperate, fluster, agitate, harass, upset, disturb, discompose, perturb, unsettle, disconcert, worry, alarm, trouble, confuse, *inf.* rattle, shake up, hassle.

rugged *adj.* **1 rough,** uneven, irregular, bumpy, rocky, stony, broken up, jagged, craggy, precipitous. **2 wrinkled,** furrowed, lined, gnarled, irregular, weather-beaten, leathery. **3 unrefined,** unpolished, uncultured, crude, unsophisticated, graceless, inelegant. **4 tough,** hardy, robust, sturdy, strong, vigorous, stalwart, hale and hearty, muscular, brawny, solid, mighty, burly, well-built, *inf.* husky, beefy. **5 tough,** harsh, austere, spartan, exacting, taxing, demanding, difficult, hard, arduous, rigorous, strenuous, onerous. **Ant.** smooth; refined; feeble.

ruin *n.* **1 ruination,** destruction, devastation, havoc, wreckage, demolition, disintegration, dilapidation, desolation, decay, disrepair. **2 ruination,** downfall, overthrow, defeat, undoing, conquest, elimination, termination, end. **3 ruination,** loss, failure, bankruptcy, insolvency, financial failure, deprivation, penury, impoverishment, indigence, destitution, calamity, disaster. **4 remains,** relics, remnants, vestiges, wreckage, wreck, remainder, debris, detritus.

▸ *v.* **1 damage,** spoil, wreak havoc on, mar, injure, wreck, botch, make a mess of, mess up, smash, shatter. **2 bring to ruin,** bankrupt, make insolvent, impoverish, pauperize. **3 destroy,** devastate, lay waste, raze, demolish, crush. **Ant.** create; restore; enhance; enrich.

ruinous *adj.* **1 disastrous,** devastating, calamitous, catastrophic, cataclysmic, dire, injurious, damaging, crippling, destructive. **2 in ruins,** ruined, dilapidated, decaying, in disrepair, derelict, ramshackle, broken-down, decrepit.

rule *n.* **1 ruling,** law, bylaw, regulation, statute, ordinance, tenet, canon, order, court order, decree, commandment, directive, guideline. **2 principle,** precept, standard, axiom, truth, truism, maxim, aphorism, motto. **3 practice,** procedure, routine, custom, habit, wont, convention, standard, form. **4 reign,** dominion, sovereignty, kingship, queenship, regime, government, administration, jurisdiction, authority, control, direction, mastery, leadership, command, ascendancy, supremacy, power, sway, influence.

▸ *v.* **1 reign,** sit on the throne, wear the crown, wield the scepter. **2 be in power,** be in control, be in authority, be in command, be in charge, govern, *inf.* be at the helm. **3 order,** decree, direct, pronounce, make a judgment, judge, adjudge, adjudicate, lay down, decide, determine, resolve, settle, establish. **4 prevail,** obtain, hold sway, predominate, preponderate.

ruling *n.* **judgment,** adjudication, finding, verdict, resolution, decree, pronouncement.

▸ *adj.* **1 reigning,** regnant, on the throne. **2 dominant,** controlling, governing, commanding, leading, in charge, upper. **3 prevalent,** predominant, main, chief, principal, widespread, general, popular, universal.

rumor *n.* **1 gossip,** hearsay, talk, *inf.* the grapevine. **2 report,** story, whisper, canard, information, word, news, tidings, *inf.* buzz.

▸ *v.* **say,** report, think, give out, put about, circulate, spread, pass around, noise abroad, disseminate, gossip, hint, suggest.

run *v.* **1 race,** rush, hasten, hurry, dash, sprint, bolt, dart, gallop, career along, tear along, charge along, speed along, jog along, scurry, scamper, scramble, travel, traverse, go over, complete, finish, *inf.* scoot, step on it, get a move on, hotfoot it. **2 abscond,** flee, take flight, take oneself off, make off, decamp, bolt, beat a retreat, make a run for it, clear out, make one's getaway, escape, *inf.* beat it, vamoose, skedaddle, split, cut and run, hightail it. **3 move,** go, get along, travel. **4 glide,** course, roll, slide. **5 go,** operate, function. **6 operate,** be in operation, be valid, be current, continue. **7 be staged,** be presented, be performed, be on, be put on. **8 go,** continue, proceed, extend, stretch. **9 compete,** take part, enter, be in the race. **10 stand,** stand as candidate, be a contender, put oneself forward.

11 flow, issue, stream, pour, gush, cascade, spurt, jet, trickle, leak. **12 be wet with,** stream with, flow with, drip with, be flooded by. **13 turn on,** switch on. **14 spread,** be diffused, bleed. **15 melt,** dissolve, liquefy, thaw. **16 go on,** do, carry out, perform, fulfill, execute. **17 publish,** print, feature, carry. **18 own,** operate, conduct, carry on, direct, manage, administer, be in charge/control of, control, head, lead, look after, organize, coordinate, supervise, superintend, oversee, *inf.* boss. **19 drive,** transport, convey. **20 smuggle,** traffic in, deal in, bootleg. **21 chase,** drive, propel, hunt, put to flight. **22 go,** pass, dart, flow, slide. **23 pass,** slide, flick. **24 unravel,** tear, be snagged. **25 stream,** exude, secrete, ooze, tear. *Ant.* saunter; stroll.

▸ *n.* **1 jog,** sprint, dash, gallop, canter, headlong rush, scamper. **2 trip,** route, way, course, itinerary. **3 period,** spell, stretch, streak, chain, string, round, cycle, sequence, series, succession. **4 demand,** rush, clamor. **5 kind,** variety, type, sort, class, category, order. **6 tendency,** trend, tide, course, direction, movement, drift, current, stream. **7 enclosure,** pen, coop. **8 rip,** tear, snag.

runner *n.* **1 racer,** sprinter,

hurdler, jogger, athlete. **2 branch,** shoot, offshoot, tendril, sucker. **3 messenger,** courier, dispatch rider, bearer, errand boy/girl.

rupture *n.* **1 break,** fracture, crack, split, burst, rent, tear, rift, fissure, breaking, fracture, cracking, splitting, bursting. **2 rift,** estrangement, schism, breakup, breach, division, alienation, variance, disagreement, quarrel, feud, *inf.* falling-out. **3 hernia.**
▸ *v.* **1 break,** fracture, crack, split, breach, burst, rend, tear, puncture. **2 sever,** cut off, break off, disrupt, breach.

rural *adj.* **country,** countryside, pastoral, rustic, agricultural, agrarian, Arcadian. *Ant.* urban; city; town.

rush *v.* **1 hurry,** make haste, hasten, run, race, dash, sprint, bolt, dart, gallop, career, tear, charge, speed, scurry, scamper, *inf.* step on it, get a move on, hotfoot it. **2 attack,** assault, charge, storm, take by storm, capture, seize. **3 hurry,** hasten, expedite, speed up, accelerate, advance, hustle, press, push. *Ant.* dawdle; delay.
▸ *n.* **1 onslaught,** attack, assault, charge. **2 surge,** flow, gush, stream, flood. **3 hurry,** haste, speed, swiftness, rapidity,

dispatch. **4 demand,** clamor, run (on). **5 activity,** bustle, hubbub, flurry.

rushed *adj.* **hurried,** hasty, speedy, quick, fast, swift, rapid, expeditious, prompt.

rustle *v.* **1 swish,** whisper, whoosh. **2 steal,** purloin, filch, plunder, abduct, kidnap.

rusty *adj.* **1 rusted,** rust-covered, corroded, oxidized. **2 rust-colored,** reddish, reddish-brown, russet, brick-red, brick. **3 deficient,** impaired, diminished, weak, below par, unpracticed, out of practice, neglected, not what it was. **4 hoarse,** croaking, cracked.

rut *n.* **1 furrow,** groove, track, crack, hollow, hole, pothole, trough, gutter, ditch. **2 humdrum existence,** routine job, boring routine, *inf.* daily grind, treadmill, dead end.

ruthless *adj.* **merciless,** unmerciful, pitiless, compassionless, relentless, unrelenting, remorseless, unforgiving, unsparing, inexorable, implacable, heartless, unfeeling, hard, harsh, severe, stern, grim, cruel, vicious, brutal, barbarous, callous, savage, fierce, ferocious. *Ant.* merciful; compassionate; gentle.

Ss

sabotage *n.* **1 deliberate destruction/damage/wrecking/ impairment/incapacitation,** subversive destruction, vandalism, subversion, treachery. **2 disruption,** spoiling, ruining, ruination, wrecking, *inf.* fouling up.
▸ *v.* **1 deliberately destroy/damage/ wreck,** impair, incapacitate, cripple, vandalize, *inf.* foul up. **2 disrupt,** spoil, ruin, wreck, *inf.* throw a monkey wrench in the works of, put the kibosh on, foul up.

sack[1] *n.* **bag,** pack, pouch, shopping bag, tote bag, knapsack, backpack.

sack[2] *v.* **discharge,** dismiss, terminate (someone's) employment, give the sack; *inf.* kick out, boot out.

sack[3] *v.* **plunder,** ransack, raid, loot, strip, rob, rifle, pillage, maraud, harry, forage, lay waste, wreak havoc on, destroy, ruin, devastate, ravage, vandalize, despoil, rape.
▸ *n.* **plunder,** ransacking, raid, looting, stripping, robbing, pillage, marauding, harrying, destruction, ruin, ruination, devastation, ravaging, vandalization, vandalism, despoliation, rape, rapine.

sacred *adj.* **1 holy,** blessed, blest, hallowed, consecrated, sanctified. **2 religious,** spiritual, devotional, church, churchly, ecclesiastical. **3 godly,** divine, deified, supreme, venerated. **4 sacrosanct,** inviolable, inviolate, unimpeachable, invulnerable, protected, defended, secure, safe, unthreatened. *Ant.* profane; secular; temporal.

sacrifice *n.* **1 giving up,** renunciation, abandonment, surrender, relinquishment, yielding, ceding, forfeiture. **2 renunciation,** relinquishment, loss, self-sacrifice. **3 offering,** gifts, oblation, burnt offering, immolations, hecatomb.
▸ *v.* **1 give up,** forgo, renounce, abandon, surrender, relinquish, yield, cede, forfeit. **2 offer up,** offer, immolate.

sacrilege *n.* **desecration,** profanity, profaneness, profanation, blasphemy, impiety, irreverence, irreligion, godlessness, disrespect.

sad *adj.* **1 unhappy,** miserable, sorrowful, gloomy, melancholy, blue, mournful, woebegone, wretched, dejected, downcast, despondent, in low spirits, low-spirited, low, downhearted, depressed, doleful, glum, cheerless, dispirited, disconsolate, heartbroken, brokenhearted, sick at heart, grief-stricken, grieving, *inf.* down, down in the dumps, down in the mouth, in the pits. **2 unhappy,** unfortunate, sorrowful, miserable, sorry, depressing, upsetting, distressing, dispiriting, heartbreaking, heart-rending, pitiful, pitiable, grievous, tragic, disastrous, calamitous. **3 sorry,** wretched, deplorable, lamentable, regrettable, unfortunate, pitiful, pitiable, pathetic, shameful, disgraceful. *Ant.* happy; cheerful; fortunate.

sadden *v.* **cast down,** deject, depress, dispirit, dampen one's spirits, cast a gloom upon, desolate, upset, distress, grieve, break one's heart, make one's heart bleed.

sadness *n.* **unhappiness,** misery, sorrow, gloom, melancholy, wretchedness, dejection, despondency, low spirits, depression, dolefulness, glumness, cheerlessness, disconsolateness, brokenheartedness, heartache, grief.

safe *adj.* **1 safe and sound,** secure, protected, sheltered, guarded, defended, free from harm/danger, out of harm's way. **2 unharmed,** all right, alive and well, well, unhurt, uninjured, unscathed, undamaged, out of danger, *inf.* OK, okay, out of the woods. **3 secure,** sound, risk-free, riskless, impregnable, unassailable. **4 reliable,** dependable, responsible, trustworthy, tried and true, reputable, upright, honest, honorable, cautious, circumspect, prudent, unadventurous, conservative, timid, unenterprising. **5 harmless,** innocuous, nontoxic, nonpoisonous. *Ant.* insecure; dangerous; unreliable; harmful.

▸ *n.* **safety-deposit box,** safe-deposit box, cashbox, repository, depository, locker, vault, crypt.

safeguard *n.* **protection,** defense, preventive, precaution, security, surety.

▸ *v.* **protect,** look after, defend, guard, preserve, secure. *Ant.* endanger; imperil.

safety *n.* **1 safeness,** security, secureness, soundness, impregnability. **2 shelter,** sanctuary, refuge.

sag *v.* **1 sink,** subside, curve down, slump. **2 hang unevenly,** droop. **3 fall,** flag, fail, wilt, falter, weaken, languish. **4 fall,** decline, decrease, diminish, sink, plummet, tumble, *inf.* take a nosedive.

saga *n.* **epic,** chronicle, legend, history, romance.

sail *v.* **1 boat,** cruise, yacht, ride the waves, go by water, go on a sea voyage, voyage. **2 set sail,** embark, put to sea, leave port/ dock, hoist sail, raise sail, put off, shove off. **3 steer,** captain, pilot, navigate. **4 glide,** drift, float, slide, sweep, skim. **5 soar,** wing, fly.

sailor *n.* **seaman,** seafaring man/ woman, seafarer, mariner, marine, (old) salt, sea dog, boatman, yachtsman, yachtswoman, *inf.* tar, gob.

saintly *adj.* **saintlike,** sainted, holy, godly, pious, God-fearing, religious, devout, blessed, virtuous, righteous, good, moral, ethical, unworldly, innocent, sinless, blameless, pure, angelic.

sake *n.* **1 good,** well-being, welfare, behalf, benefit, advantage, interest, gain, profit, consideration, regard, concern, account, respect. **2 cause,** reason, purpose, aim, end, objective, object, goal, motive.

salary *n.* **pay,** earnings, remuneration, fee, emolument, stipend, honorarium.

sale *n.* **1 selling,** vending, bargaining. **2 deal,** transaction. **3 market,** outlet, demand, buyers, purchasers, customers, consumers.

salubrious *adj.* **healthy,** health-giving, healthful, beneficial, good for one's health, wholesome, salutary, refreshing, invigorating, bracing. *Ant.* unhealthy; unwholesome.

salute *n.* **greeting,** salutation, address, welcome.
▸ *v.* **1 greet,** address, hail, acknowledge, pay one's respects to. **2 pay tribute to,** pay homage to, honor, recognize, acknowledge, *inf.* take one's hat off to.

salvage *n.* **1 rescue,** saving, recovery, reclamation, salvation. **2 waste material,** waste paper, scraps, remains.
▸ *v.* **rescue,** save, recover, retrieve, reclaim, get back.

salvation *n.* **1 redemption,** deliverance, saving, rescue. **2 lifeline,** preservation, conservation. *Ant.* damnation; downfall; destruction.

same *adj.* **1 identical,** the very

same, selfsame, one and the same, the very. **2 identical,** alike, duplicate, twin, indistinguishable, interchangeable, corresponding, equivalent. **3 selfsame,** aforesaid, aforementioned. **4 unchanging,** unchanged, changeless, unvarying, unvaried, invariable, unfailing, constant, consistent, uniform. **Ant.** different; dissimilar.

sample *n.* **1 specimen,** example, instance, illustration, exemplification, representative type, model, pattern. **2 cross section,** sampling, test.
▸ *v.* **try,** try out, test, examine, inspect, taste, partake of.

sanctify *v.* **1 consecrate,** make holy/sacred, bless, hallow, set apart, dedicate. **2 free from sin,** absolve, purify, cleanse, wash (someone's) sins away. **3 sanction,** ratify, confirm, warrant, legitimize, legitimatize.

sanctimonious *adj.* **self-righteous,** holier-than-thou, overpious, pietistic, unctuous, smug, mealy-mouthed, hypocritical, pharisaic, *inf.* goody-goody.

sanction *n.* **1 authorization,** warrant, accreditation, license, endorsement, permission, consent, approval, seal of approval, stamp of approval, go-ahead, approbation, acceptance, thumbs-up, backing, support, *inf.* the green light, OK. **2 ratification,** validation, confirmation. **3 penalty,** punishment, penalization, penance, sentence. **4 embargo,** ban, boycott.
▸ *v.* **1 authorize,** warrant, accredit, license, endorse, permit, allow, consent to, approve, accept, give the thumbs up to, back, support, *inf.* give the green light to, OK. **2 ratify,** validate, confirm. **3 penalize,** punish. **Ant.** prohibit; ban; reject.

sanctity *n.* **1 sacredness,** holiness, inviolability. **2 holiness,** godliness, saintliness, spirituality, religiosity, piety, devoutness, devotion, righteousness, goodness, virtue, purity.

sanctuary *n.* **1 holy place,** church, temple, shrine, altar, sanctum. **2 refuge,** haven, shelter, retreat, hide-out, hiding place. **3 safety,** safekeeping, protection, shelter, security, immunity. **4 preserve,** reserve, wildlife reserve, reservation.

sane *adj.* **1 of sound mind,** in one's right mind, compos mentis, rational, lucid, in possession of one's faculties, *inf.* all there. **2 sensible,** reasonable, sound, balanced, levelheaded, judicious, responsible, prudent, wise, politic, advisable. *Ant.* insane; mad; foolish.

sanguine *adj.* **1 optimistic,** confident, assured, hopeful, buoyant, cheerful, spirited. **2 florid,** ruddy, red, rubicund. *Ant.* pessimistic; gloomy.

sanitary *adj.* **hygienic,** clean, germ-free, antiseptic, aseptic, sterile, unpolluted, salubrious, healthy.

sanity *n.* **1 saneness,** soundness of mind, mental health, reason, rationality, lucidness. **2 sense,** sensibleness, common sense, good sense, reasonableness, rationality, soundness, judiciousness, prudence, wisdom, advisability.

sap *n.* **1 vital fluids,** life fluid, juice. **2 vigor,** energy, vitality, vivacity, enthusiasm, spirit, *inf.* pep, zip, oomph. **3 fool,** idiot, simpleton, nincompoop, ninny, *inf.* twit, nitwit, chump, jerk, sucker, dupe, schnook.

▸ *v.* **1 drain,** enervate, exhaust, weaken, enfeeble, debilitate, devitalize. **2 erode,** wear away, deplete, impair, drain, bleed.

sarcasm *n.* **derision,** scorn, mockery, ridicule, sneering, scoffing, gibing, taunting, irony, satire, lampoon, causticness, trenchancy, acerbity, acrimony, asperity, mordancy, bitterness, spitefulness.

sarcastic *adj.* **derisive,** derisory, scornful, mocking, sneering, jeering, scoffing, taunting, ironic, sardonic, satirical, caustic, trenchant, acerbic, acrimonious, mordant, bitter, spiteful.

sardonic *adj.* **dry,** wry, derisory, scornful, mocking, cynical, sneering, jeering, scoffing, contemptuous, ironic, sarcastic, caustic, trenchant, acerbic, mordant, bitter, spiteful.

satanic *adj.* **diabolical,** fiendish, devilish, demonic, demoniac, demoniacal, hellish, infernal, accursed, wicked, evil, sinful, iniquitous, malevolent, vile, foul.

satire *n.* **1 burlesque,** parody, travesty, caricature, lampoon, skit, pasquinade, *inf.* takeoff, spoof, send-up. **2 mockery,** ridicule, irony, sarcasm.

satirical *adj.* **mocking,** ridiculing, taunting, ironic, sarcastic, sardonic, caustic, biting, cutting, stinging, trenchant, mordant, acerbic, pungent, critical, censorious, cynical.

satirize *v.* **mock,** ridicule, hold up to ridicule, deride, make fun of, poke fun at, parody, lampoon, burlesque, travesty, criticize, censure, *inf.* take off, send up.

satisfaction *n.* **1 fulfillment,** gratification, pleasure, enjoyment, delight, happiness, pride, comfort, content, contentment, smugness, appeasement, assuagement, achievement. **2 damages,** compensation, recompense, amends, reparation, redress, indemnity, restitution, requital, atonement, reimbursement, remuneration, payment. **Ant.** dissatisfaction; discontent; loss.

satisfactory *adj.* **adequate,** all right, acceptable, fine, good enough, sufficient, competent, up to standard, up to the mark, up to par, up to scratch, passable, average, *inf.* OK, okay. **Ant.** inadequate; unacceptable; poor; unsatisfactory.

satisfy *v.* **1 satiate,** sate, slake, quench. **2 fulfill,** gratify, appease, assuage, meet, indulge. **3 solve,** resolve, answer, be the answer to, meet, serve the purpose of, be sufficient/adequate/good enough for. **4 fulfill,** meet, comply with, answer. **5 pay,** settle, discharge, square up. **6 make reparation for,** atone for, compensate for, recompense. **7 convince,** persuade, assure, reassure, remove/dispel doubts from, put one's mind at ease/rest.

saturate *v.* **1 wet through,** wet, soak, souse, steep, douse, drench. **2 permeate,** imbue, pervade, suffuse. **3 overfill,** surfeit, glut, satiate, sate.

sauce *n.* **1 gravy,** relish, dressing, condiment. **2 impudence,** impertinence, insolence, rudeness, disrespect, audacity, presumption, temerity, boldness, brazenness, gall, cheek, pertness, brashness, *inf.* sauciness, sass, brass, lip, freshness, back talk.

saucy *adj.* **impudent,** impertinent, insolent, rude, disrespectful, audacious, presumptuous, bold, brazen, cheeky, pert, brash, *inf.* fresh, sassy.

saunter *v.* **stroll,** amble, wander, meander, traipse, walk, ramble, roam, promenade, *inf.* mosey.
▸ *n.* **stroll,** meander, walk, turn, airing, promenade, constitutional.

savage *adj.* **1 vicious,** ferocious, fierce, brutal, cruel, bloody, murderous, bloodthirsty, inhuman, harsh, grim, terrible, merciless, ruthless, pitiless, sadistic, barbarous. **2 fierce,** ferocious, wild, untamed, undomesticated, feral, rough, rugged, uncivilized, barbarous, barbaric. **3 primitive,** uncivilized, uncultivated, wild. **Ant.** mild; tame; civilized.
▸ *n.* **1 barbarian,** wild man/ woman, native, primitive, heathen. **2 barbarian,** boor, churl, yahoo. **3 brute,** beast, monster, barbarian, ogre.

save *v.* **1 rescue,** free, set free,

liberate, deliver, snatch, bail out, salvage, redeem. **2 protect,** safeguard, guard, keep, keep safe, shield, screen, preserve, conserve. **3 prevent,** obviate, forestall, spare, make unnecessary, rule out. **4 put aside,** set aside, put by, put away, lay by, keep, reserve, conserve, salt away, stockpile, store, hoard. **5 economize,** practice economy, be thrifty, be frugal, scrimp, budget, husband one's resources, cut costs, cut expenditure. **Ant.** endanger; cause; waste; spend.

savings *pl. n.* **capital,** assets, resources, cache, reserves, funds, nest egg.

savior *n.* **rescuer,** liberator, deliverer, emancipator, champion, knight in shining armor, Good Samaritan, friend in need.

savor *n.* **1 taste,** flavor, tang, piquancy. **2 smell,** aroma, fragrance, scent, perfume, bouquet, odor. **3 hint,** suggestion, touch, vein, tone. **4 enjoyment,** joy, excitement, interest, zest, spice, piquancy.
▸ *v.* **taste,** enjoy, enjoy to the full/fullest, enjoy to the hilt, appreciate, delight in, take pleasure in, relish, revel in, luxuriate in.

savory *adj.* **1 appetizing,** mouthwatering, fragrant, flavorsome, flavorful, palatable, tasty, delicious, delectable, luscious, toothsome, *inf.* scrumptious. **2 salty,** piquant, tangy, spicy. **Ant.** unpalatable; sweet.

say *v.* **1 speak,** utter, mention, voice, pronounce, put into words, give utterance to, give voice to, vocalize. **2 state,** remark, announce, affirm, assert, maintain, declare, aver, allege, profess, avow, *lit.* opine, *inf.* come out with. **3 express,** put into words, tell, phrase, articulate, communicate, make known, convey, reveal, divulge, disclose. **4 recite,** repeat, deliver, declaim, orate, read, perform, rehearse. **5 indicate,** specify, designate, tell, explain, give information (about), suggest. **6 estimate,** judge, guess, hazard a guess, predict, speculate, conjecture, surmise, imagine, assume, suppose, presume. **7 state,** suggest, allege, claim, put about, report, rumor.
▸ *n.* **1 opinion,** view, right to speak, chance to speak, turn to speak, vote, voice, *inf.* (one's) two cents, (one's) two cents worth. **2 share,** part, influence, sway, weight, input.

saying *n.* **proverb,** maxim, aphorism, axiom, adage, saw, epigram, dictum, gnome, apothegm, platitude, cliché.

scaffold *n.* **1 scaffolding,** frame, framework, gantry. **2 gallows,** gibbet.

scale[1] *n.* **plate,** flake, coating, coat, crust, incrustation, covering.

scale[2] *n.* **1 scales,** weighing machine, balance. **2 graduated system,** calibrated system, measuring system, progression, succession, sequence, series, ranking, register, ladder, hierarchy; *inf.* pecking order. **3 extent,** scope, range, degree, reach. **4 ratio,** proportion.

scale[3] *v.* **climb,** ascend, go up, clamber, mount, clamber up, escalade.

scaly *adj.* **flaky,** scurfy, rough, scabrous, squamous.

scamp *n.* **rascal,** rogue, imp, devil, monkey, wretch, scalawag, mischief-maker, troublemaker, prankster, miscreant.

scan *v.* **1 study,** examine, scrutinize, survey, inspect, take stock of, search, scour, sweep. **2 skim,** look over, have a look at, glance over, run one's eye over, read through, leaf through, thumb through, flick through, flip through.

scandal *n.* **1 wrongdoing,** impropriety, misconduct, offense, transgression, crime, sin. **2 outrage,** disgrace, embarrassment. **3 disgrace,** shame, dishonor, disrepute, discredit, odium, opprobrium, censure, obloquy. **4 scandalmongering,** slander, libel, calumny, defamation, aspersion, gossip, malicious rumors, dirt, muckraking, smear campaign. **5 disgrace,** shame, pity, crying shame.

scandalous *adj.* **1 disgraceful,** shameful, dishonorable, outrageous, shocking, monstrous, disreputable, improper, unseemly, discreditable, infamous, opprobrious. **2 slanderous,** libelous, defamatory, scurrilous, malicious, gossiping.

scant *adj.* **little,** minimal, limited, barely sufficient, insufficient, inadequate, deficient. ***Ant.*** abundant; ample; sufficient.

scanty *adj.* **meager,** scant, sparse, small, paltry, slender, negligible, skimpy, thin, poor, insufficient, inadequate, deficient, limited, restricted, exiguous. ***Ant.*** abundant; ample; copious.

scapegoat *n.* **victim,** dupe, whipping boy, *inf.* fall guy, patsy.

scar *n.* **1 mark,** blemish, blotch, discoloration, cicatrix, disfigurement, defacement. **2 damage,** trauma, shock, injury, suffering, upset.

▸ *v.* **1 mark,** blemish, blotch, discolor, disfigure, deface. **2 damage,** traumatize, shock, injure, upset.

scarce *adj.* **1 in short supply,** short, meager, scant, scanty, sparse, paltry, not enough, too little, insufficient, deficient, inadequate, lacking, at a premium, exiguous. **2 rare,** infrequent, few and far between, seldom seen/found, sparse, uncommon, unusual. ***Ant.*** plentiful; abundant; frequent.

scarcely *adv.* **1 hardly,** barely, only just. **2 hardly,** certainly not, definitely not, surely not, not at all, on no account, under no circumstances, by no means.

scarcity *n.* **1 dearth,** shortage, undersupply, paucity, scantness, meagerness, sparseness, insufficiency, deficiency, inadequacy, lack, exiguity. **2 rarity,** rareness, infrequency, sparseness, uncommonness, unusualness.

scare *v.* **frighten,** make afraid, alarm, startle, make fearful, make nervous, terrify, terrorize, petrify, horrify, appall, shock, intimidate, daunt, awe, cow, panic, put the fear of God into, scare stiff, make one's blood run cold, make one's flesh crawl/creep, make one's hair stand on end, *inf.* scare the living daylights out of, scare the pants off.

▸ *n.* **fright,** alarm, start, fearfulness, nervousness, terror, horror, shock, panic.

scathing *adj.* **virulent,** savage, fierce, ferocious, brutal, stinging, biting, mordant, trenchant, caustic, vitriolic, withering, scornful, harsh, severe, stern. ***Ant.*** mild; gentle.

scatter *v.* **1 disseminate,** diffuse, spread, sow, sprinkle, strew, broadcast, fling, toss, throw. **2 break up,** disperse, disband, separate, dissolve. ***Ant.*** collect; gather; assemble.

scavenge *v.* **search,** look for, hunt, forage for, rummage for, scrounge.

scenario *n.* **1 plot,** outline, synopsis, summary, précis, rundown, story line, structure, scheme, plan. **2 chain of events.**

scene *n.* **1 place,** location, site, position, spot, setting, locale, whereabouts, arena, stage. **2 background,** backdrop, setting, set, mise en scène. **3 event,** incident, happening, situation, episode, affair, moment, proceeding. **4 scenery,** view, outlook, landscape, vista, panorama, prospect. **5 fuss,** exhibition, outburst, commotion, to-do, upset, tantrum, furor, brouhaha. **6 area of interest,** field of interest, field, interest, sphere, world, milieu.

scenery *n.* **1 view,** outlook, landscape, vista, panorama, prospect. **2 set,** stage set, setting, background, backdrop, mise en scène.

scenic *adj.* **1 picturesque,** pretty, beautiful, pleasing. **2 landscape,** panoramic.

scent *n.* **1 aroma,** perfume, fragrance, smell, bouquet, redolence, odor. **2 track,** trail, spoor. **3 hint,** suggestion, whiff, implication. **4 perfume,** fragrance, toilet water, eau de cologne.
▸ *v.* **1 smell,** sniff, be on the track/trail of, track, trail. **2 detect,** discern, recognize, become aware of, sense, get wind of, sniff out, nose out.

schedule *n.* **1 timetable,** plan, scheme, program, diary, calendar, social calendar, itinerary, agenda, docket. **2 list,** catalog, syllabus, inventory.
▸ *v.* **time,** timetable, arrange, organize, plan, program, book, slot (in).

scheme *n.* **1 plan,** program, project, course of action, line of action, system, procedure, strategy, design, device, tactics, contrivance. **2 arrangement,** system, organization, disposition,

schema. **3 outline,** blueprint, design, delineation, diagram, layout, sketch, chart, map, schema. **4 plot,** ruse, ploy, stratagem, maneuver, machinations, subterfuge, intrigue, conspiracy, *inf.* game, racket.
▸ *v.* **plot,** conspire, intrigue, maneuver, plan, lay plans.

scheming *adj.* **calculating,** designing, conniving, wily, crafty, cunning, sly, tricky, artful, foxy, slippery, underhand, underhanded, duplicitous, devious, Machiavellian. **Ant.** ingenuous; honest; aboveboard.

schism *n.* **division,** breach, split, rift, break, rupture, separation, splintering, disunion, scission, severance, detachment, discord, disagreement.

scholar *n.* **man/woman of letters,** learned person, academic, intellectual, pundit, savant, *inf.* bookworm, egghead, highbrow.

scholarly *adj.* **learned,** erudite, academic, well-read, intellectual, scholastic, literary, studious, bookish, lettered, *inf.* egghead, highbrow. **Ant.** illiterate; ignorant.

scholarship *n.* **1 learning,** book learning, knowledge, education, erudition, letters, academic achievement/attainment/

accomplishment. **2 fellowship,** endowment, award, grant, support.

school *n.* **1 educational institution,** nursery school, primary school, secondary school, comprehensive school, grammar school, high school, academy, seminary, public school, private school, vocational-technical school, votech, college, university. **2 department,** faculty, division. **3 group,** set, proponents, adherents, devotees, circle, class, sect, clique, faction, followers, following, disciples, admirers, votaries, pupils, students. **4 school of thought,** outlook, persuasion, opinion, point of view, belief, faith, creed, credo, doctrine, stamp, way of life.
▸ *v.* **1 educate,** teach, instruct. **2 train,** coach, instruct, drill, discipline, direct, guide, prepare, prime, verse.

scientific *adj.* **systematic,** methodical, orderly, regulated, controlled, exact, precise, mathematical.

scintillating *adj.* **sparkling,** dazzling, vivacious, effervescent, lively, animated, ebullient, bright, brilliant, witty, exciting, stimulating, invigorating. ***Ant.*** boring; dull; pedestrian.

scold *v.* **1 rebuke,** reprimand, chide, reprove, reproach, remonstrate with, upbraid, berate, censure, lecture, castigate, rake/haul over the coals, read the riot act to, rap over the knuckles, *inf.* tell off, give a talking-to to, give a dressing-down to, bawl out. **2 nag,** lay down the law, rail, carp, criticize, find fault, complain, *inf.* go on.

scoop *n.* **1 ladle,** spoon, dipper. **2 exclusive story,** revelation, exposé.
▸ *v.* **1 hollow out,** gouge out, dig, excavate. **2 gather up,** pick up, lift.

scope *n.* **1 extent,** range, sphere, area, field, realm, compass, orbit, reach, span, sweep, confine, limit. **2 opportunity,** freedom, latitude, capacity, room to maneuver, elbowroom.

scorch *v.* **1 burn,** singe, char, sear, discolor. **2 burn,** dry up, wither, discolor, brown.

score *n.* **1 total. 2 result,** outcome. **3 basis,** grounds, reason, account, count. **4 notch,** mark, scratch, scrape, groove, cut, nick, chip, gouge, incision, slit, gash. **5 bill,** tally, reckoning, amount due, debt, obligation, *inf.* tab. **6 dispute,** grievance, grudge, injury, a bone to pick, a bone of contention.
▸ *v.* **1 win,** gain, achieve, *inf.* chalk

up, notch up. **2 win a point/goal,** gain a point. **3 keep count,** keep a record, keep a tally. **4 achieve success,** win, triumph, gain an advantage, make an impression, *inf.* be a hit. **5 notch,** make a notch in, mark, scratch, scrape, make a groove in, cut, nick, chip, gouge, slit, gash.

scorn *n.* **contempt,** contemptuousness, disdain, haughtiness, disparagement, derision, mockery, contumely. *Ant.* admiration; praise.
▸ *v.* **1 hold in contempt,** look down on, disdain, disparage, slight, deride, mock, scoff at, sneer at. **2 rebuff,** spurn, shun, refuse, reject, turn down.

scornful *adj.* **contemptuous,** disdainful, haughty, supercilious, disparaging, slighting, scathing, derisive, mocking, scoffing, sneering, contumelious.

scoundrel *n.* **villain,** rogue, rascal, miscreant, reprobate, scapegrace, cad, good-for-nothing, ne'er-do-well, wastrel.

scour[1] *v.* **scrub,** rub, clean, cleanse, abrade, wash, wipe, polish, buff, burnish.

scour[2] *v.* **search,** comb, go over, look all over, ransack, hunt through, rake through, rummage through, leave no stone unturned in.

scourge *n.* **1 bane,** curse, affliction, plague, trial, trial and tribulation, torment, torture, suffering, burden, cross to bear, thorn in one's flesh/side, nuisance, pest, punishment, penalty, visitation. **2 whip,** horsewhip, bullwhip, switch, lash, cat-o'-nine-tails, thong, flail, strap, birch.
▸ *v.* **1 whip,** horsewhip, flog, lash, strap, birch, cane, thrash, beat, leather, *inf.* belt, wallop, lambaste, tan someone's hide. **2 curse,** afflict, plague, torment, torture, make (one) suffer from, burden, punish.

scout *n.* **1 advance guard,** vanguard, lookout man/woman, outrider, spy. **2 talent scout,** talent spotter, recruiter.

scowl *v.* **frown,** glower, glare, lower, look daggers, grimace.
▸ *n.* **frown,** glower, glare, dirty look.

scraggy *adj.* **scrawny,** thin, skinny, gaunt, bony, angular, rawboned. *Ant.* fat; plump.

scramble *v.* **1 clamber,** climb, crawl. **2 struggle,** hurry, hasten, rush, race, scurry. **3 jockey,** struggle, jostle, strive, contend, compete, vie. **4 mix up,** jumble, tangle, throw into confusion, disorganize.
▸ *n.* **1 clamber,** climb, trek.

2 hurry, rush, race, scurry.
3 jockeying, struggle, tussle, jostle, competition, vying.
scrap[1] *n.* **1 fragment,** piece, bit, snippet, remnant, tatter, morsel, particle, sliver, crumb, bite, mouthful. **2 bit,** grain, iota, trace, whit, snatch. **3 waste,** junk, rubbish, scrap metal.
▸ *v.* **throw away,** get rid of, discard, toss out, abandon, jettison, dispense with, shed; *inf.* ditch, junk, throw on the scrap heap. *Ant.* keep; retain; restore.
scrap[2] *n.* **fight,** quarrel, argument, squabble, wrangle, tiff, row, fracas, brawl, scuffle, disagreement, clash, *inf.* set-to, run-in.
▸ *v.* **fight,** quarrel, bicker, argue, squabble, row, wrangle, brawl, disagree, *inf.* fall out, have a set-to.
scrape *v.* **1 scour,** rub, scrub, file, sandpaper. **2 clean,** remove, erase. **3 grate,** rasp, grind, scratch. **4 creak,** grate, squeak, screech, set one's teeth on edge. **5 graze,** scratch, abrade, skin, cut, lacerate, bark. **6 scratch,** gouge, damage, deface, spoil, mark.
▸ *n.* **1 grating,** rasping, grinding, scratching, creaking, squeaking. **2 graze,** scratch, abrasion, cut, laceration, wound. **3 scratch,** mark, defacement. **4 trouble,** difficulty, straits, distress, mess,

muddle, predicament, plight, tight spot, tight corner, *inf.* fix.
scratch *v.* **1 graze,** scrape, abrade, skin, cut, lacerate, bark. **2 rub,** scrape, tear at. **3 scrape,** grate, rasp, grind. **4 cross out,** strike out, delete, erase, remove, eliminate. **5 withdraw,** take out, pull out, remove, eliminate.
▸ *n.* **1 graze,** scrape, abrasion, cut, laceration, wound. **2 scrape,** mark, line, defacement.
scream *n.* **1 shriek,** howl, shout, yell, cry, screech, yelp, squeal, wail, squawk, bawl, *inf.* holler. **2 comedian,** comic, joker, laugh, wit, clown, *inf.* hoot, riot, barrel of laughs, card, caution.
▸ *v.* **1 shriek,** howl, shout, cry out, call out, yell, screech, yelp, squeal, wail, squawk, bawl, *inf.* holler. **2 clash,** not go together, jar.
screen *n.* **1 partition,** (room) **divider. 2 mesh,** net, netting, curtain, blind. **3 shelter,** shield, protection, guard, safeguard, buffer. **4 sieve,** riddle, strainer, colander, filter, winnow.
▸ *v.* **1 shelter,** shield, protect, guard, safeguard. **2 conceal,** hide, cover, cloak, veil, mask, camouflage, disguise. **3 check,** test, examine, investigate, scan. **4 sieve,** riddle, sift, strain, filter, winnow.

scribble *v.* **dash off,** jot down, scrawl.

  ► *n.* **scrawl,** illegible handwriting.

scrimp *v.* **skimp,** economize, be frugal, be thrifty, husband one's resources, tighten one's belt, draw in one's horns.

script *n.* **1 handwriting,** writing, hand, pen, calligraphy. **2 text,** book, libretto, score, lines, words, manuscript.

scrounge *v.* **cadge,** beg, borrow, *inf.* sponge, bum.

scrounger *n.* **cadger,** beggar, borrower, parasite, *inf.* sponger, freeloader.

scrub *v.* **1 rub,** scour, clean, cleanse, wash, wipe. **2 cancel,** scratch, drop, discontinue, abandon, call off, give up, do away with, discard, forget about, abort.

  ► *n.* **brushwood,** brush, copse, coppice, thicket, scrublands, chaparral, maquis.

scruples *pl. n.* **qualms,** twinge of conscience, compunction, hesitation, second thoughts, doubt, misgivings, uneasiness, reluctance, restraint, wavering, vacillation.

scrupulous *adj.* **1 meticulous,** careful, painstaking, thorough, rigorous, strict, conscientious, punctilious, exact, precise, fastidious. **2 honest,** honorable, upright, righteous, right-minded, moral, ethical. ***Ant.*** careless; slapdash; dishonest; unscrupulous.

scrutinize *v.* **examine,** study, inspect, survey, scan, look over, investigate, go over, peruse, probe, inquire into, sift, analyze, dissect.

scrutiny *n.* **examination,** study, inspection, survey, scan, perusal, investigation, exploration, probe, inquiry, analysis, dissection.

sculpture *n.* **statue,** statuette, bust, figure, figurine.

  ► *v.* **sculpt,** sculp, chisel, model, fashion, shape, cast, carve, cut, hew.

scum *n.* **1 film,** layer, froth, foam, crust, algae, filth, dirt. **2 lowest of the low,** dregs of society, riff-raff, rabble, canaille.

scurrilous *adj.* **abusive,** vituperative, insulting, offensive, disparaging, defamatory, slanderous, gross, foul, scandalous.

scurry *v.* **hurry,** hasten, make haste, rush, race, dash, run, sprint, scamper, scramble.

  ► *n.* **hurry,** haste, rush, bustle, racing, dashing, scuttling, scampering.

seal *n.* **1 emblem,** symbol, insignia, badge, crest, token, mark, monogram. **2 sealant,**

sealer, adhesive. **3 assurance,** attestation, confirmation, ratification, guarantee, proof, authentication, warrant, warranty.
▸ *v.* **1 fasten,** secure, shut, close up, seal up, make airtight, make watertight, close, shut, cork, stopper, stop up. **2 close,** shut, cordon, fence. **3 secure,** clinch, settle, decide, complete.
4 confirm, guarantee, ratify, validate.

seam *n.* **1 joint,** join, junction.
2 layer, stratum, vein, lode.
3 furrow, line, ridge, wrinkle, scar.

sear *v.* **1 burn,** singe, scorch, char.
2 burn, scorch, dry up, wither, discolor, brown. **3 anguish,** torture, torment, wound, distress, harry.

search *v.* **1 go through,** look through, hunt through, rummage through, forage through, rifle through, scour, ransack, comb, go through with a fine-tooth comb, sift through, turn upside down, turn inside out, leave no stone unturned in. **2 examine,** explore, investigate, inspect, survey, study, pry into. **3 examine,** inspect, check, *inf.* frisk.
▸ *n.* **1 hunt,** rummage, forage, rifling, scour, ransacking.
2 exploration, pursuit, quest, probe.

season *n.* **period,** time, time of year, spell, term.
▸ *v.* **1 flavor,** add flavoring to, add salt/pepper/herbs/spice(s) to, spice, pep up, *inf.* add zing to.
2 enliven, leaven, spice, pep up.
3 mature, mellow, prime, prepare.
4 temper, moderate, qualify, tone down.

seasonable *adj.* **1 usual,** appropriate to the time of year.
2 opportune, timely, well-timed, appropriate, suitable, apt.

seasoned *adj.* **experienced,** practiced, well-versed, established, habituated, long-serving, time-served, veteran, hardened, battle-scarred. *Ant.* inexperienced; callow; green.

seat *n.* **1 chair,** bench, settee, stool. **2 headquarters,** location, site, whereabouts, place, base, center, hub, heart. **3 bottom,** buttocks, posterior, rump, hindquarters, *inf.* behind, backside, butt, tail, fanny, *vulg.* ass. **4 grounds,** cause, reason, basis, source, origin.
▸ *v.* **1 place,** position, put, situate, deposit. **2 hold,** take, have room for, accommodate.

secluded *adj.* **sheltered,** concealed, hidden, private, unfrequented, solitary, lonely, sequestered, out-of-the-way, remote, isolated, off the beaten track/path, tucked away, cut off. *Ant.* public; busy; accessible.

seclusion *n.* **privacy,** solitude, retreat, retirement, withdrawal, sequestration, isolation, concealment, hiding, secrecy.

second[1] *adj.* **1 next,** following, subsequent, succeeding. **2 additional,** extra, further, other, alternative, backup, substitute. **3 secondary,** lower, subordinate, lesser, lower-grade, inferior. **4 other,** duplicate, replicate.

second[2] *n.* **assistant,** attendant, helper, supporter, backer, right-hand man/woman.

second[3] *v.* **1 assist,** help, aid, support. **2 formally support,** give one's support to, back, approve, give one's approval to, endorse, promote.

secondary *adj.* **1 lesser,** subordinate, minor, ancillary, subsidiary, nonessential, unimportant. **2 derived,** derivative, indirect, resulting, resultant. **3 second,** backup, reserve, relief, auxiliary, extra, alternative, subsidiary. *Ant.* primary; prime; main.

secondhand *adj.* **used,** worn, nearly new, handed down, *inf.* hand-me-down.
▶ *adv.* **at second hand,** indirectly, *inf.* on the grapevine.

second-rate *adj.* **1 second-class,** low-class, inferior, lesser, unimportant. **2 inferior,** substandard, poor-quality, low-quality, low-grade, shoddy, *inf.* tacky.

secret *adj.* **1 confidential,** private, unrevealed, undisclosed, under wraps, unpublished, untold, unknown, *inf.* hush-hush. **2 hidden,** concealed, camouflaged, disguised. **3 hidden,** clandestine, furtive, conspiratorial, undercover, surreptitious, stealthy, cloak-and-dagger, covert, *inf.* closet. **4 hidden,** mysterious, cryptic, abstruse, recondite, arcane. **5 secluded,** concealed, hidden, sheltered, private, unfrequented, solitary, lonely, sequestered, out-of-the-way, remote, tucked away. **6 secretive,** reticent, uncommunicative. *Ant.* public; open; obvious.
▶ *n.* **1 confidential matter,** confidence, private affair. **2 mystery,** enigma, puzzle, riddle. **3 recipe,** formula, key, answer, solution.

secrete[1] *v.* **discharge,** emit, excrete, exude, ooze, leak, give off, send out. *Ant.* absorb.

secrete[2] *v.* **hide,** conceal, cover up, stow away, sequester, cache, *inf.* stash away. *Ant.* reveal; show.

secretive *adj.* **secret,** reticent, uncommunicative,

unforthcoming, reserved, taciturn, silent, quiet, tight-lipped, close-mouthed, close, playing one's cards close to one's chest, clamlike, *inf.* cagey. **Ant.** open; communicative; chatty.

secretly *adv.* **1 in secret,** confidentially, privately, behind closed doors, in camera, sub rosa, clandestinely, furtively, conspiratorially, surreptitiously, stealthily, on the sly, covertly, *inf.* on the q.t. **2 privately,** in one's heart, in one's innermost thoughts.

sectarian *adj.* **doctrinaire,** partisan, factional, bigoted, prejudiced, narrow-minded, parochial, insular, hidebound, extreme, fanatic, fanatical, *inf.* clannish. **Ant.** tolerant; liberal; broad-minded.
▶ *n.* **bigot,** partisan, fanatic, zealot, dogmatist, extremist.

section *n.* **part,** segment, division, component, piece, portion, bit, slice, fraction, fragment, component, chapter, department, branch.

sector *n.* **1 part,** division, area, branch, category, field. **2 zone,** quarter, district, area, region.

secular *adj.* **lay,** nonreligious, nonspiritual, nonchurch, laical, temporal, worldly, earthly. **Ant.** holy; religious; sacred.

secure *adj.* **1 safe,** free from danger, out of harm's way, invulnerable, unharmed, undamaged, protected, sheltered, shielded. **2 fastened,** closed, shut, locked, sealed. **3 stable,** fixed, steady, strong, sturdy, solid. **4 safe,** unworried, at ease, comfortable, confident, assured. **5 safe,** reliable, dependable, settled, fixed, established, solid. **Ant.** insecure; precarious.
▶ *v.* **1 make safe,** make sound, fortify, strengthen, protect. **2 fasten,** close, shut, lock, bolt, chain, seal. **3 tie up,** moor, anchor. **4 assure,** ensure, insure, guarantee, underwrite, confirm, establish. **5 acquire,** obtain, gain, get, get hold of, procure, get possession of, come by, *inf.* get one's hands on, land.

sedate *adj.* **calm,** tranquil, placid, dignified, formal, decorous, proper, demure, sober, earnest, staid, stiff. **Ant.** wild; excitable; fast.
▶ *v.* **give a sedative to,** put under sedation, calm down, tranquilize.

sedative *n.* **tranquilizer,** calmative, depressant, sleeping pill, narcotic, opiate, *inf.* downer.
▶ *adj.* **calming,** tranquilizing, soothing, calmative, relaxing, assuaging, lenitive, soporific, narcotic.

sedentary *adj.* **sitting,** seated, deskbound, inactive. ***Ant.*** active; mobile.

sediment *n.* **lees,** dregs, grounds, deposit, residue, precipitate, settlings.

seduce *v.* **1 lead astray,** corrupt, deflower, ravish, violate. **2 attract,** allure, lure, tempt, entice, beguile, ensnare.

seductive *adj.* **1 attracting,** alluring, tempting, provocative, exciting, arousing, sexy. **2 attractive,** appealing, inviting, alluring, tempting, enticing, beguiling.

see *v.* **1 make out,** catch sight of, glimpse, spot, notice, observe, view, perceive, discern, espy, descry, distinguish, identify, recognize. **2 look at,** regard, note, observe, heed, mark, behold, watch, *inf.* get a load of. **3 watch,** look at, view. **4 understand,** grasp, get, comprehend, follow, take in, know, realize, get the drift of, make out, fathom, *inf.* latch on to. **5 find out,** discover, learn, ascertain, determine, ask, inquire, make inquiries into/about, investigate. **6 think,** consider, reflect, deliberate, give thought, have a think. **7 see to it,** take care, mind, make sure, make certain, ensure, guarantee. **8 foresee,** predict, forecast, anticipate, envisage, imagine, picture, visualize. **9 meet,** encounter, run into, stumble upon, chance upon, recognize. **10 visit,** pay a visit to, consult, confer with. **11 meet,** arrange to meet, meet socially (with). **12 go out with,** take out, keep company with, court, *inf.* go steady with, date. **13 escort,** accompany, show, lead, take, usher, attend.

seed *n.* **1 ovule,** germ. **2 sperm,** spermatic fluid, semen, spermatozoa. **3 source,** origin, root, cause, reason, grounds, basis, motivation, motive. **4 child,** children, offspring, progeny, issue, descendant(s), scion(s).

seek *v.* **1 search for,** try to find, look for, be on the lookout for, be after, hunt for, be in quest of, be in pursuit of. **2 ask for,** request, solicit, entreat, beg for. **3 try,** attempt, endeavor, strive, aim, aspire.

seem *v.* **appear,** appear to be, have the appearance of being, give the impression of being, look, look like, look to be, have the look of.

seep *v.* **ooze,** leak, exude, drip, drain, percolate.

seesaw *v.* **fluctuate,** go from one extreme to the other, swing, oscillate.

seethe *v.* **1 boil,** bubble, fizz,

foam, froth, ferment, churn. **2 be furious,** be livid, be incensed, be in a rage, rant and rave, storm, fume, foam at the mouth, breathe fire.

segment *n.* **section,** part, division, component, piece, portion, slice, wedge.

segregate *v.* **separate,** set apart, isolate, dissociate, cut off, sequester, ostracize, discriminate against.

segregation *n.* **separation,** setting apart, isolation, dissociation, sequestration, discrimination, apartheid, partition.

seize *v.* **1 grab,** grab hold of, take hold of, grasp, take a grip of, grip, clutch at. **2 confiscate,** impound, commandeer, appropriate, take possession of, sequester, sequestrate. **3 snatch,** abduct, take captive, kidnap, hijack. **4 catch,** arrest, apprehend, take into custody, take prisoner, *inf.* collar, nab.

seizure *n.* **1 confiscation,** commandeering, appropriation, sequestration. **2 snatching,** abduction, kidnapping, hijacking. **3 arrest,** apprehension, *inf.* collaring, nabbing.

seldom *adv.* **rarely,** hardly ever, scarcely ever, infrequently, only occasionally, *inf.* once in a blue moon. *Ant.* often; frequently.

select *v.* **choose,** pick, hand-pick, single out, opt for, decide on, settle on, prefer, favor.
▸ *adj.* **1 choice,** hand-picked, prime, first-rate, first-class, finest, best, high-quality, top-quality, supreme, superb, excellent. **2 exclusive,** elite, limited, privileged, cliquish, *inf.* posh. *Ant.* inferior; second-rate; common.

selection *n.* **1 choice,** pick, option. **2 anthology,** variety, assortment, miscellany, collection, range.

self-centered *adj.* **egocentric,** egotistic, egotistical, self-absorbed, self-seeking, wrapped up in oneself, selfish, narcissistic.

self-confidence *n.* **self-assurance,** confidence, self-reliance, self-dependence, self-possession, poise, aplomb, composure, sang-froid.

self-conscious *adj.* **awkward,** shy, diffident, bashful, blushing, timorous, nervous, timid, retiring, shrinking, ill-at-ease, embarrassed, uncomfortable.

self-control *n.* **self-restraint,** restraint, self-discipline, willpower, strength of will.

self-important *adj.* **pompous,** vain, conceited, arrogant, swell-headed, egotistical, presumptuous, overbearing, overweening, haughty, swaggering, strutting.

self-indulgence *n.* **self-gratification,** lack of self-restraint, unrestraint, intemperance, immoderation, excess, pleasure-seeking, pursuit of pleasure, sensualism, dissipation.

selfish *adj.* **self-seeking,** self-centered, egocentric, egotistic, egoistic, self-interested, self-regarding, self-absorbed, *inf.* looking out for number one. *Ant.* unselfish; altruistic; selfless.

selfless *adj.* **unselfish,** altruistic, generous, self-sacrificing, self-denying, magnanimous, liberal, ungrudging. *Ant.* selfish; self-centered; egoistic.

self-respect *n.* **self-esteem,** self-regard, pride in oneself, pride in one's abilities, belief in one's worth, faith in oneself, amour propre.

self-righteous *adj.* **sanctimonious,** holier-than-thou, pietistic, pharisaic, unctuous, mealy-mouthed, *inf.* goody-goody.

self-sacrifice *n.* **self-denial,** selflessness, self-abnegation, unselfishness, altruism.

self-seeking *adj.* **self-interested,** opportunistic, looking out for oneself, ambitious, mercenary, out for what one can get, fortune-hunting, gold-digging, *inf.* on the make, looking out for number one.

sell *v.* **1 put up for sale,** put on sale, dispose of, vend, auction off, trade, barter. **2 trade in,** deal in, be in the business of, traffic in, stock, carry, offer for sale, market, handle, peddle, hawk. **3 be bought,** be purchased, go, move, be in demand, *inf.* go like hot cakes. **4 retail,** go, be found. **5 get acceptance for,** win approval for, get support for, get across, promote. **6 sell down the river,** betray, cheat, swindle, defraud, fleece, deceive, trick, double-cross, bilk, gull, *inf.* con, stab someone in the back. *Ant.* buy; purchase.

seller *n.* **vendor,** retailer, salesman, saleswoman, salesperson, shopkeeper, trader, merchant, dealer, agent, representative, *inf.* rep.

semblance *n.* **appearance,** outward appearance, show, air, guise, pretense, façade, front, veneer, mask, cloak, disguise, camouflage, pretext.

send *v.* **1 dispatch,** forward, mail, post, remit. **2 transmit,** convey, communicate, broadcast, televise, telecast, radio. **3 throw,** fling, hurl, cast, let fly, propel, project. **4 drive,** make, cause one to be/become. **5 excite,** stimulate, titillate, rouse, stir, thrill, intoxicate, enrapture, enthrall, ravish, charm, delight, *inf.* turn one on. **Ant.** receive; get.

senile *adj.* **doddering,** decrepit, failing, in one's dotage, in one's second childhood, mentally confused.

senior *adj.* **1 high-ranking,** higher-ranking, superior. **2 older,** elder. **Ant.** junior; subordinate; inferior.

sensation *n.* **1 feeling,** sense, awareness, consciousness, perception, impression. **2 stir,** excitement, agitation, commotion, furor, scandal. **3 great success,** *inf.* hit, smash hit, wow.

sense *n.* **1 feeling,** sensation, faculty, sensibility. **2 feeling,** atmosphere, impression, aura, sensation, awareness, consciousness, perception. **3 feeling,** sensation, awareness, consciousness, perception. **4 appreciation,** awareness, understanding, comprehension. **5 common sense,** practicality, wisdom, sagacity, sharpness, discernment, perception, wit, intelligence, cleverness, understanding, reason, logic, brain, brains, *inf.* gumption. **6 meaning,** definition, import, signification, significance, implication, nuance, drift, gist, purport, denotation. **7 intelligibility,** coherence, comprehensibility, logic, rationality, purpose, point.
▸ *v.* **feel,** get the impression of, be aware of, be conscious of, observe, notice, perceive, discern, grasp, pick up, suspect, divine, intuit, *inf.* have a feeling about.

senseless *adj.* **1 nonsensical,** stupid, foolish, silly, inane, idiotic, mindless, unintelligent, unwise, irrational, illogical, meaningless, pointless, absurd, ludicrous, fatuous, asinine, moronic, imbecilic, mad, *inf.* daft. **2 unconscious,** insensible, out cold, out, cold, stunned, numb, numbed, insensate. **Ant.** sensible; wise; conscious.

sensible *adj.* **1 practical,** realistic, down-to-earth, wise, prudent, judicious, sagacious, sharp, shrewd, discerning, perceptive, farsighted, intelligent, clever, reasonable, rational, logical, *inf.* brainy. **2 perceptible,** discernible, appreciable, noticeable, visible, observable, tangible, palpable. **Ant.** foolish; silly; unaware.

sensitive *adj.* **1 delicate,** fine, soft, easily damaged, fragile. **2 responsive,** receptive, perceptive, discerning, discriminatory, sympathetic,

understanding, empathetic.
3 oversensitive, easily upset, thin-skinned, touchy, temperamental.
4 delicate, difficult, problematic, ticklish. ***Ant.*** insensitive; coarse; tough.

sensual *adj.* **1 physical,** carnal, bodily, fleshly, animal, nonspiritual, epicurean, sybaritic.
2 voluptuous, sexual, sexy, erotic. ***Ant.*** spiritual; ascetic.

sensuous *adj.* **aesthetic,** pleasing, pleasurable, gratifying.

sentence *n.* **1 judgment,** verdict, pronouncement, ruling, decision, decree. **2 prison sentence,** jail sentence, penal sentence, prison term, *inf.* time.
▸ *v.* **impose a sentence on,** pass judgment on, mete out punishment to, punish, condemn, doom, punish, penalize.

sentiment *n.* **1 emotion,** emotionalism, finer feelings, tender feelings, tenderness, softness. **2 feelings,** attitude, belief, opinion, view, point of view. **3 sentimentality,** emotionalism, overemotionalism, mawkishness.

sentimental *adj.* **1 emotional,** overemotional, romantic, mawkish, maudlin, soppy, *inf.* mushy, slushy, soppy, schmaltzy, corny. **2 emotional,** nostalgic, affectionate, loving, tender,

warm. ***Ant.*** dispassionate; practical; hardheaded.

sentiments *pl. n.* **feeling,** attitude, belief, thoughts, way of thinking, opinion, view, point of view, idea, judgment, persuasion.

sentry *n.* **guard,** lookout, watch, watchman, sentinel.

separate *adj.* **1 individual,** distinct, different, particular, autonomous, independent.
2 unconnected, unattached, distinct, different, disconnected, unrelated, detached, divorced, divided, discrete. ***Ant.*** united; same.
▸ *v.* **1 disconnect,** detach, sever, uncouple, divide, disjoin, sunder.
2 come apart, come away, break off, divide, disunite. **3 divide,** come between, stand between, keep apart, partition. **4 part,** part company, go their separate ways, go different ways, diverge, split, divide. **5 break up,** split up, part, become estranged, divorce.
6 divide, sort, sort out, classify, categorize. **7 set apart,** segregate, single out, put to one side, isolate. ***Ant.*** join; unite; marry; mix.

separately *adv.* **1 apart,** individually, independently, autonomously. **2 individually,** one by one, one at a time, singly, severally, independently.

septic *adj.* **infected,** festering,

poisoned, putrefying, putrefactive, putrid.

sequel *n.* **follow-up,** development, result, consequence, outcome, issue, upshot, end, conclusion.

sequence *n.* **chain,** course, cycle, series, progression, succession, set, arrangement, order, pattern.

serene *adj.* **calm,** composed, tranquil, peaceful, placid, still, quiet, unperturbed, imperturbable, undisturbed, unruffled, unworried, unexcited, unexcitable, unflappable.

series *n.* **succession,** progression, sequence, chain, course, string, train, run, cycle, set, row, arrangement, order.

serious *adj.* **1 solemn,** earnest, unsmiling, unlaughing, thoughtful, preoccupied, pensive, grave, somber, sober, long-faced, dour, stern, grim, poker-faced. **2 important,** significant, consequential, of consequence, momentous, of moment, weighty, far-reaching, urgent, pressing, crucial, vital, life-and-death. **3 acute,** grave, bad, critical, alarming, grievous, dangerous, perilous. **4 earnest,** in earnest, sincere, honest, genuine, firm, resolute, resolved, determined, fervent. ***Ant.*** cheerful; trivial; minor; flippant.

sermon *n.* **1 preaching,** teaching, speech, homily, address, oration. **2 lecture,** moralizing, declamation, tirade, harangue, ranting, diatribe, reprimand, reproof, remonstrance, castigation, *inf.* talking-to, dressing-down.

servant *n.* **domestic,** help, domestic help, helper, maid, housekeeper, butler, steward, valet, handyman, menial, drudge, slave, vassal, serf, attendant, lackey, flunky.

serve *v.* **1 be in the service of,** work for, be employed by, have a job with. **2 be of service for,** be of use to, help, give help to, assist, give assistance to, aid, lend a hand to, do a good turn to, benefit, support, foster, minister to, succor. **3 have/hold a place,** be, sit, perform duties, carry out duties, fulfill duties. **4 be useful to,** be all right for, be good to/for, be adequate for, suffice, serve a purpose for, meet requirements for, *inf.* fill the bill for, do. **5 spend,** go through, carry out, fulfill, complete, discharge. **6 dish up,** give out, distribute, set out, present, provide. **7 wait,** wait table(s), waitress. **8 attend to,** attend to the wants of, look after, take care of, assist. **9 treat,** act toward, behave toward, conduct oneself toward, deal with, handle.

service *n.* **1 work,** employment, period of employment, labor, duties. **2 good turn,** assistance, help, advantage, benefit. **3 ceremony,** ritual, rite, sacrament. **4 servicing,** overhaul, check, maintenance check, repair. **5 serving,** waiting at table, waiting, waitressing. **6 treatment,** behavior, conduct, handling.
▸ *v.* **check,** go over, overhaul, give a maintenance check to, repair.

serviceable *adj.* **1 functional,** utilitarian, practical, nondecorative, plain, useful, durable, hardwearing, tough, strong. **2 usable,** of use, functioning, operative, repairable. *Ant.* impractical; inoperative.

servile *adj.* **1 menial,** low, lowly, humble, mean, base. **2 subservient,** obsequious, sycophantic, fawning, toadying, groveling, submissive, *inf.* bootlicking.

serving *n.* **helping,** portion, plateful, bowlful.

session *n.* **1 period,** time, spell, stretch. **2 meeting,** sitting, assembly, conference, discussion, *inf.* get-together. **3 semester,** school term, term.

set[1] *v.* **1 put,** put down, place, lay, lay down, deposit, position, rest, locate, lodge, situate, station, posit, *inf.* stick, park, plunk. **2 fix,** embed, insert, lodge, mount, arrange, install. **3 put,** apply, lay, place, bring into contact with, touch. **4 apply,** direct, aim, turn, address, focus, concentrate, zero in on. **5 adjust,** regulate, synchronize, coordinate, harmonize, collimate, calibrate, rectify, set right. **6 fix,** make ready, prepare, arrange, organize. **7 lay,** arrange. **8 fix,** style, arrange, curl, wave. **9 decorate,** adorn, ornament, deck, bedeck, embellish, furbish, bejewel. **10 put,** cause to be, start, actuate, instigate. **11 solidify,** stiffen, thicken, gel, jell, harden, cake, congeal, coagulate, crystallize, gelatinize. **12 go down,** sink, dip below the horizon, vanish, disappear, subside, decline. **13 set off,** start, begin, motivate (to be), cause (to be). **14 set up,** establish, fix, create, bring into being, bring into existence, institute. **15 fix,** settle (on), agree on, appoint, decide on, name, specify, stipulate, determine, designate, select, choose, arrange, schedule, confirm. **16 lay down,** impose, establish, define, determine, stipulate, prescribe, ordain, allot. **17 assign,** allocate, allot, give, give out, distribute, dispense, mete out, deal out, dole out, prescribe. **18 evaluate,** valuate, value, assess, price, rate, estimate, reckon, calculate. **19 direct,** steer, orientate, point, incline, bend, train, aim.

▸ *adj.* **1 fixed,** prescribed, scheduled, specified, predetermined, prearranged, determined, arranged, appointed, established, decided, agreed. **2 customary,** regular, normal, usual, habitual, accustomed, everyday, common. **3 stock,** standard, habitual, routine, rehearsed, unspontaneous, hackneyed, conventional, stereotyped. **4 fixed,** firm, rooted, immovable, deep-seated, ingrained, entrenched, rigid, inflexible, hidebound. **5 ready,** prepared, equipped, primed, fit.

set[2] *n.* **1 collection,** group, assemblage, series, batch, arrangement, array, succession, progression, assortment, selection. **2 circle,** crowd, clique, group, gang, coterie, faction, band, company, sect, *inf.* crew. **3 bearing,** carriage, cast, posture, position, altitude, turn, inclination. **4 stage set,** stage setting, setting, stage scene, scene, scenery, backdrop, wings, mise en scène.

setback *n.* **reversal,** reverse, upset, check, stumbling block, hitch, holdup, hindrance, impediment, obstruction, disappointment, misfortune, blow.

setting *n.* **1 environment,** surroundings, milieu, background, location, place, site. **2 stage setting,** set, scene, stage, scenery, backdrop, mise en scène. **3 mounting,** frame. **4 setting.**

settle *v.* **1 make one's home,** set up home, take up residence, put down roots, establish oneself, go to live, move to, emigrate to, colonize, occupy, people, inhabit, populate. **2 settle/calm/quiet down,** be quiet, be still, relax. **3 calm,** calm down, tranquilize, quiet, soothe, compose, pacify, lull, sedate, quell. **4 make comfortable,** bed down, tuck in. **5 alight,** light, land, come down, descend, repose, rest. **6 resolve,** clear up, make peace in, patch up, reconcile, conclude, bring to an end. **7 put in order,** arrange, set to rights, straighten out, organize, regulate, adjust, clear up, systematize. **8 pay,** discharge, square, clear, liquidate. **9 settle out,** sink, subside, fall, gravitate. *Ant.* agitate; disturb.

settlement *n.* **1 establishing,** founding, pioneering, peopling, colonization. **2 community,** colony, town, village, hamlet, encampment, outpost.

3 resolution, patching up, reconciliation, conclusion.
4 agreement, contract, pact, compact. **5 ordering,** arrangement, organization, regulation, adjustment, systematization. **6 payment,** discharge, defrayal, liquidation.

settler *n.* colonist, colonizer, pioneer, frontiersman, immigrant.

sever *v.* **1 cut off,** chop off, lop off, hack off, break off, tear off. **2 divide,** split, cleave, rive, dissect, halve. **3 break off,** discontinue, suspend, dissolve, end, bring to an end, terminate, stop, cease, conclude. *Ant.* join; maintain; begin.

several *adj.* **1 some,** a number of, a few. **2 separate,** different, diverse, disparate, divergent, respective, individual, own, particular, specific, various, sundry.

severe *adj.* **1 harsh,** hard, stringent, rigorous, unsparing, relentless, merciless, ruthless, painful, sharp, caustic, biting, cutting, scathing, serious, extreme, stern, strict, grim, inflexible, uncompromising, inexorable, implacable, relentless, unrelenting, merciless, pitiless, ruthless, brutal, inhuman, cruel, savage, hard-hearted, iron-fisted, iron-handed, autocratic, tyrannical, despotic. **2 harsh,** hard, stern, rigorous, stringent, strict, grim, inflexible, uncompromising, inexorable, implacable, relentless, unrelenting, merciless, pitiless, ruthless, brutal, inhuman, cruel, savage, hard-hearted, iron-fisted, iron-handed, autocratic, tyrannical, despotic. **3 extreme,** very bad, serious, grave, acute, critical, dire, dangerous, perilous. **4 fierce,** strong, violent, intense, powerful, forceful, very bad, harsh, extreme, inclement, cold, freezing, frigid. **5 demanding,** taxing, exacting, tough, difficult, hard, fierce, arduous, rigorous, punishing, onerous, burdensome. **6 stern,** grim, cold, chilly, austere, forbidding, dour, disapproving, tight-lipped, unsmiling, somber, grave, sober, serious. **7 austere,** stark, ultraplain, spartan, ascetic, plain, simple, modest, bare, blank, unadorned, undecorated, unembellished, restrained, functional. *Ant.* mild; lenient; ornate.

sew *v.* **stitch,** seam, embroider, mend, darn.

sex *n.* **1 gender. 2 sexuality,** sexual attraction, sexual chemistry, sexual desire, desire, sex drive, sexual appetite, libido. **3 facts of**

life, sexual reproduction, reproduction, *inf.* the birds and the bees. **4 intimacy,** coitus, coition, coupling, copulation, carnal knowledge, making love, mating, fornication.

sexuality *n.* **1 sex,** gender, sexual characteristics. **2 sexual desire,** sexual appetite, sexiness, carnality, physicalness, eroticism, lust, sensuality, voluptuousness, sexual orientation, sexual preferences.

sexy *adj.* **1 erotic,** titillating, suggestive, arousing, exciting, stimulating, provocative, seductive, sensuous, slinky, sexually attractive, alluring, seductive, shapely. **2 exciting,** appealing, sensational.

shabby *adj.* **1 dilapidated,** broken-down, run-down, tumbledown, ramshackle, in disrepair, scruffy, dingy, seedy, squalid, tatty, slumlike, slummy, *inf.* tacky. **2 worn,** worn-out, threadbare, ragged, frayed, tattered, faded, scruffy, tatty, the worse for wear. **3 contemptible,** despicable, dishonorable, disreputable, mean, base, low, dirty, odious, shameful, ignoble, unworthy, cheap, shoddy, *inf.* rotten, low-down. *Ant.* smart; neat; honorable.

shackle *v.* **1 chain,** fetter, put in irons, manacle, tie up, bind, tether, hobble, handcuff. **2 deter,** restrain, restrict, limit, impede, hinder, hamper, obstruct, encumber, check, curb, constrain, tie the hands of.

shade *n.* **1 shadiness,** shadow, shadowiness, shadows, shelter, cover. **2 dimness,** dusk, semidarkness, twilight, gloaming, darkness, gloom, gloominess, murkiness, murk. **3 color,** hue, tone, tint, tinge. **4 screen,** shield, curtain, blind, canopy, veil, cover, covering. **5 nuance,** degree, gradation, difference, variety. *Ant.* sunlight; light.
▸ *v.* **1 shut out the light from,** block off light to, cast a shadow over, screen, darken, dim. **2 cover,** obscure, mute, hide, conceal, veil, curtain.

shadow *n.* **1 shade,** shadowiness, shadows, shelter, cover. **2 dimness,** dusk, semidarkness, twilight, gloaming, darkness, gloom. **3 silhouette,** outline, shape. **4 gloom,** gloominess, cloud, blight, sadness, unhappiness. **5 constant companion,** inseparable companion, close friend, bosom friend, intimate, alter ego, *inf.* sidekick. **6 watch,** follower, detective, *inf.* tail.

shadowy *adj.* **1 shady,** shaded, dim, dark, gloomy, murky, crepuscular, tenebrous, tenebrious. **2 indistinct,** indeterminate, indefinite, unclear, vague, nebulous, ill-defined, indistinguishable, unsubstantial, ghostly, phantom, spectral. *Ant.* bright; sunny; distinct.

shady *adj.* **1 shaded,** shadowy, screened, sheltered, covered, dim, dark, leafy, bowery, umbrageous, tenebrous, tenebrious. **2 disreputable,** of dubious character, suspicious, suspect, questionable, dishonest, dishonorable, untrustworthy, devious, shifty, slippery, tricky, underhand, underhanded, unscrupulous, *inf.* crooked, fishy. *Ant.* bright; sunny; reputable; aboveboard.

shaft *n.* **1 passage,** duct, tunnel, well, flue. **2 ray,** beam, gleam, streak, pencil. **3 pole,** stick, rod, staff, shank, stem, handle, upright.

shaggy *adj.* **hairy,** hirsute, long-haired, rough, coarse, matted, tangled, unkempt, untidy.

shake *v.* **1 rock,** bump, jolt, bounce, roll, sway, swing, oscillate, wobble, rattle, vibrate, jar, jerk, joggle, jounce. **2 shiver,** tremble, quiver, quake, shudder. **3 jiggle,** joggle, jolt, jerk, rattle, agitate, jounce. **4 agitate,** upset,

distress, shock, alarm, disturb, perturb, fluster, unsettle, discompose, disquiet, disconcert, unnerve, ruffle, jolt, flurry, confuse, muddle, *inf.* rattle. **5 undermine,** weaken, lessen, impair, harm, hurt, injure. **6 brandish,** wave, flourish, swing, wield, raise.
▸ *n.* **1 shaking,** rocking, bump, jolt, bounce, roll, swaying, rattle, vibration, jarring, jerk. **2 shaking,** shivering, trembling, tremor, quiver, quivering, convulsion. **3 jiggle,** joggle, jolt, jerk, rattle. **4 upset,** shock, jolt. **5 brandish,** wave, flourish, swing.

shaky *adj.* **1 shaking,** trembling, tremulous, quivering, quivery, unsteady, wobbly, weak. **2 shaking,** unsteady, faltering, wobbly, tottering, teetering, doddering, staggering. **3 infirm,** unsound, unwell, ill, below par, indisposed, *inf.* under the weather. **4 questionable,** dubious, tenuous, unsubstantial, flimsy, weak, nebulous, unsound, unreliable, undependable, ungrounded, unfounded. **5 rickety,** wobbly, flimsy, ramshackle, dilapidated, gimcrack, jerry-built. *Ant.* steady; sound; stable.

shallow *adj.* **frivolous,** foolish, unintelligent, unthinking, trivial, insincere, superficial, unsubstantial, trifling, trivial, petty, empty, meaningless. *Ant.* serious; profound.

sham *v.* **fake,** pretend, feign, counterfeit, put on, simulate, affect, imitate, dissemble, malinger, make believe.
▸ *n.* **1 fake,** pretense, feint, feigning, counterfeit, imposture, simulation, forgery, copy, imitation, hoax. **2 impostor,** fake, fraud, pretender, masquerader, dissembler, wolf in sheep's clothing, charlatan, *inf.* phony. **3 counterfeit,** fake, forgery, imposture, copy, imitation, hoax.

shamble *v.* **shuffle,** hobble, limp, falter, totter, dodder, toddle.

shambles *pl. n.* **chaos,** muddle, mess, confusion, disorder, disarray, disorganization, anarchy, *inf.* disaster area.

shame *n.* **1 humiliation,** ignominy, mortification, loss of face, remorse, guilt, compunction, shamefacedness, embarrassment, discomfort, discomposure. **2 disgrace,** dishonor, scandal, discredit, degradation, ignominy, disrepute, infamy, odium, opprobrium, condemnation, reproach, blot, smirch, stain, blemish, stigma. **3 pity,** misfortune, bad luck, ill luck, source of regret. *Ant.* pride; honor; credit.

shamefaced *adj.* **1 ashamed,** embarrassed, guilty, conscience-stricken, remorseful, contrite, penitent, regretful, humiliated, mortified, shamed. **2 shy,** bashful, timid, timorous, shrinking, coy, sheepish.

shameful *adj.* **1 disgraceful,** base, mean, low, vile, outrageous, shocking, dishonorable, unbecoming, unworthy, discreditable, deplorable, despicable, contemptible, reprehensible, scandalous, atrocious, heinous. **2 shaming,** humiliating, mortifying, embarrassing. *Ant.* admirable; honorable; laudable.

shameless *adj.* **1 unashamed,** without shame, unabashed, uncontrite, unpenitent, impenitent, unregretful. **2 brazen,** impudent, bold, brash, forward, audacious, immodest, unseemly, improper, unbecoming, indecorous, wanton, abandoned, indecent.

shape *n.* **1 form,** figure, configuration, formation, conformation, contour, outline, silhouette, profile, outward form, external appearance, shadow, body, apparition. **2 form,** guise, appearance, likeness, look,

semblance, image, aspect.
3 condition, state, health, trim,
fettle, kilter.

▸ *v.* **1 form,** fashion, make, create,
design, mold, model, cast, frame,
block, carve, sculpt, sculpture,
produce, influence, guide,
determine, define. **2 plan,** devise,
prepare, develop, organize, line
up. **3 adjust,** adapt, accommodate,
alter, modify, tailor.

shapeless *adj.* **1 amorphous,**
formless, unformed, unshaped,
unfashioned, undeveloped,
embryonic. **2 formless,** sacklike,
ill-proportioned, inelegant,
misshapen, battered, deformed.

shapely *adj.* **well-formed,** well-
shaped, well-proportioned,
elegant, curvaceous, curvy.

share *n.* **division,** quota,
allowance, ration, allocation,
allotment, portion, part, lot,
measure, helping, serving, *inf.* cut,
piece of the cake, piece of the
action.

▸ *v.* **1 divide (up),** split, *inf.* divvy
(up). **2 divide (up),** distribute,
apportion, parcel out, deal out,
dole out, give out, *inf.* divvy (up).

sharp *adj.* **1 cutting,** serrated,
knifelike, edged, razor-edged,
keen. **2 pointed,** needlelike, spear-
shaped, barbed, spiky. **3 steep,**
sheer, abrupt, precipitous,

vertical. **4 sudden,** abrupt, rapid,
unexpected. **5 clear,** clear-cut,
distinct, marked, well-defined,
crisp. **6 intense,** acute, keen,
piercing, cutting, extreme, severe,
stabbing, shooting, stinging.
7 pungent, biting, bitter, acid,
sour, tart, vinegary, acrid,
pungent, burning. **8 piercing,**
shrill, high-pitched, earsplitting,
harsh, strident. **9 harsh,** curt,
brusque, bitter, hard, cutting,
scathing, caustic, biting, barbed,
acrimonious, trenchant, sarcastic,
sardonic, venomous, malicious,
vitriolic, hurtful, unkind, cruel.
10 sharp-witted, intelligent,
bright, clever, quick. **11 keen,**
acute, quick, ready, smart,
knowing, comprehending,
shrewd, discerning, perceptive,
penetrating. **12 unscrupulous,**
dishonest, cunning, wily, crafty,
artful. **13 smart,** stylish,
fashionable, chic, elegant, *inf.*
dressy, snappy, natty. ***Ant.*** blunt;
gentle; indistinct; mild.

▸ *adj.* **promptly,** punctually, on
time, on the dot, *inf.* on the nose.

sharpen *v.* **put an edge on,** edge,
whet, hone, strop, grind.

shave *v.* **1 cut off,** trim, snip off,
crop, pare, plane, shear. **2 brush,**
graze, touch, scrape, rub.

sheath *n.* **1 scabbard,** case,
casing, cover, covering, envelope,

wrapper. **2 condom,** contraceptive, *inf.* rubber.

shed[1] *n.* **hut,** outhouse, lean-to, shack.

shed[2] *v.* **1 let fall,** let drop, cast off, slough off. **2 take off,** remove, strip off, doff. **3 pour forth,** let flow, spill, discharge, exude. **4 diffuse,** send forth, radiate, disperse, scatter. **5 discard,** get rid of, dispense with, drop, declare/make redundant, dismiss, *inf.* sack, fire.

sheen *n.* **shine,** luster, gleam, sparkle, gloss, burnish, polish, patina.

sheer *adj.* **1 utter,** complete, thoroughgoing, total, absolute, veritable, downright, out-and-out, unqualified, unconditional, unmitigated, unalloyed, unadulterated. **2 steep,** abrupt, sharp, precipitous, vertical, perpendicular. **3 diaphanous,** transparent, see-through, translucent, filmy, gossamer, gauzy, ultrafine, fine, thin. **Ant.** qualified; gradual; thick.

▸ *v.* **swerve,** change course, slew, veer, drift, yaw.

sheet *n.* **1 bedsheet,** bed linen. **2 layer,** stratum, overlay, surface, lamina, covering, coating, coat, facing, veneer, film, piece, pane, panel, plate, slab.

shell *n.* **1 carapace,** case. **2 casing,** case, husk, pod, integument. **3 bullet,** grenade, shot, cartridge, case. **4 framework,** frame, structure, chassis, hull, skeleton.

▸ *v.* **1 husk,** shuck. **2 bomb,** bombard, blitz, torpedo, strafe, fire on, open fire on.

shelter *n.* **1 protection,** shield, cover, screen, safety, security, defense, refuge, sanctuary, asylum. **2 refuge,** sanctuary, retreat, haven, harbor.

▸ *v.* **1 protect,** provide protection for, shield, cover, screen, safeguard. **2 protect,** shield, screen, safeguard, provide refuge/sanctuary for, guard, harbor, conceal, hide. **Ant.** expose; endanger.

sheltered *adj.* **1 shady,** shaded, protected, screened, shielded, secluded. **2 secluded,** quiet, withdrawn, retired, isolated, protected, cloistered, reclusive.

shepherd *v.* **escort,** conduct, usher, convoy, guide, marshal, steer.

shift *v.* **change,** alter, vary, modify, reverse, do an about-face, *inf.* do a U-turn.

▸ *n.* **1 change,** alteration, variation, modification, about-face, reversal, sea change, *inf.* U-turn. **2 days,** evenings, nights, stint, spell of work.

shifty *adj.* **evasive,** slippery,

devious, duplicitous, deceitful, underhand, underhanded, untrustworthy, double-dealing, dishonest, wily, crafty, artful, sly, scheming, contriving. **Ant.** honest; open; trustworthy.

shimmer v. **glisten,** glint, flicker, twinkle, sparkle, gleam, glow, scintillate, dance.

▸ n. **glistening,** glint, flicker, twinkle, sparkle, gleam, glow, luster, iridescence, scintillation.

shine v. **1 emit light,** give off light. **2 gleam,** sparkle, glisten. **3 gleam,** glow, glint, sparkle, twinkle, flicker, glitter, glisten, shimmer, flash, dazzle, beam, radiate, illuminate, luminesce, incandesce. **4 glow,** beam, radiate, bloom, look healthy, look good. **5 polish,** burnish, buff, wax, gloss, brush, rub up. **6 excel,** be expert, be brilliant, be very good, be outstanding. **7 stand out,** be outstanding, be conspicuous, be preeminent, excel, dominate, star.

▸ n. **1 light,** brightness, gleam, glow, glint, sparkle, twinkle, flicker, glitter, glisten, shimmer, flash, dazzle, glare, beam, radiance, illumination, luminescence, luminosity, lambency, effulgence. **2 polish,** burnish, gleam, gloss, luster, sheen, patina.

shiny adj. **shining,** polished,

burnished, gleaming, glossy, satiny, lustrous. **Ant.** dull; lusterless.

shirk v. **avoid,** evade, dodge, sidestep, shrink from, shun, get out of, inf. duck (out of).

shirker n. **dodger,** slacker, truant, malingerer, layabout, loafer, idler.

shiver v. **tremble,** quiver, shake, shudder, quaver, quake, vibrate.

▸ n. **tremble,** quiver, shake, quaver, shudder.

shock[1] n. **1 impact,** blow, collision, crash, clash, jolt, bump, jar, jerk. **2 surprise,** blow, upset, disturbance, state of agitation, source of distress, source of amazement/consternation, revelation, bolt from the blue, bombshell, eye-opener. **3 state of shock,** trauma, traumatism, prostration, stupor, stupefaction, collapse.

▸ v. **appall,** horrify, scandalize, outrage, repel, revolt, disgust, nauseate, sicken, offend, traumatize, distress, upset, perturb, disturb, disquiet, unsettle, discompose, agitate, astound, dumbfound, stagger, amaze, astonish, stun, flabbergast, stupefy, overwhelm, bewilder.

shock[2] n. **mass,** mop, mane, thatch.

shoddy adj. **poor-quality,** inferior,

second-rate, cheapjack, tawdry, rubbishy, trashy, junky, gimcrack, jerry-built, *inf.* tacky, tatty.

shoot *v.* **1 hit,** wound, injure, shoot down, bring down, bag, fell, kill, slay, *inf.* pick off, pump full of lead, plug. **2 fire,** discharge, launch, let off, let fly, send forth, emit. **3 race,** dash, sprint, bound, charge, dart, fly, hurtle, bolt, streak, flash, whisk, run, speed, hurry, hasten, *inf.* scoot. **4 film,** photograph, take photographs of.
▶ *n.* **bud,** offshoot, slip, scion, sucker, sprout, branch, twig, sprig, cutting, graft.

shop *n.* **1 store,** boutique.
2 workshop, plant, factory, machine shop, auto body shop, auto repair shop.
▶ *v.* **go shopping,** look to buy, be in the market for.

shore[1] *n.* **seashore,** seaside, beach, coast, seaboard, waterfront, waterside, strand.

short *adj.* **1 small,** little, slight, petite, tiny, wee, squat, stubby, dwarfish, diminutive, dumpy, Lilliputian, *inf.* pint-sized, pocket-sized, knee-high to a grasshopper. **2 low,** stubby, miniature. **3 small,** little, tiny, minuscule. **4 brief,** concise, succinct, to the point, compact, terse, summary, crisp, pithy, epigrammatic, abridged, abbreviated, condensed, summarized, contracted, curtailed, truncated. **5 brief,** momentary, temporary, short-lived, impermanent, short-term, cursory, fleeting, passing, transitory, transient, ephemeral, fugacious, evanescent, meteoric. **6 direct,** straight. **7 deficient,** lacking, wanting, insufficient, inadequate, scarce, scanty, meager, sparse, unplentiful, tight, low. **8 curt,** sharp, abrupt, blunt, brusque, terse, gruff, surly, testy, tart, rude, discourteous, uncivil, impolite. *Ant.* tall; long; abundant.
▶ *adv.* **abruptly,** suddenly, all of a sudden, unexpectedly, without warning, out of the blue.

shortage *n.* **dearth,** scarcity, lack, deficiency, insufficiency, paucity, deficit, inadequacy, shortfall, want, poverty. *Ant.* abundance; surfeit; surplus.

shortcoming *n.* **defect,** fault, flaw, imperfection, failing, drawback, weakness, weak point, foible, frailty, infirmity.

shorten *v.* **1 abbreviate,** condense, abridge, cut, cut down, contract, compress, reduce, lessen, decrease, diminish, curtail, duck, trim, pare down. **2 get shorter,** grow shorter, grow less. *Ant.* lengthen; extend; elongate.

shortly *adv.* **1 soon,** in a short

while, in a little while, presently, before long, directly, *inf.* before you know it, before you can say Jack Robinson. **2 curtly,** sharply, abruptly, bluntly, brusquely, tersely, gruffly, testily, tartly, rudely, discourteously, uncivilly, impolitely.

shortsighted *adj.* **1 myopic,** nearsighted. **2 lacking foresight,** uncircumspect, ill-considered, unwary, imprudent, injudicious, unwise, ill-advised, thoughtless, unthinking, heedless, rash, incautious.

shot *n.* **1 gunfire,** report (of a gun), crack, bang, blast, explosion. **2 pellet(s),** bullet(s), slug(s), lead, projectile(s), ammunition. **3 throw,** toss, lob, fling, hurl. **4 shooter,** marksman, markswoman, rifleman. **5 photograph,** photo, snap, snapshot, picture, *inf.* pic. **6 attempt,** try, effort, endeavor, *inf.* go, stab, crack, whack. **7 turn,** chance, opportunity, *inf.* go. **8 injection,** vaccination. **9 comment,** remark, statement, utterance, *inf.* crack.

shout *v.* **cry out,** call out, yell, roar, howl, bellow, scream, bawl, call/yell at the top of one's voice, raise one's voice, *inf.* holler.
▸ *n.* **cry,** call, yell, roar, howl, bellow, scream, *inf.* holler.

shove *v.* **push,** thrust, drive, force, shoulder, elbow, jostle, jolt.
▸ *n.* **push,** thrust, jostle, jolt.

shovel *v.* **scoop up,** spade, dig, excavate, clear.

show *v.* **1 be visible,** be seen, be in view, appear, put in an appearance. **2 exhibit,** display, present, demonstrate, set forth, uncover, reveal. **3 indicate,** express, manifest, reveal, make known, make plain, make obvious, evince, evidence, disclose, betray, divulge. **4 demonstrate,** point out, explain, expound, clarify, elucidate, teach, instruct in, give instructions in, tutor in, indoctrinate in. **5 escort,** accompany, usher, conduct, attend, guide, lead, direct, steer. **6 show up,** appear, put in an appearance, make an appearance, turn up, come, arrive, be present. *Ant.* conceal; suppress; withhold.
▸ *n.* **1 display,** array, arrangement, exhibition, presentation, exposition, spectacle. **2 exhibition,** demonstration, display, exposition, presentation, *inf.* expo. **3 performance,** theatrical performance, production, *inf.* gig. **4 appearance,** outward appearance, air, guise, semblance, pretense, illusion, pose, affectation, profession, parade. **5 display,** ostentation, affectation, window-dressing. **6 organization,**

operation, establishment, undertaking, enterprise, business, venture.

shower *n.* **1 fall,** drizzle, flurry, sprinkling. **2 volley,** raining, barrage, fusillade. **3 abundance,** profusion, plethora, flood, deluge.
> *v.* **1 rain,** fall. **2 deluge,** inundate, overwhelm. **3 lavish,** pour, load, heap.

show-off *n.* **exhibitionist,** extrovert, swaggerer, bragger, braggart, boaster, braggadocio, *inf.* blowhard.

showy *adj.* **ostentatious,** flamboyant, elaborate, fancy, pretentious, overdone, glittering. ***Ant.*** discreet; restrained; plain.

shred *n.* **1 scrap,** fragment, wisp, sliver, bit, piece, remnant, snippet, tatter. **2 scrap,** bit, iota, whit, particle, atom, modicum, trace, speck.
> *v.* **cut up,** tear up, rip up, grate.

shrewd *adj.* **1 astute,** sharp, clever, intelligent, smart, alert, quick-witted, discerning, perspicacious, perceptive, discriminating, wise, sagacious, farseeing, canny, cunning, artful, crafty, wily, calculating, *inf.* with all one's wits about one. **2 astute,** clever, wise, judicious, farsighted, cunning, artful, crafty, wily, calculated. ***Ant.*** stupid; unwise; ingenuous.

shriek *v.* **scream,** screech, squeal, yell, howl, shout, cry out, call out, whoop, wail, *inf.* holler.
> *n.* **scream,** screech, squeal, yell, howl, shout, cry, call, whoop, wail, *inf.* holler.

shrill *adj.* **high-pitched,** high, sharp, piercing, ear-piercing, penetrating, earsplitting, screeching, shrieking. ***Ant.*** low; soft; dulcet.

shrine *n.* **1 memorial,** monument, cenotaph. **2 holy place,** temple, church. **3 reliquary,** burial chamber, tomb, sepulcher.

shrink *v.* **1 get/become/grow smaller,** contract, diminish, lessen, reduce, dwindle, narrow, decline, fall off, drop off, shrivel. **2 draw back,** pull back, start back, back away, shy away, recoil, retreat, withdraw, flinch, cringe, wince. ***Ant.*** stretch; expand; confront.

shrivel *v.* **dry up,** wither, desiccate, dehydrate, wrinkle, pucker up.

shroud *n.* **cover,** covering, pall, cloak, mantle, blanket, cloud, veil, screen.
> *v.* **cover,** enshroud, swathe, envelop, cloak, blanket, cloud, veil, screen, conceal, hide.

shuffle *v.* **1 hobble,** limp, drag one's feet, scuff one's feet. **2 scrape,** scuff, drag. **3 mix,**

intermix, shift, rearrange, reorganize, jumble. **4 hedge,** equivocate, be evasive, prevaricate, fence, parry, beat about the bush, beg the question, *inf.* pussyfoot around.

shun *v.* **avoid,** evade, eschew, steer clear of, shy away from, recoil from, keep away from, keep one's distance from, cold-shoulder, give a wide berth to.

shut *v.* **close,** fasten, bar, lock, secure, seal. ***Ant.*** open; unlock.

shy *adj.* **bashful,** diffident, reserved, reticent, retiring, self-effacing, shrinking, withdrawn, timid, timorous, fearful, nervous, hesitant, wary, suspicious, chary, unconfident, self-conscious, embarrassed, abashed, modest. ***Ant.*** bold; brash; confident.

sick *adj.* **1 unwell,** ill, ailing, indisposed, poorly, below par, out of sorts, laid up, *inf.* under the weather, on the sick list. **2 seasick,** nauseous, nauseated, queasy, bilious, *inf.* green around the gills. **3 vomit,** retch, be sick to one's stomach, *inf.* throw up, puke. **4 angry,** annoyed, displeased, disgruntled, distressed, disgusted, *inf.* fed up. **5 morbid,** macabre, ghoulish, gruesome, sadistic, perverted, cruel. ***Ant.*** well; healthy.

sicken *v.* **make sick,** nauseate, turn one's stomach, revolt, disgust, repel, shock, appall.

sickening *adj.* **nauseating,** nauseous, revolting, disgusting, repellent, repulsive, loathsome, distasteful, stomach-turning, shocking, appalling, offensive, vile, foul.

sickly *adj.* **1 unhealthy,** in poor health, chronically ill, delicate, frail, weak, feeble, puny. **2 pale,** wan, pallid, peaky, anemic, bloodless, languid, listless, *inf.* bilious, washed-out. **3 sentimental,** cloying, mawkish, maudlin, slushy, mushy, syrupy, *inf.* soppy, schmaltzy.

sickness *n.* **1 illness,** disease, disorder, ailment, complaint, affliction, malady, infirmity, indisposition, *inf.* bug. **2 vomiting,** retching, upset stomach, stomach upset, *inf.* throwing up, puking. **3 nausea,** queasiness, biliousness.

side *n.* **1 edge,** border, verge, boundary, margin, rim, fringe, skirt, flank, brink, brim, periphery. **2 part,** quarter, section, sector, neighborhood. **3 surface,** face, part, facet. **4 aspect,** angle, facet, point of view, viewpoint, view, opinion, standpoint, position, slant. **5 camp,** faction, caucus, party, wing, splinter group, sect. ***Ant.*** center; heart.

▸ *adj.* **1 lateral,** wing, flank. **2 minor,** lesser, secondary, subordinate, subsidiary, ancillary, marginal. **3** sidelong, oblique, indirect. ***Ant.*** central; major; primary.

sidelong *adj.* **side,** sideways, oblique, indirect, covert.

sidetrack *v.* **divert,** deflect, distract, lead away from.

sideways *adv.* **1 crabwise,** to the side. **2 side first,** edgeways, edgewise. **3 obliquely,** indirectly, sidelong.
▸ *adj.* **sidelong,** side, oblique, indirect.

sieve *n.* **strainer,** sifter, filter, colander, riddle, screen.
▸ *v.* **1 strain,** sift, filter, riddle, screen. **2 separate out,** remove, winnow.

sift *v.* **1 filter,** strain, screen. **2 shake,** sprinkle, distribute, scatter, strew. **3 separate out,** remove, winnow.

sigh *v.* **1 breathe out,** exhale. **2 whisper,** rustle. **3 yearn,** pine, long, mourn.

sign *n.* **1 indication,** symptom, hint, suggestion, mark, clue, manifestation, token, evidence, proof. **2 signpost,** notice, placard, board, marker. **3 gesture,** signal, motion, movement, wave, gesticulation. **4 symbol,** mark, cipher, code, hieroglyph. **5 omen,** portent, warning, forewarning, augury, presage.
▸ *v.* **1 write,** inscribe. **2 autograph,** initial, endorse, certify, validate, authenticate. **3 signal,** indicate, beckon, gesture, motion, gesticulate, wave, nod.

signal *n.* **1 sign,** indicator, cue, indication, token, evidence, hint. **2 incentive,** impetus, stimulus, motive, cause, reason.
▸ *v.* **1 sign,** give a sign, indicate, beckon, gesture, motion, gesticulate, nod, show, express, communicate. **2 be a sign of,** mark, signify, designate.

significance *n.* **1 meaning,** sense, import, signification, purport, point, gist, essence, implications. **2 importance,** consequence, moment, momentousness, weight, weightiness, magnitude, impressiveness, seriousness.

significant *adj.* **1 meaningful,** eloquent, expressive, indicative, pregnant, knowing. **2 important,** of importance, of consequence, momentous, of moment, weighty, material, impressive, serious, vital, critical. ***Ant.*** insignificant; meaningless; minor.

signify *v.* **1 be a sign of,** indicate, mean, denote, betoken, suggest, point to, portend, represent, symbolize, stand for. **2 indicate,** show, exhibit, express, communicate, intimate, announce, proclaim, declare, pronounce. **3 matter,** be of importance, be of consequence, be important, be significant, be of significance, carry weight, count.

silence *n.* **1 still,** stillness, quiet, quietness, hush, peace, peacefulness, tranquillity, noiselessness, soundlessness. **2 speechlessness,** wordlessness, voicelessness, dumbness, muteness, taciturnity, reticence, uncommunicativeness. **3 secrecy,** secretiveness, concealment, reticence, taciturnity, uncommunicativeness. ***Ant.*** noise; speech; communication.

▸ *v.* **1 quiet,** hush, still, calm, pacify, subdue, quell. **2 muffle,** deaden, abate, extinguish. **3 put an end to,** put a stop to, cut short, gag, prevent.

silent *adj.* **1 still,** quiet, hushed, peaceful, tranquil, noiseless, soundless. **2 speechless,** unspeaking, wordless, voiceless, dumb, dumbstruck, mute, taciturn, reticent, uncommunicative, mum, tight-lipped, tongue-tied, *inf.* struck dumb. **3 unspoken,** wordless, unvoiced, unsaid, unexpressed, unpronounced, tacit, implicit, understood, implied. ***Ant.*** noisy; loquacious; spoken.

silhouette *n.* **outline,** contour, profile, delineation, form, shape.

▸ *v.* **outline,** stand out, etch, delineate.

silky *adj.* **silken,** smooth, sleek, velvety, diaphanous.

silly *adj.* **1 foolish,** stupid, unintelligent, idiotic, brainless, mindless, witless, imbecilic, doltish; imprudent, thoughtless, rash, reckless, foolhardy, irresponsible; mad, scatterbrained, featherbrained; frivolous, giddy, inane, immature, childish, puerile, empty-headed; *informal* crazy, dotty, scatty, loopy, wingy, ditzy, screwy, thick, thickheaded, birdbrained, pea-brained, dopey, dim, dimwitted, halfwitted, dippy, blockheaded, boneheaded, lamebrained; daft, chowderheaded; *dated* tomfool. ***Ant.*** sensible. **2 unwise,** imprudent, thoughtless, foolish, stupid, idiotic, senseless, mindless; rash, reckless, foolhardy, irresponsible, injudicious, misguided, irrational; *informal* crazy; daft. ***Ant.*** sensible. **3 trivial,** trifling, frivolous, footling, petty, small, insignificant, unimportant; *informal* piffling, piddling, small-bore. ***Ant.*** important. **4 senseless,**

insensible, unconscious, stupid, into a stupor, into senselessness, stupefied.

similar *adj.* **like,** alike, much the same, comparable, corresponding, analogous, parallel, equivalent, kindred, approximate. ***Ant.*** dissimilar; unlike; different.

similarity *n.* **resemblance,** likeness, sameness, similitude, comparability, correspondence, analogy, parallel, parallelism, equivalence, approximation, closeness, affinity, kinship.

similarly *adv.* **likewise,** in the same way, in like matter, correspondingly, by the same token.

simmer *v.* **1 cook gently,** boil gently, bubble, stew. **2 fume,** seethe, smolder, chafe, smart, be angry, be furious.

simple *adj.* **1 easy,** uncomplicated, straightforward, uninvolved, effortless, manageable, elementary, facile, *inf.* like falling off a log, a piece of cake, a cinch, no sweat. **2 clear,** plain, intelligible, comprehensible, understandable, lucid, direct, straightforward, uncomplicated, uninvolved. **3 plain,** classic, clean-cut, unelaborate, unadorned, undecorated, without ornament/ ornamentation, unembellished,

unfussy, uncluttered, austere, stark, spartan, unpretentious, restrained, natural, casual, informal. **4 noncomplex,** uncompounded, uncombined, unmixed, unblended, unalloyed, pure, basic, single, simplex, elementary, fundamental. **5 plain,** straightforward, frank, direct, candid, honest, sincere, absolute, unqualified, unvarnished, bald, stark, unadorned, unembellished. **6 unsophisticated,** natural, unaffected, wholesome, innocent, artless, guileless, childlike, naïve, ingenuous, gullible, inexperienced, *inf.* green. **7 ordinary,** commonplace, unpretentious, modest, homely, humble, lowly, rustic. ***Ant.*** difficult; complicated; fancy; compound.

simplify *v.* **make easy/easier,** make plainer, clarify, decipher, disentangle, explain, paraphrase, translate, abridge, shorten, condense, streamline, reduce to essentials.

simplistic *adj.* **oversimple,** oversimplified, facile, shallow, superficial, naïve.

simply *adv.* **1 clearly,** plainly, intelligibly, lucidly, directly, straightforwardly. **2 plainly,** classically, unelaborately, without adornment/decoration/ornament/

ornamentation/embellishment, unfussily, without clutter, austerely, starkly, spartanly, with restraint, naturally, casually, informally. **3 unpretentiously,** modestly, humbly. **4 purely,** solely, merely, only, just. **5 absolutely,** unreservedly, positively, certainly, unconditionally, categorically, utterly, completely, altogether, totally, wholly.

simultaneous *adj.* **concurrent,** contemporaneous, concomitant, coinciding, coincident, synchronous, coexistent, parallel.

sin *n.* **wrong,** wrongdoing, act of evil/wickedness, crime, offense, misdeed, misdemeanor, transgression, error, lapse, fall from grace, evil, evildoing, wickedness, badness, iniquity, crime, immorality, transgression, error, unrighteousness, ungodliness, irreligiousness, irreverence, profanity, blasphemy, impiety, sacrilege, *lit.* trespass. ***Ant.*** virtue; good.

▸ *v.* **commit a sin,** do wrong, commit a crime, offend, commit an offense, transgress, break the law, misbehave, transgress, go astray, stray from the straight and narrow, go wrong, fall from grace.

sincere *adj.* **1 genuine,** real, true, honest, unfeigned, unaffected,

bona fide, honest, wholehearted, heartfelt, serious, earnest, fervent. **2 honest,** aboveboard, trustworthy, frank, candid, straightforward, plain-dealing, no-nonsense, genuine, undeceitful, artless, guileless, ingenuous, *inf.* up-front. ***Ant.*** insincere; false; dishonest.

sincerely *adv.* **1 with all sincerity,** wholeheartedly, with all one's heart, earnestly, fervently. **2 genuinely,** really, truly, in truth, without pretense, without feigning, honestly, in good faith.

sinful *adj.* **wrong,** evil, wicked, bad, iniquitous, criminal, immoral, corrupt, unrighteous, ungodly, irreligious, irreverent, profane, blasphemous, impious, sacrilegious, wrongdoing, evildoing, erring, errant, immoral, dissolute, corrupt, depraved.

sing *v.* **1 carol,** trill, warble, pipe, quaver, croon, chant, yodel, chirp. **2 inform,** act as informer, tell tales, rat, *inf.* squeal, blow the whistle, spill the beans, fink.

singe *v.* **scorch,** burn, sear, char, blacken.

single *adj.* **1 one,** one only, sole, lone, solitary, unique, isolated, by itself, exclusive. **2 individual,** particular, separate, distinct. **3 unmarried,** unwed, unwedded, wifeless/husbandless, spouseless, partnerless, a bachelor, unattached, free. *Ant.* double; married.

single-handed *adv.* **by oneself,** alone, on one's own, solo, independently, unaided, unassisted, without help.

single-minded *adj.* **unswerving,** unwavering, undeviating, set, fixed, devoted, dedicated, committed, determined, dogged, tireless, purposeful, obsessive, monomaniacal.

singular *adj.* **1 extraordinary,** exceptional, rare, unusual, unique, remarkable, outstanding, notable, noteworthy, striking, conspicuous, distinctive.
2 strange, unusual, odd, peculiar, curious, queer, bizarre, weird, abnormal, atypical. *Ant.* ordinary; common; run-of-the-mill.

sinister *adj.* **1 evil-looking,** wicked-looking, menacing, threatening, frightening, terrifying. **2 evil,** wicked, bad, villainous, malevolent, criminal, base, vile, vicious, cruel, malicious, malign. **3 ominous,** ill-omened, inauspicious, portentous. *Ant.* benevolent; good; innocent; auspicious.

sink *v.* **1 fall,** drop, descend, go down, go lower, plunge, plummet, slump. **2 go under,** submerge, founder, capsize. **3 collapse,** cave in, fall in. **4 decline,** fade, fail, deteriorate, weaken, grow weak, flag, degenerate, decay, *inf.* go downhill. **5 stoop,** lower oneself, debase oneself, be reduced. **6 lower,** become/get lower, drop, become softer. **7 dig,** bore, drill, excavate. **8 drive,** place, put down, plant, position. **9 destroy,** ruin, cause the downfall of, be the ruin/ruination of, demolish, devastate, *inf.* put the kibosh on. **10 invest,** put, venture, risk. *Ant.* rise; ascend; improve.

sinner *n.* **wrongdoer,** evildoer, criminal, offender, miscreant, transgressor, reprobate, *lit.* trespasser.

sit *v.* **1 sit down,** take a seat, settle down, be seated, *inf.* take a load off, take the load off one's feet. **2 be placed,** be positioned, be situated, rest, perch. **3 set down,** place, put, deposit, rest, position, situate. **4 be convened,** meet, assemble, be in session. **5 babysit.** *Ant.* stand; rise; lift.

site *n.* **1 location,** situation, position, place, locality, setting, scene. **2 ground,** plot, lot.

situate *v.* **place,** position, locate, site.

situation *n.* **1 place,** position, location, site, setting, milieu, environment. **2 circumstances,**

affairs, state, state of affairs, condition, case, predicament, plight, *inf.* kettle of fish, ball game. **3 status,** station, standing, footing, rank, degree. **4 post,** position, place, job, employment.

size *n.* **dimensions,** measurements, proportions, bigness, largeness, magnitude, vastness, bulk, area, expanse, extent.

▸ *v.* **sort,** categorize, classify.

skeptic *n.* **1 questioner,** doubter, doubting Thomas, disbeliever, dissenter, scoffer, cynic. **2 agnostic,** unbeliever, doubter, doubting Thomas.

skeptical *adj.* **doubting,** doubtful, dubious, questioning, distrustful, mistrustful, suspicious, hesitant, disbelieving, misbelieving, incredulous, unconvinced, scoffing, cynical, pessimistic, defeatist. ***Ant.*** certain; credulous.

skepticism *n.* **1 doubt,** doubtfulness, dubiety, distrust, mistrust, suspicion, hesitancy, disbelief, misbelief, incredulity, scoffing, cynicism, pessimism, defeatism. **2 agnosticism,** unbelief, doubt.

sketch *n.* **1 drawing,** preliminary drawing, outline, diagram, plan, representation, delineation. **2 outline,** summary, abstract, précis, résumé, skeleton, bare

bones, draft, plan. **3 short play,** skit, act, scene.

▸ *v.* **draw,** rough out, outline, pencil, represent, delineate, depict.

sketchy *adj.* **1 preliminary,** provisional, unfinished, unrefined, unpolished, rough, crude. **2 slight,** superficial, cursory, perfunctory, meager, skimpy, insufficient, inadequate, imperfect, incomplete, deficient, defective.

skill *n.* **skillfulness,** ability, accomplishment, adeptness, competence, efficiency, adroitness, deftness, dexterity, aptitude, expertise, expertness, art, finesse, experience, professionalism, talent, cleverness, smartness.

skilled *adj.* **1 skillful,** able, good, accomplished, adept, competent, masterly, expert, talented, first-rate. **2 trained,** qualified, expert, experienced, practiced.

skim *v.* **read quickly,** glance at, scan, run one's eye over, flip through, leaf through, thumb through.

skimp *v.* **do hastily,** do carelessly, dash off, cut corners with. ***Ant.*** squander; lavish.

skin *n.* **1 integument,** epidermis, cuticle, corium, derma. **2 hide,** pelt, fleece, fell, integument,

tegument. **3 peel,** rind, hull, husk.
4 film, coating, coat, layer, crust.
▸ *v.* **1 peel,** pare, hull, decorticate.
2 scrape, graze, abrade, cut, bark,
excoriate.

skinny *adj.* **thin,** lean, scrawny,
emaciated, skeletal, *inf.* skin and
bone. **Ant.** fat; plump; obese.

skip *v.* **1 bound,** jump, leap,
spring, hop, bounce, dance,
caper, prance, trip, cavort,
gambol, frisk, bob. **2 move
quickly,** go rapidly, pass quickly,
flit, dart, zoom. **3 omit,** leave out,
pass over, bypass, skim over.
4 play truant from, miss, not
attend, dodge, *inf.* cut, play hooky
from.

skirmish *n.* **battle,** fight, clash,
conflict, encounter,
confrontation, engagement,
combat, contest, tussle,
scrimmage, fracas, affray, melee,
quarrel, altercation, argument,
dispute, *inf.* set-to, scrap.
▸ *v.* **fight,** engage, combat, clash,
collide, have a confrontation,
come to blows, tussle, quarrel,
argue, have a dispute.

skirt *v.* **1 border,** edge, flank. **2 go
around,** walk around, circle,
circumnavigate. **3 evade,** avoid,
dodge, steer clear of, sidestep,
circumvent, bypass.

skittish *adj.* **highly strung,**
nervous, restive, jumpy, fidgety,
excitable, restless, skittery. **Ant.**
calm; laid-back.

sky *n.* **atmosphere,** heaven,
firmament, blue, blue yonder, *lit.*
ether.

slab *n.* **hunk,** chunk, lump, slice,
wedge, piece, portion, plank,
piece.

slack *adj.* **1 not tight,** loose, baggy,
bagging, easy, hanging, flapping.
2 not taut, relaxed, limp, flaccid,
flabby. **3 not taut,** not rigid,
relaxed, flexible, pliant. **4 not
busy,** slow, quiet, inactive,
sluggish. **5 lax,** negligent, remiss,
neglectful, careless, inattentive,
offhand, slapdash, slipshod,
sloppy, disorderly, disorganized.
Ant. tight; taut; meticulous.
▸ *n.* **1 looseness,** play, *inf.* give.
2 surplus, excess, inessentials,
leeway.

slacker *n.* **idler,** shirker, loafer,
dawdler, dallier, layabout,
malingerer, gold brick, *inf.* clock-
watcher.

slam *v.* **1 bang,** bang shut, bang
closed. **2 slap,** bang, thump, hurl,
fling, throw. **3 criticize,** attack,
pillory, vilify, damn, *inf.* slate, pan,
lambaste, run down, blast.
4 defeat utterly, rout, trounce,
thrash, vanquish, conquer, crush,
overwhelm, give a drubbing to,
inf. wipe the floor with, clobber,
slaughter, hammer.

slander *n.* **defamation,** misrepresentation, calumny, libel, aspersion, vilification, verbal abuse, muckraking, smear campaign/campaigning, backbiting, obloquy, disparagement, denigration.
▸ *v.* **defame,** blacken the name of, libel, cast aspersions on, malign, vilify, verbally abuse, muckrake about, smear, slur, backbite, calumniate, disparage, denigrate, decry, run down.

slanderous *adj.* **defamatory,** damaging, libelous, abusive, muckraking, malicious, backbiting, calumnious, disparaging, denigrating.

slang *n.* **jargon,** colloquialism, lingo, cant, argot, *inf.* gobbledygook, technospeak, mumbo-jumbo.

slant *v.* **1 slope,** tilt, be askew, lean, dip, shelve, list. **2 give a slant to,** give a bias to, bias, angle, distort, twist.
▸ *n.* **1 slope,** tilt, dip, leaning, inclination, shelving, listing. **2 bias,** leaning, one-sidedness, prejudice, angle, distortion, twist. **3 angle,** point of view, view, opinion, attitude.

slanting *adj.* **slanted,** aslant, at an angle, sloping, oblique, tilting, tilted, askew, leaning, dipping, shelving, listing, diagonal. *Ant.* straight; plumb.

slap *n.* **smack,** blow, hit, whack, thump, cuff, spank, *inf.* wallop.
▸ *v.* **1 smack,** strike, hit, whack, cuff, spank, *inf.* wallop, swipe, belt. **2 plunk,** plop, slam, bang, fling, hurl, toss, throw. **3 daub,** plaster, spread.

slapdash *adj.* **careless,** slipshod, sloppy, untidy, messy, hasty, hurried, cursory, perfunctory, disorganized, offhand, thoughtless, heedless, negligent, neglectful, remiss. *Ant.* careful; meticulous; painstaking.

slaughter *v.* **1 butcher,** kill, massacre, murder, put to death, put to the sword, slay, assassinate, liquidate, exterminate, annihilate. **2 defeat utterly,** rout, trounce, thrash, vanquish, conquer, crush, overwhelm, give a drubbing to, *inf.* wipe the floor with, clobber, slam, hammer.
▸ *n.* **massacre,** murder, butchery, killing, putting to death, slaying, liquidation, extermination, annihilation, bloodshed, carnage.

slave *n.* **1 bondsman,** bondswoman, bondservant, serf, vassal. **2 drudge,** laborer, menial worker, servant, *lit.* scullion.
▸ *v.* **toil,** drudge, slog, labor, grind, work one's fingers to the bone,

work day and night, work like a Trojan/Turk.

slavery *n.* **1 enslavement,** bondage, servitude, subjugation, thralldom, thrall, serfdom, vassalage. **2 drudgery,** toil, hard labor, grind. *Ant.* freedom; liberty; emancipation.

slavish *adj.* **1 servile,** subservient, obsequious, sycophantic, deferential, groveling, fawning, cringing, menial, abject. **2 imitative,** unoriginal, uninspired, unimaginative.

slay *v.* **1 kill,** murder, slaughter, put to death, assassinate, do away with, *inf.* rub out. **2 amuse/ entertain greatly,** *inf.* have one rolling in the aisles, be a hit with, wow.

sleek *adj.* **1 smooth,** glossy, shiny, lustrous, silken, silky, satiny, burnished. **2 well-fed,** thriving, prosperous, well-groomed, *inf.* well-heeled. *Ant.* dull; rough; unkempt.

sleep *v.* **be asleep,** slumber, doze, nap, drowse, *lit.* rest in the arms of Morpheus, *inf.* snooze, crash, count sheep, catch some Z's, have forty winks, be in the land of Nod.
▸ *n.* **slumber,** doze, nap, rest, siesta, drowse, *inf.* snooze, forty winks, (bit of) shut-eye.

sleepiness *n.* **drowsiness,** tiredness, somnolence, somnolency, languor, languidness, lethargy, sluggishness, inactivity, heaviness, lassitude, torpor, torpidity, comatoseness.

sleepless *adj.* **1 without sleep,** wakeful, restless, disturbed. **2 unsleeping,** wakeful, insomniac.

sleepy *adj.* **1 drowsy,** tired, somnolent, languid, languorous, lethargic, sluggish, inactive, heavy, torpid, comatose. **2 inactive,** quiet, peaceful, slow-moving, slumberous. *Ant.* awake; alert; active.

slender *adj.* **1 slim,** thin, slight, lean, narrow, svelte, willowy, sylphlike. **2 slight,** small, little, meager, scanty, paltry, insubstantial, inadequate, insufficient, deficient, negligible, trifling. **3 small,** slight, slim, faint, remote, feeble, flimsy, tenuous, fragile. *Ant.* fat; substantial; considerable.

sleuth *n.* **detective,** private detective, investigator, private investigator, *inf.* private eye, dick, gumshoe.

slice *n.* **1 piece,** portion, segment, sliver, wedge, chunk, hunk. **2 share,** part, piece, proportion, allotment, allocation.
▸ *v.* **cut up,** cut through, carve, divide, segment, cut, sever, separate.

slick *adj.* **1 smooth,** smooth-running, well-organized, streamlined, efficient, polished. **2 smooth,** glib, fluent, plausible, specious. **3 smooth,** efficient, skillful, deft, adroit, masterly, professional, smart, sharp, shrewd. **4 suave,** urbane, sophisticated, polished, smooth-speaking, glib, smarmy, unctuous. *Ant.* clumsy; inept; unsophisticated.
▸ *v.* **smooth,** flatten, plaster.

slide *v.* **1 slip,** skid, slither, skate, glissade. **2 slip,** glide, slither. **3 pass/move quickly,** slip, steal, slink.

slight *adj.* **1 small,** little, tiny, minute, inappreciable, imperceptible, subtle, modest. **2 little,** minor, unimportant, petty, inconsiderable, insignificant, inconsequential, negligible, irrelevant, trivial, trifling, paltry, meager, scant. **3 slightly built,** slim, slender, small, spare, delicate, frail. **4 fragile,** frail, flimsy, rickety, jerry-built. *Ant.* large; substantial; considerable.
▸ *v.* **snub,** insult, affront, rebuff, treat disrespectfully, give the cold shoulder to, keep at arm's length, disregard, ignore, neglect, take no notice of, disdain, scorn.

slightly *adv.* **a little,** a bit, somewhat, rather, to some degree.

slim *adj.* **1 slender,** thin, slight, lean, narrow, svelte, willowy, sylphlike. **2 slight,** small, slender, faint, remote, feeble, flimsy, tenuous, fragile. *Ant.* fat; thick; substantial; strong.
▸ *v.* **lose weight,** shed weight, lose pounds, reduce, diet, go on a diet.

slime *n.* **sludge,** muck, ooze, mud, *inf.* goo, gunk.

slimy *adj.* **1 sludgy,** mucky, oozy, muddy, slippery, sticky, viscous, mucous. **2 despicable,** contemptible, shameless, detestable, vile, low, scurvy.

sling *v.* **1 toss,** fling, throw, cast, hurl, heave, pitch, lob, *inf.* chuck. **2 hang,** suspend, dangle, swing.
▸ *n.* **support bandage,** support, bandage, strap.

slink *v.* **steal,** sneak, creep, slip, skulk, lurk.

slip[1] *v.* **1 skid,** slither, lose one's footing, lose one's balance. **2 fall,** slide, drop. **3 steal,** slide, creep, sneak, slink, break free from, escape, get away from, break away from, evade, dodge. **4 untie,** unfasten, undo, unbind, untangle, unsnarl. **5 drop,** fall off, decline, deteriorate, degenerate, *inf.* go downhill, go to the dogs.
▸ *n.* **slipup,** mistake, error, blunder, miscalculation, oversight; *inf.* boo-boo.

slip[2] *n.* **1 slip of paper,** piece of

paper; sales slip, receipt.
2 cutting, offshoot, scion, sprout, sprig.

slippery *adj.* **1 slick,** greasy, oily, slimy, icy, glassy, smooth, soapy, *inf.* slippy. **2 shifty,** devious, deceitful, duplicitous, crafty, cunning, foxy, tricky, sneaky, treacherous, perfidious, two-faced, dishonest, false, unreliable, untrustworthy.

slit *v.* **cut,** split open, slash, gash, rip, make an incision in, tear, rend, pierce, knife, lance.
▸ *n.* **cut,** split, slash, gash, rip, incision, tear, rent, fissure, opening.

slither *v.* **slide,** slip, skid.

sliver *n.* **chip,** flake, splinter, shred, fragment, scrap.

slobber *v.* **slaver,** drool, dribble.

slogan *n.* **motto,** logo, catchword, jingle, rallying cry.

slop *v.* **spill,** overflow, splash, slosh, splatter, spatter.

slope *v.* **drop away,** slant, incline, lean, tilt, dip.
▸ *n.* **1 slant,** inclination, angle, skew, tilt, dip, gradient. **2 hill,** hillside, hillock, bank, rise, scarp, mountain.

sloping *adj.* **slanting,** oblique, leaning, inclining, inclined, angled, askew, tilting, dipping. *Ant.* straight; plumb.

sloppy *adj.* **1 watery,** wet, soggy, splashy, slushy, sludgy. **2 careless,** slapdash, slipshod, disorganized, unmethodical, untidy, messy, slovenly, hasty, hurried, offhand. **3 sentimental,** overemotional, mawkish, maudlin, gushing, gushy, effusive, banal, trite, *inf.* soppy, mushy, wet, schmaltzy. *Ant.* careful; meticulous; unemotional.

slot *n.* **1 slit,** crack, hole, opening, aperture, groove, notch. **2 place,** position, niche, space, opening, time, period.

sloth *n.* **laziness,** indolence, idleness, sluggishness, inertia, inactivity, lethargy, languor, slothfulness, torpor, torpidity, fainéance.

slothful *adj.* **lazy,** indolent, idle, sluggish, inert, inactive, lethargic, languid, languorous, torpid, fainéant. *Ant.* industrious; active.

slovenly *adj.* **1 slatternly,** untidy, dirty, unclean, messy, unkempt, disheveled, bedraggled, tousled, rumpled. **2 careless,** sloppy, slapdash, slipshod, disorganized, unmethodical. *Ant.* tidy; neat; careful.

slow *adj.* **1 slow-moving,** unhurried, leisurely, measured, deliberate, ponderous, creeping, dawdling, loitering, lagging, laggard, sluggish, snail-like, tortoiselike. **2 backward,** retarded, slow-witted, dull-witted, dull, unintelligent, stupid, thick, dense, *inf.* dumb, dopey, slow on the uptake. **3 slow-moving,** delayed, dilatory, unpunctual, tardy. **4 long-drawn-out,** drawn-out, time-consuming, protracted, prolonged, interminable. **5 dull,** uninteresting, tedious, boring, tiresome, wearisome, monotonous, uneventful. **6 sleepy,** unprogressive, behind-the-times, backward, stagnant, *inf.* not with it, one-horse. **7 not busy,** slack, quiet, sluggish, slow-moving, dead. **8 reluctant,** hesitant, loath, unwilling, disinclined. *Ant.* fast; quick; brisk; bright.

slowly *adv.* **1 at a slow pace,** unhurriedly, at a leisurely pace, steadily, ploddingly, taking one's time, in one's own good time, with heavy steps, at a snail's pace. **2 at a slow pace,** gradually, bit by bit, by degrees.

sluggish *adj.* **1 inactive,** inert, heavy, lifeless, apathetic, listless, lethargic, languid, languorous, torpid, phlegmatic, indolent, lazy, slothful, drowsy, sleepy. **2 slow,** slow-moving, slack, inactive, stagnant. *Ant.* active; energetic; busy.

slump *n.* **plummeting,** plunge, nosedive, collapse, fall, falling-off, drop, downturn, downswing, slide, decline, decrease, lowering, devaluation, depreciation, depression.
 ▸ *v.* **1 collapse,** sink, fall, subside. **2 plummet,** plunge, nosedive, fall, drop, go down, slide, decline, decrease, devalue, deteriorate, degenerate, *inf.* go downhill, go to the dogs. *Ant.* rise; soar; improve.

slur *v.* **mumble,** stumble over, stammer, drawl.
 ▸ *n.* **1 insult,** slight, aspersion, imputation, slanderous statement, libelous statement, misrepresentation, smear, stain, stigma. **2 insult,** affront, defamation, slander, libel, calumny.

sly *adj.* **1 cunning,** crafty, wily, artful, foxy, tricky, conniving, scheming, devious, underhand, underhanded, shrewd, smart, astute. **2 furtive,** insidious, underhand, underhanded, shifty, stealthy, sneaky, secret, surreptitious, covert, undercover, clandestine. **3 roguish,** impish, mischievous, playful, arch, knowing. *Ant.* frank; honest; aboveboard.

smack[1] *n.* **1 slap,** blow, hit, whack, thump, cuff, punch, spank, buffet, rap, bang, *inf.* wallop, clout, clip, swipe, belt, sock. **2 thud,** thump, bang, wham, *inf.* wallop.

▸ *v.* **slap,** hit, strike, whack, thump, cuff; *inf.* wallop, clout, clip, swipe, belt.

▸ *adv.* **headlong,** right, straight, directly, bang, plumb, exactly, precisely, suddenly.

smack² *n.* **1 taste,** flavor, savor. **2 suggestion,** hint, trace, tinge, touch, overtone, hallmark, resemblance, air.

▸ *v.* phrase: **smack of 1 taste of,** have the flavor of. **2 suggest,** hint at, have overtones of, have the hallmark of, resemble, seem like, have the air of.

small *adj.* **1 little,** tiny, teeny, teeny-weeny, wee, petite, slight, minute, miniature, mini, minuscule, diminutive, undersized, puny, *inf.* pocket-size, pint-sized, teensy-weensy. **2 slight,** minor, unimportant, trifling, trivial, insignificant, inconsequential, inappreciable. **3 humble,** modest, lowly, simple, unpretentious, poor, inferior. **4 narrow,** narrow-minded, mean, petty. ***Ant.*** big; large; substantial.

smart *adj.* **1 clever,** bright, intelligent, gifted, sharp, quick-witted, nimble-witted, shrewd, ingenious. **2 well-dressed,** well turned out, fashionably dressed, fashionable, stylish, modish, elegant, chic, neat, spruce, trim, *inf.* natty, spiffy. **3 brisk,** quick, fast, swift, lively, energetic, spirited, vigorous, jaunty. ***Ant.*** scruffy; stupid; slow.

▸ *v.* **sting,** nip, burn, bite, pain.

smash *v.* **1 break,** shatter, crash, shiver, pulverize, splinter. **2 crash,** demolish, wreck. **3 destroy,** ruin, shatter, devastate.

▸ *n.* **breaking,** shattering, crashing.

smattering *n.* **bit,** modicum, dash, rudiments, elements.

smear *v.* **1 spread,** daub, slap, plaster, smudge, streak, blur. **2 sully,** tarnish, blacken, taint, stain, slur, defame, defile, vilify, slander, libel, calumniate.

▸ *n.* **1 daub,** spot, patch, splotch, smudge, streak. **2 taint,** stain, slur, blot.

smelly *adj.* **smelling,** evil-smelling, foul-smelling, stinking, malodorous, fetid, mephitic, *lit.* noisome.

smirk *v.* **leer,** sneer, simper, grin.

smog *n.* **haze,** fog, pollution.

smoke *v.* **1 smolder,** reek. **2 cure,** dry, preserve.

smoky *adj.* **1 smoke-filled,** reeky, hazy, foggy, smoggy, murky. **2 begrimed,** grimy, smoke-stained, smoke-darkened, sooty. **3 dark,** gray, black.

smolder *v.* **1 smoke,** reek. **2 burn,**

seethe, simmer, fester. **3 seethe,** fume, burn, boil, rage, smart.

smooth *adj.* **1 even,** level, flat, plane, flush, unrough, unwrinkled. **2 glossy,** shiny, sleek, silky, satiny, velvety, polished, burnished. **3 calm,** still, tranquil, flat, glassy, mirrorlike. **4 easy,** effortless, trouble-free, simple, plain sailing. **5 steady,** regular, rhythmic, uninterrupted, flowing, fluid. **6 soft,** soothing, mellow, dulcet, mellifluous, melodious, musical. **7 clean-shaven,** smooth-shaven, shaven, hairless. **8 smooth-tongued,** suave, urbane, sophisticated, courteous, gracious, glib, persuasive, slick, oily, ingratiating, unctuous, *inf.* smarmy. ***Ant.*** uneven; rough; irregular.
▸ *v.* **1 level,** even, flatten, plane, press down, steamroll. **2 ease,** soothe, pacify, calm, tranquilize, alleviate, assuage, appease, palliate. **3 get rid of,** remove, eliminate. **4 ease,** make easy/ easier, facilitate, clear the way for, pave the way for, open the door for, expedite, assist, aid, help, help along.

smother *v.* **1 suffocate,** stifle, asphyxiate, choke. **2 overwhelm,** shower, inundate, envelop, surround. **3 extinguish,** dampen, damp down, put out, snuff out, stamp out. **4 stifle,** muffle, repress, suppress, keep back, conceal, hide.

smudge *n.* **dirty mark,** mark, spot, smear, streak, stain, blotch, blot, blur, smut, splotch.
▸ *v.* **mark,** dirty, soil, blacken, smear, streak, daub, stain, besmirch, blur.

smug *adj.* **self-satisfied,** complacent, content, pleased with oneself, superior, proud of oneself, conceited.

snack *n.* **light meal,** refreshments, bite, nibbles, tidbit, *inf.* bite to eat, little something.
▸ *v.* **eat between meals,** nibble, munch, *inf.* graze.

snag *n.* **1 catch,** drawback, hitch, stumbling block, obstacle, disadvantage, inconvenience, unseen problem, problem, complication. **2 rip,** tear, run, hole.
▸ *v.* **catch,** rip, tear.

snap *v.* **1 break,** break into two, fracture, splinter, separate, come apart, crack. **2 have a nervous breakdown,** break down, collapse, lose one's mind, lose one's reason, go mad, go insane. **3 crack,** click, crackle. **4 bite,** gnash the teeth. **5 hurry,** hasten, rush, race.
▸ *n.* **1 crack,** click, crackle. **2 bite,**

gnashing, clenching. **3 spell,** period, time, stretch, interval. **4 liveliness,** animation, sparkle, verve, vitality, vivacity, spirit, vigor, sprightliness, zest, *inf.* pizzazz, zip, zing, pep, oomph.

snappy *adj.* **1 irritable,** irascible, ill-tempered, cross, touchy, testy, crabbed, crotchety, grumpy, grouchy. **2 smart,** fashionable, up-to-date, stylish, chic, up-to-the-minute, modish, dapper, *inf.* natty, spiffy, trendy.

snare *v.* **trap,** entrap, catch, springe, net, ensnare, trap, catch, get hold of, seize, capture.
▸ *n.* **1 trap,** gin, springe, net, noose. **2 trap,** pitfall, trick, catch, danger, hazard, peril.

snatch *v.* **1 seize,** grab, take hold of, pluck, wrest, wring, secure. **2 grab,** steal, make off with, appropriate, *inf.* nab, swipe. **3 kidnap,** abduct, grab, hold for ransom, take as hostage.
▸ *n.* **1 grab,** pluck, grip, clutch. **2 fragment,** snippet, bit, scrap, piece, part. **3 spell,** period, time, fit, bout.

sneak *v.* **1 steal,** creep, slip, slide, slink, sidle. **2 creep,** skulk, lurk, prowl, pad. **3 snatch,** take, catch.
▸ *n.* **rascal,** rogue, scoundrel, cheater, cheat.

sneaking *adj.* **secret,** private, hidden, concealed, unexpressed, unvoiced, undisclosed, undivulged, unconfessed, unavowed.

sneer *v.* **curl one's lip,** smirk, snicker, snigger.
▸ *n.* **1 smirk,** snicker. **2 jeer,** jibe, taunt, insult, slight.

sniff *v.* **1 snuffle,** inhale, breathe in. **2 smell,** detect the smell of, catch the scent of, get a whiff of.
▸ *n.* **1 snuffle,** sniffle. **2 smell,** scent, whiff.

snip *v.* **cut,** cut into, nick, slit, notch, incise, clip, dock, trim, crop, prune.
▸ *n.* **1 cut,** nick, slit, notch, incision. **2 scrap,** cutting, bit, piece, fragment, remnant, tatter.

snippet *n.* **bit,** piece, scrap, fragment, particle, shred, snatch.

snivel *v.* **1 weep,** cry, sob, whimper, *inf.* blubber. **2 sniffle,** snuffle, run at the nose, have a runny/running nose.

snobbish *adj.* **snobby,** arrogant, proud, condescending, haughty, disdainful, supercilious, patronizing, *inf.* snooty, uppity, stuck-up, hoity-toity.

snoop *v.* phrase: **snoop into pry into,** spy on, interfere with, meddle with, *inf.* poke one's nose into.
▸ *n.* **snooper,** pryer, busybody, interferer, meddler.

snooze *v.* **doze,** nap, catnap,

drowse, sleep, slumber, *inf.* take forty winks, catch some Z's.

▸ *n.* **doze,** nap, catnap, siesta, sleep, slumber, *inf.* forty winks.

snub *v.* **ignore,** disregard, take no notice of, shun, rebuff, repulse, spurn, slight, give the cold shoulder to, cold-shoulder, insult, affront, *inf.* cut dead, give the brush-off to, give a slap in the face to, put down.

▸ *n.* **rebuff,** repulse, slight, insult, affront, *inf.* brush-off, slap in the face, put-down.

snug *adj.* **1 cozy,** comfortable, warm, homelike, homely, sheltered, *inf.* comfy. **2 close-fitting,** tight, skintight.

snuggle *v.* **nestle,** cuddle, curl up, nuzzle.

soak *v.* **1 drench,** wet through, saturate, make sopping. **2 steep,** immerse, souse. **3 permeate,** penetrate, infuse, imbue.

soaking *adj.* **soaking wet,** soaked (to the skin), wet through, drenched, sodden, saturated, sopping wet, dripping wet, wringing wet, streaming wet.

soar *v.* **1 fly,** take flight, take off, ascend, climb, rise, mount. **2 rise/increase/climb rapidly,** spiral.

sob *v.* **weep,** cry, shed tears, blubber, snivel, howl, bawl, *inf.* boohoo.

sober *adj.* **1 abstemious,** teetotal, abstinent, temperate, moderate, *inf.* on the wagon, dry, having signed the pledge. **2 serious,** solemn, thoughtful, grave, earnest, calm, composed, sedate, staid, dignified, steady, levelheaded, self-controlled, strict, puritanical, important, crucial, weighty, ponderous. **3 factual,** low-key, dispassionate, objective, rational, logical, well-considered, circumspect, lucid, clear. **4 dark,** dark-colored, somber, quiet, restrained, drab, severe, austere. *Ant.* drunk; lighthearted; flamboyant.

sociable *adj.* **social,** friendly, affable, cordial, neighborly, companionable, gregarious, convivial, communicative, conversable, genial, outgoing, approachable, accessible. *Ant.* unsociable; unfriendly; uncommunicative; solitary.

social *adj.* **1 community,** civil, civic, public, societal. **2 entertainment,** recreational, amusement. **3 friendly,** affable, cordial, companionable, gregarious, convivial, communicative.

socialize *v.* **be social,** be sociable, mix, mingle, keep company, fraternize, consent, hobnob, get together, get out and about.

society *n.* **1 mankind,** humankind, humanity, civilization, the public, the general public, the people, the population, the world at large, the community. **2 community,** group, culture, civilization. **3 high society,** polite society, the aristocracy, the gentry, the nobility, the upper classes, the elite, the smart set, the beau monde, haut monde, *inf.* the privileged classes, the upper crust, the top drawer. **4 company,** companionship, fellowship, friendship, camaraderie. **5 association,** club, group, band, circle, body, fraternity, brotherhood, sisterhood, league, union, alliance, federation.

sodden *adj.* **soaked,** soaking wet, drenched, saturated, sopping, dripping, wringing wet, soggy, boggy, swampy, waterlogged.

soft *adj.* **1 mushy,** squashy, doughy, *inf.* gooey. **2 spongy,** swampy, boggy, miry, quaggy. **3 pliable,** pliant, supple, elastic, flexible, ductile, malleable, plastic. **4 smooth,** velvety, cushiony, fleecy, downy, leathery, furry, silky, silken, satiny, *inf.* like a baby's bottom. **5 gentle,** light, mild, moderate, calm, balmy, delicate. **6 low,** faint, dim, shaded, subdued, muted, mellow. **7 pale,** light, pastel, subdued, muted, understated, restrained, dull. **8 hushed,** whispered, murmured, stifled, inaudible, low, faint, quiet, mellow, melodious, mellifluous. **9 vague,** blurred, fuzzy, ill-defined, indistinct, flowing, fluid. **10 sympathetic,** kind, gentle, soothing, tender, affectionate, loving, warm, sweet, sentimental, romantic, *inf.* mushy, slushy, schmaltzy. **11 easygoing,** tolerant, forgiving, forbearing, lenient, indulgent, permissive, liberal, lax. **12 tender-hearted,** docile, sensitive, spineless, feeble. **13 flabby,** flaccid, limp, out of condition. **14 easy,** comfortable, cozy, pampered, privileged, indulged, *inf.* cushy. **15 feebleminded,** simple, silly, *inf.* daft, nutty. **Ant.** firm; hard; harsh; strict.

soften *v.* **1 ease,** cushion, temper, mitigate, assuage. **2 abate,** moderate, lessen, diminish, calm down. **3 modify,** moderate, temper, tone down.

soggy *adj.* **wet,** soaking, saturated, sodden, sopping wet, boggy, swampy, waterlogged.

soil *n.* **1 earth,** ground, clay, dirt. **2** land, country, terra firma.
▸ *v.* **dirty,** stain, muddy, spot, smear, splash, smudge, sully, taint, besmirch, blot.

soldier *n.* **fighter,** foot soldier, infantryman, warrior, trooper, warmonger, *inf.* GI, grunt, cannon fodder.

solemn *adj.* **1 serious,** grave, important, profound, formal. **2 dignified,** ceremonious, stately, majestic, imposing, impressive, grand. **3 serious,** somber, unsmiling, pensive, thoughtful, gloomy, glum, grim, *inf.* moody, blue. **4 earnest,** sincere, honest, genuine, committed, heartfelt. *Ant.* frivolous; lighthearted; insincere.

solicit *v.* **1 ask for,** request, apply for, seek, beg, plead for, crave. **2 ask,** beg, beseech, implore, entreat, petition, importune, supplicate. **3 work as a prostitute,** engage in prostitution, accost people, make sexual advances, *inf.* hustle.

solicitous *adj.* **1 concerned,** caring, attentive, considerate, anxious, worried, nervous, uneasy, apprehensive. **2 eager,** keen, anxious, desirous, enthusiastic, avid, zealous.

solid *adj.* **1 firm,** hard, thick, dense, concrete, compact, compressed, condensed. **2 complete,** pure, unalloyed, unmixed, unadulterated, genuine. **3 sound,** substantial, strong, sturdy, stout, durable, well-built, well-constructed, stable. **4 sound,** well-founded, well-grounded, concrete, valid, reasonable, logical, cogent, weighty, authoritative, convincing, plausible, reliable. **5 reliable,** dependable, trustworthy, stable, steadfast. **6 sensible,** levelheaded, down-to-earth, decent, law-abiding, upright, upstanding, worthy. **7 sound,** worthy, staid, unexciting, unimaginative, uninspired. **8 financially sound,** sound, solvent, creditworthy, in good standing, in the black, secure. **9 continuous,** uninterrupted, unbroken, undivided. **10 unanimous,** united, undivided, of one mind, of the same mind, in unison, consentient. *Ant.* liquid; hollow; flimsy; unsound.

solidarity *n.* **unity,** unification, union, unanimity, singleness of purpose, like-mindedness, team spirit, camaraderie, harmony, esprit de corps.

solidify *v.* **harden,** go hard, set, gel, jell, congeal, cake.

solitary *adj.* **1 lonely,** lonesome, companionless, friendless, antisocial, unsocial, unsociable, withdrawn, reclusive, cloistered, introverted, hermitical. **2 lonely,** remote, out-of-the-way, isolated, secluded, hidden, concealed,

private, unfrequented, unvisited, sequestered, retired, desolate.
3 lone, single, sole, alone, by oneself/itself. *Ant.* sociable; gregarious; busy.

▸ *n.* **loner,** lone wolf, introvert, recluse, hermit, eremite, anchorite, stylite, cenobite.

solitude *n.* **loneliness,** remoteness, isolation, seclusion, privacy, retirement, desolation.

solution *n.* **1 answer,** result, key, resolution. **2 solving,** resolving, explanation, clarification, elucidation, unraveling, unfolding. **3 suspension,** emulsion, mixture, mix, blend, compound.

solve *v.* **find the solution to,** answer, find the answer to, resolve, work out, figure out, fathom, find the key to, decipher, clear up, get to the bottom of, unravel, disentangle, unfold, *inf.* crack.

solvent *adj.* **financially sound,** debt-free, creditworthy, *inf.* in the black.

somber *adj.* **1 dark,** dark-colored, dull, dull-colored, drab, dingy. **2 gloomy,** depressed, sad, melancholy, dismal, doleful, mournful, joyless, cheerless, lugubrious, funereal, sepulchral. *Ant.* bright; cheerful.

somehow *adv.* **by some means,** in some way, in one way or another, no matter how, come what may, by hook or by crook, *inf.* come hell or high water.

sometimes *adv.* **occasionally,** on occasion, on occasions, now and then, now and again, from time to time, once in a while, every so often, off and on.

somnolent *adj.* **1 sleepy,** drowsy, half-asleep, heavy-eyed, dozy, groggy, comatose, *inf.* dopey. **2 soporific,** sleep-inducing.

sonorous *adj.* **1 deep,** rich, full, round, resonant, resounding, booming, ringing, reverberating, vibrating, pulsating. **2 impressive,** imposing, majestic, lofty, high-sounding, grandiloquent, declamatory, orotund, euphuistic, fustian.

soon *adv.* **1 shortly,** in a short time, in a little while, before long, in a minute, in a moment, any minute, in the near future, in a twinkling, in the twinkling of an eye, *inf.* before you know it, before you can say Jack Robinson, pronto, in two shakes of a lamb's tale. **2 quickly,** promptly, speedily, punctually, early.

soothe *v.* **1 quiet,** calm, calm down, pacify, settle, settle down, hush, lull, tranquilize, mollify. **2 ease,** assuage, alleviate, allay, moderate, mitigate, temper,

palliate, soften, lessen, reduce.
Ant. agitate; disturb; aggravate.

sophisticated *adj.* **1 worldly-
wise,** worldly, experienced,
seasoned, suave, urbane, cultured,
cultivated, polished, refined,
elegant, stylish, cosmopolitan,
blasé. **2 advanced,** highly
developed, ultramodern,
complex, complicated, elaborate,
intricate. *Ant.* unsophisticated;
naïve; crude.

sorcerer *n.* **magician,** wizard,
enchanter, warlock, necromancer,
magus, thaumaturgist.

sorcery *n.* **black magic,** magic,
witchcraft, witchery, wizardry,
necromancy, black art,
enchantment, thaumaturgy.

sordid *adj.* **1 vile,** foul, base, low,
debased, degenerate,
dishonorable, disreputable,
despicable, ignominious, ignoble,
abhorrent, abominable. **2 mean,**
greedy, avaricious, covetous,
grasping, mercenary, miserly,
niggardly, stingy. **3 filthy,** dirty,
foul, unclean, grimy, squalid,
shabby, seedy, seamy, slummy,
sleazy. *Ant.* immaculate;
honorable; noble; generous.

sore *adj.* **1 painful,** in pain, aching,
hurting, tender, inflamed, raw,
smarting, stinging, burning,
irritated, bruised, wounded,
injured. **2 distressed,** upset,
resentful, vexed, aggrieved,
offended, hurt, pained, annoyed,
angry, irritated, irked, nettled, *inf.*
peeved. **3 dire,** urgent, pressing,
desperate, critical, acute, extreme.
▸ *n.* **wound,** scrape, abrasion, cut,
laceration, graze, boil, abscess,
swelling.

sorrow *n.* **1 sadness,**
unhappiness, grief, misery,
distress, heartache, heartbreak,
anguish, suffering, pain, woe,
affliction, wretchedness,
dejection, heaviness of heart,
desolation, depression,
disconsolateness, mourning.
2 trouble, worry, woe, misfortune,
affliction, trial, tribulation. *Ant.*
joy; delight; pleasure.

sorrowful *adj.* **1 sad,** unhappy,
tearful, heartbroken, wretched,
woebegone, miserable, dejected,
desolated, depressed,
disconsolate, mournful, doleful,
melancholy, lugubrious. **2 sorry,**
wretched, miserable, pitiful,
piteous, pitiable, moving,
affecting, pathetic, heart-rending,
deplorable, lamentable.

sorry *adj.* **1 regretful,** apologetic,
repentant, penitent, remorseful,
contrite, ashamed, conscience-
stricken, guilt-ridden, in sackcloth
and ashes, compunctious.
2 sympathetic, pitying, full of
pity, compassionate, moved,

commiserative, empathetic. **3 sad,**
unhappy, distressed, grieved,
regretful, sorrowful, miserable,
wretched. **4** wretched, miserable,
pitiful, piteous. ***Ant.*** impenitent;
unrepentant; shameless.

sort *n.* **1 kind,** type, variety, class,
category, style, group, set, genre,
genus, family, order, breed, make,
brand, stamp. **2 person,**
individual, soul, *inf.* fellow, guy,
character, customer.
  ▸ *v.* **1 classify,** class, categorize,
catalog, grade, rank, group,
divide, arrange, order, put in
order, organize, assort,
systematize, methodize. **2 clear
up,** tidy up, put straight, put in
order, deal with.

sortie *n.* **sally,** foray, charge, rush,
onrush, raid, attack.

soul *n.* **1 spirit,** psyche, inner self,
true being, vital force, animating
principle. **2 personification,**
embodiment, incarnation,
essence, epitome. **3 person,**
human being, being, individual,
creature. **4 essential part,** essence,
heart, core, center, vital force,
driving force. **5 feeling,** emotion,
intensity, fervor, ardor, vitality,
animation, vivacity, energy,
inspiration.

sound[1] *n.* **1 noise,** utterance, cry,
music, note, chord. **2 impression,**
idea, thought, concept. **3 hearing,**
distance, earshot, range. ***Ant.***
silence; hush.
  ▸ *v.* **1 play,** blow. **2 resound,**
reverberate, resonate. **3 operate,**
set off, ring. **4 pronounce,** utter,
voice, enunciate, articulate,
vocalize. **5 utter,** express, voice,
pronounce, declare, announce.

sound[2] *adj.* **1 healthy,** in good
health, in good condition,
physically fit, disease-free, hale
and hearty, undamaged,
uninjured, unimpaired, in good
shape, in fine fettle. **2 solid,**
substantial, sturdy, well-
constructed, intact, whole,
undamaged, unimpaired. **3 solid,**
well-founded, well-grounded,
concrete, valid, reasonable,
logical, cogent, weighty,
authoritative, convincing,
plausible, reliable, orthodox.
4 reliable, dependable,
trustworthy, fair, good, sensible,
intelligent, wise, judicious,
sagacious, astute, shrewd,
perceptive, foresighted. **5 solvent,**
creditworthy, in good financial
standing, in the black, solid,
secure. **6 deep,** undisturbed,
unbroken, uninterrupted,
untroubled, peaceful. **7 thorough,**
complete, without reserve,
unqualified, out-and-out, drastic,
severe. ***Ant.*** unsound; unhealthy;
flimsy.

sound³ *v.* **plumb,** fathom, probe.

sour *adj.* **1 acid,** acidy, acidlike, acetic, acidulous, tart, bitter, sharp, vinegary, vinegarlike, unpleasant, distasteful, pungent. **2 turned,** curdled, fermented, rancid, bad. **3 embittered,** nasty, unpleasant, disagreeable, bad-tempered, ill-tempered, ill-natured, sharp-tongued, irritable, crotchety, cross, crabbed, testy, touchy, snappish, peevish, grumpy, *inf.* grouchy. **Ant.** sweet; fresh; amiable.
  ▸ *v.* **embitter,** make bitter, disenchant, alienate, *inf.* turn off.

source *n.* **1 wellspring,** wellhead, headspring. **2 origin,** derivation, commencement, beginning, start, rise, cause, wellspring, fount, fountainhead, provenance, author, originator, begetter. **3 reference,** authority, informant.

sovereign *n.* **ruler,** monarch, supreme ruler, king, queen, emperor, empress, czar, crowned head, potentate.
  ▸ *adj.* **1 supreme,** absolute, unlimited, chief, paramount, principle, dominant, predominant, ruling. **2 independent,** self-ruling, self-governing, autonomous. **3 ruling,** kingly, queenly, princely, royal, regal, majestic, noble. **4 efficient,** effective, efficacious, effectual, excellent, outstanding.

sow *v.* **1 scatter,** disperse, strew, bestrew, disseminate, distribute, spread, broadcast, plant. **2 implant,** plant, lodge, initiate, instigate, foster, promote, foment, invite.

space *n.* **1 room,** expanse, extent, capacity, area, volume, amplitude, spaciousness, scope, elbowroom, latitude, margin, leeway. **2 interval,** gap, opening, interstice, break. **3 blank,** empty space, gap. **4 empty seat,** seat, place, berth, accommodation. **5 unoccupied area,** empty area, expanse, stretch, sweep. **6 time,** duration, period, span, stretch, interval. **7 empty space,** the blue, the vacuum, the void. **8 outer space,** the universe, the galaxy, the solar system, infinity.
  ▸ *v.* **place at intervals,** arrange, line up, range, order.

spacious *adj.* **1 roomy,** commodious, capacious, sizable, large, big, ample. **2 extensive,** broad, wide, expansive, ample, large, vast. **Ant.** cramped; close.

span *n.* **1 length,** extent, reach, stretch, spread, distance. **2 time,** duration, period, space, stretch, interval.
  ▸ *v.* **1 extend over,** stretch across, cover, range over. **2 bridge,** cross,

traverse, pass over, arch over, vault over.

spare *adj.* **1 extra,** additional, reserve, supplementary, auxiliary, surplus, supernumerary. **2 free,** leisure, unoccupied. **3 lean,** thin, slim, slender, without an ounce of fat, skinny, wiry, lank, *inf.* skin and bones. **4 meager,** frugal, scanty, skimpy, modest. **5 sparing,** economical, frugal. *Ant.* essential; occupied; fat.
▸ *v.* **1 afford,** part with, give, provide. **2 dispense with,** do without, manage without, get along without. **3 be merciful to,** show mercy to, be lenient to, deal leniently with, pardon, leave unpunished, *inf.* let off, go easy on. **4 save,** protect, guard, defend.

sparing *adj.* **economical,** frugal, thrifty, careful, saving, prudent, cautious, parsimonious, niggardly, *inf.* stingy, tight-fisted. *Ant.* extravagant; lavish.

spark *n.* **1 flicker,** flash, flare, glint. **2 bit,** flicker, glimmer, trace, scrap, vestige, touch, hint, suggestion, suspicion, jot, whit, iota. **3 sparkle,** vivacity, liveliness, animation, energy, spirit, enthusiasm, wit.

sparkle *v.* **1 twinkle,** flicker, shimmer, flash, glitter, glint, blink, wink, dance, shine, gleam, glow, coruscate. **2 be sparkling,** be vivacious, be lively, be animated, be ebullient, be effervescent, be witty, be brilliant. **3 bubble,** give off bubbles, effervesce.
▸ *n.* **1 twinkle,** flicker, shimmer, flash, glitter, glint, blinking, winking, dancing, shining, gleam, glow, coruscation. **2 vivacity,** liveliness, life, animation, energy, vitality, spirit, enthusiasm, dash, élan, panache, *inf.* pizzazz, vim, zip, zing.

sparse *adj.* scanty, meager, slight, thinly distributed. *Ant.* abundant; plentiful.

spartan *adj.* **austere,** harsh, frugal, stringent, rigorous, strict, severe, bleak, grim, ascetic, abstemious, self-denying.

spasm *n.* **1 contraction,** convulsion, cramp, twitch. **2 fit,** paroxysm, convulsion, attack, bout, seizure, outburst, access.

spasmodic *adj.* **intermittent,** fitful, irregular, sporadic, erratic, periodic, recurring, recurrent.

spatter *v.* **bespatter,** splash, spray, shower, daub.

speak *v.* **1 utter,** voice, express, say, pronounce, articulate, enunciate, state, tell. **2 give a speech,** give a talk, talk, lecture, deliver an address, hold forth, discourse, orate, harangue, sermonize, *inf.* spout, spiel, speechify. **3 mean,** convey, signify, impart, suggest, denote, indicate, demonstrate.

speaker *n.* **public speaker,** speech-maker, lecturer, orator, declaimer, haranguer, demagogue, *inf.* spieler.

spearhead *n.* **vanguard,** van, forefront, driving force.
▸ *v.* **lead,** head, be in the van/vanguard of, set in motion, initiate, launch, pioneer.

special *adj.* **1 exceptional,** remarkable, unusual, rare, out-of-the-ordinary, extraordinary, singular, distinctive, notable, outstanding, unique. **2 specific,** particular, individual, distinctive, exact, precise, definite. **3 especial,** extra special, particular, exceptional, out-of-the-ordinary. **4 significant,** momentous, memorable, festive, gala, red-letter. **5 specific,** particular, custom-built. **6 particular,** chief, main, major, primary. *Ant.* ordinary; usual; run-of-the-mill.

specialist *n.* **expert,** authority, professional, consultant, master.

specialty *n.* **1 area of specialization,** field of study. **2 distinctive feature,** forte, métier, talent, gift, pièce de résistance, claim to fame. **3 specialty of the house,** house special, chef's special.

species *n.* **sort,** kind, type, variety, class, category, group, breed, genre.

specific *adj.* **1 well-defined,** clear-cut, unambiguous, unequivocal, exact, precise, explicit, express, detailed. **2 particular,** specified, fixed, set, determined, distinct, definite. *Ant.* vague; general.

specify *v.* **state,** mention, name, stipulate, define, set out, itemize, designate, detail, list, spell out, enumerate, particularize, catalog, be specific about.

specimen *n.* **sample,** representative, example, illustration, exemplification, instance, type, exhibit.

specious *adj.* **plausible,** seemingly correct, misleading, deceptive, fallacious, unsound, casuistic, sophistic.

speck *n.* **1 spot,** fleck, dot, speckle, stain, mark, smudge, blemish. **2 particle,** bit, piece, atom, iota, grain, trace.

speckled *adj.* **mottled,** flecked, spotted, dotted, dappled, brindled, stippled.

spectacle *n.* **1 sight,** vision, scene, picture. **2 display,** show, exhibition, pageant, parade, extravaganza. **3 laughingstock,** fool, curiosity.

spectacular *adj.* **1 striking,** picturesque, impressive, magnificent, splendid, eye-catching, breathtaking, glorious, dazzling, sensational, stunning, dramatic, *inf.* out of this world. **2 striking,** impressive, remarkable, outstanding, extraordinary, sensational, dramatic, astonishing, singular. *Ant.* ordinary; run-of-the-mill; simple.

▸ *n.* **extravaganza,** display, exhibition, performance.

spectator *n.* **watcher,** beholder, viewer, observer, onlooker, looker-on, witness, eyewitness, bystander, *inf.* rubberneck.

specter *n.* **apparition,** ghost, phantom, spirit, vision, revenant, *inf.* spook.

speculate *v.* **conjecture,** theorize, hypothesize, guess, take a guess, surmise.

speech *n.* **1 communication,** talk, conversation, discussion, dialogue, colloquy. **2 diction,** articulation, enunciation, pronunciation. **3 talk,** lecture, address, discourse, oration, sermon, harangue, diatribe, tirade, philippic. **4 language,** tongue, idiom, dialect, parlance, *inf.* lingo. **5 utterance,** remarks, comments, observations, declarations, assertions.

speechless *adj.* **1 struck dumb,** dumbstruck, dumbfounded, astounded, thunderstruck.

2 tongue-tied, inarticulate, dumb, struck dumb. **3 silent,** unspoken, unexpressed, unsaid, unvoiced, tacit. *Ant.* loquacious; verbose.

speed *n.* **rapidity,** swiftness, quickness, fastness, haste, hurry, hurriedness, expeditiousness, expedition, alacrity, promptness, fleetness, celerity, velocity.

▸ *v.* **1 hurry,** hasten, make haste, rush, race, dash, sprint, scurry, scamper, charge, *inf.* tear. **2 drive too fast,** break the speed limit, exceed the speed limit, *inf.* put one's pedal to the metal, step on it. **3 expedite,** hasten, hurry up, accelerate, advance, further, forward, facilitate, promote, boost, aid, assist.

speedy *adj.* **rapid,** swift, quick, fast, expeditious, fleet, high-speed, prompt, immediate, express. *Ant.* slow; leisurely; dilatory.

spell[1] *v.* **mean,** signify, amount to, add up to, signal, denote, result in, cause, bespeak, portend, augur, presage.

spell[2] *n.* **1 time,** period, interval, stretch, course, extent, span, patch. **2 bout,** fit, access. **3 turn,** stint, term, stretch, shift.

spell[3] *n.* **1 incantation,** conjuration, charm. **2 trance,** state of enchantment, entrancement, enthrallment, bewitchment. **3 irresistible influence,** magnetism, allure, charm, attraction, pull, draw, enticement, beguilement.

spellbound *adj.* **riveted,** entranced, enthralled, enraptured, transported, rapt, bewitched, fascinated, captivated, mesmerized, hypnotized, *inf.* hooked.

spend *v.* **1 pay out,** lay out, expend, disburse, *inf.* fork out, shell out, dish out. **2 occupy,** fill, take up, use up, pass, while away. **3 use,** use up, employ, put in, apply, devote. **4 use up,** consume, exhaust, finish off, deplete, drain. *Ant.* save; keep; hoard.

spendthrift *n.* **squanderer,** prodigal, profligate, wastrel, *inf.* big spender.
▸ *adj.* **extravagant,** thriftless, squandering, prodigal, profligate, wasteful, improvident.

spent *adj.* **1 used up,** consumed, exhausted, finished, depleted, drained, emptied, *inf.* played-out, burnt-out. **2 exhausted,** worn-out, tired-out, fatigued, weary, wearied, weakened, *inf.* all in, done in, dead on one's feet, bushed, fagged out.

sphere *n.* **1 globe,** ball, orb, globule. **2 planet,** star, moon, celestial body. **3 area,** field, range, scope, extent, compass,

jurisdiction. **4 field,** discipline, specialty, domain, realm, province. **5 social class,** social level, social stratum, station, rank, status, social circumstances, walk of life.

spherical *adj.* **globe-shaped,** globular, globoid, round, orblike, orbicular.

spice *n.* **1 flavoring,** seasoning, herb, condiment, relish. **2 spiciness,** flavoring, flavor, seasoning, piquancy, pungency, relish, tang, bite, zest, savor, *inf.* punch, kick. **3 excitement,** interest, color, piquancy, zest, gusto, pep, *inf.* zip, zing.

spicy *adj.* **1 spiced,** seasoned, flavorsome, well-seasoned, sharp, tart, hot, peppery, piquant, pungent. **2 lively,** spirited, suggestive, risqué, racy, off-color, improper, indecent, offensive, *inf.* raunchy. *Ant.* bland; tasteless; boring.

spill *v.* **1 pour,** pour out, flow, overflow, brim over, run over, slop over, well over. **2 reveal,** disclose, divulge, leak, make known, *inf.* let out, blab.
▸ *n.* **fall,** tumble, *inf.* header, nosedive.

spin *v.* **1 revolve,** rotate, turn, turn around, circle, whirl, gyrate, wheel, twirl, twist, swivel, pirouette. **2 go around,** whirl,

reel, swim, be giddy. **3 tell,** unfold, relate, narrate, recount, concoct, make up, invent, fabricate.
▸ *n.* **1 turn,** revolution, rotation, whirl, gyration. **2 drive,** ride, trip, run, jaunt, journey, outing, turn, *inf.* joyride.

spine *n.* **1 spinal column,** vertebrae, vertebral column, backbone, dorsum. **2 mettle,** grit, pluck, pluckiness, spirit, firmness of purpose, determination, resolution, fortitude, courage, braveness, bravery, valor, manliness. **3 needle,** spike, barb, quill.

spiral *adj.* **coiled,** corkscrew, winding, twisting, whorled, helical, cochlear, cochleate, voluted.
▸ *n.* **coil,** twist, whorl, corkscrew, wreath, curlicue, helix, volute.

spirit *n.* **1 soul,** psyche, inner self, ego. **2 breath of life,** vital spark, animating principle, life force. **3 apparition,** ghost, phantom, specter, wraith, revenant, *inf.* spook. **4 character,** temperament, temper, disposition, humor, complexion, quality, constitution, makeup. **5 attitude,** way, state of mind, mood, frame of mind, point of view, reaction, feeling, humor. **6 prevailing tendency,** motivating force, animating principle, dominating characteristic, ethos, essence, quintessence, embodiment, personification, quiddity. **7 courage,** bravery, braveness, valor, mettle, pluck, grit, pluckiness, willpower, motivation, backbone, stouteartedness, manliness, vigor, energy, determination, firmness of purpose, resoluteness, *inf.* guts, spunk. **8 animation,** liveliness, vivacity, enthusiasm, fervor, fire, passion, energy, verve, zest, dash, élan, *inf.* pizzazz, zing, zip. **9 implication,** underlying message, essence, gist, tenor, drift, meaning, sense, purport.

spirited *adj.* **1 courageous,** brave, valiant, valorous, heroic, mettlesome, plucky, gritty, determined, resolute. **2 animated,** lively, vivacious, enthusiastic, fervent, fiery, passionate, energetic. *Ant.* timid; apathetic; lifeless.

spiritual *adj.* **1 nonmaterial,** incorporeal, ethereal, intangible, otherworldly, unworldly.
2 religious, sacred, divine, holy, nonsecular, churchly, ecclesiastic, devotional, devout. *Ant.* material; corporeal; secular.

spit *v.* **1 expectorate,** hawk.
2 discharge, issue, eject. **3 hiss,** rasp, snort.
▸ *n.* **spittle,** saliva, sputum.

spite *n.* **malice,** maliciousness, ill-will, malevolence, venom, malignance, hostility, evil, resentment, resentfulness, snideness, rancor, grudgingness, envy, hate, hatred, vengeance, vengefulness, vindictiveness. *Ant.* benevolence; goodwill; charity.
▸ *v.* **injure,** harm, hurt, wound, annoy, harass, irritate, vex, offend, provoke, peeve, pique, thwart, foil, frustrate.

spiteful *adj.* **malicious,** ill-natured, malevolent, venomous, poisonous, malignant, malign, hostile, resentful, snide, rancorous, grudging, envious, vengeful, vindictive, splenetic, *inf.* bitchy, catty.

splash *v.* **1 spatter,** sprinkle, spray, shower, splatter, squirt, slosh, slop, bespatter. **2 dash,** beat, batter, buffet, break, wash, surge. **3 paddle,** wade, wallow, dabble. **4 blazon,** display, exhibit, plaster, publicize, broadcast, headline, flaunt, trumpet.
▸ *n.* **1 splashing,** dashing, beating, battering. **2 spot,** splotch, daub, smudge, smear, stain. **3 display,** exhibition, splurge, sensation, impact. **4 patch,** burst, streak.

splendid *adj.* **1 magnificent,** imposing, superb, grand, sumptuous, resplendent, opulent, luxurious, plush, deluxe, rich, costly, lavish, ornate, gorgeous, glorious, dazzling, brilliant, showy, elegant, handsome. **2 distinguished,** impressive, glorious, illustrious, brilliant, notable, noted, remarkable, outstanding, eminent, celebrated, renowned, noble, venerable. **3 glorious,** brilliant, bright, gleaming, glowing, lustrous, radiant, dazzling, refulgent. **4 excellent,** fine, first-class, first-rate, marvelous, wonderful, *inf.* fantastic, terrific, great, fabulous, fab. *Ant.* drab; inferior; ordinary; undistinguished.

splendor *n.* **1 magnificence,** grandeur, sumptuousness, opulence, luxury, luxuriousness, richness, lavishness, gloriousness, elegance. **2 illustriousness,** brilliance, notability, eminence, renown, venerableness. **3 gloriousness,** brilliance, brightness, gleam, glow, luster, radiance.

splice *v.* **1 interweave,** braid, plait, intertwine, interlace, join, unite, connect, bind, fasten. **2 join,** unite, connect, overlap.

splinter *n.* **sliver,** fragment, shiver, shard, chip, shaving, shred, piece, bit.
▸ *v.* **break into pieces,** break into fragments, break into smithereens, shatter, shiver,

fracture, split, disintegrate, crumble.

split *v.* **1 break,** chop, cut, hew, lop, cleave, rend, rip, tear, slash, slit, splinter, snap, crack, rive.
2 divide, separate, sever, sunder, bisect, partition, set apart, disunite. **3 share,** divide, halve, apportion, distribute, dole out, parcel out, allot, allocate, carve up, slice up, *inf.* divvy. **4 divide in two,** divide, fork, bifurcate.
5 leave, depart, take off, decamp, exit, *inf.* push off, shove off.
▸ *n.* **1 break,** cut, rent, rip, tear, slash, slit, crack, fissure, breach.
2 division, rift, schism, rupture, partition, separation, breakup, alienation, estrangement.

spoil *v.* **1 damage,** impair, mar, blemish, disfigure, deface, injure, harm, ruin, destroy, wreck.
2 upset, mess up, disorganize, ruin, destroy, wreck. **3 pamper,** overindulge, mollycoddle, cosset, coddle, baby, spoonfeed, wait on hand and foot, kill with kindness.
4 go bad, turn, go sour, become rotten, rot, become tainted, decompose, decay.

spoilsport *n.* **killjoy,** damper, dog in the manger, *inf.* wet blanket, party pooper.

spoken *adj.* **oral,** verbal, uttered, voiced, expressed, by word of mouth, unwritten.

sponge *v.* **clean,** wash, wipe, mop, rub, swab.

sponsor *n.* **patron,** backer, promoter, subsidizer, guarantor, supporter, *inf.* angel.
▸ *v.* **be a patron of,** back, put up the money for, fund, finance, promote, subsidize, act as guarantor of, support, lend one's name to.

spontaneous *adj.* **1 voluntary,** unforced, unconstrained, uncompelled, unprompted.
2 unplanned, unpremeditated, unrehearsed, impromptu, extempore, spur-of-the-moment, extemporaneous, *inf.* off-the-cuff.
3 natural, instinctive, involuntary, automatic, impulsive, impetuous.
Ant. forced; premeditated.

sporadic *adj.* **irregular,** intermittent, scattered, random, infrequent, occasional, on and off, isolated, spasmodic. *Ant.* frequent; regular; steady.

sport *n.* **1 physical activity,** physical exercise, physical recreation, athletics, pastime.
2 amusement, entertainment, diversion, play, fun, pleasure, enjoyment.
▸ *v.* **wear,** exhibit, display, have on show, show off.

sporting *adj.* **sportsmanlike,** fair, just, honorable, generous.

spot *n.* **1 mark,** dot, speck,

speckle, fleck, smudge, stain, blotch, splotch, patch. **2 pimple,** pustule, papule, boil, pock, whitehead, blackhead, blemish. **3 stain,** taint, blemish, defect, flaw, brand, stigma. **4 area,** place, site, location, scene, setting, situation, position, niche. **5 difficulty,** mess, trouble, plight, predicament, quandary, tight corner, *inf.* hot water, fix, jam.

▸ *v.* **1 catch sight of,** see, notice, observe, espy, discern, detect, make out, pick out, recognize, identify. **2 mark,** stain, dirty, soil, spatter, besmirch.

spotless *adj.* **1 clean,** ultraclean, snowy-white, whiter-than-white, spick-and-span, immaculate, shining, gleaming. **2 pure,** flawless, faultless, blameless, unstained, unsullied, untainted, unblemished, unimpeachable, above reproach. *Ant.* dirty; filthy; blameworthy; tainted.

spotlight *n.* **limelight,** public eye, glare of publicity, publicity, public attention, public interest.

▸ *v.* **highlight,** point up, draw attention to, focus on, zero in on, accentuate, underline, stress, emphasize, give prominence to, bring to the fore.

spotted *adj.* **dappled,** mottled, pied, piebald, speckled, polka-dot, flecked.

spouse *n.* **husband,** wife, partner, mate, companion, consort, helpmate, *inf.* better half, old man/lady, missis.

spout *v.* **1 spurt,** gush, spew, squirt, jet, emit, erupt, disgorge, pour, stream, flow, spray. **2 declaim,** orate, hold forth, ramble, rant, harangue, speechify, sermonize, *inf.* spiel.

sprawl *v.* **1 stretch out,** lounge, lie around, repose, recline, slump, flop, loll, slouch. **2 spread,** stretch, spill, ramble, straggle, trail.

spray[1] *n.* **1 shower,** jet, mist, drizzle, foam, froth. **2 atomizer,** vaporizer, aerosol, sprinkler.

▸ *v.* **disperse,** disseminate, sprinkle, shower.

spray[2] *n.* **sprig,** posy, bouquet, nosegay, corsage, wreath, garland.

spread *v.* **1 stretch,** extend, open out, unfurl, unroll. **2 stretch out,** extend, enlarge, grow bigger, widen, broaden, grow, develop, branch out. **3 stretch out,** unfold, be on display, be exhibited, be on show, uncover, be unveiled, be revealed. **4 lay,** put, apply, smear, *inf.* plaster. **5 cover,** coat, layer. **6 mushroom,** extend, increase, advance, proliferate, escalate. **7 disseminate,** circulate, transmit, make public, make known, broadcast, publicize, propagate, promulgate, bruit. **8 set,** lay, arrange.

▸ *n.* **1 extent,** stretch, span, reach, compass, sweep. **2 period,** time, term. **3 increase,** advance, expansion, mushrooming, proliferation, escalating, diffusion. **4 dissemination,** circulation, transmission, broadcasting, publicizing, propagation. **5 bedspread,** bedcover, cover, coverlet, counterpane, throw. **6 feast,** banquet, repast, *inf.* blowout.

spree *n.* outing, fling, revel, drinking bout, orgy, debauch, bacchanal, bacchanalia, *inf.* binge, bender, jag.

sprightly *adj.* spry, lively, energetic, active, agile, nimble, supple, animated, vivacious, spirited, brisk, vital, lighthearted, cheerful, merry, jolly, blithe, jaunty, perky, frisky, frolicsome, playful, sportive. ***Ant.*** doddering; sluggish; lethargic; inactive.

spring *v.* **1 jump,** leap, bound, vault, hop, descend, originate, derive, issue, stem, arise, emanate, proceed, start. **2 appear,** come into view, crop up, *inf.* pop up. **3 present unexpectedly,** introduce suddenly, reveal suddenly, announce without warning.

▸ *n.* **1 jump,** leap, bound, vault,

hop, rebound, recoil. **2 springiness,** bounciness, elasticity, resilience, flexibility, stretch, stretchiness, tensility. **3 bounce,** bounciness, buoyancy, liveliness, lightheartedness, merriment.

springy *adj.* **1 bouncy,** elastic, resilient, flexible, stretchy, tensile. **2 bouncy,** lively, lighthearted, merry.

sprinkle *v.* **1 spray,** shower, splash, trickle, spatter. **2 scatter,** strew. **3 dust,** powder, dredge.

sprinkling *n.* **1 scattering,** dusting. **2 handful,** trickle.

sprint *v.* **run,** race, rush, dash, hotfoot it, *inf.* scoot, tear.

sprout *v.* **1 send forth,** put forth, grow, develop, bud, germinate. **2 shoot up,** spring up, grow, develop, appear, mushroom, proliferate.

spruce *adj.* **neat,** well-groomed, well turned-out, smart, trim, dapper, elegant, chic, *inf.* natty. ***Ant.*** scruffy; untidy; disheveled.

spur *n.* **1 goad,** prick, prod. **2 stimulus,** stimulant, incentive, inducement, encouragement, impetus.

▸ *v.* **1 goad,** prick, prod. **2 stimulate,** incentivize, induce, encourage, motivate, prompt, urge, impel.

spurious *adj.* **counterfeit,**

fraudulent, fake, bogus, sham, mock, feigned, pretended, make-believe, imitation, contrived, fictitious, deceitful, specious, *inf.* phony, pseudo. **Ant.** authentic; genuine; real.

spurn *v.* **reject,** turn away, repulse, rebuff, repudiate, snub, slight, treat with contempt, disdain, look down one's nose at, scorn, despise, condemn, *inf.* kick in the teeth, give the air.

spurt *v.* **gush,** squirt, shoot, surge, well, jet, spring, pour, stream, flow, issue, emanate.
  ▸ *n.* **1 gush,** surge, jet, spray, outpouring. **2 burst,** outburst, fit, surge, access. **3 burst of speed,** burst of energy, sprint, rush.

spy *n.* **enemy agent,** foreign agent, secret agent, undercover agent, secret service agent, intelligence agent, double agent, fifth columnist, *inf.* mole.
  ▸ *v.* **catch sight of,** spot, see, notice, observe, glimpse, make out, discern, descry, espy.

squabble *n.* **quarrel,** fight, row, dispute, argument, difference of opinion, tiff, wrangle, brawl, *inf.* scrap, set-to, run-in, spat.
  ▸ *v.* **quarrel,** fight, row, argue, bicker, have a dispute/tiff, have a difference of opinion, have words, wrangle, brawl, *inf.* fall out, scrap.

squalid *adj.* **1 dirty,** filthy, dingy, grubby, grimy, mucky, slummy, slumlike, foul, vile, low, wretched, mean, nasty, seedy, sordid, sleazy, slovenly, repulsive, disgusting, neglected, dilapidated, ramshackle, broken-down, tumbledown, *inf.* grungy. **2 sordid,** vile, nasty, repulsive, horrible, disgraceful, shameful, abominable, odious, filthy, indecent, depraved. **Ant.** clean; spotless; pleasant.

squander *v.* **waste,** misspend, dissipate, fritter away, run through, lavish, splurge, be prodigal with, spend like water, pour down the drain, *inf.* blow.

square *n.* **1 town square,** village square, market square, quadrangle, quad. **2 fogy,** old fogy, conservative, traditionalist, conventionalist, conformist, *inf.* stick-in-the-mud, fuddy-duddy.
  ▸ *adj.* **1 fair,** just, equitable, honest, straight, upright, aboveboard, ethical, *inf.* on the level. **2 old-fashioned,** behind the times, conservative, ultraconservative, traditionalist, conventional, conformist, bourgeois, straitlaced, stuffy, unadventurous, *inf.* fuddy-duddy.

squash *v.* **1 crush,** squeeze, flatten, compress, press, smash, pulp, mash, pulverize, macerate.

2 crowd, crush, cram, pack tight, pack like sardines, jam, squeeze, wedge. **3 put down,** quash, quell, crush, suppress, squelch, nip in the bud, *inf.* put the kibosh on.

squat *v.* **crouch,** sit on one's haunches, sit on one's heels.
▸ *adj.* **dumpy,** stubby, chunky, thickset, stocky, short.

squeak *n.* **squeal,** peep, pipe, yelp, whimper.
▸ *v.* **1 squeal,** peep, pipe, yelp, whimper. **2 creak,** scrape, grate.

squeamish *adj.* **1 queasy,** nauseous, sickish, sick, queer. **2 fastidious,** particular, punctilious, finicky, fussy, scrupulous, prudish, straitlaced, *inf.* persnickety, prissy.

squeeze *v.* **1 wring,** twist, press. **2 extract,** press, force, express. **3 compress,** crush, squash, mash. **4 grip,** clutch, pinch, press, compress. **5 crowd,** crush, cram, pack tight, pack like sardines, jam, squash, wedge. **6 embrace,** hug, cuddle, clasp, hold tight. **7 extort,** wring, wrest, extract, milk, *inf.* bleed. **8 bring pressure to bear on,** pressure, pressurize, strong-arm, blackmail, *inf.* put the squeeze on, lean on, bleed, put the screws on, put the bite on.
▸ *n.* **1 embrace,** hug, cuddle, clasp, hold. **2 clasp,** grip, grasp, clutch. **3 crowd,** crush, jam, squash,

press, congestion. **4 drop,** droplet, dash, spot, bit.

squirm *v.* **wriggle,** wiggle, writhe, twist, turn, shift.

squirt *v.* **1 discharge,** expel, shoot, spurt. **2 eject,** emit, discharge, spew out, spurt, spout, jet, stream, spray, gush, surge, pour, flow, issue. **3 splash,** wet, spray, bespatter, shower, sprinkle, besprinkle.
▸ *n.* **1 jet,** stream, spray, flow. **2 insignificant person,** *inf.* pipsqueak, twerp.

stab *v.* **knife,** pierce, puncture, run through, stick, skewer, gash, slash.
▸ *n.* **1 puncture,** gash, slash, incision. **2 pain,** shooting pain, pang, twinge, ache, throb, spasm. **3 try,** attempt, endeavor, essay, effort, venture, *inf.* go, shot, crack.

stability *n.* **1 firmness,** solidity, steadiness, secureness, strength, fastness, stoutness, sturdiness. **2 secureness,** solidity, strength, steadiness, firmness, sureness, durability, constancy, permanence, reliability, dependability. **3 soundness,** sense, responsibility, self-control, sanity.

stable *adj.* **1 firm,** solid, steady, secure, fixed, strong, fast, stout, sturdy, moored, anchored, immovable. **2 secure,** solid, strong, steady, firm, sure, steadfast, unwavering, unfaltering, unswerving, established, long-lasting, long-lived, deep-rooted, well-founded, well-grounded, abiding, durable, enduring, lasting, constant, permanent, reliable, dependable, true. **3 well-balanced,** balanced, sound, mentally sound, steady, reasonable, sensible, responsible, equable, self-controlled, sane. **Ant.** rickety; insecure; unstable.

stack *n.* **1 heap,** pile, mass, accumulation, collection, hoard, store, stock, stockpile, mound, mountain. **2 haystack,** rick, hayrick, cock, shock. **3 abundance,** amplitude, *inf.* great deal, lot, load, heap, ton, oodles, scads.
▸ *v.* **heap,** pile, pile up, amass, accumulate, collect, hoard, store, stockpile.

staff *n.* **1 rod,** pole, walking stick, stick, cane, crook. **2 rod,** mace, scepter. **3 employees,** workers, workforce, personnel.
▸ *v.* **man,** people, equip, fit out, supply, furnish, provide.

stage *n.* **1 point,** period, step, juncture, time, division, level. **2 lap,** leg, phase, step. **3 platform,** dais, rostrum, podium. **4 setting,** scene, site, arena, background, backdrop.
▸ *v.* **1 put on,** produce, direct, perform, mount, present. **2 arrange,** organize, engineer, orchestrate, put together, lay on.

stagger *v.* **1 reel,** sway, teeter, totter, wobble, lurch, pitch, roll. **2 amaze,** astound, dumbfound, astonish, flabbergast, shock, shake, confound, nonplus, take aback, stupefy, stun, *inf.* strike dumb. **3 alternate,** vary, step.

stagnant *adj.* **1 still,** unflowing, motionless, standing, foul, stale, dirty, filthy, polluted, putrid, putrefied, brackish. **2 sluggish,** slow-moving, quiet, inactive, dull, static. **Ant.** flowing; fresh; active.

stagnate *v.* **1 stand,** vegetate, become stagnant, fester, putrefy. **2 become stagnant,** do nothing, be sluggish, lie dormant, be inert. **3 vegetate,** idle, be idle, laze, loaf, hang about, languish.

staid *adj.* **sedate,** quiet, serious, serious-minded, grave, solemn, somber, sober, proper, decorous, formal, prim, demure, stiff, starchy, *inf.* stuffy, stick-in-the-mud. **Ant.** frivolous; flighty; informal.

stain *v.* **1 soil,** mark, discolor, dirty, spot, blotch, blemish, smudge, smear, besmirch, begrime. **2 blacken,** tarnish, sully, blemish, damage, mar, injure, defame, denigrate, dishonor,

besmirch, defile, taint, blot, slur.
3 varnish, dye, paint, color.
▸ *n.* **1 mark,** spot, blotch, blemish,
smudge, smear. **2 blemish,**
damage, injury, taint, blot, slur,
stigma. **3 varnish,** dye, paint,
colorant.

stake[1] *n.* **post,** pole, stick,
upright, rod, spike.
▸ *v.* **1 support,** prop up, hold up,
brace, tether. **2 establish,** declare,
state.

stake[2] *n.* **1 wager,** bet, ante.
2 financial interest, interest,
share, investment, involvement,
concern.
▸ *v.* **wager,** bet, place a bet of, put,
gamble, pledge, chance, venture,
risk, hazard.

stale *adj.* **1 unfresh,** dry, dried
out, hard, hardened, moldy.
2 unfresh, stuffy, close, musty,
fusty. **3 flat,** sour, turned, spoiled.
4 hackneyed, tired, worn-out,
threadbare, banal, trite, stock,
stereotyped, clichéd, run-of-the-
mill, commonplace,
platitudinous, unoriginal,
unimaginative, uninspired, flat,
insipid, vapid, *inf.* old hat. ***Ant.***
fresh; original.

stalemate *n.* **deadlock,** impasse,
standstill, stand-off.

stalk[1] *n.* **stem,** branch, shoot,
twig.

stalk[2] *v.* **pursue,** chase, give chase

to, follow, shadow, trail, track
down, creep up on, hunt, *inf.* tail.

stall *n.* **1 booth,** stand, kiosk.
2 pen, coop, sty, corral,
compartment, cubicle.
▸ *v.* **1 play for time,** use delaying
tactics, delay, beat about the bush,
hem and haw, *inf.* drag one's feet.
2 hold off, stave off, keep at bay,
keep at arm's length, evade, avoid.

stalwart *adj.* **1 strong,** sturdy,
robust, hardy, muscular, brawny,
strapping, powerfully built, burly,
rugged, lusty, *inf.* husky. **2 brave,**
courageous, valiant, valorous,
intrepid, fearless, manly, heroic,
indomitable, bold, daring, plucky,
spirited, adventurous, *inf.* gutsy.
Ant. puny; frail; timid.

stamina *n.* **endurance,** staying
power, indefatigability,
resistance, resilience, fortitude,
strength, vigor, energy,
staunchness, robustness,
toughness, *inf.* grit, guts.

stammer *v.* **stutter,** stumble,
mumble, splutter, hesitate, falter,
pause.
▸ *n.* **stutter,** speech impediment,
speech defect.

stamp *v.* **1 imprint,** inscribe,
engrave, emboss, mark, sign,
impress, fix. **2 brand,** characterize,
designate, identify, categorize,
style, term, label, dub, name, tag.
▸ *n.* **1 mark,** hallmark, label,

brand, tag, characteristics, quality.
2 kind, sort, type, variety, class,
classification, form, breed, kidney,
mold, cast, cut.

stampede *n.* **charge,** rush, flight,
scattering.
▸ *v.* **charge,** rush, flee, take flight,
dash, race, run.

stance *n.* **stand,** standpoint,
position, line, policy, attitude,
angle, slant, viewpoint, point of
view, opinion.

stand *v.* **1 be upright,** be erect,
rise, rise to one's feet, get to one's
feet, get up. **2 be situated,** be
located. **3 set,** place, put, position.
4 stop, halt, come to a halt, come
to a standstill. **5 remain/be in
force,** remain/be valid, remain/be
effective, hold, hold good. **6 put
up with,** tolerate, bear, take,
endure, abide, suffer, brook,
countenance, cope with, handle,
inf. stomach. ***Ant.*** sit; lie.
▸ *n.* **1 standstill,** halt, stop,
stoppage, rest. **2 firm stand,**
defensive position, resistance,
opposition. **3 stance,** standpoint,
position, line, policy, attitude.
4 stall, booth, kiosk, cubicle.
5 display case, shelf, rack, frame.
6 platform, stage, staging, dais,
rostrum.

standard *n.* **1 yardstick,**
benchmark, gauge, measure,
criterion, guide, guideline, norm,
touchstone, model, pattern,
example, exemplar, paradigm,
ideal, archetype, specification,
requirement, rule, principle, law,
canon. **2 level,** grade, quality,
evaluation, worth, merit. **3 flag,**
banner, pennant, streamer,
ensign, colors. **4 support,** prop,
post, pole, cane, upright.
5 principle, code of behavior, code
of honor, morals, ethics, ideals.
▸ *adj.* **1 usual,** ordinary, average,
normal, common, regular, stock,
set, fixed, conventional.
2 definitive, established, classic,
recognized, approved, accepted,
authoritative, official. ***Ant.***
abnormal; unusual; uncommon.

standardize *v.* **make uniform,**
regulate, systematize, normalize,
homogenize, regiment, bring into
line.

standing *n.* **1 status,** rank,
ranking, social position, position,
station, footing, place,
circumstances. **2 reputation,** good
reputation, repute, eminence,
prominence, note,
noteworthiness. **3 duration,**
length of time, existence,
continuance, endurance.
▸ *adj.* **1 upright,** erect, vertical,
upended, perpendicular, rampant.
2 still, stagnant, static,
motionless. **3 permanent,** fixed,
regular, perpetual, constant.

stand-off *n.* **deadlock,** impasse, stalemate.

standpoint *n.* **point of view,** viewpoint, opinion, perspective, angle, slant, frame of reference.

staple *adj.* **chief,** primary, main, principal, foremost, leading, basic, fundamental, essential, indispensable, necessary, important, vital.

star *n.* **1 heavenly body,** celestial body, planet, planetoid, asteroid. **2 astral influence,** destiny, fate, fortune, lot. **3 horoscope,** forecast, augury. **4 principal,** leading lady, leading man, lead, name, superstar. **5 celebrity,** dignitary, notable, name, somebody, *inf.* VIP, bigwig, big shot, big cheese, big wheel.
▸ *adj.* **brilliant,** great, talented, gifted, celebrated, illustrious, renowned, famous, distinguished, prominent, eminent, preeminent, principal, chief, leading, major.

stare *v.* **1 gaze,** gape, look, *inf.* gawk. **2 be conspicuous,** be obvious, be blatant, stand out, be prominent, stick out, glare.

stark *adj.* **1 sharp,** sharply delineated, sharply defined, obvious, evident, clear, clear-cut. **2 desolate,** bare, barren, arid, vacant, empty, forsaken, bleak, dreary, depressing, grim, harsh, *lit.* drear. **3 austere,** severe, plain, simple, unadorned, unembellished, undecorated. **4 sheer,** utter, absolute, downright, out-and-out, outright, total, complete, thorough, thoroughgoing, pure, unmitigated, unqualified, consummate, unmissable, patent, palpable, rank, arrant. **5 bald,** bare, simple, blunt, straightforward, unadorned, unembellished, harsh, grim.
▸ *adv.* **completely,** totally, entirely, wholly, altogether, utterly, absolutely, quite.

start *v.* **1 begin,** commence, get underway, go ahead, get going; *informal* kick off. **Ant.** finish. **2 arise,** come into being, begin, commence, be born, come into existence, appear, arrive, come forth, establish oneself, emerge, erupt, burst out, originate, develop. **Ant.** clear up, end. **3 establish,** set up, found, create, bring into being, institute, initiate, inaugurate, introduce, open, launch, float, kick-start, jump-start, get something off the ground, pioneer, organize, mastermind; *informal* kick something off. **Ant.** end. **4 commence,** make a start, begin, take the first step, make the first move, get going, go ahead, set things moving, start/get/set the

ball rolling, buckle to/down, turn to; *informal* get moving, get cracking, get down to, get to it, get down to business, get the show on the road, take the plunge, kick off, get off one's backside, fire away. ***Ant.*** stop, give up, procrastinate. **5 set off,** set out, start out, set forth, begin one's journey, get on the road, depart, leave, get underway, make a start, sally forth, embark, sail; *informal* hit the road. ***Ant.*** arrive, stay. **6 activate,** set in motion, switch on, start up, turn on, fire up; energize, actuate, set off, start off, set something going/moving. ***Ant.*** stop, shut down, close down. **7 begin working,** start up, get going, spring into life. ***Ant.*** stop. **8 flinch,** jerk, jump, twitch, recoil, shy, shrink, blench, wince.
▸ *n.* **1 beginning,** commencement, inception. ***Ant.*** end. **2 onset,** commencement, emergence, (first) appearance, arrival, eruption, dawn, birth; *informal* square one. **3 lead,** head start, advantage. ***Ant.*** handicap. **4 flying start,** helping hand, lift, assistance, support, encouragement, boost, kick-start; *informal* break, leg up. ***Ant.*** handicap. **5 jerk,** twitch, flinch, wince, spasm, convulsion, jump.
startle *v.* **make one jump,** disturb,

agitate, perturb, unsettle, scare, frighten, alarm, surprise, astonish, shock, *inf.* give one a turn.
startling *adj.* **disturbing,** unsettling, alarming, surprising, unexpected, unforeseen, astonishing, amazing, staggering, shocking, extraordinary, remarkable.
starvation *n.* **extreme hunger,** lack of food, death from lack of food, fasting, famine, undernourishment, malnourishment.
starving *adj.* **starved,** famished, ravenous, very hungry, faint from lack of food, dying from lack of food, fasting, *inf.* able to eat a horse.
state[1] *n.* **1 condition,** shape, situation, circumstances, state of affairs, position, predicament, plight. **2 condition,** mood, humor, spirits, frame of mind, attitude. **3 state of agitation,** anxiety, nerves, panic, distressed state, fluster, pother, *inf.* flap, tizzy. **4 untidiness,** mess, chaos, disorder, disarray, disorganization, confusion, clutter. **5 country,** nation, land, realm, kingdom, republic, territory, federation, commonwealth, body politic. **6 government,** parliament,

administration, establishment.
7 pomp, ceremony, display, dignity, majesty, grandeur, glory, splendor.

state² *v.* **express,** voice, utter, say, tell, declare, set out, lay down, affirm, assert, announce, make known, reveal, disclose, divulge, pronounce, articulate, aver, proclaim, present, expound, promulgate.

stately *adj.* **ceremonial,** dignified, solemn, majestic, royal, regal, magnificent, grand, glorious, splendid, elegant, imposing, impressive, august, lofty, pompous, slow-moving, measured, deliberate.

statement *n.* **declaration,** account, recitation, report, affirmation, assertion, announcement, revelation, disclosure, divulgence, pronouncement, articulation, averment, proclamation, presentation, expounding, promulgation.

static *adj.* **unmoving,** unvarying, undeviating, changeless, constant, stable, steady, stationary, motionless, at a standstill, frozen. *Ant.* mobile; variable.

station *n.* **1 stop,** stopping place.
2 terminus, terminal, depot.
3 base, office, headquarters, seat.
4 post, place, position, location,

site. **5 class,** level, rank, grade, standing, status, caste.

stationary *adj.* **1 unmoving,** motionless, at a standstill, parked.
2 changeless, unchanging, constant, unvarying, invariable, undeviating. *Ant.* moving; variable.

statue *n.* **statuette,** sculpture, effigy, figure, figurine, representation, likeness, image, bust, head.

statuesque *adj.* **dignified,** stately, majestic, noble, magnificent, splendid, imposing, impressive, regal, well-proportioned, handsome, beautiful.

stature *n.* **1 height,** tallness, size, altitude. **2 status,** importance, import, standing, consequence, eminence, preeminence, prominence, note, fame, renown.

status *n.* **standing,** rank, level, grade, degree, position, importance, reputation, consequence.

staunch *adj.* **loyal,** faithful, dependable, reliable, steady, constant, stable, firm, steadfast, unswerving, unwavering, unhesitating, unfaltering. *Ant.* disloyal; unfaithful; unreliable.

stay *v.* **1 remain,** wait, stay put, continue, linger, pause, rest, delay, tarry. **2 remain,** continue to

be, go on being. **3 put off,** postpone, suspend, adjourn, defer, hold over, hold in abeyance, delay, prorogue.
4 check, curb, arrest, stop, delay, hold, prevent, hinder, impede, obstruct. *Ant.* leave; depart.
▸ *n.* **1 visit,** sojourn, stop, stopover, vacation.
2 postponement, suspension, adjournment, deferment, delay.
3 prop, underprop, support, brace, bolster, buttress.

steadfast *adj.* **1 faithful,** loyal, true, constant, devoted, dedicated, trustworthy, dependable, reliable, staunch.
2 steady, firm, determined, resolute, unchanging, unwavering, unfaltering, unswerving, unyielding, inflexible, uncompromising, relentless, implacable. **3 steady,** fixed, intent, immovable, unwavering, unfaltering. *Ant.* disloyal; irresolute.

steady *adj.* **1 firmly fixed,** firm, fixed, stable, secure, immovable.
2 still, unshaking, motionless, unmoving, sure. **3 steadfast,** fixed, immovable, unwavering, unfaltering. **4 constant,** unchanging, changeless, unvarying, invariable, undeviating, continuous, continual, unceasing, ceaseless,

perpetual, persistent, unremitting, unwavering, unfaltering, unfluctuating, undying, unending, endless.
5 uniform, even, regular, rhythmic, consistent. **6 regular,** habitual, usual, customary. **7 well-balanced,** balanced, sensible, levelheaded, rational, settled, down-to-earth, calm, equable, imperturbable, reliable, dependable, serious-minded, serious. *Ant.* insecure; inconstant; uneven; sporadic.
▸ *v.* **1 make steady,** hold steady, stabilize, secure, balance, support.
2 calm, calm down, settle, compose, tranquilize, control, get a grip on.

steal *v.* **1 take,** appropriate, misappropriate, pilfer, purloin, filch, walk off with, embezzle, pocket, abstract, shoplift, peculate, *inf.* pinch, swipe, lift, rip off. **2 plagiarize,** copy, pirate, appropriate, poach, *inf.* lift.
3 kidnap, snatch, abduct, carry off, make off with, seize, shanghai. **4 snatch,** obtain stealthily, get surreptitiously.
5 slip, slide, tiptoe, sneak, creep, slink, slither, flit, glide.
▸ *n.* **bargain,** good buy, *inf.* giveaway.

stealthy *adj.* **secret,** furtive, surreptitious, sly, sneaky, clandestine, covert, shady, underhand, underhanded, undercover. *Ant.* aboveboard; open.

steam *n.* **1 vapor,** fume, smoke, exhalation. **2 energy,** vigor, vitality, stamina, power, force.
▶ *v.* **rush,** race, run, dash, charge, sprint, hurry, speed, hasten, *inf.* tear, zoom, zip.

steamy *adj.* **1 humid,** muggy, sticky, moist, damp, sweltering, boiling, like a Turkish bath, like a sauna. **2 erotic,** sexy, passionate, tempestuous, sensuous, lustful, wanton.

steep *adj.* **1 sheer,** abrupt, precipitous, sudden, sharp, perpendicular, vertical, declivitous, acclivitous. **2 sharp,** rapid, sudden, precipitate. **3 high,** costly, expensive, dear, unreasonable, excessive, exorbitant, *inf.* over the top. *Ant.* gradual; gentle; reasonable.
▶ *v.* **1 soak,** saturate, immerse, submerge, wet through, drench, souse. **2 marinate,** marinade, soak, souse.

steeple *n.* **spire,** tower, church tower, bell tower, campanile, turret, minaret.

steer *v.* **1 guide,** navigate, drive, pilot, be in the driver's seat of, be at the wheel of. **2 guide,** lead, direct, conduct, usher.

stench *n.* **stink,** foul smell/odor, reek, mephitis, *inf.* whiff.

step *n.* **1 stride,** pace. **2 footstep,** footfall, tread. **3 footstep,** footprint, print, impression, track. **4 walk,** gait, bearing, carriage. **5 short distance,** pace, stone's throw, spitting distance. **6 rung,** tread. **7 course of action,** move, act, action, deed, measure, maneuver, procedure, expedient, effort. **8 step forward,** advance, advancement, development, progression, stage, move. **9 stage,** level, grade, rank, degree.
▶ *v.* **walk,** tread, stride, pace, move, advance, proceed, *inf.* hoof it.

stereotype *n.* **cliché.**
▶ *v.* **typecast,** pigeonhole, conventionalize, standardize, label, tag, categorize.

sterile *adj.* **1 infertile,** barren, infecund, unprolific. **2 infertile,** unproductive, unfruitful, unyielding, arid, dry, barren, unprolific. **3 unproductive,** unfruitful, fruitless, useless, futile, vain, idle, unsuccessful, ineffectual, ineffective, worthless, abortive, unprofitable, unrewarding. **4 sterilized,** germ-free, germless, antiseptic, disinfected, aseptic, uninfected, uncontaminated, unpolluted, pure, clean. *Ant.* fertile; fruitful; septic.

sterilize *v.* **1 disinfect,** purify, fumigate. **2 make infertile,** make barren, make infecund, castrate, vasectomize, geld, neuter, emasculate, spay, *inf.* fix.

stern *adj.* **1 strict,** harsh, hard, severe, rigorous, stringent, rigid, exacting, demanding, cruel, relentless, unsparing, inflexible, unyielding, authoritarian, tyrannical, despotic, draconian. **2 severe,** forbidding, frowning, unsmiling, somber, sober, austere. *Ant.* lenient; lax; friendly.
▸ *n.* **back,** rear, tail, poop.

stew *v.* **1 simmer,** boil, fricassee. **2 be anxious,** be nervous, be agitated, worry, fret, agonize, get in a panic, get worked up, get overwrought, *inf.* be/get in a flap, be/get in a tizzy.
▸ *n.* **1 casserole,** ragout, fricassee. **2 state of agitation,** nervous state, fluster, panic, dither, pother, *inf.* flap, tizzy.

stick¹ *n.* **1 piece of wood,** branch, twig, switch, cane, pole, post, stake, upright, birch, rod. **2 cudgel,** truncheon, blackjack, baton.

stick² *v.* **1 thrust,** push, insert, jab, poke. **2 glue,** paste, tape, fasten, attach, fix, pin, tack. **3 remain,** stay, linger, dwell, lodge, persist, continue. **4 become bogged down,** become embedded, become

lodged, become clogged up, be fixed, become immobilized, be unable to move. **5 jam,** become jammed, come to a standstill, stop, halt, come to a halt, cease to work, become inoperative. **6 put,** set down, place, lay, deposit, drop, position, locate, plant, *inf.* plunk, stuff. **7 be valid,** be sound, be well-founded, be well-grounded, be convincing, be cogent, be persuasive, be relevant.

sticky *adj.* **1 adhesive,** adherent, gummy, gluey, tacky, glutinous, viscous, viscid, *inf.* gooey. **2 humid,** muggy, clammy, sultry, sweltering, oppressive. **3 awkward,** difficult, tricky, ticklish, delicate, thorny, touch-and-go, embarrassing, *inf.* hairy.

stiff *adj.* **1 rigid,** inflexible, unyielding, inelastic, firm, hard, hardened, brittle. **2 unsupple,** tight, tense, taut, aching, arthritic, rheumatic, *inf.* creaky. **3 difficult,** hard, arduous, tough, laborious, exacting, demanding, formidable, challenging, tiring, fatiguing, exhausting, Herculean. **4 severe,** harsh, hard, stringent, rigorous, drastic, strong, heavy, draconian. **5 strong,** vigorous, determined, resolute, dogged, tenacious, unflagging, stubborn, obdurate. **6 formal,** ceremonial, ceremonious, dignified, proper, decorous, pompous. **7 formal,** unrelaxed, prim, punctilious, chilly, cold, *inf.* starchy. **8 strong,** potent, alcoholic. **9 strong,** vigorous, powerful, brisk, fresh. ***Ant.*** flexible; supple; lenient; mild.

stiffen *v.* **1 become stiff,** thicken, set, gel, jell, solidify, harden, congeal, coagulate. **2 strengthen,** harden, fortify, brace, steel, reinforce. **3 tighten,** become stiff, tense, become taut, begin to ache, become arthritic/rheumatic, *inf.* become creaky.

stifle *v.* **1 smother,** check, restrain, keep back, hold back, hold in, withhold, choke back, muffle, suppress, curb, silence, prevent. **2 suppress,** quash, quell, put an end to, put down, stop, extinguish, stamp out, crush, subdue, repress. **3 suffocating,** very hot, sweltering, airless, close.

stigma *n.* **shame,** disgrace, dishonor, slur, stain, taint.

still *adj.* **1 motionless,** unmoving, without moving, immobile, unstirring, inert, lifeless, stock-still, stationary, static. **2 quiet,** silent, hushed, soundless, sound-free, noiseless, undisturbed. **3 calm,** mild, tranquil, peaceful, serene, restful, windless, wind-free, halcyon, stagnant. ***Ant.*** moving; noisy; windy.

▸ *n.* **quietness,** quiet, silence, hush, soundlessness, noiselessness, calmness, calm, tranquillity, peace, peacefulness, serenity.

stilted *adj.* **1 stiff,** unnatural, wooden, forced, labored, constrained, unrelaxed, awkward. **2 pompous,** pretentious, high-flown, high-sounding, grandiloquent, pedantic, bombastic. ***Ant.*** natural; spontaneous; unpretentious.

stimulant *n.* **1 tonic,** restorative, reviver, energizer, excitant, analeptic, *inf.* pep pill, upper, pick-me-up, bracer. **2 stimulus,** incentive, impetus, fillip, spur.

stimulate *v.* **act as a stimulus/ incentive/impetus/fillip/spur to,** encourage, prompt, spur on, activate, stir up, excite, whip up, kindle, incite, instigate, foment, fan.

stimulating *adj.* **1 tonic,** restoring, restorative, reviving, energizing, analeptic, *inf.* pick-me-up. **2 interesting,** exciting, stirring, thought-provoking, inspiring, exhilarating, rousing, intriguing, provoking, provocative. ***Ant.*** sedative; uninteresting; boring.

stimulus *n.* **stimulant,** incentive, fillip, spur, push, drive, encouragement, inducement, incitement, goad, jog, jolt, *inf.* shot in the arm.

sting *n.* **1 prick,** inflamed area, wound, injury. **2 irritation,** smarting, tingling, tingle, pain, hurt. **3 pain,** hurt, distress, anguish, agony, torture, torment. **4 sharpness,** bite, edge, pungency, causticity, acrimony, malice, spite, venom. **5 swindle,** fraud, cheating, fleecing, *inf.* rip-off.

▸ *v.* **1 prick,** wound, injure, hurt. **2 smart,** tingle, burn, be irritated. **3 hurt,** wound, distress, grieve, vex, pain, anguish, torture, torment, harrow. **4 swindle,** defraud, cheat, fleece, gull, overcharge, *inf.* rip off, take for a ride.

stingy *adj.* **mean,** miserly, parsimonious, niggardly, tight-fisted, penny-pinching, *inf.* tight, cheap. ***Ant.*** generous; liberal; magnanimous.

stink *v.* **1 smell bad,** reek, *inf.* smell to high heaven. **2 be very bad,** be unpleasant, be nasty, be vile, be foul, be abhorrent, be despicable, be dishonest, be corrupt.

▸ *n.* **1 bad smell,** foul smell, stench, reek, malodor, malodorousness. **2 fuss,** to-do, commotion, outcry, uproar, brouhaha.

stipulate *v.* **specify,** set down, lay down, state clearly, demand, require, insist upon, make a condition of, make a point of, make a precondition/proviso of.

stipulation *n.* **specification,** demand, requirement, condition, precondition, provision, proviso, prerequisite.

stir *v.* **1 mix,** blend, beat, whip. **2 move,** quiver, tremble, twitch. **3 move,** disturb, agitate, rustle. **4 move,** move an inch, budge, get up. **5 get up,** get out of bed, rise, rouse oneself, bestir oneself, move about, be up and about, be active, *inf.* be up and doing, shake a leg, look lively. **6 stimulate,** excite, rouse, awaken, waken, kindle, quicken, electrify, inspire. **7 stir up,** rouse, incite, provoke, inflame, goad, spur, egg on, urge, encourage, motivate, drive, impel.

▸ *n.* **excitement,** commotion, disturbance, fuss, uproar, to-do, bustle, flurry, ferment, brouhaha.

stirring *adj.* **exciting,** dramatic, thrilling, gripping, riveting, spirited, rousing, stimulating, moving, lively, animated, heady, passionate, impassioned. ***Ant.*** boring; pedestrian.

stitch *n.* **sharp pain,** stabbing pain, stab of pain, shooting pain, pang, twinge, spasm.

▸ *v.* **sew,** baste, sew up, repair, mend, darn.

stock *n.* **1 store,** supply, range, selection, assortment, variety, collection, quantity. **2 supplies,** goods, merchandise, wares, items/articles for sale, commodities. **3 store,** supply, stockpile, reserve, reservoir, accumulation, pile, heap, load, hoard, cache. **4 equipment,** apparatus, machinery, implements, appliances. **5 livestock,** cattle, cows, beasts, herd, sheep, flock, pigs. **6 shares,** investment, holding, money. **7 standing,** status, reputation, repute, position. **8 descent,** line of descent, lineage, ancestry, extraction, family, parentage, relatives, pedigree, genealogy, strain, breed, background. **9 bouillon,** broth. **10 handle,** haft, grip, shaft, shank.
▸ *adj.* **1 standard,** regular, average, readily available, widely available. **2 regular,** common, customary, staple, basic, fundamental, necessary, essential, indispensable. **3 usual,** routine, run-of-the-mill, commonplace, conventional, traditional, stereotyped, clichéd, hackneyed, overused, worn-out, banal, trite. *Ant.* irregular; uncommon; original.

stockpile *v.* **collect,** gather, accumulate, amass, pile up, store, lay in, put away, put down, deposit, *inf.* put away for a rainy day, squirrel away, salt away, stash.

stocky *adj.* **heavyset,** thickset, dumpy, stubby, stumpy, squat, chunky, solid, sturdy, mesomorphic. *Ant.* slender; willowy.

stodgy *adj.* **dull,** uninteresting, boring, staid, sedate, stuffy, dull as dishwater/ditchwater, tedious, dry, wearisome, unimaginative, uninspired, monotonous, labored, wooden, turgid. *Ant.* light; interesting; lively.

stoical *adj.* **impassive,** dispassionate, unimpassioned, unemotional, self-controlled, self-disciplined, forbearing, patient, long-suffering, resigned, philosophical, fatalistic, imperturbable, calm, cool, unexcitable, unflappable, phlegmatic. *Ant.* emotional; impassioned; melodramatic.

stolid *adj.* **impassive,** unemotional, apathetic, uninterested, unimaginative, indifferent, dull, stupid, bovine, lumpish, wooden, doltish, thick, dense. *Ant.* emotional; lively; imaginative.

stomach *n.* **1 abdomen,** belly, paunch, potbelly, *inf.* tummy, gut, insides, pot, bread basket.

2 appetite, taste, hunger, desire, inclination, liking, fancy, mind, fondness, relish, zest, gusto.

▸ *v.* **1 eat,** digest, swallow, find palatable. **2 stand,** put up with, bear, take, tolerate, abide, endure, suffer, swallow, submit to, *inf.* weather.

stone *n.* **1 pebble,** cobble, rock, boulder. **2 precious stone,** jewel, gem, *inf.* rock. **3 tombstone,** gravestone, headstone, memorial stone, monument. **4 kernel,** pit, nut, seed, pip.

stony *adj.* **1 rocky,** pebbly, gravelly, gritty, rough, hard. **2 cold,** chilly, frosty, icy, frigid, hard, stern, severe, rigid, fixed, expressionless, blank, poker-faced, deadpan, sphinxlike. **3 unfeeling,** uncaring, unsympathetic, insensitive, callous, heartless, tough, unmoved, unemotional, dispassionate, unresponsive, stern, severe, harsh, hard, cruel, cold-hearted, merciless, pitiless, ruthless, unforgiving, inflexible, unbending, unyielding, adamant, obdurate. ***Ant.*** friendly; sympathetic.

stooge *n.* **1 butt,** foil, straight man. **2 underling,** subordinate, assistant, deputy, right-hand man/woman, girl/man Friday, *inf.* sidekick.

stoop *v.* **1 bend down,** lean over, lean down, crouch down, bend, bow, lower, duck. **2 slouch,** slump, walk with a stoop, be round-shouldered, hunch one's shoulders, bend one's head forward. **3 condescend,** deign, lower oneself, humble oneself, demean oneself, sink, descend, resort.

▸ *n.* **1 bending,** bow, lowering, ducking. **2 round-shoulderedness,** hunch, droop/sag of the shoulders.

stop *v.* **1 bring to a stop,** halt, bring to a halt, end, bring to an end, put an end to, finish, bring to a close, terminate, bring to a standstill, wind up, discontinue, cut short, interrupt, nip in the bud. **2 discontinue,** cease, refrain from, desist from, leave off, break off, quit, forbear from, *inf.* knock off. **3 come to a stop,** come to a halt, end, come to an end, finish, come to a close, be over, cease, conclude, terminate, come to a standstill, pause. **4 prevent,** hinder, obstruct, impede, block, check, hamper, curb, frustrate, thwart, foil, stall, restrain, bar, *inf.* put the kibosh on. **5 break one's journey,** stay, remain, sojourn, lodge, rest. ***Ant.*** start; begin; continue; expedite.

▸ *n.* **1 halt,** end, finish, close, cessation, conclusion, termination, standstill, stoppage, discontinuation, discontinuance. **2 stopping place,** terminus, terminal, depot, station. **3 stopoff,** stopover, stay, sojourn, overnight, rest.

stopgap *n.* **temporary substitute,** substitution, fill-in, makeshift, improvisation, expedient, last resort.

store *n.* **1 supply,** stock, stockpile, reserve, accumulation, pile, heap, load, amassment, cache, deposit, reservoir. **2 storeroom,** storehouse, warehouse, repository, depository. **3 shop,** department store, supermarket, retail outlet, emporium.
▸ *v.* **1 stock up with,** get in supplies of, stockpile, collect, gather, accumulate, amass, lay in, put away, put down, deposit, hoard, *inf.* put away for a rainy day, squirrel away, salt away, stash. **2 put into storage,** put in store. **Ant.** use; discard; scrap; jettison.

storm *n.* **1 gale,** hurricane, cyclone, tempest, squall, cloudburst, downpour, torrent. **2 outcry,** outburst, commotion, furor, brouhaha, clamor, tumult, row, disturbance, fight, trouble, *inf.* to-do, rumpus. **3 assault,** attack, offensive, onslaught, charge, raid, foray, sortie, siege.
▸ *v.* **1 attack,** conduct an offensive on, make an onslaught on, charge, rush, make a raid/foray/ sortie on, take by storm. **2 charge,** rush headlong, flounce, stride, stamp, *inf.* stomp. **3 rage,** rant, rave, rant and rave, fume, bellow, thunder, shout, *inf.* fly off the handle, blow one's top, blow up, raise the roof, raise hell.

stormy *adj.* **1 blustery,** blustering, windy, gusty, squally, rainy, wild, tempestuous, turbulent. **2 angry,** emotional, violent. **Ant.** calm; still.

story *n.* **1 short story,** tale, fairy tale, fable, myth, legend, anecdote, novel, novella, romance, narrative, chronicle, *inf.* yarn. **2 account,** report, recital, record. **3 story line,** plot, plot development. **4 news item,** news report, article, feature, *inf.* scoop. **5 lie,** white lie, untruth, falsehood, fib, piece of fiction.

stout *adj.* **1 fat,** fattish, plump, portly, tubby, obese, corpulent, rotund, big, heavy, thickset, overweight, bulky, burly, brawny, fleshy, *inf.* beefy. **2 strong,** heavy, solid, substantial, sturdy. **3 stouthearted,** brave, courageous, valiant, valorous, gallant, fearless, unafraid, intrepid, bold, plucky, manly, heroic, lionhearted, daring, tough, doughty, *inf.* gutsy, spunky. **4 firm,** determined, resolute, staunch, steadfast, unyielding, unbending, unfaltering, unswerving, unwavering. **5 vigorous,** forceful, spirited, energetic, strenuous. *Ant.* thin; cowardly; weak.

stow *v.* **place,** deposit, put, put away, pack, store, load, bundle, stuff.

straggle *v.* **1 wander,** ramble, stray, roam, meander, rove, range, spread out. **2 trail behind,** fall behind, lag, string out, linger, loiter. **3 grow untidily,** be messy, be disheveled, be unkempt.

straight *adj.* **1 direct,** undeviating, unswerving, uncurving, unbent, straight as an arrow. **2 successive,** consecutive, in a row, running, uninterrupted, solid, nonstop. **3 level,** symmetrical, even, true, in line, aligned. **4 in order,** orderly, neat, tidy, spruce, shipshape, in place, organized, arranged, sorted out. **5 direct,** honest, faithful, sincere, frank, candid, forthright, straightforward, plainspoken, plain-speaking, plain, matter-of-fact, outspoken, straight from the shoulder, unequivocal, unambiguous, unqualified, unmodified. **6 logical,** rational, sound, intelligent, unemotional, dispassionate. **7 respectable,**

upright, upstanding, honorable, honest, sincere, decent, fair, just, righteous, right-minded, law-abiding, conventional, orthodox. **8 unmixed,** undiluted, unadulterated, pure, neat. *Ant.* bent; indirect; askew; evasive.
▸ *adv.* **1 directly,** by a direct route, without deviating, without delay. **2 straight out,** directly, honestly, frankly, candidly, outspokenly, plainly, straight from the shoulder, with no holds barred, unequivocally, unambiguously, *inf.* pulling no punches. **3 logically,** rationally, intelligently, unemotionally, dispassionately.

straighten *v.* **1 make straight,** adjust, arrange, put in order, make tidy, tidy up, neaten, put to rights. **2 uncurl,** untangle.

straightforward *adj.* **1 straight,** direct, honest, frank, candid, forthright, plain-speaking, unambiguous, straight from the shoulder. **2 uncomplicated,** easy, simple, elementary, effortless, undemanding, unexacting, routine, *inf.* easy as falling off a log, easy as pie. *Ant.* evasive; devious; indirect; complicated.

strain[1] *v.* **1 draw tight,** tighten, make taut, tauten, stretch, extend, elongate, distend. **2 pull,** wrench, twist, sprain, wrick, injure, hurt, damage, weaken,

impair. **3 tax,** overtax, exert to the limit, exert something excessively, overwork, push to the limit, fatigue, tire. **4 make every effort,** make a supreme effort, strive one's utmost, push/drive oneself to the limit, struggle, labor, *inf.* pull out all the stops, go all out, give it one's all. **5 pull,** tug, heave, haul, jerk, *inf.* yank. **6 distort,** falsify, garble, misrepresent, invert, stretch, exaggerate, embroider, overdraw. **7 tax,** overtax, be too much for, go beyond the limit of, exceed the range/scope of, overstep. **8 sieve,** filter, percolate, sift, screen, riddle, separate.
▸ *n.* **1 tightness,** tautness, tension, tensity, distension. **2 wrench,** twist, sprain, wrick. **3 demands,** exertions, burdens, pressure, stress, tension. **4 stress,** pressure of work, tension, overwork, exhaustion, anxiety.
strain² *n.* **1 stock,** descent, lineage, ancestry, family, extraction, blood, breed. **2 variety,** kind, type, sort. **3 trait,** disposition, characteristic, tendency, susceptibility, propensity, proclivity, proneness, inclination. **4 streak,** vein, element, strand, trace, indication, suggestion, suspicion. **5 vein,** way, tone, style, manner. **6 music,**

tone, melody, air, song. **7 line,** snippet, fragment, scrap, bit.
strained *adj.* **1 forced,** artificial, unnatural, false, constrained, labored, wooden, stiff, self-conscious. **2 awkward,** embarrassed, uneasy, uncomfortable, tense, unrelaxed. **3 under a strain,** tense, troubled, uneasy, hostile. *Ant.* natural; relaxed; friendly.
strainer *n.* sieve, colander, filter, sifter, screen, riddle.
strand¹ *n.* **1 thread,** cord, fiber, filament, length. **2 lock,** wisp, tress. **3 element,** component, strain, story line, theme.
strand² *n.* shore, seashore, beach, coast, seaside, waterfront.
stranded *adj.* **1 left helpless,** left penniless, in dire straits, in difficulties, left in the lurch, left high and dry, abandoned, forsaken. **2 grounded,** beached, shipwrecked, wrecked, marooned.
strange *adj.* **1 peculiar,** odd, bizarre, unusual, atypical, abnormal, surprising, weird, funny, unfamiliar. **2 previously unencountered,** unknown, unfamiliar. **3 inexplicable,** anomalous, unexpected, extraordinary. *Ant.* normal; ordinary; familiar.
stranger *n.* **1 unknown person,** alien. **2 new person,** outsider, new

arrival, newcomer, incomer, foreigner.

strangle *v.* **1 throttle,** choke, strangulate, garrote. **2 suppress,** inhibit, repress, check, restrain, hold back, curb, stifle, gag.

strap *n.* **band,** belt, thong, cord, tie.
▸ *v.* **1 fasten,** secure, tie, bind, lash, truss, pinion. **2 bind,** bandage. **3 flog,** lash, whip, scourge, beat, *inf.* belt.

strategic *adj.* **1 tactical,** diplomatic, politic, calculated, planned, plotted, cunning, wily. **2 crucial,** key, vital, critical, essential, important.

strategy *n.* **1 policy,** approach, program, scheme, plan of action, master plan, schedule, blueprint, game plan. **2 art of war,** martial art, military science, military tactics.

stray *v.* **1 wander,** roam, rove, go astray. **2 go astray,** go wrong, do wrong, stray from the straight and narrow, err, sin, transgress, go down the primrose path.
▸ *n.* **homeless animal,** stray dog/cat, homeless person, waif, foundling.

streak *n.* **1 line,** band, strip, stripe, slash, smear. **2 strain,** vein, element, trace, touch, dash. **3 bolt,** flash, beam. **4 smear,** smudge, mark. **5 spell,** period, course, stretch, series.
▸ *v.* **1 band,** stripe, mark, slash, striate, fleck, daub, smear. **2 smear,** smudge, mark. **3 race,** rush, speed, dash, sprint, hurtle, scurry, fly, flee, flash, whistle, zoom, zip, *inf.* tear, whiz.

stream *n.* **1 river,** brook, creek, rivulet, rill, freshet, run, fork. **2 flow,** rush, gush, surge, jet, outpouring, efflux, current, cascade. **3 flow,** current, tide, course, drift.
▸ *v.* **1 flow,** run, pour, course, spill, gush, surge, flood, cascade, well. **2 emit,** issue, shed, spill. **3 flow,** float, swing, flap, flutter. **4 surge,** pour, crowd.

streamlined *adj.* **1 smooth,** sleek, elegant. **2 efficient,** smooth-running, well-run, modernized, rationalized, slick.

street *n.* **road,** thoroughfare, boulevard, avenue, drive, lane.

strength *n.* **1 power,** might, force, brawn, muscle, muscularity, sturdiness, robustness, vigor, toughness, stamina. **2 health,** robustness, healthiness, vigor. **3 fortitude,** courage, bravery, pluck, firmness, stamina, backbone, *inf.* grit, guts. **4 solidity,** toughness, resistance, impregnability. **5 force,** forcefulness, intensity,

vehemence, ardor, fervency.
6 cogency, potency, weight,
effectiveness, efficacy, soundness,
validity. **7 mainstay,** chief support,
tower of strength, anchor,
foundation stone. **8 advantage,**
asset, strong point, forte. **9 size,**
extent, magnitude, bigness,
largeness, greatness. *Ant.* frailty;
infirmity; weakness; failing.
strengthen *v.* **1 make strong,**
make stronger, give strength to,
make healthy, nourish, build up.
2 grow strong, grow stronger,
gain strength, intensify, heighten.
3 make stronger, give strength to,
fortify, give a boost to, harden,
stiffen, toughen, steel. **4 give
strength to,** reinforce, support,
back up, bolster, authenticate,
confirm, substantiate,
corroborate.
strenuous *adj.* **1 arduous,**
laborious, taxing, demanding,
difficult, hard, tough, uphill,
heavy, weighty, burdensome,
exhausting, tiring, fatiguing.
2 energetic, active, vigorous,
forceful, strong, spirited, bold,
determined, resolute, tenacious,
earnest, keen, zealous. *Ant.* easy;
effortless; halfhearted.
stress *n.* **1 strain,** pressure,
tension, worry, anxiety. **2 worry,**
anxiety, trouble, difficulty,
distress, trauma. **3 emphasis,**

priority, importance, weight,
significance, value, worth, merit.
4 emphasis, accent, accentuation.
5 strain, tension, tensity,
tightness, tautness, stretching.
▶ *v.* **1 lay stress on,** emphasize,
place emphasis on, give emphasis
to, accentuate, underline,
underscore, point up, highlight,
spotlight, press home, dwell on,
harp on, belabor, place the accent
on. **2 tax,** overtax, pressurize,
overwork, overstretch,
overburden, push to the limit,
push too far.
stretch *v.* **1 be stretchy,** be elastic,
be tensile. **2 extend,** elongate,
lengthen, expand, draw out, pull
out. **3 get larger,** get bigger,
enlarge, expand, pull out of
shape. **4 reach out,** hold out, put
forth, proffer, offer. **5 unbend,**
extend, elongate. **6 extend,**
spread, unfold, cover, range. **7 be
a challenge to,** challenge, extend,
tax, push to the limit. **8 strain,**
overstrain, exaggerate, overdraw,
push too far. *Ant.* shorten;
contract.
▶ *n.* **1 expanse,** area, tract, extent,
spread, sweep. **2 period,** time,
spell, term, space, run, stint.
strict *adj.* **1 precise,** exact, close,
faithful, true, accurate,
scrupulous, meticulous,
conscientious, punctilious.

2 stringent, rigorous, severe, harsh, hard, stern, authoritarian, rigid, narrow, austere, illiberal, inflexible, unyielding, uncompromising. **3 absolute,** utter, complete, total, perfect. **4 orthodox,** fundamentalist. *Ant.* loose; moderate; liberal; lenient.

stride *v.* **step,** pace, walk, stalk.
▸ *n.* **step,** pace.

strident *adj.* **harsh,** raucous, rough, grating, discordant, rasping, jarring, shrill, loud, screeching, unmelodious, unmusical, stridulous, stridulant, stridulatory. *Ant.* soft; musical; dulcet.

strife *n.* **conflict,** friction, discord, disagreement, dissension, dispute, argument, quarreling, wrangling, bickering, controversy, contention, ill feeling, hostility, animosity. *Ant.* peace; harmony.

strike *v.* **1 bang,** beat, hit, pound, batter. **2 hit,** slap, smack, beat, batter, thrash, thump, thwack, punch, cuff, box, knock, rap, buffet, smite, cane, lash, whip, *inf.* wallop, belt, tan someone's hide, clout, whack, bash, clobber, bop, lambaste, sock, plug. **3 run into,** knock into, bang into, bump into, smash into, collide with, dash against. **4 hit,** drive, propel, *inf.* swipe, smack, knock. **5 light,** ignite. **6 attack,** launch an attack upon, charge, make an assault on, assault, storm, set upon, fall upon. **7 hit,** come upon, affect, afflict, smite. **8 reach,** achieve, arrive at, find, attain, effect. **9 agree on,** come to an agreement on, settle on, sign, endorse, ratify, sanction. **10 assume,** adopt, take on, affect, feign. **11 discover,** find, come upon, light upon, chance upon, happen upon, stumble upon, unearth, uncover, turn up. **12 occur to,** come to, come to the mind of, dawn on, hit. **13 seem to,** appear to, impress, affect, have an impact on. **14 go on strike,** protest, walk out. **15 delete,** cross out, erase, rub out, obliterate.
▸ *n.* **1 hit,** slap, smack, thump, thwack, punch, cuff, box, knock, *inf.* wallop, clout, whack, bop, plug. **2 discovery,** find, unearthing, uncovering. **3 air strike,** air attack, attack, assault, bombing, blitz. **4 walkout,** protest.

striking *adj.* **1 noticeable,** obvious, conspicuous, evident, visible, distinct, prominent, clear-cut, unmistakable, remarkable, extraordinary, incredible, amazing. **2 impressive,** imposing, grand, splendid, magnificent, superb, marvelous, wonderful, dazzling, *inf.* great, smashing. **3 attractive,** good-looking, beautiful, glamorous, stunning, gorgeous. *Ant.* inconspicuous; ordinary; unremarkable.

string *n.* **1 twine,** cord, yarn, rope, cable, line. **2 chain,** series, succession. **3 line,** row, queue, procession, file, column, stream, succession, sequence. **4 strand,** necklace.

▸ *v.* **1 hang,** suspend, sling. **2 stretch,** sling, run, fasten, tie, secure. **3 thread.**

stringent *adj.* **1 strict,** firm, rigid, rigorous, severe, harsh, tough, tight, exacting, demanding, inflexible, hard and fast, uncompromising. **2 difficult,** tight, hard, harsh, tough. *Ant.* lenient; mild; easy.

stringy *adj.* **1 straggly,** straggling. **2 lanky,** gangling, spindly, skinny, wiry. **3 tough,** fibrous, gristly, leathery.

strip[1] *v.* **1 strip naked,** undress, take one's clothes off, remove one's clothes, disrobe, unclothe. **2 peel,** pare, skin, excoriate. **3 remove,** take off, peel off, flake off. **4 dismantle,** break down (to pieces), take apart. **5 clear out,** empty out, clean out, plunder, ransack, rob.

strip[2] *n.* **piece,** bit, band, belt, ribbon, stripe, bar, swathe, slip, fillet.

stripe *n.* **strip,** band, belt, bar.

striped *adj.* **banded,** barred, striated, variegated.

stripling *n.* **youth,** adolescent, youngster, boy, lad, teenager, child, juvenile, minor, young man, *inf.* kid, young'un, shaver.

strive *v.* **try,** try hard, attempt, endeavor, make an effort, make every effort, exert oneself, do one's best, do all one can, do one's utmost, labor, toil, strain, struggle, bend over backward, *inf.* go all out, give it one's best shot.

stroke *n.* **1 blow,** hit, slap, smack, thump, thwack, punch, cuff, box, knock, rap, buffet, smite, *inf.* wallop, clout, whack, bop. **2 movement,** action, motion. **3 accomplishment,** achievement, feat, attainment, coup. **4 movement,** action, mark, line. **5 touch,** detail, bit, addition. **6 striking,** peal, ring, knell, ding-dong, boom. **7 thrombosis,** embolism, cerebral vascular accident, CVA, transient ischemic attack, TIA, seizure, shock, apoplexy.

▸ *v.* **caress,** fondle, pat, touch, rub, massage, soothe.

stroll *v.* **saunter,** amble, wander, meander, ramble, dawdle, promenade, go for a walk, take a walk, stretch one's legs, take the air, *inf.* mosey (along).

▸ *n.* **saunter,** walk, amble, wander,

turn, airing, constitutional, promenade, perambulation.

strong *adj.* **1 powerful,** mighty, brawny, muscular, well-built, strapping, sturdy, burly, robust, vigorous, tough, rugged, stalwart, hardy, lusty, Herculean, strong as an ox/horse/lion. **2 healthy,** well, robust, vigorous, hale and hearty. **3 courageous,** brave, plucky, firm, resolute, strong-minded, determined, forceful, high-powered, self-assertive, tough, formidable, aggressive, redoubtable, *inf.* gutsy. **4 solid,** well-built, heavy, tough, secure, well-fortified, well-defended, well-protected, impregnable, impenetrable. **5 heavy-duty,** solid, sturdy, durable, hard-wearing, long-lasting, enduring. **6 keen,** eager, deep, acute, dedicated, passionate, fervent, zealous. **7 forceful,** intense, vehement, passionate, fervent. **8 keen,** eager, enthusiastic, dedicated, staunch, loyal, steadfast, passionate, fierce, fervent. **9 powerful,** cogent, potent, weighty, compelling, convincing, plausible, effective, efficacious, sound, valid, well-founded. **10 marked,** pronounced, distinct, definite, clear-cut, obvious, evident, unmistakable, notable, remarkable. **11 deep,** intense, vivid, graphic. **12 bright,** brilliant, intense, radiant, gleaming, dazzling, glaring. **13 firm,** energetic, active, forceful, severe, drastic, extreme, draconian. **14 concentrated,** undiluted, highly flavored. **15 alcoholic,** spirituous, intoxicating, heady. **16 potent,** powerful, effective, efficacious. **17 sharp,** pungent, biting, spicy. *Ant.* weak; frail; timid; mild.

structure *n.* **1 building,** edifice, construction, erection, pile, complex. **2 construction,** form, configuration, conformation, shape, constitution, composition, makeup, organization, system, arrangement, design, frame, framework.

▶ *v.* **construct,** build, put together, assemble, shape, design, organize, arrange, order.

struggle *v.* **1 strive,** try hard, endeavor, make every effort, exert oneself, do one's best, do all one can, do one's utmost, battle, labor, toil, strain, bend over backward, *inf.* go all out, give it one's best shot. **2 fight,** grapple, wrestle, scuffle, brawl, *inf.* scrap. **3 fight,** compete, contend, vie, clash, lock horns, cross swords. **4 make one's way with difficulty,** battle, battle one's way, fight one's way.

▶ *n.* **1 striving,** battle, endeavor,

effort, exertion, labor, toiling, pains. **2 fight,** wrestling match, wrestling bout, scuffle, brawl, tussle, *inf.* scrap, set-to. **3 battle,** fight, combat, conflict, contest, hostilities, clash, skirmish, brush, competition, contention, vying, rivalry, trial, labor, problem, trouble, *inf.* grind, hassle.

strut *v.* **swagger,** prance, parade, flounce, sashay.

stubborn *adj.* **obstinate,** headstrong, willful, strong-willed, pigheaded, mulish, dogged, persistent, adamant, inflexible, uncompromising, unbending, unyielding, unmalleable, obdurate, intractable, refractory, recalcitrant, contumacious. *Ant.* compliant; docile; malleable.

stuck *adj.* **1 glued,** fixed, mired, fastened. **2 immovable,** immobile, fast, fixed, rooted. **3 baffled,** beaten, stumped, at a loss, perplexed, nonplussed, at one's wits ends, *inf.* up against a brick wall.

student *n.* **pupil,** schoolboy, schoolgirl, undergraduate, trainee, apprentice, probationer.

studied *adj.* **deliberate,** willful, conscious, calculated, purposeful, studious, contrived, affected, forced, feigned, artificial. *Ant.* unpremeditated; natural; spontaneous.

studious *adj.* **1 scholarly,** academic, intellectual, bookish, book-loving, serious, earnest. **2 diligent,** careful, attentive, industrious, assiduous, painstaking, thorough, meticulous, punctilious, zealous, sedulous. **3 studied,** deliberate, willful. *Ant.* careless; negligent.

study *n.* **1 learning,** scholarship, education, academic work, research, book work, reading. **2 investigation,** inquiry, research, examination, analysis, review, survey, scrutiny. **3 office,** workroom, studio, library. **4 paper,** work, essay, review.
▸ *v.* **1 apply oneself,** revise, burn the midnight oil, *inf.* cram. **2 learn,** read up on, read, work at, *inf.* bone up on. **3 investigate,** inquire into, research, conduct research into, look into, examine, analyze, review, survey, conduct a survey of, scrutinize. **4 watch,** keep watch on, look at, observe, keep an eye on, keep under surveillance.

stuff *n.* **1 material,** fabric, matter, substance. **2 things,** objects, articles, items. **3 things,** luggage, baggage, belongings, possessions, goods, goods and chattels, paraphernalia. **4 facts,** information, data, subject, discipline.

▸ *v.* **1 fill,** pack, pad, load, cram, squeeze, crowd, stow, press, force, compress, jam, wedge. **2 thrust,** shove, push, ram. **3 fill,** gorge, overindulge, satiate, *inf.* make a pig of oneself. **4 block,** stop up, bung up, obstruct, choke.

stuffy *adj.* **1 airless,** close, muggy, stifling, suffocating, musty, stale. **2 dull,** boring, dreary, staid, sedate, stiff, formal, pompous, starchy, prim, priggish, straitlaced, conventional, conservative, stodgy, *inf.* fuddy-duddy, square. **3 stuffed-up,** blocked. *Ant.* airy; exciting; informal.

stumble *v.* **1 trip,** lose one's balance, slip. **2 blunder,** lumber, lurch, stagger, reel. **3 stammer,** stutter, hesitate, falter, *inf.* fluff one's lines.

stump *n.* **end,** stub, tail end, butt, remnant, remains.
▸ *v.* **1 baffle,** be too much for, put at a loss, nonplus, mystify, outwit, foil, perplex, puzzle, confound, bewilder, *inf.* flummox, stymie. **2 clomp,** clump, stamp, stomp, lumber, blunder.

stun *v.* **1 daze,** stupefy, knock senseless, knock unconscious, knock out, lay out, knock stupid. **2 shock,** astound, dumbfound, stupefy, overwhelm, overcome, overpower, devastate, stagger, amaze, astonish, take one's breath away, confound, bewilder, confuse, *inf.* flabbergast, hit one like a ton of bricks.

stunning *adj.* **1 impressive,** imposing, remarkable, extraordinary, staggering, incredible, amazing, astonishing, marvelous, splendid, *inf.* mind-boggling, mind-blowing. **2 sensational,** ravishing, dazzling, wonderful, marvelous, magnificent, glorious, exquisite, impressive, splendid, beautiful, lovely, *inf.* gorgeous, out of this world, fabulous, smashing. *Ant.* ordinary; run-of-the-mill; average.

stupendous *adj.* **1 amazing,** astounding, astonishing, extraordinary, remarkable, wonderful, prodigious, phenomenal, staggering, breathtaking, *inf.* fantastic, mind-boggling, mind-blowing. **2 colossal,** immense, vast, gigantic, massive, huge, enormous, mighty. *Ant.* run-of-the-mill; ordinary; slight.

stupid *adj.* **1 unintelligent,** foolish, dense, brainless, mindless, dull-witted, dull, slow-witted, slow, duncelike, doltish, simpleminded, halfwitted, gullible, naïve, *inf.* thick, dim, dumb, dopey, moronic, imbecilic, cretinous. **2 foolish,** silly, unintelligent, idiotic, brainless, mindless, crackbrained, nonsensical, senseless, irresponsible, unthinking, ill-advised, ill-considered, inept, unwise, injudicious, indiscreet, shortsighted, inane, absurd, ludicrous, ridiculous, laughable, fatuous, asinine, pointless, meaningless, futile, fruitless, mad, insane, lunatic, *inf.* crazy, cockeyed. **3 dazed,** stupefied, unconscious. ***Ant.*** intelligent; sensible; prudent; conscious.

stupidity *n.* **1 lack of intelligence,** unintelligence, foolishness, denseness, brainlessness, mindlessness, dull-wittedness, dullness, slow-wittedness, slowness, doltishness, *inf.* thickness, dimness, dumbness, dopiness. **2 foolishness,** folly, silliness, idiocy, brainlessness, senselessness, irresponsibility, injudiciousness, ineptitude, inaneness, inanity, absurdity, ludicrousness, ridiculousness, fatuousness, fatuity, asininity, pointlessness, meaningfulness, futility, fruitlessness, madness, insanity, lunacy, *inf.* craziness.

sturdy *adj.* **1 well-built,** well-made, muscular, athletic, strong, strapping, brawny, powerfully built, powerful, solid, substantial, robust, vigorous, tough, hardy, stalwart, mighty, lusty. **2 strong,** vigorous, stalwart, firm, determined, resolute, tenacious, staunch, steadfast, unyielding, unwavering, uncompromising. ***Ant.*** puny; frail; weak.

stutter *v.* **stammer,** stumble, speak haltingly, hesitate, falter, splutter.

style *n.* **1 kind,** type, variety, sort, design, pattern, genre. **2 technique,** method, methodology, approach, manner, way, mode, system. **3 stylishness,** smartness, elegance, polish, suaveness, urbanity, chic, flair, dash, panache, élan, *inf.* pizzazz, ritziness. **4 comfort,** elegance, chic, affluence, wealth, luxury. **5 fashion,** trend, vogue, mode. **6 mode of expression,** phraseology, wording, language. ▶ *v.* **1 design,** fashion, tailor, make, produce. **2 designate,** call, term, name, entitle, dub, address, denominate, label, tag.

stylish *adj.* **fashionable,** smart, elegant, chic, modish, à la mode, voguish, modern, up-to-date, *inf.* trendy, dressy, trendy, natty, classy, nifty, ritzy, snazzy, snappy, with it. ***Ant.*** unfashionable; dowdy.

subdue *v.* **1 conquer,** defeat, vanquish, get the better of, overpower, overcome, overwhelm, subjugate, master, gain the upper hand at, triumph over, crush, quash, quell, tame, humble, bring to his/her knees, hold in check. **2 control,** curb, restrain, check, hold back, inhibit, rein in, repress, suppress, stifle. *Ant.* arouse; incite; provoke.

subdued *adj.* **1 dim,** muted, toned down, softened, soft, lowered, shaded, low-key, subtle, unobtrusive. **2 quiet,** hushed, noiseless, soundless, silent, still, calm. **3 low-spirited,** downcast, dejected, depressed, down in the mouth, restrained, repressed, inactive, spiritless, lifeless, dull, passive, unexcited, unemotional, unresponsive. *Ant.* bright; noisy; lively.

subject *n.* **1 subject matter,** topic, theme, question, substance, gist, text, thesis. **2 branch of study,** branch of knowledge, course of study, course, discipline. **3 case,** client, patient, participant, *inf.* guinea pig. **4 occasion,** basis, grounds, source. **5 citizen,** national. **6 liege,** subordinate, underling, vassal.

subjective *adj.* **personal,** personalized, individual, biased, prejudiced, bigoted, nonobjective. *Ant.* objective; impartial.

subjugate *v.* **gain mastery over,** gain ascendancy over, gain control of, bring one to his/her knees, bring under the yoke, conquer, vanquish, defeat, crush, quell, quash, overpower, overcome, subdue, tame, break, humble, tyrannize, oppress, enslave.

submerge *v.* **1 go under water,** dive, sink, plummet. **2 immerse,** dip, plunge, dunk. **3 flood,** inundate, deluge, engulf, swamp, overflow (into, onto/upon). **4 overwhelm,** inundate, deluge, swamp, bury, engulf. **5 hide,** conceal, veil, cloak, repress, suppress. *Ant.* surface; come to light; reveal

submission *n.* **1 yielding,** capitulation, agreement, acceptance, consent, accession, compliance. **2 surrender,** yielding, laying down one's arms. **3 observance,** adherence, regulation, subjection. **4 presentation,** presenting, proffering, tendering, proposal, proposing, introduction. **5 sending in,** entry, referral. **6 argument,** assertion, contention, statement, averment, claim. **7 submissiveness,** yielding, compliance, malleability, acquiescence, tractability, manageability, unassertiveness, nonresistance, passivity, obedience, biddability, dutifulness, docility, meekness, patience, resignation, humility, self-effacement, deference, subservience, obsequiousness, servility, subjection, self-abasement, *inf.* bootlicking.

submissive *adj.* **yielding,** compliant, malleable, acquiescent, accommodating, tractable, manageable, unassertive, nonresisting, passive, obedient, biddable, dutiful, docile, meek, patient, resigned, subdued, humble, self-effacing, deferential, obsequious, servile, self-abasing, *inf.* bootlicking. ***Ant.*** headstrong; obstinate; intractable.

submit *v.* **1 put forward,** present, proffer, tender, advance, propose, suggest, introduce, move. **2 put in,** send in, hand in, enter, refer. **3 argue,** assert, contend, state, claim, aver, propound.

subordinate *adj.* **1 lower-ranking,** junior, lower, lesser, inferior. **2 lesser,** minor, secondary, subsidiary, ancillary, auxiliary, subservient. ***Ant.*** superior; major; central.
▸ *n.* **junior,** assistant, second, deputy, aide, underling, inferior, second fiddle, *inf.* sidekick.

subsequent *adj.* **following,** ensuing, succeeding, later, future. ***Ant.*** previous; prior; former.

subservient *adj.* **servile,**

submissive, deferential, obsequious, sycophantic, groveling, fawning, ingratiating, toadying, unctuous, *inf.* bootlicking. ***Ant.*** overbearing; domineering; superior.

subside *v.* **1 abate,** let up, moderate, quiet down, calm, slacken, die down/out, peter out, taper off, recede, lessen, diminish, dwindle. **2 go down,** get lower, sink, fall back, recede. ***Ant.*** intensify; rise.

subsidize *v.* **pay a subsidy to,** give a grant to, contribute to, make a contribution to, give money to, back, support, invest in, sponsor, finance, fund, underwrite, foot the bill for, *inf.* pick up the tab for.

subsidy *n.* **grant,** contribution, backing, support, aid, investment, sponsorship, finance, funding, subvention.

subsist *v.* **1 live,** exist, eke out an existence, survive. **2 be in existence,** exist, be alive, live, survive, continue, last.

substance *n.* **1 matter,** material, stuff, medium, mass, fabric. **2 solidity,** body, corporeality, reality, actuality, materiality, concreteness, tangibility. **3 solidity,** meaningfulness, significance, weight, power, soundness, validity, pith.

4 character, backbone, mettle, strength of character. **5 subject matter,** subject, theme, topic, content, text, burden, essence, gist, sense, import. **6 wealth,** affluence, prosperity, money, capital, means, resources, assets, property.

substantial *adj.* **1 real,** true, actual, existing, material, concrete. **2 real,** material, weighty, sizable, considerable, meaningful, significant, important, notable, major, marked, valuable, useful, worthwhile. **3 sizable,** considerable, significant, large, ample, goodly, *inf.* tidy. **4 solid,** sturdy, stout, strong, well-built, durable, large, big, hefty, bulky. **5 solid,** meaningful, significant, weighty, powerful, sound, valid, pithy. **6 successful,** profit-making, prosperous, wealthy, affluent, moneyed, well-to-do. **7 essential,** basic, fundamental. *Ant.* insubstantial; slight; paltry; flimsy.

substitute *n.* **replacement,** deputy, relief, proxy, reserve, surrogate, fill-in, stand-in, standby, locum, stopgap.

subterfuge *n.* **1 trick,** ruse, wile, ploy, stratagem, artifice, dodge, maneuver, pretext, expedient, intrigue, scheme, deception.

2 trickery, intrigue, deviousness, evasion, deception, duplicity.

subtle *adj.* **1 elusive,** delicate, faint, understated, low-key, muted, toned down. **2 fine,** fine-drawn, nice, slight, minute, tenuous, indistinct, indefinite. **3 perceptive,** discerning, sensitive, discriminating, penetrating, astute, keen, acute, shrewd, sagacious. **4 clever,** ingenious, skillful, adroit, complex, intricate, strategic, cunning, crafty, wily, artful, devious. *Ant.* obvious; obtrusive; crude; artless.

subtract *v.* **take away,** take, deduct, *inf.* knock off.

suburb *n.* **outlying district,** residential area, bedroom community.

suburban *adj.* **provincial,** unsophisticated, parochial, insular. *Ant.* sophisticated; cosmopolitan.

subversive *adj.* **undermining,** discrediting, destructive, disruptive, troublemaking, inflammatory, seditious, revolutionary, treasonous.

subvert *v.* **1 overthrow,** overturn, wreak havoc on, sabotage, ruin, destroy, demolish, wreck, upset, disrupt, undermine, weaken. **2 corrupt,** pervert, warp, deprave, contaminate, vitiate.

subway *n.* **underground (railroad),** tunnel, metro, *inf.* tube.

succeed *v.* **1 be successful,** turn out well, work, work out, *inf.* pan out, do the trick. **2 come after,** follow, follow after, replace, take the place of, supplant, supersede. **3 achieve success,** be successful, do well, make good, prosper, flourish, thrive, triumph, *inf.* make it, do all right for oneself, arrive. ***Ant.*** fail; flop; precede.

success *n.* **1 accomplishment,** achievement, attainment, fulfillment, victory, triumph. **2 successful outcome,** favorable result, positive result, victory. **3 prosperity,** affluence, wealth, life of ease, fame, eminence. **4 best seller,** winner, *inf.* hit, sensation. **5 box-office success,** winner, sell-out, triumph, *inf.* hit, box-office hit, smash hit, sensation. **6 celebrity,** big name, somebody, VIP, star. ***Ant.*** failure; flop; disaster; poverty.

successful *adj.* **1 victorious,** triumphant. **2 prosperous,** affluent, wealthy, well-to-do, famous, eminent, at the top, top. **3 flourishing,** thriving, booming, profitable, profit-making, moneymaking, lucrative. ***Ant.*** unsuccessful; vain; ineffective; poor.

succession *n.* **1 sequence,** series, progression, course, cycle, chain, train, run, continuation. **2 accession,** inheritance, assumption, elevation. **3 line of descent,** descent, ancestral line, dynasty, lineage.

successor *n.* **heir,** heir apparent, next-in-line, replacement, supplanter. ***Ant.*** predecessor; precursor.

succinct *adj.* **short,** brief, concise, compact, condensed, crisp, terse, tight, to the point, pithy, summary, short and sweet, in a few well-chosen words. ***Ant.*** lengthy; long-winded; verbose.

succulent *adj.* **juicy,** moist, luscious, mouthwatering. ***Ant.*** dry.

sudden *adj.* **1 immediate,** instantaneous, abrupt, unexpected, unforeseen, unanticipated, unlooked-for, without warning. **2 rapid,** swift, speedy, fast, quick, meteoric. ***Ant.*** gradual; gentle; prolonged.

suddenly *adv.* **all of a sudden,** all at once, instantaneously, abruptly, unexpectedly, without warning, *inf.* out of the blue.

sue *v.* **take one to court,** take legal action against, bring an action against, prefer/bring charges against, charge, bring a suit against, prosecute, bring to trial, summons, indict, *inf.* have the law on.

suffer v. **1 be in pain,** feel pain, be racked with pain, endure agony, hurt, ache. **2 be distressed,** be in distress, experience hardship, be upset, be miserable, be wretched, be hurt, hurt, be handicapped. **3 experience,** undergo, sustain, encounter, meet with, endure. **4 be impaired,** deteriorate, fall off, decline, get worse. **5 put up with,** tolerate, bear, stand, abide, endure, stomach.

suffice v. **be enough,** be sufficient, be adequate, do, serve, meet requirements, satisfy (demands), answer/fulfill/meet one's needs, inf. fill the bill, hit the spot.

sufficient adj. **enough,** adequate, plenty of, ample, inf. plenty. **Ant.** insufficient; inadequate; sparse.

suffocate v. **1 smother,** stifle, asphyxiate. **2 be breathless,** be short of air, be too hot.

suffuse v. **spread over,** cover, bathe, mantle, permeate, pervade, imbue.

suggest v. **1 propose,** put forward, move, submit, recommend, advocate, inf. throw out. **2 put one in mind of,** bring to mind, evoke. **3 indicate,** lead (one) to believe, give the impression, give the idea. **4 insinuate,** hint, imply, intimate.

suggestion n. **1 proposal,** proposition, plan, motion, submission, recommendation. **2 hint,** trace, touch, suspicion. **3 insinuation,** hint, implication, intimation.

suggestive adj. **1 provocative,** titillating, sexual, sexy, indecent, indelicate, improper, off-color, smutty, dirty, ribald, bawdy, racy, blue, risqué, lewd, salacious. **2 redolent,** indicative, evocative, reminiscent.

suit n. **1 set of clothes,** outfit, costume, ensemble. **2 lawsuit,** court case, action, proceedings, prosecution. **3 petition,** appeal, request, plea, entreaty. **4 courtship,** wooing, addresses, attentions.
▸ v. **1 become,** look attractive on, enhance the appearance of, go well with, look right on. **2 be suitable for,** be convenient for, be acceptable to, meet requirements, satisfy demands, be in line with the wishes of. **3 be agreeable to,** agree with, be good for, be healthy for. **4 make appropriate,** make fitting, tailor, fashion, accommodate, adjust, adapt, modify.

suitable adj. **convenient,** acceptable, satisfactory, right, appropriate, fitting, apt, becoming, seemly, decorous, proper, well qualified, ideal. *Ant.* unsuitable; unfit; inapt.

sulk *v.* **mope,** pout, be sullen, have a long face, be in a bad mood, be put out, be out of sorts, be grumpy, *inf.* be in a huff.

sulky *adj.* **moping,** pouting, moody, sullen, piqued, disgruntled, ill-humored, grumpy.

sullen *adj.* **morose,** unresponsive, uncommunicative, unsociable, resentful, sulky, sour, glum, gloomy, dismal, cheerless, surly, cross, angry, frowning, glowering, grumpy. *Ant.* outgoing; sociable; responsive.

sultry *adj.* **1 airless,** stuffy, stifling, suffocating, close, oppressive, muggy, humid, sticky, hot, sweltering. **2 sensual,** sexy, voluptuous, seductive, provocative, alluring, tempting, passionate, erotic.

sum *n.* **1 sum total,** grand total, tally, aggregate, answer. **2 amount,** quantity. **3 arithmetic/ arithmetical problem,** problem, calculation, reckoning, tally. **4 entirety,** totality, total, whole, *inf.* whole shebang, whole (kit and) caboodle, whole shooting match.

summarize *v.* **give/make a summary of,** sum up, give a synopsis of, précis, give a précis of, give a résumé of, give an abstract of, abridge, condense, epitomize, outline, sketch, give the main points of, give a rundown of, review.

summary *n.* **synopsis,** précis, résumé, abstract, abridgment, digest, epitome, outline, sketch, rundown, review, summing-up. ▸ *adj.* **1 immediate,** instant, instantaneous, direct, prompt, speedy, swift, rapid, without delay, sudden, abrupt, hasty, peremptory, without discussion, without formality. **2 abridged,** abbreviated, shortened, condensed, short, brief, concise, succinct, thumbnail, cursory. *Ant.* dilatory; slow; lengthy.

summit *n.* **1 top,** peak, crest, crown, apex, vertex, apogee. **2 peak,** height, pinnacle, culmination, climax, crowning point, zenith, acme. *Ant.* bottom; base; nadir.

summon *v.* **1 send for,** call for, bid, request the presence of, demand the presence of. **2 order,** call, convene, assemble, convoke, muster, rally. **3 summons,** serve with a summons, cite, serve with a citation, serve with a writ, subpoena.

sumptuous *adj.* **lavish,** luxurious, deluxe, opulent, magnificent, gorgeous, splendid, rich, costly, expensive, dear, extravagant, *inf.* plush, ritzy. **Ant.** humble; plain; cheap.

sundry *adj.* **1 several,** various, varied, miscellaneous, assorted, diverse. **2 several,** some, various, different.

sunken *adj.* **1 at a lower level,** below ground level, lowered. **2 hollow,** hollowed, concave, drawn, haggard.

sunlight *n.* **sun,** sunshine, light, daylight, light of day.

sunny *adj.* **1 sunshiny,** sunlit, bright, clear, fine, cloudless, unclouded, without a cloud in the sky. **2 happy,** cheerful, cheery, lighthearted, bright, glad, gay, merry, joyful, buoyant, bubbly, blithe, hopeful, optimistic. **Ant.** dull; shady.

sunrise *n.* **dawn,** crack of dawn, daybreak, sunup, first light, morning, *lit.* aurora.

sunset *n.* **sundown,** nightfall, close of day, evening, twilight, dusk, gloaming.

sunshine *n.* **1 sun,** sunlight, sun's rays. **2 happiness,** laughter, cheerfulness, gladness, gaiety, merriment, joy, joyfulness, blitheness.

superb *adj.* **1 superlative,** excellent, first-rate, first-class, outstanding, remarkable, dazzling, brilliant, marvelous, magnificent, wonderful, splendid, exquisite, *inf.* fantastic, fabulous, A-1. **2 magnificent,** gorgeous, splendid, sumptuous, opulent, lavish, luxurious, deluxe, *inf.* plush, ritzy. **Ant.** poor; inferior; dreadful.

supercilious *adj.* **arrogant,** haughty, conceited, proud, vain, disdainful, scornful, condescending, superior, patronizing, imperious, overbearing, lofty, lordly, snobbish, snobby, *inf.* hoity-toity, high-and-mighty, uppity, snooty, stuck-up.

superficial *adj.* **1 surface,** exterior, external, outer, outside, peripheral, slight. **2 cursory,** perfunctory, hasty, hurried, casual, sketchy, desultory, slapdash. **3 outward,** apparent, evident, ostensible. **4 shallow,** empty-headed, trivial, frivolous, silly. **5 lightweight,** insignificant, trivial. **Ant.** deep; profound; thorough.

superfluous *adj.* **1 spare,** surplus, extra, unneeded, unrequired, excess, in excess, supernumerary. **2 unnecessary,** needless, unneeded, inessential, uncalled-for, unwarranted, gratuitous. **Ant.** necessary; essential.

superhuman *adj.* **1 Herculean,** phenomenal, prodigious, stupendous, heroic, extraordinary. **2 divine**, godlike, holy. **3 supernatural,** preternatural, preterhuman, paranormal, otherworldly.

superior *adj.* **1 better,** greater, better-class, more expert, more skillful, more advanced, higher, higher-ranking, higher-up, higher-grade, greater, surpassing, good-quality, high-quality, first-rate, top-quality, high-grade, of the first order, choice, select, prime, upmarket, fine. **2 haughty,** disdainful, condescending, supercilious, patronizing, lofty, lordly, snobbish, snobby, *inf.* high-and-mighty, hoity-toity, uppity, snooty, stuck-up. **Ant.** inferior; low.

▸ *n.* **boss,** manager, chief, supervisor, foreman. **Ant.** inferior; subordinate.

superlative *adj.* **best,** greatest, supreme, consummate, first-rate, first-class, of the first order, of the higher/highest order, brilliant, excellent, magnificent, outstanding, unsurpassed, unparalleled, unrivaled, peerless, matchless, transcendent, *inf.* crack, ace. **Ant.** poor; mediocre; unexceptional.

supernatural *adj.* **1 otherworldly,** unearthly, spectral, ghostly, phantom, magical, mystic, unreal.

2 paranormal, supernormal, hypernormal, psychic, miraculous, extraordinary, uncanny.

supersede *v.* **1 take the place of,** replace, take over from, displace, supplant, oust, usurp. **2 replace,** take the place of, take over from, succeed. **3 discard,** cast aside, throw out, dispose of, abandon, jettison, *inf.* chuck out. **Ant.** precede; antedate.

supervise *v.* **1 superintend,** be in charge of, direct, administer, manage, run. **2 oversee,** keep an eye on, watch, observe, inspect, be responsible for, guide.

supervision *n.* **1 administration,** management, direction, control, charge, superintendence. **2 observation,** inspection, guidance.

supervisor *n.* **1 director,** administrator, manager, overseer, controller, boss, chief, superintendent, *inf.* honcho. **2 overseer,** observer, inspector, guide, adviser.

supplant *v.* **take the place of,** take over from, replace, displace, supersede, oust, usurp, overthrow, remove, unseat.

supple *adj.* **1 lithe,** loose-limbed, limber. **2 pliant,** pliable, flexible, bendable, stretchable, elastic. **Ant.** stiff; rigid.

supplement *n.* **1 addition,** supplementation, additive, extra, add-on. **2 appendix,** addendum, back/end matter, tailpiece, codicil, rider. **3 pullout,** insert, special-feature section, magazine section.
▸ *v.* **add to,** augment, increase, complement.

supplementary *adj.*
1 supplemental, additional, extra, add-on, complementary. **2 added,** appended, attached, extra.

suppliant *n.* **supplicant,** petitioner, pleader, beseecher, applicant, suitor, beggar, appellant.

supplication *n.* **plea,** pleading, entreaty, beseeching, begging, imploration, petition, appeal, solicitation, request, prayer, invocation.

supplies *n.* **provisions,** stores, rations, food, victuals, provender, equipment, materials, matériel.

supply *v.* **1 provide,** give, furnish, contribute, donate, grant, come up with, equip, outfit, *inf.* fork out, shell out. **2 satisfy,** meet, fulfill.
▸ *n.* **1 supplying,** providing, provision, furnishing. **2 stock,** store, reserve, reservoir, stockpile, heap, pile, mass, hoard, cache.

support *v.* **1 bear,** carry, hold up, prop up, bolster up, brace, keep up, shore up, underpin, buttress.

2 maintain, provide for, provide sustenance for, sustain, take care of, look after. **3 give moral support to,** give strength to, be a source of strength to, comfort, help, sustain, encourage, buoy up, hearten, fortify, *inf.* buck up.
4 back up, substantiate, give force to, bear out, corroborate, confirm, verify, validate, authenticate, endorse, ratify. **5 back,** contribute to, give a donation to, give money to, subsidize, fund, finance.
6 back, champion, give help to, help, assist, aid, be on the side of, side with, vote for, stand behind, stand up for, *inf.* stick up for.
7 back, advocate, promote, further, champion, be on the side of, espouse, espouse the cause of, be in favor of, recommend, defend. **8 bear,** put up with, tolerate, stand, abide, suffer, stomach, brook. **Ant.** neglect; abandon; oppose; contradict.
▸ *n.* **1 base,** foundation, pillar, post, prop, underprop, underpinning, substructure, brace, buttress, abutment, bolster, stay. **2 keep,** maintenance, sustenance, subsistence, aliment.
3 moral support, friendship, strengthening, strength, encouragement, buoying up, heartening, fortification, *inf.* bucking up. **4 backing,**

contribution, donation, money, subsidy, funding, funds, finance, capital. **5 backing,** help, assistance, aid, vote, advocacy, promotion, championship, espousal, recommendation, comfort, tower of strength, prop, backbone, mainstay.

supporter *n.* **1 backer,** contributor, donor, sponsor, patron, friend, well-wisher. **2 backer,** helper, adherent, follower, ally, voter, apologist. **3 backer,** adherent, advocate, promoter, champion, defender, apologist. **4 fan,** follower.

supportive *adj.* **helpful,** encouraging, caring, sympathetic, understanding.

suppose *v.* **1 dare say,** assume, take for granted, presume, expect, imagine, believe, think, fancy, suspect, guess, surmise, reckon, conjecture, theorize, opine. **2 take as a hypothesis,** hypothesize, postulate, posit, *inf.* let's say. **3 presuppose,** require, imply.

supposed *adj.* **presumed,** assumed, believed, professed, so-called, alleged, putative, reputed.

supposition *n.* **1 assumption,** presumption, suspicion, guess, surmise, conjecture, speculation, theory. **2 assumption,** hypothesis, postulation.

suppress *v.* **1 conquer,** vanquish, put an end to, crush, quell, squash, stamp out, extinguish, put out, crack down on, clamp down on. **2 restrain,** keep a rein on, hold back, control, keep under control, check, keep in check, curb. **3 keep secret,** conceal, hide, keep hidden, keep silent about, withhold, cover up, smother, stifle, muzzle. *Ant.* encourage; incite; publicize.

supremacy *n.* **1 ascendancy,** predominance, paramountcy, dominion, sway, authority, mastery, control, power, rule, sovereignty, lordship. **2 preeminence,** dominance, superiority, ascendancy, incomparability, inimitability, matchlessness, peerlessness.

supreme *adj.* **1 highest-ranking,** highest, leading, chief, foremost, principal. **2 extreme,** greatest, utmost, uttermost, maximum, extraordinary, remarkable. **3 final,** last, ultimate. *Ant.* subordinate; minimum.

sure *adj.* **1 certain,** definite, positive, convinced, confident, decided, assured, free from doubt, unhesitating, unwavering, unfaltering, unvacillating. **2 assured,** certain, confident, with no doubts, guaranteed, inevitable, irrevocable, *inf.* in the bag. **3 true,** certain, undoubted,

absolute, categorical, well-grounded, well-founded, proven, unquestionable, indisputable, incontestable, irrefutable, incontrovertible, undeniable.
4 certain, unfailing, infallible, never-failing, reliable, dependable, trustworthy, tested, tried and true, foolproof, effective, efficacious, *inf.* sure-fire.
5 true, reliable, dependable, trusted, trustworthy, trusty, loyal, faithful, steadfast. **6 firm,** steady, stable, secure, confident, unhesitating, unfaltering, unwavering. **Ant.** unsure; uncertain; doubtful.

surface *n.* **1 outside,** exterior, top. **2 outward appearance,** superficial appearance, façade.
▶ *adj.* **superficial,** external, exterior, outward.

surge *n.* **1 gush,** rush, outpouring, stream, flow, sweep, efflux. **2 upsurge,** increase, rise, upswing, escalation. **3 rise,** swell, swelling, heaving, billowing, rolling, eddying, swirling.
▶ *v.* **1 gush,** rush, stream, flow.
2 rise, swell, heave, billow, roll, eddy, swirl.

surly *adj.* **bad-tempered,** ill-natured, crabbed, grumpy, crotchety, grouchy, cantankerous, irascible, testy, crusty, gruff, abrupt, brusque, churlish, uncivil,

morose, sullen, sulky. **Ant.** good-natured; friendly; pleasant.

surmise *v.* **guess,** conjecture, suspect, deduce, assume, presume, gather, feel, be of the opinion, think, believe, imagine.

surmount *v.* **1 get over,** overcome, conquer, triumph over, prevail over, get the better of, beat. **2 climb,** ascend, scale, mount. **3 top,** cap, crown. **4 rise above,** tower above, overtop, dominate.

surname *n.* **last name,** family name, patronymic.

surpass *v.* **be greater than,** be better than, beat, exceed, excel, transcend, outdo, outshine, outstrip, overshadow, eclipse.

surplus *n.* **excess,** remainder, residue, surfeit. **Ant.** dearth; shortage; lack.
▶ *adj.* **excess,** in excess, superfluous, leftover, unused, remaining, extra, spare.

surprise *v.* **1 astonish,** amaze, nonplus, take aback, startle, astound, stun, flabbergast, stagger, leave open-mouthed, take one's breath away, *inf.* bowl over, blow one's mind. **2 take by surprise,** catch unawares, catch off guard, catch red-handed, catch in the act, catch napping, burst in on, spring upon, catch with his/her pants down.

▸ *n.* **1 astonishment,** amazement, incredulity, wonder. **2 shock,** bolt from the blue, bombshell, revelation.

surprised *adj.* **astonished,** amazed, nonplussed, startled, astounded, stunned, flabbergasted, staggered, open-mouthed, speechless, thunderstruck.

surprising *adj.* **astonishing,** amazing, startling, astounding, staggering, incredible, extraordinary, remarkable, *inf.* mind-blowing.

surrender *v.* **1 give up,** relinquish, renounce, forgo, forsake, cede, abdicate, waive. **2 hand over,** give up, deliver (up), part with, let go of, relinquish. **3 give in,** give oneself up, yield, submit, capitulate, lay down one's arms, raise/show the white flag, throw in the towel. **4 give way,** yield, succumb, capitulate, give up, abandon, leave behind, lose. *Ant.* resist; withstand; defy.
▸ *n.* **1 surrendering,** relinquishment, renunciation, forgoing, ceding, cession, abdication, waiving. **2 yielding,** capitulation, submission.

surreptitious *adj.* **stealthy,** clandestine, secret, sneaky, sly, cunning, furtive, underhand, underhanded, undercover, covert. *Ant.* open; honest; blatant.

surround *v.* **go around,** encircle, enclose, encompass, ring, gird, girdle, fence in, hem in, confine.

surrounding *adj.* **neighboring,** nearby.

surroundings *plural noun* **environment,** setting, milieu, element, background.

survey *v.* **1 look at,** take a look at, observe, view, contemplate, regard, examine, inspect, look over, scan, study, consider, review, examine, inspect, scrutinize, take stock of, *inf.* size up. **2 make a survey of,** value, carry out a valuation of, estimate the value of, appraise, assess, prospect, triangulate.
▸ *n.* **study,** consideration, review, overview, examination, inspection, scrutinization, scrutiny, valuation, appraisal, investigation, inquiry, research, probe, questionnaire.

survive *v.* **1 live on,** be extant, continue, remain, last, persist, endure, exist, be. **2 outlive,** outlast, live after, remain alive after. **3 remain alive,** live, hold out, pull through, cling to life.

susceptible *adj.* **1 impressionable,** likely to be taken in, credulous, gullible, innocent, defenseless, vulnerable, receptive, easily led. **2 subject,** liable, prone, inclined, predisposed, disposed. *Ant.* skeptical; immune; resistant.

suspect *v.* **1 feel,** have a feeling, be inclined to think, fancy, surmise, guess, conjecture, have a suspicion, speculate, have a hunch, suppose, believe, think, conclude. **2 doubt,** have doubts about, harbor suspicions about, have misgivings about, be skeptical about, distrust, mistrust, regard as guilty, regard as a wrongdoer.

suspend *v.* **1 hang,** put up, swing, dangle, sling. **2 adjourn,** interrupt, cut short, bring to an end, cease, discontinue, break off, arrest, put off, postpone, delay, defer, shelve, pigeonhole, table, put on the back burner, *inf.* put on ice. **3 debar,** shut out, exclude, keep out, remove. *Ant.* continue; resume.

suspense *n.* **uncertainty,** doubt, doubtfulness, anticipation, expectation, expectancy, excitement, tension, anxiety, nervousness, apprehension, apprehensiveness.

suspicion *n.* **1 feeling,** surmise, guess, conjecture, speculation, hunch, supposition, belief, notion, idea, conclusion, *inf.* gut feeling. **2 trace,** touch, suggestion, hint, soupçon, tinge, shade.

suspicious *adj.* **1 doubtful,** unsure, wary, chary, skeptical, distrustful, mistrustful, disbelieving. **2 guilty-looking,** dishonest-looking, strange-looking, queer-looking, funny-looking, *inf.* shifty, shady. **3 questionable,** doubtful, odd, strange, irregular, queer, funny, *inf.* fishy, shady. *Ant.* trustful; upright; innocent.

sustain *v.* **1 bear,** support, carry, keep something up, prop up, shore up. **2 keep something up,** keep something going, continue, carry on, maintain, prolong, protract. **3 support,** give strength to, be a source of strength to, be a tower of strength to, comfort, help, assist, encourage, buoy up, cheer up, hearten, *inf.* buck up. **4 keep alive,** keep going, maintain, continue, preserve, feed, nourish, nurture. **5 experience,** undergo, go through, suffer, endure. **6 uphold,** validate, ratify, vindicate, confirm, verify, corroborate, substantiate, bear out, prove, authenticate, validate.

sustained *adj.* **continuing,** steady, continuous, constant, prolonged, perpetual, unremitting. *Ant.* broken; intermittent; sporadic.

sustenance *n.* **1 food,**

nourishment, daily bread, provisions, victuals, rations, aliment, comestibles, *lit.* provender, *inf.* grub, chow. **2 living,** livelihood, means of support, maintenance, support, subsistence.

swagger *v.* **1 strut,** parade, prance. **2 boast,** brag, bluster, *inf.* show off.
▸ *n.* **1 strut,** parading, prancing. **2 boasting,** bragging, bluster, swashbuckling, braggadocio, vainglory, *inf.* showing-off, swank.

swallow *v.* **1 gulp down,** eat, consume, devour, ingest, *inf.* scarf (down). **2 gulp down,** drink, swill down, *inf.* swig, chug (down). **3 put up with,** tolerate, endure, stand, bear, suffer, abide, stomach, brook. **4 believe,** accept, *inf.* fall for, buy. **5 repress,** restrain, hold back, choke back, control, rein in, eat.

swamp *n.* **marsh,** bog, quagmire, mire, morass, fen, quag.
▸ *v.* **1 flood,** inundate, deluge, wash out, soak, drench, saturate. **2 inundate,** flood, deluge, overwhelm, engulf, snow under, overload, overburden, weigh down, besiege, beset.

swap *v.* **1 exchange,** interchange, trade, barter, switch. **2 exchange,** trade, bandy.

swarm *n.* **crowd,** multitude, horde, host, mob, throng, stream, mass, body, army, flock, herd, pack, drove.
▸ *v.* **flock,** crowd, throng, stream, surge.

swarthy *adj.* **dark,** dark-colored, dark-skinned, dark-complexioned, dusky, tanned. *Ant.* pale; fair.

swashbuckling *adj.* **swaggering,** dashing, daring, adventurous, bold, gallant.

swathe *v.* **wrap,** envelop, bind, swaddle, bandage, bundle up, cover, shroud, drape.

sway *v.* **1 swing,** shake, bend, lean, incline, roll, stagger, wobble, rock, oscillate. **2 waver,** hesitate, fluctuate, vacillate, oscillate. **3 influence,** affect, persuade, prevail on, bring around, win over, induce. **4 rule,** govern, dominate, control, direct, guide.
▸ *n.* **1 jurisdiction,** rule, government, sovereignty, dominion, control, command, power, authority, ascendancy, domination, mastery. **2 control,** domination, power, authority, influence, guidance, direction.

swear *v.* **1 promise (under oath),** solemnly promise, pledge oneself, vow, give one's word, take an oath, swear on the Bible. **2 vow,** insist, be emphatic, pronounce, declare, assert, maintain, contend, aver. **3 curse,**

blaspheme, be blasphemous, utter profanities, be foul-mouthed, use bad language, take the Lord's name in vain, swear like a trooper/sailor, *inf.* cuss.

sweat *n.* **1 perspiration,** *Tech.* diaphoresis. **2 fluster,** fret, dither, fuss, panic, state of anxiety/agitation/nervousness/worry, *inf.* state, flap, tizzy, stew, lather. **3 labor,** effort, chore, backbreaking task.
▸ *v.* **1 perspire,** exude perspiration, drip with perspiration/sweat, break out in a sweat. **2 fret,** dither, fuss, panic, be on tenterhooks, be in a state of anxiety/agitation/nervousness, worry, lose sleep, *inf.* be on pins and needles, worry, agonize, be in a state/flap/tizzy/stew/lather. **3 work hard,** work like a Trojan, labor, toil, slog.

sweaty *adj.* **sweating,** perspiring, clammy, sticky.

sweep *v.* **1 brush,** clean. **2 carry,** pull, drag, drive. **3 glide,** sail, stride, flounce. **4 race,** hurtle, streak, whip, spread like lightning/wildfire, *inf.* tear.
▸ *n.* **1 gesture,** movement, move, action, stroke, wave. **2 curve,** curvature, bend, arc. **3 span,** range, scope, compass, reach. **4 stretch,** expanse, extent, vastness.

sweet *adj.* **1 sweetened,** sugary, sugared, honeyed, syrupy, saccharine, ripe, mellow, luscious. **2 sweet-smelling,** fragrant, aromatic, perfumed, scented, balmy. **3 sweet-sounding,** musical, tuneful, dulcet, mellifluous, soft, harmonious, euphonious, silvery, silver-toned. **4 pleasant,** pleasing, agreeable, delightful, welcome. **5 good-natured,** amiable, pleasant, agreeable, friendly, kindly, charming, likable, appealing, engaging, winning, winsome. **6 attractive,** beautiful, lovely, comely, glamorous. **7 dear,** dearest, darling, beloved, loved, cherished, precious, treasured. *Ant.* sour; harsh; disagreeable.

sweeten *v.* **1 sugar. 2 make agreeable,** soften, ease, alleviate, relieve, mitigate. **3 soften,** soften up, mellow, pacify, appease, mollify. **4 purify,** freshen, ventilate, deodorize.

sweetheart *n.* **1 girlfriend,** boyfriend, lover, suitor, admirer, beau, paramour, inamorato, inamorata, *lit.* swain, *inf.* steady, flame. **2 dear,** dearest, darling, love, beloved, *inf.* honey, sweetie, sugar, baby.

swell *v.* **1 expand,** bulge, distend, become distended, inflate, become inflated, dilate, become bloated, blow up, puff up, balloon, tumefy, intumesce. **2 increase,** grow larger, grow greater, rise, mount, escalate, accelerate, step up, snowball, mushroom. **3 grow loud,** grow louder, intensify, heighten. *Ant.* shrink; contract; decrease. ► *n.* **1 billowing,** undulation, surging. **2 increase,** rise, escalation, acceleration, stepping-up, snowballing, mushrooming.

swelling *n.* **bump,** lump, bulge, blister, inflammation, protuberance, tumescence.

swerve *v.* **change direction,** go off course, veer, turn aside, skew, deviate, sheer, twist.

swift *adj.* **1 fast,** rapid, quick, speedy, fleet-footed, fleet, swift as an arrow, brisk, lively, expeditious, express. **2 rapid,** sudden, abrupt, hasty, hurried, meteoric, prompt, immediate, instantaneous. *Ant.* slow; leisurely; unhurried.

swill *v.* **gulp down,** drink, quaff, swallow, down, drain, guzzle, *inf.* swig, knock off. ► *n.* **1 gulp,** drink, swallow, *inf.* swig. **2 waste,** slop, refuse, scourings.

swim *v.* **1 float,** tread water. **2 be saturated in,** be drenched in, be soaked in, be steeped in, be immersed in.

swindle *v.* **defraud,** cheat, trick, fleece, dupe, deceive, scam, rook, exploit, *inf.* con, rip off, take for a ride, pull a fast one on, bilk. ► *n.* **fraud,** trick, deception, scam, exploitation, *inf.* con job, con, rip-off.

swindler *n.* **fraud,** cheat, trickster, rogue, mountebank, exploiter, *inf.* con man, con artist, shark, bilker.

swing *v.* **1 hang,** be suspended, dangle, be pendent. **2 move back and forth,** sway, oscillate, wag. **3 curve,** veer, turn, lean, incline, wind, twist. **4 march,** stride, stroll. **5 change,** fluctuate, oscillate, waver, seesaw, yo-yo. **6 achieve,** obtain, acquire, get, maneuver. ► *n.* **1 swaying,** oscillation, wagging. **2 rhythm,** beat, pulse. **3 move,** change, variation, turn-around.

swirl *v.* **whirl,** eddy, circulate, revolve, spin, twist, churn, swish.

switch *n.* **1 shoot,** twig, branch. **2 cane,** rod, stick, whip, thong, cat-o'-nine-tails. **3 change,** shift, reversal, turn-around, about-face, swerve, U-turn, changeover, transfer, conversion. **4 exchange,** trade, *inf.* swap. ► *v.* **1 change,** shift, reverse. **2 exchange,** interchange, trade, barter, *inf.* swap.

swollen *adj.* **expanded,** bulging,

distended, inflated, dilated, bloated, blown-up, puffed-up, puffy, tumescent.

swoop *v.* **pounce,** dive, descend, sweep down, drop down.

sycophant *n.* **toady,** flatterer, Uriah Heep, *inf.* bootlicker, yes-man, suck-up.

sycophantic *adj.* **servile,** subservient, obsequious, toadying, fawning, flattering, ingratiating, unctuous, truckling, *inf.* bootlicking.

symbol *n.* **1 emblem,** token, sign, badge, representation, figure, image, type. **2 sign,** character, mark. **3 stamp,** emblem, badge, trademark, logo, monogram.

symbolic *adj.* **1 emblematic,** representative, typical. **2 representative,** illustrative, emblematic, figurative, allegorical.

symbolize *v.* **be a symbol of,** stand for, be a sign of, represent, personify, exemplify, typify, betoken, denote, signify, mean.

symmetrical *adj.* **1 balanced,** well-proportioned, proportional, in proportion, regular, even, harmonious. **2 regular,** even, uniform, consistent, in agreement. *Ant.* asymmetrical; uneven; disproportionate.

sympathetic *adj.* **1 compassionate,** commiserating, commiserative, pitying, condoling, consoling, comforting, supportive, caring, concerned, solicitous, considerate, kindly, kind, kindhearted, warm, warmhearted, understanding, charitable, empathetic. **2 pleasant,** agreeable, likable, congenial, friendly, sociable, companionable, neighborly, easy to get along with, *inf.* simpatico. *Ant.* unsympathetic; unfeeling; indifferent; unfriendly.

sympathy *n.* **1 compassion,** commiseration, pity, condolence, consolation, comfort, solace, support, caring, concern, solicitude, solicitousness, consideration, kindness, kindheartedness, warmth, warmheartedness, charity, charitableness, understanding, empathy. **2 affinity,** empathy, rapport, fellow feeling, harmony, accord, compatibility, closeness, friendship. **3 favor,** approval, approbation, good will, commendation, support, encouragement. *Ant.* indifference; hostility; disapproval.

symptom *n.* **1 sign,** indication, signal, warning, mark, characteristic, feature. **2 expression,** sign, indication, signal, mark, token, evidence, demonstration, display.

synthesis *n.* **1 combination,** combining, union, unification, merging, amalgamation, fusion, coalescence, integration. **2 combination,** union, amalgam, blend, compound, fusion, coalescence.

synthetic *adj.* **manufactured,** man-made, fake, artificial, mock, ersatz. ***Ant.*** real; genuine; natural.

system *n.* **1 structure,** organization, order, arrangement, *inf.* setup. **2 method,** methodology, technique, process, procedure, approach, practice, line, attack, means, way, modus operandi. **3 systematization,** methodicalness, orderliness, planning, logic, tightness, routine.

systematic *adj.* **structured,** organized, methodical, orderly, well-ordered, planned, systematized, logical, efficient, businesslike. ***Ant.*** disorganized; haphazard; chaotic.

Tt

table *n.* **1 counter,** bar, buffet, bench, stand. **2 food,** fare, meal, victuals, *inf.* spread, nosh, grub, chow. **3 tableland,** plateau, flat, mesa. **4 list,** catalog, tabulation, inventory, digest, itemization, index. **5 chart,** diagram, figure, graph, plan.
▸ *v.* **postpone,** defer, suspend, shelve, *inf.* put on ice.

tablet *n.* **1 slab,** panel, stone. **2 pill,** capsule, lozenge. **3 pad,** notepad, memo/scratch pad, notebook.

taboo *adj.* **forbidden,** prohibited, banned, proscribed, vetoed, ruled out, outlawed, not permitted, not acceptable, frowned on, beyond the pale. *Ant.* acceptable; permitted.
▸ *n.* **prohibition,** proscription, veto, interdiction, nonacceptance, interdict, ban.

tacit *adj.* **implicit,** understood, implied, taken for granted, unstated, undeclared, unspoken, unexpressed, unmentioned, unvoiced, silent, wordless. *Ant.* explicit.

taciturn *adj.* **unforthcoming,** uncommunicative, reticent, secretive, untalkative, tight-lipped, closemouthed, quiet, silent, mute, dumb, reserved, withdrawn, aloof, cold, detached. *Ant.* communicative; loquacious.

tack *n.* **1 nail,** pin, staple, rivet. **2 course/line of action,** method, approach, process, way, policy, tactic, plan, strategy, attack.
▸ *v.* **1 nail,** pin, staple, fix, fasten, affix, put up/down. **2 stitch,** baste, sew. **3 change course/direction,** alter one's approach, change one's mind/attitude, have a change of heart, do an about-face, *inf.* do a U-turn. **4 add,** attach, append, tag, annex.

tackle *n.* **gear,** equipment, apparatus, rig, outfit, tools, implements, accouterments, paraphernalia, trappings, *inf.* things, stuff.
▸ *v.* **1 undertake,** attempt, apply/ address oneself to, get to grips with, set/go about, get to work at, busy oneself with, embark on, set one's hand to, take on, engage in. **2 grapple with,** seize, take hold of, confront, face up to, *inf.* have a go at. **3 speak to,** confront, accost, waylay, remonstrate with.

tacky[1] *adj.* **sticky,** gluey, gummy, *inf.* gooey.

tacky[2] *adj.* **tawdry,** tasteless, kitsch, vulgar, crude, garish, gaudy, flashy.

tact *n.* **diplomacy,** discretion, savoir faire, sensitivity, understanding, thoughtfulness, consideration, delicacy, subtlety, finesse, skill, adroitness, dexterity, discernment, perception, judgment, prudence, judiciousness, *inf.* savvy. **Ant.** indiscretion; tactlessness.

tactful *adj.* **diplomatic,** politic, discreet, sensitive, understanding, thoughtful, considerate, delicate, subtle, skillful, adroit, discerning, perceptive, prudent, judicious. **Ant.** tactless; indiscreet.

tactic *n.* **maneuver,** expedient, device, stratagem, trick, scheme, plan, ploy, course/line of action, method, approach, tack, means.

tactical *adj.* **strategic,** politic, planned, shrewd, skillful, adroit, clever, smart, cunning, artful.

tactless *adj.* **undiplomatic,** impolitic, indiscreet, insensitive, inconsiderate, indelicate, unsubtle, rough, crude, unskillful, clumsy, awkward, inept, bungling, maladroit, gauche, undiscerning, imprudent, injudicious. **Ant.** tactful; diplomatic; discreet.

tag *n.* **1 label,** ticket, sticker, docket. **2 tab,** loop, flap.
▸ *v.* **1 label,** put a ticket/sticker on, mark. **2 name,** call, nickname, title, entitle, label, dub, term, style, christen. **3 add,** attach, append, affix, tack.

tail *n.* **1 brush,** scut, dock, *Tech.* cauda. **2 bottom,** rump, buttocks, *inf.* butt, backside, rear. **3 tail-end,** close, end, conclusion, termination. **4 track,** trail, scent. **5 detective,** investigator, private investigator, shadow, *inf.* sleuth, private eye, gumshoe. **Ant.** head; front.
▸ *v.* **follow,** shadow, stalk, trail, track, dog the footsteps of, keep under surveillance.

tailor *n.* **outfitter,** dressmaker, couturier, clothier, costumier.
▸ *v.* **fit,** suit, fashion, style, mold, shape, adapt, adjust, modify, convert, alter, accommodate.

take *v.* **1 get/lay hold of,** get into one's hands, grasp, grip, clutch. **2 get,** receive, obtain, gain, acquire, secure, procure, come by, win, earn. **3 seize,** catch, capture, arrest, carry off, abduct. **4 remove,** appropriate, make off with, steal, filch, pilfer, purloin, pocket, *inf.* pinch, swipe. **5 buy,** purchase, pay for. **6 reserve,** book, engage, rent, hire, lease. **7 pick,** choose, select, decide on, settle on, opt for. **8 use,**

make use of, utilize. **9 consume,** eat, devour, swallow, drink, imbibe. **10 be effective,** have/take effect, be efficacious, work, operate, succeed. **11 use,** use up, require, call for, need, necessitate. **12 carry,** fetch, bring, bear, transport, convey, cart, *inf.* tote. **13 escort,** accompany, conduct, guide, lead, usher, convoy. **14 experience,** be affected by, undergo, suffer. **15 find out,** discover, ascertain, determine, establish. **16 understand,** interpret as, grasp, gather, comprehend, apprehend, assume, believe, suppose, consider, presume. **17 receive,** deal with, cope with. **18 accept,** receive, adopt. **19 enter upon,** undertake, begin, set about. **20 study,** learn, be taught, take up, pursue. **21 perform,** execute, effect, do, make, have. **22 engage in,** occupy oneself in. **23 hold,** contain, have the capacity for, have space/room for, accommodate. **24 bear,** tolerate, stand, put up with, stomach, brook. **25 derive,** obtain, come by. **26 extract,** quote, cite, excerpt, derive, abstract. **27 subtract,** deduct, remove. **28 captivate,** enchant, charm, delight, please, attract, win over, fascinate. **29 catch on,** become popular, gain popularity, be successful, succeed.

▶ *n.* **1 catch,** haul, bag. **2 takings,** proceeds, returns, receipts, profits, winnings, purse, pickings, earnings, gain, income, revenue.

takings *pl. n.* **proceeds,** returns, receipts, earnings, winnings, pickings, profit, gain, income, revenue.

tale *n.* **1 story,** short story, narrative, anecdote, legend, fable, myth, parable, allegory, epic, saga, *inf.* yarn. **2 talk,** rumor, gossip, hearsay, report, allegation. **3 lie,** fib, falsehood, untruth, fabrication, piece of fiction, *inf.* story, tall story, cock-and-bull story, whopper.

talent *n.* **gift,** flair, aptitude, facility, knack, bent, ability, capacity, faculty, aptness, endowment, strong point, forte, genius.

talented *adj.* **gifted,** accomplished, able, capable, apt, deft, adept, proficient, brilliant, expert, artistic. **Ant.** incapable; hopeless; inept.

talk *v.* **1 speak,** give voice/ utterance, chat, chatter, gossip, prattle, prate, gibber, jabber, babble, rattle on, *inf.* yak, gab. **2 speak,** say, utter, voice, express, articulate, pronounce, enunciate, verbalize. **3 communicate,** converse, speak to each other, discuss things, confer, consult

each other, have negotiations, have a tête-à-tête, parley, palaver, confabulate, *inf.* have a confab, chew the fat, jaw, rap. **4 tell,** reveal all, tell tales, give the game away, open one's mouth, let the cat out of the bag, *inf.* blab, squeal, spill the beans, sing.
5 gossip, spread rumors, pass comment, make remarks, criticize. **6 give a talk,** give/make/ deliver a speech, speak, lecture, discourse. **7 speak,** speak out, speak up, give voice, tell the facts, divulge information, reveal all.
▸ *n.* **1 talking,** speaking, chatter, chatting, gossiping, prattling, gibbering, jabbering, babbling, gabbling, *inf.* yakking, gabbing.
2 words, speech, language, dialect, jargon, cant, slang, idiom, idiolect, patois, *inf.* lingo.
3 conversation, chat, discussion, tête-à-tête; dialogue, *inf.* confab, rap. **4 lecture,** speech, address, discourse, oration, sermon, disquisition. **5 gossip,** rumor, hearsay. **6 chat,** conversation, discussion, gossip, subject, theme.
talkative *adj.* **loquacious,** garrulous, voluble, chatty, gossipy, conversational, long-winded, gushing, effusive, *inf.* gabby, mouthy, bigmouthed. **Ant.** taciturn; uncommunicative.

tall *adj.* **1 big,** colossal, gigantic, lanky, rangy, gangling, high, lofty, towering, soaring, sky-high, skyscraping. **2 in height,** high.
3 exaggerated, unlikely, incredible, far-fetched, implausible. **Ant.** short; small; low.
tally *n.* **count,** record, running total, reckoning, enumeration, register, roll, census, poll, score, result, total, sum.
▸ *v.* **1 add (up),** total, sum (up), count (up), reckon. **2 agree,** accord, concur, coincide, conform, correspond, match, fit, harmonize.
tame *adj.* **1 domesticated,** gentle, docile. **2 subdued,** docile, submissive, compliant, meek, obedient, tractable, amenable, manageable, unresisting.
3 unexciting, uninteresting, uninspired, dull, bland, flat, insipid, vapid, run-of-the-mill, mediocre, prosaic, humdrum, boring, tedious, wearisome. **Ant.** wild; fierce.
▸ *v.* **1 domesticate,** break, train, gentle. **2 subdue,** discipline, curb, control, master, overcome, suppress, repress, humble.
tan *adj.* **yellowish-brown,** brownish-yellow, light brown, pale brown, tawny.
tangible *adj.* **1 touchable,**

palpable, tactile, visible.
2 concrete, real, actual, solid, substantial, hard, well-documented, well-defined, definite, clear, clear-cut, distinct, unmistakable, positive, discernible. **Ant.** intangible; abstract.

tangled *adj.* **1 entangled,** twisted, snarled, raveled, knotted, knotty, matted, tousled, messy, *inf.* mussed-up. **2 confused,** jumbled, mixed-up, messy, chaotic, complicated, involved, convoluted, complex.

tank *n.* **1 container,** receptacle, vat, cistern. **2 armored car/vehicle,** combat vehicle.

tantalize *v.* **tease,** torment, torture, frustrate, disappoint, thwart, make one's mouth water, lead on, entice, titillate, allure, beguile.

tape *n.* **1 band,** strip, string, ribbon. **2 adhesive tape,** insulating tape, masking tape, strapping tape, duct tape, *Trademark* Scotch tape. **3 tape recording,** cassette, videotape, videocassette, video, audiotape, audiocassette.
▸ *v.* **1 bind,** tie, fasten, stick, seal, secure, *Trademark* Scotch tape.
2 record, tape-record, video-record, video. **3 seal,** mark with tape.

taper *v.* **narrow,** thin, become narrow/thinner, come to a point.

target *n.* **1 mark,** bull's-eye.
2 prey, quarry, game. **3 objective,** goal, object, aim, end, intention, desired result. **4 butt,** victim, scapegoat.

tariff *n.* **1 price list,** schedule.
2 menu, bill of fare. **3 tax,** duty, toll, excise, levy, impost.

tarnish *v.* **1 dull,** dim, discolor, rust. **2 lose its shine/luster,** discolor, rust. **3 sully,** besmirch, blacken, stain, blemish, blot, taint, befoul, drag through the mud. **Ant.** brighten; polish; enhance.
▸ *n.* **1 discoloration,** oxidation, rust. **2 black mark,** slur, stain, blemish, blot, taint, stigma.

tart[1] *n.* **pastry,** pie, quiche, strudel.

tart[2] *adj.* **1 sharp,** sharp-tasting, sour, tangy, piquant, pungent, bitter, acid, acidulous, vinegary.
2 astringent, caustic, sharp, biting, cutting, stinging, mordant, trenchant, incisive, piercing, acrimonious, barbed, scathing, sarcastic, sardonic. **Ant.** sweet; kind.

task *n.* **job,** duty, chore, charge, odd job, assignment, commission, mission, engagement, occupation, undertaking, exercise, errand, quest.

taste *n.* **1 flavor,** savor, relish, tang. **2 bit,** morsel, bite, mouthful, spoonful, sample, sip, drop, swallow, touch, soupçon. **3 liking,** love, fondness, fancy, desire, preference, penchant, predilection, inclination, partiality, leaning, bent, hankering, appetite, palate, thirst, hunger. **4 discrimination,** discernment, judgment, cultivation, culture, refinement, polish, finesse, elegance, grace, stylishness. **5 decorum,** propriety, correctness, etiquette, politeness, tact, tactfulness, diplomacy, delicacy, nicety, discretion.
▸ *v.* **1 sample,** test, try, nibble, sip. **2 make out,** perceive, discern, distinguish, differentiate. **3 eat,** partake of, consume, devour. **4 have a flavor of,** savor of, smack of. **5 experience,** undergo, encounter, meet, come face to face with, come up against, know.

tasteful *adj.* **1 in good taste,** aesthetic, artistic, harmonious, pleasing, elegant, graceful, beautiful, pretty, charming, handsome, discriminating, refined, restrained. **2 decorous,** proper, seemly, correct, polite, fitting, fit, appropriate, refined, cultured, cultivated. *Ant.* tasteless; tacky; garish; improper.

tasteless *adj.* **1 flavorless,** unflavored, savorless, bland, insipid, watery, watered-down, weak, thin, unappetizing, uninteresting, vapid. **2 vulgar,** crude, tawdry, garish, gaudy, loud, flashy, showy, cheap, gross, meretricious, indecorous, improper, unseemly, incorrect, impolite, rude, unfitting, inappropriate, unrefined, uncultured, uncultivated. *Ant.* spicy; appetizing; tasteful; seemly.

tasty *adj.* **flavorsome,** flavorful, full-flavored, appetizing, palatable, toothsome, delectable, delicious, luscious, mouthwatering, piquant, pungent, spicy, *inf.* scrumptious, yummy. *Ant.* bland; insipid.

taunt *n.* **gibe,** jeer, sneer, insult, barb, catcall, teasing, provocation, ridiculing, derision, mockery, sarcasm, *inf.* dig, put-down.
▸ *v.* **gibe at,** jeer at, sneer at, insult, chaff, tease, torment, provoke, ridicule, deride, mock, poke fun at.

taut *adj.* **1 tight,** stretched, rigid. **2 tightened,** flexed, tensed. **3 tense,** strained, stressed, drawn, *inf.* uptight. **4 in good order/ condition,** orderly, in order, shipshape, tight, trim, neat, well-ordered, well-regulated, tidy, spruce, smart. *Ant.* loose; slack.

tawdry *adj.* **showy,** gaudy, flashy,

garish, loud, tasteless, cheap, cheapjack, shoddy, meretricious, *inf.* tacky, kitsch. **Ant.** tasteful; refined.

tax *n.* **1 levy,** charge, duty, toll, excise, tariff, impost, tribute, customs. **2 burden,** load, weight, encumbrance, strain, pressure, stress, drain.
▸ *v.* **1 levy a tax on,** impose a toll on, charge duty on. **2 make demands on,** weigh heavily on, weigh down, burden, load, encumber, overload, push, push too far, stretch, strain, try, wear out, exhaust, sap, drain, enervate, fatigue, tire, weary, weaken.

teach *v.* **1 give lessons to,** instruct, educate, school, tutor, coach, train, drill, ground, enlighten, edify. **2 give lessons/ instruction in,** instill, inculcate. **3 instruct,** train, show, guide.

teacher *n.* **schoolteacher,** instructor, educator, tutor, coach, trainer, lecturer, professor, pedagogue, guide, mentor, guru.

team *n.* **1 group,** band, bunch, company, party, gang, crew, troupe, set, squad, side, lineup. **2 pair,** span, yoke.
▸ *v.* phrase: **team up join,** get/ come/band together, work together, unite, cooperate, form an alliance.

tear[1] *n.* **1 rip,** split, hole, rent, run, rupture. **2 laceration,** gash, slash, scratch, cut, mutilation, injury, wound.
▸ *v.* **1 rip,** pull apart, pull to pieces, split, rend, sever, rive, sunder, rupture. **2 lacerate,** gash, slash, pierce, stab, scratch, cut, claw, mangle, mutilate, hack, injure, wound. **3 rip,** pull, wrench, yank, wrest, extract, peel, snatch, pluck, grab, seize. **4 divide,** split, rend, disrupt, break apart. **5 disrupt,** distress, upset, harrow, torture, torment. **6 run,** race, sprint, gallop, rush, dash, bolt, career, dart, fly, shoot, hurry, speed, hasten; *inf.* hotfoot it, whiz, zoom, zip.

tear[2] *n.* **1 teardrop. 2 drop,** droplet, globule, bead.

tearful *adj.* **1 in tears,** crying, weeping, sobbing, blubbering, sniveling, whimpering, wailing, emotional, upset, distressed, *inf.* weepy, blubbing. **2 emotional,** upsetting, distressing, heartbreaking, heart-rending, sad, sorrowful, piteous, pitiful, pitiable, pathetic, poignant, mournful, melancholy, lamentable, dolorous.

tease *v.* **1 torment,** provoke, badger, bait, goad, needle, pest, bother, worry, vex, irritate, annoy, gibe, mock, ridicule, poke fun at, *inf.* aggravate. **2 joke (with),**

fool (with), rag, twit, *inf.* kid, rib, have on.

technical *adj.* **1 mechanical,** practical, scientific, applying science, nontheoretical.
2 specialist, specialized, scientific.

technique *n.* **1 method,** modus operandi, system, procedure, style of approach, manner, way, course of action, mode, fashion, means.
2 execution, performance, skill, skillfulness, proficiency, expertise, expertness, mastery, artistry, art, craftsmanship, craft, ability, adroitness, deftness, dexterity, knack. **3 skill,** ability, capability, proficiency, capacity, aptitude, expertise, knack, talent, gift, genius, *inf.* know-how.

tedious *adj.* **wearisome,** wearying, tiresome, tiring, fatiguing, soporific, long-drawn-out, overlong, long-winded, prolix, dull, deadly dull, boring, uninteresting, dry, dreary, drab, unexciting, lifeless, uninspired, flat, banal, vapid, insipid, monotonous, unvaried, prosaic, humdrum, run-of-the-mill, routine. ***Ant.*** exciting; interesting.

teem *v.* **1 abound,** be abundant, be plentiful, be copious.
2 abound, swarm, crawl, bristle, seethe, brim.

teetotaler *n.* **abstainer,** nondrinker.

telephone *v.* **call,** ring, *inf.* phone, give someone a ring/buzz, get on the blower, buzz.

telescope *n.* **glass,** spyglass, reflector, refractor, radio telescope/dish, infrared/X-ray telescope.

television *n.* **television set,** *inf.* TV, tube, boob tube, box, idiot box.

tell *v.* **1 make known,** impart, communicate, announce, proclaim, broadcast, divulge, reveal, disclose, declare, state, mention, utter, voice, say, speak.
2 narrate, relate, recount, give an account of, report, chronicle, recite, rehearse, describe, portray, sketch, delineate. **3 inform,** let know, make aware, apprise, notify. **4 assure,** promise, guarantee, warrant. **5 instruct,** bid, order, give orders, command, direct, charge, enjoin, dictate to, call upon, require. **6 talk,** tell tales, blab, give the game away, open one's mouth, let the cat out of the bag, *inf.* squeal, spill the beans, sing, rat. **7 report,** inform, *inf.* squeal, rat, blow the whistle, pull the plug. **8 reveal,** disclose, show, display, exhibit, indicate. **9 deduce,** make out, discern, perceive, see, identify, recognize, discover, understand, comprehend. **10 distinguish,**

differentiate, discriminate.
11 have an effect, make its
presence felt, count, carry weight,
have influence/force, register, *inf.*
have clout.

telling *adj.* **marked,** significant,
substantial, considerable, sizable,
solid, weighty, important,
striking, impressive, potent,
powerful, forceful, effective,
effectual, cogent, influential,
decisive. *Ant.* unimportant;
insignificant.

temper *n.* **1 temperament,**
disposition, nature, humor, mood,
character, frame of mind, cast of
mind, mind, attitude, stamp.
2 tenor, tone, attitude, vein. **3 bad
mood,** ill humor, fury, rage,
passion, fit of temper/pique,
tantrum, anger, annoyance,
irritation, irritability, irascibility,
hotheadedness, petulance,
peevishness, resentment,
surliness, churlishness.
4 composure, equanimity, self-
control, coolness, calm, calmness,
tranquillity, good humor, *inf.* cool.
▸ *v.* **1 toughen,** anneal, harden,
strengthen, fortify. **2 moderate,**
soften, tone down, modify,
mitigate, alleviate, allay, palliate,
mollify, assuage, lessen, weaken.

temperament *n.* **1 disposition,**
nature, humor, mood, character,
personality, makeup,
constitution, complexion, temper,
spirit, mettle, frame of mind, cast
of mind, mind, attitude, outlook,
stamp, quality. **2 excitability,**
emotionalism, volatility,
mercurialness, capriciousness,
moodiness, oversensitivity,
touchiness, hotheadedness,
impatience, petulance, moods.

temperamental *adj.*
1 constitutional, inherent, innate,
inborn, congenital, deep-rooted,
ingrained. **2 excitable,** emotional,
volatile, mercurial, oversensitive,
capricious, erratic, touchy,
moody, hotheaded, explosive,
impatient, petulant. *Ant.* calm;
stable; easygoing.

temperance *n.* **1 moderation,**
self-restraint, self-control,
abstemiousness, continence,
abstinence, austerity, self-denial.
2 teetotalism, abstinence,
abstention, sobriety, prohibition.

temperate *adj.* **1 moderate,** self-
restrained, restrained,
abstemious, self-controlled,
continent, austere, self-denying.
2 teetotal, abstinent, sober.
3 moderate, mild, gentle,
clement, balmy, pleasant,
agreeable. *Ant.* intemperate;
immoderate; extreme.

tempestuous *adj.* **1 stormy,**
turbulent, blustery, squally,
windy, gusty, breezy. **2 stormy,**

turbulent, boisterous, violent, wild, uncontrolled, unrestrained, passionate, impassioned, emotional, intense, fierce, heated, feverish, hysterical, frenetic.

temple *n.* **place/house of worship,** holy place, house of God, synagogue, church, mosque, shrine, sanctuary.

tempo *n.* **1 beat,** rhythm, cadence, throb, pulse, pulsation. **2 pace,** rate, speed, measure.

temporal *adj.* **1 secular,** nonspiritual, worldly, material, earthly, carnal. **2 of time,** time-related. *Ant.* spiritual; eternal.

temporary *adj.* **1 short-term,** impermanent, interim, provisional, pro tem, pro tempore. **2 brief,** fleeting, passing, momentary, short-lived, here today and gone tomorrow, transient, transitory, ephemeral, fugitive, evanescent, fugacious. *Ant.* permanent; constant.

tempt *v.* **1 try to persuade,** entice, incite, induce, egg on, urge, goad, prompt, sway, influence, persuade, cajole, coax. **2 allure,** lure, entice, attract, whet the appetite of, make one's mouth water, captivate, appeal to, beguile, inveigle, woo, seduce, tantalize. **3 fly in the face of,** risk, bait, provoke.

tempting *adj.* **alluring,** enticing, attractive, captivating, appealing, beguiling, fascinating, tantalizing, appetizing, mouthwatering. *Ant.* repellent.

tenable *adj.* **1 justifiable,** defensible, defendable, arguable, maintainable, supportable, plausible, credible, reasonable, rational, sound, viable. **2 holdable,** occupiable, available. *Ant.* indefensible; untenable.

tenacious *adj.* **1 clinging,** firm, fast, tight, strong, forceful, powerful, unshakable, iron. **2 persistent,** pertinacious, determined, dogged, resolute, firm, steadfast, purposeful, unshakable, unswerving, relentless, inexorable, unyielding, inflexible, stubborn, obstinate, intransigent, obdurate, strong-willed, contumacious. **3 retentive,** retaining, remembering, unforgetful. **4 sticky,** gluey, adhesive, clinging. *Ant.* loose; irresolute; hesitant.

tend[1] *v.* **1 have/show a tendency,** be apt/disposed/liable, be likely. **2 move,** go, head, point, gravitate.

tend[2] *v.* **look after,** take care of, care for, attend to, minister to, see to, cater to, nurse, wait on, watch over, watch, guard, keep an eye on, keep.

tendency *n.* **1 inclination,** disposition, predisposition, proclivity, propensity, proneness, aptness, bent, leaning, penchant, susceptibility, liability. **2 movement,** direction, course, drift, bias, trend.

tender *adj.* **1 succulent,** juicy, soft. **2 easily damaged,** breakable, fragile, frail, delicate, sensitive, slight, feeble. **3 young,** youthful, early, immature, callow, inexperienced, green, raw. **4 compassionate,** softhearted, kind, kindly, sympathetic, warm, caring, humane, gentle, solicitous, generous, benevolent, sentimental, emotional, susceptible, vulnerable, fond, loving, affectionate, warm, amorous, touching, moving, poignant, evocative. **5 sore,** painful, aching, smarting, throbbing, inflamed, irritated, red, raw, bruised. **6 delicate,** sensitive, difficult, tricky, ticklish, risky. ***Ant.*** tough; durable; cruel.

▸ *v.* **1 offer,** proffer, present, extend, give, volunteer, put forward, propose, suggest, advance, submit. **2 put in a bid,** bid, give an estimate, propose a price.

tense *adj.* **1 tight,** taut, rigid, stretched, strained. **2 strained,** under a strain, under pressure, nervous, keyed up, worked up, overwrought, distraught, anxious, uneasy, worried, apprehensive, agitated, jumpy, edgy, on edge, restless, jittery, fidgety, *inf.* uptight, wound up, strung out. **3 nerve-racking,** stressful, worrying, fraught, exciting, cliff-hanging. ***Ant.*** slack; calm; cool; relaxed.

tension *n.* **1 tightness,** tautness, rigidity, stretching, straining. **2 strain,** stress, stressfulness, suspense, pressure, anxiety, unease, disquiet, worry, apprehensiveness, agitation, jumpiness, edginess, restlessness, nerves, ill feeling, hostility, enmity, *inf.* butterflies in the stomach.

tentative *adj.* **1 speculative,** conjectural, experimental, exploratory, trial, provisional, test, pilot, untried, unproven, unconfirmed, unsettled, indefinite. **2 hesitant,** hesitating, faltering, wavering, uncertain, unsure, doubtful, cautious, diffident, timid. ***Ant.*** definite; confident.

tenuous *adj.* **1 fragile,** slight, flimsy, weak, insubstantial, shaky, sketchy, doubtful, dubious, nebulous, hazy, vague, unspecific, indefinite. **2 fine,** thin, slender.

term *n.* **1 word,** expression, phrase, name, title, denomination, appellation, designation. **2 period,** time, spell, interval, stretch, span, duration, space, semester.

▸ *v.* **call,** name, entitle, style, dub, label, tag, designate, denominate.

terminal *adj.* **1 fatal,** deadly, mortal, lethal, killing, incurable. **2 dying,** on one's deathbed, near death, in the throes of death, incurable. **3 boundary,** bounding, limiting, confining, end, ending. ***Ant.*** initial; incipient.

▸ *n.* **1 terminus,** last stop, depot. **2 workstation,** visual display unit, monitor, input/output device, *inf.* VDU.

terminate *v.* **1 bring/come to a close/end/conclusion,** close, end, conclude, finish, stop, wind up, discontinue, cease, discontinue, cancel, result, expire, run out, lapse. **2 abort,** end. ***Ant.*** begin; start; commence; initiate.

terminology *n.* language, phraseology, vocabulary, nomenclature, jargon, cant, argot, terms, expressions, words, *inf.* lingo.

terrible *adj.* **1 great,** extreme, incorrigible, outrageous, *inf.* awful, dreadful, frightful, impossible. **2 bad,** poor, incompetent, useless, talentless, *inf.* rotten. **3 dreadful,** terrifying, frightening, frightful, horrifying, horrible, horrific, horrendous, terrific, harrowing, hideous, grim, unspeakable, appalling, awful, gruesome. **4 extreme,** severe, harsh, unbearable, intolerable, insufferable. **5 nasty,** foul, offensive, odious, obnoxious, vile, revolting, repulsive, abhorrent, loathsome, hateful, unpleasant, disagreeable, *inf.* dreadful, awful, horrible, horrid. ***Ant.*** brilliant; wonderful; pleasant.

terrific *adj.* **1 tremendous,** great, huge, sizable, considerable, intense, extreme, extraordinary, excessive. **2 very good,** excellent, superb, remarkable, magnificent, wonderful, marvelous, great, super, sensational, *inf.* fantastic, fabulous, A-1, ace, wizard, unreal, awesome. **3 dreadful,** frightful, horrible, horrific, hideous, grim, appalling, awful. ***Ant.*** awful; dreadful.

terrify *v.* **terrorize,** frighten to death, frighten, scare stiff, scare, petrify, horrify, make one's blood run cold, make one's flesh crawl, make one's hair stand on end, alarm, panic, intimidate, dismay, appall, shock, paralyze with fear, put the fear of God into, *inf.* spook.

territory *n.* **1 country,** state, domain, county, district, region, area, terrain, tract, space. **2 area,** area of concern/activity, province, field, sector, department. **3 area,** section, route, beat, ambit.

terror *n.* **1 fright,** fear, fear and trembling, dread, alarm, panic, intimidation, dismay, consternation, shock, horror, *inf.* heebie-jeebies. **2 bogeyman,** bugbear, monster, demon, fiend, devil. **3 hooligan,** ruffian, hoodlum, villain, rogue, rascal, troublemaker, *inf.* holy terror.

terrorize *v.* **1 strike terror in/into,** terrify, frighten to death, scare stiff, petrify, horrify. **2 coerce,** browbeat, bully, intimidate, menace, threaten, *inf.* bulldoze, strong-arm.

terse *adj.* **1 concise,** succinct, compact, brief, short, to the point, crisp, pithy, elliptical, epigrammatic. **2 abrupt,** curt, brusque, laconic, short, clipped, blunt. ***Ant.*** long-winded; verbose; polite.

test *n.* **1 examination,** check, assessment, evaluation, appraisal, investigation, inspection, analysis, scrutinization, scrutiny, study, probe, exploration. **2 trial,** tryout, try, probation, assay. **3 exam,** examination, quiz, set of questions, questionnaire. **4 criterion,** touchstone, yardstick, standard, measure, model, pattern.

▸ *v.* **1 put to the test,** examine, check, assess, evaluate, appraise, investigate, scrutinize, study, probe, try, try out. **2 try,** tax, strain, put a strain on. **3 analyze,** assay, check, investigate, scrutinize, explore, probe.

testify *v.* **1 give evidence,** bear witness, attest, be a witness. **2 swear to,** attest to, corroborate, substantiate, verify, vouch for, endorse, support, back up, uphold. **3 swear,** declare, assert, affirm, state, allege, pledge, profess, avow. ***Ant.*** deny; belie.

testimonial *n.* **1 reference,** character reference, recommendation, letter of recommendation, commendation, credential, endorsement, certificate of competence. **2 gift,** tribute, trophy, memento, souvenir.

testimony *n.* **1 evidence,** attestation, sworn statement, deposition, affidavit. **2 statement,** declaration, assertion, protestation, affirmation, profession, submission, allegation. **3 proof,** evidence, verification, corroboration, support, demonstration, manifestation, indication.

text *n.* **1 main body,** contents, main matter. **2 words,** wording, script, transcript. **3 theme,** subject matter, subject, matter, topic,

issue, focus, point, motif.
4 passage, verse, quotation, extract, line, abstract, paragraph.
5 textbook, schoolbook, book, handbook, manual, reader, primer.

texture *n.* **1 feel,** touch, appearance, surface, grain.
2 weave, structure, composition, constitution, constituency.

thank *v.* **offer/extend thanks to,** express/show gratitude to, show appreciation to.

thankful *adj.* **1 grateful,** appreciative, pleased, relieved.
2 grateful, indebted, obliged, under an obligation, beholden. *Ant.* ungrateful; unappreciative.

thankless *adj.* **1 ungrateful,** unthankful, unappreciative, ungracious, unmannerly.
2 unappreciated, unrewarded, unrewarding, unacknowledged, vain, in vain, fruitless, useless.

thanks *plural noun* **gratitude,** gratefulness, appreciation, acknowledgment, recognition.
▸ *interj.* **thank you,** many thanks, thank you kindly, much obliged, much appreciated.

thaw *v.* **1 defrost,** unfreeze, melt, soften, liquefy. **2 relax,** loosen up. *Ant.* freeze; chill; solidify.

theater *n.* **1 drama,** dramatic art, dramaturgy, the stage, show business, thespian art, *inf.* showbiz. **2 hall,** room. **3 scene,** field, place of action.

theatrical *adj.* **1 dramatic,** stage, dramaturgical, show business, thespian, *inf.* showbiz. **2 dramatic,** melodramatic, histrionic, emotional, exaggerated, overdone, ostentatious, showy, affected, mannered, stilted, unreal, forced, stagy, *inf.* hammy. *Ant.* natural; unaffected; low-key.

theft *n.* **stealing,** robbery, thieving, thievery, burglary, larceny, misappropriation, pilfering, purloining, shoplifting, embezzlement, swindling, fraud, *inf.* swiping, rip-off.

theme *n.* **1 topic,** subject, subject matter, matter, thesis, text, argument, burden, idea, keynote.
2 theme song, melody, tune, air, leitmotif. **3 motif,** leitmotif, unifying idea. **4 essay,** composition, paper, dissertation.

theoretical *adj.* **conceptual,** abstract, hypothetical, conjectural, suppositional, speculative, notional, postulatory, assumed, presumed. *Ant.* practical; concrete; actual; real.

theory *n.* **1 hypothesis,** thesis, conjecture, supposition, speculation, guess, notion, postulation, assumption, presumption, opinion, view.

2 abstract knowledge, speculative thought, hypothetical situation, the abstract. **3 system,** scheme, philosophy.

therapy *n.* **1 treatment,** remedy, cure. **2 psychotherapy,** psychoanalysis.

thesis *n.* **1 theory,** hypothesis, contention, argument, proposal, proposition, premise, postulation, opinion, view, idea. **2 dissertation,** paper, treatise, disquisition, essay, composition, monograph.

thick *adj.* **1 across,** in extent/ diameter, wide, broad, deep. **2 broad,** wide, large, big, bulky, solid, substantial, fat, *inf.* beefy. **3 dense,** close-packed, concentrated, crowded, condensed, compact, impenetrable, impassable. **4 coagulated,** heavy, firm. **5 dense,** heavy, opaque, smoggy, soupy, murky, impenetrable. **6 stupid,** dense, unintelligent, dull-witted, dull, slow-witted, slow, doltish, *inf.* dim, dim-witted, boneheaded. **7 husky,** hoarse, throaty, guttural, rough, indistinct, muffled. **8 broad,** pronounced, marked, strong, rich, obvious, distinct, decided, very great, extreme. **9 friendly,** on friendly/good terms, intimate, close, devoted, hand and/in glove, inseparable, familiar, *inf.* palsy-walsy, chummy. *Ant.* thin; sparse; clever.

thicken *v.* **1 set,** gel, solidify, congeal, clot, coagulate, cake. **2 deepen,** get more profound, become more involved/ complicated/intricate. *Ant.* dilute; thin down (see thin).

thief *n.* **robber,** burglar, housebreaker, larcenist, pilferer, stealer, purloiner, filcher, shoplifter, pickpocket, embezzler, bandit, swindler, fraudster, *inf.* mugger, swiper.

thieve *v.* **steal,** rob, pilfer, purloin, shoplift, pickpocket, filch, run off with, embezzle, swindle, *inf.* swipe, rip off, knock off, lift.

thin *adj.* **1 narrow,** fine, attenuated. **2 fine,** light, delicate, flimsy, diaphanous, gossamer, unsubstantial, sheer, transparent, see-through, gauzy, filmy, translucent. **3 slim,** slender, lean, slight, svelte, light, spare, skinny, spindly, lank, lanky, scrawny, scraggy, bony, skeletal, wasted, emaciated, shrunken, anorexic, undernourished, underweight. **4 sparse,** scanty, wispy, skimpy, scarce, meager, paltry, scattered. **5 dilute,** diluted, weak, watery, runny. **6 weak,** small, low, soft, faint, feeble. **7 flimsy,** unsubstantial, weak, feeble, lame, poor, shallow, unconvincing, inadequate, insufficient. *Ant.* thick; fat; abundant.

▸ *v.* phrases: **thin down 1 become thinner/slimmer,** slim down, lose weight, reduce. **2 dilute,** water down, weaken. **thin out 1 reduce in number,** lessen, decrease, diminish. **2 become less dense,** decrease, diminish, dwindle.

thing *n.* **1 object,** article, item, *inf.* what-d'you-call-it, whatchamacallit, what's-its-name, whatsit, thingamabob, thingamajig. **2 action,** act, deed, exploit, feat, undertaking, task, job, chore. **3 idea,** thought, notion, concept, theory, conjecture. **4 statement,** remark, comment, declaration, utterance, pronouncement. **5 event,** happening, occurrence, incident, episode. **6 quality,** characteristic, attribute, property, trait, feature. **7 soul,** creature, wretch. **8 fact,** point, detail, particular, aspect. **9 style,** fashion, specimen, example.

think *v.* **1 believe,** suppose, expect, imagine, surmise, conjecture, guess, fancy. **2 consider,** deem, hold, reckon, regard as, assume, presume, estimate. **3 ponder,** meditate, deliberate, contemplate, muse, cogitate, ruminate, cerebrate, concentrate, brood, rack one's

brains, be lost in thought, be in a brown study. **4 expect,** anticipate, imagine, surmise.

▸ *n.* **consideration,** contemplation, deliberation, muse, reflection.

thinker *n.* **philosopher,** scholar, intellectual, pundit, sage, theorist, *inf.* intellect, brain.

thirst *n.* **1 thirstiness,** dryness, parchedness, dehydration. **2 desire,** craving, longing, hankering, yearning, avidity, keenness, eagerness, hunger, lust, appetite, passion, covetousness, *inf.* yen.

▸ *v.* phrase: **thirst for/after desire,** crave, long for, hanker after, yearn for, hunger after, lust after, covet.

thirsty *adj.* **1 having a thirst,** parched, dehydrated, *inf.* dry. **2 dry,** droughty, parched, dehydrated. **3 thirsting,** avid, keen, eager, hungry, greedy, covetous.

thong *n.* **strip,** belt, strap, cord, lash, rope, tie, tether.

thorny *adj.* **1 prickly,** spiky, barbed, spiny, spined, spinose, bristly, sharp, pointed. **2 problematic,** awkward, ticklish, difficult, tough, troublesome, bothersome, trying, taxing, irksome, vexatious, worrying, harassing, complicated, convoluted, involved.

thorough *adj.* **1 in-depth,**

exhaustive, complete, comprehensive, full, intensive, extensive, widespread, sweeping, all-embracing, all-inclusive, detailed. **2 meticulous,** scrupulous, assiduous, conscientious, painstaking, punctilious, methodical, careful. **3 thoroughgoing,** out-and-out, utter, downright, sheer, absolute, unmitigated, unqualified, complete, total, perfect. ***Ant.*** superficial; cursory; careless.

thought *n.* **1 powers of thinking,** faculty of reason, power of reasoning. **2 thinking,** reasoning, pondering, meditation, deliberation, cogitation, rumination, musing, mulling, reflection, introspection, contemplation, consideration, cerebration. **3 idea,** notion, line of thinking, theory, opinion. **4 intention,** plan, design, purpose, aim. **5 judgment,** conclusion, appraisal, assessment, estimation, opinion, point of view, position, stance, stand, feeling, sentiment, belief, conviction. **6 consideration,** attention, heed, regard, scrutiny, care, carefulness, thoughtfulness, concern, solicitude, kindness, kindliness, compassion, tenderness. **7 expectation,** anticipation, hope, prospect, aspiration, dream.

thoughtful *adj.* **1 pensive,** reflective, introspective, meditative, contemplative, ruminative, cogitative, absorbed, rapt/lost in thought, in a brown study. **2 profound,** deep, serious, pithy, meaty, weighty. **3 considered,** circumspect, prudent, careful, cautious, heedful, wary, guarded. **4 considerate,** attentive, caring, solicitous, helpful, kind, kindly, compassionate, tender, charitable. ***Ant.*** superficial; careless; inconsiderate; thoughtless.

thoughtless *adj.* **1 tactless,** undiplomatic, indiscreet, insensitive, inconsiderate, careless, selfish, impolite, rude. **2 unthinking,** heedless, careless, unmindful, absentminded, injudicious, ill-advised, ill-considered, imprudent, unwise, foolish, silly, stupid, reckless, rash, precipitate, negligent, neglectful, remiss. ***Ant.*** thoughtful; sensitive; considerate; careful.

thrash *v.* **1 beat,** whip, horsewhip, flog, lash, birch, cane, flagellate, scourge, spank, chastise, belt, wallop, lambaste, *inf.* tan. **2 trounce,** rout, vanquish, drub, give a drubbing to, defeat, beat, worst, crush, *inf.* lick, clobber, hammer, slaughter, wipe (up) the floor with. **3 flail,** toss and turn, jerk, twitch, squirm, writhe.

thread *n.* **1 yarn,** cotton, filament, fiber. **2 strand,** line, streak, strip, seam. **3 train of thought,** story line, drift, theme, plot, subject, subject matter, motif, tenor.
▸ *v.* **1 pass,** string, ease. **2 inch,** wind, push, squeeze, shoulder, elbow.

threadbare *adj.* **1 worn,** frayed, tattered, ragged, holey, shabby, *inf.* tatty. **2 hackneyed,** tired, stale, worn-out, trite, banal, platitudinous, clichéd, cliché-ridden, stock, stereotyped, *inf.* played out.

threat *n.* **1 threatening remark,** warning, menace, menacing, *lit.* commination. **2 warning,** menace, risk, danger, omen, foreboding, portent, hazard.

threaten *v.* **1 make threats to,** menace, intimidate, browbeat, bully, pressurize, *inf.* lean on. **2 announce one's intention. 3 be imminent,** impend, hang over, loom, foreshadow. **4 warn of,** give warning of, presage, portend, augur. **5 be a threat to,** menace, endanger, imperil, put at risk, put in jeopardy, jeopardize.

threatening *adj.* **1 menacing,** warning, intimidating, bullying, minacious, minatory. **2 ominous,** inauspicious, foreboding.

threshold *n.* **1 doorway,** doorstep, entrance, entry. **2 beginning,** commencement, start, outset, inception, opening, dawn, brink, verge, debut, *inf.* kickoff. **3 lower limit,** minimum. **4 upper limit,** maximum.

thrifty *adj.* **economical,** economizing, careful, frugal, sparing, scrimping, parsimonious, penny-pinching, miserly. ***Ant.*** extravagant; wasteful; spendthrift.

thrill *n.* **1 feeling of excitement/ stimulation,** sensation of joy, wave of pleasure, glow, tingle, *inf.* buzz, charge, kick. **2 thrilling experience,** joy, delight, pleasure, adventure. **3 throb,** tremble, tremor, quiver, flutter, shudder, vibration.
▸ *v.* **excite,** stimulate, arouse, stir, electrify, move, give joy/pleasure to, *inf.* give a buzz/charge/kick to.

thrilling *adj.* **1 exciting,** stirring, stimulating, electrifying, rousing, moving, gripping, riveting, joyful, pleasing, *inf.* hair-raising. **2 throbbing,** trembling, tremulous, quivering, shivering, fluttering, shuddering, vibrating. ***Ant.*** boring; dull; monotonous.

thrive *v.* **1 flourish,** prosper, do/go well, boom, burgeon, succeed, advance, get ahead, make progress. **2 flourish,** burgeon, grow vigorously, do well, shoot up. *Ant.* fail; decline; wither.

throb *v.* **beat,** pulse, pulsate, palpitate, pound, vibrate, go pit-a-pat, thump.

▶ *n.* **beating,** beat, pulse, pulsating, palpitation, pounding, vibration, pit-a-pat, pitter-patter, thumping.

throng *n.* **crowd,** horde, mob, mass, host, multitude, swarm, flock, pack, herd, drove, press, assemblage, gathering, congregation.

▶ *v.* **flock,** troop, swarm, crowd, mill, congregate, converge, pack, cram, jam, fill.

throttle *v.* **1 choke,** strangle, strangulate, garrote. **2 gag,** muzzle, silence, stifle, suppress, control, inhibit.

throw *v.* **1 hurl,** toss, cast, sling, pitch, shy, lob, propel, launch, project, send, *inf.* heave, chuck. **2 cast,** project, send. **3 cast,** send, dart, bestow on, give. **4 throw/hurl to the ground,** fell, floor, prostrate. **5 unseat,** dislodge. **6 disconcert,** discomfit, disturb, confound, astonish, surprise, dumbfound, discountenance. **7 operate,** turn/switch on, move. **8 shape,** form, mold, fashion. **9 pull on,** put on quickly, don quickly, slip into.

▶ *n.* **hurl,** toss, cast, sling, pitch, lob, *inf.* heave, chuck.

thrust *v.* **1 push,** shove, ram, drive, press, prod, propel. **2 force,** impose, push, press, urge. **3 stab,** pierce, stick, jab, lunge at. **4 push,** shove, press, force, shoulder, elbow, jostle.

▶ *n.* **1 push,** shove, ram, drive, press, prod, stab, jab, lunge. **2 advance,** push, drive, attack, offensive, assault, charge, onslaught, incursion, raid. **3 verbal attack/assault,** criticism, censure, hostile remark. **4 drive,** push, force, impetus, energy, assertiveness, aggression, ambition, *inf.* get-up-and-go. **5 motive force,** propulsive force, force, pressure. **6 gist,** drift, substance, essence, theme, subject, thesis.

thrusting *adj.* **forceful,** pushing, forward, energetic, assertive, aggressive, insistent, ambitious, *inf.* pushy. *Ant.* reticent; meek.

thug *n.* **ruffian,** tough, rough, hoodlum, bully, hooligan, villain, gangster, robber, bandit, murderer, killer, assassin, *inf.* hood, goon, mobster, hit man.

thunder *n.* **boom,** booming, rumble, rumbling, outburst, roar, roaring.

▶ *v.* **boom,** rumble, roar, blast, resound, reverberate, bellow, bark, yell, shout.

thunderous *adj.* **booming,**

rumbling, roaring, resounding, reverberating, deafening, earsplitting, loud, noisy, tumultuous.

thwart *v.* **frustrate,** foil, balk, check, block, stop, prevent, defeat, impede, obstruct, hinder, hamper, stymie. ***Ant.*** assist; help; facilitate.

tic *n.* **twitch,** spasm, jerk.

ticket *n.* **1 pass,** token, stub, coupon, card. **2 label,** tag, price tag.

tickle *v.* **1 stroke,** pet, touch. **2 interest,** excite, stimulate, arouse, captivate, please, gratify, delight. **3 amuse,** entertain, divert, cheer, gladden.

tide *n.* **course,** movement, direction, trend, current, drift, run, tendency, tenor.
▸ *v.* phrase: **tide over help out,** assist, aid, keep one going, see one through, keep one's head above water, keep the wolf from one's door.

tidy *adj.* **1 neat,** trim, orderly, in order, in good order, well-ordered, spruce, shipshape, well-kept, clean, spick-and-span, well-groomed, organized, well-organized, methodical, systematic, businesslike. **2 considerable,** sizable, substantial, goodly, handsome, generous, ample, largish, large,

respectable, fair, decent, healthy. ***Ant.*** untidy; messy; scruffy; unkempt.
▸ *v.* **clean,** clean up, put to rights, put in order, straighten, make shipshape, spruce up, groom, smarten, neaten.

tie *v.* **1 tie up,** fasten, attach, fix, bind, knot, hitch, bend, secure, tether, moor, lash, join, connect, link, couple, rope, chain. **2 draw,** be equal, be even, be neck and neck. ***Ant.*** untie; loosen.
▸ *n.* **1 ligature,** link, fastening, fastener, clip, catch. **2 necktie,** bow tie, cravat, neckerchief. **3 bond,** connection, relationship, kinship, affiliation, allegiance, liaison, friendship. **4 draw,** dead heat, deadlock, stalemate.

tier *n.* **row,** level, bank, line, layer, story, echelon, rank.

tight *adj.* **1 fast,** secure, fixed, clenched, clinched. **2 taut,** rigid, stiff, tense, stretched, strained. **3 tight-fitting,** close-fitting, figure-hugging, narrow. **4 compact,** compacted, compressed. **5 cramped,** restricted, limited, constricted. **6 impervious,** impenetrable, sound, sealed, hermetic, watertight, airtight. **7 scarce,** scant, sparse, in short supply, limited, insufficient, inadequate. **8 strict,** rigorous, stringent, tough, rigid,

uncompromising, exacting.
9 problematic, difficult,
precarious, hazardous, dangerous,
perilous, tricky, ticklish,
worrying, delicate, *inf.* sticky.
10 concise, succinct, terse, crisp,
straightforward, pithy,
epigrammatic. **11 close,** even,
evenly matched, neck and neck.
12 drunk, intoxicated, inebriated,
tipsy, *inf.* tiddly, under the
influence, plastered, smashed,
wasted, wrecked, pickled, stewed,
out of it, blotto, three sheets to
the wind. **13 tight-fisted,** mean,
miserly, parsimonious, stingy,
niggardly. ***Ant.*** loose; slack;
generous.

tighten *v.* **1 secure,** make fast.
2 tauten, make tight/taut, stretch,
make rigid, rigidify, stiffen, tense.
3 screw on, close. **4 increase.**
5 narrow, constrict, contract. ***Ant.***
loosen; slacken; relax.

till[1] *prep.* **1 until,** up to, as late as,
up to the time that/of. **2 before,**
prior to, previous to, earlier than.

till[2] *n.* **cash register,** cashbox, cash
drawer, strongbox.

tilt *v.* **lean,** list, slope, slant,
incline, tip, cant.
▸ *n.* **angle,** slant, slope, incline,
inclination, cant.

time *n.* **1 age,** era, epoch, period.
2 while, spell, stretch, span,
period, term. **3 occasion,** point,

juncture, moment, instant, stage.
4 lifetime, life, life span.
5 condition, circumstance,
situation, experience. **6 rhythm,**
measure, tempo, beat, meter.
7 freedom, leisure, leisure time,
spare time, moments, odd
moments.
▸ *v.* **1 schedule,** fix, set, arrange,
program. **2 clock,** measure,
calculate, regulate, count.
3 regulate, adjust, set,
synchronize.

timeless *adj.* **ageless,** enduring,
lasting, permanent, abiding,
unending, ceaseless, undying,
deathless, eternal, everlasting,
immortal, changeless, immutable,
indestructible. ***Ant.*** ephemeral;
fleeting.

timely *adj.* **opportune,** well-timed,
at the right time, convenient,
appropriate, seasonable,
felicitous. ***Ant.*** ill-timed;
inconvenient.

timetable *n.* **schedule,** program,
calendar, list, agenda.

timid *adj.* **1 easily frightened,**
timorous, fearful, apprehensive,
afraid, frightened, scared, faint-
hearted, cowardly, pusillanimous,
inf. chicken, yellow, lily-livered.
2 shy, diffident, bashful, reticent,
unselfconfident, timorous,
shrinking, retiring, coy, demure.
Ant. bold; brazen.

tingle *v.* **prickle,** prick, tickle, itch, sting, quiver, tremble.
> *n.* **1 tingling,** prickling, pricking, tickle, itch, quiver, trembling, *inf.* pins and needles. **2 quiver,** tremor, thrill, throb.

tinker *v.* **fiddle,** play, toy, tamper, fool (around), mess (about).

tint *n.* **1 shade,** color, tone, tinge, cast, tincture. **2 pastel,** pale color, soft color. **3 dye,** rinse, colorant, coloring.

tiny *adj.* **minute,** diminutive, miniature, mini, minuscule, infinitesimal, microscopic, dwarfish, midget, pocket-sized, Lilliputian, wee, petite, small, little, insignificant, trifling, negligible, inconsequential, *inf.* teeny, teeny-weeny, itsy-bitsy, pint-sized. *Ant.* huge; enormous; gigantic.

tip[1] *n.* **point,** peak, top, summit, apex, crown, end, extremity,point.

tip[2] *v.* **tilt,** lean, list, cant, slant.

tip[3] *n.* **1 gratuity,** *pourboire,* baksheesh; *inf.* little something. **2 hint,** suggestion, recommendation, piece of advice; advice.
> *v.* **give a tip to,** reward, remunerate.

tirade *n.* **diatribe,** harangue, stream of abuse, verbal onslaught, lecture, upbraiding, denunciation, obloquy, philippic, invective, vituperation, fulmination, censure, vilification.

tire *v.* **1 tire out,** fatigue, wear out, weary, exhaust, drain, enervate, debilitate, jade, *inf.* take it out of. **2 get/grow tired,** get fatigued, flag, droop, *inf.* poop out. **3 bore,** weary, irk, irritate, get on one's nerves, annoy, exasperate, *inf.* get to.

tired *adj.* **1 fatigued,** worn out, weary, wearied, exhausted, drained, enervated, debilitated, jaded, *inf.* done, done in, all in, beat, dog-tired, bushed, pooped (out), dead on one's feet, ready to drop. **2 sleepy,** drowsy, weary, *inf.* asleep on one's feet. **3 stale,** hackneyed, familiar, worn-out, outworn, well-worn, clichéd, stock, platitudinous, trite, banal, *inf.* corny. **4 bored,** wearied, irked, irritated, annoyed, exasperated. *Ant.* energetic; lively; fresh.

tireless *adj.* **untiring,** unwearied, unflagging, indefatigable, energetic, industrious, vigorous, determined, resolute, dogged.

tiresome *adj.* **1 wearisome,** laborious, wearing, tedious, boring, monotonous, dull, uninteresting, unexciting, humdrum, routine. **2 troublesome,** irksome, vexatious, irritating, annoying, exasperating, trying. **Ant.** interesting; exciting; pleasant.

tiring *adj.* **wearying,** wearing, fatiguing, exhausting, draining, enervating, arduous, laborious, strenuous, exacting, taxing, tough.

titillate *v.* **excite,** arouse, stimulate, provoke, thrill, interest, fascinate, tantalize, seduce, *inf.* turn on. **Ant.** bore; turn off (see turn).

title *n.* **1 name. 2 credit,** caption, legend, inscription, heading. **3 form of address,** designation, appellation, name, denomination, epithet, sobriquet, *inf.* moniker, handle. **4 entitlement,** right, claim, ownership, proprietorship, possession, holding. **5 deed,** ownership document, proof of ownership. **6 championship,** first place, crown, laurels.
▸ *v.* **entitle,** name, call, designate, label, tag, style, term.

titter *n.* **snicker,** snigger, giggle, tee-hee, laugh, chuckle, cackle, *inf.* chortle.

toast *v.* **1 brown,** crisp, grill. **2 warm (up),** heat (up). **3 drink (to) the health of,** drink to, pledge, salute.
▸ *n.* **1 pledge,** salutation, salute, tribute, compliments, greetings. **2 celebrity,** darling, favorite, heroine, hero.

toddle *v.* **totter,** teeter, wobble, falter, dodder.

together *adv.* **1 with each other,** in conjunction, jointly, conjointly, in cooperation, as one, in unison, side by side, hand in hand, hand and/in glove, shoulder to shoulder, cheek by jowl. **2 simultaneously,** concurrently, at the same time, at once, all at once, in unison, with one accord, synchronously. **3 in a row,** in succession, successively, consecutively, on end, one after the other, continuously, without a break, without interruption. **4 organized,** sorted out, straight, to rights, settled, fixed, arranged.
▸ *adj.* **composed,** calm, cool, well-balanced, stable, well-adjusted, well-organized, efficient.

toilet *n.* **lavatory,** bathroom, rest room, washroom, men's room, ladies' room, powder room, convenience, urinal, latrine, privy, outhouse, *inf.* john, can, head.

token *n.* **1 symbol,** sign, emblem, badge, representation, indication, mark, manifestation, expression, demonstration, recognition, index, evidence. **2 memento,** souvenir, keepsake, remembrance, reminder, memorial. **3 disk,** counter, slug, coin, substitute coin.
▸ *adj.* **1 symbolic,** emblematic.

2 perfunctory, superficial, nominal, minimal, slight, hollow.

tolerable *adj.* **1 endurable,** bearable, sufferable, supportable, brookable, acceptable. **2 fairly good,** fair, all right, passable, adequate, satisfactory, good enough, average, mediocre, middling, fair to middling, ordinary, run-of the-mill, indifferent, unexceptional, *inf.* not bad, OK, so-so, nothing to write home about. *Ant.* intolerable; unbearable; insufferable.

tolerance *n.* **1 toleration,** open-mindedness, lack of prejudice/ bias, broad-mindedness, liberalism, forbearance, patience, magnanimity, understanding, charity, lenience, lenity, indulgence, permissiveness, complaisance, laxness. **2 toleration,** endurance, sufferance, acceptance, fortitude, stamina, hardiness, resilience, toughness.

tolerant *adj.* **open-minded,** unprejudiced, unbiased, unbigoted, broad-minded, liberal, catholic, forbearing, patient, long-suffering, magnanimous, sympathetic, understanding, charitable, lenient, indulgent, permissive, free and easy, easygoing, complaisant, lax. *Ant.* intolerant; narrow-minded.

tolerate *v.* **1 permit,** allow, admit, sanction, warrant, countenance, brook, recognize, acknowledge. **2 endure,** bear, suffer, take, stand, put up with, abide, accept, stomach, submit to. **3 take,** receive, be treated with.

toll *n.* **1 charge,** fee, payment, levy, tariff. **2 cost,** damage, loss.
▸ *v.* **1 sound,** ring, peal, knell, clang, strike, chime. **2 announce,** herald, signal, warn of.

tomb *n.* **grave,** burial place/ chamber, sepulcher, vault, crypt, catacomb, mausoleum.

tone *n.* **1 sound,** sound quality, color, pitch, timbre, tonality. **2 tone of voice,** mode of expression, expression, intonation, inflection, modulation, accentuation. **3 mood,** air, attitude, character, manner, spirit, temper, tenor, vein, drift, gist. **4 style,** quality, high quality. **5 tint,** shade, tinge, cast, tincture.
▸ *v.* phrase: **tone down 1 soften,** lighten, subdue, mute. **2 moderate,** soften, modulate, play down, temper, subdue, dampen, restrain, soft-pedal.

tonic *n.* **restorative,** refresher, stimulant, analeptic, pick-me-up, boost, fillip, *inf.* shot in the arm, picker-upper.

tool *n.* **1 implement,** instrument,

utensil, device, apparatus, gadget, appliance, machine, contrivance, contraption, aid. **2 puppet,** pawn, minion, lackey, flunky, henchman, toady, *inf.* stooge.
▸ *v.* **1 shape,** work, cut, chase, decorate, ornament. **2 drive,** ride, motor.

top *n.* **1 summit,** peak, pinnacle, crest, crown, tip, apex, vertex, apogee. **2 height,** high point, peak, pinnacle, zenith, acme, culmination, climax, crowning point, prime, meridian. **3 upper part,** upper surface, upper layer. **4 cap,** lid, stopper, cork, cover. **5 shirt,** T-shirt, blouse, jersey, sweater, sweatshirt. **6 leaves,** shoots, stem, stalk.
▸ *adj.* **1 topmost,** uppermost, highest. **2 foremost,** leading, principal, preeminent, greatest, finest, chief, main, highest, ruling, commanding, *inf.* top-notch. **3 top-quality,** top-grade, best, finest, prime, choicest, quality, excellent, *inf.* A-1, top-notch. **4 maximum,** maximal, greatest, utmost.

topic *n.* **subject,** subject matter, theme, issue, matter, point, question, argument, thesis, text.

topical *adj.* **newsworthy,** in the news, current, up-to-date, up-to-the-minute, contemporary, popular. ***Ant.*** out of date, outdated.

topple *v.* **1 fall over,** tip over, keel over, overturn, capsize. **2 upset,** knock over, push over, tip over, capsize. **3 overthrow,** oust, unseat, overturn, bring down, bring low.

torment *n.* **1 agony,** suffering, torture, pain, excruciation, anguish, hell, misery, distress, affliction, wretchedness. **2 scourge,** curse, plague, bane, affliction, thorn in the flesh, irritation, irritant, vexation, annoyance, worry, nuisance, bother, trouble, pest, *inf.* pain in the neck.
▸ *v.* **1 afflict,** harrow, plague, torture, distress, worry, trouble. **2 tease,** irritate, vex, annoy, pester, harass, badger, plague, worry, be a nuisance to, bother, trouble, be a pest to.

torn *adj.* **1 ragged,** tattered, ripped, split, slit, cut, lacerated, rent. **2 divided,** split, wavering, vacillating, irresolute, uncertain, unsure, undecided.

torrent *n.* **1 flood,** deluge, inundation, spate, cascade, rush, stream, current. **2 downpour,** deluge, rainstorm. **3 outburst,** stream, volley, outpouring, barrage, battery.

tortuous *adj.* **1 twisting,** winding, curving, curvy, sinuous, undulating, coiling, serpentine, snaking, snaky, zigzag,

convoluted, meandering, spiraling, anfractuous.
2 convoluted, roundabout, circuitous, indirect, involved, complicated, ambiguous.
3 devious, cunning, tricky, deceitful, deceptive, guileful. **Ant.** straight; straightforward.

torture *n.* **1 persecution,** pain, suffering, abuse, ill-treatment, punishment, torment. **2 torment,** agony, anguish, distress.
▸ *v.* **1 persecute,** inflict pain/suffering on, abuse, ill-treat, punish, torment, *inf.* work over.
2 torment, rack, cause agony/suffering/pain to, inflict anguish on, afflict, harrow, plague, distress, worry, trouble.

toss *v.* **1 throw,** hurl, cast, sling, pitch, shy, lob, propel, launch, project, *inf.* heave, chuck.
2 thrash, wriggle, writhe, squirm, roll, tumble. **3 rock,** roll, sway, undulate, pitch, lurch, heave.
4 throw back, throw up, jerk, jolt.

total *n.* **sum,** sum total, aggregate, whole, entirety, totality.
▸ *adj.* **1 complete,** entire, whole, full, comprehensive, combined, aggregate, composite, integral.
2 complete, thorough, thoroughgoing, all-out, utter, absolute, downright, out and out, outright, sheer, rank, unmitigated, unqualified.

totalitarian *adj.* **one-party,** monocratic, undemocratic, autocratic, authoritarian, absolute, despotic, dictatorial, tyrannical, oppressive, fascist.
Ant. democratic; autonomous.

totter *v.* **1 teeter,** wobble, stagger, stumble, reel, sway, roll, lurch.
2 shake, sway, rock, lurch, shudder. **3 be unstable,** be unsteady, be shaky, be on the point of collapse, falter.

touch *v.* **1 be in contact,** come into contact, come together, meet, converge, be contiguous, adjoin, abut. **2 press lightly,** tap, brush, graze, feel, stroke, pat, fondle, caress. **3 handle,** hold, pick up, move, play with, toy with, fiddle with, interfere with.
4 eat, consume, drink, take, partake of. **5 affect,** move, make an impression on, have an impact on, influence, upset, disturb, make sad, arouse sympathy, *inf.* get to. **6 have an effect on,** affect, concern, involve, have a bearing on, be relevant/pertinent to. **7 be associated with,** concern/involve oneself in, have dealings with, deal with, handle, be a party to.
8 come near (to), come up to, compare with, be on a par with, equal, match, be a match for, be in the same league as, parallel, rival, *inf.* hold a candle to. **9 reach,**

get up/down to, attain, arrive at, come to. **10 ask,** beg, borrow from.

▸ *n.* **1 pressure,** tap, strike, hit, blow, brush, stroke, pat, caress. **2 feel,** feeling, sense of touch, tactile sense, tactility. **3 feel,** texture, grain, finish, surface, coating. **4 small amount,** bit, trace, dash, taste, spot, drop, pinch, speck, smack, suggestion, hint, soupçon, tinge, tincture, whiff, suspicion. **5 craftsmanship,** workmanship, artistry, performance, dexterity, deftness, skill, virtuosity, adroitness. **6 detail,** feature, addition, accessory, fine point. **7 skill,** skillfulness, expertise, technique, knack, adeptness, ability, talent, flair. **8 influence,** effect, hand, handling, direction, management, technique, method. **9 contact,** communication, correspondence.

touching *adj.* **moving,** impressive, affecting, warming, heartwarming, affecting, emotive, stirring, upsetting, disturbing, saddening, pitiful, piteous, poignant, pathetic, heartbreaking, heart-rending.

touchy *adj.* **1 sensitive,** oversensitive, hypersensitive, easily offended, thin-skinned, testy, irascible, irritable, grouchy, grumpy, peevish, querulous, bad-tempered, captious, crabbed, cross, surly. **2 tricky,** ticklish, delicate, precarious, chancy, risky, uncertain. *Ant.* calm; affable; good-humored.

tough *adj.* **1 strong,** durable, resistant, resilient, sturdy, firm, solid, hard, rigid, stiff. **2 chewy,** leathery, gristly, stringy, fibrous, sinewy. **3 hardy,** strong, fit, sturdy, rugged, stalwart, vigorous, strapping, robust, resilient. **4 difficult,** hard, arduous, onerous, heavy, uphill, laborious, strenuous, exacting, taxing, stressful, harsh, austere, rugged, bleak, grim, dire, rough. **5 firm,** strict, stern, severe, harsh, hard-hitting, adamant, inflexible. **6 difficult,** hard, knotty, thorny, baffling, perplexing, ticklish. **7 rough,** rowdy, unruly, disorderly, violent, wild, lawless, lawbreaking, criminal. **8 unfortunate,** unlucky, hard, regrettable, *inf.* too bad. *Ant.* soft; tender; weak; easy.

▸ *n.* **ruffian,** rowdy, thug, hoodlum, hooligan, bully, *inf.* roughneck, bruiser.

toughen *v.* **1 strengthen,** fortify, reinforce, harden, rigidify. **2 stiffen,** tighten, make stricter, make severe, *inf.* beef up.

tour *n.* **1 trip,** excursion, journey, expedition, jaunt, outing,

peregrination, guided tour, walk around, visit, inspection. **2 circuit,** ambit, round, course, beat. **3 tour of duty,** duty, stint, stretch, turn.
▶ *v.* **1 travel around/through,** journey through, explore, vacation in. **2 go around,** walk/ drive around, visit, sightsee, inspect.

tourist *n.* **visitor,** sightseer, vacationer, traveler, excursionist, journeyer, *inf.* globe-trotter.

tournament *n.* **competition,** contest, series, meeting, event, match, *inf.* tourney.

tout *v.* **hawk,** peddle, sell, offer for sale.

towering *adj.* **1 high,** tall, lofty, elevated, sky-high. **2 extreme,** mighty, fierce, terrible, intense, violent, vehement, passionate, frenzied, frantic. **3 outstanding,** extraordinary, preeminent, surpassing, superior, great, incomparable, unrivaled, peerless.

toxic *adj.* **poisonous,** venomous, virulent, noxious. *Ant.* non-toxic; harmless; safe.

trace *n.* **1 mark,** sign, vestige, indication, evidence, remains, remnants, relics. **2 bit,** touch, hint, suggestion, suspicion, trifle, drop, dash, tinge, tincture, shadow, jot, iota.
▶ *v.* **1 find,** discover, detect, unearth, uncover, track down,

turn up, dig up, ferret out, hunt down. **2 follow,** pursue, track, trail, tail, shadow, stalk, dog. **3 draw,** draw up, sketch, draft, outline, mark out, delineate, rough out, map, chart, record, indicate, show, depict.

track *n.* **1 marks,** impressions, prints, imprints, footprints, footmarks, footsteps, trail, spoor, scent. **2 trail,** path, pathway, way, course, route. **3 path,** line, course, orbit, route, trajectory, flight path. **4 rail,** line, rails. **5 course,** running track, racetrack.
▶ *v.* **follow,** pursue, trail, trace, tail, shadow, stalk, dog.

trade *n.* **1 commerce,** buying and selling, dealing, traffic, trafficking, business, marketing, merchandising, transactions. **2 line of work/business,** line, occupation, job, career, profession, craft, vocation, calling, métier; work, employment. **3 swap,** trade-off, exchange, switch, barter.
▶ *v.* **1 do business,** deal, run, operate. **2 buy and sell,** deal, traffic, market, merchandise. **3 swap,** exchange, switch, barter.

trader *n.* **merchant,** dealer, buyer, seller, buyer and seller, marketer, merchandiser, broker.

tradition *n.* **1 custom,** belief, practice, convention, ritual, observance, habit, institution, usage, praxis. **2 historical convention,** unwritten law, oral history, lore, folklore.

traditional *adj.* **1 customary,** accustomed, conventional, established, ritual, ritualistic, habitual, set, fixed, routine, usual, wonted, old, time-honored, historic, folk, familial, ancestral. **2 handed-down,** folk, unwritten, oral. *Ant.* novel; unconventional.

tragedy *n.* **disaster,** calamity, catastrophe, misfortune, misadventure, affliction, adversity, sad event, serious accident, shock, blow. *Ant.* blessing; comedy.

tragic *adj.* **1 disastrous,** calamitous, catastrophic, fatal, terrible, dreadful, appalling, dire, awful, miserable, wretched, unfortunate. **2 sad,** unhappy, pathetic, moving, distressing, disturbing, pitiful, piteous, melancholy, doleful, mournful, dismal, gloomy. **3 dreadful,** terrible, awful, deplorable, lamentable, regrettable. *Ant.* fortunate; happy; joyful.

trail *n.* **1 track,** scent, spoor, traces, marks, signs, footprints, footmarks. **2 path,** beaten path, pathway, footpath, track, road, route. **3 line,** queue, train, file, column, procession, following,

entourage. **4 train,** chain, series, sequence, aftermath. **5 stream,** tail, appendage.

▶ *v.* **1 tow,** pull, drag, draw, haul. **2 drag across,** sweep, dangle, hang down, droop. **3 trudge,** plod, drag oneself, dawdle, straggle, loiter, linger, lag, fall behind. **4 creep,** crawl, slide, slink. **5 follow,** pursue, track, trace, tail, shadow, stalk, dog. **6 lose,** be down, be behind. **7 fade,** fade away/out, disappear, vanish, peter out, die away, melt away.

train *n.* **1 tail,** appendage. **2 trail,** stream, track, path, wake, wash. **3 trail,** chain, string, series, sequence, set, progression, order, concatenation. **4 procession,** line, file, column, convoy, caravan. **5 retinue,** entourage, cortege, following, staff, household, court, followers, attendants. **6 railway train.**

▶ *v.* **1 instruct,** teach, coach, tutor, give lessons to, school, educate, drill, prepare, ground, guide, indoctrinate, inculcate. **2 study,** qualify, learn, prepare, exercise, do exercises, work out, practice. **3 coach,** drill, exercise. **4 aim,** point, focus, direct, level, line up.

trait *n.* **characteristic,** attribute, feature, quality, property, idiosyncrasy, peculiarity, quirk.

traitor *n.* **betrayer,** backstabber,

turncoat, double-crosser, double-dealer, renegade, defector, deserter, apostate, Judas, quisling, fifth columnist, *inf.* snake in the grass, two-timer.

trample *v.* **1 tramp on,** tread on, walk over, stamp on, squash, crush, flatten. **2 ride roughshod over,** treat with contempt, disregard, show no consideration for, encroach on, infringe.

trance *n.* **daze,** stupor, hypnotic state, half-conscious state, dream, reverie, brown study.

tranquil *adj.* **1 peaceful,** restful, reposeful, calm, quiet, still, serene, placid, undisturbed. **2 calm,** placid, pacific, composed, cool, calm, cool and collected, serene, even-tempered, unexcitable, unflappable, unruffled, unperturbed. *Ant.* noisy; disturbed; excitable.

tranquilizer *n.* **sedative,** barbiturate, opiate, *inf.* downer, trank.

transaction *n.* **1 business,** deal, undertaking, affair, bargain, negotiation, proceedings. **2 conducting,** performance, execution, enactment, handling, negotiation, conclusion, discharge, settlement.

transcend *v.* **go beyond,** exceed, overstep, rise above, surpass, excel, be superior to, outdo, outstrip, leave behind, outrival, outrank, outshine, eclipse, overshadow.

transfer *v.* **1 convey,** move, shift, remove, take, carry, transport, change, relocate. **2 turn over,** sign over, hand on, hand down, pass on, transmit, convey, devolve, assign, delegate.
▸ *n.* **1 move,** shift, relocation, change. **2 transfer document,** conveyance, papers, deeds.

transform *v.* **change,** alter, convert, metamorphose, revolutionize, transfigure, remodel, redo, reconstruct, rebuild, reorganize, rearrange, renew, translate, transmute, *inf.* transmogrify.

transformation *n.* **change,** radical change, alteration, conversion, metamorphosis, sea change, revolutionization, revolution, transfiguration, remodeling, reconstruction, reorganization, renewal, transmutation, *inf.* transmogrification.

transgress *v.* **1 go beyond,** overstep, exceed, infringe, breach, break, contravene, violate, defy, disobey. **2 do wrong,** go astray, misbehave, break the law, err, lapse, fall from grace, stray from the straight and narrow, sin, trespass.

transient *adj.* **transitory,** short-lived, short-term, impermanent, temporary, brief, short, ephemeral, evanescent, momentary, fleeting, flying, passing, fugitive, fugacious, mutable, here today and gone tomorrow. *Ant.* permanent; constant; perpetual.

transit *n.* **1 movement,** travel, journeying, passage, transfer, crossing. **2 transport,** transportation, conveyance, haulage, freightage.

transition *n.* **move,** passage, change, transformation, conversion, changeover, metamorphosis, shift, switch, jump, leap, progression, gradation, development, evolution, transmutation.

translate *v.* **1 construe,** interpret, render, convert, transcribe, transliterate. **2 render,** paraphrase, reword, convert, decipher, decode, explain, elucidate. **3 interpret,** take, construe, understand, read, judge, deem. **4 turn,** change, convert, transform, alter, metamorphose, transmute, *inf.* transmogrify.

transmission *n.* **1 sending,** conveyance, transport, dispatch, remission. **2 transference,** transferral, passing on, communication, imparting, dissemination, spreading. **3 broadcasting,** relaying, sending out. **4 broadcast,** program.

transmit *v.* **1 send,** convey, transport, dispatch, forward, remit. **2 transfer,** pass on, hand on, communicate, impart, disseminate, spread, carry, diffuse. **3 broadcast,** air, relay, send out, put on the air.

transparent *adj.* **1 clear,** see-through, translucent, lucid, pellucid, crystal-clear, crystalline, limpid, glassy, transpicuous, sheer, diaphanous, filmy, gauzy. **2 obvious,** patent, manifest, undisguised, unmistakable, clear, plain, visible, noticeable, recognizable, distinct, evident, apparent, perceptible, discernible. **3 frank,** open, candid, direct, forthright, plainspoken, straight, ingenuous, artless. **4 clear,** lucid, straightforward, plain, explicit, unambiguous, unequivocal. *Ant.* opaque; cloudy.

transpire *v.* **1 become known,** be revealed, be disclosed, come to light, emerge, come out. **2 come about,** take place, happen, occur, turn up, arise, chance, befall.

transport *v.* **1 convey,** take, transfer, move, shift, bring, fetch, carry, bear, haul, lug, cart, run, ship. **2 banish,** exile, deport, drive away, expatriate. **3 enrapture,**

entrance, enchant, enthrall, captivate, bewitch, fascinate, spellbind, charm, overjoy, thrill, delight, ravish, carry away.
▸ *n.* **1 transportation,** conveyance, transit, carriage, freight, vehicle, car. **2 transportation,** conveyance, vehicle, car, carriage. **3 strong emotion.**

transpose *v.* **interchange,** exchange, switch, swap, transfer, reverse, invert, rearrange, reorder, change, alter, convert, move.

transverse *adj.* **crosswise,** crossways, cross, athwart.

trap *n.* **1 snare,** net, mesh, ambush, pitfall, booby trap. **2 stratagem,** setup, play, artifice, ruse, wile, trick, device, deception, subterfuge. **3 ambush,** lure, decoy, bait.
▸ *v.* **1 snare,** ensnare, enmesh, entrap, catch, corner. **2 trick,** dupe, deceive, lure, inveigle, beguile, set up. **3 cut off,** corner, confine, imprison.

trappings *plural noun* **accouterments,** appurtenances, appointments, trimmings, paraphernalia, fittings, things, equipage, equipment, apparatus, gear, livery, adornment, ornamentation, decoration, finery, frippery, panoply.

trash *n.* **1 rubbish,** garbage, nonsense, drivel, balderdash, bunkum, twaddle, *inf.* bunk, tripe, bilge, rot, poppycock. **2 rubbish,** waste, refuse, litter, garbage. **3 riff-raff,** scum, rabble, canaille, vermin, dregs, good-for-nothings, white trash.

traumatic *adj.* **1 painful,** agonizing, wounding, shocking, scarring, disturbing, distressing, damaging, injurious, harmful. **2 unpleasant,** disagreeable, irksome, troublesome, vexatious, irritating, distressing.

travel *v.* **1 journey,** take a trip, tour, voyage, sightsee, cross, traverse, cover, wander, ramble, roam, rove, range, wend, make one's way over. **2 proceed,** progress, advance, be transmitted, carry. **3 speed,** go fast/rapidly, drive fast, go at breakneck speed, *inf.* hellbent for leather, go like a bat out of hell, tear up the miles.
▸ *n.* **traveling,** journeying, touring.

traveler *n.* **tourist,** vacationer, excursionist, explorer, passenger, voyager, sightseer, globe-trotter.

traverse *v.* **1 cross,** go/lie/ stretch/extend across, travel over, journey over, make one's way across, pass over, wander, roam, range, cut across, bridge. **2 consider,** examine, check, study, review, investigate, inspect, scrutinize, look into, look over, scan, pore over, take stock of.

treacherous *adj.* **1 traitorous,** backstabbing, double-crossing, double-dealing, disloyal, faithless, unfaithful, perfidious, duplicitous, deceitful, false-hearted, false, untrue, untrustworthy, unreliable, undependable, *inf.* two-timing. **2 precarious,** unreliable, undependable, unstable, unsafe, risky, hazardous, dangerous, perilous, deceptive, *inf.* dicey. **3 hazardous,** dangerous, unsafe, flooded, icy, ice-covered, slippery. *Ant.* loyal; faithful; reliable.

tread *v.* **1 walk,** step (out), go, pace, march, hike, tramp, stride, trek, trudge, plod. **2 trample,** tramp (on), step on, stamp (on), squash, crush, flatten, press (down).
▸ *n.* **step,** footstep, footfall, walk, tramp.

treason *n.* **high treason,** betrayal, traitorousness, treachery, disloyalty, faithlessness, perfidy, disaffection, sedition, subversion, mutiny, rebellion, lese-majesty.

treasure *n.* **1 riches,** valuables, jewels, gems, gold, silver, precious metals, money, cash; wealth, fortune; treasure trove. **2 valuable,** work of art, masterpiece, precious item. **3 paragon,** gem, angel, find, star, one of a kind, one in a million.
▸ *v.* **cherish,** hold dear, prize, value greatly; adore, dote on, love, be devoted to, worship, venerate.

treat *n.* **1 surprise,** celebration, entertainment, amusement, diversion, party, feast, banquet. **2 gift,** present, tidbit, delicacy, *inf.* goodie. **3 pleasure,** delight, thrill, joy, gratification, satisfaction, fun. **4 gift,** present, one's turn to pay.
▸ *v.* **1 act/behave toward,** deal with, handle, cope with, contend with, manage, use. **2 regard,** consider, view, look upon, deal with. **3 give treatment to,** medicate, doctor, nurse, care for, attend to, minister to, cure, heal. **4 have talks with,** talk with, confer with, negotiate with, parley with, bargain with, make terms with, come to terms with. **5 deal with,** discuss, go into, write/speak/talk about, discourse upon, be concerned with, touch upon, refer to, consider, study, review, analyze.

treatise *n.* **discourse,** exposition, dissertation, thesis, disquisition, study, essay, paper, monograph, tract, pamphlet, work, piece of writing.

treatment *n.* **1 action,** behavior, conduct, handling, management, use, dealings. **2 medical care,** medication, medicament, therapy, doctoring, nursing, first aid, care, ministration, cure, remedy, drugs, therapeutics.

treaty *n.* **agreement**, pact, deal, compact, covenant, bargain, pledge, contract, alliance, concordat, convention, entente.

trek *v.* **trudge**, tramp, hike, march, slog, plod, walk, ramble, roam, range, rove, travel, journey, *inf.* traipse.
▶ *n.* **expedition**, trip, journey, hike, march, walk, odyssey.

tremble *v.* **1 shake**, quiver, shiver, quake, twitch, wiggle, shudder, teeter, totter, wobble, rock, vibrate, oscillate, rattle. **2 fear**, be afraid, be fearful, be frightened, be apprehensive, worry, be anxious.

tremendous *adj.* **1 great**, huge, enormous, immense, massive, vast, colossal, prodigious, stupendous, gigantic, gargantuan, mammoth, giant, titanic, *inf.* whopping. **2 loud**, deafening, earsplitting, booming, thundering, roaring, resounding, crashing. **3 excellent**, very good, great, marvelous, remarkable, extraordinary, exceptional, wonderful, incredible, *inf.* fabulous, fantastic, terrific, super, ace, wizard. ***Ant.*** tiny; small; slight; poor.

tremor *n.* **1 tremble**, trembling, shake, shaking, Parkinsonism, shiver, quiver, quaver, vibration, twitch, spasm, paroxysm. **2 earth tremor**, earthquake, *inf.* quake.

trend *n.* **1 tendency**, drift, course, direction, bearing, current, inclination, bias, leaning, bent, swing. **2 fashion**, vogue, style, mode, look, craze, *inf.* fad.
▶ *v.* **move**, go, tend, head, drift, turn, incline, lean, shift, veer, swing.

trespass *v.* **do wrong**, err, go astray, fall from grace, stray from the straight and narrow, sin, transgress.

trial *n.* **1 court case**, case, hearing, inquiry, tribunal, litigation, judicial examination, legal investigation. **2 trial period**, probation, test, test/testing period, audition, testing, tryout, trial/test run, check, assay, experiment, *inf.* dry run. **3 try**, attempt, endeavor, effort, venture, *inf.* go, shot, stab, crack. **4 nuisance**, pest, bother, worry, vexation, annoyance, irritant, irritation, bane, affliction, curse, burden, cross to bear, thorn in one's flesh, *inf.* pain in the neck, hassle, plague. **5 trouble**, worry, anxiety, vexation, load, burden, cross to bear, blow, affliction, tribulation, adversity, hardship, ordeal, pain, suffering, distress, misery, wretchedness, unhappiness, sadness, woe, grief. **6 contest,** competition, field trials.

▸ *adj.* **testing,** experimental, pilot, probationary, provisional.

tribe *n.* **1 ethnic group,** family, dynasty, clan, sept. **2 group,** crowd, company, party, band, number, gang, assembly, collection, *inf.* bunch.

tribute *n.* **1 gift,** present, accolade, commendation, testimonial, paean, eulogy, panegyric, encomium, gratitude, applause, praise, homage, honor, exaltation, laudation, extolment, glorification, congratulations, compliments, *inf.* bouquets. **2 acknowledgment,** recognition, testimonial, indication, manifestation, evidence, proof. **3 homage,** payment, contribution, offering, gift, donation, charge, tax, duty, levy, tariff, ransom. *Ant.* blame; criticism; reproach; condemnation.

trick *n.* **1 stratagem,** ploy, artifice, ruse, dodge, wile, device, maneuver, trick of the trade, deceit, deception, subterfuge, swindle, fraud, *inf.* con. **2 illusion,** mirage. **3 knack,** art, gift, talent, technique, ability, skill, expertise, *inf.* know-how. **4 hoax,** practical joke, joke, prank, jape, antic, caper, frolic, lark, gambol, *inf.* leg-

pull, gag, put-on. **5 sleight of hand,** legerdemain, juggling, prestidigitation. **6 idiosyncrasy,** habit, mannerism, quirk, peculiarity, foible, eccentricity, characteristic, trait, practice.

▸ *v.* **deceive,** delude, mislead, take in, cheat, hoodwink, fool, outwit, dupe, hoax, gull, cozen, defraud, swindle, *inf.* con, pull a fast one on, put one over on, shaft.

trickery *n.* **guile,** artifice, wiliness, deceit, deception, cheating, subterfuge, craft, craftiness, chicanery, pretense, dishonesty, fraud, swindling, imposture, double-dealing, duplicity, *inf.* conning, monkey/funny business, hanky-panky. *Ant.* honesty; candor.

trickle *v.* **1 drip,** dribble, leak, ooze, seep, exude, percolate. **2 come/go/pass gradually.** *Ant.* pour; gush.

tricky *adj.* **1 difficult,** problematic, awkward, delicate, sensitive, ticklish, thorny, knotty, touchy, risky, uncertain, precarious, *inf.* sticky. **2 cunning,** crafty, wily, artful, devious, scheming, foxy, sly, slippery, subtle, deceitful, deceptive. *Ant.* straightforward; honest.

trim *adj.* **1 neat,** tidy, neat and tidy, smart, spruce, well-groomed, well-dressed, well-turned-out, dapper, elegant, orderly, in good order/condition, well-maintained, shipshape, well-looked-after, well-cared-for, spick-and-span, *inf.* natty. **2 slim,** slender, lean, svelte, streamlined, willowy, lissome, sleek, shapely, in good shape, fit, physically fit. ***Ant.*** untidy; messy; fat.

▸ *v.* **1 cut,** clip, snip, shear, prune, pare, even up, neaten, tidy up, chop, hack, remove, take off. **2 cut down,** decrease, reduce, diminish, cut back on, curtail, dock, retrench. **3 decorate,** adorn, ornament, embellish, festoon, edge, pipe, border, fringe, embroider, bespangle.

trip *n.* **1 excursion,** tour, expedition, voyage, jaunt, outing, run. **2 stumble,** misstep, false step, slip, slide, fall, tumble, spill. **3** *inf.* **hoot,** scream, laugh, card, caution. **4 hallucination,** acid trip, bad trip.

▸ *v.* **1 stumble,** lose one's footing/ balance, stagger, totter, slip, slide, misstep, fall, tumble. **2 skip,** dance, hop, prance, bound, spring, gambol, caper, frisk, cavort, waltz. **3 hallucinate,** freak out, trip out.

triumph *n.* **1 conquest,** victory, win, ascendancy, mastery, success. **2 coup,** tour de force, feat, masterstroke, achievement,

attainment, accomplishment, supreme example, sensation, *inf.* hit. **3 exultation,** jubilation, jubilance, elation, rejoicing, joy, joyfulness, pride. ***Ant.*** defeat; failure; disaster.

▸ *v.* **1 win,** succeed, come first, be the victor, be victorious, gain a victory, carry the day, take the honors/prize/crown. **2 exult,** rejoice, jubilate, celebrate, revel, glory, gloat, swagger, brag, boast.

triumphant *adj.* **1 winning,** victorious, successful, undefeated, unbeaten, prizewinning, trophy-winning. **2 exultant,** jubilant, elated, rejoicing, joyful, joyous, proud, gloating, boastful. ***Ant.*** unsuccessful; defeated; depressed.

trivial *adj.* **1 unimportant,** insignificant, inconsequential, flimsy, insubstantial, petty, minor, of no account/matter, negligible, paltry, trifling, foolish, worthless, *inf.* piddling. **2 frivolous,** small-minded, featherbrained, giddy, silly. ***Ant.*** important; significant; profound.

troops *plural noun* **armed forces,** army, military, services, soldiers, soldiery, fighting men/women.

trouble *n.* **1 worry,** bother, anxiety, disquiet, unease, irritation, vexation, inconvenience, annoyance, agitation, harassment, difficulty,

distress, problems. **2 difficulty,** misfortune, adversity, hardship, bad luck, ill luck, burden, distress, pain, suffering, affliction, torment, woe, grief, unhappiness, sadness, heartache, problems. **3 bother,** inconvenience, disturbance, fuss, effort, exertion, work, labor, attention, care, thoughtfulness, nuisance, problem, pest, *inf.* hassle, headache, pain in the neck, pain. **4 problem,** difficulty, failing, weakness, shortcoming, fault, imperfection, defect, blemish. **5 disorder,** disease, illness, dysfunction.
6 disturbance, disorder, unrest, fighting, strife, conflict, tumult, commotion, turbulence, lawbreaking. **Ant.** luck; pleasure; peace.
▶ *v.* **1 worry,** bother, disturb, annoy, irritate, vex, irk, fret, pester, torment, plague, inconvenience, upset, perturb, agitate, discompose, harass, distress, *inf.* hassle. **2 take the trouble/time,** bother, make the effort, exert/disturb oneself, go out of one's way. **3 afflict,** oppress, weigh down, burden, incapacitate. **4 bother,** disturb, inconvenience, put out, impose upon, discommode, incommode.
troublemaker *n.* **mischief-**

maker, inciter, agitator, instigator, agent provocateur, firebrand, malcontent, rabble-rouser, demagogue, stormy petrel.
troublesome *adj.* **worrying,** worrisome, bothersome, tiresome, disturbing, annoying, irritating, irksome, upsetting, perturbing, harassing, distressing, difficult, problematic, demanding, taxing. **Ant.** easy; pleasant.
truancy *n.* **absenteeism,** absence, nonattendance, French leave, shirking, malingering, *inf.* cutting, skipping.
truant *n.* **absentee,** dodger, malingerer, shirker, deserter.
truce *n.* **cease-fire,** armistice, suspension/cessation of hostilities, peace, respite, moratorium, lull, *inf.* letup.
true *adj.* **1 truthful,** accurate, correct, right, valid, factual, exact, precise, faithful, genuine, reliable, veracious, honest. **2 real,** genuine, authentic, actual, bona fide, valid, legitimate, *inf.* honest-to-goodness. **3 loyal,** faithful, trustworthy, trusty, reliable, dependable, staunch, firm, fast, steady, constant, unswerving, unwavering, devoted, sincere, dedicated, supportive, dutiful.
4 exact, precise, perfect, faithful, close, accurate, correct, unerring.

Ant. untrue; false; disloyal; inaccurate.

▸ *adv.* **1 truly,** truthfully, honestly, sincerely, candidly, veraciously. **2 accurately,** unerringly, unswervingly, without deviating, on target, *inf.* dead on.

trust *n.* **1 faith,** confidence, belief, conviction, credence, assurance, certainty, reliance, hope, expectation. **2 responsibility,** duty, obligation, commitment. **3 trusteeship,** guardianship, safekeeping, protection, charge, care, custody.

▸ *v.* **1 put/place one's trust in,** have faith/confidence in, pin one's hopes on. **2 rely on,** depend on, bank on, count on, be sure of, swear by. **3 hope,** assume, presume, expect, believe, suppose. **4 entrust,** put in the hands of, turn over, assign, consign, commit, delegate. *Ant.* distrust; mistrust; doubt.

trustful *adj.* **trusting,** unsuspicious, unguarded, unwary, unsuspecting, unquestioning, credulous, gullible, ingenuous, naïve, innocent. *Ant.* suspicious; wary.

trustworthy *adj.* **reliable,** dependable, stable, staunch, loyal, faithful, trusty, responsible, sensible, levelheaded, honest, honorable, upright, ethical, righteous, principled, virtuous. *Ant.* untrustworthy; unreliable; unfaithful.

truth *n.* **1 truthfulness,** accuracy, correctness, rightness, validity, fact, factualness, factuality, genuineness, veracity, verity, honesty, reality, actuality. **2 truthfulness,** honesty, integrity, uprightness, righteousness, honor, honorableness, sincerity, candor. **3 truism,** axiom, maxim, proverb, adage, aphorism, saw.

truthful *adj.* **1 honest,** trustworthy, veracious, candid, frank, open, forthright, straight. **2 true,** accurate, correct, right, valid, factual, exact, faithful, precise, genuine, reliable, veracious, honest. *Ant.* untruthful; lying; dishonest; inaccurate.

try *v.* **1 attempt,** aim, endeavor, make an effort, exert oneself, undertake, strive, assay, seek, struggle, do one's best, *inf.* have a go/shot/crack/stab. **2 try out,** test, put to the test, experiment with, assay, investigate, examine, appraise, evaluate, assess, experience, sample, check out. **3 tax,** strain, make demands on, sap, drain, exhaust. **4 trouble,** bother, irk, vex, annoy, irritate, harass, afflict, nag, pester, plague, torment, *inf.* drive mad. **5 hear,** adjudge, adjudicate, examine.

trying *adj.* **1 troublesome,** bothersome, tiresome, irksome, vexatious, annoying, irritating, exasperating. **2 taxing,** demanding, stressful, difficult, arduous, hard, tough, tiring, fatiguing, exhausting, upsetting. *Ant.* accommodating; easy.

tuck *v.* **gather,** push, ease, insert, stuff, fold, ruck, ruffle, pleat.
▸ *n.* **gather,** fold, ruck, ruffle, pleat.

tug *v.* **pull,** jerk, yank, wrench, wrest, draw, drag, haul, tow, trail.
▸ *n.* **pull,** jerk, yank, wrench, haul.

tumble *v.* **1 fall over/down/ headlong,** topple, fall head over heels, fall end over end, lose one's footing/balance, stumble, stagger, trip up. **2 somersault,** go head over heels, flip. **3 plummet,** plunge, slump, dive, drop, slide, fall, decrease, decline. **4 roll,** toss, pitch, heave, thrash. **5 fall headlong,** move hurriedly, blunder, stumble. **6 tousle,** dishevel, ruffle, disarrange, disorder, mess up, rumple, *inf.* muss up.
▸ *n.* **1 fall,** stumble, trip, spill, *inf.* nosedive, header. **2 plummeting,** plunge, slump, dive, drop, fall, decline, failure, collapse. **3 somersault,** flip, front/back flip, acrobatic feat.

tumbledown *adj.* **dilapidated,** ramshackle, crumbling, disintegrating, falling to pieces/ bits, decrepit, ruined, in ruins, rickety, shaky, tottering, teetering.

tumor *n.* **1 lump,** growth, swelling, excrescence, protuberance, tumefaction, intumescence. **2 cancerous growth,** carcinoma, cancer, malignancy.

tumult *n.* **1 din,** uproar, commotion, racket, hubbub, hullabaloo, clamor, shouting, yelling, pandemonium, babel, bedlam, noise. **2 disorder,** disarray, disturbance, confusion, chaos, upheaval, uproar, riot, protest, insurrection, rebellion, breach of the peace, row, brawl, fight, quarrel, altercation, affray, fracas, melee, brouhaha, *inf.* free-for-all. **3 turmoil,** upheaval, confusion, ferment.

tumultuous *adj.* **1 loud,** noisy, clamorous, ear-shattering, deafening, ear-piercing, blaring, uproarious, unrestrained, boisterous. **2 rowdy,** unruly, boisterous, disorderly, disturbed, restless, agitated, excited, fierce, obstreperous, wild, violent, lawless, vociferous, noisy, rioting. **3 passionate,** vehement, fervent, violent, raging, unrestrained, uncontrolled, frenzied, in turmoil, turbulent.

tune *n.* **1 melody,** air, song, theme,

strain, motif. **2 agreement,** accord, accordance, harmony, correspondence, congruence, conformity, sympathy. **3 mind,** attitude, view, opinion.

▸ *v.* **adjust,** regulate, pitch, bring into harmony, attune.

tunnel *n.* **1 underground/ subterranean passage,** underpass, subway. **2 burrow,** underground passage.

▸ *v.* **dig,** excavate, burrow, mine, cut, scoop out.

turbulent *adj.* **1 tempestuous,** stormy, raging, foaming, rough, choppy, agitated. **2 rowdy,** unruly, boisterous, disorderly, restless, agitated, obstreperous, wild, violent, lawless, noisy.

3 disturbed, agitated, unsettled, unstable, troubled, distraught, in turmoil. *Ant.* calm; peaceful; quiet.

turgid *adj.* **1 swollen,** enlarged, puffy, puffed up, bloated, distended, tumescent, edematose. **2 bombastic,** high-flown, high-sounding, rhetorical, oratorical, grandiloquent, magniloquent, extravagant, pretentious, pompous, flowery, fulsome, orotund, fustian. *Ant.* simple; plain.

turmoil *n.* **agitation,** ferment, confusion, disorder, disarray, upheaval, chaos, pandemonium, bedlam, tumult, disturbance, bustle, flurry, commotion.

turn *v.* **1 go around,** rotate, revolve, circle, roll, spin, wheel, whirl, twirl, gyrate, swivel, pivot. **2 turn around,** change direction/ course, go back, return, reverse direction, make a U-turn. **3 change direction/course.** **4 change position,** veer, wheel around, swing around. **5 turn over,** reverse, invert, flip over, turn upside down, turn topsy-turvy. **6 aim,** direct, point, train, level, focus. **7 change,** alter, transform, metamorphose, mutate. **8 become,** come to be, get, go. **9 go/turn sour,** sour, curdle, become/make rancid, go bad, spoil, taint. **10 be nauseated,** be upset, be unsettled. **11 nauseate,** sicken, upset, unsettle. **12 spin,** feel dizzy/giddy. **13 go/come around,** round, pass around/round, negotiate, take. **14 become,** reach, get to, pass. **15 put,** switch. **16 perform,** execute, do, carry out. **17 make,** bring in, gain, acquire, obtain, get, procure, secure. **18 shape,** mold, fashion, form, cast, construct. **19 change sides,** go over, defect, desert, renege, turn renegade, break faith, apostatize, tergiversate.

▸ *n.* **1 rotation,** revolution, circle,

spin, whirl, twirl, gyration, swivel.
2 change of direction/course,
deviation, divergence, veer.
3 turning, bend, curve, corner,
twist, winding. **4 trend,** tendency,
bias, leaning, direction, drift,
change, alteration, variation,
difference, deviation, divergence,
shift. **5 bent,** tendency,
inclination, bias, propensity,
affinity, leaning, aptitude, talent,
gift, flair, knack. **6 time,**
opportunity, chance, stint, spell,
move, try, attempt, *inf.* go, shot,
crack. **7 walk,** stroll, saunter,
amble, airing, constitutional,
promenade, drive, ride, outing,
excursion, jaunt, *inf.* spin. **8 act,**
action, deed, service, gesture,
favor. **9 shock,** start, surprise,
fright, scare.

turnover *n.* **1 gross revenue,**
volume of business, business,
financial flow, sales figures.
2 change, coming and going,
movement, replacement.

tutor *n.* **teacher,** instructor, coach,
lecturer, educator.
▸ *v.* **teach,** instruct, coach,
educate, school, train, drill,
direct, guide.

twig *n.* **branch,** stick, offshoot,
shoot, spray, stem.

twilight *n.* **1 dusk,** late afternoon,
early evening, gloaming. **2 half-
light,** semidarkness, dimness.

3 decline, ebb, waning, closing
years.

twin *n.* **1 identical twin,** fraternal
twin, Siamese twin. **2 mate,**
match, fellow, counterpart,
complement. **3 double,** look-alike,
likeness, image, duplicate, clone,
inf. spitting image, ringer, dead
ringer.

twinge *n.* **1 stab of pain,** spasm,
pain, pang, ache, throb, tweak,
tingle, cramp, stitch. **2 pang,**
uneasiness, discomfort, qualm,
scruple, misgiving.

twist *v.* **1 bend,** warp, misshape,
deform, contort, distort, wrench,
wrest. **2 contort,** screw up.
3 wrench, turn, sprain. **4 twine,**
entwine, coil, wind, weave, wrap,
plait, braid. **5 twirl,** coil, wind,
curl. **6 wind,** curve, bend, twine,
zigzag, meander, snake, worm.
7 wriggle, writhe, squirm, wiggle.
8 distort, pervert, warp, garble,
misrepresent, falsify, misquote,
misreport, change, alter. **9 swivel,**
screw, turn, rotate, spin, pivot,
revolve. *Ant.* straighten; unwind.
▸ *n.* **1 wrench,** wrest, turn,
contortion, pull, jerk, yank.
2 bend, warp, kink, deformity,
contortion, distortion, defect,
flaw, imperfection. **3 wrench,**
turn, sprain. **4 coil,** twirl, curl,
braid. **5 bend,** turn, curve,
winding, arc, zigzag, meander,

undulation. **6 aberration,** peculiarity, quirk, oddity, eccentricity, idiosyncrasy, foible. **7 development,** turn, change, alteration, variation, slant.

twitch *v.* **1 move spasmodically,** jerk, jump, quiver, shiver, quaver. **2 blink,** flutter, jump.
▸ *n.* **1 spasm,** jerk, jump, quiver, tremor, shiver, quaver. **2 blink,** flutter, jump, tic.

type *n.* **1 kind,** sort, variety, form, class, classification, category, group, order, set, genre, strain, species, genus, *inf.* ilk. **2 person,** individual, specimen, character. **3 example,** exemplar, model, pattern, essence, personification, epitome, quintessence, archetype, prototype. **4 print,** font, face, character.

typical *adj.* **1 representative,** classic, standard, stock, orthodox, conventional, true-to-type, quintessential, archetypal.

2 normal, average, ordinary, regular, general, customary, habitual, routine, run-of-the-mill.
3 characteristic, in character, in keeping, to be expected, usual, normal. *Ant.* atypical; exceptional; unorthodox; singular.

typify *v.* **1 exemplify,** characterize, personify, epitomize, symbolize, embody, sum up, incarnate.
2 exemplify, represent, indicate, illustrate, denote.

tyrannical *adj.* **despotic,** autocratic, dictatorial, absolute, arbitrary, authoritarian, high-handed, imperious, oppressive, coercive, domineering, bullying, harsh, strict, severe, cruel, brutal, unjust, unreasonable. *Ant.* democratic; liberal; gentle.

tyrant *n.* **despot,** autocrat, dictator, absolute ruler, authoritarian, oppressor, martinet, slave driver, bully.

Uu

ubiquitous *adj.* **everywhere,** omnipresent, ever-present, in all places, all over, all over the place, pervasive, universal.

ugly *adj.* **1 ill-favored,** hideous, plain, unattractive, unlovely, homely, unprepossessing, unsightly, displeasing, horrible, horrid, frightful, terrible, disagreeable, unpleasant, foul, nasty, vile, shocking, distasteful, disgusting, revolting, repellent, repugnant, loathsome, hateful, nauseating, sickening, objectionable, offensive, obnoxious, base, dishonorable, dishonest, rotten, *inf.* not much to look at. **2 threatening,** menacing, ominous, sinister, dangerous, nasty, unpleasant, disagreeable. **3 nasty,** angry, bad-tempered, ill-natured, hostile, surly, sullen, mean, sour. **4 dark,** threatening, menacing, hostile, spiteful, malevolent, evil. *Ant.* beautiful; attractive; pleasant; friendly.

ulterior *adj.* **hidden,** concealed, unrevealed, undisclosed, undivulged, unexpressed, secret, covert, unapparent. *Ant.* overt; obvious.

ultimate *adj.* **1 last,** final, eventual, concluding, conclusive, terminal, end, furthest. **2 basic,** fundamental, primary, elemental, radical. **3 topmost,** utmost, maximum, supreme, superlative, paramount, greatest, highest, unsurpassed, unrivaled. *Ant.* first; secondary; minimum.
 ▸ *n.* **last word,** utmost, height, peak, culmination, perfection, epitome, nonpareil.

umpire *n.* **adjudicator,** arbitrator, arbiter, judge, moderator, referee, *inf.* ref.
 ▸ *v.* **adjudicate,** arbitrate, judge, moderate, referee, *inf.* ref.

unable *adj.* **not able,** incapable, powerless, impotent, not up/equal to, inadequate, ineffectual, incompetent, unfit, unfitted, unqualified.

unacceptable *adj.*
 1 unsatisfactory, inadmissible, unsuitable. **2 insupportable,** intolerable, objectionable, offensive, obnoxious, undesirable, disagreeable, distasteful, improper.

unaccompanied *adj.* **alone,** on one's own, by oneself, partnerless, unescorted, solo, lone, solitary, single.

unaccustomed *adj.* unusual, unfamiliar, uncommon, unwonted, new, exceptional, out of the ordinary, extraordinary, special, remarkable, singular, rare, surprising, strange.

unanimous *adj.* **in complete agreement/accord,** of one mind, like-minded, totally in harmony, at one, with one voice, united, concordant, solid, concerted, uniform, consistent, congruent.

unassailable *adj.* **1 impregnable,** invulnerable, invincible, secure, well-defended. **2 indisputable,** undeniable, unquestionable, incontestable, incontrovertible, irrefutable, conclusive, absolute, positive, proven.

unassuming *adj.* **modest,** self-effacing, humble, meek, retiring, demure, restrained, reticent, diffident, shy, bashful, unassertive, unobtrusive, unostentatious, unpretentious, unaffected, natural, genuine, simple, artless, ingenuous. ***Ant.*** bold; brazen; pretentious.

unattached *adj.* **1 unmarried,** unwed, unwedded, unengaged, unbetrothed, wifeless, husbandless, spouseless, uncommitted, free, available, footloose and fancy free, partnerless, single, on one's own, by oneself, unescorted. **2 independent,** unaffiliated, unassociated, autonomous, nonaligned, self-governing, self-ruling.

unauthorized *adj.* **uncertified,** unaccredited, unlicensed, unofficial, unsanctioned, unwarranted, unapproved, disallowed, prohibited, forbidden, illegal.

unavoidable *adj.* **inescapable,** inevitable, bound to happen, inexorable, ineludible, ineluctable, certain, fated, predestined, necessary, compulsory, required, obligatory, mandatory.

unaware *adj.* **1 unknowing,** unconscious, ignorant, heedless, unmindful, oblivious, uninformed (about), unenlightened (about), *inf.* in the dark. **2 not perceptive,** undiscerning, incognizant, nondiscriminating, unresponsive.

unbelievable *adj.* **beyond belief,** incredible, unconvincing, far-fetched, implausible, improbable, inconceivable, unthinkable, unimaginable, impossible, astonishing, astounding, staggering, preposterous.

unbending *adj.* **1 rigid,** stiff, inflexible, unpliable, inelastic, unmalleable. **2 formal,** stiff, aloof, reserved, *inf.* uptight. **3 inflexible,** hard-line, uncompromising, tough, harsh, strict, stern, severe, firm, resolute, determined, unrelenting, relentless, inexorable.

unbiased *adj.* **impartial,** unprejudiced, nonpartisan, neutral, objective, disinterested, dispassionate, detached, evenhanded, open-minded, equitable, fair, fair-minded, just.

unbreakable *adj.* **nonbreakable,** shatterproof, infrangible, indestructible, toughened.

uncertain *adj.* **1 unknown,** undetermined, unsettled, pending, in the balance, up in the air, unpredictable, unforeseeable, incalculable, speculative, unreliable, untrustworthy, undependable, risky, chancy. **2 unsure,** doubtful, dubious, undecided, unresolved, indecisive, irresolute, hesitant, wavering, vacillating, equivocating, vague, hazy, unclear, ambivalent, in two minds. **3 changeable,** variable, irregular, fitful, unpredictable, unreliable. **4 hesitant,** hesitating, tentative, halting, unsure, unconfident.

uncharted *adj.* **unmapped,** unsurveyed, unexplored, unresearched, unplumbed, unfamiliar, unknown, strange.

uncivilized *adj.* **1 barbarian,** barbarous, barbaric, primitive, savage, wild. **2 uncouth,** coarse, rough, boorish, vulgar, philistine, uneducated, uncultured, uncultivated, unsophisticated, unrefined, unpolished.

unclean *adj.* **1 dirty,** filthy, polluted, fouled, impure, adulterated, tainted, grubby, grimy, stained, besmirched, smeared, unwashed. **2 unchaste,** impure, lustful, licentious, lewd, corrupt, sullied, degenerate, bad, wicked, evil, sinful. **3 forbidden,** impure.

uncomfortable *adj.* **1 not comfortable. 2 uneasy,** ill-at-ease, nervous, tense, edgy, self-conscious, awkward, embarrassed, discomfited, disturbed, troubled, worried, anxious, apprehensive. **3 awkward,** uneasy, unpleasant, disagreeable, painful, distressing, disturbing.

uncommon *adj.* **1 unusual,** rare, uncustomary, unfamiliar, strange, odd, curious, out of the ordinary, novel, singular, peculiar, queer, bizarre, *inf.* weird. **2 rare,** scarce, infrequent, few and far between, occasional. **3 remarkable,** extraordinary, exceptional, singular, outstanding, notable, noteworthy, distinctive, striking.

uncompromising *adj.* rigid, stiff, inflexible, unbending, unyielding, hard-line, tough, immovable, firm, determined, dogged, obstinate, obdurate, tenacious, relentless, implacable, inexorable, intransigent.

unconcerned *adj.* **unworried,** untroubled, unperturbed, unruffled, unanxious, insouciant, nonchalant, carefree, blithe, without a care in the world, serene, relaxed, at ease.

unconditional *adj.* **complete,** total, entire, full, plenary, outright, absolute, downright, out-and-out, utter, all-out, thoroughgoing, unequivocal, conclusive, definite, positive, indubitable, incontrovertible, categorical, unqualified, unlimited, unreserved, unrestricted.

unconscious *adj.* **1 senseless,** insensible, comatose, knocked out, stunned, dazed, *inf.* blacked out, KO'd, out like a light, laid out, out cold, out. **2 unaware,** heedless, ignorant, in ignorance, incognizant, oblivious, insensible. **3 unintentional,** unintended, accidental, unthinking, unwitting, inadvertent, unpremeditated. **4 instinctive,** automatic, reflex, involuntary, inherent, innate, subliminal, subconscious, latent.

unconventional *adj.* **unorthodox,** irregular, informal, unusual, uncommon, uncustomary, unwonted, rare, out of the ordinary, atypical, singular, individual, individualistic, different, original, idiosyncratic, nonconformist, bohemian, eccentric, odd, strange, bizarre, *inf.* offbeat, freakish, way-out.

uncouth *adj.* **rough,** coarse, uncivilized, uncultured, uncultivated, unrefined, unpolished, unsophisticated, provincial, crude, gross, loutish, boorish, oafish, churlish, uncivil, rude, impolite, discourteous, unmannerly, bad-mannered, ill-bred, vulgar. ***Ant.*** refined; cultivated; sophisticated.

uncover *v.* **1 expose,** lay bare, bare, reveal, unwrap. **2 discover,** detect, unearth, dig up, expose, bring to light, unmask, unveil, reveal, lay bare, make known, divulge, disclose.

undaunted *adj.* **undismayed,** unalarmed, unafraid, unflinching, unfaltering, indomitable, resolute, unflagging, intrepid, bold, valiant, brave, courageous, heroic, doughty, plucky, *inf.* spunky.

undemonstrative *adj.* **unemotional,** impassive, restrained, self-contained, reserved, uncommunicative, unresponsive, stiff, reticent, aloof, distant, remote, withdrawn, cool, cold, unaffectionate.

underestimate *v.* **miscalculate,** misjudge, set too low, underrate, rate too low, undervalue, set little store by, not do justice to, misprize, minimize, hold cheap, belittle, disparage, look down on, deprecate, depreciate, *inf.* sell short.

undergo *v.* **go through,** experience, sustain, be subjected to, submit to, endure, bear, tolerate, stand, withstand, put up with, weather.

underground *adv.* **1 below ground,** below the surface. **2 into secrecy,** into seclusion, into hiding, behind closed doors.
▸ *adj.* **1 subterranean,** subterrestrial, below-ground, buried, sunken, hypogean.
2 secret, clandestine, surreptitious, covert, undercover, concealed, hidden.
3 unconventional, unorthodox, experimental, avant-garde, alternative, radical, revolutionary, subversive, counterculture.

undermine *v.* **1 weaken,** impair, damage, injure, sap, threaten, subvert, sabotage, *inf.* throw a monkey wrench in/into the works of, foul up. **2 tunnel under,** dig under, burrow under, excavate.
3 wear away, erode, eat away at.

underprivileged *adj.*
disadvantaged, deprived, in need, needy, in want, destitute, in distress, poor, impoverished, impecunious, badly off.

understand *v.* **1 comprehend,** apprehend, grasp, see, take in, perceive, discern, make out, glean, recognize, appreciate, get to know, follow, fathom, get to the bottom of, penetrate, interpret, *inf.* get the hang/drift of, catch on, latch on to, figure out.
2 appreciate, accept, commiserate with, feel compassionate toward, sympathize with, empathize with.
3 gather, hear, be informed, learn, believe, think, conclude. *Ant.* misunderstand; be ignorant of (see ignorant); ignore.

understanding *n.*
1 comprehension, apprehension, grasp, perception, discernment, appreciation, interpretation, belief, perception, view, notion, idea, fancy, conclusion, feeling.
2 intelligence, intellect, mind, brainpower, brains, powers of reasoning, *inf.* gray matter.
3 compassion, sympathy, empathy, insight. **4 agreement,** gentleman's agreement, arrangement, bargain, pact, compact, (verbal) contract. *Ant.*

ignorance; misunderstanding; indifference.

▶ *adj.* **compassionate,** sympathetic, sensitive, considerate, kind, thoughtful, tolerant, patient, forbearing, lenient, merciful, forgiving.

understate *v.* **downplay,** play down, make light of, minimize, de-emphasize, *inf.* soft-pedal.

undertake *v.* **take on,** set about, tackle, shoulder, assume, enter upon, begin, start, commence, embark on, venture upon, attempt, try. ***Ant.*** neglect; forgo, forego.

undertone *n.* **1 low tone/voice,** murmur, whisper. **2 undercurrent,** hint, suggestion, intimation, inkling, insinuation, trace, tinge, touch, atmosphere, aura, tenor, flavor. ***Ant.*** shout; bellow.

undervalue *v.* **underestimate,** underrate, set little store by, rate too low, think too little of, not do justice to, belittle, disparage, *inf.* sell short.

underwear *n.* **underclothes,** undergarments, underclothing, lingerie, underlinen, *inf.* underthings, undies, unmentionables.

undesirable *adj.* **unpleasant,** disagreeable, nasty, unacceptable, unwanted, unwished-for, foul, objectionable, offensive, obnoxious, disliked, hateful, repugnant, repellent, distasteful, unsavory.

undisciplined *adj.* **unruly,** disorderly, disobedient, obstreperous, recalcitrant, refractory, uncontrolled, unrestrained, wild, willful, wayward, capricious, unsteady, untrained, unschooled, disorganized, erratic, lax.

undisguised *adj.* **open,** obvious, evident, patent, manifest, transparent, overt, unconcealed, unhidden, unmistakable.

undistinguished *adj.* **ordinary,** common, plain, simple, commonplace, everyday, mediocre, run-of-the-mill, pedestrian, prosaic, unexceptional, indifferent, unimpressive, unremarkable, unnoticeable, inconspicuous, *inf.* nothing special, no big deal, no great shakes, nothing to write home about.

undo *v.* **1 unfasten,** unhook, unbutton, untie, unlace, unbind, unfetter, unshackle, loosen, loose, disentangle, release, free, open, unlock. **2 cancel,** annul, nullify, invalidate, revoke, repeal, rescind, reverse, set aside, wipe out. **3 destroy,** ruin, wreck, smash, shatter, annihilate, eradicate, obliterate, defeat, conquer, overthrow, overturn, topple, upset, quash, squelch, crush.

undoubted *adj.* **undisputed,** not in doubt, uncontested, unquestioned, not in question, certain, unquestionable, indubitable, incontrovertible, irrefutable.

undress *v.* **take off one's clothes,** remove one's clothes, strip, disrobe, unclothe.

undue *adj.* **unwarranted,** unjustified, unreasonable, inappropriate, unsuitable, unseemly, unbecoming, improper, ill-advised, excessive, immoderate, disproportionate, inordinate, fulsome, superfluous, too much, too great, uncalled-for, unneeded, unnecessary, nonessential, unrequired. *Ant.* due; appropriate; proper.

undying *adj.* **deathless,** immortal, eternal, infinite, perpetual, unending, never-ending, unceasing, ceaseless, incessant, permanent, lasting, enduring, abiding, continuing, constant, unfading, undiminished, imperishable, indestructible, undestroyed, inextinguishable. *Ant.* transient; ephemeral.

uneasy *adj.* **1 ill at ease,** troubled, worried, anxious, apprehensive, alarmed, disturbed, agitated, nervous, on edge, edgy, restive, restless, unsettled, discomposed, discomfited, perturbed, upset, *inf.* jittery, nervy. **2 strained,** constrained, tense, awkward, precarious, unstable, insecure. **3 worrying,** alarming, dismaying, disturbing, perturbing, disquieting, unsettling, upsetting. *Ant.* calm; composed; tranquil; stable.

unemotional *adj.* **undemonstrative,** passionless, cold, frigid, cool, reserved, restrained, self-controlled, unfeeling, unresponsive, unexcitable, unmoved, impassive, apathetic, indifferent, phlegmatic, detached.

unemployed *adj.* **jobless,** out of work, out of a job, workless, laid off, idle, *inf.* on the dole.

unequal *adj.* **1 different,** differing, dissimilar, unlike, unalike, disparate, unidentical, varying, variable, not uniform, unmatched, uneven, asymmetrical, unsymmetrical, unbalanced, lopsided, irregular, disproportionate, not matching. **2 not up to,** inadequate, insufficient, found wanting. **3 unfair,** unjust, inequitable, uneven, one-sided, ill-matched.

unequivocal *adj.* **unambiguous,** clear, clear-cut, crystal-clear, unmistakable, plain, well-defined, explicit, unqualified, categorical, outright, downright, direct, straightforward, blunt, point-blank, straight from the shoulder, positive, certain, decisive.

unethical *adj.* **immoral,** unprincipled, unscrupulous, dishonorable, dishonest, disreputable, dirty, unfair, underhand, underhanded, bad, wicked, evil, sinful, iniquitous, corrupt, depraved, *inf.* shady.

uneven *adj.* **1 rough,** bumpy, lumpy. **2 variable,** varying, changeable, irregular, fluctuating, erratic, patchy. **3 unequal,** asymmetrical, unsymmetrical, unbalanced, lopsided, irregular, disproportionate, not matching. **4 unequal,** unfair, unjust, inequitable, one-sided, ill-matched.

uneventful *adj.* **unexciting,** uninteresting, monotonous, boring, dull, tedious, routine, unvaried, ordinary, run-of-the-mill, pedestrian, commonplace, everyday, unexceptional, unremarkable, unmemorable.

unexpected *adj.* **unforeseen,** unanticipated, unlooked-for, unpredicted, not bargained for, sudden, abrupt, surprising, startling, astonishing, out of the blue, chance, fortuitous.

unfair *adj.* **1 unjust,** inequitable, partial, partisan, prejudiced, biased, one-sided, unequal, uneven, unbalanced. **2 undeserved,** unmerited, uncalled-for, unreasonable, unjustifiable, unwarrantable, out of proportion, disproportionate, excessive, extreme, immoderate. **3 foul,** unsporting, unsportsmanlike, dirty, below-the-belt, underhand, underhanded, unscrupulous, dishonorable, *inf.* crooked.

unfaithful *adj.* **1 disloyal,** false, false-hearted, faithless, perfidious, treacherous, traitorous, untrustworthy, unreliable, undependable, insincere. **2 faithless,** adulterous, fickle, untrue, inconstant, *inf.* cheating, two-timing.

unfamiliar *adj.* **unknown,** new, strange, alien, unaccustomed, uncommon.

unfasten *v.* **undo,** open, loose, detach, disconnect, untie, unwrap, unbind, unlace, unhitch, untether, unlock, unbolt.

unfavorable *adj.* **1 adverse,** critical, hostile, inimical, unfriendly, negative, discouraging, poor, bad. **2 disadvantageous,** adverse, unfortunate, unhappy, detrimental. **3 inconvenient,** inopportune, untimely, untoward.

unfeeling *adj.* **uncaring,** unsympathetic, hard-hearted, hard, harsh, heartless, apathetic, cold, callous, cruel, pitiless, inhuman.

unfit *adj.* **out of condition,** in poor condition/shape, out of kilter, flabby, unhealthy, debilitated, weak.

unfold *v.* **1 open out,** spread out, stretch out, flatten, straighten out, unfurl, unroll, unravel. **2 narrate,** relate, recount, tell, reveal, make known, disclose, divulge, present. **3 develop,** evolve, grow, mature, bear fruit.

unforgivable *adj.* **inexcusable,** unpardonable, unwarrantable, unjustifiable, indefensible, reprehensible, deplorable, despicable, contemptible, disgraceful, shameful.

unfortunate *adj.* **1 adverse,** disadvantageous, unfavorable, unlucky, untoward, unpromising, hostile, inimical, disastrous, calamitous. **2 unlucky,** out of luck, luckless, ill-starred, star-crossed, hapless, wretched, miserable, unhappy, poor. **3 regrettable,** deplorable, ill-advised, inappropriate, unsuitable, inapt, tactless, untactful, injudicious, awkward, clumsy.

unfriendly *adj.* **1 unamicable,** uncongenial, unsociable, inhospitable, unneighborly, unkind, unsympathetic, aloof, cold, cool, distant, disagreeable, unpleasant, surly, sour, hostile, inimical, antagonistic, aggressive, quarrelsome. **2 unfavorable,** disadvantageous, unpropitious, inauspicious, hostile, inimical, alien.

ungainly *adj.* **awkward,** clumsy, ungraceful, graceless, inelegant, gawky, gangling, maladroit, inept, bungling, bumbling, lumbering, uncoordinated, hulking, lubberly. *Ant.* graceful; elegant.

ungrateful *adj.* **unthankful,** unappreciative, impolite, uncivil, rude.

unhappy *adj.* **1 sad,** miserable, sorrowful, dejected, despondent, disconsolate, brokenhearted, down, downcast, dispirited, crestfallen, depressed, melancholy, blue, gloomy, glum, mournful, woebegone, long-faced, joyless, cheerless. **2 unfortunate,** unlucky, luckless, hapless, ill-starred, ill-fated, star-crossed, wretched, miserable, disadvantageous, adverse. **3 unfortunate,** regrettable, inappropriate.

unhealthy *adj.* **1 in poor health,** unwell, ill, ailing, sick, sickly, poorly, indisposed, unsound, weak, feeble, frail, delicate, debilitated, infirm.

2 unwholesome, unnourishing, detrimental, injurious, damaging, deleterious, noxious, insalubrious.

3 unwholesome, morbid, undesirable.

unheard-of *adj.* **1 unknown,** little-known, undiscovered, obscure, nameless, unsung.

2 unprecedented, unexampled, exceptional, extraordinary, out of the ordinary, uncommon, unusual, unparalleled, unrivaled, unmatched, unequaled, singular, unique, unbelievable, inconceivable. **Ant.** famous; common.

unhurried *adj.* **leisurely,** leisured, easy, slow, slow-moving, slow-going, slow and steady, deliberate, sedate, lingering, loitering.

unidentified *adj.* **nameless,** unnamed, unknown, anonymous, incognito, obscure, unmarked, undesignated, unclassified.

uniform *adj.* **1 constant,** consistent, invariable, unvarying, unvaried, unchanging, undeviating, stable, regular, even, equal, equable. **2 same,** alike, like, selfsame, identical, similar, equal. **Ant.** changeable; variable; varied; different.

▸ *n.* **livery,** regalia, habit, suit, dress, costume, garb, regimentals.

unify *v.* **unite,** bring together,

merge, fuse, amalgamate, coalesce, combine, blend, mix, bind, link up, consolidate. **Ant.** separate; split; sever.

unimaginable *adj.* **unthinkable,** inconceivable, incredible, unbelievable, unheard-of, unthought-of, implausible, improbable, unlikely, impossible, undreamed of, fantastic, beyond one's wildest dreams, *inf.* mind-boggling, mind-blowing.

unimportant *adj.* **of little/no importance,** insignificant, of little/no consequence, inconsequential, of no account, nonessential, immaterial, irrelevant, not worth mentioning, not worth speaking of, minor, slight, trifling, trivial, petty, paltry, insubstantial, inferior, worthless, nugatory, *inf.* small-fry, no great shakes, dinky.

uninhabited *adj.* **vacant,** empty, unoccupied, untenanted, unpopulated, unpeopled, unsettled, abandoned, deserted, forsaken, unfrequented, barren, desert, desolate.

uninhibited *adj.* **1 unreserved,** unrepressed, unconstrained, unselfconscious, spontaneous, free and easy, relaxed, informal, open, candid, outspoken.

2 unrestrained, unrestricted, unrepressed, unconstrained, uncontrolled, uncurbed, unchecked, unbridled.

unintelligible *adj.*
1 incomprehensible, meaningless, unfathomable, incoherent, indistinct, inarticulate, confused, muddled, jumbled. **2 illegible,** indecipherable.

unintentional *adj.* unintended, accidental, inadvertent, unplanned, unpremeditated, uncalculated, chance, fortuitous, unconscious, involuntary, unwitting, unthinking.

uninterested *adj.* **1 indifferent,** unconcerned, uninvolved, apathetic, blasé, unresponsive, impassive, dispassionate, aloof, detached, distant. **2 bored,** incurious.

uninteresting *adj.* unexciting, dull, unentertaining, boring, tiresome, wearisome, tedious, dreary, flat, monotonous, humdrum, uneventful, commonplace, dry, pedestrian, prosaic, hackneyed, stale.

uninterrupted *adj.* unbroken, undisturbed, continuous, continual, constant, steady, sustained, nonstop, unending, endless, ceaseless, unceasing, incessant, interminable, unremitting.

union *n.* **1 joining,** junction, merging, merger, fusion, amalgamating, amalgamation, blend, mixture, coalition, combining, combination, consolidation, confederation. **2 coupling,** joint. **3 association,** alliance, league, coalition, consortium, syndicate, guild, confederation, federation, confederacy. **4 marriage,** wedding, coupling, intercourse, coition, coitus, copulation. **5 agreement,** accord, concurrence, unity, unison, unanimity, harmony, concord. **Ant.** separation; parting; divorce; disagreement.

unique *adj.* **1 only,** one and only, single, sole, lone, solitary, sui generis, exclusive, in a class by itself. **2 unequaled,** without equal, unparalleled, unexampled, unmatched, matchless, peerless, unsurpassed, unexcelled, incomparable, beyond compare, inimitable, second to none. **Ant.** common; ordinary; usual.

unit *n.* **1 entity,** whole.
2 component, part, section, element, constituent, subdivision, portion, segment, module, item, member. **3 measurement,** measure, quantity.

unite *v.* **1 join,** link, connect, combine, amalgamate, fuse, weld, splice. **2 combine,** mix, commix, admix, blend, mingle, homogenize. **3 marry,** wed, join in

wedlock, tie the knot between.
4 join together, join forces,
combine, amalgamate, band
together, ally, cooperate, work/
act/pull together, work side by
side, pool resources. *Ant.*
separate; split; divorce.
united *adj.* **1 combined,**
amalgamated, allied, cooperative,
concerted, collective, pooled. **2 in
agreement,** agreed, in unison, of
the same opinion/mind, of like
mind, like-minded, at one, in
accord, unanimous.
unity *n.* **1 oneness,** singleness,
wholeness, entity, integrity.
2 union, unification,
amalgamation, coalition, alliance,
cooperation, undividedness.
3 agreement, harmony, accord,
concord, concurrence, unanimity,
consensus, concert, togetherness,
solidarity. *Ant.* division; discord;
disunity.
universal *adj.* **general,** all-
embracing, all-inclusive,
comprehensive, across the board,
worldwide, global, widespread,
common, predominant,
preponderate, omnipresent,
ubiquitous, catholic. *Ant.*
particular; restricted; local.
unjust *adj.* **1 unfair,** inequitable,
prejudiced, biased, partisan,
partial, one-sided. **2 unfair,**
wrongful, wrong, undue,

undeserved, unmerited,
unwarranted, uncalled-for,
unreasonable, unjustifiable.
unjustifiable *adj.* **1 indefensible,**
inexcusable, unforgivable,
unpardonable, uncalled-for,
blameworthy, culpable,
unwarrantable. **2 groundless,**
unfounded, without foundation,
baseless, without basis,
unsupported, unsubstantiated,
unreasonable.
unkempt *adj.* **untidy,** disheveled,
disordered, disarranged, tousled,
rumpled, windblown, uncombed,
ungroomed, messy, messed up,
scruffy, slovenly, *inf.* sloppy,
mussed up. *Ant.* tidy; neat; trim.
unkind *adj.* **1 unkindly,** unfriendly,
unamiable, uncharitable,
unchristian, inhospitable,
ungenerous, nasty, mean, cruel,
vicious, spiteful, malicious,
malevolent, harsh, pitiless,
ruthless, unsympathetic,
unfeeling, hard-hearted, heartless,
cold-hearted. **2 inclement,** harsh,
intemperate.
unknown *adj.* **1 untold,**
unrevealed, undisclosed,
undivulged, undetermined,
undecided, unestablished,
unsettled, unascertained, in the
balance, up in the air.
2 unidentified, unnamed,
nameless, anonymous, incognito.

3 unfamiliar, unexplored, uncharted, untraveled, undiscovered. **4 unheard-of,** little-known, obscure, undistinguished, unrenowned, unsung.

unlawful *adj.* **against the law,** illegal, illicit, illegitimate, criminal, felonious, actionable, prohibited, banned, outlawed, proscribed, unauthorized, unsanctioned, unwarranted, unlicensed.

unlikely *adj.* **1 improbable,** doubtful, dubious, faint, slight, remote, not likely, unexpected. **2 improbable,** implausible, questionable, unconvincing, incredible, unbelievable, inconceivable, unimaginable.

unlimited *adj.* **unrestricted,** unconstrained, uncontrolled, unrestrained, unchecked, unhindered, unhampered, unimpeded, unfettered, untrammeled, absolute, total, unqualified, unconditional, limitless, illimitable, boundless, unbounded, immense, vast, great, extensive, immeasurable, incalculable, untold, infinite, endless.

unloved *adj.* **unbeloved,** uncared-for, uncherished, unwanted, unpopular, forsaken, rejected, jilted, disliked, hated, detested, loathed.

unlucky *adj.* **1 luckless,** out of luck, down on one's luck, unfortunate, hapless, ill-fated, ill-starred, star-crossed, wretched, miserable. **2 unsuccessful,** failed, ill-fated. **3 adverse,** disadvantageous, unfavorable, unfortunate, untoward, unpromising, inauspicious, unpropitious, doomed, ill-fated, ill-omened.

unmarried *adj.* **single,** unwed, unwedded, spouseless, partnerless, divorced, unattached, bachelor, celibate, husbandless, wifeless.

unmistakable *adj.* **clear,** plain, obvious, evident, manifest, apparent, patent, palpable, distinct, distinctive, conspicuous, well-defined, pronounced, striking, glaring, blatant, undoubted, indisputable, indubitable, beyond a doubt, unquestionable, beyond question.

unmitigated *adj.* **absolute,** unqualified, unconditional, categorical, complete, total, thorough, thoroughgoing, downright, utter, out and out, veritable, perfect, consummate.

unnatural *adj.* **1 unusual,** uncommon, extraordinary, strange, queer, odd, bizarre, preternatural. **2 perverted,** depraved, deviant, abnormal,

aberrant, sick, immoral, *inf.* kinky.
3 affected, artificial, feigned, false, self-conscious, contrived, forced, labored, studied, strained, insincere, theatrical, stagy, mannered.

unnecessary *adj.* **needless,** unneeded, inessential, nonessential, uncalled-for, unrequired, gratuitous, useless, dispensable, expendable, redundant, superfluous.

unobtrusive *adj.* **1 self-effacing,** retiring, unassuming, modest, quiet, meek, humble, unaggressive, unassertive, low-profile. **2 low-key,** restrained, subdued, quiet, unostentatious, unshowy, inconspicuous, unnoticeable.

unofficial *adj.* **1 informal,** casual, unauthorized, unsanctioned, unaccredited, wildcat.
2 unconfirmed, unauthenticated, uncorroborated, unsubstantiated.

unorthodox *adj.* **1 heterodox,** uncanonical, heretical, nonconformist. **2 unconventional,** unusual, uncommon, uncustomary, unwonted, out of the ordinary, nonconformist, unconforming, irregular, abnormal, divergent, aberrant, anomalous.

unpalatable *adj.* **unsavory,** unappetizing, uneatable, inedible,

undelectable, nasty, disgusting, repugnant, revolting, nauseating, sickening, distasteful, disagreeable, unpleasant, offensive, obnoxious, unattractive, repulsive, repellent.

unparalleled *adj.* **without parallel,** unequaled, without equal, matchless, unmatched, peerless, unrivaled, unprecedented, unsurpassed, unexcelled, incomparable, beyond compare, singular, unique. ***Ant.*** ordinary; run-of-the-mill.

unpleasant *adj.* **1 disagreeable,** unpalatable, unsavory, unappetizing, disgusting, repugnant, revolting, nauseating, sickening, offensive, obnoxious, foul, smelly, stinking.
2 disagreeable, unlikable, unlovable, unattractive, nasty, ill-natured, cross, bad-tempered.
3 disagreeable, irksome, troublesome, annoying, irritating, vexatious.

unpopular *adj.* **disliked,** unliked, unloved, friendless, unwanted, unwelcome, avoided, ignored, rejected, shunned, out in the cold, unattractive, undesirable, out of favor.

unpredictable *adj.*
1 unforeseeable, undivinable, doubtful, dubious, uncertain,

unsure, in the balance, up in the air, *inf.* iffy. **2 erratic,** fickle, capricious, whimsical, mercurial, volatile, unstable, undependable, unreliable.

unpremeditated *adj.* **unplanned,** unarranged, unprepared, unintentional, extempore, impromptu, ad lib, spontaneous, spur of the moment, on the spot, impulsive, hasty, *inf.* off the cuff.

unpretentious *adj.* **1 simple,** plain, modest, ordinary, humble, unostentatious, unshowy, unimposing, homely. **2 unassuming,** modest, unaffected, natural, straightforward, honest.

unprofessional *adj.* **1 unethical,** unprincipled, improper, unseemly, indecorous, lax, negligent. **2 amateur,** amateurish, unskilled, inexpert, untrained, unqualified, inexperienced, incompetent.

unpromising *adj.* **unfavorable,** adverse, unpropitious, inauspicious, gloomy, black, discouraging, portentous, ominous.

unquestionable *adj.* **beyond question/doubt,** indubitable, undoubted, indisputable, undeniable, irrefutable,

uncontestable, incontrovertible, certain, sure, definite, positive, conclusive, self-evident, obvious.

unravel *v.* **1 untangle,** disentangle, straighten out, separate out, unknot, undo. **2 solve,** resolve, work out, clear up, get to the bottom of, fathom, *inf.* figure out. **Ant.** entangle; tangle; complicate.

unreal *adj.* **imaginary,** make-believe, fictitious, mythical, fanciful, fantastic, fabulous, hypothetical, nonexistent, illusory, chimerical, phantasmagoric, phantasmagorical.

unrealistic *adj.* **1 impractical,** impracticable, unworkable, unreasonable, irrational, illogical, improbable, foolish, wild, absurd, quixotic, *inf.* half-baked. **2 unreal-looking,** unlifelike, nonnaturalistic, artificial, contrived.

unreasonable *adj.* **1 excessive,** immoderate, undue, inordinate, outrageous, extravagant, preposterous, unconscionable. **2 exorbitant,** extortionate, expensive, *inf.* steep. **3 irrational,** illogical, opinionated, biased, prejudiced, obstinate, obdurate, willful, headstrong, temperamental, capricious. **4 unacceptable,** preposterous, outrageous, ludicrous, absurd, irrational, illogical.

unreliable *adj.* **1 undependable,** irresponsible, untrustworthy, erratic, fickle, inconstant.
2 suspect, questionable, open to question/doubt, doubtful, unsound, implausible, unconvincing, fallible, specious.

unrepentant *adj.* impenitent, unrepenting, unremorseful, shameless, unregenerate, abandoned.

unrest *n.* **dissatisfaction,** discontent, discontentment, unease, disquiet, dissension, dissent, discord, strife, protest, rebellion, agitation, turmoil, turbulence. *Ant.* peace; calm.

unrestricted *adj.* **unlimited,** open, free, unhindered, unchecked, unbounded, *inf.* free for all, with no holds barred.

unsavory *adj.* **1 unpalatable,** unappetizing, unpleasant, disagreeable, disgusting, loathsome, repugnant, revolting, nauseating, sickening.
2 unpleasant, disagreeable, nasty, objectionable, offensive, obnoxious, repellent, repulsive, disreputable, degenerate, coarse, gross, vulgar, boorish, churlish, rude, uncouth.

unscrupulous *adj.* unprincipled, unethical, amoral, immoral, conscienceless, shameless, corrupt, dishonest, dishonorable, deceitful, devious, exploitative, wrongdoing, bad, evil, wicked, *inf.* crooked. *Ant.* ethical; honest.

unselfish *adj.* altruistic, self-sacrificing, selfless, kind, self-denying, openhanded, generous, liberal, unsparing, ungrudging, unstinting, charitable, philanthropic.

unsightly *adj.* **ugly,** unattractive, unprepossessing, hideous, horrible, repulsive, revolting, offensive, distasteful. *Ant.* attractive; beautiful.

unskilled *adj.* untrained, unqualified, inexpert, inexperienced, amateurish, unprofessional.

unsophisticated *adj.*
1 unworldly, naïve, simple, innocent, inexperienced, childlike, artless, guileless, ingenuous, natural, unaffected, unpretentious, unrefined, unpolished, gauche, provincial.
2 crude, unrefined, basic, rudimentary, primitive, undeveloped, homespun.
3 simple, straightforward, uncomplicated, uninvolved, unspecialized.

unspeakable *adj.* **1 beyond words,** inexpressible, unutterable, indescribable, undefinable,

ineffable, unimaginable, inconceivable, unthinkable, unheard-of, overwhelming, marvelous, wonderful.
2 indescribable, indescribably bad/wicked/evil, unmentionable, appalling, shocking, horrible, frightful, terrible, dreadful, abominable, deplorable, despicable, contemptible, repellent, loathsome, odious, monstrous, heinous, execrable.

unspoiled adj. **1 preserved,** intact, as good as new/before, perfect, unblemished, unimpaired, undamaged, untouched, unaffected, unchanged. **2 innocent,** wholesome, natural, simple, artless, unaffected, pure, uncorrupted, undefiled, unblemished.

unstable adj. **1 unsteady,** infirm, rickety, shaky, wobbly, tottery, unsafe, unreliable, insecure, precarious. **2 unbalanced,** unhinged, irrational, deranged, mentally ill, crazed, insane, mad, volatile, moody, mercurial, capricious, giddy, erratic, unpredictable. **3 changeable,** variable, unsettled, fluctuating, inconstant, unpredictable.

unsuccessful adj. **1 without success,** failed, vain, unavailing, futile, useless, worthless, abortive,

nugatory, ineffective, ineffectual, inefficacious, fruitless, unproductive, unprofitable, frustrated, thwarted, foiled.
2 failed, losing, unprosperous, unlucky, luckless, out-of-luck, unfortunate, ill-starred, ill-fated.

unsuitable adj. **inappropriate,** inapt, inapposite, unfitting, unbefitting, incompatible, incongruous, out of place/ keeping, ineligible, unacceptable, unbecoming, unseemly, indecorous, improper.

unsure adj. **1 unselfconfident,** insecure, hesitant, diffident.
2 undecided, irresolute, in two minds, in a dilemma/quandary, ambivalent. **3 uncertain,** unconvinced, dubious, doubtful, skeptical, distrustful, suspicious.

unsuspecting adj. **unsuspicious,** unwary, off guard, trusting, trustful, overtrustful, gullible, credulous, ingenuous, naïve, innocent, dupable, exploitable.
Ant. suspicious; wary.

unsympathetic adj.
1 unsympathizing, unkind, uncompassionate, compassionless, unpitying, pitiless, uncommiserating, uncaring, unfeeling, insensitive, unconcerned, indifferent, unresponsive, apathetic, unmoved, untouched, heartless,

cold, hard-hearted, hard, harsh, callous, cruel. **2 disapproving of,** opposed to, against, anti.

untangle *v.* **1 disentangle,** unravel, unsnarl, straighten out. **2 straighten out,** sort out, clear up.

untenable *adj.* **indefensible,** undefendable, insupportable, unmaintainable, unsustainable, refutable, unsound, weak, flawed, defective, faulty, implausible, specious, groundless, unfounded, baseless, unacceptable, inadmissible.

unthinkable *adj.*
1 inconceivable, unimaginable, unbelievable, beyond belief, impossible, beyond the bounds of possibility, implausible. **2 not to be considered,** out of the question, absurd, preposterous, outrageous. *Ant.* imaginable; plausible; conceivable.

unthinking *adj.* **1 thoughtless,** inconsiderate, tactless, undiplomatic, injudicious, indiscreet, insensitive, blundering, careless, rude.
2 inadvertent, unintentional, unintended, mechanical, automatic, instinctive, involuntary.

untidy *adj.* **disheveled,** unkempt, bedraggled, rumpled, messy, slovenly, slatternly, disordered,

disorderly, disarranged, disorganized, chaotic, confused, muddled, jumbled, topsy-turvy, at sixes and sevens, *inf.* mussed up, sloppy, higgledy-piggledy, every which way.

untie *v.* **undo,** loose, unbind, unfasten, unwrap, unlace, untether, unhitch, unknot.

untiring *adj.* **tireless,** indefatigable, unfailing, unfaltering, unwavering, unflagging, unremitting, constant, incessant, unceasing, dogged, determined, resolute, steady, persistent, staunch.

untroubled *adj.* **unperturbed,** undisturbed, unworried, unruffled, unagitated, unbothered, unconcerned, calm, cool, collected, composed, serene.

untrue *adj.* **1 false,** fallacious, fictitious, fabricated, erroneous, in error, wrong, incorrect, inaccurate, economical with the truth, inexact, flawed, unsound, distorted, misleading. **2 disloyal,** faithless, unfaithful, false, treacherous, perfidious, deceitful, untrustworthy, double-dealing, insincere, unreliable, inconstant. **3 inaccurate,** wide of the mark, wide, off, out of true.

unusual *adj.* **1 uncommon,** out of the ordinary, atypical, abnormal, rare, singular, odd, strange, curious, queer, bizarre, surprising, unexpected, different, unconventional, uncustomary, unwonted, unorthodox, irregular, *inf.* weird. **2 extraordinary,** exceptional, singular, rare, remarkable, outstanding.

unwarranted *adj.*
1 unauthorized, uncertified, unaccredited, unlicensed, unsanctioned, unapproved.
2 unjustifiable, unjustified, indefensible, inexcusable, unforgivable, unpardonable, uncalled-for, gratuitous.

unwelcome *adj.* **1 unwanted,** undesired, uninvited, unpopular.
2 unpleasant, disagreeable, unpalatable, displeasing, distasteful, undesirable.

unwell *adj.* **ill,** sick, sickly, ailing, in poor health, unhealthy, run-down, below par, *inf.* out of sorts, poorly, under the weather.

unwieldy *adj.* **cumbersome,** unmanageable, unmaneuverable, awkward, clumsy, massive, hefty, bulky, ponderous, *inf.* hulking.
Ant. manageable; graceful; dainty.

unwilling *adj.* **1 reluctant,** disinclined, unenthusiastic, grudging, involuntary, forced.
2 reluctant, disinclined, averse, loath, opposed, not in the mood.

unwind *v.* **1 undo,** unravel, uncoil, unroll, untwine, untwist, disentangle. **2 wind down,** relax, calm down, slow down, *inf.* loosen up, let oneself go, take it easy, let one's hair down.

unwitting *adj.* **1 unknowing,** unconscious, unaware, ignorant.
2 unintentional, unintended, inadvertent, unmeant, unplanned, accidental, chance.
Ant. conscious; deliberate.

unworthy *adj.* **1 unsuitable,** inappropriate, unbefitting, unfitting, unseemly, improper, incompatible, incongruous, inconsistent, out of character, degrading, discreditable.
2 worthless, inferior, second-rate, undeserving, ignoble, disreputable, *inf.* lousy, crappy.
3 disreputable, dishonorable, base, contemptible, reprehensible.

upgrade *v.* **1 improve,** better, ameliorate, reform, enhance, touch up, rehabilitate, refurbish.
2 promote, advance, elevate, raise.
Ant. downgrade; demote.

upheaval *n.* **disruption,** disturbance, revolution, disorder, confusion, turmoil, chaos, cataclysm.

uphill *adj.* **1 upward,** ascending, climbing, mounting, rising.
2 arduous, difficult, laborious, strenuous, hard, tough, burdensome, onerous, taxing,

punishing, grueling, exhausting, wearisome, Herculean, Sisyphean.

uphold *v.* **1 confirm,** endorse, support, back up, stand by, champion, defend. **2 maintain,** sustain, hold to, keep. *Ant.* oppose; discard.

upkeep *n.* **1 maintenance,** running, preservation, conservation, repairs, keep, support, subsistence, sustenance, outlay, operating costs, costs, overheads, expenses. **2 outlay,** running/operating costs, costs, overheads, expenses.

upper *adj.* **1 higher,** further up, loftier. **2 superior,** higher-ranking, elevated, greater. *Ant.* lower; inferior.

upright *adj.* **1 erect,** on end, vertical, perpendicular, standing up, rampant. **2 honest,** honorable, upstanding, decent, respectable, worthy, reputable, good, virtuous, righteous, law-abiding, ethical, moral, high-principled, of principle, high-minded. *Ant.* horizontal; dishonorable; crooked.

uproar *n.* **1 tumult,** turmoil, turbulence, disorder, confusion, commotion, mayhem, pandemonium, bedlam, din, noise, clamor, hubbub, racket. **2 outburst,** row, rumpus, brouhaha, hullabaloo, affray,

furor, fracas, brawl, scuffle, conflict, struggle, free-for-all, *inf.* ruckus.

upset *v.* **1 overturn,** knock over, push over, upend, tip over, topple, capsize. **2 perturb,** disturb, discompose, unsettle, disconcert, dismay, disquiet, trouble, worry, bother, agitate, fluster, ruffle, shake, frighten, alarm, anger, annoy, distress, hurt, grieve. **3 disturb,** throw into disorder/confusion, disorganize, disarrange, mess up, mix up, turn topsy-turvy. **4 defeat,** beat, conquer, vanquish, rout, overthrow, overcome, triumph over, be victorious over, get the better of, worst, thrash, trounce. ▶ *n.* **1 perturbation,** discomposure, dismay, disquiet, trouble, worry, bother, agitation, fluster, alarm, distress, hurt. **2 disturbance,** disorder, confusion, disorganization, disarrangement. **3 disorder,** disturbance, complaint, ailment, illness, sickness, disease, malady, *inf.* bug. **4 defeat,** conquering, rout, overthrow, worsting.

upshot *n.* **result,** outcome, conclusion, issue, end, end result, denouement, effect, repercussion, reaction, *inf.* payoff. *Ant.* origin; cause.

upstart *n.* **parvenu,** parvenue,

would-be, social climber, status seeker, nouveau riche, arriviste.

upward *adj.* **rising,** climbing, mounting, ascending, on the rise. *Ant.* downward; downhill.

urbane *adj.* **suave,** debonair, sophisticated, smooth, worldly, elegant, cultivated, cultured, civilized, polished, refined, gracious, charming, agreeable, affable, courtly, civil, polite, courteous, well-mannered, mannerly. *Ant.* uncouth; unsophisticated; boorish.

urge *v.* **1 push,** drive, propel, impel, force, hasten, hurry, speed up. **2 spur,** incite, stir up, stimulate, prod, goad, egg on, encourage, prompt, *inf.* psych up. **3 entreat,** exhort, implore, appeal, beg, beseech, plead. **4 advise,** counsel, advocate, recommend, suggest, support, endorse, back, champion. *Ant.* dissuade; deter; discourage.
  ▸ *n.* **desire,** need, compulsion, longing, yearning, wish, fancy, impulse, itch, *inf.* yen.

urgent *adj.* **1 imperative,** vital, crucial, critical, essential, exigent, top-priority, high-priority, important, necessary. **2 vital,** crucial, exigent, top-priority, high-priority, important, pressing, serious, grave. **3 importunate,** insistent,

clamorous, earnest, pleading, begging. *Ant.* unimportant; trivial; casual.

usable *adj.* **utilizable,** available, ready/fit for use, in working order, functional.

use *v.* **1 make use of,** utilize, employ, work, operate, wield, ply, maneuver, manipulate, avail oneself of, put to use, put into service. **2 employ,** exercise, apply. **3 treat,** handle, deal with, act/ behave toward. **4 make use of,** exploit, manipulate, take advantage of, impose upon, abuse, *inf.* walk all over, play for a sucker. **5 consume,** get through, exhaust, deplete, expend, spend, waste, fritter away.
  ▸ *n.* **1 usage,** application, utilization, employment, operation, manipulation, maneuvering. **2 using,** usage, wear, wear and tear. **3 right,** privilege, prerogative. **4 exploitation,** manipulation. **5 usefulness,** good, advantage, benefit, service, help, gain, profit, avail. **6 usage,** practice, custom, habit, wont. **7 need,** necessity, call, demand, purpose, reason.

used *adj.* **secondhand,** nearly new, cast-off, *inf.* hand-me-down. *Ant.* new; pristine.

useful *adj.* **1 of use,** functional, utilitarian, of service, practical, convenient. **2 beneficial,** advantageous, of help, helpful, worthwhile, profitable, rewarding, productive, valuable. **3 effective,** efficacious, effectual, competent, capable, able. **Ant.** useless; disadvantageous; ineffective.

useless adj. **1 vain,** in vain, to no avail/purpose, unavailing, unsuccessful, futile, purposeless, ineffectual, inefficacious, fruitless, unprofitable, unproductive, abortive. **2 worthless,** ineffective, ineffectual, incompetent, incapable, inadequate, inf. no good. **Ant.** useful; beneficial; effective.

usual adj. **1 habitual,** customary, accustomed, wonted, normal, regular, routine, everyday, established, set, familiar. **2 common,** typical, ordinary, average, run-of-the-mill, expected, standard, stock, regular. **Ant.** unusual; uncommon; extraordinary.

usually adv. **generally,** as a rule, normally, by and large, in the main, mainly, mostly, for the most part, on the whole.

usurp v. **take over,** seize, expropriate, take possession of, appropriate, commandeer, lay claim to, assume.

utilitarian adj. **practical,** functional, useful, to the purpose.

utter adj. **absolute,** complete, total, thorough, thoroughgoing, positive, downright, out-and-out, sheer, unmitigated, categorical, unqualified, unconditional, perfect, consummate.
▸ v. **1 emit,** let out, give. **2 voice,** say, speak, pronounce, express, put into words, enunciate, articulate, verbalize, vocalize.

utterance n. **1 voice,** expression, articulation, enunciation, verbalization, vocalization. **2 remark,** word, comment, statement, opinion.

utterly adv. **absolutely,** completely, totally, entirely, thoroughly, positively, extremely, categorically, perfectly, consummately, to the core.

Vv

vacancy *n.* **1 emptiness,** voidness. **2 opening,** position, post, job, opportunity, slot. **3 unoccupied room,** room. **4 blankness,** lack of expression, expressionlessness, lack of emotion/interest, emotionlessness, vacuousness. **5 lack of thought/intelligence,** brainlessness, denseness, thickness, vacuousness, vacuity, inaneness, inanity, stupidity.

vacant *adj.* **1 empty,** void, without contents. **2 unoccupied,** unfilled, free, empty, available. **3 empty,** unoccupied, free, unengaged, not in use, unused, available, uninhabited, untenanted, tenantless, to let, abandoned, deserted, *inf.* up for grabs. **4 blank,** expressionless, inexpressive, deadpan, poker-faced, emotionless, uninterested, vacuous, inane. **5 without thought,** unintelligent, brainless, dense, dull-witted, thick, vacuous, inane, stupid. *Ant.* full; occupied; expressive.

vacate *v.* **leave,** quit, depart from, evacuate, abandon, desert. *Ant.* occupy; inhabit.

vacillate *v.* **shilly-shally,** waver, dither, be irresolute/indecisive, hesitate, equivocate, hem and haw, keep changing one's mind, beat about the bush, *inf.* blow hot and cold.

vacuous *adj.* **1 vacant,** blank, expressionless, deadpan, inane. **2 unintelligent,** brainless, vacant, inane, stupid.

vagrant *n.* **tramp,** hobo, beggar, itinerant, nomad, wanderer, vagabond, *inf.* bum.
▸ *adj.* **tramplike,** itinerant, nomadic, peripatetic, wandering, roving, vagabond, homeless.

vague *adj.* **1 indistinct,** indeterminate, ill-defined, unclear, amorphous, shadowy, hazy, dim, fuzzy, foggy, blurry, bleary, out of focus, imprecise, inexact, unexplicit, nonspecific, loose, generalized, ambiguous, equivocal, woolly, nebulous. **2 uncertain,** unsure, hesitant, wavering, shilly-shallying, *inf.* blowing hot and cold. **3 uncertain,** undecided, indefinite, indeterminate, doubtful, open, speculative, conjectural, *inf.* up in the air. **4 absentminded,**

abstracted, dreamy, vacuous, *inf.* with one's head in the clouds. **Ant.** distinct; precise; clear; certain.

vaguely *adv.* **1 in a general way,** in a way, somehow, slightly, obscurely, approximately, roughly, imprecisely. **2 absentmindedly,** abstractedly, vacantly, vacuously.

vain *adj.* **1 conceited,** self-loving, narcissistic, self-admiring, peacockish, egotistical, proud, haughty, arrogant, boastful, swaggering, imperious, overweening, cocky, affected, *lit.* vainglorious, *inf.* stuck-up, bigheaded, swellheaded. **2 futile,** worthless, insignificant, pointless, meaningless, nugatory, valueless, meritless, empty, hollow, insubstantial, idle, vapid. **3 unsuccessful,** futile, useless, unavailing, to no avail, ineffective, inefficacious, fruitless, unproductive, abortive, unprofitable, profitless. **Ant.** modest; successful.

valiant *adj.* **brave,** courageous, valorous, heroic, stouthearted, lionhearted, gallant, manly, intrepid, fearless, undaunted, undismayed, bold, daring, audacious, staunch, stalwart, indomitable, resolute, determined. **Ant.** cowardly; timorous.

valid *adj.* **1 sound,** well-founded, well-grounded, substantial, reasonable, logical, justifiable, defensible, vindicable, authentic, bona fide, effective, cogent, powerful, convincing, credible, forceful, weighty. **2 lawful,** legal, licit, legitimate, legally binding, binding, contractual, in force, in effect, effective. **Ant.** invalid; null; void; illegal.

validate *v.* **1 ratify,** legalize, legitimize, authorize, sanction, warrant, license, approve, endorse, set one's seal to. **2 verify,** prove, authenticate, substantiate, confirm, corroborate, justify. **Ant.** invalidate; revoke; disprove.

valley *n.* **dale,** dell, hollow, cove, vale, glen, depression.

valuable *adj.* **1 costly,** high-priced, expensive, priceless, precious. **2 useful,** helpful, beneficial, advantageous, worthwhile, worthy, important. **Ant.** worthless; cheap; useless.

value *n.* **1 monetary value,** face value, price, market price, cost. **2 worth,** merit, usefulness, advantage, benefit, gain, profit, good, avail, importance, significance.
▸ *v.* **1 set a price on,** price, evaluate, assess, appraise. **2 rate highly,** appreciate, esteem, hold in high regard, think highly of, set

store by, respect, admire, prize, cherish, treasure.

vanguard *n.* **advance guard,** point, forefront, front, front line, front rank, leading position, van, leaders, spearheads, trailblazers, trendsetters.

vanish *v.* **1 disappear,** be lost to sight/view, be/become invisible, evaporate, dissipate, disperse, fade, fade away, evanesce, melt away, recede from view, withdraw, depart, leave. **2 cease to exist/be,** pass away, die out, come to an end, end, be no more, become extinct/obsolete. *Ant.* appear; materialize.

vanity *n.* **1 conceit,** conceitedness, self-conceit, self-admiration, self-love, narcissism, egotism, pride, haughtiness, arrogance, boastfulness, braggadocio, pretension, affectation, ostentation, show, vainglory, airs, *inf.* stuck-upness, bigheadedness, swellheadedness, showing off. **2 worthlessness,** futility, futileness, insignificance, pointlessness, meaninglessness, emptiness, hollowness, insubstantiality, vapidity. *Ant.* modesty; humility; worth.

variable *adj.* **varying,** variational, changeable, changeful, changing, mutable, chameleonic, protean, shifting, fluctuating, wavering, vacillating, inconstant, unsteady, unstable, fitful, capricious, fickle, *inf.* blowing hot and cold. *Ant.* constant; uniform; steady.

variation *n.* **1 change,** alteration, modification, diversification. **2 variability,** changeability, fluctuation, vacillation, vicissitude. **3 varying,** difference, dissimilarity. **4 deviation,** divergence, departure, difference. **5 diversification,** innovation, novelty.

varied *adj.* **diversified,** diverse, assorted, miscellaneous, mixed, motley, heterogeneous. *Ant.* uniform; homogeneous.

variety *n.* **1 variation,** diversification, diversity, multifariousness, many-sidedness, change, difference. **2 assortment,** miscellany, range, mixture, medley, motley, collection, multiplicity. **3 strain,** breed, kind, type, sort, class, category, classification, brand, make.

various *adj.* **1 varying,** diverse, different, differing, dissimilar, unlike, disparate, many, assorted, mixed, miscellaneous, variegated, heterogeneous. **2 numerous,** many, several, varied, sundry, diverse, *lit.* divers.

varnish *v.* **1 lacquer,** japan, shellac, enamel, glaze, veneer.

2 embellish, smooth over, cover up, gloss over, mask, disguise.
▸ *n.* **coating,** lacquer, shellac, enamel, glaze, veneer, polyurethane, spar varnish.

vary *v.* **1 differ,** be different, be unlike, be dissimilar, deviate, diverge, depart. **2 change,** be transformed, alter, metamorphose, suffer a sea change, vacillate, fluctuate. **3 be at variance,** disagree, be in disagreement, differ, conflict, clash, be at odds, be in opposition, diverge. **4 change,** alter, modify, transform, permutate.

vast *adj.* **immense,** huge, enormous, massive, bulky, tremendous, colossal, prodigious, gigantic, monumental, elephantine, extensive, broad, wide, expansive, boundless, limitless, infinite, *inf.* hulking. *Ant.* tiny; minute.

vault[1] *n.* **1 arched roof/ceiling,** arch. **2 cellar,** basement, underground chamber, tomb. **3 safe,** strongbox, strongroom, repository, depository.

vault[2] *n.*
▸ *v.* **jump,** leap, jump over, leap over, spring over, bound over.

veer *v.* **change course/direction,** shift direction, turn, swerve, swing, sidestep, sheer, tack, be deflected.

vehemence *n.* **passion,** ardor, fervor, strength, force, forcibleness, forcefulness, emphasis, vigor, intensity, violence, earnestness, keenness, enthusiasm, zeal, zealousness, spirit, spiritedness, gusto, verve.

vehement *adj.* **passionate,** ardent, impassioned, fervent, fervid, strong, forceful, forcible, powerful, emphatic, vigorous, intense, violent, earnest, keen, enthusiastic, zealous, spirited. *Ant.* apathetic; indifferent.

vehicle *n.* **1 means of transport,** transportation, conveyance, car, bus, truck. **2 channel,** medium, means, means of expression, agency, instrument, mechanism, organ, apparatus.

veil *n.* **1 face covering,** mantilla, yashmak, purdah, hijab, burkah. **2 covering,** cover, screen, curtain, film, mantle, cloak, mask, blanket, shroud, canopy, cloud.
▸ *v.* **1 hide,** conceal, cover up, camouflage, disguise, mask, screen. **2 cover,** envelop, mantle, cloak, blanket, shroud, canopy.

vein *n.* **1 blood vessel,** *Tech.* venule. **2 lode,** seam, stratum. **3 streak,** stripe, line, thread, marking. **4 streak,** strain, trait, dash, hint. **5 humor,** mood, temper, temperament, disposition, frame of mind, attitude, inclination, tendency, tenor, tone.

veneer *n.* **1 facing,** covering, coat, finishing coat, finish. **2 façade,** front, false front, show, outward display, appearance, semblance, guise, mask, pretense, camouflage.

venerable *adj.* **venerated,** respected, revered, reverenced, worshiped, honored, esteemed, hallowed. ***Ant.*** disreputable; infamous.

veneration *n.* **respect,** reverence, worship, adoration, honor, esteem.

vengeance *n.* **revenge,** retribution, requital, retaliation, reprisal, an eye for an eye, tit for tat, measure for measure, blow for blow, quid pro quo.

venomous *adj.* **1 poisonous,** toxic, lethal, deadly, fatal, noxious. **2 spiteful,** rancorous, vindictive, malicious, malevolent, malignant, baleful, bitter, resentful, grudging, virulent, antagonistic, hostile, hate-filled, vicious.

vent *n.* **1 opening,** outlet, aperture, hole, gap, orifice, duct, flue. **2 outlet,** free passage, expression, release.
▸ *v.* **give vent/expression to,** express, air, utter, voice, verbalize, let out, release, pour out, emit, discharge, come out with.

ventilate *v.* **1 air,** aerate, oxygenate, air-condition, freshen, cool, purify. **2 air,** give an airing to, bring into the open, discuss, debate, talk over, give expression to, express.

venture *n.* **1 adventure,** exploit, mission, risky undertaking. **2 enterprise,** undertaking, project, speculation, fling, plunge, gamble.
▸ *v.* **1 dare,** be so bold as, presume. **2 volunteer,** advance, put forward, chance, risk. **3 risk,** put at risk, endanger, hazard, put in jeopardy, jeopardize, imperil, chance, gamble.

verbal *adj.* **1 oral,** spoken, said, uttered, articulated. **2 word for word,** verbatim, literal, close, faithful, exact, precise.

verbatim *adj.* **word for word,** literal, exact.
▸ *adv.* **word for word,** literally, to the letter, closely, faithfully, exactly, precisely, literatim.

verbose *adj.* **wordy,** loquacious, garrulous, long-winded, prolix, diffuse, pleonastic, circumlocutory, periphrastic, tautological. ***Ant.*** succinct; taciturn.

verdict *n.* **decision,** judgment, adjudication, finding, conclusion, ruling, opinion.

verge *n.* **1 edge,** border, margin, rim, limit, boundary, end, extremity. **2 brink,** threshold.
▶ *v.* phrase: **verge on approach,** incline to/toward, tend toward, border on, come near.

verification *n.* **confirmation,** substantiation, corroboration, attestation, validation, authentication, endorsement, accreditation, ratification, evidence, proof.

verify *v.* **confirm,** substantiate, prove, corroborate, attest to, testify to, validate, authenticate, endorse, accredit, ratify, bear out, justify, give credence to, confirm.

vernacular *n.* **everyday/spoken language,** colloquial/native speech, conversational language, common parlance, nonstandard language, jargon, cant, patois, *fml.* vulgate, *inf.* lingo, patter.

versatile *adj.* **1 adaptable,** flexible, all-around, multifaceted, resourceful, ingenious, clever. **2 adaptable,** adjustable, multipurpose, all-purpose, handy.

verse *n.* **1 poetry,** poem(s), lyric, sonnet, ode, limerick, piece of doggerel, ditty, song, lay, ballad. **2 stanza,** strophe, canto, couplet.

version *n.* **1 account,** report, story, rendering, interpretation, construction, understanding, reading, impression, side.

2 adaptation, interpretation, translation. **3 variant,** variation, form, copy, reproduction.

vertical *adj.* **upright,** erect, on end, perpendicular. *Ant.* horizontal; level.

vertigo *n.* **dizziness,** giddiness, light-headedness, loss of balance/equilibrium, *inf.* wooziness.

verve *n.* **enthusiasm,** vigor, force, energy, vitality, vivacity, liveliness, animation, sparkle, spirit, life, élan, dash, brio, fervor, gusto, passion, zeal, feeling, fire, *inf.* zing, zip, vim, punch, get-up-and-go, pizzazz.

very *adv.* **extremely,** exceedingly, to a great extent, exceptionally, uncommonly, unusually, decidedly, particularly, eminently, remarkably, really, truly, *inf.* awfully, terribly.
▶ *adj.* **1 actual,** exact, precise, unqualified. **2 ideal,** perfect, appropriate, suitable, fitting, right, just right. **3 sheer,** utter, simple, pure, plain, mere. **4 extreme,** absolute.

vessel *n.* **1 ship,** boat, yacht, craft, *lit.* barque, argosy. **2 container,** receptacle.

veteran *n.* **old hand,** old-timer, past master, master, *inf.* pro, warhorse. *Ant.* novice; apprentice.

▸ *adj.* **long-serving,** seasoned, old, adept, expert, *inf.* battle-scarred.

veto *v.* **reject,** turn down, give the thumbs down to, prohibit, forbid, interdict, proscribe, disallow, outlaw, embargo, ban, bar, preclude, rule out, *inf.* kill, put the kibosh on. *Ant.* approve; allow; endorse; authorize.

▸ *n.* **rejection,** prohibition, interdict, proscription, embargo, ban.

vex *v.* **anger,** annoy, irritate, incense, irk, enrage, infuriate, exasperate, pique, provoke, nettle, disturb, upset, perturb, discompose, put out, try one's patience, try, bother, trouble, worry, agitate, pester, harass, fluster, ruffle, hound, nag, torment, distress, tease, fret, gall, molest, *inf.* peeve, miff, bug, hassle, aggravate, rile, get one's goat, drive up the wall, get to.

viable *adj.* **workable,** sound, feasible, practicable, applicable, usable. *Ant.* impracticable; infeasible.

vibrant *adj.* **1 vibrating,** vibratory, oscillating, swinging. **2 throbbing,** pulsating, resonant, reverberating, ringing, echoing. **3 trembling,** quivering, shaking, shivering. **4 lively,** energetic, spirited, vigorous, animated, sparkling, vivacious, dynamic, electrifying. **5 vivid,** bright, strong, striking.

vibrate *v.* **1 oscillate,** swing, move to and fro. **2 throb,** pulsate, resonate, resound, reverberate, ring, echo. **3 pulsate,** tremble, quiver, shake, quaver, shiver, shudder.

vibration *n.* **1 oscillation,** swinging. **2 throb,** pulsation, resonance, reverberation. **3 pulsating,** trembling, tremble, quivering, quiver, shake, shaking, quaver, shiver, shivering.

vicarious *adj.* **indirect,** secondhand, surrogate, by proxy.

vice *n.* **1 sin,** sinfulness, wrong, wrongdoing, wickedness, badness, immorality, iniquity, evil, evildoing, venality corruption, depravity, degeneracy, transgression, offense, misdeed, error, violation. **2 failing,** flaw, defect, imperfection, weakness, foible, shortcoming. *Ant.* virtue.

vicinity *n.* **1 surrounding district,** neighborhood, locality, area, district, environs, precincts, purlieus, *inf.* this neck of the woods. **2 nearness,** closeness, proximity, propinquity.

vicious *adj.* **1 fierce,** ferocious, savage, dangerous, ill-natured, bad-tempered, surly, hostile. **2 malicious,** malevolent, malignant, spiteful, vindictive, venomous, catty, backbiting, rancorous, caustic, mean, cruel, defamatory, slanderous, *inf.* bitchy. **3 violent,** savage, brutal, fierce, ferocious, inhuman, barbarous, fiendish, sadistic, monstrous, heinous, atrocious, diabolical. **4 corrupt,** degenerate, depraved, debased, wicked, evil, sinful, bad, wrong, immoral, unprincipled, abandoned, unscrupulous, disreputable, dissolute, dissipated, debauched, profligate, libertine, vile, infamous, notorious. **Ant.** gentle; kindly; virtuous.

vicissitude *n.* **change,** alteration, transformation, inconstancy, instability, uncertainty, unpredictability, chanciness, fickleness, ups and downs.

victim *n.* **1 injured party,** casualty, sufferer. **2 dupe,** easy target/prey, fair game, sitting target, everybody's fool, *inf.* sitting duck, sucker, sap, fall guy, pushover. **3 prey,** quarry, game, the hunted, target. **4 offering,** sacrifice, scapegoat. **Ant.** attacker; assailant.

victimize *v.* **1 persecute,** bully, pick on, discriminate against, punish unfairly, *inf.* have it in for. **2 exploit,** prey on, take advantage of, swindle, dupe, cheat, trick, hoodwink.

victor *v.* **conqueror,** vanquisher, winner, champion, prizewinner, conquering hero, *inf.* champ, top dog, number one. **Ant.** loser; vanquished.

victorious *adj.* **conquering,** vanquishing, triumphant, winning, champion, successful, prizewinning, top, first. **Ant.** unsuccessful; losing.

vie *v.* **compete,** contend, contest.

view *n.* **1 sight,** field/range of vision, vision, eyeshot. **2 outlook,** prospect, scene, spectacle, vista, panorama, landscape, seascape. **3 point of view,** viewpoint, opinion, belief, judgment, way of thinking, thinking, thought, notion, idea, conviction, persuasion, attitude, feeling, sentiment, impression. **4 viewing,** sight, look, contemplation, observation, study, survey, inspection, scrutiny, scan.
▸ *v.* **1 look at,** watch, observe, contemplate, regard, behold, scan, survey, inspect, gaze at, stare at, peer at. **2 look over,** be shown over, survey, examine, scrutinize, take stock of. **3 look on,** consider, contemplate, think about, reflect on, ponder. **4 see,** consider, judge, deem.

viewpoint *n.* **point of view,** way of thinking, frame of reference, perspective, angle, slant, standpoint, position, stance, vantage point.

vigilant *adj.* **watchful,** on the lookout, observant, sharp-eyed, eagle-eyed, attentive, alert, on the alert, on the qui vive, awake, wide awake, unsleeping, on one's guard, careful, cautious, wary, circumspect, heedful. *Ant.* heedless; negligent; inattentive.

vigor *n.* **1 robustness,** healthiness, strength, sturdiness, fitness, toughness. **2 energy,** activity, liveliness, spryness, sprightliness, vitality, vivacity, verve, animation, dynamism, sparkle, zest, dash, élan, gusto, pep, *inf.* zip, zing, oomph, vim.

vigorous *adj.* **1 robust,** healthy, in good health, hale and hearty, strong, sturdy, fit, in good condition/shape/kilter, tough. **2 energetic,** lively, active, spry, sprightly, vivacious, animated, dynamic, full of life, sparkling. **3 powerful,** potent, strenuous, forceful, forcible, spirited, mettlesome, plucky, determined, resolute, aggressive, eager, keen, enthusiastic, zealous, ardent, fervent, vehement, intense, passionate. **4 strong,** forceful, effective, cogent, valid, pointed, to the point, striking, graphic, vivid. *Ant.* frail; feeble; weak.

vile *adj.* **1 foul,** nasty, unpleasant, disagreeable, horrid, horrible, offensive, obnoxious, odious, repulsive, repellent, revolting, repugnant, disgusting, distasteful, loathsome, hateful, nauseating, sickening. **2 base,** low, mean, wretched, foul, nasty, horrible, horrid, dreadful, disgraceful, appalling, shocking, ugly, abominable, monstrous, wicked, evil, iniquitous, sinful, vicious, corrupt, depraved, perverted, debased, reprobate, degenerate, debauched, dissolute, contemptible, despicable, reprehensible. *Ant.* pleasant; agreeable; admirable.

vilify *v.* **defame,** run down, impugn, revile, berate, denigrate, disparage, speak ill of, cast aspersions at, criticize, decry, denounce, fulminate against, malign, slander, libel, conduct a smear campaign against, blacken the name/reputation of, calumniate, traduce, *inf.* bad-mouth, do a hatchet job on, pull to pieces, sling/throw mud at, drag through the mud. *Ant.* praise; commend; exalt.

villain *n.* **1 rogue,** scoundrel, blackguard, wretch, cad, reprobate, evildoer, wrongdoer, ruffian, hoodlum, hooligan, miscreant, criminal, miscreant, jailbird, *inf.* bad guy, baddy, crook, rat, louse. **2 rascal,** rogue, imp, monkey, scamp, brat, *inf.* scalawag.

vindicate *v.* **1 acquit,** clear, absolve, free from blame, exonerate, exculpate. **2 justify,** warrant, substantiate, testify to, verify, confirm, corroborate. **3 defend,** support, back, fight for, champion, uphold, maintain, sustain, stand by. *Ant.* blame; convict; incriminate.

vindictive *adj.* **vengeful,** out for revenge, revengeful, avenging, unforgiving, grudge-bearing, resentful, ill-disposed, implacable, unrelenting, unconciliative, spiteful, rancorous, venomous, malicious, malevolent, malignant. *Ant.* forgiving; merciful.

vintage *n.* **1 year,** harvest, crop. **2 era,** epoch, period, time, generation.
▸ *adj.* **1 high-quality,** quality, prime, choice, select, superior, best. **2 classic,** ageless, enduring. **3 characteristic,** most typical, supreme, at his/her/its best.

violate *v.* **1 break,** breach, infringe, contravene, infract, transgress, disobey, disregard, ignore. **2 desecrate,** profane, defile, blaspheme. **3 disturb,** disrupt, intrude on, interfere with, encroach on, invade, break into, upset, shatter, destroy.

4 rape, ravish, indecently assault, abuse, deflower, molest, seduce.

violence *n.* **1 strength,** forcefulness, lack of control/restraint, wildness, passion, powerfulness, might, savagery, ferocity, destructiveness, brutality, force, brute force, roughness, strong-arm tactics. **2 wildness,** tempestuousness, turbulence. **3 strength,** intensity, vehemence. **4 sharpness,** acuteness, intensity.

violent *adj.* **1 strong,** powerful, forceful, uncontrolled, unrestrained, unbridled, uncontrollable, ungovernable, wild, passionate, raging, vicious, destructive, savage, fierce, intemperate, hotheaded, hot-tempered, bloodthirsty, homicidal, murderous, maniacal, mighty, ferocious, damaging, brutal. **2 wild,** blustery, boisterous, raging, tempestuous, turbulent, tumultuous. **3 strong,** great, intense, extreme, vehement, inordinate, excessive. **4 sharp,** acute, intense, excruciating, agonizing, biting.

virile *adj.* **manly,** masculine, male, all-male, strong, vigorous, robust, powerfully built, muscular, rugged, strapping, sturdy, red-blooded, *inf.* macho. *Ant.* unmanly; effeminate.

virtue *n.* **1 goodness,** righteousness, morality, ethicalness, uprightness, upstandingness, integrity, rectitude, honesty, honorableness, honor, incorruptibility, probity, decency, respectability, worthiness, worth, trustworthiness. **2 virginity,** celibacy, purity, pureness, chastity, chasteness, innocence, modesty. **3 good quality/point,** merit, asset, credit, attribute, advantage, benefit, strength, *inf.* plus. **4 merit,** advantage, benefit, usefulness, efficacy, efficaciousness, power, potency. *Ant.* vice; sin; failing; disadvantage.

virtuoso *n.* **master,** genius, expert, artist, maestro, wizard.
▸ *adj.* **skillful,** masterly, impressive, outstanding, dazzling, bravura.

virtuous *adj.* **1 good,** righteous, moral, ethical, upright, upstanding, honest, honorable, incorruptible, decent, respectable, worthy, trustworthy. **2 virginal,** celibate, pure, chaste, innocent, modest. *Ant.* evil; sinful; promiscuous.

virulent *adj.* **1 poisonous,** toxic, venomous, deadly, lethal, fatal, noxious, harmful. **2 severe,** extreme, violent, rapidly spreading, highly infectious/ contagious, harmful, lethal. **3 hostile,** spiteful, venomous, vicious, vindictive, malicious, malevolent, malignant, bitter, rancorous, acrimonious, abusive, aggressive, violent.

visible *adj.* **1 in view,** perceptible, perceivable, discernible, detectable, seeable. **2 apparent,** evident, noticeable, observable, detectable, recognizable, manifest, plain, clear, obvious, patent, palpable, unmistakable, unconcealed, undisguised, conspicuous, distinct, distinguishable. *Ant.* invisible; hidden.

vision *n.* **1 eyesight,** sight, power of seeing, eyes. **2 apparition,** specter, phantom, ghost, wraith, phantasm, chimera, revelation. **3 dream,** hallucination, chimera, optical illusion, mirage, illusion, delusion, figment of the imagination. **4 dream,** daydream, pipe dream, fantasy, image, mental picture. **5 perception,** perceptiveness, insight, intuition, imagination. **6 foresight,** farsightedness, prescience, breadth of view, discernment. **7 dream,** spectacle, picture, feast for the eyes, beautiful sight, *inf.* sight for sore eyes.

visionary *adj.* **1 idealistic,**

impractical, unrealistic, utopian, romantic, quixotic, dreamy, dreaming, *inf.* starry-eyed. **2 perceptive,** intuitive, insightful, imaginative. **3 farsighted,** discerning, wise, prescient. **4 unreal,** imaginary, imagined, fanciful, fancied, illusory, delusory, figmental, phantasmal, phantasmagoric, spectral, ghostly, wraithlike. **5 impractical,** unrealistic, unworkable, unfeasible, theoretical, hypothetical, idealistic, utopian.
▸ *n.* **1 mystic,** seer, prophet. **2 dreamer,** daydreamer, idealist, romantic, romanticist, fantasist, theorist, utopian.

visit *v.* **1 pay a visit to,** go/come to see, pay a call on, call on, look in on, stop by (to see), stay with, be the guest of, *inf.* pop/drop in on, look up. **2 pay a call on,** inspect, survey, examine. **3 attack,** assail, afflict, smite, descend on, trouble, harrow, torture.
▸ *n.* **1 call,** social call. **2 stay,** sojourn, stopover.

visitation *n.* **1 official visit,** inspection, tour of inspection, survey, review, scrutiny, examination. **2 affliction,** scourge, plague, pestilence, blight, disaster, tragedy, calamity, catastrophe, cataclysm.

visual *adj.* **1 seeing,** optical, ocular. **2 to be seen,** seeable, perceivable, discernible.

visualize *v.* **conjure up,** envisage, picture in the mind's eye, picture, envision, imagine, conceive.

vital *adj.* **1 life-giving,** life-preserving, life-sustaining, basic, fundamental, essential. **2 essential,** necessary, needed, indispensable, key, important, significant, imperative, urgent, critical, crucial, life-and-death. **3 lively,** animated, spirited, vivacious, vibrant, zestful, dynamic, energetic, vigorous, forceful. **4 deadly,** lethal, fatal, fateful. *Ant.* unimportant; dispensable; peripheral; listless.

vitality *n.* **life,** liveliness, animation, spirit, spiritedness, vivacity, vibrancy, zest, zestfulness, dynamism, energy, vigor, forcefulness.

vitriolic *adj.* **caustic,** mordant, acrimonious, bitter, acerbic, astringent, acid, acidulous, acrid, trenchant, virulent, spiteful, venomous, malicious, scathing, withering, sarcastic, sardonic, *inf.* bitchy.

vivacious *adj.* **lively,** full of life, animated, effervescent, bubbling, ebullient, sparkling, scintillating, lighthearted, spirited, high-spirited, gay, merry, jolly, vibrant, vivid, dynamic, vital. *Ant.* dull; languid; listless.

vivid *adj.* **1 strong,** intense, colorful, rich, glowing, bright, brilliant, clear. **2 graphic,** clear, lively, stirring, striking, powerful, impressive, highly colored, dramatic, memorable, realistic, lifelike, true to life. **3 strong,** striking, flamboyant, memorable, dynamic, lively, animated, spirited, vibrant, vital. *Ant.* dull; colorless; nondescript.

vocal *adj.* **1 voiced,** vocalized, spoken, said, uttered, expressed, articulated, oral. **2 vociferous,** outspoken, forthright, plainspoken, free-spoken, blunt, clamorous, strident, loud, noisy. *Ant.* taciturn; reticent.

vocation *n.* **profession,** calling, occupation, walk of life, career, life's work, métier, trade, craft, job, work, employment, business, line, speciality.

vogue *n.* **1 fashion,** mode, style, trend, taste, fad, craze, rage, latest thing, last word, dernier cri, *inf.* the thing. **2 fashionableness,** modishness, popularity, currency, prevalence, favor, acceptance.

voice *n.* **1 power of speech,** powers of articulation. **2 expression,** utterance, verbalization, vocalization, airing. **3 opinion,** view, comment, feeling, wish, desire, vote. **4 spokesman,** spokeswoman, spokesperson, mouthpiece, organ, agency, medium, vehicle. ▸ *v.* **put in words,** express, give utterance to, utter, articulate, enunciate, mention, talk of, communicate, declare, assert, divulge, air, ventilate, *inf.* come out with.

void *adj.* **1 empty,** emptied, vacant, without contents, bare, clear, free, unfilled, unoccupied, uninhabited, untenanted, tenantless. **2 null and void,** nullified, invalid, canceled, inoperative, ineffective, not binding, not in force, nonviable, useless, worthless, nugatory. *Ant.* full; occupied; valid. ▸ *n.* **1 empty space,** emptiness, blank space, blankness, vacuum. **2 space,** gap, lacuna, hole, hollow, chasm, abyss.

volatile *adj.* **1 mercurial,** changeable, variable, capricious, whimsical, fickle, flighty, giddy, inconstant, erratic, unstable, unsteady, unstable, irregular, fitful, explosive, eruptive, charged, inflammatory, tense, strained. **2 evaporative,** vaporous, vaporescent. *Ant.* stable; constant; calm.

voluble *adj.* **talkative,** loquacious, garrulous, chatty, gossipy, chattering, articulate, eloquent, forthcoming, fluent, glib. *Ant.* taciturn; uncommunicative.

volume *n.* **1 book,** publication, tome. **2 bulk,** capacity, quantity, amount, mass. **3 loudness,** sound, amplification.

voluminous *adj.* **capacious,** roomy, commodious, ample, full, big, vast, billowing.

voluntary *adj.* **1 of one's own free will,** volitional, of one's own accord, optional, discretional, at one's discretion, elective, noncompulsory, nonmandatory. **2 unpaid,** honorary, volunteer. *Ant.* compulsory; obligatory.

volunteer *v.* **1 offer,** tender, proffer, present, put forward, advance. **2 offer one's services,** present oneself, step forward.

voluptuous *adj.* **1 hedonistic,** sybaritic, epicurean, pleasure-loving, self-indulgent, sensual, carnal, licentious, lascivious. **2 curvy,** shapely, full-figured, ample, buxom, seductive, sexy, *inf.* curvaceous.

vomit *v.* **1 be sick,** retch, heave, spew, *inf.* throw up, puke, barf, toss one's cookies, lose one's lunch, upchuck, hurl. **2 bring up,** regurgitate, spew up, spit up. **3 belch,** eject, emit, send forth, eruct.

voracious *adj.* **1 gluttonous,**

greedy, ravenous, ravening, starving, hungry. **2 insatiable,** insatiate, unquenchable, prodigious, uncontrolled. **3 compulsive,** enthusiastic, eager.

vote *n.* **1 ballot,** poll, election, referendum, plebiscite. **2 right to vote,** franchise, suffrage.
▸ *v.* **1 cast one's vote,** go to the polls, mark one's ballot. **2 elect,** opt for, return. **3 suggest,** propose, recommend, advocate.

voucher *n.* **chit,** slip, ticket, token, document.

vow *n.* **oath,** pledge, promise.
▸ *v.* **swear,** state under oath, pledge, promise, undertake, give one's word of honor.

voyage *n.* **crossing,** cruise, passage, journey, trip, expedition, travels.
▸ *v.* **sail,** cruise, travel, journey, take a trip.

vulgar *adj.* **1 rude,** indecent, indecorous, indelicate, unseemly, offensive, distasteful, obnoxious, risqué, suggestive, off-color, blue, ribald, bawdy, obscene, lewd, salacious, licentious, concupiscent, smutty, dirty, filthy, pornographic, scatological, *inf.* raunchy. **2 rude,** impolite, ill-mannered, unmannerly, ill-bred, common, coarse, boorish, rough, crude. **3 tasteless,** gross, crass, unrefined, tawdry, ostentatious, showy, flashy, gaudy. **4 common,** ordinary, low, lowborn, ignorant, unsophisticated, unrefined, uneducated, illiterate, uncultured, uncultivated, uncouth, crude. **Ant.** decorous; genteel; mannerly; tasteful.

vulnerable *adj.* **1 open to attack,** attackable, assailable, exposed, unprotected, unguarded, defenseless, easily hurt/wounded/damaged, powerless, helpless, weak, sensitive, thin-skinned. **2 open,** wide open, exposed, liable, subject. **Ant.** invulnerable; immune.

Ww

wad *n.* **1 lump,** mass, chunk, hunk, ball, plug, block. **2 bundle,** roll.

waddle *v.* **sway,** wobble, totter, toddle, shuffle.

wade *v.* **1 ford,** cross, traverse. **2 paddle,** splash about. **3 proceed with difficulty,** work one's way, plow, labor, toil/plug/peg away.

waft *v.* **1 float,** glide, drift, be carried/borne/conveyed. **2 carry,** bear, convey, transport, transmit.

wag[1] *n.* **1 swing,** sway, vibration, quiver, shake. **2 wiggle,** wobble, wave. **3 nod,** bob.
▸ *v.* **1 swing,** sway, vibrate, quiver, shake, rock, twitch. **2 waggle,** wiggle, wobble, wave. **3 nod,** bob.

wag[2] *n.* **wit,** humorist, jester, joker, jokester, comic, comedian, comedienne, wisecracker, punner.

wage *n.* **pay,** remuneration, wages, earnings.
▸ *v.* **carry on,** conduct, execute, engage in, pursue, undertake, devote oneself to, practice.

wager *n.* **bet,** gamble, stake, pledge, hazard.
▸ *v.* **lay a wager,** bet, place/make/lay a bet, lay odds, put money on, speculate.

wail *n.* **cry,** lament, lamentation, weeping, sob, moan, groan, whine, complaint, howl, yowl, ululation.
▸ *v.* **cry,** lament, weep, sob, moan, groan, whine, complain, howl, yowl, ululate.

wait *v.* **1 stay,** remain, rest, linger, tarry, abide. **2 be patient,** hold back, stand by, bide one's time, hang fire, mark time, cool one's heels, *inf.* sit tight, hold one's horses, sweat it out. **3 await,** wait for, look/watch out for, anticipate, expect, be ready for, be in readiness for. **4 delay,** postpone, put off, hold off, hold back, defer. **5 be ready,** anticipate, expect.
▸ *n.* **period of waiting,** interval, stay, delay, holdup.

waive *v.* **1 relinquish,** renounce, give up, abandon, surrender, yield, cede. **2 set aside,** forgo, disregard, ignore. **3 postpone,** defer, put off, delay, shelve, *inf.* put on the back burner. *Ant.* claim; uphold; pursue.

wake *v.* **1 awake,** awaken, waken, wake up, waken up, rouse, stir, come to, get up, arise, rouse. **2 rouse,** stir up, activate, stimulate, spur, prod, galvanize, provoke. **3 become aware/ conscious,** become alert, become mindful/heedful. **4 awaken,** evoke, call up, conjure up, rouse, stir, revive, resuscitate, revivify, rekindle, reignite. *Ant.* sleep; snooze; doze.

wakeful *adj.* **1 unsleeping,** restless, tossing and turning, insomniac. **2 alert,** on the alert, vigilant, on the lookout, on one's guard, on the qui vive, watchful, observant, attentive, heedful, wary. *Ant.* asleep; inattentive.

walk *v.* **1 go on foot,** travel on foot, *inf.* go by shank's mare, hoof it. **2 stroll,** saunter, amble, plod, trudge, hike, tramp, trek, march, stride, step out. **3 accompany,** escort, convoy.
▶ *n.* **1 stroll,** saunter, amble, promenade, ramble, hike, tramp, march, constitutional, airing. **2 gait,** pace, step, stride. **3 road,** avenue, drive, promenade, path, pathway, footpath, track, lane, alley.

walkover *n.* **easy victory,** *inf.* piece of cake, child's play, pushover.

wall *n.* **1 partition,** room divider, enclosure. **2 fortification,** rampart, barricade, parapet, bulwark, stockade, breastwork.

wallet *n.* **purse,** billfold.

wallow *v.* **1 roll,** tumble about, lie around, splash around. **2 luxuriate,** bask, take pleasure/ satisfaction, indulge oneself, delight, revel, glory.

wan *adj.* **1 pale,** pallid, ashen, white, white as a sheet/ghost, anemic, colorless, bloodless, waxen, pasty, peaked, tired looking, washed out, sickly. **2 dim,** faint, weak, feeble, pale. *Ant.* flushed; ruddy; bright.

wand *n.* **baton,** stick, rod, staff, twig, sprig.

wander *v.* **1 ramble,** roam, meander, rove, range, prowl, saunter, stroll, amble, peregrinate, drift, *inf.* traipse. **2 wind,** meander, curve, zigzag. **3 stray,** depart, diverge, veer, swerve, deviate. **4 be incoherent,** ramble, babble, talk nonsense, rave, be delirious.
▶ *n.* **ramble,** saunter, stroll, amble.

wanderer *n.* **rambler,** roamer, rover, drifter, traveler, itinerant, wayfarer, nomad, bird of passage, rolling stone, gypsy, vagabond, vagrant, hobo, tramp, derelict, beggar, homeless/displaced person, *inf.* bum.

wane *v.* **decrease,** decline, diminish, dwindle, shrink, contract, taper off, subside, sink, ebb, dim, fade away, vanish, die out, draw to a close, evanesce,

peter out, wind down, be on the way out, abate, fail, become weak, deteriorate, degenerate. *Ant.* wax; increase; grow.
▸ *n.* **decline,** decrease, diminution, dwindling, contraction, subsidence, ebb, vanishing, evanescence, abatement, failure, weakening, deteriorating, degenerating.

want *v.* **1 wish,** wish for, desire, demand, call for, long for, hope for, yearn for, pine for, fancy, crave, hanker after, hunger for, thirst for, lust after, covet, need, *inf.* have a yen for. **2 need,** be in need of, require. **3 have need of,** lack, be without, be devoid of, be bereft of, be short of, be deficient in, have insufficient.
▸ *n.* **1 lack,** absence, dearth, deficiency, inadequacy, insufficiency, shortness, paucity, shortage, scarcity, scarceness, scantiness. **2 wish,** desire, demand, longing, yearning, fancy, craving, hankering, hunger, thirst, lust, covetousness, *inf.* yen. **3 need,** neediness, privation, poverty, destitution, penury, indigence. *Ant.* presence; abundance; wealth.

wanting *adj.* **1 lacking,** deficient, inadequate, imperfect, not up to standard/par, not good enough, disappointing, not acceptable, not up to expectations, flawed, faulty, defective, unsound, subpar, substandard, inferior, second-rate, patchy, sketchy. **2 lacking,** missing, absent, not there, short. *Ant.* sufficient; adequate; acceptable.
▸ *prep.* **lacking,** in need of, without, sans, *inf.* minus.

wanton *adj.* **1 promiscuous,** fast, immoral, loose, immodest, shameless, unchaste, unvirtuous, of easy virtue, impure, abandoned, lustful, lecherous, lascivious, libidinous, licentious, libertine, dissolute, dissipated, debauched, degenerate. **2 willful,** malicious, malevolent, spiteful, wicked, evil, cruel, unmotivated, motiveless, arbitrary, groundless, unjustifiable, unjustified, needless, unnecessary, uncalled-for, unprovoked, gratuitous, senseless, pointless, purposefulness. **3 capricious,** playful, sportive, careless, heedless, impulsive, rash, reckless, devil-may-care. **4 wild,** unrestrained, uncontrolled, immoderate, lavish, extravagant, abundant, profuse, luxuriant. *Ant.* moral; chaste; justifiable.

war *n.* **conflict,** strife, hostility, enmity, antagonism, animus, ill will, bad blood, warfare, conflict, strife, combat, fighting, struggle,

armed conflict, battle, fight, confrontation, skirmish, hostilities, campaign, crusade. *Ant.* peace; harmony; truce.
▸ *v.* **wage/make war,** be at war, conduct a war, do combat/battle, fight, take up arms, cross swords, quarrel, wrangle.

ward *n.* **1 room,** compartment, cubicle, section, division. **2 administrative district,** district, division, quarter, zone. **3 charge,** protégé, protégée, dependent.
▸ *v.* phrase: **ward off fend off,** stave off, parry, avert, deflect, turn aside, drive back, repel, repulse, beat back, rout, put to flight, scatter, disperse, keep at bay, keep at arm's length, avert, rebuff, foil, frustrate, thwart, checkmate, *inf.* send packing.

warehouse *n.* **store,** storehouse, depot, depository, stockroom.

wares *plural noun* **goods,** products, commodities, lines, merchandise, produce, stuff, stock.

warily *adv.* **1 carefully,** with care, cautiously, gingerly, circumspectly, guardedly, on one's guard, on the alert, on the qui vive, watchfully, vigilantly. **2 cautiously,** suspiciously, distrustfully, mistrustfully, charily, *inf.* cagily.

warlike *adj.* **aggressive,**

belligerent, bellicose, pugnacious, combative, militaristic, militant, martial. *Ant.* peaceful; peaceable; pacific; conciliatory.

warm *adj.* **1 heated,** tepid, lukewarm. **2 sunny,** balmy. **3 kindly,** kind, friendly, affable, amiable, genial, cordial, sympathetic, affectionate, loving, tender, caring, charitable, sincere, genuine, hearty, hospitable, enthusiastic, eager, heartfelt, ardent, vehement, passionate, intense, fervent, effusive. **4 heated,** hostile, tense, strained, explosive, dangerous, perilous, hazardous, tricky, difficult, unpleasant, uncomfortable, disagreeable. **5 close,** near. *Ant.* cold; cool; unfriendly.
▸ *v.* **warm up,** make warm, heat, heat up, reheat.

warn *v.* **1 inform,** notify, give notice, give prior notice/tell, let know, acquaint, give fair warning, forewarn, *inf.* tip off, put wise. **2 advise,** exhort, urge, counsel, caution, forewarn, prewarn, put on the alert, make aware. **3 give a warning to,** admonish, remonstrate with.

warning *n.* **1 information,** notification, notice, word, forewarning, *inf.* tip-off. **2 caution,** advice, exhortation, counseling. **3 admonition,** remonstrance.

4 omen, premonition, foretoken, token, augury, signal, sign, threat, caveat.

warrant *n.* **1 authorization,** consent, sanction, permission, validation, license, imprimatur, seal of approval. **2 authorization,** document, order, papers. **3 voucher,** chit, slip, paper.
▸ *v.* **1 authorize,** consent to, sanction, permit, license, approve of. **2 justify,** vindicate, excuse, be a defense of, explain away, account for, be a reason for, offer grounds for, support. **3 guarantee,** swear to, answer for, vouch for, testify to, bear witness to, support, endorse, underwrite, back up, stand by.

wary *adj.* **1 careful,** cautious, circumspect, chary, on one's guard, alert, on the alert/look out, on the qui vive, attentive, heedful, watchful, vigilant, observant, *inf.* wide awake, on one's toes. **2 careful,** cautious, chary, suspicious, distrustful, mistrustful, *inf.* leery. **Ant.** unwary; unsuspecting; inattentive; trustful.

wash *v.* **1 wash oneself,** bathe, shower, take a bath/shower, clean, cleanse, sponge, scrub, launder, shampoo. **2 splash,** dash, break, beat. **3 be accepted,** be plausible, be convincing, hold up, hold water, stand up, bear scrutiny, *inf.* stick. **4 carry,** bear, sweep, convey, transport. **5 erode,** abrade, wear, denude.
▸ *n.* **washing,** clean, cleaning, cleansing, bath, shower, laundry.

waste *v.* **1 squander,** dissipate, fritter away, misspend, misuse, spend recklessly, throw away, go through, run through, *inf.* blow. **2 grow weak,** wither, atrophy, become emaciated. **3 weaken,** enfeeble, sap the strength of, wither, debilitate, atrophy, emaciate, shrivel, shrink. **4 destroy,** devastate, wreak havoc on, pillage, plunder, sack, spoliate, loot, maraud, harry. **Ant.** conserve; save; strengthen.
▸ *n.* **1 squandering,** dissipation, frittering away, misspending, misuse, prodigality, unthriftiness. **2 rubbish,** refuse, garbage, trash, debris, dross, dregs, leavings. **3 desert,** wasteland, wilderness, barrenness, emptiness, vastness.

wasteful *adj.* **prodigal,** profligate, thriftless, spendthrift, extravagant, lavish. **Ant.** thrifty; frugal; economical.

watch *v.* **1 look at,** observe, view, eye, gaze at, stare at, gape at, peer at, contemplate, behold, inspect, scrutinize, survey, scan, examine. **2 keep watch on,** keep an eye on, keep in sight, follow, spy on, *inf.*

keep tabs on. **3 mind,** take care of, look after, supervise, superintend, tend, guard, protect, babysit, *inf.* keep an eye on. **Ant.** ignore; disregard; neglect.

▸ *n.* **1 wristwatch,** pocket watch, timepiece, chronometer. **2 guard,** vigil, surveillance.

watchful *adj.* **observant,** alert, vigilant, attentive, heedful, sharp-eyed, eagle-eyed, wary, circumspect. **Ant.** inattentive; careless.

watchman *n.* **security guard,** guard, custodian, caretaker.

water *n.* **1 H₂0,** tap water, drinking water, mineral water, bottled water. **2 sea,** ocean, sound, bay, river, lake, pond, pool, reservoir.

▸ *v.* **1 sprinkle,** moisten, dampen, wet, water down, douse, hose, spray, drench, saturate, sodden, flood. **2 tear,** moisten, leak. **3 add water to,** water down, dilute, thin, weaken, adulterate.

waterfall *n.* **cascade,** cataract, falls.

watertight *adj.* **1 waterproof,** sound. **2 sound,** flawless, incontrovertible, indisputable, foolproof, unassailable, impregnable.

watery *adj.* **1 aqueous,** liquid, liquefied, fluid, hydrous. **2 wet,** damp, moist, sodden, soggy, saturated, waterlogged, marshy, boggy, swampy, miry. **3 thin,** runny, weak, dilute, diluted, watered down, adulterated, tasteless, flavorless, *inf.* wishy-washy. **4 pale,** wan, insipid, *inf.* wishy-washy. **5 moist,** tearful, teary, weeping, weepy, lachrymose. **Ant.** solid; dry; thick.

wave *v.* **1 undulate,** ripple, stir, flutter, flap, sway, swing, shake, quiver, oscillate. **2 move up and down,** move to and fro, wag, waggle, flutter. **3 brandish,** swing, shake. **4 gesture,** gesticulate, signal, sign, beckon, indicate. **5 undulate,** curl, kink.

▸ *n.* **1 breaker,** billow, roller, ripple, whitecap, swell, surf. **2 stream,** flow, rush, surge, flood. **3 undulation,** curl, kink. **4 surge,** upsurge, groundswell, welling up, rush, outbreak, rash. **5 ripple,** vibration, oscillation, undulation.

waver *v.* **1 become unsteady,** falter, wobble, hesitate. **2 be irresolute/indecisive,** hesitate, dither, equivocate, hem and haw, vacillate, beat about the bush, *inf.* shilly-shally, pussyfoot around, blow hot and cold. **3 flicker,** quiver, tremble.

wavy *adj.* **undulating,** curvy, curling, squiggly, rippled, curving, winding. **Ant.** straight; unswerving.

wax *v.* **1 approach full moon,** get/ grow bigger, enlarge, increase, grow, develop, magnify, extend, widen, broaden, spread, mushroom. **2 become,** grow. *Ant.* wane; decrease; fade.

way *n.* **1 road,** roadway, street, thoroughfare, track, path, pathway, lane, avenue, drive. **2 route,** road, course, direction. **3 method,** course of action, process, procedure, technique, system, plan, scheme, manner, modus operandi, means. **4 manner,** style, fashion, mode. **5 conduct,** behavior, practice, wont, manner, style, nature, personality, temperament, disposition, character, habit, custom, characteristic, trait, attribute, mannerism, peculiarity, idiosyncrasy. **6 distance,** length, stretch, journey. **7 room,** elbowroom, space. **8 state,** condition, situation, *inf.* shape. **9 feature,** aspect, detail, point, particular, respect, sense.

wayfarer *n.* **traveler,** walker, hiker, rambler, wanderer, roamer, rover, nomad, gypsy, vagabond, vagrant.

waylay *v.* **1 lie in wait for,** ambush, hold up, attack. **2 accost,** stop and talk to, intercept, pounce on, swoop down on.

wayward *adj.* **1 willful,** self-willed, headstrong, stubborn, obstinate, obdurate, perverse, contrary, uncooperative, refractory, recalcitrant, contumacious, unruly, ungovernable, unmanageable, incorrigible, intractable, difficult, fractious, disobedient, insubordinate. **2 capricious,** whimsical, fickle, inconstant, changeable, changeful, variable, erratic, unpredictable, unstable, mercurial, volatile, flighty. *Ant.* tractable; docile; stable.

weak *adj.* **1 weakly,** frail, fragile, delicate, feeble, infirm, shaky, debilitated, incapacitated, ailing, indisposed, decrepit, puny, faint, enervated, tired, fatigued, exhausted, spent, worn out. **2 cowardly,** pusillanimous, timorous, timid, spineless, ineffectual, useless, inept, effete, powerless, impotent, namby-pamby, soft, *inf.* yellow, weak-kneed. **3 defective,** faulty, poor, inadequate, deficient, imperfect, substandard, lacking, wanting. **4 unsound,** feeble, flimsy, lame, hollow, pathetic, unconvincing, untenable, implausible, unsatisfactory. **5 faint,** low, muffled, stifled, muted, scarcely audible, dim, pale, wan. **6 understrength,** dilute, diluted, watery, waterish, thinned down, thin, adulterated, tasteless, flavorless, insipid, *inf.* wishy-washy. **Ant.** strong; powerful; flawless; convincing.

weaken *v.* **1 enfeeble,** debilitate, incapacitate, sap one's strength, enervate, tire, exhaust, wear out. **2 lessen,** reduce, decrease, diminish, moderate, temper, sap, abate, dwindle, ease up, let up. **3 impair,** undermine, invalidate. **4 relent,** give in, acquiesce, yield, give way, accede, come around. **5 dilute,** water down, thin, adulterate.

weakling *n.* **coward,** mouse, milksop, namby-pamby, *inf.* wimp, sissy, drip, doormat, chicken, yellowbelly, fraidy-cat, scaredy-cat.

weakness *n.* **1 frailty,** fragility, delicateness, delicacy, feebleness, infirmity, debility, incapacity, indisposition, decrepitude, puniness, enervation, fatigue. **2 cowardliness,** timidity, spinelessness, ineffectuality, ineptness, powerlessness, impotence. **3 defectiveness,** faultiness, inadequacy, deficiency. **4 unsoundness,** feebleness, flimsiness, lameness, untenability, implausibility. **5 faintness,** low intensity, mutedness, dimness. **6 diluteness,** wateriness, thinness, tastelessness, flavorlessness, *inf.* wishy-washiness. **7 weak point,** failing, foible, fault, flaw, defect, shortcoming, imperfection, blemish, Achilles' heel, chink in one's armor. **8 soft spot,** fondness, liking, love, passion, partiality, preference, penchant, predisposition, predilection, leaning, inclination, proneness, proclivity. **Ant.** strength; power; forte.

wealth *n.* **1 money,** cash, capital, treasure, fortune, finance, property, riches, assets, possessions, resources, goods, funds, *inf.* wherewithal, dough, bread. **2 richness,** money, affluence, prosperity, substance, means. **3 mass,** abundance, profusion, copiousness, plenitude, amplitude, bounty, cornucopia. **Ant.** poverty; dearth.

wealthy *adj.* **1 rich,** well off, well-to-do, moneyed, affluent, prosperous, of means, of substance, *inf.* well-heeled, rolling in it/money, in the money, made of money, filthy/stinking rich, loaded, flush, on easy street. **2 rich,** opulent, lavish, luxurious, sumptuous, splendid, magnificent. **Ant.** poor; penniless; impoverished.

wear *v.* **1 be dressed in,** dress in,

be clothed in, cloth oneself in, have on, put on, don, sport. **2 have,** assume, present, show, display, exhibit. **3 erode,** corrode, abrade, wash away, rub away, rub down, grind away, wear down. **4 become worn,** show signs of wear, wear thin, fray, become threadbare. **5 fatigue,** tire, weary, exhaust. **6 last,** endure, hold up, survive, bear up, stand up to wear, prove durable.

▸ *n.* **1 wear and tear,** use, service, employment. **2 clothing,** attire, apparel, wardrobe, clothes, garments, outfits, *inf.* gear. **3 use,** friction, erosion, detrition, attrition, corrosion, abrasion, deterioration, degeneration, damage.

weariness *n.* **fatigue,** tiredness, exhaustion, enervation, lassitude, languor, listlessness, lethargy.

wearisome *adj.* **fatiguing,** tiring, exhausting, draining, wearing, trying, irksome, boring, tedious, dull, uninteresting, monotonous, humdrum, routine. ***Ant.*** refreshing; interesting; enjoyable.

weary *adj.* **1 fatigued,** tired, exhausted, drained, worn, worn out, spent, wearied, *inf.* dead tired/beat, dead on one's feet, dog-tired, all in, done in, fagged out, pooped (out), whacked, bushed. **2 wearisome,** fatiguing, tiring, exhausting, wearing, trying, taxing, irksome, tiresome, laborious, boring, tedious, dull. **3 bored,** fed up, discontented, jaded, uninterested, listless, lethargic, *inf.* sick and tired. ***Ant.*** energetic; refreshed; refreshing; enthusiastic.

▸ *v.* **1 fatigue,** tire, exhaust, drain, wear out, *inf.* wear to a frazzle, poop out. **2 bore,** irk, make fed up, make discontented/jaded. **3 grow weary,** tire, get bored, have enough, grow discontented/jaded. ***Ant.*** revive; refresh; invigorate.

weather *n.* **meteorological/ atmospheric conditions,** temperature, raininess, cloudiness, dryness, humidity, windiness.

▸ *v.* **1 dry,** season, expose, expose to the elements. **2 be exposed,** undergo change, erode, wear, bleach. **3 come/get through,** survive, withstand, live/pull through, bear up against, stand, endure, ride out, rise above, surmount, overcome, resist, *inf.* stick out.

weave *v.* **1 interlace,** intertwine, interwork, intertwist, twist together, entwine, braid, plait, interknit. **2 make up,** fabricate, put together, construct, invent, create, contrive. **3 zigzag,** wind, crisscross.

web *n.* **interlacing,** lacework, lattice, latticework, mesh, net, netting, network, tissue, tangle, knot, complex.

wed *v.* **1 get married,** marry, become man and wife, take as one's wife/husband, join in matrimony, make one, unite, *inf.* get hitched, tie the knot, hitch. **2 unite,** join, merge, amalgamate, fuse, link, ally. **3 dedicate,** devote. *Ant.* divorce; separate.

wedge *n.* **chunk,** lump, block, chock.
▸ *v.* **1 thrust,** stuff, pack, ram, force, cram, squeeze, jam. **2 secure,** fasten, block, chock.

weep *v.* **cry,** shed tears, sob, blubber, snivel, whimper, whine, moan, lament, grieve, mourn, keen, wail, *inf.* boo-hoo. *Ant.* laugh; rejoice.

weigh *v.* **1 measure/gauge the weight of,** put on the scales. **2 have a weight of,** *inf.* tip the scales at. **3 balance,** compare, evaluate.

weight *n.* **1 heaviness,** poundage, tonnage. **2 burden,** load, onus, millstone, albatross, oppression, trouble, worry, strain, millstone around one's neck, cross to bear. **3 importance,** significance, consequence, value, substance, force, influence, *inf.* clout.

4 preponderance, main force, onus.

weird *adj.* **strange,** queer, uncanny, eerie, mysterious, mystifying, supernatural, preternatural, unnatural, unearthly, ghostly, odd, eccentric, bizarre, outlandish, freakish, grotesque, *inf.* spooky, creepy, offbeat, far-out, way-out. *Ant.* normal; ordinary; conventional.

welcome *n.* **greeting,** salutation, reception, warm reception.
▸ *v.* **1 bid welcome to,** greet, receive, embrace, receive with open arms, roll out the red carpet for, meet, usher in. **2 receive with gladness,** be pleased by, take pleasure in, feel satisfaction at. *Ant.* shun; spurn; reject.

welfare *n.* **1 well-being,** health, good health, soundness, happiness, comfort, security, prosperity, success, fortune, good fortune. **2 state aid,** public assistance, social security, support.

well[1] *adv.* **1 satisfactorily,** in a satisfactory manner/way, correctly, rightly, properly, fittingly, suitably, nicely. **2 agreeably,** pleasantly, happily, *inf.* famously, capitally. **3 ably,** competently, proficiently, adeptly, skillfully, with skill, effectively, expertly, with expertise,

admirably, excellently. **4 kindly,** in a kind/kindly way, genially, affably, generously, hospitably, civilly, politely. **5 thoroughly,** completely, efficiently, effectively, conscientiously, industriously, carefully. **6 thoroughly,** fully, deeply, profoundly, intimately, personally. **7 closely,** attentively, carefully, conscientiously. **8 highly,** admiringly, with admiration, with praise, glowingly, approvingly, favorably, warmly. **9 comfortably,** in comfort, prosperously. **10 probably,** possibly, likely, undoubtedly, certainly, unquestionably, justifiably, reasonably. **11 very much,** considerably, to a great/marked extent/degree, markedly, substantially. **12 fortunately,** luckily, auspiciously, propitiously. *Ant.* badly; poorly.
▸ *adj.* **1 healthy,** in good health, fit, strong, robust, hale and hearty, able-bodied. **2 satisfactory,** all right, (just) fine, good, thriving, flourishing, *inf.* OK, fine and dandy. **3 advisable,** fitting, proper, wise, prudent, sensible. *Ant.* ill; poorly; inadvisable.

well[2] *v.* **flow,** stream, run, ooze, seep, trickle, pour/rush forth, issue, gush, surge, spurt, spout, jet.

▸ *n.* **source,** wellspring, fount, reservoir, repository, mine.

well-advised *adj.* **sensible,** wise, prudent, judicious, circumspect, farsighted, sagacious.

well-balanced *adj.* **1 well-adjusted,** sensible, reasonable, rational, levelheaded, sound, practical, discerning, logical, sane, in one's right mind. **2 balanced,** well-proportioned, well-ordered. **3 balanced,** symmetrical, well-proportioned, proportional, well-ordered, well-arranged, graceful, elegant.

well-built *adj.* **strongly built,** strong, muscular, brawny, sturdy, robust, strapping, burly, big, *inf.* hulking, husky, hefty, beefy. *Ant.* puny; slight.

well-known *adj.* **1 known,** widely known, familiar, common, usual, everyday. **2 famous,** famed, renowned, celebrated, noted, notable, illustrious, eminent. *Ant.* unknown; obscure; unsung.

well off *adj.* **1 wealthy,** rich, well-to-do, moneyed, affluent, prosperous, of means, of substance, *inf.* well-heeled, rolling in it/money/dough, in the money, made of money, filthy/stinking rich, loaded, flush, on easy street. **2 fortunate,** lucky, comfortable, thriving, successful, flourishing.

Ant. poor; broke; badly off; unfortunate.

well-spoken *adj.* **articulate,** eloquent, fluent, silver-tongued, smooth-talking, *inf.* having the gift of the gab.

wet *adj.* **1 damp,** dampened, moist, moistened, wet through, soaked, drenched, saturated, sopping/dripping/wringing wet, sopping, dripping, soggy, waterlogged. **2 rainy,** raining, pouring, showery, drizzling, damp, humid, dank, misty. **3 aqueous,** watery, watered, sloppy. *Ant.* dry; arid.
  ▸ *n.* **wetness,** damp, dampness, moisture, moistness, condensation, humidity, water, liquid, wet/rainy/showery/damp weather, rain, drizzle, damp, rains.

wharf *n.* **pier,** quay, dock, jetty.

wheel *n.* **disk,** hoop, circle, ring, *Tech.* annulus.
  ▸ *v.* **1 turn,** go around, circle, rotate, revolve, spin. **2 push,** shove, trundle.

wheeze *v.* **breathe audibly/noisily,** gasp, whistle, hiss, rasp.
  ▸ *n.* **gasp,** whistle, hiss.

whereabouts *n.* **location,** site, position, situation, place.

whet *v.* **1 sharpen,** put an edge on, edge, hone, strop, file, grind, rasp. **2 stimulate,** excite, arouse, rouse,

kindle, quicken, stir, titillate, tempt. *Ant.* blunt.

whim *n.* **1 notion,** fancy, idea, impulse, urge, caprice, vagary, craze, passion, inclination, bent. **2 whimsy,** capriciousness, caprice, volatility, fickleness.

whimper *v.* **whine,** cry, sniffle, snivel, moan, wail, groan.
  ▸ *n.* **whine,** cry, moan, wail, groan.

whimsical *adj.* **capricious,** fanciful, fantastical, playful, mischievous, waggish, quaint, unusual, curious, droll, eccentric, peculiar, queer, bizarre, weird, freakish.

whine *v.* **whimper,** cry, complain, grumble, moan, groan, fuss, lament, *inf.* grouse, gripe, bellyache, beef.
  ▸ *n.* **whimper,** cry, wail, groan.

whip *v.* **1 lash,** flog, scourge, flagellate, birch, switch, strap, cane, thrash, beat, strike, castigate, *inf.* belt, tan, lay into, give a hiding to, beat the living daylights out of. **2 beat,** whisk, mix. **3 whisk,** flash, snatch, pull, yank, jerk, produce, remove. **4 whisk,** dart, dash, dive, dodge, shoot, tear, rush, fly, bolt, zoom. **5 beat,** defeat, overcome, overpower, overwhelm, thrash, trounce, crush, rout. **6 rouse,** stir up, incite, goad, prod, spur, prompt, agitate.

▸ *n.* **lash,** scourge, flagellum, horsewhip, bullwhip, cat o'nine tails, knout, birch, switch, thong, crop, riding crop, cane.

whirl *v.* **1 turn around,** circle, spin, rotate, revolve, wheel, twirl, swirl, gyrate, reel, pirouette, pivot. **2 speed,** rush, race, shoot, tear, charge, whip. **3 spin,** reel, feel dizzy/giddy.

▸ *n.* **1 turn,** spin, rotation, revolution, wheel, twirl, swirl, gyration, reel, pirouette, pivot. **2 activity,** bustle, flurry, to-do, hurly-burly. **3 round,** succession, series, sequence, progression, string, chain, cycle. **4 spin,** dither, state of confusion, daze, muddle, jumble. **5 try,** tryout, test, *inf.* go, shot, stab.

whirlpool *n.* **vortex,** maelstrom, eddy.

whirlwind *n.* **cyclone,** tornado, twister, waterspout *inf.* dust devil.

▸ *adj.* **lightning,** swift, rapid, quick, speedy, hasty, headlong, impulsive.

whisk *v.* **1 wave,** flick, brandish. **2 brush,** sweep, wipe. **3 whip,** snatch, pull, yank, jerk, produce, remove. **4 dart,** dash, dive, dodge, whip, shoot, tear, rush, fly, bolt, zoom. **5 whirl,** whip, snatch. **6 whip,** beat, mix.

▸ *n.* **1 wave,** flick brandish. **2 brush,** sweep, wipe. **3 beater.**

whisper *v.* **1 murmur,** mutter, speak softly, speak in muted/hushed tones, breathe, say/utter softly, say/utter under the breath. **2 murmur,** rustle, sigh, sough, swish, swoosh, *lit.* susurrate. ***Ant.*** shout; yell.

▸ *n.* **1 murmur,** mutter, low voice, hushed tone, undertone. **2 murmur,** rustle, sigh, sough, swish, swoosh, *lit.* susurration. **3 rumor,** report, insinuation, suggestion, hint, gossip, word. **4 whiff,** trace, tinge, hint, suggestion, suspicion.

whit *n.* **particle,** bit, jot, iota, mite, little, trifle.

white *adj.* **1 white as a ghost/ sheet,** chalk-white, pale, wan, pallid, ashen, anemic, colorless, bloodless, waxen, pasty, peaky, gray. **2 gray,** silver, hoary, snow-white.

whiten *v.* **make white,** make pale, bleach, blanch, fade, wash out, etiolate.

whole *adj.* **1 entire,** complete, full, total, solid, integral, unabridged, unreduced, undivided, uncut. **2 intact,** sound, flawless, in one piece, unimpaired, undamaged, unharmed, unhurt, uninjured, unmutilated. ***Ant.*** part; partial; incomplete; broken.

▸ *adv.* **in one piece,** in one.

wholehearted *adj.* **1 devoted,**

dedicated, enthusiastic, eager, keen, zealous, earnest, serious, committed. **2 unreserved,** unqualified, unstinting, complete, committed, hearty, emphatic, real, sincere, genuine. **Ant.** apathetic; halfhearted; qualified.

wholesale adj. **indiscriminate,** mass, all-inclusive, total, comprehensive, extensive, wide-ranging, sweeping, broad. **Ant.** partial; selective.

▸ adv. **indiscriminately,** all at once, without exception, on a large scale, comprehensively, extensively.

wholesome adj. **1 nutritious,** nourishing, health-giving, healthful, good, good for one, strengthening. **2 salubrious,** invigorating, bracing, stimulating, refreshing. **3 moral,** ethical, nonerotic, nonviolent, uplifting, edifying, helpful, beneficial, prudent.

wholly adv. **1 completely,** fully, entirely, totally, utterly, thoroughly, altogether, comprehensively, in every respect, perfectly, enthusiastically, with total commitment, unreservedly, heart and soul, inf. one hundred percent. **2 only,** solely, exclusively, purely.

wicked adj. **1 evil,** sinful, bad, black-hearted, villainous, base, vile, vicious, dishonorable, unprincipled, unrighteous, criminal, lawless, perverted, immoral, amoral, unethical, corrupt, dissolute, abandoned, dissipated, degenerate, reprobate, debauched, depraved, unholy, impious, irreligious, ungodly, godless, devilish, iniquitous, wrong, foul, mean, gross, odious, obnoxious, nefarious, heinous, flagitious, infamous, dreadful, dire, grim, horrible, hideous, gruesome, monstrous, atrocious, abominable, abhorrent, loathsome, hateful, detestable, reprehensible, dishonorable, disgraceful, shameful, ignoble, ignominious, unlawful, illicit, illegal, dastardly, blackguardly, impure, ungodly, godless, profane, blasphemous, irreverent, damnable, demonic, diabolic, spiteful, malicious, malignant, nasty, offensive, hurtful, distressing, galling, vexatious. **2 dangerous,** perilous, destructive, harmful, injurious, hurtful, painful, agonizing, ferocious, fierce, terrible, mighty. **3 mischievous,** impish, roguish, arch, rascally, naughty. **4 bad,** nasty, unpleasant, disagreeable, inf. dreadful, terrible, awful. **5 excellent,** expert, masterly, skillful, proficient, deft, adept, dexterous, first-rate, outstanding, superior, superlative, *inf.* top-notch. *Ant.* virtuous; good; righteous.

wide *adj.* **1 broad,** extensive, spacious, large, outspread, spread out, ample. **2 open,** dilated. **3 ample,** broad, extensive, large, large-scale, vast, far-ranging, immense, wide-ranging, expansive, sweeping, encyclopedic, comprehensive, general, all-embracing, catholic, compendious. **4 off target,** off course. *Ant.* narrow; limited; restricted.
▸ *adv.* **1 to the fullest/furthest extent,** as far as possible, fully, completely. **2 wide of the mark/target,** off target, off course, astray.

wide-eyed *adj.* **1 surprised,** amazed, astonished, astounded. **2 naïve,** impressionable, ingenuous, credulous, trusting, unsuspicious, innocent, simple, unsophisticated, inexperienced, green, *inf.* wet behind the ears.

widen *v.* **make wider,** broaden, expand, extend, enlarge, increase, augment, add to, supplement, open wide, dilate. *Ant.* narrow; restrict; limit.

widespread *adj.* **universal,** common, general, far-reaching, far-flung, prevalent, rife, extensive, sweeping, pervasive, epidemic. *Ant.* local; limited; rare.

width *n.* **wideness,** breadth, broadness, span, diameter, thickness, ampleness, scope, range, extensiveness, vastness, immensity, immenseness, expansiveness, comprehensiveness, catholicity, compendiousness.

wield *v.* **1 brandish,** flourish, wave, swing, shake, use, put to use, employ, handle, ply, manipulate. **2 exercise,** exert, be possessed of, have, have at one's disposal, hold, maintain, command, control, manage, be in charge of.

wild *adj.* **1 untamed,** undomesticated, unbroken, feral, savage, fierce, ferocious. **2 uncultivated,** natural, native, indigenous. **3 uncivilized,** primitive, ignorant, savage, barbaric, barbarous, brutish, ferocious, fierce. **4 uncivilized,** uncultivated, unpopulated, uninhabited, unsettled, unfrequented, empty, barren, waste, desolate, forsaken, godforsaken, isolated. **5 stormy,** tempestuous, turbulent, blustery, howling, violent, raging, furious, rough. **6 undisciplined,** unrestrained, unconstrained,

uncontrolled, out of control, uncurbed, unbridled, unchecked, chaotic, disorderly, rowdy, unruly, disorderly, noisy, turbulent, violent, lawless, riotous, unmanageable, ungovernable, unrestrained, excited, passionate, frantic. **7 beside oneself,** berserk, frantic, frenzied, in a frenzy, hysterical, crazed, mad, distracted, distraught, irrational, deranged, demented, raving, maniacal, rabid, *inf.* crazy. **8 angry,** infuriated, incensed, exasperated, in a temper, seething, *inf.* mad.
9 extravagant, fantastical, impracticable, foolish, ill-advised, ill-considered, imprudent, unwise, madcap, impulsive, reckless, rash, outrageous, preposterous.
10 enthusiastic, eager, avid, agog, *inf.* crazy, mad, nuts. **11 arbitrary,** random, hit-or-miss, haphazard, uninformed, unknowledgeable.
12 uncombed, unkempt, disheveled, tousled, windblown, disarranged, untidy. *Ant.* tame; civilized; calm; restrained.
wilderness *n.* **1 desert,** wasteland, waste, jungle, no-man's land, wilds. **2 confusion,** tangle, jumble, muddle, clutter, miscellany, hodgepodge, bewilderment, maze, labyrinth.
will[1] *v.* **1 wish,** want, desire, please, see/think fit, think best, choose,

prefer, opt, elect. **2 do,** have a tendency to, have a habit of.
will[2] *v.* **1 impose one's will on,** try to make/cause. **2 decree,** order, ordain, command, direct, bid, intend, wish, desire. **3 bequeath,** leave, give, hand/pass down to, pass on to, transfer to.
▸ *n.* **1 volition,** choice, option, decision, discretion, prerogative. **2 desire,** wish, preference, inclination, fancy, mind. **3 decree,** ordinance, dictate, wish, decision. **4 willpower,** determination, resolution, resolve, firmness of purpose, purposefulness, doggedness, single-mindedness, commitment, moral fiber, pluck, mettle, grit, nerve. **5 last will and testament,** testament; last wishes. **6 feeling,** disposition, attitude.
willful *adj.* **1 deliberate,** intentional, intended, conscious, purposeful, premeditated, planned, calculated. **2 headstrong,** strong-willed, obstinate, stubborn, stubborn as a mule, mulish, pigheaded, bullheaded, obdurate, intransigent, adamant, dogged, determined, persistent, unyielding, uncompromising, intractable, refractory, recalcitrant, disobedient, contrary, perverse, wayward, self-willed. *Ant.* accidental; unintentional; docile.

willing *adj.* **1 ready,** eager, keen, enthusiastic, avid. **2 prepared,** ready, disposed, content, happy, so-minded, consenting, agreeable, amenable, in the mood, compliant, *inf.* game. **3 cooperative,** gladly given, cheerful, accommodating, obliging. ***Ant.*** unwilling; reluctant.

willingly *adv.* **1 voluntarily,** of one's own free will, of one's own accord, by choice, by volition, spontaneously, unforced. **2 cheerfully,** happily, with pleasure, readily, without hesitation, ungrudgingly, with all one's heart.

wilt *v.* **1 droop,** wither, shrivel, lose freshness, sag, feel weak/faint, languish. **2 diminish,** dwindle, lessen, grow less, flag, fade, melt away, ebb, wane, weaken, fail. ***Ant.*** grow; thrive.

wily *adj.* **crafty,** cunning, artful, sharp, astute, shrewd, scheming, intriguing, shifty, foxy, sly, guileful, deceitful, deceptive, fraudulent, cheating, underhand, underhanded, *inf.* crooked.

win *v.* **1 achieve,** attain, earn, gain, receive, obtain, acquire, procure, get, secure, collect, pick up, come away with, net, *inf.* bag. **2 be victorious (in),** be the victor (in), achieve success in, come first in, gain the victory, overcome, achieve mastery, carry the day, finish first, come out ahead, come out on top, succeed, triumph, prevail, *inf.* win out. **3 charm,** attract, lure, disarm. ***Ant.*** lose; fail; repel.
▸ *n.* **victory,** conquest, success, triumph.

wind[1] *n.* **1 air current,** current/stream of air, puff of wind, light air/wind, zephyr, breeze, gust, blast, gale. **2 breath,** respiration, *inf.* puff. **3 empty talk,** talk, babble, blather, boasting, bluster, braggadocio, *inf.* hot air, baloney, gas. **4 rumor,** gossip, hint, suggestion, inkling, intimation, news, information, report, intelligence.

wind[2] *v.* **1 twist,** twist and turn, curve, bend, loop, zigzag, snake, spiral, meander, ramble. **2 curl,** spiral, wreathe, snake. **3 twist,** twine, coil, wrap, roll. phrases: **wind down 1 unwind,** relax, become less tense, ease up, calm down, cool off. **2 bring to a close/end,** make less active, ease up on. **3 slacken off,** ease up, taper off, dwindle, diminish, lessen, decline, come to an end/close. **wind up 1 make tense,** strain, make nervous, work up, put on edge, agitate, fluster, disconcert, discompose. **2 bring to**

an end/conclusion, end, conclude, terminate, finish; *inf.* wrap up.
3 end up, finish, find oneself.
windfall *n.* **piece/stroke of good luck,** unexpected gain, godsend, manna (from heaven), bonanza, jackpot.
wink *v.* **1 blink,** flutter, bat, nictate, nictitate. **2 flash,** twinkle, sparkle, glitter, gleam.
▸ *n.* **1 blink,** flutter, bat, nictation. **2 flash,** twinkle, sparkle, glitter, gleam. **3 moment,** minute, second, instant, *inf.* jiffy, jiff, two shakes of a lamb's tail.
winner *n.* **champion,** victor, vanquisher, conqueror, conquering hero, cup winner, prizewinner.
winning *adj.* **1 victorious,** successful, triumphant, vanquishing, conquering. **2 captivating,** enchanting, bewitching, beguiling, disarming, taking, engaging, endearing, winsome, charming, attractive, fetching, alluring, sweet, lovely, delightful, darling, amiable, pleasing.
wintry *adj.* **1 cold,** chilly, icy, frosty, freezing, frozen, snowy, arctic, glacial, biting, piercing, nippy. **2 unfriendly,** cool, chilly, cold, distant, remote, bleak, cheerless.
wipe *v.* **rub,** brush, dust, mop,

sponge, swab, clean, dry, swipe.
▸ *n.* **rub,** brush, dust, mop, sponge, swab, clean.
wiry *adj.* **1 lean,** spare, sinewy, tough, strong. **2 strong,** coarse, tough. **3 bristly,** prickly, thorny, stiff, rigid. *Ant.* frail; smooth.
wisdom *n.* **1 sageness,** sagacity, cleverness, intelligence, erudition, learning, education, knowledge, enlightenment, reason, philosophy, discernment, perception, insight. **2 sense,** common sense, prudence, judiciousness, judgment, shrewdness, astuteness, smartness, circumspection, strategy, foresight, reasonableness, rationality, logic, soundness, saneness. *Ant.* folly; stupidity.
wise *adj.* **1 sage,** sagacious, clever, intelligent, erudite, learned, educated, well-read, knowledgeable, informed, enlightened, philosophic, deep-thinking, discerning, perceptive, experienced, *lit.* sapient. **2 sensible,** prudent, well-advised, judicious, politic, shrewd, astute, smart, strategic, reasonable, rational, logical, sound, sane. *Ant.* stupid; silly; foolish.
wish *v.* **1 want,** desire, long, yearn, aspire, have an inclination. **2 desire,** demand, bid, ask,

require, instruct, direct, order, command.

▶ *n.* **1 desire,** liking, fondness, longing, hope, yearning, want, fancy, aspiration, inclination, urge, whim, craving, hunger, thirst, lust, *inf.* hankering, yen. **2 want,** desire, demand, bidding, request, requirement, instruction, direction, order, command.

wistful *adj.* **yearning,** longing, forlorn, disconsolate, melancholy, sad, mournful, dreaming, dreamy, daydreaming, in a reverie, pensive, reflective, musing, contemplative, meditative.

wit *n.* **1 intelligence,** intellect, cleverness, wisdom, sageness, sagacity, judgment, common sense, understanding, comprehension, reason, sharpness, astuteness, shrewdness, acumen, discernment, perspicacity, perception, percipience, insight, ingenuity, brains. **2 wittiness,** humor, jocularity, funniness, facetiousness, drollery, waggishness, repartee, badinage, banter, raillery. **3 humorist,** wag, funny person, comic, jokester, banterer, farceur, *inf.* card. *Ant.* stupidity; gravity.

witch *n.* **1 sorceress,** enchantress, magician, necromancer. **2 hag,** ogress, crone, gorgon, virago, termagant, shrew, harridan.

witchcraft *n.* **witchery,** sorcery, black art/magic, magic, necromancy, wizardry, occultism, the occult, sortilege, thaumaturgy, wonder-working.

withdraw *v.* **1 take back,** pull back, take away, extract, remove, retract, recall, unsay, revoke, annul, nullify, declare void, rescind, repeal, abrogate. **2 draw back,** go back, absent oneself, detach oneself. **3 pull back,** fall back, retire, retreat, disengage, depart, go, leave, *inf.* make oneself scarce. *Ant.* keep; proffer; stay; proceed.

withdrawn *adj.* **retiring,** reserved, uncommunicative, nonforthcoming, unsociable, taciturn, silent, quiet, introverted, detached, aloof, self-contained, distant, private, shrinking, timid, timorous, shy, bashful, diffident. *Ant.* outgoing; sociable.

wither *v.* **1 dry up/out,** shrivel, go limp, wilt, die, desiccate, kill off. **2 destroy,** ruin, kill off, blight, blast. **3 wilt,** decline, fade, ebb, wane, disintegrate, die, perish.

withhold *v.* **1 hold back,** keep back, restrain, hold/keep in check, check, curb, repress, suppress. **2 refuse to give/grant/ allow,** refuse, decline, keep back.

withstand *v.* **hold out against,** stand up to, stand firm against, resist, fight, combat, oppose, endure, stand, tolerate, bear, put up with, take, cope with, weather, brave, defy. *Ant.* surrender; yield.

witness *n.* **1 eyewitness,** observer, spectator, onlooker, looker-on, viewer, watcher, beholder, bystander. **2 testifier,** attestant, deponent. **3 evidence,** testimony, confirmation, corroboration, proof.
▸ *v.* **1 see,** observe, view, watch, look on at, behold, perceive, be present at, attend. **2 endorse,** countersign, sign, notarize.

witticism *n.* **witty remark,** clever saying, flash of wit, bon mot, quip, sally, pleasantry, riposte, joke, jest, epigram, *inf.* wisecrack, crack, one-liner.

witty *adj.* **clever,** original, ingenious, sparkling, scintillating, humorous, amusing, jocular, funny, facetious, droll, waggish, comic. *Ant.* boring; dull.

wizard *n.* **1 sorcerer,** warlock, enchanter, witch, necromancer, magician, magus. **2 expert,** master, adept, genius, virtuoso, maestro, star, *inf.* ace, whiz, wiz.

wizened *adj.* **withered,** shriveled (up), dried up, shrunken, wasted, wrinkled, lined, gnarled, worn.

wobble *v.* **1 rock,** sway, seesaw, teeter, shake, vibrate, totter, stagger, waddle, waggle. **2 shake,** tremble, quiver, quaver. **3 be undecided,** be uncertain, waver, vacillate, hesitate, dither, shilly-shally.
▸ *n.* **1 rocking,** swaying, teetering, shaking, teeter, totter, stagger. **2 shaking,** trembling, tremor, quiver, quaver.

woe *n.* **1 misery,** wretchedness, misfortune, disaster, grief, anguish, affliction, suffering, pain, agony, torment, sorrow, sadness, unhappiness, distress, heartache, heartbreak, despondency, desolation, dejection, depression, gloom, melancholy. **2 trouble,** misfortune, adversity, trial, tribulation, ordeal, burden, affliction, suffering, disaster, calamity, catastrophe, trials and tribulations. *Ant.* happiness; joy; luck.

woebegone *adj.* **miserable,** sad, unhappy, sorrowful, sorrowing, disconsolate, mournful, downcast, dejected, doleful, desolate, depressed, despairing, tearful.

woeful *adj.* **1 sad,** saddening, unhappy, sorrowful, miserable, dismal, wretched, doleful, gloomy, tragic, pathetic, grievous, pitiful, plaintive, heart-rending, heartbreaking, distressing, anguished, agonizing, dreadful, terrible, wretched, harsh, tragic, disastrous, ruinous, calamitous, catastrophic. **2 poor,** bad, inadequate, substandard, lamentable, deplorable, disgraceful, wretched, disappointing, feeble, *inf.* rotten, appalling, terrible, lousy, shocking.

woman *n.* **1 female,** lady, girl, she, *derog. inf.* chick, dame. **2 girlfriend,** female friend, lady love, sweetheart, partner, lover, wife, spouse.

wonder *n.* **1 wonderment,** awe, surprise, astonishment, amazement, bewilderment, stupefaction, fascination, admiration. **2 marvel,** phenomenon, miracle, prodigy, curiosity, rarity, nonpareil, sight, spectacle.
▶ *v.* **1 think,** speculate, conjecture, ponder, meditate, reflect, deliberate, muse, ask oneself, puzzle, be curious about, be inquisitive about. **2 be surprised,** express surprise, find it surprising, be astonished/amazed. **3 marvel,** stand amazed, stand in awe, be dumbfounded, gape, stare, goggle, look agog, *inf.* be flabbergasted, gawk, boggle.

wonderful *adj.* **marvelous,** awe-inspiring, awesome, remarkable, extraordinary, phenomenal, prodigious, miraculous, fantastic, amazing, astonishing, astounding, surprising, incredible, unprecedented, unparalleled, unheard-of, superb, magnificent, brilliant, sensational, stupendous, excellent, first-rate, outstanding, terrific, tremendous, admirable, very good, *inf.* great, super, fantastic, fabulous, tip-top, ace, A-1, wizard, bad, wicked, *lit.* wondrous. *Ant.* ordinary; indifferent; awful; dreadful.

woo *v.* **1 court,** pay court/suit to, seek the hand of, pursue, chase after, set one's cap at, make love to. **2 seek,** seek to win/gain, pursue, chase after. **3 seek the support/favor of. 4 importune,** press, urge, entreat, beg, implore, supplicate, solicit, coax, wheedle.

wood *n.* **lumber,** timber, firewood, kindling, fuel.

wooded *adj.* **woody,** forested, tree-covered, tree-clad, timbered, sylvan.

wooden *adj.* **1 made of wood,** of wood, wood, timber. **2 stiff,** stolid, stodgy, expressionless, graceless, inelegant, ungainly, gauche, awkward, clumsy, maladroit. **3 expressionless,** inexpressive, blank, deadpan, empty, vacant, vacuous, glassy, impassive, lifeless, spiritless, unanimated, emotionless, unemotional, unresponsive.

woolly *adj.* **1 fleecy,** fluffy, shaggy, hairy, furry, flocculent. **2 woolen,** (made of) wool, wool. **3 fuzzy,** blurred, hazy, cloudy, foggy, indistinct, unclear, ill-defined. **4 vague,** hazy, indefinite, muddled, confused, disorganized.

word *n.* **1 term,** expression, name. **2 remark,** comment, statement, utterance, expression, declaration. **3 word of honor,** solemn word, promise, pledge, assurance, guarantee, undertaking, vow, oath. **4 chat,** talk, conversation, discussion, tête-à-tête, consultation, exchange of views, *inf.* confab, chitchat, powwow. **5 news,** intimation, notice, communication, information, intelligence, tidings, message, report, account, communiqué, dispatch, bulletin, *inf.* low-down. **6 rumor,** talk, hearsay, gossip, *inf.* grapevine. **7 command,** order, signal, go-ahead, thumbs up, *inf.* green light. **8 command,** order, decree, edict, mandate, bidding, will. **9 slogan,** watchword, password, catchword.
▸ *v.* **express,** phrase, couch, put, say, utter, state.

wordy *adj.* **long-winded,** verbose, loquacious, garrulous, voluble, prolix, protracted, discursive, diffuse, rambling, digressive, maundering, tautological, pleonastic.

work *n.* **1 effort,** exertion, labor, toil, sweat, drudgery, trouble, industry, *lit.* travail, *inf.* grind, elbow grease. **2 job,** task, chore, undertaking, duty, charge, assignment, commission, mission. **3 employment,** occupation, business, job, profession, career, trade, vocation, calling, craft, line, field, métier, pursuit. **4 achievement,** accomplishment, deed, feat, handiwork, fulfillment, performance, production. **5 composition,** creation, opus, piece, oeuvre, masterpiece. **6 workmanship,** art, craft, skill. **Ant.** leisure; play; holiday; retirement.
▸ *v.* **1 be employed,** have a job, hold down a job, be engaged, earn one's living, do business, follow/ply one's trade. **2 exert oneself,** put in effort, make efforts, labor, toil, sweat, drudge, slave, peg away, *inf.* grind, plug away, knock oneself out. **3 operate,** control, drive, manage, direct, use, handle, manipulate, maneuver, ply, wield. **4 go,** operate, function, perform, run. **5 succeed,** be successful, have success, go well, be effective, be effectual. **6 cultivate,** till, dig, farm. **7 bring about,** achieve,

accomplish, perform, carry out, execute, create, cause, contrive, effect, implement. **8 arrange,** handle, manipulate, maneuver, contrive, bring off, carry off, pull off, *inf.* fix, fiddle, swing. **9 knead,** shape, form, mold, fashion, model. **10 maneuver,** manipulate, negotiate, guide, engineer, direct, edge. **11 maneuver,** progress, penetrate, move, make, push, elbow. *Ant.* rest; play; fail.

workable *adj.* **practicable,** practical, viable, doable, feasible, possible.

worker *n.* **1 employee,** hand, workman, workwoman, working man/woman/person, blue-collar worker, white-collar worker, laborer, artisan, craftsman, craftswoman, wage-earner, proletarian. **2 doer,** performer, perpetrator, executor, operator. **3 hard worker,** toiler, workhorse, busy bee, *inf.* workaholic.

working *adj.* **1 in work,** employed, in a job. **2 functioning,** operating, going, running, in working order. **3 effective,** viable. *Ant.* unemployed; broken.
▸ *n.* **1 functioning,** operation, running process, modus operandi. **2 doing,** performing, performance, perpetration, execution, operation. **3 mechanism,** machinery, works.

workmanship *n.* **craftsmanship,** craft, artistry, art, handicraft, handwork, expertise, skill, technique, work.

workshop *n.* **1 factory,** plant, mill, garage. **2 workroom,** studio, atelier, shop. **3 seminar,** study/discussion group, class.

world *n.* **1 earth,** globe, sphere, planet. **2 whole world,** world at large, mankind, man, humankind, humanity, people everywhere, people, everyone, everybody, public, general public. **3 universe,** creation, cosmos, all existence. **4 planet,** satellite, moon, star, heavenly body, orb. **5 society,** sector, section, group, division, area, field, department, sphere, province, domain, realm. **6 age,** epoch, era, period, times. **7 vast/huge amount,** *inf.* great deal, immensity. **8 secular interests,** earthly concerns, human existence.

worldly *adj.* **1 earthly,** terrestrial, secular, temporal, material, materialistic, human, carnal, fleshly, corporeal, physical. **2 worldly-wise,** experienced, knowing, sophisticated, cosmopolitan, urbane. *Ant.* spiritual; naïve; unsophisticated.

worldwide *adj.* **universal,** global, international, pandemic, general, ubiquitous, extensive, widespread, far-reaching, wide-ranging.

worn *adj.* **1 worn-out,** threadbare, tattered, in tatters, ragged, frayed, shabby, dilapidated, crumbling, broken-down, run-down, tumbledown, decrepit, deteriorated, on its last legs. **2 haggard,** drawn, strained, careworn, worn out, exhausted, overtired, tired out, fatigued, weary, wearied, spent, *inf.* all in, done in, dog-tired, dead on one's feet, played out, bushed, pooped. **3 well-worn,** worn-out, obsolete, antiquated, old, hackneyed, stale, *inf.* played out. ***Ant.*** new; mint; energetic; fresh.

worried *adj.* **anxious,** disturbed, perturbed, troubled, bothered, distressed, concerned, upset, distraught, uneasy, ill at ease, disquieted, fretful, agitated, nervous, edgy, on edge, tense, overwrought, worked-up, distracted, apprehensive, fearful, afraid, frightened, *inf.* uptight, on tenterhooks, antsy. ***Ant.*** carefree; calm; unconcerned.

worry *v.* **1 be worried,** be anxious, fret, brood. **2 cause anxiety to,** make anxious, disturb, trouble, bother, distress, upset, concern, disquiet, discompose, fret, agitate, unsettle.
▸ *n.* **anxiety,** disturbance,

perturbation, trouble, bother, distress, concern, care, upset, uneasiness, unease, disquiet, disquietude, fretfulness, agitation, edginess, tenseness, apprehension, fearfulness.

worsen *v.* **1 aggravate,** exacerbate, damage, intensify, increase, heighten. **2 take a turn for the worse,** deteriorate, degenerate, retrogress, decline, sink, slip, slide, *inf.* go downhill. ***Ant.*** improve; ameliorate.

worship *n.* **1 reverence,** veneration, homage, respect, honor, adoration, devotion, praise, prayer, glorification, exaltation, laudation, extolment. **2 service,** religious rites/acts. **3 adulation,** admiration, adoration, devotion, idolization, hero-worship.
▸ *v.* **1 revere,** venerate, pay homage to, honor, adore, praise, pray to, glorify, exalt, laud, extol. **2 attend a service,** pray. **3 adore,** be devoted to, cherish, treasure, admire, adulate, idolize, hero-worship, lionize, *inf.* be wild about. ***Ant.*** blaspheme; loathe; despise.

worth *n.* **1 value,** price, cost, valuation, price, assessment, appraisal. **2 value,** use, usefulness, advantage, benefit, service, gain, profit, avail, help, assistance, aid. **3 worthiness,** merit, credit, value, excellence, eminence, importance.

worthless *adj.* **1 valueless,** of little/no value, rubbishy, trashy. **2 valueless,** useless, of no use, of no benefit, to no avail, futile, ineffective, ineffectual, pointless, nugatory. **3 good-for-nothing,** useless, despicable, contemptible, base, low, vile, corrupt, depraved, *inf.* no-good, no-account. *Ant.* valuable; precious; useful.

worthwhile *adj.* **worth it,** worth the effort, valuable, of value, useful, of use, beneficial, advantageous, helpful, profitable, gainful, productive, constructive, justifiable. *Ant.* worthless; useless; pointless.

worthy *adj.* **1 virtuous,** good, moral, upright, righteous, honest, decent, honorable, respectable, reputable, trustworthy, reliable, irreproachable, blameless, unimpeachable, admirable, praiseworthy, laudable, commendable, deserving, meritorious. **2 deserving,** meriting. *Ant.* disreputable; unworthy.
▸ *n.* **dignitary,** notable, celebrity, personage, luminary, official, *inf.* VIP, big shot, bigwig, big cheese, big gun.

wound *n.* **1 lesion,** cut, graze, scratch, gash, laceration, tear,

puncture, slash, injury, sore. **2 blow,** injury, insult, slight, offense, affront, hurt, harm, damage. **3 injury,** hurt, pain, pang, ache, distress, grief, trauma, anguish, torment, torture.
▸ *v.* **1 cut,** graze, scratch, gash, lacerate, tear, puncture, pierce, stab, slash, injure, hurt, damage, harm. **2 hurt,** harm, damage, injure, insult, slight, offend, affront. **3 hurt,** distress, grieve, mortify, pain, shock, traumatize. *Ant.* heal; boost; gladden.

wrap *v.* **envelop,** enfold, encase, enclose, cover, swathe, bundle up, swaddle, fold, swathe, bundle, draw, arrange, wrap up, package, do up, tie up, gift-wrap.
▸ *n.* **shawl,** stole, cloak, cape, mantle.

wrath *n.* **anger,** ire, rage, fury, annoyance, indignation, exasperation, dudgeon, high dudgeon, bad temper, ill humor, irritation, crossness, displeasure, irascibility.

wreathe *v.* **1 cover,** envelop, festoon, garland, adorn, decorate. **2 twist,** wind, coil, twine, entwine, curl, spiral, wrap. **3 coil,** wind, spiral, curl.

wreck *n.* **1 shipwreck,** sunken ship, derelict. **2 wreckage,** debris, rubble, detritus, ruins, remains, remnants, fragments, pieces,

relics. **3 wrecking,** wreckage, destruction, devastation, ruination, ruin, demolition, smashing, shattering, disruption, disintegration, undoing.
▸ *v.* **1 smash,** demolish, ruin, damage, *inf.* write off. **2 destroy,** devastate, ruin, demolish, smash, shatter, disrupt, undo, spoil, mar, play havoc with. **3 shipwreck,** sink, capsize, run aground, founder. *Ant.* build; create; save; repair.

wreckage *n.* **1 wreck,** debris, ruins, remains, remnants, fragments. **2 wreck,** wrecking, destruction, ruination, ruin, demolition, smashing.

wrench *n.* **1 twist,** pull, tug, yank, wrest, jerk, jolt. **2 sprain,** twist, strain. **3 pain,** ache, pang, anguish, distress, trauma.
▸ *v.* **1 twist,** pull, tug, yank, wrest, jerk, tear, rip, force. **2 sprain,** twist, strain.

wrest *v.* **twist,** wrench, pull, snatch, take away, remove.

wretch *n.* **1 poor creature/soul/thing,** miserable creature, unfortunate, poor devil. **2 scoundrel,** villain, ruffian, rogue, rascal, blackguard, reprobate, criminal, delinquent, miscreant, *inf.* creep, jerk, louse, rat, swine, skunk.

wretched *adj.* **1 miserable,** unhappy, sad, brokenhearted, sorrowful, sorry, distressed, disconsolate, downcast, down, downhearted, dejected, crestfallen, cheerless, depressed, melancholy, gloomy, mournful, doleful, forlorn, woebegone, abject. **2 ill,** unwell, sick, sickly, ailing, below par, *inf.* under the weather, out of sorts. **3 miserable,** unhappy, poor, hard, harsh, grim, difficult, unfortunate, sorry, pitiful, tragic, unlucky, hapless, pitiable. **4 contemptible,** despicable, base, low, vile. **5 poor,** bad, substandard, low-quality, inferior, pathetic, worthless. *Ant.* happy; well; fortunate.

wriggle *v.* **1 twist,** squirm, writhe, jiggle, jerk, twist and turn, zigzag, wiggle, snake, crawl, slink. **2 avoid,** evade, dodge, duck, extricate oneself.
▸ *n.* **squirming,** writhing, jiggling, jerk.

wring *v.* **1 twist,** squeeze. **2 extract,** force, coerce, exact, extort, wrest, wrench, screw.

wrinkle *n.* **crease,** fold, pucker, gather, furrow, ridge, line, corrugation, crinkle, crumple, rumple, crow's-foot.
▸ *v.* **crease,** pucker, gather, furrow, line, corrugate, crinkle, crumple, rumple.

write *v.* **1 write down,** put in

writing, put in black and white, commit to paper, jot down, note, set down, take down, record, register, list, inscribe, scribble, scrawl. **2 compose,** draft, create, pen, dash off. **3 write a letter,** correspond, communicate, *inf.* drop a line/note.

writer *n.* **author,** wordsmith, penman, hack, novelist, essayist, biographer, journalist, columnist, scriptwriter, scribe, *inf.* scribbler, pen/pencil pusher.

writhe *v.* **twist about,** twist and turn, roll about, squirm, wriggle, fidget, jerk, thrash, flail, toss, struggle.

writing *n.* **1 handwriting,** hand, penmanship, script, print, calligraphy, chirography, scribble, scrawl. **2 work,** opus, book, volume, publication, composition.

wrong *adj.* **1 incorrect,** inaccurate, in error, erroneous, mistaken, inexact, imprecise, unsound, faulty, false, wide of the mark, off target, *inf.* off beam, barking up the wrong tree. **2 unsuitable,** inappropriate, inapt, inapposite, undesirable, infelicitous, unacceptable, unfitting, improper, unseemly, indecorous, unconventional. **3 unlawful,** illegal, illicit, lawless, criminal, delinquent, felonious, dishonest, dishonorable, corrupt, unethical, immoral, bad, wicked, evil, sinful, iniquitous, blameworthy, culpable, *inf.* crooked. **4 amiss,** awry, out of order, not right, faulty, defective. **5 inside,** reverse, opposite, inverse. **Ant.** right; correct; appropriate; legal.
▸ *adv.* **1 wrongly,** incorrectly, inaccurately, erroneously, mistakenly, inexactly, imprecisely, falsely. **2 badly,** amiss, awry, astray.

wrongdoer *n.* **lawbreaker,** criminal, delinquent, culprit, offender, felon, villain, miscreant, evildoer, sinner, transgressor, malefactor.

wrongful *adj.* **unfair,** unjust, improper, unjustified, unwarranted, unlawful, illegal, illegitimate, illicit.

wry *adj.* **1 twisted,** distorted, contorted, crooked, lopsided, askew. **2 ironic,** sardonic, mocking, sarcastic, dry, droll, witty, humorous.

Yy

yank *v.* **pull,** tug, jerk, wrench.
▸ *n.* **pull,** jerk, wrench.

yardstick *n.* **measure,** standard, gauge, scale, guide, guideline, touchstone, criterion, benchmark, model, pattern.

yarn *n.* **1 thread,** fiber, strand. **2 story,** tale, anecdote, fable, *inf.* tall tale/story, cock and bull story.

yawning *adj.* **wide,** wide open, gaping, cavernous, chasmic.

yearly *adj.* **annual,** once a year, every year.
▸ *adv.* **annually,** once a year, per annum.

yearn *v.* **long,** pine, have a longing, crave, desire, want, wish, hanker, have a fancy, hunger, thirst, *inf.* have a yen.

yell *v.* **shout,** cry out, howl, scream, shriek, screech, squeal, roar, bawl, whoop, *inf.* holler.
▸ *n.* **shout,** cry, howl, scream, shriek, screech, squeal, roar, bawl, whoop, *inf.* holler.

yes *adv.* **all right,** of course, by all means, sure, certainly, in the affirmative, *inf.* yeah, yep, uh-huh, OK.

yield *v.* **1 produce,** bear, give, give forth, supply, provide. **2 give,** return, bring in, fetch, earn, net, produce, supply, provide, generate, furnish. **3 give up,** surrender, relinquish, part with, deliver up, turn over, give over, remit, cede, renounce, resign, abdicate, forgo. **4 admit/concede defeat,** surrender, capitulate, submit, lay down one's arms, give in, give up the struggle, succumb, raise/show the white flag, *inf.* throw in the towel, cave in. **5 give,** bend, stretch, be flexible/pliant. ***Ant.*** resist; withstand; defy.

yoke *n.* **1 harness,** collar, coupling. **2 oppression,** tyranny, enslavement, slavery, servitude, bondage, thrall. **3 tie,** link, bond.
▸ *v.* **1 harness,** hitch up, couple, join up. **2 join,** unite, link, bond, tie.

yokel *n.* **rustic,** countryman, countrywoman, peasant, country bumpkin, provincial, *inf.* country cousin, hayseed, hillbilly.

young *adj.* **1 youthful,** juvenile, junior, adolescent, in the springtime of life, in one's salad days. **2 new,** recent, undeveloped, fledgling, in the making. ***Ant.*** old; elderly; mature.

▸ *n.* **offspring**, progeny, family, issue, little ones, babies, litter, brood.

youngster *n.* **young adult/person**, youth, juvenile, teenager, adolescent, young hopeful, lad, boy, young man/woman, lass, girl, *inf.* kid, shaver, young 'un.

youth *n.* **1 young days**, early years, teens, early life, adolescence, boyhood, girlhood.
2 boy, girl, young man/woman/lady, lad, youngster, juvenile, teenager, adolescent, *inf.* kid.
3 young people, young, younger generation, *inf.* kids. **Ant.** age; old age.

youthful *adj.* **1 young**, juvenile.
2 fresh-faced, young-looking.
3 young, active, vigorous, spry, sprightly. **Ant.** old; elderly; doddering.

Zz

zany *adj.* **eccentric,** peculiar, odd, ridiculous, absurd, comic, clownish, madcap, funny, amusing, *inf.* weird, wacky, daft, screwy, kooky. ***Ant.*** ordinary; run-of-the-mill; conventional.

zeal *n.* **1 ardor,** fervor, fervency, passion, fire, devotion, vehemence, intensity, enthusiasm, eagerness, keenness, earnestness, vigor, energy, verve, gusto, zest, fanaticism, *inf.* zing. **2 zealotry,** fanaticism, extremism. ***Ant.*** apathy; indifference.

zealot *n.* **enthusiast,** fanatic, extremist, radical, militant, bigot, *inf.* fiend.

zealous *adj.* **ardent,** fervent, fervid, passionate, impassioned, devoted, intense, enthusiastic, eager, keen, earnest, vigorous, energetic, zestful, fanatical. ***Ant.*** apathetic; indifferent.

zenith *n.* **highest/high point,** crowning point, height, top, acme, peak, pinnacle, climax, prime, meridian, apex, apogee, vertex. ***Ant.*** nadir; bottom.

zero *n.* **1 naught,** nothing, cipher. **2 nothing,** naught, nil, *inf.* zilch, zippo. **3 lowest point,** nadir, rock bottom.
▸ *v.* phrase: **zero in on focus on,** center on, concentrate on, home in on, pinpoint.

zest *n.* **1 relish,** gusto, enthusiasm, eagerness, zeal, vigor, liveliness, energy, enjoyment, joy, delectation, appetite, *inf.* zing, oomph. **2 piquancy,** spice, pungency, flavor, relish, tang, savor, interest, *inf.* kick. ***Ant.*** apathy; indifference; distaste.

zone *n.* **area,** sector, section, belt, district, region, province.

zoom *v.* **1 fly,** buzz. **2 rush,** dash, pelt, race, tear, shoot, fly, scurry, speed, hurry, hasten, *inf.* whiz, zip.

Language Guide

CAPITALIZATION

Beginnings

The first word in a sentence is capitalized:

> <u>Dozens</u> of spectators lined the street.

The first word in a direct quotation is capitalized:

> Andy stood by the window and remarked, "<u>The</u> view from here is spectacular."

If a colon introduces more than one sentence, the first word after the colon is capitalized:

> We went over our findings, one piece of evidence at a time: <u>The</u> custodian had discovered the body just before midnight. The keys to the victim's office were found in the stairwell. In the adjoining office, three file cabinets had been overturned.

If a colon introduces a formal and distinct statement, the first word after the colon is capitalized:

> All my years on the basketball court have taught me one thing: <u>Winning</u> is more of a process than an outcome.

If a colon introduces a complete statement that is merely an extension of the statement preceding the colon, the first word after the colon is usually lowercased:

> Everything in the house was a shade of pink: <u>the</u> sofa was carnation blush, the tiles were misty mauve, and the carpet was dusty rose.

If a colon introduces an incomplete statement, the first word after the colon is lowercased:

> The caterer provided three choices: <u>chicken</u>, beef, and shrimp.

Proper Names

Proper names are capitalized. This is true of all proper names, including those of persons, places, structures, organizations, vessels, vehicles, brands, etc. Notice from the following examples that when a properly named entity is referred to in a "non-named" general sense, the general sense is almost always lowercased:

> Eleanor Roosevelt
> J.D. Salinger
> Carson City / a city in Nevada
> Ural Mountains / a view of the mountain
> New York Public Library / borrowing books from the public library
> Washington Monument / our photos of the monument
> Calvin Leete Elementary School / the rear entrance of the school
> Amherst Historical Society / when the society last met
> Boeing 747
> USS *Missouri* [note that the names of specific ships, aircraft, spacecraft, etc., are italicized]
> Chevy Malibu
> Slinky

Titles

The titles of works are capitalized. Titled works include:

- written material (books, periodicals, screenplays, etc.)
- components of written material (chapters, sections, etc.)
- filmed and/or broadcast works (movies, television shows, radio programs, etc.)
- works of art (paintings, sculptures, etc.)
- musical compositions (songs, operas, oratorios, etc.)

There are certain rules of convention regarding which words in the titles are capitalized.

Capitalize:

- first word in the title
- last word in the title
- nouns and pronouns
- adjectives

- verbs
- adverbs
- subordinating conjunctions (*although, as, because, if, since, that, whenever,* etc.)

Do not capitalize (unless they are first or last words in the title):

- articles (*a, an, the*)
- coordinating conjunctions (*and, but, for, nor, or, so, yet*)
- prepositions (although some guides suggest capitalizing prepositions of more than four letters)
- the word *to* in infinitives

> The King, the Sword, and the Golden Lantern
> A Room within a Room (*or* A Room Within a Room)
> Seventy Ways to Make Easy Money from Your Home
> The Stars Will Shine Because You Are Mine

If a subtitle is included, it typically follows a colon. It follows the capitalization rules of the main title, thus its first word is always capitalized:

> Aftermath Explored: The Confessions of a Nuclear Physicist

The first element in a hyphenated compound is always capitalized. The subsequent elements are capitalized unless they are articles, prepositions, or coordinating conjunctions. But if the compound is the last word in the title, its final element is always capitalized, regardless of its part of speech:

> Nineteenth-Century Poets
> Over-the-Top Desserts
> The Love-in of a Lifetime
> The Year of the Love-In

An element that follows a hyphenated prefix is capitalized only if it is a proper noun or adjective:

> Pre-Columbian Artifacts
> Memoirs of a Semi-independent Child

Education

An academic title is capitalized (whether it is spelled out or abbreviated) when it directly accompanies a personal name. Otherwise, it is lowercased:

Professor Sarah McDonald
Assoc. Prof. Brown
my chemistry professor

An academic degree or honor is capitalized (whether it is spelled out or abbreviated) when it directly accompanies a personal name. Otherwise, it is lowercased:

Harold L. Fox, Ph.D.
Charles Gustafson, Fellow of the Geological Society
working toward her master's degree

Academic years are lowercased:

the senior prom
he's a sophomore
the fourth grade

The course name of a particular school subject is capitalized. A general field of study is lowercased (unless the word is normally capitalized, such as "English"):

Astronomy 101
Algebra II
taking classes in psychology, French literature, and chemistry

Calendar Terms and Time

The names of the days of the week and months of the year are capitalized:

Sunday	October
September	Tuesday
Monday	November

The names of the four seasons are lowercased:

winter	spring
summer	fall *or* autumn

The names of holidays (religious and secular) and periods of religious observance are capitalized:

Arbor Day	Lent
Easter	Memorial Day
Halloween	Ramadan

TIP

Which titles should be set in italics, and which should be set off by quotation marks? In printed material, the distinction can be significant. Here's a handy list of the most common categories of titles and their standard treatments in type:

italics:

- books
  Crossroads of Freedom: Antietam, by James M. McPherson
- pamphlets
  Thomas Paine's *Common Sense*
- magazines
  Popular Mechanics
- newspapers
  USA Today
- movies
  One Flew Over the Cuckoo's Nest
- television or radio series
  This Week in Baseball
- plays
  Neil Simon's *Lost in Yonkers*
- long poems
  Beowulf
- collections of poems and other anthologies
  The Collected Poems of Emily Dickinson
- operas, oratorios, and other long musical compositions
  Madame Butterfly
- paintings, sculptures, and other works of art
  Thomas Cole's *Mount Etna from Taormina*

quotation marks:

- articles
  "How to Remove Wallpaper"
- chapters
  "Betsy Saves the Day"

- short stories
  "The Pit and the Pendulum," by Edgar Allan Poe
- short poems
  "Tree at My Window," by Robert Frost
- essays
  Emerson's "Spiritual Laws"
- television or radio episodes
  "Lucy Does a TV Commercial"
- songs and other short musical compositions
  "Are You Lonesome Tonight?"

The names of time zones and the time systems they designate are lower-cased (except for any words that are proper names). Their abbreviations are capitalized:

eastern daylight time (EDT)
Greenwich mean time (GMT)
Pacific standard time (PST)

Legislation, Treaties, etc.

The formal name of a policy, treaty, piece of legislation, or similar agreement is capitalized. A general reference to such is lowercased:

Volstead Act
the act sponsored by Congressman Volstead
Treaty of Versailles
the treaty at Versailles
Bottle Bill
Articles of Confederation
Connecticut Constitution
Connecticut's constitution
North American Free Trade Agreement

Military Service

A military title or rank is capitalized (whether it is spelled out or abbreviated) when it directly accompanies a personal name. Otherwise, it is lowercased:

Gen. George Patton
Ensign Irene Mahoney
promoted to admiral
James Kirk, captain of the USS *Enterprise*

There are two significant exceptions to the preceding rule: the U.S. military titles "Fleet Admiral" and "General of the Army" should always be capitalized, even when not directly accompanying a personal name:

became General of the Army in 1950
a visit from the Fleet Admiral

The full official name of a military group or force is capitalized. A general reference to a military group or force is lowercased:

the Royal Air Force
the British air force
the Army Corps of Engineers
the Third Battalion
our battalion
the U.S. Navy
joined the navy

The full name of a battle or war is capitalized. A general reference to a battle or war is lowercased:

the Russian Revolution
fought in the revolution
the Spanish-American War
the war in Vietnam
the Battle of the Bulge
the first battle of the campaign
the Norman Conquest

The official name of a military award or medal is capitalized:

the Purple Heart
the Silver Star
the Victoria Cross
the Congressional Medal of Honor

Science

The capitalization rules governing scientific terminology cover a wide range of categories and applications. Some of the basic rules are discussed here.

Taxonomic nomenclature—that is, the scientific classification of plants and animals—follows specific rules for both capitalization and italics.

The names of the phylum, class, order, and family of a plant or animal are capitalized and set in roman type. This format also applies to the intermediate groupings (suborder, subfamily, etc.) within these divisions:

> The North American river otter belongs to the phylum Chordata, the subphylum Vertebrata, the class Mammalia, the order Carnivora, and the family Mustelidae.

The divisions lower than family—that is, genus, species, and subspecies—are set in italic type. Of these, only the genus is capitalized. When a plant or animal is identified by its "scientific name" or "Latin name," the name given is the genus and species (and, when applicable, the subspecies):

> The scientific name of the river otter is *Lutra canadensis*.
> The Manitoban elk (*Cervus elaphus manitobensis*) is a subspecies of the North American elk.

The common names of plants and animals, as well as their hybrids, varieties, and breeds, are lowercased and set in roman type. A part of the name may be capitalized if that part is a term normally capitalized (that is, a proper name). If there is doubt, a dictionary should be consulted.

> Alaskan malamute
> Christmas cactus
> Johnny-jump-up
> maidenhair fern
> rainbow trout
> rose-breasted grosbeak
> Swainson's hawk
> Vietnamese potbellied pig

The names of astronomical entities, such as planets, stars, constellations, and galaxies, are capitalized:

> Alpha Centauri
> Canis Major

Crab Nebula
Ganymede
Mercury
Milky Way
Orion
Sirius

TIP

The names *sun*, *moon*, and *earth* are frequently lowercased. It is customary to capitalize them only when they are being referred to as components of the solar system. Also noteworthy is the fact that, in any context, the words *sun* and *moon* typically are preceded by the definite article, *the*. In non-astronomical contexts, the word *earth* often is preceded by *the*, but it is never preceded by *the* when used specifically as the name of a planet. Hence, *the Earth* would not be an appropriate use of capitalization.

We enjoyed the warmth of <u>the sun</u>.
The glow of <u>the moon</u> has inspired poets for centuries.
Countless species inhabit <u>the earth</u>.
What on <u>earth</u> are you doing?
In size, Venus is comparable to <u>Earth</u>.
The eclipse of <u>the Moon</u> will be visible from the night side of <u>Earth</u>.
They made observations of Neptune's orbit around <u>the Sun</u>.

The names of geological eras, periods, epochs, etc., are capitalized. When included with the name, the words *era*, *period*, *epoch*, etc., are lowercased.

Mesozoic era
Quaternary period
Oligocene epoch
Upper Jurassic

Abbreviations

Although the use of abbreviations in formal writing should be limited, abbreviations are legitimate components of the language and deserve the same attention to spelling as do other words. Certain capitalization guidelines for a few types of abbreviations are given below. Because the possible variations are numerous, a standard dictionary should be consulted for more thorough guidance on the spelling, capitalization, and punctuation of a specific abbreviation.

When a capitalized term is abbreviated, the abbreviation is capitalized. If the abbreviation is comprised of initials, all the initials are capitalized:

Professor J. Leggett / Prof. J. Leggett
Sergeant David Potter / Sgt. David Potter
Master of Business Administration / MBA
United States Marine Corps / USMC

When a lowercased term is abbreviated as a simple shortening, the abbreviation is usually lowercased. But if the abbreviation is comprised of initials, all the initials are usually capitalized. When there is a compound word in the term, the initials may include the first letter of the root word:

especially / esp.
teaspoon / tsp.
deoxyribonucleic acid / DNA
monosodium glutamate / MSG
most favored nation / MFN

Usually, an abbreviation that ends in a capital letter is not followed by a period. An abbreviation that ends in a lowercase letter usually is followed by a period, although the period may be optional, depending on the prevailing style of the particular piece of writing.

One group of abbreviations that never ends with a period is the set of chemical symbols. Also, these abbreviations are always initially capitalized even though the terms they represent are lowercased:

Ar	argon	Na	sodium
Dy	dysprosium	Sb	antimony
H	hydrogen	Sn	tin
Kr	krypton	U	uranium
Lr	lawrencium	Xe	xenon

Note that some chemical symbols appear to be straightforward abbreviations (*Ca* for *calcium*) while others seem unrelated to their corresponding terms (*Au* for *gold*). In fact, these symbols are abbreviations of the official scientific, or Latin, names (*Au* for *aurum*, which is Latin for *gold*).

TIP

If the name of an entity such as an organization, institution, or movement is to be abbreviated, its full name should be identified. Upon first mention, both abbreviation and full name should appear together, with either one being set within parentheses. (Usually the lesser known format goes in the parentheses.) Thereafter in the text, only the abbreviation need appear:

> In February 1909, a group of activists founded what would become the NAACP (National Association for the Advancement of Colored People). For more than ninety years, the NAACP has persevered to honor its founders' vision of racial equality and social justice.

> Plans to rebuild at the site of the World Trade Center (WTC) are being discussed today. Various designs for new office space are expected to be considered. Thousands of suggestions for a WTC memorial have already been submitted.

PUNCTUATION

Punctuation is an essential element of good writing because it makes the author's meaning clear to the reader. Although precise punctuation styles may vary somewhat among published sources, there are a number of fundamental principles worthy of consideration. Discussed below are these punctuation marks used in English:

comma	apostrophe
semicolon	quotation marks
colon	parentheses
period	dash
question mark	hyphen
exclamation point	

Comma

The **comma** is the most used mark of punctuation in the English language. It signals to the reader a pause, which generally clarifies the author's meaning and establishes a sensible order to the elements of written language. Among the most typical functions of the comma are the following:

1. It can separate the clauses of a compound sentence when there are two independent clauses joined by a conjunction, especially when the clauses are not very short:

   It never occurred to me to look in the attic, and I'm sure it didn't occur to Rachel either.

   The Nelsons wanted to see the Grand Canyon at sunrise, but they overslept that morning.

2. It can separate the clauses of a compound sentence when there is a series of independent clauses, the last two of which are joined by a conjunction:

   The bus ride to the campsite was very uncomfortable, the cabins were not ready for us when we got there, the cook had forgotten to start dinner, and the rain was torrential.

3. It is used to precede or set off, and therefore indicate, a nonrestrictive dependent clause (a clause that could be omitted without changing the meaning of the main clause):

   I read her autobiography, which was published last July.

   They showed up at midnight, after most of the guests had gone home.

   The coffee, which is freshly brewed, is in the kitchen.

4. It can follow an introductory phrase:

   Having enjoyed the movie so much, he agreed to see it again.

   Born and raised in Paris, she had never lost her French accent.

   In the beginning, they had very little money to invest.

5. It can set off words used in direct address:

   Listen, people, you have no choice in the matter.

   Yes, Mrs. Greene, I will be happy to feed your cat.

6. It can separate two or more coordinate adjectives (adjectives that could otherwise be joined with *and*) that modify one noun:

The cruise turned out to be the most entertaining, fun, and relaxing vacation I've ever had.

The horse was tall, lean, and sleek.

Note that cumulative adjectives (those not able to be joined with and) are not separated by a comma:

She wore bright yellow rubber boots.

7. It is used to separate three or more items in a series or list:

    Charlie, Melissa, Stan, and Mark will be this year's soloists in the spring concert.

    We need furniture, toys, clothes, books, tools, housewares, and other useful merchandise for the benefit auction.

    Note that the comma between the last two items in a series is sometimes omitted in less precise style:

    The most popular foods served in the cafeteria are pizza, hamburgers and nachos.

8. It is used to separate and set off the elements in an address or other geographical designation:

    My new house is at 1657 Nighthawk Circle, South Kingsbury, Michigan.

    We arrived in Pamplona, Spain, on Thursday.

9. It is used to set off direct quotations (note the placement or absence of commas with other punctuation):

    "Kim forgot her gloves," he said, "but we have a pair she can borrow."

    There was a long silence before Jack blurted out, "This must be the world's ugliest painting."

    "What are you talking about?" she asked in a puzzled manner.

    "Happy New Year!" everyone shouted.

10. It is used to set off titles after a person's name:

    Katherine Bentley, M.D.

    Martin Luther King, Jr., delivered the sermon.

Semicolon

The **semicolon** has two basic functions:

1. It can separate two main clauses, particularly when these clauses are of equal importance:

   The crowds gathered outside the museum hours before the doors were opened; this was one exhibit no one wanted to miss.

   She always complained when her relatives stayed for the weekend; even so, she usually was a little sad when they left.

2. It can be used as a comma is used to separate such elements as clauses or items in a series or list, particularly when one or more of the elements already includes a comma:

   The path took us through the deep, dark woods; across a small meadow into a cold, wet cave; and up a hillside overlooking the lake.

   Listed for sale in the ad were two bicycles; a battery-powered, leaf-mulching lawn mower; and a maple bookcase.

Colon

The **colon** has five basic functions:

1. It can introduce something, especially a list of items:

   In the basket were three pieces of mail: a postcard, a catalog, and a wedding invitation.

   Students should have the following items: backpack, loose-leaf notebook, pens and pencils, pencil sharpener, and ruler.

2. It can separate two clauses in a sentence when the second clause is being used to explain or illustrate the first clause:

   We finally understood why she would never go sailing with us: she had a deep fear of the water.

   Most of the dogs in our neighborhood are quite large: two of them are St. Bernards.

3. It can introduce a statement or a quotation:

His parents say the most important rule is this: Always tell the truth.

We repeated the final words of his poem: "And such is the plight of fools like me."

4. It can be used to follow the greeting in a formal or business letter:

Dear Ms. Daniels:

Dear Sir or Madam:

5. It is used in the United States to separate minutes from hours, and seconds from minutes, in showing time of day and measured length of time:

Please be at the restaurant before 6:45.

Her best running time so far has been 00:12:35.

Period

The **period** has two basic functions:

1. It is used to mark the end of a sentence:

It was reported that there is a shortage of nurses at the hospital. Several of the patients have expressed concern about this problem.

2. It is often used at the end of an abbreviation:

On Fri., Sept. 12, Dr. Brophy noted that the patient's weight was 168 lb. and that his height was 6 ft. 2 in.

(Note that another period is not added to the end of the sentence when the last word is an abbreviation.)

Question Mark and Exclamation Point

The only sentences that do not end in a period are those that end in either a question mark or an exclamation point.

Question marks are used to mark the end of a sentence that asks a direct question (generally, a question that expects an answer):

Is there any reason for us to bring more than a few dollars?

Who is your science teacher?

Exclamation points are used to mark the end of a sentence that expresses a strong feeling, typically surprise, joy, or anger:

I want you to leave and never come back!

What a beautiful view this is!

Apostrophe

The **apostrophe** has two basic functions:

1. It is used to show where a letter or letters are missing in a contraction.

   The directions are cont'd [continued] *on the next page.*
   We've [we have] *decided that if she can't* [cannot] *go, then we aren't* [are not] *going either.*

2. It can be used to show possession:

   The possessive of a singular noun or an irregular plural noun is created by adding an apostrophe and an *s*:

   the pilot's uniform
   Mrs. Mendoza's house
   a tomato's bright red color
   the oxen's yoke

   The possessive of a regular plural noun is created by adding just an apostrophe:

   the pilots' uniforms [referring to more than one pilot]
   the Mendozas' house [referring to the Mendoza family]
   the tomatoes' bright red color [referring to more than one tomato]

Quotation Marks

Quotation marks have two basic functions:

1. They are used to set off direct quotations (an exact rendering of someone's spoken or written words):

   "I think the new library is wonderful," she remarked to David.

   We were somewhat lost, so we asked, "Are we anywhere near the gallery?

"In his letter he had written, "The nights here are quiet and starry. It seems like a hundred years since I've been wakened by the noise of city traffic and squabbling neighbors."

Note that indirect quotes (which often are preceded by that, if, and whether) are not set off by quotation marks:

He told me that he went to school in Boston.

We asked if we could still get tickets to the game.

2. They can be used to set off words or phrases that have specific technical usage, or to set off meanings of words, or to indicate words that are being used in a special way in a sentence:

The part of the flower that bears the pollen is the "stamen."

When I said "plain," I meant "flat land," not "ordinary."

Oddly enough, in the theater, the statement "break a leg" is meant as an expression of good luck.

What you call "hoagies," we call "grinders" or "submarine sandwiches."

He will never be a responsible adult until he outgrows his "Peter Pan" behavior.

Note that sometimes single quotation marks, rather than double quotation marks, may be used to set off words or phrases:

The part of the flower that bears the pollen is the 'stamen.'

What is most important is to be consistent in such usage. Single quotation marks are also used to set off words or phrases within material already in double quotation marks, as:

"I want the sign to say 'Ellen's Bed and Breakfast' in large gold letters," she explained.

Parentheses

Parentheses are used, in pairs, to enclose information that gives extra detail or explanation to the regular text. Parentheses are used in two basic ways:

1. They can separate a word or words in a sentence from the rest of the sentence:

On our way to school, we walk past the Turner Farm (the oldest dairy farm in town) and watch the cows being fed.

The stores were filled with holiday shoppers (even more so than last year).

Note that the period goes outside the parentheses, because the words in the parentheses are only part of the sentence.

2. They can form a separate complete sentence:

Please bring a dessert to the dinner party. (It can be something very simple.) I look forward to seeing you there.

Note that the period goes inside the parentheses, because the words in the parentheses are a complete and independent sentence.

Dash

A **dash** is used most commonly to replace the usage of parentheses within sentences. If the information being set off is in the middle of the sentence, a pair of long (or "em") dashes is used; if it is at the end of the sentence, just one long dash is used:

On our way to school, we walk past the Turner Farm—the oldest dairy farm in town—and watch the cows being fed.

The stores were filled with holiday shoppers—even more so than last year.

Hyphen

A **hyphen** has three basic functions:

1. It can join two or more words to make a compound, especially when doing so makes the meaning more clear to the reader:

We met to discuss long-range planning.

There were six four-month-old piglets at the fair.

That old stove was quite a coal-burner.

2. It can replace the word "to" when a span or range of data is given. This kind of hyphen is sometimes keyed as a short (or "en") dash:

John Adams was president of the United States 1797–1801.

Today we will look for proper nouns in the L–N section of the dictionary.

The ideal weight for that breed of dog would be 75–85 pounds.

3. It can indicate a word break at the end of a line. The break must always be between syllables:

> *It is important for any writer to know that there are numerous punctuation principles that are considered standard and proper, but there is also flexibility regarding acceptable punctuation. Having learned the basic "rules" of good punctuation, the writer will be able to adopt a specific and consistent style of punctuation that best suits the material he or she is writing.*

Commonly Misspelled Words

abbreviated
absence
absolutely
acceptance
accessible
accidentally
accommodate
accompany
accuracy
ache
achieve
achievement
acquaintance
acquire
acre
across
actually
administration
admittance
adolescent
advantageous
advertisement
advisable
affectionate
affidavit
aficionado
afraid
again
aggravate
aghast

aisle
allege
allotment
ally
amateur
analysis
analyze
anesthetic
angel
angle
annihilation
annually
answer
anticipate
anxiety
apartheid
aperitif
apology
apparatus
apparent
appearance
appetite
appreciate
approach
appropriate
approximately
argue
argument
arithmetic
arrangement

ascend
ascertain
assistant
athletic
attendance
authority
auxiliary
available
awkward
bachelor
because
beggar
beginning
behavior
believe
benefit
benefited
bicycle
bouillon
boundary
bulletin
bureau
buried
business
cafeteria
calendar
campaign
cancellation
captain
carburetor

career
ceiling
cemetery
census
certificate
chamois
changeable
character
characteristic
chauffeur
chic
chief
chocolate
choice
choose
chose
Christian
clothes
collateral
colonel
color
column
commercial
commission
committee
community
compel
competitor
completely
conceivable

concentrate
condemn
confidence
confidential
confusion
connoisseur
conscience
conscious
continuous
controlled
controversial
conversant
convertible
cooperate
copyright
corps
correspondence
counterfeit
courageous
courteous
criticism
criticize
cruelly
curiosity
curious
cylinder
dealt
debtor
deceive
decision
definite
dependent
describe
despair
desperate
despise
develop
difference

dilemma
diphthong
disappearance
disappoint
disastrous
discipline
discrepancy
disease
diuretic
doctor
duplicate
easily
ecclesiastical
ecstasy
effect
efficient
eighth
elementary
eligible
embarrass
eminent
emphasize
encouragement
encumbrances
enforceable
entirely
entourage
envelope
environment
equipped
escape
especially
essential
et cetera
   (*abbreviated*
   etc.)
exaggerate
excellent

exciting
exercise
exhilarating
exhort
existence
expense
experience
experiment
extraordinary
extremely
facsimile
familiar
fantasy
fascinate
fashionable
fasten
fatal
favorite
February
field
fiery
finally
financial
fluorescent
forehead
foreign
forfeit
fortunately
forty
forward
fourth
freight
friend
fulfill
further
gauge
genius
gourmet

government
governor
gracious
grammar
guarantee
guerrilla
guess
guidance
gymnasium
gypsy
handsome
hangar
hanger
happened
happiness
harass
Hawaii
heavily
height
heinous
heroine
hors d'oeuvre
hospital
humor
humorous
hungrily
hygiene
hypocrisy
hypocrite
hysterical
ignorance
illiterate
imagine
immediately
impossible
incidentally
increase
indefinite

independent
indictment
indispensable
individually
inevitable
influence
ingredient
innocence
inoculate
insurance
intelligence
intelligent
interference
interrupt
iridescent
irrelevant
itinerary
jealous
jewelry
knowledge
laboratory
laborer
laid
legitimate
leisure
liaison
library
license
lieutenant
lightning
likely
liquefy
liquidate
listener
literature
livelihood
lively
loneliness

luxury
magazine
magnificent
maintenance
maneuver
manufacturer
marriage
marvelous
mathematics
meant
mechanic
medical
medicine
melancholy
merchandise
millionaire
miniature
minimum
minuscule
minute
miscellaneous
mischief
mischievous
Massachusetts
misspell
mortgage
muscle
mysterious
narrative
naturally
necessary
nickel
niece
ninety
noisily
non sequitur
noticeable
obstacle

occasionally
occurrence
offensive
official
often
omission
omit
omitted
once
operate
opponent
opportunity
optimistic
orchestra
ordinarily
organization
originally
outrageous
pageant
paid
parallel
paralleled
paralyze
parliament
particular
pastime
peaceful
peculiar
performance
permanent
perseverance
personality
personnel
perspiration
persuade
pessimistic
phenomenal
Philippines

philosophy
physical
picnicking
pleasant
politician
Portuguese
possession
possibility
practically
practice
prairie
preferred
prejudice
preparation
presence
pressure
pretension
privilege
probably
procedure
proceed
procure
professor
proffered
promissory
pronunciation
propaganda
psychic
psychology
pumpkin
punctual
punctuation
pursuit
questionnaire
quiet
quite
quotient
raspberry

realize	safety	statistics	tragedy
really	satisfied	straight	transferred
realtor	scarcely	strength	traveled
realty	scarcity	stretch	tremendous
receipt	scene	strictly	truly
recipe	schedule	stubborn	twelfth
recognize	scholar	substitute	typical
recommend	scissors	subtle	unanimous
referred	scurrilous	succeed	unnecessary
reign	seance	successful	useful
relevant	secretary	suede	useless
relieve	seize	sufficient	usually
religious	semester	summary	vacillate
removal	separate	superintendent	vacuum
rendezvous	sergeant	supersede	vague
repertoire	shepherd	surgeon	valuable
repetition	siege	surprise	variety
rescind	similar	susceptible	various
reservoir	sincerely	suspense	vegetable
resistance	skein	swimming	vengeance
resource	skiing	sympathetic	vilify
responsibility	skillful	synonym	villain
restaurant	sophomore	temperamental	warrant
rheumatism	soufflé	temperature	weather
rhythm	source	tendency	Wednesday
ridiculous	souvenir	therefore	weird
roommate	specialty	thorough	whether
sachet	specifically	though	whole
sacrifice	specimen	thoughtful	yacht
sacrilegious	sponsor	tomorrow	yield

Clichés to Avoid

acid test

to go against the grain

to be all ears

all hell breaks/broke loose

for all intents and purposes

all time high/low

the American dream

and then some

A-OK

the apple of one's eye

armed to the teeth

as luck would have it

as the crow flies

at a snail's pace

to be at loggerheads

at one's beck and call

at the crossroads

at the drop of a hat

an ax to grind

back to the salt mines

one's back to the wall

ballpark figure

bane of one's existence

boldfaced lie

basket case

beat a dead horse

beat around the bush

off the beaten track

beg, borrow, or steal

believe (with) one's own eyes

to go belly up

below the belt

beside oneself

best/worst case scenario

best/greatest thing since sliced bread

be that as it may

between a rock and a hard place

big fish in a little pond

birds of a feather

bite off more than one can chew

bite the bullet

black sheep

blessed event

blind as a bat

blithering idiot

blow your stack

blow the whistle on someone

blow to smithereens

boil down to

bone dry

bone of contention

boon companion

bore to tears

bottom line

boys will be boys

get down to brass tacks

breath of fresh air

bright and early

win brownie points

burning desire

burn the midnight oil

bury one's head in the sand

business as usual

busy as a bee

open a can of worms

can't hit the broad side of a barn

can't hold a candle to

can't see the forest for the trees

cardinal sin

cast in stone

catch someone napping

to chomp at the bit

a change of heart

to change one's tune

cite chapter and verse

easy as child's play

chilled to the bone

chill out

chip off the old block

when the chips are down

clean as a whistle

to clear the air

cliffhanger

a close call

to coin a phrase

to give the cold shoulder to

come on board

come out of one's shell

come to a head

cool as a cucumber

cramp someone's style

crazy like a fox

crystal clear

cut and dried

cutting edge

a dark horse

to dawn on someone

dead in the water

dead set against

den of thieves

play devil's advocate

dime a dozen

to do a number on

dog eat dog

don't hold your breath

doom and gloom

double-edged sword

dressed to kill

drive someone up the/a wall

drunk as a skunk

dull as dishwater

eager beaver

easy as pie

eat like a bird

eat one's heart out

ego trip

elbow room

everything but the kitchen sink

to face the music

fair and square

fall by the wayside

famous last words

a far cry

fast and furious

feast one's eyes on

to have a field day

fifth wheel

fight fire with fire

a fighting chance

fight tooth and nail

figment of the imagination

to go over with a fine-toothed comb

at first blush

a fish out of water

fit like a glove

fly-by-night

to come off/out with flying colors

to foam at the mouth

food for thought

for better or worse

from bad to worse

to lead down the garden path

to get a handle on something

to get a kick out of something

to get down to brass tacks

to get into hot water

to get one's act together

to get one's feet wet

give and take

to give the shirt off one's back

a glutton for punishment

to go around in circles

to go ballistic

to go hog wild

to go overboard

the gory details

to go with the flow

to grasp at straws

the great unwashed

grist for the mill

hand in glove

hands down

happy as a clam

hard act to follow

hard as nails

head and shoulders above

have a heart of stone/gold

hell freezes over

hit below the belt

hit or miss

hit the ground running

hit the hay

hit the nail on the head

cannot hold a candle to

hook, line, and sinker

hot under the collar

no ifs, ands, or buts

ignorance is bliss

in a heartbeat

in a nutshell

in a pinch

in no uncertain terms

in one ear and out the other

in over one's head

in the cards

in the driver's seat

in the long run

in this day and age

in your face

jump down someone's throat

jump the gun

jump to conclusions

keep a straight face

keep your eyes peeled

keep your shirt on

to handle with kid gloves

kill two birds with one stone

a kindred spirit

know someone like a book

know the ropes

labor of love

lap of luxury

larger than life	make a long story short
last but not least	make heads or tails of something
last laugh	make no bones about it
last straw	make one's hair stand on end
leave out in the cold	make one's mouth water
leave well enough alone	make waves
leave to one's own devices	mind over matter
lesser of two evils	moment of truth
letter perfect	money talks
lie through one's teeth	more than meets the eye
life of the party	more than one bargained for
light as a feather	in the nick of time
like a ton of bricks	nip in the bud
like it was going out of style	nodding acquaintance with
like taking candy from a baby	no great shakes
lion's share	no laughing matter
pay lip service to	nose out of joint
lock horns with	not all black and white
a loose cannon	nothing to write home about
lost in the shuffle	no two ways about it
make a beeline for	nuts and bolts

off the wall

old hat

on an even keel

one foot in the grave

one/a picture is worth a thousand words

on pins and needles

on the level

on the ropes

on the sly

on/at the spur of the moment

on the tip of one's tongue

on the warpath

out of a/the clear blue sky

out on a limb

out to lunch

over the hill

paid one's dues

par for the course

pay through the nose

pick a bone with someone

pick someone's brain

piece of cake

plain as day

play with fire

plumb the depths of

powers that be

praise to the skies

pretty as a picture

pride and joy

prime of life

pull no punches

pure and simple

push the envelope

put one's foot down

put on hold

quantum leap

rack one's brain

rain or shine

read between the lines

red carpet treatment

red herring

red-letter day

rest is history

right off the bat

be on the right track

right up one's alley

ring of truth

risk life and limb

rock the boat

roll with the punches

rub elbows with

rub the wrong way

ruffle someone's feathers

run like clockwork

run out of steam

sacred cow

salt of the earth

saving grace

scratch the surface

scream bloody murder

see eye to eye

see the light

sell like hotcakes

separate the men from the boys

set one's sights on

shadow of one's former self

sharp as a tack

shed light on

short and sweet

show one's true colors

sight for sore eyes

sign of the times

sink one's teeth into

sink or swim

sitting pretty

skin and bones

sleep like a log

smart as a whip

smoke like a chimney

smooth as silk

soaked to the skin

spanking new

spread like wildfire

start from scratch

stiff as a board

stubborn as a mule

take a shine to

take by storm

take it in stride

take the bull by the horns

take the wind out of one's sails

talk one's head off

tall, dark, and handsome

tear one's hair out

the big picture

tight as a drum

tip of the iceberg

tongue in cheek

tough nut to crack

towering rage

turn a blind eye to

ugly as sin

under one's belt

under the weather

unvarnished truth

up in arms

up to snuff

vanish into thin air

vicious circle

walking encyclopedia

wall-to-wall

war of nerves

wet blanket

what goes around comes around

whole new ball game

whole nine yards

window of opportunity

with a grain of salt

without batting an eye

work one's fingers to the bone

worth one's salt

you can't make an omelet without breaking eggs